Sword of the Spirit, Shield of Faith

Sword of the Spirit, Shield of Faith

RELIGION IN AMERICAN WAR AND DIPLOMACY

ANDREW PRESTON

ALFRED A. KNOPF · NEW YORK · TORONTO
2012

THIS IS A BORZOI BOOK
PUBLISHED BY ALFRED A. KNOPF

Copyright © 2012 by Andrew Preston
All rights reserved. Published in the United States by Alfred A. Knopf,
a division of Random House, Inc., New York,
and in Canada by Random House of Canada Limited, Toronto.
www.aaknopf.com

Knopf, Borzoi Books, and the colophon are
registered trademarks of Random House, Inc.

Library of Congress Cataloging-in-Publication Data
Preston, Andrew, 1973–
Sword of the spirit, shield of faith : religion in American war and diplomacy /
by Andrew Preston.—1st ed.
p.   cm.
Includes bibliographical references and index.
ISBN 978-1-4000-4323-1
1. United States—Foreign relations. 2. United States—Foreign relations—
Religious aspects. 3. Religion and international relations—United States—History.
4. United States—Military policy—Religious aspects. 5. United States—
History, Military—Religious aspects. I. Title.
E183.7.P74 2012
322'.10973—dc23   2011035138

www.randomhouse.ca
Knopf Canada and colophon are registered trademarks.
Library and Archives Canada Cataloguing in Publication
Preston, Andrew, 1973–
Sword of the spirit, shield of faith : religion in American war and diplomacy /
Andrew Preston
Includes bibliographical references.
Issued also in electronic format.
ISBN 978-0-676-97742-4
1. Religion and international relations—United States—History.
2. Religion and politics—United States—History.
3. United States—Foreign relations—Religious aspects. I. Title.
BL65.I55P74 2012
201'.727   C2011-904068-9

Jacket design and calligraphy by Mary Jane Callister

Manufactured in the United States of America
First Edition

To my parents, Harry and Mary,

who have given me so much

CONTENTS

Preface

New Haven, Connecticut, March 2003. Along with the rest of the world, the student body at Yale University stood riveted by the confrontation between the United States and Iraq, George W. Bush and Saddam Hussein. War would start any day now—that much was certain. Whatever one's opinion on the war, supporters and opponents alike, at Yale as elsewhere, had over a year and a vast amount of information to argue their case. Through the summer and fall of 2002 and into the new year, the Bush administration and its supporters made several arguments for war, from national security to democracy promotion and much else in between.

Including faith. From his initial response to the terrorist attacks of September 11, 2001, to the days before the Iraq War, Bush consistently framed the crisis in terms of religion. Not necessarily in terms of who America would be fighting: despite the occasional slip of the tongue, Bush was careful not to portray the war as a crusade against Islam. But according to news reports that fateful winter and spring of 2003, the president believed he was spiritually motivated by an obligation to God and that God directed his actions and protected America in its time of crisis. "The liberty we prize is not America's gift to the world," he proclaimed in his 2003 State of the Union address, which laid out a case for war, "it is God's gift to humanity." In the giving of such gifts, the United States was God's instrument on earth: "We Americans have faith in ourselves, but not in ourselves alone. We do not know—we do not claim to know all the ways of providence, yet we can trust in them, placing our confidence in the loving God behind all of life and all of history. May He guide us now." "We're being challenged," Bush told an audience in Nashville a month later. "We're meeting those challenges because of our faith." He then justified war with Iraq as a matter of self-defense against freedom-hating fundamentalists who received support and encouragement from Saddam Hussein. "They hate the thought of the fact that in this great country, we can worship the Almighty God the way we see fit. And probably what makes them even angrier is, we're not going to change."[1]

For his part, Saddam Hussein also framed the coming war in religious terms. Unlike the decadent, infidel Americans, Iraqis belonged to a "glo-

rious faith," he declared. "Allah does not like weaklings." With encouragement from the presidential palace, Iraq's clerics also tried to rally the
faithful to arms. And though he was an avowed enemy of Ba'athist, secular Iraq, Osama bin Laden struck a characteristically religious note. The
Americans were "crusaders" who wanted "to occupy a former capital of
Islam," the al Qaeda leader warned in an audio message shortly before
the war. "This crusade war is primarily aimed at the people of Islam" to
subjugate their faith and steal their oil, and so "Muslims as a whole, and
in Iraq in particular, should pull up their sleeves and carry jihad against
this oppressive offensive and to make sure to stock up on ammunition
and arms. This is a duty for them." It was a message bin Laden had been
propounding since 9/11, indeed, since he had first begun his jihad against
the United States in the 1990s.[2]

I was then a young lecturer in the History Department at Yale, not far
removed from finishing a doctoral dissertation on McGeorge Bundy and
the origins of the Vietnam War. In the fall of 2002, I taught a large lecture
class on Vietnam; in the spring semester, I led a smaller seminar on U.S.
foreign policy during its most tumultuous Cold War period, from John
F. Kennedy and the Bay of Pigs to Jimmy Carter and the Iran hostage
crisis. It was a surreal experience, examining the Cold War while a very
similar history was unfolding before us in real time. Yet despite the trauma
of 9/11, the year 2003 was also very different from 1973. The United
States was not vulnerable, but seemed invincible; it was not reeling from
a disaster like Vietnam, but coming off a series of triumphs in the Cold
War, the Gulf War, the Balkan wars, and, apparently, driving the Taliban
from power in Afghanistan. While Lyndon Johnson and Richard Nixon
had watched Indochina consume their presidencies, here was George
W. Bush, seemingly as strong a president in living memory, deciding to
remake the Middle East in a democratic American image. For a specialist
in U.S. diplomatic history, it was a fascinating time.

My students and I debated the War on Terror, Afghanistan, and Iraq
almost as much as we pored over the record on Cuba and Chile, Vietnam
and Cambodia, the Iranian hostages and the Soviet invasion of Afghanistan. I encouraged it, so long as they avoided polemical grandstanding and
grounded their arguments about the confusing present in a careful understanding of an equally complicated past. But one thing puzzled them all:
the presence of religion in the normally hardheaded world of diplomacy,
especially American diplomacy. Why did Bush use religious imagery and
rhetoric to justify his foreign policy? Was this usual? Did other presidents of the past hundred years invoke God and Christ to explain themselves? Or was Bush a premodern aberration in a postmodern world? I
told them what I knew, which was not all that much: that some presidents
had deployed religion as a political tactic, that religion was often invoked

as a way to explain or justify intervention, but that most of the time religion was background noise and political filler and not especially important to the study of American diplomatic history. I referred them to the usual suspects—Woodrow Wilson, John Foster Dulles, Jimmy Carter—leaders who happened to be personally religious and happened, on occasion, to use religious rhetoric. A couple of scholars had looked a little bit into the broader connections between religion and diplomacy, and I recommended their books. But otherwise, I did not give it much thought.[3]

I cannot say precisely when, but at some point that spring I did begin to give religion some further thought. Intrigued, I consulted bibliographic guides, library catalogues, and journal databases. To my surprise, the existing literature did not much go beyond the usual suspects I had already mentioned to my students. There were, however, some notable exceptions just then emerging. Three colleagues, Seth Jacobs, Melani McAlister, and Andrew Rotter, had recently published exciting, innovative accounts of religion's influence on America's Cold War diplomacy: Jacobs on Vietnam, McAlister on the Middle East, Rotter on India and Pakistan. But they seemed to be one-offs, religious exceptions to a generally secular rule. Little did I know that they were on the cutting edge of a major trend in American diplomatic history.[4]

I was also familiar with American religious history, and so turned there next. But when I consulted that body of literature, I discovered something very interesting: religious historians examined diplomacy just as infrequently and unsystematically as diplomatic historians examined religion. Yet their work was littered with intriguing discussions of religion in times of war and diplomatic crisis, albeit with a focus on how foreign policy affected religion rather than the other way around. And unlike diplomatic historians, historians of religion did not simply concentrate on the usual suspects.

This was an exciting but odd and unsettling discovery. It is difficult to think of two subjects that have shaped the United States more than religion and foreign affairs, and it is difficult to find two bodies of literature that are as large, diverse, or controversial; perhaps, as categories of historical analysis, only race and economics compare. The problem, at least for me, was that historians of religion were interested in religious issues; their discussions of, say, World War I did not intend to shed light on the war, but on how religion reacted to or was changed by the war. In the same way, historians of American foreign policy were not especially interested in religious issues. Sporadic references to the other abounded in each discipline, but only a rare few scholars integrated them in a sustained and meaningful fashion. Yet there were obvious historical moments when the two subjects would have had to meet in interesting and revealing ways. Armed with this insight, I set out to write a book that would answer my students' questions—and my own.

Sword of the Spirit, Shield of Faith

Introduction

Finally, my brethren, be strong in the Lord, and in the power of his might.

Put on the whole armour of God, that ye may be able to stand against the wiles of the devil.

For we wrestle not against flesh and blood, but against principalities, against powers, against the rulers of the darkness of this world, against spiritual wickedness in high places.

Wherefore take unto you the whole armour of God, that ye may be able to withstand in the evil day, and having done all, to stand.

Stand therefore, having your loins girt about with truth, and having on the breastplate of righteousness;

And your feet shod with the preparation of the gospel of peace;

Above all, taking the shield of faith, wherewith ye shall be able to quench all the fiery darts of the wicked.

And take the helmet of salvation, and the sword of the Spirit, which is the word of God . . .

—Ephesians 6:10–17

SWORD OF THE SPIRIT, *Shield of Faith* was written under the assumption that religion played an important role in shaping American perceptions of the world and in contributing to domestic debates on how the United States should engage with other nations. It is an exploration not of *whether* religion influenced U.S. foreign relations, but *how*. It is a logical assumption: few would argue that religion has not played a consistently important role in American life, for better or worse.

This last qualifier—for better or worse—is important, for this book also operates under the assumption that religion is just like any other historical topic. It is not my desire, and certainly not my intention, to make a case either for or against a role for religion in public life. Readers will of course use the material in this book to support their own beliefs that religion is either a productive or a pernicious force in American foreign relations. Partisans on both sides of the acrimonious debate over religion's place in the public square—and increasingly over the nature of religion itself—will find plenty of evidence to back up their competing claims. But such quarrels are not my concern. Religion provokes intense emotions, and no historian is free of bias. Nonetheless, I have sought to treat my subject as objectively as possible.

Doing so has meant recognizing that there was not one religious influence upon American foreign relations, but many: nationalist but also internationalist, exceptionalist but also cosmopolitan, nativist but also tolerant, militant but also pacifist. The religious influence was neither monolithic nor consensual but a product of intense dialogue, debate, and controversy. Nor did it always push U.S. foreign policy in the same direction. It is a fascinatingly complex story, but its very complexity makes its unraveling all the more important and worthwhile.

BUT WHY FOCUS on religion at all? Why does it matter to American diplomatic history? Aside from the personal faith of individual policymakers, religion has been integral to American politics and culture, and to America's sense of itself, and thus also to the products of politics and culture, such as foreign policy. More specifically, religion has had an almost uniquely intimate relationship with American war and diplomacy. In times of war, religious liberals and conservatives, militants and pacifists, have all called upon God to sanctify their cause, and all have viewed America as God's chosen land. As a result, U.S. foreign policy has often acquired the tenor of a moral crusade.

Moreover, the religious mindset was geographically limitless; those who possessed it were concerned not only with their community, state, or country, but the entire world. As immigrants, generations of American Christians, Jews, and Muslims thought of themselves as members of a transnational faith that transcended national boundaries. They kept in regular contact with coreligionists overseas and followed the political affairs in foreign countries that affected these spiritual kinfolk. They sought to spread the gospel to people who had never heard of Christ and endured incredible hardship in doing so. They were more likely to live and travel abroad and more likely to have a foreign correspondent. Unlike most of their fellow citizens, then, religious Americans inherently thought of themselves as citizens of the world. They paid closer attention to foreign affairs and were more likely to allow international developments to affect their political views. Thus while religious faith helped create an American nationalism, it also fostered a powerful sense of internationalism.

Since the late sixteenth century, long before the United States existed, religion has played an important role in shaping Americans' perceptions of the wider world. In both popular debates about American engagement with the world and the foreign policies that have emerged from these debates, religion has been a major factor. The religious influence—indeed, religious faith itself—has not always been strong or consistent. But though it has ebbed and flowed, it has always been there.

This seems to be a basic point—religion matters, and always has—yet it is an important one to make because it has been so neglected in explaining the history of American war and diplomacy. Historians have emphasized a wide array of factors, from traditional concerns such as economics, national security, and military strategy, to newer theories based on race, gender, culture, and postmodernism. All are important grounds for inquiry, and all have yielded a rich understanding of the American past. Yet until very recently, religion was seen as a mystifying sideshow, an irrational impulse born of a "paranoid style" that clouded the realist assumptions of high diplomacy. Even after diplomatic history's cultural turn—an exciting development over the past two decades that has pushed scholars to incorporate race, class, and gender into the American diplomatic tradition—and its international turn, which portrays the United States as "a nation among nations," religion remains peripheral or nonexistent. This is true for otherwise superb overviews of U.S. foreign policy that purport to examine American "ideals," "style," "ideology," "mission," "Wilsonian idealism," "core values," even "why America fights"—normative topics, in other words, that are ideally suited to religious ideas and values and incomplete without them. In fact, until very recently religion was sidelined in most fields of modern American history. Be it the history of politics, immigration, or civil rights, religious faith was pushed to the margins when it made any appearance at all. It seemed that only historians of American religion took religion seriously, an absurd situation when one considers the prevalence and importance of religion in American life.[1]

SWORD OF THE SPIRIT, SHIELD OF FAITH aims to help fill this gap in our understanding of how Americans have engaged the wider world. It presents a new survey of the history of American foreign relations, told predominantly through a religious lens. Readers should remember that this is not a new master narrative of U.S. foreign policy but a new perspective that aims to complement and enrich existing interpretations without necessarily replacing them. I have begun my story at the onset of England's settlement of North America in the late sixteenth century and ended it with a brief look at the presidencies of George W. Bush and Barack Obama in the early twenty-first. My chronological scope should not be taken as an argument for the essential continuity of an unchanging history, yet there has been continuity: time and again, many of the same themes appear and reappear down the years.

Many of these themes—cultural habits that informed the making of policy—originated in the colonial period and then crystallized in later years. To say that this book is an examination of U.S. foreign policy is to elide the fact that our story begins before there was a United States that could even have a foreign policy. But the colonial era was crucial, a period in which many of the premises of an American worldview were established and developed. To begin in 1776 or 1783 or 1789, then, is to join the story after it has already begun. Many other syntheses of U.S. foreign relations do precisely this, and while they have much to offer they miss much that is vital in the formative years. Ignoring the colonial period in an otherwise comprehensive overview assumes that habits and ideas began anew with the creation of the United States of America, when we know that this was impossible.

Yet while the earliest eras of American history matter greatly, they do not, in the history of American foreign policy or international relations more generally, matter nearly as much as more recent periods. Of the four centuries since Europeans crossed the Atlantic to settle the eastern shore of North America, it was only in the last hundred years that America became a great power of truly world historical importance. As late as the 1880s, the United States was little more than a minnow in the diplomatic ocean; from then on, it grew steadily to become one of the largest whales the world has ever seen. For this reason, I pay more attention to the period since the United States announced itself on the global stage by routing Spain in the war of 1898. Not coincidentally, this also marked the period when American religion became more pluralistic, more complicated, and more diffuse.[2]

To uncover the habits and ideas that gave shape to America's interactions with the wider world, I focus not only on the traditional aspects of diplomatic history—elites in closed rooms conducting national security policy in secret—but also on the popular pressures brought to bear upon diplomats and policymakers. This book is a study of how religion shaped America's engagement with the wider world, including the overseas efforts of private citizens, missionaries, and other nongovernmental organizations, in addition to the use of diplomatic and military power. It is not just about U.S. foreign *policy*, then, but U.S. foreign *relations*. The distinction is critical: the former term examines only the formulation and execution of actual government policy, while the latter includes policy but also a wider array of American interactions with the world, from missionaries to voluntarist and philanthropic initiatives to corporate and economic interests. The only way to capture the richness of the religious influence—and to find it where it would otherwise remain hidden—is to blend "high" and "low" versions of history, from the top-down perspective of policymaking elites to the bottom-up view of religious Americans who do not make policy themselves but influence it collectively, through political pressure and activism abroad. As the historian Akira Iriye sensibly observes, "to understand American diplomacy, one must know something about American culture."[3] Thus while *Sword of the Spirit, Shield of Faith* is predominantly a work of religious and diplomatic history, it is also, where relevant, an exercise in cultural, intellectual, and social history. Similarly, this is also why I pay attention to domestic developments that at first glance may not seem to have a clear link to foreign affairs. As I explain later in this Introduction, politics is central because it formed a bridge between popular religion and elite policy.

Readers should always bear in mind that while this is a history of the influence of religion, I do not argue that religion was the only factor in the history of American foreign relations. It was but one among many. Sometimes it was a critically important factor; other times, it played a relatively minor role. I have focused on religion not because it offers a unified theory or single-cause explanation of U.S. foreign policy but because it is a missing link, a vital but unrecognized, even undiscovered, part of the story. And in discovering it, I hope, we will reach a fuller, more complete understanding of the role America has played in the world.

"CHANGE OVER TIME." "The past is a foreign country." These are perhaps the first rules of history, imparted as a warning to those naïve enough to search the past for lessons for our world today. But though we know that history is not linear, that it does not remain the same, and that it does not necessarily march forward to progress and enlightenment, we can also sometimes allow fear of what scholars call "presentism" to blind us to *continuity* over time. For as we shall see throughout this book, while the religious influence on American foreign relations changed dramatically, it also retained core features developed early on. Many of the themes that animate my narrative have been remarkably durable, not merely over decades but down through the centuries.

First and foremost, religion acted as the conscience of American foreign relations. U.S. foreign policy itself has never really been idealistic, and certainly not altruistic. But policymaking elites often had to pursue foreign policy initiatives under an idealistic banner because of popular religious pressures that were themselves idealistic. They had to merge the moralism and progressivism of religion with the normally realist mindset of international politics. Thus the U.S. government was often led to pursue a normative foreign policy—of human rights promotion, of democracy promotion, of humanitarian intervention, and so forth—by religious pressures emanating from below.[4]

Americans, largely but of course not exclusively acting upon a religious impulse, pushed their government not only to be a citizen of the world, but to be a model citizen. As St. Paul instructed the Ephesians, sometimes this meant brandishing the "sword of the Spirit." In the American context, this has often meant waging war in the name of God, or at least in the name of serving him and fulfilling his will. This is familiar rhetoric in the history of American exceptionalism: the stuff of providence, manifest destiny, a New Jerusalem, and a shining city upon a hill. But St. Paul told the Ephesians they must also carry the "shield of faith." And just as often in American history—in fact, as we shall see, probably more often—this has led to the promotion of peace: Christian pacifism, anti-interventionism, anti-imperialism, and internationalism.

The tendency to wield both the sword of the spirit and the shield of faith created an idealistic synthesis, as governments, faced with a crisis or war, found themselves buffeted by lobbying from highly moralistic, values-driven Americans. Due in part to this dynamic, when American governments have gone to war, they have felt the overwhelming need to do so in the name of protecting universal values and human rights or bringing progress to areas of the world suffering under poverty and tyranny. While historians have concentrated heavily on the "sword of the Spirit," they have mostly ignored the less-sensationalistic "shield of faith" of pacifism and antiwar movements.

But why would policymaking elites even care? Why would they listen to the churches and synagogues, especially if they themselves were conditioned to pursue the secular national interest? There are three important reasons why it was impossible for policymakers to ignore religion. The first is intuitively straightforward: religion mattered to individuals, and many of these individuals became policymakers, either as politicians or as diplomats. This is so simple that it is easy to ignore or dismiss, and diplomatic historians have done so countless times. It has been easy—too easy—to discount the public piety of a William McKinley or a Franklin Roosevelt or a John Foster Dulles as cynical window dressing that obscures the "real" political or strategic motives behind their foreign policies. It has been easy because historians have done so without first understanding the religious biographies of policymakers and appreciating the religious context in which they developed. Their portrayals of these and other figures are not so much inaccurate as incomplete, and thus inadequate. Much of my task is therefore dedicated to recovering the lost dimensions and exposing the hidden depths of the individuals who made U.S. foreign policy.

The other two reasons why policymaking elites had to care about the religious influence are both more structural in nature. Second is the nature of American politics. Since 1783, the United States has been a democracy—an imperfect and incomplete democracy, to be sure, given the lack of voting rights for women, the monstrously immoral institution of slavery, and the genocidal treatment of Native Americans, to mention only the most obvious limitations, but a democracy nonetheless. By the 1820s, all white male Americans could vote, an unprecedented extension of the franchise. (By contrast, in Great Britain, the other leading practitioner of mass democracy, not only were most white males denied a vote, many parts of the country—including major cities such as Manchester—were not even represented in Parliament.) Mass democracy in America meant that political elites—and by extension, diplomatic elites—could not ignore the will of the people. They might not always like it, or agree with it, or even listen to it, but they could not simply ignore it. Thus even when leaders wanted to ignore popular opinion and pursue their own policy, they had to make allowances for and adjustments to sentiment from below. To do otherwise was to risk political suicide.[5]

For its part, religion in America has always been popular, widely adhered to in one form or another by the vast majority of its people. There is little reason to reject the conclusions of Alexis de Tocqueville's *Democracy in America*, published in 1835 but still relevant today. Of the American people, he noted that "some profess Christian dogmas because they believe them, others because they are afraid of not looking like they believe them. Christianity therefore reigns without obstacles, on the admission of all."[6] Ever since, religion has remained an important part of the language of politics. Just as important, religion in America has also been popular in the sense that it is of the people; thanks to the First Amendment and widespread religious pluralism, the church has been disconnected from the state and thus beholden only to its members. From that basis, religion provided the source and ideas for many popular movements in American history, most obviously revivals and awakenings but also Populism, Progressivism, civil rights, and voluntarism. The political implications are so clear that they sometimes go unnoticed: religion has been vital to American politics because so many Americans have believed in it and believed further that religion should be applied to politics and policy, including international politics and foreign policy.

Where popular religion and elite diplomacy met, then, was in politics. Religious communities were highly devoted and motivated, but they themselves usually lacked political power. When they sought to influence foreign policy, they did so by pressuring their elected representatives. To apply such pressure, they used the tools at their disposal: newspapers, magazines, journals, radio and television, letters, pamphlets, and petitions. And at this, they were extremely effective. For their part, policymakers often worked the system from their end. When seeking support for a given policy, they wanted to speak to large bodies of people, such as religious communities. In addition to speeches, which were usually assured wide media coverage, elites used the same means of communication as the churches. A large number of Americans were (and still are) members of a religious grouping, be it a denomination, church, synagogue, or mosque. Like any large, cohesive grouping, they represent political power that can be mobilized to support or oppose a given policy. It was this latent power that elites wanted to tap into, and because religion had captured the hearts and minds of many if not most Americans, politicians had to pay them attention. Religious communities and elites spoke to each other in a continual effort to try to convince one another of what should be done in U.S. foreign policy. The religious influence, then, was the product of this continual dialogue. It was at heart a political process.

This leads us to our third explanation, also structural, of why religion has mattered so much to the conduct of American foreign relations: free security. Simply by America's very position in the international system between 1815 and 1941, Americans were allowed to develop a foreign policy of almost pure choice, free from the atavistic fears of physical security that have motivated other countries. Not coincidentally, this was the period in which the United States first became a great power, and then the world's preeminent power. To the east and west lay vast oceans, conveniently controlled by the one power, Britain, that was to some extent temperamentally and politically sympathetic to American dominance of the Western Hemisphere. To both the north and south lay relatively weak neighbors in Canada and Mexico; in the rest of the Western Hemisphere, no other nation could pose even a theoretical threat to America's physical safety. As analysts of free security have noted, the absence of threat enabled Americans to devise foreign policies almost as they pleased. This was a truly unique condition in the history of geopolitics. For example, the foreign policies of France and Russia, Japan and China, were determined largely by what their neighbors and rivals were doing. In the case of smaller and more vulnerable nations, such as Poland, foreign policy was determined *entirely* by what its rivals were planning. But even the great powers had to act within the constraints imposed by others. British foreign policy was thus formulated not only in London, but also in Berlin, Paris, Istanbul, and Tokyo. These systemic constraints would soon enmesh and entangle Washington, but not until over a century of foreign policymaking habits had been formed. Echoes of its enduring influence continue to be heard today.[7]

In an atmosphere of almost pure choice, concerns about self-defense and fears of invasion and occupation were absent not only from the general American worldview but also from U.S. foreign policymaking. But a nation needs a foreign policy—even the most insular countries have to think about the wider world, and the United States has certainly never been insular. The freedom to choose enabled other factors, based not on physical danger but ideals and values, to influence foreign policy decisions. Americans worried little about threats from the world as it actually was, but dreamed about how the world should really be. Free security also allowed democracy—and by extension, religion—to play an inordinate role in shaping America's response to the world, for leaders could not suppress the popular will in the name of a clear and present danger. The religious impulse—ever-present, morally driven, highly activist, indefatigable, politically connected, deeply concerned with the wider world—had little to block its path to the White House, Foggy Bottom, and Capitol Hill.

THERE ARE ALSO other continuities in the history of religion's influence on American war and diplomacy. If religious Americans acted as the moral conscience and progressive imagination of U.S. foreign policy, which ideas gave shape to the conscience and the imagination? In turn, which ideas and values motivated religious Americans? Such questions cannot be answered easily because they did in fact greatly change over time. Still, there are some major watchwords that have persisted and interacted throughout most of American history, broad themes that the reader should bear in mind and that are thus worth introducing here: morality, liberty, progress, and nationalism.

All, to some extent, were products of America's peculiar religious heritage. Crucially, colonial America was established as a Reformation society, founded by Protestant radicals who took refuge from the religious wars and economic crises of Europe (and came mostly from the British Isles, Holland, Germany, and France). Unlike all other Reformation societies, the American colonies never underwent a counterreformation. They never confronted a backlash, and thus never had to accommodate themselves to an alternative worldview in the name of domestic and international peace. From there, many of the American colonies developed as Reformation Protestant societies. When they came together in 1776 to become an independent nation, they did so as a Reformation Protestant nation; they did not necessarily intend to establish a religious republic, but they could not escape the cultural trappings of their Protestant inheritance. Even as the United States became more religiously and culturally pluralistic, new peoples and their faiths had to adapt to a political culture that was overwhelmingly Protestant. Not unusually for American history, this has produced something of a paradox: a nation founded and built upon religious tolerance and pluralism that has been inordinately shaped by a strongly exceptionalist Protestant identity. This milieu nurtured the themes that animate this book.[8]

If our first theme is religion as a source of morality, and from it, religion as a source of a moral foreign policy, our second theme is liberty. Produced by an intense combination of republicanism and Protestantism, a strong libertarian ethos pervaded U.S. foreign policy. This was expressed variously as isolationism, unilateralism, and suspicion of international organizations such as the United Nations. A large number of Americans showed a consistent aversion to centers of concentrated power, be they political or religious. Concentrated power—wielded by a monarch, despot, or small ruling clique—was by its very nature unrepresentative and undemocratic. It was assumed to be inherently hostile to American values and democracy, and thus a threat even if it could not strike directly at the United States. Here again, religion served as both a diagnosis and a cure, for it could identify hostile concentrations of power and then be wielded against them. The democratic peace—the idea that democracies go to war reluctantly, as a last resort, and do not go to war against one another—is an example of such thinking in action. Religion was vital to the democratic peace, for freedom of conscience was believed to be the foundation of democracy, and religion was assumed to be the source of conscience. A threat to freedom of religion was thus a threat to freedom of conscience—and, eventually, a threat to American democracy itself.

Crucially, the sanctity of liberty was also shaped by the separation of church and state. The establishment and free exercise clauses of the First Amendment that enshrined the legal separation of church and state produced a thriving but almost completely deregulated marketplace of faith. This allowed American religion to flourish, because it protected the church from the worldly compromises and interference of the state. While the separation of church and state was enacted to protect politics from religion, it was also deemed just as vital to protect religion from politics. By keeping the government out of religion, the First Amendment created competition among inherently equal, nonfavored denominations, which in turn pushed American religion to be innovative and entrepreneurial. This encouraged nonconformist and eccentric sects to invent and reinvent themselves, from evangelicalism to Mormonism to Pentecostalism, as they responded to the wishes of their adherents. It also allowed for the gradual and relatively peaceful absorption of Catholics and Jews in an overwhelmingly Protestant nation. The result of the separation of church and state was the growth of highly autonomous religious communities that harbored an innate hostility to government regulation. In foreign policy terms, the separationist mindset has led to suspicion and outright hostility not only toward concentrated power, but also international organizations and other forums for multilateral diplomacy. Isolationism and unilateralism, then, can in large part trace their origins and continued vibrancy to the power of religious ideas.[9]

Next is progress. Protestant Americans associated their faith with the hallmarks of material progress—technological innovation, industrialization, trade, commerce, finance—because they believed that free religion allowed for free economics, just as it allowed for free politics. Released from the interference of the state and an established church, Americans, it was assumed, were able to behave more or less as they thought best, within reason. This, they believed, enabled them to create economic prosperity as well as political liberty. Indeed, the two were assumed to be inseparable. (Perhaps not surprisingly, Americans also believed in Max Weber's theory of a thrifty, industrious, and dedicated "Protestant work ethic" long before he was around to devise it.)

But to religious Americans, progress meant something more than just economic prosperity. It also meant the general improvement of society, which of course included material advancement but was not limited to it. In this view, progress meant the creation and perfection of a society that respected the dignity of the individual, that cared for its poor and indolent in addition to rewarding its creators of wealth, and that sought to improve living conditions for all. It aimed, in other words, to balance personal freedom with social obligation and individual rights with group rights. At home, this faith-based progressive mindset led to campaigns against slavery, poor working conditions, alcohol, prostitution, and other vices. Abroad, it led to a mission to reform the world—though sometimes this was actually implemented at the barrel of a gun. On matters of foreign policy, religious Americans were rarely static and conservative; most often, they were aggressively progressive, at times even radical. The progressivist impulse was complicated and could lead to the adoption of seemingly contradictory policies. Within a few decades of the nineteenth century, for example, religious Americans were at the forefront in calling for the end of white supremacy at home but the spread of it abroad: first for the abolition of slavery in the South, then for the imposition of an empire overseas. Or consider the role of missionaries, who were simultaneously some of the earliest advocates of universal human rights but also practitioners of cultural imperialism. Yet whether they were missionaries, abolitionists, or imperialists, they all sincerely believed themselves to be motivated by the purest, most progressive of motives.

Our final theme is nationalism, and its attendant civil religion. Religion has for centuries been an incubator of national pride, and not just America's. But in American history, the relationship between faith and patriotism has been especially close and durable. Protestant exceptionalism helped breed American exceptionalism and led to a consistent belief in America as a chosen nation and in Americans as a chosen people. The implications this held for foreign relations are obvious. Under nationalism's spell, Americans believed themselves to be responding to a higher calling, to be executing God's plan, to be fulfilling his providence. As God's chosen nation, the United States was bound to do right. This belief underpinned U.S. intervention and imperialism in North America and around the world, a story historians have often told and one that animates this book. But many religious Americans, including the most devout, also used national exceptionalism as a spur to charity and peace. If they elevated America onto a spiritual plane, they did it not to convert others but to hold the nation to a higher moral standard. While nationalistic excep-

tionalism supported wars, it also damned them in the name of a powerfully dogmatic and equally patriotic pacifism.[10]

Nationalism, especially the belief in America as a chosen nation, has
been sustained by an American civil religion. Politics, like religion, is a
ritualistic activity, and both use ritual and ceremony as a means to codify
social relations. In a highly religious nation like the United States, it has
been relatively easy to blend the beliefs in God and country into a single,
cohesive ideology. For a long time—until the early twentieth century—this
American civil religion was grounded in political institutions and civic
values. Its purpose was to sanctify the virtues of American democracy
by linking them to the higher virtues of Christianity. But as the nation
became more pluralistic—that is, less Protestant—civil religion became
more inclusive, its mission more ecumenical, its meaning grounded more
in people than institutions. It ceased to be Protestant and instead became
"Judeo-Christian," a term rarely used before the twentieth century. This
Judeo-Christian civil religion celebrated religious liberty not only as a
source of political freedom, but also as a source of tolerance.[11]

There is no official hierarchy in the American civil religion, but as
the nation's head of state as well as its chief executive—and, not irrelevant for our purposes, its commander-in-chief—the president has acted
as its de facto pope. Since George Washington, the president has been the
interpreter of the rites, symbols, and meanings of the civil religion, with
some—particularly Abraham Lincoln, Franklin Roosevelt, and Harry
Truman—significantly recasting it under the pressure of war. Moreover, presidents were instrumental in applying the civil religion to foreign policy. As such, they and their religious rhetoric feature prominently
throughout our story here.

"Next to each religion is a political opinion that is joined to it by affinity," observed Tocqueville. "Allow the human mind to follow its tendency
and it will regulate political society and the divine city in a uniform manner; it will seek, if I dare say it, to *harmonize* the earth with Heaven."[12]
This, he concluded, was precisely what had happened in America, where
both free politics and free religion thrived together, in tandem. A consequence, explored in the pages that follow, was a powerfully enduring religious influence on the conduct of American war and diplomacy, enabled
above all by the centrality of religion to American politics and political
thought. Whether it meant wielding the sword of the spirit, the shield
of faith, or both, America's foreign relations have always been, to some
extent, rooted in religion.

PART I

In the Beginning

Jamestown, Virginia, March 1622. After fifteen years of tension, open war between English colonial settlers and their Indian neighbors had finally come to Virginia. Relations had never been friendly and violent clashes were common since the English colonists had managed to establish themselves along the tidewater peninsulas of the Virginia shore. In the five years leading up to 1622, when the proprietors of the Virginia Company discovered the lucrative crop of tobacco, the colony's population stabilized, and then tripled. With the population surge came the expansion of colonial farming, including the need for pastureland to raise pigs and cattle. Alarmed at this invasion, the Powhatan Indians who had long dominated the region decided to eliminate the threat once and for all. Catching the English settlements of Virginia by surprise on March 22, 1622, Indian attackers swiftly killed 347 colonists—roughly a third of the colony's population—and completely destroyed several villages and farms.[1]

While the ensuing war, which lasted intermittently for a decade, pitted against each other two groups of people seeking to inhabit the same territory, it was much more than a competition for land. The colonists and the Powhatans were two very distinct groups of people, divided by language, custom, technology, race—and probably above all, religion. Christianity was utterly foreign to the Powhatans, incomprehensible, even nonsensical. They resented the colonists' promises to win them to Christianity as much as they did the crowding of their space. Not only did the Indians already have their own indigenous faith, they realized that conversion to Christianity was the first step toward total assimilation and the loss of their traditional way of life. Understandably, the Powhatans feared and hated the English nation and the Protestant faith in equal measure. The famed Pocahontas, after all, had involuntarily converted to Christianity, married an Englishman, adopted an English name, and moved to England—where she died in 1617, less than a year after arriving.[2]

And the Powhatans had reason to fear. The Virginia Company had been established with an intense Protestantism typical of the religious hothouse that was seventeenth-century England. As God's chosen people, their faith gave the English confidence that the land they settled in the New World was rightfully theirs. "The first objection," the Reverend Robert Gray preached in a 1609 sermon to christen the Virginia Company's initiative, "is by what right or warrant we can enter into the land of these Savages, take away their rightfull inheritance from them, and plant ourselves in their places, being unwronged or unprovoked by them." Believing that only the Devil stood in their way, the English assumed that the Indians were in league with the forces of Hell. "Satan visibly and palpably raignes there, more then in any other known place of the world," claimed one settler. Another concluded that the Indians had "great witches among them" and were "very familiar with the Devill."[3] Thus when war broke out in 1622, it promised to be a holy war, a contest over identity as well as land.

While the Indians possessed the element of surprise, the colonists had the greater advantages of superior military technology and a steady transatlantic supply of provisions and reinforcements. Because the colonists had believed they were at peace with the Indians, a deep sense of betrayal fueled their anger. The "miserable wretches," railed one, had "despised Gods great mercies" bestowed so kindly by the Virginians. No longer. Reeling from a single-day loss of a third of their number, the colonists held little back in retaliating. They were careful not to exterminate the Indians entirely—their annual corn harvest was too valuable a source of food—but over the next ten years Virginia militiamen waged a war of societal attrition by burning Indian villages and crops and targeting Indian noncombatants as well as warriors. In one infamous episode, after inviting several hundred Powhatans to negotiate peace terms, English officials poisoned the tea drunk to celebrate the signing of a treaty. Over 250 Indians died.[4]

In a war fought with little regard to limits, the use of faith to outline the objectives and methods of fighting was in keeping with the religious traditions of early colonial America. Protestantism provided the colonists a mental map of the world, both Old and New, and helped them navigate the cultural and physical challenges of their transplanted society. Faith also provided a bedrock of moral support through incredibly trying times. Both before and after the 1622 war, Virginia's authorities declared holy days—of fasting and thanksgiving—to celebrate victory, remember the dead, and praise God for deliverance. But the Indians could also use Christianity as a weapon against the colonists. The next (and last) large-scale war between Virginians and Indians came in 1644, when Powhatan warriors gained total surprise by attacking on Maundy Thursday, a holy day before Easter when they knew the colonists would be at rest and unprepared. The Indians knew just how central religion was to colonial society.[5]

Exemplified by Virginia's wars with the Powhatans, the first decades of English colonization established some of the foundational principles of what would later become American foreign relations. The English who agitated for the establishment of American colonies, and especially those who actually sailed across the Atlantic to build a new society, were motivated by a set of core assumptions about the value of who they were and what they did. These assumptions, what might be called an ideology of securing liberty and prosperity through expansion, acted as an extremely powerful motor that drove the colonists' engagement with the wider world. Most crucially, the English settlers believed, much as their American descendants would for centuries afterward, in their own exceptional virtue. They thought of themselves as more enlightened not only than the native peoples of the New World, but also their fellow Europeans, especially Roman Catholics. Just as important, this sense of innate moral superiority led the English to perceive their motives and actions as defensive, magnanimous, progressive, even benevolent. Often they were, but just as often these exceptionalist attitudes justified the expansion of empire and the most brutal means to achieve it.

Though religious faith varied widely throughout England's American colonies, the fundamental faith-based ideology of expansion was not all that different in Boston than it was in Jamestown or Charleston. Indeed, despite its diversity in detail, a shared Christian faith was in general the only thing that tied virtually all the British colonists together. The (mostly) Protestant colonists believed themselves to be on a holy mission, blessed by God, to spread the Protestant faith through their own migration, the conversion of Indians, and the containment of Catholicism. English Protestants saw themselves as a chosen people destined to preserve their liberties by cultivating a new England overseas. The most important result of this endeavor was that it led the English to conflate the survival of a religious ideology—specifically, Protestantism—with the survival of the nation. Their own sense of physical security, in other words, became inextricably bound up with the fate of an idea. England could only be its true self if it remained Protestant, and it could only remain Protestant in a world where it was protected from the domineering ambitions of the Catholic Church. Should Catholicism prosper or Protestantism suffer, anywhere, the very security of England itself would be in danger—hence the "Protestant Cause" of solidarity between the English and their beleaguered fellow Protestants in Europe. Inhabiting the world's one true bastion of political and religious liberty, the English had both a moral imperative and a defensive duty to spread their way of life as widely as they could. They owed themselves—and the world—no less.[6]

This Protestant exceptionalism would continue into the eighteenth century—the subject of Chapter 3—in a series of wars between Great Britain and its Catholic and Indian enemies that would last from 1689 to 1763. In the process of forever destroying the threat of the Catholic Antichrist and the Indian Satan, the British American colonists would begin to devise a more general theory of liberty, uniquely American in its conception and application, that married a libertarian Protestant church to a free republican government. Not coincidentally, the wars for empire unfolded within a framework of religious revivals known collectively as the Great Awakening.

CHAPTER ONE

Defenders of the Faith

L IKE THE SPANISH BEFORE them, the English who sought to colonize North America in the late sixteenth century did so in the name of God. Spreading Christianity through two means—transplanting the English and converting the Indians—helped drive these first efforts at imperialism. Upon touring the coast of California in 1579, the famed explorer Sir Francis Drake, whose father was a minister, wanted to open the "blinded eyes" of the local Indians by introducing them to "the right knowledge and obedience of the true and everliving God." A copy of John Foxe's *The Book of Martyrs*—among Protestants a book almost as sacred as the Bible itself—reportedly sailed with Drake to provide shipboard inspiration. A hardened explorer and jaded pirate, Drake was not entirely motivated by a desire to spread Christianity. But so great was the urge to enlarge the faith that even he felt the need to justify his exploits in terms of religion.[1]

Indeed, the very fact that the New World had been revealed to Europeans was itself thought to be an act of God. These new lands offered Europe a chance to resettle people from its growing populations, and in the process spread Christianity. But—in a development that would set England, and later America, apart—following the Reformation it was imperative that the type of Christianity be Protestant. John Jewel, the Protestant bishop of Salisbury, agreed with Catholics that the Indians lived a life of inherent sin, "going naked, having no manner sense, nor knowledge of God, but falling down either before an old tree, or before the sun, and the moon, or whatsoever thing they saw first in the morning." But their salvation could never come from the Catholic faith. Even in their state of idolatrous ignorance, Jewel declared to a Catholic adversary in 1570, the Indians "might see both your and our religion set open before them, I doubt not, but nature herself would lead to judge, that ours is the Light, and yours Darkness."[2]

England's leading intellectual architect of colonial expansion, a man who seamlessly blended the objectives of church and state, was Richard Hakluyt, a well-connected graduate of Christ Church, Oxford, and an ordained Church of England minister. Religious faith did not solely shape Hakluyt's considerable scholarship—classical learning and the new humanism were just as important—yet it did play an immensely significant role in the widespread propagation, promotion, and legitimation of his views on New World settlement. Like many of his contemporaries, Hakluyt was as fiercely opposed to the Catholic Church, which he feared as a source of despotism, as he was devoted to Protestantism. With his tales of foreign adventure and discovery—not only of English exploration but travels by Europeans in general—Hakluyt became his era's most famous and authoritative chronicler of European expansion. Very much in tune with the spirit of the times, he was just as interested in geography as he was in theology. In Hakluyt's worldview, which came to shape England's early colonization of America, geography and theology would combine in a spiritual geopolitics of transatlantic expansion. Catholics, he believed, aimed to extinguish the passionate, reformed fires of liberty Protestantism had lit. As the leading Protestant power, England's very fate hung in the balance of its conflict with Spain. In his twin quests to spread Protestantism and English power, Hakluyt portrayed the New World as the decisive theater of conflict between the two rival Christian faiths. Given its century-long head start, Spain held a dangerous advantage.[3]

Fearing that England was falling behind its Catholic European rivals in the New World, Hakluyt combined the strategic urgency of spreading England's trade and territory with the zeal to spread its Protestant faith into a compelling argument for overseas expansion. His message was a powerful blend of territorial, ideological, and commercial ambition that many of his Elizabethan countrymen found impossible to resist. One of the most important tasks, something that would justify the imperial enterprise overall, was the conversion of the benighted savages who had lived for too long without God. It was necessary, Hakluyt wrote in his widely influential 1584 tract, *Discourse of Western Planting*, "for the salvation of those poore people which have sitten so longe in darkenes and in the shadowe of deathe, that preachers should be sent unto them." The kings and queens of England, he pointed out, "have the name of Defendors of the Faithe," which obliged them not only to protect Protestantism at home but also "to inlarge and advaunce" it beyond England's shores. And while Hakluyt appreciated that any colony would have to be commercially successful to survive and could not rely on faith alone, he thought faith would be its most important and ultimately determining trait. "Firste seek the kingdome of God and the righteousness thereof," he instructed, "and all other thinges shalbe mynistred unto you." Politics and economics were thus intimately mixed with faith.[4]

The infamous "Black Legend," in which English writers detailed (and exaggerated) the uncommon barbarism and cruelty of Spanish colonialism in Latin America, played a large part in creating this worldview and provided English colonial activists with a powerful ideological weapon that endured well into the eighteenth century. The Black Legend contrasted sharply with England's supposed benevolence and concern for the welfare of the indigenous peoples. In a moral and ideological sense, it was an important rhetorical tool to justify England's overseas expansion. The Spanish, Hakluyt charged, were "pretending in glorious words" in their missionary efforts, but "in deed and truth sought not them [the Indians], but their goods and riches." The virtuous English, on the other hand, would educate, enlighten, and Christianize the ignorant peoples who had the good fortune to find themselves under English rule.[5]

The Black Legend's power stemmed from the notion, prevalent in England's domestic politics as well as its foreign relations, that Catholics were inherently expansionist. Abroad, Catholics threatened English liberties and security with the might of the Spanish and French militaries; at home, they did so through a fifth column of Catholic traitors. Catholicism sought power and influence, especially at the expense of those who challenged its moral authority; it could not tolerate rival religions. Fear and loathing of Catholicism fueled England's foreign policy to such an extent that English patriotism became suffused with, even indistinguishable from, Protestantism. Sure enough, Spain's attempted invasion of England in 1588, and then its sponsorship of the Catholic League of France afterward, simply confirmed its innate aggressiveness and rapaciousness. The English had to remain vigilant, a stance that took them to Holland, where they fought alongside their fellow Protestants, the Dutch, against Spanish rule (just as Irish Catholics went to Holland to fight with the Spanish against the Protestants).[6]

What seemed to make the papist conspiracy so dangerous was that all Catholic roads led to Rome. England, virtuous but isolated, was up against a worldwide conspiracy orchestrated by the Vatican. "It is most certaine and true that the king of Spaine is wholie addicted to the Pope," the explorer Sir Humphrey Gilbert warned Elizabeth in 1577. In thrall to a despotic pope, the Spanish were duty-bound to promote the Vatican's agenda and were "thereby an enemie to all others that not be of the same religion." So long as the Spanish "be of that religion and we of ours there can be betwene us and them no good friendship." Sir Humphrey's solution was for England to go on the offensive in the Caribbean and seize the islands of Hispaniola and Cuba. This was an unfeasibly ambitious and, given the strength of the Spanish navy at the time, foolish plan that Elizabeth sensibly ignored. Yet three decades later, after a string of victories in the Atlantic and the Caribbean, the colony of Virginia fit neatly into this strategy of defensive expansionism.[7]

Thanks in part to Samuel Purchas, so too would New England. Purchas was Hakluyt's successor as chief propagandist for the expansion of

English power and the Protestant faith. Even more than Hakluyt, Purchas was passionately committed to the spread of the gospel. Like Hakluyt, he was a minister in the Church of England; like Hakluyt, he thought of Catholicism as a threat to England's security, its political freedom, and its religious faith; and like Hakluyt, Purchas thought that England's best defense was the offense of New World settlement. "[S]o little a part of the World in name *Christian*!" he lamented, "and so not little covered over . . . with Antichristian Heresie!"[8]

The main difference between them was timing. Hakluyt wrote in the final decades of the sixteenth century, when England was just beginning to mount its colonial enterprise. Purchas wrote in the 1620s, after the establishment of Virginia and the migration of the Pilgrims to Plymouth Colony. Thus Purchas knew, as Hakluyt could not, the difficulties that English colonists would face as they built their new lives in the New World. Accordingly, he portrayed the native peoples of North America as just as great a threat—albeit of a different kind—as Roman Catholics, branding them "Outlawes of Humanity," "unnaturall Naturalls" who were "like Cain, both Murtherers and Vagabonds." In a tremendously important conclusion that would justify the seizure of Indian territory for centuries to come, Purchas argued that the Indians had forfeited their claim to the land by not cultivating or taming it for permanent settlement. In the book of Genesis, God had given people the right to cultivate, and own, any vacant land they encountered, and so the wild and untamed New World, Purchas informed his audiences, was rightfully there for the taking.[9]

Before he became a successful author, Purchas had been renowned as a gifted storyteller. He would regale the people of his local parish in Eastwood, in the Puritan heartland of Essex, with tales of foreign adventure—though not his own, for he had had none—and exotic lands. He would tell them about the Virginia Company, whose members were trying to establish a godly Protestant community among the heathen savage. For his stories, his standing, and his piety, which was not exactly Puritan but not all that far off, he was a frequent guest at the local manor, Rochford Hall. One evening in 1606, one of his listeners was a young man by the name of John Winthrop, son-in-law of the family who lived at Rochford Hall. A few decades later, Winthrop would become the founding governor of Massachusetts, the driving force behind the English colony that most successfully blended faith and fortune. As Winthrop's biographer Francis Bremer writes, Purchas's riveting tales "resonated with his godly audience," for although they emphasized the economic and strategic benefits of overseas expansion, they were first and foremost "wrapped in a call to religious service."[10]

· · ·

ENGLAND'S INITIAL ATTEMPTS at North American colonization were fitful, amateurish, and, as a result, spectacularly unsuccessful. One of the main problems was that expectations for English settlement on the North American shore had been shaped by the Spanish experience in Mexico and South America, where armies of conquistadores and Catholic missionaries were reaping untold riches in both gold and souls. Conditions further north were far different, although this was at first lost on English explorers. Hakluyt had been infuriated by the second and third expeditions of Martin Frobisher, who in the 1570s had looked for gold instead of the Northwest Passage. If "we had not been led with a preposterous desire of seeking rather gaine than God's glorie," Hakluyt chastised other New World adventurers, England would not be losing its imperial race with Spain. Yet at Roanoke, a lost island colony established off the North Carolina coast in 1585 and mysteriously abandoned five years later, even the godly met with a similar fate; this complete failure led to the postponement of other plans for American settlement. Still, the men who had headed the venture were devout Protestants who hoped to establish a godly realm in the name of the English crown. As one of them put it, their objectives were simple: "1. To plant Christian religion. 2. To trafficke. 3. To conquer."[11]

For a brief time, war with Spain and the fate of Roanoke deterred other would-be colonists. But peace finally came in 1604 and opened the flow of money for colonial enterprise and shipping lanes for commercial sailing. In 1607, having been granted an exclusive charter to settle all the land between present-day North Carolina and New York, the Virginia Company established a permanent settlement, Jamestown, in the coastal, malarial swampland of lower Chesapeake Bay. While they again hoped to find precious metals and other riches, this time the colonists were careful to frame their enterprise as a religious mission. Expansion would bring with it spiritual as well as material wealth because it would spread properly Christian—that is, Protestant—values to the Indians. In a perfect marriage of merchant and missionary zeal the colonists, declared the Governing Council, would "buy" from the Indians "the pearles of earth, and sell to them the pearles of heaven." Richard Hakluyt was an original charter member of the Virginia Company, while Samuel Purchas was among its most fervent supporters in England.[12]

Profit was important, but Virginia was in large part a missionary enterprise and the colonists, backed by sponsors in England, regarded their journey to the New World as a sacred mission. Although it would wane as the years passed, Virginia was founded in a spirit of intense religious fervor. Relative to population, the colonists enjoyed an even higher concentration of trained ministers than did the mother country, and religious observances were officially mandated and strictly enforced. Everyone involved in the project was swept along by the holiness of its mission. As the poet John Donne, a member of the Virginia Company who encouraged his son to emigrate there, instructed a group about to embark for the colony, "Your principal end is not gain, nor glory, but to gain souls to the glory of God. This seals the great seal, this justifies itself, this authorises authority, and gives power to strength itself."[13]

In the eyes of the first generation of colonists, the marriage between faith and nation was bound to be a happy one, for God had already baptized Virginia as a promised land that, in the words of one settler, would "flow with milk and honey." This was an important vision, central to the idea of expansion, for the promised land meant that the settlers of Virginia must be a chosen people. It could be no other way: only God's chosen few could inhabit the land promised to his people. In the Bible (Luke 12:32), Jesus speaks of his followers as a "little flock," a faithful, special minority whose mission was to spread the gospel to the rest of world; they would lead, and others would follow. Despite the trials of the first settlement efforts, Virginians perceived their colony as blessed, a refuge and repository for Christian civilization. "So then here is a place," John Smith wrote in 1612, "a nurse for souldiers, a practise for marriners, a trade for marchants, a reward for the good, and that which is most of all, a businesse (most acceptable to God) to bring such poore infidels to the true knowledge of God and his holy Gospell."[14]

But the promised land had to be free from contagion, and so containment was as important as conversion. Thus in addition to saving the souls of lost Indians, the need for geopolitical advantage over Spain drove English expansion forward. Just as it had shaped the initial push for colonization among Hakluyt and his contemporaries, anti-Catholicism added necessity, not to mention a great deal of urgency, to the settling of Virginia. In making this point, many of Virginia's advocates invoked the Black Legend; others played upon England's own schismatic sectarian turmoil. William Symonds, for example, combined patriotism with Protestantism when he admonished Virginia's leaders "to carry thither no Traitors, nor Papists that depend on the Great Whore."[15]

Toward the end of his life, Hakluyt reflected on Virginia with evident pride. The settlers had founded a free, patriotic, and faithful Protestant society where the "Preachers shall be reverenced and cherished, the valiant and forward soldiour respected, the diligent rewarded, the coward emboldened, the weake and sick relieved, the mutinous suppressed, the reputation of the Christians among the Savages preserved, our most holy faith exalted, all Paganisme and Idolatrie by little and little utterly extinguished"—in short, a promised land. The establishment of Virginia had been an enormously difficult enterprise, and its survival would not be assured for several decades. Hakluyt would have been forgiven had he despaired, but his faith in an English, Protestant Virginia never wavered. This was the nature of his ideological commitment and religious zeal, traits that helped cast in iron an emerging colonial self-perception that America was a different and special place.[16]

IF VIRGINIANS THOUGHT THEMSELVES EXCEPTIONAL, the intensity of their self-confidence was nothing compared to the unshakeable self-righteousness of their English neighbors further north. Everything that had helped to form the worldview of Virginia was magnified several times in the godly colonies of New England. A key difference was their brand of Protestantism: instead of the establishment Anglicanism of Virginia, the people who founded and settled New England were reformed Calvinists—mostly Puritan Congregationalists—who believed that the Church of England had become almost as corrupt as the Roman Catholic Church. Theirs was a purer form of worship that relied only on the word and spirit of God, not a decadent, liturgically driven hierarchy. Puritans who rejected Anglican ways were more passionate, rigorous, and dogmatic than their fellow Protestants. The Puritans of New England, observed an astonished Dutch trader and fellow Calvinist, had established a moral code of "stringent laws" that they "maintain and enforce very strictly indeed." It was this uncompromising theological rigor that drove them across the Atlantic in 1630.[17]

Few addresses in American history have been as exhaustively quoted as John Winthrop's sermon, delivered on the deck of his ship *Arbella* while en route to Massachusetts, that invoked the image of a Puritan "city on a hill" to instill unity and purpose. The Puritans thought of themselves as exceptional. They believed they were different from, and better than, not only Catholics and Indians, but also Anglicans and even other Protestants, such as Quakers and Baptists. They were, Winthrop reminded them, God's chosen people who sought a freer life. Using the favorite Puritan trope of the covenant, Winthrop told his fellow migrants that they had formed a pact with God: he would deliver them safely to the New World, while they had to build and maintain a properly Christian community. So long as they upheld their end of the covenant, Winthrop promised,

> the Lord will be our God and delight to dwell among us, as his own
> people and will commaund a blessing upon us in all our wayes . . . wee
> shall finde that the God of Israell is among us, when tenn of us shall
> be able to resist a thousand of our enemies, when hee shall make us a
> prayse and glory, that men shall say of succeeding plantacions: the lord

make it like that of New England: for wee must Consider that wee shall
be as a Citty upon a Hill, the eies of all people are upon us . . .[18]

Should they betray God, Winthrop warned that the Puritans would be
cast out and made a terrible example of dealing falsely with the Lord.
An embattled minority of a spiritual elite, the Puritans saw themselves as
conductors of a noble experiment that must be defended at all costs. They
were God's chosen ones; now they must live like it.

As historians have pointed out, Winthrop's sermon, so famous today,
generated little comment at the time because its themes and allusions
were so commonplace among Calvinist Puritans. Chosenness provided an extremely powerful motivation for the move to New England,
and subsequent expansion within it, precisely because it was so commonplace. Massachusetts would of course have its own dissenters and
nonconformists—competing "orthodoxies," in Janice Knight's telling, as
opposed to Winthrop's illusion of consensus—but for the most part the
notion that the Puritans had embarked upon a mission from God went
unquestioned.[19]

The Puritans left England, their home, reluctantly. Suffering the persecutions of Bishop William Laud's Church of England, they felt they had
little choice but to go into exile; and like all exiles, they hoped one day
to return to their homeland. However, though they did not always enjoy
it, once in exile they sought to establish a truer, purified style of worship, modeled on the early Christians, that would eventually reform the
mother church itself. The allure of erecting a reformed church in New
England was strong, and it played a significant factor in drawing the Puritans across the Atlantic. Many began to perceive New England as a haven
of religious liberty. It was the exile's refuge, a sacred space to wait while
the fury of religious tyranny exhausted itself back home—"a refuge,"
Winthrop believed, "for many whom [God] meanes to save out of the
general callamity." Or as Thomas Hooker, the founder of Connecticut,
remarked after the first wave of Puritans had sailed from England, "God
begins to ship away his Noahs. God makes account that New England
shall be a refuge for his Noahs . . . a rock and a shelter for his righteous
ones to run unto."[20]

While Hakluyt, Purchas, and others argued that God had anointed
England as a chosen nation, the Puritans gave this familiar conceit a new
twist. Instead of looking solely to the book of Genesis for inspiration, they
saw their own plight as a sequel to the book of Exodus. New England was
their promised land. In this idea lay the seeds of permanent settlement,
of the transition from exile to migration, and of the idea that America,
not England, was the land of the chosen people. If the Puritans obeyed
the terms of their covenant with God, their new home would be the site

of a New Israel. While the topography and climate of New England were physically daunting, the land itself could also be spiritually liberating. Sheltered from the evils of a fallen Europe plagued by Turks and Catholics, and from an England that had been corrupted by an Anglican church that had lost its way, New England was not only vacant but untainted, waiting to be used by a pious and hardworking people. It was a promised land that quickly became *the* promised land. Massachusetts, described by one of the first settlers as "our new paradise,"[21] was just such a place, and would provide all of the Puritans' spiritual and material needs. Only America could provide refuge for the godly.

The Puritans knew this because God had revealed it to them. Providential thinking played a large part in the everyday life of early modern England. People from all ranks of society invested ordinary occurrences with sacred meaning about God's intentions for the future, and acted accordingly. But while providence was taken seriously by most English people, nobody invested it with as much significance as the Puritans. As strict Calvinists who believed in predestination and a God who was an active participant in the daily life of earthly matters, the Puritans thought they could determine God's will and guidance when he chose to reveal it to them through miraculous signs in everyday life. Thus the offer of a religious refuge across the ocean, the fact that it was to be a community peopled entirely by the godly (at least, that was the intention), and the colony's early success were all signs, in Edward Johnson's timeless phrase, of God's "wonder-working providence." As John Cotton preached in his 1630 sermon "God's Promise to His Plantations" to those who were about to sail for New England, "God assigned out such a land for such a posterity, and for such a time." Or as he later explained to a skeptical colleague who did not see the need to move, God had "shutt a dore" in England while "openinge a dore to us" in Massachusetts.[22]

OVER A CENTURY had passed between the European discovery of the Americas and the Puritan migration to Massachusetts, and so by the 1620s the question of native peoples was nothing new. It would, however, prove to be no less perplexing. The first generation of migrants to New England believed much of their effort would be focused on converting Indians to the gospel. The founding charter of the Massachusetts Bay Company stated that its primary goal was "to incite the natives . . . to the knowledge and obedience of the onlie true God and Saviour of mankinde." Tellingly, instead of a scriptural quotation or other biblical injunction, the official seal of the Massachusetts Bay Colony pictured an Indian pleading, "Come Over and Help Us," an allusion to an episode in the Book of Acts (16:9) when Paul has a vision of the Macedonians crying out to him with these same words. (Not coincidentally, the Puritans gave the Wampanoag chief Metacom the name of Philip, half-brother to the Macedonian ruler Alexander the Great.) Converting the Indians, moreover, would have the additional effect—perhaps more important than conversion itself—of checking Catholic advances in the New World, by Spain to the south and, increasingly as the century wore on, France to the north. As Winthrop recorded, by converting the native population New England would act as a "bullwarke" against the "kingdom of Antichrist which the Jesuites laboure to rear."[23] Hakluyt and Purchas could not have put it any better.

But as the decades passed, it became clear that succeeding generations of colonists lacked the fervor of their founding ancestors. In the words of the historian Jon Butler, the middle decades of the seventeenth century marked a "starving time" for institutional Christianity in the colonies. In Virginia, greater numbers of immigrants arrived with trade and agriculture instead of religion on their minds. Fewer people attended church and observed religious occasions, the ratio of ministers to the general population fell, and those ministers who did continue to preach were often just as profane as their impious congregants. Christian belief endured, but the colonists' fealty to institutional religion was altogether much more fragile. Even in the "Bible Commonwealth" of Massachusetts, church membership plummeted sharply: in 1650, for example, only a third of Boston's residents were members of the church; by 1677, only 15 percent of Northampton residents claimed church membership.[24]

In both Virginia and Massachusetts, the conversion of Indians to Christianity was a major casualty of the ebb of organized religion. Henrico College, established solely to convert and educate Virginia's Indians, closed in 1619 even before it could open. By the 1640s, the numbers of colonists engaged in farming and trade had long passed those involved in missionary work. The evangelists of New England fared better than their counterparts in Virginia, but not by much: while the Indian College at Harvard actually opened its doors to Indians, only five were educated there, and the college was quickly closed. Thanks to the ravages of war and disease, actual missionary endeavors did not really get under way in Massachusetts until the 1640s. True, the indefatigable John Eliot, famed for his painstaking translations of the Bible into Algonquin languages and his establishment of several "praying towns" inhabited by converted Indians, had some success in bringing the gospel to the native peoples of Massachusetts. There was also Thomas Mayhew, who converted hundreds of Indians on Martha's Vineyard. But in both instances, and despite some evidence of genuine, faithful conversions, Indians often converted for their own, largely secular reasons—usually for material or political gain—and blended Christianity with local religious beliefs and customs to create a syncretic faith that bore little relation to Christianity and no resemblance at all to the rigid, doctrinaire Protestantism practiced by the

Puritans. So while Indians were converting to a kind of Christianity, it was not the Puritans' kind.[25]

As a result of unconverted Indians, converted but insincere Indians, cultural segregation, and war, the colonists' attitudes toward native peoples steadily hardened. Once perceived as essential goals of colonization itself, by the late seventeenth century conversion and assimilation were no longer considered possible and all but disappeared as colonial priorities. Inauspiciously for the Indians, this repeated a pattern established by the English conquest of Ireland in the latter half of the sixteenth century. Like the Irish, the Indians came to be considered too barbaric to undergo complete conversion to Protestant Christianity and adhere to civilized codes of conduct. Both the Irish and the native peoples of North America were considered recalcitrant savages too ignorant to even realize the benefits they were spurning. First impressions of innocence thus gave way to the notion that the New World must be conquered, its wild, unknown evils tamed and defeated.[26]

Negative stereotypes about the Indians thrived in such an atmosphere. Native Americans provided English colonists with a "social mirror" that reflected the English religious, social, and political ideals with their complete, ghastly opposites. And to early modern Europeans, the main thing that distinguished them from the Indians was not race, but religion, from which conceptions about racial, ethnic, and cultural difference flowed. While English Protestants were enlightened by a Christian God and the Protestant faith, the Indians worshipped inauthentic pagan gods of dubious morality; while English families and communities were harmonious, organic models of charitable order and Christian virtue, Indian society was disordered, chaotic, and oppressive; while the English cultivated God's land, the Indians allowed it to lie fallow, untamed and unproductive; while the English inhabited bodies—with fair skin and fine hair—that were assumed to be a reflection of God's image, Indians and African slaves had dark skin that was further blemished by tattoos and other markings of the devil; and while the English enjoyed knowledge and certain natural rights that went with it, the Indians lived a life of ignorance and enslavement. The Indians were barbaric, and barbarians could be easily distinguished from the English, and dealt with accordingly.[27]

The notion of the promised land, then, could be read in two ways, as both promising and perilous. After the colonists had lived in the New World for a few years, they could see for themselves that it had not necessarily been given to them through God's grace—or, if it had, that God was intent on making them earn it. Indeed, the haunted "wilderness," an inverted image of the "land of milk and honey," dominated the thoughts and stoked the fears of the colonists across English North America. The land was potentially a promised land, but first it must be cleansed of the evil influences that already lurked there. To the people of Massachusetts Bay, the woods that surrounded their towns and villages provided a home for dark forces, both Indian and French, that were committed to their destruction. The wilderness, threatening and malevolent, must be tamed if the Puritan experiment was to survive. "So Sathan may stir up and combyne many of his Instruments against the Churches of Christ," declared the New England Confederation in 1645, but "the Lord of Hostes, the mighty one in battaile," will defend his people and bring about their salvation.[28]

CHAPTER TWO

God Is an Excellent Man of War

R ELIGIOUS FAITH WAS CENTRAL to the colonial way of warfare. It provided ideological glue in times of tremendous social stress, gave its adherents a set of beliefs and assumptions that allowed them to fight for legitimate and worthy causes, and freed them to use methods that would otherwise have been deemed immoral. Here the concept of holy war, grounded paradoxically in the theory of the just war, played a decisive role. Convinced of their own righteousness and their enemy's evil, in two major Puritan-Indian wars—the Pequot War of 1636–37 and King Philip's War of 1675–76—the colonists' bloody tactics rivaled the atrocities found on the early modern battlefields of Europe. For their part, the Indians also fought for their values, beliefs, and religion, and they too waged war without restraint. This was the process that the historian J. H. Elliott aptly describes as war "for the sacralization of American space."[1]

War, both literally and as metaphor, was central to the Puritan mind, just as military establishments were central to Puritan society (despite the wary ambivalence some Puritans, such as John Winthrop, felt toward a standing militia). The church and the militia were not competitors, but partners. As John Cotton explained to his congregation during the Pequot War, "the rulers of the people should consult with the ministers of the churches upon occasion of any war to be undertaken." Although the Puritans' politics were radical, their instincts were at the same time conservative. They cherished an ordered society and, at the individual level, admired discipline. Above all, they sought devotional rigor and an orderly church, so it is not especially surprising that they viewed the military regiment as a secular counterpart to the church. The English Puritan Richard Sibbes, one of the most influential spiritual mentors to the New Englanders, saw something divine in the strict discipline of the military. "The people of God," he wrote of his fellow Puritans, "are beautiful, for order is beautiful. . . . An army is a beautiful thing, because of the order and the well-disposed ranks that are within it. In this regard the church is beautiful." When it came time to establish a colonial militia, the Massachusetts authorities initially decreed that soldiers must also be members of the Congregational Church.[2]

But militias were common everywhere in colonial America; the Puritans' true innovation was to legitimize their use. Whether it was resisting Catholicism in Europe, subduing unruly subjects in Ireland, waging civil war in England, or fighting various Indian tribes in New England, the Puritans legitimized the practice of warfare and broadened its acceptability. True to their educated and disciplined traditions, they justified the expansion of war through their biblically inspired revision of the European just war tradition.

Just war theory covers the two primary stages of warfare: cause (*jus ad bellum*) and conduct (*jus in bello*). To satisfy the requirements of *jus ad bellum*, a nation's reasons for going to war must be legitimate; and to be legitimate, they must be sanctioned by a duly recognized authority, pursued for a just and righteous purpose, and intended to secure a noble and lasting peace. To satisfy the requirements of *jus in bello*, a nation must fight with proportionate and discriminate force and must not deliberately target civilians. By the early modern period, just war theory aimed to place limitations, by way of explicit moral boundaries, on why and how people wage war. It is, and has been for centuries, an attempt to impose rules and order on an inherently chaotic and disorderly practice.[3]

Despite its familiarity to the modern sensibility, just war theory is by no means a recent development. Nor is it necessarily Western or Christian, let alone Puritan: attempts to codify the rules of war were hallmarks of ancient Chinese and Greek philosophy and Hindu spirituality. In the European tradition, just war theory emerged in the fifth-century theology of St. Augustine and was later refined in the medieval writings of St. Thomas Aquinas. In the centuries that followed, the concept of the just war developed into a sophisticated school of thought that outlined when, why, and how it was morally acceptable for nations to wage war. The Puritans' contemporaries in early modern Europe, most famously Hugo Grotius, the Dutch legal philosopher and founder of international law, tested and adapted the just war concept along such lines. Many others were Spaniards, such as Bartolomé de Las Casas and Francisco de Vitoria, who were appalled by their own country's brutal conquest of the New World. When English Puritans turned their attention to just war theory in the late sixteenth and early seventeenth centuries, efforts to limit the scope of warfare, perhaps leading to the end of war itself, had been present in European philosophy, politics, and theology for a thousand years and prominent for at least a hundred.[4]

Indeed, the Puritans formed their own ideas on warfare at the precise historical moment when the just war tradition that had descended from Augustine to Thomas Aquinas through precedent, custom, scripture, and Christian doctrine was forming into a fairly cohesive body of international law and acknowledged if not always accepted practice. Yet while the Puritans were aware of this development—just war theory was debated avidly by English clergy of all denominations, and Grotius was closely read by New England's churchmen—they chose a characteristically different, self-righteous path. They decided to use just war theory to expand rather than limit the scope of war, and in doing so turned just war theory on its head: if the cause be just, the methods did not matter.[5]

While this was quite a departure from the just war tradition, the Puritans did not invent offensive war. In fact, for all its intentions to limit the scope of war, at the heart of just war theory lies a paradox: Augustine first devised it in order to legitimate warfare. After all, Christianity is an innately pacifistic religion, and so establishing acceptable rules of making war would enable Christians to fight when their religious beliefs otherwise forbade them from doing so. After Emperor Constantine's conversion, the newly Christian Roman Empire was not secure enough to allow it to abandon the use of force, and so theology had to find a way to accommodate reality. Several centuries later, the Vatican issued a series of elaborate doctrinal justifications to support the Crusaders' campaigns to seize the Holy Land from the heathen Muslim. This, for the first time, was the just war as holy war, which justified war without mercy if the enemy proved beyond the outer limits of civilization, and thus redemption. Nonetheless, despite its aggressive uses during the late Roman Empire and the Crusades, by the early seventeenth century just war theorists were attempting to limit the spread of war and constrain methods of fighting. This was certainly the prevailing view, eventually solidified and secularized as the "rule of law" by Grotius toward the end of the Thirty Years' War. By 1648, the just war had effectively begun to replace the holy war.[6]

But not among the Puritans. Following the Crusaders' example, Puritan divines resurrected the idea of holy war against the unfaithful. Belligerent in the name of spreading the sacred and eradicating the profane, holy warriors explicitly called for offensive war. A nation could—indeed, should—initiate war in the pursuit of its mission. For the first time since the Crusades, prominent European thinkers, led by English Puritans, used the concept of the just war to expand, rather than limit, the boundaries of *jus ad bellum*. War was evil, they acknowledged, but a necessary evil—though as the sixteenth century gave way to the seventeenth, the Puritans began to think of war less frequently as evil and more fervently as necessary. In doing so, they relied on the fire-and-brimstone bellicosity of the Old Testament and ignored Christ's pacifist teachings in the New. They even began to think of war as a glorious endeavor and of God as the ultimate warlord. "God is an excellent Man of War," preached Alexander Leighton, and the Bible was "the best handbook on war." For Puritans, scripture provided literal guidance on all earthly matters, and warfare was no different. There was, Leighton explained, "No better Philosophy,

Logick, or Metaphysick, then in the book of God. No better counsel or direction for war or peace . . . there is to be found." Unwilling to let their militaristic fervor be diluted by their religious contemporaries, they rejected the antiwar arguments of their fellow Protestants, particularly Anabaptists, Baptists, and Quakers; in the 1640s, the Massachusetts General Court felt it necessary to pass a law directed against Baptists for denying "the lawfulness of making war."[7]

But the Puritans did not simply argue that war was lawful; they viewed it as a sacred duty to campaign against the enemies of God, with whom there could be no neutrality or lenience. In the European context, this meant extending Protestantism at the expense of the satanic Catholic conspiracy, both internal (recalcitrant Catholics in the British Isles) and external (France, and especially Spain). Leading Puritan ministers in England, such as Leighton and William Gouge, argued the case for waging war in the name of God, which in the 1620s meant intervening in the Thirty Years' War. God, according to the Puritan minister Thomas Sutton, was closest to those who would wage war in his name. "Above all creatures," Sutton preached, God "loves souldiers; above all exercises, commends fighting; above all actions, he honors warlike and martiall designes." Even Christ was a warrior, and the angels his army. Evil was a fact of life, a daily presence, but this did not mean one should simply accept its existence. Indeed, it was the Puritan's duty to identify evil and eradicate it ruthlessly.[8]

The extreme turn in the Puritans' views on war had as much to do with the polarization of political and religious life in England, a dynamic that by the 1640s would explode in the incendiary violence of the English Civil War. In particular, the first decades of the seventeenth century witnessed the renewal of English Catholicism, the refusal of the Church of England to reform, and the increasing persecution of the Puritans themselves, especially after the rise of Bishop Laud in the 1620s. Against this backdrop, Puritan justifications for offensive holy war reached a crescendo in England at precisely the moment Winthrop and his colleagues were planning to set sail for America. Had they not emigrated when they did—say, several decades earlier, or after the Stuart Restoration in 1660— it is doubtful they would have carried with them such an intensely radical worldview.[9]

Just as the Puritans' expansion of just war theory made it easier for them to condone and initiate war, so too did it allow them to widen the scope of what was acceptable on the battlefield, or *jus in bello*. Michael Walzer, a leading just war theorist, has observed that the component parts of just war theory are not necessarily complementary—a nation can launch a just war and yet wage it unjustly, and vice versa. The Puritans simplified matters by expanding what was permissible according to both. In other words, they removed many of the constraints that tended to limit the intensity and violence of warfare. Because their wars would be fought over nonnegotiable religious principles, the Puritans did not, at least in theory, recognize or protect civilian noncombatants. This was not an inconsistency—quite the opposite, for if a Christian saw fit to wage holy war in the name of God, why should he restrain himself when fighting the enemies of God? Though Puritans rejected realism, and claimed that it "is a shame for a Christian" to heed the teachings of Machiavelli, they did believe that achieving a holy end often required the use of unholy means—and even that a holy end legitimated normally unholy means. Accordingly, as England's warring factions demonized and delegitimized each other, the most brutal, grisly acts of holy war violence intensified the fighting of the Civil War.[10]

This extremism easily crossed the Atlantic, in both directions—radicals who had migrated to New England in the 1630s rushed to return home to rally sentiment against Charles I a decade later—and it pushed the ideas of many over the edge of civilized discourse. Referring to the Indians and Catholics who already inhabited the New World, John Cotton, one of the most respected and beloved of New England's ministers, declared that God *"would drive out the Heathen before them."* This "course of warring against others, & driving them out without provocation," he told a group of Puritans departing for Massachusetts, "depends upon speciall Commission from God, or else it is not imitable." Needless to say, the Puritans felt they had been given such a commission. Later, Cotton defended his English brethren against the shocking and previously unthinkable crime of regicide, telling his Boston congregation that the beheading of King Charles I in 1649 was gruesome but necessary, perhaps even deserved.[11]

Given the close intellectual and political ties between Puritans on both sides of the Atlantic, and given its easy applicability to conflicts with the supposedly savage, godless Indians of the New World, it is easy to see why the concept of holy war found a receptive audience in New England. The Puritans of New England must "take, kill, burn, sink, destroy all sin and Corruption which are professed enemies to Christ Jesus," the Reverend Joshua Moodey preached in 1674 on the eve of King Philip's War with the Wampanoag Indians, "and not to pity or spare any of them."[12] As we shall see, the colonists proved themselves adept at appealing to God to justify unremitting, unsparing acts of war against their heathen enemies.

WITHIN A FEW years of migrating to America in 1630, the Puritans of Massachusetts had already expanded into Connecticut, in two separate colonies at Hartford and New Haven, and by the outbreak of war in 1636 several new Puritan settlements dotted the shores of the Connecticut River between Hartford and the open water of Long Island Sound. The Pequots, feared even by the other Indian tribes along the Atlantic coast—their name means "destroyers of men"—presented a particular challenge that was military and political as well as economic. After desultory negotiations, which included a 1634 treaty of mutual assistance that went largely unobserved by both sides, the colonists moved to reinforce their settlements by building a fort at the mouth of the Connecticut River at what is today the town of Old Saybrook and on land the Pequots considered rightfully theirs. They besieged the fort in the summer of 1636 but could not overrun it. As the siege continued, the Indians of nearby Block Island, allied to the Pequots, murdered John Oldham, an English trader. This had not been the first such killing; indeed, one of the terms of the 1634 treaty was that the Pequots would relinquish the perpetrators of past murders, though they never did.[13]

Although the actual circumstances of the murder were unclear, this further provocation convinced the authorities in Boston that they had to react. Winthrop claimed that Puritan forces would seek the Pequots "not to make war upon them, but to do justice." Yet it was a funny sort of justice, purely punitive in nature and in response for the most uncertain of crimes. Motivated as much by revenge as by concerns for safety and security, a raiding party under the command of John Endecott sailed from Boston in August 1636. Endecott was ideally suited to the task. Violent by nature and exceedingly zealous in his Puritanism, he represented the worst of Massachusetts's moral and ideological absolutism. But his attempts to put it into action failed miserably. Although the Indians had anticipated an attack and hid themselves, Endecott's men obliterated the Block Island community, razing its crops and burning its houses to the ground. They then sailed to the main Pequot village on the Connecticut shore, with the same result. Dispirited and discouraged, they returned to Boston. All Endecott and his men had done, complained Lion Gardiner, the commander of the Saybrook fort, was rouse the Pequots for an escalation of the conflict.[14]

Knowing they could not defeat the English colonists alone but realizing that the Connecticut River settlements were vulnerable, the Pequots approached their neighbors to the north, the Narragansett tribe in what is today Rhode Island, to form an alliance. The Puritans learned of the negotiations and sent Roger Williams, the Baptist exile from Puritan orthodoxy who was on fairly good terms with the Narragansetts, to prevent the alliance from happening. Not only did Williams succeed in splitting the Pequots from the Narragansetts, he secured an alliance between the Puritans and the Narragansetts against the Pequots. Puritan observers credited divine intervention with this turn of events. John Mason, the commander of Connecticut's forces, said that God, "by a more than ordinary providence," had kept the Indians divided at a moment of colonial vulnerability.[15]

The alliance waited until the following spring to assault the Pequot settlements. As they prepared, the Puritans turned to God's grace for protection and the tenets of holy war for instruction. One minister assured Mason's troops that they were acting on the will of the Lord and thus had every right "to execute those who God, the righteous judge of all the world, hath condemned for blaspheming his sacred majesty, and murthering his servants." They should, he preached, "execute vengeance upon the heathen [and] binde their Kings in chaines, and Nobles in fetters of Iron [and] make their multitudes fall under your warlike weapons." The normal restraints of civilized warfare, in other words, were now removed. The Pequots had proven themselves capable of evil that lay beyond what a Christian could rightfully accept; they were nothing but servants of the devil and could be treated as such. Thomas Hooker, the spiritually stalwart minister who had founded Hartford, urged Winthrop and his colleagues in Boston "to hasten execution" of war against the Pequots and "not to do this work of the Lords revenge slackly." In sermons, he exhorted the soldiers of Connecticut to do the same.[16]

With hearts thus hardened, and with the Pequots isolated thanks to the diplomatic heroics of Roger Williams, the Puritans taught the Pequots, and all other Indian tribes in the region, a harsh lesson in divine justice. The colonial authorities in Massachusetts and Connecticut raised small but sufficient armies totaling 250 men. In the spring of 1637, they marched under the guidance of their Narragansett allies toward the Pequot village of Fort Mystic on the Connecticut shore. Though outnumbered, the Puritans had the element of surprise, and they quickly breached the village's fortified walls. After wreaking havoc, they lit the settlement ablaze and withdrew from the walls of the village where they could kill anyone fleeing the inferno. It was a grisly scene, the first time that fighting in North America matched the brutality of European warfare. It was, in fact, uncommonly savage even for the supposed savage Indians, and the Narragansetts, bitter enemies of the Pequots and now allied to the Puritans, begged the English to stop. Many Pequots, from Fort Mystic and neighboring settlements, fled further west along the shore, away from the Puritan fighters and the Narragansetts' home territory in Rhode Island. But the Puritans tracked them down outside New Haven, where hundreds of Pequots were hiding in an impenetrable swamp. The Puritans offered safe passage for any noncombatants who left the swamp voluntarily; about two hundred did so, mostly women and children who were later sold into slavery. Unable to escape and unwilling to surrender, the recalcitrant warriors who remained were annihilated by the musket fire of the surrounding Puritans, whose advanced military technology proved too much for the Indians. A handful of the Pequot leadership fled during the tumult, but they could not escape the fact that, as a people, the Pequots had effectively been eradicated. It was, exulted the Reverend Thomas Shepard, a "divine slaughter."[17]

The Pequot War was undoubtedly a conflict over land and resources, a clash between two peoples who distrusted each other but wanted to occupy the same geographical space. Yet as Shepard acknowledged, from the Puritans' standpoint it was also a religious conflict, a holy war for control of spiritual space that the Puritans believed to be divinely sanctioned and, despite its violence, eminently just. Captain John Underhill of Massachusetts, who had previously fought with the English volunteers defending Protestantism against Spanish Catholic forces in the Netherlands, later reflected on the conflict's ferocity. Underhill acknowledged that "it may be demanded" of the Puritans: "Why should you be so furious . . . should not Christians have more mercy and compassion?" They should—but only if their enemy was similarly inspired by the word of God. "I would referre you to *Davids* warre," he argued, "when a people is grown to such a height of bloud, and sinne against God and man" that they lose all claim to honorable treatment. The Pequots had behaved not as men but like evil spirits ("wicked imps") and animals ("roaring lions, compassing all corners of the country for their prey"). By contrast the Puritans, brutal as they had been, had acted honorably and righteously. Claimed Underhill: "We had sufficient light from the word of God for our proceedings."[18]

The Puritans knew this to be true because, time and again, God had clearly favored his chosen people. Just as providence had ensured the survival of the Puritan settlements in the howling wilderness of New England, so too would he protect them against their savage, satanic enemies. A few pious malcontents, such as the free grace, antinomian heretic Anne Hutchinson, opposed the war as unnecessary and therefore unjust. But though these antiwar activists triggered a short-term enlistment crisis, they were very much rare exceptions to the general rule. Armed with God's righteousness and intent on establishing their unquestioned dominance over all the Indian tribes of New England, the Puritans negotiated the Treaty of Hartford in 1638 with the few surviving Pequots. Their terms were harsh, even by the standards of the time: the Pequot tribe was disbanded forever (even the very name "Pequot" was to be purged from human discourse); all Pequot settlements left standing after the war were razed; women and children were either sold into slavery in the Caribbean or given to other tribes in New England, such as the Mohegans and Narragansetts; and the heads of any Pequot warriors who had killed English soldiers had to be turned over to the colonial authorities.[19]

In both war and peace, the Puritans had ensured the total destruction of the Pequot nation. But the war's historical importance goes beyond questions of whether it amounted to an early instance of what we would today call genocide. The Puritans had settled Massachusetts and Connecticut under the sway of powerful myths, centered on faith, about their role in the world. They saw themselves as God's specially anointed people who had been chosen for their virtue, their faith, and their righteousness. Through its violence but, more important, through its themes of a holy war justly prosecuted, the Pequot War corroborated, even sanctified, these Puritan myths. Rather than wage war indiscriminately, so the Puritans thought, they had done so against a clear threat and according to the clearly defined laws of war. If Puritan exceptionalism had been strong before the war, it emerged stronger afterward.[20]

IN THE 1640s, another war, this time on English soil, gripped the colonial imagination. It was natural for the English Civil War to command the attentions of English colonists in America, for its central issues, particularly its religious core, were those that had brought them to the New World in the first place. For one thing, the conflict pitted Puritans and other dissenting sects against the Anglican Church; for another, its central cause pivoted upon the issue of political liberty, and whether sovereignty derived from the king's divine right to rule or from the people. The Pilgrims of Plymouth and the Puritans of Massachusetts and Connecticut had been most concerned with such questions that were at once both religious and political. Though the violence of the Civil War was not exported to the colonies—even dogmatic New England Puritans maintained a cautious neutrality knowing that their very existence depended upon London's prerogative, no matter who was in charge—many colonists took an active interest in its unfolding. The people of New England generally favored Parliament, while largely Anglican Virginia openly expressed its Royalist sympathies. Others, such as Roger Williams, criticized the dictatorial aspirations of both Royalists and Parliamentarians, Anglicans and Puritans. One way of cutting through the distracting calculations of political expediency to measure the colonies' true loyalties is to trace where the war's participants took refuge when their side was out of favor: between the regicide of Charles I in 1649 and the Restoration of the monarchy in 1660, Royalist Cavaliers sought asylum in Virginia; after the Restoration, Puritans and Parliamentarians fled to New Haven, where the revolutionary presence of John Dixwell, William Goffe, and Edward Whalley, who had signed Charles I's death warrant, endures in the names of three of the city's major thoroughfares.[21]

Authorities in New England strove to enforce neutrality, but they could do little to disguise the overwhelming sympathy of their people for Oliver Cromwell's Parliamentarians. Cromwell himself was a Puritan of the same theological and ideological stock as Winthrop and the other founders of Massachusetts. Although many prominent New Englanders refused Parliament's call to arms despite sympathizing with its cause, others returned to England to support Cromwell and the Puritan cause. In fact, the 1640s and '50s witnessed more emigration *from* than immigration *into* New England, with most leaving for England. Galvanized by the outbreak of war, politically motivated ministers such as Hugh Peter, Samuel Eaton, and Thomas Weld hurried from their pulpits in Massachusetts and Connecticut to sail back across the Atlantic. As one of Cromwell's closest advisers and the New Model Army's main chaplain, Peter became the most senior participant from the colonies. He was also something of a one-man Puritan revolution, having fought in Holland against the Spanish, preached in Massachusetts, and marched as a Roundhead alongside Cromwell in England.[22]

Faith-based arguments about political liberty found a receptive audience among New Englanders. One of the most radical arguments in nonconformist politics was that no earthly power had the right to come between God and his people. Owing their ultimate allegiance to God alone, only the people could impose government on earth. Anything else was artificial interference, and contrary to the will of God. Here we find an early expression of American republicanism, with its emphasis on government by the consent of the governed, that would later have a deep impact on the conduct of U.S. foreign policy. A radical, subversive group called the Fifth Monarchists, named for the reign of Christ that would follow the overthrow of the Antichrist's corrupt Fourth Monarchy under the Churches of Rome and England, advanced this argument further than most others dared. Among their leaders were Thomas Venner and William Aspinwall, Massachusetts Puritans who also returned to serve God's cause in England. By imbibing the heady Fifth Monarchist millennialism that flourished in New England, Venner and Aspinwall's time in the colonies had been vital in the formation of their religious and political radicalism. Especially important were the sermons and writings of John Cotton, who had written a 1636 legal code for Massachusetts that based the law on the teachings of the church rather than the interests of the state. The Fifth Monarchists' unorthodox theology would cost them support in Massachusetts (they were unabashed antinomians), but their arguments about the true sources of political legitimacy were an important precursor to the ideas of the American Revolution.[23]

New Englanders' revolutionary fervor ebbed as it became clear that Cromwell and the dream of godly reform had failed. Under a new king, Charles II, they did not dare challenge the monarchical rule that could end their very existence. Yet sympathy lingered still. As he passed through Boston on inspection a few years into the Restoration, Edward Randolph, a royal customs official, reported back to the Lords of Trade in London that New Englanders may have reconciled themselves to Charles II's rule, yet they nonetheless "held fast to the anti-monarchical principles spread among them." Religious and political liberty had already been intertwined together in the English colonial imagination, but if Randolph's testimony is reliable, the English Civil War entrenched the ideology of faith-based republicanism deeper still. Though it would lie dormant for years, Christian republicanism would again burst forth a century later to help shape the politics and foreign policy of a new nation.[24]

WITH THE COLONISTS' attention turned to events in the British Isles, an uneasy peace descended upon Puritan-Indian relations following the Pequot War. The colonists had demonstrated strength and ruthlessness in battle and the destructive power of their advanced weaponry. But just as important, they felt confident they had proved to the remaining tribes the superiority of their religion and way of life. Although it would take another four decades for open warfare to erupt again, the Puritans moved to take advantage of their newfound preeminence by expanding their settlements and, not coincidentally, playing various other tribes off against one another. Yet when war broke out again, in 1675, it surpassed the Pequot War for its violence, duration, and size.[25]

The year 1675 began with a single death that would ultimately lead to thousands more. John Sassamon, an Indian who had converted to Christianity and had even fought alongside the Puritans against the Pequots, was an aide to the Wampanoag chief, Metacom, better known to the English colonists as King Philip. Metacom had let it be known that he felt Sassamon had betrayed him, once in the drafting of a will—Sassamon wrote it for the illiterate Metacom and had apparently included himself as a beneficiary—and again by telling the authorities of Plymouth Colony that the Wampanoags were planning an attack. When Sassamon was found under the ice of Assawampsett Pond in January, suspicion naturally fell upon Metacom. With no direct evidence to implicate him, the Wampanoag chief was absolved of any wrongdoing. But several months later, a witness emerged to claim he had seen three of the chief's closest advisers haul Sassamon away and kill him. Solely upon this flimsy evidence, the advisers were tried, convicted, and executed at Plymouth. On June 24, Metacom's forces responded with an assault on the Plymouth town of Swansea. King Philip's War had begun.[26]

During the sanguinary battles of the summer and fall of 1675, Metacom's warriors devastated town after town throughout Plymouth; neighboring tribes in Massachusetts soon suffered the same fate. In all, allied Indian tribes attacked fifty out of ninety English towns in Plymouth, Massachusetts, and Rhode Island, utterly laying waste to twelve of them. (Though it sent troops, Connecticut escaped the fighting, much to the chagrin of the authorities in Boston.) Colonists were at first stunned by the breadth of the offensive; they were then shocked at the devastation wrought on their godly communities. Into the autumn of 1675, they appeared to be in danger of total destruction.

True to form, the colonists turned to religion for guidance, comfort, resolve—and above all, answers. As they did in their daily lives, they looked for providential signs of God's will in unfolding events. And for reasons unknown, it became clear they had strayed from the path of righteousness and provoked God's wrath. As the Massachusetts government, reeling from one defeat after another, declared in proclaiming a "Day of publick Humiliation, with Fasting and Prayer," the war had been caused by "*the Apostacy of many from the Truth unto Heresies.*" Another government proclamation lamented the colonists' "Backsliding" from godly ways, reflected most depressingly in the continually sagging rates of church attendance. "Why should we suppose that God is not offended with us," asked Increase Mather, a prominent minister and writer who informally served as the war's chief propagandist and apologist, "when his displeasure is written, in such visible and bloody Characters?" Thus the war did not trigger widespread soul-searching of a more reflective kind: land policies were not reexamined, treatment of the Indians went unquestioned. On the contrary, in August the Christian Indians of Massachusetts were ordered confined to the praying towns; in October, those who had not been sold into slavery or hanged were forcibly removed to Deer Island in Boston Harbor, where they waited out the war in the most miserable, diseased conditions. In arch-Calvinist fashion, the war was instead perceived as a divine test of the Puritans' own commitment: to God, and to the survival of their godly enterprise. Along with the Puritans' lives, the fate of their New Jerusalem was at stake.[27]

To the Puritans, the Indians served a dark purpose as God's unlikely messengers. But as displeased as he might be with his chosen people, in the end the Puritans were confident that God would not let them perish. He would teach them a lesson, a harsh lesson to be sure, but one they would survive to learn. The colonists believed they were experiencing their very own "Passions" of suffering, and ultimately redemption, that Jesus himself had endured. Puritan survivors accordingly praised "Gods marsi" in sparing them. "The Lord hath a great Interest in this Land which he will not easily part with," Mather declared confidently. It "hath pleased the Lord to make us his people." Despite their suffering, God would not forsake his people.[28]

The Puritans had sacrificed plenty; now, in the fall of 1675, the tide of battle would slowly begin to turn in their favor. A small success in October, the repulsion of a Nipmuck attack on Hatfield in western Massachusetts, was followed by a major offensive against the powerful Narragansetts of Rhode Island, accused of aiding and abetting Metacom's Wampanoags, in

December. While the charges of Narragansett perfidy were thin, Narragansett provisions were not. To colonists who had lost nearly everything in war and were facing the approach of a harsh winter, the Narragansetts presented a target of opportunity that was simply too good to pass up. A joint force from the colonies moved into Narragansett territory and, aided by a traitorous scout, marched to the Great Swamp near Rhode Island's southern shore. Inside the secreted, virtually impassable swamp was a large island; on it was an emergency Narragansett village, housing mostly noncombatant refugees fleeing the conflict. The scout was able to guide the English army directly to the island village, connected to the boggy mainland by a single felled log. The colonists penetrated the village, withdrew, set fire to it, and shot all who tried to escape the flames. This strategy ensured a rout—a massacre, really—but it also meant that the objectives of the attack, the food and supplies, were lost. Beset by freezing temperatures and intermittent blizzards, several English soldiers died on the journey home.[29]

It was a pyrrhic victory, but a victory nonetheless. Yet the brutality of the war continued, with several more English towns coming under attack in the spring of 1676; among other towns, Providence was completely destroyed. By the early spring, the war had become a stalemate. Yet Indian losses, coming from a much smaller population and weaker economic base compared to the colonists', were becoming unsustainable. Puritan thrusts into Indian territory in western Massachusetts and up from Connecticut into Rhode Island and Plymouth deepened the Indians' plight. By the summer, it was but a matter of time before the Puritans would prevail. The war finally came to an end in August, when an Indian fighting for the English shot and killed Metacom himself. A grisly war had come to a grisly end.

The savagery of the war astonished observers at the time and has continued to do so ever since. Indian warriors scalped many of their victims alive, while English troops disemboweled and drew and quartered theirs. Both sides adopted a scorched-earth strategy of retributive, total war. Few colonists considered their own brutality to be unnecessarily brutal: their enemies, after all, were servants of the devil and behaved accordingly. In February, a Nipmuck assault on Lancaster, Massachusetts, resulted not only in the deaths of several townspeople but also the capture of Mary Rowlandson. Her captivity, which she later recounted in a bestselling memoir, lasted three months and gave her an unprecedented glimpse into life among the Indians. Her "bloody heathen" attackers were little more than "hell-hounds" and "ravenous beasts" who "went without any scruple" and "acted as if the devil had told them that they should gain the victory." The Indians committed unspeakably cruel atrocities, such as scalping and skinning their captives alive. To the English, who believed they were the very embodiment of God with faces "wherein the glory and Image of God doth shine forth," the mutilation of bodies, heads, and faces were acts of blasphemy. The Indians even tortured livestock, the Puritans observed incredulously, on one occasion mutilating a cow by cutting off its horns and cutting out its tongue. It was the fiery Increase Mather who best expressed the Puritans' view of the malevolent evil of the "*vile Indians*" that contrasted with their own virtue:

> That the Heathen People amongst whom we live, and whose Land the Lord God of our Fathers hath given to us for a rightfull Possession, have at sundry times been plotting mischievous devices against that part of the English Israel which is seated in these goings down of the Sun, no man that is an Inhabitant of any considerable standing, can be ignorant.

What was more, the devilish Indians taunted the Puritans with deliberate blasphemies, such as when a party of Nipmucks taunted a group of besieged colonists to "Come and pray, & sing Psalmes," or when another attack ended in the Indians disemboweling a Puritan and carefully placing his "Bible in his Belly."[30]

Against such an enemy, the Puritans unleashed their righteous fury. The carnage of the Great Swamp was followed by further atrocities, against warriors and noncombatants alike, for the duration of the war. If "God is with us, and fights for us, and will deliver us out of the hands of these Heathen," as one English captain cried, then anything was justified. But although King Philip's War was deemed necessary and just, it was not exactly popular; support was broad, but not quite unanimous, and an important minority of ministers and writers raised troubling questions. Their numbers were small, and so they did not exactly constitute an antiwar movement. Moreover, many of them raised initial objections only to rally to the cause once fighting had broken out. Yet some were critical not only of the need for war, but of the Puritan authorities. Quakers, who had suffered under the stern rule of the Puritans, obviously had an interest in pointing out the shortcomings of officials in Massachusetts. (Puritan officials responded in kind by blaming their plight on the heresy of the Quakers.) John Easton, the deputy governor of Rhode Island, and Edward Wharton, a resident of Salem who had been exiled to London, accused the people of Massachusetts and Plymouth, and their intolerant ambition, for bringing the crisis upon themselves. But some Puritans also questioned the need for war at all. John Eliot and others complained that the true aggressor was Plymouth due to its rough justice in dealing with Metacom and the Wampanoags. Critiques such as these came closest to undermining the Puritans' rationale that theirs was a defensive war. Yet despite such reservations the scale of fighting, and the atrocities committed against the English people and their towns, mobilized all but the most hardened skeptics behind the war effort. And in the end, the image of a just, necessary, and righteous war prevailed.[31]

The war had been the biggest conflict yet in colonial North America. Approximately 1,250 members of the allied Indian tribes died in the fighting, 625 died later from battle wounds, and another 3,000 died of disease. All told, almost half of the prewar Indian population of 11,600 died during the war; the rest either became refugees or were sold into permanent slavery elsewhere in the English colonies. According to Nathaniel Saltonstall, a Puritan who lived through the war, over 800 English colonists, out of a total population of approximately 50,000—a mere 1.6 percent—died in the fighting. Whether or not the war was necessary and just, it was hardly proportionate.[32]

In addition to its personal and geographical scars, King Philip's War left a permanent imprint upon colonial American identity. A vivid and romanticized memory of the conflict would linger well into the late nineteenth century, its legacy shaping an American view of warfare that was grounded in the noble cause and the selfless spread of freedom. In this sense, perhaps the most important legacy of England's Protestant divines and holy warriors was to supply the raw material for an ideology of American exceptionalism that would emerge much later.[33]

God's specially chosen people did not behave as the tyrannical Spanish or the barbaric Indians. Instead, they were permitted to act without virtue under extreme circumstances, so long as they had no choice and fought for righteousness. Ideals and interests—the mix between the two has driven American war and diplomacy since. Christians—that is, proper Christians: Protestants—had been embattled for over a century, first by the Catholic conspiracy in Europe and then the heathen onslaughts in America. But now, in 1676, it appeared that the Protestant New Jerusalem had survived its ultimate trial. Thus tested, it would spend the next century pushing back Catholics and Indians, and all others who would deny them their sacred errand.[34]

CHAPTER THREE

Wars of Permanent Reformation

BRITISH IMPERIAL WARS were also American colonial wars, with local origins, local grudges, local ways of warfare, and local consequences. They were European great power wars but in the colonies remained quintessentially North American in character. Nothing better reflected the local character of imperial wars than the names the colonists gave them. From 1689 to 1763, Britain fought a series of wars, often global in scale and reach, against varying combinations of French-led alliances. Conflicts of European origin and byzantine European causes had European names—except in colonial British America, where they were known for the reigning British monarch. Thus the War of the League of Augsburg (1689–1697) was familiar to British colonists as King William's War; the War of the Spanish Succession (1701–1713) as Queen Anne's War; and the North American phase of the War of the Austrian Succession (1744–1748) as King George's War. Names such as these reflected another ambivalence among the colonists: proud as they were of being royal subjects of a mighty empire, they also at times resented the mother country's imperial pretensions and impositions. And as the eighteenth century aged, colonial sensibilities matured. Though the colonists continued to fight as Britons, for Britain, and for the promotion of British liberties, they increasingly came to believe that Britain's interests were not always the same as their own. Naming wars for their rulers was the colonists' way of paying monarchical tribute, but it was also a way of reminding themselves that the costs of war had been forced upon them. Yet the battles they fought for William, Anne, and George were not the colonists' only wars. If the great imperial wars had a North American component, the colonists ensured that their own interests—especially their insatiable appetite for land—were addressed. And they sometimes even sparked their own wars, with Indian and European rivals, on the contested margins of their domain.[1]

Though religion did not always determine animosity at the great power level—the English fought three wars against their Protestant brethren the Dutch, which resulted in the elimination of Dutch influence from North America and the renaming of New Netherland to New York, and France and Spain continued to be fierce imperial rivals, especially in North America, despite their shared Catholicism—all of colonial America's wars had an important religious coloring. Thus while their causes were often distant and secular, the colonists' wars were in large part shaped by faith. For example, though the fact that British North America's great rival was New France was not determined by religion, the battles the colonists fought were driven by anti-Catholic fear and an intense Protestant patriotism. And though England occasionally allied with Spain against France, as it did during King William's War, this did nothing to dilute the colonists' hatred of the Spanish they faced in the disputed borderlands of the southern territories. Overall, the series of wars with the French and Indians, beginning with King William's War in 1689 and culminating in the Seven Years' War of 1756–1763 (to the colonists, the French and Indian War), sanctified colonial America's mission of promoting Protestant liberty.

Protestantism stood at the very heart of what it meant to be British. But religion was central to the colonial American view of the world in other ways besides Protestant exceptionalism and anti-Catholicism. Most important was a series of intense religious revivals known collectively as the Great Awakening, which gripped the colonies in the midst of imperial warfare. Religion was also at the heart of the first sustained antiwar movement in American history, as Quakers and other peace churches opposed warfare and territorial expansion on grounds of Christian pacifism.

Unsurprisingly, then, in the colonies imperial wars were as much contests over the "correct" or "true" definition of nonnegotiable values such as liberty and identity as they were about territorial expansion. In such an ideologically heated climate, fighting often assumed an intensity that mirrored that of earlier Indian conflicts. In all the imperial wars, the churches rallied people to the cause; chaplains accompanied the troops into battle, steeled their nerve, and urged them forward; and colonial soldiers uncharacteristically ransacked Catholic churches and smashed Catholic icons. These would be wars to purify the soul of humanity. They would be wars of permanent reformation.[2]

FEARS OF CATHOLICISM resonated so powerfully because a threat to British America's very identity—political and religious—seemed to accompany the physical threat of the French army and navy. Protestants alleged that Catholicism's earthly powers were tightly centralized, inherently autocratic, expansionist, and aggressive. Yet there was little here that was new. Indeed, with the colonies increasingly prosperous and populous, the era's virulent anti-Catholicism should have become irrelevant, a curious echo of insecurity from a fading Puritan past.

What gave it potency and brought it to life was a series of events that seemed to corroborate anti-Catholic theories and ideas. Beginning in the

1680s, Louis XIV of France, whose extreme centralization of state power was unusually worrying even by the standards of Europe's monarchs, sought to bring both the European and colonial worlds under French influence. This bid for dominance was alarming enough, but in 1685 Louis infuriated and frightened Protestants everywhere by revoking the Edict of Nantes, a century-old law that had protected the rights of French Protestants by guaranteeing religious freedom. The termination of the edict led to a severe repression of a Protestant sect called the Huguenots. These French Calvinists, whose persecution made them heroes to Protestants everywhere, became refugees seeking shelter from Catholic persecution. They found it in the great Protestant capitals of Europe, such as London and Amsterdam, but also in the American colonies, especially in Massachusetts, New York, and Carolina, where the locals admired what the historian Jon Butler has aptly called the Huguenots' "piety of suffering": faith, courage, and steadfast resistance to Catholic tyranny. During an official day of fasting for the Huguenots, Increase Mather proclaimed that France's "great Persecution" was an ominous "token" of Protestant "destruction," while his precocious son, Cotton, warned that the fate of the Huguenots in France could easily portend the fate of Protestants everywhere—especially in the American colonies.[3]

Almost simultaneously, England and its American colonies were convulsed from within by their own Catholic bids for power, both real and imagined. In England, James II ascended the throne on the death of his brother, Charles II, in 1685. The problem was that James was a Catholic who wanted to restore the official power, prerogatives, and prestige of English Catholicism. During the English Civil War, James spent his exile in France, admiring in equal measure the Catholic faith and absolutist rule of Louis XIV. By the time he became king, England had already been gripped by sporadic bouts of anti-Catholic paranoia, including the fantastically bizarre—and entirely fictional—Popish Plot of 1678, in which Jesuits and their allies were said to have conspired to murder Charles II and restore Catholicism as the official religion.[4]

Just as Louis XIV had radically centralized monarchical authority in France, James moved to consolidate his own power at home. And just as Louis had torn up the tolerant edict that had protected the Huguenots, James declared null and void the colonial charters that had ensured local governance and political autonomy since the founding of the first colonies eight decades before. In their place, he created the Dominion of New England, a supercolony cobbled together through the forced union of Massachusetts, Plymouth, Connecticut, Rhode Island, New Jersey, and New York. Worse still, this vast territory, nearly twice the size of England itself, came under the rule of a single powerful royal appointee, Governor Sir Edmund Andros. Determined to bring the colonists to heel, Andros prohibited much of the political culture, such as local town meetings, that New Englanders held so dear. Despite Andros's support for the Church of England, the colonists conflated his rule, and the Dominion of New England, with a Catholic plot emanating from London. In justifying their right to rebel, the people of Boston recalled the Popish Plot and claimed that the "bloody Devotees of Rome had in their Design and Prospect no less than the extinction of the Protestant Religion." Andros, they charged, was actually "a branch of the Plot to bring us low" and was setting up New England and New York to be "attaqu'd by the French," who of course would then treat "the English with worse than Turkish Cruelties."[5]

True or not, the ambitions of James and his colonial agents triggered revolutionary upheavals on both sides of the Atlantic. The mother country led the way with the Glorious Revolution of 1688 by ousting an English Catholic, James, and allowing a Dutch Protestant, William, to mount a cross-channel invasion virtually unopposed. Here, faith was powerful enough to trump nation because it promised to deliver what politics could not: freedom. As one historian has put it, instead of the "poverty and slavery" of Catholicism, William gave the English "the priceless gifts of true religion, liberty, and prosperity." Increase Mather had said something similar in his sermon upon the death of William in 1702. When "God made him our King," Mather eulogized, "he was the great Instrument delivering us from popery and Slavery."[6]

Inspired by the Glorious Revolution, the colonies followed suit with their own rebellions the following year. In Boston, where according to a bystander the people "did this day rise as one man," Andros was ignominiously bundled up, imprisoned, and put on a boat back to England. In Maryland, long governed as a Catholic haven in America, Protestants—actually the majority—ousted their Catholic governors. And in New York, where many of the ruling elite were Catholic but the bulk of the population was Reformed or Anglican Protestant, Jacob Leisler—a fiery, ultraorthodox Calvinist who had recently helped resettle French Huguenots in the colony—mobilized widespread resentment of Catholics in New York and shaped it into an uprising that swept out the "Popish affected" authorities in the name of those "who would defend and Establish the true Religion."[7]

KING WILLIAM'S WAR, a ragged, pointless affair, pitted the English and the Iroquois against the French and their own Indian allies, the Abenakis of present-day Maine. While brutal, the fighting was intermittent: long periods of uneasy calm would suddenly be punctuated by bursts of spectacular violence. Though they both scored notable victories, neither side acquitted itself particularly well. The French captured the colony of Newfoundland, constantly besieged the Maine coast, and destroyed the towns of Albany and Schenectady in New York and Salmon Falls in New

Hampshire. For their part, the English successfully captured Port Royal, the main French base in Acadia (now Nova Scotia), and launched assaults on the main French towns of Montreal and Quebec. While the French fought their battles with regular troops sent from France, London left the colonies to fend—and fund—for themselves. The war was so damaging to the finances of Massachusetts that the colony became the first in North America to issue paper money, bills of credit that would be reimbursed after the imposition of higher taxes could make up for the shortfall.[8]

For the American colonists, King William's War was first and foremost a struggle to resist the domination of Catholic New France. They accused the French not only of territorial ambition but also religious persecution. Giving the ancient anti-Semitic "Christ-killer" myth a New World twist, French Jesuit missionaries taught their aboriginal converts that the Virgin Mary was French and that Jesus had been crucified by the English. French troops paid special attention to symbols of religious authority, desecrating a Dutch Protestant church in their sack of Schenectady; assassinating the Protestant minister of York, Maine, on his own doorstep; and justifying their attack on another Maine town—which included the butchering of nearly a hundred noncombatants, children among them, as they tried to surrender—as a legitimate response to the Glorious Revolution. The French could not even be trusted to be French: Cotton Mather, for one, was disgusted that the attack on Salmon Falls, New Hampshire, was led by a profane, mongrel army of "half Indianized French and . . . half Frenchified Indians." This was a terrible English nightmare come to life. But perhaps most startlingly, English soldiers and other men taken captive were brought north to Montreal, where Catholic nuns purchased them as indentured servants and prospective converts. Thus riled at these deliberate erasures of gendered norms and religious identity, colonial American soldiers purged their ranks of suspected Catholics and lashed out at symbols of French Catholicism. When they came upon the Roman Catholic church in Port Royal, for example, they embarked on the kind of iconoclastic spree not seen in England since the Civil War.[9]

These passions spun even more out of control and led to the war's greatest tragedy. Even in the context of the times, the Salem witch trials of 1692 were an irrational, unjustified bout of social paranoia that resulted in the executions of twenty-one innocent people. Decades of sporadic but grisly fighting with Indians had induced something of a collective psychosis among New Englanders. The outbreak of King William's War, which brought the scalping, torturing, and killing of entire villages, merely heightened these internal tensions. As the historian David Lovejoy has observed, by the early 1690s "it was time for some kind of reckoning between New Englanders and their God." And unfortunately for the eccentrics of Salem, mostly women, the reckoning took the form of a ferocious witch-hunt. Witch-hunters pointed to the supposed partnership of witches with French Catholics and Indian devil-worshipers—not coincidentally, many of the accusers had been traumatized residents of villages destroyed by Indian attacks during King Philip's and King William's wars before they had moved to the relative safety of Salem.[10]

By 1697, with England and France and their respective allies exhausted in Europe, fighting in the desultory North American theater had ground to a halt. The resultant Treaty of Ryswick restored everything in North America—all territorial gains and losses—to their prewar status. England had prevailed from a European standpoint, but the terms of its victory—official French recognition of William III's reign and the checking of Louis XIV's bid for hegemony—were hardly adequate compensation for eight years of war.

Still, New Englanders took solace in the fact that their godly errand had been tested and confirmed. Ever eager to control the image of America, Cotton Mather used the horrific ordeal of Hannah Dustin to confirm English virtue and French and Indian blasphemies—and thus to sanctify an emerging national identity based on the twin pillars of Protestantism and liberty. Hannah Dustin had been captured by a raiding party of Abenakis in one of the war's final acts, a 1697 raid on Haverhill, Massachusetts. While the rest of her family managed to flee to safety, Dustin and the midwife to her newborn baby were seized and taken 150 miles into the New England woods. Worried that the newborn's cries would alert English rescue parties to their presence, the Abenakis—Catholic converts, no less—killed it on the spot by bashing its head against a tree. Dustin exacted her revenge one night at camp by stealing an Indian hatchet and killing—and scalping—ten of the twelve members of her host Abenaki family in their sleep. When she finally made it back to Massachusetts, the government not only paid her a bounty of £5 per scalp, it celebrated her as a true colonial heroine. Relying, by Mather's account, on "the singular providence of God" and "nothing but fervent prayers to make their lives comfortable or tolerable," and enduring the Abenakis' religious taunting of her Puritan faith, Dustin's escape was interpreted as a deliverance straight from God. In their attempts to desecrate Hannah Dustin's virtue, the French Catholic Abenakis—whom Mather described variously as "raging dragons," "idolaters," and "savages"—had only confirmed it. Despite all its problems, God still smiled down upon the chosen people of New England.[11]

BRITAIN AND ITS American colonies had only a few years of respite before war with France, this time allied with Spain, broke out again. While the causes of Queen Anne's War in Europe and North America were different, British aims were identical: preventing French dominance and ensuring

British commercial expansion by preserving a balance of power. Waged between 1702 and 1713, Queen Anne's War would prove to be even more frustrating, inconclusive, and unproductive than King William's War. In a recurring pattern that would escalate and eventually spark a rebellion in 1775, London for the most part took its American colonies for granted. Only slowly did the priorities of British foreign policy become imperial as well as European—and even then, American objectives were often sacrificed in the name of European ambitions.[12]

Queen Anne's War expanded the geographical scale of imperial warfare, engulfing New England and Canada in the north and Florida and Carolina in the south. Religion was not a cause but a condition that shaped the war's contours and meaning; faith did not provide the spark that set war alight but the wood that fueled its burning. Foremost among the advocates for a robust colonial defense was the Reverend Solomon Stoddard, who feared another round of God's tests at the hands of the heretical Catholic Antichrist. Through their actions, the French fanned the hysteria. They used Indian allies, of course, but more galling to Puritan sensibilities in New England was their high proportion of Catholic converts: to take one example, a combined force attacking Haverhill, Massachusetts, had three times as many Catholic Indians as Frenchmen. After the fall of Port Royal in 1710, Jesuit missionaries encouraged their Indian converts to live under British rule but sabotage it from within. And male British captives were once again humiliatingly paraded in the markets of Montreal, often purchased by nunneries and other Catholic holy orders. New Englanders railed at such apostasy and hoped this war, finally, would bring an end to the Catholic threat in New France. "There are terrible troubles and calamities hastening upon the World," Samuel Clough declared in his wartime almanac, "which may be a means to bring on those Happy Times promised to the people of God, and to the Destruction of their Enemies." The war with France, he believed, would "make way for the downfall of Popery."[13]

Combatants in the south waged an especially intense holy war. Carolinian forces wreaked "horrifying carnage," in the words of one historian, in targeting Franciscan missions in Spanish Florida. After having his eyes and tongue cut out and his ears cut off, one priest was burned alive while tied to the foot of a cross. Against such ferocity, many Indians fled their mission villages and defected to the marauding invaders from the British colony. Some tried to save themselves by renouncing Catholic baptism, the only Christianity they knew and a marker of their fealty to the Spanish, by crying, "Go away water! I am no Christian!" Though a Franciscan missionary presence would cling desperately to the Floridian swamps, Spanish Catholicism had nearly been wiped out.[14]

But as in King Philip's and King William's wars, to British sensibilities it was the Indians who committed the worst atrocities, particularly in their custom of carrying away captives, for ransom, slavery, or—worse still—assimilation. In Hannah Dustin's ordeal, the Puritans had found a tale of courage and redemption. But in Queen Anne's War, a 1704 raid on Deerfield, Massachusetts, undermined basic notions of good and evil, right and wrong. A redemption of sorts would come, but it would be spoiled by a maddening ambiguity. As the historian John Demos notes, the most important thing about Deerfield was that it resulted in an "unredeemed captive"—one who did not wish to return, who freely chose barbarism over civilization.[15]

Long a site of Indian attacks—it had been the scene of vicious fighting in King Philip's War—the village of Deerfield was strategically located as the northernmost English settlement in the Connecticut River Valley. Close to the present-day border between Massachusetts and Vermont, in the early eighteenth century it sat alongside an unmarked frontier, perennially contested by English and French, Iroquois and Abenaki. As the home of the venerable Reverend John Williams, a noted divine in his own right but also related by marriage to the Mather clan, it was also one of the more famous of the Puritan villages. As such, Deerfield symbolized a blend of Protestant piety and territorial expansionism that represented to the French and Indians a particularly obnoxious English challenge—and a particularly enticing target. If their ultimate goal was to push the English back from the frontier, perhaps one day even off the continent itself, Deerfield was an excellent place to start. For these reasons, Reverend Williams had joined Reverend Stoddard in prodding the colonial authorities in Boston to strengthen the defenses of the Connecticut River Valley settlements.[16]

With these goals in mind, a war party of fifty French troops and two hundred Abenakis—most of them Catholic converts—crept into Deerfield on a cold, clear night toward the end of February 1704. Using the towering snowbanks that had imprudently been allowed to gather alongside the village's fortified walls, a smaller party of French and Indian raiders climbed into Deerfield and opened the main gate to let the rest inside. The night watchman had fallen asleep and did not awake until the gate had been opened. The villagers had little chance against such a perfect surprise attack, and the invaders had little trouble in utterly destroying Deerfield. Fifty-three villagers died; another 111 were force-marched into the wilderness, destined for sale in Montreal or a new life among the Indians. Either way, they faced the pressures of conversion from Jesuit priests. Among the captives were several members of the Williams family, including the Reverend John, his wife, and those children not already killed in the raid. Mrs. Williams died shortly afterward.[17]

After Massachusetts paid a ransom, the Reverend Williams returned from his Indian captivity in November 1706, nearly three years after being seized. As Mary Rowlandson had done following her captivity during King Philip's War, Williams wrote a captivity narrative—colonial America's singular contribution to the genres of Western literature—about his ordeal. As would be expected from a Puritan divine, Williams's account was heavily informed by Calvinist notions of piety, grace, suffering, and ultimate redemption. It was also predictably infused with fear and loathing for the French and Indians, who had not only destroyed his home, his church, and his village, but who had also, in the isolated wilderness, tried to steal his faith. Even worse than the Indians, who could not really be expected to know any better, was the power behind them: Catholic Quebec. The French represented the worst sort of threat to the New England soul—autocratic, superstitious, corrupt, venal—and intended to conquer Protestant, English America. Williams's account of his family's ordeal, entitled *The Redeemed Captive*, sounded the alarm.[18]

Though Williams and dozens of other Deerfielders were freed, one of the captives chose to remain: Reverend Williams's daughter, Eunice. For her, life was no longer Puritan, or even English: she had assimilated fully to Abenaki ways, would take an Abenaki husband, and bear Abenaki children. She would even renounce her godly ways and embrace instead the Catholic faith. She was the "unredeemed captive," a living embodiment of Cotton Mather's nightmare of assimilation and miscegenation. If little Eunice Williams, who from both her parents was made of the very flesh and blood of New England Puritanism, could lose her way, what did that say of the Puritan errand into the wilderness? Of its ability to resist Indian paganism? Or of its strength against Catholic heresy and tyranny? Such agonizing questions bedeviled the New England mind and elicited a redoubled resolve. After his release, Reverend Williams delivered a sermon to the Massachusetts General Assembly exhorting the politicians to mount a new offensive against the French. Little would actually come of Queen Anne's War, but not for a want of effort among the Protestant British colonists.[19]

WHILE THE TREATY of Utrecht brought the War of the Spanish Succession and its colonial theater to an end in 1713, true peace eluded the people of North America. In fact, over the next fifteen years the British colonists would fight several wars with the French, Spanish, and their Indian allies, wars that were fueled by religious fear, difference, and grievance. While religious strife was waning in Europe, the continuation of sectarian violence in North America reflected its more pervasive and permissive colonial condition.

War continued to set the southern hinterland alight, with British Protestants fighting Catholic Spanish and their pagan Indian allies, the

Yamasees. War continued in the north, too, with the usual sites playing host to the usual contests. French and Abenakis fought the British from western Massachusetts to the coast of Maine. Among British colonists, the war was known by two different names, both for the regional villain and alleged instigator of the war: in the west, colonists called it Grey Lock's War, named for an enemy Indian chief; in the east, where much more fighting occurred, it was known as Father Rale's War, after a Jesuit missionary who lived among the Abenakis and stirred them to resist British encroachments.[20]

There was some truth to this. Rale was a true believer "steeped," a sympathetic historian notes, "equally in French nationalism, personal piety, and deep interest in the spiritual foundations of apostolic work." So steeped was Rale in his role as apostle to the Indians that he assimilated to Abenaki life—to the British colonists, an unthinkable act of cultural treason. "We must indeed conform to their manners and customs," Rale once wrote, "so as to deserve their confidence and win them to Christ." Fears of Indians partnering the French to wipe out the British rushed back to the surface of colonial America's fervid imagination. Sporadic Indian raids culminated in several major attacks through the summer of 1723 to the following spring; one celebrated incident saw the Reverend Joseph Willard, a product of Yale, killed in an ambush near Rutland, in central Massachusetts. Further west, Grey Lock led a series of bloody raids against the towns of the Connecticut River Valley. Besieged on two fronts, Massachusetts decided once and for all to rid itself of the Catholic threat in its midst. In the west, the colonists built a series of fortifications to keep Grey Lock and his warriors at bay. In the east, a group of over two hundred militiamen sailed up the Atlantic coast to the Abenaki village of Norridgewock, in Maine. Easily overcoming its meager defenses, the New Englanders cleared the village, set upon the Catholic church and destroyed its altar and icons, and then killed and scalped Father Rale himself. In this, as on most occasions, Cotton Mather had the last word: "The Barbarous and Perfidious Indians in our Eastern Country, being Moved by the Instigation of the Devil and Father Rallee; have begun Hostilities upon us. They did it, when the French Hopes of a Fatal Revolution on the British Empire, deceived them. And it was not long before the Hairy Scalp of that Head in the House of the Wicked, paid for what Hand he had in the Rebellion, into which he Infuriated his Proselytes."[21]

WARS WOULD UNFOLD, and as they did the colonists would interpret their meaning largely through a lens crafted by two remarkable Protestant ministers who together brought about a series of intercolonial revivals in the 1730s and '40s that historians have since called the Great Awakening. The era's key religious figures, the intellectual theologian Jonathan

Edwards and the emotional evangelist George Whitefield, were both revivalists and anti-Catholic activists. Their anti-Catholicism led them to champion the cause of what the historian Thomas Kidd calls "the Protestant interest," an international endeavor, with global connections and worldwide implications, to advance the cause of Protestantism. The Great Awakening, their awesome religious mass movement that would have tremendous political and social consequences, was part of this campaign to advance the cause of the Protestant interest.[22]

Edwards, a descendant of a venerable Puritan family in the Connecticut River Valley who could trace their roots to the Winthrop, Mather, and Hooker families, was a complex man and an unlikely pioneer of evangelical revivalism. Although emotive, he was not a "noisy" preacher, a contemporary noted, but "grave, sentimental, searching, and pungent." He was a strict Calvinist who sought to reinvest the ritualistic doctrine of predestination with meaning. He was also a staunch defender of hierarchy, tradition, and experience—a most unlikely disposition for a revivalist whose followers imbibed, quite understandably, a more informal, individualistic, and accessible faith. Above all, he was an intellectual, a serious theologian who also based his biblical exegeses upon the rigorous scientific logic of Isaac Newton and John Locke. Yet he also prioritized emotion, especially the importance of the conversion experience—what we would today refer to as being "born again"—although he still held fast to the traditional Puritan beliefs in the elect and a covenant of grace. He had his own conversion experience as a student at Yale, recalling that "there came into my soul, and was as it were diffused through it, a sense of the glory of the divine being." He emphasized morality and piety in equal measure. He warned of eternal damnation for those who rejected God's law on earth but stressed that salvation was possible for all. Edwards, then, spoke to the heart as well as the head. And in him, American religion had its first great innovator of evangelicalism.[23]

From childhood, Edwards learned other core values that he would maintain for the rest of his life. As a Calvinist and English Protestant, he learned that the world played host to a struggle between God's chosen people and their enemies, Catholics and pagans. The Vatican, he believed, was nothing more than a base for the Antichrist. Though he was a great proponent of missions to convert the Indians to Christianity and believed that individually they were as capable of receiving God's grace as anyone else, he also distrusted the political intentions of Indian tribes. The wars that would devastate the colonial frontier on which Edwards was raised—especially the Indian raid on Deerfield that tore apart his extended family—impressed upon him the fragility and resilience of Protestant colonial society and the untrustworthiness of Indians. And with a father who had served as a chaplain to troops in Queen Anne's War and an uncle who was a career military officer and commander of New England's frontier defenses in King George's War, he also learned the value of patriotism, military preparedness, and the importance of armed strength. For Edwards, everything, war included, was part of God's plan; politicians and the military were but servants to God's will. "'Tis God, and he only, that determines the event of war and gives the victory," Edwards later preached during King George's War. On another occasion, he proclaimed that the "affair of war is one of the most important of all the affairs of the universe: the state of the world of mankind principally depends on it." As his biographer George Marsden puts it, Edwards believed that "Christ used human military forces as (sometimes unwitting) agents of his justice."[24]

Whitefield could not have been more different. Though their theology was similar, Edwards and Whitefield differed remarkably in preaching style and tone. Unlike Edwards—indeed, unlike most other ministers—Whitefield spoke without notes. And unlike Edwards, Whitefield's delivery was very emotional, even melodramatic. He would often weep during his sermons, and just as often he would move his audience to weep with him. He would adopt a tone of voice that suited the moment, and even do dramatic impressions of Satan and Jesus. While Edwards was most comfortable behind a pulpit and in front of a church congregation, Whitefield preferred to speak to thousands—sometimes tens of thousands—in the open air. He was, in other words, not just a preacher, but an actor; not necessarily insincere, but a showman whose theatrics were as much a part of God's message as the words themselves. While the intense Edwards produced emotion from logical argumentation, Whitefield used ostentatious displays of emotion, making him an equally important pioneer of American evangelicalism.[25]

Whitefield was also a believer in the international Protestant interest. He had, in fact, little choice: as an Englishman who launched several wildly popular tours of the American colonies, Whitefield *was* the Protestant interest. Perhaps even more than Edwards, Whitefield was motivated by a defensive mentality that saw Roman Catholicism as the root of all evil. Whereas Catholicism was authoritarian, Protestantism was decentralized, libertarian, run mostly by the people themselves, and thus the source of Britain's unique political and religious freedom. "I hope I shall always think it my bounded duty," Whitefield declared in one sermon, "to exhort my hearers to exert themselves against the first approaches of Popish tyranny and arbitrary power."[26]

Edwards and Whitefield's preaching touched off the Great Awakening. Usually led by emotional preachers loudly, extravagantly, and theatrically proclaiming that everyone was a sinner at heart and that only Jesus could save one's soul from the torments of eternal damnation, religious revivals often grew out of one particular church to spread across a region and gather souls into the denomination leading the revival. People whose faith had lapsed, or who had never had any to begin with, were brought into the church with enthusiastic joy. They had, truly for the first time in their lives, been brought to Christ. Such awakenings, as revivals were often called, were nothing new on the American religious landscape, and had with some regularity consumed the colonies, especially parts of New England, since the middle of the seventeenth century. But the Great Awakening represented something different altogether. If revivals themselves were nothing new, a series of overlapping, concurrent revivals, across the colonies from New England to Georgia, was. Newer still was the unprecedented interdependence of the revivals—no longer parochial affairs that affected the life of part of a single colony, the revivals of the Great Awakening were coordinated using the emerging phenomenon of the religious celebrity and the innovative use of printed media. Rather than a spontaneous surge of widespread piety, the Great Awakening was crafted, nurtured—"invented," in the words of one historian—into the first intercolonial mass movement. All this was novel, and it helped create a newly emerging colonial identity—"American" for lack of a better word, though the colonists still very much thought of themselves as British subjects—and sense of colonial solidarity. Moreover, the Great Awakening was not simply a colonial affair: it was transatlantic, international, and bound the Protestant interest closer together than ever before.[27]

Yet politically, from the 1740s on the Great Awakening would also have a tremendously divisive effect. Its main theological innovation was to spread the notion of individual salvation to a wide audience. Established churches shook to their very foundations at such an individualistic—some would say democratic—spirituality, for it threatened to put them out of touch with churchgoing people. The doctrinal divisions within denominations between New Lights and Old Lights—or New Sides and Old Sides to Presbyterians—pitted radicals who supported the awakenings and their mass rallies promoting a doctrine of easily accessible faith, against conservatives who cherished the stately traditions of the established church. Edwards, with his deference to traditional conduct and elite authority, was thus a most unlikely revivalist. Official, government-supported churches, such as the Anglicans of Virginia or the Congregationalists of Connecticut, were especially critical of the Great Awakening's disruptive revivalism because it sapped the stately, established churches of their power as well as their congregants, and more informal denominations, such as the Baptists, benefited at their expense.

For the time being, the implications of the new egalitarianism were as fleeting as they were unsettling. Revivalism undermined traditional sources of social authority even as the broad scope of the awakenings kindled a new social and cultural solidarity across colonial lines. But British society—including colonial British society—was still tremendously deferential to hierarchy and rank, and colonists still looked for guidance and example to the mother country first before they did to one another. Still, the Great Awakening built upon a newly emerging American version of a much older English worldview: hostile to external sources of concentrated power, fiercely protective of individual liberties, grounded in an exceptionalist belief that nowhere else did such freedoms exist, and driven by an unbending, crusading sense of righteous morality. Though relatively diffuse for now, these aspects of the American worldview would bond tightly together through two major wars: for empire in the 1750s and for independence in the 1770s.

THE GREAT AWAKENING coincided with another, equally familiar, mass movement: war. Conflict among the European powers erupted yet again, yet again it embroiled the North American colonies, and yet again it quickly assumed a faith-based crusading zeal to purge the colonies of spiritual corruption and contamination. Known to the American colonists as King George's War, the conflict pitted Britain and its colonies against Spain in 1739, then also against France in 1744; it did not end until 1748.[28]

In this renewed battle with Roman Catholic tyranny—the first time authorities in London referred to the colonists collectively as "Americans"—the southern colonists had a particular grievance. Franciscan missions in Florida were sheltering Yamasee Indians—converts to Catholicism, no less—and encouraging African slaves in South Carolina to flee south to St. Augustine, into the arms of Spanish protection. The slaves of course needed little additional encouragement beyond freedom. But many had come from parts of West Africa that had already been converted to Catholicism by the Portuguese in the fifteenth century, and in St. Augustine they could pray freely in a Catholic church. As galling as this irony was to the British Protestant self-image as the defender of liberty, it paled in comparison to the raids that freed slaves and Spanish troops had jointly carried out against South Carolina throughout the 1730s. Yet worse was still to come. Almost exactly as war with Spain was declared in the fall of 1739, British North America's first major slave uprising erupted in South Carolina. The Stono Rebellion—named for its location along the Stono River south of Charleston—threatened South Carolina's political stability and social fabric. Though the rebellion was swiftly repressed, the South Carolinians suspected it would not be the last attempt by an unholy alliance of Spanish and black Catholics to upend British colonial life. Given that many of the rebellious slaves were African Catholics who had been converted by the Portuguese, the colonists fears were not entirely unreasonable. South Carolina's Anglican hierarchy moved to contain the religious security threat from within by converting Catholic slaves to Protestantism. Yet the irony of their slaves embracing Catholicism as a religion of liberation seems to have escaped South Carolina's planters.[29]

In 1744, North American imperial politics took on a familiar look with the outbreak of another war between New France and New England. And again, for the American colonists it was in large part a religious war. The clergy had always used religion to propel popular enthusiasm for war, either by sanctifying the righteousness of the British cause or demonizing the motives of papist and pagan enemies, but rarely had it been as coordinated on such a wide scale. Broadly symbolic but relatively anodyne measures, such as public fast days, suited a wide spectrum of people, from the passionately devout to the agnostic deists. Others took a harder line, believing that French ambitions heralded the apocalypse because they were merely the tools of the Antichrist in its bid for world domination. This hard line transcended intra-Protestant divisions in the colonies. New Lights and Old Lights in Connecticut, for example, could agree on attacking French Catholics even when they failed to find any common ground on tenets of their shared Protestant faith. Characteristically, Edwards promoted this more rigorous worldview. Church and colony, faith and nation, he believed, would best march forward together. The advance of religion would come through politics, and few political causes were as glorious as an advance on a Catholic stronghold like New France. Mobilization for victory in King George's War, Edwards hoped, might even sustain the Great Awakening's waning revivalist fervor. Surely it meant something that Whitefield returned to the colonies, for the first time in several years, just as war was breaking out.[30]

Edwards's grand vision of war and revival as complementary struggles dovetailed perfectly with that of the colonial leadership. Many of the strategists in charge of the war were themselves deeply pious, and their religious backgrounds strongly influenced the way they prepared for war. The Puritan grandee John Stoddard, Jonathan Edwards's uncle and patron, had survived the 1704 raid on Deerfield and was now in charge of New England's defenses. In keeping with the political views of his father, the Reverend Solomon Stoddard, Colonel John Stoddard advised a combined policy of strong defensive fortifications along the French and Indian frontiers to the north and west and strong offensive operations against New France. Stoddard hoped and planned, though in vain, that colonial forces could capture Montreal. Like many New Englanders, he did not trust the French—frustrating negotiations with Jesuit priests and Quebec's colonial officials over the fate of the unredeemed Eunice Williams had ensured his mistrust. Nor did he entirely trust the Indians, even those who were allied to the British. Others, such as Sir William Pepperrell, another evangelical admirer of Edwards and Whitefield, and Roger Wolcott, a militia commander and orthodox Puritan, led the colonial charge against the mighty French fortress of Louisbourg.[31]

Pepperrell, in fact, consulted closely with Whitefield about the expedition, a remarkable fact that reflects its amateurish implausibility and godly pretensions. And Whitefield did even more. In February 1745, he surveyed a crowd of over 3,500 amateur militiamen from Massachusetts and Connecticut gathered alongside the docks of Boston Harbor. The soldiers waited to board ships that would take them north to Louisbourg; Whitefield's dockside sermon would bless their dangerous mission. Finding the Protestant militiamen "stirred up to God" and eager to fight the French papists, Whitefield did not disappoint. Drawing on the biblical tale of David and Goliath, he promised his listeners that like David they would prevail against the odds if they remained true to their faith. He then exhorted them with a prayer to God to "give us Cape Briton. Lord prepare us either for Victory or defeat. But if it be thy will grant it may be a Garrison for Protestants and thy dear Children who will worship thee in spirit and in truth!" Whitefield finished with a blessing of the expedition's flag and the pronouncement of its official motto: "No need to fear with Christ as our leader." The expedition, wrote one historian, had assumed "the air of a crusade."[32]

Apparently God *did* favor the American colonists. Despite tackling the most formidable military installation in North America that contained the battle-hardened troops of the most potent military power on earth, the Americans stunned the world—including their own government in London—by taking Louisbourg after a relatively brief siege in the spring of 1745. The British colonies erupted in joyful celebration, and a rare unanimity brought New Lights and Old Lights together. Gilbert Tennent, a Presbyterian revivalist from New Jersey, exclaimed that the victory at Louisbourg preserved "our civil and religious liberties" from an enemy "who unweariedly labours to rob us of our civil and religious Liberties, and brings us into the most wretched vassalage to arbitrary Power and Church Tyranny." Thomas Prince, a New England revivalist, preached that the colonists fought not merely for land and glory, but for a political and religious ideal that resisted "the absolute, hereditary, and unalienable Right of Kings," against *"Papists"* who would "rule *arbitrarily*, illegally, tyrannically, and cruelly." But the reflected glory of Protestantism's great military victory did not belong to any one faction. Charles Chauncy, the minister at Boston's First Church and a major Old Light opponent of the Great Awakening, celebrated the colonists' triumph over the French "Antichrist" and the Catholic "Man of Sin, that Son of Perdition." Only Louisbourg, it seemed, could heal America's religious wounds.[33]

"God gave [Louisbourg] into our hands," Edwards wrote. Victory was "a dispensation of providence, the most remarkable in its kind, that has been in many ages, and a great evidence of God's being one that hears prayer." But the war continued, and so more than two years later, in December 1747, another architect of the colonial war, Benjamin Franklin of Philadelphia, also found himself relying on the grace of God. Although they possessed starkly different religious beliefs, the evangelical Whitefield of the Great Awakening and the rational scientist Franklin of the Enlightenment were friends and collaborators. Franklin's key business was publishing, and few authors on either side of the Atlantic could sell as many pamphlets as Whitefield. Perhaps this was why Franklin, who feared the Spanish and especially the French but who faced considerable opposition to the war from Pennsylvania's ruling class of pacifist Quakers, turned to religion to stimulate voluntary militia recruitment. Drawing on his upbringing in Puritan Boston, where such events were regular, Franklin proposed Pennsylvania's first ever official day of thanksgiving to support the war. "Calling in the Aid of Religion," Franklin later wrote in the pages of his *Autobiography*, "I propos'd . . . the Proclaiming a Fast, to promote Reformation, and implore the Blessing of Heaven on our Undertaking." He also worked closely with another evangelical revivalist, the Presbyterian Gilbert Tennent, to drum up support for a militia among Pennsylvania's large population of Scotch-Irish. To appease the Quakers, Franklin called for conscientious objectors to be protected by law. By combining such faith-based initiatives with appeals to the colonists' more secular interests, Franklin built more than enough popular support for a militia, which eventually had more than ten thousand men under arms—no small feat for a distant, provincial outpost of the British Empire.[34]

The North American theater came to a close in 1748 in an unequivocal British victory. Edwards, Whitefield, and Franklin had prevailed. Yet when Britain and France made peace in 1748 and drew King George's War to a close, British negotiators thought it better to placate the infuriated French and return Louisbourg at the bargaining table in exchange for the French returning their capture of Madras, an important port in India. While the relinquishing of Louisbourg was unpopular in Britain, Americans were completely dumbfounded. Had they not proved their worth? Had they not sacrificed, in lives and money—both in relatively short supply—for the imperial cause? Edwards, of course, could fall back on a Calvinist providentialism that could explain everything by fitting it into the infinitely wise, mysterious, and unknowable plans of the Almighty. But most others were not as sanguine. Though it was still far too early for the American colonists to think of themselves as a nation apart from Great Britain, it was becoming increasingly clear that their interests were not always the same as the mother country's. Among the Americans, new doubts arose over the willingness of kings and queens—the very monarchs in whose names the colonists fought and died in three imperial wars since 1689—to safeguard their sacred rights and freedoms. If they still fought to safeguard Protestant liberty in the world, they now began adding republicanism to the mix.[35]

EVEN AT THE TIME, people sensed that the boom-bust cycle of Anglo-French warfare that had begun in 1689 would continue to grow until it had consumed Europe's New World colonies. Before, the British competed with the French for land and resources; by the outbreak of the last and grandest of these wars, in 1754, many feared that the competition was for survival itself. The population and prosperity of the British colonies continued to expand rapidly. Logically enough, this economic and demographic boom drove a new wave of territorial expansionism into the fertile valleys beyond the Appalachian mountains that up to this point had served as the colonies' natural western border. But the French population and economy grew, too, albeit at a smaller rate and with a lower overall result, and with them grew French ambitions for the same land in the Ohio Valley coveted by British colonists. Both peoples felt they must expand or expire; neither could live in harmony under the threat of domination by the other.

These strategic maneuverings triggered the Seven Years' War, a titanic struggle for imperial supremacy that spilled over into new sites of contest, such as West Africa and the Philippines, in addition to the more traditional theaters of Europe and the Caribbean. Alternately dubbed "the great war for empire" and the "first world war," the British colonists in North America simply called it the French and Indian War, as if to say that the scope of previous colonial wars, which had also pitted them against varying combinations of French and Indians, paled in comparison to the events of 1754–1763. American colonists and British redcoats fought an unholy alliance of French, Indian, and Spanish enemies across the continent and beyond, from Quebec in the north to Havana in the south. Like previous European great power wars, the Seven Years' War had a North American theater that was separate from, yet also connected to, other theaters, particularly in Europe and the Caribbean. And like other imperial wars, the fighting actually began in the American colonies as British, French, and Indians vied for control of strategically and economically valuable land. The only main difference was that the contest had shifted westward. Though fighting would again envelop New England, New York, and Nova Scotia, the fulcrum of war would now be found in the Ohio River Valley.[36]

The Seven Years' War stimulated colonial religion, reviving passions of the Great Awakening that had subsided for a decade or more. The war also politicized the population, especially the most religious people in society, the clergy, who now found themselves pressed into service of the state. Women, also among the most faithfully pious of people, similarly became politicized and actively supportive of the war as colonial religion itself mobilized. The effect was symbiotic, as religious colonists rallied with near unanimity in support of the British cause. Even the pacifistic Moravians of Pennsylvania built armed forts and garrisoned them with men prepared to fight. In 1755, when Pennsylvania's Quaker-dominated assembly proved unwilling to prosecute the conflict growing on its western frontier, its people, led by Benjamin Franklin, summarily replaced it and prepared for war anyway. (Nonetheless, on behalf of the Quakers Franklin also pushed through tougher legal guarantees for religious conscientious objectors. Franklin not only recognized that compelling Quakers to fight was politically unwise in Pennsylvania, he also believed that "due Regard might be had to scrupulous and tender Consciences.")[37]

Quakers aside, the colonists fervently believed that the cause they supported could not be more necessary or more glorious. The rivalry, at least to the American colonists, between British Protestant liberty and French Catholic tyranny had never subsided. Peaceful periods in between their monarchs' earlier colonial wars had only brought pause and respite, not a permanent end to hostilities. "The prejudice of their religion," warned the Reverend Isaac Stiles of New Haven, made the French "mortally to hate us, and seek our overthrow." Similar fears pervaded Protestant communities from New England to New York and south to Virginia. New France already extended across the vast stretches of land north of the St. Lawrence River and Great Lakes (what are now the Canadian provinces of Ontario and Quebec), and with its port of New Orleans the French also controlled the strategically and economically vital mouth of the Mississippi River. Should the two territories ever link up—as they would if the French gained control of the Ohio Valley and adjacent lands—the British colonies would be encircled, unable to expand, and vulnerable to French advances. The Reverend Aaron Burr Sr.—founder of Princeton University and father of a future vice president—painted a grim picture of the colonists' possible fate: "Our Sea-port Towns sack'd, and land in Ashes!—Our Country ravaged! our Houses plunder'd! Our *Wives* and *Daughters* delivered to the Lusts and Fury of a lawless Soldiery!—Our helpless Babes dashed against the Stones!"[38]

Naturally, such hysteria both produced and reflected an intensified resurgence of anti-Catholicism that couched the war not as a contest between the competing land claims of two European empires but as a moral struggle between the darkness of Catholic tyranny and the virtuous light of Protestant liberty. As the visionaries and prophets of the Protestant interest, the colonial clergy played an inordinately important role in mobilizing and maintaining popular support for the colonial cause. And the people responded, filling churches to capacity and widely observing fast days of thanksgiving. Because Protestantism was widely regarded as the original source of political liberty and economic prosperity, it could provide an ideological glue to bind together disparate colonies with different interests. "Should we succeed," declared William Hobby in 1758, "then our Liberty, Property, Life & Religion are continued." But should they falter, "farewell Liberty: Now to be exchanged for slavery! Farewell Property! Nothing hence to be called our own. Farewell Religion; the Sun sets upon the Sanctuary; which is left dark and desolate!"[39]

If they remained faithful, the preachers generally proclaimed, the American colonists could expect protection from God's providence. They should resist but not hate their French and Indian enemies, said Joseph Parsons, a minister from Bradford, Massachusetts, because their enemies were but God's way of testing his chosen people. Such a classically Calvinist theme—adversity as a godly test that his people must simply endure—enabled the colonists to persevere through the war's difficult initial years with their self-confidence still intact. Clergy also used lessons from the Bible to frighten their listeners into line. Using the biblical example of the city of Nineveh, which God destroyed in the Book of Jonah for the sinful, unrepentant pride of its people, the Reverend Joseph Lathrop of West Springfield foresaw destruction and ruin for the people of New England if they did not recognize their inherent sinfulness and utter helplessness in the face of God's power. But if they renewed their true Christian—that is, Protestant—faith, Nineveh's fate would befall the French, not the British, and the godly would emerge stronger than ever. When British soldiers and the colonial militia stumbled, as they did early on in the war, it was simply God's way of punishing his people for their sins and warning them to repent. "God hath awfully rebuked us," Jonathan Edwards noted quietly on hearing word of a defeat. The New Light Gilbert Tennent preached a similar message in Pennsylvania. But it was also a warning that, when heeded, would ensure future glory and victory.[40]

Future glory and victory that would be Christ's as well as his people's—little wonder that many colonists interpreted the war and its outcome in millennial terms. With an almost biblical rhythm, the cycle of wars between French Catholics and British Protestants seemed to be reaching its conclusion in this, an imperial war to end all wars. The final, climactic battle with the Antichrist—coinciding, amazingly enough, with a rare New England earthquake—could only portend the end of days. At the time, most colonists believed to some degree in postmillennialism, which took the Book of Revelation to mean that it was up to people on earth to prepare the way for Christ's triumphal return and his thousand-year reign of peace. Slaying the Antichrist, embodied by the French, would be an important step. So too would ensuring the survival and spread of

Protestant liberty that would follow the conquest of the French. Edwards could be so confident in the face of military disaster precisely because of his postmillennial beliefs.[41]

George Whitefield also supported the war. From his home in England, Whitefield worked with the government to build support for the war among all Britons, but especially the American colonists. To Whitefield, such efforts on behalf of the British cause and the Protestant interest came naturally. In a bestselling 1756 sermon, he charged that the French intended to invade and occupy the colonies so they could impose their autocratic political and religious system devised by Rome. "O *America*," he lamented, "how near dost thou lie upon my heart! GOD preserve it from popish tyranny and arbitrary power!" Whitefield urged colonists of all religious persuasions to support the war effort. The arguments of pacifists, in particular, had no moral standing because France had initiated the conflict under the most spurious and dishonorable circumstances in order to dominate the colonies' western edge and, eventually, the colonies themselves. Those pacifists, such as the Quakers, who still refused to support a necessary and eminently just war would suffer the "curse of Meroz," a biblical tale (Judges 5:23) of cowardly villagers whom God punished for their refusal to fight in defense of Israel. The curse had long been a staple of colonial Calvinism, a favorite scare tactic of Puritan divines such as Thomas Hooker and more recently a rhetorical device used by Jonathan Edwards to attack the Old Lights during the Great Awakening. Colonial clergy followed Whitefield's lead and the "curse of Meroz" became a common way to marginalize the war's dissenters.[42]

Millennialism and anti-Catholicism were nothing new in American theology, but republicanism was. Building on the disquiet following King George's War, for the first time since the English Civil War a century earlier the colonists began contemplating life without a king. At least, they began to equate, albeit abstractly, the arbitrary tyrannical rule of Catholicism with that of monarchs in general. Whitefield, a monarchist, may not have meant to include British kings in his charges against "arbitrary power," but in theory it could certainly apply—after all, few political orders are as arbitrary as those vesting concentrated monarchical power in the hands of a single individual who derives his authority solely through hereditary rule. So when the colonists rallied to fight arbitrary power in the name of individual liberty—not coincidentally, the same rallying call of the Great Awakening—it was only the immediate crisis that averted their gaze from London. And as the historian Mark Noll points out, the new mood was not merely found among the usual suspects of the Calvinist New England clergy. Christian republicanism could now be detected throughout the colonies, including in the habitually Anglican—and thus instinctively monarchical—confines of Virginia. Indeed, what was so powerful about these beliefs was their conflation of religious and political millennialism: final victory over the French and Indians would usher forth a new, uniquely free era of civil and religious liberty.[43]

As chaplains, now more widespread and integrated into the armed forces than at any other time in colonial history, the clergy also accompanied the militias into the field. Regular soldiers imported directly from Britain were less moved by the motivating power of faith, with the colonial militia clergy often outnumbering chaplains to the redcoats by a ratio of fourteen to one. Drawing upon the widely disseminated doctrines of Calvinism, chaplains could base everything on God's design—and upon it, they could steel resolve, explain away defeat, and foresee glory in a way no others could. The vast majority of colonial militia members were not trained, professional soldiers, but irregular reservists who fought only upon the outbreak of war. Thus while they were there as counselors and confidants, their most important function was to deliver stirring sermons to rally the frightened, often wavering citizen soldiers of the militia into battle. War was evil, the Reverend James Beebe of Woodbridge, Connecticut, preached to a group of soldiers before battle, but against the "outrages of the barbarians and the cruel laws of violence," it was at times "necessary in a Christian state and allowable by the laws of Christianity." War was hell, Beebe warned, and would consume the fainthearted and irresolute who did not put their complete trust in God: "And *you* my brethren may be called to look upon your enemies in the face. When their glittering armor and burnished shields may even dazzle your eyes. You may see the battle set in array and be called upon to face your enemies *front to front.*" In the midst of such carnage, only "the truly spiritual soldier will be able to bear up under all the hardships . . . with an unbroken and steady mind."[44]

In addition to rallying troops to battle, religion could also provide justification for outrageous acts of war that we would now call ethnic cleansing. In the case of the Acadians, a French Catholic people living in the British colony of Nova Scotia, perceptions of threat collided with religious prejudice and fear to produce draconian war measures. Nova Scotia had been a French colony, Acadia, until its conquest by the British in Queen Anne's War. But while the British had little trouble conquering Acadia, it had immense difficulties in both subjugating the Acadians and persuading Britons to settle there. British authorities presented an ultimatum to the Acadians—pledge allegiance to the British king or be exiled from your homes and land—several times between 1713 and 1754, but to no avail: the Acadians would not relent and the British did not have the stomach to enact a policy of forced migration. But the outbreak of the Seven Years' War changed the dynamic of the Acadians' situation, and in the process hardened British attitudes. Already hostile to Roman

Catholics, the British came to fear the special role Catholicism played in Acadian life despite the fact that few Catholic priests remained in Nova Scotia to provide for the spiritual needs of its French people. From this, the unusually cohesive Acadian people came to be seen as a security threat, a fifth column that would ally with the local Mi'kmaq Indians who were already implacably hostile to British claims to the land. In the years shortly before the war, the British had begun a policy of settling "foreign Protestants," initially in the village of Lunenburg, as a way to gain social and cultural control of the colony. The American colonists began agitating for sterner measures—pamphleteers in Boston shrilly warned that tolerating the presence of an Acadian enemy within would enable French papists to stab British Protestants in the back—which coincided with a new resolve of the authorities in Halifax. In 1755, the year of several British defeats, the Acadians were presented with another ultimatum. This time, those who refused were packed on British ships and forcibly moved to other parts of the British Empire.[45]

The expulsion of the Acadians in the years following 1755 perfectly captures the diverging fates of North American Catholicism and Protestantism that resulted from the Seven Years' War. For this conflict, more than any, was a battle to determine the religious complexion—and with it the political and economic character—of an entire continent. In 1762, Spain intervened on the side of the French. British forces seized the opportunity to attack their new Spanish enemy, weak and indecisive, and quickly mounted an expedition against Havana, the important Cuban port. Their ranks were swelled with thousands of enthusiastic volunteers from traditionally anti-Catholic New England, long accustomed to fighting papists and Indians on behalf of the British crown. Spanish belligerency also brought Florida into the war, where British victory brought an effective end to Floridian Catholicism until its Cuban renewal in the twentieth century.[46]

Naturally, the war had a more positive effect on colonial Protestantism by acting as a spur to social cohesion and religious endeavor. Frontier Indian missions in New England, New York, and elsewhere that had floundered at the onset of war, forgotten by all but their most dedicated participants, rejuvenated in the wake of the Protestant triumph. Piety among the colonists also revived. The Great Awakening's exhaustingly intense revivalism, impossible to sustain beyond a few years, was reawakened in service to the war effort, and became more broadly popular as it became more avowedly political and nationalistic. In responding to the unrelenting ideological demands of the war, the colonial clergy enhanced, entwined, and then entrenched the meaning of colonial identity, Protestant exceptionalism, and millennial expectation more than even the Great Awakening itself ever did. The war also spread the boundaries of colonial religion by merging its interests—especially frontier defense—with those of the state.[47]

After a wobbly start, the war resulted in a complete British, Protestant victory. In succeeding years, important French and Spanish imperial cities fell into British hands: Louisbourg (again) in 1758, Quebec in 1759, Montreal in 1760, Havana and Manila in 1762. Neither Paris nor Madrid could afford to suffer any further losses like these, and in 1763 they sued for peace. The settlement ended the imperial French influence in North America, which to many American colonists seemed to herald the end of the French presence itself despite the thousands of Québécois now living under British rule.

The French defeated once and for all, their Indian allies humbled and prone to British domination, the Spanish humiliated on the southern fringes of Britain's North American empire—no wonder colonists from Maine to Georgia looked upon victory in the Seven Years' War as the greatest event of their lifetimes, the dawn of an era of permanent peace and prosperity. And as usual, the clergy rose with a rare ecumenical unity to provide spiritual meaning for the imperial grandeur. Having emerged from a "State of War," Izrahiah Wetmore, a Congregational minister from Stratford, Connecticut, thanked "Providence" and "the great God of his infinite Goodness and Mercy" for rewarding the godly for their fidelity during a time of testing. But to others, victory meant something more: everywhere they looked, people of God pointed to the very earthly progress that seemed to follow victory. The Seven Years' War had won the American colonists a permanent freedom in all aspects of life, a freedom whose component parts were now indivisible and indissoluble. "Methinks I see Towns enlarged, Settlements increased, and this howling Wilderness become a fruitful Field, which the Lord hath blessed," preached Congregational minister Eli Forbes as early as 1760; "and to complete the Scene, I see Churches rise out of the Superstitions of Roman Bigotry." No less fulsome was Virginia's James Horrocks, an Anglican minister, who rejoiced in the "Blessing now given us," the "Security of Our Civil Liberty, a Happiness we justly glory in . . . Oh Liberty! Thou art the Author of every good and perfect Gift, the inexhaustible Fountain, from whence all Blessings flow."[48]

Thus finished the twin processes of imperial warfare and religious revivalism that transformed British colonial America between 1689 and 1763. The colonies had grown and matured, their numbers and prosperity expanding at astonishing rates. But their sensibilities matured in a strangely paradoxical way, becoming more assertive, autonomous, even on occasion advocating outright independence—more "American," the clergy pointedly noted on occasion—yet also still proudly British. The paradox is best explained by the uncomfortable fact that the kind of British exceptionalism of which the colonists were so proud was not necessarily any longer the same British identity in which the people of the mother country believed. The most important, mutually reinforcing components to colonial identity were robust notions of political freedom and the Protestant religion, forged together through a series of imperial wars that had starkly different meanings for the American colonists than they did for Britons. Crucially, colonial religion expanded and flourished alongside these developments, providing a distinctively pious tenor to an emerging American worldview.[49]

PART II

The American Revelation

Newburyport, Massachusetts, September 1775. On the eve of mounting the American Revolution's first major offensive, a thousand soldiers from the newly formed Continental Army marched into Newburyport. The New England seaside town would be the launching point for their audacious attack against the city of Quebec. More than 350 miles of rugged terrain lay between them and their target, and so before departing the soldiers requested a special church service to bless their endeavor and ask for the assistance of God's providence. With the townsfolk cheering along a packed parade route, the soldiers made their way to Newburyport's First Presbyterian Church. Everyone, townsfolk and soldiers together, filed into the church and filled it to capacity. Without notes, Reverend Samuel Spring, the army chaplain, preached from a passage in Exodus (33:15): "If thy spirit go not with us, carry us not up hence." The choice of text was fitting: few of those present did not believe that the Lord marched alongside the amateur colonial soldiers. The Book of Exodus was also appropriate, for the soldiers knew that by conquering Quebec they would lead thousands of people out from under the dual tyranny of the Catholic Church and the British Parliament. More important, by defeating the mighty British in such an important battle, the Americans would help bring about their own deliverance from imperial rule. One listener that day thrilled to Spring's sermon on "the marvelous and daring expedition on which they were about to set forth." Another who would never forget the occasion was the expedition commander, Colonel Benedict Arnold.[1]

Reverend Spring found the experience thrilling as well, though for a different reason: "I preached over the grave of Whitefield." Buried beneath the stone tiles of the church floor, beneath the altar itself, lay the tomb of George Whitefield. Five years before, in September 1770, he had died suddenly of an early morning asthma attack while staying in Newburyport. The minister of First Presbyterian, Jonathan Parsons, refused to relinquish Whitefield's body and instead had him buried in a special tomb in the church crypt. Knowing this, after his sermon Chaplain Spring asked if he could visit the tomb to pay homage to Whitefield; several soldiers joined him. They prised open the crypt and stared at Whitefield's

71

remains. His flesh had decomposed, but his clothes had not. The soldiers carefully removed Whitefield's collar and wristbands and tore off small pieces for each of them, so that they may have "a precious relic" for the arduous journey and difficult battle that awaited them.[2]

By 1783, eight years later, the American colonists had defeated Great Britain and won their independence. Joyful celebrations erupted throughout the new nation of the United States, including in Newburyport. From the same pulpit in the same church, Reverend John Murray channeled the spirit of George Whitefield to consecrate the victory. "Joy dances in every eye," Murray proclaimed. "Pleasure beams in every countenance; and every bosom beats high with the emotions peculiarly fitted to hail the auspicious day that declares the clouds of horror fled, to return no more for ever."[3] Whitefield's posthumous influence on the course of revolution had come full circle.

Whitefield was in high demand, and not merely for his comforting theology of a new birth that was available to anyone who would accept Christ into their heart. During his career, Whitefield had also, in the words of one historian, "preached politics." Until his death, he had been strongly supportive of American independence. On the many issues that had split the American colonists from the British government, Whitefield sided with the colonists. Fearing the baroque excesses and political power of the Church of England, his own denomination, throughout the 1760s he had opposed the installation of an Anglican bishop in America. In 1764, he was among the first to warn the colonists of the hated Stamp Tax. "My heart bleeds for America," he lamented to a private gathering of New Hampshire clergymen. "O poor New England! There is a deep laid plot against both your civil and religious liberties, and they will be lost." Two years later, Whitefield accompanied his good friend Benjamin Franklin to the House of Parliament, where Franklin was arguing the colonies' case against the Stamp Act. It said much about Whitefield's reputation—and Franklin's—that the famed evangelist was there not only to persuade British politicians, but to shield Franklin from the criticism of American colonists. Having spent his career warning about the dangers posed by Catholicism's concentrated, arbitrary power, Whitefield found himself applying the same libertarian logic to his own church and his own country.[4]

Revolutions fundamentally alter the political climate of regions and continents as well as individual nations, and revolutionary states often seek to export their utopian ideas to foreign countries still living under oppression. Thus while normally thought of as an internal affair, the American Revolution also marks one of the most important episodes in the history of American foreign relations. Indeed, given their colonial status and experience with imperial and Indian wars, the revolutionaries themselves made little distinction between what was foreign and what was domestic. Though the Revolution determined the political independence of the United States, it also created new or cemented existing ideas about the wider world regarding liberty, slavery, expansion, exceptionalism, and how the United States should apply its newly won independent power abroad.[5]

And of course the Revolution immediately created the need for an independent American foreign policy. Even before the creation of the United States, American diplomats negotiated possible peace terms with the British throughout the war, and they used these negotiations as a ruse to pressure other European powers to weaken Great Britain by supporting the Patriot cause. Without these foreign allies—notably France, but also Spain—the Americans would likely never have defeated Great Britain in the first place. Conducting international negotiations and managing alliances during and after the Revolutionary War, while also maintaining national autonomy, established an enduring tradition of U.S. diplomacy. George Washington may have codified this tradition in his famous 1796 Farewell Address, but it had been already flourishing for twenty years.[6]

As the life and death of Whitefield illustrate, the role of religion was instrumental in the unfolding of America's revolution and worldview alike. As with Whitefield, American religion in general helped initiate, sustain, and celebrate revolutionary fervor. Colonial religion and politics changed alongside one another in profound ways—what the historian Rhys Isaac aptly calls "the double revolution in religious and political thought and feeling"—that would attitudinally shape not only a new American nation and its political character, but that nation's relationship with the rest of the world.[7]

Religion, deeply allied to the cause of independence, made the outbreak of revolution more likely, helped steer its course, influenced its outcome, and contributed to shaping the peace. In the decades before the outbreak of revolution, developments in American religion helped nurture new ways of thinking about established authority and its relationship to individual liberty. In particular, the Great Awakening's radical individualist ethos of personal salvation helped sanctify the political ideas—particularly regarding monarchy, concentrated power, and republican liberty—that provided the fuel to power the revolutionary engine. The Great Awakening was in many ways itself revolutionary, an inherently subversive phenomenon that undermined traditional patterns of established hierarchy. There was no straight line from Awakening to Revolution, but the revivals did create a new context that enabled a revolution for individual liberties against established authority to flourish. Revivals empowered colonists, especially among the lower classes, to challenge establishments that unjustly or arbitrarily stood between the people and the free expression of their religious identity. For the first time in their lives, colonists could seize control over their own religious choices—and often they did so emphatically, even violently, in a manner that was highly destabilizing to the traditional boundaries of society and politics. Given that religion, especially Christianity, is inherently a matter of individual conscience, it was natural that this development would have political ramifications. That it happened on a mass scale in several colonies, and not just New England, made the Awakening even more politically consequential. "It seems evident," the historian Gordon S. Wood sensibly concludes, "that in one way or another the Great Awakening helped prepare American society and culture for the Revolution, but of course not in any direct, deliberate, or intentional manner."[8]

This included religious culture and habits that had long ceased to express any specifically sacred meaning. In New England, what the historian Edmund S. Morgan calls "the Puritan Ethic" of championing austerity, modesty, and frugality as the sources of virtue became translated from ideas that were once deeply spiritual but, by the 1760s, could stand on their own, largely independent of religious belief. Other Puritan practices were easily transferable to politics. The Calvinist belief in original sin, to take one example, led many colonists to doubt that a single individual could be incorruptible enough to avoid the luxuries of power and rule justly and effectively. To take another, the Revolutionary spirit broadened the Puritan errand into the wilderness into a more generic "American" sacred mission to spread the blessings of liberty. Channeling the ghost of John Winthrop, during the war John Adams boasted to General Nathanael Greene that "America is the City, set upon a Hill." Or consider the covenant, God's pact with his chosen people, that also formed the basis of Puritan government in the form of a covenant, or contract, between ruler and ruled. God, almost by definition, could never violate his end of the bargain with the godly, but his chosen people had to work strenuously to live a pious, God-fearing life in order to uphold theirs; yet civil rulers could fail, and often did, and thus could be removed from office, as Winthrop discovered when he was temporarily stripped of the Massachusetts governorship in 1634. Similar to, and certainly compatible with, John Locke's liberal theory of government as a contract between the government and the people that can be broken if one side fails to uphold its terms of the contract, in 1775 New Englanders believed their king had violated the terms of their covenant.[9]

At the same time religious ideas became secularized, politics became sacralized. Political discourse in the Revolutionary era assumed a moralistic tenor, a tone of absolute good battling absolute evil for the souls of the colonists. The language of liberty, in other words, owed much to the rhetorical rhythms and sacred ideas of the church. Consider the stirring oratory of Patrick Henry, who converted many to the cause of independence by modeling his rhetoric upon the revival sermon and plagiarizing his words from the Bible. Begun by the Puritans and evangelized by the Great Awakening, this organic process of exchange between the sacred and the secular produced an emotionally, morally, and ideologically powerful case for American independence. It was probably the Patriots' greatest weapon.[10]

Yet it was not only the secularization of religion and the sacralization of politics that influenced the cause for independence: methods mattered too. Rhetoric and forms of mass communication pioneered by the media-savvy innovators of revivalism made it possible for Patriot leaders to disseminate a message of insubordination to a wide spectrum of colonists. The Awakeners' means of transmitting their own revolutionary rhetoric—especially through large, informal, spontaneous, open-air sermons and the rapid publication and distribution of pamphlets and newsletters—invented networks of communication that later enabled Patriot leaders to win the battle for colonial hearts and minds. Publishing skills developed in the seventeenth century by highly literate New England Puritans and later perfected on a mass scale by revivalists during the Great Awakening were especially notable—by 1776, Patriot clergy in New England were publishing at a rate four times greater than secular pamphleteers.[11]

In ideas, values, and modes of communication, then, the Patriots used religion to shape their Revolutionary moment and achieve independence. In the process, they discovered a new national identity at the same time they created a new national polity—and in both, faith played an influential role. In turn, they helped to give shape to what would soon become a distinctly American foreign policy.

CHAPTER FOUR

The Harmony of the World Confounded

R ELIGION WAS CENTRAL TO the outbreak and course of the Revolutionary War. It was not quite a religious war, though a religious war raged within it as colonists drew battle lines with a cross as well as a sword. Overall, though there were significant exceptions, religious controversies burned brightest of all among the proponents of independence. Rebellious sentiment clustered within dissenting Protestant churches that resented London's increasingly interventionist manner of ruling the colonies, especially on questions of territorial expansion, taxation, and religious authority. Most crucially, faith lay at the heart of the ideals and interests that would give shape to a new American style of foreign relations. The clashes that resulted from the long push for independence convinced the new Americans that they, and they alone, were destined to spread the blessings of Protestant liberty far beyond their own borders.

Ironically, the Peace of Paris in 1763 triggered strife between colonists and Britain even as it brought an end to the Seven Years' War. Defeat in the war stimulated a great awakening of sorts among several Indian tribes of the Great Lakes region. Led by a Delaware prophet named Neolin, the Indian religious revival spread an empowering message that the Great Spirit had bequeathed the land to the Indians and that the Europeans had stolen it from them. In turn, Neolin's revival helped fuel Pontiac's Rebellion, a widespread revolt that caught the British authorities and colonial settlers completely off-guard. Aided by the element of surprise and driven on by their own visions of divine glory, Pontiac and his followers captured several British forts along the Great Lakes and killed over two thousand colonists.[1]

Rather than launch a new major war against a broad alliance of Indians, British authorities issued the Royal Proclamation of 1763, which drew a sharp red line on the map of British North America all the way down the spine of the Appalachian mountains from Maine to Georgia's southern border with Florida, beyond which colonial settlement was prohibited. But while the Proclamation Line appeased the Indians, it infuriated the American colonists, who coveted the vast expanses of "unused" arable land beyond the mountains. Echoing a long line of thought descending from Samuel Purchas and the Puritans, Charles-Jeffrey Smith, a Long Island evangelist, spoke for many in looking forward to "that glorious Day . . . when the Wilderness shall blossom as a Rose, & the Tawny Inhabitants thereof bow to the Scepter of King Jesus." Rebellion, mostly in the backcountry, was not long in coming, and it assumed a religious tone that mirrored socioeconomic divisions: rough-edged, New Light, frontier Presbyterianism fighting for its liberties against the domineering, genteel Anglicanism of royal colonial officials. In one gruesome episode in Pennsylvania in 1763, a largely Presbyterian mob going by the name of the Paxton Boys murdered dozens of Indians in the name, as one Thomas Barton put it, of "our pure Protestant faith, our equitable Laws, and our sacred Liberties." They then marched from the interior to Philadelphia, where they planned to protest the imposition of new taxes and prohibition on settling new land by killing off the hundreds of Indians who had fled and sought refuge in the city. Only the opposition of Quakers and Moravians, and the timely intervention of Benjamin Franklin, averted an even greater massacre. A similar revolt erupted in the Carolina backcountry, where the Regulator movement pitted colonial Presbyterians against governing Anglicans.[2]

At the same time, the Church of England exacerbated colonial fears by launching a new campaign to convert the Indians to Christ through its missionary arm, the Society for the Propagation of the Gospel in Foreign Parts (SPG). To many colonists, especially the large numbers of Presbyterians, Baptists, and Congregationalists who wanted to move inland from New England, Pennsylvania, and the South, the SPG was simply out to entrench the property holdings of the Church of England at their expense. Samuel Adams, James Otis, and John Hancock, three Bostonians who would lead the charge for independence, began their resistance to British authority by forming a committee in 1762 to promote Congregationalist missionaries to compete with those of the dreaded SPG. Even more outrageous were the SPG's efforts, officially encouraged, to convert souls to Anglicanism among the *colonists*—including those who already belonged to other Protestant denominations, and including in places where few if any Indians lived, such as Boston and Cambridge. In its pretensions to dominate territory, faith, and identity, the Church of England was fast beginning to replace the Vatican in the minds of colonists as the ultimate source of arbitrary government. The so-called "Bishops Plot," when the Church announced it would send bishops to America for the first time in colonial history, fanned these flames even higher.[3]

The Stamp Act, introduced without consultation in 1765 to make the colonists pay for an expensive global war from which they had singularly benefited, further heightened the transatlantic argument over the nature of liberty. The Stamp Act confirmed what the colonists had already suspected: London was the new Rome. By acting in such an arbitrary, unrepresentative manner, the British government had shown itself to be as fond of tyranny and as contemptuous of liberty as was the Catholic Church. And as they did during the Bishops Plot, the clergy took the lead in shaping opposition to the Stamp Act. New England's ministers attacked the Stamp Act with a righteous fury they had previously saved for Catholic priests and Indian warriors. Typical was an August 1765 sermon by Jonathan Mayhew, scourge of Anglicanism, that touched off a cause of mob violence in Boston resulting in the destruction of Deputy Governor Thomas Hutchinson's home. And the clergy did more than simply preach. In Boston, the Reverends Charles Chauncy and Samuel Cooper played important, clandestine roles in setting up the Sons of Liberty; in Lyme, Connecticut, Reverend Stephen Johnson did the same. This connection to the clergy explains the Sons of Liberty's millennial rhetoric, based on John's visions in the Book of Revelation, that the Stamp Act had been imposed upon the colonists by "monsters in the shape of men, who under a pretence of governing and protecting mankind, have enslaved them."[4]

Yet another eminent clergyman, none other than George Whitefield, offered his services to the anti–Stamp Act resistance. Through a mutual friend, Whitefield corresponded with Sam Adams, the driving force behind the Sons of Liberty; both men, it turned out, believed in the inseparability of political and religious liberty, and both were eager to apply Whitefield's reputation and skills to the defense of colonial liberties. Now living in England, the aging Whitefield had retained his affection for the American colonies that had once made him among the most famous men in the Atlantic world. Despite his British nationality and Anglican faith, Whitefield did not hesitate to link the arbitrary power of Catholicism that he had long warned about with the imperious authority of Parliament and the Church of England. Neither did Adams, who argued that the "Religion and public liberty of a People are intimately connected . . . and therefore rise and fall together." On a more tactical level, Adams also wanted to take advantage of Whitefield's contacts in Britain to advance the American case. And though the "Great Itinerant" would have disapproved of the use of violence, in an important way Adams was in fact following in Whitefield's footsteps. Before Whitefield and the Great Awakening, large outdoor rallies had been rare in colonial America. Through the 1740s, Whitefield pioneered and perfected the art of holding a mass revival, down to its publicity and organization, and it was this skill that Adams emulated. According to the historian Gary Nash, this approach, combined with Adams's fiery rhetoric and extremist tactics and the unusual degree of clerical consensus supporting the Patriot cause in Boston, enabled Adams "to turn the resistance movement into a kind of religious crusade."[5]

It was against this backdrop of unwanted bishops and unwarranted taxes that a young Boston lawyer, John Adams, wrote his first revolutionary tract. The rather ungainly titled *Dissertation on the Canon and Feudal Law*, published in six serialized parts in Boston newspapers between May and October 1765, laid out the historical drama of the English struggle for freedom against the "Lust of Tyrants" and "Arbitrary Government." In a drama that unfolded across the centuries, Adams argued that it was eventually "this great struggle, that peopled America." The Puritans guarded their religious liberty zealously, but it "was not religion *alone*, as is commonly supposed," that made them choose exile over conformity but "a love of *universal Liberty* . . . Tyranny in every form, shape, and appearance was their disdain, and abhorrence." The looming specter of the Bishops Plot, and its threat to both civil and religious liberty, is not difficult to detect. Adams warned Americans about the "Confederacy between the two Systems of Tyrany"—church and state, especially working in tandem—that would see government officials "contribute every Thing in their Power to maintain the Ascendancy of the Priesthood" and the clergy "employ that ascendancy over the Consciences of the People, in impressing on their Minds a blind, implicit obedience to civil Magistracy." It was up to the leaders of the colony, the lawyers and educators especially, to lead the charge against tyranny. And, Adams declared, the colonial clergy had a special role to play as well: "Let the pulpit resound with the doctrines and sentiments of religious liberty. Let us hear the danger of thraldom to our consciences, from ignorance, extream poverty and dependance, in short from civil and political slavery . . . God almighty has promulgated from heaven, liberty, peace, and good-will to man!" Adams, we shall see, went on to become one of the founders of American diplomacy, and he would use these ideas of civil and religious liberty when forging a new doctrine of U.S. foreign policy.[6]

Adams's dissent reflected another, related fear of Anglican bishops, one that went to the heart of the ideas, just then emerging, about liberty and republicanism that would drive the colonists' revolutionary fervor and shape their subsequent political union. Drawing upon two different (and not necessarily compatible) traditions of political thought on republicanism—classical and Renaissance on one hand, more recent liberal on the other—Patriot leaders believed that a republic could only succeed if it was led by enlightened rulers whose authority stemmed from the consent of the governed. But this begged the question: how would one tell if leaders were properly enlightened? The answer, which Patriot thinkers again drew from the political thought of ages past, was virtue: leaders needed to be virtuous, free from corruption, and attuned to the needs and desires of the people. And, a consensus felt, one of the best sources of virtue was Christianity in general, and Protestantism in particular. A leader who lacked virtue—and to the colonists, it was obvious this applied to Anglican clergy and British officials—was inherently corrupt, selfish, and aggressive, and an obvious danger to the peace.[7]

In 1774, as the colonies approached an open break with the mother country, Thomas Bradbury Chandler, a prominent Anglican minister from New Jersey, issued a "friendly" plea to "all reasonable Americans." Citing a verse from Romans 13, in which Paul declared that even the tyrannical rule of Roman Emperor Nero deserved compliance and respect, Chandler argued that the colonists "are bound, by the laws of Heaven and Earth, not to behave undutifully." Independence would not guarantee liberty but unleash chaos and tyranny. "The bands of society would be dissolved, the harmony of the world confounded, and the order of nature subverted," Chandler warned, "if reverence, respect, and obedience might be refused to those whom the constitution has vested with the highest authority." British Anglicanism, it seemed, was not especially well suited to American republicanism.[8]

As Chandler's plea illustrates, not everyone agreed that God Almighty smiled upon the cause of independence. Many colonists—estimates range between a fifth and a third—remained loyal to British rule. Many of these Loyalists fled the American colonies, moving north to Canada, south to other British colonies in the Caribbean, or back to Great Britain itself. Some were royal tax collectors or port and customs authorities; others were officials in the imperial bureaucracy. But naturally, a large percentage of Loyalists were Anglicans who had not only pledged allegiance to King George III but had also sworn an oath of fealty to the Church of England. Many Anglican Loyalists joined other Tory refugees on their flight into exile, forever changing the religious, cultural, and political complexion of Canada as well as America. But many others remained—under the threat of harassment, torture, and even death—to argue the British case to their fellow Americans. Yet few Patriots felt they could trust the elitist pretensions of the Church of England and its Loyalist adherents. Anglicans, it was said, "prefer basking in the sunshine of British royalty and court favour, to the simple practice of the pure religion of their forefathers."[9]

Patriots might be suspicious, but loyalty was a matter of conscience to Anglican Tories, and a matter of faith. Not only had they sworn an oath to King and Crown, they also fervently believed that monarchical government was the best way of ordering society. They feared chaos and disorder, and in the Sons of Liberty they saw the sovereignty of the people as little more than the tyranny of mob violence. Much of this view was socially conditioned, the product of habits, traditions, and a cherished history of providing for prosperity and good government. But much of it was also based in the Anglican reading of scripture. Most ministers in the Church of England believed that monarchical rule was preferable to republicanism because the Bible commanded submission to authority. They envisioned society in almost feudalistic terms, as an organic whole that prospered and suffered together regardless of an individual's wealth or social standing. They had a communalistic view of society that was incompatible with the individualistic republicanism of Patriot ideology. Anarchy was the only substitute for deference to rulers; of the two, Anglicans strongly preferred the stability assured by deference.[10]

Methodism, soon to be America's largest Protestant denomination but still a new, unnamed outgrowth of reformed Anglicanism in 1775, also stood fast with the mother church and country. In England, John Wesley, John Fletcher, and other Methodist leaders spoke out against revolution and appealed for imperial unity. Wesley mocked the Patriots' melodramatic and purely metaphorical claims of being "enslaved" by British "tyranny" by pointing out the awkward fact that the colonists, including several Patriot leaders, owned actual African slaves. Wesley also observed that even as an Englishman, living in England, he too was denied the vote and was thus being taxed without representation. In Virginia, where revivalistic Methodism exploded in popularity just as the Revolution was breaking out, early Methodists heeded their founder's call. Some could not bear to break with the Church of England; others were pacifists who refused to countenance the use of force. However, Methodist Loyalists were still a small fraction of the overall population and did not make much of an impact on the course of revolution, and most of their leaders, mainly English missionaries, returned to Britain or moved to Canada when it was clear that war was coming.[11]

While Methodist pacifism was often augmented by residual loyalty to the Church of England, the motives of the peace churches—most prominently the Society of Friends, or Quakers, but also various German Pietist sects, such as the Moravians—were not so mixed. Both groups were concentrated mostly in Pennsylvania, but Quakers could be found throughout the colonies, especially in the South. Some Quakers were indeed motivated by loyalty to the Crown, and many of the Germans harbored vestigial gratitude to the British for sheltering them from the persecutions of the Old World. Many other Quakers defied their coreligionists and openly supported the Patriots (and were expelled from the Society for doing so); some, such as General Nathanael Greene, even took up arms against the British. But for most Quakers, pacifism rather than politics established their firm neutrality. Grounding their pacifism in scripture, especially the New Testament, they argued that no political end could ever be justified or achieved through violent means. Like the Anglicans and Methodists, Quakers also adhered to the Bible's injunction that Christians had a duty to respect and obey civil authority. Most colonial governments tolerated pacifism by respecting it as a form of conscientious objection. But tolerance extended only as far as actual military service, and so most colonial governments also demanded that pacifists compensate by paying a tax that would go toward military service. Quakers refused to abide by such an obvious breach of their Christian pacifist creed, and many served prison time for their stand. Other pacifist sects, such as the Mennonites, Schwenkfelders, and Dunkers, were extremely pious, grateful to the British, and thus even more consistently strident in their pacifist witness. But their small numbers were confined to a few isolated pockets of Pennsylvania and Delaware and did not pose any threat to either the Patriots or the British.[12]

Perhaps the most interesting case is that of the Moravians, a German sect who had arrived from Saxony in the 1730s and quickly adapted to colonial American life better than any other religious refugees from middle Europe. The Moravians embraced an early form of capitalism and prospered as a result. As we saw during the Seven Years' War, they also were willing to compromise their pacifism and bear arms in the name of self-defense. Many sympathized with the Patriots' Whig ideology and calls for liberty from British oppression. Yet their pacifism remained strong nonetheless, and many Moravians were reluctant to break openly with the British. Ambivalence aside, the examples of the Anglicans, Quakers, Methodists, and Moravians illustrate just how divisive the forces of revolution could be. American devotion did not always lead to American Revolution.[13]

FAITH MAY HAVE acted as a powerful motivator to people on both sides of the conflict, but on balance it favored the Patriots. While most but not all Anglicans, Quakers, and Moravians opposed violent rebellion against British rule, other denominations threw their weight behind the Patriot cause. Most enthusiastic were the dissenting denominations—such as Presbyterianism and Congregationalism—and their spin-offs, such as Unitarianism—that for a decade had already been providing much of the ideological and moral propulsion of the anti-British insurgency. Baptists, be they Separatists or moderates, also by and large favored independence as a means to stimulate a revival and achieve their own religious liberty through it. Many things united these denominations, but three in particular stand out: in religion, their hostility to ecclesiastical hierarchy and liturgical artifice (other than their own, of course); in politics, their libertarian outlook; and in both, their sturdy antiauthoritarianism and localism, grounded in the belief that sovereignty should come from the people rather than distant rulers. In both faith and life, then, they preferred autonomy to external control.[14]

Yet even within these confines, religion did not decide whether a colonist supported or opposed the Revolution. Every denomination suffered a schism between Patriots and Loyalists. Presbyterians and Congregationalists were overwhelmingly Patriotic, but in the Carolina and New England backcountries rural folk harbored lingering distrust of the elite merchants and urbanites who were pushing hardest for independence. Similarly, Baptists had endured harsh treatment for dissenting from the established (and fiercely Patriotic) Congregational churches in Connecticut and Massachusetts. And although Anglicans were by and large Loyalists behind the Crown and Church of England, many of them supported the Revolutionary cause, especially in the South. Indeed, if Anglicans had united as one behind the king, the Revolution would have been deprived of the services of George Washington and Patrick Henry.[15]

Still, many more Anglicans supported the Patriots than Presbyterians and Congregationalists supported the British. Despite exceptions, then, in general the cause of independence enjoyed a preponderance of religious backing. Though they are a crude measurement, these denominational generalizations largely held. And within them, the clergy served an extremely important function. During the divisive upheaval of the Revolutionary era, religion acted as a critical social bond. Unity, even consensus, was hard to find in any colony, but on the whole religious support for independence was a vital piece of the puzzle of a developing "American" worldview and way of warfare. This was the clergy's message. Though they did no fighting, they were a vital resource. Unlike any other cohort or profession in society—certainly not the bulk of the Patriot leadership—the clergy could command a vast, captive audience on a weekly basis (and sometimes more often). While the Patriot leaders drew on support from the cities and the aristocratic rural gentry, the clergy's audience cut across almost all forms of identity: the backcountry as well as the coast, villages and farms as well as cities, poor as well as rich. Even though some churches remained silent—most notably the Lutherans of backcountry Pennsylvania—in general, support for the Patriots drew on nearly all Protestant denominations, too, including among Anglicans.[16]

Above all, the clergy were trusted as interpreters of events, both spiritual and earthly, theological and political. This was an awesome responsibility that in wartime carried tremendous social and political power. Wars are inherently destructive and divisive events, even when they go well. Even the most consensual wars in American history have not been as free of tensions or factions as people care to recall after victory, and the Revolutionary War, one of the most divisive in American history, was certainly no different. The Patriots had set themselves an incredibly difficult undertaking, and victory was uncertain until very late in the war. Military stalemate and a collapsing economy caused many to question whether their goal was worth the sacrifice. Though a war-weary people remained committed to the cause, often morale dipped and confidence plummeted during the war's precarious moments. The clergy's widely respected role as interpreters of the day's movements, people, and events enabled them to maintain support for the Patriots at moments when the excessively rational or frightened might have abandoned the cause.[17]

Perhaps most important, the clergy also functioned as political advocates during the Revolution. Thus they not only recruited people and maintained their overall morale, they also argued the Patriot case and mobilized popular opinion behind it. Loyalists and royal officials complained bitterly of the powerful "black regiment" of pro-Patriot clergy who manipulated gullible colonists into supporting independence. "It is your G–d damned Religion of this Country that ruins the Country," a British officer shrieked at a Patriot minister. "Damn your Religion." Ambrose Serle, aide to a British officer, relayed a similarly frustrated message to the Earl of Dartmouth: "Your Lordship can scarcely conceive, what Fury the Discourses of some mad Preachers have created in this Country." Combining covenant theology with the Whig liberalism of John Locke, the "black regiment" absolved the faithful from their obligation to obey king and Parliament since these rulers had imposed despotism upon the colonies. Some joined Reverend Jonathan Edwards Jr., son of the famous theologian and himself a pastor in New Haven, in urging the colonists to take up armed resistance to the British. Against John Wesley's critique of slavery, Reverend Samuel Hopkins promised that independence would lead to moral uplift, which in turn would sweep away America's enslavement of blacks as it was demolishing Britain's enslavement of the colonies.[18]

Other clergy mobilized colonial women—who comprised 70 percent of all churchgoers—in nonimportation boycotts and home manufacturing drives that were vital to the colonial economy as Patriots attempted to shut down trade with Britain; in turn, these same women became revolutionary leaders within their own households, motivating husbands and sons who might otherwise have been indifferent. Abigail Adams was one such woman: her arguments in favor of revolution had as much to do with her minister father's preaching as they did her husband's Whig politics. Continuing their work from the opposition to the Stamp Act and Bishops Plot, America's "mad Preachers" spread a gospel of religious and political liberty throughout the colonies. By 1770, they were even among the first to call for outright separation from Great Britain. It was an indispensable contribution to the cause of independence.[19]

Chaplains performed similar functions in the Continental Army. Their ability to sustain morale under arduous conditions and their willingness to supplement the cause of Christ with the cause of America ensured them an important role in the army. In this they needed simply to carry on the work of civilian ministry, as many who volunteered for duty in the Continental Army believed they were serving simultaneously in two armies: Christ's and America's. Chaplains constantly stressed these links between religion and nation and proclaimed that patriotism was an integral part of true Christianity. Many if not most of the militiamen and army troops were not professional soldiers and were thus unused to killing. Chaplains helped them overcome this morally disquieting but mandatory task by emphasizing that the Americans fought, in the words of a Baptist chaplain, a "defensive war in a just cause sinless." They fought for self-protection and fundamental rights, not plunder or unnecessary glory. More immediately, faith provided comfort during grueling overland marches, chronic food shortages, and the miserable conditions of camp. It also enabled chaplains and officers to sustain the inexperienced Continental Army soldiers' courage in battle against an enemy with experience, expertise, and superior military technology. Soldiers preferred warm, informal sermons to didactic, scholarly treatises, which made evangelical preachers especially popular and effective. George Washington appreciated the chaplains' contributions to maintaining discipline and morale and, as commander-in-chief of the American forces, made regular chapel services mandatory for both officers and soldiers. In the dark days of September 1777, the Continental Congress expressed a similar appreciation by appropriating scarce funds to purchase twenty thousand Bibles for the army.[20]

As a military tactician, Washington was good; as a leader of men and reader of human nature, he was great. Despite his own lukewarm, formless faith and aversion to institutional religion, Washington realized that many of his troops required the comforts of religious belief. Faith provided reassurance to the Continental Army's mostly amateur soldiers, particularly those who were entering battle for the first time in their lives. "If it is my fate to survive this action, I shall; if otherwise, the Lord's will must be done," Major John Jones wrote his wife in October 1779. "Every soldier and soldier's wife should religiously believe in predestination." When the army's morale plummeted as it faced seemingly insurmountable odds and suffered through dwindling food and supplies and dreadful weather, many turned to religion. The confessions of a young corporal were typical: "I find God has a Remnant in this Depraved and Degenerated and gloomy time." Without such inner belief, so common among the American colonists, it is uncertain whether the Americans would have continued to press for what must have seemed like an improbable victory.[21]

Popular among people, soldiers, and clergy was the use of providential self-confidence and millennial expectation in interpreting the great events that unfolded before them. With varying degrees of radicalism, and with New England leading the way, belief in a Revolutionary millennium flourished throughout colonies. Many shared the conceit that theirs was the era in which the end times, and most joyously Christ's return to earth, were approaching, and that resistance to British rule was an important sign of the millennium's unfolding. The millennium was above all a battle between Christ and the Antichrist, between good and evil, and thus provided a worldview in which the struggle against a corrupt, tyrannical British monarch—who was betraying the ancient principles of English liberty, no less—fit particularly well. It was a terrifying vision, to be sure, because it foretold imminent death and destruction. But it was also comforting because it gave the colonists reassurance that theirs was the cause that would ultimately prevail; when the battles had finished, it was they who would remain to build a better society. Even the radicalism of Thomas Paine's *Common Sense*—"We have it in our power to begin the world over again"—must be read in light of the end-of-history millennialism that pervaded the Revolutionary era.[22]

While distinct from millennialism, providentialism provided a similar fillip to the Revolution. Just as earlier generations of American colonists had believed they were being guided and protected by the hand of God, so too did many Patriots act with confidence in the knowledge that they were safely in pursuit of an undeniable destiny. Belief in providence provided colonists with an impressive degree of self-confidence in their otherwise implausible challenge to the world's mightiest military and economic power because it fostered, in the words of historian Charles Royster, "a unique enthusiasm that encouraged Americans to defy rational calculations of the probability of success." As both a believer in the supremacy of a heavenly creator and a military commander who needed to maintain the morale of his troops in their fight against the odds, Washington understood this well. During the war, he made several appeals to providence to intervene on America's behalf. Using his General Orders of May 1778 to celebrate the announcement of the alliance with France, Washington proclaimed: "It having pleased the Almighty ruler of the Universe propitiously to defend the Cause of the United American-States . . . it becomes us to set apart a day for gratefully acknowledging the divine Goodness & celebrating the important Event which we owe to his benign Interposition." Or as a number of preachers asked during the war, "If God be with us, who can be against us?" It took a brave soul to answer in the negative. With such innate self-belief, who among the Americans could doubt their ultimate victory? And after victory, who would deny them their mission to the rest of the fallen world?[23]

CHAPTER FIVE

Liberation Theology

R ELIGION'S INFLUENCE WAS NOT without further paradox, because
most of the Founders—certainly the most influential Founders—were
themselves not especially religious. Some major Revolutionary figures
were devout Christians—John Witherspoon and Benjamin Rush immediately spring to mind—but many others were not, among them Benjamin
Franklin, Thomas Jefferson, James Madison, Alexander Hamilton, and
John Adams. An engineer of the American Enlightenment as much as
he was of American independence, Franklin possessed a warm, ecumenical spirit that was almost totally devoid of spiritual content. Though he
admired the morality of Jesus and believed in an Almighty God, Jefferson
doubted Jesus's divinity and loathed institutional religion as a profane,
earthly artifice that came between humanity and the heavens and kept the
people subservient to the clergy. Despite receiving an education grounded
in religious ideas and values as a student at Princeton, James Madison felt
much the same. A nominal Presbyterian and proto-Anglican for much of
his life, Alexander Hamilton found true faith only in his later years. Finally,
having grown up in the "Bible Commonwealth" of Massachusetts—and to
an old, established Puritan family who had crossed the ocean in the 1630s,
no less—John Adams simply could not escape his religious heritage; in
addition, his father-in-law was a Congregationalist minister. But Adams
wore his religion lightly, often skeptically, and found in it a source of ideas,
values, and useable history rather than spiritual comfort.[1]

Of the principal architects of American independence, Washington
was the most fervently religious, but his Anglican faith was hardly conventional. He almost never spoke of Christ, had little interest in even the most
rudimentary aspects of theology, and rarely attended church. Though he
neglected Jesus, he paid inordinate attention to the role of God as the
"Governor of the Universe." But neither was he a deist, one who believes
in a distant God, a heavenly watchmaker who created the world and has
stood back ever since. Instead, Washington's God—America's God—was
a providential Supreme Being who regularly intervened in the world on
behalf of the righteous and the virtuous.[2]

Yet despite all their skepticism and eccentricity, religion mattered to the Founders nonetheless. They may have been agnostics, deists, or spiritually vacuous, but they lived in an era and in a nation in which religion played a central role in politics and culture. As the historian Robert Middlekauff puts it, many of the Founders "may not have been moved by religious passions. But all had been marked by the moral dispositions of a passionate Protestantism. They could not escape this culture; nor did they try." Though products of Enlightenment rationalism, they still worked with, not against, the religious currents of their time and place. They also freely used biblical ideas and scriptural passages to popularize and justify their political views. For all their knowledge of classical, Renaissance, and Enlightenment philosophy, they also appreciated that the Bible—the most widely read and deciphered book in the colonies—contained the Western world's most extensive discussions of equality and liberty. They epitomized the "religious Enlightenment." One of the secrets to their success, in fact, was their early recognition that faith and modernity were two sides to the same American coin, complementary rather than contradictory. Thus the pursuit of religious liberty mattered as much to Jefferson and Madison as did political liberty—indeed, in their minds the two were inseparable. Nor did they try to eliminate religion or reduce religion's influence upon Americans—quite the opposite, in fact, as the Founders, Jefferson and Madison included, were unanimous in believing that religion had a constructive role to play in American political culture.[3]

RELIGIOUS ATTITUDES mattered in war and diplomacy, too, but in more indirect and subtle ways. Despite the eccentricities of the faith of the Founders, religion was an integral part of colonial American politics and culture. Many of the Founders, even those who were not conventionally devout, sought to infuse politics with religion, but even those who did not found it impossible to avoid the religious influence. In particular, by fusing their Revolutionary objectives with the common fires of faith, the Founders crafted three libertarian principles that would have a lasting impact upon the conduct of U.S. foreign policy: unilateralism, republicanism, and separationism.

Dislodging the British proved to be more difficult than the Americans initially appreciated. Perhaps they were thinking of New England's improbable success in capturing the mighty fortress of Louisbourg in 1745; perhaps they assumed that because they had God and right on their side, they would conquer an ostensibly superior enemy. Whatever the reason, the Patriots began the war with a certain misplaced—or at least not entirely justified—confidence. Though the first years of the war were not a complete disaster, and though they recorded significant victories at Trenton and Princeton, Washington's forces suffered several humiliating defeats in New York and Canada that stalled the drive for independence. It was clear they needed outside help. And in a North American war against the British, who better to turn to than France? The French were certainly willing, but in 1776 they did not feel able to take on the British in tandem with a ragtag bunch of rebellious colonists. Loans and supplies made their way from France to America, but little else; and what the French did send was never enough. But in October 1777, the Americans' stunning victory over the British at Saratoga transformed the diplomatic climate, and with it the war. The ragtag bunch proved they could fight. Thus while Saratoga did not ensure Britain's defeat, it did prevent America's. Most important, it made an alliance between the French and the Americans possible.[4]

Culturally as well as militarily, this was a surprising turn of events. Protestant Britons, especially the American colonists, had demonized the papist French for the past two centuries. France represented the tyranny of superstition and ignorance—how could the enlightened, godly people of America put their fate in Catholic hands? In truth, there was little debate about whether to ally with France simply because the rebels' situation was still desperate, even after Saratoga. As Benjamin Franklin said at the time, the colonies had been "*forc'd* and *driven* into the Arms of France." Thus in February 1778, with the Americans in need of a partner and the French convinced they could use the Americans to wound the British, Benjamin Franklin and the Comte de Vergennes, the French foreign minister, concluded a Treaty of Alliance with the aim of severing the colonies' ties to Britain forever.[5]

Still, a virulent strain of anti-Catholicism lingered in the colonies, and while there was little protest over the alliance with France, it caused discomfort nonetheless. After all, only a few years had passed since the 1774 Quebec Act, which guaranteed Catholic rights in the British-held province and had been one of the American colonists' main grievances leading them to revolt. And even after the partnership was announced, riots broke out between ostensibly allied French and American sailors based in Boston Harbor. John Adams could never let go of his own suspicions of Catholicism because he could never quite separate the sources of political and ecclesiastical tyranny. In Catholic countries, he explained in a 1761 diary entry, "the gross Impostures of the Priesthood" kept the people under the "Yoke of Bondage. But in Protestant Countries . . . Freedom of Enquiry is allowed to be not only the Priviledge but the Duty of every Individual." Many years later, he told his daughter-in-law Louisa that "Liberty and Popery cannot live together." John Dickinson, the legendary "Pennsylvania Farmer" whose Revolutionary War writings promoted the American cause but who also hesitated when it came to outright independence, worried that the Americans were helping to turn France into the dominant power in Europe. "Suppose we shall ruin" Britain, Dickinson wondered. "France must rise on [Britain's] Ruins. Her Ambition.

Her Religion. Our danger from thence. We shall weep at our victories."
John Jay, a descendant of Huguenots who had fled Catholic persecution in
France for the safety of America, felt the same. Such reservations did not
trump the advantages of a French alliance, but they did make the Americans tread carefully.[6]

With all this in mind, Adams set to work drafting a template for foreign alliances, now and in the future. The result was the Model Treaty, an
often overlooked document that was never used but nonetheless codified,
for the first time, the objective of unilateralist independence in American diplomacy. An alliance was a necessity, and necessity is the diplomat's
most important virtue. But the Model Treaty also aimed to keep foreign
powers—namely, France—at arm's length. Focusing mostly on free trade
as the foundation for durable peaceful relations as well as the source of the
Revolution's immediate needs, Adams deliberately rejected the forging of
political ties, hosting foreign troops on American soil, or establishing a
permanent alliance. Of France, Adams insisted that Congress "Submit
to none of her Authority—receive no Governors, or officers from her."
Facts on the ground would override Adams's concerns. But such facts were
temporary; principles were abiding. Adams did not create the American
fear of entangling alliances or faith in unilateralism that flowed from
much deeper fears of Catholic tyranny or absolutist monarchy; he merely
reflected them. In turn, his Model Treaty established a precedent of diplomatic independence that George Washington later sanctified in his influential 1796 Farewell Address. Not until 1949, with the creation of NATO,
would the United States join a permanent foreign alliance.[7]

As early as 1763, Patriots—or those who would become Patriots—had
criticized British colonial rule with steadily increasing frequency and
ferocity. By the war's first skirmishes in Lexington and Concord a dozen
years later, this criticism had developed into a sophisticated, cohesive
political ideology that stressed the sanctity of individual liberty from arbitrary, ineffectual, and unjust rulers. The clergy had played a vital role in
forming the Patriot response, both in terms of forming an argument to
counter British rule and in mounting a violent challenge to overthrow it.
But as any body of opposition knows, it is one thing to criticize, another
thing entirely to win the argument and then be responsible for creating
a new political order. This was precisely the difficult position in which
the architects of independence found themselves in 1783: how would the
colonies replace the unity, stability, and prosperity of Britain's imperial
governance? And how would they collectively protect themselves and
safeguard their interests in a world of hostile foreign powers?

Though it would take eight agonizing years to complete, the answer,
of course, was the construction of a democratic, federal republic. And part

of the answer—a large part—came from Protestant history and doctrine. This does not mean that the Founders sought to establish a Christian republic or that they envisioned America as an exclusively, immutably Christian nation. Most of the Founders, especially the most important contributors to American political thought, were men of the Enlightenment, rational empiricists who disdained what they disparagingly thought of as religion's superstition. Rationalists in religion as well as politics and science, most of them ridiculed the emotional excesses of revivalism and evangelicalism. With the notable exception of Jefferson, most were not hostile to organized religion, but indifferent. Yet most Americans at the time were not at all indifferent; even Jefferson appreciated the salience and relevance of Christian faith in American culture and politics. Religion could not simply be ignored.[8]

Not for the first or last time in American history, religious and political ideas combined to form a powerful, irrepressible ideology: Christian republicanism, a blend of Protestant theology and democratic politics. Republicanism had other sources than Christianity. The political thought of ancient Rome that Renaissance philosophers had retrieved and revived was vital, as was the liberalism of John Locke. But in America, classical and liberal ideas about republicanism could not have been as effective or broadly accepted had Patriots not ingeniously wedded them to Christianity. It was this amalgam of diverse ideas, religion included, that endowed American republicanism with such strength.[9]

Christian republicanism had two components that were identical to classical, or what might be called "secular," republicanism. The first was the most obvious: sovereignty should be vested in the people and their duly chosen representatives, not in a hereditary monarch. Even the most benevolent, enlightened king could, in theory, act solely according to his desires. Thousands of people thus relied purely on the whim and favor of a single individual's arbitrary rule. Without them necessarily realizing it, this idea provided the colonists with the notion that they were "slaves" living under British "tyranny," despite their relatively high levels of freedom and autonomy. It also led them to conflate the "arbitrary" concentrated power of the Roman Catholic Church with that of George III, the British Parliament, and the Church of England. The second component was less apparent but just as important: if they were not to descend into anarchy and tyranny, a sovereign people had to be a virtuous people. Without virtue and its attendant benefits, American politics simply could not function.

For most political philosophers of the early modern world—and indeed, for many since—Christianity and republicanism could not coexist, let alone combine to form a stable political system, because they seemed inherently at odds with each other. As the Loyalist Anglicans illustrated, traditional views assumed that Christianity demanded obedience to divinely empowered authority; republicanism demanded precisely the opposite. But deference to authority was commonly found in other strands of Protestantism, too—even a revolutionary spirit like John Calvin decreed that individuals had neither the right nor the responsibility to defy those in power. Moreover, tradition also held that Christians owed their ultimate allegiance to God, and in turn to God's political representative on earth, the sovereign monarch. Most thinkers followed these assumptions and concluded that a republic could not exist with a strong Christian dimension.[10]

If American Christianity had been so hierarchical, it is plausible it would have been in conflict with republican liberty. But American religion was in fact not rigidly hierarchical; the Great Awakening had radically diffused and dispersed ecclesiastical authority in the 1740s, and even those denominations that rejected or escaped the revivals still had to contend with a much different religious landscape afterward. Even earlier, by 1700, Britain's North American colonies constituted one of the most pluralistic religious societies on earth. Almost every variety of Protestantism, smaller communities of European Catholics and Jews, and Native American and African faiths all lived alongside one another in the colonies. This diversity emerged in an entirely ad hoc fashion and stemmed mostly from the uncoordinated, often disorganized, and proprietary nature of British imperialism in the seventeenth century. Even in Massachusetts and Connecticut, undeniably hierarchical and nearly theocratic societies until the 1680s, Baptists and Quakers vied with Puritans for the colonists' affections. When the non-Puritan churches were persecuted, they could escape to nearby Rhode Island or New York and worship freely there. Thus geography and diversity combined to create a Christian world where religious autocracy was difficult to sustain.[11]

Yet even within those colonies that were for a time tightly controlled, republicanism thrived. Puritan New England, after all, had supported Oliver Cromwell during the English Civil War of the 1640s and despaired of a king, Charles I, who embraced ecclesiastical authority with such passion that Puritans suspected him of secretly being a Catholic. Puritans on both sides of the ocean were also suspicious, if not dubious, about Charles's claim to a divine right of kings, which struck them not only as dictatorial but blasphemous. In so doing, English revolutionary propagandists provided a counterargument to the apostle Paul's command that Christians obey authority. It was, in fact, this rich republican legacy that helped provide anti-British Patriots with a solution to the riddle of Christian republicanism in the 1770s and 1780s. By the time of the Revolution, this legacy had been widely accepted throughout the colonies, even when it was not acknowledged as such. Instead of seeing Christianity and republicanism as contradictory, Patriots argued that Christianity instead provided the basis for republicanism. Christians owed their ultimate allegiance to God, and nothing should come between them. A king, particularly one who interposed himself between heaven and earth by ruling arbitrarily and unjustly, stood between the Lord and the people. Thus two doctrines emerged to justify revolution: the Bible stated that people received their natural rights from God, and from God alone; the Bible also laid the foundations for each side, ruler and ruled, to abide by the terms of a covenant, and that if the king violated the covenant's terms he automatically forfeited his right to rule. Neither doctrine bode well for monarchical authority in Revolutionary America.[12]

One of the most important links between the Puritan republicanism of the English Civil War and the Christian republicanism of the American Revolution was the poet John Milton. A propagandist for both republicanism and reformed Protestantism, in the decades during and following the Civil War Milton articulated a theory of politics that the American Founders accepted and adopted. Like them, Milton joined British American colonists in damning Anglican bishops as an affront to civil and religious liberty. And like them, he believed that people automatically lived a life of enslaved servitude if they lived at the mercy of a single individual, especially one not chosen by the people and their representatives. Milton also believed that laws and rights, duties and privileges had been devised by God, not kings. "Shalt thou give law to God," he wrote in his epic poem *Paradise Lost*,

> *shalt thou dispute*
> *With him the points of liberty, who made*
> *Thee what thou art, and formed the powers of heaven*
> *Such as he pleased, and circumscribed their being?*

Finally, Milton believed that ecclesiastical corruption aided and abetted monarchical tyranny, and that secular authorities could not function properly without being propped up by the tyranny and superstition of an unreformed church, such as the Catholic or Anglican churches. In Milton's day, the excesses of Charles I and Bishop Laud, justified in the name of the divine right of kings, illustrated the need for both republican government and reformed religion. In the early 1650s, with Charles executed and the Church of England humbled, and a republican Commonwealth established in their place, Milton exulted in his conviction that "the most praiseworthy of all mortals [are] those who imbue the minds of men with true religion, even more to be praised than those who founded, with whatever distinction, kingdoms and republics according to human laws." To a political and religious reformer such as Milton, only a republic could safeguard the people's political and religious liberty.[13]

Not coincidentally, Milton happened to be one of the colonists' favorite writers, and *Paradise Lost* one of their favorite works. As a writer, Milton had few equals in the English language; at the time, perhaps only Shakespeare was as esteemed. But Milton's faith and politics also strongly appealed to the colonial philosophers, politicians, and activists who pushed for independence from Britain. It was his epic Christian poetry and the republican ideas of his contemporaries that fostered an "ideology of dissent" handed down from English revolutionaries to American. Adams, Washington, and especially Jefferson cited Milton to justify or explain their political views, and they applied Miltonic history and philosophy to their own revolutionary times and republican ambitions. Even more than the Founders, the Patriot clergy advanced Miltonic ideas about Christian republicanism and made them indispensable to the structure of American politics. One of the only groups in colonial society that could transcend divisions of class and region, the Patriot clergy argued to a wide audience that the British monarchy was unjust because it had exceeded its authority, abused its power, and placed its illegitimate rule between the people and their God. Their message was clear: the only legitimate kings who could rule absolutely were God and Jesus; everyone else needed the consent of the people.[14]

But liberty provided only half of the republican formula; the other was virtue. Without virtue, a republic could not properly function. It would, like all other forms of human government, descend into tyranny and cease to be a republic. And the best source of virtue was not commerce or politics, but religion; indeed, the benefits of commerce and politics flowed from an uncorrupted faith. One thing Americans could agree upon was that they could pledge allegiance to a monarchy of God and Christ. As John Jay pointed out in the *Federalist* papers, religious faith provided a common denominator for Americans, a people united in "professing the same religion." Though it had the virtue of being a sincere reflection of his own beliefs, this was the reason Washington referred to God in ambiguous terms—"Governor of the Universe," "Higher Cause," "Great Ruler of Events," "All Wise Creator," "Supreme Dispenser of all Good"—to which no American could object.[15]

THE RISE OF Christian republicanism, especially its virtuous foundations, was of course integral to the emergence of American politics. But it also marked an important development in the birth and early development of American foreign relations. In a very modern sense, Americans believed that a state's internal character influenced its external behavior. In other words, nations that were corrupt within would behave rapaciously toward other nations. The British had threatened the Americans' liberty and security because they had become corrupt and tyrannical. Though the English themselves had learned this lesson at the hands of Spanish and French Catholics, they had clearly forgotten it; the Americans had not. Virtue, then, was not simply its own reward; it was a valuable predictor of state behavior in the international system. Echoing Montesquieu and anticipating Kant, this aspect of America's Revolutionary republicanism marked one of the earliest formulations of what has come to be known as "the democratic peace," or what Madison called "the universal peace": driven by the grandiose ambitions of kings and queens, monarchies were aggressive; restrained by the peaceful, agrarian, commercial desires of the common people, republics were not.[16]

This truly revolutionary idea did not just diagnose problems, it also offered a cure. If Americans could not feel safe in a world without republican virtue, the solution was obvious: spread the virtue and its attendant blessings of liberty—which to many Americans also meant the spread of Christianity. "It is only necessary for republicanism to ally itself to the Christian religion to overturn all the corrupted political and religious institutions in the world," Benjamin Rush predicted to Jefferson in 1800. "I think we have reason to conclude," the Reverend Abraham Keteltas preached from the pulpit in Newburyport's Presbyterian Church, above the resting place of George Whitefield,

> that the cause of this American continent, against the measures of a cruel, bloody, and vindictive ministry, is the cause of God. We are contending for the rights of mankind, for the welfare of millions now living, and for the happiness of millions yet unborn.
> . . . It is God's own cause: It is the grand cause of the whole human race, and what can be more interesting and glorious. If the principles on which the present civil war is carried on by the American colonies, against the British arms, were universally adopted and practiced upon by mankind, they would turn a vale of tears into a paradise of God.

Keteltas was prescient indeed, as Indians, Canadians, Mexicans, Cubans, Filipinos, and others were to discover in the next century, although their vale of tears rarely disappeared as a result.[17]

But those living outside America's virtuous circle would not have to wait that long. America's clergy, the Revolutionary War's most able propagandists, carried the mission with them into battle. Reverend Ammi Robbins, a Connecticut chaplain with the force invading Quebec in 1776, exulted in the "pleasing views" as he and the troops crossed into foreign territory, "of the glorious day of universal peace and spread of the gospel through this vast extended country, which has been for ages the dwelling of Satan, and reign of Antichrist." A chaplain with the Virginia Brigades in Washington's camp at Valley Forge, writing rhyming poetry to boost morale, went further still:

> *AMERICA shall blast her fiercest foes!*
> *Out-brave the dismal shocks of bloody war!*
> *And in unrival'd pomp resplendid rise,*
> *And shine sole empress of the Western world!*[18]

From the outset, the Revolution created a character of American foreign relations that was deeply rooted in religious ideals.

JUST AS SIGNIFICANT was the Founders' decision to ensure the separation of church and state in the First Amendment of the Bill of Rights. The same common denominator of faith that was so vital to republicanism also made the disentangling of faith and politics a national priority. And as with republicanism itself, the unfolding of the Revolution gave shape, color, and meaning to what had before been an abstract idea.

Though the Founders squabbled constantly about many things, they were nearly unanimous on the importance of religious liberty. Whether they were devout believers or Enlightenment skeptics, whether they would become Republicans or Federalists, they all agreed that a republic could not function properly if it did not safeguard this fundamental principle. Religion was more than a matter of faith; it was a matter of conscience. The relationship between people and God was among the most personal and individual. It was also one of the most private and inviolable sources of ideas and values. To interfere with a person's religion, then, was to intrude into the deepest recesses of their mind. Almost by definition, this would introduce the very worst sort of tyranny, the kind of papist absolutism that Americans feared. As sources of personal conscience, religious liberty and diversity were indispensable to freedom overall, an argument made by Tom Paine in *Common Sense* and William Livingston, Patriot governor of New Jersey, in a 1778 speech. Thus even Catholics—and Anglicans and Jews—had a rightful place in the new nation, so long as they did not coerce others into practicing their religion. Preparing for the invasion of Canada in 1775, Washington ordered the expedition's commanders to "avoid all Disrespect or Contempt of the Religion" of the French. "While we are Contending for our own Liberty, we should be very cautious of violating the Rights of Conscience in others; ever considering that God alone is the Judge of the Hearts of Men and to him only in this Case they are answerable." He repeated this commitment in a public message to the people of Canada. Later, in an address to a Rhode Island synagogue during his first year as president, Washington boasted that the key to the new republic's success was that all Americans, regardless of their faith, "possess alike liberty of conscience and immunities of citizenship."[19]

Even before 1776, James Madison believed in the need to separate church from state. As a student at Princeton, his mentor had been the Patriot preacher and educator John Witherspoon, who blended Scottish commonsense philosophy with Presbyterianism and came up with a doctrine of individual rights that stressed the separation of church and state as a safeguard to both religious and political liberty. From Witherspoon, Madison also absorbed the Calvinist doctrine—though without Calvinist faith—of original sin and the inherent depravity of man, a vision that helped shape his views on the political necessity of checks and balances. Once back in his home state, Madison championed the rights of Virginia's Baptists and other religious minorities—not coincidentally, groups whose support Madison needed in the cause of independence. In 1779, he encouraged his friend Thomas Jefferson in the drafting of the Virginia Bill for Religious Freedom, though the bill never passed. In 1785, Madison authored, anonymously, a pamphlet under the title of "Memorial and Remonstrance against Religious Assessments" in a successful attempt to stop the reestablishment of religion in Virginia. He did so not from the convictions of his own faith, of which there was little, but because he too believed that religion was the wellspring of conscience, and that if the state could interfere with this, the most personal domain of thought, it could interfere, arbitrarily, in anything. To those who were concerned with the fate of virtue and pushed for the establishment of the Christian faith but not a particular church, Madison retorted that if the legislature could make one establishment one day, it could make another the next. Once down that road, there was little to stop such interference in religious affairs. Madison won this argument, and his "Memorial" became the template for the Virginia Statute for Religious Freedom later that year, which in turn provided a model for the establishment and free exercise clauses of the First Amendment. In order to protect the church from the state and the state from the church, Madison enshrined their perpetual separation.[20]

But separation was a necessity as well as an ideal. Had the Founders wanted to establish a national church or otherwise regulate national religion, they would have had a difficult time doing so—indeed, even at this early time, the breathtaking diversity of the religious landscape would have made it all but impossible. Already the Northwest Ordinance of 1787, an important piece of legislation that paved the way for westward expansion, had guaranteed religious liberty in land still to be politically organized. But even here, in Ohio, the sheer variety of faiths among the settlers made the decision against establishment a foregone conclusion. The Revolution, moreover, had sharpened the edges of pluralism. Authority had been subverted, hierarchy undermined, and establishments weakened in church as well as state. Revolutionary fervor destabilized American politics, and it had the same effect on religion. As one wary New Englander observed, soldiers coming home from the war returned with "looser ideas of religious liberty" and a conviction that they were masters of their own faith. This development should have surprised nobody. After all, these very soldiers had just risked their lives over abstract notions of egalitarianism and popular sovereignty. Who could blame them if they sought to practice what their leaders preached? In many cases, this had been literally true: one of the Patriot preachers' main themes was freedom from British—namely Anglican—religious tyranny. Yet the effect was to undermine not only the British authorities, but authority in general. The power and glory of the Anglican Church suffered, but so did that of the other major denominations, even the ardently Patriot Congregationalists and Presbyterians. By 1790, only 25 percent of Americans belonged to the once-dominant Anglican and Congregationalist churches, down from nearly half only thirty years before. Less formalistic evangelicals, particularly Baptists, were only too eager to step into this breach and drive the "democratization of American Christianity" forward.[21]

Moreover, many Patriot clergy outside Massachusetts and Connecticut had made the separation of church and state one of their key objectives. William Tennent, who had done the Continental Congress' bidding in the Carolina backcountry, agitated for separation during his recruiting drives. Baptists in Virginia did much the same, with Madison defending their efforts. And even within New England, a significant minority pushed for disestablishment. Jonathan Parsons, the minister who had his friend George Whitefield interred in Newburyport, believed that complete religious liberty was a prerequisite for American national unity. For Isaac Backus, a Massachusetts Baptist, the establishment of the Congregationalist Church in some New England states was fundamentally incompatible with the liberties for which Americans fought, indeed, little better than "the abominations of Popery." At the First Continental Congress in October 1774, Backus met with John and Sam Adams and other members of the Massachusetts delegation to drive home the Baptist call for religious liberty within America, and not just from Britain. How, Backus pointedly asked, was the Congregational establishment any different than the appointment of an Anglican bishop?[22]

He had a point. And though a few of the states clung to an official church, others were in agreement and dissolved their religious establishments as they became states within a national union free from British control. The dissolution of official Anglicanism in the southern states was not especially difficult, despite lingering sympathies in Virginia even among

Patriots such as Patrick Henry. New York, New Jersey, and Pennsylvania had long traditions of tolerant eclecticism; disestablishment there was never a matter for debate but a simple fact of life. Ironically, the only controversial aspect of separating church from state was the fear that it would lead to the separation of religion from politics. Few Americans—with not even Thomas Jefferson or Tom Paine among them—believed that Christian faith was irrelevant. If the republic was essential for liberty, and virtue was essential for a republic, and religion was essential for virtue, then religion was essential to a healthy republic. Viewed in this light, Patrick Henry's drive to continue tax support for the churches in post-Revolutionary Virginia had very little to do with lingering affections for the established Anglican Church and everything to do with a perceived decline of public morality that seemed to accompany a decline in morality during the war. Even Backus, the arch-separationist Baptist, conceded that "Christianity is essentially necessary to the good order of civil society is a certain truth."[23]

The solution was not to banish religion, or to regulate it, but to encourage it by enabling all Americans to worship as they chose. Religious liberty, freed from government interference: it was a fairly basic but nonetheless revolutionary principle, its genius rooted in the knowledge that religion did not have to be uniform to be vibrant. As Washington put it, "the path of true piety is so plain as to require but little political direction." The virtues of Christian republicanism did not always lead to disestablishment at the state level. But nationally, nearly everyone recognized that the only way forward was to keep church and state apart.[24]

The libertarian ethos of disestablishment fit beautifully with James Madison's theory of government based on the separation of powers, as both Madison and Hamilton themselves recognized. In the very first *Federalist*, Hamilton launched the defense of the Constitution by arguing that "in politics as in religion, it is equally absurd to aim at making proselytes by fire and sword." In the more famous fifty-first *Federalist*, which for the first time elaborated a theory of the separation of powers, Madison wrote: "In a free government, the security for civil rights must be the same as for religious rights." This also left the states, which may not be as religiously diverse as the nation, to maintain church establishments in order to safeguard public morality, and thus virtue.[25]

The effects of disestablishment were profoundly ironic: in the absence of a state sponsor, religion did not wither, but flourished. Even Anglicans—Americanized as the rebranded Protestant Episcopal Church—did not find it especially difficult to integrate themselves into the politics and culture of the United States. They were even permitted to consecrate their own bishop without harassment or protest, as if the Bishops Plot had never happened. But it was the children of the Great Awakening who would benefit most. Unsurprisingly, evangelicals largely became Anti-Federalists in the debates over the Constitution, such was their hostility to consolidations of elite power. They lost that argument, but their presence ensured that religion would continue to be a powerful voice in the new republic. In addition to these evangelical upstarts who would soon dominate American Protestantism, faith-based voluntary societies and even new denominations, such as the Mormons, emerged and thrived in the libertarian climate of the early nineteenth century—even in strongly Federalist Massachusetts, where voluntarism was often seen as a divisive attack on the social fabric and body politic.[26]

As we shall see in several chapters, the impact upon the new nation's foreign affairs was equally profound. In politics, religion, and economics, Madison and the Founders feared concentrations of power and, through federalism, church disestablishment, and the free market, sought to diffuse power as widely as possible. It was an ingenious solution to a great political quandary, and its influence was long-reaching. Coming after centuries of anti-Catholicism and a new strain of anti-monarchy, the new political order newly codified a very old and very Protestant tradition of hostility to arbitrary power. In American diplomatic thought and practice, this Protestant libertarian ethic made Americans suspicious about other nations that relied too heavily upon concentrations of power, be they religious (the Catholic Church) or political and economic (the Communist Party). Just as English Protestants in the sixteenth century had lived under the assumption that they could not live safely as the world's only Protestant refuge, Americans in the eighteenth century assumed they must tread carefully, alone, as one of the world's only republics. Unsurprisingly, religious liberty became intimately bound with the American critique of concentrated, arbitrary power, and a rallying cry in the centuries to come. Though it would not always determine U.S. foreign policy, it usually helped Americans define who were their friends in the world and who were their foes. This was a most important American revelation.

PART III

Imperial Destinies

The House of Representatives, Washington, D.C., February 1846. Two weeks shy of his seventy-ninth birthday, Congressman John Quincy Adams of Massachusetts sat quietly as debate roared around him. Ostensibly the issue was the Oregon Country, a huge territory on the Pacific coast that stretched for nearly a thousand miles from the northern boundary of California to the southern fringe of Russian Alaska. Both Great Britain and the United States laid claim to Oregon, but until then neither country had been willing to run the risk of war to assert its exclusive sovereignty. By the 1840s, however, Americans were gripped by expansionist fever and guided by a belief in their God-given manifest destiny to conquer and settle the entire North American continent. Texas, annexed the year before, was the first step, Oregon the next; the territory between Texas and the Pacific, then part of Mexico, would follow after. Few disputed expansionism in the abstract. But in the real world, expansion raised an uncomfortable question: where the flag went, would slavery follow? The Pacific Northwest was obviously unsuitable for plantation agriculture, and thus economically infeasible for slavery. Still, Southerners worried that annexing Oregon, and its several future states, would empower the antislavery North by providing it with allies—and more crucially, votes—in Congress. With its rich soil and natural harbors, Northerners wanted Oregon as farmland and a gateway to Asia, but they also wanted it to offset the acquisition of slaveholding Texas. The debate over Oregon, in other words, was actually a debate over slavery.

In frail health, Adams watched as Southerners who had pushed through the annexation of Texas called for moderation on Oregon, while Northerners did the opposite. As an opponent of slavery and an ardent nationalist, Adams knew he would vote to give President James K. Polk authority to push America's claims to Oregon to the brink of war. But to protect his failing health, he had also vowed not to participate in the increasingly heated exchanges on the House floor. Yet as a former president himself, and as the secretary of state who had agreed to disagree with the British and postpone settlement of the Oregon controversy twenty years before, how could he not? This at least was the opinion of Thomas Butler King, congressman from Georgia, who challenged Adams to defend his record, past and present. "This direct call from Mr. King," Adams recorded in his diary, "I could not resist."[1]

America's claim to all of Oregon, Adams responded, "is clear and unquestionable." After another exchange with King, Adams asked the House clerk if he could read aloud three pieces of evidence supporting this bold claim. The first was the book of Genesis, specifically chapter 1, verses 26–28, in which God created Adam and Eve in his own image and gave them, and their descendants, "dominion . . . over every living thing that moveth upon the earth." These passages from Genesis, Adams explained after the clerk finished reading, provided "the foundation not only of our title to Oregon, but the foundation of all human title to all human possessions." But if Genesis applied universally, it hardly explained whether Britain or America was the worthier claimant to Oregon. So Adams asked the clerk to read his next piece of evidence, the eighth verse of the second Psalm: "Ask of me, and I shall give thee the heathen for thine inheritance, and the uttermost parts of the earth for thy possession." Now, Adams instructed the clerk, "turn back a verse or two, and you will see to whom it is said He would give them." Though most of those present knew exactly what the second Psalm contained, the clerk continued reading before a hushed House:

6. Yet have I set my King upon my holy hill of Zion.
7. I will declare the decree: the Lord hath said unto me, Thou art my son; this day have I begotten thee.
8. Ask of me, and I shall give thee the heathen for thine inheritance, and the uttermost parts of the earth for thy possession.

In case they needed it, Adams reminded his colleagues that "the speaker of this promise was God Almighty, and the person to whom the promise was made was Jesus Christ." Because Americans were God's chosen people, a notion Adams took very seriously, their claim to earth's dominion came directly from Jesus. After this bit of drama, the third piece of evidence—Matthew 28:18–20, which enjoined the godly to "Go ye therefore, and teach all nations"—was superfluous, and Adams refrained from asking the clerk to read it aloud as well. The British did not want to civilize and Christianize the land. Instead, they wanted "to keep it in a savage and barbarous state for her hunters—for the benefit of the Hudson Bay Company for hunting." For Adams, "therein consists the difference between her claims and our claims. We claim that country—for what? To make the wilderness blossom as the rose, to establish laws, to increase, multiply, and subdue the earth, which we are commanded to do by the first behest of

God Almighty." Congressman Adams could not have been clearer: while the United States had God on its side, Great Britain did not.[2]

A national figure had come out strongly in favor of territorial expansion, couching it in religious, messianic language as America's destiny—so far, so familiar. But of course Adams was no ordinary politician. The son of a president and an accomplished diplomat, he had already served as James Monroe's secretary of state before ascending to the presidency himself. He was also an ardent patriot, a nationalist whose own life embodied the life of the nation. As a boy, he had witnessed the first Revolutionary battles at Lexington, Concord, and Bunker Hill. As a young man, he had represented the United States in the capitals of Europe; later, he was among the diplomats who negotiated the end of the War of 1812 with Britain. Perhaps above all, Adams had made it his life's work to expand the geography of the United States, from north to south and from sea to sea, and with it American power in the world.

Adams was also a deeply religious man, an ecumenist whose spiritual curiosity led him to study the Bible daily and attend three different church services every Sunday—usually Unitarian, Presbyterian, and Episcopalian—even during his hectic days as the nation's chief diplomat and head of state. As secretary of state, he also managed to find time to serve as president of the American Bible Society. Adams was theologically curious but not skeptical, and he rejected the deist theory of an almighty heavenly creator who had left humanity to its own devices. He believed in the divinity of Jesus and that biblical miracles had unfolded exactly as the Bible described them. Though he joined the Unitarian Church in Quincy in 1826, he found the philosophical wanderings of Unitarianism interesting but often cold. Like his father, he distrusted Catholicism as an inherently authoritarian system of faith that created political despotism wherever it predominated. He equally distrusted the emotional excesses of evangelicalism, at the time the dominant influence in American Protestantism.[3]

Religion exerted a profound, if varied, influence upon the worldview of John Quincy Adams. Even more than his father—perhaps because he took matters of faith much more seriously than did John Adams—John Quincy believed that religious liberty protected freedom of conscience and thus acted as the best guarantor for republican liberty. Democracy flowed from religion, just as religious liberty was made possible by democratic freedoms: to Adams, the two were inseparable. Thus when Spain's colonies in the Americas mounted republican revolutions of their own, Adams reacted with caution rather than euphoria. Roman Catholicism, he thought, would stifle any expressions of true republican liberty. In his instructions to the American minister in Colombia, Adams explained that "liberty of conscience and of religious worship . . . have been seldom admitted in Roman

Catholic countries, and are even interdicted by the present constitution of Spain. The South American Republics have been too much under the influence of the same intolerable spirit," though he hoped that Colombia, which had made provisions for religious liberty, would be the exception. Later, in outlining American objectives for an inter-American conference in Panama, Adams told the Senate that he wished to exert "the moral influence of the United States" toward pursuing "the advancement of religious liberty" and the end of "religious bigotry and oppression" in Latin America. Without such efforts, the Western Hemisphere would never be free of tyranny. At least Latin America was Christian, even if Roman Catholic, which gave the region hope for enlightened democratic reform. Non-Christian lands were not so lucky. China, for example, could never understand "the Christian precept to love your neighbour as yourself," and thus could never fully join America and Europe in a world system based on the reciprocal benefits of free commerce and the rule of law. For this reason, he supported imperial Britain in the Opium War, even as the Chinese struggled to maintain their rightful sovereignty.[4]

Possibly the most revealing thing about the faith of John Quincy Adams was his love of the Old Testament during his time as a diplomat and then secretary of state and his preference for the New Testament after. Not coincidentally, this period also marked a watershed between his ardent expansionism and his support for abolitionism. Even had he wanted to—and he confessed he did not—Adams could not escape his Calvinist Puritan heritage. He retained a belief in predestination, in original sin, and in America as a New Israel. Above all, Adams believed that God's special providence watched over and protected the United States. And it was America's divine mission, "as much a law of nature" he believed, to spread its republican liberty and prosperity across the North American continent. In 1802, in words that would return to haunt him decades later, he supported expansion south and west into "uncultivated" Indian lands, asking, "Shall the fields and valleys, which a beneficent God has formed to teem with the life of innumerable multitudes, be condemned to everlasting barrenness?"[5]

As secretary of state, Adams was responsible for fulfilling much of this destiny. Through the skillful negotiation of the 1819 Transcontinental Treaty, he prised Florida away from the Spanish Empire and successfully succeeded the Spanish claim to the Oregon Country—which meant that a European imperial power recognized that American sovereignty extended as far as the Pacific coast; soon even the British would tacitly agree. Upon concluding negotiations with Luis de Onís, the Spanish ambassador to the United States, Adams privately expressed his "fervent gratitude to the Giver of all good. . . . What the consequences may be of the compact this day signed with Spain is known only to the all-wise and all-beneficent Disposer of events, who has brought it about in a manner utterly unexpected and by means the most extraordinary and unforeseen." The Transcontinental Treaty was "the work of an intelligent and all-embracing Cause." Even if he did not always understand Providence, Adams was happy to put himself at its disposal.[6]

But as slavery expanded in the 1830s, Adams began to have second thoughts about the true nature of America's manifest destiny. This ambivalence coincided with the end of his national political career, in which compromise was a virtue, and the beginning of his tenure as a congressman from Massachusetts, where antislavery passions ran high. It also marked the emergence of the New Testament Adams. He remained an expansionist, but by now he had also become an antislavery partisan, which meant opposing expansion where it would necessarily extend slavery into new territories and entrench its foundations where it existed already. Given his efforts to win Florida and his earlier support for Indian Removal, his opposition to expansion into Texas and Mexico earned him charges of hypocrisy. His critics intensified their attacks when the Old Testament Adams invoked Genesis and the second Psalm to argue for the annexation of all of the Oregon Country. Though much of Oregon did become American, Adams lost the larger argument: Texas entered the union, the United States seized over a third of Mexico in a war for outright conquest, and the latent problem of slavery awoke with a fury that nearly consumed the nation in recriminating bloodshed. Adams did not live to see it, but only the Civil War could reconcile the warring biblical visions of manifest destiny and benevolent justice in a new religious patriotism that would stretch the American imperium across the oceans.[7]

Adams's career was representative of a broader development. Based largely on the voluntarist ethic that religious fervor and the separation of church and state had incubated, antebellum America became "a nation of joiners." Dedicated to reforming the United States, voluntary organizations, a majority with a religious basis, flourished in the years leading to the Civil War. But there was no consensus over how to go about reforming the nation. The antebellum era in fact pitted two visions of progress against each other: "externalists," who wanted to improve the American system with the expansion of territory, versus "internalists," who sought a national commitment to improve the regions already under U.S. sovereignty. The externalists largely won out, but in order to do so they had to take into account and in some way absorb the moral tenor of the internalists, whose goals included education, moral reform measures like temperance, and economic development. But there was one subject on which they could not agree, slavery, and it was this tension that eventually brought the nation to civil war. And then there were the faith-based externalists who mostly shared the internalists' abhorrence of slavery—the overseas missionaries and their legions of home supporters, and the peace activists who called for America to adopt a diplomacy of pacifism.[8]

True to form, Adams embraced the reforming ethos of his age—as a pious New Englander of old Puritan stock, he could scarcely avoid it. "Progressive improvement in the condition of man," he once remarked, was "the purpose of a superintending Providence." This belief in progress was one of the reasons Adams rejected the doctrinaire Calvinism of his upbringing. Although he retained a belief in original sin, he believed even more strongly that people could transcend it through good works. Adams announced his reformist intentions in his inaugural address of March 1825 and his first Annual Message to Congress later that year. Americans had a sacred duty, he told them, to improve their country, for themselves, for future generations of Americans, and for the world. But shortly after, he embraced both external and internal improvement on the condition that they not lead to the expansion of slavery. This proved to be an unsustainable contradiction that Adams struggled to maintain, for how could one support expansion in one direction (to the northwest, where plantation slavery was not viable) and not in another (to the southwest, in places like Texas, where slavery was sure to flourish)? In his support for acquiring Oregon but opposition to annexing Texas and waging war on Mexico, Adams was never able to reconcile the two halves of such a schizophrenic manifest destiny.[9]

Between the War of 1812 and the Civil War, Adams's dilemma would also become America's dilemma. How would the United States reconcile democracy with slave power? Economic development with slavery? Expansionism with republicanism? Empire with liberty? In keeping with the nation's political and cultural habits, religion played a large role in shaping these debates and the bloody outcome in which they all eventually converged—and which also shaped America's approach to the rest of the world. Religious Americans—in and out of the church, in and out of politics, in war and at peace—dominated the antebellum landscape. Whether they won or lost the argument, they ensured that piety and morality would become part of the very fabric of U.S. foreign policy.

CHAPTER SIX

Absolutist Apostasies

BEFORE EXPANSION COULD EVEN be considered, at least on such a grand, cosmic scale, the new United States first had to secure its own freedom of maneuver in the world system. What this meant exactly was still unknown and thus was always an ongoing process. The first test came soon after the ratification of the Constitution and Bill of Rights when France embarked upon its own republican experiment. Yet the French Revolution followed a much different path than the American: more radical, more destabilizing, and much more violent. Other European monarchies, which naturally feared that the French were setting a dangerous example for their own people, united to suppress the revolutionary fervor. They also came to fear French ambitions to liberate the oppressed people of Europe, and dominate the continent in the process. In 1793, a general European war broke out. Unsurprisingly, the French looked to the Americans to honor at least the spirit of their 1778 alliance.[1]

At first, Americans welcomed the French Revolution with near unanimity, a rare thing in the political life of the early republic. Their own liberties had spread to Europe, they boasted; their republican model would spark the reordering of a freer world. Partly because of millennial expectations that the revolutionary events in Paris were heralding a new age, perhaps even the return of Christ, the American clergy were particularly euphoric. The publication of eschatological books and pamphlets soared in the early 1790s along with hopes for a world free of absolutist monarchy. And not only monarchy—Americans rejoiced that the French had thrown off their despotic church as well as their despotic king. Unlike the rebellious Patriots in America, the French revolutionaries were anticlerical as well as antimonarchical and attacked the Roman Catholic Church with as much fervor as they did the Palace of Versailles. Many Americans hoped—and some even expected—that a full-blown reformation would engulf France and pave the way for the triumph of Protestantism, a glorious turn of events that would in turn launch the rest of Europe, still tyrannized by arbitrary Catholic rule, on the road to Protestant reform. Overall, most Americans agreed with Reverend Joseph Lathrop that France was undergoing a "transition from slavery to liberty—from a dungeon to open day—from total blindness to perfect vision."[2]

They were not expecting what actually happened. Instead of replacing their king with a bourgeois, liberal, God-fearing republic, France descended into a bloody orgy of internal violence and external war. Death squads, lawlessness, and above all the prolific use of the guillotine led Americans to think twice about the French Revolution. Opinion turned slowly in response to the horror stories coming out of France, but turn it did when French revolutionaries imposed an absolutist dictatorship of the people to replace the absolutist dictatorship of an individual. Just as shocking was the Revolution's atheistic iconoclasm. It was one thing to overthrow the Catholic Church; it was another entirely to try to overthrow God himself.

But it was not just the French who were giving radical republicanism a bad name. In Haiti, a successful slave revolt led to a race war between freed slaves and their former masters, which in turn caused hysteria in the United States, especially among Southerners, that racial rebellion and violence could soon spread to their own plantations. In Pennsylvania, the Whiskey Rebellion of 1794 stoked simmering fears about popular revolt and anarchy in the United States itself. And in American religion, deism and skepticism spread rapidly in the 1790s, leading to worries that American morals and republican virtue were being corrupted by the misdirected anticlericalism in France. Thus while many Americans continued to support the French revolutionaries—most notably Thomas Jefferson—the intense ardor for France had begun to cool by 1795. Was radical revolution better than no revolution at all? Many Americans now had their doubts.[3]

In response, American politics became more divisively partisan, with conservative Federalists arguing with populist Republicans over who best represented America's true republican spirit. The Federalists were the party of Washington, Adams, Jay, and Hamilton, and favored a strong central government; they found their strongest backing in the North and in the seaboard commercial cities. By contrast, as the party of Jefferson and Madison, the Republicans promoted robust states' rights at the expense of a relatively weak national government; they enjoyed support in the South and the expanding western hinterland, and among farmers. Terrified by the specter of mob rule, Federalists preferred the reasonableness of British parliamentary democracy. Republicans, by contrast, sympathized closely with the French Revolution, even as it lurched into its most violent phase.[4]

Thus the resumption of hostilities between Britain and France in 1793 confronted U.S. foreign policy with its first crisis at a time when Americans themselves were deeply divided. Under President Washington, the

Federalists controlled foreign policy. Though Washington did not adopt a pro-British stance—and could not, given the lingering bitterness of the Revolutionary War—he announced a policy of neutrality and reiterated the rights of neutrals to trade freely, even in wartime. The British suspected the United States of hiding a pro-French policy behind a legalistic cloak of neutrality; as the world's premier naval power, preventing trade with France was one of Britain's key strategic weapons. The British refused to recognize American neutrality and preyed on U.S. merchant shipping in the Atlantic and the Caribbean. Few Americans enjoyed these depredations, but fewer still wanted to pick a war at sea with the Royal Navy—or even in their own Northwest, where British troops and their Indian allies were spoiling for a fight. To calm nerves, uphold the principle and practice of neutrality, and settle once and for all the outstanding tensions from the Revolutionary War, Washington decided to negotiate a new settlement with Britain. As his negotiator, he sent John Jay to London in 1794; within a year, Jay negotiated what quickly came to be known as the Jay Treaty. Insulted and then incensed by what it believed to be a supreme act of betrayal, France vowed to get even with the Americans. From 1798 to 1800, with John Adams now president, the United States and France fought the inelegantly but accurately named Quasi War, an undeclared conflict fought mostly on the high seas. The result, as many Republicans pointed out, was a Federalist foreign policy that favored the British. Rarely has the politics of American foreign policy been so bitterly contested.[5]

Both politics and diplomacy split along religious lines, too. The anticlericalism, deism, and atheism of the revolutionary turn in France did not much trouble theologically skeptical Republicans like Jefferson and Madison. On the other hand, Federalist—and not coincidentally Calvinist—New England had never really overcome its suspicions of Catholicism or tolerated deism, much less atheism. When confronted with the radical turn of events in France, the largely Federalist New England clergy found it natural to turn these suspicions into fears of the anarchy and violence that seemed to accompany a revolt against God as well as king. Conservative churchmen across the country, and not only Federalists, nodded in agreement. To the people and the clergy, the French Revolution seemed to herald another epoch in the coming of the millennium and Christ's return to earth. The clergy's opposition to the French Revolution—and to honoring the 1778 treaty with France—was not simply a matter of preserving their own privileges at home, but a panicky defensive measure to protect the American republic. The Protestant faith, they argued, provided the best insurance, and as a result religious passions intensified in New England and elsewhere. Alexander Hamilton rediscovered his own faith at this time and promoted initiatives, such as the Christian Constitutional

Society, to preserve America's religious virtues and patriotism against the radical contagion of the French Revolution.[6]

This unusually pious moment for Hamilton reflected a more general reassertion of Christian republicanism, especially the identification of the United States as God's chosen nation and Americans as his chosen people. Protestant clergy teamed up with the Federalists to promote opposition to the radicalism of the French Revolution as a form of patriotism. As the New England clergy argued following the rise of violence in France, no revolution was better than one that unleashed anarchy and popular tyranny. Taking advantage of this shift in the public's mood and indifferent to the strictures of separating the activities of church and state, President Washington proclaimed a national day of prayer and holy thanksgiving, the model for many regional celebrations on a smaller scale. While the renewal of Christian republicanism generated considerable hostility to radical French revolutionary violence in the 1790s, it also helped lay the foundations for both the expansive ideology of manifest destiny and the crusading reformist zeal of abolitionism and pacifism in the decades to come. This was precisely the internal contradiction that would later torment John Quincy Adams.[7]

Yet also infused with this Protestant mindset, albeit in a more subtle form, were some of the most important figures in early American diplomacy. John Adams, vice president until 1797 and then president until 1801, loathed Britain—but he loathed French absolutism and radicalism even more. His ideas and perceptions about France—even a republican France—were rooted in a typically Puritan, visceral anti-Catholicism, and he viewed this erstwhile ally as a threat to American security, interests, and values. In 1776, Adams had drafted the Model Treaty as the safest way for America to ensure its interests and protect its ideals in foreign relations, particularly its relations with France; in the 1790s, he updated this vision through neutrality, and then a resort to war when the principle and practice of neutrality needed enforcement. In the time between, he had been one of the first Americans to criticize the French Revolution. These old cultural suspicions provided the ideological bedrock for Adams's hard-line policy during the Quasi War.[8]

Adams was not alone in harboring a vestigial distrust of French absolutism and Catholicism. French diplomats could not have been pleased when Washington sent John Jay to London to negotiate his eponymous treaty with the British. Jay did not wear his spirituality lightly: his faith was evangelical, and later in life he served as president of the American Bible Society. Nor his religious identity: his grandparents were French Huguenot refugees who escaped to the American colonies with England's blessing and encouragement. Jay never forgot this act of Protestant solidarity, even at the outbreak of an anti-British war for independence that he supported. "I wish it well," he said of Great Britain in 1778; "it afforded my ancestors asylum from persecution." Jay was horrified by the violence of the French Revolution, and though he welcomed its outbreak in 1789, he was among the first Americans to turn against it. Jay's 1795 treaty with the British proved to be explosively controversial, with even some of his fellow Federalists believing that he had conceded the British too much, too easily. But it should not have come as a shock. Jay acted as a patriotic American, but he also acted upon a visceral fear of France and a deep, sentimental attachment to Britain—and both emotions were rooted in the two countries' different attitudes toward religious liberty.[9]

As AMERICANS WRESTLED with the problems of foreign alliances, neutrality, and the desirability of republican revolutions elsewhere, they were also confronted with a crisis from another region that would become all too familiar in years to come: the Middle East. Though the term itself is anachronistic—nobody in the late eighteenth or early nineteenth centuries yet called it "the Middle East"—its challenges were not. Pirates and raiders from the states of North Africa's notoriously lawless Barbary Coast—Morocco, Algiers, Tunis, and Tripoli, stretching from present-day Morocco to Libya—had been preying on European shipping for centuries. Even when they were still British colonists, American merchants and traders had crossed the globe in search of profit, and the Mediterranean world was one of their most lucrative destinations. Until the Revolution, American ships could count on the awesome might of the Royal Navy for protection from Barbary pirates. But independence severed all ties with the mother country, and American ships suddenly realized just how difficult navigating the Mediterranean could be. The pirates not only seized cargo and money, they captured American seamen, either to ransom or to sell into slavery. Dependent upon overseas trade, American officials could hardly let piracy go unopposed. After fruitless attempts to placate the Barbary rulers with tribute and ransom payments, they instead built a navy and sent it to the shores of North Africa to defend American shipping and assert the right to trade.[10]

Without realizing it, the Barbary pirates had provoked America's first military conflict with Islam. Though religion did not spark the Barbary Wars that ran intermittently from the 1780s until 1815, it did give them color, texture, and purpose, leading to a clash of civilizations despite the best efforts of the U.S. government not to mix religion and foreign policy. The "United States of America is not in any sense founded on the Christian Religion," proclaimed a 1797 treaty between the United States and Tripoli, "as it has in itself no character of enmity against the laws, religion or tranquility of Musselmen [Muslims]." By the terms of the treaty, the governments of the United States and Tripoli further pledged not to allow religion to become a cause of war. Two years later, President John Adams appointed William Eaton as consul to Tunis. Eaton sailed for the Mediterranean on a cresting wave of optimism, believing that "Universal Love" would disprove "the idea that Mahometans and Christians are *natural enemies.*" Though Adams's successor, President Thomas Jefferson, wanted to punish the Barbary states and uphold American credibility through the use of military force, he did so in pursuit of trading rights, national honor, and reforming the international system rather than in the name of a Christian crusade against Islam.[11]

Yet events, powered by religious (and racial) prejudices on both sides, would ultimately scuttle Eaton and Jefferson's hopes. Despite the fine language of the 1797 treaty, the people of Barbary instinctively thought of Americans as Christians—and loathed them for it. Often they would add religious insult to economic or military injury, such as Tripoli's decision to rename the captured ship USS *Philadelphia* as *The Gift of Allah.* But Americans were just as steeped in religious ideology and identity. Shortly before he ratified the 1797 treaty, and thus its clause denying America's status as a Christian nation, Adams concluded his presidential inaugural address with a ringing endorsement of the political and social virtues of Christianity. With this Christian identity came a deep-rooted fear of Islam. The Puritans of colonial New England had thought of Muslims as a satanic force and the Ottoman Empire as a hellish source of earthly evil, and it was their view that had prevailed widely throughout the American colonies. Muslim Turks had always figured prominently alongside Catholics in the colonists' millennial theology. These millennial beliefs intensified with the escalation of tensions between America and the Barbary states, giving Turks a more central role as anti-Christian forces who would provoke Christ's return. Muslims, moreover, were thought to believe in a faith that was the very opposite of America's virtuous Christian republicanism: lazy, decadent, corrupt, and despotic. Islam, Americans said, encouraged tyranny because it kept its believers ignorant and servile. Muslim potentates were even more all-powerful than the absolutist Catholic kings of Europe, their arbitrary power able to keep "the lives of millions on the footing of a lottery," according to one bestselling book on Islam. Noah Webster accused the potentates of Barbary of posing a threat to the Christian faith, and with it freedom of conscience and political liberty, much as atheism in revolutionary France and deism in America did. Even the optimists despaired. After a few years serving as America's envoy to Barbary, Eaton himself changed his view. "Her subjects have neither relish nor stimulus to ambition," he reported on conditions in Algiers, because "Her religious system favors indolence" and superstition instead of "the Gift of reason."[12]

But what the Americans feared most was captivity, because it almost always led to slavery. This was not the virtual, purely theoretical "slavery" in which the British had supposedly kept their taxpaying but unrepresented colonists, but the real thing. American fears about Barbary captivity were so visceral because they were so deep-rooted, echoing back to the horrors of Indian captivity along the unstable borderlands of colonial New England and New York. Indian heathens and Barbary Muslims both represented an antithesis to the American ideal; captivity among such "barbarians"—a revealing word that Americans used to describe both peoples—was an inversion of the normal balance of social power. Bondage was thus spiritual and cultural as well as physical. As Mary Rowlandson, Hannah Dustin, and especially the family of Eunice Williams could attest, captivity did not just mean a loss of freedom—it threatened assimilation into an alien culture and a total loss of identity.[13]

Loss of physical freedom, Americans assumed, would lead directly to a loss of their Christian faith, probably through forced conversion to Islam. It was widely assumed that seizure by the Barbary pirates could make one an unredeemed captive, condemned, as was little Eunice Williams, to a life of savagery and ignorance among the heathens. Such fears were not unreasonable: for centuries, Muslim slave masters, throughout the Ottoman Empire and along the Barbary coast, had been notorious for forcibly converting enslaved Europeans to Islam. Estimates vary, but by the time of America's conflict in the Mediterranean, up to a million white Europeans had lived a life of Barbary slavery. Americans had also suffered Barbary captivity since the early seventeenth century, albeit on a much smaller scale. Cotton Mather, who played an important role in shaping the memory of colonial Indian captivity, claimed in 1703 that Muslim Barbary states boasted "the most horrible *Captivity* in the world." Islamic law justified the enslavement of infidels, and while Americans did not think of themselves as blasphemous unbelievers, the Barbary pirates certainly did. "Now I have got you, you Christian dogs," hissed Ali Hassan, the ruler of Algiers, at his American captives. Several American captives were unable to withstand the pressures to convert and completely transform their identities forever.[14]

After years of broken treaties, unending ransom and tribute payments, and the occasional feckless use of armed force, in 1815 President James Madison put an end to the conflict by dispatching a powerful fleet to the Mediterranean. No longer would Barbary pirates harass American shipping. Only military power, Americans believed, could redeem their captives in the Middle East—and the nation itself.

IT WAS NO coincidence that Madison felt free to act against Barbary in 1815. Only a few months before, the War of 1812 between the United States and Great Britain had come to an end. The U.S. Navy, a minnow before the war, grew substantially in size and ability in holding its own against the famed prowess of the Royal Navy and was better positioned to take on the Barbary pirates once hostilities with Britain had ended. But more important, Barbary and Britain posed many of the same challenges to the United States, over trading rights, freedom of the seas, and national honor. Having upheld America's rights against the British, it was natural—and politically imperative—for Madison to send the same message to Barbary. American ideology and values had been battle-tested in both wars, and settling scores with these two enemies settled Americans' views about the wider world. It also laid the foundations for Americans to turn inward and expand their own continental holdings and imperial ambitions.

With the renewal of war in Europe in 1803, the two main antagonists, Britain and France, each sought to freeze the other's economy by blocking the import and export of raw materials and finished goods. As it did in the 1790s, this meant the harassment of American shipping, which traded with both nations. In 1806, Napoleonic France instituted the "Continental System," effectively shutting Britain off from Europe; the British responded by blockading European ports to strangle the continent's vital trade with the outside world. In a conflict with such dynamics, the United States, which as a neutral aimed to continue trading with everyone, was always going to run into trouble with Great Britain. The British compounded American anger with their policy of impressment: searching for runaways from the Royal Navy by boarding American vessels and conscripting American seamen. Having been bullied continually by British, French, and Barbary ships since winning their independence in 1783, nothing was more humiliating to Americans. But as important as freedom of the seas and trading rights were, especially to a nation that relied heavily upon maritime commerce, the main cause of war in 1812 was westward expansion. And here, too, tensions assumed a familiar face. Much as it had done in issuing the Proclamation Line in 1763 and the Quebec Act in 1774, London angered American settlers and farmers by supporting the right of Indian sovereignty in the Northwest, the huge swath of territory bounded by the Great Lakes to the north, the Ohio River to the south, and the Mississippi River to the west. Although the Jay Treaty was supposed to have settled the issue of Britain's presence in the American frontier—which of course was originally supposed to have been settled by the 1783 Anglo-American peace treaty—British officials and troops in Canada continued to encourage Indian resistance to American expansion and settlement.[15]

Behind both causes for war—whether Americans could secure freedom of the seas and settlement of the west without British interference—lay the more delicate issues of national honor and the viability of republicanism. And deeper still, behind them lay an even more delicate national self-esteem that was in large part rooted in America's religious traditions, values, and culture, which were inseparable from nationalism, republicanism, honor, and credibility. In this sense, religion had two roles: it helped give shape to the reasons for war, and thus to the war itself; and it provided Americans with a convenient, comprehensible, and powerful way of expressing their views.[16]

In general, American opinion divided deeply—more deeply, even, than during the French Revolution or any other crisis until the Civil War—along partisan lines of prowar Republicans and antiwar Federalists. So hostile to war was New England that its political leaders convened in Hartford in 1814 and only narrowly rejected a motion to secede from the United States. Luckily for Madison, though, a clear majority of Americans supported the Republican march to war, possibly because by this time a clear majority of Americans were Republicans themselves. Yet one thing united all Americans: the use of religious rhetoric and imagery either to damn or to sanctify the war. Both sides argued their case with a pious stridency and moral urgency that only religious faith could sustain.

Based mostly in the South and along the nation's western borderlands, the so-called "war hawks" agitated for war as a way of both redeeming national honor and clearing the way for westward settlement. Renowned for his role in separating church and state but desperate for public support for a controversial war, President Madison set a providential national tone. By taking America to war, he told the nation in his War Message of June 1, 1812, he would "commit a just cause into the hands of the Almighty Disposer of Events." Madison set aside August 20 as a national fast day of thanksgiving and prayer, the first of several during the war, so that a penitent America could appease the Lord's "divine displeasure," evidenced by his unleashing the British upon a backsliding nation, and ask for His "merciful forgiveness" in the form of victory.[17]

Other prominent Americans used religion to sanctify war with Britain. "Parson" Mason Weems, an ordained Episcopal minister and one of the era's bestselling authors, believed that war would not only restore America's virtue, it would also instill the virtues of self-control and hard work among its people. A celebrated biographer of George Washington, Weems contrasted the Christian republican values of the United States with the decadent "modern Goths" of Great Britain. Benjamin Rush, a noted physician, signer of the Declaration of Independence, respected public intellectual, and devout evangelical, made a similar argument. In doing so, Rush even repudiated a cause close to his heart: Christian pacifism. War as a godly test of national character, war as a cleansing agent for the nation's sins and weaknesses, war as a righteous instrument to redeem national virtue—these powerful ideas, pronounced constantly by Madison, Weems, Rush, and others, were quickly absorbed into a narrative of national patriotism, heroism, and justice that propelled the War of 1812 onward.[18]

Religious advocates for war also cast a covetous gaze westward. David Jones, a Baptist chaplain during the Revolutionary War, rabid Anglophobe, passionate supporter of war with Britain, and friend of President Madison, reported from his travels through Ohio, Pennsylvania, and Virginia that "never were people more unanimous" than they were in supporting the war. Jones especially encouraged the president to seize Protestant English Canada but not Catholic French Quebec, which would enable the United States to achieve its most important objective: subduing the Indian tribes who barred the way to westward settlement. "We must humble the Savages," Jones advised Madison; "they must as a Conquered People ask for Peace" that would be contingent upon "their engaging to cultivate the Land, and abandon the former mode of Life."[19]

But not everyone agreed that war was necessary, or even wise. The antiwar camp was strongest in the Federalist redoubt of New England, where it commanded overwhelming support. New England clergy, Congregationalists mostly, proclaimed that by waging war unjustly and unwisely, "without the approbation of heaven," Madison had broken his sacred covenant with the people, just as George III had in 1776. The war was "execrable," spat a Massachusetts minister, its mindless, unthinking supporters guilty of "tame, African, slavish deportment." Many New Englanders looked wistfully upon their Puritan heritage for guidance and examples of moral courage in the face of a wicked government. In this latest incarnation of the Puritan jeremiad, clergy and state officials accused the Madison administration of betraying America's true principles. Invoking the Puritan founders, Governor John Cotton Smith of Connecticut addressed the state's General Assembly in October 1814, when secessionist dissent was at its peak, and promised to "imitate their virtues" in the hope "that God who supported them in the darkest hours will not forsake their descendants." Even Baptists, mostly Jeffersonians and Madisonians and thus not usually sympathetic to Federalist causes, protested the war, which helped blunt Republican efforts to tie New England, and its established churches, to the suppression of religious liberty. Isaac Backus, like the Republicans a champion of the separation of church and state and a fierce opponent of Federalist New England's religious establishments, railed against "calamities and multiple evils of War." That Americans "may learn righteousness" from their humiliations and depredations would be the only good to come from war with Britain.[20]

While military officials in New England may not have believed that war in general was always evil, they shared the general hostility to this particular war with Britain. Few rituals in New England's religious culture were as celebrated as the annual artillery election sermon, delivered by an esteemed minister to the Ancient and Honorable Artillery Company, a Boston-based militia founded by the first Puritan settlers. The same day Madison delivered his War Address to Congress, Reverend Eliphalet Porter of Roxbury, Massachusetts, delivered the 1812 election sermon. As the "threatening clouds" of war gathered, Porter preached that war was just only if it was necessary and defensive. "They who are called to assume the character of the soldier," Porter warned, "can never be indifferent to the moral nature of their cause." Two years later, Reverend Samuel Cary used his election sermon to accuse Madison of betraying the ideals of the Revolution, for stooping low to emulate the sinful ambitions of European kings. Reflecting the Federalists' habitual suspicion of mob rule, Cary concluded that the wars in North America and Europe had shown that the untrammeled popular will could be a source for anarchy as well as freedom. The war was "so unexpected, so appalling" that it "baffled all our calculations and all human foresight." But God would see to it that America and Europe would both soon be at peace, able then to let the true Christian spirit flourish in resurrecting a godly society.[21]

Though it was a minority view in many parts, opposition could also be found nationwide thanks to the emergence of a "greater New England" populated by thousands of inland migrants who moved from Massachusetts and Connecticut to establish transplanted towns, villages, and farms in western New York, Ohio, and beyond. Reverend S. P. Robbins, a preacher in Marietta, Ohio, wrote to his family back in Connecticut that though "the war is far more popular here than with you," he resisted it nonetheless, "on account of its being so *unnecessary* and *unjust*." Robbins confessed to harboring other, more radical thoughts: "were I *drafted* . . . I should not go—and should think I was more *justifiable* in refusing." He blamed Madison for an especially unenlightened foreign policy and for visiting the horrors of a tyrannical war upon republican America. "To what extent," Robbins concluded in words that would echo down through future debates over war, slavery, and civil rights, "ought we to obey the civil constituted authorities of our country?" Antiwar sentiment could also be found wherever Federalists lived—even in as unlikely a place as South Carolina, where the expansion of slavery and plantation agriculture and the prevalence of land speculators made it a particularly strong supporter of war with Britain. Here, too, antiwar activists believed that God was on their side. The "*Finger of* HEAVEN *points to* PEACE!!!" screeched one South Carolina Federalist; another damned the war as "the scourge of an avenging God" who was disappointed that His people had diverted from the path set down by the "virtuous WASHINGTON."[22]

Yet while the antiwar movement may have called upon God, few of its members were Christian pacifists. Like many Loyalists during the Revolution, antiwar Federalists were opposed to this particular war, not to all wars as a matter of principle. Until the War of 1812, almost all American thinking on war lacked consistency. After all, Jefferson and Madison, the architects of wars against Barbary and Britain, had argued that war was the enemy of liberty because it led to higher taxes, standing armies, and ambitious governments. Still, the War of 1812 marked an important turning point in American history because it gave birth to the first truly pacifistic antiwar movement. Once confined to the traditional peace sects, predominantly the Society of Friends and the Moravians, pacifists emerged from other denominations as well. Activists such as David Dodge, a wealthy New York merchant and active Presbyterian layman, and Reverend Noah Worcester, a New Hampshire Unitarian, established small antiwar followings and spawned local peace societies. Most significant was the branching out of Christian pacifism—at that time the basis for virtually all pacifism in the United States—beyond its usual Quaker and Moravian confines. Equally significant was pacifists' ability to gain recognition for their status as conscientious objectors even if they failed to win broad acceptance or sympathy. And though they failed to slow the march to war, or even influence policy, during the War of 1812 Christian pacifists managed to present a credible moral and political alternative to war. No longer could the state claim a monopoly on righteousness. It was a fateful development that would push future U.S. foreign policy to further heights of moralistic purpose, even when it also resorted to the use of brutal, bloody force.[23]

When news of the war's end arrived in the winter of 1815, Americans celebrated as if they had won a tremendous victory. On the face of it, this was absurd: the national capital had been sacked and burned, the British had officially conceded nothing on impressment, and one of the main objectives of the war, the conquest of Canada, had ended in total failure. All this mattered little, though. Somewhat chastened by their flirtations with secession, antiwar protesters were relieved that their bitter nightmare of war and dissent was over. And despite the failure of the war to achieve anything tangible, Madison's supporters claimed they had fought and won a "second war of independence" from the domineering British. Americans had always wanted to act alone in the world and remain free from the contaminating corruptions of Europe, but since 1783 Britain and France had not allowed them any such liberty. Now, having matched the British in war, few would dare challenge the United States in the Western Hemisphere. "God had tested Americans and their government," a writer from the popular magazine *Niles' Weekly Register* boasted, "to *secure* future peace and *establish* our mild and benevolent institutions." They could all be *"proud in the belief that America now stands in the first rank of nations."*[24]

During the war, all sides invoked the guiding hand of providence to illustrate the righteousness of their cause. The war's opponents saw it as God's way of chastising his people for electing the Republicans to power.

The failed invasion of Canada and the burning of Washington, D.C., were sure signs, in the words of a New Hampshire preacher, of "the indignation of Heaven." Supporters, however, could just as plausibly point to a series of naval victories against the Royal Navy on Lake Erie, the defeat of a British invasion at Lake Champlain, and of course General Andrew Jackson's glorious triumph at the Battle of New Orleans as proof that the "God of Battles is surely on our side." America, a Vermont newspaper concluded at war's end, had fought "a holy war, for the Lord has fought for us the battles, and given us the victories." In both these readings of God's providence, America had endured a test of its will and character—and most important, its faith. In a strange way, then, the end of the war not only treated the nation's sectional and political wounds, it vindicated and enhanced a vision of the United States as divinely destined for peace, prosperity, and above all, national greatness. As Americans like David Jones turned their attentions inland and focused their unceasing energies on conquering and settling the west, they did so confident in the knowledge that they were doing the Lord's work. They were fulfilling America's destiny, though the consequences for Native Americans would be disastrous. "It appears evident that God has been on our side," a Methodist preacher from Brooklyn announced in 1815. "If God be for us, who can stand against us?"[25]

CHAPTER SEVEN

The Benevolent Empire, at Home and Abroad

THE PERIOD following the War of 1812 was known, somewhat misleadingly, as the "era of good feelings." True, the end of the war had stimulated a powerful resurgence of patriotism, Federalist New England sheepishly set aside its secessionist complaints, and Americans throughout the nation reveled in their ability to match the world's greatest power in battle. But bipartisanship remained elusive. In the 1820s, the political rivalry between supporters of Andrew Jackson and John Quincy Adams would prove to be every bit as bitter and divisive as the old feud between Jeffersonians and Hamiltonians.

Yet in another sense the slogan was accurate. The end of war and the onset of national reconciliation enabled Americans to focus on internal economic development and overseas trade. Building on its earlier capitalist foundations, after 1815 the United States underwent something of a "market revolution"—or more properly a "communications revolution," given that the true innovations of the period were in linking people across vast distances—a period of explosive economic growth based on the emergence of an increasingly sophisticated economy. The agricultural basis of the American economy had changed little since the colonial era, but now farmers were producing crops with the intention of selling them to distant consumers in American towns and cities and in Europe. To service this integrated national economy with a global reach, the federal and state governments built canals and roads; in the 1840s and '50s, they built telegraph wires and railroads, propelling growth further still. Productivity and consumption soared as farms became more efficient and factories churned out high-quality finished goods. Fueling this expanding economy was a population that grew just as rapidly, mostly through increased immigration. Capitalism and immigration were of course nothing new in American history, but rarely before had they experienced such tremendous expansion in such a short space of time. America was entering the industrial age. By the outbreak of the Civil War, the United States was not only a prosperous and dynamic nation, it was also a powerful one.[1]

But in international relations, economic power does not automatically translate into military and political power. Though the United States was an economic power of the first rank by the mid-nineteenth century, it was at most a regional power in the international system. Still, while economic prosperity does not by itself bring international power, it does make it possible. Accordingly, in the decades before the Civil War, Americans became attracted to the idea of wielding their power abroad, if only in the Western Hemisphere. This was nothing new, but in the decades following the War of 1812, they broadened the scope of U.S. foreign policy in significant and enduring ways.[2]

That they did so between 1815 and 1861 was no simple accident of timing. Political figures such as John Quincy Adams and Henry Clay staked their careers on establishing the "American System," an ambitious plan for internal progress with the federal government at the helm. Adams, Clay, and others promoted a crucial, guiding role for the government in assisting industry and building infrastructure such as canals, telegraph lines, and railroads. Though governmental reformism was not always popular—Andrew Jackson and the Democrats based much of their success in opposition to the American System—it attracted the support of many, especially in the Northern states where religious reform was most prevalent. Indeed, most Northern religious reformers were Whigs—the party of reform—while many Southerners and others hostile to a "benevolent" hegemony of Protestant reformers, especially Catholics, were Jacksonian Democrats. Though many within both parties were evangelicals, attitudes toward worship divided the faithful along political lines, with the churchgoing formalists of the North becoming Whigs and the autonomous, antiformalists of the South supporting the Democrats. Still, as we shall see, both parties supported activist foreign policies, albeit on very different terms.[3]

That they did so largely under the banner of Christ was no coincidence, either. As America itself changed economically and socially, American religion changed as well. After 1789, with the Enlightenment's ambivalence toward religion fading from the collective memory, Christianity recaptured its dominance within the broader culture. In response to the market revolution, religion also began a period of innovation, as religious Americans confronted the problems of capitalism and strove to balance Christian selflessness with economic self-interest. So began a period Jon Butler calls the "antebellum spiritual hothouse." And as the American religious landscape underwent its own dramatic changes, religious ideas about American war and diplomacy changed with it. The Second Great Awakening, whose fires of religious passion consumed American society in the first decades of the century and dwarfed its colonial predecessor in geographical reach and number of adherents, thrust evangelicalism into the vanguard of American religion. Alongside this evangelical "explosion," as the historian Mark Noll describes it, arose a vast array of social movements that aimed to improve American society through moral reform. Encompassing temperance, education, prison conditions, and other aspects of personal moral betterment—the abolition of slavery above all, explored later in this chapter—the agenda of politically active evangelicals sought to remake the United States in a progressive Christian image.[4]

Their ability to do so and maintain theological consistency was due to the innovations of several Protestant ministers. The contribution of Nathaniel W. Taylor, a scholar of divinity at Yale, was probably most significant. Building upon the revisions of Edwardsean theology by Samuel Hopkins and Lyman Beecher, who were among the first clergy to push for benevolent social action, Taylor modified the doctrines of original sin and predestination that still formed the key tenets of Calvinism. In its place, his revised Calvinism, known as the New Haven Theology, reconciled predestination and inherent sin with people's ability to act in a moral and godly way, what Taylor called "complete moral agency." Taylor acknowledged that people were born with original sin, but he did not believe it was binding. In other words, people could transcend humanity's original sin and work toward a more godly, humane society. If this was the free will of Arminianism, scourge of Puritans and Calvinists for centuries, then so be it. By finding room for both "the consistency of exhortation to immediate duty" and "the doctrine of the sinner's dependence" on God, Taylor made it possible, indeed imperative, for Christians to make their world a better place. Another pioneer of American Protestantism, Charles G. Finney, a revivalist with an emotional style resembling that of George Whitefield, took this notion further by dispensing with predestination altogether. Finney's Oberlin Theology, named for the college where he taught, promised that anybody could be saved so long as they accepted Christ into their heart and worked to apply Christian love to earthly society. The objective was to improve life on earth. Taylor and Finney agreed on little, but on this they concurred.[5]

Evangelical reformers believed they were in the vanguard of the most glorious movement humanity had witnessed since the days of Christ. They saw their efforts to improve America and the wider world as hastening the events foretold in the Book of Revelation, especially the millennium's thousand years of peace, the second coming of Christ, and his victory over the Antichrist. They were millennialists, but more specifically they were postmillennialists who believed that Christ's return would follow the millennium. In order to bring about the second coming, life on earth had to improve. Hence their belief that reform would not only extend Christian charity where it was most needed, but that reform would also usher in the most profound spiritual rebirth the world would ever see. Popularized by the Second Great Awakening and flowing from traditional American notions of providence, millennialism became one of the dominant religious currents of an unusually religious era. Its significance guided the thoughts and actions of clergy and laity, churches and circuit riders, Northerners and Southerners—indeed, even of the skeptical and irreligious, so pervasive was the belief that "America" represented the culmination of historical progress.[6]

Other Christian reformers were not so concerned with theological consistency or the end of the world because they rejected conventional Protestant theology—particularly evangelical emotionalism—outright. These Christian rationalists, Unitarians and Universalists, had broken away from New England Congregationalism. Just like many evangelicals, Unitarians could trace their theological and cultural roots back to the original Puritan colonists. They saw their faith in Enlightenment terms, as a reflection of scientific principles guided by the spirit of problem solving. Unitarian reformers such as William Ellery Channing mounted their own drive to bring about America's moral improvement.[7]

Even further along the religious spectrum stood the Transcendentalists. A radical experiment in communal, spiritual utopianism that had split from Unitarianism, Transcendentalism celebrated the promise and potential of America even as it decried Americans' reliance on slavery, ill treatment of Indians, and tolerance of war. It was, in fact, a spiritualist rebellion against the cold rationalism of the Unitarians. As Ralph Waldo Emerson once complained to his wife, "The Unitarian church forgets that men are poets." Transcendentalism embodied a campaign for serious social reform as much as it represented a literary school or spiritual movement. And though most Transcendentalists rejected the divinity of Christ, there was no doubting their spiritual core and application of Christian ethics and love to the corruptions of a swiftly modernizing America. Any consideration of the Transcendentalists without reference to their Christian origins and context would be incomplete.[8]

WHETHER THEY BE evangelical or millenarian, Unitarian or Transcendentalist, Protestant reformers included the application of Christian love to foreign policy as well as domestic society. Foremost were two ideas—one very old, pacifism, and one relatively new, humanitarian intervention, though it was not yet called that—grounded in the belief that Christian, republican America stood for something different, something better in the world.

Pacifism had been present in America since the colonial era. In the 1790s, Benjamin Rush had proposed a faith-based Department of Peace to balance the War Department—only to undermine himself by later supporting the War of 1812. After the war, Christian pacifism became more acceptable to a wider body of people, including the major Protestant denominations, which in turn began founding local peace societies. With the establishment of regional and national organizations, such as the American Peace Society in 1828 and the more radical New England Non-Resistance Society in 1838, the crusade to end war found a wider audience. Not every member of the peace societies was an evangelical. Unitarians, the evangelicals' bitter rivals, and of course Quakers were active participants. But almost everyone was a practicing Protestant of one sort or another. In conjunction with other religious reform agendas of the era, international peace seemed a natural fit: it would eliminate the major source of violence in the world and reflect America's Christian virtues in the process. More than that, pacifism suited the era's great missionary endeavors: if war really was unchristian, then the spread of the Christian faith would spread peace.[9]

The link between international peace and Protestant missions was not coincidental. Most ministers believed that the spread of universal Christian love would also bring about universal peace. In yet another American formulation of democratic peace theory, Protestants argued that true Christians would not wage war on one another. As one Baptist put it, the acceptance of Christianity "puts a restraint upon those passions which prompt to war." Instead, preached a Boston minister, "a higher Christian morality will ultimately render this scourge of the human race universally unpopular and odious." In an oft-repeated 1830 sermon about everlasting judgment, a young Ralph Waldo Emerson, then a Unitarian minister, promised that war had been condemned by Jesus and thus one day "shall come to an end."[10]

To Christian peace activists, it was self-evident that war was a sin "contrary to the gospel." Christianity was a religion of peace—the world's only religion of peace, claimed some—but Christians had lost their way in applying its true principles. War, William Ellery Channing proclaimed shortly after the War of 1812, was the "worst vestige of barbarism, this grossest outrage on the principles of Christianity." It brought only material and spiritual destruction and corrupted the innocence of young men by apprenticing them in the "trade [of] butchery." It impoverished communities and nations and tore apart families. And, Channing said, it eroded the religious and republican foundations upon which American democracy rested. Channing's Unitarian colleague Theodore Parker agreed. "War is a violation of Christianity. If war be right, then Christianity is wrong," he preached. "Nothing is so hostile to a true democracy as war." War brought no benefit, only the capacity to destroy—on this, all peace activists agreed. After tallying up the total costs of America's wars between 1776 and 1815, a writer for the *Family Christian Almanack* concluded that the vast sums could have been better spent "to furnish every family in the world with a Bible; to provide the means of common education for all its children, and to support one minister of the Gospel for every thousand souls." In

Rochester, New York, George Washington Montgomery, a Universalist minister, advanced the liberal goal of disarmament, claiming that arms were a cause rather than a symptom of tensions. If nations got rid of their weapons, they could do away with war altogether.[11]

Reform evangelicals were an especially interdenominational, ecumenical lot. They were more interested in societal improvement than doctrinal disputes—indeed, their preoccupation with the here and now at the expense of the hereafter was one of the main criticisms leveled at them by religious conservatives. Reform-minded evangelicals loosely, and unofficially, joined together in an informal "Evangelical United Front." Under this banner, evangelicals of most denominations threw their energies together behind a common cause, be it temperance, education, or peace. When combined, their ecumenism (an effort to bring denominations and religions together) and their pacifism led them to the innovative conclusion that the act of coming together would itself facilitate peace. If they resolved to talk instead of fight, an anonymous pacifist with the American Peace Society argued, "they can as easily find some peaceable method of settling their difficulties, as professors of religion find a way to settle difficulties in the church, without resorting to personal violence." International arbitration would be one method of bringing countries together, or better still "a congress of nations" that "might take the place of war." This dream, said a prominent Tennessee Baptist, was "the desire of all nations." In New England, Congregationalists, Baptists, and Methodists joined together to call for the convening of a Congress of Nations to settle international disputes, and perhaps even prevent them before they occurred. Similarly, Elihu Burritt of the *Christian Citizen* magazine joined with Theodore Parker and the evangelical abolitionist William Lloyd Garrison in an attempt to establish a League of Universal Brotherhood. They would take some time to germinate, but the seeds of collective security and international organization had been planted in the American mind.[12]

Conservative Christians, on the other hand, criticized the peace societies for paying too much attention to earthly concerns and not enough to more important spiritual matters. The pacifists' focus on improving life in the here and now—and on themselves—was little more than "idolatry," one critic charged. Benevolent campaigns to eradicate war were hopelessly idealistic because they tried to improve humanity without paying attention to the underlying causes of original sin and human depravity. They "aim to do away the evil by striking at the *branches*—not at the *root*." This was an important criticism, one of the first salvos in what would become a running dispute between liberals who sought earthly reform as a means to grace and conservatives who retained the traditionally Calvinist view that grace was God's alone to dispense and could only come through faith in Christ. The dispute would affect all faith-based plans for reform for at least the next century, including America's role in matters of international war and peace.[13]

Despite such critics, pacifism had introduced a powerful moral voice into antebellum debates about America's proper role in the world. But it was not the only voice stemming from reformist Christian moralism. If pacifism was a very old Christian idea, the other to have a significant impact was rather modern: humanitarian intervention. It was every bit as radical as the peace movement but decidedly not as pacifistic. Occasionally the two groups overlapped—humanitarian intervention, after all, did not always have to mean military intervention. But most advocates of humanitarian intervention did not fool themselves into thinking that military force would never be used to uphold the natural, democratic rights of oppressed foreigners.

The earliest colonists had occasionally applied concepts similar to humanitarian intervention when it suited their material or political interests. In sending an armed force into Rhode Island to snuff out a sect of heretics, John Winthrop spoke of protecting persecuted minorities and extending the rule of law to an otherwise lawless region. Similar language pervaded the wars against various Indian tribes in the colonial era, from Pequots to Iroquois. But the concept of genuine humanitarianism did not really emerge until Americans discovered the plight of the Greeks in the 1820s. Since the Renaissance, Greece had held a very special place in the Western imagination as the birthplace of Western civilization. Virtually all educated Americans were steeped in classical thought, and Greek ideas about democracy exerted a strong influence upon the Founders. But by then, Greece was a Christian province of the Islamic Ottoman Empire. In 1821, when the Greeks rebelled against Ottoman rule, the call for America to help was difficult to ignore. "Greek fever" swept across the United States.[14]

Greece was not only the cradle of civilization; it was a Christian land under the oppressive thumb of Muslim Ottoman Turks, and thus a battle, declared a Harvard classics professor, of "the cross versus the crescent." Greeks lived under both civil and religious tyranny, a plight Americans believed they knew much about from their days in the British Empire. Fittingly, popular support for Greek independence was emotional and overwhelming. A women's group in Brooklyn, for instance, erected a giant cross emblazoned with a slogan, "Sacred to the Cause of Greece," that was visible in Manhattan. Freeing the Greeks from their tyranny would enable American missionaries to spread the gospel in Muslim lands. Missionaries, the Reverend Sereno Dwight argued, "will feel their way into the farthest retreats of Mohammedan darkness." It would also extend republican democracy at an important crossroads between two bastions of authoritarianism, Europe and the Ottoman Empire. "Humanity, policy, religion—all demand it," war hero and future president William Henry Harrison declared in summing up the case for American intervention. "The star-spangled banner must wave in the Aegean."[15]

Perhaps no American pushed for humanitarian intervention as vigorously as Daniel Webster. A congressman from Massachusetts in 1823, and later a senator and secretary of state, Webster deployed all of his famed rhetorical skills in an attempt to get the United States to midwife the birth of Greek independence. Webster was thoroughly grounded in the orthodox Congregationalism that still typified New England's spiritual and cultural life. Though he was not an evangelical, Christian imagery, phrases, and ethics infused his oratory with a crusading, moralistic zeal. Webster based his argument on behalf of the Greeks partly on a universal, natural right to liberty, but his most stirring rhetoric came in contrasting civilized Christian Greece with its barbaric Muslim oppressor. The Greeks, he declared to Congress, were suffering "a bitter and unending persecution of their religion" and the "habitual violation of their rights of person and property." With its blend of religious and civil liberty with property rights, this was about as strong a case as an American could make. Yet Webster continued. He pointed to the lack of separation of church and state in the Ottoman Empire, with the "religious and civil code of the state being both fixed in the Koran, and equally the object of an ignorant and furious faith." And he argued, perhaps lost in the moment and forgetting about America's own slaves, that nowhere else was freedom so violated. "In short, the Christian subjects of the Sublime Porte feel daily all the miseries which flow from despotism, from anarchy, from slavery, and from religious persecution. . . . In the whole world, Sir, there is no such oppression felt as by the Christian Greeks." Webster concluded with a flourish. The Greeks

> stretch out their arms to the Christian communities of the earth, beseeching them, by a generous recollection of their ancestors, by the consideration of their desolated and ruined cities and villages, by their wives and children sold into an accursed slavery, by their blood, which they seem willing to pour out like water, by the common faith, and in the name, which unites all Christians, that they would extend to them at least some token of compassionate regard.[16]

But while nearly all Americans wanted to save the Greeks, not everyone believed it was America's task to do so. In fact, while Reverend Dwight and others hoped to evangelize the Holy Land by going to war alongside the Greeks, missionaries themselves feared that angering the Turks would bring an end to American missions within the Ottoman

Empire, which covered almost the entire Middle East. Their experiences in Greece, moreover, convinced many Protestant missionaries that the Greek Orthodox Church was just as bad as the Roman Catholic Church. American business interests, especially the largely New England–based merchant marine, feared losing access to their lucrative trade with the Ottomans. Secretary of State John Quincy Adams was sensitive to both constituencies. While he agreed with the morality of the Greek cause, he felt that American strategic and economic interests were even more important. Thus while he did nothing to stop Americans from privately supporting the Greek cause, officially the U.S. government did little more than mouth anticolonial platitudes about freedom and democracy. Adams partly defused the emotional furor over Greece by penning an 1823 presidential speech that reiterated the independent, unilateralist principles of Washington's 1796 Farewell Address and his father's 1776 Model Treaty. Later known as the Monroe Doctrine, Adams's speech warned Europeans not to interfere in the Western Hemisphere's affairs, such as the independence revolutions in Latin America, just as it promised that the United States would not interfere in European quarrels.[17]

The case of Greece illustrated both the uses and limited influence of religion in U.S. foreign policy: while it introduced Americans to humanitarian interventionism, it also revealed that when they clashed, presidents and diplomats would usually prioritize national interests ahead of national ideals. This was true of pacifism's influence as well. Religion demonstrated utility, but not control; it could shape foreign policy, but not determine it. Yet as we shall see, it continued to push American foreign relations in a moralistic, crusading, and sometimes humanitarian direction that helped establish a tradition of what was and was not desirable in U.S. foreign policy.

Few initiatives, secular or religious, encompassed issues of war, peace, and empire as directly and comprehensively as overseas missions. Combining virtually all aspects of moral improvement, from temperance to education to peace, and applying them on a global scale, missionaries were the ultimate agents of benevolent reform. Unique among New World colonizers, Americans did not have much of a missionary tradition; aside from the limited but successful missions of Quakers and Moravians, colonial missionaries to the Indians had by and large met with more failure than success. Nonetheless, in the nineteenth century, as American power and piety grew in equal measure, the missionary enterprise grew with them. Most denominations sent missionaries abroad, but as with many innovations in American religion the impetus came mostly from New England Protestants, specifically Congregationalists. In 1810, they set up the interdenominational American Board of Commissioners for Foreign

Missions (ABCFM) and headquartered it in Boston. The ABCFM quickly became one of the best-funded mission boards in the world, sending thousands of Protestant missionaries to live and proselytize all over the world. Moreover, missionaries, including Catholic missionaries, also continued to seek converts within the United States, especially among immigrants and in the western borderlands that were increasingly coming under U.S. sovereignty and settlement.[18]

Protestant missionaries were not simply Americans abroad. Their stated aim was to convert foreign peoples to the gospel—specifically the Protestant version of the gospel, as many of their targets were other Christians, especially in the Middle East where Islamic and Ottoman law forbade the conversion of Muslims under pain of death. Sustained by their consuming and crusading faith and an allure of mysterious foreign cultures—what H. Richard Niebuhr called the missionaries' unusual "love of the distant"— American missionaries were a highly motivated group whose sole aim was to spread the blessings of civilization to "savage" lands. Motivation had to be high, for missionary life was tough. Mission death rates, mostly from disease but occasionally violence, were often as high as a third; the median life expectancy of some missions in the Ottoman Empire was as low as thirty-nine years. "You go where death may soon arrest you," an 1835 ABCFM handbook for prospective missionaries warned; "where illness may unnerve your strength; where an exhausting climate, without your accustomed advantages of health, almost invariably produces some degree of bodily languor and mental depression." Missionaries would also have to contend with the supposedly corrupting influence of foreign cultures that had not yet been enlightened by Protestantism and Western science. They would be confronted with "perverted notions of right and wrong," "aversion of mind to objects which demand sacrifices and efforts, and yield no visible advantage"—the stupidity of sloth, in other words—"blind attachment to their superstitions," and "rooted and cherished habits of iniquity" in addition to the usual "dishonesty, deceit, treachery, cruelty, tyranny, and extreme selfishness" found among "savage" peoples. Why then did missionaries do it? Because, the handbook's author revealed, "I know of no life more desirable than that of a devoted missionary."[19]

The missionary's difficult life was desirable because it pursued the most glorious cause: reforming and soul-saving the entire world. Nothing could make a committed American Protestant of the era happier than this almighty application of Almighty love. Throughout Asia and the Middle East, antebellum missionaries built libraries, medical centers, and schools; later in the century, they founded hospitals and universities. They taught the English language and imparted republican and democratic theories of government. Secular reform, then, was an essential part of the missionaries' proselytizing agenda. Yet their influence overall, especially in the Middle East, was rather limited, mostly because their numbers were at first so few and their foreign audiences not especially captivated. Only in Hawaii, and later China, did they enjoy much success—and even then, success was limited by low numbers, adverse local conditions, and competition from missionaries of other Christian faiths and nations.[20]

Almost by definition, missionaries were expansionists; many were also nationalists. They were often the first Americans to reach a foreign region and were usually its only permanent American residents. In the Middle East, missionaries traveled under the explicit protection of the U.S. flag, carrying with them an 1842 letter from Secretary of State Daniel Webster saying so; a decade later, in 1852, he extended and enhanced protections when American Protestant missionaries came under pressure in Orthodox Greece. In Hawaii, missionaries were responsible for bringing the islands into the American orbit at the expense of imperial rivals, France in particular. They were therefore a part of America's emerging globalism, its initial search for trade, prestige, and strategic influence. Claimed an early missionary during the Napoleonic Wars, the "world is in arms and opposed to our national prosperity and existence. We must, therefore, like the Israelites, fight our way to empire, in opposition to the power, and policy, and disengaging principles of the most formidable nations on earth." No matter how delicate their movements or sensitive their message, their profession was innately domineering and invasive: missionaries sought to change foreign peoples, to change their very cultures and identities, and condemned them as forever damned if they resisted. They believed in America's righteousness and worked to bring about its manifest destiny. One missionary saw his goal as "reforming the world," while another spoke of fulfilling "God's plan for this world's recovery."[21]

And yet even the most zealous American missionaries were not necessarily deliberate agents of U.S. foreign policy. They believed in republican democracy and America's righteousness, but they believed in the divinity of Christ and the power of God even more. They usually did not see a conflict between the two, but when the needs of Americanism and Christendom collided, almost all chose church over state. They were of course Americans themselves, and so could not avoid implanting American culture and custom alongside the gospel. Yet though they may have been nationalists, they were not always nativist. Forget books and proper grammar, an American in Beirut advised a fellow missionary, and "just learn the language as the people use it." Moreover, the horizon of the missionary vision stretched far beyond the interests of the U.S. government. Protestant churches in the United States avidly followed American missionary activity, but they saw themselves in partnership with Protestant missions of other nationalities: Danish, Dutch, German, and especially British. Declared a Presbyterian missionary from Virginia, the "rapid aggrandisement of Protestant nations, both in *Europe and America* has already wrought wonders for the people that sat in darkness," bringing them "pure religion" and "a brighter day."[22]

This was also the view of Rufus Anderson, the ABCFM's senior secretary and the nation's leading theorist of missions. Anderson naturally supported "the conversion of the heathen," but he also admonished American missionaries not to impose their own cultural or political views. The goal, he said, was to convert foreign peoples to Christ, not America. Missions, he instructed his charges in Ceylon (Sri Lanka), were "exclusively evangelical work and no alliance with secular powers can be otherwise than injurious." Accordingly, Anderson instructed his missionaries to work in the local language and not teach locals English; nor should they seek to impose American cultural or political values; and nor should they assume themselves to be superior to the locals. "As a missionary society, and as a mission," Anderson wrote missionaries in Hawaii in 1847, "we cannot proceed on the assumption, however plausibly stated, that the Saxon is to supersede the native races." If a missionary had a political goal, it was to encourage local independence, not American domination. Missionaries should therefore aim to train promising locals in the pastorate, ordain them, and then get on with their work; when this task was done, missionaries should leave and let this new, local offshoot of Christianity flourish in isolation. As the historian William Hutchison writes, Anderson's theory of missions was amazingly straightforward: "The Kingdom of God is a seed. The missionary is a planter. The missionary plants the seed. The missionary leaves. Yankee go home!"[23]

Amos Starr Cooke, an ordinary missionary, reflected the everyday dilemmas between the sacred and the secular and church and nation because he lived with them every day. An earnest, ABCFM-sponsored Congregationalist missionary to Hawaii, Cooke totally devoted himself to his two main concerns, classroom teaching and gospel preaching. Like many of his fellow New Englanders, he was a Calvinist who believed in the guiding hand of God's providence. "I am more and more convinced that I am in the path of duty," he assured his worried sister Mary in Danbury, Connecticut. But though he spoke of missing "our beloved America," he also told her that where "God would have us there, is our home." Amos complained about the "ignorance" of the Hawaiians, especially their rulers, but he reveled in his young pupils' progress. He worried most of all that "Heathens have souls, and those souls are perishing." The Hawaiians were as capable as Americans, or any people, of receiving God's grace: this was his preoccupation, and he never wrote of nationalist concerns. But Cooke was not oblivious to international politics and acknowledged that the Hawaiians could not keep Western domination indefinitely at bay. He did not favor American annexation, and anyway doubted that it was possible. He disapproved of British imperialism, but disapproved of French Catholics even more and hoped that if anybody colonized Hawaii it would be Britain. His preference, however, was for the islands to remain independent, and, if that proved impossible, that they be administered by a consortium of all three countries, France included, which would ensure Hawaiian sovereignty and appease the great powers. While Cooke disapproved of the Royal Navy's gunboat diplomacy, which he witnessed in action in 1843, he was under no nationalistic illusion that his country behaved any better: "It makes an American's blood run cold as he sees what is doing," he told Mary, "tho' when he thinks of the poor Indian and slave of his own beloved land, his mouth is shut." Similarly, Cooke lamented the intimidating, militaristic presence of the U.S. Navy in Honolulu Harbor. When, he plaintively asked a friend in Danbury, "will they cease to carry instruments of death, and carry Bibles and missionaries" instead?[24]

Antebellum missionaries such as Amos Starr Cooke saw themselves as marching under the banner not of the American interest, but an even older Protestant interest that had moved the spirits of George Whitefield and Jonathan Edwards a century before. They were part of a transatlantic evangelical community in which cooperation with British missionaries was more likely than it was with American Catholics or U.S. diplomats. Missionaries, to be sure, spread Americanism wherever they went, but it was not always their intention to do so. Often their political influence was inadvertent. In Armenia and Syria, for example, missionary schools inculcated Armenian and Arab nationalism that only decades later would lead to rebellion against Ottoman rule. Missionary policy supported local independence and opposed foreign imperialism, including American. "For a long time," a hostile French diplomat in Beirut reported back to the Quai d'Orsay, "I have sought to determine the objectives of the Americans in coming to evangelize here. At long last I am persuaded that their sole motivation was religious propaganda. I simply do not perceive any ulterior political motive." Still, along with merchants they played a crucial role in expanding American horizons beyond the North American continent, indeed, beyond the Western Hemisphere. But unlike merchants, they brought with them sanctified ideals about civil and religious liberty and a crusading mentality to see them successfully exported. They introduced Americans to the world and the world to America. Christian exceptionalists to their core, they were also America's accidental imperialists.[25]

CHAPTER EIGHT

Manifest Destiny and Its Discontents

MISSIONARIES WERE NOT THE only antebellum Americans with their gaze fixed on the distant horizon. Seeing their prosperity growing, their power gathering, and their confidence surging, Americans of the era did not see why their country could not keep expanding, too. It would be futile, silly even, to resist expansion, for it was destined to happen. Expansionists believed that America had a duty to conquer and civilize the North American continent—and possibly beyond—because God's providence had decreed it. They, and thus presumably God, had their eyes on the Republic of Texas and vast swaths of lightly populated territory governed by Mexico—nothing short of present-day Arizona, New Mexico, Utah, Colorado, Nevada, and California—as well as the Oregon Country.

This belief had a name—"manifest destiny"—that had overtones of the same Calvinist millennialism that had succored the colonial wars against the French and Indians and during the American Revolution. And the name had an author, John O'Sullivan, a partisan Jacksonian Democrat, ardent expansionist, newspaper editor, and talented writer. To him, the United States was a "vigorous" nation "fresh from the hand of God" that had been sent on a "blessed mission to the nations of the world," while American democracy was "Christianity in its earthly aspect—Christianity made effective among the political relations of men." In 1845, as the nation argued over the merits of expansion and Congress debated how much of Oregon to claim, O'Sullivan pointed to "the right of our manifest destiny to overspread and to possess the whole continent which providence has given us for the development of the great experiment of liberty and federated self government."[1]

The idea was not new, of course. From the very first colonial settlements in Virginia, Plymouth, and Massachusetts, Americans had been looking to expand. When they did, they almost always justified it in the name of God, as in the Puritan "errand into the wilderness." As traders extended their networks throughout the Western Hemisphere and beyond, to Europe, Africa, the Mediterranean, and China, as the domestic economy boomed, and as the colonial population grew, Americans believed they could not help but expand into the vast "empty space" that hemmed them in against the Atlantic coast. Yet the space was hardly empty, filled not only with hundreds of thriving Indian tribes but also other European colonizers. But when matched against the American colonists' relentless hunger for land, their greater numbers, and their growing economic power, these neighbors posed little challenge to American expansion. Religious ideas and values, foremost providence and the conceit that America was a chosen nation, the New Israel, had given expansionism an emotive power and righteous justification long before O'Sullivan put his pen to paper.[2]

Expansion, then, had long been portrayed as central to the American and Christian civilizing mission. For many, the territorial imperative was a more important goal, a higher calling, than the rights of Indians or slaves because it meant the spread of liberty—republican and Christian—to a barren land and its benighted people. Some of the more thoughtful expansionists realized there was a contradiction here, between the spread of republican liberty alongside the spread of slavery. Methodist home missionaries in Alabama and Mississippi, for example, acquiesced in and even defended the slave system but tried to reform its worst abuses and excesses; they also sought to educate slaves. But such moral compromises were at best only marginally effective, and rarely that, and instead of sowing doubt among the faithful they led to a fuller embrace of expansionism. The mission board of the Episcopal Church was unsure about slavery, but it was certain that acquiring Texas could only be a good thing. "To earnest, devoted, self-denying men, capable of 'enduring hardness' in the cause of Christ, there is scarcely a more promising field in the whole range of our Missionary operations than that presented by Texas," reported the bishop responsible for missions to the national church body in 1847.[3]

But most others could not even see a contradiction, or, if they could, did not care. Southern whites were a diverse lot, especially in terms of class and wealth, and had few common causes to bind them together. White supremacy was important, but not all Southern whites owned slaves. Many white Southerners were evangelicals, though, and so when evangelicalism embraced slavery—or at least defended it from Northern interference—the South's social bond became an unholy mix of faith-based racial superiority. Southerners had once felt defensive about their peculiar institution, but by the 1840s they proudly boasted about the benefits of slavery's civilizing influence on an otherwise savage, unchristian people. This was a significant development, for racialized theories of manifest destiny had never been all that comfortable with the Christian doctrine of a universal humanity in which all men and women, created in God's image, had descended from Adam and Eve; indeed, this reading of scripture was precisely the ground on which black abolitionists argued for racial equality. In response, Southern clergy such as the Virginia Baptist Thornton Stringfellow deployed scripture to argue that slavery was not an unfortunate evil—Thomas Jefferson's view—but a positive good. The "conviction is forced upon the mind, that from Abraham's day, until the coming of Christ," Stringfellow wrote in reply to an antislavery Baptist in Rhode Island, "this institution found favor with God." Slavery was Christianizing Africans who would otherwise be condemned to a life of sin and darkness, and Southern planters treated their slaves better than Northern industrialists treated their workers; rather than being a system of oppression, "slavery is full of mercy." South Carolinian James Henley Thornwell, perhaps the South's most renowned theologian, flatly declared that Southerners "cherish" slavery "not from avarice, but from principle."[4]

Stringfellow and Thornwell were not alone in their indignation. Angered by their Northern members' hostility to slavery, Southern Baptists and Methodists anticipated the sectional split of 1860–61 by breaking away from their national organizations in the 1830s and '40s; Southern Presbyterians followed suit in 1861. Both halves of these once-national bodies could now pursue what one historian has aptly called "the foreign policy of slavery" in states of ideological purity. Presciently, John C. Calhoun feared that after the church schisms "nothing will be left to hold the States together except force." Each side saw itself as the true heir to the American republican tradition. But for all sides of the dispute, the foreign policy of slavery was fundamentally about territorial expansion, which in turn posed fundamental problems of war and empire. For Southerners like John Rice, a contributor to the *Southern Presbyterian Review*, the opening of the westward settlement at precisely the moment the invention of the cotton gin rejuvenated the stagnating institution of slavery was nothing short of providential. Simply put, God favored slavery because he had made it possible. Thus the South must "never to consent that her social system . . . be confined and restrained by any other limits than such as the God of nature interposes."[5]

Likewise, many religious Americans supported Indian Removal as a way to gain territory as well as an extension of Christian benevolence without necessarily seeing a clash between the two. Home missionaries pursued Indian assimilation through American education by bringing southern Indians to schools up north. This would, a Connecticut-based missionary with the ABCFM explained to Secretary of War John C. Calhoun, serve both "the cause of humanity and national policy" by reconciling "Christian Benevolence . . . with the best policy of the Government." Many missionaries, from virtually all denominations, believed that by stubbornly standing between Americans and free land, Indians were simply ensuring the death of their own way of life. Through education and moral uplift, they sought to Christianize, civilize, and save Indians. In the 1820s, a Baptist missionary, Isaac McCoy, was one of the first to argue that the only place left to do so was west of the Mississippi, paving the way for Andrew Jackson's policy of Indian Removal in the following decade.[6]

Jackson himself couched expansion in terms of divine inevitability. A morally imperfect yet profoundly religious man, Jackson believed in America's God-given manifest destiny. Two of the great influences in his life, his mother and his wife, were both devout Presbyterians, and from them Jackson constructed a worldview based on a strict fundamentalist interpretation of Calvinist predestination. Like his great rival John Quincy Adams, Jackson attended a variety of Protestant churches (though he naturally steered well clear of Congregationalists and Unitarians). He justified Indian Removal by noting that the "god of the universe had intended this great [Mississippi] valley to belong to one nation." Who could withstand such a force? Apparently not even the indomitable Jackson—in which case the messiness of expansionism, such as war and Removal, could be explained, even justified, as unavoidable byproducts of the inevitable. Jackson packaged this theme with another powerful religious trope, America as a chosen land, in his final remarks as president. "You have the highest of human trusts committed to your care. Providence has showered on this favored land blessings without number, and has chosen you as the guardians of freedom, to preserve it for the benefit of the human race," he said in his farewell address in 1837. "May He who holds in His hands the destinies of nations make you worthy of the favors He has bestowed and enable you, with pure hearts and pure hands and sleepless vigilance, to guard and defend to the end of time the great charge He has committed to your keeping."[7]

Few Americans were as genuinely committed to expansion as the Reverend Jedidiah Morse. An orthodox Congregationalist minister and charter member of the ABCFM, Morse was also the early republic's foremost geographer. His book *The American Geography* was the standard work on the subject for Americans and Europeans alike and went through several revised editions between its first appearance in 1789 and his death in 1826. A protégé of Reverend Timothy Dwight, Morse was a staunch Federalist who believed that democracy simply could not function properly without a Christian foundation. Morse was also a proud patriot, a nationalist who foresaw America's boundaries expanding across the continent—and with them its enlightened systems of religion and government. The first edition of *American Geography* informed readers that "it is well known that empire has been travelling from east to west. Probably her last and broadest seat will be America." Americans "cannot but anticipate the period, as not far distant, when the AMERICAN EMPIRE will comprehend millions of souls, west of the Mississippi." As an orthodox Calvinist, Morse believed this as a matter of faith: God had made it so. In 1820, Morse received a commission from Secretary of War Calhoun to survey the

Indian nations that lived along what was then the northwestern frontier, near the Great Lakes. Though he believed in the capacity of Indians to receive God's grace, Morse did not believe that they could continue living their traditional life and also be citizens of the United States. The only way to reconcile American expansionism with Indian welfare, Morse reported to Calhoun, was to Christianize the Indians. And the only way to do that was to remove them to sovereign zones of safety west of the Mississippi, where they could receive a proper tutelage in American Christian republicanism.[8]

Protestant clergy and missionaries, such as Isaac McCoy, continued to promote Jedidiah Morse's plan for territorial expansion after his death, but it was actually his son, Samuel Morse, who smoothed America's westward passage. Best known as the inventor of the telegraph, Samuel Morse was also a Romantic painter, devout Calvinist, anti-Catholic nativist, defender of slavery, and fervent expansionist imbued with an inordinate sense of religious mission and a grandiose vision of America's future. His artwork aimed to inspire Americans to fulfill their God-given manifest destiny. In art and literature, the early nineteenth century marked the emergence of Romanticism in the United States, an aesthetic that questioned Enlightenment rationalism just as rationalism had once questioned faith. Samuel Morse's art reflected this Romanticism, as did other American painters of the era. Epitomized by the Hudson River School, Romanticist landscape paintings portrayed a boundless, bountiful, mythic America, a latter-day Garden of Eden. The Romantic sensibility overlapped considerably with evangelical theology and manifest destiny ideology, and few captured all three strands more perfectly than Samuel Morse.[9]

It was not Morse's paintings, however, but his invention of the telegraph in 1844 that helped enable Americans to realize their manifest destiny. For thousands of years, communications could travel only as quickly as the fastest form of transportation. The telegraph revolutionized communications by making them nearly instantaneous across the greatest of distances. Almost immediately, Americans grasped the importance of the new device, and telegraph wires soon crisscrossed the nation. Morse certainly realized what he had done—or rather, in the famous words of his first message, WHAT HATH GOD WROUGHT. The telegraph would enable the United States to spread its sovereignty and American Protestants to spread their faith. Morse's dream was on the cusp of fulfillment as a holy trinity of patriotism, Christianity, and innovation would march together westward.[10]

But manifest destiny, in all its various forms, was not the antebellum era's only faith-based imperial project. The fervent enthusiasm and energetic voluntarism sparked by the First Amendment's religious libertarianism and fueled by the Second Great Awakening led to a wave of innovation in American Christianity. New denominations, such as the Disciples of Christ, popped up across the religious landscape to add to the already bewildering diversity of American Protestantism. Another new Christian faith that emerged at this time, Mormonism, became intimately, if independently, bound up in westward expansion. From its earliest beginnings in the 1830s in western New York's "burned over district"—so-called because it had been charred by raging fires of religious passion—to its westward migrations, Mormonism was a millennial, prophetic faith with an expansive earthly vision. Joseph Smith, the Mormon founder, led his Latter-day Saints west, first to Ohio, then Missouri, and then to the muddy banks of the Mississippi, where they founded the town of Nauvoo, Illinois. Like the Puritans before them, the Mormons kept moving because of their tendency to attract violent opposition. Also like the Puritans, Mormons conceived of their journey as part Genesis, part Exodus, and part New Israel. After a series of pitched battles and Smith's murder in 1844, Brigham Young led the Mormons further west to the ultimate safety of Great Salt Lake, then a part of Mexico. There the Mormons settled permanently, cultivating the land, warding off any other Americans who also thought of settling near them, and blazing the Mormon Trail that would lead thousands more of the faithful out west. Following earlier patterns of white migratory settlement, the Mormons dealt with the local Ute Indian nation with a mixture of "noble savage" wonderment, acceptance and embellishment of their traditions, and, finally, violent conflict that resulted in American settler dominance. In 1850, the United States organized the land as the Utah Territory; in 1852, Young was appointed its first governor. Mormon history is a peculiarly American tale of religious diversity and innovation, Christian revivalism and millennialism, and westward expansion and imperialism—and yet another interpretation of manifest destiny.[11]

As GLORIOUS AND inevitable as it seemed, however, not all Americans were expansionists. Some were anti-expansionist or would support expansion only under certain conditions. In an era when benevolent reform dominated social and cultural politics, the cause of antislavery dominated benevolent reform. More than temperance, more than education, more than pacifism, more even than missions, the goal to end American slavery was the greatest reform movement of them all. The antislavery cause made for strange bedfellows, bringing together emotive evangelicals and unemotional Unitarians. In turn, opposition to slavery provoked a popular response to manifest destiny and a rival to the territorial ambitions of politicians, diplomats, and farmers: the foreign policy of abolitionism. In opposing the annexation of Texas, Eli Hawley Canfield, a low-church, evangelical Episcopal minister from Brooklyn, spoke for most abolitionists: "There is such a thing as *over-growth*." It was time instead to perfect what Americans already had.[12]

Emerging out of New England but found widely throughout the antebellum North, evangelicals and other religious reformers opposed westward expansion because it would almost certainly lead to the expansion of the two great evils of American society: war and slavery. The causes of peace and antislavery were often inseparable: for many Christian abolitionists, such as the influential editor of *The Liberator* magazine William Lloyd Garrison, pacifism led to abolitionism, which in turn led to anti-expansionism, itself already a cause embraced by pacifists. This progressive Christian view of equal human nature and a firm belief in universal humanity led many to equate antiviolence with antislavery, an innovation Garrison called "nonresistance," as in non*violent* resistance. Such an egalitarian worldview also led pacifists and abolitionists to oppose Indian Removal and support women's rights; indeed, women comprised a disproportionate share of the peace and antislavery movements. In mobilizing an implacable hostility to slavery, then, abolitionists also applied their fearsome moral energy to resisting territorial expansion as America's manifest destiny. This applied theology influenced many Americans as they decided whether slave-suitable lands, such as Texas, should be brought into the Union. Using Matthew 16:26 as the scriptural basis for his sermon—"What Shall a Man Give in Exchange for His Soul?"— during the controversy over Texas, one Ohio Presbyterian undoubtedly spoke for many: "*It is the extreme of folly to barter away our souls for the purpose of gaining the world.*" In 1837, in an open letter to Senator Henry Clay, William Ellery Channing disputed America's right to annex Texas mostly because he damned slavery as unchristian, immoral, and a violation of divine, natural rights. Stunned by Channing's "arrogance and presumptuousness," Clay complained to a friend that he was being asked to exchange "the sober practical wisdom" of logic and custom "for the vain and visionary theories of Dr. Channing" and his allies. But Channing had won the argument, for now, and Texas remained independent, outside the Union.[13]

Benevolent reformers proposed foreign policy initiatives as well. In an era when Britons and Americans were first constructing their fitful "special relationship" through cordial diplomacy and cooperative missionary work, evangelical abolitionists called for Washington and London to mount a joint effort in humanitarian intervention to eliminate, once and for all, the now-illegal but still thriving Atlantic slave trade. Ineffectual in stopping slave trading but successful in raising public awareness and applying popular pressure, the World Anti-Slavery Convention, held in London in 1840, symbolized both the potential and the limitations of a "foreign policy of antislavery." Moreover, on their own British and American evangelicals joined forces to advance transatlantic theological, political, and social concerns. The result, at a conference in London in 1846, was the formation of the Evangelical Alliance. The Alliance solidified ties between reform-minded evangelicals on both sides of the Atlantic and advanced the cause of a progressive U.S. foreign policy.[14]

In a spirit similar to abolitionism, Christian reformers of the antebellum period vigorously protested Andrew Jackson's policy of Indian Removal. Quakers and Moravians unsurprisingly disapproved, but so too did evangelical abolitionists like Garrison and Unitarian pacifists like Channing. But a broader-based opposition stemmed also from large missionary investments of time, manpower, and money—investments they would lose with Removal. The ABCFM mounted a particularly vehement opposition to Indian Removal, which was fitting because it at once symbolized an alignment of anti-expansionist Whigs, missionaries, abolitionists, and Northerners against proslavery and mainly Southern Jacksonian Democrats. Jeremiah Evarts, a leading figure with the ABCFM, attacked the morality of Indian Removal and the claims to righteousness of those—including some church leaders, such as Isaac McCoy—who claimed that Removal was simply in the best interests of the Indians. Using Evarts's arguments, Theodore Frelinghuysen, a senator from New Jersey and future president of the ABCFM whom Garrison lauded as "the Christian statesman," attacked Indian Removal from the floor of the Senate as a betrayal of America's Christian character and its true manifest destiny. When he learned of the government's plans to remove the Cherokees, Ralph Waldo Emerson wrote a furious, pleading letter to President Martin Van Buren. "In the name of God, sir, we ask you if this is so?" Emerson charged that such a "dereliction of all faith and virtue, such a denial of justice, and such deafness to screams for mercy" were incompatible with the Christian nature of American ethics.[15]

Naturally, African Americans, freed and enslaved, shared the religious reformers' emancipatory vision. Free blacks, many of them antislavery preachers, intellectuals, and activists affiliated with the emergent black Protestant churches, traveled throughout the North and pursued their own foreign policy of antislavery by carrying their message on speaking tours of Great Britain. They also seized on Swedenborgian theories of the millennium that centered on Ethiopia and African Christianity as the "true church" that would eventually redeem the world and end slavery. But in the South, black opposition to slavery and expansion had to be covert. Those who spread its subversive message were usually the articulate and literate slaves who had received their informal education from missionaries, preachers, and stray Bibles. Subjected to the horrors of bondage, they were hardly enthusiastic about its spread.[16]

By the middle of the antebellum period, American slave communities had stabilized. With the African slave trade outlawed in 1808, slave living conditions improved as their owners realized they could not replace valuable slaves with cheap imports; in turn, the slave population began a steady upward climb through higher birth rates and longer life expectancies. As brutal and dehumanizing as it remained, American slaves now possessed a measure of stability and permanency they had never known: kinship networks formed, slave couples secretly married, and tightly knit slave families grew. Slave churches—often informal and open-air, because they were usually illegal—also grew. One of the most important consequences of the Second Great Awakening was the vast expansion of the Christian religion among slaves, who embraced evangelicalism, synthesized it with African traditions, and built it into a formidable support network of cultural autonomy. Christianity, the faith of the masters, had also become the slaves' salvation.[17]

But the closing of the slave trade also brought about a new trauma: the Second Middle Passage. The original Middle Passage had been the name for the slaves' horrific Atlantic crossing from West Africa to the New World; its successor described the involuntary journey of slaves from the upper South—Delaware, Maryland, North Carolina, and especially Virginia—to the booming cotton plantations of the Deep South. Slave auctions did a brisk trade as masters of smaller tobacco farms in Virginia found themselves with more slaves than they needed and an eager market of cotton farmers in Alabama, Mississippi, and Louisiana. As a result, wives were separated from husbands, children from parents. The Second Middle Passage was a main cause of the most serious slave revolt, in Southampton County, Virginia, in 1831. Its leader, Nat Turner, an unchurched but literate Baptist slave preacher who believed he was a prophet who spoke to God, had lost his wife to the Second Middle Passage. In retaliation and the hope of liberation, Turner led a fire-and-brimstone uprising that ultimately failed but killed sixty whites in the process. Despite lacking a political voice, religious blacks also found a way to oppose American expansionism.[18]

Yet sympathy for the plight of black slaves led some antislavery activists—among them Abraham Lincoln—to support an altogether different, but no less racist kind of expansionism: African colonization. Not all opponents of slavery believed that freedom for blacks in American society was the solution. Slaves, they argued, were not only an inferior race, they had been brutalized for over a century by whites. How could the two races possibly live together in peace? Their opposition to slavery was based on a fear of what slavery was doing to America rather than a humanitarian concern about the conditions of forced servitude. Slavery must end, they argued. But how? The solution was to resettle freed slaves as semi-Americans in Africa or Central America, "to convey," in the words of Unitarian Jonathan Blake, "the African race back to the land of their nativity and to the home of their Fathers . . . where our Beneficent Creator at first located them." The problem was that very few blacks actually wanted the freedom of permanent exile. They were Americans, born and raised for generations, and understandably did not see Africa, much less Central America, as "the home of their Fathers." A group of freed American slaves did establish Liberia, in West Africa, as a U.S. colony in 1822, but it marked the end rather than the beginning of the colonization experiment. While African colonization was not an exclusively religious initiative, Christian antislavery activists gave it a critical boost of moral fervor. Their religious imprimatur was important, for it was evangelicals who had been pushing hardest the arguments that slavery was immoral and colonization was a morally acceptable alternative. In colonization, religious abolitionists also saw an opportunity. Samuel Hopkins, the divine who had scolded John Wesley that the American Revolution would bring an end to slavery for colonials and their African slaves, envisioned African colonization as a grand missionary enterprise to spread American Christianity.[19]

Moreover, not all antislavery activists were opposed to expansion. Manifest destiny exerted a strong pull on America's religious imagination, especially the notions that the United States was a blessed land, that its citizens were God's chosen people, and that America was providentially ordained to spread its blessings of liberty far and wide. These ideas had been embedded in the religious mind of virtually every Protestant denomination, including Unitarians, with the notable exceptions of Quakers and Moravians. Surprisingly, the prince of the indefatigably abolitionist Beecher family, Henry Ward Beecher, believed in the divinity of manifest destiny, even after the Mexican War had reopened the wound of slavery. As one of the most famous men in the nation and probably his era's most renowned religious figure—and, not least of all, as Harriet Beecher Stowe's younger brother—Beecher's opinion carried tremendous weight. And on this occasion, Thanksgiving Day 1847, he preached a message of manifest destiny. "I rejoice that Christians are disposed to take the West to their hearts," he told his congregation at Plymouth Congregational Church in Brooklyn as the Mexican War drew to a close, for the "fate of the West is to be the fate" of the United States. "We cannot circumscribe the territorial bounds which God hath appointed, nor diminish the swelling flood of population which rushes there to find its level." Education was critical—and something of a family crusade, begun by his father Lyman—and Beecher gloried that benevolent societies ensured that proper Christian schools followed the settlers out west. Yet while expansion was part of God's plan, slavery was not. The result would be calamitous, Beecher warned, if slavery accompanied the spread of an otherwise virtuous America. "It is not by accident that evil accompanies

despotism, and that good attends upon liberty. So God ordained it to be."
While Beecher may have distrusted the slave-neutral ideology of manifest
destiny, he had no doubts about America's providential mission to spread
civilization and education across the continent.[20]

Because it was so perfectly suited to the Romantic spirit of the age,
the notion of a providentially guided, expansive United States was simply
impossible to resist, even for many antislavery and anti-Removal religious
intellectuals. Evangelicals, such as James Knowles of Boston's Second Baptist Church, believed expansion would bring the United States—and the
world—immense spiritual and material rewards, but not if slavery played
a part. The Reverend George Cheever of the Church of the Puritans in
Manhattan offered a particularly shrill version of an antislavery manifest
destiny in his book *God's Hand in America*. "Our whole existence shall be
a lofty course of freedom and piety," exulted Cheever, "expansive as the
world, and lasting as the continent we inhabit." Though he had opposed
the annexation of Texas in 1845 and worried that the anarchy of the frontier would corrupt the virtues of America's Christian republicanism, Horace Bushnell, a theological liberal, antislavery activist, and preacher of
national renown, announced in 1847 that Americans "will not cease, till a
Christian nation throws up its temples of worship on every hill and plain;
till knowledge, virtue and religion . . . have filled our great country with
a manly and happy race of people, and the bands of a complete Christian
commonwealth are seen to span the continent." Just not with slavery.[21]

Though they were often loathe to admit it, even the Transcendentalists and Unitarians were susceptible to the lure of manifest destiny. Emerson hated slavery and Removal, yet he too embraced an almost mystical
vision of America as master of the continent and redeemer of the world.
He believed in fate and that it was America's fate to tame and civilize all of
North America. In 1844—after Removal and in the midst of manifest destiny fervor—Emerson gave a celebrated lecture on the "Young American,"
the name of a Romantic expansionist movement of American youth. On
behalf of Young America, he proclaimed confidently that the "bountiful
continent is ours, state on state, territory on territory, to the waves of the
Pacific sea . . . and new duties, new motives await and cheer us." Americans
must "appreciate the advantages opened to the human race in this country,
which is our fortunate home." Contrasting a stagnant and static Europe
with a dynamic America, Emerson noted that because of the railroad,
"the nervous, rocky West is intruding a new and continental element into
the natural mind. . . . It seems so easy for America to inspire and express the
most expansive and humane spirit; new-born, free, healthful, strong, the
land of the laborer, of the democrat, of the philanthropist, of the believer,
of the saint, she should speak for the human race. It is the country of the
Future." His prediction that fate would also ensure the gradual death of

slavery and that future generations of Americans would be racially mixed tempered but could not disguise his ardent imperialism. Other Romantically inclined Unitarian and Transcendentalist abolitionists, such as William Henry Channing (nephew of William Ellery) and Theodore Parker, shared Emerson's conflicted vision of America's mission.[22]

And they were not alone. In one of history's more pointed ironies, their vision was essentially the same as that of the author of manifest destiny himself, John L. O'Sullivan. While he was his era's most effective propagandist of expansion, O'Sullivan was no less a reformer than the evangelicals, Unitarians, and Transcendentalists—and no less a pacifist. Under his editorship, the *Democratic Review* supported the cause of peace by publishing articles on Christian pacifism by Protestant clergy. O'Sullivan promoted arbitration as an antidote to war and called, in 1841, for the creation of a "Congress of Nations." His expansionist ideology was not rooted in conquest; as the embodiment of the future and God's chosen nation, America would never need to go to such trouble. He was instead a true believer in providence, arguing consistently that America's superior culture, politics, and religion would irresistibly, inevitably—and peacefully—overwhelm the continent. Just like Emerson and Parker, O'Sullivan opposed war and the spread of slavery but welcomed the expansion of America. Little could any of them appreciate, however, that such carefully calibrated impulses would be impossible to control. "Representative government is really misrepresentative," a disillusioned, betrayed Emerson would complain, in 1856, about the turmoil in Kansas. "Manifest Destiny, Democracy, Freedom, fine names for an ugly thing." But by then, it was too late.[23]

WAR OR PEACE, empire or republic, slavery or abolition—these were the explosive political, sectional, and religious choices that had been lingering, unresolved, since the War of 1812. They erupted once more in 1846, having again been provoked by a controversial war. War with Mexico officially lasted for two years, from 1846 to 1848, though most of the fighting was over in little more than a year. The Mexican War was America's first modern war, the conflict in which the modern weapons and tactics that would define warfare until World War II were first tested. It also marked a watershed, the culmination of old forces and the introduction of new dynamics, in how domestic politics and culture affect the course of war and diplomacy. The issue of slavery, the lure of manifest destiny, the role of immigrants, the reemergence of Catholicism in America's foreign relations, the protests of Christian pacifists, and the bitterly partisan nature of the war all combined to produce an ideologically explosive, divisive conflict that ensured Mexico's ruin and nearly led to America's. By reopening the link between expansion and slavery, the Mexican War was actually the first skirmish in the Civil War.[24]

Mexico had suffered a turbulent early history since winning its independence from Spain in 1821. Its most northeasterly province, Texas, fought and won its own war of independence with Mexico in 1835–36. If the residents of Texas had had their way, they would have been annexed almost immediately by the United States. Many Americans shared the same goal, but slavery, which was widespread in Texas by the time of independence, complicated matters, for annexing Texas would also mean expanding slavery within the United States. For nearly a decade, no president would endorse annexation for fear of the tensions and emotions it would unleash. What was more, in 1836 the Mexican government announced that annexation would be a cause for war. Though war did not immediately follow in 1845, when Texas finally did join the United States, a year later the two largest countries in North America found themselves in battle for control of the continent. By that time, having absorbed Texas, President James K. Polk decided America should also conquer California and everything in between. In this, he was fantastically successful. Though the war was somewhat more treacherous than Americans had expected, the United States quickly took possession of California and the disputed borderlands between Texas and Mexico. When Mexican authorities still refused to surrender, the U.S. Army marched deep into Mexican territory and occupied Veracruz and the capital, Mexico City, in 1847. Stung by these humiliating defeats, Mexico agreed to the even more humiliating Treaty of Guadalupe Hidalgo in 1848 that forced it to relinquish more than a third of its national territory.[25]

Unlike his predecessors going back to Andrew Jackson, Polk was an unequivocal expansionist. Slavery did not affect his stance; as a Southerner from Tennessee and slave master himself, Polk had no qualms about its extension or enhancement. But Polk's expansionism was driven more by his extreme nationalism than by slavery. From the British he wanted all of the Oregon Country, a goal supported by most Northerners, and from the Mexicans he wanted California, which most Americans hoped for. And of course he had also supported the annexation of Texas, wildly popular in the South. Elected in 1844 on a platform of manifest destiny, Polk was determined to expand the Union, and expand he did. Tensions with Britain and Mexico arose almost simultaneously in 1845–46. Despite his bluster, Polk was reluctant to go to war with Britain over Oregon, especially considering that the British were willing to settle for half of the territory and leave the southern half, where Americans had settled, to the United States. Britain in fact seemed to provide the key to unlocking the entire expansionist deadlock, because it was assumed that London had its own designs not only on Oregon, but also on California, Texas, and Cuba. A settlement with Britain over Oregon thus paved the way for a war against Mexico that would in turn block Britain's own designs in

Mexico and Cuba. It was no coincidence that these events occurred almost simultaneously.[26]

Polk was a devoutly religious man and he did not hesitate to invoke providence in service to his cause. Sacred logic also made for good rhetoric that would draw wide acceptance as Christian as well as American doctrine. The piety of manifest destiny, in other words, made for good politics. And it fit with an aspect of his Calvinist upbringing that he still very much believed in: predestination. "No country has been so much favored, or should acknowledge with deeper reverence the manifestations of the divine protection," Polk declared in his Third Annual Message, in 1848, with victory in sight. "An all-wise Creator directed and guarded us in our infant struggle for freedom and has constantly watched over our surprising progress until we have become one of the great nations of the earth." As Polk had made plain, the Mexican War, and with it the acquisition of California, was the culmination of the manifest destiny impulse.[27]

Advocates for war also couched their support in terms of God's plan for his people. On June 1, 1846, Captain R. A. Stewart, a Louisiana planter and ordained Methodist minister, preached the war's first American sermon on Mexican soil. Using Jeremiah 7:7 as his text—"I will let you dwell in this place, in the land that I gave of old to your fathers for ever"— Stewart rejoiced in the "blessings of freedom" and true Christian civilization the U.S. Army was importing into Mexico. That it could happen at all was an "order of Providence" fulfilled by the "children of destiny." Conquering Mexico's sovereign territory seemed little different than Indian Removal, as some of the war's supporters pointed out. Even Unitarians could be swept up in the crusading fervor of wartime. Reverend Henry Whitney Bellows, pastor of the First Unitarian Church in New York and one of the nation's leading Unitarian voices, said he had little respect for the Mexicans' "weaker blood," which Americans could "regard with as much certainty as we do the final extinction of the Indian races, to which the mass of the Mexican population seem very little superior." The Mexicans of course practiced a weaker religion, too, which promised to open up vast new missionary opportunities for American Protestants.[28]

MANY OF THE war's participants also viewed it through the lens of faith. Mormons placed the war within the context of their prophetic faith and formed their own battalion—the only faith-based regiment in American military history—as a way to strengthen their church. Others saw it as another battle in a war between Protestants and Catholics. Southern Baptists and Southern Methodists championed it as a straightforward crusade against Latin Catholicism. Echoing the colonial Black Legend and fears of Catholicism's purported corrupt and authoritarian tendencies, many U.S. soldiers who invaded and occupied Mexico wrote home contemptuously about the backwardness of Catholic mysticism and superstition and justified America's cause in these terms. While the Mexican people starved in destitution, Private Ralph Kirkham informed his wife, the "rascally priests live well enough." They "might dress in rags," but it was still "easy enough to recognize them by their fat, well-fed bodies. They are a grand set of rogues." In another letter, Kirkham complained that "the more I see of Romish religion in this country, the more I am convinced that it is real idolatry" that did nothing but keep the people "in a state of perfect ignorance." Not surprisingly, many Mexicans feared they faced a war of religious extermination and forced conversion, an invasion of Yankee Protestants determined to wipe out Mexican Catholicism.[29]

But while disdain for Catholicism spurred many Americans to support a Protestant crusade against Mexico, others feared that conquering Mexican territory would bring a great Catholic horde into the United States. The influence of religion, then, could cut both ways. If the United States took Mexican land, shrieked the *Daily Star* of Philadelphia, scene of some of the worst anti-Catholic nativist riots, Americans would unwittingly welcome *"eight millions of foreigners*, not only entirely ignorant of our institutions, but ignorant of everything, uncultivated in mind, brutal in manners, steeped in the worst of all superstitions, and slaves to the tyranny of monks."[30]

Anti-Catholicism had of course motivated "American" foreign policy under British colonial rule, but it now had a new urgency. Thanks to the arrival of large numbers of Catholic immigrants (especially Irish Catholics), by the eve of the Civil War Americans were no longer a Protestant people. Protestantism retained its dominance, but not its monopoly. Rising immigration, the revival of Protestantism in the Second Great Awakening, and a resurgent American nationalism that identified closely with Protestantism reawakened anti-Catholicism and thrust it once again to the front ranks of American public life. Protestants, the vast majority of the population, worried about the compatibility of the new immigrants' Catholicism with republicanism, especially the lack of separation between church and state in traditional Catholic thought and practice. The Reverend Lyman Beecher, a titan of American Protestantism and architect of reform, issued "a plea for the West" in 1835 that urged Americans to push westward but ensure that Catholics and their authoritarianism did not follow along. Alexander Campbell, leader of the Restoration movement, advanced similar arguments. By the 1850s, with the founding of the American Party, a political front for the nativist movement, anti-Catholicism was threatening to hijack the national agenda—or at least a significant portion of it. In the antebellum North, Protestant angst and social instability were reflected by violent anti-Catholic riots in several American cities that accompanied the rise of nativism in the 1850s. As a contrast to Irish

Catholics, who mostly joined the Democrats, anti-Catholicism became an important aspect of the newly formed Republican Party's appeal in the 1850s. The Mexican War unfolded within this context and, in turn, contributed to the nativist return of anti-Catholicism.[31]

Some Catholics reacted forcefully to the politics of prejudice, opposing an imperialist war against their fellow Catholics. The most vocal was Orestes Brownson, editor of the Boston-based *Quarterly Review*. But nowhere did Catholics—namely, Irish Catholics—resist more dramatically than on the battlefields of Texas and Mexico. Though their role has become embellished in myth, it is clear that some Catholics deserted the U.S. Army out of anger at nativist mobs in the North and in frustration with being forced to do battle against their coreligionists in the name of a Protestant-themed manifest destiny. "As they were Roman Catholic," one immigrant soldier recalled, "they imagined they were fighting against their religion by fighting the Mexicans." Moreover, Catholic soldiers in the U.S. Army received degrading treatment that included punishments for refusing to worship in Protestant services. Mexican authorities encouraged these desertions with religious appeals against the "heretic country" of the United States. "Irishmen! Listen to the words of your brothers, hear the accents of a Catholic people," pleaded one of the Mexican Army's surrender leaflets. "Can you fight by the side of those who put fire to your temples in Boston and Philadelphia? . . . If you are Catholic, the same as we, if you follow the doctrines of Our Saviour, why are you seen sword in hand murdering your brethren? Why are you antagonistic to those who defend their country and your own God?" The leaflets worked surprisingly well. Led by John Riley, a tall Irishman who had emigrated from County Galway to Michigan via service in a British Army regiment stationed in Canada, several hundred Catholic deserters formed the St. Patrick's Battalion in the Mexican Army, known to their comrades as *los San Patricios*.[32]

Nonetheless, most American Catholics supported the Mexican War. Standing firmly behind the Polk administration was a way of blunting nativist charges and Protestant stereotypes of dual loyalty by affirming their allegiance to America. It was also an act of partisan political solidarity with the Democratic Party. If the interests of church and state clashed—a distinct possibility given the Vatican's open hostility to the war—the *Catholic Telegraph* urged every American Catholic to "enter with all his heart into the conflict" on America's side, even "if war should be proclaimed by the United States against the Sovereign Pontiff." For American Catholics, there would be no divided loyalties.[33]

EVEN AMONG PROTESTANTS, the conflict was proving to be every bit as contentious as the War of 1812. As the most reliable bellwether of antebellum values and morals, religion was an important factor in expressing and measuring dissent. In this sense, the St. Patrick's Battalion was emblematic of deep divisions among Americans that exceptionalist ideologies like manifest destiny could not conceal. While supporters perceived the war as the fulfillment of manifest destiny, opponents damned it as an immoral abomination, an act of rapacious aggression, and a blasphemous affront to the very principles of Americanism and Christianity. No government would tolerate such "sins" from one of its own citizens, Reverend Eli Hawley Canfield charged in an emotional 1847 Thanksgiving sermon. How could there be one code of morals for people and another for nations? "There is no concealing the fact that our war with a feeble sister republic is iniquitous in every point of view," for not only had Americans launched an unjust war, they were also strengthening the South's slave power. Contrasting Polk's treatment of Britain over Oregon with his war against Mexico, Canfield railed that the president would not have gone to war if "Mexico had been in a northern instead of a southern latitude." Unease simmered throughout the nation. A divinity student at Yale worried about the effects of Mexico's "sickly climate" and violent people who "never gave or took quarter." An Episcopal priest in Washington belittled Polk's "war for a wilderness" and feared that the president was inviting upon America "the deep damnation sooner or later to be visited in the retributive justice of God."[34]

Providence, then, cut both ways. While expansionists used religious arguments to support the fulfillment of America's manifest destiny— providentialism writ large—opponents feared that the nation's avaricious lust for land would come back to haunt it. Statesmen not normally known for millennialism or piety invoked the wrath of God when protesting the war. In his polemic *Peace with Mexico*, former Secretary of the Treasury Albert Gallatin accused Polk of abandoning America's true mission and distorting its destiny. Senator John C. Calhoun, who had only recently been secretary of state and had earlier served as secretary of war, was a more surprising antiwar partisan given his affection for slavery, but the South Carolinian feared competition from new slave states and the depressive effect on the price of land that acquiring vast new territories was bound to have. He also feared the war would not unfold as smoothly as Polk had promised. "Providence has cast my lot," Calhoun said of his opposition to the war, and warned of the "disastrous consequences" that would befall an aggressive and prideful America should it attempt to conquer and acquire so much Mexican land.[35]

Some religious opponents believed in America's exceptional virtue and criticized the war for its betrayal of the nation's democratic, Christian promise. To wreak destruction upon Mexico was bad enough, lamented Henry Ward Beecher, "but to do it for the sake of *civilization and religion*," as the war's supporters claimed, was simply rank "*hypocrisy*." Here, the intellectual and spiritual journey of Theodore Parker is most illustrative. This Congregationalist who became a Unitarian minister and prophet of Transcendentalism had long been a pacifist. Through the 1840s, he became an increasingly vocal abolitionist; not coincidentally, he also became a strident opponent of expansion to the south and west. Even in America's moment of triumph, with the war and the west won, Parker condemned it as expensive, bloody, and unjust. The war had been an immoral enterprise from the beginning, he claimed; victory, no matter how rewarding, could not erase that simple fact. Parker's opposition was an important litmus test, for while his pacifist convictions had been firm his abolitionism had not always been so robust. But as slave power seemed to grow, his American exceptionalism diminished—or at least, he divorced it from causes that would enhance or entrench slavery. By 1848, his opposition to militaristic expansion was complete.[36]

By the time of the Mexican War, Parker's fellow Transcendentalist Henry David Thoreau had retained little of his own faith. But like the New England Transcendentalists who had made a spiritual journey from Congregationalism to Unitarianism, his views retained a profoundly religious framework and his morality remained grounded in a system of Christian ethics. Thoreau was fiercely opposed to both slavery and war in the abstract, and the reality of the Mexican War appalled him. With his "resistance to civil government"—what later became known as "civil disobedience"—Thoreau refused to pay taxes that would help fund the war. Though he went to jail for his act of defiance, Thoreau had established a precedent that would shape the peaceful resistance movements of later reformers and antiwar activists like Martin Luther King Jr. Stemming from a faith-based moral and political climate that divided issues into sharp distinctions of right and wrong, Thoreau's protest was an expression of antebellum Christian values even if they were completely devoid of Christian spirituality and religious belief.[37]

But ideas and values often follow facts on the ground, and after victory—and the seizure of California and all the land between it and Texas—it was very difficult to resist reveling in the triumph of American righteousness. A naval commander was asked why the United States had won. "It is because the spirit of our pilgrim fathers is with us," he replied. "It is because of the God of armies and Lord of hosts is with us." America's mission had been sanctified, its horizons perhaps now extended even further. As Amariah Kalloch of the West Rockport Baptist Church preached to the Maine state legislature in 1849, "Our territory now stretches from sea to sea, and from the river in the south, almost to the Arctic regions of the north, with the strong prospect that the whole of British America will yet swell the number of our States; and even Mexico may yet find her chords of sympathy so frequently and sweetly touched by our own, as to induce her to become a part and parcel of this nation." But it was Polk, in one of his last speeches as president, who put it best. Americans had triumphed "under the benignant providence of Almighty God," he announced in December 1848. "The gratitude of the nation to the Sovereign Arbiter of All Human Events should be commensurate with the boundless blessings we enjoy." America was now a model for everyone. "Peace, plenty, and contentment reign throughout our borders, and our beloved country presents a sublime moral spectacle to the world."[38]

If the Mexican War vindicated the advocates of manifest destiny and apologists for slavery, it also galvanized and then radicalized antislavery and anti-expansionist forces in the North. Ironically, it was the end of war and the coming of peace between Mexico and the United States that actually hastened the demise of the American peace movement and smoothed the path to the outbreak of war in 1861. Christian pacifists and abolitionists did not welcome war, but as they began to realize that peaceful, nonviolent resistance could only go so far in bringing about the end of slavery, they also began to compromise their pacifist principles. Some, pledging their allegiance to the redemptive "violent messiahs" Abraham Lincoln and John Brown, abandoned their pacifism in support of armed rebellion. Theodore Parker helped arm and supply Brown for his 1859 raid on Harpers Ferry, while Emerson declared that Brown "joins that perfect puritan faith" with the "ardor of the Revolution. He believes in two articles . . . The Golden Rule, and the Declaration of Independence." Even Garrison's peace advocacy buckled after Harpers Ferry; he called for "Success to every slave insurrection" and envisioned slaves "breaking the head of the tyrant with their chains." Others, truer to their pacifist witness, could only provide comfort and sympathy, but even they could sympathize with revolutionary violence. Lydia Child, a radical Unitarian abolitionist and women's rights advocate, wrote to Brown in prison. "Believing in peace principles, I cannot sympathize with the method you chose to advance the cause of freedom," she chided the abolitionist revolutionary. "But I honor your generous intentions—I admire your courage, moral and physical. I reverence you for the humanity which tempered your zeal. I sympathize with you in your cruel bereavement, your sufferings, and your wrongs. In brief, I love you and I bless you."[39]

Out of such love, smashed against the hate of slavery, would spring the Civil War. American religion's moral vision—from humanitarian intervention to manifest destiny—now turned the nation upon itself.

PART IV

America's Mission

The White House, Washington, D.C., October 1898. Only a few months had passed since William McKinley had steered the United States to a stunning victory over Spain, and now he was faced with the most important decision of his presidency. In April, Congress declared war upon Spain for its brutal repression of a rebellion in Cuba. Though most of the fighting took place in the Caribbean, in Cuba and Puerto Rico, American war planners ordered the U.S. Navy's Pacific squadron to sail for Manila Bay, in the Spanish colony of the Philippines, and destroy the fleet there. Both campaigns went extremely well for the United States, and the war—"a splendid little war," in John Hay's famous appraisal—was over by August. Dealing with Cuba was fairly straightforward: the island became ostensibly independent but in reality was dominated by the United States through indefinite military occupation. But in the Philippines, what had been a relatively minor sideshow quickly overwhelmed U.S. foreign policy and domestic politics, provoking an intense, emotional, and acrimonious debate that lasted for several years.

Having routed the Spanish and demolished their claims to empire, McKinley was now faced with the problem of what to do with the Philippines. It was a difficult decision, bound to be controversial whatever course he chose. Even arch-imperialists like Massachusetts senator Henry Cabot Lodge and naval strategist Alfred Thayer Mahan were not convinced that the United States should seize all the islands of the Philippine archipelago. But returning the islands to Spain was unthinkable, as was handing them over to another colonial power, and few believed the Filipinos capable of governing themselves. Most Americans understood that McKinley would claim at least the city and harbor of Manila, and possibly all of the island of Luzon on which Manila was located. Such a limited protectorate would be unusual but not unprecedented: the Hawaiian Islands, after all, had finally come under American rule earlier that year, and the government had purchased Alaska in 1867. But all the Philippines? With no future possibility of gaining statehood? This was a bold step, for it would mean that the United States had unequivocally become an overseas colonial power. It would mean that Americans had joined Europe's unseemly imperial scramble.

In the fall of 1898, representatives from the governments of Spain and the United States met in Paris to hammer out a peace treaty. McKinley had chosen his negotiators but had not yet given them clear instructions for the Philippines. While the rest was clear—Cuba would become nominally independent, Puerto Rico and Guam U.S. protectorates—a solution to the Filipino dilemma was not. "When next I realized that the Philippines had dropped into our laps I confess I did not know what to do with them," McKinley told a visiting delegation from the General Missionary Committee of the Methodist Episcopal Church—his own church—just over a year later. "I sought counsel from all sides—Democrats as well as Republicans—but got little help." But then, late one night in October, he had an epiphany. Worldly politicians may have offered no guidance, but a higher power did: "I walked the floor of the White House night after night until midnight; and I am not ashamed to tell you, gentlemen, that I went down on my knees and prayed Almighty God for light and guidance more than one night. And one night late it came to me this way—I don't know how it was, but it came." He would not return the Philippines to Spain, which would be "cowardly and dishonorable." He would not hand them over to a power less squeamish about empire, such as France or Germany, which would be "bad business and discreditable." He would not grant the Filipinos independence, for they were "unfit for self-government" and would "soon have anarchy and misrule over there worse than Spain's." After ruling out these alternatives, McKinley concluded that "there was nothing left for us to do but to take them all, and to educate the Filipinos, and uplift and civilize and Christianize them, and by God's grace do the very best we could by them, as our fellow-men for whom Christ also died." After that, finally at peace with his decision, McKinley "went to bed, and went to sleep, and slept soundly," and upon waking the next morning instructed the War Department's chief map designer "to put the Philippines on the map of the United States, and there they are, and there they will stay while I am President!"[1]

It is a familiar episode in American diplomatic history, and a much derided one. For Akira Iriye and most other historians, McKinley's moment of divine inspiration rings false. Given the stakes involved—the Philippines as independent nation or colony? America as republic or empire?—few take him at his word. Historians have instead portrayed his faith-based decision as one marked by "incongruity and frivolousness," "superficiality," and a "lack of sincerity." McKinley, Iriye and others assume, could not possibly have meant what he said. Surely other factors, based on power or trade or imperial glory, must have been at work. Religion was little more than high-minded cover for more hardheaded motives.[2]

Or so it would seem. To modern historians whose worldview is not framed by religious faith, McKinley's decision to seek guidance through prayer is incomprehensible. But to McKinley himself, it made perfect sense; indeed, it would have been so natural, so intuitive, that he probably did not even pause to think whether it was incongruous or frivolous. And whether one disapproves of his ultimate decision to annex the Philippines, it was extremely unlikely that McKinley acted superficially or insincerely. In fact, given his personal history, the scene he related to the Methodist missionaries was the most likely one possible. His decision to seek guidance and solace through prayer was perfectly consistent with his religious faith and political ideology. It would have been odd, and totally uncharacteristic of the man, had McKinley *not* prayed to God for guidance.

For William McKinley was one of the most pious presidents ever to hold office. He was an evangelical Methodist and a deeply felt religious faith framed his outlook from childhood until death. He was raised in Ohio by an intensely devout mother and grew up listening to Methodist circuit riders sermonize about fighting off sin through the Holy Spirit. He entered Republican politics, as any good Northern Methodist reformer would, first in Ohio and then nationally. And along the way, he never lost this pure evangelical faith or a belief that it formed the basis of progress, order, and moral conduct. "My belief embraces the Divinity of Christ and a recognition of Christianity as the mightiest factor in the world's civilization," he wrote in a private note to himself at the height of the furor over the Philippines. "We need God as individuals and we need Him as a people." Years earlier, he had arrived in Washington with a verse from the Book of Micah as his motto: "What doth the Lord require of thee, but to do justly, and to love mercy, and to walk humbly with thy God?" This was entirely in keeping with both his religion and his politics.[3]

From adolescence to the presidency, almost everything McKinley did was informed by the crusading, reformist ideology of Northern Methodism. Like many evangelicals, benevolent reform, and not the pro-business policies he would later adopt, brought him to the Republican Party. He had a progressive, Social Gospel mentality—albeit a fairly conservative one—long before his election as president in 1896. As a student, he volunteered at the local YMCA, eventually becoming president of its branch in Canton, Ohio. He then fought in the Civil War, including in the Battle of Antietam, regularly attended soldiers' prayer meetings and participated in camp revivals, and praised emancipation as a morally just cause worthy of a Union victory. His service in the war convinced him that war was hell, to be avoided if at all possible and waged only for truly noble causes, like the abolition of slavery and the preservation of the Union. After the war, he favored Reconstruction and was bitterly critical of the South's treatment of freed slaves. In 1876, as a young Ohio lawyer, he defended striking miners in court when few others dared to do so. Around the same time, McKinley and his wife became prominent activists in the Midwest temperance movement. As a congressman in the 1880s, he denounced Jim Crow as it was beginning to take root throughout the South; he also voted several times for inflationary silver measures, such as the Bland-Allison Free Coinage Act and the Sherman Silver Purchase Act. Later, as governor of Ohio, he refused to stay in a New Orleans hotel that did not allow African Americans to meet him there.[4]

As president—more specifically, as a pro-business Republican president during a time of unprecedented social upheaval—McKinley tempered his reformist instincts. The nation polarized sharply during the 1890s, and as strikes became increasingly violent, as farmers stormed across the Plains to protest their poverty and powerlessness, as white Southerners began to build a segregated society, and as big business grew in size and power, McKinley usually found himself on the side of the establishment. He championed "sound money" policies, especially economic policies, that suited industrialists and angered farmers. His egalitarian views on race lay dormant, and as president he let segregation go unchallenged in a way that would have shamed the moralistic young congressman. His party was shifting, and he felt he had no choice but to shift with it. Partly this stemmed from the temper of the times; partly it was a matter of political expediency. The progressive Methodist within him did not disappear entirely. In some matters, where it was politically feasible, he continued to champion benevolent Christian reform. He still, for example, promoted temperance and moral individual living. But by the 1890s, such openings were rare for a Republican politician.[5]

On foreign policy, however, it was still possible for McKinley to be a Christian reformer. He came to the war with Spain slowly, so slowly that it seemed as if public opinion, driven relentlessly by the bombastic New York papers, was dragging him along. But he was careful, as most successful politicians are, not reluctant. And while he did not seek war, once he decided the United States had no other choice, he pursued it on moral grounds. There were of course other reasons for war, but for McKinley only humanitarian considerations could sanctify the resort to war and empire. For as distasteful as it now seems, McKinley and other Americans of his era did not see a conflict between benevolence and empire; they did not see the term "progressive imperialist" as inherently contradictory. He believed he was doing a great service for the Philippines, selflessly progressive, that would also benefit the rest of the world. The annexation of the Philippines, and the grisly war it caused there, were thus not at odds with his work for the YMCA, his service in the Civil War, his support for missions, or his advocacy of temperance. It was a war for the betterment of others, whether they wanted it or not. McKinley and others like him may have been misguided, but they were hardly insincere. In keeping with his own ideals, and with the spirit of his age, McKinley extended America's mission abroad and set it on the path to globalism.[6]

Along the way, he was aided by pious policymakers, Protestant and Catholic missionaries, and a newly activist sensibility among American Jews. Together, they fostered an international consciousness for America, a sense of being one part of an interconnected, global whole. In the twentieth century, the world system would be managed by American hegemony, economic, political, and cultural as well as military. It was this regulatory world order, a kind of informal American imperialism, which they helped create. But first, Americans had to sort out the issue of slavery. And to do that, they needed to fight a bloody, apocalyptic war against one another. The consequences would be profound, not only for America but also for the rest of the world.

CHAPTER NINE

Abraham Lincoln and the First War of Humanitarian Intervention

T HE CIVIL WAR IS the great paradox in the history of American foreign relations, at once the nation's least important foreign war and
yet also one of its most consequential. Overall, the stakes involved were
entirely national. Sectional interests battled for control of America's destiny, not the world's. Americans fought over slavery and their clashing
views of republicanism, not the fate of nations. Foreign policy was largely
peripheral to a conflict that lacked a significant international dimension;
few other countries were directly affected, including America's continental neighbors, and none intervened in the fighting. Yet the outcome of
this peculiarly insular war deeply affected the nation's ideology, especially Americans' general worldview and sense of world mission, in ways
that would shape both U.S. foreign policy and international politics for
decades to come.

To be sure, the causes and course of the Civil War were shaped by
wider currents in world history. The United States of the 1850s and '60s
was not simply an isolated outpost of the world system unaffected by
global trends. And foreign policy was not unimportant during the Civil
War. Both the Union and the Confederacy invested considerable amounts
of time and energy in trying to persuade, or compel, other nations to
aid their cause—or at the very least, not to aid the other side. Mostly
this centered upon whether the European powers, especially Britain and
France, would extend official diplomatic recognition to the Confederacy,
which would give Southerners precious international legitimacy and
access to vast amounts of capital and military aid. Abraham Lincoln and
his secretary of state, William Seward, spent most of their time on foreign affairs beating back Southern efforts to secure European recognition and mediation of the Civil War, real possibilities in 1861 and 1862
that would have given the Confederacy a much better chance of winning
the war. The South had several advantages, including British and French
economic reliance on Southern cotton and a European desire to see the
United States weakened through division. But the possibility of recogni-

tion turned to implausibility after September 1862, when the North won a bloody victory at the Battle of Antietam, demonstrating to the Europeans two important facts: the South would probably not win, and the North would definitely not give up. Afterward, foreign policy crises continued to flare during the remainder of the war, but there was never any prospect of foreign military intervention and, compared to the scale of the war itself, diplomacy was confined mainly to the margins.[1]

Religion, however, did play a large role simply because Protestantism had infused nearly every aspect of antebellum life. Though Americans differed over religion, often vehemently and sometimes violently, most agreed that it was central to politics, culture, and society. The Second Great Awakening, the emergence of voluntary benevolent societies in the North, the growth of evangelicalism, and even the flourishing of Unitarianism signaled the breadth and depth of the Protestant influence in America. But the nineteenth century also witnessed the first real diversification of American faith, with the creation of Mormonism and the sharp rise in Catholicism due to Irish and German immigration. Statistics, imperfect measurements though they are, bring the religious presence in the United States into sharper relief. In 1860, there were perhaps as many as four times the number of churchgoers as there were voters in the presidential election; twice as many clergy as military personnel; and thirty-five churches for every bank. Most astonishingly, the income of the nation's churches nearly equaled that of the federal government.[2]

Then came war. In some ways, such as theological innovation by elites, religion remained relatively unchanged; but in others, such as the intensification of faith at a popular level, the war deeply affected the course of American religion. But overall, the centrality of religion continued—in fact, deepened—during the Civil War years. Stemming from the schismatic fury and ideological purity of the Presbyterian, Baptist, and Methodist divisions, American clergy on both sides of the Civil War sanctified their cause and demonized the other, in effect calling for their countrymen to wage total, holy war. Political rhetoric had always been replete with religious language and imagery, but under the compressive forces of war the religious component of political discourse increased and hardened. The Benevolent Empire of evangelical reformism shifted its focus to alleviate wartime suffering through a new agency, the Christian Commission. Expressions of faith among soldiers increased on both sides as well. The Civil War thus had a galvanizing effect on a people who were already overwhelmingly faithful.[3]

Nowhere was this more true than in the mind and morals of Abraham Lincoln. Before he became president, Lincoln had experienced life at both ends of the spectrum of faith: his parents (and later, stepmother) were hard-shell fundamentalist Baptists who harbored an extreme Calvinistic theology; yet in early adulthood, Lincoln himself exhibited a skepticism that at times bordered on atheism. His lack of orthodox faith in an era of widespread Christian orthodoxy and overwhelming evangelical hegemony hampered his early political ambitions, and he had to work hard to refute charges of deism and disbelief. There was something to this Christian critique; as the historian Richard Carwardine notes, Lincoln's religious views often resembled deism, Unitarianism, possibly even Universalism, but never evangelicalism. Most of all, he accepted the existence of a Supreme Being but doubted the divinity of Jesus Christ. However, though Lincoln would never come to embrace the Protestant orthodoxy of his day, he did become increasingly—and more conventionally—spiritual. The one constant throughout his life was a devout conviction in God's providence. During the Civil War, when he underwent not only the most profound moral traumas of the war itself but also the personal pain of losing his young son Willie to typhoid fever, Lincoln's faith grew markedly; his references to God became much more noticeable and frequent, his attendance at Washington's New York Avenue Presbyterian Church more regular. He met with church leaders often, much to the consternation of his advisers and generals, and increasingly pitched his speeches and messages in biblical language and Christian values. In so doing, he helped solidify—even re-create—the link in the American mind between Christianity and republicanism. And throughout, he demonstrated a depth of religious understanding that surpassed that of any of the formally trained clergy. Generations later, Reinhold Niebuhr said it was Lincoln, and not a minister, priest, or bishop, who was America's "greatest theologian of the war years."[4]

Based partly on Lincoln's rechristening of America's civil religion and partly on the moral absolutism of preachers in the victorious North, Civil War faith helped form the ideological core of U.S. foreign policy into the twentieth century. Comprised of two key ideas, this ideology of universal redemption was not always exclusively religious in character, but religion provided its most important source. Nor were either of these ideas necessarily new, though their testing in the Civil War changed them significantly. The first of these ideas was humanitarian intervention, the second America's role as God's chosen nation. When blended with the culture of progressive benevolence, missionaries, and the dictates of the national interest, the ideology of universal redemption enabled American leaders to follow a more interventionist, activist, and ultimately globalist foreign policy.

ABRAHAM LINCOLN did not go to war in 1861 intending to end slavery in the South. His principal war aim—initially his only war aim—was simply to keep the United States intact. This was a worthy enough goal in itself, he believed, even more so than abolition, and most Northerners agreed. After all, while the Constitution did not recognize the legitimacy of secession, it did protect slavery. Like most of his fellow Republicans, Lincoln's antislavery views were free soil rather than abolitionist—that is, he worried that slavery had made the South aristocratic and undemocratic, which in turn corrupted the rest of the nation as it expanded westward. Betraying the prevailing attitudes of his day and especially of his home state, Lincoln also considered blacks an inherently inferior race and believed that, as a result, Americans could never achieve racial equality and harmony in the event of complete emancipation. Unsurprisingly, his support for African and Latin American colonization continued into the Civil War. By the outbreak of war, then, Lincoln was concerned more by what slavery did to whites rather than the evil it inflicted upon blacks.[5]

But Lincoln also knew slavery was fundamentally immoral. Though he believed blacks were inherently inferior, he respected their humanity and recognized that involuntary bondage was the highest form of tyranny. And toward the end of his life, he came to embrace the notion of innate racial equality. Slavery was "a great & crying injustice [and] an enormous national crime," a young Lincoln told his close friend Joseph Gillespie. Later, as a politician striving for success in a highly polarized atmosphere, from a free state that was deeply hostile to African Americans, Lincoln's antislavery views could not outpace those of his constituents; had they done so, he would never have become president. "I am naturally anti-slavery," he wrote Albert Hodges, a Kentucky newspaper editor, in a letter intended for publication. "If slavery is not wrong, nothing is wrong. I can not remember when I did not so think, and feel. And yet I have never understood that the Presidency conferred upon me an unrestricted right to act officially upon this judgment and feeling. It was in the oath I took that I would, to the best of my ability, preserve, protect, and defend the Constitution of the United States."[6]

Crucially, however, Lincoln's antislavery views changed profoundly during the course of the war, from free soil to outright emancipation. By the summer of 1864, he was ready to confer equal importance upon "the integrity of the whole Union, and the abandonment of slavery."[7] If Lincoln did not begin the war as an abolitionist, he certainly ended it as one. Thus as much as he had sought to avoid it, Lincoln presided as commander-in-chief over the nation's first war of humanitarian intervention: by the North, against the South, to free the slaves. Emancipation, much less human rights, was not always a central objective for the North, but in time it became one.

Yet for some Northerners, destroying slavery had always been the primary war aim. As we have seen, abolitionists had been pressing for a total end to American slavery since at least the 1820s, and they did so out of concern for the equal rights of blacks and only secondarily for what it did to the rest of the nation. And as we have also seen, the vast majority of abolitionists were Protestant activists, ranging from emotional evangelicals to rationalist Unitarians. Without necessarily sympathizing with slavery but remaining loyal to the Democratic Party—which in general did not oppose slavery in the South or its spread to the territories—American Catholics and Jews were divided on the issue, and few were outright abolitionists. More than any other competing ideology, then, Protestant theology and ethics provided abolitionism's moral center.[8]

The abolitionist clergy in the vanguard of the antislavery movement may not have been popular, but in the end it was their vision that triumphed. Throughout the North, even in New England, hostility to the South's "slaveocracy" rarely made common cause with abolitionism. Still, abolitionist preachers pressed their case. And from the very beginning, far ahead of their fellow Republican Abraham Lincoln, it was they who framed the war as a case of humanitarian intervention. Reverend S. H. Tyng, one of the most prominent Episcopalians in antebellum America, branded the tyranny of slavery as the greatest threat to republican liberty. "There is a feeling," he wrote in 1861, "that despotism, bloodshed, fraud, oppression and unbridled lust, have, in defiance of heaven, rioted long enough, and that a righteous God will soon rise in his wrath and make short work" of slavery. "Babylon is toppling to her fall," proclaimed Tyng, and Union victory would bring the culmination of "human freedom." Similarly, Hollis Read, a renowned historian, rejoiced that "Satan's empire is to be broken up." But Americans could not take down Satan through preaching alone. Slavery could "only be broken to pieces by the sledge-hammer of WAR"; in turn, war was the only way to bring about the "reorganization of society" and the "triumph of Christianity." To such minds, it was obvious that a war for the Union also had to be a war for abolition. "Thank God, the word has at last been spoken," exclaimed an evangelical soldier in the Union Army after receiving news of the Emancipation Proclamation. "Light begins to break through. Let the sons of the earth rejoice. Sing paeans to Liberty. Let tyranny die." For Christian abolitionists, it was always a war for reformation, not restoration.[9]

This is not to say that the slaves themselves were passive in the process of emancipation. Even before Lincoln's conversion, they took advantage of the upheaval of war to free themselves in what has been likened to the largest and most successful slave rebellion in history. And naturally, their fellow African Americans in the North, led by free black preachers, passionately supported the cause as a holy war of freedom. The Second Great Awakening had given birth to African American Christianity, at least on a large scale, and stimulated the creation of the first black churches. Blacks had seen, often at first hand, how entrenched was Southern slavery and how racist were most Northerners. They feared that emancipation would not come gradually, and they were certain it would never happen voluntarily. "Who has sent this great deliverance?" thundered Daniel Payne, the presiding bishop of the African Methodist Episcopal Church, shortly after the outbreak of war in 1861. "The answer shall be, the Lord; the Lord God Almighty, the God of Abraham and Isaac and Jacob." Only God alone "couldst have moved the heart of this Nation to have done so great a deed for this weak, despised and needy people!" Later in the war the *Christian Recorder*, an AME Church publication, portrayed slavery as sin and war as punishment. "God has a controversy with this nation. He is chastising us severely, by civil war." In the Union armies, moreover, many black soldiers perceived the cause of emancipation as divinely inspired. In the eyes of African Americans, it was self-evident that God's cause was a war for abolition.[10]

For both whites and blacks, Christian-inspired humanitarian intervention infused cultural expressions of the antislavery cause, both before and during the war. Thus even before most Northerners were willing to admit that theirs was a war for emancipation, they had absorbed the ideology and imagery of emancipation. Consider two wildly popular examples, a prewar novel and a wartime hymn. As early as 1852, before John Brown's violent antislavery crusades and the South's equally violent proslavery defense had begun to divorce pacifism from abolitionism, came Harriet Beecher Stowe's incendiary novel *Uncle Tom's Cabin*. Daughter and sister of two of America's most famous preachers—Lyman Beecher and Henry Ward Beecher—Stowe combined a penchant for optimistic but apocalyptic millennialism with a passionate abolitionism to create the most effective antislavery propaganda ever written. Christ, she reminded her theologically informed readers, would return to earth to bring justice, and then peace, to the world—and with them the sin of slavery would be cleansed from the American soul, by righteous violence if need be.[11]

Stowe's novel had prepared the ground, but it was a song, Julia Ward Howe's "Battle Hymn of the Republic," that spread Christian abolitionism beyond its usual hard core of believers. Howe and her husband had been members of Theodore Parker's Unitarian congregation, and they had absorbed their minister's morally absolutist abolitionism. Howe was a Unitarian, and therefore religious but not especially spiritual, much less millennial. Yet her stirring hymn, based as it was on the Book of Revelation, emphasized the apocalyptic significance of the Civil War and thus reflected the prevailing millennialism of the mid-nineteenth century. By setting it to the tune of "John Brown's Body," another popular wartime song that celebrated the martyred abolitionist and his cause, Howe ensured her hymn would be an anthem for emancipation. She placed the cause of abolitionism at the war's very heart, particularly in the hymn's final stanzas:

> *He has sounded forth the trumpet that shall never call retreat;*
> *He is sifting out the hearts of men before his judgment-seat;*
> *Oh, be swift, my soul, to answer him! be jubilant, my feet!*
> *Our God is marching on.*
>
> *In the beauty of the lilies Christ was born across the sea,*
> *With a glory in his bosom that transfigures you and me:*
> *As he died to make men holy, let us die to make men free,*
> *While God is marching on.*

Written in 1862, a few months before Lincoln announced the Emancipation Proclamation, "The Battle Hymn of the Republic" became by far the Union's most popular wartime song. And with each rendition, Northerners announced their moral intentions.[12]

But emancipation was still unpopular in 1862; most Northerners thought it either unnecessary or unwarranted, and often both. Since the 1840s, the majority of Northern clergy had conceded that slavery was a sin, but most also thought it was too deep-rooted to be ended peacefully. In any event, if slavery was a sin, war was an even greater sin. But after the bloody battles of 1862 and 1863, especially at Antietam and Gettysburg, it became clear that the struggle for the Union had already let slip the dogs of war, and that adding emancipation as a war aim would allow the North to reform, even recast, the United States in a more charitable, Christian image. The redemptive blood of war would even, many came to believe, wash away the sin of slavery. Slowly but definitively, galvanized by war, the Northern clergy came round to supporting emancipation. And as they did, they embraced the idea of the Civil War as a war of liberation: for slaves from their masters, and for the nation from slave power. Not coincidentally, the adoption of emancipation occurred alongside the transformation of the conflict from limited war to total war, even holy war. "Was the Church established without blood and slaughter?" asked the Reverend William Carden in 1863. The answer, of course, was no, as shown by the bloody struggles of the very first Christians. "It was something to be a Christian then," Carden exclaimed breathlessly. "It called for honesty, and manliness, and self-sacrifice—nay, death." A war to free the slaves provided a similar calling to a new generation of Christians.[13]

When Lincoln adopted emancipation as a primary war aim in 1862, he also adopted its Christian core. For him no less than others, the war to preserve the Union became a war of liberation and humanitarian intervention. Abolition, however, contradicted his pledge, uttered in the First Inaugural Address, not to interfere with slavery where it already legally existed. Moreover, as a wartime president fighting not only to bring the South back into line but also to keep Unionist but wavering border states in the fold, he had to act cautiously. But he knew he had to act: by the summer of 1862, after so much blood spilled in a string of military defeats, most Northerners had decided it would be impossible to reintegrate the South *and* slavery into the Union. Lincoln's first step was the Emancipation Proclamation, drafted in June and July of 1862; yet he could not announce it until the North claimed a significant battlefield victory. After yet more failure in August, the Battle of Antietam in September, the single bloodiest day of the war, offered a difficult, sanguinary victory—but victory nonetheless, which was certainly enough for Lincoln. As Secretary of the Navy Gideon Welles recorded in his diary after Antietam, Lincoln had "made a vow, a covenant, that if God gave us the victory in the approaching battle, he would consider it an indication of Divine will, and that it was his duty to move forward in the cause of emancipation. . . . God had decided this question in favor of the slaves."[14]

Five days after Antietam, Lincoln issued the Emancipation Proclamation and announced it would take effect on January 1, 1863. Later, he confided to his friend Joshua Speed that it was his greatest achievement, "something," Speed recalled, "that would resound to the interest of his fellow man." And though the Proclamation itself was a cautious, officious, almost timid document, Lincoln spent the duration of the war affirming and reaffirming the principle of emancipation, both as a means to national reunion and as a worthy moral goal in itself. In this, he was not only reframing the terms of the war, but also the terms of American patriotism, even the nation. According to Lincoln, America was a sacred endeavor, an experiment in republican liberty, and a perfection of human governance that would one day save the world. But Americans would be worthy of carrying such a weighty torch only if they transcended the merely political. This at least was the idea behind Lincoln's December 1862 Annual Message to Congress, which envisioned emancipation as America's salvation and, in turn, America as the world's. "In *giving* freedom to the *slave*, we *assure* freedom to the *free*—honorable alike in what we give and what we preserve." But only the survival of America, whole and intact, could fulfill this potential. "We shall nobly save, or meanly lose, the last best hope of earth," Lincoln said of the United States in his closing passage. "Other means may succeed; this could not fail. The way is plain, peaceful, generous, just—a way which, if followed, the world will forever applaud, and God must forever bless." Among Northerners, Lincoln's recasting of the Civil War from a struggle for the Union to a war of national liberation found strongest support among the clergy. With emancipation, declared a Pittsburgh Presbyterian, the purposes of God were now "inevitably interwoven with that of the Government."[15]

Lincoln reinforced the centrality of emancipation time and again between 1862 and the end of the war. In the process, the war's cause—indeed, its very nature—shifted in his mind from secession to slavery. As he told a group celebrating victory at Gettysburg, "we have a gigantic Rebellion, at the bottom of which is an effort to overthrow the principle that all men are created equal." In 1864, when Congress turned to drafting what would become the Thirteenth Amendment to abolish slavery once and for all, Lincoln supported it enthusiastically and pressured wavering members of Congress to do the same. To Lincoln, the war was simply God's plan to bring about justice on earth. "We hoped for a happy termination of this terrible war long before this; but God knows best and has ruled otherwise," he told the Quaker activist Eliza Gurney a year later. "He intends some great good to follow this mighty convulsion, which no mortal could make, and no mortal could stay." These were not idle words, and it is clear that this period also marked the time of Lincoln's ever-increasing piety. His moral conversion on slavery was mirrored by a spiritual conversion on faith. Religion now formed the heart of both his moral vision and his wartime rhetoric.[16]

The apotheosis of Lincoln's public faith came in one of his most famous speeches, the Second Inaugural Address of March 1865. The explicit religiosity of the Second Inaugural marked something of a departure for Lincoln, whose speeches were embedded in religious phrasing but did not normally appropriate religious doctrine for their content. Yet this departure was also a culmination, mainly of Lincoln's own struggle to sort out the true meaning of the war. Frederick Douglass, among the audience who heard the speech, said that it was "a sacred effort" that "sounded more like a sermon than a state paper." Philip Schaff, one of the nation's leading theologians, pronounced that no "royal, princely, or republican state document of recent times can be compared to this inaugural address for genuine Christian wisdom and gentleness." Observes the historian Mark Noll, "none of America's respected religious leaders . . . mustered the theological power so economically expressed in Lincoln's Second Inaugural." Or, as another historian put it, the Second Inaugural was Lincoln's Sermon on the Mount.[17]

Mentioning God several times and quoting directly from scripture, the Second Inaugural called for Americans to end the war through an embrace of both justice and reconciliation. "All knew" that slavery, not secession, "was somehow the cause of the war." While nobody could pretend to know the will of God—"The Almighty has His own purposes"—it was clear to Lincoln that whatever Americans' past differences, God had used the Civil War as punishment for the sin of slavery and a means to bring it to an end:

> If we shall suppose that American slavery is one of those offenses which, in the providence of God, must needs come, but which, having continued through His appointed time, He now wills to remove, and that He gives to both North and South this terrible war as the woe due to those by whom the offense came, shall we discern therein any departure from those divine attributes which the believers in a living God always ascribe to Him?

In the end, only emancipation, even more than Union, would cleanse the nation's soul. "Fondly do we hope, fervently do we pray, that this mighty scourge of war may speedily pass away," Lincoln declared in one of the speech's more memorable passages. "Yet, if God wills that it continue until all the wealth piled by the bondsman's two hundred and fifty years of unrequited toil shall be sunk, and until every drop of blood drawn with the lash shall be paid by another drawn with the sword, as was said three thousand years ago, so still it must be said 'the judgments of the Lord are true and righteous altogether.'" Once a war for national unity, Lincoln had rechristened the Civil War as a struggle for liberation. Through presidential rhetoric and military victory, the moral radicalism of the abolitionists had been vindicated.[18]

LINCOLN'S ELEVATION OF the United States as "the last best hope of earth" and his effort, in the Second Inaugural, to heal sectional scars with the salve of moral righteousness signaled the emergence of the second idea behind the new ideology of universal redemption. To the victors, the Civil War's ultimate meaning transcended the struggle between union and secession. Restoring the Union was only an initial step, for a divided America could never be as effective as the United States. If it was the North's duty to bring freedom to the South, it was also America's duty to protect and promote freedom wherever it could. Victory over the South convinced Northerners that America's purpose was not only heaven-sent, but also unlimited. God had spared the United States for a reason: to save the world.

This revision and significant expansion of manifest destiny was held widely in the North. Whereas John L. O'Sullivan's manifest destiny envisioned territorial expansion, the new version of manifest destiny foretold the global expansion of American values because the United States, strengthened through its test of blood and will in the Civil War, was now destined to spread republican liberty and Christian virtue to all humanity.

Americans were now beholden to a manifest destiny of limitless expanse. There was, of course, already a prevailing belief that the United States was God's chosen nation and the world's leader in freedom. "I feel sure that the hour has not come for this great nation to fall," William Seward, soon to be Lincoln's secretary of state, declared on the Senate floor in January 1861. "This Union has not yet accomplished what good for mankind was manifestly designed by Him who appoints the seasons." Even as specific doctrines of Calvinism, especially predestination, came in for new scrutiny and criticism, belief in providence and in a special national mission, which were rooted in Calvinism, had never been stronger. Thus the fervent millennialism and providentialism of the Civil War reflected rather than created this aspect of American civil religion. Nonetheless, the sacrifices of war tremendously deepened Americans' sense of mission, renewing it for generations to come.[19]

Once again, the Northern Protestant clergy made a significant contribution to the fusion of American patriotism and religious faith. The failure of politicians, who had lost control of the national agenda during the crises of the 1850s, created a predominant influence for Northern preachers in the political debates of the 1860s. Some were abolitionist, others were free soil, but all stressed the urgency of preserving the Union. In so doing, they sanctified, in the most explicitly religious terms, both the Northern cause and the United States itself. American civil religion had already pervaded public life, and the Northern clergy had praised America's mission before the war. But by blending patriotism and faith in the most shrill terms, the Civil War transformed it into an overwhelming, almost suffocating presence.[20]

To the Northern clergy, as well as to many lay Northerners, secession was tantamount to sin—"an unholy rebellion," in the words of one Pennsylvania soldier—because it aimed to destroy God's chosen instrument for human perfection, the United States. In this interpretation, America was "the last best hope" not only of Americans, but of people everywhere. Reverend Horace Bushnell, whose preaching was famed throughout the United States, saw the sanctification of America's mission as one of the main outcomes of the war. "In these rivers of blood we have now bathed our institutions, and they are henceforth to be hallowed in our sight," he told the Yale graduating class in July 1865. "Government is now become Providential,—no more a mere creature of our human will, but a grandly moral affair." Contrasting the United States to the monarchies of Europe, Bushnell promised that Americans "have not fought this dreadful war to a close, just to put our government upon a par with these oppressive dynasties!" God intended something altogether more glorious for America. Similarly, Daniel Payne of the AME Church spoke for many newly freed slaves as well as whites when he compared the United States to "the right arm of God—of God, who lifts up and casts down nations according as they obey, or disregard the principles of truth, justice, liberty." If the Civil War had been a war of humanitarian intervention, in other words, it was to be the first of many. This was now America's task.[21]

American patriotism, and with it the American sense of mission, had always possessed a defiantly Protestant soul, but the Civil War led to a more inclusive civil religion. When American Catholics and Jews fought in the war—which they did, on both sides, in large numbers—they shared in a collective sacrifice for the greater good of the nation. The Union and Confederate governments also used Catholic emissaries to plead their cases in European capitals and the Vatican. War was thus a powerful way of Americanizing non-Protestants, especially immigrant groups, like Irish Catholics, who had not lived in the United States for very long. The process was not an easy one for Catholics, especially in the North, where the war effort was dominated by Protestant Yankees. Just as awkward for the overwhelmingly Democratic Irish Catholics were the Republicans' efforts to use the war to further party interests, especially through support for big business, internal improvement, and New England shipping. Moreover, the transformation of war aims from union to emancipation troubled laboring Irish Catholics: not only did they share the traditional Democratic tolerance of slavery, they feared competition for unskilled labor from freed slaves. Still, despite the 1863 draft riots, sparked by Irish Catholic outrage at emancipation, conscription, and Protestant prejudice, and despite widespread anti-Catholicism, American Catholics successfully used the Civil War as a fulcrum for Americanization and as a starting point for full participation in the rites of American civil religion. Indeed, by the 1880s the triumphal memory of the Civil War, rather than the more complicated reality, served as a powerful Americanizing force among American Catholics, including recent Catholic immigrants.[22]

The same was true for Jews, albeit on a smaller scale because mass Jewish immigration was still decades away. For them, the turning point came when Lincoln rescinded General Ulysses Grant's notorious General Order No. 11, which blamed Jews, "as a class," for profiting from the smuggling of Southern cotton. Grant punished Jews en masse by expelling them from areas under Union Army control, such as northern Mississippi and most of Tennessee. Confederates used Grant's rank anti-Semitism as a way to attack the hypocrisy of Northerners who professed to fight a war for black liberty while violating the most basic of religious freedoms. As soon as he learned of it, Lincoln revoked Grant's order for collective punishment. He then reassured Cesar Kaskel, a Jew forcibly removed from Paducah, Kentucky, that "to condemn a class is, to say the least, to wrong the good with the bad. I do not like to hear a class or nationality condemned on account of a few sinners." Anti-Semitism did not disappear, and American Jews, no less than American Catholics, continued to endure discrimination. But a threshold had been crossed. Through Civil War, civil religion was becoming more ecumenical.[23]

Traditional notions of providence—of God protecting the United States and anointing it with a glorious destiny—rested heavily upon Americans' sense of mission. As during previous conflicts, providential thinking intensified in wartime. Already a providential people, Americans on both sides of the Mason-Dixon Line became more trusting in God's mysterious ways, more willing to accept their fate in his heavenly plans. This was no less true of America's leaders, whose invocations of providence in victory and appeals to providence in defeat increased sharply during the war. General Stonewall Jackson, hero of the South, became something of a cult figure in both the South and North for his total belief in God's providence. Yet at the time, the Civil War caused a crisis in providential thinking. For if America was God's chosen nation, why was he punishing his chosen people through the uniquely terrible scourge of civil war? Ministers and leaders had several answers, ranging from the sin of slavery to the sin of secession to the sin of interfering in states' rights—but nobody could know for sure, especially during the Union's darkest days of 1861–62 and the Confederacy's during 1864–65.[24]

As usual, it was Lincoln who provided the answer. Biographers have noted that Lincoln was unusually fatalistic, probably a vestige of his ultra-Calvinist Baptist parents and a product of his particularly brooding, depression-prone personality. Of all the religious tenets he believed in, his faith in providence was the firmest and most enduring. Unlike the nation's preachers, Lincoln did not pretend to know the will of God. As he reminded Americans in the Second Inaugural, the "Almighty has His own purposes." And as he argued several times during the war, both sides claimed that God was on their side, yet God could not possibly be acting on behalf of both sides in such a terrible conflict. Yet Lincoln firmly believed that God dictated the course of the war, even if mortals could not grasp his ultimate purpose. Most important, Lincoln believed that *he* was an instrument of providence, God's agent on earth at a particularly significant moment in history. Lincoln's providentialism—his fatalism—did not amount to passivity. Lincoln might not know the ultimate end, but he was certain he was acting as the Lord's means, and he was not about to fail in his duty. In this fashion, Lincoln explained his actions, such as emancipation, not merely as wartime necessity but divine intention.[25]

In this light, the Civil War stands not only as a struggle for the nation but as a redemptive platform for America to save the world. In November 1863, Lincoln reinforced this idea of a larger purpose in the Gettysburg Address, where he dedicated the battlefield not to the dead—only God could do that—but to the living, whose task remained incomplete. Unlike the Second Inaugural, the Gettysburg Address was not overtly religious. But its evocation of supreme sacrifice touched upon increasingly popular religious notions of living soldiers as "angels," dead soldiers as "martyrs," and the Union cause as "holy." Lincoln's theme of birth and rebirth, moreover, was grounded in both the ideal of immaculate conception and the Christian conversion narrative, as if the United States itself had been born again. The "baptism of blood" at Gettysburg, the theologian Philip Schaff said at the time, enabled America "to hope for a glorious regeneration." Lincoln's speech was conceptually and emotionally similar to the Protestant clergy's incessant appeals to a civil religion of the highest patriotism, such as Henry Ward Beecher's characteristic claim that the "battle on the Potomac for our Constitution, as a document of liberty, is the world's battle. We are fighting, not merely for our liberty, but for those ideals that are the seeds and strength of liberty throughout the earth." And of course it was consistent with Lincoln's own perception of the war as a divine test and his own role as an instrument of God.[26]

The United States was a nation "conceived in Liberty, and dedicated to the proposition that all men are created equal," Lincoln declared at Gettysburg. Yet Americans were "engaged in a great civil war, testing whether that nation, or any nation so conceived, and so dedicated, can long endure." Lincoln then imbued the Civil War with a meaning that extended far beyond American shores. "The world will little note, nor long remember what we say here," he said of the soldiers who fought at Gettysburg, "but it can never forget what they did here." Instead, it remained for the living "to be here dedicated to the great task remaining before us . . . that this nation, under God, shall have a new birth of freedom—and that government of the people, by the people, for the people, shall not perish from the earth." As Lincoln made clear, this "new birth of freedom" belonged not only to America, but to the rest of the planet. Just as the Union and emancipation had been America's salvation, a reformist America would be the world's.[27]

CHAPTER TEN

Missionaries and the Imperialism
of Human Rights

HUMANITARIAN INTERVENTION and a renewed sense of American mission: it was around these ideas, incubated by the Civil War, that an ideology for American globalism formed. Beginning in the 1890s and continuing fitfully through the next century, Americans embraced a new foreign policy: savior of the world. Yet the application of this new—or rather, rechristened—ideology did not immediately follow the Civil War for an obvious reason: Reconstruction. Before Americans could devote themselves to imperialism and internationalism, they first needed to sort out their own society. The end of Reconstruction in 1877—which ended white sectional conflict, tragically at the expense of black liberty—freed the United States to pursue burgeoning interests beyond its own shores.

Just as important in America's rise to world power was its economic transformation. Industrialization had begun in earnest in the antebellum years, principally with the construction of a vast infrastructure that enabled the market and communications revolutions to proceed apace. First paved roads and canals, then railroads and the telegraph, drew the nation ever-closer together and eased the flow of interstate commerce. In effect, the prewar improvements in infrastructure not only increased American prosperity but also widened access to overseas markets. The Civil War both hindered and advanced industrialization. Unprecedented suffering and destruction clearly acted as hindrances to economic growth. Yet mobilizing for war enabled the Lincoln administration to centralize executive power and pass legislation that Southerners would normally have opposed, such as higher tariffs to protect U.S. industry and the Homestead Act to speed the westward migration of free labor. By the 1880s, freed from the burdens and divisions of war and Reconstruction, economic growth in the United States galloped along at a previously unimaginable pace. Three phenomena, all interlinked and mutually reinforcing, supplied fuel for this continual growth: industrialization, immigration, and urbanization. Breakneck industrial growth required vast pools of unskilled labor, supplied by a surge in immigration and concentrated in the rapidly

175

expanding cities, where most factories were located. Rampant economic growth encouraged equally rampant levels of immigration and urbanization. In response to the complexity of growth, and as a resumption of the wartime centralization of governmental power, the federal bureaucracy grew alongside the economy and population. All this provided foreign policymakers with the requisite tools to manage a world role.[1]

By the late nineteenth century, then, Americans were poised to assume great power status. With its plentiful supplies of natural resources, weak continental neighbors, mobile and industrious population, constant influx of immigrants, and enormous internal market and economies of scale, the United States of the late nineteenth century was uniquely positioned to become a world power. As the historian Paul Kennedy notes, by the outbreak of the Spanish-American War in 1898 the United States "seemed to have *all* the economic advantages which *some* of the other powers possessed *in part*, but *none* of their disadvantages."[2]

But a large economy does not automatically translate into an activist foreign policy, a truism proved by nineteenth-century America itself. Until the 1890s, despite the purchase of Alaska from Russia in 1867 and sporadic disagreements over minor matters with South American and European countries, the United States focused on healing internal wounds, propelling the domestic economy, and absorbing millions of new immigrants. Yet as America rose to economic power, its pretensions to world power grew as well. Increased overseas trade brought with it increased contact with foreign peoples and their governments, for better and worse. Americans imported products from all over the world, and in the process were introduced to exotic lands and people the world over. Even more fervently, Americans believed foreigners should be introduced to the United States, and especially to the blessings of superior American technology, economics, and culture. The power of ideas here was crucial. Americans no less than Europeans had a vision of how the world should properly function, and their sectional tranquility and economic prosperity afforded them a new opportunity to extend the horizons, and ambitions, of U.S. foreign policy. For all these reasons, often reinforcing each other in a complex of motivations, once fiercely nationalistic Americans were becoming internationalists, citizens of the world, by shedding the limitations of a parochial worldview and replacing them with the ambitions of a truly global consciousness. As they did, the faith-based ideology from the Civil War provided foreign policymakers with a ready platform for action.[3]

MISSIONARIES WERE IN the vanguard of America's internationalist turn for they were, by their very nature, citizens of the world. The Civil War had enforced a pause in the American missionary enterprise, but the end of Reconstruction meant that American missions could resume their work. Between Reconstruction and World War I, missionary growth was explosive: there were sixteen missionary societies in America in 1860, more than ninety by 1900; in 1869, there were an equal number of European and American overseas missionaries but twice as many Americans by 1900. Except for a brief lean period following the depression of 1893, missionaries were also fairly prosperous: by 1900, a fifth of all direct U.S. investment in China was missionary property. Most important, no other group of Americans was as thoroughly internationalist. And over the next four decades, no other group would combine the visions of humanitarianism and American mission as fully.[4]

At the same time, American religion was experiencing another of its periodic awakenings, including Dwight L. Moody's evangelistic revivals but also the emergence of new American faiths such as Pentecostalism. Missionaries benefited from this general revival of piety, but they were also influenced by political and social developments that were sharply at odds with traditionalist religion. Shaken by Darwinism and the penetrating critiques of German biblical criticism, and nurtured by the excellence of their institutions of higher learning, America's liberal Protestants were determined to preserve their faith through incorporating, rather than rejecting, the new scientific empiricism. This crisis and renewal of faith led to a decreasing faith in scripture alone and an increasing dependence on ethical interpretations of the Bible and Christian doctrine. American Protestantism was in the midst of a modernist turn, with missionaries at the helm. Reflecting the theological evolution of their leaders, the major mission boards embraced the new modernism and its emphasis on doing good works rather than only on saving souls. Ostensibly their chief objective remained the conversion of the heathen in places like China, the Middle East, and Africa. But in reality, they ended up spending more time building hospitals and schools, and working as doctors, nurses, and teachers. Protestant mission theorists cleverly justified the shift from evangelism to social work—and thus the rejection of everything Rufus Anderson had stood for—as actually the best way to spread the gospel. If missionaries were still as enthusiastic as ever about "evangelizing the world in this generation," as they had famously promised, their means of doing so were distinctly earthbound.[5]

American Protestant missions were thus an international extension of the Social Gospel, itself a faith-based wing of the Progressive movement. Extensive industrialization, immigration, and urbanization may have brought unprecedented wealth to America—this was, after all, the Gilded Age—but they also brought unprecedented poverty, and with it misery. Appalling living conditions in overcrowded immigrant slums and dangerous working conditions in factories led to terrible living conditions in many cities, which in turn often led to labor strife and social unrest. In response, the Progressives, heirs to the antebellum reformist tradition of the Benevolent Empire, worked to improve living and working conditions. Building on the insights of Horace Bushnell, Social Gospelers based their reform efforts on the conviction that people were not inherently evil or depraved but were conditioned by their surrounding environment. Improve the environment, and you improve the person, which in turn would open the way to Christ. Josiah Strong, among others, was instrumental in shaping a robust worldview of salvation and redemption by fusing together the Social Gospel, muscular Christianity, and missionary work. Though they were not part of the Protestant Social Gospel, Catholic missionaries undertook their work in a similar spirit.[6]

By no means did religion have a monopoly on such thinking, which was very much consistent with pragmatist Progressives, such as John Dewey and William James. Yet Christian faith suffused the reformism of the Progressive era. Many Progressives, such as the settlement house leader Jane Addams, were motivated in large part by Christian ethics, even though their aim was not predominantly religious. Others may have been robustly skeptical and thoroughly modern but nonetheless adopted the religious reformers' crusading style and pious moralism. And some reformers adopted explicitly religious themes and rhetoric to shape and justify their Progressivism; nowhere was this truer than in the foreign policies of two Progressive presidents, Theodore Roosevelt and Woodrow Wilson. More explicitly, the loose collection of religious reformers known as the Social Gospel saw its mission to improve America through faith. While missions were not a direct product of the Social Gospel, they shared the same liberal theology, the same sense of social crisis, the same belief in progress, and the same faith in the power of a progressive Christ. As Walter Russell Mead rightly observes, missionaries were the first Wilsonians. Or in the words of one missionary, they were "enlisting the whole Church in the supreme work of saving the world."[7]

Yet it was precisely this modernist, reformist, postmillennialist impulse within American missions that troubled the other heirs to the American religious tradition: conservative, premillennialist Protestants who would a few decades later claim the label "fundamentalist" for their defense of traditional religious principles. For a time, certainly into the first decade of the twentieth century, a shared enthusiasm for missions, and even for Social Gospel reform, overcame theological differences between liberals and conservatives, and even these theological differences were initially not so great. But the seeds of future conflict had been planted. Modernists spoke of various theories, while conservatives thought only of the Bible: if it was not in "the book," it simply was not Christian. Shocked by ideas such as future probation, biblical literalists and conservatives saw the Social Gospel ethos of most American missions as pure heresy. If missionaries did not prioritize evangelism, if they instead built schools and health clinics, what right did they have to be called missionaries? By what right could they even claim to be Christian? As L. W. Munhall, a fundamentalist preacher from Germantown, Pennsylvania, argued in 1901, it was essential to distinguish between heaven and God's earthly kingdom. "It is very clear to my mind," declared Munhall, "that the Gospel of the kingdom is no Gospel at all if it does not include the gospel of the grace of God." Conservatives and premillennialists were just as enthusiastic about missions, so long as they focused on actual conversions rather than good works. As one disciple of Arthur Pierson, a Presbyterian minister and prominent conservative, declared upon his arrival in Japan, "Gentlemen, I have not time to take the superintendence of your schools. I have given myself to the preaching of the gospel." If the majority of American missionaries were proto-Wilsonians, the early architects of a liberal world order of collective security and international organizations, conservative missionaries were the recalcitrant unilateralists who stood for basic, traditional values and the absolute preservation of their own—and their nation's—autonomy. Conservatives did not want to make the world safe for anything other than Christ.[8]

Despite the era's prevailing ethos of muscular Christianity, women were an important part of the progressive missionary moment, just as they were vital contributors to the Progressive movement overall. Following the Civil War, Protestantism became increasingly male-dominated, especially at the leadership level. Mission boards were no exception, and missionaries embraced the spirit of muscular Christianity as an essential ingredient for success in an arduous profession. Interestingly, however, women came to predominate in overseas missions. Forced to set up their own all-female mission boards, Protestant women became the most successful missionaries of all, effectively colonizing the missionary movement itself. By 1915, more than forty women's missionary societies counted over three million members. Of course, only a very small percentage were actual missionaries who actually went overseas, but those who did had an enormous and enthusiastic audience when they returned home to introduce the world to America. Changes in mission practice that allowed lay missionaries to practice overseas gave women—very few of whom had been ordained—a large, direct role in American missions. By the early twentieth century, 70 percent of all American missionaries were laypersons, of whom a solid majority were female. Yet women still had to defer to a masculine ideal, which forced them to rely on their supposed strengths of domesticity and motherhood. This in turn made them the strongest, and most effective, advocates for missions as vehicles for progressive reform. Indeed, it was their "gospel of gentility" that provided American missions with the impetus for much if not most of their reformist intentions.[9]

FOR ALL THEIR Social Gospel good intentions, missionaries were also participants in America's imperialist turn. Progressivism, missions, and imperialism all originated from a similar source in the American imagination: a belief in progress. Even more, missionaries shared with their fellow Americans an equally fervent belief that they alone knew *the* path to progress. But in the missionary mind, their way was the only way because it was both American and Christian. All other faiths were drags to progress. "The world needs the social message and redemption of Christianity," argued Robert Speer of the Student Volunteer Movement, an organization founded in 1886 to recruit missionaries, simply because no other political or spiritual force was capable of improving people's lives. Dwight Moody's revivals at home and missions abroad, in which Speer played a large role, were thus part of the same glorious movement to uplift the world. But other nations were hindrances to progress, as well; only the United States could spread Christian change. According to the ostensibly ecumenical organizers of the World's Parliament of Religions, held at the 1893 Chicago World's Fair, "building up the Kingdom of Christ in America is to engage with fresh ardor in efforts to Christianize India and Africa, Turkey and China." What was good for America was also good for the world.[10]

As internationalists, missionaries were significantly ahead of their fellow Americans' thinking on foreign affairs. They were expansionists and perceived the world as fundamentally interconnected much earlier than most others did. Indeed, as Americans and as Christians, they could be no other. They abhorred the parochial limitations of isolationism and unilateralism. "Do not tell us that we must avoid entangling alliances," shrieked a missionary newspaper during the Chinese Boxer Rebellion. Others, such as the Union Missionary Training Institute of Brooklyn, celebrated "the Cross that turns not back." The whole world was the Christian's mission field, Reverend R. L. Bachman reminded his congregation at the First Presbyterian Church of Utica, New York, as established by Christ's command to "Go ye into all the world, and preach the gospel to every creature" (Mark 16:15). Christ's command "did not pertain to one people, or to some favored section of the globe," Bachman exhorted. "In its reach and scope it took in the whole earth."[11]

Americans had of course always been expansionist, both ideologically and territorially, since the earliest colonial days. The difference was that by the 1890s Americans had run out of land to expand into. At a time when the frontier had officially closed (according to the 1890 census), Americans began casting their gaze from the western horizon to the vast oceans that surrounded them. In 1893, the historian Frederick Jackson Turner first published his "frontier thesis," which argued that expansionism had become an immutable part of American identity, and that the closing of the frontier would simply push these basic, undeniable impulses further westward still: across the Pacific. But missionaries had long viewed the oceans not as moats that sealed the United States off from other nations but as highways that connected the entire world.[12]

Merchants and traders also shared this expansive worldview, yet they did not contribute to the formation of an internationalist consciousness. Their worldview, albeit global in scope, was driven by material interests, not universal values. They were less concerned with spreading human rights than with making a profit. Missionaries, by contrast, sought the spread of values above all else, be they religious, political, social, or economic. They were interest-driven, too, but they were also ideals-driven in a systematic and comprehensive way. Their interconnected world could only function if based on a secure foundation of enlightened privileges and duties. Religious faith was thus an essential ingredient in the formation of American internationalism. Indeed, the only other Americans with such a values-based internationalist outlook—the only other Americans to recognize the importance of ideas in an increasingly globalized world—were also religious. These were the millions of Catholic and Jewish immigrants from Europe who, even as they simultaneously pursued acceptance into the American mainstream, saw themselves as part of a larger, international community. Like the advocates of the Protestant interest in the colonial Atlantic world, they positioned the United States within a densely connected web of international rights and responsibilities.[13]

For Protestant missionaries, moreover, a globalist, expansionist mindset was deeply ingrained because of the simple fact of their faith. Even more than Americanism, Christianity is an inherently expansive faith, territorially, demographically, and ideologically. Concluded one ABCFM missionary to Hawaii, "Christianity won its throne by proving its universality." And, of course, by not making concessions to heathens. The Christian faith, said William Newton Clarke, "is not one of compromise, but of conflict and of conquest." It seeks "to displace the other religions," for the good of everyone. Unlike other world religions, Christianity's center of gravity shifted over time: from the Middle East at its formation, to the Near East after the conversion of Constantine, to Europe after the fall of Rome, and then to the Americas. Just like the United States, Christianity expanded always westward, bringing with it enlightenment, progress, and civilization. Growth and conversion are the avowed aims for all professing Christians; though they aim to do so peacefully, expansionism lies at the heart of the Christian worldview. As a result, the Christian spirit was often in communion with that of imperialism.[14]

Missionaries thus combined internationalism and nationalism, cosmopolitanism and parochialism, in highly combustible and unpredictable ways. Above all, many conflated Americanism with Christianity and foresaw these two great forces marching together for the world's redemption in a partnership that must not fail. But they also feared that the United States was the driving force, and that it was up to the church to keep up. "Woe to the future of the Church if it fails to expand with the expanding nation!" warned an Episcopal minister in 1901. Similarly, the United States was "first and foremost the chosen seat of enterprise for the world's conversion," claimed a professor at Andover Theological Seminary, a Congregationalist institution in Massachusetts and a leading center of liberal Protestantism. "Forecasting the future of Christianity as statesmen forecast the destiny of nations, we must believe that it will be what the future of this country is to be." Even more blunt was Robert Speer. "There cannot," he asserted in perhaps one of the first rejections of moral relativism, "be such different tribal or racial gods as are avowed in the ethnic religions of the East, and assumed in the ethnic politics of the West. Whatever God exists for America exists for all the world, and none other exists."[15]

Such confidence struck many as arrogance. While religion continued to penetrate nearly all layers of American society, for the first time in a century skepticism became a popular rival to faith and spirituality. The Civil War may have entrenched religion at a popular level, but for many elites, such as Oliver Wendell Holmes Jr., it completely undermined their faith in God. Moreover, while the implications of Darwinism caused soul-searching and reflection among liberal theologians, it completely destroyed faith in Christianity among many intellectuals. An early warning was an 1895 editorial in *The Nation* chastising missionaries for their intolerance and jingoism. To Mark Twain, shocked by the corruption of an American mission in China, missionaries represented little more than a domineering imperialism hypocritically dressed up in a pious but empty Christian moralism. African American intellectuals had an even sharper perspective on missionaries and imperialism. Decrying the colonialism and racism that often followed missionaries around the world, W. E. B. Du Bois called attention to the consequences of conversion. "Let not the cloak of Christian Missionary enterprise be allowed in the future, as so often in the past, to hide the ruthless economic exploitation and political downfall of less developed nations," he told delegates to the first pan-African conference, meeting in London in 1900.[16]

· · ·

YET THE MISSIONARY'S tale was not as simple as either its advocates or opponents assumed it to be. Often the expansion of Americanism and Christianity was an explicitly imperial project. But just as often, missionaries displayed a unique sensitivity to the concerns of native peoples that superseded their national prejudices. Many home missionaries, such as those from the American Missionary Association and the YWCA, expressed a gospel of tolerance for whites by preaching the gospel to blacks, in both the North and the South. Overseas missionaries then extended this spirit of tolerance abroad. "A great deal is said of men having the courage of their convictions," wrote a Southern Methodist missionary with experience in Japan and China. "Courage is a good quality, an indispensable quality. Convictions are necessary. They lie at the base of enthusiasm and intelligent purpose. Stubbornness is not courage. Prejudice [and] bigotry . . . are not convictions." Tolerance, both religious and racial, was an important component of the missionary endeavor (though of course not all missionaries practiced what they preached). Not coincidentally, missionaries were among the most vocal critics of America's anti-immigrant Chinese Exclusion Acts.[17]

Local custom, moreover, often prevailed over America's civilizing ways. Some male missionaries in China, for example, wore Chinese clothes in deference to local sensitivities and so they could blend in with the population more effectively. According to an 1889 Presbyterian primer, missionaries "should, when on the missionary field, be willing to adopt the native dress and live in native houses . . . with the idea of bridging over as much as possible the chasm which lies between the foreigner and the Chinamen." The language was vulgar, but it was not intended as an epithet or insult. More interesting is the idea that it was incumbent upon the Americans, and not the Chinese, to bridge the chasm between them by making cultural allowances. (Women, however, kept to a Western dress style.) And just as often, missionaries appreciated that they needed to accept locals on their own terms. Charles Henry Brent, the Episcopal Church's first missionary bishop to the Philippines, instructed the church's mission headquarters in New York that the "very first thing that workers must be prepared to do is to learn the native languages. Spanish is necessary in Manila and will be of limited service everywhere in the Archipelago; but it is absurd to think that you can understand the lives and ambitions of these people unless you are able to communicate with them through the medium of their own dialects." To provide an example, Brent himself took lessons in Spanish and Tagalog.[18]

Language sensitivity was only one part of Bishop Brent's report. He worried even more about Americans who claimed to have an expertise on the Philippines based on little or no actual knowledge of the country or contact with its people. "The audacity which some men have had to spend a few weeks or months in the Islands with no knowledge of Spanish, much less with any of the tribal languages, and then go home all primed to speak dogmatically on the political and religious conditions that obtain, may be a truly American feat but it is none the less astounding and reprehensible," he complained. "It is inexplicable to me that thinking men at home should give heed to their maunderings, or at any rate take them seriously." Missionaries often sympathized with the locals in recognition that Americans themselves could be pushy, overbearing, and even dangerous to local traditions and values. As one Episcopal missionary to the Philippines pointed out, missionaries were needed because the "inevitable immediate effect of the touch of America and Americans there will be to secularize, to demoralize, to disintegrate."[19]

For every missionary who wanted to force the spread of the Christian faith, then, there was a counterpart who sympathized with the plight of the subjugated. For every missionary who only wanted to convert the heathen, there were many more who wanted to educate and heal the locals regardless of their faith. For every missionary who wanted to enable American empire, there were those, as in Japanese-held Korea, who promoted anticolonialism and self-determination. And for every missionary who wanted to dominate, there was one who wanted to empower the overpowered. "A man white, black or yellow; Christian, Jew, Mohammedan or heathen, may enter and enjoy all the advantages of this institution . . . and go out believing in one God, in many Gods, or in no God," declared Daniel Bliss, the missionary founder of Syrian Protestant College, at its grand opening. Instead of exploiting local resources for America's benefit, Bliss had established the college in an attempt to halt the brain drain of talented Arabs to U.S. universities.[20]

In keeping with such practices and visions, the missionary impulse itself was deliberately constructed upon ecumenical foundations. Exemplified by John R. Mott, who later won the Nobel Peace Prize for his efforts to further international understanding and cooperation, most of the leading lights of the missionary movement were steadfast ecumenists who thought denominational rivalries were not only counterproductive but pointless. This also helps explain the religious curiosity and empathy of many missionaries. There was of course a fundamental tension between missionary conversion and ecumenical tolerance, but few at the time recognized it. Ecumenism was important, for it nourished a kind of American internationalism that saw the world as interconnected, interdependent, and responsive to universal values—with Christianity as the common denominator. (Not coincidentally, in 1887 American and Canadian churches established the Foreign Missions Conference of North America to promote a more ecumenical and less nationalistic missionary worldview. For the next seventy years, American and Canadian Protestant missionaries proved to be inseparable.) Nations were members of a global community in which they had rights and responsibilities, much as Americans did within their own communities. This was the basis for peace, be it religious or international. As Josiah Strong put it on numerous occasions, technology, industry, and communications had made "the whole world a neighborhood and every man a neighbor." Ecumenists saw one church, internationalists one world. The visions were essentially the same.[21]

John Mott, through his work in the YMCA, Student Volunteer Movement, and other organizations, embodied these visions interchangeably. Mott saw himself as a citizen of Christ—and thus automatically of the world. "The work of Mr. Mott has contributed powerfully to the development of what I have described as the international mind," wrote his friend and colleague Nicholas Murray Butler, president of Columbia University and head of the Carnegie Endowment for International Peace. "The possession by any people of an international mind is, I think, the necessary starting point for its highest contribution to the peace and progress of the world. Mr. Mott [sic] by helping various nations to develop the international point of view . . . has exercised and is constantly exercising a powerful influence in behalf of the peace and good order of the world." Mott himself claimed his goal was "to weave together all nations." Togetherness, built on notions of obligation and responsibility to all people but grounded firmly in the universal salvation of Christ, was the key to an ecumenical peace. Only missionaries could facilitate this process of cultural exchange. Only Christianity, Mott claimed, could "interpret the East to the West and the West to the East."[22]

Thus the American missionary enterprise was not a straightforward handmaiden of empire. The relationship between missions and imperialism was instead complicated and ambivalent, a limited partnership that usually did not unfold as most of its members intended. From their belief in social justice and emphasis on modernization, missionaries provided "a moral equivalent for imperialism," or even, in Samuel McCrea Cavert's echo of William James, "the moral equivalent of war." They aimed to "convert colonialism" from a one-way relationship that benefited only the United States to a mutual exchange for mutual benefit. Even its most belligerent proponents, led by the arch-nationalist Josiah Strong, decreed that missions could spread Christianity only through persuasion and voluntary conversion, not conquest or force. By 1907, moreover, mission theorists back home noted approvingly that contact with foreign religions was making American missionaries, and through them American Protestantism, more tolerant and ecumenical.[23]

Even normally skeptical U.S. diplomats were won over. From his dealings with missionaries in Turkey, Henry Morgenthau, an American ambassador to Istanbul, observed: "I had hitherto had a hazy notion that

missionaries were sort of over-zealous advance agents of sectarian religion. They were, I discovered, in reality advance agents of civilization." In
a private letter to a military official, Charles Denby, the U.S. minister to
Beijing, drew similar conclusions. "I am not particularly pro-missionary,"
he confessed; "these men and women are simply American citizens to me
as Minister. But as a man I cannot but admire and respect them." While
Denby did not care much about the missionaries' efforts to spread the
Gospel of Christ, he was impressed by their determination to spread a
gospel of progress:

> Outside of any religious question, and even if Confucianism, or Bud-
> dhism, are more divine than Christianity, and better for the human
> race . . . these people are doing a great work in civilizing, educating,
> and taking care of helpless thousands. They are the forerunners of
> Western methods and Western morality. They are preparing the way
> for white-winged commerce and material progress, which are knock-
> ing so loudly at the gate of the Chinese wall.

Indeed, while Christianity often paved the way for colonialism, many local
populations in Africa and China adopted the Christian faith and successfully adapted it to suit their own purposes, particularly modernization
initiatives and education programs. Missionaries were neither heroes nor
villains, then, but agents of what they were certain would be progressive
change.[24]

THE IMPULSE TO spread the Social Gospel to all corners of the earth was
so strong that it included some of the most unlikely participants. The missionary project was a tangle of paradox, but nowhere was it sharper than
in African American missionaries who brought Christianity to Africa in
an imperial age of the white man's burden. Some African American Christians simply ignored this contradiction; some thought they could transcend it; others still believed they could shatter such contradictions, and
white supremacy itself, by spreading the gospel. Claimed the Synod of the
Atlantic, an African American Presbyterian body in the segregated South:
"Christianity will bring a nation to the front so that it will be recognized
by the foremost nations of the world. We have Japan as our witness,"
which reflected widespread assumptions that American missionaries could
uplift a nonwhite people to equality with the Western powers. But it was
Africa that presented black American Christians with their most complicated problem. Most identified to some degree with pan-Africanism and
an international racial consciousness. But to the Western powers, and certainly to almost all white Americans, Africa represented the very depths of

human existence and epitomized the lack of civilization. Black Christians' solution was Christianity itself, a universally moral force that had the potential to spread political and economic progress and eventually bridge racial divides. Christianity had been the solution to slavery in West Africa before the Civil War, and it would be the continent's salvation now. By the end of the nineteenth century, led by the African Methodist Episcopal Church, black missionaries from the United States saw Africa as their own special calling.[25]

Ironically, however, evangelism also required American blacks to appropriate Anglo-Saxonist imagery of a benighted Africa and its savage people. While many American imperialists reveled in the triumph of the white race over all others, black missionaries believed in a civilizing mission that would overcome racial difference. Overcoming this dilemma through Christ pervaded African American nationalism. In the antebellum years, the AME Church and other black Christian churches had provided a community for free blacks and empowered them to interact with the dominant, and usually hostile, white culture. At the close of the century, with slavery behind them, the AME Church entered into a major partnership with black South African Christians, to provide them with the senses of solidarity and empowerment American blacks had already fostered among themselves. Black intellectuals like Pauline Hopkins similarly thought Christianity could be distinguished from white Western imperialism, and thus be beneficial to native peoples not only in Africa but Asia and the South Pacific as well. Most eloquent, and yet haunting, were black hymns such as Joseph Wheeler's "Missionary Hymn for Africa":

> *O, Africa, in darkness*
> 　*Thy land shall all be bright;*
> *Thy people shall be favored*
> 　*With hallowed Gospel light.*
> *The coming years will bring thee*
> 　*Great Blessings yet undreamed;*
> *Thy people shall be numbered*
> 　*Among the earth's redeemed.*
>
> *. . . They cry to God in pity,*
> 　*Send, Christians, to their need,*
> *O, labor for the Master!*
> 　*Sow now the precious seed!*[26]

SUCH TENSIONS DID NOT trouble the white mission boards. Instead, their preoccupation was to tie the practice of American diplomacy to the protection of American values, presumed to be universal, with the durable tether of religious liberty. In other words, they practiced an imperialism of ideas, and an imperialism of human rights, based on the dignity of the individual and the sanctity of his or her own conscience. ABCFM missionaries in China, for example, complained that Chinese girls were kept in a state of enforced destitution and ignorance. According to one missionary survey of a Chinese town, only 8 out of 800 girls could read. Missionaries singled out foot-binding as cruel and unnecessary, but they also pointed out that Chinese widows were forced to disfigure themselves instead of remarrying and that wealthy Chinese women were denied an education and were forced to live an indolent, soul-destroying lifestyle. American missionaries were determined to resolve these problems for Chinese women. "Shall we not come to the rescue of these poor souls without God and without hope?" asked one. This vigorous promotion of universal human rights at the expense of local custom may have been cultural imperialism, but it was a kind we easily recognize today.[27]

From the original founders of New England through to the Revolution, freedom of worship had been one of the foundational principles of American politics and society. But until the end of the nineteenth century, its application to foreign relations had been episodic, inconsistent, and, in the case of the Greeks in the 1820s, ineffective. However, by the 1890s, in China, the Ottoman Empire, British-occupied Egypt, and elsewhere, American missionaries pushed the cause of religious liberty close to its breaking point and in the process established this domestic political principle as a worthy goal of U.S. foreign policy. As a missionary to Egypt recalled, to their horror Americans "found Islam utterly opposed to the idea of religious liberty,"[28] even basic provisions like the separation of church and state. Partly this stance was a matter of principle, but in general the application of an abstraction arose simply as a matter of survival; once set, the principle would prove to be enduring.

Missionaries, both Protestant and Catholic, advanced religious freedom on two fronts. The first aimed to protect Christian minorities, such as converts in China, from persecution by ruling, non-Christian authorities. This was a particular irritant for Chinese officials, but it was not an issue that found much sympathy in the corridors of power in Washington. Foreigners, however oppressed, were still foreigners, and in the end could be forsaken to the dictates of the national interest. It was the missionaries' second method of advancing religious liberty that proved to be more influential and enduring. Their increasingly frenetic activities brought them into conflict with local authorities and nationalists, which required the U.S. government to protect its citizens abroad and assert itself on behalf of their right—presumably natural and universal—to religious liberty. Sometimes, of course, diplomats ostensibly spoke the language of liberty while actually using missionary penetration to enlarge secular national interests, especially economic and strategic; China is perhaps the best example. But this does not explain the power, resonance, or endurance of religious freedom as a legitimate goal for American diplomacy.

Nor does it account for the occasions in which the State Department acted on behalf of persecuted missionaries in countries where the U.S. government was not likely to have imperial ambitions, such as France, Germany, Holland, Norway, and Denmark. In Europe, for example, Mormon missionaries from the United States faced official harassment, sometimes imprisonment, even if they abided by local laws. Without exception, the U.S. consulates in Europe, and also in Turkey, strenuously protested the harsh treatment of Mormons and asserted their rights not only as Americans, but as Americans practicing their faith. This was a remarkable stance given the recent tensions over polygamy between the Latter-day Saints and the federal government, which had settled only after the Supreme Court upheld an antipolygamy law in 1879, Congress passed a series of laws constraining Mormon practices in the 1880s, and the Church itself officially renounced "plural marriage" in 1890. Once Mormons had conformed to the laws of the United States, they were entitled to its full protections wherever they traveled. "I shall protect them with all my power," vowed a diplomat presented with cases of French persecution of Mormon missionaries in 1895—a pledge that effectively committed American diplomats to assert the applicability of their own values, such as religious liberty and protection of Mormonism, in foreign countries.[29]

This vow quickly became official U.S. policy, set down in 1899 by Secretary of State John Hay following a dispute between the Chicago Methodist Ministers' Meeting and the governments of Bolivia, Peru, and Ecuador. As North American Protestants who sought to change the religion of deeply Catholic South America, Methodist missionaries were accustomed to official harassment. What they could not abide was a government decree in each country prohibiting Protestants from legally marrying or Protestant clergy from legally presiding over a marriage ceremony. In sending their protests to President William McKinley, the missionaries had the support of former president and missions advocate Benjamin Harrison, who echoed the Black Legend in protesting that "the religious liberty which is now universally given by Protestant countries to citizens and residents of the Roman Catholic faith calls for reciprocal treatment in Roman Catholic countries." Hay agreed, and based his decision upon a broad application of religious freedom not normally embraced by habitually cautious diplomats. "This Government, practicing as it does at home the largest principles of freedom of thought and belief, is natu-

rally desirous to see its citizens enjoy in other countries a reasonable freedom from restrictions or disabilities imposed by reason of religious faith,"
Hay instructed the U.S. legation in La Paz. Americans "may be relieved
from discriminations affecting their individual life, liberties, and domestic
relations in a manner at variance with the tendencies of this liberal age."
Facing the relentlessness of missionary zeal and the admonishment of the
United States, and the promise of continuing U.S. protection for meddle-
some Protestant missionaries, sovereign republics altered the law of their
land according to the wishes of the United States.[30]

Such disdain for national independence and international borders,
the bases of world politics for the previous 250 years, was a thoroughly
modern sensibility. It was grounded not in laws designed by humans,
but in a higher natural law, universal human rights, that superseded state
sovereignty. After World War II such rights were considered to have a
secular basis, but a major source were Christian—specifically, American
Christian—notions of a common humanity through the grace of God.
According to missionaries, all people, regardless of their color or creed,
could accept God's grace, and thus all people were part of the same human
family. However, according to missionaries this common humanity, and
with it universal human rights, could only be accessed through Christianity, and not other world religions. According to James S. Dennis, a leading
theorist of liberal Protestant missions writing in 1889, a "conflict between
Christianity and Islam is coming on apace; it will not be a conflict of arms,
but a struggle for moral supremacy." In its "great ministry of instruction
and reformation," he continued, Christianity

> is the embodiment of the highest authority in the universe. She cannot
> concede that any earthly authority has the moral right—although it
> may for a time have the power—to forbid her entrance or banish her
> agencies, if she is true to her message and limits herself to the simple
> methods and the spiritual weapons she is entitled to use. The world is
> slow to recognize the fact that the consciences of all men are free. No
> authority has been given to any human power of church or state to rule
> the moral nature. God has created it free. Its freedom is essential to its
> moral accountability.

This was heady stuff, a firm rebuke to any regime that did not reflect the
will of the people or the wishes of God, but Dennis's next prescription had
even more revolutionary implications for the international system:

> When, therefore, a civil power undertakes to prohibit by force all con-
> tact of Christian truth with the consciences of its subjects, it is assum-
> ing an attitude which is an offense to the highest moral rights of the

race, and usurping a function which does not rightly belong to human governments.

Universalism through the particular faith of Christianity: though Dennis did not realize it, he had identified the contradiction at the heart of Christian missions—though we should bear in mind today that Western notions of what constitutes universal values are no less contradictory, or contested.[31]

ULTIMATELY, missionaries—white and black, male and female—shaped America's role in the world in three important ways. First, as they were often the first Americans whom people in the colonial world would meet, they brought America to the world. As such, they were the first to introduce American political, economic, and religious values to peoples beyond Europe and Latin America. In many places missionaries acted as America's de facto foreign service. Often this meant that missionaries dragged diplomats into a more active role than they otherwise would have preferred, thus expanding the scope of U.S. activities abroad.

Second, the reverse was also true: missionaries were among the first to bring the world to Americans. Through countless books, articles, and pamphlets, sermons, lectures, and exhibitions, missionaries told Americans of new peoples and cultures—or, in the case of China and India, foreign peoples they knew only dimly. As U.S. power expanded, missionaries were there to tutor both ordinary Americans and elite policymakers about the wider world.

Third, and perhaps most important, missionaries fully realized their role as brokers of a global cultural exchange in which America would change as much as the rest of the world. By bringing America to the world, they hoped to spur progressive development; by introducing the world to America, they hoped to educate and enlighten Americans about their responsibilities in an increasingly connected world system. From such enlightenment would come grace, not just for the heathen, but for Americans themselves. "We need to save the world in order to save American spirituality," said Samuel Capen, a layman and president of the ABCFM.[32] This was the missionary's highest calling.

The missionary enterprise was therefore based upon a paradox: it sought to spread enlightened ideas about tolerance and progress, even where such ideas were not welcome. Missionaries were cosmopolitans who nonetheless believed that Christ's way was the only way. With the wisdom of hindsight, the Protestant ecumenical leader A. L. Warnshuis best captured the missionary's ambivalence. Warnshuis served as a missionary in China during the Boxer Rebellion and witnessed the recriminations that followed. During this time, he traveled throughout China with a Bible in one hand and a rifle in the other. But he was nonetheless steeped in the Social Gospel and became a leader of the most liberal, modernist wing of mainline Protestantism. "As I look back on it now," he told an interviewer in 1951,

> we were only partially informed and only partially understanding of conditions in China and the custom of the people and their beliefs; but it was our conviction in those days that whatever their beliefs might be, they were not to be considered as good as those of the Christian religion, and that the people there needed and would be greatly blessed by a knowledge and faith in the Christian religion. We went out with that idea of propagating the Christian faith among the people of China. It was a mission of goodwill.

Sherwood Eddy, another pioneer of liberal evangelical missions, summed it up differently. "We did not evangelise the world 'in this generation,'" he reflected in 1934, "but we sowed seed and launched movements which will in time transform the life of all the peoples of Asia and Africa." The great tensions embedded in the missionary enterprise—in the careers of Warnshuis and Eddy—were those between progress and local custom, tolerance and conversion, internationalism and nationalism, liberty and empire.[33]

Overall, then, missionaries were the advance agents of American imperialism—just not the formal colonialism practiced by the European powers and the United States in places like the Philippines. Rather, missionaries developed a prototype for the kind of informal imperialism, based as much on the power of ideas and human rights as on armed force, that the United States would practice in the twentieth century, especially following World War II. They introduced American ways of life around the world, not with the intention of establishing formal political and military dominance over foreign peoples, but in order to remake the world in an American image. The informal imperialism of spreading cultural, political, economic, and religious values would make the world more like America, and more receptive to Americans themselves. Informal imperialism, in other words, would make formal colonialism unnecessary. Whether missionaries themselves realized their role in changing the world system is somewhat beside the point. The importance of their legacy rests instead on the liberal global order, based on the safeguarding of individual liberties and the inculcation of American values, they helped create.

THREE IMPORTANT CASE STUDIES—China, the Ottoman Empire, and Hawaii—illustrate the paradoxical role of missionaries in the age of overseas American imperialism. (Similar patterns occurred in other important mission fields, such as Japan, Korea, and India, though not as starkly.) Missionaries generally did not seek to expand national influence or advance strategic interests, though of course there were significant exceptions. Yet they nonetheless found themselves caught in a cycle of violence that entrenched U.S. national interests at the expense of the missionaries' religious purpose. The missionaries' main objective was the conversion of local populations. But of course this usually meant also imbuing locals with ideas about republicanism, capitalism, and liberalism, which threatened to destabilize societies that were based on political and economic principles of monarchy, mercantilism, and communalism. This provoked a fierce, often violent backlash, which forced missionaries to seek protection from U.S. diplomats and the military—which in turn fomented even greater resentment among locals for the missionaries.

This unintentional cycle of recrimination was strongest in China, where U.S. missionaries were numerous and relentlessly activist. The Chinese held Western missionaries largely responsible for their humiliating subservience to the West, especially the most successful of them—American missionaries. The threat of nativist Chinese violence against missionaries was constant through the 1880s and '90s. Antiforeigner riots erupted in 1885, 1886, 1891, 1895, and 1896, resulting in the total destruction of missionary property—churches, schools, houses—and the killing of Christians, including missionaries but especially their Chinese converts and collaborators. The Chinese saw missionaries as the tip of the American imperial spear and thus had little time or patience with missionary protests that they simply wanted to bring progress to China. Christianity seemed to bring only dependence upon the West. "Death to the Devil's Religion," exclaimed an antimissionary pamphlet from Hunan in 1892. A decade later, one anti-Western nativist group adopted the motto "Uphold the Ch'ing [Qing dynasty], exterminate the church, kill foreigners." Violence against Westerners peaked in the Boxer Rebellion of 1900, in which Chinese nationalists killed thirty-two U.S. missionaries and hundreds of Chinese Christian converts.[34]

In response to the escalating violence, American missionaries appealed to their government for help. This required the difficult application of a fairly straightforward diplomatic principle. As much as possible, governments seek protections for their citizens worldwide, but missionaries were no ordinary citizens. They lived abroad, more or less permanently, and lived among foreign populations. Their interactions with foreigners were much more intimate, and invasive, than those of a tourist, merchant, or student. They were also extremely assertive about protecting what they believed were their inviolable rights, even in a foreign country. Understandably, U.S. diplomats were ambivalent about these missionaries who consumed increasing amounts of their time and energy—by one estimate, the U.S. legation in Istanbul spent about 90 percent of its time on missionary affairs. Missionaries were "troublesome and influential," complained diplomat Whitelaw Reid. William W. Rockhill, the State Department's China expert, concurred. "That our Protestant missionaries require restraining in their ardor there can be no doubt," he pondered in 1901. "How is it going to be done? The Lord only knows." Even at a time when keeping China accessible was official U.S. policy—the famed Open Door—missionaries were dragging diplomats and soldiers deeper onto the Asian mainland than they would otherwise have preferred. Indeed, missionaries applauded the Open Door Notes of 1899–1900 and interpreted them more broadly than Washington had intended. In this sense, the U.S. government followed a path missionaries had already blazed.[35]

As Reid had noted, though, missionaries were not only troublesome but influential; they could not be ignored or dismissed. Their domestic audience was simply too large, their connections to Congress and state capitals too close. When missionaries asked for diplomatic and military protection, even if it risked incurring the wrath of the Chinese government or stoking further violence, they could scarcely be refused. And of course the protection of U.S. citizens abroad was an important principle to uphold, however difficult or irritating it could be. Thus beginning in 1895 and continuing into the first two decades of the next century, U.S. diplomats demanded from the Chinese government full protection for missionaries and full indemnity for their losses. Missionaries were granted the privilege of extraterritoriality, so that they remained subject to American instead of Chinese law even as they lived and worked in China to undermine the Chinese government and Chinese customs. The State Department also acceded to missionaries' requests for continual passport renewal, even though at the time renewal was normally refused to U.S. citizens who intended to live outside the United States. "The peace and safety of the missionaries who are in China pursuing their calling under sacred treaty rights must be assured, good order among your people should be preserved, and respect for authority and compliance with law ought to be enforced" so that "the missionaries may peaceably teach and practice their faith," the American legation scolded the Chinese government in 1898. When diplomatic niceties failed, as they did in 1900, American gunboats reinforced these demands. Missionaries who looked forward to the day when "a just and righteous vengeance has been meted out to this barbarous country" told impressionable U.S. officials that the Chinese only understood, and thus only respected, the use of military force.[36]

Given that missionaries were sometimes the only Chinese experts available—and were the only ones who actually lived in China, more or less permanently—Washington looked to them for advice. Missionaries often had a salutary effect, effectively acting as filters between alien but clashing cultures. But just as often, missionary learning was refracted through a prism of racist assumptions and imperialist aggression. Arthur H. Smith, a China missionary much in demand on the U.S. lecture circuit, popularized notions of an inherently lazy, untrustworthy, and backward Orient in his book *Chinese Characteristics*, first published in Shanghai in 1890 and republished four years later for the American market. Richard Olney, secretary of state in the 1890s and an early advocate of an American imperium in the Pacific, especially relied on Smith's book. Diplomats in China, such as John Russell Young, consulted closely with missionaries before and during their service in China. And some diplomats had even been missionaries themselves, such as Chester Holcombe, author of *The Real Chinaman* and the chargé d'affaires at the American legation in Beijing. It was no coincidence that Holcombe's Christian faith, American nationalism, and view of Chinese inferiority were all equally strong.[37]

Not all American missionaries in China were strictly racist or imperialist, however. By their very nature, to some extent all missionaries were cultural imperialists; but simultaneously, they were also nurturers of Chinese nationalism and instigators of modernization. The burden of both nationalism and modernization would then be transferred to and borne by Chinese Christians whose highly activist, evangelical faith stood as a challenge to traditional authority. American Protestant missionaries therefore perceived themselves, quite rightly, as a modernizing influence, even though the effects of their modernization theories were not always beneficial to the Chinese people. The Taiping Rebellion, which lasted for fourteen years, until 1864, and resulted in the deaths of at least twenty million people, was triggered by a Chinese mystic who had been converted to Christianity by missionaries and tutored in the ways of Christ by a Southern Baptist from Shelbyville, Tennessee. Fortunately, most missionary encounters did not have such disastrous results. Mission schools and colleges educated a new generation of Chinese leaders and trained them in modern variants of political and economic thought. Many Chinese nationalists and revolutionaries accepted a Christian baptism and absorbed whatever lessons could help shape a modernist reform movement. For some, such as the convert Sun Yat-sen, the alchemic recipe of Chinese and American Christian ideas worked well—so well that in 1911, Sun and his followers used them to topple the Qing dynasty and establish a Chinese republic. Other nationalists, such as the future foreign minister Wellington Koo, had also been educated by American missionaries. And by the early twentieth century, Chinese Christians were confident enough to go their own way, leaving foreign missionaries behind.[38]

The same pattern held in the Ottoman Empire. Missionaries operating there were forbidden to proselytize Muslims—except in Egypt, where the British occupation of 1882 protected Christian missionaries and enabled them to pursue conversions freely—and the ancient Christian communities of the Middle East did not warm to the Americans' evangelical Protestantism. But everyone wanted an education, especially an American education, and so when missionaries established hundreds of schools throughout the empire, they found a steady demand for their services. The missionary enterprise in the Middle East was thus almost entirely driven by the Social Gospel, with the gospel itself largely absent. In Robert College and Constantinople Woman's College (both in Istanbul) and Syrian Protestant College (later the American University of Beirut), American missionaries founded prestigious centers of higher education that flourished under Ottoman rule.[39]

College instructors did not preach Protestantism, but they did teach modern empirical science, capitalism, and republican politics, which had their own destabilizing effects. Perhaps most radically, they also taught women. As in China, American missionaries were agents of modern change and nurturers, however unwitting or inadvertent, of anticolonial nationalisms. Bulgarian, Albanian, Arab, and especially Armenian nationalists thought of themselves as autonomous peoples and learned how to apply these new values to imperial politics under missionary tutelage. The cry of "Autonomous Armenia," noted the missionary Collins Denny, was the best "remedy" for Armenian-Turkish tensions within the Ottoman Empire. Unsurprisingly, the ruling Turkish authorities did not agree. Antimissionary violence erupted in 1885 and sporadically through the 1890s, prompting menacing patrols of the Turkish coast by U.S. warships.[40]

More tragically, in 1894–96 the stirring of Armenian nationalism provoked a genocidal rampage by the Turks, in which as many as fifty thousand Armenians died. Another seventy thousand fled to the United States, where they pressed Washington to intervene on behalf of Armenian Christians persecuted by Turkish Muslims. Led by the ABCFM, American missionaries in Turkey also applied pressure, writing home for funds to alleviate Armenian suffering and calling on Washington to intervene. "The Church everywhere has a duty to perform for the honor of Jesus Christ," one pro-Armenian missionary wrote anonymously in a widely circulated newsletter. "Can it not force the Government to remove the swords from the hands of Islam?" "Unless Christendom acts instantly and overwhelmingly to arrest this infamy," said another, "this century of enlightenment will be marked in history as the one in which a Christian people was destroyed, with the full knowledge, and before the eyes of Christendom, no Christian nation being sufficiently moved by the spectacle to lift a hand to prevent it." Mission enthusiasts were no less active at home. Spurred by Josiah Strong, William Lloyd Garrison, Julia Ward Howe, and other luminaries from the Civil War struggle for equal rights signed an anti-Turkish petition calling for immediate U.S. intervention.

But they were to be disappointed: 1895 was not 1861, Turkey was not the Confederacy, and in the end Washington did little other than express its disapproval and concern.[41]

Things turned out differently in the Hawaiian Islands, which became an American protectorate in 1898. Missionaries, we have already discovered, had been an integral part of the Westernization and Americanization of Hawaii in the decades before the Civil War. As the century drew to a close, and as American strategists and merchants envisioned China and Japan as the center of gravity for international security and prosperity, Hawaii acquired an ever-larger importance in the American imagination, and in 1893 American planters, many of them descendants of missionaries, staged a coup that they hoped would result in American annexation. Yet as we have also already seen, missionaries were deeply conflicted about Hawaii's political future. Most wanted the islands Christianized, of course, but most missionaries did not conflate this religious goal with American colonial dominance, strategic advantage, or monetary profit. Some missionaries did call for annexation, but in general their relationship to American dominance was more complex. In other words, even though formal imperialism eventually resulted, missionaries continued—mostly unwittingly—to pursue forms of informal imperialism, based on the notion of openness, access, and autonomy. Alexander Twombly, a Congregationalist missionary in Honolulu, argued that the solution to the problem was "a unique state, wholly unlike any existing Republic," one that would preserve Hawaiian independence while at the same time recognizing that "Chinese, Japanese, Portuguese, Hawaiians, and Americans must be provided for, & the stronger foreign powers"—including the United States—"be kept from interference." American strategists, planters, and traders might "all cry annexation," Twombly complained in a letter to home, "but I am not yet convinced that it is best." Little did Twombly or other missionaries realize, but their religious initiatives had already paved the way for the triumph of the altogether more secular forces for annexation.[42]

CHAPTER ELEVEN

An Also Chosen People

MISSIONARIES PROVED JUST HOW complicated America's mission could be, with private and public interests often differing on how it should be implemented throughout the world. Though the United States did not intervene on behalf of Armenian Christians, missionaries ensured that religious liberty had become an important issue for U.S. foreign policy. But they were not America's only human rights advocates—indeed, they were not even the most persistent. More strenuously and urgently than Protestant missionaries, American Jews promoted the cause of religious liberty abroad. As with the missionaries, their invocation of a universal ideal and a natural right stemmed from a very particular concern for the immediate safety of Jews in Europe. And as with missionaries, once the U.S. government took the cause of religious liberty seriously, governments abroad, even international law itself, had little choice but to follow suit.

The place of Jews in American society changed dramatically following the Civil War and Reconstruction, mostly due to the arrival of waves of Jewish immigrants from eastern Europe after the first of the Russian pogroms in 1881 following the assassination of Czar Alexander II. Between 1881 and 1914, when the outbreak of World War I in Europe closed off their avenue of escape, over two million Jews migrated to the United States from Galicia, Lithuania, Poland, Hungary, and especially Russia and Romania; the Jewish population of New York City alone soared from 80,000 to 1.4 million. Some fled pogroms, but most moved for the same reasons that have driven migrants throughout human history: economic distress and poor living standards. Russian and Romanian Jews in particular endured horrible living conditions, high unemployment, and negligible wages simply because Russian and Romanian governments had made it so. Jews had suffered such miseries for decades, but in the 1880s conditions deteriorated sharply, mostly for political reasons: in Russia, people blamed Jews for the assassination of the czar and the rise of socialist radicalism, while the government of newly independent Romania feared its Jews were a fifth column that would undermine state and nation. Eastern European Jews were desperate to leave, but no other European country would take them in. The ease with which people could now cross the Atlantic—in a matter of days rather than weeks or months, and for a relatively small sum—made the United States a realistic destination, while its religious tolerance and booming industrial revolution made it an attractive one. Russian Jews wanted to move to only two places: either the Holy Land (Palestine) or the Golden Land (America). Until World War I, almost all made their way to the Golden Land.[1]

At roughly the same time, American Jews were undergoing profound changes of their own. Up to the Civil War, Jews in the United States saw Americanization as their objective: they sought to erase the differences, or at least the most obvious ones, between themselves and the national mainstream. But after the Civil War, groups of Jews in Philadelphia and New York undertook efforts to recover their Jewish identity as a complement to their American nationality. At first, such efforts simply meant prioritizing Jewish religious festivals and ceremonies; the celebration of Hanukkah as a major holiday, for example, began in the 1870s. But the recovery of identity, when it unfolded against the backdrop of bloodthirsty pogroms in Russia and the naked anti-Semitism of the Dreyfus trial in Paris, assumed a harder, more assertive edge. By the 1890s, with the formation of the Federation of American Zionists and the Knights of Zion, Zionism was becoming a powerful force among American Jews. So too were other forms of Jewish nationalism, such as Bundist socialism, that conceived of the Jewish diaspora as a single nation consisting of a single people. Just as Protestant missionaries were helping create an international consciousness for Americans, Zionists and other Jewish nationalists were fusing an international consciousness for American Jews, a development enriched and accentuated by the arrival of millions of European Jewish immigrants. This global outlook propelled Jewish concerns about events in eastern Europe, which in turn brought humanitarian pressures to bear upon U.S. foreign policy.[2]

As Jews became more prominent, they attracted increasing attention from gentile Americans, for good and ill. Anti-Semitism was nothing new, but by the late nineteenth century it had infected, according to the subject's leading historian, "practically every stratum in society." This included the loftiest strata as well as the lowliest, as anti-Semitism increased among the patrician elites and governing class who feared that grasping, aspirational Jews aimed to supplant the traditional role of Protestantism in establishing a national code of conduct and mores. Brooks and Henry Adams, grandsons of John Quincy and two of America's leading historians and public intellectuals, hated Jews because of their supposedly conspiratorial skills and malignant ambitions to harness American power to the cause of world Jewry. They also despised the Gilded Age's nouveaux riches, who lacked style and sophistication and whose worst traits the Jews were assumed to epitomize. Writing from Paris at the height of the Dreyfus affair in the winter of 1898, Brooks blamed "a gang of dirty Jews" for stirring up controversy about Dreyfus's probable innocence. A few months later, he could barely contain himself as Émile Zola's impassioned defense of Dreyfus forced the controversy into the open. "The Jews and the monied class have outdone themselves," he hissed in a letter to Henry. Henry's feelings were just as maliciously succinct as his brother's. "I loathe the Jew," he confessed in a letter the following year.[3]

The sources of American anti-Semitism, then, could be refined as well as rough, genteel as well as crude. In such circles, Jewish immigration was unwanted and undesirable, even harmful. "You want to keep the Russian Jews out of America, a wish which, according to me, you are right." So wrote Reverend Edward Everett Hale, Unitarian minister, chaplain to the U.S. Senate, and one of the nation's leading liberal religious intellectuals, to his friend Henry Cabot Lodge, senator from Massachusetts. Jews in the United States and Russia "say that new and very stiff statutes [pogroms] are to be made in Russia this next summer, which as things go, will send a few hundred million more of them over here." Russian Jews fleeing the pogroms should be steered away from America and toward Palestine, in the interest of all concerned, Hale argued. The Russians would not care, the Jews would be happy, and the purity of America would be maintained. Only the Turks would object, but perhaps they could be persuaded by Secretary of State Hay's negotiating skills. As Hale's prejudice illustrated, one did not have to be a Christian Zionist to favor the return of the Jews to Israel.[4]

Unsurprisingly, anti-Semitism could be found lurking in nearly all institutions of privilege and power—including the State Department. The thoughts of William R. Castle, who would finish a distinguished diplomatic career as Under Secretary of State, swam in the most polluted currents of patrician anti-Semitism and reflected the innate hostility to Jews of many career foreign service officers in the late nineteenth and early twentieth centuries. Generalizing from the Jews of Poland, Castle vented to his diary that the Jews "are an incubus on the state. They are not producers. They live on driving hard bargains, on usury. They clutter the streets, because they have nothing to do except to discuss the theology of the Talmud." Jews "are dirty and harbingers of all diseases; immoral and servants of immorality; absolutely unpatriotic." Worse still, they were all in league with one another, all over the world, and advanced the cause of international Jewry over the interests of their home countries.[5]

But the anti-Semitic venom of the Adams brothers, Hale, and Castle did not monopolize American attitudes toward Jews. As Jewish immigration increased, and as American horizons stretched into the Middle East, American perceptions of Jews also became more positive, benign, even favorable. Much of this stemmed from an increasingly popular ecumenical outlook, especially among liberal mainline Protestants. Much also stemmed from the overarching inclusivity of a battle-tested civil religion. Christians and Jews should celebrate their broader "common humanity," an Episcopal minister wrote to a Jewish rabbi in 1876, instead of concentrating on narrower points of difference. Others saw anti-Semitism as a symptom of even more serious diseases: irreligion and tyranny. The Dreyfus case, a Southern Methodist bishop explained to students, was the direct result of centuries of Catholic oppression in France, which had produced an equally strong reaction among skeptics, atheists, and other people of dubious morality. Unless France "can right her iniquity, and relearn the lessons of justice and integrity and bring herself forward, she will yet reap the full results of revolution." Political liberty could not exist without religious tolerance, especially to those faiths and sects most vulnerable in society.[6]

Americans were also becoming fascinated with the Jews as a people of the Bible, and as a fellow chosen people touched by God and protected by providence. Spurred by missionary activity, and ironically also by the advent of biblical criticism, which did much to undermine the immutable authority of the Bible but stimulated interest in biblical history, post–Civil War Americans became infatuated with the Middle East and infected with Holy Land mania. In addition to the ever-present missionaries, thousands of European and American tourists embarked on a "Peaceful Crusade" to experience the ancient sites and "sacred geography" of the Bible firsthand. Others chose to move to the Holy Land, most prominently Horatio and Anna Spafford, Chicago evangelicals who established the American Colony in Jerusalem in 1881 as a place of respite for Christian pilgrims from the West. Even intellectuals like Herman Melville and Mark Twain, eccentric and skeptical in matters of faith, explored the Holy Land in person and in print, even if only to put the culture of the American mission into sharper relief. Many Americans were repelled by what they encountered in the Middle East—or rather, what they perceived they encountered—from fetid smells to lurid manners to abject poverty and religious superstition. But they were at least becoming familiar with the region, and known to it. Even if their perceptions were skewed by cultural stereotypes, parochial exceptionalism, and ignorance, Americans increasingly felt as if they had some sort of a commitment to the Middle East.[7]

People like the Spaffords were not mere tourists, however. They were committed to a new evangelical interpretation of the Bible, one that took prophecy, and especially the Second Coming of Christ, literally. Within British and American Protestantism, these doctrines of premillennialism (that Jesus would return to earth before the millennium, and thus imminently) and dispensationalism (that history is divided into distinct eras, or dispensations, that would culminate in the return of Christ) led to the formation of Christian Zionism, or Restorationism (to restore the Jews to Israel). Like Jewish Zionists, premillennial dispensationalist Christians agitated for the return of the Jews to the lands of ancient Israel, where they could establish a new Jewish state. Unlike Jewish Zionists, however, Christian Zionists saw the return—or ingathering, as they called it—of the Jews not as an end in itself but a necessary step in fulfilling the prophecy of Christ's return as told in the Book of Revelation. Jews had been persecuted ruthlessly for centuries yet survived against the odds, a leading Christian Zionist observed in 1901. Why else would God spare them if not to play a providential role in the fulfillment of prophecy? "This is the reason and the only reason for the marvelous preservation of the Jews. No other can be assigned."[8]

Restorationism found especially strong support among Christian conservatives. Building on the ideas of the British evangelical John Nelson Darby, American evangelicals promoted Jewish immigration to the Middle East as an essential part of God's plan and pushed the U.S. government to assist the return of the Jews, mostly from Russia and eastern Europe, to the Holy Land. As early as 1863, Secretary of State—and ardent Restorationist—William Seward instructed U.S. diplomats to extend protection not just to American Jews, but to all "Israelites" in the Middle East; diplomats in the following decades continued Seward's policy. In 1878, the annual Niagara Bible Conference devoted itself to returning the Jews to Israel. In 1891, William Blackstone, a wealthy Chicago evangelical, petitioned the federal government to fund and assist the resettlement of as many as two million Russian Jews in Palestine. In addition to the usual grandees of Protestant fundamentalism, signatories to this "Blackstone Memorial" of March 5, 1891, included John D. Rockefeller, J. P. Morgan, the publisher Charles Scribner, and then-congressman William McKinley. Two years later, Arthur T. Pierson, a leading Protestant conservative, published a booklet, *Israel, God's Olive Tree*, that gave Blackstone's cause some theological substance. Cyrus I. Scofield, an evangelist and friend of Dwight Moody and Pierson, provided a theological structure for premillennial dispensationalism with his annotated Scofield Reference Bible, first published in 1909. On a higher plane, Christian Hebrew scholars in the nation's best universities, such as William Rainey Harper, the founding president of the University of Chicago, inculcated a philo-Semitic, biblical, Old Testament worldview among their students.[9]

Overall, then, there was no single view of Jews but many competing perceptions that ranged from malicious to benign, and from indifferent to ambivalent to passionate. But of course American Jews themselves held strong views about their place in society and their people's role in the world. And underpinning them was a belief both straightforward and complicated: equality. American Jews believed they merited, and could demand, the same protections as any other U.S. citizen, and this applied abroad no less than it did at home. To Jews, it seemed as straightforward a proposition as could be; to others, it was anything but. Yet it was on this point that American Jews advanced the cause of religious liberty and helped enshrine universal human rights at the heart of American foreign policy.

THE NEED TO defend religious liberty arose from the oppression of Jews in eastern Europe, particularly Romania and Russia, in the late nineteenth century. Officials in both countries targeted Jews as threats to the political and cultural fabric because, authorities in Bucharest and St. Petersburg charged, they refused to assimilate into society as a whole. Romania, independent only in 1878 and forced by the great powers to codify religious liberty in its founding charter, felt especially insecure and vulnerable. Aside from acts of violence, calculated or otherwise, Romanian and Russian Jews suffered from severe government restrictions on their political and economic activities. Many fled to the United States and provided Jewish leaders in America with firsthand accounts of persecution, even genocide, in Europe. Already in 1870, the U.S. government protested Russia's maltreatment of its Jewish population. In 1881, when the pogroms against Jews began, the State Department urged Russia to allow Jews to emigrate to Palestine and pressed Turkey to let them do so. Neither the Russians nor the Turks would budge, however, and the United States continued to receive Jewish refugees from Romania and Russia. That the vast majority of all Romanian and Russian immigrants in the late nineteenth century were Jews—90 percent in Romania's case—indicated the scale and depth of the problem.[10]

And American officials did see it as a problem, a Jewish problem, in two rather contradictory ways: for the Jews and of the Jews. The problem *for* the Jews was clearly one of religious freedom: nobody doubted that they were being brutally persecuted, and humiliated as a people, purely because of their faith. In August 1902, Secretary of State John Hay issued a stiff protest on these grounds to the Romanian government. He chastised Bucharest for tolerating, even encouraging, "wrongs repugnant to the moral sense of liberal modern peoples" and pointed out that "by the cumulative effect of successive restrictions, the Jews of Roumania have become reduced to a state of wretched misery." Hay was also unstinting in his condemnation of Romania's affront to universal human rights. "This Government can not be a tacit party to such an international wrong," he told American diplomats throughout Europe, who then pleaded the case of Romanian Jews to foreign offices in London, Paris, Berlin, and Vienna. Hay stressed that the U.S. government was issuing its protest "against the treatment to which the Jews of Roumania are subjected . . . in the name of humanity," because the values and rights in question "are the principles of international law and eternal justice."[11]

Hay similarly deplored Russia's "needlessly repressive treatment" of the Jews and arranged for Jewish leaders Oscar Straus, Leo Levi, and Simon Wolf to meet with President Theodore Roosevelt in the White House to present a petition to the Russian government. Not coincidentally, this period saw a sharp shift in American Christians' perceptions of the Russian Orthodox Church. Where once Orthodoxy had been hailed as a civilizing bulwark against Muslim hordes, it was now seen as a degenerate, despotic force allied with czarist tyranny. Protestant, Catholic, and Mormon missionaries began flocking to Russia, potentially the greatest of all mission fields, where they joined the Jews in persecution.[12]

Hay furthermore disputed Russian distinctions between classes of foreign citizens, which extended domestic anti-Semitic laws to foreign Jews and thus denied the customary protections to visiting Jews holding American citizenship. The U.S. government "can admit no such discrimination among its own citizens, and can never assent that a foreign State, of its own volition, can apply a religious test to debar any American citizen from the favor due to all." The harassment of American Jews traveling in Russia became one of the main sources of tension between a United States that prioritized religious freedom and a Russia that feared Jews as subversive enemies of both the Russian state and the Christian faith. In April 1904, Congress adopted a joint resolution—passed unanimously in the House—calling on Russia to respect American passports regardless of the bearer's religious faith; Hay duly passed on the news to the U.S. embassy in St. Petersburg. More remarkably, in his 1904 Annual Message to Congress President Roosevelt openly criticized Russia's maltreatment of Jews, and especially American Jews wishing to travel to Russia, as "unjust and irritating." This radically moralistic contravention of normal diplomatic protocol angered but did not surprise the Russians, or other Europeans. "If such words had been employed in a speech from the throne at Berlin or Vienna it would have resulted in the recall of the Russian Minister at those courts," a U.S. diplomat told the *New York Times*. "As it is, nothing will now occur. The powers have come to regard the United States as entitled to exceptional toleration in matters of this kind." In 1911, after a continually growing torrent of criticism and effective coordinated action by Jewish rights groups, Congress unilaterally abrogated an 1832 treaty with Russia on mutual freedom of travel and commerce. The American rebuke to Russia could not have been any clearer.[13]

Behind the high-minded appeals to universal human rights, however, lay colder calculations of political and national interest. By the turn of the century Jews had gained political influence and with it an audience in

Washington. During the Russian pogroms of 1905, Hay's successor as secretary of state, Elihu Root, cabled his ambassador in St. Petersburg with a request for information because of the pressure from "many influential Hebrews" for news from Russia. Not for the last time, American Jews mobilized to provide relief to their Russian coreligionists and to pressure their own government to act. Fed up with the usual silence from Washington and fearful that Congress might begin to restrict Jewish immigration, activists formed the American Jewish Committee in 1906 to channel the voices of over three million American Jews in one direction. This mattered to American politicians from both parties, but especially to the Republicans, who hoped to win the allegiance of a valuable voting bloc. Such an elemental fact of political life was certainly not lost on Roosevelt.[14]

More astonishingly, religious prejudice also lay at the root of Hay's appeals to Russia to respect universal human rights. This was the problem *of* the Jews—to America. Hay was no anti-Semite, but many within the State Department were. And what concerned them was not necessarily the immorality of Romanian anti-Semitism, but the inconvenience. Thus in his instructions of August 1902, Hay lamented that whenever the Romanians persecuted their Jewish population, the Romanian Jews fled en masse to the United States. He reminded the Romanian government that "the social law holds good that the right of each is bounded by the right of the neighbor," which made the United States an interested party to Romania's domestic problems. Hay did not object to Jewish immigrants per se, but "when they come as outcasts, made doubly paupers by physical and moral oppression in their native land, and thrown upon the long-suffering generosity of a more favored community, their migration lacks the essential conditions which make alien immigration either acceptable or beneficial." Romanian Jews, in other words, were feared as a potential strain on the American body politic. Other European nations refused to accept any Jewish immigrants, which funneled them all across the Atlantic. "America," Hay noted, "was their only goal" because "the hospitable asylum offered by this country is almost the only refuge left to them." In a bid to stem the tide of Jewish immigration, the State Department pleaded with the Romanian government to put an end to its cause. In essence, the U.S. government promoted religious liberty abroad partly in deference to religious prejudice at home.[15]

Still, for everyone involved, the end justified the means. American Jews were delighted with Hay—so delighted that the B'nai B'rith planned a monument in his honor in Washington—and his efforts to extend universal notions of religious liberty into the dark recesses of anti-Semitic European politics. "As the world champion of Justice," a Jewish memorial to Hay declared upon his death in 1905, "he stood ready to inaugurate a new diplomacy—a diplomacy of humanity—which will forever mark an epoch in the affairs of nations."[16] The Republican Party was equally delighted with Hay for making a gesture to a constituency it was trying to win over. Others applauded Hay's attempt to limit the immigration of a most destitute and desperate people. Yet none of this had done anything to alleviate the plight of Europe's beleaguered Jews. Rarely had fulfilling America's mission been so complicated. Little did American politicians and diplomats realize, but such collisions of domestic politics, religion, and human rights would set the standard from now on.

CHAPTER TWELVE

Cuba, the Philippines, and the First Crusade

The end of the nineteenth century witnessed a sharp rise in national assertiveness. Though it occurred partly as a way to account for the traumas of modern change—the violent swings of boom and bust in the economy, the emergence of women in public life, the relentless pace of industrialization, immigration, and urbanization—its underlying message was one of intense pride in the United States and confidence that it would soon become the world's leading power.

The new self-assurance was no less active within religion than it was in other aspects of society. One example was the renewal of muscular Christianity, an assertive, sometimes aggressive religious outlook that did not compromise or retreat. Coinciding with the nation's imperial turn and first foreign war of humanitarian intervention, American Christians refigured the image of Christ as athletic and active, even defiant. Rejecting what one Episcopal priest condemned as the traditional "feeble, mawkish, sickly" portraits of Jesus dying helplessly on the cross, American clergy invoked a Christ who was literally muscular, ready to battle for the cause. Social Gospel ministers in particular latched on to the example of a fearless, powerful, heroic Jesus who tackled the toughest social problems and embraced the poor no matter what the consequences. Another was the sudden revival of the Puritan "city on a hill" and "New Jerusalem" motifs in American writing. Novelists and chroniclers portrayed the United States as a chosen nation and Americans as a chosen people. This was nothing new, of course, but the end of the century saw a dramatic increase in the use of such themes. Echoing John Winthrop, one writer even concluded that the eyes of the world were "riveted" upon Denver, destined as it was to become the global hub of railway traffic. A final example comes from the rise of "Anglo-Saxonism," a belief that the white, Protestant, English-speaking peoples were destined to rule the world because they came from inherently superior racial and religious stock.[1]

Surging nationalism and a sense of duty to spread the blessings of Christian civilization permeated most aspects of American thought, but it particularly saturated foreign affairs. The great paradox of the age, between reform and empire, emerged from the mindset of a generation of foreign policymakers that was Progressive but nonetheless interventionist and imperialistic. And at the heart of this paradox was a religious ideology that espoused, to its core, that Christian America had a responsibility to God to make the world a better place.

Elihu Root certainly believed it. Between 1899 and 1915, during the Spanish and Philippine wars and the outbreak of war in Europe, Root served as secretary of state and secretary of war before being elected to the U.S. Senate. Born in 1847, Root was raised in the town of Clinton, on the edge of upstate New York's "burned-over district." The nickname came in the nineteenth century, when central and western New York were the scenes of intense evangelical revivalism, fervent millennialism, and the creation of new faiths, such as Mormonism and Seventh-day Adventism. Not unusually for the antebellum North, this burning religious devotion brought with it an equally intense commitment to social reform, including abolitionism and women's rights (a movement born in nearby Seneca Falls in 1848). Root was born into an intensely religious family. As an idealistic student at Hamilton College, he was active in the local branch of the YMCA. He remained a devout churchgoing Presbyterian and active member of the YMCA after moving to Manhattan to study law at New York University; he also taught Sunday School in his local midtown church. "We have duties to ourselves that are owed to God," he once wrote. Especially "clear and imperative is the duty of improvement. . . . We give ourselves to Christ—little enough, surely, in return for what He has done. Should not each one strive to make this the gift of as perfect and fully developed a man as possible?" A conservative Republican in most matters domestically, Root, like McKinley, saw in America's burgeoning global role the perfect outlet for his reformist impulses. And like McKinley, he did not seem aware of any contradictions between Progressivism and imperialism.[2]

Alfred Thayer Mahan, the preeminent strategist of his day, also believed it. Unusually for a professor at the Naval War College in Rhode Island, he was closely consulted not only by American leaders but also by the kings and queens, presidents and prime ministers of Europe. His doctrine of "the influence of sea power upon history" argued that great power status depended heavily, if not exclusively, upon the ability to command the seas. At the same time Mahan was writing, American leaders were beginning to look to Asia, particularly China, as a new center of strategic and economic gravity. If the United States was, in the apt phrase of Secretary of State John Hay, intent on maintaining an Open Door to China, it had better have the means to keep it open—ultimately by force—if its rivals moved to slam it shut. At the close of the nineteenth century, then, Mahan's theories offered an elegant formula for a United States that now held ambitions to be a great power on a global scale.[3]

Above all, Mahan thought religion—in fact Christianity, and specifically Protestantism—was indispensable to the moral grounding that was required for national greatness. He was certain that Britain's rise to global hegemony in the nineteenth century was directly related to the Christian devotion of the Victorians. He was just as convinced that the fervent Christian faith of his fellow Americans would enable them one day to complement—and perhaps even supplant—British power. Fittingly, he believed that people of a suitably devout Christian character could rely upon the guiding hand of a watchful God to steer them toward glory. A devout Episcopalian, Mahan was as close a student of theology as he was of history—he published a book, *The Harvest Within: Thoughts on the Life of a Christian*, about the centrality of religion in his life—and for him the two were inseparable. His appreciation of the lessons of history stemmed in large part from the historical and political insights offered by his faith. "I may add that my general thought," he confessed to his friend Silas McBee during the emotional debate over U.S. imperialism in the Philippines, "depends upon my convictions as a Christian and a Churchman—the strongest convictions that I entertain; for to me the Church is a greater fact than any State, and Christianity is more than any political creed."[4]

For Mahan, Christianity not only represented more than any political creed, it was the basis for any proper form of politics. Christianity was the source of civilization, and all that civilization produced. For this reason, Mahan was a proponent of overseas missions, and was honored to have a mission school in China, the Mahan School, named for him. Without faith—Christian faith—progress, justice, and liberty could not exist. To skeptics, usually secular critics, Mahan replied that they need only "compare the conditions of the countries in which Christianity has existed with those where it has only begun to touch, in such matters as the status of women, the administration of Justice, the conditions of settled government" to uncover Christianity's earthly blessings. Mahan's understanding of the world was based upon a simple truth: "God rules all."[5]

Mahan and Root were by no means alone in their application of a religious sensibility to grand strategy. Indeed, it was a close friend of theirs who did the most to implement such ideas, first as an official in the Navy Department and eventually as president of the United States. Theodore Roosevelt possessed the religious ideology, political instincts, and global ambitions to create a foreign policy of the Social Gospel. He was also a living exemplar of muscular Christianity and lived his life accordingly. His beloved father, Theodore Sr., had been a pious member of the evangelical Dutch Reformed Church, an active reformer in the Benevolent Empire, and a follower of Dwight L. Moody. As a young man, especially during his days as a Harvard undergraduate, Roosevelt approached religion with a serious intent, devouring the Bible and attending church services regularly. And though he lost much of this ardor as he matured into adulthood, he retained for the rest of his life a progressive sense of moral righteousness. With his "bully pulpit," Roosevelt envisioned himself a national preacher and the role of the president as a kind of modern-day prophet. While the depth of his faith was a matter of conjecture, the relevance of his religious ideas were not. He was a devout Christian but had little time for Christians who did not apply their faith to the real problems of the real world. "I am mighty weak in the Lutheran and Calvinistic doctrine of salvation by faith," he once commented, but "I do believe in the gospel of works as put down in the Epistle of James."[6]

Theodore Roosevelt's righteous Progressivism is easily seen in his domestic achievements on corporate regulation, working conditions, food safety, and environmental conservation. And it was on these issues that his biblical rhetorical flourishes would often get carried away, particularly after he left the White House in 1909 and, four years later, ran for president on a third-party ticket. "Our cause is based on the eternal principles of righteousness; and even though we who now lead may for the time fail, in the end the cause itself shall triumph," he proclaimed, apocalyptically, at the founding convention of the Progressive Party in 1912. To his followers who marched with him "in the endless crusade against wrong, to you who face the future resolute and confident, to you who strive in a spirit of brotherhood for the betterment of our Nation, to you who gird yourselves for this great new fight in the never-ending warfare for the good of humankind," Roosevelt promised: "We stand at Armageddon, and we battle for the Lord."[7]

On foreign policy Roosevelt is normally thought of as a realist, someone who distinguished between central and peripheral interests and who calculated the national interest objectively, without the input of confusingly imprecise morals and values. Yet Roosevelt's worldview was very much rooted in the same Social Gospel ideology as his domestic policies. He was an internationalist who believed that the United States had no choice but to entangle itself with the rest of the world. But even more, he believed that American foreign policy should be rooted in righteousness, especially in policies that would bring progress not only to the United States but others as well. Roosevelt outlined his worldview in a letter to the missionary leader John Mott:

> Our aim in international affairs should be as our aim in private affairs. An upright man will not wrong his neighbor; and so all upright men should strive to see that the nation to which they belong refuses to wrong any neighbor, does justice to all within its gates as well as to the world outside, and makes the precepts of the golden rule its guide, exactly as it should be the guide of individuals in private life. The state

must be practical and efficient; but the state should ever show its fealty to lofty ideals.

"We cannot help playing a great part in the world," Roosevelt said on another occasion, "but we can very easily help playing that part well." If this meant wielding a "big stick," then so be it. Roosevelt believed not only in the blessings of civilization, but that they should be spread as widely as possible. The building of the Panama Canal, in which he aggressively separated the region of Panama from the nation of Colombia in order to win concessions so America could build and own the canal, is a case in point: Roosevelt got what he wanted through sordid intrigue and outright bullying, but he did so because he thought Colombia's selfish refusal to cooperate denied the world a clearly progressive benefit. And to a progressive Christian, there were few sins worse than selfishness.[8]

In the waning of the nineteenth century and into the dawn of the twentieth, Root, Mahan, and Roosevelt embodied a robust but reform-minded American foreign policy. A sense of duty weighed heavily upon them all, and through them upon America. Because of them, very old notions of providence and mission were adapted to a very new age of globalism.

IF THE CIVIL WAR became America's first war of humanitarian intervention, war with Spain over Cuba was from the outset the nation's first such foreign crusade. Other factors in causing war were also important, and historians have made the case for the influence of strategic imperatives, gender politics, party rivalry, economic interests, the sensationalism of the yellow press, and a general crisis of national confidence. All indeed played a role, but none was decisive. What linked them all together was the clear humanitarian crisis unfolding in slow motion on the island of Cuba. Moreover, few could agree on other motives for war: the business community and the major political parties, for example, were all sharply divided on the question of war. What got the public's attention, and what led them to apply massive amounts of pressure on their elected representatives to do something about Cuba, were not narrow questions of policy but the broadest possible considerations of humanity.[9]

In 1895, Cuban revolutionaries resumed their campaign to win independence from Spain. But the heavy-handed Spanish response—including the first use of the concentration camp, or *reconcentrado*, to incarcerate a civilian population—created a humanitarian crisis on top of a political one. General Valeriano Weyler, the architect of the *reconcentrado* policy, prosecuted a counterinsurgency war of unrelenting brutality that resulted in the deaths of close to 100,000 civilians, most of them women and children. Until this point, American officials supported Spanish rule because they too feared Cuban independence; Washington had rued Haitian inde-

pendence for nearly a century and wanted to avoid another black nationalist regime coming to power on its doorstep. Yet Americans could hardly
ignore the crisis. By the winter of 1898, with the insurgency flourishing
and the Spanish floundering, the United States began to contemplate life
alongside a free Cuba.

Already shaken by Turkish atrocities against the Armenians only a few
years before, Americans were appalled, almost unanimously, by Weyler's tactics and Madrid's obstinate refusal to consider Cuban liberty. But
their disapproval turned to fury when the Spanish-Cuban war dragged
Americans into the fighting. By the early spring of 1898, McKinley and
his administration realized that the only way Spain could be forced from
Cuba—and the crisis lifted—would be for the United States to do so
with force. McKinley neither sought nor avoided war, but was instead
resigned to it finding him. As a first step to demonstrate American power
and intent, he sent the USS *Maine*, a battleship, to anchor in the harbor of
Havana: not to fight, simply to observe. On February 9, the sensationalist
and ardently prowar *New York World* published a letter from the Spanish
ambassador in Washington, Enrique Dupuy de Lôme, to friends in Cuba,
in which Dupuy de Lôme belittled McKinley as weak and indecisive. On
February 15, less than a month after arriving in Havana and less than a
week after the Dupuy de Lôme affair, the *Maine* sank to the ocean floor,
destroyed by a mysterious explosion; 266 U.S. sailors died in the blast.
Most Americans blamed Spain for bombing or mining the ship, even
though Spain had nothing to gain and everything to lose from antagonizing the United States. But even more reasonable observers blamed the
Spanish for allowing the situation to spiral out of control to the point
where the *Maine*'s presence was even necessary.

Characteristically, religious groups led the way in both justifying
American intervention on moral grounds and rallying Americans to the
cause. The relief of Cuban suffering, the challenge to Spanish tyranny,
and the promotion of American justice and liberty were all simply too
irresistible for religious Americans to pass up. As with abolitionism before
and during the Civil War, religious groups were the most vocal advocates
for a war of humanitarian intervention. Beginning in the 1880s Christian
intellectuals argued, in forums religious and secular, that the Civil War
had been a righteous war of justice against slavery. Now, in 1898, came an
opportunity to export America's humanitarian justice. In this sense, Cuba
offered a chance for Social Gospelers and other reformers to vindicate
their progressive, interventionist beliefs first forged in the earlier crusade
against slavery.[10]

"This war is the *Kingdom of God coming*!" proclaimed the *California
Christian Advocate*, a Methodist publication, as McKinley prepared to evict

Spain from Cuba. Religious periodicals were every bit as shrill as New York's yellow press—but with a much longer, national reach. Denominational and ecumenical newspapers, pamphlets, broadsides, and newsletters informed their readers across the nation that a war for Cuba would be just and necessary. It was, they asserted, the only way to stop the bloodshed of innocents and ensure Cuban liberty. The *Methodist Review* envisioned war as "one of God's most efficient agencies for the advancement of true Christian civilization and the ushering in of brighter times for the human race." The *Congregationalist* declared its support, "For this war is to be God's means of hastening the time when all shall know him." The *Evangelist*, a Presbyterian magazine, declared that "if it be the will of Almighty God, that by war the last trace of this inhumanity of man to man shall be swept away from this Western hemisphere, let it come!"[11]

Prominent Social Gospelers, those who were able to sway not only a congregation but entire denominations, campaigned heavily for American intervention. They actively sought the burdens of humanitarian intervention, even those who were involved in the reawakening peace movement. Washington Gladden, a nationally revered Congregationalist minister from Columbus, Ohio, supported war as the only cure for Spanish barbarism and cruelty. Intervention was justified, he argued, purely because it was grounded in the progressive, selfless ideals "of a large humanity, of a pure philanthropy"—and only if McKinley intended "the holiest war that was ever waged on the face of the earth, a war into which lust of conquest and bloodthirsty passion never is permitted to enter." Even a socialist like Walter Rauschenbusch, a Baptist theologian and leading Progressive intellectual, portrayed war as a mission of mercy. Women progressives, at the center of the reform movement, were particularly important supporters of war. The Women's Christian Temperance Union (WCTU), one of the largest Protestant reform organizations and one of the most important national women's groups, supported intervention as the only means to relieve the suffering of the thousands of Cuban women and children penned into General Weyler's *reconcentrado* camps; affiliated organizations like the Christian Rescue Temperance Union followed suit. Emily Allen, a Southern Methodist home missionary and Southern progressive, also called for a war of humanitarian intervention. Though they shared the idealism of genuine pacifists, they were peace crusaders who could in good conscience support war—but only a progressive war, and intervention in Cuba seemed to be both noble and necessary.[12]

Particularly striking was the conversion of the venerable Lyman Abbott, who had succeeded Henry Ward Beecher in the pulpit of Brooklyn's famous Plymouth Church in 1885. As editor of *The Outlook*, the largest-selling Christian periodical, which had an avid secular readership,

Abbott was also one of the most influential journalists of the time. Until the war with Cuba, his views on international relations had been typical of a progressive Christian: he abhorred war and opposed virtually every instance in which the United States might use military force. But *Cuba libre* changed him. To Abbott, the plight of the Cubans at the brutal hands of the Spanish was as clear a case of Christian charity as there could be. "It is a crusade of brotherhood," he explained to readers who had grown accustomed to his antiwar polemics. "It is the answer of America to the question of its own conscience: Am I my brother's keeper?"[13]

Perhaps the nation's holiest warrior also happened to be one of its most prominent politicians: William Jennings Bryan. Known as the "Great Commoner" for his people's touch and Populist views, Bryan was a beloved figure in late-nineteenth-century America, despite having lost the 1896 presidential election to McKinley. Bryan was also a deeply devout Presbyterian, so devout that he would become an important lay leader of the emerging fundamentalist movement by attacking Darwinian evolution in the famous 1925 Scopes "monkey" trial. As his biographer Michael Kazin points out, Bryan was a Cumberland Presbyterian, a small revivalist denomination named for its birthplace in Kentucky that rejected the traditional Calvinistic doctrines of predestination and limited salvation. This optimistic, individualistic theology helped shape Bryan's progressive outlook, just as his fundamentalism kept him in communion with the ordinary and downtrodden people of rural America. He was a Christian friend and Progressive colleague of Gladden and Rauschenbusch, among many others. And as a progressive, deeply devout Christian, Bryan favored war with Spain, even though he too had supported the peace movement; 1898 was no ordinary time, and Bryan felt that the United States, as a civilized Christian nation, had a duty to uphold. He even volunteered for enlistment in the Nebraska National Guard, placing himself at Commander-in-Chief McKinley's mercy. Needless to say, Bryan did not find opportunity for a martyr's death or a hero's glory because McKinley ensured that his regiment did not see any action. Instead, Bryan spent the entire war at a camp in Florida, beating back mosquitoes and fighting off tropical disease.[14]

The most important Christian warrior was, of course, the president himself. The necessity of redeeming Cuba was one of the few views he and Bryan shared. Their presidential campaign duel in 1896 remains one of the most captivating in American political history. It was also one of the most important because it offered a stark ideological difference on vital policy issues during a time of widespread unrest and crisis. Bryan, the Democratic nominee, favored policies that would benefit the poor, especially farmers, including a currency based on silver instead of gold that would stimulate inflation and thereby reduce the value of debt. Though he had mixed feelings and had occasionally supported silver measures in the past, McKinley stood for the exact opposite: a solid, stable, gold-backed dollar. Cuba thus offered a moment of rare agreement. But they agreed on one other topic: the centrality of religion. As the religious historian Sydney Ahlstrom has observed, 1896 witnessed an unusually pious campaign: "As in no other election, both candidates virtually personified American Protestantism." The Presbyterian Bryan and the Methodist McKinley, both evangelicals and both fluent in the language of Protestant benevolence, represented perhaps the most religious presidential rivalry ever.[15]

By the 1890s, American Methodism had begun to diverge into high- and low-church branches. The high-church variant, representing the establishment and at home in big business and the corridors of power but still rooted in traditional Methodist ideals of progressive benevolence, included McKinley; the low-church strands formed the more radical holiness and Pentecostal movements. Though he could claim a theological inheritance from both strands, this division within Methodism dovetailed perfectly with the high-church McKinley's religious and political sensibilities. As a Republican, he was conservative on economics, particularly fiscal policy. But on social and cultural matters, the Republican Party had long been the home of reform, from antislavery, abolition, and Reconstruction to the crusade against alcohol. And on foreign policy, the Republicans were even more fervent moral crusaders than the Democrats. President Grover Cleveland, a Democrat who was in the White House when the 1895 Cuban revolt broke out, had steadfastly refused even to consider any policy other than an adherence to Spain's colonial sovereignty. As the party of American Catholics, moreover, the Democrats faced inherent constraints upon their ability to launch a crusade against a Catholic power. McKinley did not face any of these obstacles. Though he was not eager for war, when it came he framed it in the moralistic terms of Protestant benevolence, responsibility, and uplift.[16]

McKinley also faced differing pressures from his church. In general, Methodists agreed that there was a severe humanitarian crisis in Cuba and that the Spanish were guilty of causing it. But American Methodism also had a long history of wartime ambivalence, beginning in the Revolution and continuing through the War of 1812 and the Mexican War. While they almost unanimously supported McKinley—especially his caution and refusal to be coerced into war by the yellow press—in the winter and spring of 1898 Methodist churches mainly called for patience to find a peaceful solution. McKinley could not have helped but be affected by the sincerity of his coreligionists' calls for peace. If he was to fight a war, said his fellow Methodists, he would have to wage it on behalf of the highest ideals of Christian charity.[17]

But he would not necessarily wage a war for freedom. While Christian reform was not always simply a form of social control, it did contain a significant paternalistic strain. Protestant reformers, in other words, believed they knew what was best for other people, whether those people realized it or not, and were often eager to impose solutions upon the unwilling masses. This, we have seen, helps explain how Progressivism could fit so comfortably with imperialism and missionaries could be such ardent champions of empire.

These were the moralistic themes—Protestant reformism, humanitarianism, and paternalism—McKinley invoked in his April 11 war message to Congress, when he laid out a case for American belligerence and requested a declaration of war against Spain. To the fury of many lawmakers, McKinley emphasized humanitarian concerns, but he did not once mention Cuban independence or self-determination, not even in passing. He wanted to relieve Cubans' suffering and improve their lives, but he did not believe they could do it on their own. He castigated Spain's "cruel, barbarous, and uncivilized practices of warfare," which "shocked the sensibilities and offended the humane sympathies of our people." He argued that the "horrors of the strife" had entered "a new and inhuman phase, happily unprecedented in the modern history of civilized Christian peoples." The development of the *reconcentrado* "was not civilized warfare," he lamented in an unusually eloquent passage. "It was extermination. The only peace it could beget was that of the wilderness and the grave." Instead of harnessing Cuba's potential and improving the lives of its people, the Spanish had merely satisfied their own corrupt and selfish desires. For these reasons, U.S. intervention was justified by "the large dictates of humanity." The United States would go to war, McKinley explained, to alleviate human suffering, provide a better life for the Cuban people, and safeguard American interests in the region. "In the name of humanity, in the name of civilization, in behalf of endangered American interests which give us the right and duty to speak and to act, the war in Cuba must stop."[18] Left unmentioned was Cuban liberty, because McKinley never intended for Americans to fight for *Cuba libre*.

PROTESTANT ARDOR for a righteous, reformist war was not much of a surprise. More unexpected was the broad support it found among American Catholics. The last time the United States had fought a predominantly Roman Catholic country—against Mexico half a century before—Protestant nativism had threatened to transform it into a crusade against a papist Antichrist. But though anti-Catholicism had by no means disappeared, much had happened since the Mexican War. Thanks to immigration, there was simply a much larger population of American Catholics by 1898. Their political clout was enormous, especially in the major cities of the Northeast and Midwest, as was their political confidence. And the Civil War had broadened the terms of a more inclusive American civil religion, offering Catholics new avenues for a patriotic role in public life. One was service in the military, which Catholics joined in disproportionate numbers; indeed, well over half of the *Maine*'s casualties were Roman Catholic.[19]

As the spring of 1898 unfolded, and as war with Spain became increasingly likely, Catholics engaged in thoughtful debate about how to respond. The issues at stake were part of a wider debate about what it meant to be Roman Catholic in America. Fragmented by immigration and dispersed by geography, American Catholics were more diverse and autonomous than their European or Latin American counterparts. The Vatican disapproved of many American customs that were thought to be contaminating the church, especially the individualist, liberal ethos that permeated American culture and the separation of church and state codified in American law. It also worried that American Catholics were more likely to follow Washington than Rome. The Vatican had good reason to worry. Led by modernizing "Americanist" bishops and priests such as John Ireland, the Archbishop of St. Paul, Minnesota, many U.S. Catholics began to assert their independence in matters political, cultural, and social, though of course not ecclesiastical. Under the leadership of two conservative popes, Leo XIII (1878–1903) and Pius X (1903–1914), the Vatican tried to rein in its increasingly wayward American church. A series of papal encyclicals laid down the law, demanding that Americans reaffirm their ties to Rome. The Americanists ultimately bowed to Vatican pressure, promising to bridge the gap between their loyalties to church and country, but this could not erase the differences of American life. The Americanist strain quieted down but did not disappear.[20]

Catholic views on war with Spain were accordingly more complex than they had been during the Mexican War. Nearly every facet of the conflict with Spain would have ramifications for Catholicism. The United States would fight one of the world's preeminent Catholic powers for control of a traditional hub of New World Catholicism. But the people being oppressed by Spanish colonialism—not only Cubans, but Puerto Ricans and Filipinos as well—were also mostly Catholic. Thus any war would be a campaign *against* Catholics *for* Catholics—and largely by Catholics, too, as the *Maine* casualty figures suggest.

These opposing Catholic impulses did not cancel each other out, but they did create space for America's Catholic hierarchy to fashion a measured yet patriotic response. Leo XIII offered the Vatican's services as an intermediary between Spain and the United States and commissioned Archbishop Ireland to act as peacemaker. Deeply versed in just war theory, Ireland had his doubts that war against Spain was necessary, but he kept them mostly to himself. After his peace mission failed, this conflicted Catholic supported the war as a loyal American, though privately he was less sure. Sounding like a Protestant Social Gospeler, Ireland declared in a sermon that God had given "to this republic the mission of putting before the world the idea of popular liberty, the ideal of the high elevation of all humanity." Congressman John F. Fitzgerald, a Massachusetts Democrat and grandfather of a future president, also pledged Catholic loyalty to the American cause. "If war does come," he declared on the House floor shortly before the outbreak of war, "no more valiant, brave and heroic defenders of the national honor . . . will be found than the members of the Catholic church." Among the laity, support came from Irish and Polish Catholic immigrant communities, who equated Cuba's campaign against Spanish tyranny with their own struggles against British and Russian imperialism.[21]

The war made it easier for other marginalized religious groups to assimilate, as well, which in turn helped create an overwhelming national consensus. Since the founding of the Mormon Church, the relationship between the Latter-day Saints and the United States had been a complicated one, soured by anti-Mormon prejudice and marred by Mormon practices, such as polygamy, that contravened U.S. law. In the 1870s and 1880s, Congress passed a series of laws, capped by the Edmunds Act of 1882 banning polygamy, designed to curb Mormon autonomy; the Supreme Court duly upheld them all. Sixteen years later, a patriotic crusade in a foreign war offered Mormons a perfect opportunity to reconcile themselves with the federal government and their fellow Americans. Some Mormons opposed the war, but most church leaders encouraged voluntary enlistment in the army and called for Cuba's freedom. The Spanish-American War thus provided Mormons with an entry point into the American mainstream.[22]

As a debut on the world stage of great power politics, the Spanish-American War—a misleading name that robs the Cubans themselves of their pivotal role—could not have gone any better for the United States. It lasted for only three months, destroyed Spanish authority in the Western Hemisphere, kept Cuban revolutionaries at bay, and boldly asserted American power in both the Caribbean and the Pacific.

However, the most fateful events took place on the other side of the world, in the Spanish colony of the Philippines. In the event of war with Spain, American contingency plans called for the Pacific fleet to sail to the Philippine Islands and decimate the Spanish fleet in Manila Bay. With the outbreak of fighting in Cuba, Commodore George Dewey, the U.S. naval commander in the Pacific then based in waters off the Chinese coast, duly set course for the Philippines. The ensuing seven-hour battle resulted in a heavily lopsided American victory: ten Spanish ships and 381 sailors lost in action against no U.S. ships damaged and no American deaths. Tactically, the Philippine attack was a masterstroke. This crippling naval blow convinced the Spanish just how improbable it would be to defeat the United States, and how costly it could be if they prolonged the fighting nonetheless. But afterward, the United States also found itself controlling the fate of another Spanish colony.[23]

In 1899, when anti-Spanish Filipino insurgents under Emilio Aguinaldo—who had been fighting the Spanish for years—realized that the United States intended to keep the islands for itself and not grant them independence, they launched a vigorous anticolonial war against the occupying U.S. forces. In the United States, the anti-imperialists' concerns transformed into furious opposition that fueled the first anti-war movement in half a century. The Philippine-American War began badly for the Filipinos, who mounted open assaults against technologically superior American troops. Later that year, they switched tactics and adopted what is now a classic strategy of guerrilla warfare based on the tactics of hit-and-run, surprise attack, and support from the local population. In turn, U.S. forces waged a heavy counterinsurgency campaign that has been typical of occupying and technologically superior powers. Unsurprisingly, much of the war unfolded among civilians. The Americans had assumed the imperial role once held by the Spanish.[24]

Many supporters of the war for Cuba now found themselves opposing a war for empire, and thus opposing ratification of the Treaty of Paris. Indeed, colonialism in the Philippines injected new life into the pacifist strain in American religion that had been discredited and then silenced by the emancipation of the slaves and the liberation of the Cubans. For decades, Christian peace activists had to content themselves with promoting vague, idealistic mechanisms for world peace, such as international arbitration. Now they had an actual war, a manifestly unjust war, to crusade against.[25]

While the anti-imperialist movement was not centered in the churches, it had a strong and important religious dimension. Social Gospelers and other progressive Christians had infused the Cuban cause with sacred meaning, and their defection undermined imperialist claims to benevolence. But it did not destroy them. Instead, the defection of prowar Christians forced imperialists to claim a progressive stance of their own, thus transforming American imperialism into an expressly humanitarian endeavor, at least rhetorically. When progressive clergy who had supported a war over Cuba balked at colonizing the Philippines, they presented imperialists seeking to extend America's mission with a difficult problem, morally and politically. The Reverend Leonard Woolsey Bacon, a Congregationalist from Boston, told audiences in Massachusetts and Connecticut that while he had made his peace with a war "in the spirit of philanthropy and for the greater glory of God," he could not come to terms with an imperial policy that seemed so at odds with America's republican, anticolonial heritage. "Shall we lay down the American policy and adopt the Spanish policy?" Bacon implored his listeners. Shall Americans "lay down the policy of Washington and Hamilton" only to adopt the Black Legend atrocities "of Charles V and Philip II?" These were questions the imperialists could not simply ignore, especially when influential national organizations like the WCTU abandoned the McKinley administration over the change in mission from Cuba to the Philippines.[26]

African American clergy who had supported a war to free oppressed nonwhites in Cuba became uneasy with an annexationist policy that claimed the divine right to rule "savage" nonwhites unfit for self-government. Angered by the McKinley administration's silence on lynching and other instruments of terror in the Jim Crow South, they saw little difference in American white supremacy whether it was practiced in Atlanta, Birmingham, or Manila. As a result, influential black ministers such as Henry M. Turner, a bishop in the African Methodist Episcopal Church, turned sharply against McKinley's foreign policy.[27]

Mainline Protestant clergy, and not only from the traditional peace churches, also opposed what they believed was a nakedly racist war of conquest. If the United States had gone to war in the name of fighting Spanish imperialism, the Reverend H. M. Simmons told an anti-imperialist rally in Minneapolis, how could American imperialism possibly be justified? It was not unpatriotic to oppose imperialism; rather, "true patriotism seeks to make our country just, not big." Simmons also compared the U.S. Army's counterinsurgency tactics in the Philippines with Southern lynching of blacks. McKinley might denounce lynching at home, railed Simmons, "but has instead been sending great armies around the world . . . to lynch a people for merely wanting to practice the principles which we have taught." Simmons had little patience for self-proclaimed progressive imperialists: "Humanity is a queer name for burning homes and butchering people who were in peace before."[28]

American Catholics, understandably, were less comfortable with a war for annexation of the Philippines than they had been with a war for the liberation of Cuba. After the outbreak of war in the Philippines, their worst suspicions were confirmed by reports of U.S. soldiers desecrating Catholic churches. By 1899, despite continuing Protestant nativism and the Americanist controversy, Catholics generally felt confident enough to be able to assert their patriotism in promoting their anti-imperialism. Especially prominent was Bishop John Lancaster Spalding, a founder of the Catholic

University of America, who announced at a rally of the Anti-Imperialist League that Christians had "a higher love than love of country—the love of truth, the love of justice, the love of righteousness." Other Catholics agreed, though for more complex reasons. The same Irish and Polish Catholic immigrants who had favored war to free the oppressed people of Cuba now confronted a painful question: was their adopted country, the guarantor of their own religious liberty, actually no better than Russia or Britain? Moreover, the zeal of many Protestant missionaries seemed to confirm Catholic fears that the Philippines would provide the initial proving ground for a Protestant manifest destiny. Why else would missionaries announce their plans to Christianize the already-Catholic Filipinos? To many Catholics, the war was little more than manifest hypocrisy.[29]

Anti-imperialist lay Christians, including Protestants, took up the theme of religious hypocrisy to expose the unchristian nature of American policy. How, they asked, could a righteous nation, a redeemer nation, deceive itself into believing that its aggressive war of empire was an act of benevolence? To cast doubt on a holy war, they invoked holy gospel. When the secretary of the navy compared McKinley's actions to those of Christ, Edward Atkinson, the antislavery veteran and indefatigable founder of the Boston-based Anti-Imperialist League, exploded with incredulous rage. It was "blasphemy," Atkinson cried, "to cite the authority of Jesus Christ in justification of the slaughter of the Filipinos." Senator George Frisbie Hoar of Massachusetts—lion of the Senate, old abolitionist, staunch anti-imperialist, and president of the National Unitarian Conference—was similarly appalled that the United States had "made war on the only Christian people in the East," which "converted a war of glory into a war of shame." Not least as a Christian nation, Hoar declared on another occasion, the Philippines deserved national liberty no less than any other, "by the laws of nature and of nature's God."[30]

Some of Hoar's anti-imperialist allies were decidedly less principled. South Carolina Senator "Pitchfork" Ben Tillman, a rabid segregationist and opponent of annexation on racist and protectionist grounds (he worried about cheap agricultural imports from the Philippines), taunted Northern reformers that a "remarkable change . . . has come over the spirit of the dream of the Republicans. Your slogans of the past—brotherhood of man and fatherhood of God—have gone glimmering down through the ages." Now, Tillman rejoiced, the "brotherhood of man exists no longer." Though Hoar loathed all Tillman stood for, he lamented that he could not argue the point. Unfortunately for Southern blacks, Tillman and other Jim Crow racists could now use the white man's burden of imperialism as a justification to shoulder the white man's burden in the South.[31]

A corollary to racist anti-imperialism was not quite as poisonous, but it was powerful nonetheless: how the brutality of war and contact with Asian

Catholics and heathens would pervert the faith of Protestant America. Such fears had haunted America's missionaries since the earliest colonial days, and they returned with some force for America's imperial turn. "This is not civilization. This is barbarism," complained Representative Joseph C. Sibley, a Pennsylvania Republican, about U.S. military tactics in the Philippines. "We are taking the boys who left Christian homes, full of love of country, of patriotism, and of humanity, and brutalizing them." Sibley's clever inversions of America's customary civilizing role and the heathen's barbarian condition undermined imperialism's strongest claims: benevolence and progress.[32]

William Jennings Bryan, man of the people, agreed. He supported the conflict with Spain, but he could not support a war for conquest against a people who wanted nothing more than national self-determination. Though Bryan had lost the 1896 election to McKinley, he fully expected to be the Democratic Party's standard-bearer again in 1900. On domestic matters, the two would repeat their platforms of 1896, with Bryan running on Populist promises and McKinley in favor of sound money measures that favored industry. On foreign policy, McKinley appeared to have gained a decisive advantage with a virtually costless victory in the "splendid little war" with Spain. But on the Philippines, Bryan sensed an opening. Believing that most Americans shared his revulsion of empire, and especially of a war for empire, he attacked McKinley over annexation and began constructing his campaign for 1900 around the issue. His approach, however, was most unconventional: he urged Democrats in the Senate to vote *for* ratification of the Treaty of Paris; this way, the war would end, U.S. troops would be demobilized and sent home, and Bryan could run on a promise to use U.S. sovereignty over the Filipinos to grant them their immediate freedom.[33]

For Bryan in general, political strategy always had to possess the virtue of being true; he had to believe in his cause. Such was the case with colonialism in the Philippines, which not only offended his democratic, republican sensibilities but blasphemed against his Christian faith. Bryan was no pacifist—recall his voluntary enlistment in the war for Cuba—but he was a peace activist, mostly on traditional Christian grounds. When the United States waged war, it had to be either in self-defense or for the purest humanitarian motives—and to Bryan, empire clearly did not qualify. A war for annexation, he declared repeatedly, was un-American and unchristian, one of the deepest possible betrayals to the values of both. This was one of the main themes of his 1900 presidential campaign, punctuated by a thoughtful but unsparingly critical acceptance speech at the Democratic convention in Indianapolis. In waging a war of conquest, McKinley and the Republicans violated the nation's deepest principles; in waging a war of independence, even one against U.S. soldiers, Aguinaldo and the Filipino nationalists proved themselves truer heirs of the American republican tradition. Bryan even compared the Filipinos to Revolutionary War heroes and the Founders of 1776, and McKinley to King George III. But even "if it were possible to obliterate every word written or spoken in defense of the principles set forth in the Declaration of Independence, a war of conquest would still leave its legacy of perpetual hatred, for it was God Himself who placed in every human heart the love of liberty."

To pro-annexationist missionaries, Bryan charged that the Bible's command to " 'preach the gospel to every creature' has no Gatling-gun attachment." Forced conversions would never last because they would breed hatred rather than true Christianity. "Let it be known," Bryan rang out in an echo of Rufus Anderson, "that our missionaries are seeking souls instead of sovereignty; let it be known that instead of being the advance guard of conquering armies, they are going forth to help and to uplift," wearing only "the breastplate of righteousness, and carrying the sword of the Spirit." McKinley, a devout Christian himself, resented his policies being damned as unchristian as much as he did the comparison to George III. But the president had cause to worry, for Bryan had launched an effective attack on imperialism's claims to charity.[34]

LUCKILY FOR McKINLEY, not everyone abandoned the interventionist cause. The Spanish had behaved just as badly in the Philippines as they had in Cuba, and so many Americans did not see a difference between a war of humanitarian intervention for Cubans and a war on behalf of Filipinos. Of course, the United States had not campaigned in the Philippines on humanitarian grounds as it had in the Caribbean. But once they were there, and once they began considering the alternatives, a majority of Americans became convinced they had a moral obligation to safeguard Filipino sovereignty, through colonization of the islands if necessary because the Filipinos themselves were presumed to be incapable of self-government. If the war for Cuba had always to a great extent been motivated by humanitarian concerns, the war in the Philippines quickly became one. In this sense, in the minds of many there was no contradiction between a progressive war and a war for empire. They were one and the same.[35]

Because of their vital support for a moral crusade in Cuba, and because of their vast national constituencies, churches and missionary groups were pivotal in framing colonialism as a just cause. According to one poll, conducted in July 1900—long after the outbreak of colonial war in the Philippines—Protestant clergy were the most ardent supporters of imperialism. Bryan had recognized the allure of the faith-based case for humanitarian intervention and devoted part of his Indianapolis speech to refuting "the religious argument." So did the Anti-Imperialist League, which published a special issue of its *Broadside* specifically to discredit "The Moral and Religious Aspects of the So-Called Imperial Policy." But it was all to no avail. Some Christian leaders may have opposed the war, but most did not.[36]

Leading the way were Protestant missionaries, marching together in rare unanimity over a unique opportunity to spread the gospel in almost perfect solitude. American missionaries' ecumenical, internationalist outlook had been essential in places like China and the Ottoman Empire, where they were a minority in terms of both faith and citizenship. In the Philippines, however, they could realistically expect to have the mission field all to themselves, where they could sweep away the last vestiges of centuries of Catholic superstition and ecclesiastical tyranny. Their imperialist vision was somewhat different than the prevailing view—they still sought to spread the Protestant faith over and above secular American values—but this was a very fine distinction easily lost in the din and clamor of the emotional debate over the Philippines. The mission to the Philippines echoed—and borrowed heavily from—home missions to the Indians, an important part of the U.S. government's pacification program during the Indian wars of the 1860s and '70s. Yet mission boards saw even greater potential in the Filipinos, whom the YMCA missionary Sherwood Eddy praised as "progressive, bright and keenly interested in politics, with a natural aptitude for the fine arts and music, for draftsmanship, engineering and almost every class of fine handiwork."[37]

For most missionaries, then, the Philippines represented the apotheosis of their purpose on earth, the very essence of spiritual uplift. Denominational mission boards and interdenominational groups like the Student Volunteers grasped their chance. But they also appreciated the Philippines' strategic significance. Sounding like a strategist, or an industrialist with an eye on the fabled "China market," John Mott emphasized the Philippines' pivotal geographical location, especially its potential as a launching pad for missions all across Asia. Josiah Strong agreed in his bestselling book *Expansion Under New-World Conditions*, and added that America was now a world power and thus had little choice other than to grasp its civilizing mandate. "Such a world policy," he wrote, "is not only justified, but required, by the world life on which we have entered." The American Board of Commissioners for Foreign Missions went even further, urging McKinley to seize not only the Philippines but all Spanish colonial possessions in the Pacific. From the missionary's vantage point, the Philippines presented endless evangelistic possibilities.[38]

Like missionaries, Social Gospelers did not see a contradiction between empire and progress. And like McKinley, they saw little difference between the task America confronted in Cuba and the Philippines. In both cases, Americans had an obligation to spread the blessings of liberty, progress, and true religion. The abstemious women of the WCTU could not abide a war for empire, but most other progressive Christians could. Social Gospelers embraced the strident language of empire, most evidently in the political theology of Washington Gladden, Walter Rauschenbusch, and Lyman Abbott. Gladden even thought the Philippines marked the beginning of a new era of American Christian uplift throughout Asia. "To take control of these territories," he wrote in the pages of Abbott's *Outlook*, "means that we shall give the people a thousand times more liberty than they ever dreamed of possessing, and more than they could secure for themselves." In the Philippines, Americans could "make every man's life safe, every man's house secure," and "fill the land with schools." Concluded Gladden: "If this is imperialism, I am an imperialist." Abbott himself proclaimed a "new imperialism—the imperialism of liberty," and most progressive Christians rallied to his call. Even the activists of the WCTU, with prostitution and alcoholism in their sights, would eventually embrace social control in the Philippines even if they could not bring themselves to condone imperial control.[39]

Abbott and other progressive Christian imperialists believed they did not face an opportunity, but an obligation. Building an empire of liberty was their duty, demanded directly by God, as a specially blessed chosen people. Renouncing this sacred command was simply not an option. Mere mortals, Christian imperialists claimed, simply could not resist God's providence, leading one anti-imperialist to bemoan the "phenomenal . . . epidemic of Calvinism which has broken out among the expansionists." Josiah Strong spoke of "our duty to the world in general and to the Filipinos in particular." The Filipinos were entitled to the benefits of modern progress, but how could they possibly achieve them alone? Here, enlightened Americans would succeed where the decadent Spanish had failed. War—unsought, selfless, providential war—had forced upon the United States this humanitarian obligation. "On whom is that duty more incumbent than on ourselves?" asked Strong. The Right Reverend William Lawrence, Episcopal Bishop of Massachusetts, was conflicted about imperialism but argued that once Americans found themselves in the Philippines, they had to embrace the challenges before them with all the strength that muscular Christians could summon. "No one of us," Lawrence declared, "has a right, when those responsibilities are clear, to evade them. A timorous character makes a weak people," and Americans were neither timorous nor weak. The United States had not sought sovereignty over the Philippines, the prestigious Church Club of New York argued similarly in a statement signed by a certain Episcopal Church layman, Alfred Thayer Mahan: "Political responsibility carries with it spiritual and ecclesiastical duty."[40]

Senator Orville H. Platt of Connecticut, a deacon and Bible-school teacher in the Congregational Church and author of an eponymous leg-islative amendment that gave the United States control over Cuba just short of outright annexation, also viewed the Philippines as a sacred, unavoidable duty. Though neither Cubans nor Filipinos were capable yet of self-government, God had left it to the United States to help them achieve their full human potential. "Does not Providence, does not the finger of God unmistakably point to the civilization and uplifting of the Orient, to the development of its people, to the spread of liberty, educa-tion, social order, and Christianity there through the agency of American influence?" this architect of empire asked a skeptic in 1898. "Can you fail to see that in the Providence of God the time has come when the institu-tions of the English-speaking peoples are in final conflict with the institu-tions of despotism and irreligion, and that China is the battleground?" The United States, Platt declared, was "first in the family of nations; the head of the family has no right to disclaim an interest in the welfare of the other members."[41]

Why had this duty fallen upon the United States? And why now? As Strong, Platt, and others indicated, the answers were deceptively simple: because America was God's chosen nation, and Americans his chosen people; because they had perfected their own system of government, and could now tutor less fortunate people everywhere. We now know that the colonization of the Philippines marked the end of America's experiment in formal overseas empire. But at the time, people thought they stood at the very beginning of the greatest experiment in human relations since the birth of Christ, and that the United States had the leading role to play. From the Pilgrims and Puritans seeking liberty in the 1630s through to the Civil War, God had been preparing his people for this moment. Now, with their final task at hand, they were poised to complete their mission to the world. "Providence has given the United States the duty of extending Christian civilization, and we propose to execute it," proclaimed Sena-tor Knute Nelson of Minnesota, an abolitionist and decorated Civil War veteran. Americans were not in the Philippines "to enslave the Filipinos, but to uplift them."[42]

Yet despite Nelson's assurances, missionary progressivism and Social Gospel optimism flowed all too easily into Anglo-Saxonism and other forms of racism. Strong argued that the Filipinos were no more prepared for self-governance than children were for freedom from their parents. "As a part of the great world life," he wrote in justification of the war against Aguinaldo's forces, "these people cannot be permitted a lawless independence." And since the Filipinos were "subject to the limitations of childhood, we may also claim for them the rights of childhood." The burdens of duty could not be avoided or neglected; any attempts to do so would be an irresponsible betrayal of the Christian mission. Gladden certainly thought so. Granting the Philippines independence was "a morally unthinkable proposition," he stated flatly during the debate over the treaty. Of anti-imperialists like Bryan, Gladden lamented that it was "simply amazing that grown men, with the pages of history open before their eyes, should go on applying the maxims of our Declaration of Independence to populations like those of the Philippines." Framed in this way, such literal forms of paternalism proved impossible for progressives, deeply committed to notions of Christian responsibility and charity, to resist.[43]

Anglo-Saxonism and white supremacy had an even darker side, too, for if Americans represented the elevation of the human race, Filipinos represented its degeneration. And this darker side had a religious component, what might be called "Protestant supremacy." Most American Protestants, McKinley included, called for the "Christianization" of the Filipinos. This objective either ignored the fact that approximately 90 percent of them were already Roman Catholic or, more likely, acknowledged it but did not consider Catholicism to be a true Christian faith. The other 10 percent of Filipinos were mostly Muslim, sometimes "heathen"—usually Buddhist or animist—which made them prime targets for a proper Christian conversion. The United States could not retreat from its obligation to govern such "half-caste Christians" and "warlike Muslims," vowed Theodore Roosevelt, who became president after the assassination of McKinley, at the height of the war in 1901.[44]

And yet it did not take long for Americans to take a more cooperative approach toward Filipino Catholics. In the sliding scale of civilization, what the historian Michael Hunt has called a "hierarchy of race," Catholics were always above Muslims and other faiths. In relative terms, Catholicism could be a civilizing influence too, and U.S. officials were willing to co-opt the Filipino Catholic elite if it helped subdue the insurgency among peasants and Muslims. The establishment of the Bureau of Non-Christian Tribes in 1900 was an important part of the hardening division between semi-civilized Catholics and completely uncivilized heathens. Domestic political pressures also forced a change of attitude toward Catholics, as well as a general toning down of Protestant ambitions to launch a Filipino reformation.[45]

Addressing American Catholic concerns in the overheated atmosphere of Protestant supremacy was no simple task. If the United States was to remake the Philippines in a more progressive and democratic image, it would have to remake the role of religion in the islands while also preserving Catholicism's role. In 1899, McKinley sent the president of Cornell University, the erstwhile anti-imperialist Jacob Gould Schurman, to the Philippines to investigate possible reforms. "The very thing they [the Filipinos] yearn for is what of all others our Government will naturally desire to give them," the Schurman Commission reported, especially "religious liberty, fundamental personal rights, and the largest practicable measure of home rule," though Schurman rejected outright independence in the near term. Specifically in religious matters, this meant separating church from state, a political condition which was second-nature to Americans but completely alien to Spanish and Filipino Catholics. Nonetheless, this was bound to be popular among Filipinos—indeed, among Aguinaldo's main targets were the hated Spanish Catholic friars. Long a source of repression, the Catholic Church in the Philippines had trained very few indigenous priests and so was quite out of touch with the local population. The Church was also the islands' largest landowner, and so disestablishment provided an opportunity for mass land reform that would help alleviate poverty as well as iniquitous food shortages. In 1900, to solve such matters and smooth the transition to stable colonial rule, McKinley appointed the renowned and respected jurist, and future president, William Howard Taft as the first governor of the Philippines.[46]

While separating church from state was uncontroversial for most Americans, and while it promised to be popular with most Filipinos, it was a source of concern for the Vatican and American Catholics. The Holy See opposed any attempts to disestablish the Catholic Church, anywhere, and so its opposition was unsurprising. American Catholics were not necessarily opposed to disestablishment in principle, but they worried that it would come at the hands of zealous Protestant officials and thus destroy the Church in the Philippines. Simultaneously, back home Catholics were also in the midst of heated battles with state and local officials over the funding of school boards. Roosevelt recognized the Philippine church issue as a political danger that threatened to spark wider, explosive unrest between American Protestants and Catholics. While McKinley wanted to Christianize Filipinos—that is, convert them to Protestantism—Roosevelt believed that moral uplift "must come chiefly through making them better Catholics and better citizens."[47]

As governor, Taft quickly defused incipient tensions between Protestants and Catholics, and the United States and the Vatican. Disestablishment of the Philippine Catholic Church proceeded, as did the sale of its vast estates, but Taft traveled to the Vatican to consult with Pope Leo XIII over the best way to do so; he also consulted widely with American Catholic leaders. Through Taft, Roosevelt arranged for the repatriation of the Spanish friars and proper compensation of their monastic orders. Pleased with Washington's sensitivities to the Vatican's concerns, Leo issued an encyclical in January 1903 that reorganized the Filipino church based mostly on local authority and autonomy, though at the highest level four American bishops replaced the outgoing Spanish bishops. The Vatican singled Taft out for praise "for all the great good he has done . . . for the

interests of Catholicity in those islands." The policy of religious reform
and reconciliation proved so successful that it robbed Aguinaldo's insurgency of critical support and led many Filipino Catholics, especially the
urban and commercial elite, to collaborate with the U.S. occupation.
American Catholics agreed; within a decade, they were among the most
steadfast imperialists and consistently spoke out against Filipino independence. The result was as ironic as it was surprising: Filipinos enjoyed
religious freedom even as they lacked political independence. Religious
pluralism began to replace the enforced Roman Catholic monopoly, with
the Philippine Independent Church forming a breakaway, populist variant of Catholicism and Protestant churches being established. Beginning
with religion, the United States was already remaking the Philippines in
its own image.[48]

ALL THESE RELIGIOUS IDEAS—from providence and duty to Protestant supremacy—mattered because politicians, diplomats, and strategists
repeatedly deployed them to convince Americans to embrace a progressive
colonial mandate. They had little choice, for if the anti-imperialists established a monopoly of the moral high ground, America's imperial moment
would be short-lived indeed. This did not require much effort, for most if
not all of the influential Christian imperialists believed in America's divine
calling.

Imperialist politicians of all ideological persuasions and on both sides
of the aisle used religion to justify and explain America's paternal duty
to the Philippines; so too did influential, pro-imperialist newspapers.
Providence had long informed Americans' foreign policy and military
decisions, and thus offered the imperialists a widely familiar and popular
argument. According to Dewey, now promoted to admiral for his heroics
in the Battle of Manila Bay, it was not superior technology or the element
of surprise that won the day but "the hand of God." Such proclamations
were not unusual. Of course, providence could also be interpreted differently to mean that an embrace of imperialism was a betrayal of God's
providential mission for America. But such nuanced readings of theology were never going to be popular amid the triumphalism of victory
and in an atmosphere of global manifest destiny, social Darwinism, and
Anglo-Saxonism. Thus could a religious worldview, in the service of progress, justify war and imperialism. As the editors of the *Chicago Tribune*
wrote in a sharp rebuke of Senator Hoar that quoted his own words, it
would be difficult to find "a single great civilizing, moralizing, Christianizing movement in history . . . that has not triumphed by 'vulgar physical
force,'" of which the Civil War was the clearest example. Even a normally level-headed Unitarian like Taft could get caught up in the spirit
of a divine, progressive manifest destiny. His contact with American mis-

sionaries in the Philippines convinced him that nobody could "study the movement of modern civilization from an impartial viewpoint and not realize that Christianity, and the spread of Christianity, are the only basis for hope of modern civilization."[49]

Mahan and other strategists favoring a large foreign policy also invoked God's guiding hand in defense of empire. Though Mahan was initially "doubtful" about whether the United States stood to gain anything from seizing the entire archipelago, he eventually came round to the annexationist view. America had a duty, he believed, to uplift the human race, and God had chosen the Philippines as its first test. It now fell to Americans "to address themselves to the duty of the day," he argued in defense of imperialism, and "to see in each event the calling of God, not always clear at first, but sure to be made clear to honest search—the Christian will add, to earnest prayer." Just as God's "Personal Will, acting through all time," had assured Britain's rise to naval dominance, Mahan wrote, it was "the hand of Providence" that had enabled America to acquire the Philippines, with its natural harbors and secure access to the Asian continent. " 'Chance' said Frederick the Great. 'Deus vult' say I," he wrote to George Sydenham Clarke in the summer of 1898. "It was the cry of the Crusader and the Puritan, and I doubt if man ever utters a nobler."[50]

In the Senate, Christian imperialism found its most zealous proponent in Albert J. Beveridge, a freshman Republican from Indiana. The United States, he declared on countless occasions in purple prose that blended the most extreme forms of nationalism and providentialism, was God's chosen nation and its destiny was to build a benevolent empire for the betterment of all the world. He was the most assertive, and usually the most obnoxious, of imperialists. What few historians notice, however, is that Beveridge had essentially the same background, and emerged from the same cultural milieu, as McKinley. Like the president, then, Senator Beveridge was a progressive imperialist. Though Beveridge was a generation younger—he was born in 1862, the same year McKinley fought at Antietam—he too was born in Ohio into a morally strict, fervently patriotic, staunchly Republican, evangelical Methodist household. He also grew up listening to intensely moralistic Sunday sermons by Methodist circuit riders, and later imbibed the revivalist atmosphere as a student at Indiana Asbury University (later rechristened DePauw University), a Methodist denominational college. "Love of country was instilled with love of God," writes Beveridge's biographer, "and the youth grew up in the belief that the G.O.P. was God's helper in building a happier, nobler land." Later in his career, Beveridge would temporarily leave the Republican fold to join the upstart Progressive Party.[51]

"God's hour has struck," Beveridge declared at the outbreak of war with Spain in 1898. "The American people go forth in a warfare holier than liberty—holy as humanity." So arrived Beveridge's own historical moment. The Philippines, he believed, was God's test for Americans. This was the main theme of his 1898 senatorial election campaign, and it formed the platform throughout his first term in the Senate. "And of all our race He has marked the American people as his chosen nation to finally lead in the regeneration of the world," Beveridge said of God's providential errand in the Philippines. "This is the divine mission of America, and it holds for us all the profit, all the glory, all the happiness possible to man." Beveridge's intense nationalism was unusually strong, even in the context of his era. But it was not out of step with the times, and it was certainly not inconsistent with the man. Beveridge was a progressive—a conservative progressive, to be sure, but a progressive nonetheless, and his vision for the Philippines was based not simply on acquisitive lust or martial glory but an extreme form of Protestant reformism that would usher the entire world into the golden age of a new millennium. Beveridge genuinely believed, as did his fellow progressive imperialists, that their actions were for the good of all, for America and the world.[52]

Which returns us to McKinley. For this business-friendly Republican, foreign policy offered an outlet for his Christian reformism in a clear, simple, moralistic way that economics could not. Viewed in this light, his progressive framing of America's Philippine policy makes more sense. It echoed strongly with the voices of Christian reformers from the Benevolent Empire to the missionary enterprise. As he declared in December 1898, Americans had embarked upon a "mission . . . of benevolent assimilation," of bringing Filipinos to a culture of enlightened, Christian civilization. Annexation was "a holy cause," he proclaimed on another occasion. The "Philippines, like Cuba and Puerto Rico, were entrusted to our hands by the providence of God," he told a crowd in Boston, the headquarters of the anti-imperialist movement, during the national debate over ratification of the treaty. No doubt McKinley had other factors in mind when he decided to make the Philippines an American colony, but religious values gave him the strongest incentive.[53]

With pious foot soldiers like Mahan, Strong, Roosevelt, and Beveridge behind him—to say nothing of the thousands of churches and millions of faithful—McKinley launched America on a crusade in Cuba and the Philippines. It would be the first of many. Clearly he did so for the advantage of America. But this did not preclude a war for the betterment of humanity in the name of universal rights and freedoms as well. McKinley and his holy warriors genuinely believed, in keeping with their long-held religious beliefs, that they advanced justice and progress. The Spanish-American and Philippine-American wars were aggressively nationalistic wars fought on behalf of the entire world's welfare. As we have seen through events unfolding down the centuries, this was very much in keeping with the religious traditions of American foreign relations. The Spanish-American and Philippine-American conflicts were not America's first holy wars; they would certainly not be the last.

PART V

Woodrow Wilson and the Second Crusade

New York City, Easter Sunday, April 8, 1917. It was a difficult day for every American, but it was particularly fraught for the Reverend Henry Sloane Coffin. As the pastor of Madison Avenue Presbyterian Church, one of the more prestigious pulpits in the nation and, as a professor at Union Theological Seminary, one of the leading centers of religious learning in the world, Coffin had used the authority of his positions to condemn the war raging in Europe, pray for peace, and dissuade his own country from joining the mindless slaughter. For nearly three years, Coffin railed against the folly and obsolescence of war, against the Europeans who had brought it upon themselves, and against the "preparedness" campaign in the United States to build up the military in case the war reached America's shores. During a Christmas sermon in 1914, he told his congregation that the Europeans had proven themselves to be little better than "silly children" who petulantly, selfishly waged war with the very worst of motives: "with self-seeking patriotism, with nationalism based on brute might, with force as the arbitrament of justice." In May 1916, at the height of preparedness hysteria, he lambasted the American militarists who would commit the nation to Europe's folly. A boisterous, nationalistic ticker-tape parade down Fifth Avenue for Preparedness Day was, Coffin proclaimed, nothing but "a march into yesterday." War was a betrayal of true patriotism and true religion, and totally unnecessary for such a rich, powerful nation far removed from the fighting. In words that a year later would be considered treasonous and that would echo half a century later as his nephew William protested against Vietnam, Coffin called on his listeners to "let us as American patriots and as loyal believers in Jesus Christ resist to the utmost this attempt to deamericanize our beloved America and dechristianize our Christianity."[1]

But now that day had come, in the midst of Eastertide no less, and it placed Coffin in an awkward position. Less than a week earlier, on April 2, President Woodrow Wilson had addressed a joint session of Congress to ask for a declaration of war against Germany. Congress obliged,

233

and war was officially pronounced on April 6, Good Friday. Across the United States, Coffin and thousands of other antiwar ministers knew they would have to address the war in their Easter sermons. And they also knew they had a difficult decision: either abandon their antiwar beliefs and support the war, or maintain their dissent and face the inevitably harsh consequences from both church and state. Presbyterians were not Quakers or Unitarians: there was no pacifist tradition in Coffin's church to shield him. President Wilson himself was a devoted Presbyterian elder, and so to oppose the war was also to oppose not only the president, but also the church. Yet these considerations did not enter into Coffin's thinking. He hated war, but he was no pacifist, and his stature in the church and at Union gave him considerable authority to withstand attacks upon his reputation. He would make up his own mind.

Coffin had actually been reconsidering his position on the war for some time. "Circumstances are certainly changing," he confessed in a New Year's sermon for 1917, "and we find ourselves facing new questions, fronting new outlooks, feeling new impulses. What fresh problems each year of this awful war has forced on our thinking!" By late March, in light of these changing circumstances—especially Germany's resumption of unrestricted submarine warfare in the Atlantic, including against U.S. ships—he had decided to change course. War is "irrational," he preached on March 25, as the nation anticipated Wilson's war address, and "hellishly brutal." Coffin had been "eager to go to great lengths to avoid it, to do nothing that would make it easy for us to enter it. And lo, it is waged upon us." Just as Christ had done centuries earlier, it was now America's turn to bear the world's burden and unselfishly sacrifice for a greater good. The "cross is apparently forced on our nation," he said. This war "is not 'glorious war'; it is the senseless, hideous, butchery of brother by brother. It is everything we loathe; but so was the cross." Above all, Coffin told his rapt congregation, Americans "must set forth unmistakably for what we are contending," a cause that would be "worth the spilling of the blood of American citizens to achieve." Americans "covet nothing for ourselves" except "a world so ordered that there can be no repetition of these frightful years" and "peace . . . goodwill and brotherhood among the nations." Only for these noble goals "are we prepared to make what is to us scarcely less than a descent into hell."[2]

Thus when he mounted the pulpit on Easter Sunday, Reverend Coffin had already resolved to support the war—specifically, Wilson's call for a new world order to establish permanent peace. Wilson had tried to remain neutral, to keep America above the fray, but now war had been forced upon him. Coffin had come to believe that though all parties to the war had sinned, Germany's sins in Belgium and on the high seas were much greater than those of Britain and France. While the British and

French had imperfect democracies and ruled their global empires through the coercion of armed force, they were still democracies and much preferable to aggressive German dictatorship. Wilson's notion of a disinterested United States, with no empire or alliances to maintain, fighting not for its own interests but those of the world, struck Coffin as the most Christian foreign policy possible. To the cynics who scoffed that war was endemic to human nature, or to the selfish isolationists and steadfast pacifists who refused to bear their share of the burden, Coffin replied that this war was different. It would be a truly progressive war, a war to end all wars. On Resurrection Sunday, Coffin could see the reformation of the world unfolding, with a millennium of permanent peace at its end. Easter, he rejoiced, "is taking us back to a grave where just such idealistic hopes as ours were once buried." The world's resurrection was now in America's hands.[3]

Coffin fully converted to the cause. He joined one of the most important religious bodies participating in the war, the General War-Time Commission of the Churches, and supported the YMCA's relief programs on the Western Front. And at war's end, he was jubilant at the triumph of right over might. "Our consciences, so often puzzled by the seeming victories of iniquity and the tortures of good, find themselves exulting in a manifestly just universe," he preached on November 10, 1918, a day before the official armistice. "The defeat of a sinister world-domination has been worth everything which has been paid for it." Germany was powerful, and by many measurements should have won the war, but because its cause was unjust it lacked the favor of God. Americans had sacrificed, but it was God's providence, his designs for a more peaceful world, which in the end prevailed. America was but God's instrument, and better times lay in store for all. The Social Gospel was bringing about the kingdom of God in the United States, and Wilson was doing the same for the world. "It is a great thing," Coffin beamed a week after the war had ended, "to be able to recognise the presence of the Christian God in the events of life."[4]

Coffin's conversion from advocate of peace to crusading warrior—from wielding the shield of faith to brandishing the sword of the spirit—had been personally difficult, confusing, at times painful. But it was not unusual. Throughout the United States, ministers, priests, and rabbis who had scorned war as immoral and evil in 1915 and 1916 hailed its power to cleanse and renew the nation, and the world, in 1917 and 1918. In New York alone, Coffin underwent his own conversion alongside many others.

Monsignor Michael J. Lavelle, the venerable rector of St. Patrick's Cathedral, had prayed for peace as fervently as Coffin and had enjoined the city's Roman Catholics to follow suit. In 1915, he officiated a special mass for peace. "Americans have special reason for gratitude," he prayed at the end of 1916, "because of the peace, prosperity and stability which

have been ours, and which we hope will abide and increase with us for-
ever." Yet a year later, Father Lavelle could be found blessing a Service
Flag for U.S. troops bound for Europe and calling on Congress to grant
Wilson extraordinary powers to prosecute the war. Lavelle's superior,
James Cardinal Farley, the archbishop of New York, made a similar jour-
ney from dove to hawk.[5]

No less dramatic was the transformation of Rabbi Stephen Wise. A
deeply committed social reformer, Wise founded the Free Synagogue of
New York in 1907 to enable him to spread a progressive agenda free from
Conservative or Orthodox interference. Progressivism brought him into
the Democratic Party fold, which in turn made him a strong supporter of
Woodrow Wilson. Though he sympathized with the British and French
before 1917, Wise was desperate to keep the United States out of the
war, and he mobilized Jewish sentiment behind Wilson's policy of neutrality. To further this goal, he had been a founder of the Anti-Preparedness
Committee and a spokesman for the antiwar group American Union
Against Militarism. Indeed, before 1914 Wise had been a major advocate for international cooperation and predicted the eventual abolition
of war. Wilson's embrace of preparedness in late 1915 came as a shock
to Wise that bordered on betrayal. The rabbi wrote Wilson "how deeply
I deplore" the fact that the president was "accepting and advocating a
preparedness program." Yet by early 1917, Wise had come to believe that
only the United States could impose a peace settlement, and in order to
do that the country would have to enter the war. On that same fateful
Sunday in April 1917, he delivered a prowar sermon that, like Coffin's,
threw support behind American intervention while continuing to abhor
war in general. The break with his progressive, pacifist friends was bitter and painful, but Wise saw no other choice. It was also a complete
break, and he was soon denouncing antiwar protesters for having "served
the interests of Germany." Like the vast majority of American clergy that
weekend, he would only sanction a progressive war, hopefully for the last
time in history. Wise, however, also had other motives: as a Zionist, he
hoped the war would now hasten the establishment of a Jewish homeland
in Palestine.[6]

The personal stories of Reverend Coffin, Monsignor Lavelle, and Rabbi Wise are representative of broader trends in the religious influence on
American foreign relations, and in American life. As we shall discover,
their motives were not always identical, or at times even similar, but
mostly they addressed the world crisis in compatible and complementary
ways. First, the fusion of Protestant-Catholic-Jew in American civil religion, now instantly familiar, was of course nothing new, but the Great
War marked its period of maturation: for the first time, Catholic and
Jew were becoming full partners in, rather than adjuncts to, an American

Creed. These developments began in the World War I era and not, as is commonly assumed, World War II and the Cold War.

Second, Coffin, Lavelle, and Wise were indicative of religion's importance in thinking about the morality, ethics, and ultimate meaning of the war. Americans were by no means alone in turning to faith for answers—religion played a central role in European and Canadian attitudes, as well—but clergy in the United States faced a different set of circumstances and pressures and responded to them differently.[7]

Third, these three religious leaders epitomized the American response to war, from outright opposition to enthusiastic support. Americans had been reluctant to intervene in Europe, for a variety of reasons. When they finally did, it would be not in the name of national interests but for the good of humanity. Religious leaders, and through them their congregations, invested America's role in the war with transcendent meaning and millennial yearning. They provided the moral platform from which the United States would launch a new world order.

CHAPTER THIRTEEN

The Idealistic Synthesis

T HE WAR THAT ERUPTED in the heart of Europe in August 1914 was the most significant event in world history in a century. It tore apart the existing order throughout Europe and beyond and dramatically altered the international system itself. Though the United States at first remained aloof from the fighting, it could not help but be affected by the Great War. Soon, even daily life in America would also become subsumed by the effects of war.

The response of the nation's religious communities was important, for they commanded the attention and respect of millions of Americans, though it was also mixed. Some opposed war, any war, on principled grounds of Christian pacifism. Others, mainly immigrants from belligerent nations in Europe, opposed an American war against their native land. But many supported a war to aid what they unequivocally saw as a noble struggle of the democratic Allies—led by Britain and France—against German aggression and militarism. These ultrapatriotic war hawks envisioned a righteous America intervening on the side of civilization and enforcing a settlement upon Germany and its partners in crime. In 1914, there was little clarity in the conflict between American pacifists and war hawks. But as the war continued, as a settlement seemed ever more distant, and as neutrality became more difficult to sustain, pacifists and hawks hardened their positions into irrevocable moral claims that had a spiritual core. Pacifists saw no nation as justified in waging war, while war hawks celebrated Britain—and by extension America—and vilified Germany. Though they could not admit it, each side represented a kind of idealism that conditioned their response to war, and in particular to this war.

By 1917, however, neither pacifists nor war hawks could command a majority of Americans, even within the churches. What they did instead was combine to produce an idealistic synthesis that borrowed elements from both to produce something different and more relevant to the needs of the time. This third group mirrored the Wilson administration's own response to the war, and in the process helped to condition it. Like the pacifists, they opposed military intervention—until, that is, they believed the United States had no other realistic choice. Like the war hawks, they advocated fighting alongside the Allies in a war for democracy against the authoritarian warmongering of Germany—while also acknowledging America's own sins and part in bringing the world to war. Like the pacifists, they were internationalists; but like the war hawks, they were also nationalistic patriots who, in 1917, accepted war as unavoidable. They were neither doves nor hawks, but both. They were something completely new and different: America's first-ever liberal internationalists.

THE PERIOD BETWEEN 1914 and 1916 was the high-water mark for the American peace movement. After that, as the United States inched closer every day to joining the war, opponents of American belligerency had an increasingly difficult case to make without sounding unpatriotic, even seditious. By 1917, they had dwindled down to a small cast of hard-core activists who were willing to serve prison time for their beliefs. Throughout, the vast majority of American pacifists were motivated by religious conviction.

This was even more the case before 1914, when the peace movement was almost exclusively a Christian—indeed, Protestant—endeavor. Clergy, churches, and laymen and -women dominated American pacifism, be it through organizations like the venerable American Peace Society or through regular venues such as the annual Lake Mohonk conferences and Chautauqua meetings, both in upstate New York. The traditional peace churches, led by the Society of Friends, played an inordinately large role in the peace movement, but also important were other liberal denominations, especially the Unitarians and Universalists. Established mainline churches did as well, especially Congregationalists, Episcopalians, and Methodists. They emphasized the ethics of the New Testament and a politics of the Social Gospel, and they muted Calvinism in favor of the more diffusive "Fatherhood of God" and "Brotherhood of Man" that would become staples of the American civil religion. The peace movement, discredited by its inability to solve the problem of slavery, lay dormant between the Civil War and the Spanish-American War, but the annexation of the Philippines brought it back to life and swelled its ranks with newcomers. Some, such as the industrialist Andrew Carnegie, had a similarly liberal, ecumenical outlook and adapted their faith to science. Others were also faith-based but Catholic or Jewish, although their participation in dissent was muted by fears of appearing un-American and unpatriotic. And many others were not religious at all, including skeptics like the novelist Mark Twain and secular socialists. Still, despite these modest inroads, on the eve of war in Europe the American peace movement remained a pious, mostly Protestant affair.[1]

The dramatic events of August 1914 sent shock waves through the peace movement and galvanized it for a massive antiwar crusade. This war, pacifists realized, would confront them with their greatest challenge since 1860. Christian pacifists from a variety of backgrounds moved quickly to establish national organizations devoted to pursuing two aims: an end to the fighting in Europe and U.S. neutrality. To serve these ends, Fannie May Witherspoon and Tracy Mygatt, active laywomen in the Episcopal Church, combined political radicalism with a faith in the New Testament to form the Christian Socialist League in 1914. Later that same year, Andrew Carnegie plowed several of his millions into forming the Church Peace Union, an avowedly ecumenical initiative that aimed to promote both international and ecclesiastical harmony. With encouragement from British Quakers who had founded their own peace group, American peace advocates also established the American Fellowship of Reconciliation in 1915, which embraced the New Testament as its guiding philosophy; within a year, it would become the dominant peace group in the United States. In turn, groups such as these spawned others. In 1915, for example, Church Peace Union used its Carnegie money to fund the establishment of the American League to Limit Armaments under the leadership of Hollingsworth Wood, a Quaker attorney. The next year, Church Peace Union hosted a massive "Conference of Peacemakers" in New York that brought together all the main peace groups, including the Woman's Peace Party, the American Peace Society, the League to Enforce Peace, the American Neutral Conference Committee, and the World Peace Foundation.[2]

Prominent antiwar Americans cooperated with these and other groups, but they were perhaps even more effective when drawing attention to the cause by freelancing on their own. Combining a strong Social Gospel commitment to justice and reform with a mordant critique of modern American life, most of these pacifist celebrities advanced some form of socialism or radicalism, especially as the war dragged on. Some—such as Stephen Wise; John Haynes Holmes, president of the Unitarian Fellowship for Social Justice; or Kirby Page and Harold Gray, Disciples of Christ evangelicals and YMCA workers—were prominent within the religious community. Others, such as A. J. Muste, represented a new generation who would use their opposition to the Great War as a basis for future pacifist crusades.[3]

The Great War also marked the emergence of Norman Thomas, one of the American Century's most persistent dissidents. Thomas would become better known to later generations as a perennial Socialist Party candidate for president of the United States, but he got his start in the heady Christian socialism then fashionable among young Social Gospelers. Of the older generation, only Walter Rauschenbusch—whom Thomas greatly admired and avidly read—had seriously engaged with socialism and Marxism, but around the time of the war the Social Gospel was in the midst of taking a sharp leftward turn. After graduating from Princeton, where he met not only Wilson's future aide Raymond Fosdick but Woodrow Wilson himself, Thomas enrolled as a student at Union Theological Seminary, where he came into contact with Henry Sloane Coffin. At Union, Thomas trained for the ministry, and afterward was ordained as a Presbyterian minister. He then apprenticed at a Manhattan church before taking up the pastorate at East Harlem Presbyterian, a mission church with close ties to Union Theological; he was at East Harlem when the war broke out. He later claimed to not only "being a pacifist on religious grounds," but also that World War I "was an imperialist war." Union had been a haven for young, idealistic pacifists, but that was before April 1917—before, that is, America entered the war—when most of the student body mobilized in support of Wilson and the war. When Thomas continued his peace advocacy, the Presbyterian Home Missions Council, with the help of those at Union, eased him out of his position at East Harlem.[4]

Other peace activists had a more national following, though their stance on the war would tarnish them irrevocably. For more than two decades, Jane Addams had been a leader of social reform and women's rights in America. She was also one of the nation's most renowned and respected pacifists, a conviction that largely stemmed from her commitment to reform, which itself had been stimulated by a trip to England in 1888 and visits with the evangelical reformers of Toynbee Hall in London's notoriously destitute East End. Although she had been raised in a pious household and attended Rockford Female Seminary in Illinois, Addams had not received the theological training that Muste, Thomas, and others had. After a period of doubt and aimlessness, she had something of a mild born-again experience and was baptized into the Presbyterian Church. She would always wear her faith lightly, and at Hull House, her settlement house that administered to the poor of Chicago, the new discipline of sociology and the theory of pragmatism would eventually supplant the Social Gospel. But faith nonetheless remained central to her own reformist outlook and a source of her pacifism, especially the teachings of Jesus. She had opposed war with Spain and the annexation of the Philippines, and would renew her peace vows during the Great War. She worked with the Quakers, Church Peace Union, and the Fellowship of Reconciliation to bring an end to the war and prevent American entry. Her wartime pacifism landed her in trouble several times and, in the year after April 1917, eventually ruined her reputation among most Americans. Yet she continued to insist that the teachings of Jesus could not possibly be seditious.[5]

Concerned about the health of world Christianity and the future of missions and eager to find a constructive role for the YMCA, John

Mott traveled to Europe between September and December 1914. Taking advantage of America's official neutrality, he visited Britain, France, and Germany, and was appalled by the militarist fervency of the people, including their Christian leaders. But he was also heartened by the amount of serious, thoughtful reflection on the meaning of the war and on plans to ensure that it would never happen again. Upon his return, he told one of his patrons, John D. Rockefeller Jr., of the "holy war" mentality that prevailed on the continent and the "indescribably awful" suffering that flowed from "rivers of pain." In a meeting with his friend Woodrow Wilson, Mott urged the president to maintain American neutrality. The United States must "keep our moral powder dry," which would give Wilson an "absolutely unique opportunity" to broker an enduring peace settlement once the Europeans had exhausted themselves on the battlefield. What he witnessed in Europe, followed by counsel from Quaker friends in Britain, convinced Mott to become a founding member of the American Fellowship of Reconciliation.[6]

During the first phase of the conflict, in 1914 and 1915, antiwar activists had little trouble making their case. All they needed to do was point to the gruesome, hellish warfare in the trenches of Europe to illustrate how tragically pointless it all was. "Contrary to our fervent prayers and earnest hopes, the Great War is still raging," preached the Reverend Harry E. Stocker in the Moravian Church of Charlottesville, Virginia. Stocker pointed out that the "work of destruction" was costing Europe over one hundred million dollars a day. If the war paused for only ten days, he claimed, the nations at war could use the savings to fund "all Christian work at home and abroad for a whole year." Even worse was the toll of death and human suffering, with millions "killed or maimed" and even more "shut up in prison camps in Europe and Asia." The war had no redeeming purpose or attendant benefits, lamented Stocker, and had to stop at once. At the very least, America must avoid involvement in such collective madness.[7]

In 1916, as the war continued in Europe and as the preparedness campaign at home gained momentum, peace crusaders found that their message was becoming increasingly controversial. But they continued nonetheless. Scarred by their support of unjust wars in the recent past, even some who sympathized with the Allied cause fiercely opposed preparedness. In particular, imperialism in the Philippines had embarrassed many of its Social Gospel supporters and made them doubt that war could ever be progressive. "One shudders to recall the temper of the time," Washington Gladden recalled of 1898. "I wonder if we have not moved forward a little since that day." Preparedness, he and many other Social Gospelers felt, was the first step down the road to war, and they opposed it with all the moral authority at their command.[8]

One of the most pugnacious antipreparedness speeches came from the Reverend Martin D. Hardin, pastor of the Third Presbyterian Church in Chicago. Speaking to the Union Ministers' Association in February 1916, in a speech quickly entered into the *Congressional Record*, Hardin could not believe that Americans were even contemplating participation in the war. If "every cabinet and council over there [in Europe] had been made up of members taken from their lunatic asylums," Hardin chided, "it is doubtful if they could have brought such havoc and universal misery." No nation, not even America, could win such an apocalyptic contest. But if it waited, patiently and peacefully, the United States "at the close of this stupid struggle . . . will stand forth incomparably [as] the great nation of the world" and, free of the taint of war, would be able to impose its own enlightened settlement on the unreformed nations of Europe. And what kind of peace did Hardin envision? A settlement based on "real democracy" and a "federated world in which all men may be comparatively free and safe."[9]

Many conservative Christians were also suspicious of preparedness and strongly opposed U.S. intervention. Some were Protestant separatists who zealously guarded their autonomy from the state. Others were Holy Spirit charismatics who loved the New Testament above all else. Many were both, antigovernment nonconformists who also believed that taking human life, especially in a dubious cause, was morally wrong. A. J. Tomlinson, founder of the Church of God, a Pentecostal denomination in Tennessee, called the preparedness campaign an "iron hand" and a "cruel monster" that would split American families apart by robbing them of husbands, fathers, and sons.[10]

Immigrant communities also opposed preparedness and intervention, albeit for very different reasons. In particular, German-Americans endured their own persecutions just for being German. Communities where the German language was still widely spoken, mostly in the Midwest, were particularly harassed. "Church Germans" who worshiped in their native tongue, mainly Lutherans and Catholics, saw their basic religious liberties curtailed while living in the United States. A young Reinhold Niebuhr lamented that his fellow German-Americans clung desperately to old customs that were unsuited to American life and unwelcome in a time of war, but it was in their churches that they found solace, solidarity, and safety in numbers.[11]

Walter Rauschenbusch felt this resentment more keenly than most, especially when many of his Social Gospel comrades began to turn against Germany. Rauschenbusch had turned his back on the very idea of progressive warfare after the war in the Philippines. Following the outbreak of war in Europe, he joined the Fellowship of Reconciliation, where his socialism and pacifism could flourish in a protected environment. But he was also of German ancestry, had lived for a decade in Germany, spoke the language, and remained close to German culture. Thus in addition to his peace witness, Rauschenbusch refused to back a war against his native country, especially when the British and French, with their empires, aristocracies, and deeply unequal industrial societies, were no freer of sin than the Germans. "The current of public opinion has been so overwhelmingly hostile," he wrote his friend Thomas Hall in November 1914, "that a man feels like a Protestant in Spain if he stands up for Germany." His friends did not discuss the war in his company, "which means they don't like to remind me that I belong to a disreputable family." Later, Hall would be dismissed from his teaching post at Union for expressing pro-German views. "It is indeed a cross which we have to bear just now because of our German names and affiliations," Charles W. Wendte, general secretary of the International Congress of Free Christians and other Religious Liberals, complained in a letter to Rauschenbusch. "Such is the spirit of Militarism!"[12]

Irish-American Catholics also supported neutrality, though for different reasons. They may have been agnostic about Germany, but they loathed Protestant Britain for its domination of Catholic Ireland and found it difficult to imagine waging war in partnership with the British Empire. Irish-American Catholics exploded in anger when the British suppressed the nationalist Easter Rising in Dublin in 1916 and executed its leaders, which of course complicated any possible American approach to the Great War. These sentiments, expressed by mainly Democratic communities in an election year, at a time when the country was drifting toward war and an alliance with Britain, severely constrained Wilson's freedom to maneuver. Moreover, a majority of the Catholic hierarchy, and of laymen's groups like the Knights of Columbus, were Irish-American. Yet so concerned was the Catholic hierarchy with Americanization and patriotism that they pledged support for Wilson no matter which path he chose. It was every Catholic's duty, declared James Cardinal Gibbons, the widely recognized leader of the American church, in a 1916 speech, "to take an active, personal and vital interest in the welfare" of the United States, and that it should take priority over affections or loyalties to any other country.[13]

YET DESPITE ALL the unease, the war began to draw the United States into its orbit, and the pacifist initiative became increasingly difficult to maintain. To counter an Allied blockade of Europe, in February 1915 Germany declared the waters around the British Isles to be a war zone and any vessel within them to be a legitimate target for German submarines. This blanket declaration covered passenger ships the Germans suspected of carrying supplies for the Allies. One of the first ships to be sunk by German U-boats, the British steamship *Falaba*, resulted in one

American death and confronted the Wilson administration with the possibility of more to come. More—many more—did come six weeks later, when U-boats struck and sank another British passenger ship, the *Lusitania*. This time 1,200 noncombatants died, among them 128 U.S. citizens. Even though the *Lusitania* was carrying Allied munitions, American opinion was universally appalled by what many condemned as German savagery and inhumanity. Germany, of course, saw things differently: the United States had always traded heavily with Great Britain, and the war only increased this relationship. While U.S. merchants lost little by complying with the British blockade of Germany, they could not afford to obey a German blockade of Britain. The Wilson administration's policy of neutrality, in other words, was not really neutral at all.[14]

Wilson's initial response was a classic example of Americanism blended with Christian imagery of turning the other cheek, of mixing Lincoln and Christ. "The example of America must be a special example," he said in a speech in Philadelphia three days after the sinking of the *Lusitania*, "not merely of peace because it will not fight, but of peace because peace is the healing and elevating influence of the world, and strife is not." There is, he piously declared, "such a thing as a man being too proud to fight. There is such a thing as a nation being so right that it does not need to convince others by force that it is right." However, he soon bowed to public outrage and pressure from within his own administration and issued three stern warnings to Germany not to repeat such an atrocity. Berlin took note, but the U-boats continued to prowl the waters of the North Atlantic.[15]

This firmer stance caused a bitter rift between Wilson and America's most prominent Christian peace advocate and anti-interventionist—who also happened to be the nation's chief diplomat. Secretary of State William Jennings Bryan had already embarked on his own peace crusade before the war. One of his first initiatives as secretary of state was the launch of the Peace Treaties, a series of bilateral agreements that would allow the United States to manage world peace by mediating disputes before they were allowed to escalate into war. The Peace Treaties, thirty in all with eventually twenty ratified by 1914, were something of a forerunner to the League of Nations, but their failure to prevent the outbreak of World War I seriously undermined their credibility. Undeterred, the ever-optimistic Bryan redoubled his efforts after August 1914. As we saw during the Spanish-American War, Bryan was no pacifist. But the imperialist turn in the Philippines forced him to rededicate his Christian peace advocacy and brought him to a more uncompromising position. Yet for all his oratorical gifts and political glory, Bryan's religious appeal was by now fairly limited. His gentle, optimistic belief in human progress was ill-suited to the hard-shell, premillennialist fundamentalism that was then coalescing, and his simple faith in traditional religion was increasingly out of step with the forward march of Social Gospel modernism. By being sympathetic to the political and theological claims of both fundamentalists and Social Gospelers, Bryan merely ensured that he would not persuade many of his fellow Christians to follow him on his latest mission. In foreign policy, one historian has aptly termed his clashing, oxymoronic ideals "missionary isolationism." In his characteristically quixotic crusade, Bryan converted few who were not already committed against the war. When he discovered he could not convert his president and fellow Presbyterian, Bryan resigned and returned to the political wilderness.[16]

But Wilson also ran into trouble with pro-Allied militarists who did not find his policies firm enough. Like the peace crusaders, the militarists deployed Christian imagery and idealism in service to their cause. Most religious supporters of preparedness also strongly supported the British, for they identified Britain, and to a lesser extent France, with democracy and Germany with tyranny. For Anglophiles, such as Episcopalians, this was a natural position to take. In a January 1915 sermon, for example, the minister of Grace Episcopal Church in Medford, Massachusetts, damned Germany's "challenge of a definitely anti-Christian philosophy of the state," which presented a "far greater danger which threatens our democratic institutions" than war. "In her mad lust for domination Germany has sent forth a ringing challenge to the heroic soul of Christendom. . . . We are being driven to a decision. The world of easy-going tolerance is passing away." William M. Walton, the Episcopal Archdeacon of Arkansas, angrily protested to Walter Rauschenbusch that "the crimes of Germany are only surpassed by her mendacity. If it were in my power, I would place a gun in the hands of every man, woman and child" living in the Allied countries so that "Germany might be taught the lesson that she cannot defy and ignore the Christian sentiment of the world." Other mainline Protestants also felt the emotional pull of old England, especially from those denominations—Congregationalist, Presbyterian, Methodist—that had originated in the British Isles. Reverend Henry A. Stimson of the Manhattan Congregational Church—whose namesake and nephew Henry L. had been President Taft's secretary of war and would later serve as secretary of state to Herbert Hoover and secretary of war to Franklin Roosevelt—argued in a 1915 book on the war's "ethical factors" that "England, with whom we in America are most closely related, has steadfastly maintained the duty of peace, and respect for treaty obligation toward weaker states" by coming to the aid of Belgium, "and has done everything in her power to maintain this position." Charles Henry Parkhurst of the Madison Square Presbyterian Church in New York went even further and called on Wilson to intervene in a "humanitarian contribution to the security of the public."[17]

Nobody pushed the divinity of intervention harder than the antithesis to William Jennings Bryan: Theodore Roosevelt. Incensed by what he deemed Wilson's timidity, Roosevelt agitated constantly for America to side with justice and right against Prussian autocracy. Continuing the biblical rhetoric from his 1912 Bull Moose campaign, Roosevelt appealed for a progressive policy based on a potent blend of muscular Christianity and the Social Gospel. A 1916 essay, "Fear God and Take Your Own Part," outlined his message. Calling on Americans to "love God, respect God, honor God" by "obeying . . . the great and immutable law of righteousness," the former president argued that those who feared God were those who unselfishly obeyed his law and furthered his kingdom on earth. This was the proper Christian basis for industrial relations as well as foreign relations, for personal as well as national conduct.

It was a distinctly Old Testament view, with Roosevelt assuming the role of a fearsome prophet ready to do battle and bear hardship in service to a glorious cause. "When we sit idly by while Belgium is being overwhelmed," he proclaimed in a biting, thinly veiled critique of Wilson,

> and rolling up our eyes prattle with unctuous self-righteousness about "the duty of neutrality," we show that we do not really fear God; on the contrary, we show an odious fear of the devil, and a mean readiness to serve him. But in addition to fearing God, it is necessary that we should be able and ready to take our own part. The man who cannot take his own part is a nuisance to the community, a source of weakness, an encouragement to wrongdoers and an added burden to the men who wish to do what is right.

Yet Roosevelt also weaved New Testament themes of justice and eternal peace on earth with the fire-and-brimstone prophecy. He claimed to be rescuing the New Testament from the pacifists, for "the Gospels do not deal with war at all." The result was a peculiar appeal to the idealism of both war and peace—or, more accurately, peace through war. If the democratic promise of America really was the world's last best hope—and Roosevelt very much believed it was—then it was up to its people to fear God and take their own part in the Great War. "We are the citizens of a mighty Republic consecrated to the service of God above, through the service of man on this earth," he concluded. Now it was time for God's people to fulfill their almighty obligation.[18]

THIS WHIPSAW of idealisms, between the extremes of Bryan's sacred peace and Roosevelt's righteous war, produced a synthesis that eventually accepted intervention but only on the most avowedly progressive terms. It also produced a foreign policy that was both nationalist and internationalist. As we have seen, this was a common feature of American history. Not coincidentally, this was where Wilson himself ended up by 1917. However, the liberal internationalists and ecumenists of the mainline churches had envisioned this new world order from the very beginning of the war.

The liberal internationalist position anticipated Wilson's because they all responded to the same events from a similarly theological-moral perspective. Wilson was a politician—a supremely successful politician—and so not only had to balance a variety of concerns and commitments, he also had to be willing to compromise and moderate his own views if necessary. No successful politician can defy this iron rule of democratic politics. And of course, as his biographer John Milton Cooper reminds us, Wilson did not take the nation into war for a specifically religious reason or because God told him to. Nonetheless, it is striking how similar, identical even, his response to the European war was to that of his fellow mainline, ecumenical Protestants. Neither wanted the United States to join the war; both wanted to maintain some form of neutrality, even if their sympathies tended toward Great Britain and away from Germany; both envisioned the United States brokering a peace settlement that had a world federation at its core; and in 1917, both would accept war as a last resort. For Wilson as for the churches, this would be a war for the good of the world to ensure perpetual peace. It was an ideological, theological blend of William Jennings Bryan and Theodore Roosevelt, and it would produce what one historian has aptly called a "war for righteousness." For Lyman Abbott, it would be nothing less than a "twentieth century crusade."[19]

As internationalists, mainline Protestants envisioned a world in which nations were fundamentally interconnected and mutually dependent; contrary to its mythic tradition of isolationism, the United States was no exception. However, as nationalists, they also assigned the leading role in managing this interconnected world system to the United States. Without America's political, economic, moral, and spiritual guidance, the world system would collapse in a fury of competing petty interests and jealousies. Liberal, mainline internationalists were thus among the first to recognize a complex phenomenon that, after the interruptions of two world wars and the Great Depression, would reorder the world and its inhabitants: globalization.

It was no coincidence that religious Americans were among the first to recognize the emergence of a new global community. Christianity, after all, is a world religion that claims universal adherence; Jesus died not only for Christians, but for everyone. For over a century, American Protestant missionaries had been living life on the cutting edge of globalization, while the Protestant ecumenical movement had been cooperating intimately with sister churches in Europe, Canada, and elsewhere. In both enterprises, missionaries and ecumenists had benefited from the increasing speed of travel and communications, from swifter telegraph lines to faster shipping. They thought in global terms because they lived global lives. From these experiences, they perceived the technological changes that were bringing the world closer together. As early as 1891, Josiah Strong had pointed out that a traveler in midcentury could expect a journey from Boston to Oregon to take up to eight months; by 1891, the same journey had been cut to under a week. Three decades later, Harry Emerson Fosdick, a Baptist minister in a Presbyterian church and one of the most important religious figures of the first half of the twentieth century, reinforced the same point by observing that a single telegraph message from New York could circle the globe, making stops en route in Denver, San Francisco, Manila, India, and England—"around the world in nine minutes!"[20]

However, the outbreak of World War I, and especially its spread to the world beyond Europe, demonstrated that the new global interconnectedness could also be destructive. The challenge was to fix the broken world system by replacing it with a new global order, grounded in Christian principles of love and brotherhood and underwritten by American leadership. Rather than vindicate the smug self-righteousness of American isolation, the war had merely shown liberal Christian internationalists how inescapable world problems really were—and how necessary the United States was to solving them. Together, and only together, Christianity and Americanism could save the world. The "Christian social order," concluded a wartime Protestant study group, "includes all the world. It transcends, reconciles, and unites all nations and all races." This was something of a paradoxical worldview, based as it was on cosmopolitanism and tolerance that could only be safeguarded by the Christian faith, but it helps explain why religious internationalists claimed that their "new task . . . is to Christianize America's international relations."[21]

Mainline Protestants had even more to offer to a foreign policy based on interconnectedness: peace through mutual dependence. Since the interdenominational cooperation of the antebellum Benevolent Empire and Evangelical Alliance, Protestants had been searching for ways to further religious harmony. By the end of the nineteenth century, their endeavors had acquired a new urgency: not only were the new Catholic and Jewish immigrants challenging Protestantism's demographic dominance, and not only were industrialization and urbanization undermining social cohesion, but Darwinism and biblical criticism were threatening the bases of faith itself. In such an atmosphere of crisis, denominational rivalries seemed petty indeed. Abroad, Protestant missionaries were too small in numbers and authority and could not really function alone; they found that cooperation with other denominations and foreign missionaries was a matter of survival. The same was true for the Social Gospel at home, where interdenominational cooperation furthered the pursuit of an equitable and just society. Finally, the ecumenical spirit of strength and efficiency in numbers suited the Progressive era's "search for order." As a means for conflict resolution, church unity was ideal. After all, asked one ecumenist, "What does Christian union amount to if it will not enable us to confer with brotherly freedom upon the points of difference between us?" This was the impulse that produced the Federal Council of Churches (FCC) in 1908. And to the ecumenists, the implications for world politics were obvious: if an interdenominational organization (such as the FCC) could bring about religious peace, then surely an international organization (such as the League of Nations) could bring about world peace.[22]

Independently, then, the mainline churches had already sketched out the principles that would soon be better known as Wilsonianism—peace without victory, democracy promotion, self-determination, cooperation through international organization—long before the United States had entered the war. Much of this stemmed from the Social Gospel and its plans for a just and equitable industrial democracy. Walter Rauschenbusch was the Social Gospel's foremost theorist, and though he could not support a war against Germany his writings supplied the ideological justification in applying Social Gospel ecumenism to international relations. The first principle was the tolerance of pluralism as a way to achieve progress. The "Christian Church," he wrote in a treatise on the premises of the Social Gospel, "can tolerate a large diversity of religious forces and forms of expression, provided they all serve the common good." This did not mean that all religions or denominations were equal, only that the largest and strongest faiths should respect the smallest and weakest in the name of justice and fairness. But in respecting diversity, the largest faiths had a duty to lead the others toward justice. The second principle was the importance of democracy as the foundation for peace and progress. "Despotic government" lacked consent and could only resort to the use of "plentiful force to keep its unnatural structure erect." In contrast, the "spread of democracy has brought a great softening of the horrors of criminal law and it will yet bring us a great lessening of militarism." Rauschenbusch wrote for a domestic audience looking for answers to the questions of industrial relations, but the principles could just as easily be applied to international relations. Indeed, on the eve of war he recognized the utility of the Social Gospel in the wider world, what he called the "demands for social righteousness and fraternity on the largest scale."[23]

Despite the pro-Allied sympathies of many liberal Protestant clergy, the mainline ecumenical worldview was predicated upon a peace without victory for the benefit of all. Nationalism survived as the necessity of American leadership, but to the ecumenists this was not a contradiction. Progress required action, and action would not just happen on its own. As a disinterested nation, a powerful nation, a responsible nation—above all as a Christian nation—the United States was obligated to assume the mantle of leadership. To Theodore Roosevelt, this meant Americans taking their own part. But to the liberal internationalists, it meant embracing that staple of Christianity, sacrifice. If war were to come, it must not be waged for selfish, sinful reasons, but in a spirit of sacrifice for the good of others. Just as Christ had suffered for humanity, the United States would suffer too. For Sherwood Eddy, the renowned YMCA missionary and advocate for a global Social Gospel, world peace would only come "when suffering has been accepted and borne in the right spirit." Writing in 1916, Eddy was in the process of making the painful transition from advocate of peace to progressive warrior. Within a year, most of his fellow liberal internationalist clergy would make the same spiritual and political journey. At the point of U.S. entry into the war, Reverend William Adams Brown of Union Theological Seminary and the FCC told a devotional meeting full of skeptical anti-interventionists, "We who have borne the least, surely upon us the responsibility rests most heavily."[24]

CHAPTER FOURTEEN

Onward Christian Soldiers

O N THE EVENING OF April 2, 1917, Woodrow Wilson set off from the White House and made his way through the crowded, expectant streets of Washington. He was bound for Capitol Hill, where he addressed a joint session of Congress to ask for a declaration of war against Germany. The United States, he explained, had been backed into a corner; much as he hated it, there was no option left except war. Americans sought nothing for themselves, only "the vindication of right, of human right." They would fight in response to German provocations, but they would seek something far greater than Germany's defeat. "The world must be made safe for democracy," he declared in ringing terms that have become the speech's, and perhaps Wilson's, most memorable phrase. "Its peace must be planted upon the tested foundations of political liberty. We have no selfish ends to serve. We desire no conquest, no dominion." The United States was "but one of the champions of the rights of mankind. We shall be satisfied when those rights have been made as secure as the faith and the freedom of nations can make them." Wilson's concluding paragraph summarized America's noble case for war in stirring, eloquent language. He finished by paraphrasing Martin Luther's riposte to his accusers at the Diet of Worms, a rebuttal to ecclesiastical tyranny that touched off the Reformation. This was likely not an incidental reference—a man of Wilson's religious background and knowledge would surely have realized that 1917 marked the four hundredth anniversary of Luther's "Ninety-five Theses" protesting the indulgences of the Catholic Church. America, Wilson said, would wage war for its highest ideals. "God helping her, she can do no other."[1]

Sacrifice, intervening not only for America but for all the world, fighting for the highest ideals of democracy and liberty—these were the themes that Wilson stressed repeatedly to explain why America fought. Invoking a Calvinistic sense of providence, chosenness, and Christian unselfishness, Wilson told another audience in June that Americans at war were now "an instrument in the hands of God to see that liberty is made secure for mankind." The United States had been "allowed to become strong in the Providence of God that our strength might be used to prove, not our selfishness, but our greatness." Sounding a note that the churches would ring constantly for the next two years, Wilson declared himself "thankful for the privilege of self-sacrifice, which is the only privilege that lends dignity to the human spirit."[2]

"Through no choice of our own the American people has been drawn into the world war, and we must now bear our share of the burden and sacrifice." To Samuel Zane Batten, a Baptist preacher and secretary of the Northern Baptist Convention's War Commission, the United States had come to war reluctantly, unenthusiastically, and regretfully. This had long been a common theme among American clergy who favored war, from 1812 to Spain and the Philippines. According to Batten, the stakes were clear: "This war for the destruction of injustice and inhumanity is a holy crusade and a continuation of Christ's sacrificial service for the redemption of the world." Only the most committed of pacifists dissented from Batten's view. The only questions remaining for the vast majority of American Christians centered on execution: How would the churches mobilize their congregants? How would they administer to the pastoral needs of soldiers in the field? How would they help coordinate plans for a postwar peace settlement? To these questions, the nation's churches and synagogues now turned their attention. Their answers—Protestant, Catholic, and Jew alike—were largely synergistic with Wilson's, providing the president with a key base of support, encouragement, and moral authority at a moment of confusion and controversy. In so doing, they were literally answering Wilson's call for support from the nation's pulpits.[3]

In general, Protestants supported the cause in two ways: by rallying public support and by providing organization and infrastructure. Both were equally important to the war effort, particularly at home, for they gave it the moral imprimatur of nearly all the national churches and many important regional ones. Yet objectives within Protestantism differed, especially between liberals and conservatives, in ways that would help determine the confines of U.S. foreign policy for some time to come.

CONSERVATIVE EVANGELICALS and the emerging fundamentalist movement did not respond to the war with one voice. Some adhered to an unusually strict separation of church from state; these separatists viewed the government as a corrupting influence upon the church, and so refused to have anything to do with invocations of patriotism and wartime service. Others continued to embrace the New Testament's pacifist injunctions against war and reacted to preparedness and the pre-1917 debate over U.S. intervention in much the same way as liberal pacifists. Others were more interventionist, because they despised German authoritarianism and its meddling in church affairs, or because they expressed a patriotism that demanded support for the United States in a time of crisis.

Still, with their nation at war, the majority of conservatives set aside any doubts and threw their support behind Wilson. The shift by the emerging Pentecostal churches, the Assemblies of God and the Church of God in Christ, is indicative. Led by one of the founders of the faith, Aimee Semple McPherson, habitually pacifistic and anti-statist Pentecostals accommodated themselves to the government's wartime needs and patriotically supported its war aims.[4]

There was, however, one key difference between liberal and conservative Protestants: conservatives were less concerned with internationalism than they were with a more straightforward patriotism and drive to win the war. Conservatism remained diverse, yet the exigencies of war also created a standardizing effect, at least in reactions to the war and American participation, a reaction that was true of liberal modernism as well. Yet unlike liberals, fundamentalists were just beginning to assert themselves as a distinct force in American life, and their response to the war differed in important ways from the elite modernists who dominated the national discussion on religion. Conservative Protestants could be just as nationalistic and militantly anti-German as mainline modernists, but for different reasons.

Conservatives were not as preoccupied with the potential terms of a postwar settlement, and did not outline plans for world federation, collective security, or international organization. They were nationalists rather than internationalists, and so did not share the liberal view of the world as interconnected, much less interdependent. Conservatives may have distrusted the state, but they loved their country. With a strong adherence to the separation of church and state as a way to guard against the government regulation of religion and thus protect their autonomy, conservative evangelicals, premillennial dispensationalists, fundamentalists, and Pentecostals were wary of statist solutions for human frailty. As one fundamentalist put it, they feared a world order in which "government will control religion, trade, and the people themselves," leaving "no room for freedom of thought, or independence of action in any direction whatever." Instead, the world would be controlled by a dictator, "Satan's super-man," at the head of a world state. Building a postwar parliament of nations would only create a system of "centralized power in the hands of a few," warned *Presbyterian* magazine, which would simply mean "the realization of the German idea by another and less direct route."[5]

Fundamentalist preachers commanded large audiences and national followings. The most famous of them was Billy Sunday, a bombastic evangelist who took an especially hard, crowd-pleasing stance on the war. A former left-fielder for the Chicago White Stockings, Sunday had pledged his life to Christ one summer afternoon after hearing the old-time hymns and simple gospel of Chicago street preachers. He became a preacher himself, and rose to fame on a message that was even simpler and more direct than Dwight Moody's and a style even more emotional than George Whitefield's. He was also, like most conservative evangelists, an American nationalist, and his support for the American war effort was just as bombastic as his preaching. "If you turn hell upside down," he bellowed at revivals across the nation, "you will find 'Made in Germany' stamped on the bottom." Sunday would also outline his wartime philosophy in somewhat more detail. "I tell you it is Bill [Kaiser Wilhelm II] against Woodrow, Germany against America, Hell against Heaven," he railed. "Either you are loyal or you are not, you are either a patriot or a black-hearted traitor." Gentler talk "about not fighting the German people is a lot of bunk. They say we are fighting for an ideal. Well, if we are we will have to knock down the German people to get it over."[6]

More thoughtful but no less bellicose was John Roach Straton, pastor of the Calvary Baptist Church in New York City and one of the early leaders of fundamentalism. Americans, he outlined in a sermon, waged holy war against Germany's "system of autocracy and tyranny . . . founded upon the idea that men are not capable of ruling themselves." Conversely, libertarian American democracy was based on the premise "that men are essentially capable of self-direction" and that "the soul is a holy thing, and that it is competent to act under God's guidance for itself." The American way "believes that the voice of the people is the voice of God." These two systems, Straton concluded, "are the practical expressions of the forces of good and evil." American democracy protected freedom of conscience and freedom of worship, liberties that nonconformist Christians such as Baptists relied on for their very existence. If the state controlled religion in America, as it purportedly did in Germany, Straton and other fundamentalists feared their form of worship would be the first to go.[7]

Nationalistic, conservative Protestants did not hesitate to oppose German authoritarianism, but their animus had two important additional motivations. The first was a reaction to the corrupting influence of German theology. Fundamentalists had recently begun to resist the modernist challenge to absolute biblical authority. Evolution was a primary target, but so too was biblical criticism, then en vogue in the established, usually liberal theological seminaries and divinity schools. The Bible, claimed fundamentalists, was the literal word of God, and nothing else. The innovators of biblical criticism—and thus of modernist heresy, said American fundamentalists—were German theologians and scholars. Germany's culture, "including her destructive criticism of the word of God, is as false as hell because its fruits are as vile as hell!" pronounced Straton. How could anyone explain the "abominable utterances" of the "hitherto highly esteemed critics, theologians, and philosophers" of Germany, asked Reuben A. Torrey, dean of the Bible Institute of Los Angeles and another important founder of Protestant fundamentalism, "except by discerning a very brainy, very astute Devil back of them?" The war had simply verified "the terrible results of the evolutionary hypothesis when carried to its logical conclusions" and the "appalling results of German rationalism and destructive criticism."[8]

Second, just as important to the fundamentalist mind was the war's role in elevating premillennial dispensationalism to the front ranks of fundamentalism. Liberal, optimistic postmillennialism had long dominated the American religious landscape and had fueled reformist movements from abolition to temperance. Christ, the postmillennialists claimed, would return to earth only after humanity had been able to reform and perfect the world. Premillennial dispensationalists believed exactly the opposite: Christ's return depended upon the world's degradation. Jesus would then return to lead the armies of the Lord in battle against Satan, and a millennium of peace would follow their victory. Premillennialism had been gaining in popularity since the late nineteenth century; by seeming to fulfill biblical prophecy, the Great War gave the movement a tremendous boost, much to liberal dismay and alarm. Several books of the Bible, especially Daniel and Revelation, foretold the end of the world as a series of battles between the forces of light and the forces of darkness. The Great War quickly assumed apocalyptic significance for most Christians, but for many conservative Protestants it seemed to be literally true. Germany nicely filled out the role of the Antichrist, succeeding earlier versions such as the Catholic powers Spain and France. Torrey took the lead in arguing that the war proved the validity of the word of God by fulfilling millennial prophecy. Most important was the British capture of Jerusalem from the Turks (allied to Germany) and the Balfour Declaration declaring British support for a Jewish homeland in Palestine, which created waves of premillennialist excitement because an essential prerequisite to the end times was the Jews returning to govern the ancient land of Israel. The end was nigh, and premillennialists had the war to thank for it.[9]

Premillennial evangelicals and fundamentalists were also natural partners of the emerging Zionist movement. Indeed, they became Zionists before most American Jews had themselves converted to the cause. The defeat of the Ottoman Empire, the British capture of Jerusalem, the prospect of a restored state of Israel—all these apparent fulfillments of biblical prophecy moved conservative Christian Zionists to back Jewish nationalist plans for a new homeland in Palestine. William Blackstone, the de facto leader of Christian Zionism in America, and theologians like Charles Blanchard of Wheaton College lobbied the Wilson administration to support Zionist plans. Blackstone deemed it providential that the United States had remained on the sidelines of the war until the moment it could participate and dictate the terms of peace. Louis Brandeis and

Stephen Wise, Jewish Zionists who accepted support wherever they could find it, encouraged these Christian sympathizers. Brandeis bestowed upon Blackstone the title "Father of Zionism" because, he explained to the Christian leader, "your work antedates [Theodor] Herzl." Brandeis and Wise even orchestrated a second Blackstone Memorial, a petition presented to Wilson in June 1917. It was no coincidence that American Zionism and premillennial dispensationalism were maturing at precisely the same moment.[10]

Finally, the war politicized conservative Protestants as they never had been before. Partly this was because the war politicized everyone in America. Aside from raising the most important questions of war and peace, the Wilson administration mobilized public opinion to support intervention, and persecuted those who refused to go along. But conservative politicization also resulted from wartime battles with modernists, early skirmishes that would later explode in the theological civil wars of the 1920s. Modernists attacked fundamentalists for their pessimistic premillennialism, branding it little more than a way to attack needed social reform and an excuse to ignore the squalid living conditions of many Americans. Fundamentalists attacked modernists for accepting empiricist, skeptical German philosophy and theology, which, they charged, had led to the popularity of Darwinian evolution, the rise of social Darwinism, competition among the great powers, and eventually the terrible world war. Cities with significant centers of both modernism and fundamentalism, such as New York and Philadelphia, became battlegrounds for the soul of American Protestantism. Chicago saw some of the most intense, emotional arguments as the liberal University of Chicago Divinity School and the conservative Moody Bible Institute violently denounced each other for holding beliefs that were tantamount to heresy. Both sides then used the war to attack the other, charging their adversaries with insufficient patriotism or culpability in causing war in the first place. For both sides, then, expressing their utmost support for the war, its grand objectives, and the nation was not only patriotic duty but a matter of survival.[11]

LIBERAL PROTESTANTS also passionately supported the war, but in different ways and for different reasons. Their rallying of support was important as well, and they elevated their postmillennial rhetoric about a reformation of the world system, but they were even more instrumental in providing voluntarist institutional solutions to many of the federal government's unprecedented organizational problems.

Pacifist exceptions remained, although by April 1917 they were very much exceptions to the overwhelmingly prowar norm. The power of the peace crusade lingered—in June, for example, Wilson withdrew plans to co-opt church services to support the war lest they become a platform for pacifist antiwar protest—but then quickly faded. The mainline churches more or less abandoned what little pacifism they had tolerated, which left it in the hands of the traditional peace churches, Christian socialists, famous individual exceptions such as Jane Addams, and fundamentalist sects that resisted all involvement with the state. This loss of support from the religious establishment made pacifism all the more ineffective. Christian pacifists in the mainline churches, moreover, were confronted with an agonizing choice of conformity or defiance. Most conformed, but some, like Arthur Dunham with his resignation from the Presbyterian Church, became independent liberal Christians who stood on conscience alone. Pacifist societies continued their work, but only a much harder core of idealists remained. While their purity may have been intact, their effectiveness was completely destroyed. The Fellowship of Reconciliation offered aid and comfort to conscientious objectors, but they also adopted a much more strident political stance, fully embracing socialism and partnering with the antiwar socialist union, the Industrial Workers of the World. Given that the IWW was anathema to most liberals, all conservatives, and both political parties, it was evident that the main pacifist organizations had fallen out of touch with the mainstream.[12]

In May, Congress brought in the draft when it passed the Selective Service Act. Though draft boards only recognized the most well-established pacifist denominations, such as the Society of Friends and the Mennonites, as legitimate conscientious objectors, others came forward to claim exemption from the obligations of military service, including African American Pentecostals, Jehovah's Witnesses, and the Molokan Church of Arizona. Their claims were ignored, they were punished by the government, and they suffered popular ridicule and persecution as "shirkers" and "cowards." Even Mennonites, duly recognized as legitimate pacifists, came under fierce attack for their alleged cowardice and lack of patriotism, particularly those who still worshipped in German; some were even flogged, tarred, and feathered. But conscientious objectors from established denominations, such as Episcopalians and Presbyterians, received even harsher treatment for selfishly turning against their brethren and country. In all, only 65,000 men claimed conscientious objector status—0.3 percent of the total number drafted. Most of these claims were recognized, and the claimants performed alternative service on farms, in hospitals, or with relief agencies such as the YMCA or the Red Cross. Nearly four thousand men were imprisoned for their beliefs because they refused to participate at all, including alternative service, and of them the vast majority—over 90 percent—were Christian pacifists. Conscientious objectors established their own relief agencies; the most celebrated, successful, and enduring was the American Friends Service Committee, which worked in tandem with Herbert Hoover, himself a practicing Quaker, in administering post-war reconstruction efforts in Europe well into the 1920s.[13]

As Christian pacifists discovered at their peril, a principled refusal to fight had become an overwhelmingly unpopular belief by 1917—even among Christians. Even if the kaiser and Teddy Roosevelt worshipped the same militaristic God, as the pacifist Frederick Libby charged, it was now a more popular deity than the Prince of Peace. Indeed, preaching a peace sermon from the gospels of the New Testament bordered on treason. In a contest of good versus evil, pacifism seemed an ignoble, selfish, sinful response to a crisis that demanded faith, sacrifice, and suffering. Referring to the Espionage Act of 1917 and the Sedition Act of 1918, which effectively criminalized dissent, one critic of "pagan" pacifism rejoiced that all "forms of peace propaganda are at present justly and properly repressed by the Government as a war measure." The New Testament was noble, but it was "not meant to play into the hands of the evil Power." Instead of aiding the cause of Christ, pacifism "only gluts the ravenous maw of inhuman soulless tyranny" in a worldwide crisis "when incarnate evil sits in the very temple of God, setting itself forth as God, a time when the law of violence is openly avowed and exalted above the law of mercy and right, a time of the beast and false prophet."[14]

Where these extremes met in the middle, they produced an early form of Christian realism, one of the most important politico-religious doctrines of the last century. Associated with Reinhold Niebuhr and his fight to secure U.S. intervention in World War II, the rough outlines of Christian realism, at least as it applied to questions of war and peace, were already visible in 1917. It was essentially another form of compromise between pacifism and militarism; though few at the time said so, it was also a revival of just war theory. As Harry Emerson Fosdick put it, "Force and love are not necessarily antithetical" so long as Americans wielded "the judicious application of force in the hands of love." This insight was based upon two profound recognitions: that war was evil, but that sometimes injustice, tyranny, and aggression posed even greater evils than war. The world was a place of innate sin as well as progress, argued these early Christian realists. Or, as Henry Sloane Coffin lectured to students at Yale, the world was "tragic," not necessarily hopeful, and a place of "judgment and redemption." Christian realism offered a subtle yet powerful justification for those liberals who came to believe in America's duty to fight in Europe. Though they would later go their separate ways, Fosdick and Coffin were two of Christian realism's early apostles. So was Shailer Mathews of the University of Chicago's Divinity School, one of the most intellectually pugnacious supporters of the war. Mathews once accosted a former friend, the pacifist Kirby Page, by accusing him of playing the

Good Samaritan by simply waiting for the thieves to beat and rob the traveler before helping him. What use was such a timid faith? "If the religion of the Quakers had become the religion of the world, war would have ceased," Mathews reasoned elsewhere. "But it has not become the religion of the world or even an appreciable section of the world."[15]

Aside from a hard core of the most idealistic Christian pacifists, then, most liberals joined the crusade against Germany, even those who themselves had once been advocates of peace (or, like Fosdick, would be in the future). Their conversion to the nobler purposes of war was especially important, as it sanctified intervention and infused it with the intense, burning idealism of Christian pacifism. Reverend Hardin was one such convert: he moved to Paris in 1918 to work for the Red Cross and believed that "all that America is doing . . . in this grand struggle" proved it was "the hope of humanity." Another was Sherwood Eddy, who called himself in 1918 a "Christian militant" who claimed a "right to fight." Eddy redefined his position as one of "peace, based upon a law of right, supported when necessary by the use of force." Against such an immoral, aggressive enemy as Germany, "armed defence" became a "moral obligation" higher even than peace. Yet another convert was John Mott, a founding member of the ultra-pacifist Fellowship of Reconciliation; in 1917, he supported U.S. intervention and oversaw the YMCA's relief programs in Europe. Frederick Lynch now firmly supported Wilson, too, and brought the organization he headed, Church Peace Union, along with him. Washington Gladden made a similar conversion. But most astonishing was William Jennings Bryan, who despite his fifty-seven years of age immediately wrote Wilson to volunteer his services as a private in the U.S. Army.[16]

A critical element in mobilizing liberal Protestant support for the war, especially among those who had opposed preparedness and intervention, was the belief that the United States would use victory in war to bring nations together in a permanent settlement of world peace. In this view, the United States would have no credibility or legitimacy at all, and thus no influence, if it remained out of the war. This was an article of faith for almost all liberals, from Southern Methodist missionaries to Unitarians. If America had maintained its selfish neutrality, claimed a Minnesota Unitarian minister, it would mean that "every man's hand would be against us" and the "world would despise us." Instead, "America has given her answer," to itself and to the world, by taking its rightful place "with the hosts that are battling for a great human ideal." What was more, Americans would ennoble themselves in the eyes of the world, and of God. Robert Speer, now head of the FCC's General War-time Commission of the Churches, framed American intervention as a progressive war "in defense of human rights, of weak nations, of innocent and inoffensive peoples, an unselfish war in which the nation seeks absolutely nothing for itself and is willing to spend everything in order that all men, including its enemies, may be free."[17]

Just as critical was the conviction that the United States had intervened unwillingly, as an absolute last resort. Even if they were not committed pacifists, many mainline liberals would never support war in the first instance. War not only had to be waged with the highest, purest motives, it also could not be a matter of choice. To traditional antiwar denominations, such as the Unitarians, this was a vital distinction. "Now, in this universal Armageddon, in which we find ourselves compelled to bear our part, the choice incessantly is forced upon us," intoned Alfred Hussey of the First Unitarian Church in Lowell, Massachusetts, in a sermon shortly before the war. "Will you throw in your lot with the forces of light or those of darkness? Will you champion truth, or falsehood, the things seen or the things unseen, God or devil?" To traditionally antiwar Unitarians, these were extraordinary questions for an extraordinary time.[18]

Liberals also demonized Germany as the world's main source of tyranny and militarism, and thus as the antithesis of all that America stood and fought for. Mainline clergy sponsored boycotts of German products and turned their backs on German theology. That indefatigable crusader Lyman Abbott used the pages of *The Outlook* to attack the Germans mercilessly as "the Predatory Potsdam Gang." He could not, Abbott announced, pray to "forgive them for they know not what they do" simply because "it is not true. I do not hate the Predatory Potsdam Gang because it is my enemy," he confessed in remarkably unchristian language. "I hate it because it is a robber, a murderer, a destroyer of homes, a pillager of churches, a violater of women. I do well hate it." When Speer, a firm supporter of the war, had the temerity to lecture an audience at Columbia University in early 1918 that the United States also had its own sins to answer for, and that Americans should love their enemies even though they fought them, he was wrongly condemned as either a seditious German sympathizer, a cowardly pacifist, or both.[19]

The liberal critique of German culture, however, was less straightforward than it was for conservatives because liberals had long admired Germany's contributions to science, theology, and higher learning. Indeed, many had studied at one of the great universities in Germany and had embraced a thoroughly German approach to scholarship and Bible reading; others, including Woodrow Wilson in the doctoral program at Johns Hopkins, had imbibed German scholarship and methods from German-trained mentors. As dean of the Divinity School at the University of Chicago, Shailer Mathews was one of liberal Protestantism's most influential figures; as an educator at Chicago, a nerve center of modernism, he was also steeped in the empiricism of higher education. When

Dean Mathews of Chicago spoke, America's liberal Protestants listened. Which made his stunning 1918 attack on German intellectualism all the more important in the service of war. The conflict, Mathews explained, had illustrated for Americans that German thought "was born of a malignant political philosophy" which had been "implanted within our intellectual life. Liberty [was] then forgotten at the shrine of a new god, Teutonic Efficiency" while "Germans sanctified anti-internationalistic patriotism by appeal to their *Kultur.*" This was a significant attack, for it was Germany's vaunted culture that had elevated its status among liberal theologians in the first place. The war had revealed Germany's worst authoritarian tendencies, and German *Kultur's* subservience to the whims of a tyrant. "A religion that thus yields itself to the will of the state is certainly far enough from the Christianity of Jesus," an argument that enabled Mathews not only to criticize Germany but rescue modernism for American Protestants.[20]

Woodrow Wilson actually knew this story well: Princeton, both the University and the neighboring and more conservative Theological Seminary, had been the source of some of the fiercest attacks on German biblical criticism. Just as Wilson's affection for Britain was rooted in his own personal history and in the heritage of Presbyterianism, then, his animus for Germany was theological as well as political.[21]

MAINLINE PROTESTANT SUPPORT for the war was not confined merely to individuals. Churches believed their country was fighting a heavenly fight in a righteous cause, and acted accordingly. Many decorated their churches with American flags and patriotic bunting. Typical was the Second Presbyterian Church of Richmond, Virginia, which alone sent eighty-one men into military service and four women into relief work (two were field nurses, two worked for the YWCA). Most were sent into action in Europe, and two of the men died in battle; several others, noted the church's minister, Russell Cecil, had been gassed or severely wounded. Reverend Cecil described the attitude of his congregation as "enthusiastic" yet grounded in "the spirit of self-sacrifice." Every Sunday, he read out a special prayer to those serving overseas; often he gave a special sermon on the moral aims of the war. For the duration of the war, a Service Flag graced one side of the pulpit, an American flag the other. Many of the church's women volunteered for the Red Cross in a room set aside especially for that purpose. Cecil recorded this information as an everlasting testament to Second Presbyterian's wartime devotion and sacrifice. "Finally," he wrote, "it should be said that the members of the church and congregation evinced a true patriotic spirit; and did not spare themselves or their means when called upon by the country to defend its honor in the war, and to assist in the efforts of the entente Allies in resisting the organized attempts of Prussianism to over-run the nations of Europe and dominate the world." Second Presbyterian had given much, but it was for a noble cause.[22]

Almost without exception, the large organizations of liberal Protestantism placed their services in the hands of the Wilson administration and its war campaign. This was crucial assistance for a government that had only recently decided to take on the monumental challenge of waging a world war for world peace. Protestant organizations were national in scope, with memberships and activities that reached from coast to coast; though they were concentrated in the Northeast, their presence extended into every region, including the South. Their reach was lengthened by the fact that many supporters of the ecumenical movement were laymen who were either leaders of industry (Andrew Carnegie, John D. Rockefeller, Jr.) or government (Woodrow Wilson, John Foster Dulles). Their overall memberships were not small, either—at its height, for example, the FCC alone represented thirty-three major denominations comprising as many as two-thirds of all American Protestants—and they were able to magnify their influence by speaking through their members, the clergy, who would pass on messages and information through sermons and other communications to their congregations. By allying itself to the national mainline Protestant institutions, then, the Wilson administration found itself with a direct line to possibly the largest captive audience in the United States.[23]

No group benefited more than the Federal Council of Churches. Established in 1908 as the national Protestant body, the ecumenical FCC did not initially prosper, despite having the support of nearly every major mainline denomination. What plagued the FCC was the same irony that had undone ecumenical councils before it: a body devoted to religious unity could not overcome strong denominational identities and different, often contradictory, approaches to theology and politics. Before the war, these issues had not extended much into the realm of foreign affairs. The FCC had been established not only as a means to promote Protestant unity, but also as a forum to advance the Social Gospel. Yet it was mostly ineffective, a national debating society that could not command an authoritative voice even among its member churches. That is, until the war. The Great War presented the most serious challenge to Western society on all fronts. If the Protestant churches were to be politically relevant, something they desperately wanted, they needed to have a coordinated response. This desire led naturally to the FCC, which seized its opportunity.[24]

The Federal Council responded to the outbreak of war in Europe by sympathizing with the Allied cause but also firmly supporting American neutrality. Though its concerns had been mostly domestic, the FCC had been supportive of the pre-1914 peace movement. Its natural tendencies, then, were toward peace. After the outbreak of war in Europe, it moved quickly to send a prayer for "brotherhood and peace" to 130,000 churches in the United States and a missive to Wilson about America's opportunity to broker a cooperative peace. A year later, Charles Macfarland of the FCC's Executive Committee toured Europe in a vain effort to promote an early peace settlement. But the Federal Council also saw the war in stronger, moralistic terms of right and wrong, and eventually of good and evil. To their minds, Germany had clearly violated international peace, and though the British and French were not free of sin themselves, they had responded in a measured and justifiable way. Without sensing a contradiction, many members supported both peace and preparedness. The Federal Council was thus the perfect vehicle to rally "middle ground" Christians who were neither pacifists nor militarists but somewhere in between and to some extent sympathetic to both. This was the idealistic mindset that eventually led many to support American involvement in a progressive war.[25]

By 1917, the Federal Council was ready for war even before America joined. "I regret to urge war," the FCC's Worth M. Tippy counseled Wilson in March, "but I think the time has come to go in with all our power." The Federal Council thus needed little encouragement to rally around the flag once Wilson had planted it in the soil of France and Belgium. In order to coordinate its relief and chaplaincy programs in Europe and manage its communications and prowar message in America, in 1917 the FCC established the General War-Time Commission of the Churches. Comprised of over a hundred major Protestant leaders, including clergy and laymen, the General War-Time Commission acted as the lead agency on wartime issues affecting American Protestantism. It was chaired by Robert Speer, the missionary organizer whose work with the Presbyterian mission board and the Student Volunteers had made him one of America's leading religious figures. Speer was an ideal choice to lead an ecumenical commission: he believed in Social Gospel reform yet was also a proto-fundamentalist who prioritized the word of God above all else; he was a mainline Presbyterian who could communicate sympathetically with conservative evangelicals; he was supportive of the war but was not a militarist; and he was a missionary leader with contacts the world over. His deputy, and the true driving force behind the General War-Time Commission's dynamic activism, was William Adams Brown of Union Theological Seminary. Members included not only other middle ground liberals like Harry Emerson Fosdick and John Mott, but also both sides of the prewar debate, including the fervent prowar advocate Shailer Mathews and the antipreparedness dissenter Henry Sloane Coffin. Speer worked hard to secure cooperative, active participation with other groups who would not assume full membership in an FCC body, such as the Southern Baptist Convention. Aware that the war had the power to transform faith in unforeseen ways, Speer also established a study group, the Committee on the War and the Religious Outlook, to consider its ramifications for American religion.[26]

The FCC and its General War-Time Commission were not the only ecumenical Protestant groups active during the war. Church Peace Union, flush with Carnegie's millions, also followed a classic middle-ground path to the war, from promoting European peace in 1914–15 and opposing preparedness in 1916 to supporting U.S. intervention in 1917. Throughout, Church Peace Union tried to maintain an uneasy balance between peace advocacy and righteous war. It sponsored, for example, a peace convention in the spring of 1917 that pledged support for Wilson's policies but also established a legal defense fund for conscientious objectors. Yet once America was at war, its tendencies became increasingly supportive of war and it pledged its assistance to fulfilling Wilson's ambitious postwar peace agenda.

To this end, Church Peace Union and the FCC entered into something of an unholy alliance with the League to Enforce Peace and the government's own notorious propaganda machine, the Committee on Public Information, to establish the National Committee on the Churches and the Moral Aims of the War. Frederick Lynch, Church Peace Union's director, had misgivings about facilitating government propaganda, but justified the new committee on the grounds that it promoted the "lofty and disinterested character" of American war aims and fostered "an overwhelming resolution in the hearts of our people to insist that out of this war must come some new international order" that would make such wars "improbable, if not impossible, forever." Even for the progressive clergy, the ends could justify the means.[27]

While the Federal Council and Church Peace Union acted as bridges between the Protestant churches and the government, it was another ecumenical organization, the interdenominational Young Men's Christian Association (YMCA), that took the lead in administering actual war work. For this reason, it was probably the best-known American religious group during the war. Along with its sister organization the YWCA, the YMCA was also deliberately less political and did not really take a stand on the war other than to support the American and Allied efforts after April 1917. This did not, however, stop it from receiving state support. In 1915, Secretary of State Bryan did not see why Americans should be protected while traveling into a war zone, but he still put the State Department to work to secure nonbelligerent status for American Y workers in Europe. In 1917, Bryan's successor Robert Lansing approved the Y's plan to assist not only American soldiers, but Italian and Russian troops too. The moral and physical welfare of soldiers were the Y's main concerns. Sherwood Eddy, by 1917 a traveling secretary for the Y, wrote from "somewhere in

France" of the "enormous moral danger" to which American troops "are exposed in this far away foreign land." Y workers aimed to furnish these lost souls with a Bible and keep them away from the usual temptations of the war camp, from prostitutes and venereal diseases to the spiritual doubts arising from alcoholism and loneliness. But State Department officials also hoped the Y's work in Russia could act as an antidote to Bolshevism. When Mott cabled Wilson to offer the YMCA's services the day Congress declared war on Germany, Wilson immediately accepted. A few weeks later, he issued General Order No. 57 informing the military that "official recognition is hereby given to the Young Men's Christian Association as a valuable adjunct and asset to the service."[28]

However, not all Protestant groups flourished under the pressure of war. The success of Speer at the Federal Council and Mott at the YMCA could not disguise the suffering of overseas missions. Indeed, it was no small irony that the two driving forces behind the Student Volunteer Movement, Speer and Mott, were busy with other agencies at a time when the SVM's own health was deteriorating rapidly. By the end of the war, the Student Volunteers had entered a downward spiral of irreversible decline. Essentially, the war made missionary work impossible. Not only was much of the world at war, including traditional mission fields and the pivotal sea lanes that linked North American missionaries to the rest of the world; money now became an issue, as funds dried up and American churches and their patrons shifted donations to wartime relief. Only a week after war broke out in 1914, Mott warned missionaries in the field that mission boards and home agencies would soon be burdened under "very large and seriously crippling financial debt" and that activities would have to be drastically scaled back. With the war distracting the YMCA, the Federal Council, and denominational organizations, missions floundered. The SVM wholeheartedly supported Wilson and the war and promised to use the global reach of its missionaries to "broadcast the life-giving principles of liberty, of the infinite worth and inalienable rights of every individual child of God," but it was of little use. After the war, with a younger generation coming into its own, the Student Volunteers underwent a self-confessed "marked change in attitude" and focused increasingly on solving "racial and international problems," a shift that was radical even in the liberal context of modernist mainline missions. This was too much for conservatives, but strangely not enough for many increasingly skeptical liberals, who drifted out of missions altogether. For the first time since the Civil War, missions were not at the forefront of American Protestantism.[29]

Overall, the war had an oddly disjointed effect on mainline Protestantism. It invigorated faith, especially at the highest levels and especially by stimulating further ecumenical cooperation. The FCC and Church Peace

Union, for example, cooperated together in the creation of yet another group, the inelegantly named World Alliance for the Promotion of International Friendship through the Churches, in London in 1914. In a rare partnership with the National Catholic War Council (NCWC), the Federal Council also designed a single official Church Flag to be hung in churches during the war. With the YWCA, the YMCA's National War Work Council orchestrated the United War Work Campaign to raise funds for religious relief efforts; among its cooperating agencies was the NCWC, and by 1919 the campaign had raised the staggering sum of $188,644,230. Yet as the fate of missions illustrates, not everyone thrived. Moreover, even despite the manifest successes of the YMCA and the FCC, Protestantism was becoming even more schismatic, fractious, and disillusioned than before 1914. The war provided motivation, and then cover, for modernists and fundamentalists to wreak havoc upon the very notion of a united Protestant endeavor.[30]

ROMAN CATHOLICS WERE no less active than Protestants, though their efforts were tempered by the fact that America's Catholics had to conform to a domestic culture that was still overwhelmingly Protestant. Yet paradoxically, the complexity of their status in American society ensured that the Catholic response to the war was fairly straightforward. In general, Catholics supported the government, initially by favoring neutrality and then by mobilizing behind a president who, they believed, had been forced to fight a war he had not wanted. In April 1917, not long after Congress declared war, most of the archbishops in the church gathered at Catholic University in Washington to pledge unanimously their "most sacred and sincere loyalty and patriotism toward our country, our government, and our flag" and promise to work for "the welfare of the whole nation." James Cardinal Gibbons, archbishop of Baltimore and the church's leading voice on foreign affairs, called on every Catholic to maintain "an absolute and unreserved obedience to his country's call." To his flock in the Baltimore archdiocese, Gibbons passed on even clearer instructions: "Let it not be said that we were weighed in the balance of patriotism and found wanting."[31]

More, however, was needed, at least if the Catholic hierarchy was going to fulfill these promises within the whole church, throughout the nation, because American Catholicism was too diffuse and diverse to coordinate. The best way Catholics could assist the war effort and demonstrate their patriotism was through an organization like the Protestant Federal Council. Up to this point, the Catholic Church had a well-defined hierarchy and far-reaching ecclesiastical network, but it lacked a national body that could efficiently tackle social and political as well as religious questions. There was only one Catholic Church, but within it clamored many voices, and so in some ways American Catholicism was as diverse as Protestant-ism. Poles, Germans, and Italians all had their own liturgical styles; many of them continued to worship in their mother tongue. (They were united, however, in their resentment of Irish dominance of the church hierarchy in the United States.) There were also authoritative Catholic laymen and lay groups—such as the Knights of Columbus, the Catholic Young Men's Association, and the Society of St. Vincent de Paul—that worked inti-mately with the church and yet stood outside its official hierarchy. But the war demanded a cohesive response; without one, Catholics' voices would be drowned out. There already existed the American Federation of Catholic Societies, but it was too large and unwieldy, its constituent mem-bers too autonomous. The solution was the establishment of the National Catholic War Council, with Cardinal Gibbons as president, at a grand convention meeting at Catholic University in August 1917. The NCWC was officially incorporated in November, and with it the Catholic Church had a single agency to coordinate the massive task of assisting the national war effort.[32]

American Catholics strongly supported Wilson's program, especially his decision to fight the war as an "Associate" and not an "Ally" of Britain and his vision for a League of Nations to administer a fair and perma-nent peace settlement. In other words, Catholics were particularly well suited to a patriotic war in defense of American interests and in pursuit of internationalist ideals because they were not especially well suited to an alliance either *with* Britain and Russia or *against* Germany. Catholics were sincere in their American patriotism, and they took pains to dem-onstrate that sincerity whenever they could. But many were also first- or second-generation immigrants who maintained close ties to friends and relatives in Europe. In 1916, there were nearly sixteen million Roman Catholics living in the United States. Many had recently immigrated from eastern and southern Europe, especially Poland and Italy, but many more had come from Ireland. Moreover, older Catholic populations had moved mostly from Ireland and Germany in the middle decades of the nineteenth century. Between 1851 and World War I, more than 7.5 million Irish moved to the United States, the overwhelming majority of them Roman Catholic. Figures for the population at large are imprecise, but among the hierarchy who would set the Catholic agenda during the war, the for-eign connection was even stronger: 40 percent of American bishops were foreign-born, of whom half (or 20 percent of the overall total) had been born in Ireland; in total, including American-born bishops, approximately 60 percent were Irish. The connection deepens when one considers edu-cation: two-thirds of American bishops had received their training abroad, of whom 28 percent had been trained at one of the colleges or seminaries in Rome. Their American patriotism was evident, but the bishops—the same group who ran the NCWC during the war—also retained an Irish, German, or Polish perspective, and were reluctant to fight for Britain and Russia or against Germany. They would instead fight for America.[33]

Couched in these terms, and with the question of loyalty lingering menacingly in the national air, American Catholics were unstinting in their support of the United States and the Wilson administration at war. Catholic leaders therefore stressed many of the same themes of American patriotism and Christian unity, suffering, and righteousness as their Protestant counterparts. Archbishop John Ireland, who had supported the Spanish-American War as a way to Americanize Catholicism, threw his considerable weight behind the Great War for much the same reason (though he also decried the Germans' destruction of Catholic churches in France and Belgium). "If we fight like heroes and pray like saints," ran a typical Catholic statement, "soon America will overcome by greater force and conquer lust of power by the nobler powers of sacrifice and faith." The only major difference in Catholics' support for the war was the absence of belligerent, anti-German vitriol.[34]

Particularly striking was the absence of Catholic pacifism, but perhaps the most notable feature of Catholic wartime thought was the abstention, or acquiescence, of just war theory. Long abandoned by Protestant theologians and ethicists, the just war tradition had become an almost exclusively Catholic concern, at least in the United States. Before 1917, several leading authorities on just war theory had doubted whether the war in Europe qualified. As a result, they also concluded that American intervention would fail the just war test. But the combination of Wilson's efforts to maintain neutrality with the more immediate need to demonstrate an unqualified patriotism silenced such doubts. To satisfy the requirements of just war theory, it was particularly important for Catholic leaders to portray America's actions as defensive and reactive and its motives as disinterested and unselfish. In 1915, Father John Burke, editor of *The Catholic World*, had condemned war as "by no means a Christian tradition" and argued that to be "Christian means that we are pacifists." In April 1917, however, he told his national readership that war "has been literally forced upon our country, and she is compelled to take up arms for her own honor and for justice among men." Father Thomas J. Campbell of St. Patrick's Cathedral in New York reminded his parishioners that "as Catholics" they "must be conscious of the justice and the necessity of the war in which we have engaged." The Great War, now an American war, was now also a just war.[35]

Nothing illustrates the depth of American Catholic support for Wilson more than the reaction to Pope Benedict XV's peace proposal of August 1917. Using his papal authority, Benedict called for a very Wilsonian-sounding peace without victory in order to bring an immediate end to

Christendom's ultimate civil war. Europe was being ground down under the heel of war, and the Vatican worried about the consequences to European society and the Christian faith. Most of all, Benedict feared the ideological rivals that would seek to reorder a devastated continent: secularism, modernism, and communism. But even though he too had once sought a peace without victory, Wilson summarily rejected the pope's peace proposal as unwittingly favoring Germany and Austria, who stood to benefit from an early peace now that the United States had entered the war against them. Dictates from the Vatican normally commanded instant respect from American Catholics, but this time Catholics followed Wilson. Father John A. Ryan, a progressive Catholic intellectual, was virtually alone in calling for consideration of Benedict's peace plan. Other Catholic leaders resolved their conflicting loyalties between Rome and Washington by favorably comparing the unselfish, disinterested nature of Benedict's vision of peace with Wilson's but ultimately siding with the president's position that the United States and its partners first needed to defeat the forces of German authoritarianism.[36]

Catholic organizations, newly consolidated because of the demands of war, also rallied to the cause. Mostly in parallel, sometimes in partnership, and occasionally in conflict with the national Protestant organizations, the National Catholic War Council and the Knights of Columbus assisted the American war effort. Nativist Protestant fears of Catholics' dual loyalties and concerns about the separation of church and state strained relations between Catholics and the FCC and YMCA, but for the most part Protestants and Catholics maintained good relations simply by staying out of each other's way. The Knights, along with smaller Catholic agencies, already had a wealth of experience of relief work in war-torn Europe, especially Belgium. From April 1917, they began ministering to the needs of U.S. soldiers serving in Europe. The NCWC, headquartered in Washington, was an especially important innovation because it enabled the Catholic Church to coordinate its efforts on a national basis. The NCWC ensured that Catholic views were represented and heard in the Wilson administration and that Catholic concerns were respected and addressed. In return, the NCWC mobilized American Catholic support for the war effort, both in the United States and in Europe. Given the large number of Catholics in both the general population and U.S. forces in Europe, this was an important contribution. But just as important for American Catholicism, the war galvanized the church into becoming a cohesive national institution.[37]

AMERICAN JEWS ARRIVED at much the same position but from a different, more circuitous route. As with Catholics, the Jewish population was composed of a small, Americanized minority with a much larger, aspirational immigrant and second-generation majority. Unlike German, Austrian, and Irish Catholics, these Jews did not face charges of dual loyalty: almost without exception, they had little affection for the pogroms and official anti-Semitism of their homelands and felt no residual ties to any European country. And though it was gathering steam, Zionism was still an inchoate movement, dominated by Europeans, and did not pose a rival to American patriotism. The war would help change this by providing hopes for a Jewish homeland in Palestine, and by fostering Zionist sentiment among American Jews. Still, during the war few doubts emerged about Jews' attachment to the United States.[38]

However, other trends within Judaism, mostly political rather than religious, complicated Jewish reactions to the Great War. Many Jews, especially recent immigrants, were active socialists. In Manhattan, where Jewish participation in left-wing and radical politics was especially pronounced, Jews ran in city elections as candidates for the Socialist Party. Backed by the predominantly Jewish United Cloth and Cap Makers Union and United Hebrew Trades, Jewish Socialist candidates won several seats to the New York State legislature and New York City council in the elections of 1917. They ran on the usual socialist platform of redistributed wealth, workers' rights—and peace. In New York, as in many cities, those members of the peace movement not affiliated with a Protestant denomination were usually socialists. (In the case of some, such as Norman Thomas, they were both, but Thomas had received his entry into Socialist Party politics from Jewish mayoral candidate Morris Hillquit.) As Socialists, many Jews denounced what they saw as the capitalist and imperialist origins of the war. Through organizations such as the People's Council, the Jewish Socialist Federation, and the Emergency Peace Federation, Jews helped merge antiwar politics with radical polemics.[39]

Moreover, Jews of all political persuasions—conservative and socialist, Zionist and anti-Zionist—protested American aid to the Allies not only on traditional grounds of pacifism but also in opposition to aiding czarist Russia. "What right have the Allies even to expect the sympathy of American Jews with their cause as long as Russia fails to make any pronouncement with regard to the Jewish question?" asked Rabbi Stephen Wise in 1914. "There is no disguising the fact that American Jews will not swallow with any great degree of pleasure the cause of the Allies," wrote Cyrus Adler, a prominent conservative Jew, to his friend Solomon Schechter. "I have a decided feeling against Germany and her allies in this war and believe that the general cause of justice and human rights will be advanced by her defeat. I have a great feeling of friendliness for England and France but for the life of me I cannot get any enthusiasm about Russia and I think it a blot upon England and France that they have allied themselves with that barbarous country."[40]

The Jewish peace movement was short-lived, however, and by the fall of 1917 most American Jews were firm supporters of the war and ardent promoters of their patriotism. This reversal was sudden but not surprising given the dramatic turn of events at home and in Europe. First and perhaps foremost, Jews feared that with the United States now at war, antiwar dissent would trigger a nativist, anti-Semitic backlash. Many had firsthand memories of Russian and Romanian pogroms and other, less-deadly forms of official harassment; the last thing they wanted to do was provoke a similar reaction in their adopted Golden Land. Second, like Catholics Jews were reliably loyal to the Democratic Party and were loathe to oppose Wilson—the first president to nominate a Jew, Louis Brandeis, for the Supreme Court—on an issue of such political, diplomatic, and moral importance.

Third, with the war having dragged on for three years, American Jews also worried about the fate of their fellow Jews in Europe, who endured even greater miseries than they had known in peacetime. In response, Jewish relief agencies were created to meet the need. The American Zionist Medical Unit sent volunteers to the Middle East to relieve the suffering of Jews living there, while the Jewish Welfare Board, a similar body to the YMCA or Knights of Columbus, solicited donations to fund pastoral care for Jewish American soldiers in Europe. It served, in the words of Vice Chairman Cyrus Adler, as a "method of providing religious services and comfort for the Jewish men" in the service. American Jews, moreover, made up the largest national contingent in the Jewish Legion, an all-volunteer unit of the British Army serving in the Middle East. American immigrants and their descendants felt lucky to have escaped the daily horrors and indignities of Jewish life in eastern Europe, and they felt a conscientious urge to assist those who were not so fortunate. "It is now our turn to do our share," wrote labor leader Joseph Schlossberg in *Advance*, a Jewish newspaper in New York. "Most of us come from those very countries where this terrible conflagration is now raging," he reminded his readers. "We have found a home of refuge in this country. Let us show that we are worthy of the advantages we enjoy in this country by responding to the cry of despair coming from our fellow human beings on the other side of the globe."[41]

Finally, events in Europe and the tottering Ottoman Empire electrified American Jewish opinion and caused many to reverse their stance on the conflict. A war that was once perceived as benefiting only industrialists and imperialists was instantly transformed into a war for liberty, justice, and national self-determination. The hated Czar Nicholas II of Russia had been deposed in February 1917, and American Jews overwhelmingly supported the Menshevik revolutionaries who took power in his place. An alliance with that "barbarous country" Russia was no longer unpalatable.

Cyrus Adler may not have had much enthusiasm for Zionism, but this was a cause he could now support. The communist Bolshevik revolution that followed in November complicated matters but strengthened the Jewish commitment to the war: the Bolsheviks had relinquished to Germany vast amounts of Russian territory, including most of the land settled by Russian Jews, and no Jew wanted to oust the Russian czar only to be ruled by a German kaiser.[42]

Even more important, in November 1917 British Foreign Secretary Arthur Balfour proclaimed Britain's support for the creation of a Jewish homeland in Palestine. American Jews had never before been especially passionate Zionists, but now, with a Jewish-ruled Israel in sight for the first time in more than two thousand years, they rallied to the cause. "The Zionist movement in this country has become another thing since the war began," Wise reported excitedly to a friend in England. Initially wary of charges of dual loyalty and sensitive to the "100% Americanism" campaign, the American Jewish Committee found enough confidence to endorse the Balfour Declaration in early 1918. National self-determination, that very Wilsonian concept, became part of the Jewish nationalist crusade and Jewish objectives in the war across the ideological and theological spectrum, from organized labor and capital to Reform and Orthodox. "I am happy," Alexander Marx, a professor at the Jewish Theological Seminary in New York, wrote to a friend in November 1918, "that we are actually approaching the end of this awful war and that we can look forward to a real restoration of our people to their homeland."[43]

CHAPTER FIFTEEN

The Wilsonian Creed

O N JANUARY 8, 1918, Woodrow Wilson used an address before a joint session of Congress to unveil his Fourteen Points, the list of American war aims that has come to be seen as the definitive statement of Wilsonianism. Though he would refine these original Fourteen Points over the next eighteen months, his January speech to Congress set out an independent course for U.S. war aims and outlined one of the most liberal programs for a postwar settlement on either side of the Atlantic. Eight of the Fourteen Points dealt with specific issues, mainly territorial, such as where the proper borders of Poland, Belgium, and France should lie. But the other six outlined a remarkably progressive vision for the future of world politics. With little specificity, Wilson outlined six principles that placed mutual dependence and reciprocity—Christianity's Golden Rule, which also happened to form the heart of Social Gospel progressivism—at the heart of international relations: open diplomacy, freedom of the seas (an abiding American concern since the Quasi War with France and War of 1812 with Britain), free trade, disarmament, national self-determination, and a league of nations. The Fourteen Points represented Wilson's vision for permanent peace; some said they were hopelessly idealistic, their messenger irredeemably arrogant. "The good Lord Himself required only ten points," complained French Prime Minister Georges Clemenceau. "Wilson has fourteen."[1]

Fittingly, the Fourteen Points received ecstatic support from the American churches. It represented the perfect combination of right and might that underpinned the Christian concept of a progressive crusade. And it seemed to mark the culmination of millennial hopes of a new world. "The world that existed before the War has disappeared forever," declared Wilson's friend John Mott. "For the world it is a new birth, a great day of God such as comes only once in 100 or 1000 years." Shailer Mathews agreed, arguing that it was now "beyond belief" that the world "will ever revert permanently to conditions as they were before 1914." Most appealing was the notion that this, finally, was a plan to end all war. Christianity had led the way in abolishing slavery a half century earlier, Harry Emerson Fosdick pointed out, so why not war? The Great War was this generation's stern test, its Civil War. Just as many abolitionists had abandoned pacifism and nonresistance, by 1917–18 most liberal clergy believed that war was the only answer to tyranny and injustice. Argued Mathews, "non-resistance to evil might sometimes be the greatest of crimes." The churches' task, the FCC argued, was "to quicken the spirit of America in support of the President's policies in prosecuting the war for Democracy, International Justice, and a League of Nations." This was not a peace movement but "emphatically a war campaign."[2]

To the ecumenical mind, collective security and international organization seemed to offer the best means of ensuring permanent peace. Independent of Wilson, ecumenists had been promoting this same vision of a permanent peace for years. Recall the antebellum evangelical peace societies' dream of a "Congress of Nations" and a "League of Universal Brotherhood"; in 1911, Frederick Lynch called for the creation of a "United Nations of the World." Recall also their support throughout the nineteenth century for permanent international arbitration panels that would resolve disputes before they led to war. Such visions of institutionalized global cooperation had become central to the American Christian worldview. So it is little wonder that Christian figures turned to the biblical concept of "the brotherhood of man" as a way out of the European war. Indeed, Andrew Carnegie had spent millions in setting up Church Peace Union for this very purpose. "Surely," Carnegie wrote in his New Year's greeting card for 1915,

> after an armistice is established between the nations now unfortunately at war, the majority of enlightened people in all civilized lands will realize that permanent world peace would be Earth's greatest blessing and is entirely practicable through a union of a very few powerful nations pledged to maintain it, and inviting all other civilized lands to become members thereof, each nation contributing to the cost of such union in proportion to its population and wealth.

In this way, wrote Carnegie, the "Brotherhood of Man would then have arrived, and life on this Earth flash forth glimpses of Heaven."[3]

Carnegie's plea was not unusual, for the concept of a managed peace along cooperative lines flowed naturally, inevitably, out of the ecumenical project. Groups such as Church Peace Union and the World Alliance for the Promotion of International Friendship through the Churches were established to build global links and foster a spirit of transnational cooperation and integration that would lead to peace. This was a variant of the liberal worldview, best described as ecumenical internationalism, that stemmed from concerns about globalization and interdependence, biblical ethics, and traditional Christian peace advocacy. In 1915, the YMCA leader D. Willard Lyon proposed a peace settlement established on "the law of cooperation" and a "federation of the world" guided by Christianity's ideals and "universal values." Such a settlement, he claimed, was the "Christian equivalent of war." A year later, the World Alliance called for a "New Internationalism" to be founded after the war on the principle of "the equal right of all nations and races, small and great, to share in the world's resources" under the watchful eye of "a family of nations—an international brotherhood" that would manage the new peaceful, equitable order.[4]

Calls for some form of a league of nations accelerated in 1917, when it became clear that the United States would hold the initiative in any peace conference and that Wilson was sympathetic to a permanent postwar international organization. This was the ecumenists' moment, when secular groups sympathetic to a Wilsonian basis for peace were still coming to terms with its meaning, and they did not hesitate to seize it. In the ecumenical mind, if the Christian faith was universal, if the gospel was universal, and if the church was universal, then the ultimate sin was what one ecumenist condemned as "isolation and exclusiveness." Cooperation through integration was something of an article of faith for Social Gospelers. Washington Gladden had warned of the "errors of individualism," while Walter Rauschenbusch encouraged "the cooperative principle" because it facilitated communication, prevented misunderstanding, and reduced tension and conflict. So it was no surprise that liberal Protestant clergy would view barriers to recognition of a common humanity, such as state sovereignty and racism, as the root of all evil, and the sanctification of a transnational society based on reciprocal obligation as the source of an endless, postmillennial peace. The spread of a global society of brotherhood, declared the Home Missions Board of the Presbyterian Church, was an "incomparable missionary opportunity" for the "world's greatest Republic [and] Christian democracy." Other denominations, such as the Episcopalians, made similar declarations of Wilsonian intent, while a minister with the American Baptist Foreign Mission Society hailed the president's plan for peace as the moment marking the "birth of [a] world consciousness." Even ecumenical clergy in the Jim Crow South argued that racial integration and international organization were both necessary and mutually supportive.[5]

When Wilson himself announced his own Wilsonian vision with his January 1918 Fourteen Points address, and when he baptized the League of Nations as the vehicle for its success in a major speech in New York in September, mainline ecumenical clergy mobilized en masse in support. To them, the League represented "the political expression of the Kingdom of God on earth." The reformation of the world could now begin in earnest. From this new world order, the reformation of America could also begin.

Despite the wartime fervor, liberal internationalist clergy warned that even though the United States had been chosen to lead, Americans were not free from sin. Thus the "world must not only be made safe for America," Reverend Robert Denison preached even before Wilson's September speech, "democracy must also be made sure and complete in America. We must go on and perfect a League of Nations," but Americans must also eliminate the injustices within their own society.[6]

As the largest and broadest of the ecumenical organizations, the Federal Council of Churches and Church Peace Union led the way in promoting the application of ecumenism to world politics. From the very beginning of the war in Europe, they envisioned cooperation and mutual dependence as the pillars of peace. Ironically, in August 1914 they had teamed up to sponsor a peace conference in Konstanz, Germany, near the Swiss border. While en route from Paris, delegates were roused from the train and told they could not continue because the Germans had torn up the railroad tracks and closed the border with France. The Americans made it to Konstanz eventually, but just as Europe was beginning its agonizing descent into the depths of an unusually hellish war. Powerless to stop the spread of war, the FCC and Church Peace Union delegates relocated to London and devoted themselves to the promotion of an ecumenical peace settlement once the fighting stopped. Their first step was both audacious and characteristically bureaucratic: they set up yet another organization, the World Alliance. Little did they know that the war would last another four years.[7]

The FCC and Church Peace Union, either individually or in tandem, promoted ecumenical solutions for the duration of the war and through the subsequent debate over the terms of peace. Their only real difference was whether peace should take precedence over justice: the FCC accommodated itself to the demands of preparedness, while Church Peace Union steadfastly remained committed to peace advocacy until the United States entered the war. Yet as ecumenists and as internationalists, they both argued that it was essential that human relations—be they economic, social, or diplomatic—be organized along the principle, in the words of Reverend Linley Gordon of the World Alliance, that "general human interests should take precedence over special national interests, and a nation no less than an individual must recognize that it lives as a member of a larger whole." This principle represented the crucible of peace, and for the remainder of the war the ecumenical groups made the League their top priority.[8]

Crucially, ecumenists saw international peace and religious peace as two sides of the same coin. Nations needed to adopt cooperative, collective security, but churches needed to practice what they preached by continuing to further the ecumenical project. Such was the intensity of wartime ecumenism that U.S. intervention in turn stimulated further initiatives for church union as a natural complement to efforts to spur international peace through collective security. If Christians did not lead, they reasoned, the world would not follow. In the mission field, this meant supporting another tenet of the Wilsonian creed, national self-determination. In Korea, for example, American Protestant missionaries were instrumental in encouraging nationalists to press Wilson to support Korean independence from Japan.[9]

Even pious captains of industry saw no conflict between the gospel of wealth at home and the Social Gospel abroad. Carnegie had done much to promote both causes, and ecumenists hailed him as someone who could create the "United Churches of the World." Carnegie was joined by his fellow captain of industry, John D. Rockefeller Jr. A devout Baptist and avid philanthropist, Rockefeller supported the League and pushed for greater church unity as the two best means to preserve lasting peace. Invoking scripture and the Christian aim of a "Brotherhood of Men and Nations" in a wartime speech in Denver, Rockefeller declared that modern technology and communications meant that "No longer can any man live to himself alone, nor any nation. The world has become a unit." Just as the "peace and prosperity of any nation depend upon the happiness and the welfare of all of the people in that nation," so the "peace and prosperity of the world are dependent upon the happiness and welfare of all the nations of the world. And no force will be so powerful in conserving universal peace and good will after the war is over as the spirit of Brotherhood among men and nations." With stage one of his plan on track, Rockefeller then donated funds to establish the Interchurch World Movement in 1919. In matters of faith and diplomacy, Rockefeller's golden capitalist touch let him down: American participation in both the League of Nations and the Interchurch World Movement failed. Later, no less committed to ecumenism, the Rockefellers stopped donating money directly to the Baptist church and pledged to give only to nondenominational, interdenominational, or ecumenical groups.[10]

Christian liberal internationalists enhanced the Wilsonian creed by adding further provisions. They all agreed that open diplomacy, freedom of the seas, free trade, and collective security were worthwhile endeavors and indispensable to peace, but they supplemented Wilsonianism's democratic thrust with religious liberty. This was a peculiarly American preoccupation and had little resonance elsewhere, particularly in Europe where an established church was not only the norm but thought to be essential to social stability. Wilson was committed to religious liberty nonetheless and did what he could to promote it in Paris. In the Council of Four at the Paris conference, it was he who pressed—and personally drafted clauses—for the guarantee of religious liberty in the newly independent nations to be created from the dismemberment of the Austro-Hungarian and Russian empires. Wilson, for example, insisted that Poland be compelled by treaty to respect the freedoms of conscience and worship, a move designed to protect Poland's beleaguered Jewish minority.[11]

Wilson's allies on both ends of the theological spectrum were even more assertive. On behalf of American missionaries, Mott implored Wilson to include a commitment to religious liberty in the terms of any peace treaty. The Southern Baptist Convention, at this stage deeply internationalist despite its theological conservatism, placed the First Amendment's nonestablishment and free exercise clauses above all other freedoms and urged their worldwide application. The Federal Council of Churches urged the framers of the League Charter to protect religious liberty as a "fundamental feature . . . of vital democracy and essential to the peace of the world." Unitarian layman and former president William Howard Taft, founder of the League to Enforce Peace and the leading Republican advocate for the League of Nations, went a step further, arguing that the essence of the League meant it would automatically protest violations of religious liberty even if religion had not been explicitly codified. To Americans, there were few if any principles as valuable as the freedoms of conscience and worship, from which all other human rights flowed.[12]

IT WAS NO ACCIDENT that the mainline churches and Wilson expressed the same millennial visions of a postwar peace based on collective security and world federation. As his aide Ray Stannard Baker commented to Wilson after the war, the churches represented by the FCC "are the sincerest supporters of your principles," and the president thanked them for their support. Wilson did not turn to the clergy for advice or guidance on the Fourteen Points. His trusted adviser Colonel Edward House and the Inquiry, a confidential team of journalists and scholars who served as special advisers on postwar order, helped give shape to Wilson's scattered images of a just peace. But the churches were not unimportant, and Wilson did not turn to them because he did not need to; he was so thoroughly steeped in mainline Protestant theology, so familiar with the premises of the Social Gospel, that it would have been surprising had his foreign policy resembled anything else. Wilsonianism was essentially an expression of Christian reformism, of the global application of progressive Christianity, not because of a conscious vision but simply because Wilson could not escape who he was.[13]

Throughout his life, Woodrow Wilson was a devoted Presbyterian. He was the son, nephew, and grandson of Presbyterian ministers on both sides of his family, and he took his spiritual heritage very seriously. In particular, Wilson used Calvinism as a prism through which to perceive the secular world. His belief in the comforting dictates of providence and the guiding hand of God was especially strong and would not have been out of place had he lived among the first generation of Puritans in Massachusetts Bay. "There is a spirit that rules us," he declared on the stump during his first run for the presidency in 1912. "If I did not believe in Providence I would feel like a man going blindfolded through a haphazard world." Wilson marveled at those "small," futile people who would "intrigue against Providence. How God must laugh!" Or as he told a confidant during the Senate fight over the Treaty of Versailles: "If I were not a Christian, I think I should go mad, but my faith in God holds me to the belief that He is in some way working out His own plans through human perversities and mistakes." Another vestige of his Calvinism was his belief that the United States was the chosen nation. "I believe that God presided over the inception of this nation," he boasted during the 1912 presidential election campaign. "I believe that God planted in us the visions of liberty" and "that we are chosen and prominently chosen to show the way to the nations of the world how they shall walk in the paths of liberty."[14]

Presbyterianism, learned at the feet of his father, impressed upon Wilson other ideas that had political as well as religious meaning. Perhaps the most important was covenant theology, a central tenet of the Presbyterian Church, especially the Scottish strain that guided the faith of both sides of his family. According to covenant theology, God had made a compact, a covenant, with his people. In return for their obedient faith, God would protect them and forgive their sins. This had particular resonance for American political thought, in which Jefferson's Declaration of Independence had based the right to self-determination upon the idea that ruler and ruled were bound by a contract, and that George III had violated his end of the contract by ruling arbitrarily and tyrannically. The Scottish Covenanters of the 1630s, whom Wilson considered his intellectual and spiritual ancestors, grounded their faith and politics in the idea of God's covenant, which motivated both their Presbyterianism and challenge to the English crown. Covenant theology informed Wilson's thinking on history, law, education, and politics, and it followed him when he became a graduate student at Johns Hopkins, a professor at Princeton, and president of the United States.[15]

From his religious background, Wilson also developed a sharply defined appreciation of right and wrong, good and evil. Covenant theology left no room for ambiguity or moral relativism: a person either obeyed God's law or did not. To Wilson, recalled Secretary of Agriculture David F. Houston, "God was an immanent presence. He was with Him in the White House, and if he could discern what He wanted, he gave no heed to what anybody else or everybody else wanted or thought." Wilson possessed a clarity of moral vision that struck observers, particularly foreigners, as unusually dogmatic and inflexible. Most often, others used religious metaphors when describing him. Constantin Dumba, the Austrian ambassador to Washington, found Wilson to be "doctrinaire." To Sir Cecil Spring Rice, the British ambassador, Wilson was a "hardened saint." The economist John Maynard Keynes, a member of the British delegation to the 1919 Paris Peace Conference, shrewdly likened Wilson to "a Nonconformist minister, perhaps a Presbyterian. His thought and his temperament were essentially theological not intellectual." Keynes worried most of all that Wilson's "theological temperament" sometimes "became dangerous" because it was so dogmatic. Harold Nicolson, another member of the British delegation, viewed Wilson as "a prophet." David Lloyd George, the British prime minister who should have been Wilson's natural ally in Paris, later wrote that the president "regarded himself as a missionary whose function it was to rescue the poor European heathen from their age-long worship of false and fiery gods." "I can get on with you," Clemenceau confided to one of Wilson's advisers. "You are practical . . . but talking to Wilson is something like talking to Jesus Christ!" Saint, minister, prophet, missionary, messiah—Wilson's contemporaries were certainly not agnostic about his manner, bearing, and temperament.[16]

For Wilson, religion formed the basis for politics: from religious liberty flowed political liberty, and from religious justice flowed political justice. This is not to say that he sought to impose a particular religious vision or belief upon the nation. He had no pretensions of being a theologian or making a contribution to religious thought. As one of his biographers notes, Wilson's "religious concerns were preeminently moral, not theological, in character; the Christian life was merely the task of acting out God's certain commands in a world of good and evil." But like Washington, Madison, and Lincoln before him, Wilson saw in religious faith the basic requirements for democratic citizenship, patriotism, and political responsibility. As a Christian republican, he believed that only God and Christ could claim the right of divine rule; people owed them their allegiance, and thus could only rule one another through accountable, democratic procedures. A denial of this belief was what made materialist political systems, such as communism, so undemocratic. "Some men make themselves the centre of the universe instead of making God the centre," Wilson told his secretary of the Navy, Josephus Daniels, which gave them the "wrong outlook upon the world." On another occasion, President Wilson told a Fourth of July audience that the "way to success in this great country" was "to show that you are not afraid of anybody except God and His final verdict. If I did not believe that, I would not believe in democracy. If I did not believe that, I would not believe that people can govern themselves."[17]

Also very much in the tradition of Jefferson and Madison, Wilson saw religion as a vital source of liberty because it was the wellspring of individual thought and conscience. Religious faith provided "each man a magistracy over himself by insisting upon his personal, individual responsibility to God." A former student from Princeton spoke of Wilson's lectures on political freedom, in which the Scottish Covenanters had a starring role. "It was here that freedom of conscience took root," the student recalled. It was "a steppingstone by which the past made its way into a future of wider justice."[18]

A final element to Wilson's civil religion, particularly after his adoption of progressivism, was the importance of religion to the spread of progress and the protection of justice. To be sure, his Southern Presbyterian heritage, with its instinctive separating of church from state, had always kept him somewhat at odds with the Social Gospel. The "*object of the church as an organization* [is] *the salvation of souls*" and "only indirectly *the purification of Society*," he wrote in 1900. Despite an exposure to Social Gospel teachings as an undergraduate at Princeton, and despite having many mainline Protestant friends who discovered their calling in social reform, Wilson found the political activism of religious ministers distasteful and unappealing. As he explained to his friend John Mott, "I have had the fear in recent years that the ministers of our churches, by becoming involved in all sorts of social activities . . . have too much diverted their attention from the effectual preaching of the Word." The "danger" was that "individual churches will become great philanthropic societies instead of being what it seems to me they ought to be, organizations from which go forth the spiritual stimulation which should guide all philanthropic effort." But religion, with its prophetic insights and timeless moral precepts, was essential to a healthy society. Thus while Wilson found the preaching of politics distasteful, he was also an enthusiastic supporter of Protestant missions as agents of civilization and faith through progressive change. And of course, most crucially of all, Wilson himself was not a preacher. As a politician, unlike a minister, he was free to use faith as a guide to the implementation of political solutions to social problems. Thus while he could not strictly be considered a Social Gospeler, in a looser sense he shared many of their aims. To Wilson, the Christian religion was a progressive force, and he was, through and through, a Protestant reformer. "No doubt Christianity came into the world to save the world," he proclaimed in 1909. "We are privileged to live in the midst of many manifestations of the great service that Christianity does to society, to the world that now is."[19]

Politically and theologically, then, Wilson was an ecumenical internationalist. Moreover, from his devoutly Protestant background and contacts with mainline religious leaders, especially in the Presbyterian Church and within various branches of the missionary enterprise, he was already familiar with the principles of the ecumenical movement. Indeed, stemming from his Presbyterian-influenced affinity for order, organization, and governance, his theology was nearly identical to the ecumenists'. Moreover, Wilson was no stranger to ecumenical councils, and he had worked with and supported the Federal Council in its infancy. While president of Princeton University, he had given a speech on aspects of religious cooperation at the FCC's founding convention in New York. "Cooperation is the vital principle of social life; not organization merely," he declared in another speech to the FCC on "the translation of doctrine into life." "But if the object of the organization is to afford a mechanism by which the whole community can cooperatively use its life, then there is a great deal in it." From his many offers of "spiritual mediation" before 1917 to his vision for a League of Nations afterward, Wilson's diplomacy was steeped in the ideas of ecumenical internationalism.[20]

Most important, perhaps, the League of Nations and a codified set of principles such as the Fourteen Points fit naturally into the very basics of Wilson's religious and political philosophy. His historical heroes, the Scottish Covenanters, had staked their claims to just authority and as protectors of liberty upon the notion of a compact—a written contract—between ruler and ruled. God, infallible and almighty, was unique in that only he could break the compact; only he was above reproach. Yet because he was wise and loving, God would reward the faithful with blessings on earth and everlasting life after death. Such compacts were always written down—be it the Bible or the Constitution, the Ten Commandments or the Fourteen Points—so that all knew their place, role, and obligations. For Wilson, the Bible was "the Magna Charta of the human soul," and thus the foundation of democracy. Written compacts were supremely important because they prevented arbitrary rule, circumvented monopoly power, and undermined secret diplomacy.[21]

This was not an exclusively religious concept, of course, as the work of political philosophers such as Thomas Hobbes and John Locke attests. But for Wilson, it had a crucially important historical and religious component, one that strengthened his faith that the League of Nations and Fourteen Points would be the means to end war forever. According to Jan Smuts, a South African delegate in Paris who was one of the original architects of the League, it was Wilson who personally insisted on the term "covenant." So it was no coincidence that Wilson often invoked the Covenanters when promoting the League. "The stern Covenanter tradition that is behind me sends many an echo down through the years," he said in London in December 1918. "I wish that it were possible for us to do something like some of my very stern ancestors did, for among my ancestors are those very determined persons who were known as the Covenanters," he remarked a few days later to an audience in Manchester. "I wish we could . . . enter into a great league and covenant, declaring ourselves, first of all, friends of mankind and uniting ourselves together for the maintenance and the triumph of right." It was no coincidence that the League's founding rules and principles would not be recorded in a charter, or a constitution, but a covenant. Indeed, neither was it a coincidence that the League would be headquartered in Geneva, the birthplace of Calvinism and the seat of Reformed Protestantism.[22]

MAINLINE PROTESTANTS MAY have dominated postwar planning, but Catholics and Jews supported the Fourteen Points and the League of Nations for reasons of their own. Both Catholics and Jews favored internationalist solutions to the problems of world politics, and both had Wilsonian idealists and philosophers of international relations within their ranks. Advocates of social thought represented the majority of those Catholics who thought seriously about the postwar order. Father John Ryan was the Catholic internationalists' leader, but he was not alone. "There is no longer any dream of a nation at peace," wrote Father William J. Kerby, a Catholic socialist. "There is vision now only of the world at peace." Similarly, Moses Baroway, a young Jewish nationalist with the American Zionist Medical Unit in Palestine, expressed the Wilsonianism typical of American Jews. From Jerusalem, now in British hands, Baroway wrote his family in New York of his hope that an "international program that spells orderly living for a long time to come" would happen as a result of the Fourteen Points, especially the League of Nations. This was also the cause Brandeis and Wise supported.[23]

But other, more particular concerns motivated Catholics and Jews as well, and it was no coincidence that Baroway penned his letter while visiting Palestine. For Catholic and Jew alike, national self-determination promised an end to imperial subjugation abroad. For Catholics, it was sure to mean Irish home rule and freedom from the British—most Irish Catholics insisted that Ireland would be the standard by which Wilsonianism would be judged—though some worried that the League's protections of national sovereignty might also be a way for the British to maintain their domination of Ireland. It was, William Cardinal O'Connell declared to the Irish County Clubs of Boston, "to God and America that Ireland must look for the vindication of all that her dead have died for. American intervention promises to help small nations. Be Irish and doubly be Americans." Stephen Wise concurred, and wrote Wilson a week after the declaration of war to urge the president to issue another declaration, in the name of oppressed peoples everywhere, for Irish home rule. Not all Irish progressives and internationalists were also Wilsonians—Irish Catholic labor unions, for example, argued that the League of Nations would simply be beholden to the same monied powers that had kept Ireland under Britain's thumb—but on the whole most saw Wilson as the best means to achieve independence.[24]

Though it was left unsaid, Rabbi Wise obviously had other causes in mind besides a free Ireland. For Jews, the League of Nations was sure to lead to a Zionist homeland in Palestine. Once an almost exclusively European endeavor, Zionism was becoming increasingly popular, and as a result assertive, in the United States. The Federation of American Zionists was founded in 1897, but it remained small and ineffectual until the war. In 1914, Louis D. Brandeis was elected president of the Federation. A Supreme Court judge and brilliant legal mind, Brandeis was also close to the president who nominated him to the Court, Woodrow Wilson. Because Brandeis's immigrant connection to Europe was many years past—his parents fled Bohemia in 1848 and eventually settled in Kentucky, where he was raised—he possessed a thoroughly American identity that instantly infused Zionism with patriotic credibility in the United States. And beyond—when Balfour traveled to the United States, the man he wanted to confer with most was not Wilson, but Brandeis.[25]

But Wilson himself was also sympathetic to Zionism, for political but above all moral reasons. He shared the Progressive vision that Brandeis had for the "social and political laboratory" that was to be the Jewish home in Palestine. He also saw in anti-Semitism an ominous political bellwether of tyranny and oppression. In voicing his support for Zionism in Paris, Wilson told Lloyd George and Clemenceau that he "not only had a friendly feeling towards the Jews" but that "it was perfectly clear that one of the most dangerous elements of ferment arose from the treatment of Jews." Furthermore, the Inquiry recommended "religious determination" in the former Ottoman Empire instead of national or ethnic self-determination. In an August 1918 letter to Wise, Wilson endorsed the Balfour Declaration. This did not resolve the issue, of course, which Wilson would discover in Paris, where his support for Zionism unnerved Secretary of State Robert Lansing and other American peace commissioners. But for now, American Zionists were among the most devoted of Wilsonianism's disciples. For Brandeis, Wise, and others, the war was not only America's, but Israel's.[26]

AFTER SUCCESSFULLY HOLDING their lines against a German offensive and launching a vigorous attack of their own in the summer of 1918, the war officially ended on November 11. Fearful of losing ground and opening the way for war to devour their own country, the Germans sued for peace directly to Wilson, for a settlement based upon the Fourteen Points. In December, Wilson traveled to Paris for the peace conference the world had been anticipating for the past four years. Wilson's overseas journey was unprecedented for a sitting president, but his ambitions were unprecedented as well, and he dared not leave his cabinet secretaries and assistants in the hands of cynical, experienced European diplomats.

Ecstatic throngs greeted Wilson in Europe, where he was hailed by the public as a messiah more than a president. Back home, the Protestant churches continued their crusade to move "From World War to World Brotherhood."[27]

Protestants were not the only Wilsonians on crusade. American Zionists joined other Jewish nationalists from Europe to present their case directly to Wilson and the victorious great powers. Louis Brandeis, Stephen Wise, and Felix Frankfurter, a professor at Harvard Law School and another future Supreme Court justice, sailed across the Atlantic in search of a Jewish homeland in Palestine. First they had to stop in France, where they queued with other nationalist leaders—the young Vietnamese nationalist Ho Chi Minh, the professorial Czechs Thomas Masaryk and Edvard Beneš, the august Arab King Faisal, and the patrician Greek statesman Eleftherios Venizelos—who sought a hearing on their freedom. To Brandeis, the peace conference was "the most auspicious moment in [the] history of [the] Zionist Movement." Thanks to Balfour and Prime Minister David Lloyd George, the British had already staked their claim to a Jewish homeland in Palestine. Wilson was sympathetic—after all, the twelfth of the Fourteen Points called for the dismantling of the Ottoman Empire—and the Inquiry had looked upon Zionist plans favorably. "To think that I," Wilson exulted to Wise, "a son of the manse, should be able to help restore the Holy Land to its people!" Wilson was also sympathetic to the Armenians, another unhappy Christian people living under Turkish Muslim rule, and supported the idea of an independent Armenia in eastern Turkey.[28]

Yet in the end, they all failed. Armenians could not win an independent state of their own, and neither could Zionist Jews—at least, not yet. The United States had not declared war against Turkey and had no troops anywhere in the Middle East—and thus had no leverage. Irish Catholics did eventually gain their autonomy, but this came in spite of great power politics, not because of it, and they resented Wilson's reluctance to pressure Britain to apply national self-determination to Ireland. Most important of all, Wilson and the ecumenical internationalists could not convince the United States Senate to abandon the unilateralist diplomatic tradition. Permanent peace would have to wait if it meant entering into permanent alliances. The Senate voted against the ratification of the Treaty of Versailles, ending any hopes of America leading the world in a League of Nations toward the millennium of unending peace.[29]

While Protestants, modernist and fundamentalist, had been mostly united against Germany during the war, they were deeply divided over the potential terms of the peace. Theologically liberal ecumenists favored integration and the erasure of individual sovereignties, be they denominational or national, in pursuit of a greater good. To conservatives, however, ecumenism in religion and collective security in geopolitics were tantamount to blasphemy. This difference cut to the heart of the modernist-fundamentalist dispute, for fundamentalists decried the compromises that modernists were willing to make in the name of social justice and harmony. These might be worthy goals, conservatives agreed, but they were not necessarily reflections of the true religion. The very label *fundamentalist*, coined and worn with pride by conservatives themselves, perfectly conveyed the importance they attached to remaining faithful to the original essence of the Christian faith as outlined in the Bible—hence their belief in biblical literalism and hostility to evolution. "We will never get together on minimums of faith but only on maximums of faith," warned Baptist pastor John Roach Straton in words that could have served as the fundamentalist creed. This was not a theology comfortable with compromise, religious, political, or diplomatic. In religion, conservative evangelicals and fundamentalists attacked ecumenical initiatives, especially the Federal Council and Rockefeller's Interchurch World Movement, as watered-down versions of Christianity. The FCC "united on a social creed instead of a religious one" that "would make a praiseworthy platform for a political party" but was "quite inadequate" for a church body, accused fundamentalist author John Horsh. Unless a religious institution "stands for the fundamentals of the Christian faith . . . it does not sustain a distinctly Christian character." Instead, "modern religious unionism stands for ignoring every fundamental of the Christian faith." Because modernism lacked purity, it also lacked spirituality and the relevance it sought.[30]

Fundamentalists easily transferred this aversion to compromise on core principles from theology to foreign policy, and from the Federal Council to the League of Nations. Sensitive to the preservation of traditional morals and identity, conservatives cherished denominational autonomy. As society's nonconformists and self-appointed guardians of heritage, they feared government regulation of religion and fiercely defended the separation of church and state. Their opposition to the Social Gospel stemmed from this raw anti-statism, even though many fundamentalists sympathized with the social reformist intentions of liberal clergy. Similarly, while many conservatives also favored the promotion of democracy after the war, they did not want the United States to be subservient to a cooperative international organization—analogous to an ecumenical organization—such as the League of Nations. They wanted to preserve America's autonomy in the world system. As Wilson was putting the finishing touches on the peace settlement in Paris, James M. Gray of the Moody Bible Institute was attacking the League of Nations by linking it to the Interchurch World Movement. Reuben Torrey went further, equating the League with the socialist internationalism of the Industrial Workers of the World. Ignoring their own strictures against mixing religion and politics, Gray, Torrey, and other leading fundamentalists mounted a national campaign against Senate ratification of the League. Collective security under the aegis of an international organization, Gray charged, would be "national suicide."[31]

Ever conscious of purity as well as identity and autonomy, fundamentalists also objected to joining a League in which the United States would be recognized as the moral and political equal of other nations. Membership in an international organization would require Americans to participate as partners of nations that were Catholic or Muslim. What good was such an organization? And what could it ever hope to accomplish? "How," demanded an indignant Arno Gaebelein, a leading Methodist fundamentalist, "can God bless these nations, who continue in idolatries, who defy His laws? Can He bless professing Christian nations, banded together in pact with heathen nations?" J. C. Massee, a Baptist preacher and fundamentalist insurgent who led the attack on modernism in the Northern Baptist Convention, denounced the League as the very worst sort of ecumenism, "a deliberate effort to dethrone God in the earth. . . . We who are a professedly Christian nation are about to enter a league of nations, and into an international alliance, with nations that are altogether pagan." Americans would incur the wrath of God, Massee warned, because, as Christians, the Bible explicitly put them "under obligation to foreswear any alliance with a pagan nation." Mirrored across the South and Midwest, and in the booming churches of urban fundamentalism in Chicago, Philadelphia, Detroit, and New York, such concerns helped severely erode popular support for the League.[32]

Perhaps Wilson should have listened to the reservations of the most prominent conservative American Protestant at the Paris peace conference, a man who also happened to be his secretary of state. In 1915, Wilson rid himself of one fundamentalist Presbyterian secretary of state, William Jennings Bryan, only to appoint another, Robert Lansing. But despite their shared Presbyterianism and dour personalities, Wilson and Lansing did not get along. A specialist in international law with a suitably pedantic mind, Lansing agreed with Wilson that some sort of new world order had to emerge from the ashes of war. And in theory, he thought a league of nations could work. But the League Wilson envisioned made no allowances for traditional American diplomatic doctrine, especially the Monroe Doctrine, or even the Constitution. From a very early point, Lansing feared that a treaty containing the League would never pass through the Senate intact. Not coincidentally, Lansing was also a quasi-fundamentalist Presbyterian: not active enough in religious politics to earn himself a label, but nonetheless a firm believer in biblical inerrancy, miracles, and the virgin birth of Christ in addition to being an avid reader of scripture. Like most conservative Protestants, Lansing did not like to deviate from the written word. Nor was he comfortable with watering down the essence of identity, be it denominational or national, in pursuit of a common objective. He thought the League could work only if it consisted of like-minded democracies, a concern shared by many other evangelicals and fundamentalists. Lansing pressed his concerns in Paris, but Wilson ignored him, and in early 1920 the two parted ways.[33]

By that time, Wilson's dream of world peace had ended. The Senate rejected the Treaty of Versailles, and with it the League of Nations. The Wilsonian creed would have to wait until another world war, more terrible than the first, had vindicated its prophecy.

PART VI

Franklin Roosevelt and
the Third Crusade

The State Department, Washington, D.C., January 18, 1941. Distressed by the collapse of basic living conditions and the spread of starvation and disease in his country, Gaston Henry-Haye, the French ambassador to Washington, requested an emergency meeting with Secretary of State Cordell Hull. The emotional ambassador spoke "very earnestly and strongly," Hull wrote afterward in his notes, "about the urgency of obtaining food" for France—including the northern half of France occupied by the Nazis—through U.S. aid and assistance. America was still officially neutral, Henry-Haye and the government of unoccupied France reasoned, and had traditionally sympathized with foreign people suffering through humanitarian disasters. And they had received encouragement from no less a figure than former President Herbert Hoover, who was in the midst of organizing relief efforts for Europe. Yet Hull was unmoved. He did not especially care for the ambassador, whom he described as "a little man with ruddy cheeks and a truculent mustache," and he certainly did not care for his government, the Vichy-based regime under Marshal Philippe Pétain that had capitulated to the Germans and was actively collaborating with the Nazis. Hull acknowledged the "ancient friendship" between the French and American people, but that was about all he would concede. "I said that it must be made clear," he recorded, "that we feel deeply that the future welfare of France like that of our own country makes it all the more important for Great Britain to successfully resist the Hitler onslaught," and that naïvely shipping food and medical supplies through the British blockade to French civilians would simply end up feeding and supplying the Nazis. It was Germany's responsibility to feed the people of France, Hull lectured the sheepish ambassador, not America's—and certainly not Herbert Hoover's.[1]

Hull was not a hard-hearted man. Nor was he uninformed of the situation in Europe. A year earlier, Polish diplomat Ludwik Rajchman had warned the State Department of widespread food shortages that had led to malnutrition and starvation. A few months later, after the German conquest of western Europe, King Leopold III of Belgium wrote Franklin Roosevelt that his people "live in anguish, scattered, without shelter, in dire distress," and that their plight was "even more dreadful" than in 1914. And in the summer of 1940, the French, including Henry-Haye himself, had warned that hardship and hunger would only cement fascism's grip on France. Pétain even sent a personal letter to Roosevelt pleading for "relief and assistance" from "your generous country, which is bound to mine by century-old friendship."[2]

Here was a classic moral dilemma of international politics. Clearly, the humanitarian objective should be to aid the victims of aggression against starvation, disease, and other afflictions of war. But to do so might—and given the Nazis' track record, would—instead help the aggressors without helping the victims at all. This was certainly the view of the British, who were using the Royal Navy to blockade Europe and were naturally hostile to provisioning the victims of Nazism with food and supplies that the Nazis would simply take for themselves. The British decided that despite the deepening humanitarian crisis, they "must treat Germany and the territories under her occupation on the same footing." It was well within Germany's power to feed those people, claimed the British, which made them doubly suspicious that relief would never actually reach its intended recipients. Moreover, it would be "entirely mistaken," if not also immoral, to assist Germany with "the difficulties which confront her and which are of her own creation." Yet initially, in this earlier period of the winter, spring, and summer of 1940, Hull and the State Department had been more receptive to Americans sending relief into Nazi-occupied Europe, and they were at first willing to support them with the full authority at their disposal. "The American Government feels that the right of its citizens to send medical and other related supplies to victims of war should not be interfered with by the British Government," Hull instructed the U.S. Embassy in London in February 1940. This was a very different tone than the one he would use with Ambassador Henry-Haye a year later.[3]

Though the controversy over European relief was not solely a religious issue, it was fundamentally a moral concern that had religious ethics at its core. Other than the American Red Cross, the advocates of relief were mostly faith-based relief agencies, especially the American Friends Service Committee. Against tremendous odds, American Quakers had been unique in their ability to remain neutral and administer aid to both sides of the Spanish Civil War, and they aimed to do the same in war-torn Europe. Just as prominent was fellow Quaker Herbert Hoover, who worked with the AFSC but also orchestrated relief programs of his own. In 1939, Hoover founded the Commission for Polish Relief and oversaw the shipment of nonmilitary aid to Poland before German obstruction and the British blockade shut it down. The next year, after the German offensive in the west, he established the National Committee on Food for the Small Democracies (Norway, Finland, Holland, Belgium, and Poland). In announcing his relief plan for western Europe, Hoover declared that humanitarian values could not be eclipsed by military necessity or ideology "because of the teachings of Christ which have resounded down these two thousand years" and which "gave to mankind a new vision and part of that mission was mercy and compassion." Shortly after, in a major article in *Collier's*, he argued that "compassion is the woof and warp of democracy" and that the "Christian world is confronted with preserving the lives of millions" of innocent people in Europe. "We cannot as a Christian nation dismiss our concern." Instead, Americans should act like the Good Samaritan—or like Jesus Christ himself, "the Greatest Teacher of all time" who "did not allow His immortal vision to be clouded by debate" over politics or ideology.[4]

Hoover's relief efforts posed a serious problem for the British and their sympathizers in America. The blockade was seen as Great Britain's only effective weapon; to weaken it, even for the sake of Christian charity, would weaken its defenses, particularly against an enemy who would surely take advantage of any relief supplies for itself. But to let Europe's needy starve and freeze would make the British look not only uncharitable, but cruel. Hull and the State Department sympathized with the British, and even suspected Hoover of playing politics with an issue that could damage the president to whom he had ignominiously lost the White House in 1932. But politics aside, Hoover presented a danger to both Roosevelt and Britain. Roosevelt's secretary of the interior, Harold Ickes, recalled that FDR "expressed concern" about Hoover's relief plans, which would "make a very unpleasant issue in this country and would complicate the foreign situation badly."[5]

But Hoover not only had Christ on his side, he also had the blessing of some of America's most famous religious leaders. He even boasted to Lord Halifax, the British ambassador to Washington, that he could launch a campaign that would be "echoed from 10,000 pulpits." This may have been an exaggeration, but Hoover did have tremendous support from what he called "the spiritual and moral forces of this nation." Among the more than two hundred clergy who signed up to support Hoover were the prominent Catholics William Cardinal O'Connell of Boston and Archbishop Edward Mooney of Detroit; Protestants included John R. Mott and Reverend Daniel A. Poling. None could be dismissed as dreamy idealists or pacifists. Mooney, for example, was an early supporter of military preparedness, including conscription; Mott was an ally of Reinhold Niebuhr and a charter member of the pro-Allied magazine *Christianity and Crisis*; Poling had been a YMCA chaplain in World War I, was an outspoken opponent of Nazism and supporter of the Allies, and encouraged his own son, Clark, to volunteer as a chaplain in the U.S. Army. (In fact, in 1943, Lieutenant Clark Poling died aboard the stricken USS *Dorchester* as one of the famously heroic Four Chaplains—two Protestant ministers, a Catholic priest, and a Jewish Rabbi—who voluntarily gave up their life jackets and places on lifeboats to go down together with the stricken ship, braced against the railing while praying aloud and singing hymns.) Just as significant was the presence of Rabbi Edward N. Calisch: if a Jew could vouch for the integrity of Hoover's program, anyone could.[6]

Moreover, other clergy who did not join Hoover's organization also supported relief for occupied Europe. Without mentioning Hoover's group, the Federal Council of Churches endorsed the need for relief in Europe and China. Reverend Ernest Fremont Tittle, a noted Social Gospel Methodist from Evanston, Illinois, argued in the pages of *Christian Century* and *Zion's Herald*, two of the largest-circulation religious magazines in the country, that feeding Europe's hungry might also be an opening gambit for a peace settlement. But for most, the issue was one of simple Christian charity, and many were incensed that anyone could possibly disagree. "I do not see how we in America, surrounded by comforts and a large measure of security, can deliberately advocate the starvation of thirty million neutral human beings," wrote a Yale Divinity student in 1940.[7]

Yet Hoover was not the only one with Christ on his side. A group of pro-British and mostly interventionist clergy, led by Niebuhr and Henry Sloane Coffin, moved quickly to mobilize public opinion against the former president's relief plans. Hoover and the architects of relief may have been sincere humanitarians, but they were misguided, perhaps even delusional, about both their own capabilities and German intentions. Any aid sent to occupied Europe would go straight to the Nazis, the opponents of relief charged. And even if the German forces allowed American observers to monitor the shipment of aid, they would simply requisition the same amount of supplies and foodstuffs away from prying eyes. Either way, American relief would end up perpetuating, even collaborating in, the far greater crime of Nazi aggression. Niebuhr and Coffin had support from secular groups with awkward names that mirrored Hoover's, such as the Committee to Defend America by Aiding the Allies or the Century Club Group. But secular critics did so on the grounds of strategy and national security. The interventionist clergy were more effective because they could debate Hoover on his own terms: morality.[8]

Feeding and clothing the hungry, shivering people of Nazi-occupied Europe was a morally compelling cause, Hoover's opponents acknowledged, but it was also misleading. Here, they appealed to national security but, as Roosevelt himself would do on countless occasions before and during the war, they linked national security to the survival of values, morality, even religion itself. In a statement largely drafted by Coffin, Hoover's opponents deployed some Christian imagery of their own. "No one can hope to evade a share of the suffering," read their October 1940 press statement, including the victims of Nazi aggression. Two months later, another Coffin-orchestrated declaration, signed by several of the nation's most renowned religious leaders, argued that while the issue presented "a dilemma of heart-searching difficulty," relief would in all likelihood only strengthen the forces of Nazism. "What is at stake is not merely the security of Great Britain and the United States, but also the sole remaining hope of freedom." Under such pressure, the advocates of relief began to relent. While the FCC—still opposed to intervention—publicly called for relief, privately it warned Roosevelt against committing to anything that would give indirect assistance to the Germans. And in a parallel and surely much more painful effort, Rabbi Stephen Wise requested the World Jewish Congress to stop smuggling relief supplies to incarcerated Jews in occupied Europe. Claimed Wise on an earlier occasion, "To die at the hands of Nazism is cruel; to survive by its grace were ten thousand times worse. We will survive Nazism unless we commit the inexplicable sin of bartering or trafficking with it in order to save some Jewish victims."[9]

But most telling of all, and probably most helpful to the Allied war effort, the religious leaders who opposed aid to occupied Europe never pretended to be neutral. Coffin, Niebuhr, and Wise, along with all their associates, were fervently supportive of the British. Coffin even orchestrated his campaign against Hoover in secret collaboration with the British Embassy in Washington. Coffin also headed his own group, the Inter-Faith Committee to Aid the Democracies, which claimed Wise as a member. On his own and within the Jewish community, Wise was in fact a tireless champion of sending the same aid to Britain that he called on the World Jewish Congress to withhold from Jews suffering under Nazi occupation, including $18,000 worth of vitamins and $69,000 to build a children's health care center in London. Rabbi Wise and his wife even "adopted" a British boy, Dennie Edward Mitchell, as a way to highlight the plight of British children in wartime. Coffin and Wise sympathized with the people of occupied Europe. But the surest route to relief, they argued, was an Allied military victory.[10]

The United States did eventually ship some aid to Vichy France in 1941, but it was a paltry amount designed to relieve political and diplomatic pressures in Washington, not alleviate suffering in France. The British, of course, were thrilled. They had won an important political and propaganda battle over a very delicate issue on which American public opinion was sharply divided. Their blockade—their only potentially effective weapon against the military might of Nazi Germany—had begun to leak. Now it could be resealed. Just as important, in winning the battle over the blockade Britain secured a priceless political victory in the United States. That the American public, who had been staunchly anti-interventionist and whose instincts were naturally sympathetic to the beleaguered and blameless civilians of occupied Europe, acquiesced in the blockade without much protest said a great deal about their changing view of the world crisis. For the equally beleaguered British, here was an encouraging bellwether of the future direction of the war.

The struggle over relief for Europe represented more than an argument over wartime strategy. It was also a national argument about the ethics of war that provided a glimpse into the passionate debates to come. In 1940–41, advocates of both neutrality and intervention deployed religious morality in service to their cause. Both would continue to do so for the duration of the war.

CHAPTER SIXTEEN

Princes of Peace and Prophets of Realism

THE PEACE MOVEMENT had ebbed and flowed for a century, rising with the launch of unpopular wars against Mexico and the Philippines and falling when redemptive violence seemed to offer the only path to justice and salvation, as in the Civil War or Spanish-American War. This pattern sped up in the five years between 1914 and 1919, with pacifism dominant in the years before 1917 and Christian soldiers on the march during the war and the peace conference that followed. Then the failure of Wilsonianism, followed by suspicions that the war had been fought to ensure profits for bankers and weapons manufacturers and not to make the world safe for democracy, reinvigorated the faith-based peace movement. For the next twenty years, Christian pacifism was in the ascendance. No longer could one support a war to end all wars. After World War I, this was no longer an acceptable, even glorious paradox but an impossible, hateful contradiction.[1]

IN AN INTERWAR ERA of corrosive cynicism and fearful isolationism, Christian peace advocates remained true to their internationalist vision. They were not isolationists. They did not turn their back on the world, but instead increased their efforts to reform it in a more enlightened, progressive image. They would never support war; nor would they support an aggressive, nationalistic foreign policy. In other words, they could not, said Norman Thomas after World War I, abide "armed isolationism and hemispheric imperialism." The United States could still be "a constructive force toward peace," intoned Church Peace Union; the nation would be "remiss if it pursued a course of complete isolation as a means of peace." Even after the war, pacifist Christian internationalists still positioned the United States within a complex web of interconnected states with mutual rights and obligations, and they still expected Americans to lead the world to a better, warless world. Instead of being discouraged or deterred by the specter of the Great War, they used it as a lesson for what would afflict humanity if people did not join together to enforce its extinction. There were true isolationists in the country, people who desperately wanted the United States to remain free from the taint of the Old World and its aggression and avarice. But they were challenged by pacifist international-ists, mostly mainline Protestants but also larger numbers of Catholics and Jews than ever before, who wanted an activist but peaceful America.[2]

For their part, the traditional peace churches simply continued on the same peace crusade they had been following for centuries. Unlike the YMCA, which was ostensibly neutral but in reality acted as an adjunct of the Allied and American war efforts, during the war the American Friends Service Committee had proven its worth as a strictly unbiased relief agency. The AFSC continued its work through the interwar period, while individual Quakers delved into the pacifist politics of groups like the Fellowship of Reconciliation. Mennonites had almost unanimously refused to support the war effort in 1917, for which they were harshly condemned. Determined not to be caught in such a position of disorga-nized vulnerability again, their interwar pacifism was more than a contin-uation of long-held beliefs: it was a newly concentrated and coordinated effort to promote peace beyond the peace church.[3]

But whereas Quaker and Mennonite pacifism had been unfashionable, even treasonable, in the Great War, it now found itself swimming in the religious mainstream. After 1920, war became unthinkable, its permanent banishment an obsession among the mainline churches that had often associated with pacifism but were not necessarily peace churches. To those dedicated to both Christianity and pacifism, it was self-evident that war was unchristian, the most grievous of all sins. "If a thing is *wrong in prin-ciple* for Jesus, it is wrong for a Christian," claimed Kirby Page, a Disciples of Christ minister and leading pacifist, and to him it was obvious that Jesus thought war was wrong. Though he was a Socialist, Page was no radi-cal; a former Student Volunteer and YMCA secretary, his was very much a mainstream, mainline vision. He reflected the absolutist pacifism that quickly became the guiding principle for most interwar Christian paci-fists: under no circumstances, including self-defense, could a Christian use violence. "Not even when the political freedom of a nation is at stake should the Christian militant make use of an unchristian weapon," Page commanded. "*The following of Jesus Christ is infinitely more important than the maintenance of political liberty at the expense of his principles.*" Though his idealism may seem radical, it was commonplace in the shell-shocked 1920s and '30s.[4]

However, the Depression made Page's mission infinitely more diffi-cult. Economies that underpinned fragile political stability in Germany, Japan, and elsewhere collapsed, enabling extremist alternatives to liberal democracy to seize power. In such an atmosphere, militarism was once again on the march. Japan invaded Manchuria in 1931, and then China proper in 1937; Italy invaded Ethiopia in 1935; fascists in Spain launched a civil war to extinguish republican democracy; Germany rearmed. At each step, America's Christian pacifists were unable to offer a solution to the blatant use of brutal force. Enraged at the dictators and frustrated by the impotence of their own moral injunctions, many pacifists began to rethink their unbending dedication to the gospel of love. In response to the crisis in Ethiopia, Sherwood Eddy, the famed evangelist, YMCA missionary, and peace crusader, called for "a needed police power under the League of Nations by collective security and always under judicial sanctions of the League." To an incredulous pacifist friend, Eddy explained: "You might define this as war. I prefer to define it as police power." Aghast at Francisco Franco's assault on Spanish democracy, Norman Thomas vowed he would "not yield to fascism anywhere without a struggle." More startlingly, he also declared that "nonviolence is not its first and last commandment." The Japanese invasion of China, home to thousands of Social Gospel missionaries, provoked similar changes of heart.[5]

Still, though the world crises of the 1930s challenged the American peace movement, they could not destroy it. Peace seemed more and more a utopian dream, but most were unwilling to abandon it completely. The kind of internationalism that Christian pacifists and peace advocates believed in called for a peaceful, equitable world order that was becoming more unlikely with each passing year. And with each passing year, it was increasingly unrealistic, and utopian, to expect it could happen through Christian persuasion and moral example. The 1930s had made the peace crusade more difficult, which no pacifist would deny. Yet despite their depleted numbers, thanks to the defection of Eddy and others, their optimism remained intact. "The cause of the peacemakers has met with frustration and opposition, but is far from being lost," declared a Michigan pastor in a sermon that was typical of pacifism's stubborn perseverance.[6]

Of course, not all religious opponents of intervention were pacifists. Some, like the Detroit radio priest Father Charles Coughlin—who in 1935 almost single-handedly killed Senate ratification of U.S. membership in the World Court—and Gerald L. K. Smith were genuine isolationists who wanted the United States to protect its sovereignty and remain free from the taint of Europe's political and spiritual plagues. Rather than wilt under the heat of crisis, their isolationism actually hardened in the 1930s. Other Christians also opposed intervention without resorting to anti-Semitism or political extremism. From his lofty perch as the editor of the Catholic magazine *America*, Francis Xavier Talbot could survey the whole Roman Catholic community in the United States. His own views were "completely and absolutely anti-Communist and anti-Nazi" and "of moral, intellectual, cultural sympathy with the Allies." But he also did not believe there was "sufficient reason" for the United States to get involved. He confessed that most Catholic priests disagreed with him, but he also sensed that "the very great majority" of the Catholic laity shared his view.

He was probably right, especially when it came to German and Irish Catholics who were, once again, unenthusiastic about joining a European war against Germany and allied with Britain. In 1936, for example, the only Catholics to vote substantially against Roosevelt's reelection were pockets of isolationist German and Irish communities who already suspected the internationalist Democrats of secretly plotting an alliance with the British.[7]

Catholic peace activists, led by Father John A. Ryan and the organization he founded in 1927, the Catholic Association for International Peace (CAIP), also continued to oppose intervention even as they took a stand against fascism and militarism. On the surface, with its commitment to social justice and racial equality, the CAIP seemed to be cut from the same cloth as the Fellowship of Reconciliation or the Federal Council of Churches. Moreover, the CAIP also believed that modern wars were the result of runaway nationalism, materialism, political idolatry of the kind found in fascist and communist personality cults, and Western racism and imperialism. But there was a significant difference between these Catholic and Protestant organizations that went beyond denominational intricacies of tradition and liturgy. Doctrinally, Ryan and the CAIP were not pacifists. They were peace advocates, and noninterventionists, and could scarcely imagine a scenario in which they would support the use of armed force. But the difference was that they could, in theory, imagine one. As Catholics, they looked to just war theory for guidance. So long as a nation observed the constraints of *jus ad bellum* and *jus in bello*—the just cause of war and its just execution—war could be accepted as part of the Christian order. Ryan and the CAIP were alarmed by Hitler's rise, but as late as 1940 they still did not agree that the distant challenge of Nazism made U.S. involvement necessary or just. The reliance on just war theory led Catholics away from absolutist pacifism and, should events deteriorate, toward U.S. intervention, a distinction that Reinhold Niebuhr and his fellow Protestant Christian realists would borrow. There were Catholic pacifists, of course, most notably Dorothy Day and the Catholic Workers, but they set themselves apart as noble exceptions by never using, and eventually rejecting, just war theory.[8]

Nonetheless, within the broad church of religious anti-interventionism, liberal Protestants continued to predominate. And while they believed in the power of transnational Christianity, they also believed that any truly just and peaceful world order required American stewardship. This belief in the exemplary, persuasive power of American values and Christian ethics was firmly rooted in a tenet of the Wilsonian creed: people were naturally peace-loving, and appeals directly to them over the heads of unrepresentative, undemocratic leaders would constrain militarism and war. As the world's leading democracy, the United States was best suited to the task. Pacifists did not want to avoid war so that Americans could be safe; they wanted to avoid war so that uncorrupted Americans could dictate the terms of the peace. In 1938, the president of the FCC informed Roosevelt that his member churches were "profoundly convinced that strategically, historically and providentially our country is called to lead the world along the road, not of ancient bluster, but of sacrificial peace."[9]

Sometimes this belief in the power of moral suasion led pacifists to wander aimlessly down diplomatic blind alleys. But so powerful was their belief in peace, and in a natural, universal desire for peace, that they had trouble recognizing that their pacific liberal internationalism was becoming increasingly untenable. The sincere but misguided vision of Harold Fey, the executive secretary of the Fellowship of Reconciliation, serves as a poignant example. The Fellowship was perhaps the most hardline of all Christian pacifist groups; for most members, even self-defense was no justification for the use of force. In the fall of 1937, Fey found himself arguing against a rising tide of support for economic sanctions against Japan. He did not condone the Japanese invasion of China, but he also believed that coercion—even economic sanctions, which of course would likely escalate tensions and possibly spark a war—was unjustified. What else could a Christian do? Fey thought he had an answer. "Cannot American Christians go directly to influential people in Japan," he asked a skeptical Winnifred Wygal of the YWCA, "and try to get them to see how the civilized world looks at this dreadful campaign in China and try to persuade them to use their influence to stop it?" Prodded by A. J. Muste, the Fellowship was soon applying these techniques of Gandhian nonviolent resistance, conscientious objection, and Christian pacifism to race relations in the United States, including a successful 1941 drive to integrate a public swimming pool in Cleveland. From the Fellowship emerged the Congress of Racial Equality, and from CORE emerged many of the tactics that would make the civil rights movement so successful in the post–World War II decades. But Japan presented a challenge even more daunting than American racism. "Of course nothing may come of it," Fey conceded of his plan. "Of course we run the risk of being thought fools—fools of God."[10]

As always, the Federal Council of Churches led the liberal internationalist peace crusade against war, imperialism, and isolationism. This was the special mission of Walter W. Van Kirk, an Ohio-born, Boston University–trained Methodist who headed the FCC's Department of International Justice and Goodwill. The title of his 1934 book, *Religion Renounces War,* made sweeping claims of absolute certainty that were typical of modernist interwar pacifism. Using the FCC's imprimatur and national organization, Van Kirk then went on to mount a campaign to support the passage of neutrality laws that would tie Roosevelt's hands as Wilson's had not been. "Neutrality," he reminded his readers, "does not mean isola-tion." Nor was it "hostile to world cooperation." In 1935, he founded the National Peace Conference as an umbrella organization for more than thirty pacifist groups.[11]

It is important to remember that Van Kirk was not a lonely voice in the wilderness. Peace was demonstrably the preference of most Christian churches during the decade of crisis. Throughout the 1930s, the annual assemblies and conventions of the Presbyterian Church USA, the Evan-gelical Synod of North America, the Methodist Episcopal Church, and the Northern Baptist Convention all passed strong resolutions renounc-ing war. In 1930, when the Episcopalians gathered at Lambeth Palace in London with fellow Anglicans from around the world, they agreed unani-mously that war was "incompatible" with Christianity. The Northern Baptists were the least absolutist, but even they proclaimed their "unal-terable opposition to war as a means of settling international disputes, and urge non-participation except in case of invasion." Most significant were the resolutions for peace at the 1934 annual meeting of the Southern Baptist Convention. Southerners had been more willing to march to war in 1898 and 1917 and in later decades would provide bedrock support for American wars in Southeast Asia and the Middle East. But the tide of lib-eral internationalism ran high in Protestant circles in the interwar period, and for a time it washed over the souls of Southern Baptists as well. Their 1934 meeting noted that the "prospect for International Peace has not been promising," thanks mostly to the aggressively revisionist policies of Germany and Japan. But instead of calling for America to respond in kind, Southern Baptists criticized the Roosevelt administration for pursuing naval rearmament in economically crippling times. Instead of retrench-ing with an appeal to American patriotism, they urged the Senate to ratify U.S. membership in the World Court—"a necessary and valuable agency for preserving and promoting International Peace"—without delay.[12]

Nor had Van Kirk misrepresented the Federal Council. Though some were beginning to doubt the likelihood of peace and thus the effective-ness of pacifism, the overwhelming majority of ecumenists were resolutely opposed to war on the grounds of moral conviction and still believed that the principles of the ecumenical movement offered the best way forward. Yet few seemed to anticipate the irresolvable tensions within ecumenical internationalism, between collective security—which in theory was ulti-mately backed by force or some other means of compulsion if peaceful order broke down—and an absolutist desire for peace. And they would not appreciate it until the dilemma had been solved for them by Japan and Germany in 1941. Even as late as October 1939, the FCC could write to FDR with "support . . . in your purpose that our government shall not join in this war." Ecumenists instead "seek to keep the United States at peace in the hope that our nation may thereby render a greater service to mankind."[13]

Nor, finally, were Van Kirk and the FCC out of step with the peace mission of the worldwide ecumenical movement as a whole. In 1937, ecumenists from North America and Europe met at Oxford University in England to convene the Universal Christian Council for Life and Work Conference and lay the groundwork for erecting a World Council of Churches. Like the American FCC, the global WCC intended not only to manage harmonious Protestant relations but to foster world peace through ecumenical communication, understanding, and tolerance. It would, claimed its leading American light, William Adams Brown of Union Theological Seminary, "emphasize the things that men share in common above those which divide them and so make a peaceful solution of international questions easier." Only the international church, WCC planners claimed in the summer of 1939, "has shown that it can transcend national barriers in a time of crisis."[14]

BY 1940–41, the main adversary of American Christian pacifists was not a war leader like Hitler or Churchill, or dictators like Stalin or Franco, or even Franklin Roosevelt, who was slowly, surreptitiously leading America into the war. It was Reinhold Niebuhr, a professor at Union. Liberal loathing for Niebuhr was intense—had his critics not been pacifists, it would have been understandable had Niebuhr feared for his life. Feeling betrayed, one former student chastised Niebuhr for letting "your basic point of view justify you in taking unchristian positions." He doubted Niebuhr's views "as being even Christian" and was left "wondering what you do with Jesus." Reverend Rufus Ansley of the First-Pilgrim Congregational Church in Buffalo dismissed Niebuhr's writings as "British propaganda." Ralph Brandon, a minister from Covington, Ohio, expressed his "disgust" with Niebuhr and his fellow "back-sliders" who "refuse to practice the faith in Jesus Christ." Just because "you have cold feet and are afraid to take the 'Way of Jesus' in overcoming evil," he charged, "is no reason why you should try to destroy the force of the Christian methods by coaxing others to be cowards with you." Charles Lyttle, a church historian at Meadville Theological School in Chicago, reached "the point where I can no longer be silent at your shocking disregard for the fundamental decencies of your Christian ministry and professorship." Lyttle castigated Niebuhr's "very feeble yet sinister sophistries about never being perfect or ever being able to achieve our ideals in their perfection," which were antithetical to the true spirit of Christianity. Niebuhr's opinions were "apostasy, brazen and shameless, from your vows as a Christian minister and your duties as a professor in your field." But perhaps the worst insult came from Reverend Albert Edward Day of the First Methodist Church of Pasadena, California. When Reverend Day received a flyer advertising subscriptions to a magazine Niebuhr had recently founded, *Christianity and Crisis*, he wrote Niebuhr personally to say that he was immediately sending a check for $25—to a rival magazine, *Christian Century*.[15]

What had Niebuhr, a fellow progressive, said to enrage the pacifists? How exactly had he betrayed them? Felix Frankfurter thought he had the answer. "Too many liberals," the Supreme Court justice and ardent interventionist gleefully wrote Niebuhr, "are still enslaved by their romantic illusions, and cannot face your clean, surgeon-like exposition of reality." Frankfurter was right; Niebuhr's incisions had inflicted traumatic pain upon his fellow liberals. But why?[16]

To begin with, for over a decade Niebuhr had been one of them—indeed, in many respects he was still one of them. He always remained a liberal Protestant who believed in empirical, scientific inquiry and did not believe in the Bible as the inerrant word of God. So his theology had not changed. Nor had his commitment to ecumenical and interfaith cooperation; he never broke with the Federal Council of Churches and was an important contributor to the building of a World Council of Churches. He also still believed in social democracy, and, after a brief flirtation with Marxism, remained a member of the Fellowship of Socialist Christians and Norman Thomas's Socialist Party throughout the 1930s. Moreover, Niebuhr continued to devote his time to Socialist pet projects, such as the Delta Cooperative Farm in Mississippi that he and Sherwood Eddy helped organize in tandem with the Southern Tenant Farmers' Union and the leftist Fellowship of Southern Churchmen. At the end of the decade, his views on political economy remained much further to the left than many of his friends and colleagues at Union, such as Henry Sloane Coffin and Henry Pit Van Dusen. He remained pro-labor and pro–civil rights at a time when many white liberals, religious or otherwise, were hastily abandoning both causes. So in many ways, Niebuhr's liberalism remained intact.[17]

However, Niebuhr had also been a pacifist, and it was this that changed dramatically. In the 1920s and early '30s, Niebuhr edited the pacifist magazine *World Tomorrow*, wrote prolifically for that great organ of absolute pacifism and liberal Protestantism, *Christian Century*, and was a senior member of the Fellowship of Reconciliation. Two of his closest friends, Kirby Page and Sherwood Eddy, were leaders in the peace movement, and of course Norman Thomas made pacifism one of the major planks in the Socialist Party platform. Thus Niebuhr's repudiation of pacifism—flowing freely from his caustic, abrasive, withering pen—came as a painful betrayal.

But what had changed for Niebuhr? What had led him to abandon his commitment to a universal peace through Christian love? Based on his experiences in America and his reading of the international scene, Niebuhr saw, earlier than many others, that one could only be a true Christian pacifist if one lived beyond the margins of modern society. In the real world, it was sometimes necessary to use coercive means to achieve a just end. Christian ethics remained central to politics because they would help determine the acceptable limits of coercion and distinguish between just and unjust causes. Though Niebuhr was not its creator, this essentially Niebuhrian vision of politics quickly became known as Christian realism. With it, Niebuhr also criticized American exceptionalism and national self-righteousness. In the depths of the world crisis of the 1930s, he maintained that Americans were no more free of guilt and responsibility than others. Sin was universal and nobody, certainly not Americans, was free of it. But crucially, Christian realism did not prevent Niebuhr from identifying those who bore more culpability than others. There were no heroes in the Niebuhrian world, but there were definitely villains.[18]

At home, even before the Depression, the role of villain was played by ruthless industrialists like Henry Ford. After an upbringing in the Midwest, a divinity degree at Yale, and ordination in the German Evangelical Church, Niebuhr moved to a pastorate in Detroit, Bethel Evangelical Church, in 1915. There, he found himself in the thick of America's industrial strife. Despite the bourgeois status of his congregation, Niebuhr leaped into the fray on behalf of workers in the automotive industry. Against the muscle of the Ford Motor Company, he discovered that nonresistance and nonviolence were in fact noneffective, especially if the government sided with industry over labor. For now, he was still willing to give peace a chance, but the seeds of doubt had been sown.

In 1928, Niebuhr left his congregation in Detroit to take up a professorship at Union Theological Seminary. Union was then a leading center of pacifism; indeed, peace was the one issue upon which conservatives like Henry Sloane Coffin and radicals such as Harry F. Ward could agree. Yet even here, Niebuhr's faith in pacifism continued to erode. The Depression had convinced him that workers would never overcome the combined power of capital and state without sometimes resorting to coercive measures. He argued that force should remain an option for organized labor, a controversial stance that led to his resignation from the Fellowship of Reconciliation. In the beginning, then, Niebuhr's realist turn away from pacifist idealism was rooted more in domestic turmoil and social democracy than in foreign affairs.[19]

Differences over foreign affairs, however, would provide the breaking point between Niebuhr and his erstwhile comrades, just as the international crisis would crystallize and sharpen the emerging dogma of his Christian realism. Ironically, it was international relations, specifically the carnage of World War I and the apparent iniquity of the Versailles settlement, that had originally inspired Niebuhr's pacifism. But a decade and more later, things had changed; Germany's brutality against Jews and Christians particularly moved him. Niebuhr decided that the democracies—Britain and France—might be tainted by imperialism and imperfect democracy, but they were infinitely better than the totalitarian alternatives of fascism, communism, and Nazism. Unlike the moral absolutists of the peace movement, Niebuhr perceived foreign policy as a series of realistic choices between relative goods and lesser evils.[20]

Personal experience also played its part. In the intervening years, Niebuhr married an Englishwoman, Ursula Keppel-Compton. At Union, he mentored a young exchange student and rising star of German theology, Dietrich Bonhoeffer, who opposed Hitler and was later executed by the Nazis. Niebuhr also traveled to Britain in the summer of 1939; a side trip to Holland was cut short, another to Sweden canceled outright, all because Europe was paralyzed by the imminence of war. Niebuhr then found himself in London for two momentous events that confirmed beyond doubt his realist view of the world: Joseph Stalin's cynical but utterly realistic pact with Hitler on August 23, and Germany's invasion of Poland on September 3. All around him, it seemed, Britain was moving closer to his own code of personal Christian ethics while Germany, his ancestral homeland, was moving further away.[21]

His friend Sherwood Eddy found such logic persuasive, even morally compelling, and he followed Niebuhr's conversion to realism. Eddy's friends in the peace movement chided him that Gandhi was proving that nonviolence could be an effective political tool. Eddy was unconvinced, because the British Empire, as bad as it was, was still run by the British, who were completely different from Soviet communists or German Nazis. Eddy knew what he was talking about, for in 1930 he had briefly acted as an intermediary between the British and Gandhi; he had also traveled extensively in the Soviet Union and Nazi Germany. Religion, he told his pacifist friends, was important because it was the source of ethics and morals, the stuff of which the human conscience is made. For nonviolence to work, the powers that be had to have at least some ethical and moral boundaries. Conscience, therefore, was the pacifist's secret weapon. But where the human conscience had died, as in the Soviet Union and Germany, nonviolence was simply a form of surrender. Pacifists were "completely ineffectual against Stalin and Hitler, who promptly put them to death," Eddy pointed out. "I believe that Gandhi would never have been heard from in Russia or Germany."[22]

NIEBUHR GROUNDED HIS politics in theology—realists claimed that the political failings of religious liberalism demanded a return to original theological foundations—and here he made another significant break with most mainline liberals by championing neo-orthodoxy. First developed by European theologians Karl Barth and Emil Brunner in the wake of World War I, neo-orthodoxy challenged liberalism's belief in human progress shepherded by an immanent God dwelling within the world. The Social Gospel had built its political foundation upon this and from it the idea that progress was not only possible but inevitable. As Progressives, they believed that immorality was not an innate personal defect but a product of circumstance. Drunkenness, prostitution, and theft were conditions of poverty, manifestations of a broken society; cure the poverty, repair society, and you would see the end of immoral, destructive behavior. To Social Gospelers, sin was a product of human activity that could in turn be ended through human activity. Sin was historical; love was eternal, and the cure for sin.[23]

Niebuhr doubted if such an optimistic theology could possibly be true. In its place, he turned to neo-orthodoxy, from which the politics and geopolitics of Christian realism grew. God was transcendent, not immanent. More important, sin was original, not historical; it was unbound by time or space and could only be mitigated, never eliminated. Humanity, Niebuhr argued from here, was inherently depraved, lustful, and ignorant, motivated by power and greed as much as by peace and justice. People everywhere, including Americans, were essentially self-interested, and no amount of reform could change that basic fact of human nature. Society could limit sin, but never end it. Society itself often enabled sin because groupings of people were less likely to behave in a moral way than individuals. This was the central thesis of his seminal book *Moral Man and Immoral Society*, which marked an early break with both the practicality and ethics of pacifist idealism. The glorious promise of Christianity was that it alone offered salvation for humanity's inherent wickedness. As Niebuhr explained in a 1940 essay on "Why the Christian Church Is Not Pacifist," Christianity held that "though Christ is the true norm (the 'second Adam') for every man, every man is also in some sense a crucifier of Christ. The good news of the gospel is not the law that we ought to love one another. The good news of the gospel is that there is a resource of divine mercy which is able to overcome a contradiction within our souls, which we ourselves cannot overcome."[24]

Those close to Niebuhr were changing, too, and it was they who devised a philosophical architecture for Christian realism in the United States, closer to politics than European neo-orthodoxy but more grounded in the tenets of traditional faith than mainline Protestantism. In the pages of a 1933 issue of *Christian Century* (ironically enough), Niebuhr's close friend John Coleman Bennett, a professor at Auburn Theological Seminary in upstate New York, first criticized liberal Protestantism's failure to account for the pervasive influence of original sin. Inspired by Bennett's critique, Walter Horton, a young theologian at Oberlin College, provided a fuller exposition in his 1934 book *Realistic Theology*. That same year, Reinhold's younger brother, H. Richard, published a major scholarly article that made some of the strongest claims yet for a realistic religion grounded in original sin. And a year after that, Bennett expanded upon his Christian realism in his book *Social Salvation*.[25]

Perhaps without realizing it—there is scant evidence that the effort was deliberate—Niebuhr and his fellow realists also borrowed from Roman Catholic theology by applying just war theory to their Christian realism. For John Ryan and other noninterventionist Catholic theologians, war was theoretically justifiable under the right circumstances and if fought the right way, yet international events had not yet reached such a critical point. The Protestant realists used similar logic about the justness of the Allied cause, especially in comparison with Nazi Germany's unusual barbarity. In 1936, John Bennett suggested some categories of war that would be just, including self-defense and the enforcement of League of Nations decisions. The realists also took pains to ensure that advocates of war agreed upon necessary limitations, which complicated straightforward realism by saying that the end did not necessarily justify all means. Christian realism was not simply a doctrine practiced by Christians but an ethical worldview that nonetheless sanctioned war under certain circumstances. This was just war theory for Protestants.[26]

In keeping with neo-orthodoxy, Niebuhr and his allies warned of the dangers of national self-righteousness that could lead to war fever, hysteria, and jingoism and end in a form of American militarism that might not be all that different from European fascism. With the humiliating legacy of the Great War foremost in his mind, Niebuhr's colleague Henry Van Dusen emphatically impressed this point upon the authors of a Federal Council statement against U.S. intervention shortly after the outbreak of war in Europe in 1939. The "grave danger" was that if war came without proper preparation, Americans would be "swept" away on a tide of "Hun-hating" and "glorification of War." Such a war, even against the Nazis, would not be wholly just. "Extreme begets extreme," Van Dusen warned. "An unsound pacifism and isolationism now . . . are dooming us first to a bitter struggle" within Protestantism that could only end in "jingoism within the churches." Van Dusen added a caustic concluding remark, designed to shame his friends within the FCC into realizing how isolated they really were. "On all sides I run into a rising tide of resentment because the organs of public expression within the churches have so largely fallen into control of pacifists and isolationists who are held to be unrepresentative of great numbers of laity and ministry." Politically, Van Dusen was saying, it was time to be realistic.[27]

The logic of both neo-orthodoxy and just war theory, then, flowed naturally toward Christian realism, and vice versa. The "utopians" of the *Christian Century*, as Niebuhr usually branded them, did not understand that their vision of absolute rights and absolute wrongs was an illusion—and a supremely dangerous illusion because it contributed to American lethargy and negligence as Nazism increased in strength. By continuing to champion pacifism and nonintervention, even after the fall of France in 1940, Charles Clayton Morrison, *Christian Century's* imperious editor, who had once been Niebuhr's publisher, was guilty of spreading a "doctrine [that] is politically dangerous but morally very bad." But to Niebuhr's unending frustration, Morrison, like Kirby Page an ordained Disciples of Christ minister, remained dogmatically committed to peace. Morrison and his fellow pacifists, Niebuhr wrote to Bennett, were "simply the end of a Christianity which tries to find a vantage point of guiltlessness from which to judge a guilty world." This had been bad enough in the 1930s, but after the Nazi conquest of Europe it was unforgivable. Yet ever the realist, Niebuhr continued to warn against self-righteousness. Britain, France, and America were not free of sin either, and not only because of their dereliction in failing to stop Hitler before it was too late. "Of course," he told Bennett, "our spiritual task is not an easy one because we must defend a civilization which has been digging its grave for decades and has the right to live only because the alternative is so horrible." Yet fools like Morrison deluded the people into believing they could have redemption without sacrifice. "Americans simply don't know what kind of slavery the Nazis will enforce upon the world," Niebuhr feared. Tyranny such as that could not survive for very long, but it could still "destroy everything before it is destroyed."[28]

Pacifist anger was therefore understandable, for Niebuhr and his partners were contradicting—indeed, repudiating, even humiliating—the postmillennial optimism that had lifted the liberal Protestant worldview above the turbulence and ugliness of the interwar years. Through the FCC, in 1920 a group of leading Christian pacifists had declared that "Christianity does not deny that there is radical evil in human nature." But Christians could not "accept it as final." Human nature "is there to be changed and it can be changed, if only for a long enough time and in a thorough enough way we bring to bear upon it the principles of Christ." This remained the liberal lodestar in the intervening decades. Now, in 1940, Niebuhr was telling his fellow liberals: no, human nature cannot be changed, or at least not so easily. Christianity did have a role to play in the nurturing and promotion of morality and human rights, but it simply could not do so without recognizing that evil would always exist and that it would sometimes need to be met in kind, with violence. After the Nazi conquest of western Europe, it was a difficult argument to refute.[29]

· · ·

NIEBUHR HAD MADE a significant contribution to a shift in American opinion, but he could not have done it alone. In fact, neither the theology of neo-orthodoxy nor the politics of Christian realism were his innovations. At Union and through countless periodicals and organizations, not all of them religious, Niebuhr surrounded himself with fellow Christian interventionists. Once a sanctuary for pacifism, under the sway of Niebuhr's celebrity Union slowly became a bastion of realism. Seminary president Henry Sloane Coffin, who had not always appreciated Niebuhr's socialism and who had championed pacifism before 1917 and through the 1920s, embraced the realist creed, as did emeritus professor William Adams Brown. So too did Henry Van Dusen, occupant of one of Union's most prestigious chairs. Paul Tillich, a refugee from Hitler's Germany, one of the most influential Protestant theologians of the century, and a leading light of neo-orthodoxy, moved to Union in 1933 at Niebuhr's behest. All this marked an important development, for Union was still home to two of the nation's most eminent Christian pacifists, Harry F. Ward and Harry Emerson Fosdick. It also had close ties to other leading theologians, its sister divinity schools, and leading ecumenical organizations like the Federal Council. Thus the realist critique of pacifism was much more effective as a result of its capture of Union. Many of Niebuhr's other comrades, moreover, such as Sherwood Eddy, had also been erstwhile pacifists. Others, like John Mott, were titans of the Protestant establishment in general and the ecumenical movement in particular. Not all of them were realists, and not all subscribed to neo-orthodoxy. But they did all share a commitment to defeating Nazism with American power, because though it might be a sin to use violent means it was entirely justifiable if deployed for the noble end of defeating Nazi Germany. "To refuse to fight does not necessarily mean to make peace," the venerable, avuncular Brown chided pacifists in 1938. "If we doubted this before, what happened at Munich has made it impossible to doubt it any longer." They all shared a prophetic vision of reformed Wilsonianism, of the United States leading the world through the horrors of war and into an enduring, ecumenical, but realistic peace. From the halls of Union and Yale Divinity School, and in new settings such as the Theological Discussion Group, they were, in one historian's resonant phrase, "theologians of a new world order." And by the late 1930s, they were poised to eclipse pacifism within mainline Protestant politics.[30]

This was particularly true of the ecumenical movement. Just as Niebuhr and his allies aimed to reform liberal, modernist Protestantism to make it more relevant and useful for modern times, they sought to capture and remake ecumenism in a realist image. As hard-boiled as Niebuhr and the realists could be, they remained committed to interdenominational and interfaith cooperation in religion and to international organization in geopolitics. Only the institutions of cooperation could help manage peace. Liberals and pacifists erred in assuming that institutional cooperation could lead to the eradication of sin and the establishment of permanent peace. Ecumenism could help manage international tensions but not eliminate them. Thus realists also saw potential in the 1937 Oxford Conference, and the plan for the World Council of Churches that emerged from it. Niebuhr told the Oxford delegates to remember that while Christian love was essential, it could also be destroyed if sin was left to grow unopposed. Bennett followed suit with his own speech. Edwin Ewart Aubrey, a conference delegate and ally of Niebuhr's, confessed that many of the speeches at Oxford bored him, especially those by pacifists who did not yet realize how obsolete and irrelevant they had become. "Just as the decadent Protestantism of the seventeenth century gave rise to pietism on the one hand and rationalism on the other," Aubrey mused while staring at the Sheldonian Theatre's beautiful, Christopher Wren–designed ceiling, "so the present crisis is met at this conference in two ways that are continually in tension. Can any significant results be hoped for?" Indeed there would be, at least for Aubrey and his fellow realists, but not until American participation in the war would give them the opportunity.[31]

Niebuhr had a doctrine. He had surrounded himself with allies and followers. His task now was to organize it all in such a way that would influence hearts and change minds, from church pews to the halls of Congress. One way was through a new organization to combat the noninterventionism of the Socialist Party, so in 1941 Niebuhr and his allies established the Union for Democratic Action. But as a successful author of bestselling books and leading articles in national magazines such as *The Nation, The New Republic,* and *The Atlantic Monthly,* Niebuhr also turned to what he understood best and knew would be most effective: the printed word. He had already edited two journals with some success, *The World Tomorrow* and *Radical Religion,* and devoted his efforts to founding a periodical that would be dedicated solely to promoting Christian realism as the solution to the crises of the 1930s. Niebuhr intended the result, *Christianity and Crisis,* to be an antidote to the pacifism that continued to prevail in Morrison's widely read *Christian Century.* Launched in 1941 with a powerhouse list of editorial sponsors that included Bennett, Brown, Coffin, Eddy, Horton, and Mott, *Christianity and Crisis* paid attention to economics, religion, and domestic politics. But its main focus was international relations, and its editorial line was robustly interventionist, anti-Nazi, and pro-Allied. The sponsors pledged to "adhere to the historic Protestant faith that men must choose between relative goods and that the attempt to practice an absolute perfection in historic decisions only serves to betray men into subjection to tyranny." They then asked prospective subscribers to "enlist their resources in defense of democratic civilization."[32]

Hesitantly, stung by Niebuhr and the Christian realists and shocked by militarism's easy advance across Europe and China, the major Protestant organizations began to reconsider just how effective their pacifist witness could really be against determined, aggressive dictators. At the 1938 Foreign Missions Conference, the largest annual gathering of modernist missionaries in North America, Reverend Luman J. Shafer of the Reformed Church proclaimed support for peace through world federation, but he also pointed out that it needed to be backed by force. He still believed in the collective, but went further and called for security as well. Japan and Italy, he said, had uncovered the League's "helplessness," which led Shafer to the "vivid discovery" of "increased appropriations for armaments in order that future diplomatic protests may be more effective because there will then be behind them the threat of a greater force than at present." It was a logical discovery, but one that shocked pacifists nonetheless: Shafer had damned their most sacred cow, disarmament. "There is an element of futility in our Christian protest against the building of ever larger and more powerful armaments," Shafer chastised his fellow missionaries, because it left the world community at the mercy of dictators.[33]

Whether they learned it from Niebuhr and the Christian realist leadership, clergy throughout the country began expounding much the same message as Germany marched through Europe in 1939 and 1940. In Sunday after Sunday, sermon after sermon drove home the same message: the United States is at risk and America's values are in danger. Just as English and colonial American Protestants believed they could not live in a world surrounded by Catholic tyranny and survive as Protestants, an increasing number of Americans in 1940–41 believed they could not survive as an isolated outpost of democracy in a world dominated by tyranny. At some point, the protective seal of isolation would break, and America would be overrun.

Consider two sermons in two different parts of the country delivered right after the turn of the new year in 1941. Reverend Harold Cooke Phillips, pastor of the First Baptist Church in Cleveland, had until this point supported the pacifists. But now, he changed his mind. If Britain were defeated, "America would find herself standing alone in a world in which every strong nation would be . . . aggressively hostile to her way of life." This would preserve isolation, but "with a vengeance." Phillips repeated pacifist warnings that going to war would create "a war psychology" and lead to the irony of American democracy being killed at home as Americans fought for its survival abroad. Yet the risks of a Nazi victory were now greater than the domestic dangers of war. The pacifists were correct in theory, he maintained, but "unfortunately the situation we face is not a theoretical one but one of stark reality. We are set down in a world in which our absolute Christian idealism . . . has to do business with a pagan world. We agree completely with the absolute pacifist that war is a colossal evil." Yet that was not the issue: "what now," Phillips demanded, "actually, realistically, is the alternative to war, to this war?"[34]

Across the country, before an audience at the Rotary Club of Portland, Oregon, in January 1941, Reverend Edgar Raymond Attebery of Seattle's Grace Methodist Episcopal Church delivered a similar message. Attebery had become a staunch interventionist, a belief that would cost him his life when the unit he served as chaplain came under Japanese fire while trying to land on Biak Island in New Guinea. The past twelve months, Attebery told the Rotarians in early 1941, had witnessed "the greatest crises in all human history since Christianity began" that "may be greater in consequences, depending on whether we play the ball right at this juncture of human history." He painted a grim portrait for his listeners. The "slumbering democracies of the world" would either "have to rise up" and "challenge the dictatorships" or "receive the inevitable consequence of slavery and serfdom." While the United States could once monitor events from afar, the "security due to wide oceans is gone." Those who continued to advocate an obsolete and morally suspect isolationism were forfeiting a long tradition of freedom that had been won in battle by generations past. This was not only dangerous, but a betrayal to both the past and the future. Americans were now "compelled to retreat from our neutrality" and to "face the fact that if democracy goes down in this hour of crisis, in all probability neither we nor our children, nor our children's children, will have the privilege of the spiritual heritage with which we were born and which by the Grace of God for 150 years we have preserved and expanded in this republic." The Americans of 1941 must learn from their forebears of 1861, a "gallant bunch of men and women" who may have "hated war" but "loved decency, truth, and humanity more." This was heady, powerful stuff, and it was being repeated by increasing numbers of clergy across the nation.[35]

With the German advance in 1940 and the continuing Japanese onslaught in China, the American mood was quickly shifting. Suddenly, the rise of totalitarianism abroad did seem like a direct threat to Americans. For such an occasion, in such an atmosphere, Christian realism was ideally suited. Even if people did not understand the exegesis of neo-orthodox theology—and even if pastors did not deploy it in their sermons—Christian realism's message that war was evil but that totalitarianism was a greater evil still could not have been more powerful or timely. For two decades, the idealism of the Christian peace movement had provided the moral core of noninterventionism. But now noninterventionism, to say nothing of strict isolationism, was itself morally dubious. Into this uncertain, ambiguous breach stepped the doctrine of Christian realism. It assured Americans that intervention was moral, in keeping with God's will. Its refusal to believe in moral absolutes beyond the pure evil of Nazism was strangely reassuring, for by recognizing moral uncertainty and ambiguity, and yet also recognizing the severity of the world crisis, Christian realism seemed to be the only sane voice in an increasingly insane world. More important, it provided Americans with a theology and a morality for military intervention.[36]

CHAPTER SEVENTEEN

The Simple Faith of Franklin Roosevelt

F OR HIS CONTEMPORARIES as well as historians, Franklin Delano Roosevelt's personality and motivations have been difficult to capture, let alone analyze. He was not an intellectual, unlike his mentor, Woodrow Wilson, or his hero and distant cousin, Theodore Roosevelt, and left only a faint impression of his formative ideas and influences. Yet for all of FDR's enigmatic traits, and for all the neglect it has suffered at the hands of historians, it is perhaps easiest to define his religious faith. Not since Abraham Lincoln had a president embodied America's civil religion so naturally. Others had refined it, but they either lacked Lincoln and FDR's transcendent virtues or were too self-consciously theological in presenting it to the American people. Roosevelt also succeeded in enshrining religious pluralism at the heart of the American national faith. Wilson and Theodore Roosevelt had moved Americans closer to this goal, but for all their political gifts their personalities were too complicated, and too intellectual, to succeed. FDR was neither prophet nor priest. Instead, he possessed a serene and simple faith that was more accessible to the people because it so closely resembled their own.

Fittingly, Roosevelt was an Episcopalian. In terms of social standing, the members of the Episcopal Church stood at the pinnacle of the mainline Protestant elite, much wealthier than the average Presbyterian or Congregationalist and much better educated than the average Methodist or Baptist. Perhaps as a result, Episcopalians were also far less schismatic than Methodists, Presbyterians, or Baptists. Yet despite the Church's wealth and conservative reputation, there has always been a strongly progressive strand within the mainline Protestant Episcopal Church. Represented by the women's leaders Ellen Gates Starr, Fannie May Witherspoon, and Tracy Mygatt, and by the pacifist John Nevin Sayre, Episcopalians stood at the very center of the Social Gospel movement. They led the "institutional church movement," which aimed to revitalize slums for its poor, working-class residents. They formed the Church Socialist League and founded the Church League for Industrial Democracy and marched at the front of campaigns for workers' rights, women's rights, and an end to nationalism and war. More relevant in the case of Franklin Roosevelt was the church's very strong ethos of noblesse oblige. Many wealthy Episcopalians, such as the Roosevelts, recognized their privileged status in society, and were determined to give something back, especially through philanthropy and public service. For a young aristocrat with a social conscience and internationalist horizon such as Franklin Roosevelt, it was an ideal spiritual home.[1]

This is not to say that Roosevelt's religion was theologically profound or sophisticated. His contemporaries noted how deeply faith mattered to him, but they also noted that it lacked any intellectual depth. The president's son James recalled that his father held fast to a "basic, simple, rather unquestioning religious faith." Frances Perkins, who would later become FDR's secretary of labor and the first-ever female cabinet official, formed a similar impression. At an official reception one evening, when Roosevelt was still governor of New York, he continued to chat with guests and listen to their problems late into the night, even though he was clearly exhausted. Perkins marveled not only at Roosevelt's perseverance but his empathy with the problems of total strangers. Standing beside Eleanor Roosevelt, who was also watching the scene, Perkins said, "You know, Franklin is really a very simple Christian." Eleanor pondered the notion and, "with a quizzical lift of her eyebrows," replied, "Yes, a *very simple* Christian." Roosevelt's faith was simple because it was uncomplicated, pure, and sincere. "As far as I can make out," Perkins concluded, "he had no doubts. He just believed with a certainty and simplicity that gave him no pangs or struggles." James Roosevelt agreed. To his father, "religion was a real and personal thing from which he drew much strength and comfort. Piety was not something he put on like a cloak at election time; his feelings were deep and unshakeable." Eleanor, herself an agnostic who argued with FDR over whether their children should attend Sunday school, marveled at her husband's serene spirituality. "I think he felt guided in great crises by a strength and a wisdom higher than his own," she recalled several years after his death, "for his religious faith was simple and direct. . . . He had a strong religious feeling and his religion was a very personal one. I think he actually felt he could ask God for guidance and receive it."[2]

Franklin Roosevelt was born into the Episcopal Church. He was a thoroughly liberal mainline Protestant for whom the essence of Christianity could be captured by the teachings of Jesus and a handful of basic biblical lessons, such as the brotherhood of man and the Golden Rule. As a young man, he attended an elite private school in Groton, Massachusetts. The headmaster there, Reverend Endicott Peabody, was a rector in the Episcopal Church and a powerful, formative influence on the future president. Peabody emphasized the duties of Christian citizenship, particularly service to God and country. The bond between them was close and enduring: Peabody officiated at Roosevelt's marriage to Eleanor and at the new president's inaugural ceremonies in 1933.[3]

As his son, wife, and colleagues knew, religion was important to Roosevelt. Many of those around him observed that his legendary self-confidence, geniality, and serenity rested upon a bedrock of faith. His speechwriter Robert Sherwood noted that while Roosevelt could be "utterly cynical, worldly, illusionless . . . his religious faith was the strongest and most mysterious force that was in him." He was also a loyal Episcopalian. In 1906, he followed in the footsteps of his father and became a vestryman at St. James Church in his hometown of Hyde Park, New York; later, he was appointed senior warden, the Church's highest lay position, and became a trustee of the Episcopal Cathedral of St. John the Divine in Manhattan. Yet Roosevelt also detested the pedantry of narrow, doctrinal disputatiousness, which ran counter not only to his temperament but also to his view of religion's essence and purpose in life. He was a Protestant Christian who respected faith in general, and thus was the most instinctively ecumenical president since Lincoln. He appointed more Catholics and Jews than his predecessors. Calling himself "very Low Church," he preferred the simpler services of Baptists, Methodists, and Presbyterians to the rituals of the Episcopal Church. "In the dim distant past they may have been Jews or Catholics or Protestants," he said of his own ancestors, in an allegory that also embodied his overall attitude toward religion. "What I am more interested in is whether they were good citizens and believers in God. I hope they were both."[4]

In wearing his theology lightly but holding his faith closely, Roosevelt was closely in tune with the religious sentiments of most Americans, who valued religion as much for its social utility and spiritual comforts as for any deeper philosophical meaning. Roosevelt offered Americans a flattering reflection of their own religious beliefs and practices, be they Protestant, Catholic, or Jew. Indeed, except for Lincoln and possibly Washington, Roosevelt's respect for non-Protestants and non-Christians was at the time higher than any other president's. His practice of the American civil religion was successful because it seemed genuine. Catholics and Jews were naturally attracted to his social democratic vision for society: for Catholics, it was simply a governmental extension of Catholic social thought and concern for the welfare of the poor and indigent. Though some Catholics worried about the New Deal's secular incursion into the charitable duties of the church, most became and remained loyal Democrats. Jews were similarly attracted to social democracy and statist solutions to economic problems. As predominantly urban ethnic groups heavily tied to organized labor, Catholics and Jews also appreciated the New Deal's provisions for workers and the poor. Ever the political tactician, Roosevelt realized he could tap into a vast reservoir of Catholic and

Jewish electoral support, and he cultivated both groups assiduously. One quarter of all his judicial appointments went to Catholics, an appointment rate six times greater than those of his Republican predecessors, and he broadened Catholic patronage to include not only Irish but also Italians. So closely were Jews associated with the president that his anti-Semitic enemies branded his program for economic recovery the "Jew Deal."[5]

In turn, Americans of all kinds invested religious significance in Roosevelt himself: to his supporters, he appeared as an angel or saint; to his detractors, the Antichrist. Roosevelt's faithful compared him to a "Moses who is leading us out of the wilderness" of the Depression. William Cardinal O'Connell of Boston believed the president had been "God-sent." In 1933, before his bitter break with Roosevelt, Father Coughlin proclaimed that "the New Deal is Christ's deal!" Even FDR's rival for the 1932 Democratic presidential nomination, Newton D. Baker, called Roosevelt "a providential person at a providential moment." But for all the same reasons, Roosevelt was unpopular with the devout and the doctrinaire. Fundamentalist Protestants in particular detested his watered-down ecumenism, passionately objected to his repeal of Prohibition, and distrusted the New Deal's expansion of government power. Criticism from conservative Protestants was typically unsparing. James M. Gray accused Roosevelt of being in league with "the big dictator, the superman, the lawless one," while Gerald B. Winrod variously branded the "wet radicals" of the Roosevelt administration "sinister," "socialistic," and bent on "dictatorship." They were a minority, however; most Americans warmed to Roosevelt's tolerant, simple faith. This was one of the secrets to his extraordinary political success.[6]

To the mainline Protestants, Catholics, and Jews who made up a majority of the population and together formed the New Deal coalition, Roosevelt's confident, optimistic religion was a source of soothing stability in a world of menacing dictators and rampant extremism. Realizing that his faith was an integral part of his political appeal, Roosevelt frequently used religious imagery, symbolism, and language in his official duties. All four of his inaugural addresses were riddled with biblical rhetoric, as were many of his famous radio fireside chats to the nation. In 1935, he wrote to more than 120,000 "representative clergymen" asking them for their advice and opinions about the New Deal. Later, during the war, he established several official days of thanksgiving and prayer, resurrecting a long American tradition that began with the Puritans and continued through the various colonial wars, the Revolutionary War, the War of 1812, and the Civil War. And as we shall see, he constantly framed the world crisis, and especially the conflict between democracy and totalitarianism, in explicitly religious terms. FDR may have been less theologically informed than Woodrow Wilson, but his public faith was more pronounced. The

Federal Council was quite right to declare, during the darkest depths of the war, "We rejoice that in this time of crisis we have as our national leader a man of Christian faith and purpose, reared in the Church and continuing in its service."[7]

ROOSEVELT WAS INDEED a man of Christian faith, and it was this faith that grounded his political beliefs. Perhaps without realizing it, he shared the Christian republican view that religion was the source of democratic freedom because it was the source of conscience and private belief. Freedom of conscience was the bedrock upon which liberty was built, because if the state could interfere with individual conscience, there was no stopping its power or potential for tyranny. Protecting religious faith and the freedom of worship were therefore essential prerequisites for democracy. Moreover, Roosevelt also believed other tenets of the Christian republican tradition, especially that religion was a source of virtue and community spirit, and that it encouraged a sense of responsibility to the welfare of others. For these reasons, in foreign affairs religion could provide an early warning of hostile states and threats. Roosevelt believed, as have most American leaders since the anti-Catholicism of the colonial era and the republicanism of the Revolutionary era, that undemocratic nations are hostage to the whims of their rulers. If religious liberty was the ultimate source of democracy, then the absence of religious liberty would indicate the absence of democracy, which would in turn identify which states were prone to aggression and conquest. The spread of religious liberty would bring with it the spread of democracy, and also peace. Faith, then, could not only provide a diagnosis for international threats, it could also provide the cure. As Roosevelt told the Chair of the Democratic National Committee and Postmaster General Jim Farley in 1933, a "proper attitude toward religion, and belief in God, will in the end be the salvation of all peoples."[8]

That same year, religious liberty shaped Roosevelt's approach to one of his first major foreign policy initiatives, the establishment of diplomatic relations with Moscow. Within the Cabinet and the State Department, there were serious concerns about recognizing a country that did not respect freedom of religion. Secretary of State Cordell Hull distrusted the Soviet Union on these grounds and feared that Roosevelt could lose the 1936 election if he did not deal with the religion question, but ultimately he favored recognition if it could be sorted out. William C. Bullitt, Roosevelt's choice as the first U.S. ambassador to Soviet Moscow, took a somewhat harder line and insisted upon official guarantees of civil and religious rights as a prerequisite of recognition. Jim Farley, a staunch Irish Catholic, reflected the nearly unanimous opposition of the Catholic Church to recognition. Father Edmund A. Walsh of Georgetown University, an expert on foreign affairs, led the public outcry against any deal with Soviet communism. While FDR was determined to recognize Moscow, he was also determined to manufacture consensus behind his foreign policy initiatives. Thus he reassured doubters that he would trade recognition for a Soviet guarantee to relax its prohibitions on freedom of worship. In a private meeting with Walsh, Roosevelt promised he would secure religious liberty for American citizens in the Soviet Union, a policy that stretched back to John Hay and Theodore Roosevelt's efforts on behalf of American Jews.[9]

But Franklin Roosevelt did not need anyone to remind him of the importance of religious liberty, or of its resonance with a large number of American voters. The president agreed that Moscow had to promise that it would at least respect the religious liberty of American citizens visiting or living in the USSR as a condition of establishing relations with Washington. When the Soviet foreign minister, Maxim Litvinov, ignored Roosevelt and instead submitted a plan for diplomatic relations that did not include religious liberty, the president firmly insisted. Roosevelt hoped to tame Soviet communism and bring it properly into the family of nations, and he believed the influence of faith would have a reforming effect on Soviet society. If an American priest, minister, or rabbi administered religious rites to Soviet citizens—including, Roosevelt specified, "baptismal, confirmation, communion, marriage and burial rites," in any language, and in any building, including private houses—communist officials would have no choice but to stand back and allow it to happen, or intervene and incur the wrath of the United States. This was exactly how American missionaries had expanded their influence around the world, and Roosevelt hoped it would work in the Soviet Union. "Let me add," FDR warned Litvinov at the conclusion of negotiations, "that American diplomatic and consular officials in the Soviet Union will be zealous in guarding the rights of American nationals."[10]

Roosevelt personally took part in the negotiations over the normalization of diplomatic relations, often meeting directly with Litvinov in Washington. In one awkward session, Roosevelt used the religious question to throw Litvinov off balance. "Well now, Max," FDR remarked casually,

you know what I mean by religion. You know what religion gives a man. You know the difference between the religious and the irreligious person. Why, you must know, Max. You were brought up by pious parents. Look here, some time you are going to die, and when you come to die, Max, you are going to remember your old father and mother—good, pious Jewish people who believed in God and taught you to pray to God. You had a religious bringing up, and when you come to die, Max, that's what is going to come before you, that is what you are going to think about, that's what you are going to grasp for. You know it's important.

Litvinov, Roosevelt recalled, "got red and fumbled and seemed embarrassed." He was also probably frightened at the thought of Stalin's reaction. But Roosevelt was a shrewd bargainer, and he got what he wanted: the Kremlin agreed to respect the right to religious liberty of Americans in the Soviet Union. It was a vital concession, for it protected not only U.S. Embassy staff, but also the activities of any American ministers, priests, or rabbis who entered the Soviet Union.[11]

Though Roosevelt referred to these ideas domestically, they did not become a major theme of his presidential rhetoric until the full emergence of the Nazi threat became clear in 1936. From then on, and especially in the critical period between the outbreak of war in Europe in 1939 and Pearl Harbor, religion became one of the dominant ideological themes of his foreign policy. In so doing, Roosevelt was drawing upon at least 150 years of American political thought. Yet how he applied it was startlingly new, and provided the basis for his reformulation of American civil religion. Roosevelt embraced what had essentially been Protestant ideas—individual autonomy, the separation of church and state, hostility to concentrated power—but included America's other main religions, Catholicism and Judaism, as believers in them. Building on Lincoln's ecumenical civil religion, Roosevelt was the first president to prioritize faith itself, as opposed to Protestantism or even Christianity, as the essence of American democracy. Others before him—Washington, Lincoln, and Wilson especially—had spoken of the importance of religious toleration and of the need for an inclusive civil religion, but none had done as much to make non-Protestants an integral part of it. Roosevelt's toleration, however, was limited in a way that was typical for American religion and politics. While he tolerated all faiths, he could not tolerate a lack of faith. Without faith, there was no morality, and without morality no democracy.

At the 1936 Inter-American Conference in Argentina, Roosevelt praised the stability of the peoples of the Western Hemisphere and attributed it to their common faith in democracy. "But this faith," he warned, "will not be complete if we fail to affirm our faith in God." Given the overwhelming Roman Catholic setting, this was a surprising claim coming from an American Protestant. After all, only a few decades earlier William McKinley had claimed the need to "Christianize" the already Catholic Filipinos as a justification for imperialism. But in Buenos Aires, Roosevelt pointedly did not differentiate between faiths. "In the whole history of mankind," he declared, "the human race has been distinguished from other forms of life by the existence—the fact—of religion. Periodic attempts to deny God have always and always will come to naught." One of those periodic attempts was of course occurring at that very moment, in Germany and the Soviet Union. By contrast, he told his fellow republicans of the Americas, embedded in "the constitutions and in the practice of our nations is the right of freedom of religion. But this ideal, these words presuppose a belief and a trust in God."[12]

That same year, in a radio address on religious tolerance sponsored by the National Conference of Christians and Jews, Roosevelt made the same appeal to Americans in even more explicit terms. "We who have faith cannot afford to fall out among ourselves," he said at a time of rising anti-Semitism and continuing anti-Catholicism. "The very state of the world is a summons to us to stand together. For as I see it," he continued with Nazi Germany obviously in mind,

> the chief religious issue is not between our various beliefs. It is between belief and unbelief. It is not your specific faith or mine that is being called into question—but all faith. Religion in wide areas of the earth is being confronted with irreligion; our faiths are being challenged. It is because of that threat that you and I must reach across the lines between our creeds, clasp hands, and make common cause.

This was probably the clearest expression of the American civil religion yet given. And it was central to Roosevelt's view of democracy at home and security abroad.[13]

Protestant though he was, Roosevelt was often frustrated with the bigotry of his coreligionists. Just as Nazism and communism represented threats to religious liberty, so did intolerance. Anti-Catholicism and anti-Semitism were simply anti-American, and not problems only for Catholics and Jews but for all Americans. In 1939, he named Myron C. Taylor as his unofficial envoy to the Vatican—unofficial because Congress had prohibited official relations between Washington and the Holy See nearly a century before, and more immediately because of the anti-Catholic hostility Taylor's appointment was bound to provoke. When George Buttrick of the Federal Council wrote to express his "misgivings" about Taylor's mission to the Vatican on the grounds that it favored the Roman Catholic Church and thus violated the constitutional separation of church and state, Roosevelt exploded with uncharacteristic anger. He first sent a polite but terse reply. Then, in an extraordinary burst of fury, he quickly penned a second reply to accompany the first. "I am sending this additional personal letter" because of the FCC's "completely ridiculous . . . objection to a sincere effort on my part to mobilize the moral and religious forces of the world on behalf of peace." He then confessed that he was also seeking an interlocutor from the Muslim world. Presumably Buttrick would oppose that too, but just "because they were non-Christians,"

Roosevelt could "see no reason why a Christian President should not seek their aid in strengthening a world-wide desire for peace." Most incredible, and insulting, was Buttrick's charge that "by some wild and utterly crazy stretch of the imagination that I am disregarding the separation of Church and State." Roosevelt closed by observing that religious bigotry had been common when he was a boy; he even recalled reciting an Episcopal prayer "calling down divine wrath on 'Jews, Turks and other infidels.' I think that most American Christians have advanced considerably in their religious thought in the past half-century."[14]

As the crises in Europe and Asia escalated, Roosevelt intensified his faith-based vision of politics and peace. Following the appeasement at Munich, he began to prepare Americans for a European war in which they would not necessarily fight but which the United States could not possibly avoid. Roosevelt's public relations campaign, a role that is almost uniquely the president's, relied on identifying the rise of totalitarianism as a threat to American security. Often he did so by claiming that once it had conquered Europe, Germany intended to conquer Latin America as a springboard to invading the United States. Isolationists and other anti-interventionists had a relatively easy time parrying such predictions as unrealistic. So FDR took a different approach: he warned Americans that they risked being surrounded in a world of tyranny and that they could not long survive as a free people under such conditions. A "nation whose origins go back to Jamestown and Plymouth Rock," he said in 1940, could not live as "a lone island in a world dominated by the philosophy of force."[15]

In January 1939, in his annual State of the Union address to Congress, Roosevelt gave his most explicit warning yet about the threat to American security and American values. "Storms from abroad directly challenge three institutions indispensable to Americans," he cautioned at the beginning of his speech. "The first is religion. It is the source of the other two—democracy and international good faith." For those perplexed by the links between faith and foreign policy, Roosevelt explained what he meant:

> Religion, by teaching man his relationship to God, gives the individual a sense of his own dignity and teaches him to respect himself by respecting his neighbors.
>
> Democracy, the practice of self-government, is a covenant among free men to respect the rights and liberties of their fellows.
>
> International good faith, a sister of democracy, springs from the will of civilized nations of men to respect the rights and liberties of other nations of men.
>
> In a modern civilization, all three—religion, democracy and international good faith—complement and support each other.

Where freedom of religion has been attacked, the attack has come from sources opposed to democracy. Where democracy has been overthrown, the spirit of free worship has disappeared. And where religion and democracy have vanished, good faith and reason in international affairs have given way to strident ambition and brute force.

An ordering of society which relegates religion, democracy, and good faith among nations to the background can find no place within it for the ideals of the Prince of Peace. The United States rejects such an ordering, and retains its ancient faith.

He then applied this concept of liberty as indivisible—that its component parts could not exist without each other—to the practice of foreign policy:

There comes a time in the affairs of men when they must prepare to defend, not their homes alone, but the tenets of faith and humanity on which their churches, their governments and their very civilization are founded. The defense of religion, of democracy and of good faith among nations is all the same fight. To save one we must now make up our minds to save all.

We know what might happen to us of the United States if the new philosophies of force were to encompass the other continents and invade our own. We, no more than other nations, can afford to be surrounded by the enemies of our faith and our humanity.[16]

As tensions mounted and war broke out in Europe, and as he edged the United States closer and closer to supporting the enemies of Nazism, Roosevelt escalated his religious rhetoric. In his 1940 State of the Union address, he accused Germany of trying to establish a world order in which people everywhere "were compelled to worship a god imposed by a military ruler, or were forbidden to worship God at all." In May, as western Europe was coming under German occupation, he warned that "the Americans might have to become the guardian of Western culture, the protector of Christian civilization." A year later, in announcing an "unlimited national emergency," he feared that "the whole world is divided between human slavery and human freedom—between pagan brutality and the Christian ideal." And in one of his most important speeches, an ominous October 1941 Navy Day address proclaiming the existence of a state of armed hostility between the United States and Germany, Roosevelt alleged that Hitler had a secret "plan to abolish all existing religions—Catholic, Protestant, Mohammedan, Hindu, Buddhist, and Jewish alike," and replace them with an "International Nazi Church." *Mein Kampf* would replace the Bible and be "enforced as Holy Writ," while the swastika would replace the cross—claims he repeated in his 1942 State of the Union. "The god of

Blood and Iron will take the place of the God of Love and Mercy," Roosevelt preached. "Let us well ponder that statement which I have made tonight."[17]

At moments of grave crisis, Roosevelt turned to faith to explain the need for an anti-Nazi foreign policy. This was entirely understandable: religion offers solace in times of turbulence and danger, it stirs passions and can thus act as a call to arms, and it provides orators with some of the most moving yet instantly familiar and accessible rhetoric in the English language. It also provides a morally compelling and politically useful platform. But Roosevelt did not merely confine religion to the phrases of speeches. He codified it as policy, consistent with the principles of his political philosophy, in some of the most important statements of American war aims. Most notably, Roosevelt reduced the cause for which Americans would fight to four essential values, his Four Freedoms, the second of which was the "freedom of every person to worship God in his own way—everywhere in the world." In perhaps the fullest expression yet of a global Social Gospel, he also listed the freedom of speech and expression, the freedom from want, and the freedom from fear as the other Freedoms. He did not feel it necessary to mention democracy; according to him, democracy would exist wherever religious liberty could be found. Similarly, at Roosevelt's insistence and despite the risk of arousing Soviet resentment, the State Department ensured that "religious freedom" was listed in the inaugural 1942 Declaration of the United Nations.[18]

Following Roosevelt's example, efforts to promote and protect religious liberty permeated U.S. foreign policy for the rest of the war. In particular, the State Department used religion in much the same way as the president had to justify American participation in the war on ideological grounds. Like Roosevelt, Secretary of State Cordell Hull believed that Americans "have a desperate need for more religion and morality as the background for Government. The religious and moral foundations for thought and conduct require strengthening here" in America, "as well as throughout the world. There is no higher civilizing influence than religious and moral concepts." Assistant Secretary of State Adolf Berle spread a similar message of the indivisibility of liberty. "Life, liberty, independence, religious freedom, human rights," he told a wartime audience at Columbia University. "These are the essential conditions of free men and free minds." Under Secretary Sumner Welles concurred. On June 23, 1941, the day after the Germans invaded the Soviet Union, Welles reminded Americans that the Roosevelt administration "has often stated, and in many of his public statements the President has declared, that the United States maintains that freedom to worship God as their consciences dictate is the great and fundamental right of all peoples. This right has been denied to their peoples by both the Nazi and the Soviet Governments." Thus the first official American response to the most important development of the war was to observe that both Nazism and communism were opposed to religion. "Neither kind of imposed overlordship can have, or will have, any support or any sway in the mode of life, or in the system of Government, of the American people." It was a strange choice of words under the circumstances, but not out of character for Roosevelt or his officials. In March 1942, Welles attempted to rally South American republics to the cause of the United Nations by invoking shared responsibility. "We, the American nations," he declared in a speech in Rio de Janeiro, "are trustees for Christian civilization."[19]

Such efforts continued after Roosevelt's death in April 1945. In May, at the San Francisco Conference to establish the United Nations, Secretary of State Edward Stettinius pushed the U.S. delegation to include "freedom of worship" as one of the UN's official goals. A few months later, in August, Roosevelt's successor, Harry Truman, promised that Germany would be reconstructed along liberal democratic lines, with a political system built specifically upon the foundations of "free speech, free press, freedom of religion, and the right of labor to organize." Religion, long a part of the fabric of American culture and politics, was now automatically a part of U.S. foreign policy.[20]

Religious faith was of course not the only driving force within Franklin Roosevelt's diplomatic thought and foreign policy. But by offering moral clarity in a confusing world at war, Roosevelt's religion—a simple faith to which nearly all Americans of all faiths could relate intuitively—provided America's quickly expanding world role with direction and purpose.

CHAPTER EIGHTEEN

The Holocaust and the Moral Meaning of the War

So MUCH HAS BEEN said and written about Adolf Hitler that today his evil is self-evident; it is astonishing to people today that not everyone initially recognized it. Americans were not at first worried about Nazi genocide, which was still in a scarcely imaginable future. Instead, they focused on exploding the myths of the Great War, when exaggerated reports of German atrocities concocted by the British were accepted at face value. In the conclusion to his 1933 book *Preachers Present Arms*, a relentless exposé of church complicity in whipping up nationalist frenzy during World War I, Ray Abrams claimed to see history repeating itself. Where the kaiser was once vilified, Hitler was now cast as the ultimate enemy. "Thus," Abrams charged, "does the campaign of hatred go on." He acknowledged that the Nazis were meting out "excessively cruel and heinous treatment" upon Jews and that Hitler was no democrat. "But is persecution in one country remedied by stirring up hatred and vilification in another?" he asked. "Instead of laying all the blame on Hitler, might it not be more reasonable to try to understand and account for the present German situation?" The one thing nearly everyone wanted to avoid—at all costs—was another world war.[1]

This was especially the case among liberal Protestants of the peace movement. Like Abrams, they recognized Hitler as a special, perhaps unique, danger. They had no love for Nazism and feared it would reach into American life as the nation suffered through the Depression. Immediately after Hitler came to power in 1933, John Haynes Holmes, the Unitarian pacifist, condemned Nazism as "savagery," "barbarianism," and "tyranny." Later in the decade, Kirby Page denounced Nazi Germany's ambitions as "aggressive, atrocious, and suicidal." But as with the Japanese challenge, Christian pacifists continued to believe that the crisis would only get worse if the United States tried to solve it with force. Through the 1930s, even after the invasion of Poland, they continued to stick to neutrality as the only sensible policy.[2]

Unsurprisingly, American Jews felt otherwise. They were among the earliest to warn of Nazism's threat, they were the staunchest supporters of Britain's isolated stand against Germany in 1940, and they were among the first to suggest a firm U.S. response that might even lead to war. This time, Rabbi Stephen Wise would not need to make an emotionally wrenching conversion from dove to hawk. He spent the summer of 1933 traveling in Europe, only a few months after Hitler had come to power. In Paris, Geneva, Vienna, and Prague, he met refugees, mostly Jews but also some dissident German Christians, who had fled the new order. At Munich in 1938, when the British and French passed up an opportunity to stand up to Hitler over Germany's demands for the Czechoslovakian Sudetenland, Wise knew a dangerous threshold had been crossed. "You may not feel as I do," he wrote his close friend John Haynes Holmes, who also loathed the Nazis but was not willing to abandon the peace crusade, "but to me this is one of the saddest days of history." Contrary to the claims of American pacifists, appeasement did "not mean England and France are opposed to war." It meant instead that they were willing to sacrifice others to save their own skins, probably in the hope that Germany would now turn on the Soviet Union. "Human liberties are fled, democracy is a sham, standards have gone, the moral realm of mankind is laid waste. God help us!"[3]

Wise was so upset, he quickly penned another letter to Holmes that serves not only as a moving testament to Jewish anguish but also to the moral dilemma then racking Christian internationalists over the use of force. "I know you will feel that we have been saved from the horror of horrors which is war," he wrote. "But the evil day has only been put off." Instead, "representatives of the two democracies have sat in conference with the two cruellest, foulest Dictators of earth." Worse still: "They have yielded." Most disturbingly, the Munich conference met "in the absence of Czecho-Slovakia, and without her consent! Jesus at least had the dignity of being crucified in his own presence." And this would not be the last the world would hear from Hitler. "Don't think we have escaped war," Wise insisted to his Christian pacifist friend. "We have war without sacrifice. We have victory with shame!"[4]

WISE'S DESPAIR IS understandable, especially in light of what happened in the ensuing seven years, but he did not realize that the tide of American opinion was slowly beginning to shift in his favor. While the specter of the Great War loomed large in the American imagination, the fear that Hitler was bent on starting another began to grow, and with it the determination that he must be stopped.

Vital to this development, at least for Christians, was the perception that Nazism was both a pagan movement and a threat to all religion, including Christianity—not just to religious liberty, and thus to democracy, but to faith itself. In the eyes of many Americans, Nazism assumed many of the worst characteristics of communism, yet was even more aggressive, militant, and dangerous. According to a 1938 poll, 94 percent of Americans disapproved of Germany's treatment of the Jews, while 97 percent disapproved of its treatments of Catholics. In 1940, *Time* dramatized the plight of European religion under Nazi occupation by publishing pleas from persecuted Christians. "Many parishes invaded, churches bombed and burnt . . . pastoral families ruined," said one. Cried another, "Where is America? We need your help and prayers more than ever." Protestant groups began asking themselves, "Can Christianity Survive?" Catholics may have been ambivalent about fascism in Italy and Spain, which promised to protect the church from atheists and communists, but they were overwhelmingly hostile to Nazism in Germany. "Nazism will seek to exterminate Christianity if Nazism dominates Europe," warned Father Raymond Feely, a California Jesuit. If Americans allowed that to happen, it would only be a matter of time before the same attack on democracy and religion reached them, too.[5]

Hitler and the Nazis not only conjured up images of another, more catastrophic world war, they also revived awful memories of genocides past. Greek and Armenian Christians under the Turks, Jews in Russia and Romania, Cubans under Spanish tyranny, and slaves in the Old South had all provoked American religion's righteous indignation. But compared with these historical atrocities, and even alongside the spread of religious persecution during the 1930s—Stalin's communist atheism, Franco's repression of Spanish Protestants, and Japan's brutality against Chinese Christians—the Nazi hounding of German Jews raised the specter of something far more sinister. To the socialite Nancy Astor, who doubted that the Germans were capable of committing such crimes, Felix Frankfurter warned that "Hitler's brutality and cruelty . . . make the old Russian pogroms seem kind by comparison." Wise was similarly aghast at Americans who said they could reason with Hitler: "in truth," he wrote despairingly during a visit to Geneva, "the Jews of Germany are finished."[6]

Jewish relief agencies sprang into action, of course, but so too did many Christian organizations, both Protestant and Catholic. With the U.S. government still unwilling to admit Jewish refugees from Europe or take tougher measures against Germany, it was left to private relief efforts to aid European Jews and resettle them as best they could. Zionist groups saw this as an opportunity to augment Palestine's Jewish population, while older, anti-Zionist Jewish organizations just wanted Jews to leave Germany for anywhere possible. "I would rather have him go to China than stay in Germany," a non-Zionist Jew said of a German family member; his other suggestions included Central America, South Africa,

Zanzibar, and of course the United States. For American Christians sympathetic to the plight of European Jews, the politics of Zionism were less of an issue than the politics of intervention. Deeply sympathetic to Jewry, Reinhold Niebuhr was one of the first to warn of the Nazi menace, and his advocacy for Jews became another part of his anti-Nazi campaign. But for others concerned with the fate of German Jews, it was vital that Jewish relief not lead to U.S. intervention. Thus could John Haynes Holmes plead for peace through tolerance of Jews, at home and abroad; thus could Harry Emerson Fosdick, who renounced war even in self-defense and would oppose World War II even after Pearl Harbor, rail from the pulpit against Hitler's anti-Semitism and produce a fund-raising film for German refugees; thus could the FCC sponsor a nationally broadcast report on CBS radio, featuring Harold Ickes, about the notorious Nazi rampage of *Kristallnacht*. All Jews and an increasing number of Christians could agree on one end: stop the Nazi persecution of German Jews. They simply differed on the means.[7]

Yet this sense of urgency over the fate of European Jewry did not extend into the Roosevelt administration. Severe immigration restrictions imposed in 1924 were still in force, and though the Ku Klux Klan had diminished by the 1930s, other racist groups arose to take its place. Even respectable public opinion was overwhelmingly in favor of maintaining low levels of immigration. In addition, noninterference was government policy. A decade earlier, against the backdrop of renewed pogroms in Romania, Secretary of State Frank Kellogg told a distraught Rabbi Wise that the U.S. government might privately deplore human rights abuses abroad but it had no business telling another sovereign nation how to run its domestic affairs, a policy the Roosevelt administration maintained when faced with crises over persecution of the Catholic Church in Mexico and Spain. Moreover, there were no American lives or property to protect in Germany or Austria, so the example of pushing the Soviets to respect religious liberty in exchange for recognition did not apply. For now, at least, Roosevelt felt he could do little to stop the rape of European Jewry. Instead, in 1938 he proposed an international conference, to convene at Évian-les-Bains in France, to address the refugee crisis. Despite Hull's insistence that America's "purpose is to alleviate the lot of these unfortunate people," the Évian Conference achieved nothing because Roosevelt and his special envoy for refugees, Myron C. Taylor, could not convince other nations to adopt immigration measures the United States itself was unwilling to consider. Nor was the State Department willing to pressure the British to consider Palestine as an outlet for Jewish refugees from Europe. Only the Dominican Republic, for cynical reasons of its own rather than out of any humanitarian concern, agreed to accept Jewish refugees, but even this meager measure ended in failure. In the face of sclerotic official inaction and deafness to the plight of Europe's persecuted Jews (and Christians), it was left to churches, synagogues, and voluntary organizations to shape the nation's conscience instead.[8]

While the Roosevelt administration remained inert, private individuals, sometimes including government officials acting independently, launched their own operations to help Jewish refugees fleeing Europe. One of the more remarkable of these rescue missions was a clandestine, and for the most part illegal, scheme code named Operation Texas and run through the office of a young, little known Texas congressman named Lyndon Baines Johnson. In 1937, LBJ was about to begin a torrid, seven-year affair with Alice Glass. A beautiful Southern belle who just happened to be married to Johnson's political patron, the publishing baron Charles Marsh, Glass was a well-educated lover of the arts. She and Marsh spent that summer in Europe. In Austria, they heard not only the beauty of Mozart but the disturbed ravings of Hitler. They also met a talented young Jewish conductor, Erich Leinsdorf, who soon fled Austria, found work with the Metropolitan Opera in New York, and later took refuge at Longlea, Marsh's sprawling estate in northern Virginia. With Leinsdorf's U.S. visa about to expire and the immigration authorities determined to expel him from the country, Marsh and Glass turned to Johnson for help. LBJ immediately gained Leinsdorf a six-month reprieve, told him to go to Cuba, and from there apply for asylum in the United States as a political refugee. This feint inspired Johnson to launch Operation Texas, which used the Leinsdorf scheme to smuggle Jewish refugees from Europe to Texas via Latin America. Johnson's collaborators were a wealthy Jewish businessman from Austin who had immigrated from Russia twenty-five years before; the state head of the National Youth Administration (NYA), a New Deal program with which Johnson was heavily involved; and the head of the Texas Railroad Commission. Once safely in Texas, the refugees took shelter in local NYA camps. Leinsdorf went on to have one of the most distinguished careers of any American conductor, while Operation Texas rescued forty-two Jews and resettled them in the Austin area.[9]

The sense of humanitarian crisis in Europe was exacerbated by the rise of fascism and virulent anti-Semitism in the United States. Fascists were never poised to seize control of Washington as they had in Berlin, Rome, and Madrid, but domestic far-right groups surged in popularity in the 1930s as the twin specters of financial collapse and big government cast a shadow over the minds of many Americans. Among conservatives, the Depression raised economic fears of poverty, destitution, and anarchy, while the New Deal raised political fears of dictatorship and social engineering. To right-wing extremists, it was clear that Jews lay behind both developments, from the international bankers who manipulated the world's money to the New Dealers who planned a takeover of the country.

Between 1933 and 1941, in response as much to the example set by Hitler and the ambitions of the New Deal as to the deprivations of the economic crisis, more than a hundred anti-Semitic groups were established in the United States. Religious extremists were not the cause of the new, harder-edged anti-Semitism, but they were certainly at its helm. To begin with, during the era of the Great War the second coming of the Ku Klux Klan coincided with the emergence of fundamentalism and was ideologically bound up with extremist Protestantism's hatred for communism and Catholics as well as Jews. Not long afterward, in the 1930s, fundamentalist preachers like William Bell Riley accused Jews of everything from Christ-killing to the spreading of Darwinism. Father Charles Coughlin, the radio demagogue, began attacking "communistic Jews" on his wildly popular radio program in 1938. That same year, his followers set up their own organization, the Christian Front, which would protect American liberties against communists and Jews. Not coincidentally, anti-Semites were also usually among the most hard-line isolationists—Coughlin, for example, or Senator Gerald Nye, who claimed that "the Jewish people are a large factor in our movement toward war," or the group America First, which tried but could never quite fully purge anti-Semitism from its ranks—who accused Jews of manipulating an unsuspecting America into a European war on behalf of world Jewry and Zionism.[10]

But of course not every Christian—not even every fundamentalist—was anti-Semitic. Premillennial dispensationalists, for example, rejected Nazism not only as the most dangerous form of pagan autocracy, but also because the Bible revealed that the Antichrist would make himself known by attacking the Jews. Many Southern Baptists who did not necessarily believe in prophecy shed their cultural anti-Semitism in light of the Nazis' threat to human rights and democracy. Ecumenical modernists were also quick to assist and defend Jews. Against a backdrop of crisis, dictatorship, and militarism in Europe, anti-Nazi activists in the United States formed interfaith coalitions to defeat the surge of domestic anti-Semitism as an unpatriotic perversion of American democracy. In response to anti-Semitism at home and abroad, interfaith leaders harked back to a very long American tradition of grounding democratic liberty within the freedoms of conscience and worship.[11]

As Mark Silk and Wendy Wall have pointed out, these leaders also constructed a new national identity of America as a "Judeo-Christian" country. The National Conference of Christians and Jews, the nation's leading interfaith organization, played an especially large role in spreading this message, and Jews spread it through the American Jewish Committee. Liberal Protestants set up the American Christian Committee for German Refugees, which aimed to help persecuted Christians as well as Jews, while Catholics established their own staunchly pro-Jewish group, the Committee of Catholics for Human Rights, which pledged to resist Coughlin's Christian Front and assist Jewish refugees from Europe. For interventionists like Niebuhr, this argument fed nicely into arguments in favor of aiding the Allies, even of America joining the war itself. To fight Nazism at home, went the argument, it was also necessary to fight it abroad. In fact, American fascists, anti-Semites, and Nazi sympathizers made it easier to discredit respectable pacifism and anti-interventionism. Anti-fascists and opponents of anti-Semitism thus began a process of blurring ideological distinctions between domestic and foreign enemies. Said one interfaith partisan, the struggle was not really between Germany and the United States or Christians and Jews but "Nazis vs. Civilization."[12]

Not all interfaith and ecumenical Jewish sympathizers favored U.S. intervention. Philo-Semitic pacifist clergy like John Haynes Holmes and pacifist groups such as the American Alliance of Christians and Jews comfortably walked a moral tightrope of aiding Jewish refugees and denouncing Hitler, but refusing to do anything more. Nonetheless, the logic of anti-anti-Semitism ran irrepressibly toward a clash with Nazi Germany. And even peace crusaders were increasingly conflicted. "Most of us feel that the Democracies cause is just yet we wonder whether Jesus would call any war righteous," wrote one morally torn Baptist a few days after Germany invaded Poland. "I don't know. But I am sure that liberty is bought at a great price. Perhaps peace—a really honorable peace—is a greater sacrifice than war."[13]

As Roosevelt well knew, religious persecution was not an abstract problem in political theory but a pressing humanitarian crisis. American Jews were careful not to press the plight of their coreligionists as the reason for their country to join the war. The Depression-stricken United States had just come through perhaps its worst-ever bout of domestic anti-Semitism, and nothing would revive it more than if Jews appeared to be manipulating Roosevelt into war on their behalf. Yet the situation became even more critical after the outbreak of war in September 1939. Many Christians and Jews pointed to Nazi attacks on European Jews as but one example of Hitler's general threat to religious liberty, and thus to democracy. In a nationwide address over CBS Radio, for example, Rabbi Abba Hillel Silver warned that the fate of the Jews was an early warning signal of the more general fate of freedom in the world, including in America. In December 1941, Japan's attack on Pearl Harbor and Germany's declaration of war provided all the evidence Silver needed.[14]

During the war, the ecumenical conflation of religion and democracy, and of Christians and Jews, was not confined to the nation's rabbis. Roosevelt himself had ideologically grounded America's purpose as a struggle to preserve religious freedom, and by extension political freedom, and he deliberately defined religious liberty as broadly as possible. The Nazis attacked all "monotheistic religions," he told a Jewish audience in 1942, which was why it was "important for the lovers of freedom to work harmoniously together in mutual understanding." Now, with the nation at war, Protestant ministers and Catholic priests similarly rallied their parishioners to the wartime crusade for faith and freedom by portraying the attack on the Jews as a more general attack on religion itself. Detecting a new ethos of interfaith tolerance that resulted directly from the war effort against antireligious Nazism, a scholar at the University of Chicago concluded that the "three great religious groups have become increasingly aware that they are allies in a common cause," dedicated not only to securing military victory but to "upholding those basic principles of faith in God and man to which they are committed as Christians and Jews, and upon which the meaning and strength of the nation's cause depend." Perhaps the best example of the emergence of a truly interfaith civil religion was found in Congress. By overwhelming majorities, both the House and the Senate passed wartime resolutions explicitly condemning the Nazi persecution of the Jews and calling upon Roosevelt to do more to protect them. Anti-Catholicism and anti-Semitism remained repugnant features of American life, and tensions between Protestants and Catholics over schools and other issues continued. But religious bigotry was increasingly discredited by its association with Nazi extremism—which itself seemed to stand against everything the American ideal was supposed to represent. Such efforts to breathe life into a truly interdenominational, Judeo-Christian civil religion were critical, not only for the war effort but for fundamental changes in the complexion of American religious culture.[15]

For the interfaith vision of religious liberty as a human right to flourish, it was vital for Christians to rally to the cause. And rally they did. The precise details of the Holocaust were still largely unknown, yet Americans sensed that an unusual catastrophe was befalling Europe's Jews. For example, in 1943 a Protestant chaplain at the University of Michigan asked enlisted students to name their most pressing moral quandaries. Of nineteen submitted, the most common question was, understandably, "If God is good and also powerful, why this war?" The next most pressing question, ahead of democracy and more everyday concerns like marriage and moral living, was: "What will be the place of the Jews after the war?" For some, such as Peter Maurin of the Catholic Worker movement, that place should be the United States. "America is big enough to find a refuge for persecuted Jews," he declared in opposition to immigration restrictions that were kept in place throughout the war.[16]

The interfaith civil religion was even more tightly embraced by the nation's leading Christians. In 1943, Catholic bishop Fulton J. Sheen, whose radio program the *Catholic Hour* reached over four million listeners, declared the war to be "not merely a political and an economic struggle but rather a theological one" that pitted the forces of democracy and faith against "the totalitarian world view which is anti-Christian, anti-Semitic and anti-human." Americans fought not only out of self-defense but for "the Christian world view which grounds the human and the democratic values of the western world on a moral and religious basis." Crucially, according to Bishop Sheen, the "Christian view includes not only Christians but also Jews who historically are the roots of the Christian tradition and who religiously are one with the Christian in the adoration of God and the acceptance of the moral law as the reflection of the eternal reason of God." Bishop James Cannon Jr., a leading Southern Methodist, followed suit by calling upon America to save the Jews who "wrote the Scriptures we read every Sunday, but whom we allow to be murdered by the diabolical wretches of Naziism."[17]

Government officials also joined in. Vice President Henry A. Wallace linked his vision of leftist politics with the fate of European Jews by declaring that "the efforts to destroy the Jews are only part of the war to crush the spirit of the common man all over the world." Other notable lay leaders, such as Supreme Court justice Frank Murphy, an active Roman Catholic, established organizations like the National Committee Against Persecution of the Jews. Similarly, a sold-out rally at Madison Square Garden to "Stop Hitler Now," assist the "five million Jews threatened with extermination by Adolf Hitler," and "halt the liquidation of European Jewry by the Nazis" was orchestrated by Rabbi Stephen Wise, cosponsored by the American Jewish Congress and Church Peace Union, and featured speeches by New York City mayor Fiorello La Guardia, New York governor Thomas Dewey, Supreme Court justice William O. Douglas, British ambassador Lord Halifax, and the heads of the American Federation of Labor and the Congress of Industrial Organizations. The *New York Times* gave the rally front-page coverage.[18]

This was an encouraging turn of events for American Jews, but it still did not reflect the emergency of what was unfolding in Nazi-occupied Europe. When Jewish leaders warned of "the complete annihilation of the Jews in Europe and wherever else the Nazis can reach them," as Abraham Duker did in the summer of 1942, they were not speaking of political theory or of threats to values and ideas. Duker drove the point home: "Few people believe that under certain circumstances Jewish survival is even possible in case of a Hitler victory." Yet Duker directed his criticism not toward gentiles, but his fellow American Jews. Complacent, parochial, fearful of reawakening dormant anti-Semitism at home—for whatever reason, many Jews *in* the United States felt that the Jews *of* the United States were deaf to the pleas of their fellow Jews in Europe.[19]

The Roosevelt administration was not much better, though its members were preoccupied with the overriding task of winning a world war on two transoceanic fronts. Precise figures may not have been known, but administration officials, President Roosevelt included, certainly knew the Holocaust was unfolding. In 1942, Myron Taylor, FDR's envoy to the Vatican, referred to "the Nazi plan of extermination" and verified for Roosevelt and Cordell Hull that "the atrocities in France, Poland and Yugoslavia are confirmed as generally reported." Sumner Welles also acknowledged the Nazis' systematic destruction of European Jewry. Yet a solution proved elusive. The Allied militaries were powerless to rescue Jews from Nazi-occupied Europe, while Roosevelt and Hull acknowledged that Congress would never relax immigration quota restrictions to accommodate refugees. Still, by 1943, the evidence—and bodies—of the Holocaust had mounted to such an extent that officials from London and Washington met in Bermuda to come up with a rescue plan. Political pressure at home, moreover, also helped push the State Department into action; Hull, for example, saw the meetings in Bermuda as a way to respond to the massive "Stop Hitler Now" rally at Madison Square Garden. Much like the 1938 Évian Conference, however, the Bermuda Conference could offer only modest rescue proposals for a meager number of Jewish refugees—in the low thousands, not millions—who had made it to neutral Spain and could go no further. And even those proved controversial, with the Joint Chiefs of Staff adamantly opposing any diversion of ships or troops from the military campaign. In the end, little was accomplished.[20]

WHILE FACTS on the ground were moving faster than the U.S. government recognized, the reality of the unfolding Holocaust was crystal-clear to most American Jews, especially those who were most committed to Zionism. The Pioneer Women's Organization of St. Louis, a Jewish group, wrote their senator, one Harry S. Truman, of their "deepest distress" at the "unabated" and "deliberate extermination of the Jews in Nazi occupied Europe." Because the civilized world had failed to prevent "these wholesale slaughters of human beings," immediate rescue and evacuation to Palestine for permanent resettlement offered the Jews their only hope of survival as a people. The "very dignity of mankind is at stake," feared the pro-Zionist Emergency Conference to Save the Jewish People of Europe in words that Roosevelt himself could have said. "Action cannot be postponed until after the war. In the case of the Jews, rehabilitation after the war will come too late. There may be only corpses to rehabilitate." Stephen Wise, a leading Zionist as president of the American Jewish Congress, warned Sumner Welles in 1943 that more "than three million

Jews have been brutally done to death by the Nazis and there is every reason to believe that unless halted by the action of the United Nations, the
Axis powers will fulfill their pledge of complete extermination." Not only
were Zionists more active in issues affecting transnational Jewry, and thus
closer to events in Europe, they also made an instant connection between
the persecution of Jews in Europe and the existence of a possible safe
haven in Palestine. Not all American Jews were Zionists, of course, but
the Holocaust gave those who envisioned Palestine as the site of a future
Jewish nation-state powerful moral leverage.[21]

This group also included many Christians, and not simply evangelicals
who supported a Jewish state as the fulfillment of prophecy. The plight of
European Jewry moved many anti-Nazi liberals to throw their considerable political and moral weight behind Zionism. It was, they believed,
the least they could do. Reverend Henry A. Atkinson, a Congregational
minister and leading modernist, pledged that "the Christian conscience
cannot rest" until something had been done for the Jews. The "shocking
scandal" of the Bermuda Conference proved that Washington and London were unable, perhaps even unwilling, to rescue the Jews of Europe,
which prompted Atkinson to urge his fellow Christians to support a
Jewish homeland in Palestine. Since 1939, he wrote in a 1943 issue of
Niebuhr's magazine *Christianity and Crisis*, "two to three million Jews have
been relentlessly hounded to death. The remaining four to five million
in Europe today are doomed as the victims of an avowed policy of extermination." In the face of Anglo-American inaction, "Palestine is the only
feasible solution to offer an immediate haven of refuge in this desperate
emergency." The consequences of further inaction, or of outright opposition to Zionism, were profoundly immoral, for the "only alternative is
death." By way of justification, Atkinson also applied the Social Gospel to
Palestine. European Jews, he claimed, would bring the blessings of civilization to the benighted Middle East, and thus would improve the living conditions of the Arabs already living there. This was a double-sided
humanitarianism, and it was not atypical for Protestants with Atkinson's
anti-fascist, progressive worldview.[22]

Secular foreign policy analysts also supported Zionism as the solu-
tion to the Holocaust. Upon hearing persistent rumors of genocide, the
New York–based Council on Foreign Relations, the most established of
Establishment think tanks, launched an investigation into the plight of
the Jews. Hamilton Fish Armstrong, the imperious editor of the Council's
journal, *Foreign Affairs*, reported the study group's findings in May 1943:
"Probably a third of the 6,000,000 Jews formerly in Nazi-held sections of
Europe have now been destroyed; many more are likely to perish." This
was a humanitarian problem of the greatest magnitude, something the

world had never before witnessed. Its solution, Armstrong reported, was simple, readily available, and relatively straightforward. "The root of the Jewish problem is the homelessness of the Jews. Hence a home in Palestine offers the only satisfactory solution. Palestine is already a Jewish land. The Arab-Jewish problem can be solved if Great Britain and the United States will tell the Arabs to come to terms with the Jews who want only to be left alone but are ready to cooperate with the Arabs." *Foreign Affairs* also published an article by the leader of world Zionism, Chaim Weizmann, that portrayed "a Jewish state in Palestine" as a "moral need" and a "decisive step towards normality and true emancipation." The Christian democracies, Weizmann argued, owed the Jews nothing less.[23]

This was certainly consistent with the thinking of Franklin Roosevelt, at least until he ran into a wall of opposition from both Arabs and his own State Department in the winter of 1945. As president, Roosevelt needed to tread a careful line on Palestine: it was, after all, a British mandate with a sizable Arab population that drew intense interest across the Arab region—the same Arab region that controlled much of the world's oil resources. And because Zionism was a powerful transnational phenomenon that would help determine the future of the Holy Land, Palestine attracted widespread attention throughout Europe, especially in the Vatican. Whatever his own preference, then, Roosevelt had to move cautiously. Yet his own preferences favored the Jews. As early as 1939, FDR was certain enough of this to tell Abdul Aziz ibn Saud, the king of Saudi Arabia and one of Zionism's most implacable opponents, that Palestine was not simply about individual rights but fundamentally an issue of "a spiritual character." (Perhaps not coincidentally, "a spiritual problem" was precisely how Sumner Welles defined Zionism.) Roosevelt also referred the king to a 1938 State Department declaration that pointed to "American sympathy in a Jewish Homeland in Palestine" as a principal basis for U.S. policy. Much later, in 1944, Roosevelt declared in a letter to Senator Robert Wagner that Zionism was "in keeping with the spirit" of the Four Freedoms. Most intriguingly, at the Yalta Conference with Stalin and Churchill in February 1945, Roosevelt had a revealing exchange with the Soviet leader over dinner one evening. "THE PRESIDENT said he was a Zionist and asked if Marshal Stalin was one," Charles Bohlen of the State Department recorded in his notes. "MARSHAL STALIN said he was one in principle but recognized the difficulty."[24]

Within a few days, Roosevelt would discover exactly what Stalin meant. After Yalta, where the bizarre exchange between Roosevelt and Stalin was the only reference to Palestine, the president sailed across the Mediterranean, through the Suez Canal, to the Great Bitter Lake, where he received King Saud aboard the USS *Quincy* for the first-ever American-Arab summit meeting. Saud was passionately opposed to a Jewish state in Palestine and wanted Roosevelt to support the immediate cessation of Jewish immigration. Should the Jews persist with American backing, it would only lead to war. Before his meeting with Roosevelt, the king had told U.S. diplomats in the region that he "would be honored to die on battlefield himself, a champion of Palestine Arabs." On another occasion, King Saud explained that he would "see to the execution of any Jew that might seek to enter his dominion" because, as head of the "Moslem sect that is the spearhead of the true pan-Islam movement," he was "unwilling to have any dealings with Infidels, not to say Jews." For American and British Christians, however, he would make an exception. Yet the king's patience with the Allies was not infinite. "As to Palestine," he warned, "America and Britain have a free choice between an Arab land of peace and quiet or a Jewish land drenched in blood." At their shipboard summit, Roosevelt's Zionism wavered in the face of King Saud's relentless opposition. If the Nazis had killed so many European Jews, asked the king, then why not resettle displaced Jews in Europe, where they were from? Astonishingly, Roosevelt agreed. He even pointed to Poland, where the "Germans appear to have killed three million Polish Jews, by which count there should be space in Poland for the resettlement of many homeless Jews." He also promised King Saud "that he would do nothing to assist the Jews against the Arabs." Later, he confirmed these views to a State Department aide.[25]

Yet this was simply another instance of Roosevelt's habit of telling his audience—in this case, the Arabs and U.S. foreign service officers—exactly what they wanted to hear. Once back in Washington, with his own death imminent, Roosevelt reiterated his faith in Zionism as a just remedy for the persecution of the Jews and as a way to reaffirm his pledge to defend religious liberty. Only a month after his meeting with King Saud, Roosevelt repeated the pledges he had given to Rabbi Wise and Senator Wagner of official U.S. support for the lifting of Britain's restrictions on Jewish immigration to Palestine. The State Department was unsettled by the inconsistency as much as the substance of the president's policy, but by then it was too late to reverse it.[26]

This was where matters stood when Roosevelt died on April 12, 1945. As the new president, Harry Truman did little to settle the controversy of Palestine, but he did assert himself in the making of U.S. policy toward it. Temperamentally, if anything, Truman was even more favorable to Zionism than Roosevelt had been. As we shall see, throughout his Cold War presidency Truman continued—enhanced—FDR's promotion of religious liberty as a source of democracy and antidote to tyranny. And his benchmark was not only how the Soviets treated their Christians, but how the world treated its Jews. Political calculations also played a role—Democrats like Truman lived or died on election day by mobilizing their base, which included the bulk of American Jewry. But for Truman, at least as important as politics was morality. In 1942, while still a senator from Missouri, he was one of the signatories to an advertisement in the *New York Times*—two full pages—on "the moral rights of the stateless and Palestinian Jews." A year later, at a rally in Chicago "To Demand Rescue of Doomed Jews," he called for the establishment of "a haven and place of safety" for those who had been tormented by "Nazi butchers." Of the Jews who had been exiled within their own countries, he declared: "Free lands must be opened to them." After becoming president, Truman reviewed the relevant files on Palestine and was struck by the near-unanimity of the State Department's objections to Zionism. "I was skeptical," he recalled in his memoirs, "about some of the views and attitudes assumed by the 'striped-pants boys' in the State Department. It seemed to me that they didn't care enough about what happened to the thousands of displaced persons who were involved." The diplomats did indeed care about "displaced persons," but their sympathies lay with the displaced Arabs of Palestine rather than the displaced Jews of Europe. This was decidedly not Truman's view. "It was my feeling that it would be possible for us to watch out for the long-range interests of our country while at the same time helping these unfortunate victims of persecution to find a home."[27]

Truman moved quickly. At the Potsdam Conference in July, his first summit meeting and his first journey abroad as president, he pressed a reluctant Britain to relax its quotas on Jewish immigration to Palestine. In August, he announced that the United States wanted "to let as many of the Jews into Palestine as it is possible." He then wrote to Churchill's successor as prime minister, Clement Attlee, to urge the British to grant an additional 100,000 visas for Palestine to European Jews as "a sound solution" to the Holocaust. "There isn't a reason in the world why One Hundred Thousand Jews couldn't go into Palestine," he vented elsewhere. Lest anyone doubt his resolve on the issue, in September Truman publicly denied that FDR had ever made a pledge to King Saud that the United States would act impartially. He also endorsed the Harrison Report, drafted by legal scholar and presidential envoy Earl G. Harrison, which called for much greater levels of Jewish migration from Europe to Palestine as both a practical way to solve the postwar refugee crisis and a matter of basic human rights. "I know you will agree with me," Truman wrote Gen. Dwight D. Eisenhower, who was officially in command of Allied-occupied Germany,

> that we have a particular responsibility toward these victims of persecution and tyranny who are in our zone. We must make clear to the German people that we thoroughly abhor the Nazi policies of hatred

and persecution. We have no better opportunity to demonstrate this than by the manner in which we ourselves actually treat the survivors remaining in Germany.[28]

Under Franklin Roosevelt and Harry Truman, the new Judeo-Christian sensibility combined powerfully with the more traditional promotion of religious liberty. On Israel, the implications were profound, and set the United States on a different course from much of the rest of the world.

CHAPTER NINETEEN

Spiritual Diplomacy

T HE RELATIONSHIP between religion and diplomacy was consistently strong throughout American history, but it had never been more direct than during World War II. In part this stemmed from a president who had made religious faith and the freedom of worship central aspects of his worldview. In part it stemmed from the vigor with which religious communities in the United States, particularly Catholics but also Protestants and Jews on certain issues, contested the Roosevelt administration's diplomacy. And in part, it stemmed from the unusual salience of religious matters in the war, from the Holocaust to the revival of religion in the Soviet Union. In particular, America's spiritual diplomacy was active in its dealings with the Vatican, Great Britain, and the Soviet Union.

FITTINGLY, Roosevelt was the first president to involve the Vatican in American diplomacy. This is not to say that FDR allowed the Vatican a role in the formulation of U.S. foreign policy, which would not only have flouted the natural laws of national self-interest but would have been wholly unacceptable to nearly every Protestant in the country. Instead, Roosevelt treated the Vatican as he would any other sovereign state—that is, as a place to send diplomats so they could exchange views on important issues of mutual interest. Though Stalin dismissed the influence of the Holy See—"Oho! The Pope! How many divisions has *he* got?" he once scoffed when reminded of the pontiff's concern for Roman Catholics in Russia—the Vatican was a hive of diplomatic intrigue. It was literally in the middle of Fascist Italy, it commanded the allegiance of millions of Germans, Italians, Spaniards, and others throughout Europe, and it had experience in navigating the labyrinthine politics of European diplomacy. And in Pius XII, the Vatican had a pope who was not only politically engaged but also diplomatically savvy.[1]

Roosevelt recognized the Vatican's obvious importance long before the United States entered the war. If nothing else, it was at the very least a sensitive listening post in the heart of fascist Europe. But it was also much more: a critical hub of European politics, particularly Italian politics, and the spiritual lodestar of millions of Europeans on all sides of the war. Both Secretary of State Cordell Hull and Under Secretary of State Sumner Welles pressed Roosevelt to send an emissary to the Vatican, as did Francis Cardinal Spellman of New York, an ally of Pius XII who was fast becoming the single most important Catholic leader in the United States. Joseph P. Kennedy, the Hollywood mogul and prominent Catholic layman then serving as Roosevelt's ambassador to London, argued that "the Pope is the mainstay for reasonable thinking in Italy" and, if properly engaged by the White House, could act as a partner in bringing about an early end to the war. Roosevelt agreed with them all, and in December 1939 he asked Myron C. Taylor, a wealthy businessman and fellow Episcopalian, to be his envoy to the Vatican. Taylor accepted and presented his credentials as Roosevelt's personal representative in his first audience with the pope in February 1940.[2]

Taylor was well-suited to the role. He was conservative but pragmatic, and unlike many business leaders had shown a willingness to work with the New Deal rather than rail against it. As the CEO of U.S. Steel in 1937, Taylor compromised with the Steel Workers' Organizing Committee, then planning a major strike at the company's Illinois plant. His sympathies did not lie with labor, but he had shown himself to be a problem-solver, not an ideologue. A year later, Roosevelt asked Taylor to head the U.S. delegation to the ill-fated Évian Conference. It was a thankless task, but Taylor took it seriously and worked hard to secure some sort of agreement. He did not succeed—nobody could have under the circumstances—but his diligence impressed Roosevelt nonetheless, and the president asked Taylor to continue monitoring the refugee situation in Europe and begin devising relief programs. As a conservative, Taylor was politically acceptable to the Vatican. As an Episcopalian, he was theologically acceptable as a relative moderate: not as suitable as a Catholic, but far more amenable than a Protestant from a harder-edged tradition, such as a Presbyterian or a Baptist. Taylor could do business with Pius XII, an asset Roosevelt grasped intuitively.[3]

However, Taylor could only serve as the president's personal representative, not as an official U.S. ambassador. Roosevelt did not try to establish diplomatic relations with the Vatican, because he felt it would be impossible to do so without incurring significant political damage. Congress had outlawed official relations between Washington and the Holy See in 1867, and overturning this ban would have been a difficult task at the very best of times. During a world war, with anti-Catholicism still pervasive in American life, it was all but impossible. Protestant distrust of Catholicism was not simply a matter of rank prejudice, though there was plenty of it. Protestants perceived the Catholic Church, wrongly but not insincerely, as a monolithic, authoritarian institution that followed a strict chain of command that led directly to Rome. Their concerns about sending a

U.S. representative to the Vatican were rooted in fears that it would give the Catholic Church in America privileged access to the federal government and enable the Church to advance specifically Catholic interests, as opposed to American interests. As expected, even the informal nature of Taylor's mission triggered a wave of Protestant anger over violations of the separationist principle.

While the Taylor mission was a shock to Protestants, it should not have come as a surprise given Roosevelt's instinctive ecumenism, his close relationship with Catholics, and Italy's major role in the world crisis. The Roosevelt administration considered the Vatican so important that it also used several other approaches, some secret but most a matter of public knowledge. On December 23, 1939, FDR sent a Christmas peace message to Pius XII to seek the pontiff's cooperation in "the re-establishment of world peace on a surer foundation." To alleviate concerns about Catholic favoritism, he sent similar letters to Protestant and Jewish leaders in the United States—but not to an American Catholic. Protestant concerns did not deter him from making further contact with the pope. He frequently used Monsignor Michael J. Ready, head of the National Catholic Welfare Conference, as a back channel to the Vatican. Roosevelt also retained the services of an American Catholic bishop, Joseph P. Hurley, who had served as a papal nuncio (Vatican ambassador) and had personal ties to Pius. Much later in the war, Roosevelt dispatched Harry Hopkins, his most trusted adviser, to Rome. Hopkins was tasked with ensuring that there would be no lingering tensions between the Kremlin and the Vatican that could scuttle the postwar peace settlement.[4]

In 1940, Roosevelt elevated these links by sending Sumner Welles, a frequent collaborator with Ready and Hurley, to meet with the pope as part of a European fact-finding tour. Pius confessed he hoped the United States would help constrain Mussolini, who was not committed to war with France but might jump into the fray if Germany did well. After his meetings with Pius and his secretary of state, Cardinal Luigi Maglione, Welles left the Vatican "with the conviction that one of the constructive forces working for the regeneration of mankind will be the present Pope and many of those about him." Later that spring, the pope and Cardinal Maglione furiously lobbied Roosevelt, via Taylor and Welles, to write directly to Mussolini and urge him to remain out of the war. As Maglione noted, "I did not fail to remind Welles that the United States *can do a lot*" to influence the course of the war. The Vatican envisioned a secret "parallel endeavor" with the White House. Roosevelt at first refused, and then relented. His two confidential missives to Mussolini, sent at the behest of a worried pope, urged restraint in the name of an international system that was collapsing around him. But they were to no avail: on June 10, an opportunistic Italy declared war on Britain and France.[5]

Though he was faced with Protestant suspicion and a world engulfed by war, Roosevelt still did not retreat from spiritual diplomacy—instead, he widened it. If Protestants claimed Catholic favoritism, then Roosevelt would demonstrate to them exactly how committed he was to the broadest religious dialogue possible. Nazism had committed itself to replacing Christianity as the faith of Europe; Nazism was therefore an enemy to religion. In response, Roosevelt sought to marshal the global forces of faith to combat atheism, paganism, and the idolatry of the state. His religious alliance already included the Protestants, Catholics, and Jews of America, even if they did not always get along among themselves, and he had begun allying the United States to the Vatican. But he aimed for more. In March 1940, after receiving yet another tedious complaint from the Federal Council of Churches that the Taylor mission violated the separation of church and state, Roosevelt asked Assistant Secretary of State Adolf Berle "to find out whether there is somebody in the Mohammedan Church," a spiritual leader like the pope, whom he "could contact in the cause of peace." Roosevelt also wanted to know whom he could contact in the Greek Orthodox Church. In fact, he got so carried away with his plan that he asked Hull and Berle to think of religious leaders from all across eastern Europe and the Middle East who could form a spiritual coalition for peace with the United States. This led to a bizarre conversation between Berle and Mehmet Münir Ertegün, the Turkish ambassador to the United States, in which the American diplomat was gently reminded that spiritual diplomacy violated the Turkish constitution's strict separation of church and state and would require "a radical reversal of the policy of the Turkish government." The best idea Berle could come up with was an approach to the king of Saudi Arabia, which would risk upsetting the Turks. Hull pointed out that appeals to Muslims in India would upset Hindus, not to mention the British. And these were only the most obvious of religious tensions Roosevelt's coalition would probably ignite. "In view of these many considerations," Hull dryly noted, "the President abandoned his plan."[6]

Roosevelt's grand coalition of worldwide believers came to nothing, but it did anticipate a similar plan by his successor, Harry Truman, in the early Cold War. More immediately, it did nothing to blunt Taylor's diplomatic mission to the Holy See. Taylor remained at the Vatican until the United States entered the war in 1941, communicated with the pope through the apostolic delegate to Washington, and then returned to Rome in 1944 after the ouster of Mussolini. American belligerency brought relations between Washington and the Holy See close to a breaking point, particularly after Roosevelt and Churchill, meeting at the Casablanca Conference of January 1943, pronounced a policy of "unconditional surrender" that Pius XII not only considered immoral but a poor strategy that would prolong the war. Taylor handled two other sensitive issues: whether the Allies would bomb Rome and Italy's postwar future.[7]

Just as important was Taylor's message that the United States and the Holy See represented the forces of virtue and faith in the world and that they were on the same side of history. All Americans, Taylor told Pius XII in 1942, looked to the pope for moral leadership, just as the rest of the world looked to Roosevelt. "Because we know we are in the right," he declared,

> and because we have supreme confidence in our strength, we are determined to carry through until we shall have won complete victory. . . . Our cause is just. We fight, with conscience clear, for the moral rights of our nation, and for the liberties of our people; our victory will ensure these rights and liberties to the world. Even our enemies know that we seek no aggrandizement. Precisely for the reason that our moral position is impregnable, we are not open to the compromises usual to those who look for merely material gains, and who will bargain for half a loaf if they cannot have the whole.

It was a remarkably audacious bit of ideological salesmanship from the Episcopalian industrialist and novice diplomat, but it set the tone for the relations between Washington and the Vatican as they grappled with the problems of totalitarianism posed first by Nazi Germany, and then by the Soviet Union after the war.[8]

THE LINKS ROOSEVELT and Taylor labored to forge with the Vatican came much more naturally to America's alliance with Britain. Historians have long realized that the Anglo-American "special relationship" was mostly a myth, a deliberate ideological and cultural construction to serve diplomatic and political goals. Yet there was some truth to the myth; as different as they were, Americans and Britons shared a similar outlook. Often politicians on both sides of the Atlantic would play up these similarities for all they were worth, but they were built upon a shared moral and historical foundation with which both American and British elites were intuitively familiar.

Nobody played this game better than Winston Churchill. Churchill was not in any sense an orthodox Christian, though like most English people he was a nominal member of the Church of England. He did believe in providence, especially with regard to himself and his own role as a maker of history, but his Christian faith, long dominated by skepticism, was nonexistent by the 1930s. If he believed in God, it was a distant deity who had abdicated the responsibility of ruling his earthly creation. And initially, Churchill opposed Hitler's rise on classically British geopolitical grounds: no single power must be allowed to dominate the continent. But as the Nazi threat gathered pace, and as the ideological and humanitarian threat grew, Churchill began to infuse morality and religion into his anti-appeasement speeches. He pronounced that Britain wanted to protect not only Europe, but democratic civilization itself. By the Munich agreement of 1938, he conflated "democratic civilization" with "Christian civilization," a way of life in which religion was a natural part of politics.[9]

Partly this was simply a matter of rhetorical convenience: few orators in modern politics have spoken in such biblical cadences as Churchill, and the Bible provided familiar images of the most fundamental struggles between good and evil. Partly this was also a matter of political expediency, for at this time Britain was still a devoted churchgoing nation, and as the crisis deepened in the late 1930s and into 1940 Britons flocked to the churches for comfort and solace. But Churchill also recognized in religious liberty a source of democratic thought, and he recognized in Germany's essentially anti-Christian and anti-Semitic policies the denial of basic human dignities and liberties that were essential to any democracy. Perhaps most important, after the German conquest of western Europe in 1940, Churchill knew Britain's only hope of salvation lay with the United States. And he knew that by framing Britain's struggle with evil in explicitly Christian terms, his messages would resonate with the American people—and their president.[10]

For all these reasons, Churchill portrayed the conflict between Britain and Germany much as Roosevelt did the clash between democracy and totalitarianism. As the German menace became greater, Churchill's speeches increasingly invoked religion, especially its influence upon democracy. In virtually all of his major speeches at the most pivotal crisis moments, Churchill contrasted Christianity with Nazism. His speech in Parliament after Munich warned that "there can never be friendship between the British democracy and the Nazi Power, that Power which spurns Christian ethics, which cheers its onward course by a barbarous paganism, which vaunts the spirit of aggression and conquest, which derives strength and perverted pleasure from persecution, and uses, as we have seen, with pitiless brutality the threat of murderous force." In June 1940, now prime minister, Churchill used one of his most famous speeches to declare that "the Battle of France is over. I expect that the Battle of Britain is about to begin. Upon this battle depends the survival of Christian civilization." A month later, he followed with a stirring call to holy war:

And now it has come to us to stand alone in the breach, and face the worst that the tyrant's might and enmity can do. Bearing ourselves humbly before God, but conscious that we serve an unfolding purpose, we are ready to defend our native land against the invasion by which it is threatened. We are fighting by ourselves alone; but we are not fighting for ourselves alone. Here in this strong City of Refuge which enshrines the title-deeds of human progress and is of deep consequence to Christian civilization . . . we await undismayed the impending assault.

And again, in January 1941, in response to FDR's proclamation of the Four Freedoms: "It is no exaggeration to say that the future of the whole world and the hopes of a broadening civilization founded upon Christian ethics depend upon the relations between the British Empire or Commonwealth of Nations and the U.S.A."[11]

For both Churchill and FDR, though for different reasons, the moral meaning of the war was in large part religious, predicated upon the individualist and rights-based assumptions they believed were central to the Christian ethic. For Churchill as for Roosevelt, democracy was rooted in individual natural rights that transcended the state. For Churchill as well, democracy was rooted partly in faith because religion was the source of conscience and morality. And for Churchill, religion was a source of virtue and communal solidarity that acted as the glue in an otherwise atomized society. There existed profound differences between Churchill and Roosevelt, not least over colonialism and monarchy, but they were largely overridden, at least in the ideological hothouse of war, by a shared Protestant view of the world.

Americans were happy to play this game, too. By 1940—and arguably since his October 1937 "Quarantine" speech in response to the Japanese invasion of China—Roosevelt's great dilemma was that while he wanted the United States to play a part in the defeat of world fascism, the American people were still in thrall to isolationism, pacifism, and other forms of noninterventionism. In Great Britain, the lone, recalcitrant holdout to Nazi domination, he found a proxy. If Roosevelt could not yet commit America to the fight, he would at least support Britain. Assisted by Hitler's constant aggression, Roosevelt began easing the United States into a partnership with the British in which America would be an "arsenal of democracy." Once the British proved, in the Battle of Britain, that they could prevent a German invasion, Roosevelt moved to aid the anti-Nazi cause. First came the Destroyers for Bases Agreement in September 1940, in which the U.S. Navy transferred warships to the Royal Navy in exchange for basing rights in British colonies in the Western Hemisphere. The much more significant Lend-Lease program followed in March 1941, by which the United States supplied Britain and its dominions with matériel, ships, and weapons. From that point on, the United States was effectively at war with Nazi Germany.[12]

But even before Lend-Lease was finalized, Roosevelt felt it necessary to tell Churchill and the British cabinet that the United States was committed to their survival. In January, he sent Harry Hopkins to London to confer with Churchill and impress upon the British a sense of Anglo-American solidarity. "The President is determined that we shall win the war together. Make no mistake about it," Hopkins told Churchill shortly after arriving in an England under siege. "He has sent me here to tell you that at all costs and by all means he will carry you through, no matter what happens to him—there is nothing that he will not do so far as he has human power." Weeks later, at a dinner in Glasgow, Hopkins imparted the same message with a great deal more emotion. Rather than try to emulate Churchill's soaring rhetoric, Hopkins simply quoted from a passage in the Book of Ruth (1:16): "Whither thou goest, I will go; and where thou lodgest, I will lodge: thy people shall be my people, and thy God my God. Even to the end." Hopkins had meant to be reassuring, but the effect of his words was far greater than he had intended. According to Churchill's personal physician, who was at the dinner, the prime minister "was in tears. He knew what it meant." Hopkins's impromptu sermon "seemed like a rope thrown to a drowning man." Though the comments were censored for fear of antagonizing isolationists in the United States, presidential speechwriter Robert Sherwood recalled that "word of it spread all over Britain." Lord Beaverbrook, in charge of Britain's wartime industrial production, told Sherwood that Hopkins's biblical pledge "provided more tangible aid for Britain than had all the destroyers and guns and rifles and ammunition that had been sent previously."[13]

Both Roosevelt and Churchill wanted to consummate these ever-closer ties with a summit meeting. Dancing delicately around American political sensitivities and for obvious reasons of security, the Atlantic Conference met in secret, floating off the coast of Newfoundland on board the warships HMS *Prince of Wales* and USS *Augusta*, in August 1941. Roosevelt had sailed from Washington on the pretense of taking a fishing holiday off the coast of New England. Churchill's ship sailed from Britain with an eminent passenger, Harry Hopkins, who had visited both London and Moscow in advance of the Atlantic Conference. On August 12, the two leaders signed the Atlantic Charter, a statement of war aims that has been characterized as "tantamount to America's declaration of war" against the fascist powers. One could hardly blame Germany and Japan if they saw it as such, for the Charter listed eight points that stood diametrically opposed to the systems then being imposed in Europe and East Asia by German and Japanese military power. Roosevelt and Churchill eschewed territorial acquisition as a war aim and proclaimed their support for national self-determination, free trade, universal economic security, and freedom of the seas. The eighth and final point stated their shared belief "that all nations of the world, for realistic as well as spiritual reasons, must come to the abandonment of the use of force" and come together in "a wider and permanent system of general security" in a future international organization. In deference to the Soviet Union, allied to Britain since the German invasion in June, religious liberty was uncharacteristically omitted from this moral call to arms, but in a separate message to Congress Roosevelt reassured Americans that it was "unnecessary for me to point out that the declaration of principles includes . . . the world need for freedom of religion and freedom of information" because their importance was so self-evident. Later, FDR claimed that the Atlantic Charter had been designed not only to complement but to implement the Four Freedoms.[14]

As a symbol of democratic resolve and purpose, the Atlantic Charter was an enormous success. Much of this stemmed from the carefully orchestrated consecration of a new Anglo-American special relationship. Roosevelt was fond of using church services as political symbol, particularly Anglican church services to symbolize the spiritual solidarity between America and Britain. He had done so twice before—once at sea, in the Caribbean in 1934, when he personally led an Easter service for British and American seamen, and once at St. James' Episcopal Church in Hyde Park, in 1939 as Europe edged closer to war, to honor the visit of King George VI. Now, on the Sunday of the Atlantic Conference, Churchill paid Roosevelt the ultimate compliment by holding an Anglican service aboard the *Prince of Wales*. The prime minister paid close attention to every last detail, down to personally choosing the hymns and prayers. They sang the hymns "O God, Our Help in Ages Past" and "Onward, Christian Soldiers," among others. Fittingly, the verse for the sermon was from Joshua 1:5–6: "as I was with Moses, so I will be with thee: I will not fail thee, nor forsake thee. Be strong and of a good courage: for unto this people shalt thou divide for an inheritance the land, which I swore unto their fathers to give them." And of course, they prayed: "Stablish our hearts, O God, in the day of battle, and strengthen our resolve, that we fight not in enmity against men but against the powers of darkness enslaving the souls of men."[15]

The British journalist Henry Morton had been invited to observe the conference. As the man who had first reported the discovery of King Tutankhamen's tomb and as the author of several travelogues of the Holy Land, Morton could appreciate the historical and religious symbolism of Churchill's Sunday service. "In the long, frightful panorama of this War," Morton wrote afterward,

> a panorama full of guns and tanks crushing the life out of men, of women and children weeping and of homes blasted into rubble by bombs, there had been no scene like this, a scene, it seemed, from another world, conceived on lines different from anything known to

the pageant-masters of the Axis, a scene rooted in the first principles of European civilisation which go back to the figure of Charlemagne kneeling before the Pope on Christmas morning.

Roosevelt was also impressed. "It was our keynote," he said of the church service to his son Elliott, a captain in the Army Air Force. "If nothing else had happened while we were here, that would have cemented us. 'Onward Christian Soldiers.' We *are*, and we *will* go on, with God's help."[16]

Throughout the war, religious Americans, Protestants and Jews especially, reacted warmly to the concept of an organic special relationship between the English-speaking peoples. Britain was by no means free of anti-Semitism, but it was much more hospitable to Jews than the rest of Europe. Most important, until 1941 only Britain stood between the Nazis and total victory. But Protestant support for Britain was also a natural outgrowth of the ecumenical and missionary movements that had been predicated upon Anglo-American cooperation for the past century. Differences over the British Empire aside, British and American Protestants were used to cooperating with one another and to viewing the world, morally and theologically, through more or less the same normative lens. Special church services, such as "Great Britain Sunday" dedicated to rallying Americans to the defense of "the heritage of a common ideal of democracy and freedom and a common struggle to achieve it," were not uncommon, especially during the Battle of Britain.[17]

This was true even for the Christian realists, who normally shied from moralistic claims to truth and purity. Most of the realists, including Reinhold Niebuhr, John Coleman Bennett, and Henry Van Dusen, were Anglophiles who sided emotionally as well as ideologically with the British. Whether consciously or not, they used Churchill's imagery of Britain as an isolated island of democracy defying the satanic tyranny of Nazi Germany; they also viewed the war as a struggle between a relative good—Anglo-American democracy, as imperfect as it was—and the absolute, unmitigated evil of Nazi Germany. The world would only survive the crisis if it was led by a partnership of these two religious democracies. Henry Sloane Coffin tried to reassure a colleague that an Anglo-American alliance would not result in the United States supporting Britain's colonial and European ambitions. Instead, Coffin believed that "we could stand with them for a world order . . . and that we ought to work to have our country take its responsibility for the maintenance of that world order" based on the liberal democratic principles common to both the British and American political traditions. "As I read the Bible, it seems to me fellowship in righteousness is a leading idea which runs all through. That I think we can work for." Despite his suspicion of national and cultural pride, Niebuhr agreed. "The British," he argued in the summer of 1941, "are fighting for the kind of civilization which has made Protestantism possible." Flawed though they may have been, British values were infinitely superior to Nazi Germany's, and were therefore worth preserving.[18]

In spreading such an idealistic message in such realistic terms, Coffin, Niebuhr, and other Anglophile interventionists played an important role in shifting U.S. public opinion away from isolationism and pacifism. This took some effort, because they had essentially propounded the same message in World War I only to see it utterly discredited at Versailles, by the Senate, and by the interwar investigations into wartime profiteering. The unremittingly aggressive nature of the Nazi threat helped them erode widespread doubts about intervention. But so too did their access to the popular media. Coffin in particular had close ties to media and publishing elites in New York, and he used them throughout 1940 and 1941 to spread sympathy for Britain. In a September 1940 nationwide broadcast over the NBC radio network, Coffin, a Presbyterian, hosted a show featuring special prayers for Britain by a Catholic priest, a Jewish rabbi, and an Episcopal bishop. In a remarkable display of America's interfaith civil religion, they prayed for God to give the British "strength to withstand the tragic ordeal to which they are being subjected" and "that He will in due time rescue them from the ravages of ruthless totalitarianism." While Americans remained sheltered from the world crisis for now, it was "the men, women, and children of the streets of London and the cities of England who are battling to rescue for the world that concept of liberty towards which men have struggled since the exodus of the children of Israel from Egypt." Coffin himself delivered several more wartime radio addresses, including over the BBC, on the theme of Anglo-American democracy and its responsibility to lead.[19]

Yet as Coffin well knew, not everyone trusted the British. Catholics, particularly those of Irish, German, and Italian descent, were naturally wary of supporting a British crusade. "England has a natural right to defend herself," the liberal Catholic writer Thomas Merton conceded in a 1940 diary entry. "Whether what she is defending is, in any other than a very superficial sense, just, is quite another matter." Protestants of the Social Gospel tradition had similar qualms about allying too closely with the world's greatest imperial power. Though Niebuhr might be right in saying that the British Empire was better than German Nazism, this was still a relative judgment. "It will be our friends, not our enemies, that we have trouble with when the war is done," complained Reverend Marcellus Nesbitt of the First United Presbyterian Church in Beaver, Pennsylvania. "Churchill tells us specifically that he will countenance no dissolving of the British Empire," but "Pearl Buck and Stanley Jones tell us definitely that the continuance of the white man in Asia will simply mean another racial war not many decades hence." Nesbitt felt strongly about this, so strongly that he contended "that we are not supporting anything right at all. In the long last it would be better to see the war end in deadlock." It was an extreme position to take, but not a wholly unusual one. E. Stanley Jones himself, a famous missionary and longtime champion of Indian independence, certainly did not think so. "With the Britain of democracy we can go anywhere," he announced in 1944. "With the Britain of empire we cannot go unless we desire to be in perpetual wars," because imperialism was simply "incompatible with both democracy and Christianity."[20]

Moreover, missionaries, though long associated with the spread of empire, often sympathized with the people they were trying to convert rather than the Europeans they were fighting with. Minnesota congressman Walter Judd, a former medical missionary who had spent much of the previous decade in China, lamented that while "Mr. Churchill is announcing that Britain intends to adhere to her traditional policies of imperialism, the world is hungry to be reassured that America intends to stick to her traditional policies of advocating self-determination and freedom for all peoples under oppression." This applied to India as well as China.[21]

Still, the majority of religious Americans embraced the special relationship even if they acknowledged its flaws. The American religious tradition, and its civil religious offspring, simply had too much in common with the Protestant heritage of the British Isles. In a world seemingly divided between democracy and dictators, this was a most natural bond indeed.

JUST AS IMPORTANT strategically as Great Britain but even more complicated politically was the Soviet Union. Aside from a handful of preachers on the radical left, like Harry F. Ward, American Christians were almost unanimous in their condemnation of Soviet communism, not merely for its atheism and materialism but also for its embrace of violence and rejection of democracy. But then Hitler confused matters by invading the Soviet Union in June 1941. Suddenly, Americans were faced with a dilemma: whom should they support in a battle between two such evil forces? Through Destroyers for Bases and Lend-Lease, the United States had clearly sided with Britain and against Germany. And for two years, it had seemed that Nazi Germany's totalitarian cousin, the Soviet Union, stood against democracy with the forces of totalitarian darkness. But now the fate of Hitler's Germany would rest on the outcome of its war against Stalin's Soviet Union. Some Americans, watching with distaste from afar, were certain that the United States should simply watch and wait as the two tyrants destroyed each other. "If we see that Germany is winning," Missouri senator Harry Truman told a reporter shortly after the German invasion, "we should help Russia and if Russia is winning we ought to help Germany and that way let them kill as many as possible, although I don't want to see Hitler victorious under any circumstances."[22]

Truman's modest concession to the Soviet Union, apparently an afterthought, was in fact the very basis of the Roosevelt administration's response to the German invasion, and indeed its strategy for the rest of the war. Recall Sumner Welles's formulation of June 23, the day after the German invasion: the "freedom to worship to God . . . is the great and fundamental right of all peoples," a right that "has been denied to their peoples by both the Nazi and Soviet Governments." But that, Welles continued, was not the "present issue which faces a realistic America." The issue was instead something more immediate: "our own national defense and the security of the New World in which we live." As a result, it was the administration's policy that "any defense against Hitlerism, any rallying of the forces opposing Hitlerism, from whatever source these forces may spring, will hasten the eventual downfall of the present German leaders, and will therefore redound to the benefit of our own defense and security." On this basis, Roosevelt quickly wanted to extend Lend-Lease aid to the Soviet Union, under the same terms offered to Britain. This was Niebuhr's realist doctrine of the lesser evil in action, and in fact Niebuhr and the realists supported the Soviets in their defense against the Nazi onslaught of the summer of 1941.[23]

But even as he praised the Soviet resistance and urged the United States to help it, Niebuhr continued to reject communist ideology. And among religious Americans, Niebuhr was a relatively moderate anticommunist; most others were immovably hostile. Here stood the Roosevelt administration's biggest obstacle to aiding the Soviet Union and defeating Nazi Germany, for a great number of Americans simply could not abide communism, especially Soviet communism, even if they agreed that Germany presented an even greater danger to world peace and American security. Roosevelt may have wanted to move quickly to extend Lend-Lease aid to the Soviets, but first he had to contend with anticommunism in Congress—and through it, the churches.

Roosevelt appreciated the sensitivity, and severity, of this particular political challenge. The "religious question," recalled W. Averell Harriman, the president's envoy to Moscow, "was regarded by Roosevelt as a matter of the highest domestic priority." Many of his advisers agreed, among them Harold Ickes and Supreme Court justice Frank Murphy, himself a Catholic, who believed that one of the "dangers" was that "the Catholic Church will stir up among its religionists here a feeling of alarm about communism." Harry Hopkins confided to Brendan Bracken, Churchill's confidant and minister of information, that while Roosevelt would probably be able to extend Lend-Lease to the Soviets, it would be difficult. "The American people don't take aid to Russia easily," he wrote early in September. "The whole Catholic population is opposed to it" and would move to block any assistance to defend communism. If FDR was going to aid the defense of the Soviet Union, he would first have to overcome religious opposition at home.[24]

This would be no small task. Liberals and conservatives, Protestants and Catholics were divided by much, but they were nearly united by a moral unease at allying so closely with Stalin. To be sure, an overwhelming majority wanted the Soviet Union to defeat Germany. In a poll of religious Americans conducted on June 24, 79 percent of Jews preferred a Soviet victory, while only 2 percent favored the Germans. But 75 percent of Protestants also preferred the Soviets (as opposed to 4 percent for Germany), as did 65 percent of Catholics (6 percent for Germany). However, when asked in the same poll whether the "U.S. gov't should supply USSR with war materials on same basis as Britain," solid majorities responded negatively. This time, only 33 percent of Catholics and 36 percent of Protestants agreed, and even among Jews, who presumably would have been single-mindedly focused on Germany's defeat, only 41 percent replied affirmatively. Though not unanimous, Catholic opposition to extending Lend-Lease to Moscow was especially strong, encompassing the liberals of *Commonweal* magazine as well as the conservative, anticommunist extremists. Conservative Protestants naturally objected to aiding the Soviets, but so did liberal pacifists like Charles Clayton Morrison and John Haynes Holmes—who had, moreover, both been fiercely critical of Nazi Germany. In what might be called the "first Truman doctrine," it seemed that most religiously observant Americans agreed with the senator from Missouri that while a Soviet victory was preferable, a quick Soviet victory, aided by the United States, was not.[25]

Public opposition to aiding the Soviet Union was swift and shrill, especially among Catholics, but it did not come as a surprise. The Vatican had taken a firm stance against communism as early as 1846, when Pius IX condemned "the unspeakable doctrine of *Communism*, as it is called, a doctrine most opposed to the very natural law" that would result in "the complete destruction of everyone's laws," even "human society itself." This was merely the first in a series of nineteenth-century encyclicals denouncing communist ideology as antithetical to religion and morality. Most recently, American Catholics felt bound by a 1937 papal encyclical from Pius XI, *Divini Redemptoris*, on "bolshevistic and atheistic Communism, which aims at upsetting the social order and at undermining the very foundations of Christian civilization. In the face of such a threat, the Catholic Church could not and does not remain silent." Pius XII, who ascended to the papacy in 1939 and remained pope until well into the Cold War, was every bit the anticommunist his predecessors had been.

While Catholics worldwide, certainly those in the United States, were not rigidly controlled by the Vatican and did not automatically adhere to its every pronouncement, these strictures were hard to ignore.[26]

More startling, and much more worrying for the Roosevelt administration, were attempts by Protestants as well as Catholics to make U.S. aid conditional upon Stalin agreeing to ease restrictions on religion in the Soviet Union. Recall that in 1933, Roosevelt had assured anticommunist dissenters and members of his own State Department that diplomatic recognition of the Soviet Union would eventually pave the way for an increase of religious freedom. That had not happened—in fact, the situation worsened—but with the Soviets on the verge of total defeat, religious Americans sensed a unique opportunity to force liberal reform upon the USSR. Already in the summer, clergy, labor leaders, and politicians were pressing Roosevelt to offer Lend-Lease to the Soviets on the condition that they respect and protect religious liberty. And already, they suspected Roosevelt of intending to aid the Soviet Union no matter what. While FDR had spoken frequently about religious freedom as a baseline for liberty in general and its absence as a symptom of threat in the international system, and while the second of the Four Freedoms had promoted religious liberty, the Atlantic Charter's failure to mention religion struck many as a sign of Roosevelt's appeasement of Stalin. If FDR was seeking to facilitate U.S. assistance to the Soviet Union, his methods thus far had been counterproductive.[27]

Yet the Soviets' military situation was dire, and still deteriorating, and if the Nazis conquered Russia they would in all likelihood be able to dominate Europe indefinitely. If Roosevelt was going to act, he had to do so quickly. Many of his advisers—certainly the British, whose fate now rested with the Soviet Union's—thought he was moving much too slowly. "There were some impatient people," recalled Robert Sherwood, the president's speechwriter, "who thought that the President exaggerated the strength of Catholic sentiment, but it was his way to tread with extreme wariness wherever religious sensibilities were involved; he knew a lot more than his advisers did about these sensibilities." To defuse Catholic and wider religious concerns, in the late summer and fall of 1941 Roosevelt devised a three-pronged strategy targeted at the Vatican, the Kremlin, and American public opinion.[28]

In July, when rumors of possible American aid began reaching Rome, U.S. ambassador William Phillips advised the State Department that "it would be helpful" if there was "any evidence . . . of increased religious tolerance in Russia." Phillips then suggested that the United States declare that its aid would be made in the "hope that the Soviet Government would abandon its attitude of religious and political intolerance." With American clergy making the same point, Roosevelt decided, after some initial reservations about pressuring Stalin, to persuade Americans and the Vatican that he could convince the Soviets to relax restrictions on religion. And after receiving private advice from Monsignor Michael J. Ready, Edward Cardinal Mooney, and other interventionist American Catholics, via Sumner Welles, he would also stress that aid to the Soviet Union would be designed to defeat Nazism and not strengthen communism.[29]

While many were willing to approach the problem tactically—suspending, temporarily, their anticommunism in the name of defeating Nazi Germany—it seems that Franklin Roosevelt genuinely believed the Soviet Union capable of religious reform. The war had induced a relaxation, even something of a liberalization of sorts, in Russian society, including religion. Partly because Stalin and the Kremlin were so shocked and incapacitated by the Nazi invasion and partly because military victory superseded ideological purity, the people of the wartime Soviet Union found they were able to express themselves more freely than they had in decades. Hopes of a Russian reformation soared among wartime Americans, and one of the earliest believers was the president himself. Roosevelt believed in the gradual "convergence" of the American and Soviet systems. As he explained it to Welles, the Soviet Union had progressed "from the original form of Soviet Communism . . . toward a modified form of state socialism," while the United States was moving "toward the ideal of true political and social justice" advocated by communists. While Roosevelt believed that "American democracy and Soviet Communism could never meet," he felt that they were becoming increasingly similar, even complementary. The Great Depression and World War II were hastening this process, and the emergence of religious freedom in the Soviet Union was a key indicator. Hence the president's optimism, and hence his confidence that he could use the liberalization of Soviet society and religion to convince Catholics and other Christians in turn to relax their views of the Soviet Union.[30]

In September, Roosevelt sent Taylor, in Washington awaiting further instructions, back to the Vatican, thereby launching the first phase of his three-fronted strategy to extend Lend-Lease to the Soviet Union. On behalf of Roosevelt, Taylor presented Pius XII with a letter expressing the president's hope that the Vatican would soften its stance on assisting the Soviet Union. "I believe there is a real possibility that Russia may as a result of the present conflict recognize freedom of religion . . . on a much better footing than religious freedom is in Germany today," FDR wrote to Pius. More important was the urgent threat posed by the Nazis. "I believe," he cautioned, "that the survival of Russia is less dangerous to religion, to the church as such, and to humanity in general than would be the survival of the German form of dictatorship." Taylor made these points in several long conversations with Pius and Monsignor Domenico Tardini, one of the Holy See's top diplomats. But as the American minutes of a conversation between Pius and Taylor recorded, an "undercurrent of distrust of the Soviet regime was . . . present throughout." Tardini reminded Taylor of the persecution of the Polish Catholic Church under Soviet occupation between September 1939 and June 1941, and observed that the Vatican had no hard evidence that the Soviet Union yet had allowed for any increase of religious liberty.[31]

While Taylor was encouraging the Vatican to soften its view of communism, Roosevelt himself was gently prodding the Soviet Union to relax its hostility to religion. On September 11, in a meeting with Constantine Oumansky, the Soviet ambassador to Washington, Roosevelt "explained in some detail" the "extreme difficulty" of getting Congress to appropriate Lend-Lease funding for the Soviet Union due to "the unpopularity of Russia among large groups in this country who exercise great political power in Congress." He then confessed that he personally believed that religious freedom did in fact exist in the Soviet Union and suggested that if the Soviets could provide evidence to this effect it would generate "some publicity" in the United States "regarding the freedom of religion" that "might have a very fine educational effect before the next lend-lease bill comes up in Congress." Oumansky said he would attend to the issue immediately. When the ambassador asked whether Moscow could receive American credit even before the next Lend-Lease vote, Roosevelt reminded him of the political difficulties surrounding the issue of religious freedom.[32]

Roosevelt now passed the religious liberty baton to Averell Harriman, who was accompanying Lord Beaverbrook on an Anglo-American mission to Moscow. Though America was not yet at war, their goal was to convince Stalin, with whom they had three lengthy meetings, that Britain and the United States were committed to ensuring the Soviet Union's survival and to defeating Nazi Germany together. But Roosevelt also asked Harriman to impress upon Stalin how vital it was to offer concrete demonstrations of the new Soviet tolerance for religious faith. "I told Stalin of the importance of the religious question in the United States," Harriman cabled from Moscow. He also urged the Kremlin to publicize any "relaxation of restrictions" on religious worship. Stalin, of course, had already heard this from Oumansky, who reported to the Kremlin that "Roosevelt fears influential Catholics" and would not be able to extend Lend-Lease without placating religious opinion. Harriman was supported by Father Leopold Braun, an American Catholic priest and the only Catholic licensed to preach in Moscow. Braun told Harriman and Taylor of how difficult it was to be a Christian in the Soviet Union, but he also reported a recent easing of Stalinist restrictions. Braun urged them to use Lend-Lease as a wedge to pry open Soviet society, and he was confident it could work because of the Soviets' enormous need for American assistance. It was time to "beat the iron while it is hot and soft and obtain from these people what they would only be too willing to grant." Harriman was not converted and was certain the Soviets would only "give lip service and make a few gestures" rather than "give freedom of religion in the sense that we understand it." But he was hopeful this would be enough.[33]

And for a moment, it seemed like it would be. Congress had begun debating the bill to renew Lend-Lease funds on September 18. At the Vatican, Pius reluctantly conceded to Taylor that under these unique circumstances helping the Soviet Union was not tantamount to assisting communism, and thus not a violation of the 1937 encyclical. From exiled Poles living in the Soviet Union, reports were emerging of Soviet officials allowing Catholics to worship openly and priests to officiate religious services. In Washington, the Polish Ambassador informed the State Department that the Soviets had granted Poles living in Russia and Polish military units serving alongside the Red Army "full cultural freedom and freedom of worship for both Christians and Jews." In Moscow, the Kremlin officially proclaimed its respect for religious freedom throughout the Soviet Union—the gesture Harriman had predicted, but a gesture all the same. These were encouraging developments as Congress considered an extension of Lend-Lease aid.[34]

But then came the disastrous third strand of Roosevelt's strategy—changing American public opinion—which nearly sabotaged all the efforts by Taylor, Harriman, and Oumansky. Believing in "convergence" and encouraged by the preliminary reports of a new attitude toward religion among Soviet officials, Roosevelt used an October 2 press conference to announce: "Since the Soviet Constitution declares that freedom of religion is granted, it is hoped that . . . the practice of complete freedom of religion is definitely on its way." This led straight to questions from skeptical reporters. "As I think I suggested a week or two ago," Roosevelt answered,

> some of you might find it useful to read Article 124 of the Constitution of Russia.
> QUESTION: What does it say, Mr. President?
> THE PRESIDENT: Well, I haven't learned it by heart sufficiently to quote—I might be off a little bit, but anyway: Freedom of conscience—
> QUESTION: Would you say—
> THE PRESIDENT:—Freedom of religion. Freedom equally to use propaganda against religion, which is essentially what is the rule in this country; only, we don't quite put it the same way.
> For instance, you might go out tomorrow—to the corner of Penn-

sylvania Avenue, down below the Press Club—and stand on a soapbox and preach Christianity, and nobody would stop you. And then, if it got into your head, perhaps the next day preach against religion of all kinds, and nobody would stop you.

Rather than simply telling the American people what he had told the Vatican, and what most of his advisers believed—that aiding the Soviets was essential to saving the world from Nazism and was not necessarily an endorsement of communism—Roosevelt embellished matters by claiming that the Stalinist constitution of 1936 ensured religious liberty and the separation of church and state in the Soviet Union. And he did so despite recent signs that American clergy, including influential members of the Catholic hierarchy, were willing to accept a more realist calculation that Americans would simply be aiding the enemy of their enemy. Worried that he had overreached himself, immediately after the press conference Roosevelt asked the U.S. Embassy in Moscow to dig up evidence that there was in fact religious freedom in the Soviet Union.[35]

But whatever the embassy staff could dig up would not be enough, for the reaction to Roosevelt's clumsy portrayal of faith in a communist society was universally, indeed ecumenically, hostile. Religious freedom in the USSR was a "hollow mockery," declared Edmund A. Walsh, the Catholic priest and vice president of Georgetown University who had consulted with Roosevelt over Soviet recognition in 1933. The Soviets demanded American money, ships, and weapons, even American "blood if that be necessary," Walsh charged, but they would not permit Americans "to have a word to say respecting the freedoms for which you shall make these sacrifices." Roosevelt's statement would be "humorous," the Knights of Columbus intoned, "if the facts were not so tragic." The Catholic magazines *Commonweal* and *America* found rare common ground in opposing Roosevelt's statement. Protestants, including liberals, also strongly criticized the president. Raymond J. Wade, Methodist Bishop of Detroit, cut to the heart of the distrust: "Undisputed imprisonment and slaying of tens of thousands of priests . . . together with thousands of closed churches, speak louder than printed words." Luther A. Weigle, president of the FCC, said the American and Soviet traditions of a disestablished church were fundamentally different because Moscow "accepts atheism as the accepted philosophy of the State." More strident was Hamilton Fish, a congressman from New York, who suggested that Roosevelt invite Stalin to the White House "so that he might be baptized in the swimming pool." Afterward, everyone could "join the Stalin Sunday School."[36]

Roosevelt persisted nonetheless, yet he need not have gone to such lengths. By the time of his press conference, with the Soviets on the brink of defeat, most Americans had already decided it was in their national interest to aid the Soviets. While FDR wanted to oversee an arsenal of democracy, most were content to provide the arsenal for victory. In this spirit, a thousand Protestant leaders relieved the pressure on Roosevelt by presenting him with a petition calling for the defense of the USSR. On the other hand, while they accepted an alliance with the Soviets as a condition of wartime necessity, many people simply did not want their president to fool himself into believing that the Soviet Union would liberalize as a result. "To welcome Russia as an associate in the defense of democracy," warned the Soviet expert and U.S. diplomat George F. Kennan, "would invite misunderstanding of our own position and would lend to the German war effort a gratuitous and sorely needed aura of morality." Such doubts aside, Roosevelt got his wish, and in late October Congress approved new funding for Lend-Lease and allowed the president to dispense it at his discretion as commander-in-chief.[37]

SIX WEEKS LATER, the Japanese attacked Pearl Harbor, Germany and Italy declared war, and the United States found itself a full-fledged belligerent in alliance with Great Britain and the Soviet Union. Under these new conditions, religious anticommunism in the United States became deeply conflicted between a Rooseveltian optimism about Russian reform and a harder-edged pessimism based on a lingering, fundamental distrust of communist ideology and Stalinist intentions. Both religious currents would help fuel the onset of the Cold War after 1946, as American perceptions of Soviet postwar behavior outraged the optimists and vindicated the pessimists.

Strangely, though, Stalin himself complicated the debate by actually allowing a significant increase of religious freedom in the Soviet Union. Liberalization occurred in many facets of life in the wartime Soviet Union, though few benefited as much as organized religion because, unlike political dissent, the Russian Orthodox faith tended to reinforce the intense levels of patriotism needed to power the Soviet Union's colossal war effort. Stalin, moreover, was adept at making gestures toward religious freedom, especially ones that would sow dissension within the ranks of American religion. His choice as envoy to Poland, for example, was Father Stanislaus Orlemanski, a rare pro-Soviet Catholic priest from Springfield, Massachusetts, who seemed to refute the anticommunist consensus among American Catholics. Monsignor Ready condemned Orlemanski's visits to the Kremlin as a "political burlesque, staged and directed by capable Soviet agents," but Roosevelt took encouragement from Stalin's willingness to listen to Catholic opinion.[38]

Coupled with the workings of the wartime alliance, these signs of reform led to an improvement of the Soviet Union's image in the United States. Helped along by Roosevelt and his theory of "convergence," the intense anticommunist politics of the early 1920s and the late 1930s quickly receded in 1942. For one thing, it was important for Americans not to offend their new ally. For another, the Roosevelt administration courted Communist Party–led unions to forestall strikes that could cripple wartime production. Of Stalin, FDR predicted that Americans "are going to get along very well with him and the Russian people—very well indeed." Wendell Willkie toured the USSR and wrote wondrously of the Soviet system's achievements in industrial production and wartime sacrifice. Americans "do not need to fear Russia," he said. "We need to learn to work with her." The wartime spirit of collaboration influenced views of Soviet policies on religion, too. Between June 1942 and August 1944, *Time* published five major articles on religious revivals in the Soviet Union, while its sister magazine, *Life*, featured a photographic essay on the perseverance of Christianity in the Soviet Union. In early 1945, with the end of the war in sight, Roosevelt asked Edward Flynn, a Catholic layman who was head of the Democratic National Committee, to visit the Soviet Union and convince the Kremlin to relax its restrictions on religion, permanently.[39]

One American caught in the emotional whipsaw between optimism and pessimism was the practicing Presbyterian, diplomat, and Soviet expert George F. Kennan. As the founder of containment, Kennan's views will be examined more closely in a later chapter. But given his importance to the Cold War, it is striking that his views on Soviet society swung so wildly during World War II. In 1942, while he was posted to the U.S. Embassy in Lisbon, Kennan received a letter from Myron Taylor soliciting his views on the revival of religion in the Soviet Union. Kennan was skeptical, he told Taylor, because Soviet leaders "see in the Church . . . a spiritual rival" that posed a direct threat to the political supremacy of communism. Increased religious freedom was a tactic—Harriman's "lip service"—designed to help win the war rather than open up Soviet society to the forces of religion. The Kremlin, Kennan argued,

> did all in its power to build Communist ideology into something like a competing religious life in its own right, with similar requirements of spiritual devotion and even of public profession in ceremony and symbol.
>
> That this latter effort could not be successful—that Christian faith could not be adequately replaced by a materialistic economic doctrine which had no answers to the problems of suffering and death—is obvious to all of us who have been brought up in a Christian atmosphere.

For now, it was in the Kremlin's interest to tolerate greater levels of religious freedom, but would Stalin actually loosen his grip on religion once the pressure of the war had eased? Kennan doubted it. The Soviet revival, he wrote in a subsequent report for the State Department, "has little or nothing to do with the state of religion in the Soviet Union" but was instead "founded in the determination of the regime to make available for its own use every possible channel of influence in foreign affairs."[40]

By the end of the war, however, even Kennan found himself swept away by the tide of enthusiasm for the Soviet-American alliance. In May 1945, he was struck by the extent to which the Kremlin "has lost moral dominion over the masses of the Russian population." This did not mean that the people had turned against their government. "But it does mean that there are no longer many illusions among the Russian people as to the moral or spiritual quality of all that the state represents. The fire of revolutionary Marxism has definitely died out." This was an arresting conclusion from Kennan, who had built a career upon a wariness of communist ideology and Russian nationalism. But the war had had a transformative, regenerative effect on the Soviet system. And he could see the new Soviet Union most clearly in its attitude toward religion. Soviet citizens "crowd the churches and even the whole city districts surrounding them in an atmosphere of intense excitement and emotion." Certainly the Communist Party could not elicit "even a shadow of the atmosphere of real emotional excitement" that Kennan recently witnessed over Easter. "The party has been successful in retaining that which is Caesar's," he concluded, "but its initial bid to retain that also which was God's has been quietly and decisively rejected." He saw reason for hope, which in turn bred a confidence that the ultimate destruction of the Soviet system would come from within as long as it was kept in check by countervailing forces. Though he had not yet coined the phrase, Kennan had begun to construct a strategy of containment.[41]

Yet while many Americans were encouraged by Soviet-American wartime collaboration, pessimism continued to prevail among the devout. Most American Christians retained their innate suspicions of communist ideology and remained skeptical that the Soviet Union could ever really reform. A 1942 State Department survey of religious attitudes in the United States concluded that only the most liberal Protestants, mainly Unitarians, were confident that Stalin was truly and permanently liberalizing his country's religious practices. John Foster Dulles, a leading voice of mainline Protestantism, told a 1942 religious conference in England that the Soviet-American alliance was purely a matter of converging interests, not systems, and that "the feeling in America was strongly anti-Russian." As if to prove Dulles right, speakers at the 1943 founding convention of the National Association of Evangelicals equated fascism with communism as totalitarian enemies of Christian democracy. Similarly, Reinhold Niebuhr warned some of his optimistic colleagues at the FCC that "the lack of democracy in Russia is more dangerous" than they had assumed. Almost all Catholic organizations, from the conservative Knights of Columbus to the centrist NCWC to the liberal Catholic Association for International Peace, distrusted the Soviets. Even Harry F. Ward, the radical Social Gospeler and erstwhile champion of Leninism, thought Stalinism was beyond redemption. Such thinking did not bode well for the continuation of the Grand Alliance after the war.[42]

In viewing the wartime alliance between the United States and the Soviet Union, then, most Christians agreed with Edward Cardinal Mooney, archbishop of Detroit, who warned Roosevelt administration officials not to push reformist hopes too far because of the lingering "suspicion of insincerity which rightly attaches to . . . Bolshevik pronouncements on the subject of religious freedom." Mooney was willing, as almost all Americans were during the war, to provide military and financial aid to the Soviet Union. But he was unwilling to accept the Soviets as full partners in the causes for which Americans fought, including the Four Freedoms, the Atlantic Charter—even the 1942 Declaration of the United Nations, to which the Soviet Union was a signatory. "Freedom of worship, even in its most restricted sense," Mooney bluntly concluded, "does not actually exist in Russia today."[43]

It was a damning indictment that had already doomed prospects for postwar cooperation between the United States and the Soviet Union. Just as the United States had fought a war for religious liberty under Franklin Roosevelt, it would now try to forge a peace on the same basis under Harry Truman. But in his dealings with the Soviet Union, Truman would soon discover just how complicated the religious influence could be.

CHAPTER TWENTY

The Church Unmilitant

A T THE END OF THE WAR, religious Americans celebrated victory over Germany and Japan along with all other Americans. Aside from posing a seemingly existential threat to religion and democracy, the war had raised difficult questions of faith and morality, and few mourned its passing in 1945. "We lift our hearts in thanksgiving this day for the assurance that the threat of the totalitarian form of government has been destroyed," preached Benjamin Hersey, a New York Universalist, upon the death of Hitler and the capitulation of Germany. Few disagreed.[1]

But joy at war's end could not hide the divisions within the churches that resulted from the war in the first place. There is a myth, particularly powerful and enduring, that because World War II was a "good" war, it was also a war of consensus and solidarity. If they had once sought to avoid Europe's strife, the American people patriotically united as one behind a noble cause after Germany and Japan had forced war upon them. Reinforced subsequently through film and television, and maintained by the demonstrable evil of Nazism, the notion that World War II was "the best war ever" remains as popular as ever in the American imagination.[2]

And of course it *was* a good war, in the sense that the adversaries, Nazi Germany and imperial Japan, were aggressive tyrannies bent on regional if not global hegemony. (Yet even this traditional narrative has come under criticism from recent historians who have chronicled the terrible costs inflicted by the Allies.) It was not an especially good war, however, when we consider domestic solidarity and consensus. For at the time the war was deeply controversial; the tide of patriotic fervor released by Pearl Harbor did not completely wash away dissent, pacifism, anticommunism, or isolationism. If Franklin Roosevelt conceived of the war as a crusade for religion, liberty, and democracy, it was for the American people, especially the churches, a "cautious crusade" driven by "a cautious patriotism."[3]

STILL, the heady mix of patriotism and faith traditionally found in wartime was not entirely absent. Religion still had its uses in the presentation of war aims and in mobilizing support. In fact, the president himself led the way by sanctifying the war as a holy enterprise. In addition to the Four Freedoms and numerous speeches portraying America's war as a struggle for religious liberty, Roosevelt set aside national days of prayer and thanksgiving. In a 1942 fireside chat, he led Americans in prayer for "the cause of all free mankind" and "victory over the tyrants who would enslave all free men and Nations." Perhaps Roosevelt's most famous prayer, suitably couched in the lyrical, foreboding style of the King James Bible, came shortly after D-Day and the invasion of Europe. He asked God for "strength" and "Faith" in this almighty battle against "the unholy forces of our enemy." He also asked Americans not to set aside only one day of prayer, as had been his custom, but to pray continuously.[4]

Other wartime leaders used the rhetoric of faith to build support for America's war and to demonize the enemy. Vice President Henry Wallace, a modernist Social Gospeler whose dabbles in New Age spirituality would damage him politically, perceived the war in Rooseveltian terms of a "fight between a free world and a slave world," with the "ideal of freedom . . . derived from the Bible with its extraordinary emphasis on the dignity of the individual." Fascism and Nazism were antithetical to faith, while "Democracy is the only true political expression of Christianity." But Wallace also had darker, more apocalyptic visions. In this same, bizarre speech, he invoked Satan—by name—five times. Stranger still were the rhetorical links he made between fighting Nazism abroad and injustice at home. Wallace was shrill not only out of a desire for victory, but because Hitler's Nazism seemed to be a twisted, populist bid for the allegiance of the "common man," and thus a direct threat to Wallace's own Christian progressivism:

> Through the leaders of the Nazi revolution, Satan now is trying to lead the common man of the whole world back into slavery and darkness. For the stark truth is that the violence preached by the Nazis is the devil's own religion of darkness. So also is the doctrine that one race or one class is by heredity superior and that all other races or classes are supposed to be slaves. The belief in one Satan-inspired Fuhrer . . . is the last and ultimate darkness.

It was as if Wallace had channeled the spirit of William Jennings Bryan and his firebrand, fundamentalist populism. But he was just getting warmed up. "In a twisted sense, there is something almost great in the figure of the Supreme Devil operating through a human form, in a Hitler who has the daring to spit straight into the eye of God and man." Americans now realized they could never appease such evil: "No compromise with Satan is possible." Instead, the "people's revolution is on the march, and the devil and all his angels can not prevail against it. They can not prevail, for on the side of the people is the Lord." He then quoted scripture—Isaiah 40:29–31, on the awesome powers God granted to the righteous—and concluded: "Strong in the strength of the Lord, we who fight in the people's cause will never stop until that cause is won."[5]

Less dramatic but probably more effective was General Dwight D. Eisenhower, commander of D-Day, who had not yet found God—that would come later, during his presidency—but who nonetheless used religion to steel his troops for the trials that lay in store. Instead of adopting Wallace's imagery of Armageddon or Roosevelt's language of the Bible, Eisenhower invoked the ideas of an American civic religion, thought to date back to the Puritans, that fused patriotic destiny with moral virtue. Eisenhower did not quote Christ, but John Winthrop. "You are about to embark upon the Great Crusade, toward which we have striven these many months," he said to the D-Day soldiers hours before they landed on the shores of Normandy. "The eyes of the world are upon you. The hopes and prayers of liberty-loving people everywhere march with you. . . . And let us all beseech the blessing of Almighty God upon this great and noble undertaking."[6]

For their part, many churches and synagogues followed suit. While some Christians remained ambivalent about the war, others rallied to the cause and threw their support behind a war for freedom against fascism and religion against paganism and atheism. The Japanese strike on Pearl Harbor, particularly the fact that it was a surprise attack that violated treaty obligations while diplomats were still negotiating, provoked a furious response. Until then, Japan had avoided much of the American furor over religious liberty: the Japanese did not appear to have an explicitly anti-Christian program as did the Nazis and Soviets, and missionaries to Japan formed a vocal body of pro-Japanese sentiment in America. For many, Pearl Harbor changed all this. American Protestants had long prioritized the written word, an objective, lasting testament for all to read themselves, as the rock of Christian civilization. Pearl Harbor therefore seemed, in a manner perhaps only Hitler would dare, to defy all civilized behavior and Christian norms. "Japan not only slaughtered Americans last Sunday," preached Albert Day of the First Methodist Church of Pasadena, California, a week after Pearl Harbor. "She assaulted that faith in the pledged word without which neither men nor nations can achieve understanding and cooperation. She cleverly deceived us but basely betrayed that mutual trust which is humanity's only bulwark against chaos." Not surprisingly, after Pearl Harbor it did not take long to uncover Japan's supposed plot against religious freedom. *Time* reported ominously that the Japanese had abolished Christianity in Filipino schools and that Tokyo vowed to shut down Christian churches throughout Asia that did not openly support Japanese policies. It all added up, the magazine warned in a play on the phrase the Japanese used to describe their ambitions, to an "Un-Christian Co-Prosperity" sphere in East Asia. U.S. diplomats abroad reported accounts of intensifying Japanese cruelty toward U.S. missionaries and other civilians in Japan, Korea, Manchuria, and occupied China.[7]

The spirit of righteous nationalism pervaded the armed forces, as well. The ranks of the chaplaincy swelled in all three branches of the military (a separate air force did not yet exist), and among them were few if any doubters of either the faith or the cause. One of the most popular songs during the war, "Praise the Lord and Pass the Ammunition," told the story of a navy chaplain's attempts to rally troops under heavy Japanese fire. When some members of the clergy back home complained that the song was blasphemous and warmongering, a chaplain stationed in the South Pacific responded angrily that "out here" he and the fighting men sang the song "with religious zeal." He thanked God "that there are men in the ministry who still have sufficient practical and immediate faith in the Almighty . . . to stand on battleship in an hour of dark . . . and sustain the men by saying, 'Praise the Lord and Pass the Ammunition!' " This was in stark moral contrast to the comforts of home and the "ministers who are so far detached from the struggle as to be wholly unaware that it exists." Another hit song among enlisted men was the sanguinary "God Is My Co-Pilot," in which the protagonist "strafed Japs swimming from boats we were sinking" and "blew a Jap pilot to hell out of the sky."[8]

Remarkably, and crucially for the war effort overall, the patriotic, interventionist mood enveloped institutions that had for years fought against the drift to intervention. In the first of many declarations of support, the Federal Council of Churches, once steadfastly opposed to American belligerency, organized a 1942 petition in support of the war signed by nearly a hundred of the nation's leading Protestant figures. A year later, the FCC reiterated its support for the war and declared, controversially for many liberal Protestants, that peace could only come through military victory. Church Peace Union abandoned its antiwar stance to call for a "complete military victory" to secure a peace that would be "backed by an international police force." Individual denominations also pledged their support and cooperation. Methodists who had once been among the most passionately pro-labor and antiwar of the mainline churches now condemned workers' strikes as unpatriotic and called on the government to enforce a quick settlement in industrial disputes. The Catholic hierarchy had been wary of war before Pearl Harbor, but now they too presented a united front. In November 1942, the Catholic Archbishops and Bishops of the United States, the most important body of American Catholic leaders, officially declared its unreserved support for Roosevelt and the war effort (even as it expressed reservations about the administration's encouragement of women to take industrial jobs while working men enlisted in the service). Given the strongly isolationist sentiment among Catholics before the war, this was vital support indeed.[9]

Just as important was the often shrill support for the war by renowned individual clergy. The 1940s remained a time when religious leaders were national public intellectuals and could command not only audiences of millions over the radio, but access to the nation's most important secular newspapers and magazines. Because Roosevelt had declared America's cause to be virtuous and moral, it was important for the recognized guardians of virtue and morality to pronounce a similar message. And so they did. If Francis Cardinal Spellman had had his doubts about intervention in 1940, he most emphatically did not in 1942. In wonderfully purple, patriotic prose, Spellman recalled the moment when the Japanese, "with fire and brimstone," forced war upon peace-loving Americans. "America's throat was clutched, her back was stabbed, her brain was stunned," he wrote of Pearl Harbor; "but her great heart still throbbed." That day, "America began the fight to save her life." The archbishop even offered all Americans, not only members of his Catholic flock, a wartime "Prayer for Victory" that was, characteristically, equally pious and pugnacious in linking the sanctity of family and nation:

> *Lord, give us Victory.*
> *In the clearer visioning of*
> *The mission of America;*
> *The glory of manhood;*
> *The achievement of paternity;*
> *The beauty of motherhood;*
> *The sacredness of childhood;*
> *The inviolability of our souls, our homes, our*
> *nation, our altars.*
>
> *Lord, give us victory;*
> *Not alone in the might of our arms,*
> *But in the righteousness of our cause,*
> *The defense of the defenseless,*
> *The succoring of the weak*
> *The shackling of Injustice, Greed and Passion;*
> *Lord, give us Victory.*[10]

Spellman had always been a nationalist and never a pacifist, so his turn to support the war was not especially surprising. More remarkable was the change of heart by many pacifists, mostly Protestant, who renounced their peace witness to support what they deemed not only a necessary war, but a noble one. Norman Thomas, the inspirational leader of American Socialists, quietly abandoned his Christian pacifism after Pearl Harbor. Others followed his lead. "If many of us didn't see it yesterday, let it pass," pleaded a Congregationalist minister and former peace crusader from Chicago. "We see it today."[11]

Unlike Spellman and Thomas, Right Reverend William T. Manning, an Episcopal Bishop and rector at the Cathedral of St. John the Divine, FDR's preferred church in New York City, had been a consistent supporter of aid to Britain and American intervention. After Pearl Harbor, he focused his efforts not only on rallying support but on marginalizing pacifists and doubters. "We all know what the issues are in this great World Battle," he declared in an August 1942 sermon. "America, and all that America stands for in human life, is in mortal peril." The fate of the free world hung in the balance, which made reflective soul-searching, normally a most Christian quality, a form of sabotage. "No Church which is true to its principles, and to its Mission in this World, can stand lukewarm, or half-hearted, or apathetic in a conflict such as this." To those who called themselves prophets of peace, Manning had only this to say: "there will be no Peace, and no new World Order, unless our Armed Forces, and those of our Allies, win this War."[12]

Manning's excoriation of outright pacifists and ambivalent doubters was not a random outburst. As we shall see, conscientious objection and condemnation of American strategy and military tactics were common among the faithful, and not only in the traditional peace churches, which explains why Manning was so eager to mount a public relations campaign. Led by an otherwise implausible alliance of Spellman and Father John A. Ryan, Catholic leaders launched a vigorous defense of the just war tradition, and with it the idea that pacifism was not synonymous with Christianity. In a just war, explained Ryan, a Christian did not in fact have the right to follow the dictates of his or her conscience over the demands of government. And World War II was exactly such a just war. "No man who is acquainted with Catholic moral teaching can honestly be a pacifist," he concluded shortly after U.S. entry into the war. In a war to defend democratic and Christian values, said others, it was the pacifist who suffered from a shortage of morality. At Union Theological Seminary, president Henry Sloane Coffin took the highly unusual step of publicly denouncing those of his students who refused, on grounds of Christian conscience, to register for the draft.[13]

While the leaders of liberal Protestantism wrestled with their recalcitrant and unenthusiastic members, conservative evangelicals and fundamentalists had no such problems. True, many had embraced a hard-shell isolationism before 1941, while some, such as Gerald L. K. Smith, had adopted an anti-Semitic hostility toward fighting a Jewish war. But while Christian conservatives had often been opposed to the government, they were passionately patriotic, which eased their post–Pearl Harbor transition to supporting the war. Their anti-statism, moreover, instinctively alerted them to the dangers of totalitarianism in which a single leader could dominate the lives of ordinary citizens. And perhaps most important, just as Mormons, Catholics, and Jews had learned in previous conflicts, supporting the war effort would alleviate concerns among the rest of the population about the "eccentric" ways of the evangelical subculture. Youth for Christ, an important new group of young evangelicals, staged patriotic revival meetings in the United States and for U.S. forces overseas. Aimee Semple McPherson, the nation's leading Pentecostal, did likewise. In 1942, she held a war bond rally in Los Angeles that raised over $150,000 in a single hour. "How many of you would like to see Hitler covered with boils from head to foot?" she called out. "Well, I would!" This was a noteworthy conversion for a group of people who normally distrusted the growth of government power. But the most astonishing about-face came from William Bell Riley, who throughout the interwar years had accused Jews of propagating Darwinism as a way to weaken America and dominate the world. He changed his tune in 1941, when he abandoned anti-Semitism (at least in public) and accused Nazism of being "the philosophy of evolution in action" and Hitler with being "the BEAST-MAN!" Riley even revived the old World War I charge that Germany was the home of biblical Higher Criticism and atheist philosophy, which Hitler was adapting to a new era to bring about German world domination.[14]

So overwhelming and cohesive was Christian conservative support for the war, and so ambivalent were liberals, that World War II marked a decisive shift in religious attitudes toward patriotism. After two decades of being portrayed as extremists, the war offered Christian conservatives a lifeline back into the mainstream. In the interwar period, fundamentalists had stridently attacked the hedonism of American society, the plausibility of modern science, and the legitimacy of the U.S. government (especially the New Deal). Some had even flirted with fascism and anti-Semitism. But, aside from Darwinism, World War II settled many of these issues so decisively that they were no longer a matter of debate, while the ethos of wartime sacrifice brought the conservatives' stern morality back into fashion. Because Christian conservatives had always loved their country even when they hated their government, they felt completely free to support a war that provided a clear-cut crusade for religion, democracy, and American security.

On the other hand, liberals and other heirs to modernism still had difficulty overcoming their bitter experience with ultrapatriotism during the Great War. They were just as patriotic as fundamentalists and evangelicals, but they now saw dissent as a form of patriotism because it would protect Americans from their more aggressive impulses. This proved to be a most controversial stance in wartime, and Christian conservatives used it to discredit religious liberalism. Patriotism does not usually sit well with ambivalence or moral self-reflection, so it is no surprise that conservative clarity began to prevail over liberal soul-searching. For some liberals, then, it was essential that they support the war not only to preserve freedom and democracy in the great crises overseas, but to protect themselves in religious politics at home. Those "who are commonly rated as patriotic belong almost exclusively to the Fundamentalist sect," complained a United Presbyterian educator from Chicago in a letter to Niebuhr. Their patriotism "has become one of the worst incriminations against Modernism." This was why prowar liberals like Niebuhr were so important, for they showed "that not every liberal theologian is taking to the woods."[15]

World War II enabled conservatives to rescue a reputation that had been tarnished by their political and theological extremism of the previous two decades, for their uncompromising patriotism was now very much in tune with the national mood. Victory over Germany in May 1945 and Japan in August not only brought widespread celebration but also provided the best example of a civil religion of American righteousness. Purity of faith and nation had prevailed over the forces of paganism, atheism, and tyranny. God carried America to victory and ensured that the devastations of war would remain far from its shores. In this heady atmosphere, it was no surprise that evangelicalism surged in the armed forces. Writing in the *American Journal of Sociology*, the FCC's F. Ernest Johnson was astonished by the growth of faith in the military, especially when compared to civilians. The triumph of a righteous America sped the process of evangelizing the military, but it was also encouraged by evangelicals at home who now viewed the U.S. military as a mission field in itself. In turn, the armed forces encouraged religion as an ideological glue that would hold together a massive body of soldiers who had only just enlisted. To speed the process, the State Department and the newly founded United Service Organizations drafted prowar religious leaders, such as Henry Sloane Coffin and Sherwood Eddy, to produce moral propaganda for the troops.[16]

President Truman therefore spoke for many when, in announcing Germany's surrender in May 1945, he offered "thanks to the Providence which has guided and sustained us through dark days of adversity." He spoke of "the debt" that Americans "owe to our God," praised the nation's "sacrifice and devotion" that won the war "with God's help," and asked people to "give thanks to Almighty God, who has strengthened us and given us the victory." He then declared the first Sunday after VE Day to be an official day of national prayer. In August, Truman repeated these rites of civil religion in announcing the surrender of Japan. Again, he proclaimed a national day of prayer, and called "upon the people of the United States, of all faiths, to unite in offering our thanks to God for the victory we have won, and in praying that He will support and guide us into the paths of peace."[17]

THE WAR SHOULD have been a time of unbridled, triumphalist nationalism. Given that the United States achieved victory on two fronts on two separate continents a world apart, all without suffering any physical damage itself, and given how wealthy the nation emerged after fifteen years of war and Depression, it would not have been a surprise had Americans treated world events as a total vindication of their way of life. And of course, many if not most Americans felt exactly this way, and celebrated accordingly. But many others did not, and most of those who questioned that the war provided confirmation of America's goodness or disagreed that it had come at a worthwhile cost were religious Americans. Religious belief is often a source of dogmatic moral certainty, but it can also cause profound doubt and self-reflection, even among the most devoted. This seems to have been the case during World War II, for a sizable number of religious Americans did not support the war.

For obvious reasons, American Jews supported the war with near unanimity and Jewish pacifism was marginal to the point of irrelevance. Yet a sizable number of Protestants and a small but articulate and passionately motivated hard core of Catholics opposed America's participation throughout World War II, even after Pearl Harbor and even with a victory that seemed to justify it all. Just as important were the much larger numbers of Christians who believed the United States should fight but who strongly denounced the ways in which the Roosevelt administration and U.S. military did the fighting. Either through pacifist opposition, halfhearted ambivalence, or moral criticism of military strategy and tactics, Christian dissent represented a major challenge to the self-satisfied triumphalism of self-righteous nationalism.

"Whatever . . . this war is named, there is one thing it is plainly not," complained a prowar writer in the *New Republic* in June 1942. "It is not a Holy War. On the civilian front, it is being waged with less benefit of clergy than any major war of our history." This was an exaggeration: faith-based antiwar movements had been major aspects of the War of 1812, the Mexican War, and the Philippine War, to say nothing of the religious character of the Loyalists during the American Revolution. Yet it was a valid point. The clergy had formed the moral core of pacifism in the 1920s and anti-interventionism in the 1930s, and many of them simply could not abandon the cause even after Pearl Harbor and Germany's subsequent declaration of war upon the United States. With most secular pacifists abandoning the cause, absolutist pacifism became an almost exclusively faith-based phenomenon. But even those erstwhile pacifists who now supported the war did so reluctantly and with little enthusiasm or vigor. In its critique of the "church unmilitant," the *New Republic* charged institutional religion with a dereliction of duty. Instead of rallying the American people to a noble but difficult cause, the clergy, especially the mainline Protestant clergy, were in a state of "spiritual immobilization" that was "notably lame, halting and sometimes shameful."[18]

Both the State Department and the British Foreign Office were unsettled by the mood of the churches, and for good reason. In the Great War, almost all mainline Protestants, even those who had campaigned in the peace movement, had converted to the cause of the Wilsonian creed in 1917 before returning to the pacifist fold after postwar disillusionment had set in. But now, in 1941–42, thousands refused to budge from their opposition to war—all war, including this war. The traditional peace churches, among them Quakers and Mennonites, did not support World War II. Yet neither did many mainline Presbyterians, Baptists, and Methodists, which posed a significant problem for the government and helps in part to explain why Roosevelt featured religion so prominently in his wartime proclamations. The mainline churches continued to claim the nation's moral high ground and still counted millions among their flock. Though the laity did not always follow their preachers' lead, the clergy nonetheless had an influential platform at their command. They were articulate and well-connected, and they could not be moved. "I feel sure that pacifists will do better to stick to our main business," wrote Harry Emerson Fosdick to Reverend John Nevin Sayre in 1944, "proclaiming that this unspeakable horror now going on *is* war, is essentially and irredeemably war, that war reaches out for every new power and turns it to destructive purposes," and that "all military strategy is an utter denial of Christian motives." The "whole military business," Fosdick concluded balefully, "is essentially antichristian."[19]

As the *New Republic* feared, even many liberals who supported the war could not bring themselves to do so wholeheartedly. America itself was also a source of profound injustice, they said, especially on matters of race; Americans could not claim innocence or be absolved from responsibility for the world's problems. "The rise of Hitlerism is no accident," wrote one erstwhile pacifist who grudgingly supported what he called a "just war of unjust nations." The Nazis were simply the most extreme manifestation of an evil that imperial Britain and France and racist America had allowed to flourish. "Had the democracies been what they are supposed to be, they would have been impregnable. Our defects gave Hitler and his allies their chance." In a similar spirit, as late as 1944 the annual meeting of the Northern Baptist Convention passed a prowar platform but made a point of removing stridently patriotic phrases from the first draft. Perhaps learning from the FCC's controversy, the Northern Baptists also emphatically declared, "we will not bless war."[20]

Neither, for the most part, would missionaries, both Protestant and Catholic, who had always coexisted uneasily with imperialism. After the Great War, missionaries themselves began to appreciate just how closely associated their movement was with imperialism, and just how easily its conversion initiatives facilitated Western political and military dominance. Led by E. Stanley Jones, Sherwood Eddy, and other Social Gospel–minded evangelists, and prodded by the 1932 Laymen's Report that reevaluated the purpose of mainline missionaries in a strikingly radical direction, Protestant mission boards increasingly stressed their independence from, even outright opposition to, great power politics. On balance, this did not change with the war, even though many within the single largest group of evangelists overseas, the China missionaries, had come around to the idea of using military force to fend off the encroachment of Japan, and even though some liberal missionaries, like Eddy, supported the war. Throughout 1941, missionaries across the theological spectrum pressed their case for peace with Japan. Bishop James E. Walsh and Father James M. Drought of the Catholic Foreign Mission Society met privately with Roosevelt and Hull to argue that a clash was not inevitable and that Japanese had genuine grievances. Similarly, E. Stanley Jones badgered Roosevelt and the State Department to accept his services as an intermediary between Tokyo and Washington; he even entered into freelance discussions with Japanese officials, suggested that New Guinea could be turned over to Japan as a way to appease its desire for territory, and, less than a week before Pearl Harbor, vowed to bring peace to the Pacific through Christian understanding. Needless to say, none of them received much encouragement—or success—yet they refused to budge. Even in 1942, the Foreign Missions Conference, the largest body of mainline missionaries, pointedly refused to sanctify the war. Instead, as Christians they stressed their "supranational and truly ecumenical loyalty" to all peoples, ally and adversary alike.[21]

Just as novel was the emergence of a full-blown pacifist movement in the Catholic Church. By accepting the legitimacy of the Augustinian just war, Catholics essentially denied that a Christian could ever be a pacifist. The true Christian should not condone war except under certain circumstances and within certain rules outlined in just war doctrine, but this was much different from denying the validity of any war at any time under any circumstance. This was the position of the Vatican as well as the Catholic hierarchy in the United States, including those on the left such as John Ryan. Yet the Catholic Worker movement represented something different. Ryan, Spellman, and other Catholics had not supported intervention before December 7, 1941, but they had little hesitation in doing so afterward. Catholic Workers did not join them. In its first issue after Pearl Harbor, *The Catholic Worker* defiantly pledged to "continue our pacifist stand" against the surge of wartime patriotism. "We are still pacifists. Our manifesto is the Sermon on the Mount, which means that we will try to be peacemakers." Allied with like-minded souls in the Association of Catholic Conscientious Objectors, Catholic Workers extended their search for social justice by rejecting the validity of just war doctrine. No Christian could justify war, not even one against Nazi Germany.[22]

ASIDE FROM THE WAR ITSELF, four issues in particular troubled the consciences of American Christians: the draft, the Allied strategy of total war and unconditional surrender, Japanese internment, and the use of atomic weapons. On each of these issues, religion comprised the predominant strand of dissent because moralistic people of faith were much more likely to be ill at ease with the methods used to prosecute the war.

For the hard core of pacifists who refused to accept the moral meaning of the war, a clash between God's law and U.S. law was inevitable. In September 1940, Congress passed the Selective Service Act and instituted the first peacetime draft in American history. Nonetheless, conscientious objectors refused to cooperate with draft boards, and even encouraged young men to defy the law by not registering. They continued to obstruct selective service after Pearl Harbor. While much of the rest of the nation prosecuted a foreign war with Old Testament fervor, conscientious objectors adhered to a New Testament gospel of love. "When Jesus said that His disciples should not resist evil, should turn the other cheek, should love their enemies, that His kingdom is not of this world," wrote Dan West of the Church of the Brethren in 1943, "we thought He meant that for us too." Friends, Mennonites, and Brethren continued their historic stand against war, but this time they were joined by mainline Protestants, radical Catholics, and even liberal Catholics from establishment institutions like the Catholic University of America.[23]

This time, unlike during the Great War, their right to do so was supported by Christians who supported the war. When it looked as if Congress was going to resurrect the draft laws of 1917, which limited conscientious objection to the traditional peace churches, Roswell P. Barnes of the Federal Council testified before the House Committee on Military Affairs to urge lawmakers to broaden their definition. To Roosevelt and the Senate Military Affairs Committee, the FCC's Walter Van Kirk likened conscientious objection to the freedom of religion FDR had enshrined in the Four Freedoms. Other religious bodies followed suit, including the House of Bishops of the Episcopal Church and the annual meeting of the Southern Baptist Convention. Even Coffin, an ardent interventionist who had publicly censured COs at Union Theological Seminary, used his close personal ties to Secretary of War Henry Stimson to ensure that pacifists from the Fellowship of Reconciliation received a hearing on Capitol Hill. These efforts were largely successful. The Selective Service Act included a watered-down definition of who could claim CO status and provided for the establishment of alternative forms of service through domestic Civilian Public Service camps that were administered and run by the peace churches themselves. Toward the end of the war, moreover, the FCC called upon Congress to terminate the draft once victory had been achieved. More surprising was the director of Selective Service, General Lewis Hershey, whose ancestors were Mennonites and who proved sympathetic to the more capacious definition of COs.[24]

Conscientious objectors were often vilified as cowards and shirkers, but for COs the moral stakes involved were worth the sacrifice. "Bear in mind that each of us is responsible for the actions of our government," admonished one conscientious objector, "and if these actions exceed the limits" of morality "the guilt is ours." This was no idle warning. According to most COs, by 1943–44 the U.S. government was engaged in warfare of a most dubious morality. The intensity of conscientious objection actually increased as the war dragged on and as victory neared. Though the true scale of Nazi atrocities was becoming clear, the Allies' own strategy was increasingly brutal and, said an increasing number of Americans, immoral. Much to the fury of the Soviets, who had borne the brunt of the Nazi war machine, the British and Americans could not open a second European front until the invasion of Italy in 1943. Even this did little to blunt the Nazi war effort, and the Normandy invasion was still a year away. But in the skies, the Allies had superiority at a much earlier point. Their obvious recourse was to pound Germany into submission from the air. At the same time, U.S. war planners arrived upon a similar solution to their inability to mount a direct assault against Japan. But the resort to what critics called "obliterative bombing" triggered furious protests. From Europe, victims of German aggression could not fathom why the Allies would imitate their indiscriminate tactics. The British writer Vera Brittain condemned Allied bombing as immoral, while continentals who had endured years of German occupation now found themselves in a new line of fire. "How can this conduct be justified before the reason and conscience of mankind?" pleaded Cardinal Jozef-Ernest Van Roey, the head of the Belgian Catholic Church. In the United States, Fosdick led other prominent clergy in protesting the "carnival of death," while others exhorted that by allowing the killing of "innocent women and children," even if they were German or Japanese, "we Christians must stand our share of the blood-guilt."[25]

The dissent of Protestants like Fosdick and A. J. Muste called into question the Allies' claims to moral superiority, but a much more serious challenge emerged from the Catholic Church. Pope Pius XII did not much like fascism or Nazism, but while he sympathized with Allied objectives he could not bring himself to support a war that would devastate the European continent. Instead of rallying to one side or the other, Pius continued treading the careful line of neutrality he had laid down in the two years before 1941. However, in 1943–44, he leveled a strong moral condemnation of the Allied campaign. That same year, fearing a repeat of the inconclusive end to World War I, Roosevelt and Churchill vowed they would accept nothing less than Germany's unconditional surrender. However, Pius believed that unconditional surrender was unnecessarily brutal and merciless, and he criticized indiscriminate aerial bombing as tantamount to mass murder. That it was mainly Catholic countries—Germany, Italy, Belgium, France, Poland—that bore the brunt of Allied bombing made it even more difficult for the Vatican to accept, even as an unfortunate necessity of war. The Vatican's polite requests to Roosevelt that "the civil populations be spared the horrors of war" went answered but unheeded. As the war ended, the Vatican complained bitterly that the United States had never "been able to comprehend the fatal damage which they have inflicted upon this continent, casting it into the depths of misery by aerial bombardment."[26]

Following this papal lead, American Catholics condemned Allied strategic bombing. Not only antiwar pacifists but Catholic just war ethicists in the United States issued stern moral rebukes of their own and likened Allied bombing to a war crime. Perhaps the strongest, most eloquent denunciation came from John Ford, a Jesuit priest whose detailed, theologically informed article, "The Morality of Obliteration Bombing," became required reading for American Catholics and Protestants much as Vera Brittain's "Massacre by Bombing" had before.[27]

The sordid story of Japanese internment also provoked vigorous religious dissent, this time over race as well as militarism. Deemed an internal security threat, hundreds of thousands of Japanese Americans, most of whom were U.S. citizens, were forcibly imprisoned in camps scattered throughout the American West. It was a drastic thing to do, but most Americans approved of internment as a matter of wartime necessity. Typically, however, many if not most Christian leaders did not approve, including in the West. In the shadow of the rugged Sawtooth Mountains, Reverend Emery E. Andrews delivered one of the most impassioned moral protests against internment. Andrews had lost his entire congregation to the war, for his parishioners had been Japanese Americans. Speaking to the 1943 Idaho Baptist Assembly, he excoriated America for its violation of basic liberties at home while it professed to defend them abroad and pleaded that the Japanese Americans were innocent. Upon hearing that his congregants were to be locked up, Andrews confessed that "two conflicting emotions stirred within." He would either "become the most ardent and fanatical conscientious objector" or "I would seek revenge on those who were responsible for such injustice to an innocent people." In the end he did neither, though he did become one of the war's sterner critics. "What a sad commentary on our civilization," he lamented. "This we have done in Christian America to people just as loyal as you or I. How loyal would you be if you were treated the same way that these people are treated? I would not be loyal. There are some things I would not fight for, even in America." Other western Christians, such as the Colorado Council of Churches, offered lonely voices of protest amid the anti-Japanese din. But opposition to internment was not confined simply to pacifist opponents of the war or preachers of Japanese American congregations. It was "important to go before the public and make an appeal in behalf of justice for our Japanese citizens," Reinhold Niebuhr believed. "This is a time when people who keep their heads will have to work hard against the hysteria of the nation."[28]

Perhaps no other event caused as much soul-searching as the use of nuclear weapons against Japan in the very last days of the war. President Harry Truman authorized the use of two atomic bombs on Japanese targets: Hiroshima on August 6, 1945, and Nagasaki on August 9. Not long after, Tokyo sued for peace. Truman himself expressed no doubts, at least in public, although there is compelling evidence that privately he felt troubled by his decision even if he ultimately thought it was necessary. And Truman's ambivalence was by no means exceptional. As Paul Boyer has noted, Americans reacted to the news of the bombing of Hiroshima and Nagasaki with a wide variety of emotions: exultation that the war had ended victoriously, relief that it had finished quickly, vindictive satisfaction that the "Japs" had been brought so low, discomfort about atomic warfare. These were certainly some of the emotions of those sitting in the nation's pews. But from the pulpit, opinions were not so divided. Among the nation's clergy, an overwhelming majority responded to the atomic bombs with trepidation, fear, and moral outrage. Thus as Boyer has also pointed out, "the greatest concentration of critical comment on the Hiroshima and Nagasaki bombings came from the churches." There was little triumphalism among the clergy. In fact, for many of them the war's culmination in a mushroom cloud reignited their drive for world peace.[29]

Moral protest was not simply confined to the pacifist Protestant left. Supporters of a righteous, progressive war for democracy and human rights against Germany and Japan also voiced their outrage. One minister's condemnation of the bomb as "moral degeneration" reflected widespread disgust. Thirty-four prominent church leaders signed an open letter to Truman to express their opposition to "an atrocity of a new magnitude" and to Truman's "reckless and irresponsible" decision to commit "so colossal a crime." Among the signatories was the missionary leader

E. Stanley Jones, which was not surprising. Missionaries, many of whom had either lived in Japan or knew people who had, reacted to the bombings with a particular revulsion. "I am in soul agony over that Atomic Bomb dropped on Hiroshima," lamented William Axling, one of the leading Japan missionaries. "That is not war, it is mass murder. I hold no brief for the militarists who are in the saddle in Japan today but whatever Germany and they have done it is heart breaking to see my beloved America resorting to such diabolical measures."[30]

This was typical stuff from Axling, who for years had criticized American racism and condescension toward Japan. Less expected was the moral criticism from those who had actually been in charge of the war effort. Admiral William D. Leahy, chief of staff to Roosevelt and Truman during the war, believed the bomb was immoral because it killed not only through immediate destruction but through "poisonous" long-term radiation. As the first country to use nuclear weapons, Leahy charged, the United States "had adopted an ethical standard common to the barbarians of the Dark Ages." It was a way of waging "uncivilized warfare" and represented "a modern type of barbarism not worthy of Christian man."[31]

Among Protestants, the FCC used its institutional authority to assume a leading role in opposition to the bomb. Its first foray into the moral politics of nuclear weapons, an August 9 statement by John Foster Dulles and G. Bromley Oxnam, a Methodist Bishop and president of the Federal Council, was relatively tame. Writing after the attack on Nagasaki, Dulles and Oxnam hailed the wonders of American science and refrained from direct criticism of the bombings. But they also called on Truman to declare a halt to further use of the bomb and hinted that only international control of atomic energy would ensure peace. Privately, however, the FCC was much more pointed in its criticism. The same day as the Nagasaki bombing and the Dulles-Oxnam statement, Samuel McCrea Cavert, the FCC's general secretary, wrote Truman that American Christians were "deeply disturbed" by atomic weapons "because of their necessarily indiscriminate destructive effects and because their use sets extremely dangerous precedent for the future of mankind." Cavert instead urged Truman to regard the secret of splitting the atom and harnessing its power as being held in "trust for humanity" by the United States, and not as a weapon of war. Two weeks later, Richard Fagley of the FCC's Commission on a Just and Durable Peace combined the moderate internationalism of the Dulles-Oxnam statement with the stridency of the Cavert letter. The discovery and use of the bomb, Fagley said in a statement, had brought on a "profound crisis of man" that could not be solved by the United States alone.[32]

Following logically from their wartime denunciations of strategic bombing, Catholic priests were almost uniformly opposed to the atomic bombing of Japan. Much more than even the most conservative forms of Protestantism, Catholicism viewed life as sacrosanct. The taking of human life was justified according to the just war tradition, but only under the most deliberately considered and circumscribed conditions. World War II fulfilled those just war requirements, but not by much and, for most Catholics, not until the Japanese had attacked Pearl Harbor. Then it became not only a war for democracy, which was just, but a war of self-defense, which was even more clearly just. Yet as we have seen, American Catholics and the Vatican together condemned many aspects of Allied strategy, especially strategic bombing and unconditional surrender. Their denunciations of the atomic bomb were therefore unsurprising, but their tone adopted an even greater sense of urgency. *L'Osservatore Romano*, the Vatican newspaper and a reliable indicator of papal opinion, condemned the atomic bomb as a "catastrophic conclusion" to a war full of "apocalyptic surprises." Father John Ryan, who had done much to shape Catholic response to the upheavals of the 1930s, categorically condemned the bombings of Hiroshima and Nagasaki as immoral and unbecoming of American values. "Here is obliteration bombing with a vengeance and upon the largest scale," he declared in a statement. Americans "must reflect upon what is in store," in terms of both God's infinite judgment and world politics when America's adversaries obtained the atomic secret for themselves. Blunter still were Catholic pacifists, who simply condemned the atomic bombings as acts of "murder."[33]

The sudden appearance of the bomb also raised the most profound existential questions of the kind that had preoccupied the greatest minds in Christianity and Judaism for centuries. For fundamentalists such as Carl McIntire, it was second nature to conclude that the atomic bomb "makes seem more real the Biblical statements of the earth's destruction." Paradoxically, then, the scientific mastery behind the bomb merely corroborated the conservative belief in an inerrant, literally true Bible. Yet even the liberal *Christian Century* observed that the "function of Christians is to make preparation for world's end. For generations this fundamental aspect of the Christian faith has been ignored or relegated to the subconscious." But after Hiroshima, eschatology now "confounds us at the very center of consciousness." This was quite an admission for a modernist magazine that itself normally avoided eschatology—indeed, did not even realize that millions of conservative Christians believed in end times prophecies—which illustrates just how difficult it was to avoid questions about the meaning of life in the atomic age. *Fortune* magazine, not normally known for its philosophical or theological musings, predicted that the bomb would trigger a "religious awakening" and a "reaffirmation of Christian values" across America. After the war, Americans wanted to return to their normal lives, back to things the way they were before depression and war. But that was impossible, claimed Reverend Benjamin B. Hersey of the Church of the Divine Paternity in New York. "Back to what?" he asked his congregation in a sermon based around the unveiling of the four horsemen of the apocalypse in the sixth and seventh chapters of the Book of Revelation. "The world as it was? O no, things have gone too far for that. There is no going back. That possibility vaporized with the steel tower on the New Mexican desert and in the explosions over Hiroshima" and Nagasaki.[34]

AND OF COURSE, while religion influenced the war, the war in turn exerted a profound, lasting effect upon American religion. We have already examined Roosevelt's cementing of the interfaith civil religion that Washington, Lincoln, and Wilson had nurtured over the past century and a half. But the war had other effects, mostly by spurring spiritual mobilization and regeneration. While the idea that the interwar era marked a "depression" of religion has been exaggerated—only liberal mainline Protestantism declined, while fundamentalism, evangelicalism, Pentecostalism, Catholicism, and Judaism all flourished—the war nonetheless triggered a process of tremendous growth and resurgence in virtually all corners of American religious life.[35]

In particular, spiritual mobilization spurred Christian conservatives forward. Contrary to popular belief, evangelicals and fundamentalists cared deeply about wider social, cultural, and political issues. As the government expanded first with the New Deal and then with the war, they realized they too would need to consolidate and speak as one if they wanted their voices heard. The effectiveness of the liberal Federal Council, which claimed to speak for the majority of Protestants, was an unending source of frustration for conservatives. But now, instead of simply lambasting the New Deal state and the FCC, conservatives used the "united action" ethos of the war to imitate them. Led by Reverend Carl McIntire, an indomitable, extremist Presbyterian, fundamentalists established the American Council of Christian Churches in 1941. Evangelicals followed with the founding of the National Association of Evangelicals two years later. At a time when internationalism was finally coming of age, the NAE enacted a form of collective security for America's Christian conservatives. Still, by adopting "Cooperation Without Compromise" as its motto, the NAE made it clear it would not abandon the sanctity of sovereignty and autonomy that underpinned the Christian conservative worldview.[36]

Wartime spiritual mobilization also created space for political and social mobilization. For conservatives, this meant a push for moral reform. With parents away fighting or working long hours, young people had more free time on their hands than ever before. The result was a full-scale moral panic over an epidemic of juvenile delinquents. Evangelicals mobilized

Youth for Christ to divert gangs of wayward adolescents away from the boredom that led to petty crime. Not coincidentally, this mobilization coincided with the initiative to establish the NAE. Conservative missionaries made similar efforts abroad. Their champion, Walter Judd, a Minnesota congressman and former medical missionary to China, prodded U.S. diplomats to ensure that the control of opium and other drugs was enshrined in the UN Charter.[37]

For liberals, especially pacifists, wartime spiritual mobilization meant a push for racial reform. Campaigning against the war was frustrating and lonely work, and pacifists quickly decided to channel their energies and organizational skills into causes at home. The war, wrote a Presbyterian minister from Plainfield, New Jersey, was "exposing" Americans to their own "deadly perils" by making them "painfully aware of the ways in which we are defying the will of the righteous and loving God, in our treatment of minority groups like the Japanese Americans and the Negroes." Harry Emerson Fosdick pursued this line by linking domestic peace and tranquility with the success of postwar collective security. Both, he claimed, would succeed only if they respected difference by enshrining tolerance. Writing to Senator Harry Truman in 1943, Fosdick hoped that Americans would do "everything that we can do, both for the sake of our own democracy at home, and of a better understanding between the different races of the United Nations, to improve interracial relationships." African Americans certainly hoped so. According to a black Baptist preacher from Ann Arbor, Michigan, their World War II was one in which Americans "died that civilization might be saved from utter destruction by ruthless nations" and "that all peoples of the earth, all nationalities and races might be free." Similarly, Protestant and Catholic missionaries used the moral meaning of the war to push for the repeal of anti-Chinese immigration laws.[38]

Clearly, a wide gulf was opening up between religious conservatives and liberals over political rather than theological issues, foremost among them foreign policy. Though it was not yet apparent, the climate of war had been much kinder to patriotic conservatism than dissenting liberalism. However, their disputes did not dissipate after the war. On the contrary, as we shall see: they intensified, and provided Cold War policymakers with both their most ardent supporters and their sternest critics. In this sense, the religious response to the bomb was important, for it revived a liberal peace witness and critique of American power precisely at a time when victory in a righteous war might have killed it off. Instead, the Cold War began a new argument over the soul of American foreign policy.

John Foster Dulles and the Quest
for a Just and Durable Peace

THE ENDURING IDEAL OF peace, combined with the immediate fact of war, shaped wartime religious thinking more than anything else. Pacifists were active in their support of peace, of course, but they were mostly ignored by the administration. Instead, most of the interwar peace crusaders and isolationists supported the war effort. But as we have seen, many remained ambivalent and did not give the Roosevelt administration carte blanche. On the issue of postwar order, they demanded that FDR fulfill Woodrow Wilson's promise and fight a war to end all wars. War might be an ugly necessity in this instance, they agreed, but the real challenge would begin when the guns fell silent.

As in World War I, liberal Protestants played a large role in planning for a postwar world order. As one of the closest chroniclers of American internationalists has noted, "Virtually all were old-stock Protestant Americans." And as before, the Federal Council of Churches assumed the mantle of leadership. The FCC had opposed intervention well into 1941, and while Pearl Harbor may have changed its stance on the war it did nothing to dilute the FCC's pacific impulses. Thus most members of the Federal Council supported the war, and urged the United States to pursue a total victory, but they did so with certain caveats. The first was that Roosevelt should aim not simply to defeat Germany, Italy, and Japan but begin constructing an architecture for permanent peace. The second was that the war must be waged justly, proportionately, and not in a spirit of rancor or vengeance; this was a lesson learned from the misplaced patriotic fervor of the Great War. The FCC's third caveat expressed the conflicted exceptionalism of American liberals: the United States must fight the war and fashion a peace along internationalist lines of global interdependency, as a nation among nations; but that, as the world's most powerful democracy, America had a responsibility to take the lead in building a better world. Overall, then, the spirit of Walter Van Kirk and the pacifists lived on, but in harness to that of Reinhold Niebuhr and the Christian realists.[1]

. . .

To FURTHER THEIR AIMS, in 1940 the Federal Council established the Commission on a Just and Durable Peace. Over the next five years, this small group would become one of the most influential nongovernmental organizations in U.S. foreign policy. But rather than turn the Commission over to one of its illustrious theologians or preachers, the Federal Council entrusted its vision to a legalistic Presbyterian layman, John Foster Dulles. It was a momentous decision.

A cultural Calvinist of the most stubborn, puritanical kind, Dulles was not exactly blessed with charisma. After a 1942 meeting in London, British Foreign Secretary Anthony Eden, who would spar with Dulles throughout the 1940s and '50s, called him "the wooliest type of useless pontificating American. Heaven help us!" Later, a frustrated Eden called Dulles a "preacher in a world of politics" who often "had little regard for the consequence of his words." Churchill memorably classified Dulles as "the only case of a bull I know who carries his china closet with him." When he was secretary of state, Dulles's special assistant described his negotiating style as "carefully weighing every word and putting it down on the table exactly next to the last word." *Time* reported that colleagues referred to him as "dull, duller, Dulles." Yet this stern, dour, pedantic Wall Street lawyer was an ideal choice to head the Commission on a Just and Durable Peace, for he possessed a brilliant mind, religious faith, diplomatic experience, and sterling political connections.[2]

Dulles was a devout Christian who came from a family in which religion played a major formative role. His grandfather was a Presbyterian missionary to India who lived in Madras and died in Ceylon (Sri Lanka). Dulles was the son of a Presbyterian minister, like Woodrow Wilson, and grew up in Watertown, New York, listening to his father's weekly Sunday sermons, studying the Bible before and after school, and singing morning hymns on the front porch during the summer. Also like Wilson, Dulles experienced the Presbyterian milieu as a young undergraduate at Princeton. In fact, Wilson was president of the university during Dulles's time at Princeton, and he attended Wilson's lectures on constitutional government. After graduation, Dulles decided, contrary to his family's expectations, that he would not enter the ministry but instead become a lawyer. "I think I could make a greater contribution as a Christian lawyer and a Christian layman than I would as a Christian minister," he told his parents. His prescience soon became apparent: after law school at George Washington University, family connections secured him a job at Sullivan and Cromwell, one of Wall Street's most prestigious firms. There, he would specialize in matters of international law.[3]

Crucially, this Christian lawyer was a liberal Protestant. The distinction is important, for had Dulles been a theological conservative, much less a fundamentalist, he would not have become involved with the Federal Council and most likely would not have become a prominent diplomat. In Watertown, Reverend Dulles had firmly sided with the modernists. He took his Bible seriously and ensured that his children knew it intimately, but he did not take it literally. Later, during the fundamentalist-modernist battles of the 1920s, John Foster Dulles represented Harry Emerson Fosdick in a heresy trial before the Judicial Commission of the Presbyterian General Assembly. Dulles, then, was a modernist: pious, but accepting of secular society and scientific empiricism, and he did not believe that the Bible expressed the inerrant word of God. And while he was a proud Presbyterian, he was also, as his father had been, strongly ecumenical. This too was a badge of theological liberalism. Beginning in the late 1930s, after a period in which he became busy with his legal career and allowed his religious observance to lapse, Dulles became very active in church activities, not only within the Presbyterian Church but within Protestantism more generally; in 1947, an Episcopal newspaper anointed him "the most influential layman in the world." He was not just a Christian; nor was he simply a mainline Protestant—every Dulles biographer has recognized these influences. More precisely, and much more importantly, he was an ecumenical Christian. Indeed, it was his participation in the 1937 Oxford Conference, and its interdenominational cooperative spirit, that had regalvanized his faith after a period of spiritually aimless uncertainty.[4]

On foreign policy, Dulles possessed impeccable, impressive credentials. On his mother's side, both his grandfather (John W. Foster) and uncle (Robert Lansing) had been secretaries of state; both had also been successful lawyers. Unusually for diplomats of the era—who were often political appointees with more business acumen than diplomatic expertise—John W. Foster enjoyed a long and distinguished career in foreign service; in 1907, during his senior year at Princeton, young Dulles accompanied his grandfather to the Second Hague Peace Conference—where, not unusually, he was representing not the U.S. government, but the Chinese. In 1919, Dulles accompanied Lansing—his "Uncle Bert"—to the Paris Peace Conference as an official member of the U.S. delegation. In Paris, he was witness not only to the polished intricacies of diplomacy, but also to his uncle's reservations and clashes with Wilson over the League of Nations.[5]

Diplomat, international lawyer, modernist Protestant, influential layman, ecumenist—uniquely, Dulles embodied the characteristics and background best suited to advance the cause of ecumenical internationalism. It is not difficult to see why the Federal Council turned to him to lead their deliberations on the purpose of the war and the planning of the peace.

BUT DULLES was not widely known at first, at least not for his religious work, and certainly not outside the United States. Thus his participation in the Universal Christian Council for Life and Work Conference, held at Oxford in 1937, marked something of a debut on the world Protestant stage. As a lay delegate of some importance in American legal and political circles, Dulles was asked to give a nationally broadcast address about Oxford over the NBC radio network shortly before sailing for England. Henry Sloane Coffin had organized the radio talks as a way to promote a better Christian understanding of world politics, and he was hoping Dulles would be able to broaden this message beyond the avid church-going crowd. Though he lumped Soviet communism, German Nazism, and Italian Fascism together as "a false god" that had "deified" the state, Dulles pointedly did not advocate an American response, and instead called for greater sacrifice among American Christians to reduce their sins of nationalism and racial pride.[6]

In Oxford, Dulles gave this view a fuller airing. Echoing Niebuhr's call that sin could never be overcome, he told the assembled ministers, theologians, and divinity professors that war was an endemic part of the human condition. But he also believed war could one day be ended. Pacifists had erred by attempting to meet the problem of war head on, by "abolishing" or "outlawing" it through agreements like the 1928 Kellogg-Briand Pact. Dulles chided that such a quixotic approach was always bound to fail. Here, his childhood observances of his father's sermons proved helpful. "The river which periodically bursts its banks we do not hold in check by a frontal dam," he explained in a simple analogy typical of a Sunday sermon. "We go back toward the sources and canalize them so as to effect a peaceful diffusion." The solution was not to outlaw war by mere declaration, but to provide other, more productive outlets for human energy. Dulles believed that in world politics, national sovereignty functioned like a dam, artificially blocking people's aspirations and building up international tensions. So, just as he would not dam but "canalize" a river in order to tame it, he called for the dismantling of the inviolable sovereignty of nation-states. He acknowledged that the total eradication of national sovereignty was impractical and infeasible, but he urged its dilution to a level much weaker than had ever existed in the modern world. American federalism offered one possible model: after all, the United States was nothing more than a collection of previously sovereign states that had ceded some, but not all, of their autonomy to a centralized federal government. This was the worldview of an ecumenical internationalist.[7]

Overall, however, Dulles's application of religion to foreign policy was confused in the years before Pearl Harbor, and in the end only Pearl Harbor could clarify it. In part this stemmed from his attempts to fit his long-standing political views into a religious framework. He had already worked out intricate theories of foreign policy; now they were being shaped to correspond with his faith, and the result was not always coherent. He often used a Christian realist diagnosis to arrive at a liberal pacifist conclusion, and vice versa. He had a neo-orthodox appreciation of sin and a realist's grasp of the role of power in geopolitics, and he had little faith in the persuasiveness of moral authority or public opinion. Treaties were not sacrosanct, he warned: "history teaches that few treaties survive after they cease to become mutually advantageous. If they do survive, it is only because one party has such superior power that it is useless for the other to seek to extricate itself." And he was never a pacifist. Even in the period of disillusionment following the Great War, Dulles agreed with his fellow liberal Protestants that war was unchristian, but he pointedly refused to accept the conclusion that war and preparations for war were therefore "at all times and under all circumstances, evils which no Christian should at any time countenance."[8]

Yet unlike the realists, Dulles did not see the point of American belligerency until after Pearl Harbor. Though he predicted as early as October 1939 that the United States would enter the war, he felt that war was an abhorrence that should be avoided at almost any cost. "War has become so totalitarian and destructive that it is no longer tolerable," he proclaimed. "Space distances have largely lost their meaning" because "the world has been shrunk" due to "inventions of science" and "a steady increase in population and population pressures." He would go to great lengths to avoid war. In July 1939, at a meeting in Geneva with a group of European clergy, he defended appeasement and, according to one participant, "was ready to make considerable concessions" to Germany. He was hostile to Germany's aims, but he was not especially alarmed by Hitler's broken promises. Moreover, Dulles emphatically rejected Niebuhr's doctrine of the lesser evil. "I cannot believe that it is ever a Christian duty to choose that which is evil," he wrote Coffin in May 1940. "If the doctrines of Nazism are to be defeated, Christians at least should . . . try to defeat them in Christian ways and not on the theory that good will come out of evil. I have not lost faith in the power and methods which Christ taught." And he made it clear that he thought an American alliance with Britain and France would itself be an act of evil because it would mean "an effective guaranty of the British and French empires."[9]

Dulles placed Christianity at the very heart of his worldview, and thus at the center of planning for the postwar world. If peace were to be "just and durable," it would also have to be Christian, or at least based on Christian principles that could then be applied more broadly. Dulles liked to contrast the endlessly pedantic wrangling of diplomats with the goal-oriented approach and cooperative spirit of the churches, particularly ecumenical bodies. One of the reasons the Oxford Conference made such an impact upon him was his participation, shortly before Oxford, in the

Institute of Intellectual Cooperation, a Paris-based meeting held under the auspices of the League of Nations. The delegates in Paris were intellectually "barren" and "permeated with extreme nationalism." The contrast with Oxford, where people from "many nations, races, and creeds" were able to discuss their problems "frankly," was stark. To Dulles, the message was clear. While the diplomats' "self-interest" was "not to be discarded," it would only move the world forward if it was "enlightened self-interest. And if we are to be enlightened, we must have and use those qualities of mind and soul that Christ taught." Without religious faith and Christian ethics, world order would lack a moral foundation, as Nazi Germany, Fascist Italy, and the communist Soviet Union had proven. Thus Christianity could act as the "solvent of world conflict." While it was not the only spiritual force in the world, it was, said Dulles, the most widely practiced faith by the widest variety of peoples. It was a transnational force that transcended international borders and national sovereignties. If "a religion itself seeks universality, and if it seeks to spiritualize desires and inculcate a willingness to sacrifice, then it cannot fail to project more broadly the ethical solution," he wrote in his 1939 book *War, Peace and Change*. "Few religions conceive of their deity as concerned with the welfare of all mankind. Christianity has attained, at least in theory, the concept of a god whose interest is universal." Naturally, Dulles pointed to the Protestant ecumenical movement as the most universalizing force within Christianity.[10]

WHEN THE AMERICAN war began—a war he unhesitatingly and fully supported after Pearl Harbor despite his earlier doubts—Dulles stood at the crux of Protestant idealism and realism. This explains much of his appeal to a wide variety of religious constituencies and his ability to bridge the various political factions within liberal Protestantism and produce a consensus document. He was a devout Christian, a staunch internationalist, was sympathetic to neo-orthodoxy and Christian realism, but had also opposed U.S. intervention: he could work with almost anyone.

Largely at the behest of his friend and fellow Presbyterian Henry P. Van Dusen, Dulles was named head of the FCC's Commission on a Just and Durable Peace in December 1940 after presenting an outline of his worldview to the biennial meeting of the FCC. Without Dulles, the Commission would have been just another Protestant study group; with him, it became one of the most important nongovernment organizations for thinking and planning on the postwar world order. It was actually the Dulles Commission, "really a one man show" according to Van Dusen, and "a rubber stamp for John Foster Dulles' ideas." He had in fact been drafted precisely for such a role. Even though Dulles had opposed intervention, he was enough of a realist and diplomat to know that winning both the war and the peace was paramount. Van Dusen worried about the "pacifist-isolationists" who would inevitably be in "full weight" on the Commission and who could "strangle realistic discussion." Even those Commission members who had recently abandoned their pacifism, like Walter Van Kirk, could not be fully trusted. In helping to orchestrate Dulles's appointment as chair, Van Dusen hoped to neutralize the pacifists while also taking advantage of their passion for a new world order.[11]

Ever interested in foreign affairs, desperate to make an impact on the Roosevelt administration's internationalist policies, and unimpressed with other nongovernmental organizations planning for the postwar world, Dulles effectively turned the Commission into his own private think tank. He did not run it on his own; nor did he ignore the advice of his Commission colleagues. But its findings almost always reflected his own views. In turn, the FCC as a whole, which adopted almost all of the Commission's recommendations, became a forum for the promotion of Dulles's views. His lieutenant on the Commission was none other than Walter Van Kirk, the interwar peace prophet who abandoned his pacifism in 1940 so long as force was used for "establishing justice." Dulles and Van Kirk invited a wide variety of people onto the Commission, from realists to erstwhile pacifists. But Dulles was clearly in charge. Interwar pacifists Harry Emerson Fosdick—who continued to be a pacifist through the war—and Roswell P. Barnes often took part in the Commission's deliberations. Reinhold Niebuhr was also invited to join, but, busy with his own activities, only occasionally took part in the Commission's discussions.[12]

The Commission to Study the Bases of a Just and Durable Peace held its first meeting in New York in March 1941. Dulles announced that its main goal was to "arouse Christians" to their "responsibility" for world peace. More specifically, he said that the Commission would pursue two equally important objectives: first, to devise a suitable framework for a "just and durable" postwar world order that would, despite its Christian core, be applicable to all; and second, to build support among American Christians for a new, internationalist world order that would include the United States. Members of the Commission, like all American internationalists, were terrified by a possible return to isolationism after the war. This prospect also kept the latent pacifism and idealism of several Commission members in check. None had been isolationists, but many—such as Van Kirk—had been pacifists or—like Dulles himself—anti-interventionists. They saw their mission as one of drawing up an ethical, peaceful world order that was both workable and palatable to most Americans. It was a daunting task, but the churches felt up to it. A week after this first meeting, the FCC printed 450,000 copies of a handbook produced by the Commission, "A Just and Durable Peace," and distributed them throughout the country.[13]

To Dulles and his fellow FCC commissioners, an international organization that managed a system of world federalism was indispensable to a just and durable peace. Dulles had already outlined his reasons for a federated world at Oxford: only the dilution of national sovereignty could provide for a healthy flow of people, goods, and ideas across the world. Blocking these natural flows would either create pressure or stagnation; Dulles identified both as causes of war. But the unshakeable belief in international organization—indeed, in a federal world government—among liberal Protestants was also deeply rooted in their ecumenical ideology. Integration was assumed to be a means of conflict resolution because it facilitated communication and understanding. Barriers to integration, be they national or denominational, only created fear and distrust, and eventually conflict. At home, on religious matters, this was the need fulfilled by the Federal Council of Churches. It served as a neutral meeting place for disparate groups—Protestant denominations—each with their own agenda and interests. The FCC did not require denominations to forfeit all of their identities, but it did require them to sacrifice a small piece of their individual identities in the name of a common good. In U.S. domestic politics, moreover, as Dulles and fellow Commission members Richard Fagley and Justin Wroe Nixon pointed out, the relationship between the federal government and the states functioned along the same lines. Regarding world politics, the "Federal" Council's own name is telling: ecumenists argued that global anarchy would be tamed and world peace managed by a federated union of nations rather than a unitary world state. Now, with the world in crisis, it was their moment "to create a world-wide community in Jesus Christ, transcending nation, race, and class."[14]

However, when Roosevelt and Churchill issued the Atlantic Charter on August 14, 1941, Dulles and the Commission were deeply disappointed. The Charter's eight declarations of "common principles"—including national self-determination, free trade, and freedom of the seas—certainly appealed to Dulles, but they were vague and imprecise, expressions of idealistic intent rather than a detailed plan of action. They were, in Dulles's words, "tentative and incomplete." And none of them addressed what most American internationalists believed was the most important ingredient for postwar peace: a new league of nations. But at least Roosevelt was thinking internationally. Dulles's criticisms of the Atlantic Charter were therefore pointed but intended to be constructive. Published by the Commission, through the FCC, Dulles's "Long Range Peace Objectives," released a month after the Atlantic Charter, chided Roosevelt and

Churchill for their hypocrisy—though he did not use that term—of calling for measures when the "United States has in the past been a principal violator of good international practice." Great Britain, of course, was probably even worse, with its imperial possessions and preferential trading system. Dulles then criticized Roosevelt and Churchill for failing to mention international organization. World peace would only come when Americans "use our power, not to perpetuate itself, but to create, support, and eventually give way to international institutions drawing their vitality from the whole family of nations." The Atlantic Charter merely proclaimed a vague desire to return to the world as it existed before 1929, or 1933, even 1939. It was therefore not a revolutionary document but a conservative one. To Dulles, the failure to address international organization was rooted in an even greater failure to think about the fallacies of the world system as it was and had been. "It has been demonstrated, beyond doubt, that the old system of many disconnected sovereignties, each a law unto itself, inevitably breeds war," he concluded. "We must not keep humanity chained to such a wheel."[15]

Such extremes of thought were not unusual for Dulles during the war. It is interesting that while he derided plans to abolish war as unrealistic, he himself was insistent upon abolishing the system of sovereign nation-states that had prevailed for the past three centuries. While some Europeans viewed the war as a larger and more violent version of previous wars, Dulles and other Americans perceived it in millennial terms, as ushering in a totally new epoch. The war "is not just one more war in the history of the world," ran a typical wartime statement by the FCC, but instead was "bringing with it the liquidation of the old and the birth of a new world order." The Europeans found such thinking alarming, but due to U.S. power and American Protestantism's dominance of transatlantic ecumenical and missionary councils, they could do little to stand in its way. But even back in the United States, the Commission formed the vanguard of internationalist thinking. Unlikely as it was, Dulles had become a radical.[16]

In July 1942, Dulles and Van Kirk traveled together to Britain, to see the war up close and compare notes on postwar planning with their Protestant brethren in Oxford and with Cabinet ministers and government officials in London. Included on Dulles's itinerary was a meeting with Foreign Secretary Anthony Eden (it was this encounter that led Eden to dismiss Dulles as a "pontificating American"). While Van Kirk concentrated on religious matters, especially the ecumenical initiative, Dulles focused mostly on questions of war and peace. To his dismay, he found members of the Cabinet focused almost solely on winning the war against Germany; it seemed nobody had time or energy for postwar planning. Aside from victory, the British were preoccupied with maintaining their economic system of imperial preferences and protecting the integrity of the Empire itself, even though both were quickly becoming obsolete, even dangerous, in the modern world. Dulles also found it disconcerting that Britons did not appreciate the revolutionary character of the war, the "fundamental changes" that required "new planning and the birth of a new faith." Most disappointing was that he found "virtually no thinking about a revived League of Nations."[17]

At Balliol College, Oxford, Dulles and Van Kirk held meetings with British ministers and church officials, including the Archbishop of Canterbury and the Bishop of Chichester. Also present was the historian Arnold Toynbee, a deeply religious man. Dulles spoke bluntly. He said that the problems likely to emerge after the war were "insoluble except in terms of the type of spiritual approach which Christianity was able to give." But he lamented that not enough people, particularly in Britain, shared this view; he also worried that too many Europeans thought the world could return to a status quo ante after the defeat of the Nazis. If this happened, warned Dulles, "if we relapsed into the same state of mind as that of the interwar period, we should certainly lose the third world war." He then pointed to the new world order that was forming before their very eyes, whether they could see it or not: the legitimacy of colonialism was eroding, which created "the necessity of getting non-Christian assent to the proposals which we as Christians made." The ability to provide for the basic welfare of humanity was becoming easier, which made it "necessary for us to do something to raise that standard of life" in the non-Western world. Call it liberal empire or progressive imperialism, but the great powers had to begin acting out of concern for the welfare of others, and not simply dominate them. Given that he was a Republican who was close to the likely 1944 GOP presidential nominee, New York Governor Thomas Dewey, the most startling part of Dulles's appeal was his invocation of the New Deal to describe postwar planning. They needed some sort of new, regulatory order, "something like a 'new deal' . . . There was a great opportunity in the world today to raise the moral, material and spiritual standards of life in the whole world and in this there was a tremendous amount of work to be done." Pointing to the need to spread the West's prosperity more widely, Dulles closed with a progressive call to alms: "if a man became content with the world as it was, he had ceased, in fact, to be a Christian."[18]

His tour of England convinced Dulles that the world would not change—and thus would not survive, at least peacefully—without American leadership. The Soviets were too atheistic, autocratic, and economically stifled, while the British were contaminated by imperialism and exhausted by war. Only the Americans, imperfect as they were, could save the world from itself. Only the United States could bring about a truly new world order. Dulles was realistic in that he recognized the need for compromise and, if necessary, gradual reform, but he was determined that victory over Germany and Japan would also bring with it the chance to build a federal world system. Now he and the Commission on a Just and Durable Peace just had to spread the word.

THEY DID SO through the best means available to the Federal Council: publish a book, donate several hundreds of thousands of copies to churches nationwide as well as offer it for sale to the general public, and instruct member clergy to use it as the basis for their sermons on the war. Accordingly, in March 1943, before a "distinguished audience" of leaders in finance, industry, labor, religion, government, and higher education, the Commission on a Just and Durable Peace hosted a book launch on the sixty-fourth floor of Rockefeller Center's RCA Building. The book, *Six Pillars of Peace*, aimed to improve upon the generalities of the Atlantic Charter and the Four Freedoms by laying out the essential principles that would need to form the core elements of any postwar system. The first pillar, international organization, was the most important because all others would emanate from it and be managed by it. The second was more complicated: providing for economic justice by limiting the ability of states to pass domestic laws that would have global ramifications; clearly, Dulles and the Commission had the protectionist measures of the 1930s in mind. The third pillar called for political reform of the world system by making treaties more flexible to reflect changing circumstances. The fourth, fifth, and sixth pillars upheld more familiar goals of liberal Protestants: decolonization, disarmament, and the protection of individual freedoms, especially religious and intellectual liberty. Most of *Six Pillars of Peace* elaborated on these themes and linked them through the solution to them all, and Dulles's particular concern: the dilution of all national sovereignty.[19]

Six Pillars of Peace provided Dulles and the Commission with a major voice in postwar planning. The FCC's national and international reach ensured that it received attention: an initial print run sold more than eighteen thousand copies, while over a hundred regional newspapers ran feature stories on the Dulles plan. And *Six Pillars* did receive widespread attention, not merely for the prominence of its chair or the institutional strength of its sponsor but simply because it was one of the only substantive plans for U.S. postwar planning. The *New York Herald Tribune* featured an explanation of the six pillars on its front page. The *New York Times* also devoted it considerable attention and, in addition to giving it front-page coverage and printing an article by Dulles, published favorable assessments by Harry Emerson Fosdick; Minnesota Senator Joseph Ball, a Republican internationalist and leading proponent of international organization; Under Secretary of State Sumner Welles, the Roosevelt adminis-tration's leading advocate for world government; and New York Governor Thomas E. Dewey. *The Times* of London, the quasi-official newspaper of the British establishment, prominently featured *Six Pillars. Time* reported that Dulles had devised a plan for "American participation in an interna-tional alliance of all nations to preserve the postwar peace" and printed abridged versions of each of the six pillars. As the British Embassy in Washington, which tracked Dulles and the Commission closely through-out the war, reported to London, the "influence of the crusade begun by the Protestant churches, inspired by John Foster Dulles . . . is not to be underestimated."[20]

In political terms as well, *Six Pillars of Peace* catapulted the Commis-sion on a Just and Durable Peace into an important role. Dulles himself was an emerging political player, a longtime Republican with close per-sonal and political ties to Thomas Dewey. But Dulles's political ties and ambitions, either to run for office himself or to become Dewey's secretary of state, proved both a blessing and a curse for the Commission: Dulles's stature and the success of *Six Pillars* ensured it would receive a hearing from the Roosevelt administration, but it also meant that the Democrats in the White House and State Department would instinctively distrust Dulles and his motives. Still, Dulles worked with the Roosevelt adminis-tration as closely as he could. Welles had acted as an unofficial consultant to the Commission during the writing of *Six Pillars*. A week after the lav-ish Rockefeller Center book launch, President Roosevelt himself met with Dulles, Reverend Barnes, and Henry St. George Tucker, the president of the Federal Council and presiding bishop of the Episcopal Church, to discuss postwar planning. Roosevelt agreed with the six pillars in general but reminded them of the need to be realistic. He was a firm believer in the need for some form of postwar international cooperation, but he feared repeating Wilson's fatal mistake: a refusal to compromise on the specific workings of the system, both with domestic critics and interna-tional leaders.[21]

Next came several meetings between Dulles and either Roosevelt or Secretary of State Cordell Hull. In their Oval Office meeting, FDR and Dulles had agreed upon the need to be realistic in order to compromise. But it soon became clear that the president was acting much too realisti-cally for the Commission on a Just and Durable Peace, and not neces-sarily as a way to facilitate compromise. In November 1943, the United States, Britain, the Soviet Union, and Nationalist China issued the Mos-cow Declaration, which vowed that Grand Alliance cooperation would continue after the war in the name of keeping the peace. Just as important for American internationalists, the Declaration also marked the first time the Allies jointly pledged to establish a permanent international organization to maintain peace. Dulles publicly supported the Moscow Declaration's call for a permanent United Nations, which had been established earlier in 1943 as a way to manage wartime relief efforts, but privately he seethed at the Declaration's blatant reliance on traditional great power politics. In particular, Dulles bridled at the great powers' insistence that postwar peace would be "based on the principle of the sovereign equality of all peace-loving states" and that they would "consult with one another and as occasion requires with other members of the United Nations, with a view to joint action on behalf of the community of nations." In January 1944, the Commission issued a statement of reservations about the Moscow Declaration; a month later, Dulles gave a speech criticizing the administration's plans for the "perpetuation of any given status quo" as "wholly unrealistic." This earned Dulles and Tucker another invitation to the White House, where Roosevelt tried to mollify them, with little success. They urged FDR instead to seek a peace that was "curative and creative," not simply reactive. To keep up the pressure, the Commission orchestrated a petition, signed by 1,251 prominent clergy and laypeople, calling for the immediate establishment of a permanent United Nations Council to begin preparing for peace.[22]

DULLES WAS BECOMING a problem for Roosevelt: 1944 was a presidential election year, and FDR planned to run for an unprecedented fourth term. Not everyone was pleased with this, including some Democrats. As the popular governor of a populous state, Dewey was the presumed GOP nominee, and he stood a good chance of upsetting Roosevelt. Dulles had to tread a fine line between his nonpartisan role on the Commission and his political commitments to Dewey, which by April 1944 included drafting Dewey's foreign policy speeches. Unsurprisingly, the Roosevelt administration perceived Dulles's critique of its policies not merely as a contribution to the debate on postwar planning but as a real political threat at the beginning of what was going to be a long and fiercely contested presidential election campaign. In August, after wrapping up the Republican nomination, Dewey attacked Roosevelt's diplomacy on precisely the grounds Dulles and the Commission had criticized the Moscow Declaration—as a sordid sellout to the kind of great power politics at which the British and Soviets excelled. This was no coincidence: Dulles had helped Dewey write the speech. Hull lamented that Dewey's speech "suddenly shattered" the bipartisan spirit that had thus far underpinned postwar planning.[23]

Duly alarmed, Roosevelt sent Secretary of State Hull to deal with these troublesome Republicans. Hull was ideally placed to settle the dispute, and in Roosevelt's favor, for he had earned a reputation in Washington as a practitioner of bipartisan foreign policy. For Hull, more than most others, politics truly did stop at the water's edge, but he was not naïve enough to assume that domestic politics always was kept out of foreign affairs—hence his role as an intermediary between Roosevelt and Dewey. Dewey would not meet with Hull, which would have made him look like FDR's supplicant rather than his equal. In his place as Hull's interlocutor, Dewey sent the one man he could trust on foreign policy as well as politics: Dulles. Dulles, of course, was not only temperamentally stubborn but also an international lawyer with vast experience in the art of the deal. Hull and Dulles entered into several days of difficult negotiations; one afternoon was devoted to a tedious argument over the meaning of the words "bipartisan" and "nonpartisan," with an exasperated Hull at one point brandishing a dictionary. "I had hoped that we would agree within a few hours," Dulles said of the negotiations. "Actually, we had three days of almost continuous conference. The Secretary seemed to me very stubborn. Perhaps I seemed that way to him."[24]

In the end, they agreed to keep discussions of postwar planning "nonpartisan"—that is, completely out of politics, as opposed to the "bipartisanship" of two parties actively working together—for the duration of the campaign. Dulles may have been a shrewd negotiator, but Hull realized he had the upper hand. Dulles had been working for a postwar international organization, and hopefully a world federation, for four years, and would not do anything to jeopardize its fulfillment. "I emphasized to Dulles that Governor Dewey was in a position where he might destroy the movement under way to get a postwar security organization," Hull told Dulles, who of course was leading that very movement. "I added that Dulles had a real opportunity to help put over this project which meant so much to mankind." Or as Assistant Secretary of State Breckenridge Long commented, without Dewey's approval there would be no Senate approval, and "without that approval and *our* cooperation *this* time there will be *no* World Organization and we might as well get ready for World War III and the end." It was a masterstroke, but Hull did not gloat. A month later, at the conclusion of the Dumbarton Oaks conference in Washington that began constructing the United Nations Organization, he ensured that Dewey and Dulles were kept fully informed.[25]

Hull had won a major victory for internationalism, for he not only neutralized Dewey over the issue, he had also cornered Dulles and the Commission on a Just and Durable Peace into supporting the Roosevelt administration's postwar planning. This was significant because the peace planning at Dumbarton Oaks—with a permanent Security Council consisting of five great powers and an international police force to ensure the maintenance of peace—strikingly resembled the Moscow Declaration. Yet the Commission meekly issued a statement urging Americans to support Dumbarton Oaks. "There must be world organization," it declared.

Without it, the "underlying causes of war," such as the "quest for power, economic and political maladjustment, exploitation in colonial relationships, racial discrimination and the denial . . . of spiritual and intellectual freedoms" would not ease. The Commission came to terms with the use of force to maintain peace. It was only after Roosevelt's victory in the November election that Dulles felt free to attack Dumbarton Oaks as only a "beginning" to postwar planning because it "partakes too much of a military alliance."[26]

ONE PART OF the Commission on a Just and Durable Peace's mandate was to contribute specific proposals, grounded in Christian ethics, to the national debate on the structure of postwar peace. But the other part, equally important, was for Commission members to help build support for international organization among the American people, especially in the Protestant churches. And at this, they were wildly successful. There was already support, but there was also much opposition, and even much of the support was neither deep nor committed. Partly in response to the urgings of the FCC and the Commission, partly out of their own fervency for global cooperation, the Protestant churches mobilized themselves behind plans for a just and durable peace based upon a new world order.

As always, the liberal Protestant churches were boisterous in their support for a permanent United Nations. As early as January 1942, the ministers of the famous Old South Church in Boston and the Fourth Presbyterian Church of New York called for a "Superstate of Free Peoples" and a "World Brotherhood in God." Appeals to racial and religious tolerance were by now ritualistic for most liberals, but between 1943 and 1945 they mustered the old enthusiasm for an equitable world order one more time. National bodies, such as the General Assembly of the Presbyterian Church, endorsed world security through racial tolerance. Central to this message was the need to extend Christian love not just to allies but former enemies; also central was the old missionary paternalism that was strongly progressive as well. Anything less would ensure a new world war. "As we form our attitudes toward the other nations of the earth," preached a Congregationalist in Connecticut, "it will not be enough to ask, 'Will this step be good for the United States?' We must also ask, 'Will it be good for our brethren? Will it be good for England and France, for Russia and China? Yes, will it be good for Italy and Germany and Japan? Will it be good for India and Africa and all the other little people who are now exploited and oppressed?' " The worry was not over the need for a progressive international organization. It was, said a United Methodist bishop, that there "are too many people who are talking about a new world order after the war but are not willing to make any sacrifice to obtain" it.[27]

In the last two years of the war, liberal Protestant churches and inter-denominational organizations mobilized as one in support of collective security and resource sharing under the management of a world government. In terms of funding and organization, their efforts in World War II dwarfed even those during the Great War. With Sumner Welles featured as the keynote speaker, in October 1943 over five thousand Protestants gathered at New York's Episcopal Cathedral of St. John the Divine to launch the Christian Mission on World Order. This three-week campaign, devoted entirely to promoting *Six Pillars of Peace*, toured 102 cities and led to the observance of World Order Sunday by thousands of churches nationwide. World Order Sunday even attracted the support of the Southern Presbyterians, normally the careful guardians of denominational and national sovereignty.[28]

Encouraged by the results, individual denominations joined in with their own missions. Under the energetic leadership of Bishop G. Bromley Oxnam, a key Dulles ally and frequent collaborator with the Commission, the Methodists mounted a "Crusade for a New World Order" in January 1944. Every Methodist church in America was encouraged to write their local congressman and plead for a postwar united nations. This was no small undertaking, but the Methodists were confident they could pull it off; they had, after all, done something similar in leading the temperance campaign and could call upon the energies of over 8,000,000 members in 41,000 churches. According to the historian Robert Divine, Oxnam's Crusade achieved "spectacular results" that included "one of the largest outpourings of mail in [the] history" of Congress. The Northern Baptist Convention followed with its own World Order Crusade, designed to build support for "a world organization in which every nation is invited to participate" and "which will face realistically all problems that relate to human well-being." After the Baptists came the Congregational Church with its World Order Compact, built on the pro–world government conclusions of its in-house study group, the Council for Social Action, and modeled on the Mayflower Compact of 1620.[29]

Of course, interdenominational and ecumenical groups joined in as well. The Federal Council sponsored World Order Day, to be held on November 12, 1944. Using St. Paul's epistle to the Ephesians admonishing Christians to wield the sword of the spirit and don the shield of faith, the FCC called upon its 150,000 member churches to "unite their forces in a common effort to win the peace" based upon "a world settlement consistent with Christian principles." Other groups followed suit. The United Council of Church Women began campaigning for "world community" in 1944, while the World Council of Churches acted as a broker for world government from its wartime headquarters in Switzerland.[30]

But the most important thing about this new peace crusade was that this time others joined in. Indeed, if there was ever a consensus moment in American religious politics, it was over the need for a federal world order. Vice President Henry A. Wallace, a Social Gospeler by temperament and upbringing, supported an explicitly faith-based internationalism as the path to world peace. More surprising were Southern Protestants, who normally defended the principles of identity and autonomy but were just as enthusiastic about world order as liberal Northerners like Wallace. In the spring of 1944, John W. Frazer, pastor of the First Methodist Church of Opelika, Alabama, even established a new organization to further the cause. His proposed group, the Southern Council of Churchmen, would build local support "in setting up a Post War World built upon the Atlantic Charter and other principles of International justice." "Does a Persons Race Preclude Membership?" asked an SCC promotional flyer. "No!" The SCC quickly added members from across the Deep South, earning rare regional praise as politically active civic-minded ministers. Decades later, Southerners would turn angrily against politically minded ministers who marched against Jim Crow, but this time the confluence of national and international progressivisms led many to support racial tolerance. It seemed that the only thing distinctively Southern about the SCC's manifesto was its vehement rejection of pacifism.[31]

Distrust of pacifism aside, it is striking that many Protestant clergy from Jim Crow states were unequivocal in calling for a global peace based on religious—and racial—tolerance. "As we struggle against racial hatreds, poverty and disease," said the Fellowship of Southern Churchmen, "we prepare in the sorrow of the present a bulwark of faith for the world of the future." While the Southern Baptist Convention, assembled for its annual conference in Atlanta in 1944, disavowed any official role in peace planning so as not to violate the separation of church and state, it passed a world peace platform nonetheless. Given segregation's grip on Southern society, the result was astonishing. To the Southern Baptists, Christ's command to "love thy neighbor as thyself" was a clear "condemnation of the policy of isolation on the part of any nation. No nation is justified in seeking to separate itself from the rest of the world," proclaimed the habitually separatist Baptists. "We are inevitably members of one another." They called for an international organization with economic sanctions and police power at its disposal to enforce the peace, and they called for national self-determination and decolonization. But then the Southern Baptists went further still:

> Believing in the worth of every individual, we deplore race prejudices and hatreds as undermining the respect to which every individual is entitled, and as destroying the spirit of good will, which must be the

foundation of enduring peace. This is true whether we consider racial tensions in our nation or in international relationships.

Elsewhere, Southern ministers made appeals to a world order based on economic justice that harked back to the South's Populist glory days. "Let me be specific," wrote Reverend Lawrence Lay of Britton, Oklahoma, in response to a survey by another FCC commission. "I will attempt it by stating a specific core from which may radiate a thousand specific principles for which Christians can and must fight to the last ditch or all is lost. All the natural resources of this earth belong to all the people of the earth."[32]

Catholics were also strong proponents of the United Nations. Pope Pius XII had issued his own program, Six Conditions of a Just Peace, which dovetailed with both the Atlantic Charter and the FCC's *Six Pillars*. The Holy See and the White House had had their differences over wartime strategy, and they would have more during the Cold War. But on the need for the United Nations, they were of one mind. With Washington and the Vatican in agreement, the National Catholic Welfare Conference issued the Bishops' Statement on International Order, a strongly internationalist document. But even before, American Catholics, led by John Ryan and the Catholic Association for International Peace, had spent the war calling for the establishment of a just peace based on international organization and multilateral cooperation. Moreover, for social justice Catholics the pursuit of a more equitable and peaceful international order was an integral part of improving American society at home, especially on industrial and racial questions. In 1945, both the Catholic Association for International Peace and the National Catholic Welfare Conference would send high-powered delegations to the UN Conference in San Francisco, where they made important contributions to the codification of international law and a balancing between individual political rights and group social and economic rights.[33]

As staunch progressives and internationalists, and as charter members of Roosevelt's New Deal coalition, Jews were natural proponents of the United Nations as well. As the victims of Russian and German aggression during the past half century, they were also apt to support an organization that would curtail the sovereignty and power of tyrannies and keep their ambitions in check. But Zionism complicated matters. The desire to build a Jewish homeland reflected a very old-fashioned type of nationalism that ran counter to the "one world" internationalist visions of the UN's supporters. In the future, who would need nationalism in a world of diluted sovereignty and global governance? Not coincidentally, Jews who opposed Zionism proved to be some of the UN's most impassioned supporters. Rabbi Louis Finkelstein, president of the Jewish Theological Seminary in New York, was one of the leading voices of Conservative Judaism and a long-standing opponent of Zionism. When he looked at the causes of the war, he saw the specter of aggressive nationalism; when he peered into a future of peace, he saw only the bonds of universal tolerance. "The creation of an enduring peace presupposes an active cooperative relationship among nations and peoples, which makes the question of statehood less and less relevant," he wrote in 1943. On the other hand, "emphasis on national sovereignty anywhere must be fatal to civilization." Jews, including Zionists, overwhelmingly supported the creation of a permanent United Nations, but already the question of statehood in Palestine was complicating the postwar world.[34]

Thus the desire for international peace managed by the United Nations was, at least among religious Americans, nearly universal: not just interdenominational, but interfaith. In October 1943, hundreds of leaders from all of America's major faiths signed an "Interfaith Declaration on World Peace" that promoted the new internationalism. "For the first time in our history," wrote one of the declaration's key authors, Episcopal Bishop of Albany George Ashton Oldham, to President Roosevelt, "we have secured the collaboration of not only Protestants and Jews, but of leading members of the Hierarchy of the Roman Catholic Church." He did not exaggerate. Though serious Protestant-Catholic tensions would survive the war and continue into the postwar era, there was active collaboration for world order among Protestants, Catholics, and Jews. As evidence, Oldham sent FDR a seven-point plan for world peace signed by leading figures from all three faiths. Led by Roosevelt and his promotion of interfaith tolerance, the war marked a coming of age for American civil religion, and nearly everyone espoused the same message of global tolerance and pluralistic harmony.[35]

NEARLY EVERYONE, that is, but not quite everyone. Evangelicals and Southern Baptists, most Catholics and Jews, and of course mainline Protestants were now all staunch internationalists. But Protestant fundamentalists and conservative evangelicals could not bring themselves to support the construction of a regulatory global state that would herald the birth of a new world order. True to their theology, premillennial dispensationalists claimed that postwar planning was futile because the end times were approaching. Indeed, proclaimed M. G. Hatcher, a fundamentalist Baptist preacher from Muscatine, Iowa, "Scripture does prophecy" the establishment of world government, which "will make it possible for the World Dictator, the Anti-Christ, to take over control." The wartime United Nations was thus the first step in creating "a reign of suffering and terror as the world has never known." The logic of premillennialism was not entirely consistent—if world government would hasten the end times, and with them the Second Coming of Christ and the salvation of the faithful, why not encourage it?—but this did nothing to allay Christian conservatives' fears of international organization.[36]

Moreover, conservative anti-statism, based upon reflexive fears of regulation and government interference with matters that rightfully belonged to the family and the church, surged whenever people spoke of a federated world order. To many conservatives, a United Nations probably meant world government, and world government would mean foreign interference in American life. William L. Blessing, a self-styled savior of true Christianity from Denver, equated the "God-denying, Christ-rejecting, Holy Ghost–blaspheming, Bible-hating atheistic" Federal Council of Churches with the "anti-Christ world order" of a postwar international organization. Gerald Smith, an extremist preacher and sometime fringe candidate for president, mounted a protest against the planned "superstate" and "world police force" that would take away the liberties of ordinary Americans. Dan Gilbert, a Congregational fundamentalist, accused Dulles of "wiping out of the independence and sovereignty of nations" and planning a "scheme for world-wide socialism." Gilbert also equated the evils of the UN with those of the FCC. Just as the Federal Council "makes itself the mouthpiece for almost every secular and religious group," so too would the United Nations include every voice on every issue from all over the world, no matter how blasphemous or sinful. The FCC's superstructure simply ignored "the great company of millions of Bible-believers who are denominationally tied to its organization," robbing them of their voice and their autonomy. This, Gilbert charged, was just what the UN would do to Americans.[37]

BUT EVEN SOME LIBERAL PROTESTANTS—those who had adopted neo-orthodoxy—could see the wisdom of such logic. H. Richard Niebuhr, Reinhold's brother and professor of Christian Ethics at Yale Divinity School, was one of the leading architects of Christian realism and neo-orthodox theology in the United States, and his belief in original sin and humanity's innate capacity for evil made him skeptical that a world state was the best thing for peace. "Perhaps you took for granted that world government would be responsible and limited government, but these things must not be taken for granted," he warned Richard Fagley of the Commission on a Just and Durable Peace shortly after the war. "Better to die than to submit to tyranny—that motto applies to world government as well as to any other." Niebuhr agreed upon the need for the United Nations, but one that was constrained by its members, just as the U.S. government was kept in check by its reliance upon the consent of the governed. Dulles could safely ignore the fundamentalists' fears; Richard Niebuhr's hit closer to home, and he knew he would have to address it sooner or later.[38]

Older brother Reinhold's contribution to the debate on world order was more constructive because it was more amenable to the idea of international organization. With other realists, such as Henry Van Dusen, John C. Bennett, and Paul Tillich, Niebuhr cooperated with Dulles and the Commission and attended many of its meetings. He also shared Dulles's concerns about Dumbarton Oaks. In keeping with his realism, Niebuhr did not believe that international organization could eliminate war; he doubted it could even eliminate the competitive nature of states. Like all realists, Christian or otherwise, Niebuhr believed the international system was inherently, irredeemably anarchic. Only a world state, an international leviathan, could bring it under control, but this was unwise and even dangerous because to be effective it would have to wield absolute, dictatorial authority. Yet Niebuhr also agreed that international organization was necessary for the maintenance of peace and that any postwar settlement would need to be based in large part upon the establishment of an international confederation. For Niebuhr, as for Dulles and the ecumenists in general, the shrinkage of the world due to modern weapons technology had made war too dangerous, and potentially apocalyptic, to continue unregulated by the international community. But the rise of American power and the nature of the world system meant that the responsibility of establishing a new world order rested with the United States. "There is a fateful significance," Niebuhr wrote in 1943 in an article that called attention to the Dulles Commission's efforts,

> in the fact that America's coming of age coincides with that period of world history when the paramount problem is the creation of some kind of world community. The world must find a way of avoiding complete anarchy in its international life; and America must find a way of using its great power responsibly.

The most "urgent problem" facing the world was "the establishment of a tolerable system of mutual security" that would "avoid both a tyrannical unification of the world and the alternative anarchy," but such a system would be possible only "if each nation is ready to make commitments, commensurate with its power." The stakes could not be higher. "If America fails to do this, the world is lost for decades to come," Niebuhr concluded. "America must not fail."[39]

Niebuhr complemented Dulles's work by popularizing world order beyond the leadership circles of the ecumenical movement. Dulles may have had access to the corridors of power in Washington and New York, but Niebuhr was a public intellectual of international scope who wrote not only in religious periodicals but national newsmagazines. During the war, Niebuhr used *Christianity and Crisis* as a platform for international organization. The editors proclaimed they were "committed to the real-ization of a community of nations founded in justice," and their articles continually promoted the establishment of a postwar international orga-nization. Perhaps uniquely among major periodicals, the magazine also linked the guiding premises of ecumenism to a framework of collective security. Yet, ever the realist, Niebuhr warned against the American "ten-dency to oscillate between utopianism and disillusionment" that would result from a demand for "a world state or nothing." While international organization might be necessary, its powers would have to be limited to account, to some extent, for national priorities and the inevitability of power politics. Thus Niebuhr's overall contribution to the cause of ecu-menical internationalism was to merge it with the realities of power by making it less innately pacific and more beholden to American leadership. As he argued toward the end of the war, a "global civilization requires a collective and mutual defense." In a word, ecumenical internationalism was becoming realistic.[40]

As THE WAR drew to a close, and as the Allies planned to meet in San Francisco to transform the United Nations from a wartime alliance to an organization for the maintenance of postwar peace, Dulles and the Com-mission hoped to play a part in framing the American approach to world order. But thanks to his ties to the Republican Party, it was unlikely that the Roosevelt administration would consult Dulles. The State Depart-ment suspected him as the source of damaging leaks during the cam-paign and were reluctant to entrust him with a role in San Francisco. But Roosevelt was also determined to avoid what everyone acknowledged had been one of Woodrow Wilson's signature errors in 1919—a lack of bipartisanship—and sought Republican participation to prevent politics from sabotaging the conference. And so, also thanks to his ties to the Republican Party, especially to Michigan Senator Arthur Vandenberg, the party's leading voice on foreign affairs, Dulles was invited to join the U.S. delegation. Vandenberg, who had drafted the GOP's foreign pol-icy platform for the 1944 National Convention, was "greatly impressed" by Dulles's advice and negotiations with Hull, and found him "totally trust-worthy." A formerly hard-core isolationist who had converted to a cautious internationalism during the war, Vandenberg wanted to be on hand to ensure that the president signed a treaty that all Americans, conservatives included, could support. The historical irony was rich, and would not have been lost on Dulles: his "Uncle Bert," Robert Lansing, had raised precisely these concerns twenty-six years earlier.[41]

Though it would turn out to be a temporary departure, Dulles resigned from the Commission on a Just and Durable Peace and made his way to San Francisco. "The Conference will need Christian prayers and the guidance of Christian judgment," he wrote Van Kirk. To further this lofty goal, he wrote a prayer to the other members of the U.S. delegation "that the movement toward world organization shall be advanced . . . in such a way as to invoke the moral and creative forces of mankind and not rely on repressive force." Christianity did in fact play a role, though thanks less to Dulles and more to the great powers' revolutionary decision to admit nongovernmental organizations to provide expert testimony and advice. This opened the door to many NGOs, though none had the Federal Council of Churches' national and international scope or massive membership (approximately twenty-five million). The Commission was invited to attend, along with other FCC bodies. Most important was the role played by O. Frederick Nolde of the Joint Committee on Religious Liberty, a body set up by the FCC and the Foreign Missions Conference. Nolde was tasked with pushing for the inclusion of explicit human rights provisions in the UN Charter, specifically religious liberty, which, he argued, "affects all other human rights." This was a crucial fact neglected by other NGOs. "Unless man can move and speak and act in accordance with the dictates of his conscience, limited only by the well-being of his neighbor, he has no freedom," Nolde explained. As the source of conscience, religious liberty therefore held "a primary place among all human rights."[42]

Yet things did not quite turn out the way Dulles envisioned. His ecumenical internationalism rose and fell with the war itself, soaring and then peaking with American entry in 1941 and victory in 1945. With the end of the war in Europe, around the time of his departure for San Francisco, the specter of Nazism disappeared. Ominously, a new specter was emerging that would haunt Dulles for the rest of his life and completely twist his worldview.

For Dulles, Soviet communism had always been an evil at least as great as Nazism, and much greater than fascism. Its looming presence at San Francisco, not to mention in Eastern Europe, led him to recommend modifications that diluted the powers of the United Nations. The issue at hand centered on whether the members of the UN legally had the right to withdraw from the organization—a secessionist clause. Normally, Dulles would have summarily dismissed the very concept of withdrawal; as secession had once threatened the Union, it would just as surely undermine the UN. But now, faced with what seemed to be Stalin's betrayals of promises made at the Yalta Conference to respect Polish independence after the war, Dulles told Vandenberg that the United States "*must* have a withdrawal clause." Dulles had previously been unconvinced, but "he has now come to the conclusion that it must be made specific. We dealt in blunt, plain realism," Vandenberg confided to his diary that night. "Since coming to Frisco, our relations with Russia have worsened all over the world (as well as here). Russian pledges at Yalta are being everywhere defied. Yet we are proposing to enter a Peace Partnership with her based upon mutual faith—and she is getting a 'veto' . . . upon our freedom of action all round the globe to a substantial degree." Alarmed by the prospect of American interests being tethered to a Soviet-driven agenda at the UN, Dulles drafted a withdrawal clause.[43]

This must have been a painful moment for Dulles, who had worked tirelessly for an organization like the United Nations for the past five years. Now, at what should have been his moment of triumph, he was instead determined to shorten its reach. "Dulles said he has been reluctantly driven to the conclusion," Vandenberg wrote, "that America cannot enter such an arrangement without a definite right of withdrawal because we cannot foresee the future." But Dulles *had* foreseen the future: during the war, he prophesied a world flourishing in a just and durable peace; now, he foresaw a new apocalypse if atheistic, materialistic, autocratic, militaristic communism was not stopped. America—Dulles—had made the mistake of appeasing evil once. It must not do so again.[44]

Another specter appeared alongside the Soviets, though, and it too led Dulles to distort his commitment to one world: the Democrats. As his most perceptive biographer has shown, Dulles's work with Dewey awakened within him a previously dormant instinct for political partisanship. His closeness to Dewey and Vandenberg led most political observers to assume that Dulles would become the next secretary of state if the GOP captured the White House in 1944 or 1948. And while Dulles may have been a devoted internationalist, not everyone in the Republican Party was. Even those who had recently converted to the cause, like Vandenberg, still retained the conservative impulse to protect American sovereignty even as it moved to become a full member of the global community. At San Francisco, Dulles was not merely a member of the U.S. delegation—he was a member of Vandenberg's Republican cohort, there to advise the senator and other Republicans on how best to build the UN without violating American autonomy or sovereignty.[45]

Initially, Dulles tried to stick to his internationalist principles, but each time they ran up against the hard realities of international and domestic politics. For example, he defended regional security arrangements, such as the Monroe Doctrine and the Inter-American System, even though they undermined the universalism that should have provided the UN's very foundation. He also said that while he favored the unlimited "compulsory jurisdiction" of the World Court in theory and was confident that international law would evolve to a point where all cases would automatically come before the World Court, he opposed it in practice and felt it should not be codified in the UN Charter.[46]

More startling were his efforts to remove matters of purely "domestic jurisdiction" from the UN mandate, which would allow countries to violate human rights domestically so long as the consequences did not spill beyond their borders. In 1944, as head of the Commission, he had vigorously opposed "domestic jurisdiction," but in 1945, as a member of the GOP, he supported it. Interestingly, in one of his first meetings with the U.S. delegation in San Francisco, Dulles "objected" to removing domestic jurisdiction because it was "a contradiction in terms to say that a matter which threatened the peace of the world was solely a matter of 'domestic jurisdiction.' How could that be?" Vandenberg coolly explained that "without it there would be no possibility of getting the Charter approved by the United States Senate." From then on, Dulles was a staunch supporter of domestic jurisdiction. And yet its recognition would not only ensure the UN Charter's passage by an otherwise skeptical U.S. Senate, it would also have the unfortunate effect of protecting the Jim Crow South from international law and American industry from international labor standards, though these were not Dulles's motives. Perhaps it was pure politics; perhaps it was the fear of communism; or perhaps it was the ghost of Robert Lansing reminding his nephew that Wilson had failed by a refusal to compromise. But for a man who had campaigned for international organization first and foremost upon the belief that national sovereignty was the main cause of international conflict and war, it was a shocking defection from principle.[47]

Nonetheless, despite such compromises, the assembled delegates in San Francisco established the United Nations, and with it the political framework for a world community that was based on consensus and voluntary membership rather than imperial coercion. It was a momentous occasion. "If it were not for the churches of this country," Dulles reflected with evident pride in 1947, "there probably would not be a United Nations today." This extravagant claim obviously goes too far, but Dulles's pride was not entirely without justification. The publicity generated by the Commission on a Just and Durable Peace was an invaluable tool for educating both the public and elites about world order. The various FCC conferences, books, sermons, and pamphlets had spread the message to an audience wider than any other. Church and missionary links between the United States and the rest of the world ensured a symmetry of views that transcended national borders. Most important was the effect on the American people, whose support was crucial and who had absorbed the message of ecumenical internationalism. A 1941 Gallup poll listed "international federation" and "reform based on toleration and Christian principles" as the two most popular solutions to the problem of war. Thanks in large part to the FCC, by April 1945 some polls recorded 90 percent approval ratings for the establishment of a permanent United Nations. The difference between

1945 and 1919 was dramatic, and much of it had to do with the organizational effort of the churches. Rather than presenting arms or calling for peace at any price, they prepared the way for a new world order. The triumph of "anti-isolationist opinion" in America, observed the British Embassy, was due to the efforts of two groups of people: congressional internationalists, especially in the Senate; and "Dulles's influential conference of various churchmen's and Wilsonian organizations, which led to defeat of the extreme anti-imperialist and near-isolationist positions of the *Christian Century* group."[48]

The Commission on a Just and Durable Peace attended the San Francisco Conference and, like other NGOs, was invited to submit proposals. It, along with Nolde's Joint Committee on Religious Liberty, proposed nine items for inclusion into the UN Charter, of which four—a statement of moral aims; the codification of international law; a commitment to decolonization through trusteeship; and a declaration of fundamental human rights—were accepted. The Commission was not the only body to propose such measures, of course, but it was among the most adept. Rarely had religious lobbying been so effective, or so consequential.[49]

PART VII

The Cold War and the Fourth Crusade

The White House, Washington, D.C., August 1947. Wherever President Harry Truman surveyed the world scene, he saw communism on the march. In eastern Europe, occupied by the Red Army, the Soviet Union had spent the previous two years installing pliant communist governments. In Iran and Turkey, the Soviets had demanded access to strategically vital shipping lanes and oil fields. From the Kremlin, Stalin had declared that capitalism and communism could not peacefully coexist and had even predicted the outbreak of a third world war. In China, Mao Zedong and the Communist Party kept up their relentless advance against Chiang Kai-shek and the Nationalists. Even in Vietnam, the French were finding it difficult to suppress an anticolonial uprising led by an obscure communist revolutionary named Ho Chi Minh. If the United States was to avoid getting dragged into another major European war, if it was to prevent the emergence of an anarchic world that would give rise to new threats, then Truman and his advisers were sure they had to act. U.S. foreign policy had stumbled along uncertainly in the immediate postwar period, lurching from anticommunist belligerence to a willingness to negotiate. But now, in the summer of 1947, convinced that the United States must assert some control over an increasingly hostile world, Truman put the United States on the offensive.

By August, the most important parts of Truman's new Cold War strategy, known as containment for its intention to stop the spread of communism, were already in place. In March, in the Truman Doctrine, he had announced American aid to Greece and Turkey, who were then fighting communist movements of their own. In June, Secretary of State George C. Marshall announced the creation of the European Recovery Program, better known as the Marshall Plan, which delivered billions of dollars of unconditional financial aid to help Europe rebuild from World War II. And in July, Truman signed the National Security Act, which established the Department of Defense, the Joint Chiefs of Staff, the Central Intelligence Agency, and the National Security Council—and with them, a national security state that could compete with the Soviets on something

411

close to a permanent wartime footing. Politically, diplomatically, ideologically, economically, and militarily, the Truman administration was ready to do battle with communism.

Yet something was missing. Economic power and military might were considered necessary, and they played to certain American strengths. But to Truman, what ultimately distinguished the United States from the Soviet Union was not prosperity or power, but their political systems, in particular their differing attitudes toward individual freedom. And the key difference between Americans and Soviets, he concluded, the one thing that neither system could claim in common with the other, was religious faith. Truman, like Franklin Roosevelt before him, saw religion as a source of democracy because it protected freedom of conscience, and thus the individual's autonomy from the state. The Soviets, avowedly atheist and materialist, rejected faith completely. Both sides of the Cold War claimed to want peace, progress, and prosperity for the world. But only one side could claim God.

And so to politics, diplomacy, economics, and military power, Truman added religion. It was, he believed, the missing element in U.S. foreign policy, and potentially its secret weapon. When "the sages and the scientists, the economists and the statesmen have exhausted their resources in the search for peace and security in this troubled world," he explained, "one solution and only one solution will remain—the substitution of conscience for force in the government of man. The alternative is the annihilation of civilization. . . . Religion alone has the answer to humanity's twentieth century cry of despair."[1]

To wage this spiritual Cold War, Truman hoped to rally the forces of world religion—not just Protestants, not even just Christians and Jews, but all people of faith. That August, he and his advisers drafted a letter to one of the unquestioned leaders of global faith, Pope Pius XII. Pius was not only the head of the Roman Catholic Church with influential protégés in America—not least Francis Cardinal Spellman—he was also an ardent anticommunist himself. (Two years later, in 1949, the pontiff threatened to excommunicate any Catholic who belonged to or aided the Communist Party.) He was, in short, an ideal partner to demonstrate the ecumenical vitality of the religious forces arrayed against communism. "I believe that the greatest need of the world today, fundamental to all else, is a renewal of faith," the president wrote to the pope. "I seek to encourage renewed faith in the dignity and worth of the human person in all lands, to the end that the individual's sacred rights, inherent in his relationship to God and his fellows, will be respected in every land." Truman then professed "with heartfelt conviction" his belief that "those who do not recognize their responsibility to Almighty God cannot meet their full duty toward their fellow men." Later that month, Pius responded warmly to Truman's overture. The foundations of "a lasting peace among nations," he agreed, "can be secure only if they rest on bedrock faith in the One, True God, the Creator of all men." Was Truman "over-sanguine in hoping to find men throughout the world ready to cooperate for such a worthy enterprise?" the pope asked rhetorically. "We think not."[2]

Thus began Truman's quest to unite the forces of faith against the threat of "godless" communism. To make it happen, he renewed and expanded the otherwise completed wartime mission of Myron C. Taylor, presidential envoy to the Holy See. Roosevelt had toyed with the idea of assembling a religious front against Nazism, but he abandoned the idea and instead concentrated on Taylor's diplomacy with the Vatican. Now, in the midst of a global Cold War, Truman revived Roosevelt's plan and charged Taylor with putting it together. Truman and Taylor were both devout Protestants who shared a deep commitment to basic interfaith tolerance. Both saw communism as an ultimate menace to faith and democracy, and both envisioned world religion as the antidote to the poison of communism. At first, Truman wanted Taylor to form an anticommunist alliance with only the Vatican, but he quickly expanded the mission to include all the religious forces of the world with the immediate goal of gathering them all together for a spiritual summit in Washington. "Looks as if he and I may get the morals of the world on our side," the president boasted. "We are talking to the Archbishop of Canterbury, the bishop at the head of the Lutheran Church, the Metropolitan of the Greek Church at Istanbul," even "the top Buddhist and the Grand Lama of Tibet. If I can mobilize the people who believe in a moral world against the Bolshevik materialists . . . we can win this fight."[3]

However, they met with some unexpected opposition. Though it was politically motivated, Truman's plan represented one of the most ambitious ecumenical initiatives since the 1893 World's Parliament of Religions. It would also be the crowning symbol atop his vigorous promotion of America's Judeo-Christian civil religion. Yet ironically, it all proved a step too far for some of the nation's leading ecumenists, especially the normally tolerant Protestants of the Federal Council of Churches. America may have been in the throes of its Judeo-Christian moment, but Protestants of almost all denominations still feared the Catholic Church. Catholicism, they charged, was too hierarchical, too authoritarian, and too beholden to the Vatican. They agreed with Paul Blanshard, formerly one of their own but now an avowed atheist, whose bestseller *American Freedom and Catholic Power* warned of the authoritarian Catholic Church's unrivaled power to dictate the terms of American politics and government policy. The liberal Protestants of the FCC especially disliked the pope's extreme anticommunism, which threatened to stir up tensions that could lead to war, and they disliked even more the Catholic Church's oppression of Protestants in Spain and Latin America. Truman's goal was to bring "all *believers in God and human liberty* to join together to bring pressure of a common desire for peace upon the atheistic communistic government of Russia," but this proved too much for a modernist establishment that felt that containment was already too aggressive and that the Vatican was no partner for peace. Methodist Bishop G. Bromley Oxnam, one of the leading mainline voices in the country, told Truman that opening official relations with the Vatican would "precipitate a tremendous flood of unhappy controversies." Truman and Taylor were especially shocked by the opposition from the World Council of Churches. Taylor complained that the organization's title, which reflected its ambitions to the world's ecumenical voice, was a "mis-nomer" and "deceptive," but to no avail.[4]

Reluctantly, Truman and Taylor abandoned their plans for a religious world summit. But Truman was still determined to solidify the closer bonds Taylor had formed with the Vatican. In 1951, after Taylor decided to retire for good, Truman announced that he would establish official diplomatic relations with the Holy See and replace Taylor, a personal envoy, with a permanent ambassador. But the establishment of relations with the Vatican had been expressly prohibited by an act of Congress during Reconstruction; recognition would require a change in law, and thus the inevitably arduous passage of congressional legislation. Secretary of State Dean Acheson—son of an Episcopal bishop and alumnus of the staunchly Anglican Groton School—had an intuitive sense of Protestant sensibilities even if his faith was no longer as strong as his father's, and he warned Truman of the firestorm of controversy that awaited him. But most others in the State Department were eager to establish official ties with the Vatican, indeed, with all major world religions. Taylor was particularly insistent, and Truman pushed forward. To avoid controversy, he appointed a war hero, Army General Mark Clark, who was a prominent Episcopalian and Mason.[5]

American Protestants from across the theological spectrum united in opposition, ostensibly because official ties with the Vatican violated the separation of church and state but in reality out of fear and loathing of the Catholic Church. Nothing united fundamentalists and modernists, evangelicals and liberals, more since the crusade for Prohibition. After Clark's nomination, the White House received its heaviest volume of mail on record, with passionate opposition outnumbering support by more than six-to-one. Acheson recalled that Senator Tom Connally was "incoherent with rage" at the news of such a controversial appointment. Edwin T. Dahlberg, president of the Northern Baptist Convention and a renowned pacifist, complained that the United States would be "thrown into opposition to Russia" by allying with the "ecclesiastic totalitarianism" of the Vatican. Even Harry Emerson Fosdick, the lion of tolerant modernism, leader of pacifism, and champion of black civil rights, wrote Truman to protest the "tragic blunder" of Clark's appointment. Though Truman wanted to persevere, Clark wilted under the pressure and withdrew his name from consideration. Truman could not quite believe it. He was convinced that containment was a necessity, but he was also concerned that it lacked a moral and spiritual foundation. With the demise of the Clark nomination, thanks to "violently bigoted" American Protestants, Truman felt that the nation had missed an opportunity to put its religious divisions behind it once and for all. And he feared that U.S. foreign policy would suffer as a result.[6]

Faith seemed to be an obvious ideological, rhetorical, and political—and at times even diplomatic—weapon in the Cold War. More surprising was its ability to spark division as well as foster unity. On foreign policy as in domestic politics, the religious impulse did not lead only in one, presumably anticommunist, direction. Instead, the burgeoning influence of Cold War faith created several competing visions of America's proper role in the postwar world.

CHAPTER TWENTY-TWO

The Faith of Harry Truman and the Theology of George Kennan

FOR MANY AMERICANS, the Cold War was an intensely spiritual affair. For the first time since the Civil War, it raised ultimate questions about life and death, of national survival—even, thanks to apocalyptic air power and the use of the atomic bomb, the very meaning of human existence itself. But religion was important to diplomacy for other reasons. Nuclear weapons changed not only how people viewed life on earth, they altered the once-timeless character of great power rivalry and conflict. No longer could great powers fight each other directly—to do so in the nuclear age would invite the total annihilation of all humanity. This revolutionary nature of the Cold War facilitated a religious role for American diplomacy: while the era most certainly did not mark a time of peace, the risks of direct military confrontation between the United States and the Soviet Union pushed them toward a greater use of nonmilitary methods. Indeed, it is no coincidence that the Cold War marked the zenith of espionage and propaganda and the emergence of culture and foreign aid as essential tools of foreign policy. In other words, the absence of direct fighting between the superpowers created space for other means of competition and conflict. For this reason, scholars speak of a "cultural Cold War" in a way that seems foreign even to other conflicts, such as World War II, in which ideas and propaganda were central.[1]

But we would do just as well to speak of a "religious Cold War," for the same conditions that afforded a greater role for culture, propaganda, and espionage also enabled religion to play a substantive role in the framing of U.S. foreign policy. And to understand America's religious Cold War, we first need to understand the faith and motivations of its two key architects: President Harry S. Truman and diplomat George F. Kennan.

IN CHRISTIAN FAITH as in Democratic politics, Harry Truman drew his inspiration from the example set by Franklin Roosevelt. Truman was a religious man, a devout Christian, and an ecumenist at heart—in fact, more truly ecumenical than the professional ecumenists of the Federal Council of Churches. Though he cared little for theology, liturgy, or doctrine, and though he attended church infrequently, Truman was, in the words of one biographer, "deeply religious in a larger sense." Like Roosevelt's religion, Truman's was a simple faith. Raised in a staunchly Baptist household, he attended a Presbyterian Sunday school because it was closer to his family's home in Independence, Missouri. The young Truman suffered from acute myopia, which ruled out sports and other outdoor activities. Reading distracted him instead, and though he would never become an intellectual he maintained a reverence for the "great books" of the Western canon and retained a detailed knowledge of their lessons and stories. In particular, Truman read the Bible, twice from cover-to-cover by the age of twelve and several times thereafter for the rest of his life. As another of his biographers notes, Truman possessed "an almost Fundamentalist reverence for the Bible."[2]

Truman was no fundamentalist, but biblical tenets, Christian ethics, and a fierce commitment to religious tolerance did play a central role in shaping and maintaining his worldview. After his education in the Presbyterian Sunday school, at the age of eighteen he joined the Baptist Church of Grandview, Missouri. As a Baptist, Truman practiced one of the most populist of faiths. It offered, he liked to boast, "the common man the shortest and most direct approach to God." Baptists were not only the most autonomous of Protestants, they were also the least hierarchical and the least deferential to established authority. As such, they were the least tied to organized religion, and thus the least connected to formal church structures. "I've never been of the opinion that Almighty God cares for the building or the form that a believer approaches the Maker of Heaven and Earth," Truman wrote in his diary during the last year of his presidency. "Forms and ceremonies impress a lot of people, but I've never thought that The Almighty could be impressed by anything but the heart and soul of the individual. That's why I'm a Baptist, whose church authority starts from the bottom up—not the top." Baptists were also among the most ardent supporters of social reform. Truman shared these progressive and populist strains in equal measure, and they helped nurture similar instincts in his politics. His democratic faith, in other words, inspired his Democratic politics. And underpinning it all was the sanctity of the Bible and the timelessness of its moral instruction. The prophets, he once explained, "were the protagonists of the common man" because they tried "to help the underdog, and the greatest prophet was crucified because He was trying to help the underdog."[3]

The simple, democratic character of Truman's religion led naturally to one of his most important and enduring beliefs: religious tolerance. The autonomous streak of Baptists often leads to a strong denominational identity, but in Truman it created the exact opposite impulse. He was not so much a religious independent as a believer in eclectic informality. His family on both sides practiced a variety of low-church Protestantism, from Disciples of Christ to a variety of Baptist churches. And as a Baptist who had attended a Presbyterian Sunday school, ecumenism had been an inherent part of Truman's religious outlook from childhood. Later, as an aspiring Democratic politician in Jackson County, Missouri, Truman worked with the infamous Pendergast machine and allied with its boss, Tom Pendergast, a Roman Catholic. Like many Protestants of his era, and especially his class, Truman flirted with the Ku Klux Klan during his 1922 campaign to become a judge of the Jackson County court, but when a Klan organizer told Truman that, if elected, he would be expected to fire the court's Catholic employees and replace them with Protestants, he quit and demanded a refund of his $10 dues payment.[4]

Religious morality stood at the center of Truman's worldview. He was no puritan, as his fondness for off-color language and poker illustrate. But neither did he believe that American society could function properly without a clear sense of right and wrong that only religion—almost any religion—could provide. He was delighted when his daughter, Margaret, began attending Sunday school in 1936. "She ought to go to one every Sunday—I mean *a* Sunday school," he wrote his wife, Bess, while he was away at the Democratic National Convention in Philadelphia. "If a child is instilled with good morals and taught the value of the precepts laid down in Exodus 20 and Matthew 5, 6 and 7, there is not much to worry about in after years. It makes no difference what brand is on the Sunday school." "My political philosophy is based on the Sermon on the Mount," President Truman explained years later in a formulation he repeated frequently. It was also based on the Ten Commandments, delivered by Moses and recorded in Exodus 20, which offered rules for a virtuous life and the "fundamental basis for all government." When he was sworn in as president, he requested his Bible be opened to the twentieth chapter of Exodus so he could place his hand directly upon the Ten Commandments. Most important was the Golden Rule (Matthew 7:12), which taught believers to treat others as they would be treated themselves and which Truman felt was a belief common to all great religions.[5]

This applied to international politics and society as well, for without faith morals could not exist, and without morality there could be no peace. And while Truman acknowledged that the United States was not a perfect society, he believed that America practiced the world's truest application of Christian ethics. As he declared at the outset of his 1948 State of the Union message, the "basic source of our strength is spiritual. For we are a people with faith. We believe in the dignity of man. We believe that he was created in the image of the Father of us all." For the same reason,

Americans believed in the sanctity of the individual and held "a deep concern for human rights." Thus it was America's mission to spread morality and democracy the world over. "Though we may meet setbacks from time to time," he declared at a Navy Day celebration to mark the end of World War II, "we shall not relent in our efforts to bring the Golden Rule into the international affairs of the world." America's mission was providential, mandated by God, a responsibility which Americans simply could not forsake. Truman was no Calvinist, but he firmly believed in the doctrine of predestination that had become central to the American civil religion. In building support for the United Nations and the North Atlantic Treaty Organization, two international commitments that ran against the American temperament and the grain of U.S. history, Truman spoke variously of "the responsibility which I believe God intended this great Republic to assume" and the "responsibility which God Almighty" invested in the United States. This had much in common with Lincoln's sense of providence: America was God's instrument on earth, whether Americans themselves realized it or not.[6]

The emerging Judeo-Christian consensus was thus perfectly suited to Truman's religious outlook. The concept of "Judeo-Christianity" is not an ancient tradition but a relatively recent one, forged in the fires of religious conflict and war in the era of World War II. But to a person of Truman's ecumenical instincts, it seemed as timeless and natural as faith itself. And although the Cold War did not mark the creation of America's Judeo-Christian identity, it did solidify it into something permanent. For unlike World War II, when the United States was allied to the godless Soviet Union, the Cold War pitted religion against atheism in an existential struggle of indefinite duration. In such an atmosphere, it mattered little whether one was Methodist or Baptist, Protestant or Catholic, or even Christian or Jew. This more elemental distinction divided believers from nonbelievers, faith from godlessness, morality from immorality, and democracy from tyranny. As Truman himself put it, "Minor, and even major, differences in how we choose to worship God strike me as being of relatively little importance in the face of an aggressive foe threatening to destroy all freedom of worship and other individual liberties."[7]

With the application of the Golden Rule worldwide, and with ultimate faith in the peaceful instincts of a people properly educated in religious morality, Truman was a firm believer in the democratic peace. The further democracy and religion spread, together, the further away the world could push the threat of tyranny and war. "Our American heritage of human freedom is born of the belief that man is created in the image of God and therefore is capable of governing himself," Truman declared as the ideological outlines of the Cold War hardened. From it, Americans had created a government dedicated to the dignity and the freedom of man. It is a government whose creed is derived from the word of God, and its roots are deep in our spiritual foundations. Our democracy is an expression of faith in the spirit of man, and it is a declaration of faith in man as created by God.

On these spiritual foundations we have established a creed of self-government more precious to us than life itself.

If others around the world could only share in such a political system, rooted in democratic faith, there would be no cause for war. "If man could achieve self-government and kinship with his God throughout the world, peace would not tremble in the constant dread of war." Here lay America's advantage over communism. While the Soviets had "no intellectual honesty and no moral code," the United States could "organize Exodus XX, Matthew V, VI & VII to save morals in the world." If "I could succeed in getting the world of morals associated against the world of no morals," Truman vowed, "we'd have world peace for ages to come. Confucius, Buddha, Moses, our own Jesus Christ, Mahomet, all preached: 'Do as you'd be done by.' Treat others as you'd be treated."[8]

Yet peace could not prevail so long as the world faced an enemy to freedom and faith. In communism, liberty and democracy faced their antithesis, and, according to Truman, their greatest threat. However much faith he placed in the Sermon on the Mount and the Golden Rule, Truman was no pacifist. He pointed out that while the prophet Isaiah (2:4) admonished the faithful to "beat their swords into plowshares, and their spears into pruninghooks," the prophet Joel (3:10) called for the exact opposite. In the name of self-defense, Joel urged God's people to "beat your plowshares into swords and your pruninghooks into spears: let the weak say, I am strong." As Truman interpreted the Bible, a book he knew from memory, the rightfulness of war depended upon its degree of necessity, which in turn depended upon the circumstances and nature of the threat. In a religiously pluralistic nation, in the depths of the Cold War, Truman participated in the revival of the just war tradition. It was time, he decided in July 1950, shortly after the outbreak of the Korean War, to "succeed in our quest for righteousness" and, "in St. Paul's luminous phrase, put on the armor of God." Truman was not the first president to invoke the just war by quoting from the Epistle to the Ephesians. Nor would he be the last.[9]

And the Cold War *was* a just war, Truman proclaimed, because it *was* a war of self-defense. Not only did Soviet communism attack America's allies, and not only did it threaten the security of the United States, it menaced the values upon which American democracy had been founded and by which Americans lived their daily lives. If Franklin Roosevelt had warned the nation that it could not live as an island of democracy in a sea of tyranny, Truman would now do the same. "At the present time," he declared in a speech during the Korean War at Washington's New York Avenue Presbyterian Church, where Lincoln used to pray during the Civil War,

> our nation is engaged in a great effort to maintain justice and peace in the world. An essential feature of this effort is our program to build up the defenses of our country.
>
> There has never been a greater cause. There has never been a cause which had a stronger moral claim on all of us.
>
> We are defending the religious principles upon which our Nation and our whole way of life are founded. We are defending the right to worship God—each as he sees fit according to his own conscience. We are defending the right to follow the precepts and the example which God has set for us. We are defending the right of people to gather together, all across our land, in churches such as this one.
>
> For the danger that threatens us in the world today is utterly and totally opposed to all these things. The international Communist movement is based on a fierce and terrible fanaticism. It denies the existence of God and, wherever it can, it stamps out the worship of God.[10]

It was supremely ironic that Truman borrowed so heavily from Roosevelt's faith-based formula for portraying America's struggle as one of necessity against an implacable and unalterably evil enemy. Roosevelt had used religion as an ideological weapon against Germany and Japan, but he refrained from doing so when discussing the Soviets because he thought postwar peace would last only as long as the United States and the Soviet Union could work together. In emphasizing the importance of religious liberty, in stressing the threat to the ideas of religion and democracy as well as the physical security of the North American continent, in mobilizing an interfaith coalition against godless enemies, both Roosevelt and Truman rallied Americans to the fight. The only difference was their choice of enemy.

GEORGE F. KENNAN almost single-handedly established the foundations for American foreign policy in the Cold War. For better or worse, few diplomats in history have seen their ideas play such a major role shaping their geopolitical environment. That he did so in a four-year period in which he ranked no higher than a consular official in Moscow and head of the State Department's Policy Planning Staff is all the more remarkable.[11]

Kennan's main contribution was the strategy of containment, first outlined in an eight-thousand-word cable, known to history as the "Long Telegram" he sent from the U.S. Embassy in Moscow in February 1946. If the United States wanted to limit Soviet expansionism without resorting to war, he wrote under the pseudonym "X" in the July 1947 issue of *Foreign Affairs*, it should adopt "a policy of firm containment, designed to confront the Russians with unalterable counter-force at every point where they show signs of encroaching upon the interests of a peaceful and stable world." From then on, containing the global spread of communism would define, and sometimes imprison, the foreign policy of every president from Harry S. Truman to George H. W. Bush. Though they would each modify it in important ways—from Dwight D. Eisenhower's New Look to John F. Kennedy's flexible response to Lyndon Johnson's war in Vietnam to Richard Nixon's détente—until the fall of the Berlin Wall each president placed the containment of communism at the very heart of American national security. Few foreign policy doctrines have been as enduring.[12]

Containment was predicated equally upon two fundamental aspects of Kennan's character: realism and anticommunism. Yet despite the endurance of containment over four decades, the two premises were not necessarily complementary. Realism is based on identifying the national interest and pursuing it with force if necessary, but it is also grounded in a recognition of the limits of national capabilities and resources. Realists do not embark upon moral crusades on behalf of national ideals, especially if they do not conform to the national interest. Realists distrust what Kennan once derided as the "legalistic-moralistic" and "universalistic" mindsets so common among idealistic Americans. While postwar American leaders may have led the greatest power the world had yet seen, Kennan argued that they must first and foremost distinguish between what was vital and what was peripheral. He perceived Soviet communism as a national security threat, but he saw less danger in other forms of communism. For example, he later argued that while Vietnamese communists might be violent and repressive, Vietnam itself did not represent a vital strategic concern for the United States; hence his opposition to the Vietnam War.[13]

Cold War anticommunism, on the other hand, was often based on a moralistic identification of right and wrong, good and evil, that did not coexist peacefully with the idea of merely "containing" communism's growth. Anticommunists did not necessarily share Kennan's realist caution; they wished instead to "roll back" communism where it already existed, starting in Eastern Europe, and eradicate it from areas where it had since made gains, such as China, Vietnam, and Cuba. Many anticommunists possessed a moralistic streak that Kennan found worrying because it was unrealistic, unnecessary, and prone to dangerous extremes.

Kennan's most significant achievement, then, was to reconcile realism and anticommunism within a single, coherent premise. And a major reason he was able to sustain what others saw as an untenable paradox was the inherent duality of his religious belief. In fact, Kennan argued, the global conditions that made realism necessary also made Christianity indispensable, for it was religion that provided morality in a world of inherently narcissistic individuals. The problem with American society, naturally individualistic as it was, was its increasing faith in science and decreasing faith in God. "The Christian layman of our age has a far greater need for stiffening in the face of the dilemmas of personal life than did any other Christian layman in history," he claimed. Only the "Church has within its power" the ability to preserve a moral spirit that was fast disappearing in "an environment of almost unnatural abundance and luxury." When asked about the place of Christian ethics in world politics, Kennan replied that God did not care about the normal diplomatic questions regarding free trade or territorial disputes. What mattered was a higher, moral law that pervaded everything. "The moral laws which we acknowledge predicate the existence of a certain sort of world . . . in which people live," he wrote in the pages of the *Atlantic Monthly*. "This setting presumably reflects God's purpose. We did not create it; we do not have the right to destroy it." To the British historian Arnold Toynbee, whose bestselling books were infused with a powerfully devout Christian faith and who complained of Kennan's derision of "moralistic" foreign policies, Kennan protested that he had never meant to attack morality per se. Morality was essential, he told Toynbee; a moralism by which Americans believed themselves to be the unblemished moral arbiters of the world was not. This belief that *morality* was indispensable to diplomacy but that *moralism* was dangerous was what made Kennan not just a realist, but a Christian realist.[14]

In particular, Kennan held a deep faith that had been powerfully shaped by his family's centuries-long membership in the Presbyterian Church. He was an active churchgoer and frequently delivered guest sermons, including scriptural references for guidance and instruction, from the pulpit. Presbyterianism was central to his intellectual formation, especially its traditional adherence to the teachings of John Calvin. In essence, Calvinism, as theology but especially in its political applications, is based upon a contradiction: it is at once deeply pessimistic yet profoundly optimistic. Pessimistic Calvinism believes humanity to be inherently sinful and depraved (Kennan's realism); following largely from this theology but also from the severe anti-Catholic politics of the Reformation, it also has little hesitation in identifying evil in the world and calling it by name (his anticommunism). Less recognized is optimistic Calvinism, which recognizes these dangers but is confident they can overcome through faith in God and trust in providence. Evil existed, in other words, but it could eventually be overcome.

As Kennan himself readily acknowledged, pessimistic Calvinistic theology had a profound impact upon his own realist worldview. In its purest dogmatic expression, Calvinism attributes original sin to every human being and denies them any agency in rectifying their inherent sinfulness. According to Calvin and his most literal followers, life on earth is predestined according to God's will and there is absolutely nothing anyone can do about it. Kennan found such rigorous Calvinism not only distasteful but unchristian. But there was something about Calvinism that appealed to him, for he thought it explained much about human nature. People were not inherently good, but sinful. He believed that Calvin's best modern interpreter was not a theologian but the founder of psychoanalysis, Sigmund Freud. Freud also ruminated on human nature and, like Calvin, argued that people were born with certain primordial instincts that did not always conform to Christian mores or the dictates of modern society. This, Kennan reasoned, was a doctrine of original sin for the modern age.[15]

Kennan stripped away the most absurd excesses from the thought of Calvin and Freud to produce a distinctly realist view of human nature: at heart, people were selfish and self-interested; their natural tendencies were not toward charity or virtue but self-preservation. In the real world, this required both "the need for individual humility" and "the need for collective humility." Practically, it meant that people should not assume their own or their nation's moral superiority. It also meant that this world was sinful, and dangerous, and that no amount of crusading would change this basic fact. What made religion so important was its sole capacity to mediate human life above self-interest. Kennan could think of no better interpreter of Christianity than John Milton, whose epic poem *Paradise Lost* had inspired the political thought of Jefferson and Madison. In it, Kennan explained, Adam realizes what life must be like, for all time, after his expulsion from the Garden of Eden. As Adam admits to the Archangel Michael at the end of Milton's tale,

> *Henceforth I learn, that to obey is best,*
> *And love with fear the only God: to walk*
> *As in his presence: ever to observe*
> *His providence; and on him sole depend . . .*

The lesson was simple: Americans must rally to their own self-defense against communism, but they must not crusade against it. They must be righteous, but not self-righteous. "With regard to other nations," he said on another occasion, using guidance from the Book of Matthew (7:1), "let us not judge, that we not be judged. Let us not attempt to constitute ourselves the guardians of everyone else's virtue; we have enough trouble to guard our own."[16]

Calvin, Freud, and Milton were not Kennan's only theological influences. In Reinhold Niebuhr, Kennan found a kindred spirit who warned of the dangers of both Soviet communism and American exceptionalism. Though Kennan exaggerated when he described Niebuhr as "the father of us all," it is little wonder he was excited by the theologian's ideas. Kennan counted himself "more indebted" to the ideas and values of Niebuhr "than to those of any other person of our time." In turn, Niebuhr praised Kennan's exposé of the "legalistic-moralistic" approach and his brilliance in illuminating "the evils which arise from the pursuit of unlimited rather than limited ends, even by highly civilized nations in the modern era." This was a critique of precisely the kind of ideologies—pacifism, Nazism, fascism, communism—that Niebuhr had fought throughout his career. Like Niebuhr, Kennan was a Christian realist who believed in the fundamental importance of original sin. What he most appreciated in Niebuhr's thought was the realization of "the essential weakness of every such utopian approach to human affairs—of every outlook that professes to have discovered some gimmick, lying within man's own power of action, by which he could be relieved of his self-will and his estrangement from God." Kennan may not have spoken of neo-orthodox theology, but his religious views were consistent with it—so consistent that he often brought Niebuhr to Washington for consultations with the Policy Planning Staff.[17]

In 1953, in a "Laymen's Sunday" sermon to the First Presbyterian Church of Princeton, Kennan noted that while technology and science made it "hard, in our day, to be a Christian," he believed that "it is perhaps harder not to be one." The alternative to faith in God was faith in science, and blind faith in science, without the moral infusion of Christianity, would lead to totalitarianism. This explained the fate of Soviet Russia. "I am trying to draw a distinction between, on the one hand, any form of belief that accepts the existence of a divine order and a personal moral law and, on the other, the state of mind of those people who accept none of this," he explained. "Russia has long been the seat of one such experiment." In confronting communism, Americans must not be complacent or self-righteous; they must have faith in themselves and their religion, but they must not take their strength for granted. But neither, he told the congregation at First Presbyterian, should they "underestimate the strength of evil itself. Evil is a force in this world of no mean quality, a force in its own right, with its own pride and even its own desperate self-respect. That is what our ancestors meant when they believed in the reality and physical proximity of the devil."[18]

But the optimistic side of Calvinism also pervaded Kennan's diplomatic thought, especially in the ideological fulcrum of the early Cold War. Adam, Christ, and Milton had taught him there was little use in

despairing. So did Calvin. Calvinists believe themselves to be God's chosen people—the elect—and that divine providence will actively promote
and protect them in unforeseen, mysterious ways. Calvinists also reconcile
pessimism with optimism by noting that the presence of evil is simply
a way for God to test his chosen people and that by passing such tests,
they will ensure that good will ultimately triumph. The Cold War, Kennan wrote in a little-noticed passage toward the end of his *Foreign Affairs*
article, "is in essence a test of the over-all worth of the United States as a
nation among nations. . . . Surely there was never a fairer test of national
quality than this." In rising to this ultimate test, Americans would "experience a certain gratitude to Providence which, by providing the American
people with this implacable challenge, has made their entire security as
a nation dependent on their pulling themselves together and accepting
the responsibilities of moral and political leadership that history plainly
intended them to bear." John Calvin himself could not have put it any
better. Neither could Harry Truman.[19]

TRUMAN AND KENNAN could not have been more different temperamentally and politically. Instead, it was their shared spirituality and anticommunism that helped shape U.S. foreign policy in the formative early
years of the Cold War. As the historian William Inboden observes, religion offered the Truman administration both a diagnosis of the problem
of communism and its potential cure. This was, we have seen, in keeping
with the Anglo-American use of religion in world politics dating back to
the sixteenth century: what English imperialists and colonists feared in
Catholicism, Cold War Americans feared in communism.[20]

Most disturbingly, Soviet communism seemed to present not just a
rival ideology but a rival religion that threatened to destroy traditional
faith. Secretary of Defense James V. Forrestal was not alone in his uncertainty "whether we are dealing with a nation or a religion—religion after
all being merely the practical extension of philosophy." As Christians and
Jews, Americans professed ultimate allegiance to a faith and ethical tradition that was not of their making, that had lasted for thousands of years,
and that had been sanctified by the one power whom all people must obey.
Communism's moral claims rested on a doctrine of social justice similar
to Christianity's, but it emphatically rejected the institutional legitimacy
of the Christian church and denied the existence of a supernatural higher
power that had created the world and continued to guide it. It was, in
other words, so different from Christianity and yet very similar, which is
precisely what made it seem so dangerous.[21]

The Cold War, however, did not immediately follow the end of World
War II. True, many of the sources of Cold War tensions had rested uneasily within the contradictions of the Grand Alliance, and the ideological

character of the war and the postwar bore stronger similarities than differences. But after the surrender of Germany in May 1945, the Truman administration grappled uncertainly with the twin problems of postwar reconstruction in Europe and the enigma of Soviet intentions. Truman and his advisers felt that Soviet communism presented a threat, but they were still unsure what exactly their response should be. In this year of uncertainty, religion did not play much of a role in U.S. foreign policy. Myron Taylor, still officially acting as the president's envoy to the Vatican and other religious leaders in Europe, had so little to do he even contemplated retirement. In the winter of 1946, Methodist bishop Ivan Lee Holt of St. Louis told Truman he was embarking on a tour of postwar Europe and would meet with the WCC and other church officials. Did Truman have any messages he wanted conveyed to the religious leaders of Europe? Holt only received a boilerplate message of vague goodwill. Other prominent ministers received a similarly tepid response.[22]

During the fateful year 1946, the Truman administration began to reconsider its approach to the Soviet Union. Perhaps most important was the arrival of George F. Kennan's legendary "Long Telegram," sent from the U.S. Embassy in Moscow to the State Department in February. From there, Truman's national security strategy became more focused—too focused—upon containing the spread of both communist ideology and Soviet power in Europe. Not coincidentally, this period also marked the reemergence of religion and the reappearance of Taylor. In announcing his decision to continue Taylor's mission to the Vatican even after a peace treaty with Italy had been finalized, Truman told reporters that America's spiritual diplomacy would continue indefinitely. "However long it takes, we will go through with the thing to the end." When asked if "the end" meant the signing of the Italian treaty, Truman simply replied: "Peace in the world."[23]

And they were not alone. "I am for the Pope," wrote Winston Churchill in a private letter to Taylor in January 1946. "I join Him in combating Communism." Churchill wanted Taylor to convey his greetings to Pius XII, and he encouraged Taylor's efforts to provide a spiritual and moral counterpart to the West's grand strategy. Two months later, Churchill did his own part in a speech at Westminster College in Fulton, Missouri. The occasion had the feel of a small-town revival, and the British war hero, probably then the most famous person in the world, did not disappoint. A small, Presbyterian college with a strong denominational loyalty, Westminster was known locally as "the Bible School." For the thousands of Missourians who flocked to Westminster to see or hear Churchill, the women of Fulton's Methodist Church prepared a dinner of Missouri ham, twice-baked potatoes, and angel cake. With Truman sitting on the stage immediately behind him, Churchill revived his wartime religious rhetoric to deliver a call to arms that coined the phrase "Iron Curtain." The Red Army did not simply pose a threat to European security, Churchill warned; "Communist parties or fifth columns constitute a growing challenge and peril to Christian civilization." After the speech, Churchill kept crying out "God bless you all!" to the cheering throngs.[24]

The next day, Truman parted company with Churchill and traveled to Columbus, Ohio, where he addressed the annual general meeting of the Federal Council of Churches and delivered his own summons to civic and religious duty. The setting was important, for as we shall see the mainline liberals of the FCC were already questioning Truman's anticommunist foreign policy. "Dictatorship, by whatever name, is founded on the doctrine that the individual amounts to nothing," he reminded the gathering of Protestant theologians and ministers. In a world still unhealed from the scars of war, where hunger and poverty created conditions ripe for the growth of communist dictatorship and where the rule of violence and injustice seemed unbreakable, Truman presented an alternative future:

> Now that we have preserved our freedom of conscience and religion, our right to live by a decent moral and spiritual code of our own choosing, let us make full use of that freedom. Let us make use of it to save a world which is beset by so many threats of new conflicts, new terror, and new destruction.

American Christians had a responsibility, to themselves and to the world. They had no choice but to embrace it as part of God's design. To do otherwise would be to commit the greatest sin possible. To do otherwise would be unbecoming of a great people—a chosen people—at their moment of destiny.[25]

A year later, on March 12, 1947, before a special joint session of Congress, Truman issued what amounted to a declaration of Cold War. The chaplain of the House of Representatives, Reverend James Shera Montgomery, began the session with a prayer asking that God's "way may be known upon earth, Thy saving health among all nations." Americans must praise God, and be humble before Him, "for Thou shalt judge the people righteously, and govern the nations upon earth." The president's speech, known as the Truman Doctrine, promised American aid to fund the anticommunist crusade in Greece and Turkey. But its real objective was much grander, for the Truman Doctrine unveiled containment as the basis for American strategy worldwide. After explaining the immediate problems facing Greece and Turkey, Truman placed them in a global context, as early warning signals of the challenges the United States would face everywhere in the world. He divided the world into two camps, a world in which "nearly every nation must choose between alternative ways of life," although the "choice is too often not a free one."

Truman was borrowing a rhetorical and ideological tactic from Franklin Roosevelt, although he was also, intentionally or not, tapping into a much longer American religious tradition of dividing the world into forces of light and forces of darkness. This starkly moralistic worldview had been a staple of the Puritans, of the Patriots who campaigned against French Catholics and Anglican bishops, and of Lincoln's fulminations against slavery. Thus while the Truman Doctrine itself was not an explicitly religious speech, it possessed all the hallmarks of an American diplomatic sermon. Moreover, the choice facing the world was not a matter of political theory; the national security of the United States depended upon its outcome. "One way of life," he explained,

> is based upon the will of the majority, and is distinguished by free institutions, representative government, free elections, guarantees of individual liberty, freedom of speech and religion, and freedom from political oppression.
>
> The second way of life is based upon the will of a minority forcibly imposed upon the majority. It relies upon terror and oppression, a controlled press and radio, fixed elections, and the suppression of personal freedoms.

In the face of such a threat, Truman declared that "it must be the policy of the United States to support free peoples who are resisting attempted subjugation by armed minorities or by outside pressures. I believe that we must assist free peoples to work out their own destinies in their own way." To syndicated newspaper columnist Walter Lippmann, one of containment's earliest critics, it sounded as if Truman was not announcing a foreign policy but launching a "crusade."[26]

The Truman Doctrine was by no means an exception. Truman constantly linked religious rhetoric and imagery to the implementation of containment, and his pious tone suffused the rest of his administration. National Security Council Report 68 (NSC-68), one of the most important documents in American diplomatic history, is a prime example. NSC-68's phrasing and meaning derived directly from the libertarian impulse of the Reformed Protestant tradition that still held the American imagination in thrall. In presenting a blueprint for waging a more aggressive Cold War, NSC-68's language was intense, at times shrill and hyperbolically alarmist. Given that it was never aimed for public consumption—and was not declassified until 1975—it provides a reliable guide to the thinking of

American officials charged with devising a way to fight communism and win the Cold War without triggering World War III.[27]

The Soviets, wrote NSC-68's authors, presented a completely new and fatal danger, for they threatened America's ideas and values as well as its physical security. They presented a spiritual as well as a political and military challenge because they advanced a new, aggressive form of religion: communism. The Soviets were "unlike previous aspirants to hegemony," different even from the Nazis, because they were "animated by a new fanatic faith, antithetical to our own," and sought to impose "absolute authority over the rest of the world." At stake was not only "the fulfillment or destruction of this Republic but of civilization itself." Americans believed in a "free society" founded on "the dignity and worth of the individual." Soviets, by contrast, lived in a "slave state" based upon the "submission" and "degradation" of the individual "under the compulsion of a perverted faith." Under such tyranny, the individual "can only find the meaning of his existence in serving the ends of the system. The system becomes God, and submission to the will of God becomes submission to the will of the system." The individual must internalize the communist system and truly believe in it; any signs to the contrary, and the individual would be destroyed by the state. The communist state risked its own destruction if it did not crush all individual thought or conscience, "for the spirit of resistance and the devotion to a higher authority might then remain, and the individual would not be wholly submissive." After wiping out individual conscience, and with it any possible dissent, communist rulers had at their disposal "a new universal faith," practiced obediently by millions of adherents who were ready to launch "an international crusade."[28]

THE NEXT STEP was to contain communism with a moral offensive that only religious faith could muster, and Truman directed many of these efforts himself. As his speechwriter George Elsey recalled, in longhand Truman would often insert religious themes and phrasing into speech drafts that lacked a moral or spiritual dimension. This presidential lead established guidelines for the rest of his administration. The Food for Peace program, which began in 1949, exported America's agricultural surpluses via the people who knew how to distribute them best: mission boards and religious relief organizations. The United States Information Exchange programs, administered by the State Department, consulted with religious leaders like Francis Cardinal Spellman on the most effective means of deploying religion in the West's moral combat with the Soviet Union; during the debate over whether to join NATO, Truman personally called upon Spellman to drum up popular support for the North Atlantic Treaty, and the cardinal enthusiastically complied. The Psychological Strategy Board, an important new organization created by Truman, also used religion in its ideological war against communism. The "potentialities of religion as an instrumentality for combating Communism are universally tremendous," the PSB advised the Central Intelligence Agency in 1952. In Europe, Latin America, Africa, and Asia, the shield of faith could be used to defend against the growth of communist ideology; in eastern Europe, a region of traditionally intense religious devotion, the sword of the spirit could be wielded effectively against communist regimes.[29]

Truman recognized that European religion represented the one institution that not only stood for anticommunist principles but also had the wherewithal and motivation to implement them. Usually, in postwar Eastern Europe, this meant the Catholic Church, but it also meant Eastern Orthodox, Protestants, and Jews. Communist Party infringements upon religious liberty seemed to present a clear case of totalitarian aggression that aimed to dominate not only territory, but also the souls and minds of the people. Unsurprisingly, such crackdowns provoked an impassioned response in the United States, particularly among Catholics but also Protestant fundamentalists. In determining policy, the Truman administration viewed religion as an advance indicator of Soviet intentions. If communist officials allowed the churches some measure of freedom, as they had during the war, then Americans could hope for peace. But if there was a crackdown on religion, then it could only mean that the communists were on the march. A government that did not respect religious freedom could not be democratic, and an undemocratic state was likely an aggressive state. As American diplomats in Moscow, Warsaw, Budapest, and elsewhere began reporting on communist violations of religious freedom in Eastern Europe and the Soviet Union, the State Department and White House studied the evidence with growing concern.[30]

As the Cold War intensified, communist persecutions of religion took on an increasingly public profile. In 1946, the government of Yugoslavia charged Archbishop Aloysius Stepinac with wartime collaboration with the fascists and sentenced him to sixteen years of hard labor. The arrest of Stepinac was controversial in the United States, but it did not provoke a serious crisis because the Truman administration, wary of the archbishop's ties to Croatian fascism during the war, decided not to rally to his cause. Two years later, however, the new communist regime in Hungary condemned Jozsef Cardinal Mindszenty, an outspoken anticommunist with no ties to fascism, to life in prison. Hungarians reacted with "stunned amazement" and "anxious anticipation," reported the ranking U.S. diplomat in Budapest, Selden Chapin, but they were not as stunned and anxious as Chapin himself. The Mindszenty arrest, he believed, was the "worst example" of an "affront to human liberties since [the] Jewish persecution."

It also had "major significance" for the Cold War. "For if a prince of the church," he asked his superiors in Washington, "may be unceremoniously ill treated, browbeaten and broken in order [to] obtain alleged incriminating evidence, what chance for justice has [an] ordinary citizen who objects to or criticizes unlimited state power on moral or spiritual grounds?" This was not an idle philosophical problem or isolated incident, Chapin argued, but a portent of ominous things to come. In other words, it was a problem for U.S. foreign policy:

> [The] cynical arrest of Mindszenty and his probable ruthless liquidation culminates a long series of blows striking at basic human freedoms and transcends all sectarian considerations. In this issue we are faced with a direct assault on one of the most vital main streams of the western heritage. It seems to me therefore that if it becomes manifest that Communist officials who locally represent Soviet power may arbitrarily violate religious freedom and flout local opinion and conscience without arousing violent condemnation from free peoples and institutions, the declaration of human rights of which we are a signatory will be regarded as a "scrap of paper," the moral leadership of the US will suffer severely, and the foundations of hope for the 100,000,000 or more newly condemned inhabitants behind the curtain will have been destroyed. It will be obvious, moreover, that the harmful effects of this assault on western spirituality by Marxist materialism may well dishearten other peoples wavering between conflicting ideologies.

As John Foster Dulles, then a delegate to the UN, wrote to the State Department's Dean Rusk in another context that same year, the Soviets would not invade Europe as the Nazis had invaded Poland and France or the Japanese had invaded China. Instead, Soviet "aggression is primarily against individual rights and freedoms" while the communists' "use of terror" would "stifle opposition." It was a new form of conquest, and Mindszenty was one of its first casualties.[31]

Encouraged by the Vatican, which issued no fewer than three papal encyclicals on Hungary in the space of a week (comparatively, Pius XII issued forty encyclicals during his entire twenty-year papacy), the Catholic Church in America exploded with rage at the arrests and warned that they represented a form of religious persecution that heralded a new age of tyranny. In New York, Francis Cardinal Spellman excoriated the "satanic Soviet sycophants" who had arrested and tortured Stepinac in the name of the "perfidious pattern of communist godlessness, barbarism, and enslavement." Following Mindszenty's arrest, Spellman rallied Americans to the "defense of the rights of God and man against Christ-hating communists whose allegiance is pledged to Satan!" Spellman's outbursts were typical of Catholic reaction, but they were by no means isolated. Interfaith demonstrations against the arrest of Mindszenty sprang up across the country. In response to the outcry of both U.S. diplomats in Eastern Europe and American public opinion, Under Secretary of State Robert A. Lovett ridiculed the cardinal's arrest as a "sickening sham" that augured the communist domination of Europe. In a cable to London, Secretary of State Dean Acheson called it the most "flagrant" example yet of a more "systematic suppression [of] human rights and freedoms." Truman concurred, and the United States escalated its anticommunist offensive.[32]

This dichotomy between good and evil, free and enslaved, fanatical atheism and true religion, also found anticommunist expression on the ground, both in Europe and in Asia. Simultaneous to Taylor's initiative, an even more important and altogether more successful religious initiative was taking place. Washington offered support for a "third way" alternative to communism and fascism in France, West Germany, and Italy: Christian Democracy. With variants of fascism still tainting their societies and with communism an increasingly popular political movement, French, German, and Italian anticommunists turned to the traditional conservative politics of religion. Closely allied to the Vatican, Christian Democrats rejected communism and socialism by combining faith in the free market with an even greater faith in Catholic social welfare. It was, in Tony Judt's apt phrase, a movement of "politicized clericalism" that represented the antithesis of Marxism. Despite some misgivings about the movement's conservative Catholicism, this was exactly what the Truman administration was looking for to stabilize its half of postwar Europe. In France, where secularism and an anticlerical tradition were strongest, the movement stalled. But in Germany, it succeeded by entwining effectively with Protestantism. And in Italy, where the Catholic Church remained a major political player but where the Communist Party seemed poised to win the 1948 elections, the Truman administration orchestrated campaigns of support, both overt and covert, to help the Christian Democrats to victory. With Cardinal Spellman in New York teaming up with Myron Taylor in Washington, the United States ensured that communism would not expand its reach into Italy.[33]

American officials thought Christianity held similar potential for an anticommunist reconstruction in postwar Asia. American missionaries had for over a century taken the lead in spreading both the gospel of Christ and the gospel of modernity throughout Asia. They had allied themselves to anticolonial and anticommunist nationalist movements in China, Korea, India, and elsewhere, and had long been proponents of Western modernization in Japan. They saw no reason why their work should not continue after the war, and neither did Washington. In China (explored in a later chapter), where the United States ostensibly supported Chiang Kai-shek and the Nationalists but in reality washed its hands of such a corrupt ally fighting a losing battle, this task was left to the missionaries.

But in Japan, where the U.S. military maintained an indefinite occupation and controlled all aspects of Japanese political life, government and military officials took the lead in promoting Christianity as a modernizing, democratic force. Truman set the tone shortly after the Japanese surrender. If Japan was to "evolve into a peaceful nation, with an international as against a nationalistic outlook, she must understand and appreciate the religious forces of the world," he declared. Joseph Grew, a former U.S. Ambassador to Tokyo and influential American voice on Japanese affairs, was even more specific in proclaiming his belief "that democracy and progress in Japan must be based on fundamental Christian principles." In July 1946, James Forrestal, then secretary of the navy, paid a visit to Tokyo to confer with General Douglas MacArthur, who commanded the occupation. MacArthur feared the growth of communism in Asia as much as Forrestal feared it in Europe, but he also felt the United States had a secret weapon. The "two great ideas" that America could use to "oppose . . . the crusade of Communism," MacArthur revealed, "were (a) the idea of liberty and freedom, and (b) the idea of Christianity." MacArthur had been reading about the crucifixion of Christ and only now realized the purpose of his suffering: "it was there for us to learn a lesson from; that Christ, even though crucified, nevertheless persevered." According to Grant K. Goodman, a young foreign service officer and Japanese translator who had worked for MacArthur in the Philippines and followed him to Tokyo, the general "did everything possible to facilitate the evangelical activities of American missionaries and religious leaders," including the establishment of International Christian University with Grew as its general chairman. In 1947, MacArthur invited the YWCA to Japan and encouraged them to spread the values of "Christian internationalism." At home, these efforts were complemented by private religious initiatives, most often by churches and missionary societies, to facilitate Japan's postwar rehabilitation in an American image.[34]

THE RELIGIOUS ROLE in containment had mixed success, but Truman fared better with another faith-based initiative: the recognition of the state of Israel in May 1948. Of course, recognition of Israeli independence and sovereignty was not exclusively a religious concern. But while religion was not the only determinant, it was one of the most important, and it flowed from much the same religious impulses that guided Truman's thoughts on Soviet communism. Without religion, moreover, it is unlikely that Truman would have acted as he did in the face of ferocious and nearly unanimous opposition from the State and Defense Departments. Unlike the establishment of relations with the Vatican, the recognition of Israel required nothing more than a presidential directive. Understanding Truman's personal motives, then, is essential to understanding his decision.

Three motives, all connected to some degree to religion, were particularly important: domestic politics, biblical faith, and humanitarianism. National security considerations were not irrelevant, but the dictates of the national interest leaned more toward the Arab states and their vast reserves of oil than toward the recognition of Israel. For this reason, and for fear of uniting the Muslim world in anger against the United States and possibly moving them toward an alliance with the Soviet Union, the State Department vehemently opposed recognizing Israel. Secretary of State George C. Marshall, perhaps the most respected man in America and a personal favorite of Truman's, was especially adamant; so too was the highly respected James V. Forrestal, the nation's first-ever secretary of defense after a major overhaul of the government combined the War and Navy Departments. This was formidable opposition that only a president could overcome. Eventually, Marshall promised not to obstruct Truman even while refusing to endorse the president's decision (afterward, with the presidential election looming, Truman would sometimes exclude Marshall from discussions on Israel "because of their political implications"). With Marshall on board, all other internal opposition melted away. Yet even this required Truman to take a forceful stand. "All I can say," Clark Clifford, Truman's confidant and point man on Israel, warned a colleague in the State Department, "is that if anyone is going to give, it is going to have to be General Marshall because—I can tell you now—the President is not going to give an inch." On purely strategic grounds, then, the United States would likely not have recognized Israel. Instead, other factors at play in the mind of the man who alone would decide U.S. policy came to the fore.[35]

Domestic politics was certainly important, especially in an election year. Though Truman needed no reminding of the importance of the Jewish vote to the Democratic Party, American Zionists pressed their claims relentlessly; at times, they even explicitly linked the fates of Zionists and Democrats together. "You let me have the Jewish vote of New York and I will bring you the head of Ibn Saud on a platter," Democratic Party strategist and fund-raiser Bernard Baruch told a Zionist. "The Administration will sell all seven Arab states if it is a question of retaining the support . . . of the Jews of New York alone; never mind the rest of the country." The State Department, focused on the national interest, found political logic such as this "embarrassing," but Truman could not simply ignore it. He faced a difficult campaign, and after losing control of Congress in the 1946 midterms the Democrats could not afford any defections from their base. Truman deeply resented such pressure, but he could do little to avert it and nothing to deny the substance of its message. "I have to answer to hundreds of thousands who are anxious for the success of Zionism," he snapped at a dissenter from the State Department. "I do not have hundreds of thousands of Arabs in my constituents." So domestic politics was crucial, even though, in the end, it was also largely irrelevant: Truman lost New York State but won the presidency anyway.[36]

Biblical faith also played a part. Truman, we have seen, was devout but not a fundamentalist. He knew the Bible by rote, but he could also apply its meanings and lessons to current affairs. Because he did not expect the prophecies of Revelation to come true, he did not support a Jewish state in Palestine because it would help fulfill the end times. But he did know his Bible, and this was no small influence upon deciding the issue of Jewish statehood in the Holy Land. Clark Clifford noted that Truman often quoted scripture when talking about Israel, especially the passage in Deuteronomy (31:7) in which God tells the Israelites to "go and take possession of the land which the Lord hath sworn unto your fathers." Indeed, Truman enjoyed fitting his own part in Jewish history into a larger biblical narrative. "What do you mean 'helped create'?" he asked incredulously when, years later, he was introduced at a function as the man who had helped create the modern state of Israel. "I am Cyrus!" The obscure biblical reference was vintage Truman. Cyrus the Great, king of Persia, allowed the Jews to rebuild the state of Judea in the sixth century BCE, and Truman felt he was the ancient king's modern heir.[37]

The recognition of Israel also dovetailed perfectly with America's new Judeo-Christian ethic, something Truman himself had done much to cultivate. Judeo-Christian identity was biblically based in that the Bible—namely, what Christians call the Old Testament—provided the traditions, morals, and spiritual heritage for Protestants, Catholics, and Jews alike. As Vice President Truman reminded Americans only a few weeks before he became president, "It was the Hebrews who first fought the worship of pagan idols in the western world and who preached eternal faith in *one God*—the God in whom we all put our trust." There were few Muslims in the United States, and though they too partly shared this same biblical heritage they were not considered a part of America's interfaith civil religion. Truman revealed perhaps too much when he joked with King Saud that Arabs and Jews "are all cousins" because of their common lineage descended from Abraham; yet Truman did not mention that Christians, too, shared the same biblical ancestry. The joke did little to conceal the cultural gulf that lay between the president and the king. Instinctively, Truman was predisposed to seeing the world through a Judeo-Christian lens that either obscured Islamic concerns or refracted them beyond all recognition.[38]

But the most influential of Truman's motives were the twin engines of his humanitarianism: religious tolerance and the horror of the Holocaust.

The Nazis' persecution of the Jews was terrible enough, but the refugee crisis it triggered continued well into the postwar era. The Harrison Report of 1945 and consistent British obstructionism had helped convince Truman that Europe's Jewish problem could not be solved by Europeans. He could not, he confessed, simply "stand idly by while the victims of Hitler's madness were not allowed to build new lives. The Jews needed someplace where they could go." At first, this did not necessarily mean Palestine. The Jews, argued Myron Taylor, were accustomed to being a diasporic people and would adapt to their surroundings wherever they went. But as always, few places were willing to admit a large infusion of Jewish immigrants, and the Jewish refugees themselves overwhelmingly wanted to move to the Holy Land, even over moving to their traditional Golden Land of the United States. While the Allies held hundreds of thousands of Holocaust survivors in disused Nazi facilities and squalid refugee camps, the Jews of Palestine pleaded for an infusion of newcomers to strengthen their claims to statehood.[39]

Unable to escape such logic, in October 1946, on the eve of Yom Kippur, Truman pledged U.S. support for a Jewish commonwealth in the Middle East. This prompted an immediate angry response from King Saud. "I feel certain that Your Majesty will readily agree that the tragic situation of the surviving victims of Nazi persecution in Europe presents a problem of such magnitude and poignancy that it cannot be ignored by people of good will or humanitarian instincts," Truman replied. "This problem is worldwide. It seems to me that all of us have a common responsibility for working out a solution which would permit those unfortunates who must leave Europe to find new homes where they may dwell in peace and security." These were blunt words for the protector of Islam's holiest shrines and the acknowledged leader of opposition to Zionism. Yet Truman continued. The plight of the postwar Jews was "particularly tragic" because it reflected the fate of "the pitiful remnants of millions who were deliberately selected by the Nazi leaders for annihilation." These Jews "look to Palestine as a haven where they hope among people of their own faith to find refuge, to begin to lead peaceful and useful lives, and to assist in the further development of the Jewish National Home." Surely the American president could not have expected the Saudi king to be persuaded by such concerns. But to Truman, it seemed like a patently obvious solution. The Jews had to go somewhere, so why not Palestine?[40]

Why not indeed. As the State Department reminded him endlessly, and as he well knew from his communications with King Saud, the Arabs were implacably hostile to any kind of Jewish state in Palestine. Rather than providing safety and justice for Jews, Zionism seemed to be the latest in a long line of Western imperial land grabs. Bringing justice to Jews, said the Arabs, would merely result in injustice for others. Yet these were secondary concerns for Truman, who remained committed to a Jewish solution above all else. And a Jewish solution meant religious tolerance for a people who had long been denied it, even if it came at the expense of the rights of others. In a heated argument with Clifford, Forrestal pointed out that the Arabs outnumbered the Jews fifty-to-one in the Middle East. "Why don't you face up to the realities?" demanded the Secretary of Defense. "Jim, the President knows just as well as you do what the numbers are," Clifford shot back, "but he doesn't consider this to be a question of numbers. He has always supported the right of the Jews to have their own homeland, from the moment he became President. He considers this to be a question about the moral and ethical considerations that are present in that part of the world. For that reason, he supports the foundation of a Jewish state."[41]

After he had made his decision to recognize Israel, Truman remarked, "My soul objective in the Palestine procedure has been to prevent bloodshed." Whether it was a misspelling of a common homonym, a Freudian slip, or a deliberate pun, Truman's justification revealed much about the overriding priority he had given to matters of religion.[42]

High Priests of the Cold War

EISENHOWER AND THE SECOND COMING OF DULLES

A FTER A PERIOD of national uncertainty through Depression and war, the resurgent 1950s marked another of America's "great awakenings." Church membership rose from 49 percent in 1940 to 69 percent in 1960 as public religiosity reached new highs. The war had ushered in a new era of abundance, and after decades of scrimping and saving, churches and synagogues indulged in a frenzy of new building projects. What was most striking about the Cold War awakening was its ecumenicity—its interfaith formula of "Protestant-Catholic-Jew," according to the title of one of the decade's bestselling books. Critics, and not only theological conservatives, assailed the religious revival as broad but not deep, a rootless belief in God without any of the philosophical or liturgical complications of actual religion, a watered-down "faith in faith." William Lee Miller, one of the more perceptive observers of the era's religious practices, decried the ostentatious "piety on the Potomac" and criticized President Dwight D. Eisenhower in particular as "a very fervent believer in a very vague religion."[1]

Whatever its qualities, the signs of religion were absolutely everywhere in Cold War America. From politics to pop culture, the era was saturated with excessive piety as people competed to demonstrate their devotion to God, and to America as God's country. In one year alone, the Revised Standard Version of the Bible, first published in its entirety in 1952, sold more than 26.5 million copies. Music charts saw religiously themed singles race to the Top 10, while Hollywood churned out biblical epics like *The Ten Commandments*, *Ben-Hur*, *Quo Vadis*, and *Solomon and Sheba*. By leading packed revivals in cities across the country, evangelist Billy Graham became one of the most famous and admired people in America, while the Jehovah's Witnesses emulated his feat by filling Yankee Stadium for their first international assembly. Not unusually for the times, the infusion of religion and culture had explicitly geopolitical purposes, as well. Cecil B. DeMille, director of *The Ten Commandments*, described his portrayal of Moses and Exodus as based on "whether men should be ruled by God's law, or by the whims of a dictator like Ramses. Are men the property of the state, or are they free souls under God?" DeMille then elaborated in case anyone had failed to grasp his meaning: "This same struggle is still going on today."[2]

Politicians followed suit. At precisely the moment the Supreme Court— the branch of government least susceptible to popular pressure—was beginning to shore up the wall of separation between church and state in a series of cases involving religion in schools and other public venues, Congress busied itself with efforts to bring more religion into public life. Though sponsoring one religion over another was now taboo in Judeo-Christian America—a Senate bill proposing a constitutional amendment to recognize the authority and law of Jesus Christ failed to attract any support—sponsoring faith itself was most definitely not. Accordingly, Congress inserted the words "under God" into the Pledge of Allegiance in 1954 and established "In God We Trust" as the official national motto two years later. As Eisenhower said in support of changing the Pledge, "Whatever our individual church, whatever our personal creed, in our fundamental faith we are all one. Together we thank the Power that has made and preserved us as a nation." The president himself began several civil religious traditions: he was the first to say a prayer before his inaugural address, the first to begin Cabinet meetings with prayer, the first to be baptized while in office, and the first to preside over a National Prayer Breakfast. Even the Supreme Court joined in the revival. "We are a religious people whose institutions presuppose a Supreme Being," wrote Justice William O. Douglas in one of his opinions.[3]

As politics reflected religion, so too did diplomacy. Eisenhower and Secretary of State John Foster Dulles both, in differing ways and to varying degrees, applied faith to foreign policy. Their moral rectitude has not always sat well with historians. Dulles, noted Arthur M. Schlesinger Jr., was "the high priest of the Cold War" who waged an ideologically aggressive, even reckless, campaign of American exceptionalism. Schlesinger captured his subject well, and most observers have since concurred. Yet this characterization of Dulles, and by extension Eisenhower, also ignores the sources of their public piety and their reasons for applying it to foreign policy. For all their stridency and bluster, the religious views of Eisenhower and Dulles were more subtle than most portraits would suggest. They had their reasons, which went beyond the simplicities of reactionary anticommunism. Whether their stewardship of U.S. foreign policy was shrewd is another matter. To better understand what they did, however, we first need to understand their religious views more fully.[4]

As PRESIDENT, Dwight D. Eisenhower exhibited a faith that was more broadly ecumenical and less doctrinally informed than any since that of another general-turned-politician, George Washington. There is no reason to doubt the sincerity of Eisenhower's faith, though many observers do: because it was so theologically imprecise, because he spoke in almost deist generalities, and because he did not join a church until he became president at a time when religious devotion was a political necessity, his religion has been easy to deride and dismiss as a political tactic or mere rhetoric. He was, Democratic Senator Matthew Neely angrily charged in 1954, a "publican," someone who worshipped only so he could "parade" his religion "for political purposes." For a man so ostentatiously pious, Eisenhower could also be shockingly irreverent. As he said to Ezra Taft Benson, a prominent Mormon who was secretary of agriculture, "we've got to deal with spiritual matters. I feel your church connection . . . is a distinct asset." Or when reminded that he had begun a Cabinet meeting without first pausing for reflection—a custom, after all, he himself had begun—he snapped, "Oh, goddammit, we forgot the silent prayer." Such comments, as well as his habit of playing golf on Sundays instead of attending church, did nothing to allay concerns that Eisenhower's commitment to religion was not especially strong.[5]

"Although Eisenhower himself cannot be characterized as a devout man," notes one of the most astute historians of the era's religion and politics, "his rhetoric is indicative of the climate of opinion during his administration, and the president, a shrewd political animal, knew how to exploit prevailing attitudes." As with Arthur Schlesinger's portrayal of Dulles, this assessment of Eisenhower is mostly correct: the president was indeed politically shrewd, and part of this skill was knowing how to deploy religious imagery in support of his policies and his own personal appeal. But it is also incomplete. While Eisenhower's faith was neither sophisticated nor profound, it was consistent, and consistently devout. He essentially held fast to one big idea—that religious faith was the source of democratic politics—and applied it loosely throughout his presidency, especially to foreign policy.[6]

David Dwight Eisenhower—his names were switched in childhood—was born in Texas in 1890 but moved with his family to Abilene, Kansas, when he was only a few months old. Abilene, named for a biblical region mentioned in the Book of Luke (3:1), was a very small town lost in the vast remoteness of the Kansas prairie. Known initially as the fabled Wild West's most rambunctious, licentious outpost, Abilene had settled into a more sedentary lifestyle by the time the Eisenhowers arrived. The region's desolation had incubated religious movements of burning intensity for decades, and in this sense, the Eisenhowers could feel at home. Young Dwight's paternal grandfather had been not only a successful farmer but also a preacher in the River Brethren, a small, fundamentalist Protestant sect that originated among the German immigrants of Pennsylvania. His parents raised their children in a strict religious household, with

Bible readings several times a day. Even his name, Dwight, was steeped in American faith, coming not from a family member but in honor of the great evangelist, Dwight L. Moody. The River Brethren were such a tiny group that in a place like rural Kansas, far from most of their fellow believers back east, they had to worship in one another's homes. "There is no question about the regimen of religious instruction," notes Peter Lyon, an otherwise skeptical biographer, of Eisenhower's childhood. "The boys were steeped in it." Much later in life, Eisenhower reflected that he and his brothers "are all very earnestly and seriously religious. We could not help being so considering our upbringing." They continued to "devoutly believe in the extraordinary virtues of our parents," he remarked in 1954. "First of all they believed the admonition 'The fear of God is the beginning of all wisdom.' " Later in life, his parents joined another strict sect of uncompromising values, the Jehovah's Witnesses.[7]

"I am a serious and fervent Protestant and have been so throughout my career." Such a statement, issued in the spring of 1952 as Eisenhower considered a run for the presidency, smacks of special pleading and tactical savvy. And no doubt it was both. After leaving provincial Abilene for West Point and a military career that would take him around the world, Eisenhower rarely attended church. Yet special pleading and tactical savvy do not necessarily contradict, let alone eliminate room for, sincere religious devotion. Eisenhower may not have gone to church during his long military career, but churchgoing had never been a part of his life, not even in his fervent fundamentalist upbringing. As a national politician at a time of unusually strong popular religiosity, it would indeed have made great political sense for him to make an issue of his religion. But it does not mean that he lacked religion, only that he was exploiting one of his best natural assets. "I am one of the most deeply religious men I know," he claimed at a 1948 press conference at Columbia University, years before the presidency beckoned, and there is no reason to doubt him.[8]

Religious, perhaps, but not theological. In keeping with a boy who had been raised on a steady diet of uncompromising but unchurched faith, Eisenhower's religion was vague to the point of formlessness. It was an American civil religion as much as it was a Bible-based faith. At that same Columbia press conference, he explained that being deeply religious "doesn't mean that I adhere to any particular sect or organization. I do not believe that Democracy can exist without religion and I do believe in Democracy." He rarely quoted from scripture or made biblical allusions and loathed denominational identities and liturgical disputes. He became a member of the National Presbyterian Church in Washington after living an adult life without a spiritual home, but he did not become a sectarian. He explained that he had always "treasured my independence" in religious matters "because I like to note the difference in the several Protestant denominations." Eisenhower was broadly devout without being narrowly doctrinal. He was, in short, perfectly attuned to his times.[9]

This was no accident. Eisenhower was careful to cultivate his religious image, not just for partisan political advantage but as the nation's moral custodian. He felt it his duty, as president, to provide moral inspiration and guidance. And being moral meant being religious. Prodded by Clare Booth Luce to lead by example, Eisenhower decided to root his presidency in acting as the minister-in-chief for a reinvigorated civil religion. He believed he had a responsibility to serve "not only as the political leader, but as the spiritual leader of our times." With his own devout but unlimitedly broad religious faith, he was ideally suited to serving in such a role. Some of his closest aides certainly thought so. "What President Eisenhower wants for America is a revival of religious faith," wrote Stanley High, a former Republican campaign strategist who became an editor at *Reader's Digest*. "He is determined to use his influence and his office to make this period a spiritual turning point in America, and thereby to recover the strengths, the values, and the conduct which a vital faith produces in a people." As president, claimed senior White House aide Frederic Fox, who also happened to be a former Congregational minister—the first member of the clergy to be a White House staffer since the Civil War—Eisenhower "has a new responsibility. He is not only the Upholder of the Constitution; he is the 'Defender of the Faith.' "[10]

What Fox meant was that religion had a geopolitical role, too. For in the Cold War, when America seemed to face an existential threat to its values and political system as well as its physical security, religion offered both a sword and a shield. For Eisenhower, religion was important in that it alone could distinguish between the justness of America's cause and the wickedness of the Soviet Union's. Religion told Americans who they were, what they stood for, and thus also what they fought for. Though there was more on the margins, Eisenhower's religious rhetoric essentially struck a single theme over and over again: religious faith, and with it freedom of worship, was the bedrock of democracy. Here, Eisenhower was tapping into and reinventing a very old tradition of American thinking of the relationship between religious and political liberty. He was already familiar with this idea, having deployed it in the war. Nazi Germany's assault on civilization, General Eisenhower said in 1943, "constitutes a direct conflict between the forces of evil and those of Christian principles of human rights and dignity." And on this point, his belief in a civil religion of watered-down ecumenism served him well—but not without controversy.[11]

In December 1952, speaking at a meeting of the Freedoms Foundation at the Waldorf-Astoria in New York, President-elect Eisenhower reminisced about Georgi Zhukov, the Red Army general who had engineered the Soviet Union's victory over Nazi Germany on the Eastern Front much as Eisenhower had done for the British and American armies in North Africa and France. Despite their clashing views, Eisenhower spoke fondly of Zhukov and surmised that the Soviet general's postwar fall from grace stemmed from their wartime friendship. But Eisenhower also spoke of the great ideological and moral gulf that separated them. Zhukov once told him that communism was an idealistic, moral philosophy that appealed to humanity's better instincts but nonetheless required individual sacrifice for the good of all; by contrast, the United States told its people "they could do as they pleased" because it was grounded in a "materialistic and selfish" ideology. Eisenhower did not berate his Soviet friend. Instead, he pitied him, because a communist could never understand the true source of American ideas. "I knew it would do no good" to argue with Zhukov, Eisenhower told his audience at the Waldorf, because the American system "is founded on religion," and the Soviet general would not understand the importance of faith. "In other words," Eisenhower continued in words that would later come to haunt him, "our form of Government has no sense unless it is founded in a deeply felt religious faith, and I don't care what it is." Most commentators stop there, and hold up Eisenhower's words as proof of his banality or insincerity. But Eisenhower himself had not stopped: "With us of course it is the Judo-Christian [*sic*] concept but it must be a religion that all men are created equal. So what was the use of me talking to Zhukov about that? Religion, he had been taught, was the opiate of the people."[12]

Eisenhower's meaning, inelegantly expressed, was a version of the Christian republicanism that had helped shape American political thought for the previous two hundred years. People were inherently equal in the eyes of God because they had been created in his image. God, moreover, was the only being to whom they owed their automatic allegiance; below God, everyone else was equal. Eisenhower was fond of paraphrasing (he rarely quoted it accurately) the Declaration of Independence to this effect. " 'We hold that all men are endowed by their *Creator*' with certain rights," he explained to a friend a year later. "The point is that except for this equality of right, a gift from the Almighty, there was no sense, logic or reason in free government." Once people had agreed on this basic premise—fundamental to monotheistic religions such as Christianity and Judaism—as the Founders had in 1776, they could construct a democratic system built upon political equality. Atheistic societies, such as the Soviet Union or the People's Republic of China, lacked such built-in safeguards for democratic equality and were thus prone to tyranny. To Eisenhower, this was an elemental and elementary concept, almost self-evident. As he explained to the United Jewish Laymen's Committee, "Our Democracy needs Religion; our Religion also needs Democracy." It was as simple as that.[13]

Eisenhower had a very traditional fear of concentrated power, such as communism, that was particularly strong in both American and Protestant political thought. As he said in a 1948 speech, "danger arises from too great a concentration of power in the hands of any individual or group." If unchecked and "allowed to dominate," such concentrations of power were "fully capable of destroying individual freedom." In Eisenhower's mind, religious liberty and free enterprise were the most important sources of freedom, even more important than the right to vote or freedom of the press. No matter how diluted it had become, his Protestant faith—particularly his highly autonomous, anti-statist fundamentalist background—was a powerful source of these ideas. "Our Protestant beliefs and convictions," Eisenhower exclaimed in a revealing detour out from under the Judeo-Christian umbrella, provided the foundation for "our civilization and government."[14]

Religious liberty was thus an essential protector of civil liberty; without the first, the second could not exist. "The freedom of a citizen and the freedom of a religious believer are more than intimately related," he said in 1958, "they are mutually dependent. These two liberties give life to the heart of our Nation. We are politically free people because each of us is free to express his individual faith." Atheists were not only amoral, and probably immoral, but were incapable of democratic self-government. Elinor Smith, the aviator and freethinker, castigated Eisenhower's stance as "freedom of religion for everyone but agnostics. You can have any you like, but you gotta pick one." Intended to be sarcastic, her joke in fact interpreted Eisenhower's meaning perfectly. In a very impolitic statement that caused a storm of controversy, he told a delegation of Nebraska Republicans that the "one place where France has gone astray" was that "50 per cent of their people [are] agnostics or atheists. It takes no brains to be an atheist." It also meant that French "moral fiber has disintegrated."[15]

Normally, the religious complexion of France would not have been America's concern, but for Eisenhower, as for almost all policymakers at the time, the interconnected world of the Cold War was not a normal time or place. France's alleged atheism was an irritant, not a threat, but Eisenhower felt the same could not be said of Soviet communism. Perhaps the greatest concentration of power ever known, communism was in service to an expansionist Soviet state. It was not simply an ideological irritant but a geopolitical threat. He believed, as he told world leaders assembled for the United Nations' tenth anniversary celebrations in 1955, that "man—a physical, intellectual and spiritual being—has individual rights, divinely bestowed," and that "to deny any person the opportunity to live under their shelter is a crime against all humanity." The key difference between French and Soviet atheism was that France did not seek to deny anyone else from holding their own beliefs, while the Soviet Union did. Thus it was important to identify communism not merely as a military or political threat, but as a moral and religious one. "Communism denies the spiritual premises on which your education has been based," he warned Baylor University's graduating class of 1956. According to the communists, "there is no God; there is no soul in man; there is no reward beyond the satisfaction of daily needs." The implications were terrifying: "toward the human being, Communism is cruel, intolerant, materialistic." Most ominously for the United States, it was also "committed to conquest by lure, by intimidation and by force" and sought "to destroy the political concepts and institutions that we hold to be dearer than life itself."[16]

In two of his most famous speeches, Eisenhower began and ended his presidency with this same warning. His first inaugural address, in 1953, used religion to celebrate America's virtues and identify the Soviet menace. "At such a time in history," he declared,

> we who are free must proclaim anew our faith. This faith is the abiding creed of our fathers. It is our faith in the deathless dignity of man, governed by eternal moral and natural laws.
>
> This faith defines our full view of life. It establishes, beyond debate, those gifts of the Creator that are man's inalienable rights, and that make all men equal in His sight.
>
> ... This faith rules our whole way of life. It decrees that we, the people, elect leaders not to rule but to serve.

After reaffirming "our dedication and devotion to . . . the watchfulness of a Divine Providence," Eisenhower turned to the antithesis of the American creed and echoed holy war rhetoric from the Puritans to NSC-68:

> The enemies of this faith know no god but force, no devotion but its use. They tutor men in treason. They feed upon the hunger of others. Whatever defies them, they torture, especially the truth.
>
> ... This conflict strikes directly at the faith of our fathers and the lives of our sons. No principle or treasure that we hold, from the spiritual knowledge of our free schools and churches to the creative magic of free labor and capital, nothing lies safely beyond the reach of this struggle.
>
> Freedom is pitted against slavery; lightness against the dark.
>
> The faith we hold belongs not to us alone but to the free of all the world.

Almost exactly eight years later, as he prepared to depart the White House, he repeated this stark warning. In his farewell address, the same speech in which he warned against the increasingly concentrated power of America's own "military-industrial complex," he reminded Americans that they faced "a hostile ideology—global in scope, atheistic in character, ruthless in purpose, and insidious in method." America, he said, must never let down its guard.[17]

But, like his fellow Presbyterian George Kennan, Eisenhower believed that America would prevail if it remained true to itself. It would be a difficult test, but he was certain Americans could pass it. "Confronted by a militant atheism and brazen materialism, our religious institutions were never more important to our way of life," he wrote to a retired general in 1954. "It is only as we are strong in faith that we are adequate for our age." And like Kennan, he believed that communism contained the seeds of its own destruction. No political system without faith, and thus without individual autonomy, could survive against the wishes of its own people for very long. "The destiny of man is freedom and justice under his Creator," not communism, he told the Baylor students. "Any ideology that denies this universal faith will ultimately perish or be recast." Religion was an essential part of containment: it was an intangible and thus unstoppable force. It was a faithful, penitent America's secret weapon. "The free world has one great factor in common," he told a national television audience before departing for the 1955 Geneva Conference. "We are not held together by force but we are held together by this great factor. It is this. The free world lives under one religion or another. It believes in a divine power. It believes in a supreme being." Then he asked all Americans, "165 million of us," to pray for peace on Sunday. "This would be a mighty force."[18]

Through the efforts of Secretary of State Dulles, examined below, but also in other ways, the Eisenhower administration sought to apply this mighty force of faith to the practice of U.S. foreign policy. A large part of these efforts were simply through presidential rhetoric, which mobilized Americans into action by identifying their adversary and reminding them why they must struggle against it. Religion could also apply pressure to atheist regimes who did not respect faith but whose people did. In 1954, Eisenhower declared September 22 to be an official National Day of Prayer, and he invited people living throughout Europe to join in. As he explained to Senator William Knowland, the Soviets had "not succeeded in extinguishing the religious faith and aspirations of the peoples behind the Iron Curtain." Appealing to the people of Eastern Europe and the Soviet Union therefore "supports our conviction that, if the present oppressive regime were removed, we should probably quickly establish friendly relations between our nation and the peoples now so cruelly cut off from the free world." Through the universal religious impulse, Eisenhower hoped to drive a wedge between communist rulers and their people.[19]

At the World Council of Churches' second assembly, held in 1954 in Evanston, Illinois, Eisenhower used his address to call for a World Day of Prayer that would, if only for a few moments, unite the global faithful as a single community bound not by any government but only by their shared individual belief in a higher deity. Despite its logistical difficulties, the United States Information Agency was eager to launch the president's plan. "To be successful," the USIA's Abbott Washburn enthused to the White House,

> the world-wide moment of prayer must embrace not just Christians but Mohammedans, Buddhists, and all major religions—each person praying as an *individual.* Thus the great action would not be *ecclesiastical,* but *personal.* Each in his own way. Some standing. Some kneeling on prayer rugs. Some, behind the Curtain, praying only in their minds, silently. Some in services in their own familiar churches. Some at home. Some listening to and participating in a vast global radio service, led by the temporal and spiritual leaders of free countries.

This would not really be an ecumenical initiative but a weapon in the Cold War. It would be, Washburn continued, "a dramatic event of magnitude and impact" that would "give us and the Free World the initiative in the movement for *peace.* (The Soviets continually label us war-mongers.)" It would also "reveal the true spiritual foundation of our Government and our society, in contrast to the Russian. (The one thing the USSR cannot promote is *prayer* for peace.)" It would "stress the real unity of human aspirations, in spite of differences of race, culture and religion," and of course establish the United States as the guarantor of that moral unity. Above all, said Washburn, it would be "unstoppable. No man, not even a prisoner, can be stopped from prayer, providing the prayer is the prayer of the heart."[20]

Beyond propaganda, religion inflected the direction of policymaking as well. The fact that South Vietnam's Ngo Dinh Diem was Roman Catholic, for example, was a significant factor in leading Eisenhower and Dulles to support his bid for the leadership of an overwhelmingly Buddhist country. During Hungary's 1956 revolt against Soviet rule, Radio Free Europe vigorously promoted Jozsef Cardinal Mindszenty, the head not only of the country's Catholicism but perhaps also its most prominent anticommunist, as the rightful leader of the uprising. Dulles told the NSC that Mindszenty, not Imre Nagy, was the rebellion's "unifying force," while Eisenhower used a press conference to hail the Cardinal as a symbol "of freedom and the desire for liberation." When the revolt failed, the

U.S. Embassy in Budapest gave Mindszenty emergency refuge, and then granted him permanent asylum; he would not leave the embassy grounds for the next fifteen years. In more systematic fashion, religion was also an important part of the Eisenhower administration's propaganda campaign, conducted by the Operations Coordinating Board and the U.S. Information Agency, to convince the world's people of the evils of communism and the virtues of Americanism.[21]

But these were not even the most important policies to be influenced by faith. And with the second coming of John Foster Dulles, Eisenhower was not the only high priest of America's Cold War.

IN KEEPING WITH the spirit of the times, Eisenhower chose John Foster Dulles to be his secretary of state. Dulles was of course eminently qualified to serve as a spiritual statesman, having been a delegate to the peace conferences following both world wars and an architect of the United Nations. His most formative experience in world politics, we have seen, came as head of the Federal Council of Churches' Commission on a Just and Durable Peace. The ecumenical internationalism he imbibed and internalized at the Commission provided him with a coherent worldview and strategic outlook. He was a spiritual diplomat, equally adept in both worlds, and it was this versatility that appealed to Eisenhower. "There is probably no one in the world who has the technical competence of Foster Dulles in this diplomatic field," the president reflected midway through his presidency. But as much as his diplomatic skill, Eisenhower also admired Dulles's "great intellectual capacity and moral courage." Stanley High, an Eisenhower adviser during the 1952 campaign, praised Dulles's "pronounced spiritual convictions" and esteem among "church people, as no other man of this generation, as a Christian statesman." Eisenhower did not disagree.[22]

Yet Dulles in power scarcely resembled Dulles the ecumenist. Where he had once warned against the temptations of military intervention, now he seemed to advocate using force as a first resort; where he had once questioned the atomic bombing of Japan, now he seemed to flaunt a cavalier attitude toward nuclear weapons; and where he had once helped design the UN to be a forum for all people to conduct their affairs together, now he divided the world into good and evil, freedom and communism, faith and godlessness. "You may have to recognize the fact of evil," Secretary of State Dulles said in what amounted to a wholesale rebuke of both Christian pacifists and realists, "but that doesn't mean that you have to clasp it to your bosom." As secretary of state, Dulles's piety seemed to acquire a harder, more triumphalist edge. "No one in the State Department knows as much about the Bible as I do," he crowed after moving into Foggy Bottom, and he seemed intent on proving it. The "terrible things" happening around the world were because geopolitics had been "separated from spiritual content," he warned in words that bore more resemblance to a fundamentalist sermon than his usual mainline fare. "Such conditions repel us. But it is important to understand what causes these conditions. It is irreligion." How could this new Dulles have anything in common with his old self when they seemed to be two completely different people?[23]

The answer is deceptively simple: they were not so different after all. Contrary to most portraits, there was no real inconsistency between his work for the Federal Council and his stewardship of the State Department. In fact, his second coming was a product of, rather than a reaction to, his wartime work. The positions that Secretary of State Dulles took as the nation's leading holy warrior did not repudiate his earlier views so much as take them to their logical extremes. And even in the remoteness of those diplomatic extremities, when he sometimes seemed isolated from not only allies and public opinion but also his own president, Dulles privately continued to believe what his public persona could not: that war was a sin, that nuclear weapons had a greater potential for evil than good, that integration was still the best means of facilitating cooperation, and that cooperation was still the surest path to peace. Beneath a doggedly, aggressively anticommunist exterior still lurked an ecumenical internationalist.[24]

Admittedly, to say that Dulles was not completely different from his earlier self is not to say there was no difference. For after 1953—indeed, after 1946—he did adopt a much more strident, dogmatic, aggressive approach to the Cold War, and specifically to the Soviet Union. But here lies the solution to the riddle of Dulles. World War II had defeated Nazism and other forms of fascism, and Dulles was in the vanguard of fashioning a new world order that would make great power war unnecessary, and eventually obsolete. But after the war, Soviet communists seemed intent on sabotaging this new world order simply in order to advance their own expansionist and tyrannical ambitions. They acted not on behalf of humanity, but for their own selfish ends. A visceral hostility to communism now began to consume Dulles, not only because he disliked its atheism, its dictatorship of the proletariat, and its command economy, but because the Soviets—and only the Soviets—stood between the people of the world and an era of peace and prosperity. At San Francisco, Dulles confessed he had "some doubt as to whether the Soviets really wanted a world organization." Now, in the Cold War, he was sure of it.[25]

Thus from 1946 until his death in 1959, Dulles modified his ecumenical internationalism to do battle with communism in order to rescue ecumenical internationalism. First in occasional partnership with the Truman administration and Protestant ecumenists, and then much more substantially as Eisenhower's secretary of state, Dulles mounted a crusade to rid the world of communism so it could find the peace it deserved.

· · ·

UNTIL THE COLD WAR, Dulles had never been an anticommunist crusader. Before 1945–46, in fact, he had shown little interest in communism and certainly did not see it as an all-consuming threat to Western civilization. To be sure, anticommunism was part of his intellectual and personal background. While serving as Wilson's secretary of state, his uncle Robert Lansing responded to the 1917 Bolshevik revolution by denouncing "these dangerous idealists" who appealed to the world's "ignorant and mentally deficient, who by their numbers are urged to become masters." Communism, Lansing concluded straightaway, was "a very real danger in view of the present social unrest throughout the world." Unlike many mainline Protestants in the interwar period, Dulles had never admired communism's industrial achievements or commitment to social justice, and during the war he worried about America's enthusiasm for its Soviet ally. Temperamentally and intellectually, Dulles and communism were simply too unsuited to each other. Like fascism, communism abridged the freedom of worship and respect for individual liberties that Dulles believed to be indispensable to peace, justice, and democracy. But before the end of World War II, communism had never been his overriding concern. Most of the time, he simply ignored it.[26]

For at least a year after the surrender of Germany, Dulles did not abandon his dream of world peace through global governance, international organization, and world brotherhood. He still believed, very deeply, that the UN reflected the universal hopes of all humanity. That it actually reflected a very Western, indeed predominantly American view of world politics seems to have totally escaped him. In March 1946, after resuming his duties with the Commission on a Just and Durable Peace, he drafted a comprehensive statement of guidance for the Federal Council of Churches. Other than a passing reference to Stalin's meeting with Truman and Churchill at Potsdam, Dulles did not once mention communism; nor did he even allude to a Soviet threat. Instead, reprising his wartime ecumenical vision, he called for the United States to work through the UN, "accept the jurisdiction of the World Court in all legal disputes," help draft an International Bill of Rights, maintain control of nuclear policy in civilian hands, sponsor comprehensive and mutual disarmament, abolish conscription, and "seek the development of international or universal law." It was a classically mainline peace manifesto that would not have been out of place if published in the noninterventionist pages of the *Christian Century* circa 1938.[27]

As his biographer has noted, Dulles's mood changed sharply only a month later. The timing of this sudden transition in the spring of 1946 was not unusual for American officials and those, like Dulles, who had a vested interest in foreign policymaking. In the previous months, Stalin had declared capitalism and communism to be incompatible and a third world war inevitable, Churchill had declared the Iron Curtain to be descending across Europe, Kennan had written his Long Telegram from Moscow, and the Soviets had seemed to threaten a takeover of northern Iran. Witness to what he thought was communist obstructionism and expansionism as the rest of the world began the tasks of economic reconstruction and political settlement, Dulles turned sharply against the Soviet Union. First, in June 1946, courtesy of his fellow Christian cold warrior Henry R. Luce, came two major articles in *Life* magazine that sounded the trumpet for a new American crusade. According to Dulles, the Soviets had divided the world into three spheres—inner, middle, and outer—and aimed to dominate all three. They conceived the world, as did internationalist Americans such as Dulles, as interconnected and indivisible; therefore, in order to maintain Soviet security, Moscow had to spread its system into as much of the rest of the world as possible. It was a classic strategy of security through expansion, but Dulles did not have the presence of mind to note that it was a mirror image of his own American geopolitics. Like Stalin, internationalist Americans perceived the world as irreversibly interconnected, and to protect U.S. security, they would have to expand, as widely as possible, America's own political and economic system. In order to feel secure, both had to create an international environment in which they could feel at home. It was a recipe for conflict that was as natural as it was unavoidable, yet increasingly Dulles did not see it this way.[28]

The articles in *Life* provoked something of a backlash among his colleagues at the FCC. In a pivotal meeting to decide the future direction of the Commission on a Just and Durable Peace just days after the publication of the first article, Dulles faced a barrage of skeptical questions. Even Niebuhr, who as we shall see was in some ways every bit as much an anticommunist Cold Warrior as Dulles, thought he had gone too far. The Soviet Union was a danger, Niebuhr conceded, but it was acting "out of a sense of her weakness." The best thing the United States could do now would be to remove the sources of Soviet suspicion. Doing so would not end all tension, but it would alleviate the worst of it. Bishop Bromley Oxnam, perhaps the Commission member who was personally and professionally closest to Dulles, was the most bewildered. He simply could not understand why his friend had so quickly become such a hard-liner. Oxnam warned that Dulles's new stance raised the "danger of developing a holy war against Communism." The United States had enough social, racial, and economic problems of its own, Oxnam reminded Dulles, so why should Americans assume a posture of moral superiority? Niebuhr sided with Oxnam. John Coleman Bennett wanted Dulles and the Truman administration instead "to let the Russians know that we are not going to try to destroy their system." Though he did not use the term, Niebuhr then suggested that Soviet-American tensions were caused by what political scientists call the "security dilemma": when a state feels threatened, it reacts in a way that it sees as defensive but that others perceive as aggressive, thus making them feel threatened; defensive moves seem aggressive to others, triggering an escalating cycle of tension. Resolving the security dilemma requires a level of trust that is usually impossible to attain. "You are dealing with a highly organized society that feels itself imperiled but is spreading out further and further on the basis of its feeling," Niebuhr said of the Soviet Union. There "is such a thing as a vicious circle of fear. Fears of the Russians are plausible. They produce the situation which they fear. If you don't say anything about that then I don't think you can say [anything] about having peace with Russia."[29]

But Dulles would not budge. The Soviet Union was not a partner for peace—believing so was America's big mistake during the war—but a threat to be contained. Interestingly, the rhetoric of rollback—of eradicating, rather than merely containing, global communism—was not yet a part of his ideological arsenal. On this point, Dulles thought himself much more the realist than the neo-orthodox Niebuhr and Bennett. "In order to have a peaceful outcome of this thing we must realize quickly that the attack is there and if we don't do something quickly about it we shall have to surrender or go to war," he said in a rebuttal to his Commission colleagues. "The main question is, are we going to tell the American people that they face this kind of a challenge or are we going to say that the Soviet [Union] is sweetness and light? The challenge came—how are we going to parry it?" Under these new circumstances, it would be foolish for the Commission and the FCC to call for the usual mainline goals—the very same goals Dulles had reiterated as recently as March—of disarmament and unconditional dialogue. "If we were to proceed to disarm today that would leave unchecked the forces which would bring ruin on the world. Just now there is one thing which is holding the forces of the Soviets and their satellites back from complete invasion of Europe"—the Allied occupying forces. The "heart of the problem" and the "reason we face the danger of war with the Soviet Union and don't face it with other countries," Dulles continued, "is that the Russian system in its present mood is one of very extreme intolerance and of the feeling that it is right and justified to use any available method, including force and violence to eliminate those who don't share the views they think are right." Instead of negotiating with the Soviets, who would never do so in good faith, Dulles insisted on the need for "a clear and direct demonstration of the vigor and vitality of our system." When Oxnam pointed out that in fact the American system had also been guilty of intolerance, aggression, and imperialism, Dulles shot back, "Why do we have to run all that down? Why present ourselves as such a terrible species of being?" Especially at a time, he argued, when the Europeans themselves were desperate for American assurances. The United States had had its problems, Dulles admitted, but in the final analysis its record on democracy and human rights was incomparably better than the Soviet Union's. "I just don't see how we help our case at all by deprecating all that."[30]

Dulles's views on the United States and the Soviet Union were changing dramatically. In the United States, which he had once seen as a paradoxical embodiment of racist democracy and progressive empire, he now saw an exceptionally virtuous nation of faith that had committed sins of omission, not commission, and was a leading light to the rest of the world. Americans, he told a forum sponsored by the *New York Herald Tribune* in 1947, "have a great heritage." Some thought it political, some economic, but their heritage "is, in its essentials, a religious heritage" that had become "widely known as an experiment in human freedom." Instead of deriving rights from the state, the "sovereignty of man rests upon a religious estimate of his nature. Without this estimate he tends to slavery," as in a communist society.[31]

Conversely, in the Soviet Union Dulles saw an awesome military juggernaut that marched at the command of an unremittingly hostile atheist ideology and at the whim of a malevolent dictator. It was natural, he declared in a Philadelphia speech in the fall of 1946, for allies to squabble after they had defeated their common enemy. "This time, however, what is happening is more than that. We seem to be witnessing a challenge to established civilization—the kind of thing which occurs only once in centuries." Dulles compared the Soviets not to more recent hegemonic challengers, such as the Nazi Germans or Napoleonic French, but to the Islamic hordes who had "swept over much of Christendom" in the Middle Ages. "The faith and institutions of Soviet Communism differ vastly from those of the Western democracies," he explained, and it was the Soviet Union's mission to see its faith and institutions triumph over all rivals. Whereas the Soviets were materialistic, dictatorial, communistic, and violent, the West was based on religious faith, democracy, free enterprise, and a peaceful order. His colleagues on the Federal Council still called for disarmament, but Dulles wanted "to keep the United States strong militarily as long as it was under the guns of a threatening power."[32]

An awkward divide now began to separate Dulles from his erstwhile colleagues in the mainline churches. They still agreed theologically—Dulles had not become more conservative on religion. But on foreign policy, Dulles was inching toward the right, certainly in relation to the FCC. He complained that the Commission on a Just and Durable Peace—and by extension, mainline liberal Protestantism as a whole—"has been derelict in not facing up to the Russian problem." For their part, liberal Protestants felt disappointed, even betrayed, by Dulles's newfound anticommunism. James A. Crain of the mainline United Christian Missionary Society thought it was "extremely unfortunate" that Dulles, "the man who has become the symbol of Protestant thinking about World Order," would use the prominence of *Life* magazine "to express views which are so widely at variance with the spirit, if not the actual text," of the FCC's foreign policy views. Yet Dulles was still unacceptable to fundamentalist Protestants, such as Carl McIntire, who accused him of being "an effective tool" of the "extremely radical and pacifist" Federal Council.[33]

Could Crain and McIntire both be right? On almost all other matters, no. Yet it is a testament to Dulles's complexity and contradictions that on this issue they each had a point. With Dulles, both liberals and conservatives could have cause for grievance. McIntire's complaint is especially interesting, for while Dulles became a crusading Cold Warrior wielding the sword of the spirit, he also retained enough of his mainline liberalism to keep the shield of faith nearby. What McIntire recognized that many historians have not, in other words, was that Dulles had not completely repudiated his earlier views. In 1946, as a result of his debate with Niebuhr, Bennett, and Oxnam, the final version of Dulles's Commission statement on the Cold War accepted the security dilemma—and its explicit recognition of Soviet concerns as to some extent understandable, even perhaps legitimate—as a fundamental cause of tension. In 1947, in a private meeting about Security Council voting procedures with Andrei Gromyko, the Soviet Ambassador to the UN, Dulles confessed that he "could understand" that the Soviets "would be particularly sensitive" about their position in the world. A year later, he publicly recognized that "Russian leaders do not now want war and would not initiate war unless they genuinely believed that war was our intention." He also acknowledged that "Russia suffered horribly from the last war. Because she emerged victorious and because her leaders now adopt a hard attitude, we forget how deeply she was wounded." He still insisted that there was a Soviet threat, but it was one based on "penetration, propaganda, and terrorism" that could be defeated through vigilant containment. Two years after that, in 1950, he and Walter Van Kirk, an old friend and a leading light of the Protestant peace crusade, coauthored an NCC statement declaring that war with the Soviet Union was neither "inevitable nor imminent" and that "the best hope of preventing global atomic war lies in preventing the recurrence of global war itself." Moreover, his belief in racial and religious tolerance had not ebbed. "Most people of the world are not white and they are not of the Christian or Jewish tradition," he said in a 1947 statement. "In fact, no race and no religion can muster a majority of the whole. Thus no group is accepted in the world as a friend, if its members seem to be contemptuous of races or religions different from their own." Nor had he abandoned the

FCC's commitment to decolonization. He regarded "the colonial system as obsolete," he declared as a member of the U.S. delegation to the UN, "and wished to see it abolished."[34]

Rather than a simple fear of the Soviets, then, Dulles's worldview was in fact a complicated mix of anticommunism and American nationalism with ecumenical internationalism. But as the Cold War deepened, his anticommunism and nationalism began to eclipse his ecumenical internationalism. Dulles still believed that broadly integrative organizations, such as the United Nations and the World Council of Churches, could steer the world toward peace. But how could the UN and the WCC resolve international problems if the Soviets and their allies took advantage of the good faith on which they were based? To Dulles's great frustration, already in 1944, at Dumbarton Oaks, the Soviets seemed to be intent on sabotaging Dulles's six pillars of peace. Now, at the UN, the Soviet veto was proving to be an obstacle to peace and the undoing of global governance. Meanwhile, at the WCC, communist sympathizers who had the temerity to call themselves Christian were sabotaging the ecumenical project from within. Infiltration, subversion, sowing dissension— these, Dulles believed, were the hallmarks of an eventual communist takeover.[35]

The tensions between Dulles's anticommunism and his ecumenism, once buried deep within, came rushing to the surface at the World Council of Churches' founding assembly in Amsterdam in 1948. With the Czech theologian Josef Hromadka criticizing the West in general and American capitalism in particular, Dulles felt he had to counteract a dangerous threat to the unity of the Christian West. The clergy and laity who assembled at Amsterdam "represent both great diversity and great unity," he said in his address. Diversity was a strength, but not without moral unity; hence the importance of the WCC, the FCC in the United States, and the UN. But the WCC gathering "comes at a fateful hour, for, in the world, division is assuming an ominous character." Ecumenical convocations such as the WCC and international organizations such as the UN could only work if they were based on two fundamental principles that were the source of all human and civil rights: moral law and the dignity of the individual, both of which "rest on fundamental religious assumptions." For those in the audience who had not yet grasped that his address was also an attack on atheist Soviet communism, Dulles elaborated:

Marxian communism is atheistic and materialistic. Its leaders reject the concept of moral law. There is, says Stalin, no such thing as "eternal justice"; laws are merely the means whereby those in power carry out their will, and human beings have no rights that are God-given and therefore not subject to be taken away from them.

... The Soviet communist regime is not a regime of peace and, indeed, it does not purport to be.... It is inevitable that orthodox communism should reject peaceful ways, except as a matter of temporary expediency, because it rejects the moral premises that alone make possible the permanent organization of peace. Peace can never be stabilized except by institutions that seek to reflect the moral law and that respect the dignity of the individual.

For democratic, peace-loving Christians, the source of their salvation was ironic: resistance. Here, Dulles approached something of the tragic element in Niebuhr's thought, though Niebuhr abhorred Dulles's American exceptionalism. "The solution," Dulles explained, "is for those who have faith to exert themselves more vigorously to translate their faith into works." Elsewhere, he claimed that if "communism and fascism are hateful because of the consequences of their godlessness, it is equally true that they can be successfully resisted only by societies imbued with strong spiritual convictions." It was a logical point. Dulles's problem, however, was that many of those in Amsterdam agreed with Hromadka's communist logic instead.[36]

To overcome this dilemma, Dulles followed his own advice: he strove to turn faith into works. He did not abandon the ecumenical initiative, but instead sought to narrow it. Despite their universalist pretensions, the FCC and WCC themselves believed in limiting their membership by excluding Roman Catholics and Protestant fundamentalists, and Dulles had something similar in mind for world politics. Organizations, he had reminded his fellow delegates to San Francisco in 1945, "have the power to determine" whether a potential member "has or has not the characteristics that entitle it to representation." Similarly, if the Soviets sabotaged the UN then it was up to the United States to create a more workable international organization that reflected its own beliefs, and work outward from there. The UN was still necessary, Dulles conceded, but for the time it simply was not a practical solution to world problems. With democratic governments comprising only a fifth of the UN's membership, and with the Soviet Union intent on dominating the globe, world government "could not be other than despotic." It was easy to create the UN, Dulles said shortly after the WCC Amsterdam assembly; the hard part was in finding a common morality around which all the members could coalesce. It was not simply "a matter of organization" but of finding "the will, the perseverance and the capacity of the members in support of the organization." At a time when half of the world was dominated by atheists who did not believe in natural rights or religion, it was time to build a new organization of fellow true believers.[37]

This was how Dulles, one of the leading American proponents of

United Nations universalism, also came to be one of the leading American proponents of Western regionalism in the form of the North Atlantic Treaty Organization. He had of course already shown an ability to compromise his principles in the face of political pressure. What was significant about his support of NATO was a willingness to adapt his principles in a manner that was not exactly inconsistent with his earlier, universalistic views. Dulles explained away the apparent inconsistencies by claiming that the Soviets were tainting the UN with "their kind of reality," based on "the principle of unanimity" that would destroy diversity of opinion, enforce conformity, and "lead easily to the argument that world peace and security could be accomplished only on a basis of universality." Unlike the UN, which the Soviets could cynically manipulate, NATO members would be cohesive, "distinctively identified with Western civilization and its institutions of political freedom." NATO, he told an interviewer for NBC News, was thus "a logical step in the unification of Western Europe," and that "unity must come if Western civilization is to survive." Dulles was also willing to cross the partisan political divide and advise the Truman administration during NATO's planning stages.[38]

It was no idle commitment. In a quirk of politics due to the illness and sudden retirement of Senator Robert Wagner, Dulles found himself appointed to represent New York in the U.S. Senate. He began his term in July 1949, right in the middle of the contentious debate over NATO ratification. The North Atlantic treaty marked a significant change in U.S. history. Americans had always interacted with the world, but always on their own terms—more unilateralist than truly isolationist. The U.S. government had signed many treaties in the previous 150 years, but it had never bound itself to an entangling alliance of indefinite duration. Most controversially, Article 5 of the NATO Charter obligated all members automatically to the defense of all other members. NATO, in other words, seemed to take away from Congress the exclusive right to declare war. Led by Robert A. Taft of Ohio, Republican senators expressed deep reservations about committing to such an open-ended commitment and abridgment of American sovereignty. Breaking Senate etiquette against new members speaking on the Senate floor, Dulles rose to confront the members of his own party. "It is apparent now," he argued, "that security could not be achieved at a single step through a single world organization." Instead, it was now "necessary to advance progressively through a series of organizations for collective self-defense." Dulles was still very much the ecumenist, though his vision was much more narrowly defined.[39]

UNDERSTANDING DULLES in an ecumenical context is vital to understanding his anticommunist turn in the early Cold War. But it is also essential if we are to reach a fuller appreciation of his tenure as one of the nation's most influential—and controversial—secretaries of state. It is as Eisenhower's global attack dog, not his work for the Federal Council, that we remember Dulles. Yet as we have just seen, the two cannot be separated, because his anticommunist convictions sprang from an almost parental desire to protect his offspring, an international order based upon cooperation through interdependence and integration. But even more interesting was the consistency of ecumenical internationalism that continued to run through his policies as secretary of state.

Picturing Secretary of State Dulles as a foreign policy liberal does violence to the historical imagination. In 1954, he coined the phrase "massive retaliation" to explain that the United States would use its overwhelming nuclear superiority to respond to any kind of communist expansion. Massive retaliation was bad enough, but two years later Dulles made it even worse with his infamous strategy of "brinkmanship." Of diplomacy, Dulles told an interviewer from *Life* that the "ability to get to the verge without getting into the war is the necessary art. If you cannot master it, you inevitably get into a war. If you try to run away from it, if you are scared to go to the brink, you are lost." When the art of brinkmanship was joined with the doctrine of massive retaliation, it seemed as if Dulles was using America's nuclear weapons to play chicken with the Soviet Union.[40]

Such needlessly exaggerated rhetoric earned Dulles the reputation as a warmonger. It also provoked even greater distrust from religious liberals, especially those at the National Council of Churches (the FCC changed its name in 1950). Beneath the mandatory surface pleasantries, by the mid-1950s Dulles and the mainline clergy had completely lost faith in one another. As John Mackay, president of Princeton Theological Seminary, leading ecumenist, and fellow Presbyterian, reflected, Dulles lacked "a constructive approach" to America's role in the world. "I cannot but feel that in this, Mr. Dulles was not really true to his deepest self and to insights which he had formerly expressed." For his part, Dulles thought the churches had simply lost touch with the realities of geopolitics.[41]

There was some truth to these charges and countercharges, yet they obscured as much as they revealed. For beneath his anticommunist bluster, Secretary of State Dulles remained truer to his "deepest self" than the mainliners realized. He continued to hold beliefs and express doubts that were rooted in the tenets of ecumenism and liberal Protestantism. Moreover, his ecumenical instincts attuned him to the sensitivities of liberal views that he knew would be at odds with the Eisenhower administration's more conservative policies. On a surprising number of issues, especially when his ecumenism and his anticommunism complemented each other, he seemed very much his old self. Only by remembering his ecumenical background—and not simply his religious rhetoric—can we really understand his motivations and policies.

On nuclear weapons, for example, the issue on which Dulles and church leaders clashed most often, there is a great deal of evidence to suggest that he privately shared some of their concerns. The author of massive retaliation was not averse to disarmament—so long as it was monitored by the international community. Nuclear weaponry "was too vast a power to be left for the military use of any one country," he told Eisenhower in 1955. Ideally, it should instead be "internationalized for security purposes." This would not undermine America's defenses because it would simply "universalize the capacity of atomic thermonuclear weapons to deter aggression." Deterrence, in other words, would be no longer national but international. And he knew, from his intimacy with liberal Protestants, that nuclear weapons would be not only controversial but morally troubling. "Propaganda picturing us as warmongers on account of our atomic capabilities has done incalculable harm," he told a National Security Council meeting in 1954, perhaps forgetting it was he who had done the most to paint this picture. In any event, he realized that this was not in America's interests, because, as he noted to Eisenhower, U.S. strategy rested upon America's "atomic striking power. However, that striking power was apt to be immobilized by moral repugnance. If this happened, the whole structure could readily collapse."[42]

Another aspect of foreign policy that is better understood in light of Dulles's ecumenism is U.S. support for European integration. Here, there was not as much tension between his ecumenical internationalism and U.S. national interests, for most American policymakers believed that only a strong, prosperous, united Western Europe could stand as a bulwark against the spread of communism. European union fit perfectly with Dulles's old ecumenical instincts as well as his new strategy, first seen with NATO, of limiting integration by joining forces not with everyone but only those who shared vital interests and a common moral heritage. From their time on the American and French delegations to the 1919 Paris Peace Conference, Dulles was old friends with Jean Monnet, the leading inspiration behind the European community that, after years of fitful attempts, began to take definite shape in the 1957 Treaty of Rome. Again in tandem with Monnet, Dulles vigorously promoted the European Defense Community (EDC), a plan to rearm Western Europe, including West Germany, in a measured way that would not alarm people about restoring German military power. As secretary of state, he encouraged Europe's efforts in what were essentially secular forms of ecumenical integration. To Dulles, the underlying principles were certainly the same.[43]

Other issues were not so simple. Unlike many of his administration colleagues but very much like his mainline coreligionists, Dulles supported greater levels of foreign aid to the decolonizing and developing worlds. Foreign aid was not especially high on the Eisenhower administration's agenda, a stance that Democrats and modernization theorists—they were mostly the same people—denounced as shortsighted and uncharitable. Without aid, instability would grow, and with instability would almost inevitably come communism. Dulles realized he was in the minority in the administration, and that Congress was not in the mood to be generous to countries that were prone to criticizing the United States. He hoped nonetheless that Americans would "more bountifully dispense aid and comfort to those who are materially less fortunate," and he called on the NCC for help in publicizing this cause. In 1958, after consulting with the Commission of the Churches on International Affairs and backed by an NCC publicity campaign, Dulles testified before a Senate committee on behalf of increased foreign aid, even though it was neither a typical Republican concern nor a priority for the Eisenhower administration.[44]

In the final analysis, the discrepancy between Dulles the church leader and Dulles the diplomat stemmed from the fact that as a church leader he had no policymaking power and few political constraints. This was obviously not the case during his time in the Eisenhower administration. Frederick Nolde, the ecumenical missionary who led the churches' campaign for international human rights in San Francisco, was unusual among religious liberals in recognizing the constraining effect of the demands of power. The conflict between Dulles and the mainline churches was based on a "misunderstanding" because the clergy "failed to reckon with the difference between a leader of the opposition and a leader of the party in power. In a sense, the churches were always in tension with the government," which came, Nolde believed, with a responsibility of speaking truth to power. But he also conceded that Protestant ministers "have to keep in mind that the government has a responsibility and cannot take certain risks that the critical opposition calls upon them to take." Nolde was right: Dulles was not a different person, but he did carry different responsibilities.[45]

And of course, the greatest mainstay in his life was the United Nations, even though it also caused him the most grief. His view of the world as fundamentally interconnected *and* interdependent—the globalized worldview, in other words, of a liberal Protestant—had not faded even slightly in the years since his work with the Commission on a Just and Durable Peace. Indeed, globalization was what made communism so potently dangerous, for its spread could not easily be stopped in an interconnected world. Integrative organizations that pooled the moral, spiritual, and material resources of like-minded people, such as NATO, the WCC, and the European Defense Community, were vital; larger endeavors, such as the UN, would simply have to wait until the world had been purified.

Famously, Dulles the arch–Cold Warrior condemned the neutralism of the Non-Aligned Movement, a grouping of Third World nations that sought to belong to neither East nor West, communist nor capitalist. In a world divided between freedom and tyranny, between faith and atheism, nations that did not choose sides undermined international security just as much as the communists, for they refused to pool their own strengths and thus denied others a better chance to prevent their enslavement. Relying on the collective security aspects of ecumenism rather than merely its internationalist leanings, Dulles called for the "creation of power on a community basis and the use of that power so as to deter aggression." "By uniting their strength," he said elsewhere, the Europeans "can and ought to become a great citadel of freedom and well-being." As expressed in NATO and the EDC, this was a very extreme version of Dulles's ecumenism—but it was a version nonetheless.[46]

Thus the new danger of communism did not make the United Nations irrelevant or obsolete. If anything, establishing a truly cohesive world community, with a properly functioning governing body, was more important than ever. It may be an impossibility for the time being, Dulles mused at several points during his time as secretary of state, but it must not be abandoned. And if it were ever to become a success, it would be through the moral and spiritual forces of the world. The UN had "grievously disappointed" its founders, Dulles chided those gathered in San Francisco to celebrate the organization's tenth anniversary in 1955. Any successes it enjoyed were not the work of all its members but rather "have been largely due to those throughout the world who believe that there is a God, a divine Creator of us all," that faith provides the moral foundations for harmonious personal and domestic relations, and that these faith-based "moral principles" must also "govern the conduct of nations." Eventually, communism would not be able to continue to sustain its own monstrous tyranny, and would collapse. And when it did, the world could finally unite as one.[47]

Communism did not negate "the indispensability of interdependence," Dulles explained in the pages of *Foreign Affairs* two years later; it simply complicated matters. He denounced the concept of inviolable national sovereignty—a very old Dulles cause—as an "obsolete" practice that allowed selfish nations to "put what they deem to be their own national rights and interests above the need of the whole society of nations." It was no coincidence that the atheistic and materialistic nations were also the selfish ones. Americans had their faults, but selfishness and irresponsibility were not among them. "Because of our religious beliefs we attach exceptional importance to freedom," he explained. Religion enabled Americans to believe in "the sanctity of the human personality" but also that "individuals as well as governments are subject to moral law." These were the bases of the American political mind, and as such were the bases of U.S. foreign policy:

> We are as a nation unsympathetic to systems and governments that deny human freedom and seek to mold all men to a preconceived pattern and to use them as tools to aggrandize the state. We are also unsympathetic to assertions of sovereignty which do not accept the concept of social interdependence.[48]

At its very foundations, then, America's diplomacy was a spiritual diplomacy—it could be no other way, and nor should it be. This, at least, was the gospel according to John Foster Dulles.

The Great Schism and the Myth of Consensus

THE EARLY YEARS of the Cold War are remembered as a golden age of bipartisanship, when politics supposedly stopped at the water's edge and Democrats and Republicans put aside their political differences in a common pursuit of the national interest. Perhaps this was true of politics—though it almost certainly was not—but it is wildly inaccurate when we consider religious opinion in the early Cold War. Instead of a monolithic anticommunist consensus, what actually occurred was a great schism between religious liberals and conservatives, a schism that led to the kind of bitter arguments over America's role in the world normally associated with the partisanship of later decades.[1]

This great schism stemmed in large part from differences over foreign policy, but its root causes were the result more of social and cultural changes to American religion. As a religious nation, the United States underwent a profound transformation in the middle decades of the twentieth century. Two changes were especially important and had lasting effects on religious attitudes toward war and diplomacy.

First, the nature of religion altered dramatically. Although Protestantism was still the majority faith, and although it continued to be the dominant religious influence on culture and politics, it was no longer the only religion. After years of immigration and intolerance, Catholicism and Judaism had finally matured as American faiths and become part of the mainstream. Anti-Catholicism and anti-Semitism were not yet dead, but they were fading fast; by the 1960s, they would more or less be consigned to the hateful, lunatic fringe, marginalized in both religion and politics. Just as important was the rise of secularization. On the major questions in life, many Americans were turning to science instead of religion. In a wide variety of institutions—medicine, education, the law—religious authority could no longer command automatic allegiance and deference. Religion was still a force in politics, mainly because of the efforts by the faithful to keep it relevant. There was nothing inevitable about secularization, and it did not spell the end of American religion. But the increasingly wide division between the sacred and the secular in modern American life meant that religion's social importance could no longer be assumed.[2]

Second, as the nature of American religion changed, the relationship between religion and politics changed with it. Religion still mattered in politics, but its influence became much more complicated. The kind of separation between church and state established by the Founders and maintained throughout the nineteenth and early twentieth centuries had not been intended to remove religion from the public sphere. Religion was thought to be a source of community spirit and moral values, both of which were considered vital in preventing American society from becoming too fractious and self-interested. Though the notion of a hard "wall of separation" is rightly attributed to Thomas Jefferson, it did not form the legal basis of church-state separation until after World War II. Partly this resulted from the fact that America was no longer a Protestant nation, or even an exclusively Christian nation. While Protestantism had always played an intimate and unifying role in politics, its role became more contentious when not everyone was a Protestant. Newly confident postwar Jews, for example, took the lead in using the courts to tighten the First Amendment and ensure that Protestants and Catholics did not receive preferential treatment at their expense. And of course, even Protestants were divided among themselves between fiercely competing liberal and conservative factions.[3]

But perhaps most important, the balance of power between church and state had begun to shift away from the church and toward the state. With the New Deal, the Cold War national security state, and the rights revolutions of the 1960s and '70s, the federal government was increasingly responsible for things that had normally been the church's prerogative. Thus the hardening of the wall of separation contributed to, rather than caused, the empowerment of the state at the expense of the church. All this led to religious identification being determined more by political issues rather than the other way around. For example, religious liberals and conservatives were becoming defined as "liberal" and "conservative" not only by where they stood on the virgin birth or belief in miracles, but by where they stood on divisive political, cultural, and social matters such as school prayer, abortion, welfare, and women's rights. Over time, moreover, conservative Protestants and Catholics partly overcame theological differences to form once-unthinkable alliances on social and political issues. Anomalies remained, and the changes would not become fully apparent until the 1970s. But the foundations had begun to shift nonetheless.[4]

Long before the culture wars of the 1960s and after, foreign policy was probably the first of these divisive issues to provoke religious and political controversy. Most historians identify the extreme anticommunism of the early Cold War with the postwar surge in religious piety, but religious views of world politics were much more diverse and complex. They tended to divide between conservatives, who usually were ardent anticommunists, and liberals, who were not. Conservatives not only wanted Truman and Eisenhower to pursue containment, they often called for rollback. Liberals, on the other hand, thought containment was too rigid and feared that it distorted issues, such as decolonization and global poverty, that did not fit so easily into an anticommunist foreign policy. Moreover, liberals were much less willing to support the militarization of containment and much more supportive of diplomacy and the United Nations.[5]

Essentially, the great schism did not divide anticommunists from communist sympathizers, for most religious Americans were to some degree opposed to communism. Instead, a division emerged between conservatives who wanted U.S. foreign policy to promote liberty and liberals who wanted their country to pursue progress. The apostles of liberty set aside all other priorities in favor of containing and perhaps even defeating communism at home and abroad. The apostles of progress, on the other hand, believed that questions of global social justice should drive foreign policy, even if it meant working with communists, socialists, nationalists, and even the Soviet Union itself.

"THE AMERICAN PEOPLE stand firm in the faith which has inspired this Nation from the beginning," Harry Truman declared in his inaugural address of January 1949. "We believe that all men are created equal because they are created in the image of God." In the pursuit of their ideals and security, Americans "find themselves directly opposed by a regime with contrary aims and a totally different concept of life," a regime that "adheres to a false philosophy which purports to offer freedom, security, and greater opportunity to mankind." This was a dangerous new heresy, a rival vision of progress and liberty that actually threatened to destroy all hope of true progress and liberty forever. In issuing his call to arms, Truman wanted to be clear about who this enemy was. "That false philosophy," he warned starkly, "is communism."[6]

For many religious Americans, Truman was preaching to the choir. Communism represented the antithesis to everything they and America stood for: atheism instead of religion, materialism instead of spirituality, dictatorship of the proletariat instead of liberal democracy, command economy instead of free enterprise. To some liberal Protestants, communism embodied a system of violent materialism; to virtually all conservative Protestants, communism represented the ultimate nightmare of state power at the expense of individual liberty; and to most Catholics, communism represented the ultimate rejection of God and Christian ethics. To Whittaker Chambers, the ex-communist turned professional anticommunist who had dabbled in the Episcopal Church and Quaker meetings, the fundamental struggle of the modern world was between Christianity and communism. "At every point, religion and politics interlace," he wrote in his 1952 bestselling memoir, *Witness*, "and must do so more acutely as the conflict between the two great camps of men—those who reject and those who worship God—becomes irrepressible." Even more ominously, these two camps "are not only outside, but also within nations."[7]

The intense ideological atmosphere of the early Cold War—when extreme anticommunism flattened out the fine, subtle distinctions between social democracy, socialism, and outright communism—benefited religious conservatives who were unafraid to attack any form of leftist politics. Because anticommunism dovetailed so closely with the tenor of their faith, evangelicals and fundamentalists were most able to exploit the red scare climate of McCarthyism. Conservative Christians had largely faded from popular view after the 1925 Scopes trial and the end of Prohibition. They rallied during the religious fervor of the war and organized their growing numbers: moderate "neo-evangelicals" formed the National Association of Evangelicals while arch-fundamentalists, led by Carl McIntire, established the American Council of Christian Churches (its very name a deliberate patriotic challenge to the ecumenical Federal Council). Thus by the early Cold War, conservatives were poised for a major revival. Unlike liberals, conservatives felt no hesitation about attacking communist ideology or the Soviet Union, and they felt no compunction in calling for the most vigorous response that American foreign policy could muster. And unlike liberals, ambivalent and internally divided on all these questions, their patriotism was never in doubt.[8]

Their champion, and soon to be the new face of American Christianity, was a handsome young evangelist with a soft Southern drawl from Charlotte, North Carolina. By the time of his 1949 breakout revival in Los Angeles, which made him a national figure, Billy Graham was already something of a rising star in evangelical circles. He had been a regular speaker on the Youth for Christ circuit and—like evangelists from George Whitefield to Dwight Moody before him—had launched a successful revival tour of England. But the eight-week tent meeting in Southern California surpassed all expectations and reintroduced evangelicalism to mainstream America. That the L.A. revival met with success in the fall of 1949, when revivals only a year or two earlier had received a tepid response, was no coincidence: it came during a wave a hysteria over the spread of communism, bracketed between the Soviets' first successful atomic test in August and the "fall" of China to Mao and the communists in October. Graham explicitly linked the cause of Christ with the cause of America, of Christianity's struggle against Satan with America's struggle against communism. "There are communists everywhere," he proclaimed in Los Angeles, and "unless the Christian religion rescues these nations from the clutches of the unbelieving, America will stand alone and isolated in the world." Communism stood "against God, against Christ, against the Bible, and against all religion. Communism is not only an economic interpretation of life—Communism is a religion that is inspired, directed, and motivated by the Devil himself who has declared war against Almighty God." As Graham's biographer William Martin has noted, the evangelist's blend of intense patriotism, stern moralism, fervent anticommunism, sunny optimism, and simple Christian message was perfectly "geared to the times." This was an evangelism for the Cold War, and it propelled Graham to the front ranks of American public life.[9]

But Graham the Cold Warrior could display nuance and vision as well as wield fire and brimstone. He was not a fundamentalist, but something rather new on the American religious scene: a neo-evangelical, straddling the vast chasm between Carl McIntire's hard-shell fundamentalism and the Federal Council's soft-touch modernism. If Graham and his cohorts from the National Association of Evangelicals were going to have broad-based success, they would need to tailor conservative Protestantism to the modern age. They did so brilliantly, by adapting evangelicalism to contemporary society. They were masters at using the media to spread a message of born-again love rather than fundamentalist anger. The neo-evangelicals were also adept—much more adept than liberals—at appealing to young people, which gave them a critical advantage in a society that was becoming increasingly obsessed with youth. Thus Graham's message for the Cold War could be moderate as well as dogmatic. While he wanted Americans to "stand firmly" against the "incoming tide of atheistic communism and all that comes in its wake," and while he urged them to "remember that at this moment all of civilization is in the crucible," in the next breath he also called for commonsense restraint. "There are those in the United States . . . who have been talking about a preventive war," he warned. But an attack on the Soviet Union "cannot be done . . . on the basis of the principles of Western civilization and Western culture, because of our basis of Christian principles." America, he preached, must be vigilant but not vengeful. It was a message of both love and strength, and Americans adored Graham for spreading it.[10]

Rather more direct was the troublesome fundamentalist Presbyterian Carl McIntire, who was a constant thorn in the Eisenhower administration's side because even Republicans did not receive leniency in his uncompromising, all-consuming crusade against communism. Eisenhower aide Frederic Fox described McIntire's followers as "230,000 humorless souls" and, referring to Jesus's parable on the dangers of being judgmental, described McIntire himself as "a discredited Presbyterian minister with a big log in one eye and a beam on his shoulder." If Fox exaggerated, it was only slightly, for McIntire's anticommunism was harder-edged than most. But it was not unusual among fundamentalists. He ascribed the invention of communism not to Marx and Engels but Satan. Satan intended to enslave the world, and the "most brilliant scheme he has ever invented for this purpose is the totalitarian State. He is the author of it; and communism, its most highly developed form, is his brain child. It looks very much like his last trump card." If America could defeat communism, it could defeat Satan; but if Americans did not defeat communism, Satan would eventually overtake the world. At home, the danger lay in the welfare state, a form of creeping socialism that had already found expression in the New Deal. Such a government seizes power "which it actually does not have under God" and results in "great bureaucratic combines" that become "burdensome, crushing, destructive of freedom." McIntire also pointed to the objectivity of the written word as the source of all liberty, comparing the sanctity of the Bible with that of the Constitution. "The Author of liberty," God, "has given us the Book of liberty. The issue confronting the Western world is the Christ of this Book versus the Marx of Moscow."[11]

Protestant neo-evangelicals and fundamentalists were flourishing, but no group benefited more from the Cold War than Roman Catholics. For more than fifty years, Catholics had debated how their hierarchical church could function alongside the pluralism and individualism of American society. Their concern with "Americanism" subsided as time went on and Catholic immigrants successfully assimilated while maintaining their religious traditions. But nothing helped settle the issue like anticommunism. While Protestants and Jews differed among themselves as to the nature of the communist threat, Catholics did not. They were perhaps the most robustly anticommunist group at a time when communism became the nation's overriding priority and when the validity of someone's patriotism largely depended on their attitude toward communism. To be sympathetic to communism was not only to be *anti*-American, but positively *un*-American. Though he was not especially observant, Senator Joseph McCarthy, an Irish Catholic, represented the apotheosis of the Catholic anticommunist crusade. Mitigating McCarthy's buffoonery and legitimating his message was a new generation of Catholic laymen, led by the journalist and public intellectual William F. Buckley Jr., who advanced a sophisticated but no less robust anticommunism. For their part, Catholic Church leaders seemed to compete with one another to see who could issue the strongest attacks against the communist menace. In religion, Francis Cardinal Spellman paralleled McCarthy's efforts in politics. More philosophical but equally strident was Bishop Fulton Sheen, who damned communism as an ideology that "wishes to be not only a State but a Church judging the consciences of men." Catholic McCarthyism was not monolithic—Senator McCarthy found opponents in the National Catholic Welfare Conference, *Commonweal* magazine, and other prominent

Catholic laypeople such as fellow Senator Eugene McCarthy (no rela-tion)—but it was dominant. It was also durable, surviving Joe McCar-thy's ignominious downfall in 1954 only to be reinvigorated by the trials of Cardinal Mindszenty and the failed Hungarian uprising of 1956.[12]

However, if Cold War anticommunism enabled Catholics to move closer to the cultural mainstream, it had the explosive potential to do the opposite for Jews. It did not help that two of the leading fundamental-ist crusaders against communism, the Reverends Hyman Appelman and Fred Schwarz, were foreign-born Jewish converts to American Protes-tantism, leaving the mistaken impression that Jews could only be true anticommunists if they were not Jews. Schwarz's organization, Christian Anti-Communism Crusade, was especially active, and his bestselling book *You Can Trust the Communists (to Be Communists)* sold more than a million copies. Nor did it help that two of the most notorious communist spies of the era, Julius and Ethel Rosenberg, were Jewish.[13]

Unfortunately for Jews, their politics made it easy for extremist oppo-nents to tar them with the brush of anticommunism, however unfairly. Unlike Catholics, who could easily mount an anticommunist crusade because it was rooted deep in the politics and culture of their church, naturally internationalist, progressivist Jews could be accused of being soft on communism because they were indeed softer on communism. In Israel, Zionists established a socialist state, while in America polls revealed that Jews were much less confrontational toward the Soviet Union. In 1948, for example, while less than a third of Catholics and Protestants said they would "allow communists to speak over the radio," 78 percent of Jews said they would. They were also similarly out of step on Joseph McCarthy: in a November 1954 poll, after his senatorial censure, 58 percent of Catholics still held a favorable view of him while only 15 percent of Jews did. This of course did not mean that Jews were communists, or even communist sympathizers: such views reflected the importance Jews ascribed to tol-erance and dialogue, values they had prioritized after centuries of being persecuted themselves. Still, anti-Semitic anticommunists made much of the impression that Jews were closet communists and thus a danger to the nation. Reverend Gerald L. K. Smith, leader of the Christian Nationalist Crusade, maintained his virulent anti-Semitism even as he pivoted oppor-tunistically from interwar isolationism to extreme Cold War interven-tionism.[14]

Nonetheless, anti-Semitism remained confined to these marginalized extremes. Despite the best efforts of Congressman John Rankin, a noto-rious red-baiting anti-Semite, and despite the intensive investigations of the House Un-American Activities Committee, most Americans did not lump communism and Judaism together. Most telling of all was Joe McCarthy himself, who not only refused to make anticommunism a form of anti-Semitism but also supported Israel and campaigned for the rights of persecuted Jews in the Soviet Union. When asked why he was soft on Jews but hard on communism, McCarthy simply replied, "I have many friends who are Jewish." Among them was his chief investigator, Roy Cohn, who had been one of the prosecuting attorneys in the Rosenberg espionage trial, and Cohn's assistant and best friend (and possibly lover), David Schine. Notwithstanding the haunting specter of old Jew-hating ghosts, America's Judeo-Christian civil religion, one of its prime weapons in the Cold War, held together.[15]

Cohn and Schine were the unlikely exemplars of a new trend: Jewish anticommunism. American radicalism remained disproportionately Jewish, but a new generation of disillusioned Jewish leftists was moving quickly toward anticommunism. They were the first of the neoconservatives, though they were not yet known as such, moving swiftly through the political spectrum from left to right. One of their main concerns was Soviet communism, which they saw as a new form of the old totalitarianism and thus a menace to both international security and universal rights. Many Jewish public intellectuals, from Will Herberg to Irving Kristol, feared that liberals were not taking communism seriously enough and vowed to do something about it. Magazines such as *Commentary*—founded in 1945 by the American Jewish Committee—assumed a stridently anti-Soviet editorial stance; the predominantly Jewish *Partisan Review* adopted a similar tone. Also common to both magazines, stemming from a desire to assert Jewish patriotism and a fear that anti-Semitism would be roused once again if Americans began associating Jews with communism, was a desire to promote the Jewish and American identities as complementary. If Catholics found their anticommunist views to be an easy way to assimilate into a broader American culture, anticommunist Jews felt they could do the same. "As Americans of the Jewish faith we have an especially profound challenge," intoned Rabbi Norman Gerstenfeld in 1951. Because European Jews had historically been subjected to "tyranny and superstition" and denied basic liberties, American Jews, "the greatest Jewish community in the world and the freest in all the pages of historic time," had a special obligation to fight communist autocracy.[16]

IF COMMUNISM WAS anathema in theory, it was positively dangerous at home. Religious Americans worried about the power of communist ideology when deployed by the military and political might of the Soviet Union, but they were just as concerned with the encroachment of communism in the United States. This was in keeping with the general postwar hysteria over communist espionage, but religious Americans also worried that the nation's values were a communist target. They were terrified most of all by what they saw as a tightening embrace between the mainline churches of liberal Protestantism and the collectivist aspirations of communists. As early as 1945, McIntire predicted that "America faces the greatest struggle of her existence. In the postwar world the conflict between a free economy and the Russian idea of controlled economy will produce its severest conflict within the United States." Economics was a concern not because most conservative Christians were wealthy—far from it—but because liberty was considered to be absolute and indivisible: if tyranny could weaken one element of freedom, all would eventually succumb. "Liberty plus liberty equals liberty," McIntire explained elsewhere. "Tyranny plus tyranny equals tyranny. But liberty plus tyranny equals tyranny!"[17]

Either out of ideological zeal or tactical savvy—probably both—secular organizations also used the libertarian strain of Protestantism to attack communism. In 1946, the National Association of Manufacturers, the largest and most powerful lobby for American business interests, established a quarterly newsletter "devoted to cooperation between clergymen and businessmen" at a time when "Church and Industry face a common foe." Communism, claimed the NAM, "destroys all liberty—religious, economic, and political." Church and industry had to unite to stem "the rising tide of collectivism—a system in which man's dignity and independence is lost to him, and he becomes a slave to the State." The National Economic Council, a much smaller and even more conservative organization based in New York, warned of a global campaign "to marry Communism to Christianity."[18]

Conservative Protestants mounted a parallel campaign to discredit the liberalism and ecumenism of the Federal Council and its successor body, the National Council of Churches. McIntire, founder of the rival American Council of Christian Churches, railed against liberals and their "Superchurch" that "twisted Christ to propagate their perverted, revolutionary, new order." Just as Stalin and the United Nations aimed for a global political and ideological monopoly, liberal ecumenists hoped for a religious monopoly that would "produce a tyranny in ecclesiastical circles that the world has never seen." Such "one-world planning" for a "one-world social order" sought to build on earth "the Kingdom of Antichrist." To McIntire and others, the monopolistic tendencies in the FCC and NCC were but an extension of the Soviets' totalitarian methods and communist ideology. Members of the ACCC were incandescent with righteous fury when the NCC's Walter Van Kirk proclaimed that "the Christian community in the United States is unanimous in its judgment that nation states must surrender to the organized international community whatever measure of their national sovereignty is required to establish peace and justice on a global scale." Not surprisingly, they focused not only on Van Kirk's call for a world state but on the presumptuousness of his claims to unanimity.[19]

Rhetoric such as this marked only the latest round in a battle that had begun during World War I and continued during the Depression and World War II. Both modernists and fundamentalists, liberals and conservatives had regularly used world events to impugn the patriotism and religious fidelity of their opponents. But now, thanks to the Cold War, conservatives had the advantage. Liberals could of course be anticommunists, too. In 1948, Reinhold Niebuhr helped found the liberal anticommunist group Americans for Democratic Action, the logical culmination of his fiercely antitotalitarian worldview that had begun forming a decade earlier. Among liberal Democrats, Niebuhr's views were becoming the mainstream, but among liberal Protestants, they were atypical. Most did not like Soviet communism, but they either contextualized its abuses or downplayed its danger. And of course, in the interwar period many liberal clergy had either embraced socialism or flirted with communism. Their subtleties and progressive politics were easy targets for religious conservatives.[20]

As a result, liberal churches of the Social Gospel tradition came under furious attack in the late 1940s and early 1950s. Norman Vincent Peale, the Presbyterian pastor of the Marble Collegiate Church in New York and bestselling motivational author, warned as early as 1945 that the "campaign to swing American clergymen to collectivist programs is well organized" and "gaining ground." Using Galatians 5:1 for scriptural guidance—"Stand fast therefore in the liberty wherewith Christ hath made us free, and be not entangled again with the yoke of bondage"—Peale told his congregation that the current crisis was just as serious at home as it was in Europe: "The present question is whether new philosophies or old philosophies in new form, calling themselves liberal, but actually reactionary, are not further imperiling freedom." Communism in the churches represented the most dire threat to American freedom because it was in the church where children learned the stories of the Bible; it was there Americans learned their morals. For this reason, the Truman administration warned, in NSC-68, that as providers of "moral strength" the nation's churches were one of communism's "prime targets." But conservatives went even further, charging the mainline churches with complicity. *United Evangelical Action*, the official magazine of the National Association of Evangelicals, accused many of the nation's leading divinity schools and theological seminaries of teaching the ministers of tomorrow that " 'the profit motive' and 'corporate enterprise' are sinful."[21]

As they had in the antebellum period over slavery, Protestant denominations split into liberal and conservative factions, divided this time by the controversy over communism. Methodists were particularly riven. Conservative Methodist muckrakers attacked Bishop Bromley Oxnam and the Methodist Federation for Social Action for unwittingly helping the Soviets undermine the foundations of a free American society. One Methodist magazine denounced the Federation for Social Action as "subversive in character and dangerous to the future of our nation." Another warned that Oxnam was at the head of a "Communist conspiracy in religion" that was "seeking to change our traditional, American economic order." In 1953 Stanley High—once a seminary student training for the Methodist ministry, then an Eisenhower campaign strategist, now an editor at *Reader's Digest*—published the results of his investigation into communism and the churches. The resulting article, "Methodism's Pink Fringe," plunged the church into the turmoil and recriminations of a religious civil war. Unfortunately for Bishop Oxnam, High's article attracted the attentions of another Methodist layman, Congressman Harold H. Velde, an Illinois Republican who also happened to be chair of the notorious House Un-American Activities Committee. Even worse for Oxnam was the fact that one of HUAC's most tenacious investigators, J. B. Matthews, was an ordained Methodist minister and had done mission work overseas. Velde hauled Oxnam before HUAC in 1953, doing incalculable damage to the church but finding no communists.[22]

Ironically, despite the conservative assault on the FCC and NCC, splits such as the Methodists' actually spurred a new kind of ecumenism in which interdenominational cooperation on political issues blurred traditional religious identity. Liberal Baptists, Methodists, and Presbyterians closed ranks together against a similarly interdenominational front of Christian anticommunists. As was becoming customary in the Cold War, the beneficiaries of this new ecumenism were large conservative organizations such as the National Association of Evangelicals. With numbers and unity came strength, and upon such strength Christian conservatives were able to construct a new platform for a very old style of religious politics.[23]

COMMUNISM AT HOME seemed like such an imminent threat because it was seen as the tip of the Soviet spear. Even before Harry Truman and George Kennan had found it necessary to devise containment, many religious Americans were convinced of the need for an anticommunist, anti-Soviet foreign policy. Composed of an unstable coalition of Catholics, evangelicals and fundamentalists, and a handful of mainline liberals, they promoted an activist, global foreign policy, grounded in Christian values of sacrifice and responsibility. At the same time, the Truman administration appreciated such support and used religion in a battle not only of tanks and bombs, but for hearts and minds.

Once again leading the way was Reinhold Niebuhr, who saw his mission to rally the nation against Soviet communism as something of a reprise of his crusade against pacifism and Nazism in the 1930s. Now, as then, he had to convince the overwhelmingly peace-minded mainline

Protestant clergy that vigilance was required before compromise. In 1946, after a tour of Europe, he wrote a major article for *Life* calling for the reconstruction of Germany and the containment of communism. A year before the Truman Doctrine and the Marshall Plan, then, Niebuhr had already outlined his own plan for political and economic containment. But Niebuhr also sought to strike a balance between sounding the alarm and sounding alarmist. In this, he was very much a realist, like Kennan, warning of the Soviet menace but also warning of the dangers of an American overreaction. And like Kennan, who later lamented that his refined theory of containment had been militarized, bluntly and brutally, in its implementation, Niebuhr had trouble convincing his fellow Cold Warriors of the need for balance in U.S. foreign policy.[24]

As Truman was to Kennan, Henry Luce was to Niebuhr. Born in China to Presbyterian missionaries, the Time-Life publishing baron was a devout Christian, a committed believer in America's worldwide manifest destiny, and a proponent of Judeo-Christian America's duty to fend off the godless communist menace. His wife, the equally pious congresswoman Clare Boothe Luce, had converted to Catholicism under the guidance of Bishop Fulton Sheen. Encouraged by Clare, Henry Luce's abiding faith led him to espouse a particularly virulent strain of anticommunism. He was happy to publish Niebuhr's anticommunist warnings but could not understand his ambivalence about U.S. foreign policy. Niebuhr spoke of a nation "confident and even over-confident in its 'rightness,' " Luce wrote to the theologian, but "I see, at the moment, no such America." Niebuhr saw America as "a powerful country on the offensive," but to Luce it was communism that was on the march. "I think, on the contrary, that we are defensive," guilty not of aggression but timidity and faithlessness in an age of increasing materialism. America, charged Luce, was "a powerful country dissipating its power, tragically, on a false and stultifying defensive." For now, in the early Cold War, it was Luce's mission rather than Niebuhr's realism that won out.[25]

What was needed most was action by the United States, not the United Nations. In keeping with their anti-statist and ultrapatriotic worldview, evangelicals and fundamentalists were generally suspicious of a regulatory world government that would compromise American sovereignty, identity, and security for a greater, presumably socialist, good. "I am opposed to yielding to foreign dictation in regard to our own welfare," cried Anson Gustavus Melton, a Baptist preacher in Ashland, Virginia. "Are we not in the middle of a bad fix in the so called UN? If I figure rightly it is a misnomer. In fact it is an Ununited Nations." Melton found it particularly galling that the Soviets had "an honorable seat" in the UN "while they furnish arms to kill U.S. soldiers in Korea." Other conservatives criticized the world body for their own reasons. Because it seemed so closely to

resemble the armies of Satan in the prophetic books of the Bible, premillennial dispensationalists feared the UN as a harbinger of the apocalypse.
But even neo-orthodox liberals warned that the UN was not an answer to
the world's prayers. Their concerns were grounded less in fears for U.S.
sovereignty than in concerns over the UN's efficacy. Though he was a
staunch internationalist, Niebuhr was discovering just how unhelpful the
Soviets could be in global governance. Americans should not expect too
much of the United Nations, he cautioned, and certainly not a capacity
to lead. Ironically, Niebuhr warned, attempts to expand the UN's powers into something like the domestic authority of a national government
were bound to lead directly to the very thing the UN was designed to
avoid: war.[26]

APOSTLES OF LIBERTY such as Henry Luce were concerned about China
as much as they were about Europe, but there the story of Christian liberty and progress was complicated by the fact that the United States held
a decidedly weaker hand. The morality tale for China was also much
murkier than it was in Japan, where Americans had enforced unconditional surrender upon a demonstrably evil enemy. Under Mao Zedong,
the Chinese Communist Party (CCP) held the genuine loyalty of many
Chinese, while at the same time America's corrupt and ineffectual Christian ally, Chiang Kai-shek, was steadily losing whatever support he had
left. For the Chinese, World War II had begun not in 1941 or even 1939,
but in 1937, with the Japanese invasion. The civil war between Nationalists and Communists was folded into this larger international war, and
when it stopped in 1945 the factions of competing Chinese simply continued their own struggle. But though Americans were beset by a red scare
at home and pursuing containment abroad, the Truman administration
had had enough of Chiang and the Nationalists. In 1949, more than two
years after George Marshall had failed to secure a truce and fed up with
the Nationalists' mounting political and military problems, Secretary of
State Dean Acheson washed America's hands of Chiang and published a
thousand-page "white paper" illustrating that there was little Washington
could do to avert a Communist victory.

American missionaries, however, did not find it so easy to walk away
from China. It had been their biggest mission field—and, they believed,
their most promising. For its size and prestige, the conversion of China
was the missionary movement's ultimate prize—hence their reluctance to
just let it go as had the Truman administration. And once again, missionaries on the ground, many of whom were living in areas under CCP rule,
helped form American impressions of the struggle for China. The "Chinese
Communists are totalitarian, anti-religious, and anti-western," warned an
anonymous missionary in China; they were also powerful and probably

unstoppable. By contrast, "the Christian Church is pitifully vulnerable." "Communists are terrorizing the people and causing intense suffering and loss of life and property," wrote Gertrude McCulloch, a Woman's American Baptist Foreign Mission Society missionary based in Hangzhou, in a 1948 newsletter to friends and supporters in the United States. Hangzhou remained under Nationalist control for now, but the news from missionaries further north was not encouraging. "Christian work has been treated ruthlessly wherever they have come to stay," McCulloch said of the Communists, "and we are fearful for our Chinese Christians." For their part, these Chinese Christians stoked fears of a communist takeover, warning, as did one Beijing convert, of "a struggle between democracy and anti-democracy. No middle way out!" Luce thought of the Chinese Communists as the forces of the Antichrist. He was especially concerned for the fate of the American missionaries who continued to toil for Christian freedom and progress in China. So was the State Department, which had kept a close watch on CCP abuse of American missionaries since World War II. Under such conditions, the fundamentalist Independent Board for Presbyterian Foreign Missions cabled Truman, it was essential that the United States act quickly to prevent China "from falling into the complete dominance of godless communists" and enable Chiang "to preserve the nation for freedom and open doors for the preaching of the Gospel of Jesus Christ."[27]

Both ordinary Americans and the U.S. government had long turned to missionaries to explain and interpret China and the Chinese. So it was not unusual for Truman to do the same, and in 1946 he appointed J. Leighton Stuart as America's ambassador to China. As a missionary, Stuart had been issuing strong warnings against the growth of Chinese communism since the early 1930s. But despite his ties to Chiang Kai-shek, he was also a realist who recognized by 1947 that the Nationalists had virtually no chance of winning the civil war. Stuart did not believe that the Communists could reform or that they would convert to Christianity. Instead, he hoped that Mao would tolerate a missionary presence in China after the CCP took power. From there, missionaries would win over the Chinese people, and their Communist rulers, with a simple message of justice that was ideally suited to an Asia being transformed by decolonization, nationalism, and development. The "Christian faith," Ambassador Stuart explained in 1949, "as a determined effort to realize the ideal social order which Jesus described as the kingdom of heaven on earth, as the most dynamic revolutionary movement of all time, cannot fail in its appeal to the Oriental peoples."[28]

Stuart's gospel of progress, however, failed to win over the conservative apostles of liberty who wanted to oppose Chinese Communism without any compromise. Many of them, not coincidentally, also had missionary experience in China. From the floor of Congress and his seat on the House Committee on Foreign Affairs, Walter Judd had an insider's view of U.S. foreign policy. As a former medical missionary with a decade of service in China, he also held an emotional stake in its unfolding drama. And he did not agree with Stuart about the prospects for Christian missions under CCP rule, or even on the legitimacy of working with Mao at the possible expense of Chiang. "If the Communists win in China," Judd warned a missionary friend in Beijing, "there isn't going to be any missionary work anywhere in areas they control." As for Chiang, Judd accused the Truman administration of setting its expectations unreasonably high. Chiang was an anticommunist and a devoted Christian. He was the only hope for true democratic reform in China, even if prevailing conditions had made it impossible for him to fulfill this potential. Judd thought it incredible that Truman and Marshall demanded "perfection" from Chiang at a time when he was fighting for his life and China's against Communist tyranny. How could the Nationalists govern China after fifteen years of war and insurrection? "Georgia didn't recover from . . . Sherman for 50 years," he later told an interviewer. "But Chiang had to recover from 8 years of Japanese occupation in 30 minutes, so to speak. It couldn't be done." These uncharitable, unchristian "blunders" by Truman were also unwise, for they paved the way for a Communist seizure of power in China and deepened American isolation in an increasingly godless world.[29]

In June 1950, the outbreak of war in Korea seemed to confirm missionary predictions that the world's future would be determined in Asia, not Europe. The North Korean invasion stunned most observers, including an off-guard Truman administration that had, said Billy Graham, "blundered" into the war by being too soft on Asian communism. Though U.S. officials had been sending strong signals that they would not go to war over Korea, Truman did not hesitate to do just that. He committed U.S. forces to stand and fight within a day of the North's invasion, and then, with the Soviets boycotting the Security Council, quickly brought the United Nations alongside. The invasion stunned the American religious community, which reacted with rare unanimity to support Truman's policy. Religious opinion at home either supported a war for the defense of Korea against communism or a war for the defense of the United Nations against abuse and irrelevance. Even the Federal Council, a most reluctant supporter of war in 1941, endorsed the Korean War. In his annual Thanksgiving sermon, Henry Sloane Coffin condemned the Soviets "who egged on the North Koreans, their puppets," condemned also those in America who "little understood the men of the Kremlin," and endorsed the war as a matter of self-defense much as he had World War II. Even Church Peace Union endorsed the war as an example of collective security in action. If Truman's efforts "curb aggression and halt world war, then it follows that we must be ready to pay the price, specifically in Korea." This was a far cry from interwar pacifist denunciations of collective security as just another form of unchristian warmongering.[30]

In this, American religious opinion mirrored that in South Korea, where Christians, their faith and nationalism fired by American missionaries and Cold War evangelists like Graham, demanded that the faithful "Arise altogether for the emancipation of our northern brethren." As one Korean evangelical exclaimed during the war,

> We Koreans learned about liberty and the rights of man from American Christians, when they brought us the Word of God. With God's help, we shall prove our faith. Marching arm in arm with our fellow defenders of the faith, we are determined to uproot this scourge, to destroy this blight. This is the crux of the conflict—light or darkness, good or evil. Let us pray for strength.[31]

With Syngman Rhee leading South Korea, trumpet calls such as this were not at all out of place. Raised in a Confucian household, Rhee converted to Methodism while serving a prison sentence for anti-Japanese activism. He later spent several years in exile in the United States, even earning a doctorate from Princeton. Christianity was a larger part of Rhee's anticolonial nationalism than it was for Chiang Kai-shek, and it was integral to the anticommunist Korean national movement which Rhee led in the South. Like Chiang, Rhee was an autocrat, but for Americans his Christian faith and commitment to fighting communism overrode his dictatorial tendencies. His leadership was vital if the United States aimed to transform Korea into what Clare Boothe Luce called a "bulwark of Christian democracy" for a region threatened by communist domination.[32]

The Korean War also drew the energies of a new generation of evangelical missionaries who wanted to retain the conservative emphasis on doctrinal purity while at the same time pursuing good works projects that had long been the preserve of liberal mainline missions. The primary emphasis remained, as it always had, on leading lost souls to the love and light of Christ. But now, improving daily lives on earth was increasingly seen as a way to prepare for eternal life in heaven. This represented something of a shift in American religion. While the nation as a whole was experiencing a great awakening, mainline missions were declining precipitously, soon be replaced by a vastly larger cohort of evangelical missionaries who possessed an increasingly rare ability to combine conservative religion with progressive geopolitics. Spurred by the proselytizing ambitions of groups like the National Association of Evangelicals and Youth for Christ, conservative Christians were determined to win the world to Christianity, and away from communism.

The largest and most successful of these new conservative missions was World Vision, founded by Bob Pierce, a Youth for Christ worker, as a way to further several goals simultaneously. Pierce wanted to spread true Christianity, unadulterated by liberalism, and alleviate the suffering and refugee crisis caused by the conflict in Korea. But perhaps above all, he wanted to mobilize religion against communism. "All over the world the Russians are outpreaching us, outsacrificing us, outworking us, out-planning us, outpropagandising us and outdying us in order to gain their ends," he once said. The solution was for Americans to do a much better job in mobilizing their strongest resource: faith.[33]

This new breed of evangelical missionary, eager to dispense material aid as well as the gospel, thrived in the Cold War. They promised to deliver a solution to instability and the expansion of communism because the two seemed fundamentally connected. Poor living conditions in the Third World, they argued, created the necessary conditions for the emergence and growth of communism, a point many American policymakers were forced to concede. "Hunger," not communism, "is cause number one of the conditions that make wars," wrote Frank C. Laubach, a prominent missionary who ran literacy programs throughout the developing world. Thus if hunger could be ended, so too could communism, especially if the word of Christ followed to counteract the atheism and immorality that communists spread. Laubach concluded that "the moment government, church, business, and philanthropy join hands in all-out sincere, unselfish effort, the whole world will love us. . . . And when we begin this, God will be on our side." With the decline of mainline missionary enterprise, the Social Gospel's global mission was moving sharply to the right.[34]

CHRISTIAN CONSERVATISM WAS a source of crucial support for policy-makers because it was not the only religious voice on foreign policy. Over the same period, religious liberals of almost all denominations formed a powerful critique of America's role in the world and offered a compel-ling alternative. During the Truman era, they hesitated to support con-tainment; during the Eisenhower presidency, they were outright critical of U.S. foreign policy and increasingly skeptical that the United States should be pursuing containment at all. And among liberals, support for rooting out communists at home was almost nonexistent.

Instead, religious liberals offered a competing vision of America's mis-sion in the postwar world. In place of containment, they called for sub-stantive and unconditional dialogue with the communist world, nuclear disarmament, and the promotion of human rights and genuinely equitable economic development even if it meant working with leftist and nationalist regimes that were hostile to short-term U.S. national interests. Only a for-eign policy of diplomatic engagement, civil rights, and social justice, said these apostles of progress, could provide a workable alternative to communism. Like the conservatives, they promoted individual rights—freedom of worship, expression, conscience, and so forth—but they also pursued group rights, such as social justice and economic equality. As a result, they were more inclined to focus on foreign aid, decolonization, and international racial equality than on straightforward anticommunism.

Mainline Protestants comprised the largest of this dissenting contingent, but on most issues it also included leftist, social welfare Catholics. This ecumenical coalition established by the apostles of progress may not have been what Truman or Eisenhower had envisioned, but it represented an authentic alternative to the patriotic American civil religion championed by conservatives. The apostles of progress would contest the Cold War on this basis, not in moral opposition to the Soviet Union or China but their own government. Often such liberal clergy were out of step with their own congregations, and during the Cold War a large gap opened up between a liberal leadership and a more conservative laity on issues like civil rights and foreign policy.

From the very beginning of the Cold War, the apostles of progress criticized containment as excessively dogmatic and militaristic. Their view of Soviet communism was much more optimistic than that of the apostles of liberty, resembling Roosevelt's wartime theory of convergence much more than Truman's strategy of containment. In 1946, even the president of the Southern Baptist Convention, Louie D. Newton, could travel to the Soviet Union and be impressed by its commitment to social progress as well as its wartime sacrifices. Just as importantly, Newton felt that Soviet society was becoming freer and more relaxed in its treatment of religion. He was allowed to preach in several Russian churches and meet with Russians of various denominations. They all assured him that they were as free to practice their religion as any American because the Soviet constitution enshrined the very same separation of church and state as the First Amendment. Newton was not only impressed, but convinced. He published a travelogue upon his return to the United States; Bishop Bromley Oxnam provided the introduction. "I have preached the Gospel in Soviet churches," he told his undoubtedly shocked Southern Baptist flock. "I have seen and talked with the Soviet people at work, at play, and in worship; I have savored the war-born sorrows and the soaring hopes of the mighty people that first defeated Hitler."[35]

Religious liberals were unlikely to damn communism. Rather, while they criticized the Soviet Union's political abuses, they also cautiously extolled communism's social and economic virtues. Like Newton, they saw potential in the Soviet Union for religious reform and revival and did not believe the Russian Orthodox Church was merely an agent of the Kremlin. They refused to condemn communism while a very different set of evils within capitalism went unchecked. And they refused, most of all, to identify with crusades against either communism or capitalism, instead seeing them as two flawed systems whose potential for progress must be unlocked but made humane. "There are those who would mobilize the Church in a 'holy war' against communism," Oxnam proclaimed in his 1946 presidential address to the Federal Council of Churches. "There are others who would mobilize similarly against capitalism. The Church must herald a new day but it must not become the voice of reaction nor the voice of revolution. . . . We refuse to identify the Christian gospel with an economic order, whether it be capitalist, communist, or socialist." This neutralist doctrine of moral equivalence would land Oxnam in trouble with HUAC and other anticommunists, and a decade later his friend Dulles would call it immoral. But it expressed the dominant sentiment among the liberal Protestant clergy nonetheless.[36]

Two years later, at its founding convention in Amsterdam, the World Council of Churches made a similar declaration of moral equivalence and refused, despite tremendous pressure from Truman and Myron Taylor, to join forces with Washington and the Vatican in an anticommunist crusade. Josef Hromadka, the Czech theologian who argued with Dulles over the nature of communism, proved to be an effective critic of the United States and its ambitions in Europe. The West was deluding itself, he argued in Amsterdam, "when it imagined it possessed freedom and others did not." Instead of embracing containment, the architects of world Protestant unity essentially wanted to combine the individual rights of capitalism with the group rights of communism. But in doing so, the WCC acknowledged that communism was potentially redemptive. "Christians should ask why Communism in its modern totalitarian form makes so strong an appeal to great masses of people in many parts of the world," stated a WCC report on world affairs. "They should recognize the work of God in the revolt of multitudes against injustice that gives Communism much of its strength. They should seek to recapture for the church the original Christian solidarity with the world's distressed people." Both liberty and progress were possible, but only if they were treated with equal respect and priority. The World Council then issued a stark critique of capitalism that infuriated the White House. "The Christian church should reject the ideologies of both Communism and capitalism, and should seek to draw men away from the false assumption that these are the only alternatives. Each has made promises which it could not redeem." Instead, it was "the responsibility of Christians to seek new creative solutions which never allow either justice or freedom to destroy the other."[37]

This unflinching denunciation of national and ideological exceptionalism found broad appeal among liberal theologians. Even Niebuhr, also at Amsterdam and normally wary of communist political incursions, thought the WCC's declaration was "quite right." The Federal Council then used the impetus from Amsterdam to issue its own assessment of human rights. It was the churches' duty, said the FCC, to promote both individual rights (mostly through religious liberty) and group rights (through the promotion of social and economic equality). Frederick Nolde, the veteran ecumenist who had contributed to the 1945 San Francisco Conference, continued his work with the UN and ensured that its 1948 Universal Declaration of Human Rights included respect for religious liberty and struck a balance between individual and group rights.[38]

The WCC's equivalence of communism and capitalism, and mainline Protestantism's enthusiasm for the WCC, reflected the perseverance of ecumenical internationalism in the United States. The United Nations was not simply a diplomatic meeting point where governments could present their own narrow, national self-interests, but a forum for all peoples of the world to meet, discuss issues of mutual importance, realize one another's viewpoints on points of difference, and work toward peaceful solutions to world problems. And the WCC was not simply an ecumenical body for Protestants but the UN's religious counterpart in a campaign for world peace. Without the UN, said the missionary and ecumenist Henry Smith Leiper, the world would experience another war, but without the WCC, the UN would lack a soul and a conscience. Similarly, in honor of the 1948 World Congress of Religion, Harry Emerson Fosdick epitomized the spirit of ecumenical internationalism, and its enduring pacifism, in a special prayer for the UN:

> Eternal God, Father of All Souls: Grant unto us such clear vision of the sin of war that we may earnestly seek that cooperation between nations which alone can make war impossible. As man by his inventions has made the whole world into one neighborhood, grant that he may by his cooperation make the whole world into one brotherhood.

Writing for Church Peace Union, Justin Wroe Nixon said Christ would have approved of the UN because it was a worldwide mechanism for "bearing one another's burdens."[39]

Support for the UN was broad as well as deep. The United Church Women repeatedly announced it would "pray for the success" of the world body because it was the only vehicle that could truly express the hopes and fears of an entire planet. In 1948, the Federal Council–sponsored United Nations Sunday was widely observed across the nation. In November 1950—after the outbreak of the Korean War—the International Convention of the Disciples of Christ, meeting in Oklahoma City, called for the United States to join with others "to move by constitutional means as rapidly as possible toward a limited world federal government with democratically held and exercised powers." Spurred by the National Catholic Welfare Conference, the Catholic Association for International Peace, and a new UN office dedicated to Catholic concerns, American Catholics placed their faith in the UN even as they continued their anticommunist crusade. In 1956, the NCWC pronounced that the UN, despite its flaws, embodied "the hope of humankind" and offered "the only present promise we have for sustained peace in our time; peace with any approximation of justice." Throughout the era, overwhelming majorities of liberal Protestants, Catholics, and Jews expressed support for a UN that would shepherd a truly ecumenical world peace.[40]

By contrast, support for policies that were driven by American leadership, especially military leadership, or that did not reflect the ecumenists' absolute internationalism, was tepid at best. The Truman Doctrine and the North Atlantic Treaty Organization were the two main examples. Both divided the world into West and East, good and evil, free and enslaved, and both pledged to combat communist tyranny in the name of democratic liberty. As we have seen, religious anticommunists such as Dulles and Niebuhr supported NATO because they had concluded that the Soviets would always sabotage designs for a truly ecumenical new world order. But liberals would not abandon their vision so easily. In pursuing such aggressive, particularistic policies, they charged Truman with jeopardizing any chance for peaceful, universalistic solutions. He was also making Soviet intransigence a self-fulfilling prophecy, for why would Moscow ever trust Washington when the president was adopting such a hard line? No wonder the Soviets were troubled by NATO, remarked the FCC, just as surely as Americans would be by a communist alliance of Latin American republics. The Truman administration met with similar obstacles in its domestic campaign for congressional ratification of NATO. After the State Department's Charles Bohlen spent hours explaining it to the FCC's 1949 National Study Conference, after Dulles pleaded with his fellow delegates not to condemn U.S. foreign policy, and after an hour of what the *New York Times* called "heated debate," the conference would only vote "neither to endorse nor oppose" NATO.[41]

The best place to begin practicing international control was nuclear energy. Until 1949, the United States maintained an atomic monopoly. Though in reality it proved to be ineffectual, the monopoly provided American leaders with a potentially enormous source of power and leverage. Nonetheless, many Catholics, Jews, and liberal Protestants denounced nuclear weapons and called upon Truman to begin disbanding the nation's atomic arsenal. In a typical episode, a Protestant missionary in Japan challenged her fellow Americans to take a quick tour of Hiroshima and see for themselves the immoral effects of nuclear weapons. For Catholics, only the existential angst caused by nuclear arms could mitigate their hostility for communism. The nuclear monopoly was not only ineffective, said three leading Catholic just war theorists, it was provocative, and therefore dangerous. Even those charged with maintaining America's nuclear might were troubled by its power. David Lilienthal, head of the Atomic Energy Commission, was so repelled by nuclear weapons and perplexed by their spiritual challenge that he sought the counsel of Bishop Oxnam several times in 1948. Most religious opponents of the bomb realized that the nuclear genie could not simply be rebottled, and so rather than call for the abolition of nuclear energy they urged Truman to place it under international control. Only the UN's involvement could lead to both nuclear disarmament and the harnessing of nuclear energy's almost unlimited potential. Because war had become "total and diabolical," declared A. J. Muste, the United States must no longer be a part of it.[42]

That Muste could continue his career as a leading critic of U.S. foreign policy revealed much about the endurance of pacifism and the widespread unease with the onset of the Cold War. In the first years after the war, when internationalism flourished widely, Christian pacifism enjoyed something of a revival. But even during the dark days of McCarthyism and the Korean War, pacifists maintained their critique of the abuses of American power. Not even the munificent Marshall Plan could win their affections: the best thing Muste had to say was that Truman's plan to fend off destitution *and* communism presented pacifists with "a bitter dilemma." He was also a trenchant critic of his fellow Protestants, particularly liberal Christian realists, who gave support and spiritual guidance to the Truman and Eisenhower administrations.[43]

Muste's Cold War pacifism was an important precursor to the more widespread dissent of the Vietnam era, but even in the depths of the early Cold War he was not alone in calling for a pacifist foreign policy. In 1948, the Baptist Council for Christian Social Progress organized an interdenominational Conference of Church People on World Peace that called for peace through negotiations, nuclear disarmament, the UN, decolonization, foreign aid, and the permanent abolition of the draft. In classically pacifist terms, the Conference condemned war as unchristian and concluded that if Americans only acted sensibly, "war need not be either imminent or inevitable." That same year, the General Conference of the Methodist Church, which met every four years, acted as if nothing had changed in two tumultuous decades and pronounced the "sinfulness" of war and that Christianity was "utterly opposed" to it. "The task of the Church is healing, reconciliation, the removal of prejudice and hate, the cementing of bonds of brotherhood, the exalting of God as the Father and Ruler of all mankind and Christ as the Savior of all." This task could not be completed if the church supported aggressive policies such as the Truman Doctrine. Instead, only dialogue with the Soviets and a willingness to make sacrifices and compromises would bring about peace; the Methodists vowed to support nothing else.[44]

Just as the anticommunism of Christian conservatives and liberal realists gained in strength during the Truman years, religious dissent gained momentum by feeding off the energy generated by the intense fears and emotions of the early Cold War. With allies in high politics, such as former vice president and presidential aspirant Henry Wallace, the apostles of progress posed a real threat to the domestic supports that were essential for the pursuit of containment. By the winter of 1947, Niebuhr was alarmed enough to use a leader in his magazine, *Christianity and Crisis*, to attack the dissenters. In it, he relied on all the credibility he had gained in being the lonely voice to warn against Nazism and used it on his modernist colleagues without restraint. "We are told that a policy of firmness must inevitably lead to war, while conciliation could guarantee peace," Niebuhr wrote caustically. "In the Nazi days this was called appeasement." It was a blunt, harsh message that he would repeat often, with great effect, over the next few years.[45]

Despite the apparent wickedness and anti-Christian zealotry of the Chinese Communists, despite even the outbreak of the Korean War, a Cold War consensus was just as elusive on Asia as it was on Europe. Protestants were especially divided, with liberals criticizing the excessive anticommunist zeal of Catholics and conservative Protestants as well as the Truman and Eisenhower administrations. To mainline modernists, China was a classic example not of the expansionism of communism, but of the political consequences of despair. Poverty, malnutrition, a lack of education, and Nationalist tyranny and corruption were the true evils that had enabled communism to thrive. In classically Progressive, Social Gospel fashion, liberals saw the malfunctioning of Chinese society, and not the CCP, as the source of China's problems. The Communists had simply taken advantage of the situation, not created it, said the FCC in 1947. The "dynamic" was not political, but "the pressure of poverty" and the "negative and repressive measures used by the Government" of Chiang Kai-shek. Alleviate poverty, hunger, and other societal ills, and communism would cease to be a problem. While the CCP's consolidation of power in October 1949 electrified American opinion, it did nothing to change the FCC's opinion. "The fear that Russia might control Asia must not tempt us into a reliance upon military strategy when it is obvious that Communist influence cannot be arrested apart from a general effort to further the economic betterment and growing independence of Asiatic peoples," its Executive Committee explained in a December 1949 statement. "The real issue is whether or not our government is prepared to advance the greater welfare of the peoples of Asia, with higher standards of living, and with cultural, social, and political institutions which will accord with the free choice of the peoples directly concerned."[46]

American missionaries had been brutalized and harassed, and eventually deported, and many of them used their bitter experience to push for a hard-line U.S. approach to China. But interestingly, in 1948–49, as a CCP victory in the civil war seemed inevitable, many mainline missionaries continued to believe in engagement, dialogue, and forgiveness. Above all, they continued to believe that the solution to China's problems, and thus to America's problems in China, were development and national self-determination. Liberal hopes persisted even after the Communists came to power in October 1949. Only a month after the establishment of the People's Republic, the Foreign Missions Conference concluded that because the struggle for China "is not primarily a test of arms" but rather "a social and political convulsion of revolutionary proportions," the Truman administration "should promote in every way the economic well-being of the peoples of the Far East." Beijing, not Taipei, should represent China on the UN Security Council. Through the United Nations, the United States "should labor incessantly for the observance of human rights and fundamental freedoms for the peoples of Asia." Just as important was racial justice. "The status of inferiority thus far imposed upon these people by the West must come to an end. Asiatics, no less than ourselves, are children of the Heavenly Father and, as such, are entitled to be dealt with on the basis of racial equality."[47]

Above all, the apostles of progress assumed that admitting China to the United Nations would unravel Sino-American tensions and prevent future wars such as Korea. Even during the Korean War, liberal Protestants called for the seating of China at the UN. According to the Peace Council of the East Harlem Protestant Parish, a mission set up by Union Theological Seminary, it was a step that would not only end the war but "restore the United Nations as an effective agency of mediation." After the war, the Foreign Policy Commission of Christian Action kept up the pressure, arguing that Chinese inclusion in the UN would make the world body "an even more effective instrument for peace." Throughout the 1950s, the National Council of Churches joined these calls for the admission of the People's Republic to the UN. And when secular leaders such as Eleanor Roosevelt made similar appeals, they knew they would find a receptive audience among groups like the United Church Women, a national organization she described to Truman as politically important. Progress could only happen, the church women believed, when the United States admitted China into the family of nations.[48]

. . .

As the Cold War matured in the Eisenhower years, religious dissent matured with it. Indeed, many of the themes that observers found new and startling in the protest movements of the 1960s had been repeatedly tried and tested in the Truman and Eisenhower eras, and not only by radicals on the margins of American political life. The mainline churches, from a wide variety of denominations, joined Protestant and Catholic pacifists in calling for a more humane foreign policy based not on military strength but compassion and charity. The world system's increasingly globalized nature—indeed, the emergence of something akin to an international society—required the leading religious nation, the United States, to play a commensurately leading political and economic role. "If ever there were a time to beg God's help," a Catholic order wrote Eisenhower in 1956, "it is now, for the affliction of our fellow men across the ocean has become our own affliction." Social problems in one part of the world could not be kept isolated from another, and so had to be dealt with by all. And this was not simply a matter of doing good works. It also made for smart policy, because poverty, hunger, and disease were also assumed to be leading causes of communism and tyranny the world over.[49]

True to his contradictory, quarrelsome nature, Reinhold Niebuhr was one of the leading apostles of progress. The anticommunist gospel of liberty still motivated him, but by the 1950s it became clear that his anticommunism was actually a much more specific anti-Sovietism. He still had no time for communist ideology, but what he saw emerging in the Third World was not Soviet expansionism, nor even the ideological rapacity of Marxism, Leninism, and Stalinism, but a socialist means to several ends: decolonization, development, and national self-determination. Calling the North Vietnamese "communist" simply distorted the meaning of the Cold War and drew attention and precious resources away from the very real struggle with the Soviet Union.

Americans, Niebuhr wrote in a 1955 statement for Americans for Democratic Action, were dangerously blind to the "continued weight of the inheritance of 'colonialism.'" Despite the independence of the Philippines in 1946, colonialism was part of the American inheritance just as much as the European—if, that is, Americans wanted to consider themselves leaders of the West and the free world. Decolonization was a problem, partly because of its slow pace and partly because the West still acted as if it was the rest of the world's master. Niebuhr warned that instead of instilling gratitude, the "emancipation" of colonial peoples "has frequently aggravated their resentments because their new freedom did not cure them of all the ills" attributed to colonialism. Liberty was important, but so too was progress; development must follow independence. Yet Eisenhower and Dulles, who continued to fold every complex world crisis into the simplistic binary of the Soviet-American Cold War, did not seem to be able to grasp this very basic point. They instead fostered a "persistent illusion," Niebuhr complained, by giving "military strategy a false priority in our total strategy" that merely "veiled the social and political realities with which we must come to terms." The Soviets recognized what the Eisenhower administration did not, which was why they were winning the global battle for hearts and minds. Though they had once been ecumenical allies, the secretary of state particularly galled Niebuhr. "Mr. Dulles has confused the picture by his simple moral preachments and distinctions," he said elsewhere to a friend, "and thus the whole non-committed world of Asia and Africa have been alienated."[50]

Niebuhr's message—that geopolitics could not be defined simply in terms of a struggle between East and West—epitomized the liberal approach to the Cold War. No longer did world politics turn on Europe and the United States; others were now just as important and had to be considered as equals in the international system. Praising the 1955 Bandung Conference in Indonesia, which gathered dozens of noncommunist, non-Western nations to form a neutral, "nonaligned" movement, one liberal Protestant rejoiced that "the nineteenth century was decently buried, and the twentieth century was proclaimed for Africa and Asia!" "NOW is the time," declared the American Baptist Women two years later, to welcome "that rising Asian-African bloc" that was neither East nor West. "Will we make every effort to understand their fears, their needs, their ambitions, so that together we may make the world safe for the survival of ideas and way of life we hold dear?" That the Third World's fears, needs, and ambitions centered as much on such basic issues as food, water, and education made the West's preoccupation with communism seem wasteful and selfish, even perverse. The world needed more food and better access to clean drinking water, not nuclear weapons. Protestant, Catholic, and Jewish organizations all scrambled to facilitate development in the Third World, and all lent vocal support to Truman's Point Four program to increase U.S. development aid. Mission boards were particularly well-placed to inculcate modernization.[51]

Race—or more specifically, racism—in international relations was another liberal preoccupation, closely connected to global poverty and decolonization because most of the world's nonwhites constituted most of the world's poor and colonized. In the United States, Judeo-Christian appeals to tolerance had arisen out of a need to distinguish Americanism from anti-Semitism, fascism, and Nazism. But in the context of the Cold War, religious tolerance was broadened to include racial tolerance as well. It is important to remember, for example, that Truman's 1948 Executive Order desegregating the military also prohibited religious prejudice. Most of the major white liberal Protestant organizations mobilized behind the cause of racial tolerance, at home and worldwide. Since 1928, the Federal Council of Churches had sponsored Race Relations Sunday, an annual event that highlighted the evil of racial prejudice in America. These special services continued into the Cold War but assumed a new urgency. Tolerance, religious *and* racial, declared one minister in 1949, was the key to conflict resolution and thus "the only real hope for the world." This was a message all Christians must heed. After all, preached the pastor of the Parkchester Baptist Church in Brooklyn, if "God created anyone, He must have created everyone." The United Church Women issued a similar appeal on the World Day of Prayer in 1954 and drafted prayers for the UN, for poverty relief, and for racial tolerance. "Let us pray for those in areas of racial tension," appealed the church women, and "that the love of God may fill their hearts so that love of all men as brothers must follow."[52]

To further this goal, white mainline churches allied with African American Protestants campaigning for racial justice at home. Mainline Protestants, liberal Catholics, and many Jews had long sympathized with the plight of African Americans, but until now they had done little about it. Aside from large, symbolic gestures such as Race Relations Sunday, before the 1950s only radical pacifists from the Fellowship of Reconciliation and the Catholic Worker movement had actually mobilized to advance the cause of civil rights. But in the 1950s, in a development critical for the eventual success of the civil rights movement, white mainline liberals began to team up with blacks. The ideological climate of the Cold War, pitting the "free world" against communist enslavement, gave them confidence. With the Soviets and the Third World nonaligned movement able to use Jim Crow to undermine America's claims to be the leader of the free world, it was becoming increasingly more difficult to maintain segregation at home while pursuing "freedom" abroad.[53]

The most significant figure in these early bridge-building initiatives was Benjamin E. Mays, a renowned black Baptist preacher, president of Morehouse College in Atlanta, and founding member of the World Council of Churches. Mays was a commanding presence in the black community and had nurtured several generations of civil rights leaders—including one of his former students at Morehouse, Martin Luther King Jr., who called him "one of the great influences in my life." Mays had also been one of the leading thinkers of liberal Protestant theology in America, mixing company and sharing ideas with both the neo-orthodox crowd and the pacifists of the Fellowship of Reconciliation. In 1954, in Evanston, Illinois, the WCC held its first assembly since its founding in Amsterdam in 1948. This summit of world Protestantism, now including many Eastern Orthodox churches as well, featured Mays as one of its keynote speakers. Addressing the assembly in a country that still respected legally sanctioned racial persecution, Reverend Mays called for all churches, white and black, to live up to the demands of their Christian witness, unite as one, and dismantle racism everywhere in the world—including America.[54]

Blacks had of course already been campaigning for their civil rights for decades. Activists aimed to recapture the gains of Reconstruction that had been consumed by the hatred and persecution of Jim Crow. Organizations like the National Association for the Advancement of Colored People (founded in 1909) agitated for black freedom with little success. At the same time, African Americans had fought with distinction in each of the nation's foreign wars since 1898—so that foreigners could have access to the same rights denied to them at home. This cruel discrepancy fed the fires of the black freedom struggle, and as the scale and ideological stakes of the conflicts escalated from the Spanish-American War to World War I to the conflicts of the 1940s, so too did the intensity of the African Americans' struggle at home. The Cold War both hindered and helped the civil rights movement. While anticommunist red baiting could be wielded to delegitimize domestic causes as antithetical to Americanism, the stridency of Washington's Cold War claims to moral legitimacy made the gap between Cold War rhetoric and American reality too large to ignore and impossible to sustain.[55]

African Americans were thus able to use the Cold War to achieve progress in civil rights, with black churches and organizations such as King's Southern Christian Leadership Conference leading the way. But they also applied the same moral pressures to U.S. foreign policy. Beyond the United States, the Cold War world was a place of "agonized scarcity" populated by the "hungry, homeless, destitute," declared the Synod of Catawba, North Carolina, an African American body of the Presbyterian Church (USA). These were threats to world peace every bit as much as communist expansionism. But of "all the factors in the world today that militate against Christian brotherhood, race prejudice is one of the most outstanding, and the most dangerous. Out of race prejudice has grown the race problem, which is one of the most perplexing problems in the world." Without racial justice, there could be no racial peace; and without racial peace, there could be no world peace.[56]

With this in mind, American Protestants, both black and white, brought pressure to bear on the apartheid regime in South Africa at the same time they campaigned against segregation in the South. With Africa's position in world politics taking on "new significance," the AME Church focused attention on apartheid. Not unlike the segregated American South, white South Africans claimed that separate was not necessarily unequal. But just as in the South, apartheid was "not applied Justly. There are two different communities not side by side, but one which enforces its will upon the other." This was precisely the evil that Americans, of all faiths and races, had fought to eradicate in the war. It was now time to finish the job, though this time peacefully. Liberal white Protestants agreed. "The churches," declared the New York–based International Missionary Council in a 1954 report on Africa, "have a responsibility to find solutions for inter-racial conflict."[57]

But of all the liberal causes of the early Cold War, nothing earned such widespread support as the campaign against nuclear weapons. It was not yet the broad-based popular movement it would become in later decades, especially the 1960s and 1980s. But it was already a cause that earned widespread sympathy among religious liberals. And for pacifists, nuclear weapons sustained their cause in an otherwise unsympathetic age of Christian realism and anticommunist containment.

In fact, opposition to nuclear weapons was the main cause that could unite mainline liberals and pacifist radicals. Mainline Protestants were forming a fairly solid consensus on a number of foreign policy issues that would sustain a powerful moral critique not of communism, but of the U.S. government. Some, such as Reverend Robert J. McMullen of the Presbyterian Church of Chapel Hill, North Carolina, called for "the outlawing of such destructive forces and the mass annihilation of peoples and nations that can be caused by them." Others advanced slightly different proposals that included unilateral disarmament by the United States. Liberal Congregationalists acknowledged that the secret of atomic energy could not be simply unlearned or forgotten, but they suggested that the U.S. government cooperate with the Soviet Union to ensure only civilian uses prevailed. More important, they unequivocally condemned the military applications of nuclear power. "The security of the United States is a very precious thing," conceded the United Church of Christ magazine *Social Action*. "But the Christian conscience should not dare attempt to protect that security at the price of the atomized cities of another nation—*even if we could prevent the same thing happening to our country*." Some did not go quite so far—the National Federation of Temple Sisterhoods, a Reform Jewish organization, urged Eisenhower to embark upon prudent disarmament through the UN while also pushing him to embrace quicker desegregation policies at home—but overall, liberals were united in their desire for the United States to begin dismantling its awesome nuclear arsenal.[58]

And of course, pacifist opposition to nuclear weapons—and to U.S. foreign policy in general—remained even more resolute. Whereas the mainline Protestant churches could oscillate between support for some policies and opposition to others—could applaud, for example, the Korean War while criticizing its tactics—Christian pacifists were steadfast in their conviction that the United States government was perhaps the world's single greatest purveyor of violence. Nuclear arms had something to do with this, but the pacifist critique was rooted much deeper in a sense that U.S. officials had betrayed, and were continuing to betray, America's true calling in the world. Any form of containment was repugnant, any use of force an affront to God. While some veteran pacifists—most prominently Norman Thomas—lost their way after the Holocaust had vindicated military intervention and communism had vindicated containment, others kept the faith. A. J. Muste certainly did so, as did Dorothy Day and her Catholic Workers. They were a small minority, to be sure, but they were a noisy minority who raised troubling questions about America's role in the world. And just as Christian pacifists from the Fellowship of Reconciliation had teamed up with civil rights campaigners Bayard Rustin, James Farmer, and A. Philip Randolph during the war, Muste and the FOR would link up with a new generation of leaders in the black freedom struggle. In 1950, Martin Luther King Jr., still a divinity student at Crozer Theological Seminary in Pennsylvania, was "deeply moved" by a Muste lecture on nonviolence. Though initially skeptical, the young King had been introduced to pacifism, a significant turning point encouraged by the religious activists in the FOR who linked nonviolent resistance against imperialism abroad to the fight against segregation at home.[59]

As Muste, Day, and King illustrated, just as a shared anticommunism was bringing conservative Protestants and Catholics closer together, leftist dissent could also lead to ecumenical cooperation. The Cold War, then, blurred denominational boundaries on the left as well as the right. For example, when Day and other Catholic Workers deliberately got themselves arrested by refusing to participate in New York air-raid drills and nuclear shelter exercises—which contravened state law—the American Friends Service Committee stepped in to pay for their legal defense. On other occasions, Catholic Workers and Quakers worked together to protest air-raid drills as provocative to the Soviets and corrosive to American life. This hinted at the broad-based peace coalitions that would come in the following decade, not only over nuclear weapons but also civil rights and the war in Vietnam.[60]

By the 1950s, the unsettling realities of thermonuclear warfare had even stirred the consciences of the Christian realists. Once again, Niebuhr proved to be an important bellwether. Niebuhr had previously been more accepting of atomic weapons than his mainline colleagues. But the hydrogen bomb, which represented a quantum leap in destructive capacity, pushed him away from perceiving nuclear arms as simply another weapon. Especially repugnant were the strategists, like Herman Kahn and Henry Kissinger, who had declared nuclear war to be winnable. Kahn had even contemplated the number of "acceptable" American deaths in a nuclear exchange with the Soviet Union—anything under so many tens of millions of dead would be considered a success because it would likely mean greater Soviet casualties and thus a U.S. victory. Niebuhr had little patience for those, like Kissinger, who considered nuclear arms "tactical rather than strategic" and thus available for use like a conventional weapon. "I think this is monstrous," he complained to John C. Bennett after Eisenhower had likened a nuclear bomb to conventional weapons, such as a bullet or a tank, "and I am saying so."[61]

In saying so, time and again, as both an apostle of liberty and an apostle of progress, Niebuhr epitomized the contradictions and tensions of an era falsely remembered for its homogeneity. Yet these tensions were but rumblings compared to the earthquake that would hit the United States—and its foreign policy—in the decades to come.

PART VIII

Reformation and Counterreformation

Seabury House, Greenwich, Connecticut, March 1963. It was a remarkable sight and, to the liberal mainline clergy gathered for the occasion, a hopeful one. The National Conference Center of the Episcopal Church, better known as Seabury House, had played host to numerous religious gatherings over the years, but few such as this. Mingling with the leadership of the National Council of Churches and several mainline denominations were sixteen clerics from the Soviet Union, mostly Russian Orthodox and Protestant. They had spent the past month touring the United States, from Iowa to New York, on a visit of international goodwill and Christian unity. After harrowing crises over Berlin and Cuba that had twice brought the world to the brink of nuclear war, the Cold War was entering a period of reduced tension between the superpowers. Rejoicing at the new geopolitical climate, the NCC had taken it upon itself to further this cause. "If nations of the world are ever to enjoy orderly procedures and peaceful change," Reverend Stewart Herman told his Soviet-American audience at Seabury House, "surely it is incumbent upon the Christian churches to furnish practical examples in the conduct of their own national and international affairs." The NCC believed it was doing what churches do best: leading by example.[1]

However, the Soviets' visit was not a product of détente so much as its forerunner, and it was actually the return leg of an exchange with their American counterparts. Half a year before, in the late summer of 1962, the National Council of Churches sent a delegation to tour the Soviet Union. That visit, the NCC said, was "held in a spirit of Christian mutual understanding, fraternity, and cordiality." It was also intended to help "overcome some of the dangerous hostility and rigidity between our two nations" and to prove, Cold War tensions notwithstanding, that "God has not lost control of his world, which includes the Soviet Union." Despite the prevailing climate of international hostility, the American ministers wanted to make contact with their Soviet colleagues as a way to build bridges and transcend the ideological competition between communism and capitalism. Most of all, the Protestant ministers wanted to humanize and demystify the Soviet Union, and to prove to the American people that the Soviets were not inherently evil but every bit as human as themselves. As Reverend Eugene Carson Blake put it, the "real reason for a trip like this" was simple: "There are people over there."[2]

Through the State Department and the U.S. Information Agency (USIA), the federal government had already made cultural exchange a Cold War priority. After all, in a global battle for hearts and minds, it was a lot cheaper and safer, and a lot less controversial, than nuclear brinkmanship. Initially, the Truman administration promoted tourism as a way to build transatlantic anticommunist solidarity. Subsequently, the Eisenhower administration set up a wide variety of cultural exchange programs, such as the People-to-People Program, that would bring foreigners to the United States and send Americans overseas. The idea, explained the USIA, was to make "every man an ambassador." An ambassador, of course, represents his or her country and tries to advance its interests, and it was the government's intention to use public funds to send private Americans around the world to spread, either implicitly or explicitly, a pro-American and anticommunist message. But this was not quite what the NCC had in mind. These apostles of progress tended to be almost as critical of the United States and capitalism as they were of the Soviet Union and communism. They did not seek or accept government funding for their cultural exchanges; nor would they accept official direction as to what they should say or do. They wanted an ecumenical peace in which each system could respect, tolerate, and live with the other. The exchange, explained the NCC, was neither "an isolated undertaking nor the product of a quixotic impulse." Instead, it was "part of a long ecumenical process" of mutual and peaceful understanding that would hopefully contribute to an improved understanding between the superpowers. Later, the mainline churches hoped to expand their mission to include China and Cuba. Said one liberal Baptist minister in San Francisco, "We think things are changing. The world marches on. It's a very realistic thing in today's world. As Christians who believe in reconciliation, we believe God intends us to talk to Communists. We are interested in contacts of some kind. You must establish communications if you are going to reconcile."[3]

Yet it was this very purpose, with its implications of moral equivalence between the United States and the communist world, that touched a nerve among many other American Christians. The Soviets, these conservative Christians argued during the 1963 visit, were not in fact ordinary people like themselves. They were evil, and did evil things in communism's name. *New York Times* headlines like "Soviet Presses War on Religion," which ran shortly before the Soviet clergy arrived in America, certainly did not help the liberals' cause. Nor did the case of thirty-two Siberian Pentecostals, who stormed the U.S. Embassy in Moscow in hopes of finding political asylum and religious liberty only two months before the Soviet church tour of America. Nor especially did the involvement of the National Council of Churches, which the apostles of liberty reviled as an unrepresentative and apostate organization and which Carl McIntire accused of knowingly hosting KGB agents, not men of God. Whatever the reason, Christian conservatives reacted to the exchange, particularly the return visit of the Soviet clergy, with outrage. The solution, they said, was not ecumenical tolerance and dialogue, which only watered down faith to its lowest common denominator and bleached it of any true meaning. Instead, Americans must stand their ground and resist communism forever. One angry fundamentalist from Old Hickory, Tennessee, wrote that Americans needed "fewer organizations like the National Council of Churches if our Nation is to survive the onslaught of Communism." After listing the evils of communist doctrine, he outlined the dangers of the NCC exchange. "Coexistence and peace are other advocated Communist policies. Coexistence in this case means our compliance to their demands; peace means our enslavement. If we maintain our Christian civilization, we'll have to fight for it." If the NCC wanted to help the Soviet people so much, it "could do its work better by transferring its head quarters to Russia. Such a course would also be a benefit to American Churches." George McMillin, head of the Indiana Committee for Captive Nations, wondered if the NCC was "so naïve as to think that the good patriotic American does not know that the war has never ceased, either hot or cold, since its start in 1939."[4]

Was America at war? This question spoke to a profound, unbridgeable difference between religious liberals and conservatives. For liberals, the Cold War was an abomination, an artificial construction of an unnecessary and misguided foreign policy. The Cold War could only be transcended, and then overcome, through peaceful endeavor, mutual understanding, and unfettered communication. For conservatives, however, the Cold War was a necessary, unavoidable struggle against the forces of godless tyranny. Dialogue would do nothing except weaken America's vigilance. Such differences spoke to the religious, political, and cultural gap between liberals and conservatives—domestic differences that, we shall see, shaped their views of America's role in the wider world. This domestic cold war within the global Cold War carried over into the new era of the Kennedy presidency, and intensified over the next three decades. But gradually, after Vietnam, irrepressible grassroots conservatives, armed with the doctrines of patriotism, true faith, and inviolable religious liberty, gained the upper hand. Following a period of blasphemous détente, these apostles of liberty ensured that America would resume its offensive, and that a second Cold War would begin. U.S. foreign policy would not be immune to forces of reformation and counterreformation that engulfed American religion and politics.

The Revolutionary Church
in a Revolutionary Age

B Y 1960, Americans had lived for three decades with presidents who had used religion to define their political values and foreign policies. When Franklin Roosevelt, Harry Truman, and Dwight Eisenhower needed to justify or explain the purposes of diplomacy, they found a ready answer in religious faith. Central to their messages, with only slight variations in tone, were the links between faith and freedom, especially between interfaith tolerance and democratic politics. Thus the election in 1960 of the nation's first Roman Catholic president, John F. Kennedy, was in many ways the logical culmination of their efforts. And at first, JFK seemed to continue promoting their presidential civil religion. "I have sworn before you and Almighty God the same solemn oath our forebears prescribed nearly a century and three quarters ago," he declared at the outset of his inaugural address. "And yet the same revolutionary beliefs . . . are still at issue around the globe—the belief that the rights of man come not from the generosity of the state but from the hand of God." The new president pledged his support for "those old allies whose cultural and spiritual origins we share" and asked God for "His blessing and His help" while acknowledging that "here on earth God's work must truly be our own."[1]

Slain by an assassin's bullet in November 1963, Kennedy never lived to finish God's work. The task was left to his successor, Lyndon B. Johnson, who used his 1965 inaugural address to share his vision of building a Great Society in America. Under a "covenant of justice, liberty, and union," LBJ proclaimed, "we have become a nation—prosperous, great, and mighty." Yet this did not mean God's work was finished. Americans were a blessed people, but they had "no promise from God that our greatness will endure. We have been allowed by Him to seek greatness with the sweat of our hands and the strength of our spirit." Americans had work ahead of them, hard work, even in a time of plenty. Johnson, in a prophetic mood, left them with no alternative. "If we fail now then we will have forgotten in abundance what we learned in hardship: that democracy rests on faith, that freedom asks more than it gives, and the judgment of God is harshest on those who are most favored."[2]

Yet the religious rhetoric of Kennedy and Johnson marked a subtle but significant change. It seemed as pious as the language that had come before, but it was more ambivalent, less comfortable in the absolute certainties of faith. In pledging to do God's work on earth, Kennedy signaled a more humanist, even secular, approach to solving the problems of the world. Johnson's tone was even sharper, warning Americans against complacent exceptionalism and reminding them that God would not look kindly upon those who did not put their vast powers to good use. Perhaps without realizing it, Kennedy and Johnson reflected a shift that was taking place in religion's influence on politics and especially on foreign policy. In a modernizing society that was both increasingly secular and pluralistic, religion's role could never again be assumed. The presidents could look to faith, but they could not rely on it. As a result, neither Kennedy nor Johnson provided Americans with guidance on how to apply the teachings of religion to the practice of world politics.

However, religious Americans felt no such ambivalence or hesitation. In fact, under pressure from the same secular and pluralistic sources, people of faith on both the left and the right strengthened the application of their religious beliefs to public life. In an uncertain and constantly shifting world, religion seemed to provide the only remaining fixed points of moral reference. With no direction from the White House, they were left free to channel their religious energies and passions into whichever outlets they thought best. The result was chaotic. For the first time since the interwar period, the religious influence on American foreign relations, from both the left and the right, was mostly oppositional and rarely in concert with policymakers.

IT IS NO small irony that one of the least religious of presidents should have been the agent of such profound religious change. With his election in 1960, John F. Kennedy broke one of the oldest and strongest cultural prejudices in America, anti-Catholicism, simply because of his inherited faith. And yet it was this very faith that compelled him to deemphasize the role of faith in the presidency. Pierre Salinger, JFK's press secretary, recalled that Kennedy was "determined to lean over backward to disprove the suspicion that he would be a *Catholic* president." Kennedy's determination not to favor one religion meant that he would give favor to no religion.[3]

Kennedy was not irreligious, and he certainly was not an atheist. But neither was he devout—at least, not in a spiritual sense. He believed in God and the Catholic Church, but did not seek their counsel for guidance on earthly matters. On religion, his sister Eunice noted that "he was always a little less convinced about some things than the rest of us." Raised in a strongly Irish Catholic household by a mother who was deeply devoted to the church, Kennedy was proud of his Catholic identity. In Boston, a city of deep sectarian divisions, it gave him a sense of solidarity with a community that would always remain loyal. But while he remained respectful of the church, he exhibited a humanist independence, and at times a skepticism, from a young age. Thus began a strongly pragmatic, problem-solving mindset that would later characterize his presidency. Ted Sorensen, his longtime speechwriter and confidant and perhaps his closest political adviser from the Senate to the White House, noted that Kennedy was a Catholic "by heritage, habit and conviction" but "did not believe that all virtue resided in the Catholic Church" or "believe that all non-Catholics would (or should) go to hell. He felt neither self-conscious nor superior about his religion but simply accepted it as part of his life." Arthur Schlesinger, another White House aide and observer, agreed: "Kennedy's religion was humane rather than doctrinal," and he had "little knowledge of or interest in the Catholic dogmatic tradition." Perhaps his strongest belief about religion was that it should be an entirely private and personal matter.[4]

This emphasis on privacy, and by political extension on a firm separation of church and state, was to serve him well in the 1960 presidential election campaign. We may now realize that Protestant hostility to the Catholic Church had already begun its decline by 1960, but at the time the notion that a Catholic president could loyally serve the United States was controversial. Evangelicals and fundamentalists were particularly concerned, but mainline liberal Protestants expressed reservations as well. Could a Catholic avoid having two loyalties, one to church and one to state? The answer was unclear, even for racially tolerant Protestant leaders who were simultaneously championing the cause of African American civil rights. Charles Clayton Morrison, the former pacifist leader and longtime editor of *Christian Century*, charged that there were "two powerful monarchical" systems in the world, "the Communist Dictatorship and the Infallible Papacy," and Americans had to resist both if they wanted to preserve their free way of life. "How do you feel about a Catholic candidate for President?" *Look* magazine asked two of the most prominent liberal ministers in the country, Methodist Bromley Oxnam and Presbyterian Eugene Carson Blake. "Uneasy," they answered, because Kennedy would find himself confronted with tough decisions in which he would have to choose between his Catholic faith and his presidential duties. A Catholic president would also provide the Church with a means to undermine the separation of church and state by, for example, using public money to fund parochial schools. The Kennedy campaign hired James Wine, a lawyer and active Presbyterian layman, to handle the religious issue, though many Protestants thought he had made a pact with the devil. "Had John Knox felt as you do, then perhaps we would all still be held in the throes of this ecclesiastical monster," a Baptist pastor from Arkansas City, Kansas, complained to Wine. "[Y]ou are a traitor to the Protestant Religion and a contemptible scoundrel," protested another.[5]

Kennedy allayed such fears by stressing, in the strongest possible terms, that religion was strictly a private matter. This represented something of a sea change from the public piety of the Truman and Eisenhower eras, but it quelled Protestant fears of a Catholic conspiracy to take over the U.S. government. Kennedy argued his case first in the Democratic primary in West Virginia, a state with few Catholics and many devout Protestants, and then in a famed speech to the Greater Houston Ministerial Association, a grouping of the kind of conservative Protestants who were most uneasy about Kennedy's candidacy. In Houston, JFK declared his belief in the firmest possible separation between church and state. "I am not the Catholic candidate for president," he told the skeptics in Houston. "I am the Democratic party's candidate who happens also to be a Catholic." His religion was a personal matter, irrelevant to the presidency. He won over both the West Virginians and the Houstonians, critical turning points not only in his own political career but in the increasing secularization of American religion, especially its division into private and public spheres. Predictably, his stance angered some Catholic priests and intellectuals, who wondered just what kind of Catholic Kennedy was if the Church's values were personal and not applicable to politics.[6]

Most Catholics did not care about such matters on election day—at least, not as much as they hoped to send a Catholic to the White House. In fact, even though Kennedy's religion damaged his showing in the popular vote, it increased Catholic turnout in key battleground states and contributed to his victory over Richard Nixon. After the election, most Protestants buried their suspicions of the Catholic Church. Baptists, traditionally among the staunchest defenders of the separation of church and state and the denomination that had probably caused Kennedy the most trouble during the campaign, eagerly approached the new president after his inauguration. They "want the President to know they consider him *their* President," Bill Moyers reported to presidential adviser Kenneth O'Donnell. It was a widely shared sentiment that killed off anti-Catholicism as a major feature of American public life and, at least for now, effectively removed religion from presidential politics.[7]

Kennedy had helped usher in a new era. But in a strange and completely unintended way, Lyndon Johnson actually embodied the decade's religious confusion, experimentation, and dynamism much better than Kennedy. Raised in a conservative religious town in the Texas Hill Country—one resident recalled that local churches tried to "out-Baptist the Baptists"—

by a father who was religious but loathed fundamentalism and a mother who was a devout Southern Baptist, Johnson converted to the Disciples of Christ, a pious and evangelical but informal and liberal Protestant denomination, at the age of fifteen. Later, as president, he encouraged his daughter's and wife's own conversions (to the Episcopal Church). Johnson himself often dabbled in the services of other denominations, especially the Catholic Church (to which his other daughter converted), and would often carry a scriptural verse with him to suit the political moment. He was also extremely close to Billy Graham, the nation's most prominent religious figure, and leaned heavily on the evangelist for emotional support and spiritual comfort during the worst years of race riots and Vietnam. Like Truman and Eisenhower before him, Johnson was an ecumenical president, deeply religious without believing that any one denomination had a monopoly on spiritual truth: he was devout without being doctrinaire. As Jack Valenti, one of his closest advisers, observed, LBJ "believed in God" but "simply detached himself from any dogma, indeed, found rigidly-fixed doctrine as unappetizing in religion as he disavowed it in politics." As the difficulties of his presidency mounted, Johnson found solace in faith. "During his years in the White House," recalled Joseph Califano, another close adviser, "Lyndon Johnson had become increasingly religious." When confronted with issues of profound moral quandary and complexity, such as the impact of war upon Vietnamese civilians, Califano noticed that Johnson openly turned to the reassurances of religion. "Over time, the President talked more often about seeking guidance from the Almighty and praying. I had a sense that he found comfort in his relationship with God, particularly during his final year in office."[8]

THE SIXTIES ARE rightly remembered as a decade of turmoil and instability resulting from rapid social change. In matters of race, gender, and sexuality, long-held traditions came under attack from a new generation of rights campaigners. The new role of the federal government, forged by Lyndon Johnson's Great Society programs, was especially revolutionary, much more so even than Franklin Roosevelt's New Deal. Whereas FDR sought merely to stabilize the economy and create conditions for economic growth, LBJ wanted to create a more egalitarian society by establishing a new set of ground rules for how people treated one another. Despite pleas from African Americans, the New Deal had mostly ignored race relations, while gender issues were never even considered. By tackling these most sensitive of social and cultural questions, then, the Great Society proved itself to be far more radical than the New Deal—or, for that matter, any other domestic reform program since Reconstruction. The monumental ambition of Johnson's social engineering proved to be its key weakness as well as its main strength. But even though it was only a mixed success, the Great Society triggered a Rights Revolution in which the very fundamentals of American identity were no longer certain. From it spun a continuing series of subsequent "rights revolutions," largely beyond LBJ's control, on privacy, sexual orientation, and reproductive rights that lasted well into the next decade and beyond. America would never be the same again.[9]

Nor would its faith. "Nothing changed so profoundly in the United States during the 1960s as American religion," claim two leading historians of the radical decade, and it is easy to see why. Judaism largely escaped the tumult, but American Christianity underwent its greatest period of strife and restructuring in forty years. Both Protestants and Catholics challenged the very basics of what it meant to be a practicing Christian. As a result, some changed the tenets or conventions of their faith completely; others, as we shall see, reaffirmed the traditional bases of their religion. Many switched sides, by breaking the shackles of conservatism or fleeing the chaos of liberal change into the comforting assurances of traditional faith. Others simply lost their faith entirely, or embraced the new religious pluralism that resulted from the arrival of a new generation of Buddhist, Hindu, and Muslim immigrants from Africa, India, and the Middle East. As a result, many Americans embraced foreign religions—Zen, Hare Krishna, and New Age spiritualism—that only a few years before would have tested the bounds of plausibility, let alone acceptability. All told, in the decades after 1960 American religion not only radicalized and polarized between contending forces of politicized religion but diversified into a wholly new mosaic of world faith.[10]

While religion was not necessarily on the Great Society's agenda, the federal government was not inactive on matters of faith. In the early 1960s, in response to petitions by parents who were either religious minorities or atheists, the Supreme Court decided three cases that built an insurmountable wall of separation between religion and public education. In 1962, in the case of *Engel v. Vitale*, the Court decided that a nonsectarian prayer to "Almighty God," approved by an advisory board comprised of ministers, priests, and rabbis, constituted a violation of the First Amendment's establishment clause. In two cases the following year—*Abington Township v. Schempp* and *Murray v. Curlett*—the Court upheld and widened the new prohibition on prayer in public schools. In hardening and raising the wall of separation between church and state, the Supreme Court was responding to but also accentuating the secularization of American public life, a profound change in itself that in turn stoked the fires of religious reformation and counterreformation.[11]

Protestantism changed more than at any other time since the emergence of Darwinism, biblical criticism, and modernism in the late nineteenth century. In 1960, the election of John Kennedy coincided with the waning of America's Cold War great awakening. Public religiosity ebbed with the departure of Eisenhower and the acquiescence of his successor, who wanted to deemphasize the public role of his own Catholic religion. But the receding tide of religious revivalism left behind a new generation of innovative, imaginative Protestant theologians who believed their mission was to reconcile religion with the increasing pace of modern life. In doing so, they pushed the bounds of faith itself, with ramifications for U.S. foreign policy.

Protestant intellectuals advanced a radical version of Christianity that rejected its spiritualism but embraced its ethics. Philosophically burdened and emotionally troubled by the Cold War and its stalemate of nuclear terror, liberal Christians turned increasingly to existentialism. Many embraced the faith-based Christian existentialism of Paul Tillich and Dietrich Bonhoeffer, a young German minister who was executed by the Nazis at the end of World War II. But others incorporated secular ideas about death and the meaning of life, particularly from German (especially Friedrich Nietzsche) and French philosophers (Albert Camus and Jean-Paul Sartre). In 1961, Gabriel Vahanian, a French-born and Princeton-educated theologian at Syracuse University, published *The Death of God*. The modern world, he argued, had overtaken the supernatural God of the Bible; to keep God relevant, Christians must adapt their faith to the times. The "mythological world-view of Christianity," Vahanian wrote, "has been succeeded by a thoroughgoing scientific view of reality, in terms of which either God is no longer necessary, or he is neither necessary nor unnecessary: he is irrelevant—he is dead." To Vahanian, this was a positive development. From here emerged the doctrine of "secular theology," espoused by young Protestant theologians across the country. In 1963, Paul Van Buren of the University of Texas published *The Secular Meaning of the Gospel*; two years later, Harvard Divinity School's Harvey Cox followed with *The Secular City*, which sold over a million copies; a year later came *Radical Theology and the Death of God* by Thomas Altizer and William Hamilton. Speaking for most of his fellow Protestant radicals, Cox attacked the spiritual bases of Christianity by declaring that "cultic worship is no longer necessary," that "there is no otherworldliness in Jesus," and that "the barrier between the sacred and the secular is not only abolished, but in many instances completely reversed." In 1966, *Time* scandalized the nation by bringing the still-obscure notions of secular theology, and its roots in Nietzschean philosophy, to a wider public. "Is God Dead?" the establishment magazine asked in bold red letters against a stark black cover. To many disillusioned Protestants living in a paradoxical age of affluence and abundance, but also Holocaust memory, nuclear missiles, race riots, and the Vietnam War, the answer was no longer clear.[12]

"It is no longer possible for Protestantism to survive in its present form," concluded Stephen E. Rose, a young religious intellectual who issued a "Manifesto for Protestant Renewal" in 1966. And for many Americans, it did not. As the supernatural foundations of liberal Protestant belief crumbled, its fixed moral bearings collapsed as well. Most famous was the advent of "relativism," the idea that there are no moral absolutes but only a series of constantly shifting relative goods. Nobody, not even Christians, had a monopoly on truth and righteousness. In 1966, at the height of secular theology's fame, Joseph Fletcher, an Episcopal divinity school professor from Massachusetts, published *Situation Ethics*. Carrying the provocative subtitle *The New Morality*, Fletcher's book argued that it was simply impossible to reconcile traditional morality with the dynamism and pluralism of modern life. Christians should instead make moral decisions based on the circumstances and context of the situation immediately before them, not on the Bible or teachings of the church.[13]

Similarly, a new generation of black theologians, such as Union Theological Seminary's James H. Cone, adapted Christianity to suit an assertive black identity that aimed for equality but not necessarily integration with whites. First in the provocative book *Black Theology and Black Power*, published in 1969, and then a year later in the equally provocative *A Black Theology of Liberation*, Cone presented Christ as a subaltern figure of African descent, a revolutionary who fought the wickedness of authority to ensure the salvation of the oppressed. "Black Power and Christianity have this in common: the liberation of man!" he argued. "And if Christ is present today actively risking all for the freedom of man, he must be acting through the most radical elements of Black Power." Cone's message was a blend of the decade's most powerful religious ideologies of the oppressed: Black Power plus liberation theology incorporated from leftist and outright Marxist South American Catholics. It was a far cry from the more soothing message of Exodus preached by Martin Luther King, but by the end of the decade it was also a better reflection of how many African Americans felt. In books such as *The Black Messiah* and *Black Power and White Protestants*, other black Protestant intellectuals advanced similar arguments.[14]

American Catholics also underwent a process of wrenching change that was truly revolutionary. The terms of Catholicism had not changed much in the preceding century since the First Vatican Council established many of the modern Church's ground rules, even under the pressures of immigration and assimilation to American society. But in a process initiated by no less an authority than Pope John XXIII, the Second Vatican Council, or Vatican II, initiated a reformation of the Catholic faith. Meeting intermittently from 1962 until 1965, the decisions made by worldwide Catholic authorities at Vatican II liberalized many of the practices of the

Church, particularly concerning liturgy and worship. Ecumenism was also a central theme, epitomized by John XXIII's promise to tolerate and cooperate with other Christian denominations. Moreover, the Church took a more progressive stand on social and political questions, such as on issues of race and war and peace. Although some reforms, such as the marriage of priests and the use of birth control, proved too much even for the reformers, it is difficult to overestimate the significance of the changes that were approved. Vatican II modernized a church that had long taken pride in resisting modernization. As a result, by 1970 many American Catholics, for better or worse, scarcely recognized the church of 1960.[15]

Yet further changes to American religious life were still to come. In 1965, Congress passed the Immigration and Nationality Act, which lifted racist restrictions and quotas imposed by the 1924 National Origins Act. The result was a flood of new immigrants from Africa, India, the Middle East, and East and Southeast Asia who brought with them religious beliefs—traditional African faiths, Hinduism, Islam, and Buddhism—that were completely new to the vast majority of Americans. In terms of sheer numbers, adherents to the new faiths were still dwarfed by the standard Protestant-Catholic-Jew composition of American religion. But their mere presence was a startling challenge to existing norms, and they became especially popular among a younger generation of Americans who were desperate to break free from the constraints of their Judeo-Christian heritage and willing to experiment with foreign alternatives. The popularity of Eastern and New Age spiritualities that began slowly in the 1950s blossomed into a religious phenomenon in the more philosophically curious, irreverent Sixties. Islam, conducive to Black Power ideology and the emerging pan-African movement and already practiced by American variants such as the Nation of Islam, caught on among African Americans who were less willing to embrace black Protestantism's ethos of patient sacrifice and eventual salvation. The practice of traditional African faiths grew alongside the spread of Islam. As a result of this new immigration, American domestic life was quickly becoming globalized. Perhaps it was no coincidence that 1965 also marked the founding of the International Society for Krishna Consciousness, and with it the Hare Krishna movement in America.[16]

UNSURPRISINGLY, the religious liberals who had been the apostles of progress during the staid 1950s flourished in the reformation Sixties. Their quests for progressive change in religion and politics mirrored and fueled each other to the extent that crusades against poverty and racism and crusades for inclusiveness and innovation in faith became opposite sides of the same coin. The Kennedy and Johnson administrations welcomed these reformers, but not without mixed feelings, for religious liberals wanted to push a reformist agenda, at home and abroad, much further and faster than government officials thought possible.

The Kennedy administration generally shared the liberals' goals but not necessarily their moral passion or sense of urgency. The apostles of progress kept alive the internationalist Social Gospel tradition by calling for the United States, the world's wealthiest nation, to help cure socioeconomic problems around the world. Americans needed to share their wealth and lift starving billions out of destitution, but doing so would require sacrifice for the good of all humanity. "A fat and complacent and luxury-loving America can never preach Christ persuasively to a starving, struggling world," declared Reverend John M. Krumm, chaplain of Columbia University, after a 1960 tour through Asia. Instead, Americans must find solutions, "perhaps even through higher taxes," to level the global economic playing field and "lift the level of life around the world to something approaching our own incredible level." Reflecting widespread concerns about the domestic poor, in 1962 the National Council of Churches told Kennedy that "it is no longer necessary to tolerate poverty" and demanded that the president commit the nation to "an all-out effort to abolish it, both at home and abroad."[17]

Kennedy did not disagree, illustrated by the fact that foreign aid and development stood at the heart of his foreign policy, even if his efforts were not exactly all-out. Through programs such as the Peace Corps and the Alliance for Progress, he aimed to inoculate the Third World against communism by stimulating economic growth that would lead to political stability. Exiled to the banks of the Charles River during the Eisenhower administration, modernization theorists flocked to Kennedy's Washington and filled the ranks of the State Department and National Security Council. Led by Walt Rostow, who in 1960 wrote *The Stages of Economic Growth*, an avowedly "non-communist manifesto," modernization theorists believed they had unlocked the political and economic secret to steering the world toward capitalism and, in the process, winning the Cold War peacefully. As Rostow would discover in Vietnam, however, the road to modernization was not so straightforward.[18]

Neither was the role of faith. Kennedy and his advisers were committed to a reformist agenda abroad, but they remained unsure about the role religion should play. For one thing, modernization theory presupposed the fading away of religion. For another, it was not an altruistic means of delivering charity to the world's poor but a weapon in the Cold War. Thus at a basic level, modernization theory and religious reformism were incompatible, perhaps even contradictory. Moreover, Kennedy was concerned not to let it appear that his faith was determining his policies, including his foreign policy. Religious faith marked an essential difference between East and West, he acknowledged to a 1961 prayer breakfast held by the International Christian Leadership, but it was no more than that: "I do not regard religion as a weapon in the cold war." In case the assembled evangelists and apostles of liberty did not understand him the first time, he repeated himself the following year. "I do not suggest that religion is an instrument of the cold war," he declared at the 1962 prayer breakfast before largely the same audience. "Rather it is the basis of the issue which separates us from those who make themselves our adversary. And at the heart of the matter, of course, is the position of the individual—his importance, his sanctity, his relationship to his fellow men, his relationship to his country and his state." Thus it was left to the individual, not the state, to promote religious solutions to international problems.[19]

Yet religion could not be purged so easily from U.S. foreign policy, much less from American public life. As Kennedy would soon discover, voluntarist activity could not always be easily separated from public policy—at least, not without rancor. The Kennedy administration may have had a special interest in development, but it also happened to be a field in which America's large contingent of overseas missionaries and faith-based relief agencies—Protestant, Catholic, and Mormon—had tremendous experience and expertise. Missionaries from the Southern Baptist Convention and relief workers from Church World Service and Catholic Relief Services approached the Kennedy administration as partners in a global war on poverty. Some officials, such as Assistant Secretary of State for International Organization Affairs Harlan Cleveland, called for a more formal partnership between government and religious organizations, especially mission boards, but on the whole they were lonely voices in an administration preoccupied with social science and problem solving. "This is a group we need to cultivate," said Bill Moyers, an aide to then vice president Johnson, of the Southern Baptist missionaries. Few paid him any heed.[20]

Characteristically, religious groups pushed on regardless. The NCC and mainline Protestant denominations were active, but more surprising was the leading role taken by the Roman Catholic Church. The Vatican II reforms ushered in sweeping changes to the life and worship of Catholics, but it also renewed an activist mission of worldwide peace and social justice that had in recent decades been subsumed by the demands of the Church's anticommunist holy war. Now, the Vatican called for a more equitable world order and for ecumenical cooperation with Protestants, Eastern Orthodox, Muslims—even, to a degree, communists. In May 1961, Pope John XXIII issued *Mater et Magistra*, a progressive encyclical on economic life in the modern world. Rather than unfettered capitalism, John enjoined that "all forms of economic enterprise must be governed by the principles of social justice and charity." Rather than engaging in economic and political competition, "man's aim must be to achieve in social justice a national and international juridical order . . . in which all economic activity can be conducted not merely for private gain but also in the interests of the common good." The pope pointed out that the world was in the midst of being re-created by decolonization and globalization, in which "nations are becoming daily more interdependent," which in turn created the imperative for international cooperation across religious and ideological lines. The encyclical focused on economics, national and international, and John stressed one theme above all: "Economic progress must be accompanied by a corresponding social progress, so that all classes of citizens can participate in the increased productivity. The utmost vigilance and effort is needed to ensure that social inequalities, so far from increasing, are reduced to a minimum." In other words, "the economic prosperity of a nation is not so much its total assets in terms of wealth and property, as the equitable division and distribution of this wealth."[21]

Two years later, at the height of Vatican II, John XXIII extended such thinking from economics to the realm of world politics. *Pacem in Terris* ("Peace on Earth"), an encyclical addressed "to all men of good will," argued that the preservation of peace was the duty of all humanity in an age of nuclear weapons. Human rights, based upon a careful balancing of individual rights with collective social justice, must be the basis of international relations. There would naturally be differences among people over how best to achieve such a balance. Everyone, not only Catholics, had to remember that people who believed in "erroneous doctrines" such as communism were fellow human beings who sought the same objectives: peace, stability, justice, prosperity, equality. It did no good to condemn communists or damn them to the eternal fires of hell; denunciations such as these only fueled the Cold War without offering constructive solutions for its end. "Besides," asked the pope, "who can deny that those movements, in so far as they conform to the dictates of right reason and are interpreters of the lawful aspirations of the human person, contain elements that are positive and deserving of approval?" Because peace was essential, tolerance was now also essential. The pope led by example by meeting with Soviet officials, much to the consternation of the State Department.[22]

The Vatican's next step was to seek a partnership on international social justice with the world's most powerful nation. Aware that the usual American sensitivities about undue Catholic influence would be heightened during a Catholic presidency, Vatican officials and allies made discreet contact with Kennedy administration officials to see if some sort of alliance could be struck. This marked a change from Harry Truman and Myron Taylor's approaches to Pius XII, in which the United States sought an anticommunist alliance of all religious believers against the Soviet Union. Now, it was John XXIII's turn to solicit American cooperation in establishing an ecumenical peace of all peoples, communists included. Norman Cousins, the editor of *Saturday Review* and an intimate of several Kennedy administration officials, was granted a papal audience in 1962 with the knowledge that the conversation would be passed along to the White House. The pope suggested that 1962 could be a "Geo-Humanistic Year" in which the United States and the Soviet Union embarked upon a "Peace Race" that would not only ensure the "absence of nuclear conflict" but also "provide adequate education for the world's young" and "develop the creative potential of every child." Yet John's vision of peace caused concern in Washington, not hope. Kennedy officials told reporters they were "puzzled" by the Vatican peace offensive; others expressed "concern." The State Department's Bureau of Intelligence and Research concluded that the Vatican's new diplomacy "could conceivably be a dialogue and even collaboration" with regimes behind the Iron Curtain, while a CIA analysis warned that the Vatican was creating a geopolitical atmosphere that was "permissive rather than positive." By 1963, Kennedy himself was pursuing a détente of sorts with Moscow, but he and his advisers worried that the Vatican was pushing the process too quickly, and in ways that would not always be conducive to American interests.[23]

In Catholic America, the pursuit of peace had been dominated by left-liberals, such as Father John Ryan and the Catholic Association for International Peace, and radicals, such as Dorothy Day and the Catholic Workers. The hierarchy took social justice seriously, but when it came to international relations anticommunism took precedence over all else. But now, with the impetus of Vatican II, many bishops and priests embraced a peace crusade that sought the extension of global social justice to all. "Our moral responsibility," proclaimed the National Catholic Welfare Conference in 1961, "transcends the limited circle of our individual lives and the confining borders of our country. Our interests and our obligations are world-wide," especially in the developing world, which might begin with material aid but must also include "a recognition of their dignity." Other Catholic leaders were willing to go even further.[24]

Mainline Protestants, particularly those who debated the "death of God" and "situation ethics," were for the most part even more radical than Catholics. They believed that not only was the church in revolution, but the whole world was. And according to Princeton Theological Seminary's Richard Shaull, as both Christians and Americans "we may feel quite at home in the midst of revolution." Often this revolutionary critique of the Cold War was also a critique of the United States, especially on the American record on perpetuating racial and economic inequalities at home and around the world. In fact, Americans were so morally compromised, so used to tolerating human rights abuses by their own government and people, that they were no longer a truly Christian people. "We live in the time of the invalidation of the Christian gospel by Christians themselves," lamented Harvey Cox in 1963. "We have managed to prove to most of the world's people that we don't really mean what we say." Cox called for a renewal of America's belief in Christian ethics by tackling racism in all America—not just in the South—and curtailing its imperial ambitions abroad. The "first thing the church must always do," he urged his fellow Christians, "is to find out where God is on the move in his world today, and then make all possible haste to be there with him." For Cox, God's locations were obvious: Mississippi, Harlem, Latin America, Indochina, and other places where poverty and injustice thrived.[25]

While reformist Catholics and liberal Protestants cheered Kennedy's policies of international uplift, such as the Peace Corps, they despaired of his more traditional use of force. Foremost among liberal concerns was America's continuing strategic reliance on nuclear weapons—indeed, for many liberal ministers and theologians, many sins flowed from the looming shadow of nuclear terror. Because nuclear weapons threatened all life on earth, placed in human hands the power that should be God's alone, cost so much, and seemed so illogical and unnecessary, religious liberals believed that further reform was not possible unless the United States committed itself to nuclear disarmament. The Friends Witness for World Order, a Quaker peace group, sent Kennedy a petition that called for unequivocal support of the United Nations, foreign aid, and recognition of communist China, but above all pressed for a general disarmament to begin with nuclear weapons. The Central Conference of American Rabbis made a similar plea to JFK, this time linking nuclear disarmament to civil rights and support for Israel. After the Soviets resumed atmospheric nuclear testing in 1961, Kennedy felt the United States could not afford to fall behind and authorized new American tests in the spring of 1962. An incensed Thomas Merton, the celebrated American Catholic intellectual, antinuclear activist, and perhaps the world's most famous Trappist monk, typified the shock and anger of religious liberals. Merton was "convinced," he wrote not long after the resumption of testing, that America "is not only capable of starting a preemptive nuclear war but is perhaps on the way to doing it." "Is peace possible?" Church Women United asked on World Community Day in 1964. Not without disarmament. "To build international peace with justice and freedom," liberal church women across America prayed, "nations in community must not trust in armed might as their greatest resource for strength."[26]

The liberal critique of American foreign policy accelerated as the tumultuous decade wore on, race relations deteriorated, and the war in Vietnam escalated. By continuing to rely on brute force, Lyndon Johnson and his successor, Richard Nixon, seemed determined to block the historical changes sweeping the world into the postmodern age. If the

Soviet-American clashes over Berlin and Cuba in 1961–62 had appeared to be the product of mutual hostility, American interventions in the Dominican Republic (1965) and Chile (1973) seemed to be a more clearly one-sided case of wanton aggression. And they were only the most obvious cases of American imperialism. "Repression has intensified," Cox reported to friends after a 1970 tour of Latin America, due mostly to the rise of "right-wing dictatorships that often seized power with American encouragement." Cox promised that "hope is still alive," thanks not to the United States but to local grassroots resistance movements of "workers and farmers, students and intellectuals, priests and ministers." These people's movements "are trying to wrench the future of their continent away from the ruling cliques and their American sponsors," and they were succeeding due to the galvanizing effects of their "buoyant religious vision." Cox was witnessing the growth of liberation theology, a popular movement that started in Colombia in 1968 with the aim of resisting war, authoritarianism, and the United States through a powerful blend of Marxism and Catholicism.[27]

By the end of the 1960s, the renewal of the global Social Gospel was in full swing. Believing that their own society and the world at large were in the midst of revolution, liberal clergy called for immediate action producing immediate results. Like Cox, they saw their efforts as existing in opposition to the policies of the U.S. government. Though they might disagree on some issues, such as the use of birth control to slow world population growth, Protestants and Catholics promoted a global agenda of peace, human rights, and equitable economic development with equal vigor. A 1969 report on Christian missions by the United Methodist Church summed it up best: "Poverty, health, race relations, peace—you name it," said Bishop Lloyd C. Wicke. "These are the concerns of the whole church; these are the gospel's concern, the concern of the entire family of man." American Catholics launched a similar mission drive, while Catholic writers, such as Michael Novak (later a neoconservative), affirmed the radical critique of American politics and society. Pope John VI joined in with a 1967 encyclical, *Populorum Progressio*, that blasted the developed nations for hoarding their wealth and keeping the Third World in a state of dependency and destitution. The World Council of Churches, led by an American Presbyterian, Eugene Carson Blake, reaffirmed in 1968 that in "the struggle for peace and justice, the Church must bear witness" and that the clergy "must speak out where no one else dares to, or where truth is not respected, where human lives or human dignity are endangered, and where opportunities for a better future are neglected" to bring about the "application of social justice to all human relations." The following year, the WCC swore to do all it could to end racism throughout the world, even if it meant supporting leftist "national liberation" movements. Perhaps most significant was the fact that liberal Protestants and Catholics now saw each other as allies rather than competitors. In 1968, Francis Sweeney, an American priest with intimate papal ties, even invited Blake to the Vatican to present a united front in the "establishment of international order."[28]

THE MARKED AMBIVALENCE that characterized the relationship between Democratic officials and religious liberals meant that there was little synergy, or even cooperation, between the Kennedy and Johnson administrations and the apostles of progress on foreign policy. This was in stark contrast to the mostly warm relations the Eisenhower administration had enjoyed with the apostles of liberty. Kennedy was not interested in deploying religion while Johnson, who was more willing to work with religious leaders, found himself sharply at odds with liberals over the Vietnam War. But also crucial was the fact that neither Kennedy nor Johnson, nor most of their advisers, understood the new American religious landscape or grasped the importance of religious pluralism in a globalizing world. From the beginning, Arthur Schlesinger Jr., Kennedy's adviser and in-house historian, noted the difference with Eisenhower in both style and substance. "The John Foster Dulles contrast between the God-anointed apostles of free enterprise and the regimented hordes of atheistic communism bored him," Schlesinger wrote of Kennedy. "Seeing the world as an historian rather than as a moralist, he could not utter without embarrassment the self-serving platitudes about the total virtue of one side and the total evil of the other."[29]

Accordingly, the attitude of Kennedy administration officials toward religion's place in world politics ranged from indifferent to hostile. Whether Americans protested the harsh treatment of Catholics in Poland, Jews in the Soviet Union, or Protestants in Spain, they received little encouragement from Washington. As the Kennedy State Department aridly informed Congressman Walter Rogers of Texas, angered by the treatment of American Protestants in Catholic South America, the U.S. government was "obliged to recognize that these are primarily internal matters under the jurisdiction of other sovereign governments." Advocates of Soviet Jews received a similarly lukewarm response. Religious persecution of Soviet Jews was regrettable, the National Security Council wrote to one concerned individual in 1963, but "it is believed that formal United States Government representations would not be in their best interests." To Congressman Steven Derounian of New York, the State Department questioned whether persecution of Soviet Jews "has its actual basis in anti-Semitism" and, veering into anti-Semitic territory itself, suggested that Jews were simply targets of "the presently intensified campaign of the Soviet authorities to stamp out black marketeering, speculation and other

economic crimes involving illegal manufacturing, theft or misappropria-
tion of state property, bribery of officials, and other economic abuses." In
any event, life in the Soviet Union was hard for everyone. Even if Soviet
Jews were being persecuted simply for being Jewish, it was doubtful they
were being subjected to "a disproportionate amount of condemnation and
victimization."[30]

It is also doubtful whether the Kennedy and Johnson administrations
had much of a clue about the majority of the world's people who were
not Protestants, Catholics, or Jews. Given that U.S. foreign policy would
become less preoccupied with Europe and more entangled with parts of
the world that were highly religious, this was not an entirely auspicious
development. In South Vietnam, for example, the 1963 Buddhist uprising
caught the Kennedy administration completely flatfooted. "How could
this have happened?" a perplexed JFK asked his advisers about the Buddhists. "Who are these people? Why didn't we know about them before?"
They were merely the people who made up almost 90 percent of South
Vietnam's population, and the fact that Kennedy and his advisers found
their presence shocking is shocking in itself.[31]

Vietnamese religion was not an exception. In similar fashion, Secretary
of State Dean Rusk, who served throughout both the entire Kennedy and
Johnson administrations, tried to separate religion from politics in the
Middle East but was only left more perplexed as a result. Rusk had been
raised in a poor Georgia farming family but rose, by dint of education,
hard work, and a knack for making the right connections, to become a
pillar of the American establishment. His father was an ordained Presbyterian minister who had been trained at Louisville Theological Seminary, one of the South's premier centers of religious learning. A chronic
throat problem prevented him from becoming a full-time preacher, but
he nonetheless ensured that his children received a religious upbringing
that included daily Bible lessons and regular church services and Sunday
school. He also took young Dean to see the famed evangelist Billy Sunday. It seemed as if Dean would follow in his father's footsteps and pursue
a career in the ministry or become a missionary to China. At the age of
eleven, he became statewide president of the Junior Christian Endeavor,
a major honor for any young Southern Presbyterian. Later, as a senior at
Davidson College—which he described as having "the religious core of
a Presbyterian school" where there was "considerable evangelical pressure"—he served as president of the college's YMCA affiliate. But he was
not destined for a religious life. He "became skeptical" while at Davidson
and shed his religious belief; he retained Christianity's ethical core and
ideals, its doctrine of works, and willingness to confront evil, but not its
spirituality. "I gradually lost interest in questions of that sort," he later
noted, and "abandoned the idea of the ministry." As a Rhodes Scholar to

Oxford, where he wryly admitted that he "fell from grace," Rusk lived the carefree, alcohol-fueled life of a typical undergraduate. As an adult with a successful career in the Truman administration and then as president of the Rockefeller Foundation, he politely condescended to his relatives, some of whom had become Jehovah's Witnesses and wanted to convert him to the Christian faith.[32]

By the time Rusk became secretary of state, then, he was ill-disposed to linking religion to politics or diplomacy, even if the foreigners he dealt with viewed the world through a religious lens he had broken long ago. For Rusk, faith was either irrelevant or unfathomably enigmatic. This meant that the Middle East was a mystery to him, just as Vietnam was a mystery to Kennedy. The "intractable nature of the divisions between Jews and Arabs . . . almost defy solution," Rusk later remarked. "They involve deeply human passions, the holy war psychology of the Arabs and the sense of apocalypse of the Jews." For Rusk, secretary of state at the time of the 1967 Six Day War, this made diplomacy especially difficult, if not impossible:

> I never knew anybody in our government, including myself, who felt he had the answer to peace in the Middle East. When both Jews and Arabs are convinced they're speaking for God, that makes for a tough negotiation. I've been at the table when Arabs quoted the Koran while Jews quoted the Book of Moses. And I couldn't say, "Oh, come on now, don't give me any of that stuff!"

Perhaps a better understanding of the Holy Land's religious psychology would not have resolved the impasse between Muslim and Jew, but it certainly would have given Rusk a better insight into the nature of the Middle East's political problems.[33]

The issue of religious liberty, moreover, once a major and uncomplicated part of the Truman and Eisenhower administrations' anticommunism, was no longer a weapon in America's ideological arsenal. Race and civil rights, not religion, now set the agenda for national discussions on individual and collective freedom. The objectives of foreign policy had also changed. Following the Cuban Missile Crisis, both the Kennedy and Johnson administrations were committed to a policy of détente with the Soviet Union. Now remembered as the policy of Richard Nixon and Henry Kissinger, détente actually began, albeit fitfully and with little success, under Kennedy and Johnson. Protestations about Soviet atheism or violations of religious freedom threatened to scuttle the emergence of détente, and so were ignored.[34]

But perhaps most important was the fact that in Vietnam, the United States itself became a party to religious persecution. South Vietnam, an

American ally, was governed by the Roman Catholic Ngo family even though the vast majority of its people were Buddhist. This in itself would not necessarily have posed a problem had President Ngo Dinh Diem not been so undemocratic and unrepresentative. Buddhists responded politically with two major uprisings, in 1963 and 1966, that criticized American support for a regime that infringed upon the freedom of worship. In 1967, Thich Nhat Hanh, a Buddhist poet from Saigon, published *Vietnam: Lotus in a Sea of Fire*, an antiwar screed that criticized the United States for not respecting Vietnam's rights to freedom of religion and national self-determination; Thomas Merton provided an elegiac preface. Against such a backdrop, it was decidedly not in Washington's interest to promote religious liberty as an antidote to godless communist tyranny.[35]

Overall, neither Kennedy nor Johnson really knew what to make of the religious changes of the 1960s, much less what to do with them. For the first time in three decades, faith acted as a complication rather than a complement to foreign policy. In retrospect, perhaps their only saving grace was that their successors would not fare much better.

The Valley of the Shadow of Death

NOWHERE DID THE LIBERAL critique of U.S. foreign policy reach higher intensity or have greater impact than on Vietnam, which sparked the largest antiwar movement in American history. The clergy— Protestant, Catholic, and Jewish—played a key role in mobilizing dissent against the Vietnam War. Their role was critical in many ways, but three in particular stand out. First, along with student groups, they were among the earliest antiwar protesters. Second, by transferring their pre-1964 activism on nuclear weapons and civil rights to the Vietnam War, they legitimized protest over an American foreign war and continued the growth of the liberal critique of America's Cold War. Third and probably most important, the clergy were important simply because of who they were. Ministers, priests, and rabbis were pillars of American society; they were also the recognized guardians and interpreters of morality, ethics, and virtue. Their opposition to the war hindered Lyndon Johnson's efforts to justify it to the public. The national discussion over just war theory returned to the nation's pulpits and magazines, but unlike 1940–41 this was a debate the president was destined to lose. As Richard John Neuhaus, a Lutheran minister and leading antiwar critic, declared in 1970, the clergy had "succeeded in making opposition to the Vietnam War respectable." At a time when the antiwar movement was indelibly associated with radicalism, anti-Americanism, and the counterculture, this was a notable contribution indeed.[1]

However, the decade was also one of conservative renewal as well as liberal and radical rebellion. As we shall see in the next chapter, a broad grouping of Christian conservatives, better known as the Religious Right, was forming alongside the liberal churches in revolution. And just as the Vietnam War brought all the elements of protest together, it also provided a rallying point for evangelicals, fundamentalists, and conservative Catholics. In fact, conservative backing for this complicated and confusing war was not really about the war itself. Instead, conservatives rallied to support a wartime president, and by extension the honor of America. Their anticommunism and fervent patriotism made these feelings sincere, but their views were shaped just as much by a desire to check the forces of radicalism and prevent them from destroying the country as a whole. The Vietnam War, in other words, also helped spark the counterreformation.

POLITICALLY, Vietnam was an exceedingly challenging war for American leaders to justify. There was no national anticommunist consensus pushing Johnson to war in 1964–65, and it is not difficult to understand why. South Vietnam was a truculent ally, its government authoritarian and corrupt and seemingly unable to win the allegiance of its own people against the communist insurgency. Who wanted to defend a regime that drove Buddhist monks to burn themselves to death in protest? The Kennedy and Johnson administrations' arguments for supporting South Vietnam did not ring true. Secretary of State Dean Rusk spoke of the need to uphold commitments to allies even when most of those very same allies were calling for negotiations and withdrawal. On the ground, moreover, this was a war with an internal logic that made no sense. U.S. troops brought the war to Vietnamese civilians, citing the need to destroy their villages in order to save them. While it is true that public opinion supported Johnson until the North Vietnamese and Viet Cong launched the Tet Offensive in January 1968, it is also true that the support was shallow. Many who told pollsters they supported the war actually supported their president in a time of war, a very different thing.[2]

In such a climate, it was natural for clergy and religious intellectuals to raise their concerns about the war. They were, after all, already critical of what they thought was the aggressive, militaristic nature of U.S. foreign policy, especially in the Third World. They were also unafraid of communism and were quite willing to see a country become communist if that was what its people thought best. Religious Americans did not necessarily like the atheism of communist ideology, but in some circumstances it could be overlooked in favor of national self-determination and socialist progress. When liberals criticized U.S. foreign policy, they did so because they saw their country as an obstacle to international social justice. Their critique of foreign policy, then, was also a critique of America itself and of what the nation should stand for and try to achieve in the world. The illogical and brutal nature of the war, and the antiwar movement it produced, helped galvanize and then radicalize other protest movements and rights revolutions on race, gender, and sexuality. Domestic problems, especially poverty and race, became inextricably bound up with foreign problems, such as Indochina, because they seemed to emanate from the same sources of American racism, violence, greed, and empire. The Vietnam War marked the broadest and most egregious violation of American principles. As such, it marked the culmination of the liberal cause, not a new beginning.

Jews opposed the war in overwhelming numbers that, proportionally, easily exceeded those of Protestants and Catholics. Yet on the religious scene, they were overshadowed by their Christian counterparts because most Jews who resisted the war did not do so on religious grounds, and most Jewish antiwar activists were not rabbis or religious figures. Secular antiwar groups, especially in the student and New Left movements, were disproportionately Jewish, but this was mainly because Jews were numerous within the groups at the forefront of opposition to the war, namely, students and intellectuals. When Rabbi Abraham Heschel of the Jewish Theological Seminary in New York voiced the "Moral Outrage of Vietnam," his message found a greater resonance among Christian clerics than his fellow rabbis. Even so, Jewish religious leaders mostly opposed the war. Notwithstanding their staunch support for Lyndon Johnson and the Democrats, beginning in 1965 most of the major Jewish organizations in America—including the American Jewish Congress, the Synagogue Council of America, and the Central Conference of American Rabbis—passed resolutions condemning the war.[3]

Catholics were more divided, and most actually supported the war until 1968, but those who went into opposition provided a vital boost to the antiwar movement. After the anticommunist crusades of the 1940s and 1950s and the election of Kennedy in 1960, few Americans questioned the patriotism of American Catholics. Certainly nobody doubted their hostility toward communism, which gave their criticism of an anticommunist war in Southeast Asia greater legitimacy. While the upper echelons of the hierarchy, namely the bishops, largely supported the war (or at least did not oppose it), many priests and nuns were free to act according to their conscience. Thomas Merton was but one of many examples. "I think the U.S. military would do more for democracy if they got out of Vietnam than they are doing there now," he lectured LBJ shortly after the launch of the first major bombing attacks against North Vietnam in February 1965. Motivated by John XXIII's vision of world peace expressed in *Pacem in Terris*, antiwar Catholics established the Catholic Peace Fellowship (CPF); inspired by the ecumenism of Vatican II, they affiliated it with the interdenominational Fellowship of Reconciliation, the leading faith-based pacifist group since World War I. In 1965, the CPF decreed that "peace on earth" necessarily meant "peace in Vietnam," and called on Johnson to negotiate and young men to avoid the draft. Every Catholic presumably knew at least the basics of just war theory, and the CPF reminded them that the just war's "basic moral principles are consistently violated in the war in Vietnam."[4]

However, the Protestant clergy formed the bulk of religious opposition to the war. And nobody expressed the critique of American power more effectively than Reverend Martin Luther King, Jr. King's main cause was civil rights, but his politics, fueled by Christian spirituality and informed by Christian ethics, were also those of a committed social democrat. Throughout his career, and not simply after passage of the Voting Rights Act in 1965 removed the last barriers to legal segregation in the South, King and the organization that supported him, the Southern Christian Leadership Conference (SCLC), called for progressive social justice as well as political equality. We now remember civil rights as a political movement that promoted African Americans' right to vote in the South. But alongside voting rights, King and the SCLC called for blacks to have equal jobs, fair pay, better schools, decent housing, and access to affordable health care across the nation, in the North as well as the South. For King as well as for virtually all other civil rights campaigners, racial equality could never be achieved by the Civil Rights Act and Voting Rights Act alone, but only in tandem with Lyndon Johnson's Great Society, especially its War on Poverty. King finished his career—and his life—directing the Poor People's Campaign, a crusade for all Americans against the indignity and injustice of poverty. He was, through and through, a preacher of the Social Gospel.[5]

Which meant that he was also a preacher of a global Social Gospel. King was naturally preoccupied with domestic American issues, but he was just as concerned with social justice in the wider world. Not unlike most other religious liberals, he wanted the United States to promote sustained and equitable development in the Third World through foreign aid and local empowerment. He wanted the rich, mostly white Western nations to devolve power to the non-white peoples of the world. Just as he criticized white Americans for their paternalistic attitude toward African Americans, he called for a level playing field in foreign affairs. He warned that "the Peace Corps will fail if it seeks to do something *for* the underprivileged peoples of the world; it will succeed if it seeks creatively to do something *with* them." But he worried that America's leaders would not heed this advice and would instead seek to maintain control of a world system that increasingly resisted such control. "For some reason, we just don't understand the meaning of the revolution taking place in the world," he lamented to a friend after Kennedy's disastrous Bay of Pigs invasion of Cuba in 1961. "There is a revolt all over the world against colonialism, reactionary dictatorship, and systems of exploitation." Through such neocolonial adventures as the Bay of Pigs, America was in danger of having "no real moral voice to speak to the conscience of humanity."[6]

From the very outset of the war in Vietnam, then, King felt his nation had gone morally astray in Vietnam. On March 2, 1965, the same day that Operation Rolling Thunder began the continuous bombing of North Vietnam, he used a speech at Howard University to call upon Johnson to seek a negotiated settlement. Characteristically, he linked American society's three innate problems—racism, poverty, and violence—to its prosecution of an unnecessary war in Vietnam. As Johnson ignored him and escalated the war, King escalated the pace and tenor of his antiwar speeches. This supreme act of betrayal provoked LBJ's legendary wrath—after all, had he not given blacks more than any other president since Lincoln? In August, Johnson snubbed King at the signing ceremony for the Voting Rights Act and encouraged others to attack King's lack of patriotism. But though King toned down his public antiwar rhetoric, he would not support Johnson's war. It was too blatant a violation of Christian morality, too violent a betrayal of the global Social Gospel. It was also, he rightly worried, destroying the Great Society in its very infancy. King calculated that for every $53 Washington spent to help a poor person in America, it spent $500,000 to kill a person in Vietnam. Johnson was turning his back on American blacks and the Vietnamese people, condemning them both to misery and even death. "To war against your own people while warring against another nation is the ultimate in political and social bankruptcy," King railed. "The Negro who runs wild in a riot has been given the example of his own government running wild in the world."[7]

After eighteen months of fitful protest and moral brooding, King used the year 1967 to launch his own war against the war. Instead of giving speeches here and there on Vietnam, he now made it the centerpiece of his public rhetoric and linked it to the "racist decision-making" by "Men of the white West." He also used Vietnam as a general springboard to criticize all U.S. foreign policy, from its acquiescence in South African apartheid to its isolation of Communist China. On April 4, exactly a year before his death, King spelled out his views at Riverside Church in New York. Entitling his sermon "A Time to Break Silence," he called on all men and women of God to take a public stand against a demonstrably unjust war that was tearing apart the nation and deflecting it from the goals of social justice and racial equality. "If America's soul becomes totally poisoned," he cried out, "part of the autopsy must read Vietnam." King referred to himself as a man of peace as well as a man of God. "This is a calling that takes me beyond national allegiances," he declared to the assembled faithful,

> but even if it were not present I would yet have to live with the meaning of my commitment to the ministry of Jesus Christ. To me the relationship of this ministry to the making of peace is so obvious that I sometimes marvel at those who ask me why I am speaking against the war. Could it be that they do not know that the good news was meant for all men—for Communist and capitalist, for their children and ours, for black and for white, for revolutionary and conservative? Have they forgotten that my ministry is in obedience to the one who loved his enemies so fully that he died for them? What then can I say to the

"Vietcong" or to Castro or to Mao as a faithful minister of this one?
Can I threaten them with death or must I not share with them my life?

To King if not to Johnson, the answers were obvious. "I am convinced,"
King said in his final sermon, a Passion Day address at the National
Cathedral in Washington only a few days before his 1968 assassination in
Memphis, that Vietnam "is one of the most unjust wars that has ever been
fought in the history of the world."[8]

The answers were just as obvious to the many other religious liberals.
These anti-warriors included many who had once been pillars of liberal
anticommunism but had still supported progressive reform at home, especially on civil rights. One example was William Sloane Coffin, a Presbyterian minister, chaplain of Yale University, and nephew of Henry Sloane
Coffin, a leader of muscular liberalism and interventionism in the interwar
and World War II eras. William enlisted in the army during the war and
served as a CIA officer in the 1950s. Disillusioned by containment's inability to deal effectively or justly with decolonizing and developing nations,
he made the simple transition from campaigning for civil rights to campaigning against Vietnam and became, by the end of the decade, one of
the antiwar movement's most compelling voices. Another example was
Reverend Kenneth M. Johnson, the staunchly anticommunist minister of
Memorial Methodist Church in Asbury, North Carolina. In a December
1966 sermon, before a congregation that included parents of soldiers serving in Vietnam, Johnson said that America "desperately needs someone to
'guide our feet into the way of peace' " and help Americans "learn from
Jesus. . . . We must learn to forgive our enemies. We must learn to love
them." And yet another was the Episcopal bishop of California, James A.
Pike, who had once given LBJ the benefit of the doubt. Pike initially proclaimed Vietnam a "righteous conflict" but soon changed his views. "Jesus
was a revolutionary like the Vietcong," he declared one Sunday morning,
"and a freedom fighter like Martin Luther King, Jr." Only a liberal apostle
of progress could undergo such a conversion.[9]

The Christian realists made a similar journey. Despite their Cold War
anticommunism, both Reinhold Niebuhr and John Coleman Bennett
could be counted among the Vietnam War's staunchest opponents. In
the 1930s, they had been religious insurgents within their own churches.
Now, in old age and vindicated by their earlier stands against Nazism and
communism, they stood as the gatekeepers of mainline theology: by 1965,
Niebuhr towered over American religious life as its most authoritative
voice, while Bennett had become president of Union Theological Seminary. Nobody could accuse them of being cowards or of opposing any
war for the sake of opposing all wars. "I reject the pacifist interpretation

for two rather general reasons," Bennett wrote in 1965, the same year Johnson Americanized the war in Vietnam. The first was "the need of power to check power for the sake of justice and freedom. For us to leave a monopoly of the decisive form of external military power in the Soviet Union or in the communist orbit would be wrong." The second followed from the first: "any government has a responsibility for the security and well-being of a nation as interpreted by its citizens." Bennett therefore objected not to all wars on any grounds, but to this specific war in Vietnam. U.S. policies, which Bennett condemned as "this cumulative evil" in prepared testimony before a 1970 Senate Foreign Relations Committee hearing, demonstrably failed to meet the realists' just war criteria.[10]

Niebuhr felt much the same. He could never embrace the pacifism of a King or a Muste; nor could he condone radicalism. Like Bennett—indeed, like his old friend and fellow realist George Kennan, who also publicly criticized the war—Niebuhr believed in the general necessity of war but did not believe that a war for Vietnam was necessary; and because it was unnecessary, it was by definition unjust, "futile and cruel." Niebuhr's influential magazine, *Christianity and Crisis*, which had once sounded the trumpet for intervention against Nazi Germany and containment of the Soviet Union, now sounded a retreat from Vietnam. Niebuhr also decried the crusading moralism with which Johnson, Rusk, and other officials justified the war, especially "the whole argument of making these sacrifices in behalf of 'democracy' in Asia." With his oblique hints at the need to withdraw from Vietnam, Nixon offered a brief glimmer of hope. But as he pulled troops out of Vietnam, Nixon searched for "peace with honor" by escalating the bombing of North Vietnam and sponsoring the invasions of previously off-limits Cambodia and Laos. "Nixon's madness in extending an unpopular war he was elected to end" would only induce further trauma, both in America and in Indochina, Niebuhr complained to Bennett in 1970. Thanks to Nixon, Americans "must fear for the future of our nation in this crisis. May God have mercy on this nation for its combination of the pride of imperial power and the pride of virtue." Niebuhr worried about the destruction of life in Vietnam, but he also feared for "the conscience of this deeply troubled nation" that acquiesced in such unnecessary violence.[11]

In 1966, antiwar protest took a decisively radical turn, both in terms of its message and its tactics, and religious dissent was no different. Ministers, priests, and rabbis, once expected to be models of respectability, now adopted the same kind of shock tactics employed by New Left students, Black Power nationalists, and counterculture radicals. Some of the new radicalism was rhetorical, such as Stanford theologian Robert McAfee Brown's accusation that the U.S. government was committing war crimes in Vietnam; among the signers of Brown's statement were Martin Luther King, John Coleman Bennett, Harvey Cox, the religious historian Martin E. Marty, and Joseph Fletcher, author of *Situation Ethics.* The Jesuit legal scholar (and future Massachusetts congressman) Robert F. Drinan went even further, comparing the American war in Vietnam with the Nazi conquest of Europe. According to Drinan, antiwar demonstrators and conscientious objectors were compelled by morality and the law: "The American ethic not merely gives them this right but, in the light of Nuremberg, imposes this duty." Coming from the dean of the Boston College Law School, this could not be dismissed as extremism from the radical fringe. Nor could the vexing words of ordinary ministers throughout the country. "You know, this country used to be the international symbol of justice, and freedom and democracy and a lot of other related values as well," preached Reverend Waldemar Argow of the First Unitarian Church of Toledo, Ohio, in a 1965 sermon. "But lately the image has become a little tarnished and Uncle Sam has begun to appear less as a symbol of peace and freedom and more as a sort of short-sighted, fumbling giant who in his confusion is destroying scores of Vietnamese towns and villages, killing thousands of people, most of them civilians, and generally bringing the world more than a little closer to Armageddon."[12]

Other aspects of the new radicalism were based on the civil rights movement's tactics of nonviolent civil disobedience, which men and women of God justified as morally courageous acts of conscience. When Southern California clergy blockaded the entrance to Camp Pendleton, for instance, Rabbi Abraham Heschel called them "examples of great moral courage and self-denial." In Virginia, only a court order prevented an ecumenical group of antiwar clergy from holding a powerfully symbolic and deliberately provocative memorial service at Arlington National Cemetery.[13]

Much of the civil disobedience centered on the draft. New faith-based groups, beyond traditional organizations like the Friends, the Fellowship of Reconciliation, and Catholic Workers, were founded to undermine the draft and protect every American's right to conscientious objection. One of the most important of these groups was New England Resistance, which used a network of churches in Massachusetts to shelter draft resisters. In 1967, Reverend George Williams of Harvard Divinity School called on the young draft-age men of Boston to turn in their draft cards at Arlington Street Church. More than two hundred did so, while another sixty burned their draft orders in the flame of the church's altar candle. Following these leads, liberal churches, theological seminaries, and divinity schools across the nation offered "sanctuary" for those who refused to be drafted on the grounds that in protecting the right of individual conscience, a house of God was beyond the reach of the state. King's old comrade in the peace and civil rights movements, A. J. Muste, swiftly launched a new crusade against Vietnam and the draft, employing the same peacefully obstructionist tactics and message he had perfected in protests on racism and nuclear weapons.[14]

Even more shocking were the actions of the Berrigan brothers, Daniel and Philip. As Catholic priests—Daniel was a Jesuit, Philip a Josephite—the Berrigans were custodians of the just war tradition. After being drafted in 1943, Philip even received artillery training and briefly served in Germany, though he did not see any action. But they were also early champions of the civil rights and antinuclear movements. Vietnam represented an even higher perversion of morality, not only of the just war tradition but of all that Christians held sacred. Following their consciences, the Berrigans acted accordingly. First attuned to the injustices of American power during the Cuban Missile Crisis—Kennedy and Khrushchev were "deciding whether I was to live or die," Philip told an interviewer, "with no consultation whatsoever. Nobody was asked. And I thought to myself, these guys are playing God with us"—the Berrigans began to agitate for a more peaceful U.S. foreign policy. Agitation became full-scale protest with the escalation in Vietnam, which they were convinced was an extension of American brutality at home. The war, said Philip, "would not have been possible against white people. It was against a brown skinned people, and we made the transition here in this country very, very easily because of the history of racism here and because of our impressions of blacks." In November 1967, Philip and three other Catholics burst into a Baltimore Selective Service office and poured vials of their own blood over the draft files. Next May, while still awaiting trial for their bloodletting protest, Philip and Daniel seized draft files from the Selective Service office in Catonsville, Maryland, and burned them in the parking lot with a homemade version of napalm. Their actions were justified because "we have experienced intimately the uselessness of legitimate dissent," Philip wrote from his Baltimore jail cell while awaiting trial. "Americans would not quarrel with destroying German gas ovens or the Nazi and Stalinist slave camps." So why not draft boards? Their protests continued. Rather than return to prison, the Berrigans went underground to plan new raids. Catholic priests had never behaved in such fashion before. Not even the pacifists of the Catholic Worker movement resorted to such shocking and sensational tactics.[15]

In order to protect the right to protest an unjust war and the right of conscientious objection for draft-age Americans, as well as to criticize the war itself, leading religious liberals decided to seek safety and strength in numbers. In October 1965, under the direction of a Lutheran minister, John Richard Neuhaus; a Catholic priest, Daniel Berrigan; and a Jewish rabbi, Abraham Heschel; and with the encouragement of John Coleman

Bennett, in whose Manhattan apartment they first met, antiwar clerics formed Clergy Concerned About Vietnam; the name was shortly changed to Clergy and Laymen Concerned About Vietnam (CALCAV), though this new name was not especially accurate because few of the laity actually participated. Other antiwar clergy would later join, including Martin Luther King, who became CALCAV's national co-chair in 1967. It was an elite enterprise, driven by the famous theologians and ministers in its slender ranks. But CALCAV could easily compensate for lack of numbers with the star power of its members, many of whom commanded international attention and had access to national media outlets. The National Council of Churches gave them office space and logistical assistance. Many of their members could also rely on sympathy and aid from their powerful home institutions, such as Coffin's Yale Divinity School or Heschel's Jewish Theological Seminary. Whereas Union Theological Seminary had censured conscientious objectors as immoral during World War II, it actively encouraged them under Bennett's leadership during Vietnam. Meanwhile, local affiliates of CALCAV sprung up across the country, including the South.[16]

More than any other group, CALCAV provided an air of respectability to antiwar dissent. As the group's executive director Richard Fernandez—not one of its famous names—recalled, "Half the clergy I would talk to had studied with these luminaries. My little letterhead with all these names . . . opened every door in every city I wanted to go to." This came in handy as Fernandez traveled the country soliciting support from local churches that were often more conservative and reflexively patriotic than their intellectual and theological leadership. At the very least, CALCAV raised troubling questions about the war's necessity and morality, even if these local churches would not come right out in opposition to the war. And when CALCAV adopted the shrill rhetoric of the antiwar movement—such as planning a Los Angeles rally for "cleansing the spirit of America"—it was difficult for churchgoers to dismiss them, even if they did not agree or approve.[17]

CALCAV was an effective instrument for respectable dissent, but it paled in comparison to the antiwar activities of an incomparably larger and more powerful religious body: the Vatican. During the Buddhist Crisis of 1963, which pitted the majority Buddhists against the Catholics of the ruling Ngo family, the NSC encouraged the Vatican to intercede and restrain the Ngos. But if officials in Washington wanted Vatican involvement, they got much more than they bargained for. Following the start of sustained U.S. bombing in early 1965, a "deeply worried" Pope Paul VI caused headaches for the Johnson administration by constantly proposing peace initiatives or offering to broker talks between the United States and North Vietnam. "It is important that Pope Paul fully appreciate your personal dedication to peace, particularly with regard to Vietnam," Dean Rusk advised Johnson shortly before his first meeting with the pope at the UN in October 1965. But it seemed the pontiff was not convinced. In 1966, he called for a Christmas truce; the next year, he received both Soviet leaders and Lyndon Johnson to press for peace negotiations; and in 1968, he offered to broker peace talks held in Sweden. Johnson could not reject these overtures outright, even though he knew they were unlikely to lead to a settlement acceptable to both Washington and Hanoi, for who would want to be seen as sabotaging the pope's drive for peace on earth? Yet LBJ had to reject them somehow, quietly, for he knew that negotiations were unlikely to succeed and that he would be blamed for their failure. Ironically, for precisely this reason Ho Chi Minh called upon the Vatican to help end the war.[18]

IT IS IMPOSSIBLE to know definitively whether this religious opposition to the war had an effect on policy. Perhaps it limited Johnson's options by making further escalation too controversial. But most likely it did not, at least not directly. Still, there are tantalizing hints that at least one architect of the war was troubled by the moral implications raised by religious dissenters and that his troubles led to the most serious internal challenge to Johnson's war strategy. No Johnson official, not even Rusk, was as indelibly associated with the war as Secretary of Defense Robert S. McNamara. Known for his acute intelligence and almost blind faith in the power of numbers to solve almost any problem, McNamara's statistical methods formed the very basis of wartime strategy. Before taking over at the Pentagon in 1961, he had taught at Harvard Business School, helped invent the discipline of systems analysis in the 1940s, and led Detroit's "Whiz Kids" to the rescue of Ford Motor Company in the 1950s.

To most Americans, when it was not "Johnson's War" it was "McNamara's War," a label he initially wore with pride. But when the war stalemated and forced McNamara to make morally untenable decisions about life and death on a mass scale, he began to crack. In 1966 and 1967, he mounted a campaign against further escalation from within the Pentagon, applying his formidable number-crunching powers to proving the ineffectiveness of bombing. He became quietly infamous among Washington's power elite for bursting into tears whenever the subject of Vietnam came up, as it invariably did. He wept in his Pentagon office. "He does it all the time now," one of his secretaries told her friend. "He cries into the curtain." He even cried at an NSC meeting shortly before his departure from the Johnson administration. Morally shell-shocked, McNamara left the Pentagon at the beginning of 1968 a broken man. He became head of the World Bank, where his policies, especially the promotion of Third

World development and health initiatives, were liberal to a fault. Though he would never admit it, these and other demonstrably good deeds were likely his way of doing penance for Vietnam.[19]

Less well known are McNamara's religious and moral views. Despite his record on Vietnam, which earned him the reputation as a cold, calculating war planner, he had a strong moralistic sense of right and wrong which, in turn, had a firm grounding in Christian ethics. The son of a Catholic father and a devout Presbyterian mother, McNamara had attended a Presbyterian Sunday school while growing up in San Francisco. Later, while living in Michigan when he was with Ford, he became a Presbyterian elder, and as secretary of defense he and his wife regularly attended Washington's New York Avenue Presbyterian Church. He also read widely—not just the usual businessman's fare, but also books on philosophy and religious ethics. McNamara was not necessarily a profoundly spiritual man. But according to his biographer, he enjoyed learning about and then discussing the philosophical and ethical dimensions of Christian moral theology, and he took the teachings seriously. He at least was aware of the implications of immoral behavior, including doing harm to others. And this moral awareness, coupled with the moral intensity of the antiwar movement, bothered him.[20]

Nothing bothered him as much as Norman Morrison. On November 2, 1965, Morrison, a young, clean-cut Quaker pacifist, set fire to himself in protest against the Vietnam War. He did it in a Pentagon parking lot which, not coincidentally, had a clear view of McNamara's office window. His final words to his wife, who did not know his intentions that morning, were: "What can I do to make them stop the war?" From his window, McNamara saw the twelve-foot high flames engulf Morrison's body, and then the ambulances converge. It was too terrible to bear contemplating, but McNamara could not push the episode out of his mind. "Morrison's death was a tragedy not only for his family but also for me and the country," McNamara recalled in his memoir of the war. "It was an outcry against the killing that was destroying the lives of so many Vietnamese and American youth. I reacted to the horror of his action by bottling up my emotions and avoided talking about them with anyone—even my family." But those emotions would soon resurface, in the form of doubt, guilt, and ultimately his resignation. The journalist Stanley Karnow first noticed a change in McNamara, strangely subdued and lacking in his usual confidence, at a briefing in February 1966, only a few months after Morrison's suicide. By 1967, McNamara did not want the war to be his any longer. He did his best to sabotage the war from within, and then left. Soon after, reeling from McNamara's defection and the shock of the Tet Offensive, Johnson announced a halt to the bombing and an end to his political career.[21]

· · ·

ON A WARM spring day in May 1970, Gordon M. Torgersen, pastor of the First Baptist Church of Worcester, Massachusetts, mounted the steps of City Hall to make an announcement. "This is no easy thing to do," he began uneasily. "We are in a time of national peril and there is peril in what we do right now." His church members knew he had become deeply distressed by the war, but Nixon's recent invasion of Cambodia pushed him over the edge. He loved his country, he said—"I love it as a patriot"—which made what he was about to do difficult but necessary. Nixon was out of control, comparable only to Hitler. As a Christian who believed in Christ's gospel of peace, Reverend Torgersen pledged to withhold the proportion of his income tax that would otherwise go to fund the military budget.[22]

Such a stance was not unusual for liberal American clergy. But what happened next was also not unusual, and it provides the flip side of the home-front story: Reverend Torgersen then had to face his congregation. And most of them were as unhappy with Torgersen as he was unhappy with the war. Many of them acknowledged that the war posed difficult moral questions, but they were not comfortable seeing their pastor mount such a public, "undignified," and "unpatriotic" protest. The Board of Deacons of the First Baptist Church of the nearby town of Holden informed him that they "shudder to think of the consequences of thwarting the laws of the land." Some of his own church members were even angrier. At a church meeting after his City Hall theatrics, Torgersen admitted that while "so many have been very charitable in their opposition . . . there have been others who have spoken or written very harshly." And, more ominously, "there have been the anonymous notes." Only a last-minute compromise prevented his ouster from the pulpit of First Baptist, but a year later he was at it again with an unflinching antiwar sermon that condemned Americans as "self-absorbed" and "detached from humanity" because "*we* are the ones who are creating the blood bath right now." Soon, Torgersen found his position in Worcester untenable. He left his Massachusetts church for the safety of an ivory tower, Colgate Rochester Crozer Divinity School in upstate New York, where his antiwar radicalism was not so radical.[23]

In a wholly typical and oft-repeated way, the Torgersen episode reflected the activities and views of both the antiwar movement and the large number of Americans who supported Johnson, Nixon, and the war. Not all religious Americans rejected the moral bases of the war in Vietnam. Many liberal clergy marched against the war, but not all joined them. Few Catholics, and even fewer Protestant evangelicals and fundamentalists, opposed Vietnam. Moreover, when the views of the laity are considered alongside those of the clergy, religious support for the war becomes even clearer. Divisions between liberal clerics and conservative congregants had always existed, especially on matters of race, but they were rarely as wide as on Vietnam. In a 1968 poll, for example, 57 percent of Protestant clergy supported an immediate and total bombing halt, while 60 percent of the laity opposed one. Gallup polls from 1965 to 1967 revealed that a substantial majority of Protestants supported the war even if their ministers did not. Only in the extremely liberal churches—the Society of Friends, the United Church of Christ, and the Unitarian-Universalists—did those in the pews share the concerns of those in the pulpit. "Officially the churches may coo like a dove," observed a Lutheran denominational magazine, "but the majority of their members are flying with the hawks."[24]

Among evangelicals and fundamentalists, the clergy and laity agreed on the need to defend South Vietnam and support the president once he had committed U.S. troops to the fight. In the summer of 1968—in other words, after the Tet Offensive had convinced most Americans, including LBJ, that victory was a mirage and that the bombing must stop—a poll of religious opinion recorded support for continued bombing and even an *increase* in U.S. military intervention among 97 percent of Southern Baptists, 91 percent of independent fundamentalists, and 70 percent of Missouri Synod Lutherans; only 2 percent of Southern Baptists and 3 percent of fundamentalists favored a negotiated withdrawal. Similarly, a 1971 survey of Missouri college students concluded that there were strong correlations between religious conservatism and support for the war.[25]

Conservatives blamed liberal protests for undermining American morale and bolstering North Vietnamese resolve. The South Vietnamese, said religious conservatives, deserved protection from communism just as much as the Germans or Japanese, and to abandon them would be positively unchristian. America's war, trying though it was, was therefore God's war, and American sacrifices would bring salvation from godless tyranny. "In a land of bullets, bombs, and the slinking Viet Cong, God's angels are stationed also," a Pentecostal wrote of U.S. troops. "And they cannot be touched by bullets or bombs! You see, angels never go to battlefields to fight but to free." At its 1967 annual convention, the Carl McIntire–led American Council of Christian Churches passed resolutions supporting the war and condemning CALCAV and the NCC. "America must win in Vietnam," read Resolution No. 12. "There is no other acceptable course. To surrender, or show weakness before the Communist onslaught would be the greatest disaster ever to befall America. The conflict with Communism is God versus anti-God, Christ versus anti-Christ." Elsewhere, McIntire sanctified the war as "a righteous and holy cause," while Billy James Hargis, a pioneer of televangelism, praised it as a struggle "against an aggressor, fought for freedom, fought for the security and protection of the United States." Antiwar protest was therefore not only unpatriotic, but immoral. A placard at a 1970 prowar demonstration, the "March for Victory," put it best: "Why Lose When You Can Win?"[26]

As might be expected, Billy Graham supported the war. Yet he was surprisingly ambivalent, and actually supported Johnson and Nixon while harboring grave doubts about the necessity and wisdom of the war. He was not a reflexive proponent of fighting in Vietnam as he had been during World War II and Korea. Vietnam seemed different, the need less clear, the fight against a poverty-stricken, preindustrial country less morally compelling. Graham had not softened on communism, but he had softened on war, especially this "complicated, confusing, and frustrating" war. "How can we have peace?" he wondered. "I don't know. I don't have any answers." Despite his lack of answers, Graham publicly supported the war nonetheless and backed Johnson and Nixon against their tormentors. And it was this ambivalence that demonstrated just how resolutely patriotic Christian conservatives could be. If Graham's support for war was no longer reflexive, his patriotism certainly was.[27]

Graham was not unaccustomed to taking difficult political stands. He had, for example, begun to criticize Jim Crow in the late 1950s, a remarkable thing for a Southern evangelical to do. But even considering Vietnam's perplexing nature, Graham believed it sacrilegious to criticize the president—and through him, America itself—for prosecuting a war against godless communist tyranny. Jim Crow was wrong, that much was clear; Vietnam, on the other hand, was not inherently wrong, just difficult. Graham believed that the United States had not sought world leadership, but he also believed that no other nation could lead. Americans therefore had a responsibility, a duty to the nation, the world, and God, to persevere despite the difficulties. That was what God's people did in a test of their will. "We either face an all-out war with Red China, or a retreat that will cause us to lose face throughout Asia. Make no mistake about it. We are in a mess," he told an audience in Hawaii. But he was just as certain that Americans had to clean up the mess rather than turn their backs on the South Vietnamese. "I have no sympathy for those clergymen who [urge] the U.S. to get out of Vietnam," he declared during a Denver revival. "Communism has to be stopped somewhere, whether it is in Hawaii or on the West Coast. The President believes it should be stopped in Vietnam." At the invitation of U.S. commanders in South Vietnam, Graham paid two Christmas visits to U.S. troops, in 1966 and 1968, and encouraged them to keep fighting the good fight. On the Fourth of July in 1970, not long after the largest spasm of antiwar demonstrations against Nixon's invasion of Cambodia, Graham hosted an Honor America Day rally at the Lincoln Memorial. "There is just too much negativism," he told the assembled. "There are too many people knocking our institutions—the government, the church, the flag." Instead, Americans must "Honor the nation! . . . And as you move to do it, never give in. Never give in! Never! Never! Never! Never!"[28]

Graham had reasons for supporting the war other than reflexive patriotism. Like Niebuhr and Bennett, his neo-evangelicalism was based on the neo-orthodox theology of original sin. The world was not yet redeemed, and would not be so long as Christ had not returned to do battle with the armies of Satan. Until that time, the world would be locked in a struggle between good and evil. Thus to do good, God's people sometimes had to resort to a little evil themselves. They had to choose the lesser evil, and in Vietnam the lesser evil was fighting communism. Pretending that the world would improve purely through a doctrine of works and blind Christian charity was not only foolish but dangerous. "There are those who have tried to reduce Christ to the level of a genial and innocuous appeaser," Graham said in obvious reference to CALCAV and other mainline dissenters. But, he continued, paraphrasing a passage from the Book of Matthew (10:34), "Jesus said, 'You are wrong—I have come as a fire-setter and a sword-wielder.' " As the Bible instructed, sometimes God's people must beat their swords into ploughshares, and sometimes they must do the reverse. It depended on whether the need to fight was just and necessary, and Graham, despite his persistent misgivings, believed the struggle in Vietnam was both. "War is sinful, yes," he argued. "But as long as you have human nature so wild as it is, you're going to have to use force." Graham's associate Sherwood Wirt agreed. After one blocked out all the noise generated by the domestic debate over the war, the basic issue was simple. "Vietnam," he argued in 1968, "becomes rather the same basic issue that free men have faced in two World Wars and Korea: *Will a man fight for his freedom? Because if he won't, in a sinful planet he will not have it long.*"[29]

Graham and his flock were not alone. Despite the fame which Niebuhr, Bennett, King, and others brought to the antiwar cause, not all Protestant intellectuals or Christian realists opposed the war. Some of Niebuhr's allies at *Christianity and Crisis*, who used the same realist logic to support America's stand in Vietnam, felt betrayed by his antiwar turn. In fact, another authoritative Protestant theorist of Christian ethics and the just war—perhaps even more authoritative than Niebuhr—defended the war and Johnson's methods of waging it. Through the middle decades of the Cold War, Paul Ramsey taught ethics and philosophy at Princeton; his 1950 primer *Basic Christian Ethics* became the starting point for every young theologian or aspiring mainline minister. In a bracing 1965 speech to the Religious Leaders' Conference on Peace, held at the Church Center for the United Nations, Ramsey reminded his audience that they and their flock lived in the real world, in which difficult and sometimes impossible moral choices would have to be made. Vietnam was one such choice where there were no perfect moral options. Outright withdrawal would abandon South Vietnam to unwanted communist tyranny and as such would be an irresponsible abdication of leadership in the Cold War. Ramsey turned Niebuhr's anti-Nazi doctrine of the lesser evil on its head for the Vietnam dilemma. "Anyone who is impressed only by the immorality and probable ineffectiveness of interventionary action," he scolded his startled listeners, "should sensitize his conscience to the immorality and probable ineffectiveness of nonintervention." "Is Vietnam a Just War?" Ramsey asked three years later in his influential book, *The Just War.* The answer was complex, but definite: yes, in every possible sense, and it was the war's opponents who lacked a clear understanding of the relationship between morality and world politics. "There is nothing much wrong with Secretary of State Dean Rusk except that he keeps saying that this should be a world in which neighbors leave neighbors alone," Ramsey noted sardonically. "Jesus of Nazareth said something like that too."[30]

While Ramsey made the intellectual case for war, faith-based relief agencies and mission boards actually helped to implement it, if at times uncomfortably. Groups like Church World Service (Protestant) and Catholic Relief Services delivered food aid to South Vietnamese and helped clothe and house refugees in South Vietnam, and they did it all within the confines of the U.S. pacification program and with the cooperation of the government in Saigon. Church World Service (CWS), a mainline group based in the grassroots laity rather than the clerical elite, distanced itself from its partner organization, the clergy-oriented National Council of Churches, which continually leveled strong protests against the war. Though the CWS-NCC tensions never led to a rupture, they revealed the liberal-conservative divisions between the laity and the clergy and the fissures between religious liberals and conservatives that would open and widen over the next several decades. Just as important, CWS and Catholic Relief Services showed the willingness of charitable organizations to help solve the Vietnam problem, even if it meant coordinating with unsuitable partners such as the U.S. military and the regime in Saigon. Evangelicals, who mostly backed the war and could be found predominating in the American missionary enterprise and increasingly the U.S. military, found South Vietnam a particularly fruitful mission field.[31]

The efforts of Catholic Relief Services were broadly representative of another major feature of religious support for the war. Notwithstanding the Berrigan brothers, a solid majority of Catholics backed the war until the Tet Offensive. This was perhaps to be expected: South Vietnam was in part a Catholic country, and the fiercely anticommunist Catholic hierarchy had given it staunch support from its very inception, when the 1954 Geneva Accords partitioned Vietnam into northern and southern halves. One of America's only propaganda victories during its entire involvement in Vietnam came that same year, when the U.S. Navy helped nearly a million Catholics flee from communist North Vietnam to the South. In addition, South Vietnam's president, Ngo Dinh Diem, was a devout Catholic, and his brother, Ngo Dinh Thuc, was the bishop of Hue. Polls throughout the war, right up to the United States' withdrawal after the 1973 Paris Peace Accords, showed consistently higher levels of support among Catholics than among Protestants (both were far higher than among Jews). If there was ever a war American Catholics were predisposed to supporting, it was Vietnam.[32]

On foreign policy in general, and on Vietnam in particular, Catholics followed the same path as Billy Graham: protests against America's mission abroad were condemned as assaults on the nation itself. Philip Berrigan noticed that his fellow Josephite priests were willing to be radical on civil rights, but not Vietnam. The Josephites were happy to focus on the "salvation" of African Americans, Berrigan later complained, but "when I plunged into the Vietnam War and got into trouble over that, there was almost no support for that. They'd visit me in jail once in a while, but not too often, and only one or two of them." Overall, the Catholic hierarchy backed President Johnson. In 1966, the National Conference of Catholic Bishops (NCCB) tried to reconcile the pope's call for "peace on earth" with American treaty and moral obligations in Southeast Asia; in this standoff between pope and president, LBJ came out ahead. Not until 1971 did the NCCB officially come out against the war, long after the rest of the country.[33]

Few people, religious or otherwise, epitomized the continuing Catholic support for the Vietnam War better than Francis Cardinal Spellman. His support for the war was automatic simply because his support for all U.S. foreign policy was automatic. But he was especially devoted to Vietnam. This was a relatively easy position to maintain in the revivalist and anticommunist atmosphere of the Eisenhower era, but Spellman held fast to it when the communist insurgency picked up in the early 1960s and Diem was overthrown in 1963. When the ranks of antiwar protesters swelled at home, the cardinal took it upon himself to counter their moral arguments with ones of his own. The turning point came with another act of antiwar self-immolation, this time by a young Catholic Worker, Roger LaPorte, who burned himself to death on the steps of the UN. Spellman blamed the Berrigans—especially after Daniel Berrigan delivered the funeral sermon and, against Spellman's strict orders, used it to attack the war—and moved to ostracize them from Church activities. But, ironically, his immovable support for the war in Vietnam put him at odds not only with the Berrigans and Catholic Workers, but also with the institution he had faithfully served his entire career. Under John XXIII and Paul VI, the Vatican had moved away from the vitriolic anticommunism of Pius XII.

They wanted peace on earth, which included peace in Vietnam. But Spellman remained unmoved. To demonstrate his full support for the war, he paid Christmas visits to Saigon in 1965 and 1966. Billy Graham was also there in 1966, and the two shared many of the same venues. They also shared a meeting with the overall U.S. commander in Vietnam, General William C. Westmoreland—who found the cardinal "a tough man when it comes to principle"—and a White House debriefing upon their return. On these occasions, though Johnson and Westmoreland appreciated such steadfast support, even Graham was taken aback by Spellman's aggressively optimistic support for the war. The night before Spellman died of a massive stroke in December 1967, he reiterated the need for America to uphold its moral duty and maintain the defense of South Vietnam.[34]

LONG AFTER THE fighting had ended, Vietnam continued to serve a political purpose for those who had supported the war. In 1984, at the height of the conservative revival, Tim LaHaye, a fundamentalist writer, commentator, and coauthor of the spectacularly successful *Left Behind* novel series, repudiated the strategists and protesters who had all but ensured defeat. "Her failure to use military might in Vietnam was a national disgrace," he said of a troubled nation then in the throes of liberalism and secularism, "permitting the enslavement or murder of twenty million people." Rus Walton, another fundamentalist writer and professional anticommunist, took a similar view: "What must the nations of the free world think of a country that spends the lives of 58,000 splendid young men and then gives up? Just quits and walks away and says, 'Sorry, fellas, it was all a mistake.' "[35] During the war, the anti-Vietnam demonstrators, many of them led by ministers, priests, and rabbis, claimed the moral high ground. But the war's defenders, the conservatives who would fuel the Religious Right, provided a vigorous counterargument that was also grounded in morality, albeit of a sterner kind. It was this moral vision that eventually triumphed and reoriented the normative bearings of U.S. foreign policy. But before it could, its adherents first had to defeat the relativism and internationalism of their liberal adversaries. Then, in the years of Richard Nixon, they turned upon the government itself.

Get Thee Behind Me, Satan

W HEN RICHARD NIXON WAS inaugurated as president in January 1969, America's position in the world was at its lowest point in nearly a century. Vietnam was obviously the main problem, but it was not the only one: the Soviets had achieved strategic parity by equaling the U.S. nuclear arsenal; the German and Japanese economies were surging (which, ironically, was possible partly because the United States bore the heavy costs of German and Japanese security); through *Ostpolitik*, the Germans were also exploring ways to open links with Eastern Europe and the Soviet Union, thereby weakening transatlantic solidarity; and the French undermined American leadership by withdrawing from NATO's military command and leading a run on the dollar. At the same time, the U.S. economy was straining under the inflationary pressures of funding a major war without raising taxes, some of the nation's major cities lay in smoldering ruins, race relations were reaching new lows, and many universities were nearing a state of insurrection. In between the disasters of the 1961 Bay of Pigs and the 1979–80 Iran hostage crisis, Nixon inherited leadership of a nation on the verge of a collective nervous breakdown.

To manage America's decline in world politics and protect it from new vulnerabilities, Nixon and his chief foreign policy adviser, Henry Kissinger—who served first as national security adviser and then, from 1973, as secretary of state—adopted a new foreign policy based upon superpower détente. No longer would the United States follow through on Kennedy's promise to bear any burden, support any friend, and oppose any foe. With the Sino-Soviet split out in the open and Beijing and Moscow fearing each other more than they feared Washington, Nixon and Kissinger moved to triangulate world politics away from its familiar U.S.–Soviet bipolar axis. Détente with the Soviets, the sensational opening to China, negotiating an end to the Vietnam War: these were intended to be the maneuvers behind a tactical retreat that would allow the United States to come through its period of decline, reemerge with new strength, and regain the initiative. Such policies astonished the world, not least of all Americans. But they also required a certain amount of dealing with the devil and treating as equals those who had only recently been denounced as godless, autocratic butchers. It was a foreign policy that avoided the crusading moralism of previous eras. It was a foreign policy of realism.[1]

Few architects of U.S. foreign policy have been chronicled as thoroughly as Richard Nixon and Henry Kissinger. Their combustible mix of brilliance, hubris, and petty personal insecurities are legend. Less well known are the religious influences on their lives and politics. But there is good reason for this: despite coming from intensely religious households, they were not especially religious men. On August 7, 1974, with the pressure of Watergate having built to unbearable levels and facing impeachment by Congress, Nixon made up his mind to resign the presidency. Late that night, he called Kissinger in for one final conversation. Nixon was disconsolate; Kissinger, one of the only administration officials to remain free from the taint of scandal, spent the next several hours bucking up his spirits. As Kissinger, emotionally exhausted, was about to leave, Nixon asked him to pray. "Henry," he said, "you are not a very orthodox Jew, and I am not an orthodox Quaker, but we need to pray." With that, the two men knelt on the carpet of the Lincoln Bedroom, and prayed. Kissinger, feeling uncomfortable but also trapped, relieved the tension not by thinking of God but by silently reciting Greek poetry. Nixon prayed aloud, and then wept quietly. It was a supremely awkward moment for both men— "the most wrenching thing I have ever gone through in my life," Kissinger said at the time—but the awkwardness was entirely fitting.[2]

Nixon's parents, Frank and Hannah, were devout Quakers from Whittier, California, a small, dusty farming community twenty miles east of Los Angeles. Settled in the 1880s as a Friends colony, Nixon's hometown had been named for a Quaker poet, John Greenleaf Whittier. However, California Quakerism bore little resemblance to the staid style of Friends worship back in Philadelphia; having been shaped by successive waves of revivalism, by the early twentieth century California Friends were in most ways indistinguishable from evangelicals. They still retained the intense cultural and social morality of conventional Quakerism, and they still believed in an "inner light" that gave every individual a personal and direct connection with God. But they were increasingly emotional in their style of worship, they believed in an inerrant Bible, and their language increasingly assumed the pietistic tenor of evangelicalism. Hannah, Nixon's mother, set the religious tone of the household; this included the faith of her husband, Frank, who agreed to convert from Methodism. "Hannah practiced her religion in utter seriousness," observes Nixon's biographer Roger Morris, and she made sure the rest of her family did so too. Southern California was prone to evangelical revivalism, and Frank took his sons to see famous preachers who passed through Los Angeles, including the Pentecostal leader Aimee Semple McPherson. Frank also taught sessions in the local Friends Sunday school that became famous in the community for their intense piety and revivalist emotion. According to a family friend, Frank was "extremely religious, almost to the point of being fanatic."[3]

Yet almost as soon as he could, Richard Nixon shed his Quaker faith. The separation began in college, but the final break came in World War II when he joined the navy against the wishes of his traditionally pacifist Quaker mother and her side of the family. Still, Nixon could not completely let go of his religious roots—not if he wanted a career in politics. He began his ascent in postwar Southern California, a time and place where religion was a political necessity. Here, his western-style Quakerism, with its emphasis on individualism and faith, was perfectly attuned to the Cold War anticommunism of the Republican Party. In 1946, during his first successful run for Congress, his campaign ads said that Nixon's religion "typified the American way of service to God" because it was based upon "the solid heritage of Quaker faith."[4]

For Nixon, however, there is little indication that religion was anything more than a political asset. In this sense, among others, he was unlike Eisenhower, who returned to faith later in life with a full embrace as well as an astute political awareness. As president, Nixon reached out to evangelicals in an attempt to woo them to the Republican Party. He often alluded to religion, certainly more often than either Kennedy or Johnson, and much of it stemmed from his Quaker upbringing. In his first inaugural address, he made reference to two staples of the Society of Friends: peace ("The greatest honor history can bestow is the title of peacemaker. This honor now beckons America—the chance to help lead the world at last out of the valley of turmoil and onto that high ground of peace that man has dreamed of since the dawn of civilization") and inner light ("To a crisis of the spirit, we need an answer of the spirit. And to find that answer, we need only look within ourselves"). Having served for eight years as Eisenhower's vice president, Nixon also needed no reminding about the importance of civil religion. In fact, he was the first president to close an address with the words "God bless America." But his displays of piety rang hollow to those who were closest to him. Nixon struck up a very close and—for Nixon—unusually intimate relationship with Billy Graham. The evangelist had even met Hannah Nixon at a California revival before he had ever met her son. During his presidency, Nixon sought Graham's counsel frequently. But he also was fairly aggressive in trying to co-opt Graham's name for political purposes. Eventually, seeing through the constant but shallow and politically transparent displays of piety, Graham came to doubt the depth, even the sincerity, of Nixon's faith. "Where religion was concerned with him, it was not always easy to tell the difference between the spiritual and the sentimental," Graham concluded in his memoirs. "In retrospect, whenever he spoke about the Lord, it was in pretty general terms."[5]

Henry Kissinger was even less pious than Nixon, yet his religious background probably had more of an influence in shaping who he was and how he viewed the world. Born in Weimar Germany to an Orthodox Jewish family, Heinz Kissinger was a bookish but well-adjusted adolescent, serious about his religion but at home in German society. His world, like that of all German Jews, collapsed when Hitler took power in 1933. In 1938, after agonizing for several years over whether to leave their homeland, the Kissingers fled Germany for the safety of the United States. After finding a haven in America, Kissinger, now known as Henry, served in the U.S. Army, eventually returning to Germany as a conqueror rather than a victim. Following the war, the GI Bill enabled Kissinger to attend university. He was accepted at Harvard, where he would remain for two decades as he progressed from undergraduate to doctoral candidate to junior faculty to tenured professor. Here, even though his Judaism quietly dropped away, he benefited from Judeo-Christian America's newfound willingness to tolerate a certain amount of upward social mobility among Jews. Such powerful formative experiences, unique to Jews, could not help but shape Kissinger's emerging worldview. "I have never forgotten that thirteen members of my family died in concentration camps," he revealed in 1977, "nor could I ever fail to remember what it was like to live in Nazi Germany as a member of a persecuted minority." But as his biographer Jeremi Suri has pointed out, the experience of personally witnessing the Nazis come to power democratically, riding on a wave of populist discontent, mass rallies, and carefully orchestrated mob rule, instilled in young Kissinger a suspicion of democracy and its potential to create a tyranny of the majority. It also led him to a certain wariness of crusading ideology, righteousness, and moralism in public life, and instead to prioritize order and stability. Emigration to the United States illustrated the benevolence of America, while victory in the war provided as clear a demonstration as possible of the uses of power in world politics. In other words, it was no accident that Kissinger became a realist whose lodestar was the primacy of American power.[6]

NIXON AND KISSINGER may not have been especially pious, but they came to power at a time when the nation at large was becoming increasingly religious. In fact, they entered office at precisely the moment when the liberal Sixties reformation was waning and the conservative counterreformation was about to begin. Nixon was well aware of these developments, and, under the assumption that the surge of conservative religion would benefit the Republicans, did his best to encourage them. But when it came to foreign policy, this was a high-risk and ultimately counterproductive strategy because Nixon and Kissinger found themselves buffeted by contradictory pressures that each demanded its own response. On one hand, the international system demanded retrenchment, a more realistic appraisal of which interests were vital and which were peripheral (for example, Vietnam), and a recognition that American capabilities were not limitless. On the other, the resurgence of traditional religion and morality, and the emergence of conservative religion as a political force, especially within the Republican Party, demanded an assertion of American exceptionalism, righteousness, and mission in foreign affairs. World politics called for realism, while domestic politics demanded moralism. Nixon and Kissinger felt it imperative to deal with the devils of Moscow and Beijing; Christian conservatives responded with Jesus's admonition against temptation (Matthew 16:23) that was also a common refrain in gospel music: "Get thee behind me, Satan."

The counterreformation was grounded predominantly in domestic politics, and because those views would do much to shape national attitudes on foreign affairs they are worth exploring in greater detail. The counterreformation was not created by a simple backlash against liberalism and secularism. Christian conservatives had been growing in numbers and confidence since at least World War II, if not before, and they surged confidently into the mainstream comforts, suburban mores, and McCarthyite red scares of the 1950s. And while the fires of the national great awakening may have been waning by the Kennedy era, the passions of the conservatives were not. In between 1960 and 1964, the fortunes of some of the most conservative preachers soared: Billy James Hargis's publication *Christian Crusade* doubled its circulation to just over 98,000; Carl McIntire expanded his radio network from one station in 1958 to over five hundred in 1964; Fred Schwarz crisscrossed the country to host Christian Anti-Communist Crusade (CACC) rallies featuring the likes of John Wayne, Pat Boone, and Ronald Reagan; and the John Birch Society saw its annual income from donations jump from $600,000 in 1958 to $3,200,000 in 1964. "We look forward to a period of growth," boasted a CACC newsletter in 1962, as "we propose to launch the greatest anti-Communism campaign America has ever known." Other far-right Protestant groups, such as the Circuit Riders, based in Cincinnati, or the American Council of Christian Laymen, based in Madison, Wisconsin, also experienced strong growth. The Kennedy administration was aware of the danger from the right—"the radical right-wing constitutes a formidable force in American life today," concluded aide Myer Feldman in an analysis that singled out McIntire, while the president himself issued a warning, prompted by Hargis and his incessant attacks, over "those on the fringe of society" launching "crusades of suspicion"—but was powerless to stop it.[7]

Nonetheless, the 1960s marked a difficult time for evangelicals and fundamentalists. The nation they loved—a god-fearing, Christian nation—was at risk of disappearing completely. The liberal theological innovations, such as the "death of God" school, were disturbing to the evangelical mind. "There was a time earlier in the Christian era when the evangelist's best ally was the theologian," wrote a dismayed Carl Henry, the widely respected editor of *Christianity Today*. "But today many theologians themselves need to be evangelized." In the absence of the true gospel, the apostasies of the mainline clergy were inflicting untold damage on Christian America. "Their tantalizing theories and their flash fads soon disappear, leaving the modern man still in desperate need of spiritual help and salvation." Melvin Munn, a fundamentalist radio preacher in Dallas, was even more categorical: "In every major main line Christian church I know anything about," he told his listeners, "national control or direction is heavily influenced by liberal, innovative, and non-Biblical concepts and doctrines." It was a conspiracy by an elite minority, just like communism. It was time, Munn declared, for ordinary laypeople to wrest control of their faith from the clergy before they inflicted further damage.[8]

Even more troubling was the steady pace of secularization at the hands of the Supreme Court. In 1962–63, the *Engel* and *Schempp* cases on school prayer raised the wall of separation between church and state to a previously unimaginable height. Traditionally anti-statist Christian conservatives, we have seen, had always been among the staunchest defenders of the First Amendment. But that was when church-state separation kept the government out of religion, not the other way around. Until the 1960s, religion had no difficulty in playing an active, and often activist, role in public life. With its school prayer rulings, however, the Court redressed that imbalance, and religion found itself pushed into the private sphere. An explosion of anger erupted among conservatives, yet school prayer was only the first of many such controversies. For the next two decades, Christian conservatives mounted crusades against sex education, obscenity, pornography, and birth control, all of which in their view undermined the very foundations of American life and all of which were protected by the Supreme Court. In 1973, the Court's verdict in *Roe v. Wade* legalized abortion nationwide. But the ultimate insult came in 1978, when the Internal Revenue Service, backed by the Supreme Court and the newly created Department of Education, withdrew charitable tax-exempt status for thousands of Christian private schools that had avoided racial integration. Faced with this threat to their way of life, conservatives mobilized politically in a way they had not done since the temperance movement. The "social crisis today has reached proportions so acute," Henry wrote in his 1971 jeremiad *A Plea for Evangelical Demonstration*, "that Christian moral protest has become imperative." At first, conservative religious politics emerged as uncoordinated individual protest rather than as a cohesive political movement. It was not until the 1970s that right-wing religion became the Religious Right.[9]

Because of civil rights, Southern evangelicals were especially upset with the Great Society's intrusions into the local way of life. In 1963, Alabama governor George Wallace was one of the first to blend evangelicalism, populism, and racism in opposition to civil rights. "We are a God-fearing people—not government-fearing people," he declared in an infamous segregationist speech delivered at the entrance to the University of Alabama. In the 1970s, North Carolina senator Jesse Helms began to coalesce these forces and harness them not just to the conservative movement but to a Republican Party that would "resist the secular humanists who are taking over our schools, our society, our businesses, our institutions at every level." In 1979, Reverend Jerry Falwell, a fundamentalist Baptist preacher from Lynchburg, Virginia, established Moral Majority, a political pressure group for religious conservatives that completed the formation of the Religious Right. This was quite a step for Falwell, whose 1965 sermon "Ministers and Marches" had condemned politically active clergy—in other words, liberals who campaigned for civil rights and against Vietnam—and pledged never to be one himself. Falwell, like most fundamentalists, was a "separationist" who vowed to live a purified life with fellow puritans untainted by mainstream society. By 1979, however, the nation was in danger of being lost to Christianity forever; in such an emergency, strictures against mixing religion with politics no longer applied. Moral Majority would not join the mainstream, but change it one voter at a time.[10]

Falwell's timing was perfect. In the 1970s, the cultural mainstream, once a forbidding wasteland for any self-respecting evangelical, became saturated with conservative Protestantism. Already in the Sixties, despite the prevailing atmosphere of revolution, Christian conservatives had built their own national community in which evangelical youth groups, authors, and musicians could flourish. During the next decade, they successfully expanded this network and adapted it to appeal to non-evangelicals, many of whom became evangelicals themselves. By the middle of the decade, more than a third of all Americans claimed to have been born again. *Newsweek* called 1976 "The Year of the Evangelical," while the journalist Tom Wolfe labeled the entire decade the "Third Great Awakening." While mainline churches stagnated, membership in conservative congregations boomed: the Southern Baptists grew by nearly a quarter between 1970 and 1985, while mainline Methodist, Presbyterian, and Episcopal churches shrunk by an average of 15 percent. Liberal churches were also losing their political clout: moderate mainline Protestants found themselves hopelessly outnumbered in the Republican Party and not particularly respected by the increasingly secular Democrats. At the same time, conservative denominations were not only growing in size, they were becoming even more doctrinally and politically conservative. In 1979, the same year Moral Majority was founded, fundamentalists defeated moderates at the Southern Baptist Convention's (SBC) annual conference and won the right to determine the SBC's future direction. The Social Gospel–oriented SBC, the one that had endorsed integration as early as 1944, was now extinct. Southern Baptists would now look to restore a lost American Eden rather than build a progressive future.[11]

Yet a focus on Wallace, Helms, Falwell, and the SBC, however warranted, obscures equally important developments. The emerging Religious Right was not simply a product of the South; nor was it entirely a creature of Protestantism. Instead, the Religious Right was national and interdenominational; Northern and Western as much as Southern; and Catholic and Mormon as much as Protestant. The South still had a lot to do with this, of course: as the historian Darren Dochuk has observed, millions of white evangelicals and fundamentalists left the impoverished South in between the 1920s and 1950s, bringing their uncompromising Christian faith and anticommunist values with them. This white Southern diaspora then established smaller versions of Southern culture in the rest of the country, from Michigan to California. With the coming of the counterreformation, their values, now nationalized, suddenly became fashionable for Americans who had never lived in the South.[12]

But something else was happening, too: the emergence of conservative ecumenism. Catholics and Mormons held many of the same cultural values as conservative Protestants, and with the rise of a Judeo-Christian ethic and the Sixties reformation these three groups began to mobilize together on cultural-political issues such as abortion and the proposed Equal Rights Amendment for women. For example, the John Birch Society, on the fringe of the far-right fringe, called itself "nonsectarian." Anticommunism, not anti-Semitism or anti-Catholicism, must be America's priority. To a fellow anticommunist activist who focused narrowly on Jews, Kent Steffgen, the John Birch Society's coordinating secretary, retorted that the Birchers' mission was "to give any morally motivated Jew, Christian, Moslem, etc., his chance to make up his mind between 'truth and repose.' . . . Not all Jews are communists in our belief, yet this is what any anti-Semite is actually implying." This was not exactly what FDR or Truman had in mind when they sought to unite the forces of faith against the forces of atheism, but it did mean that for the first time in American history conservative religion had the potential to form a broad-based interfaith political movement.[13]

Most important was the new attitude of Roman Catholics—or rather, a new political commitment to very old attitudes—and their ability to explore alliances with Protestants on issues of common concern. Until now, Catholics had been reliable members of the New Deal coalition. In the nine presidential elections between 1936 and 1968, only once did a majority of Catholics not vote for the Democratic candidate, and that was in 1956 when Eisenhower carried most of the country; on average, during this period only 32 percent of Catholics voted Republican. However, with the new political prominence of religious-cultural issues such as abortion, combined with the growing affluence of Catholics which made conservative fiscal policies more attractive, combined with the hollowing out of many industrial cities due to deteriorating race relations and the suburbanization and more evenly spread national distribution of Catholicism, American Catholics were increasingly attracted to the Republican Party and the conservative movement. In the nine elections following the watershed year 1968, a majority of Catholics voted Democratic only three times, while on average 52 percent of them voted Republican. Essential differences remained, but throughout the period Catholics responded to the very same issues as evangelicals—abortion, education, birth control, the outrageousness of "secular theology" and the "death of God" school—in much the very same way. Under such banners as the Orthodox Roman Catholic Movement, Catholic traditionalism—the closest analogue to Protestant fundamentalism—emerged to combat the theological, liturgical, and cultural modernization of the Church. Nationwide, members of the Catholic hierarchy, such as Francis Cardinal McIntyre of archconservative Orange County, California, successfully applied conservative theology and culture to a new conservative politics and visceral anticommunism. At the same time, Catholic students at Notre Dame, Fordham, and elsewhere helped make interfaith conservative groups like Young Americans for Freedom powerhouses of grassroots political activism. And of the national leaders and organizers of the New Right, two of the most important—Paul Weyrich and Richard Viguerie—were staunch pro-life Catholics.[14]

The Republicans stood to benefit from these Catholic political wanderings, a fact not lost on the Nixon White House. In fact, Nixon had them foremost in mind when he appealed, in a November 1969 national television address, to the "silent majority" of moral, patriotic Americans who did not march in protest at every little grievance. It was "clear," wrote a Nixon aide, "that future victory for the President and the Party in the Northeast lies in . . . adding to it by the tens of thousands of 'gut' conservative, predominantly Catholic, Silent Majority Democrats." So far, media attention had focused on Nixon's "Southern Strategy" of using racially loaded code phrases like "law and order" and "states' rights" to wean the South off the Democratic Party. But the Nixon strategy was national, not regional, and it appealed to conservative instincts well beyond race. "Let the press squeal about a 'Southern Strategy' all they wish," the aide continued gleefully. "What they don't seem to realize is that in addition to adding Southern Protestants by the tens of thousands to the New Majority, we are making it a national one by adding as many Northern Catholics." The conversion of ethnic voters in the Northeast and Midwest, mainly Irish, Polish, and Italians, became such a priority that the White House established a "Catholic division" devoted solely to the task.[15]

CONSERVATIVE PROTESTANTS, and to some extent conservative Catholics, were driven to oppose the liberal revolutions of the Sixties by a powerful anti-statist ideology. Evangelicals and fundamentalists had always prized the separation of church and state because it prevented the government from regulating religious life. This meant everything to the eccentric, unconventional, and emotional churches of evangelicalism, to say nothing of even more radical offspring like Mormonism and Pentecostalism. By the twentieth century, anti-statism had become hardwired into the genes of conservative Protestants.

In the previous few decades, however, the rise of big government—first with the New Deal welfare state, which assumed the powers of charity and mercy traditionally left to the churches, then the Cold War national security state, and then finally the Great Society and the rights revolution— threatened the purpose and autonomy of religion. To be sure, many evangelicals, Billy Graham foremost among them, had no trouble supporting Great Society measures like the War on Poverty. Sherwood Wirt, editor of Graham's magazine *Decision*, invoked passages from Deuteronomy (15:7–11) and Luke (6:20) to argue that "For the Christian the 'war on poverty' is not a political option. It is a lifelong battle based on the mandate of Jesus Christ, who loved the poor." But when Great Society programs appeared to fail, and worse yet actually seemed to encourage welfare dependency and inner-city violence at the expense of decency, what support it had from Christian conservatives wilted.[16]

At the same time, they would also seek to reverse the process of secularization that was threatening to relegate religion entirely to the private sphere. To save their country, Christian conservatives, Baptists included, would launch a new crusade to bring America back to its true faith. If the forces of liberalism and secularism would not respect church-state separation, neither would they. While nationalistic Christian conservatives distrusted the federal government, they loved their country unconditionally. Indeed, they envisioned their new political activism as an attempt to rescue the nation from the state. The Williamson County Baptist Association of Marion, Illinois, put it plainly in a letter to their senator, Everett Dirksen. "Certainly, we need no crystal ball to see that our country is tearing apart at the seams," the Illinois Baptists wrote in May 1968. "The heavy problems of war, racism, poverty, and civil rights are, first of all, spiritual problems. They require solutions from men moved and motivated by God. The time for action in the cause of righteousness is now!" In many ways, all other, more specific concerns—on economics, race, and gender—stemmed from the visceral hostility to the federal government's attempts at social engineering and from the fear that the new political order threatened to destroy American freedom.[17]

Here it is difficult to separate racism from anti-statism and patriotism as motivating factors for faith-based opposition to civil rights. There was certainly an unhealthy amount of rank prejudice, and for some evangelicals white supremacy would always guide their way. But for most Christian conservatives, racist or not, civil rights legislation represented a threat to local autonomy and identity. As scholars have pointed out, evangelicals who prioritize individual autonomy and free will find it difficult to appreciate systemic social inequalities that afflict racial minorities and perpetuate racism. For them, civil rights legislation marked one of many infringements of individual and community autonomy at the hands of a liberal and increasingly secular government. The same secular, liberal elites who perverted the natural order of things by banning school prayer but allowing abortion were pushing a radical civil rights agenda that defied local tradition and the realities of daily life. Thus Christian conservatives across the country, including those who had no direct stake in the South's race relations, attacked the Kennedy and Johnson administrations' progressive ambitions. And when they did, not coincidentally, they linked the growth of American state power with the spread of world communism. When George Wallace literally barred the doorway to integration at the University of Alabama, Carl McIntire's New Jersey–based newspaper *Christian Beacon* hailed him as the "Christian Patriot of the Year," an award undoubtedly motivated in part by racism but even more by a hatred of government intervention in American life. When Falwell, undoubtedly a segregationist but also philosophically a strong anti-statist, delivered his "Minister and Marches" sermon, he excoriated the "Communists" in the civil rights movement, the Northern churches, and the federal government who would impose a foreign settlement on a sovereign Southern people. Nearly a decade later, Reverend John Book, a fundamentalist preacher, led the anti-busing campaign in Richmond, Virginia, by declaring that "the combining of all races by force is communism." The conservative argument against civil rights—that the church should not be involved in politics—was often a fig leaf to disguise racism, but it was also based on an intense desire to protect local autonomy against the encroaching forces of big government liberalism.[18]

These same developments brought many Catholics into the anti-statist camp, which marked something of a fundamental shift in Catholic thought.

Coming from a church organization steeped in ideas of corporatism, social justice, and an ordered society, American Catholics had always found it easy to live with the government's economic activism and modest social welfare provisions. Their anti-statist backlash in the 1960s and '70s was in reaction to a liberal state that had overreached in the far more intimate matters of identity, gender, sexuality, local autonomy—and especially educational matters in which the Church, not the state, had always reigned supreme. For example, Catholics throughout the country mounted furious, and sometimes violent, opposition to busing programs that aimed to integrate schools. In Boston, Louise Day Hicks, an Irish Catholic Democrat and the "Mother Superior" of the anti-busing campaign, led the charge against government interference in local affairs that set the tone for Catholics and other conservatives nationwide.[19]

THESE HARD-SHELL CONSERVATIVE views on patriotism, government, morality, and culture had a profound effect on foreign policy. Nixon invoked civil religion much more than his Democratic predecessors, but with little substance or follow-through. His religious formulations were almost entirely symbolic and had no substantive policy relevance. With Nixon continuing the Kennedy-Johnson approach of providing almost no guidance on religious questions, especially regarding foreign policy, religious groups took it upon themselves to agitate for a foreign policy that would reflect and advance America's morals and values. They revived the unilateralist tradition, which rejected the premises of liberal internationalism—interdependence, collective security, multilateralism, diplomacy—and sanctioned U.S. involvement in the world on American terms only. Indeed, it is no coincidence that popular support for liberal internationalism declined in the mid-1970s at precisely the moment evangelicalism entered mainstream politics and culture.

But the counterreformation had not waited for Nixon; by the mid-1960s, it was already in full flow. "Our world is on fire, and man without God will never be able to control the flames," Billy Graham cried out in 1965. "The demons of hell have been let loose," in America and around the world. "We seem to be plunging madly toward Armageddon." If liberals embraced the revolutionary world and saw themselves as revolutionaries, conservatives abhorred it and were proud to call themselves counterrevolutionaries. But though they feared the spread of revolution—especially in a country beset by race riots, the drug counterculture, and student protests—they also reveled in the prospect of a world in flux. Carl Henry, for one, saw opportunity in the world's time of trouble. "Our century of crisis now faces a final choice between world evangelism or world revolution," he explained in 1969. It was up to America's Christians to convert the world to Christ. Never was there a better moment to do so, for the tribulations of the developing world—famine, poverty, disease, war—had created conditions ripe for the spread of God's law, as well as his love. And, Henry warned, never was there a greater need, for failure meant unleashing the full power of the forces of hell:

> The world stands at the crossroads, at the brink of doom. The evangelical task force dare not fail the Lord who sends us and the world that needs us. Of all failures in church history, none would be more costly, none more ignominious, than this. Of all the opportunities for spiritual advance, few are more exciting and promising. Let us link minds and hearts and prayers and get on with our Lord's bidding.

Link them they did, as evidenced by the soaring numbers of evangelical missionaries who took to the mission field all over the developing world. Not even mainline missions at their height in the late nineteenth century could match the evangelizing armies of Christ America sent forth to meet the world revolution.[20]

Anticommunism, of course, featured prominently. While McCarthyism may have waned in the country at large in the mid-1950s, and while some evangelical leaders, like Billy Graham, moderated their hard-line views, it never really ended for most Christian conservatives. And even Graham continued to warn that "Communism is real and it is dangerous! The Communists believe in, they plan toward, and they work for ultimate triumph." For most Christian conservatives, all forms of communism abroad and their suspected sympathizers at home came under the closest scrutiny and suspicion. In 1965, Marion Reynolds, president of the American Council of Christian Churches, warned that the "apostasy" of liberalism's "soft attitude toward Communism" had led America straight into "civil disobedience" and "racial revolution." Faith-based groups such as Christian Youth Against Communism and Fred Schwarz's Christian Anti-Communist Crusade flourished in a supposedly liberal era. "I am convinced that Communism is winning World War III without firing a single shot or losing a single soldier," railed Billy James Hargis, thanks to a combination of Soviet strength and the (in his view) treasonous activities of American labor unions, civil rights groups, and ecumenical mainliners. Pentecostals blamed communist infiltration for the Supreme Court's decision on school prayer. Reverend Charles B. Robertson of the International Church of the Four Square Gospel warned that if "Christ-hating Communism . . . should envelop this world," then "all genuine preachers of the Gospel would be imprisoned or assassinated." By the same token, even if communists were not to blame, they would surely stand to benefit from liberal measures such as the banning of school prayer. "We feel that Communism has already reached too far in the lives of our young people," a group of conservative Philadelphia ministers protested, "and unless we can call a halt somewhere along the line of righteousness, we had just as well join them and dis-recognize God altogether."[21]

These were not merely the ramblings of the paranoid, fundamentalist right-wing fringe. Russell Kirk, the intellectual godfather of modern conservatism, also portrayed communism as a "false religion" and "caricature of Christianity." America stood for something different, yet too many Americans had lost sight of it. "Our real power," he wrote in 1963, "has its source in religious conviction, and particularly Christian doctrine," because "God has given to the essence of life certain laws" that could not be erased by any earthly ideology or tyranny. Any "politico-economic creed which denies those laws must defile mankind," and would ultimately fail. Why did some Americans doubt this simple truth? Because they lacked faith. "Communism, or any other voracious ideology," he concluded, "rushes in to fill a spiritual and intellectual vacuum." In America, the causes of that vacuum were secularism, theological modernism, and political liberalism.[22]

In addition to Vietnam, then, Christian conservatives took a hard anticommunist line on virtually all foreign policy issues. Soviet premier Nikita Khrushchev "means to rule the world and is determined to do it," preached Norman Vincent Peale in one Sunday morning sermon in 1961. "There he is as a Goliath up there shaking his spear and every time he shakes his spear we get into a dither." Instead, Americans—especially the vacillating Kennedy, to whom members of Peale's Marble Collegiate Church sent a copy of the sermon—"ought to stop being afraid of him," stop thinking of peace at any price, and start resisting his evil. Khrushchev "can pull a trigger and blow us up and we'll all die," Peale noted. "So what? Is the worst thing in life to die or is the worst thing in life to be afraid to die? At least we can die like men and we've got something to die for."[23]

Few foreign policy issues triggered as much emotion as Cuba. Cuba was a Catholic country where government had had close ties to the Church, but Fidel Castro's leftist-nationalist revolution upset the traditional order and threatened the Church's role in Cuban society. American conservatives, both Protestant and Catholic, saw Castro as an arch-villain, a godless tyrant in the mold of a Stalin or Mao. At the outset of Castro's rule, Cardinal Spellman expressed "deep concern over the Communist trend in Cuba" and derided Castro as "insane and therefore impossible to work with." In South Florida, the Catholic Church cared for refugee children who had fled Castro's revolution and nurtured a stridently anticommunist exile community. Billy James Hargis embarked on a cross-country tour in 1962, dubbed "Operation Midnight Ride," that called upon Kennedy to invade Cuba.[24]

The problem, according to conservatives, was that U.S. foreign policy under Kennedy and Johnson had lost its moral bearings by losing its religion. Thus a centerpiece of their campaign to reinvigorate America's moral purpose in the world was the Christianization of the national security state. The United States Agency for International Development and the Peace Corps came in for resounding criticism for restricting the participation of religious agencies and mission boards in distributing government aid programs overseas. "*Nothing has so stirred up the leaders of the conservative and fundamental religious organizations in the South and Southwest,*" warned Bill Moyers, then working at Peace Corps headquarters in Washington. Moyers, not only a Texan but also an active Baptist layman with a divinity degree, sensed what most of his Kennedy administration colleagues could not: religion mattered on such questions, and ignoring or marginalizing it would only lead to trouble. Yet this did nothing to prevent Sargent Shriver, head of the Peace Corps, from warning that while he was willing to work with religion, no faith-based group would receive assistance "unless it forswears all proselytizing on the project it proposes." This effectively ruled out—or at the very least severely constrained—cooperation with missionaries, who were by now mostly evangelicals.[25]

Christian conservatives had greater success infiltrating the military, where their mix of faith, patriotism, and anticommunism was wildly popular. At the Glenview Naval Air Station on Chicago's North Shore, Fred Schwarz held regular classes on the basics of Christian anticommunism, with each class attracting crowds in the hundreds. Even more important were the activities of army chief of staff general Harold K. Johnson, an evangelical who promoted Christian morality for all U.S. soldiers. Johnson was a member of several conservative religious groups for enlisted personnel, such as Protestant Men of the Chapel and the Officers' Christian Union, and held regular prayer breakfasts at various U.S. bases around the world. Schwarz and Johnson helped build a growing Christian phenomenon that would transform the armed forces over the next four decades.[26]

UNSURPRISINGLY, then, when the Nixon administration came into office and did not pursue a counterreformationist foreign policy, it came in for fierce criticism from conservatives. Détente and the opening to China headed their list of complaints. Hargis, always a good bellwether of fundamentalist attitudes, was incensed at the new relationship with Mao and the resultant betrayal of Chiang Kai-shek and Taiwan. "A Bible-believing Christian Conservative, by definition, is anti-Communist, and therefore anti-Red China," he angrily wrote shortly after Nixon's historic visit to Beijing. "In this hour," he concluded with a reference to the ancient Israelite dispute over the sacrilegious worshipping of the golden calf, America needed "more Amoses and fewer Amaziahs." The Christian Nationalist Crusade leveled a similar charge against what it condemned as the dangerous prevarications of détente: "Under the Kissinger policy, the West is foreswearing interference in the affairs of Communist bloc countries while the Soviet Union continues to undermine countries of Western Europe in an attempt to destroy the NATO Alliance system." In the words of Phyllis Schlafly, a pious, conservative Catholic from St. Louis who had become one of the Religious Right's first national leaders, Americans should be alarmed by Kissinger's "defeatism" and "surrender syndrome."[27]

According to conservatives, the answer to America's problems was not Kissingerian retrenchment but revival. Christian conservatives had always been among the most patriotic Americans. The early Cold War period, when patriotism, anticommunism, and Judeo-Christian faith became the agreed bases of Americanism, both accentuated and vindicated Christian nationalism. Americans needed to praise their country, not criticize it; they needed to assert their power abroad, not rein it in. In 1976, the year of the bicentennial, Jerry Falwell began hosting a series of "I Love America" rallies across the country; they ran every year until 1980, spreading a message of family, faith, and patriotism to audiences in the thousands. At each rally's conclusion, he would close with the same reading from scripture, II Chronicles 7:14: "If my people, which are called by my name, shall humble themselves, and pray, and seek my face, and turn from their wicked ways; then will I hear from heaven, and will forgive their sin, and will heal their land." Falwell's purpose was clear. "We are committed to revival in our time," he wrote to the White House in announcing his plan to hold the rallies. "We believe our nation must come back to God or else." If the president would not do it, someone else had to.[28]

But there was more to the conservative worldview than simple old-time patriotism. Just as conservative opposition to civil rights legislation was not solely due to racism, Christian views on foreign policy were not entirely a product of reactionary nationalism and anticommunism. Instead, as with civil rights, the conservative worldview was shaped by a deep-rooted hostility to government interference and a fear of unrepresentative bureaucratic power. Recall the issues that spurred the creation of the Religious Right—school prayer, abortion, Christian academies—and then recall the institutions that pushed these issues into the conservative consciousness and onto its political agenda—the Supreme Court and the IRS, two of the most remote forms of concentrated secular power in the American political system. It is little wonder that people who prized local autonomy above almost everything else would portray the Supreme Court and IRS—or the National Council of Churches, for that matter—as servants of the Antichrist. The editors of *Christianity Today*, America's largest evangelical magazine, asked President Gerald Ford what he planned to do about the "threat to religious liberty by big government and expanding government regulations." This visceral anti-statism found expression in evangelical views on foreign policy in support of unilateralism. It even helps explain the endurance of vitriolic anticommunism in an era when other Americans, including the Nixon administration, were pursuing détente. As one fundamentalist commentator wrote, communism "is fundamentally a monopoly. . . . When it is complete, there is no way to counteract it, no way to escape it, and no political power left to change it. It is a total control of the life style." It was the logical culmination of big government.[29]

When blended together in the Christian conservative worldview, patriotism, local autonomy, and anti-statism combined to produce an implacable hostility to international organizations and multilateral institutions, such as the World Bank, the European Economic Community, and the United Nations—derided by Edgar Bundy of the Church League of America as the "sacred cow of the one-worlders and liberals." These were international equivalents of the concentrated power wielded at home by the Supreme Court, the IRS, and the Department of Education. And like the Court and the IRS, these world bodies would enforce secularism and conformity on a people whose faith had always been defiantly populist and nonconformist. Not even UNICEF could escape the fundamentalists' wrath: the Daughters of the American Revolution banned its members from purchasing UNICEF Christmas cards lest they contribute funding to a secularist world state, while Carl McIntire commanded his followers to shun UNICEF donations on Halloween. "This plan to associate the United Nations with Christmas and have it replace the religious aspect of Christmas," explained May Gaskill of the DAR's National Defense Committee, "is believed to be part of a broader Communist plan to destroy all religious beliefs and customs so that one day we shall awaken to find that December 25 is being celebrated as a One World Peace Festival instead of the birthday of Christ." If Americans ceded too much control to the UN, they would be compelled to follow orders from non-Christians. As the Pentecostal R. A. Kerby pointed out, "the majority vote in the U.N. is now being cast by heathen peoples from Asia and Africa" who, along with American liberals and mainliners, worshipped the United Nations as a false idol. With the United States as one member nation among many, unilateralism was the conservative way of preserving America's local autonomy against the encroachments of a dreaded world state.[30]

Similarly, like the NCC at home, conservatives condemned the World Council of Churches with being too large, remote, and unresponsive to the actual views and values of practicing Christians. To conservative fury, in 1975 the WCC assembly elected Metropolitan Nikodim, the Russian Orthodox archbishop of Leningrad, to its six-member presidential council. No religious leader could advance so high in the Soviet system without being in league with the Kremlin, American evangelicals and fundamentalists charged. Allowing Nikodim to serve with the WCC proved the organization's lack of true faith. "The strategy of the Communists in the use of the Moscow clergy has been successful," concluded McIntire, not least because American mainline liberals had allowed it to happen. Worse, at the same council the WCC condemned Israel for its occupation of the West Bank and treatment of Palestinians while remaining silent on Soviet violations of human rights. "It is a case of pinkeye," stated Ohio congressman John Ashbrook on the House floor, "literally and figuratively."[31]

The United Nations attracted fear not only for its supposed capability to weaken America, but also for the future role it would play in the end of the world. Premillennialists and those who shared their belief in the imminent unfolding of biblical prophecy were certain that these world organizations would provide the vehicle for Satan's challenge to Christ, as foretold, or at least alluded to, in the Books of Daniel and Revelation. Christ would return to earth only after the forces of hell had established their rule in the Tribulation, presumably through a global tyranny. Thus institutional integration and globalization were seen as important prerequisites for the coming of the end of the world. Satan, most fundamentalists agreed, would impose "a World State, based on collectivism, the planned economy, the regimentation of the individual, and a political and religious dictatorship." Some took this to mean the UN, others that "the kingdom of the antichrist is the [European] Common Market." One of the decade's bestsellers, Hal Lindsey's 1970 prophecy book *The Late Great Planet Earth*, warned that the European Community was preparing the way for the armies of Satan. When the UN expelled Taiwan from its ranks and admitted the People's Republic of China instead—a decision made possible by Nixon and Kissinger's diplomacy—premillennialists took it as a sign that the end was near. Two decades later, in their wildly successful *Left Behind* series of apocalyptic prophecy novels, Tim LaHaye and Jerry Jenkins created the character of Nicolae Carpathia as the Antichrist. His organization? The Global Community.[32]

Prophecy belief was important, but it was not the only theological determinant of the conservative Christian distrust of liberal internationalism. Temperamentally and ideologically, evangelicalism and fundamentalism were ill-suited to the finely balanced nuances of détente, diplomacy, and liberal internationalism. Christian conservatives reacted to 1960s liberalism, and its relativistic doctrines such as "situation ethics," with horror. They spoke of the need to return to basics—of faith, family, and nation. While the notion of compromise is central to the UN's mission, it is for the most part incompatible with Christian conservatism. Indeed, the very bases of evangelicalism and fundamentalism are ideological, theological, and cultural purity grounded in a refusal to compromise with the irreligious and immoral forces of liberalism—hence the emphasis on biblical inerrancy. As Moral Majority's Ed Dobson admitted after becoming disillusioned with political lobbying, "politics is essentially the art of compromise and negotiation, and fundamentalists don't place a high value on compromise and negotiation." Yet international organizations like the UN functioned on an endless series of daily compromises, and the very premise of the General Assembly of the United Nations—that each nation is respected as an equal simply on the basis of its sovereignty—required America to deal with devils, as equals, every day. This was not an especially desirous task when the devils in question included communists, atheists, anti-Israel Arabs, and anti-Americans the world over. Any act of compromise, even with the seemingly innocuous UNICEF, was instead an act of capitulation.[33]

Such charges were nothing new. As we have seen, the religious debate between nationalism and internationalism had been raging since the antebellum era. But by the 1970s, the nationalist argument had taken on a new urgency, simply because for the first time conservatives feared for the very existence of their way of life. Bans on school prayer and protections for abortion had much to do with it; so too did the relative weakness of American power in world politics, which the morally milquetoast policy of détente did little to quell. But the changing nature of the economy was also a significant factor in powering a conservative nationalist worldview. With rapid advances in technology—especially in computers, communications, and transportation—and with the cumbersome Bretton Woods system of fixed exchange rates coming under strain and giving way to financial deregulation, the U.S. economy spent the decade undergoing a painful transition from heavy industry and manufacturing to information and services. In other words, the U.S. economy was globalizing, exporting jobs where labor was cheaper and importing highly skilled workers. Comprised predominantly of people with lower incomes and lower levels of education, evangelicals and fundamentalists felt these changes acutely. Once again, elite, remote forces of concentrated power well beyond their reach or control—in this case, international economic organizations and multinational corporations—were affecting their daily lives. "As we look at this monolithic commercial system which has controlled the world and today controls our lives, we realize that the policies of nations are formed by and for commercial interests' sake," warned Chuck Smith, pastor of the fundamentalist Calvary Chapel in Southern California, one of the fastest-growing churches in America, in 1977. "More and more our lives are being manipulated. . . . We are victims, and we are helpless to do anything about it. These men play chess with the lives of the people of the world."[34]

In 1975, the United Nations embarked on two initiatives that appeared to confirm its meddling, irreligious intent. First, the UN General Assembly passed a resolution officially condemning Zionism "as a threat to world peace," an "imperialist ideology," and "a form of racism and racial discrimination." Americans, whether Jewish or not, largely reacted with outrage; the next day, a crowd of 100,000 pro-Israel demonstrators choked the streets of midtown Manhattan. Daniel Patrick Moynihan, the U.S. ambassador to the UN, angrily noted that "there cannot since the 1930s in Germany have been as much anti-Semitism spoken in one chamber." The normally even-tempered National Conference of Christians and Jews was so shaken it called for the United States to withdraw from the UN altogether. It would have seemed a radical, shocking, even unfeasible suggestion had not Congress already been in serious deliberation to do just that.[35]

Second, in pronouncing 1975 as International Women's Year (IWY) the UN promoted a very different measure that provoked a very similar U.S. response. Americans were just then in the midst of an impassioned debate over whether to ratify the Equal Rights Amendment. When Congress passed ERA, in 1972, it seemed uncontroversial, even straightforward. But government-mandated gender equality touched the same nerve already rubbed raw by school prayer, abortion, birth control, and civil rights. Motivated largely by religion, antifeminist activists charged that ERA would undermine the sanctity of the family and force traditionally minded women to change their ways. The UN's International Women's Year was framed around a summit in Mexico City that, for good measure, also passed its own resolution condemning Zionism and equating it with South African apartheid. In turn, the Mexico City conference spawned a partner conference in Houston to meet two years hence. Dianne Edmondson, an activist from Oklahoma, called for the burgeoning ranks of conservative women to show "how as Christians we must do good as the Lord commands by opposing this evil." Phyllis Schlafly, who led the antifeminist opposition, suspected that the UN was using IWY to influence the American debate on ERA. Schlafly's interfaith coalition of female Catholics, Mormons, evangelicals, and fundamentalists mobilized against ERA and IWY simultaneously, portraying them as two sides of the same socialist coin that would destroy America's sovereignty and morality. Conservative women held a parallel conference, also in Houston, that undermined the IWY conference. But Schlafly also thought the pro-ERA camp had overreached itself. The "Women's Lib movement has sealed its own doom by deliberately hanging around its own neck the albatross of abortion, lesbianism, pornography and Federal control." She was right: IWY failed to generate much support beyond its adherents, and ERA died not long afterward when it failed to win enough state capitals to secure ratification. Local autonomy had been preserved.[36]

A Judeo-Christian Foreign Policy

O N THE WHOLE, Jews stood apart from the convulsions generated by the American reformation and counterreformation. Of course, they participated in the cultural, social, and political movements of the day, particularly on behalf of liberalism. But Judaism, as a faith, did not experience a revolution. Instead, by the 1960s, Jews were secularizing at rates higher than Christians, and in 1964 *Look* magazine featured the plight of "the vanishing American Jew."[1]

But then three developments, none of them directly related to or caused by American Jewry, reinvigorated a commitment to both Jewish cultural identity and Judaism. The first was the emergence of the Holocaust as a significant cultural and political force in American life. Jews had never exactly ignored or forgotten the Holocaust, but neither had they dwelt on it. It evoked an unsettling range of emotions—guilt, shame, remorse, anger—that they understandably wanted to avoid. And avoid them they could, so long as Germany had been rehabilitated as a faithful NATO ally against communism and so long as nothing stirred the collective memory of the awful events of only a decade or two before. In 1960, however, Israel captured one of the key architects of the Final Solution, Adolf Eichmann, in Argentina; he was tried, convicted of mass murder, and executed in 1962. Hannah Arendt, a political philosopher and theorist of totalitarianism and herself a Jew, attended the trial and published her observations in a hugely controversial book, *Eichmann in Jerusalem: A Report on the Banality of Evil.* The trial, followed by Arendt's book, reintroduced the Holocaust to a people who had thus far discussed it only privately, in hushed tones. For a younger generation of American Jews, the Holocaust was no longer taboo. Over time, it would instead become a basic common denominator of what it meant to be Jewish.[2]

The second development, equally important, reinforced the new resolve among Jews to defend their identity in the modern world. Over the course of six days in June 1967, Israel and its Arab neighbors fought a war for supremacy in the Middle East. Tensions had been ever-present since the founding of Israel in 1948, and following the Suez Crisis of 1956 Egypt and Israel began a low-level state of almost continual warfare. In

May 1967, Egypt closed the Straits of Tiran to Israeli shipping, and armies on all sides mobilized. It was unclear whether the Arab coalition—Egypt, Syria, Jordan, and Iraq—was about to invade, but to Israel and its supporters in America it seemed clear that the very existence of the Jewish state was at risk. On June 5, Israel launched a surprise preemptive attack against its main threat, Egypt, and went on the offensive; six days later, on June 10, the Arabs sued for peace. For Arabs, the war was an unmitigated disaster that resulted in Israel's capture of Jerusalem and occupation of the West Bank and Gaza. For Jews, however, it was celebrated as a resounding triumph that ensured the survival of Israel.

For American Jews, the impact was momentous. Zionism was widely applauded but its popularity had never been especially deep or profound. To most American Jews, Israel was an abstraction that held little emotional attachment. The Six Day War reversed those attitudes almost instantly. Jews, Rabbi Marc H. Tanenbaum explained to an appreciative audience at the Southern Baptist Theological Seminary in Louisville, "have experienced a profound transformation since the six-day war . . . No one can truly understand Jews or Judaism today . . . unless one takes into account the magnitude and depth of this transformation, which verges on collective *metanoia*," or spiritual conversion. At first, Jews feared that Israel would be annihilated, driven into the sea by the same atavistic forces of anti-Semitism that had fueled the Holocaust. Then, with Israel's stunningly lopsided and completely unexpected victory, Jews celebrated the victory of Jewish might and resolve. If the war began as potentially another Holocaust, it ended with a new dawn of Jewish perseverance. Among American Jews, support for Israel now became *the* identifier of both their Judaism and their Jewishness. Anti-Zionist Jewish groups, such as the American Council for Judaism, closed their doors after June 1967 for lack of support. This Jewish American identification with Israel deepened with the Yom Kippur War of October 1973, when Egypt and Syria attacked Israel on two separate fronts only to wind up with the same result: an Israeli victory. Israel, wrote social scientist Charles Liebman afterward, "provides the major symbolic content for the American Jewish religion today."[3]

Finally, the rise of multiculturalism enabled Jewish pride to flourish in a domestic climate that was receptive to ethnic assertions of a unique and not originally "American" identity. Before, the immigrant experience was based upon the melting pot and its assumptions of assimilation. However, the emergence of a powerful rights consciousness among minorities in the 1960s, pushed forward by the civil rights and Black Power movements and the removal of immigration quotas, challenged the legitimacy of the melting pot. Native Americans followed with their own "Red Power" movement and the establishment of political action groups like the American Indian Movement. Descendants of older European immigrant generations, among them Jews but also Italians, Poles, Irish, and Greeks, claimed recognition for their own special qualities, a development marked by Michael Novak's 1972 book *The Rise of the Unmeltable Ethnics*—which, not coincidentally, marked the beginning of his conversion from leftist radicalism to neoconservatism. In multicultural America, nobody doubted the patriotism of these ethnic communities. It was now safe to proclaim the virtues of old world ethnicities—and faiths. Indeed, it was not only safe but fashionable. Non-Jewish Americans, mired in their own humiliating stalemate in Vietnam, applauded Israel's decisiveness, strength, and vigor against Arab enemies who were indelibly, if not always accurately, associated with Islam. Not coincidentally, Conservative Judaism, an American innovation that had attempted to preserve Jewish traditions by subsuming them within a generic Americanism, declined in the 1960s and '70s at the expense of Orthodoxy.[4]

Moreover, Jewish self-confidence and mainstream acceptance bolstered the already considerable political influence of American Jews. Though Jewish support for Israel had already played a large role in domestic politics, it had not yet coalesced into one of the most effective lobbies in Washington. The Six Day War changed that almost overnight. Donations to the American Israel Political Action Committee and other pro-Israel groups soared; memberships to the major Jewish organizations also increased. While most Jews remained liberal despite their climb up the socioeconomic ladder—Milton Himmelfarb quipped that they lived like Episcopalians but voted like Puerto Ricans—their backing for Israel came at a time when many of their fellow liberals were becoming increasingly critical of Israel, especially its occupation of the territories seized in the 1967 war, and sympathetic to the Palestinians. Though they remained loyal Democrats, on policy toward the Middle East and the Soviet Union Jews often found common cause with the Republican Party. With an appeal in both parties, and with their population scattered throughout the country but concentrated in key states—Florida, New York, and California in particular—Jews were able to influence the domestic debate on Middle East policy, sometimes (but not always) decisively. Their opinions certainly could not be ignored, no matter which party was in the White House. From a loose collective of various Zionist organizations, the Israel Lobby was born.[5]

Thanks in large part to Israel's victories in the Arab-Israeli wars of 1967 and 1973, the new Jewish self-confidence also coincided with the sudden reemergence of Christian Zionism. Swinging wildly across the ideological spectrum, most Christian conservatives had abandoned anti-Semitism for Christian Zionism, or at the very least a pro-Israel and anti-Arab view. Whereas Jews had once been vilified as Christ-killers and money manipulators, Israel now stood at the heart of premillennialist prophecy belief in America—all other developments, be they the activities of the United Nations or the Soviet Union, were dependent upon those of the Jewish state. As evangelicalism and fundamentalism surged in popularity and numbers in the 1970s, premillennial dispensationalism and other forms of prophecy belief surged with them, even into mainstream culture. Hal Lindsey's *Late Great Planet Earth* popularized biblical prophecy and rejoiced that recent developments in Israel had brought humanity to the brink of the end times. In order to protect Israel, and thus help ensure the unfolding of prophecy, Bible-believing Christians became arch-Zionists. Already distrustful of socialist Baath parties, pan-Arabism, and Islam, evangelical Christian Zionists had little to moderate their pro-Israel views. Among non-Jews, they quickly became the Jewish state's staunchest defenders.[6]

Just as important was the rise in support for Israel among liberals. In the 1950s, pro-Israel mainline Protestants such as Reinhold Niebuhr had been anomalies; now, in the 1970s, they represented the mainstream. Several developments were responsible. The emergence of Holocaust memory had a profound impact on Christians as well as Jews. In light of the Holocaust, Israel's plight in the 1967 and 1973 wars led many newly sympathetic Christians to rally to its side. "The Yom Kippur attack on Israel, and the threat posed, are as vicious a challenge as that put by Hitler's 'final solution' just a generation ago," said the mainline group Christians Concerned for Israel in a statement typical of wider attitudes. The Judeo-Christian ethic and the civil rights movements had made prejudice against Jews—and by extension, Israel—unacceptable, even un-American. Many Christians, particularly mainline liberals, criticized Israeli occupation of the West Bank and harsh treatment of the Palestinians, but the prevailing attitude was broadly sympathetic to Israel. Overall, then, the plight of the Jews, be they Israeli or Soviet, fit perfectly into several of the major narratives of Americanism, for liberals as well as conservative evangelicals.[7]

UNDER PRESIDENTS Nixon and Ford, détente became the centerpiece of U.S. grand strategy. It was not an attempt to end the Cold War but to manage it (though that was not how Nixon and Kissinger portrayed it to the American people). Its main components included both the substantive—the expansion of East-West trade, nuclear arms limitation talks, ending the Vietnam War—and the symbolic—Nixon's stroll along the Great Wall of China, his trip to Russia in 1972, a visit by Soviet Premier Leonid Brezhnev to the United States the following year. The 1975 Helsinki Conference, a comprehensive attempt to settle the status of Europe, was a mixture of both substance and symbol and marked the climax of détente. By the time Gerald Ford left office in 1977, détente was already reeling under the strains of both domestic and international politics. It would be dead by 1979, the victim not only of great power rivalry but also the unpredictable vagaries of U.S. domestic politics.[8]

In fact, the seeds of détente's demise had been sown shortly after the Moscow summit between Nixon and Brezhnev in May 1972. Despite its potential to ease the world's nuclear nightmare, some Americans were becoming restless with détente. They had never been comfortable with the warmer, cooperative relations with Moscow that détente needed to function. Their focal point was an emotionally charged issue that ultimately led to détente's unraveling: the Soviet Union's treatment of its Jews. Because of the Soviets' semi-official persecution of Jews (not unlike Russia's semi-official pogroms in an earlier age), Soviet Jews desperately wanted to immigrate to Israel; and Israel, now a strong U.S. ally, desperately wanted to receive them. The Kremlin consented to the right of Jewish emigration, but only on individual payment of a punitive fee—by some counts as much as $30,000—which only further inflamed opinion in the United States. It was one thing for the Soviets to persecute their own people; it was another thing entirely to prevent them from fleeing such persecutions. To the rights-conscious American mind, here was as clear a violation of human rights as one could find, especially the freedoms of worship and movement.

Since the late nineteenth century, the status of Jews in Russia and the Soviet Union had been a perennial concern in the United States. But it only became a major issue capturing the attention of those beyond the Jewish community when political or geopolitical conditions gave it a wider resonance. Such was the case in the early 1970s, with the maturation of a global human rights discourse that had begun with the founding of the United Nations in 1945 and the signing of its Universal Declaration of Human Rights in 1948. Suppressed by the geopolitical exigencies of the Cold War, human rights promotion was not widespread until the 1970s when legitimacy, based on a respect for human rights, became a genuinely significant factor in world politics. Human rights activism was especially pronounced at the grassroots. With increasing domestic political support in a number of countries, NGOs dedicated to the promotion and protection of human rights grew in size, stature, and authority throughout the decade. Much of the impetus for this growth came from liberals in support of liberal causes, such as the exposing of war crimes and police brutality in right-wing authoritarian regimes. And in many cases, U.S. support for dictators became as noteworthy as the dictators' crimes themselves.[9]

However, the rise of human rights also fueled an anti-communist agenda, for fewer regimes in the world violated human rights as systematically as the Soviet Union and its satellite states in Eastern Europe. The range of communist human rights abuses was vast, but anti-détente activists focused on two in particular: religious liberty and emigration. Freedom of worship had a long history in debates over U.S. foreign policy, often emerging from the bottom up to influence policymaking elites. This was certainly the case over the treatment of Soviet Jews, an issue that Nixon and Kissinger wished would just disappear. But at a time when religion was again flourishing in the public square, when the Religious Right was in formation and flexing its muscles, when Israel gave American Jews a new confidence, and when human rights was a legitimate concern for international relations, Soviet Jews presented themselves as a perfect vehicle for the destruction of détente from within the United States. In turn, with its presumably universal relevance, religion was an ideal vehicle for the promotion of universal human rights.

For American Jews, supported by their Christian sympathizers, the status of their coreligionists in the Soviet Union was nothing new. In 1963, prompted by reports of orchestrated mob violence against Jews, the City of Philadelphia passed a resolution calling on President Kennedy "to reaffirm the unequivocal opposition of our country to acts of repression and discrimination against the Jewish people of the Soviet Union," which City Council president Paul D'Ortona then passed on to the White House. The next year, protesters marched on the Soviet UN mission in New York and listened to denunciations of Soviet anti-Semitism by Senators Kenneth Keating, Jacob Javits, and senatorial hopeful Robert F. Kennedy. In 1965, the American Jewish Conference on Soviet Jewry asked the Johnson administration for public support in its fight against the Kremlin's "policy of forced assimilation which has brought the second largest Jewish community in the world today to the brink of religious and cultural extinction." And in 1968, Republican presidential nominee Richard Nixon condemned Moscow's interference with Jewish education and religious training. Overall, however, advocates of Soviet Jews received little comfort from the White House and State Department.[10]

Much as he wanted to leave it on the campaign trail, Nixon continued to face the issue as president. In March 1969, Lewis Weinstein of the American Jewish Conference on Soviet Jewry, an organization that had strong backing from virtually every major Jewish group in the country, asked Nixon for a meeting to discuss ways to ease the burden on Soviet Jews and allow them to emigrate to Israel. And for the next eight years, the cause of Soviet Jews would simply not go away, no matter how inconvenient it was for détente. Throughout the presidencies of Richard Nixon and his successor, Gerald Ford, a wide range of groups—Jewish and Christian, religious and secular—maintained constant pressure on the White House. In 1973, on the twenty-fifth anniversary of Israel's founding, nearly 100,000 demonstrators—many of them dressed symbolically in striped pajamas to resemble both concentration camp victims and

Soviet prison inmates—chanted "Free Them Now" and marched through the streets of New York to highlight the condition of Soviet Jews. During Brezhnev's U.S. tour, supposed to be a watershed in the establishment of normal U.S.-Soviet relations, demonstrators hounded the Soviet premier in every city he visited. The National Conference of Catholic Bishops called upon the Soviet Union to respect the religious rights of its Jewish population. "The conscience of humanity is aroused," claimed Bishop James W. Malone of Youngstown, Ohio, "and the USSR must understand that its anti-Jewish policies are morally intolerable to free men everywhere." The San Francisco Labor Council made a similar appeal by focusing on the case of Mikhail Shtern, a renowned endocrinologist who had been sentenced to hard labor in a Siberian prison after his two sons had successfully fled to Israel; other defenders of Shtern publicized his case with ads in the *Washington Post*. More incongruously given his geopolitical views, Hans Morgenthau, a University of Chicago political scientist and the founder of American realism, implored Nixon not to abandon Soviet Jews to their communist-controlled fate. Détente, he said, was simply not worth it.[11]

As the issue of Soviet Jews grew, it broadened to include the rights of Soviet Christians as well. Alexandra L. Tolstoy, the daughter of the great Russian novelist who fled to America after the Bolshevik Revolution, wrote Nixon in 1970 to highlight the anguish of the Russian Orthodox community in the Soviet Union, who could practice their religion only under very tight restrictions established by the Kremlin. Ukrainian Americans did the same for the rights of persecuted Catholics in Ukraine, as did Latvian and Lithuanian Americans for persecuted Lutherans and Catholics in the Baltic states. Likewise, American evangelicals pressed the case of beleaguered Soviet Protestants, particularly Baptists and Pentecostals. Even the religious freedom of the Russian Orthodox Church, assumed by many to be a stooge of the Kremlin, became an issue. In a return to the strategy first deployed by FDR and Truman, Americans were once again turning to religious liberty as a geopolitical weapon—only this time, the pressure was coming almost entirely from below.[12]

Like Kennedy and Johnson before him, however, Nixon was unwilling to go beyond platitudes about the importance of religious liberty because, like Kennedy and Johnson before him, he was unwilling to risk détente over what was essentially an internal matter of a sovereign nation. Yet for Nixon, the stakes were much higher. Kennedy had only just begun the process of détente, while Johnson had to set it aside due to the complications of Vietnam. For Nixon and Kissinger, on the other hand, détente was central: without Soviet cooperation, they believed they could not end the Vietnam War or maintain leverage in their new relationship with China. And precisely because détente was so central to Nixon and Kissinger, it was also where they were most vulnerable. What the Soviets wanted from the United States was trade, surplus food, and credit; what they prized most was Most Favored Nation status (MFN), which would give them the same access to American goods and technology as any other country and would allow them to develop the full potential of their vast natural gas reserves. Nixon and Kissinger were happy to oblige, but these economic aspects gave détente's opponents their opening, for only Congress could authorize the executive's economic promises to Moscow.

Inconveniently for Nixon and Kissinger, the Senate's leading critic of détente was also its fiercest advocate for Soviet Jews. Senator Henry M. "Scoop" Jackson was a classic Cold War liberal from Washington State cut very much from the same cloth as Harry Truman. In domestic affairs, Jackson was a progressive, allied closely to organized labor and an early supporter of the civil rights movement. But on foreign policy, he was staunchly anticommunist and a tireless proponent of a large military, positions he stuck to into the 1970s after they had become deeply unfashionable among most other Democrats. He remained an unwavering supporter of the Vietnam War, even after Nixon was elected president and many other Democrats became full-time doves. This was to be expected for a politician from a state that relied economically on defense spending—for good reason, Jackson's nickname was "the Senator from Boeing."

But Jackson's fierce anticommunism and his commitment to America's military strength were matters of conviction, too. Colleagues and observers, allies and enemies all noted how relentlessly moralistic Jackson's political convictions were. Kissinger, himself not a pushover, marveled at Jackson's tenacity during their frequent battles over détente: "Stolid, thoughtful, stubborn, as could be expected from the combination of Scandinavian origin and Lutheran theology, Jackson mastered problems not with flashy rhetoric or brilliant maneuvers but with relentless application and undeflectable persistence." His ostentatious defense of Soviet Jews smacked of presidential posturing, especially for a non-Jew, and he made no secret about his White House ambitions for 1976. But to Jackson, Soviet Jews represented something much more than political opportunity: he was one of the Senate's strongest supporters of Israel, he genuinely sympathized with the plight of Soviet Jews, and their symbolic power offered him a devastating weapon in his fight against détente. It was no coincidence that Jackson mentored a generation of neoconservatives who were hard-line anti-Soviet and pro-Israel, among them Richard Perle, Paul Wolfowitz, Elliott Abrams, and Douglas Feith. He was, Kissinger later acknowledged, the Nixon administration's worst possible enemy: "a man of high principle" who was also "stubborn and persistent."[13]

And like Truman, Jackson abhorred religious prejudice. He was a vocal supporter of Kennedy's campaign in 1960 and came out strongly against

Kennedy's nativist Protestant critics, especially Norman Vincent Peale. He credited his feelings on religious liberty to a formative experience from his childhood in Everett, Washington. When local children taunted one of Everett's only Jewish residents with shouts of "Kike!" Jackson's mother rushed out to chase them away. "My mother was a Christian who believed in a strong Judaism," he later recalled. "She taught me to respect the Jews, help the Jews! It was a lesson I never forgot." Thus while Jackson was determined to undermine détente, the cause of Soviet Jews was a matter of principle as well as politics. Senator Jacob Javits, a Republican from New York and a key Jackson ally, claimed that their crusade was not simply a way to attack détente but a means to protect American values and the universal human right of religious liberty. Attacking détente was indeed one of Jackson's prime motivations, but the most important goal was to relieve pressure on Soviet Jews.[14]

Jackson's partner on foreign policy, his chief legislative aide Dorothy Fosdick, had strong views of her own. The daughter of Harry Emerson Fosdick, Dorothy Fosdick had been raised on debates over the role of Christian morality in international relations. She may have been the daughter of the famous pacifist from Riverside Church, but she also formed an intellectual bond with Reinhold Niebuhr at Union Theological Seminary next door. Her worldview owed something to both men but in the end resembled that of neither: she integrated her father's unbending idealism with Niebuhr's realist emphasis on original sin and willingness to deploy power. The result was a highly moralistic sense of right and wrong in international politics, and a fierce conviction that the United States had a responsibility to right the wrongs. Observers called her "hard-headed, warm-hearted." With a doctorate in international relations from Columbia, Fosdick was also a Christian intellectual in her own right. She attended the landmark 1937 Oxford ecumenical conference as a missionary delegate; that same year, she gave a nationally broadcast radio address on religious liberty and the threats it faced from Nazism, fascism, and communism. As Jackson's national security assistant, Fosdick bolstered her boss's position on religious liberty with theological and intellectual substance.[15]

While Jackson and Fosdick led from the Senate, defenders of Soviet Jews could also be found in the House of Representatives. John G. Dow of New York suggested to Nixon that the Voice of America start broadcasting its programs into the Soviet Union in Yiddish, the mother tongue of Soviet Jews. Charles Vanik of Ohio was also a relentless campaigner for Soviet Jews, and soon teamed up with Jackson to sponsor congressional legislation on their behalf. But nobody was as indefatigable as Robert F. Drinan of Massachusetts. As a Jesuit priest, Drinan had a highly developed ethical worldview; as a practicing lawyer and former dean of the Boston College Law School, he also had a finely honed legal mind. He combined both his moralism and his legalism in a fierce advocacy of universal human rights. Drinan had made his name as an outspoken opponent of Vietnam and won election to Congress in 1970 on an anti-war platform. But his other main foreign policy concern—and the most important one for his many Jewish constituents in suburban Boston—was the condition of Soviet Jewry. To Drinan, both issues were grounded in basic human rights concerns: in one case, the United States was at fault, in the other the Soviet Union. What was important was not the moral superiority of communism or capitalism but the protection of rights of those who could not protect themselves. Like Javits, he was sympathetic to the idea of détente, but not if it came at the expense of morality. Not coincidentally, in campaigning for Soviet Jews Drinan often used the peaceful civil disobedience tactics from his campaigns for the rights of Vietnamese and Cambodians. In one episode, he and New York Congressman Benjamin Rosenthal barged into the Soviet Embassy in Washington demanding to present a petition on Soviet Jews to the ambassador; after a half-hour standoff, the two left without a meeting but with a clear moral and political victory. In another, Drinan asked Kissinger to help him obtain a visa to visit the Soviet Union. He would certainly have known that the Soviets would deny his application. The important thing was to embarrass them in the process—and Kissinger with them.[16]

But Kissinger was not so easily moved. Though Jewish himself, realism was the strongest current running through his worldview. The world turned on states exercising their power, not on individual people or groups exercising their human rights. "I have no doubt that Soviet Jews as a group are severely disadvantaged," he told a colleague in April 1969, long before détente had become the overriding strategic priority, "but there is virtually no way in which we as a government can exert pressure on the Soviet Union to ease their plight. In fact," Kissinger continued in what would become a common refrain over the next eight years, American pressure would be "counterproductive" because the Soviets "are exceptionally defensive about the Jewish problem, and inevitably regard any official US Government action on the subject as an attempt to interfere in Soviet internal affairs." In late 1973, in a letter to his friend and former Harvard colleague David Riesman, Kissinger explained that "in our relations with the Soviets and in our efforts to improve those relations . . . we have recognized that differences in ideology and basic differences between our two systems will continue to exist." Crusades to remove those differences would only lead to tension, possibly even war, which was decidedly not in the American national interest and certainly not at a time when the nation's international power was at a low point. The Soviets had actually dealt with the United States quite reasonably, Kissinger said on another occasion; it was Jackson who demanded too much.[17]

Even under tremendous political pressure, Kissinger's realism remained unaffected by the protests of Jackson, Javits, Vanik, Drinan, and other advocates of Soviet Jews. The important thing was stable relations between states, especially if they were nuclear superpowers. All else, including human rights, would then follow from détente. In the meantime, Americans simply had to be patient. It was not only unrealistic but also dangerous, Kissinger protested in 1969 to Daniel Patrick Moynihan, at the time a colleague but later a great critic of détente on human rights grounds, to expect the Nixon administration to do anything more. If the Kremlin felt threatened, he said in response to Moynihan's moralistic exhortations, it "will probably act in regard to Soviet Jews exactly as it has recently in Czechoslovakia—in a cold-blooded manner designed to protect perceived Soviet national interests. If necessary, they will completely defy the UN Charter and world opinion." Be reasonable, Kissinger seemed to be saying not only to Moynihan but to all his critics: détente will draw the Soviets into a more Western orbit and thus will give the United States precious leverage. "We will be able to secure an improvement in the lot of Soviet Jewry only if we somehow can convince the Soviets that an improvement will be in their own national interest, or conversely, that they will suffer some meaningful national damage if an improvement does not take place." The promotion of justice could only be possible with the establishment of order. Détente was the first important step. But for now, Moynihan and the others would have to wait.[18]

Ironically, it was precisely the last part of Kissinger's peroration to Moynihan that advocates of Soviet Jews had in mind: make the Soviets suffer the consequences of their brutality. Jackson was the most dogmatic. He believed that national sovereignty was no defense against the violation of human rights, a commonplace idea today but a new development in world politics then. Human rights were universal, not particular, and they transcended national borders. The condition of Soviet Jews "is not just a Jewish issue," he declared, "but an American issue and a great humanitarian issue." Jackson did not suggest going to war over Soviet Jews, but he did think it entirely reasonable for the United States to use whatever leverage it had to induce the Soviets to let their Jewish population emigrate. The universality of human rights, and the confluence on this issue between American ideals and interests, made it essential. Jackson made this point with characteristic emotion, telling a crowd in Denver: "Today, while we're bargaining with the Russians over dollars and rubles, let's do some bargaining on behalf of helpless human beings. When we talk about free trade let's talk about free people, too."[19]

In private, however, Jackson doubted that this would actually work. He did not trust communist ideology, and he certainly did not trust the Soviet Union. The Kremlin would never do the right thing, even if it was in its own best interest. Despite his jeremiads, Jackson was certain that the diplomacy of quid pro quo—American capital, credit, goods, and technology in exchange for Soviet compliance on a number of geopolitical issues—would never work in America's favor. The concept that America, with its economic might, could induce changes in Soviet political behavior "is extremely doubtful," concluded a report prepared by Fosdick. Kissinger believed that expanded trade ties would make the Soviet Union beholden to the United States, but the "more likely result is Soviet leverage on the United States." Already skeptical about détente, angry at arms control (and the jobs it would cost Washington State), and convinced that trade would not relax Soviet restrictions on Jewish emigration, Jackson resolved to do all he could to scuttle the linchpin of Nixon and Kissinger's grand strategy.[20]

Neither Kissinger nor Jackson was willing to compromise to break this impasse (though to be fair to Kissinger, there was little he could do without abandoning détente, for only the Soviets could accede to Jackson's demands). When Nixon traveled to Moscow in May 1972, he and Brezhnev discussed a new trade relationship predicated on the Soviets receiving most favored nation (MFN) status. But when Nixon returned to Washington with hopes of getting Congress to pass a trade bill that would grant the Soviets MFN, Jackson moved swiftly to sabotage his plans. Jackson teamed up with Representative Vanik to sponsor an amendment explicitly forbidding MFN to any country that did not have open emigration policies. The Soviets were unlikely to change their policy, not simply because it would undermine communist control but because they could never be seen to be bowing to foreign pressure to change their own internal political system. Without the trade bill, détente was effectively dead; but thanks to the Jackson-Vanik amendment, which had overwhelming support in Congress, the likelihood of the Soviets abiding by the terms of the trade bill were virtually nonexistent. Thus by the summer of 1972, even before Watergate, the Nixon administration found itself in a Cold War standoff not with the Kremlin, but the United States Congress.

During Brezhnev's visit to the United States in June 1973, with Jackson-Vanik hanging ominously over their heads, American and Soviet officials hammered out the final details of a comprehensive trade agreement. Brezhnev made a conspicuous effort to win over distrustful senators, particularly those who had spoken out in favor of Soviet Jews. Some were indeed won over—"I think he was opening the door and saying, for goodness' sake, can't we get along?" exclaimed Vance Hartke of Indiana—but not Jackson, who said the moribund communist economy made the Soviets as vulnerable as "a crippled bird" and thus susceptible to further American pressure. Nixon, he warned, must demand more in the way of concrete, verifiable guarantees that a certain number of Soviet Jews would be allowed to emigrate annually. Jackson eventually suggested the figure of 100,000, which was more than double the number of Jews who had left in any one year previously and was totally unacceptable to the Soviets. In October 1973, the Yom Kippur War complicated matters: the Soviets were now desperate to curry favor with their beleaguered Arab allies, who were of course opposed to any increase in Israel's Jewish population, and the United States was even more firmly allied to Israel. Meanwhile, throughout the entire process, the Israeli government quietly worked behind the scenes to build support for Jackson-Vanik on Capitol Hill.[21]

Now aware of the danger to the trade bill and thus to détente as a whole, Kissinger negotiated simultaneously with Jackson to lower his demands and with the Kremlin to allow more Jews to emigrate—and his sympathies were often with the Kremlin. Neither side, however, would concede very much, certainly not enough to break the deadlock. In late 1974, with Nixon felled by Watergate only to be replaced by a relatively weak figure in Gerald Ford and with congressional assertiveness on foreign policy at fever pitch thanks to Indochina, Congress was in no mood to compromise. The trade bill passed both houses of Congress in December 1974 and became law shortly after the new year—including Jackson-Vanik. As brilliant as he was, Kissinger had severely underestimated popular American sympathy for Soviet Jews and overestimated the appeal of détente. He dealt with the issue as a peripheral concern despite mounting evidence that it had become the central domestic political issue, even more important than arms control. Ever focused on the national interest, Kissinger lost sight of national ideals; when he realized their importance, he proved ill-suited to convey their meaning to the American people. He felt trapped—"Soviet behavior will depend on the incentive they feel in maintaining good relations with us" and Jackson had destroyed all such incentive, he complained to President Ford on the eve of the trade bill's passage—but he had been caught as much by his own political obtuseness as by Jackson's maneuvering.[22]

"Probably no other single question did more to sour the atmosphere of détente than the question of Jewish emigration from the Soviet Union," the Soviet ambassador to Washington, Anatoly Dobrynin, reflected ruefully in his memoirs. Kissinger agreed. Jackson had mobilized an anticommunist crusade for human rights and religious liberty behind a coalition of liberals and conservatives, Democrats and Republicans, Christians and Jews. Only in retirement did Kissinger realize what had happened. Jackson had acted as "the indispensable link" between "conservatives who hated

Communists and liberals who hated Nixon" and brought them together "in a rare convergence, like an eclipse of the sun." Yet it was not such a freak occurrence. Religious liberty touched a nerve deep in the American worldview and was not bound by partisanship or ideology. To be sure, the atmosphere of the 1970s, especially the new emphasis on universal human rights, was unusually conducive to Jackson's promotion of Soviet Jews. But in the American tradition, religious liberty is perhaps the oldest and most sacrosanct of all human rights. Kissinger was slow to recognize this, and in the end it cost him détente. And the Soviets never did receive MFN status.[23]

THIS WAS NOT the end of the story, however. Détente was reeling, already fragile by the time Jimmy Carter became president in 1977. The Soviets cut off all negotiations over Jewish emigration because they were no longer interested in MFN. Carter's election victory brought Jackson's presidential ambitions to a sudden end. But the defenders of religious freedom behind the Iron Curtain continued their crusade nonetheless.

Nearly two years before, on August 1, 1975, the United States, the Soviet Union, and over thirty other countries signed the Helsinki Final Act, the culmination of years of intricate negotiations toward a final settlement of postwar Europe. The Helsinki Accords, historians now agree, were a watershed moment in the Cold War, perhaps even marking the beginning of the end. But nobody perceived this at the time, and they were much derided in the United States as a sellout to communist tyranny and thus the ultimate sin Kissinger had ever committed in pursuit of détente. Behind a thicket of diplomatic bureaucratese, all signatories to the Helsinki Accords essentially agreed on two basic principles: the permanency of Europe's existing boundaries—in other words, recognition of communism as the legitimate governing system of half of Europe—and the inviolability of basic human rights. The Helsinki Final Act was a document with a paradox at its heart, with its simultaneous pursuit of both order and justice. And because nobody seriously believed the Soviets and their allies would respect human rights, everybody focused on the concessions to legitimizing communist rule. Critics charged Ford and Kissinger with appeasement, and "détente" became such a dirty word in American politics that Ford banished its use during the 1976 election campaign.[24]

Yet in the long run, Helsinki's human rights provisions were far more significant than its codification of borders. For the rest of the 1970s and into the '80s, U.S.–based "Helsinki groups," foremost among them Helsinki Watch (later renamed Human Rights Watch), partnered with churches and other religious groups to investigate communist rights abuses in Eastern Europe; they then reported these abuses to the media and Congress, making it impossible for the Soviets—and the Ford administration—to ignore them. The Ford Foundation and other philanthropic agencies, in addition to Congress itself, generously funded many of the Helsinki groups, such as the Christian Committee for the Defense of Believers' Rights in the USSR. Armed with the wording of the Final Act and backed by popular opinion in America, human rights campaigners like Father Drinan traveled to Romania, Israel, and elsewhere to interview victims of "Russia's irrational and erratic" record on religious freedom.[25]

For a region where faith had once flourished and where underground churches were still active—and, in the case of Poland, were openly active—religion provided Helsinki watchers with an ideal measurement to gauge communist compliance. Unsurprisingly, they found it wanting. "Too many people," Jackson told the National Council of Jewish Women in 1979, "think that Jackson-Vanik applies only to Soviet Jewry. It does not and never has." By way of example, he referred to a family of Pentecostals who had recently sought refuge in the U.S. Embassy in hopes of fleeing the Soviet Union. "Before the Soviets can enjoy MFN and other trade benefits from the American taxpayer, these people too must have a hope of escape." With information fed to him by Helsinki Watch and Christian Solidarity International, Jackson maintained the pressure on Soviet violations of religious freedom, of Christians as well as Jews. Motivated by the case of Reverend Georgi Vins, a Soviet Baptist, Jackson sponsored a 1979 Senate resolution on behalf of "Christians and other religious believers" in the Soviet Union who were "being persecuted simply because they desire to worship God according to the dictates of their conscience and the precepts of their faith rather than according to the dictates of the state." Vins and his family were then given asylum in the United States, where they settled down in Elkhart, Indiana. Shortly after, the Senate invited Vins to offer an official prayer, in which he gave thanks "for the gift of freedom" and "the goodness of the American people." Afterward, Jackson addressed his colleagues. "Throughout history," he declared triumphantly, "there have been men and women who have said: You dare not coerce conscience. You dare not coerce worship. We must obey God rather than man." This had always been a matter of God's law and U.S. law. Now, thanks to Helsinki, it was also Soviet law, and religious liberty advocates would not let them forget it.[26]

Ronald the Lionheart

IT WAS AN OCCASION imagined for decades. Now, in 1987, shortly before Christmas, Ronald Reagan and Mikhail Gorbachev had given the
world the gift of nuclear disarmament. On December 8, the two leaders
signed the Intermediate-range Nuclear Forces (INF) Treaty whereby the
United States and the Soviet Union pledged to eliminate their stockpiles
of intermediate-range nuclear arms. It was the first time the superpowers
had agreed not only to limit their nuclear arsenals but to begin reducing
them. It was a significant moment, and, after Gorbachev had returned to
Moscow, Reagan reflected on its significance in an address to the nation.
The INF Treaty symbolized his conviction that "the postwar policy of
containment is no longer enough." But instead of the hard-line rhetoric
of rollback with which people had associated Reagan, he offered a policy of
"world peace and world freedom." He hoped that all Americans could now
work together, with the Soviets, "for a day when all of God's children will
enjoy the human dignity that their creator intended." It was not backroom
negotiators who had scored the breakthrough, but the prayers of ordinary
Americans; and "in the prayers of simple people," Reagan explained, "there
is more power and might than that possessed by all the great statesmen
or armies of the Earth." And then he said his own prayer of thanksgiving:
"Let us then thank God for all His blessings to this nation, and ask Him
for His help and guidance so that we might continue the work of peace
and foster the hope of a world where human freedom is enshrined." The
Cold War ended two years later—peacefully.[1]

How did such a miraculous turn of events come to pass, especially
during one of the most bellicose anticommunist presidencies in history?
In part, the answer lies in Reagan's handling of religion, particularly the
symbolic power of religion on both sides of the Iron Curtain. Ironically,
Reagan's greatest feat was to make his own idealistic synthesis by successfully blending the militant nationalism of religious conservatives with the
peaceful aspirations of religious liberals. After strutting onto the world
stage as a brash new crusader, a self-styled Ronald the Lionheart, he discarded the sword of the spirit for a shield of faith. Not long after, the Cold

War—and Reagan's crusade—came to an end, and he exited the stage an unlikely peacemaker.

IN 1976, FOLLOWING a tumultuous decade of war and resistance to war, religious liberals hoped for a new president who could successfully transcend the Cold War and set America on its rightful path as the world's leader in the promotion of social justice. Instead, they got Jimmy Carter.

To be fair, Carter meant well. Having inherited a deindustrializing and globalizing economy and a foreign policy in crisis, he aimed to transcend the power politics of the Cold War, particularly the strictures of containment that bound America to a static and negative approach to the world. And for religious liberals, Carter offered something more: he was one of them, a pious progressive even if he was also an evangelical. A lifelong Southern Baptist, he had been a regular fixture at the First Baptist Church in his hometown of Plains, Georgia, throughout his early life: baptized at the age of eleven, Sunday school teacher as an adult, appointed deacon in 1958 at the age of thirty-four.[2]

After losing Georgia's 1966 Democratic gubernatorial primary, Carter completely reevaluated his life. Religion had always mattered to him without necessarily being central. His faith was well-grounded, yet it offered him little solace in defeat. But with the help of his evangelical sister, he had a conversion experience, accepted Christ into his heart, and became a born-again Christian. He continued teaching Sunday school and Bible study classes, not only to children but to adults as well, and traveled to the Northeast as a Southern Baptist missionary. But evangelicalism was not Carter's only religious influence. He invested a nearly sacred meaning into the Baptists' traditionally firm separation of church and state. Curiously, he also discovered original sin through the writings of Reinhold Niebuhr and incorporated them into his evangelical outlook. The result was idiosyncratic and, except in Carter's mind, paradoxical: a worldview based equally on evangelical optimism and conviction, Niebuhrian hostility to national pride and exceptionalism, and Baptist separationism. With his mind and self-confidence settled by his newfound faith, Carter resumed his political career. In 1970, four years after his third-place primary finish, he won the governorship of Georgia in a landslide. Six years later, benefitting from a post-Watergate, anti-Republican, anti-incumbent backlash, he narrowly defeated Gerald Ford in the presidential election. Once in the White House, this Niebuhrian evangelical tried to govern as both a moralist and a realist.[3]

On foreign policy, Carter should have been the ideal Social Gospel president. He was a Democrat of deep faith who had made progressive change one of his signature campaign themes. He condemned Nixon's and

Kissinger's "Machiavellian tactics," "secret diplomacy," "excessive concern with power politics," and "neglect of principles and morality." And he sought to transcend the Cold War and recalibrate U.S. foreign policy for a new era. Foremost on his agenda was the cause of human rights. Carter came into office in 1977 claiming to have found the source of the "modern concept of human rights" in the "laws of the prophets of the Judeo-Christian tradition," and vowed to make them his administration's overriding concern. According to National Security Adviser Zbigniew Brzezinski, who admitted he did not share his president's views on the subject, the administration's "commitment to human rights reflected Carter's own religious beliefs." And indeed, Carter fulfilled many liberal dreams, such as turning sovereignty of the Canal Zone over to Panama, canceling the B-1 bomber, and granting legal amnesty to Vietnam-era draft avoiders. He also pledged to continue détente and work with the Soviets to reduce tensions that could lead to nuclear war. But while complementary in theory, little did he realize just how contradictory the twin goals of peace and justice were in practice. Emphasizing human rights, for example, was bound to upset the Soviets, thereby undermining détente. And criticizing key U.S. allies for their own human rights abuses, as Brzezinski frequently warned, was bound to complicate the pursuit of U.S. foreign policy. The result produced the occasional triumph—the Camp David Accords in 1978—with tragedy—the Iran hostage crisis. Détente, already in a fragile state, eventually collapsed under the burgeoning weight of Carter's own contradictory impulses.[4]

Ironically for a man of such faith, part of Carter's problem was that he did not comprehend the religious mood of the country. In particular, he erred in trying too stringently to separate religion from politics. The most successful presidents deftly appealed to the shared principles of the civil religion, especially in the execution of foreign policy. Carter refused to do so. He did not hide his religiosity, but neither did he promote it. Jody Powell, Carter's press secretary, noted that his boss "probably quoted less Scripture . . . than any public official we've had in a long, long time"— indeed, probably since Thomas Jefferson. On the rare occasions when Carter did invoke scripture, it was often to chastise Americans. He set the tone at the outset, quoting from the Book of Micah (6:8) at his inaugural: "He hath showed thee, O man, what is good; and what doth the Lord require of thee, but to do justly, and to love mercy, and to walk humbly with thy God." Most damagingly, Carter issued Niebuhrian jeremiads when the country looked instead for uplift and inspiration. As presidential historian Gary Scott Smith points out, Carter was more prophet than priest: he reminded Americans of their sins and warned them of the hellfire that awaited if they did not repent. "Christ admonishes us against self-pride, against the condemnation of others, since we too are sinful," he declared on one occasion. On another, he told Americans that despite their "great natural resources and great wealth," they had "no special claim to be God's chosen people."[5]

On the surface, it seems surprising that the nation's first born-again president would be so tone deaf to broader cultural developments involving religion. Yet Carter's traditional Baptist faith in the separation of church and state blinded him to the changes occurring around him. "I have never found any incompatibility between my religious convictions and my duties as a President," he told a questioner at a town hall meeting in Pittsburgh during the 1980 campaign. "Every night I read a chapter in the Bible, with my wife when we're together; we read the same chapter when we're separated. It's part of my existence. I've done it for years." But, he continued, "I have never found anything in the Bible, in the Old or New Testament, that specifies whether or not we should have a Department of Education in the Federal Government or whether you should have a B-1 bomber or the air-launched cruise missiles or whether we should share with Panama . . . operation of the Panama Canal . . . Those kinds of measuring rods to define what is an acceptable Christian are contrary to my own beliefs." Carter mentioned the biblical politics of Jerry Falwell, and by extension other leaders of the Religious Right, as embodying the antithesis of his own beliefs. But he had forgotten that the Protestant left, though smaller in number, and major institutions like the Catholic Church, also looked to religion for political guidance. To them as to the Religious Right, the Bible was in fact pretty clear on whether the United States should develop the B-1.[6]

This was not only politically unwise but also geopolitically disastrous, for the Carter administration was just as indifferent to the revolutionary changes then sweeping through world religion. Almost certainly in reaction against the overweening ambitions and central planning of the modernist secular state, conservative religion was surging not only in the United States but worldwide. Beginning in the 1960s, Shiite fundamentalists in Iran struggled against the Shah's grand modernization projects. They aimed instead to return Iran to its fundamental values and morals just as Moral Majority hoped to return the United States to what they perceived as its roots. By January 1979, Shiites had gathered enough strength and support from other Iranians to overthrow the shah and evict the "Great Satan," the United States. But the rise of Islamic fundamentalism caught the Carter administration completely off guard. From the White House to the CIA, foreign policymakers grossly underestimated the seemingly irrational religious forces fulminating in Iran. The Islamic radicals seemed too divorced from the realities of modern politics to pose much of a threat. As one U.S. official working on Iran blurted out, "Who ever took religion seriously anyway!" But if Jerry Falwell could not make

Carter or the national security bureaucracy take notice of political religion, the Ayatollah Ruhollah Khomeini could. "We will teach you about God," one of the Iranian revolutionaries told his American captives in the besieged U.S. Embassy in Tehran. It was a harsh lesson that should have been unnecessary. Thanks to the shock, the Carter administration learned it too well. When the Soviets invaded Afghanistan in December of that same year, Brzezinski and other cold warriors in the administration began assembling a coalition of Muslim nations to resist the godless communists in the belief that this would also realign the Islamic world's sympathies toward the United States.[7]

THE SOCIAL GOSPEL was still around, but its message was weighed down by an ineffectual liberal president stumbling through some of the worst international crises to hit America in two decades. But more important, religious liberals simply could not match the intensity of the surging Religious Right. In 1979 alone, Christian conservatives founded four major political action groups that aimed to coax conservative voters to the ballot box: Moral Majority, Religious Roundtable, Christian Voice, and National Christian Action Coalition; the next year saw the establishment of the Family Research Council. Abortion, school prayer, the autonomy of Christian academies, and gay rights remained their abiding concerns, but the Religious Right was immersed in foreign policy issues as well. The Soviets appeared to have retaken the offensive and were marauding all around the world. Carter was either incapable or incompetent to meet the communist threat, said Falwell and other leaders of the Religious Right, and had made it worse through his dithering, disarming, and negotiating.[8]

It did not matter that in the second half of his term, Carter embarked on a rearmament program that was unusually aggressive for peacetime. Nor did it matter that, as he re-launched the very same Cold War he had tried to suspend only two years earlier, Carter used religion to galvanize Americans for the struggle and demonize their enemies. "The Soviets represent a totalitarian nation; we are committed to peace and freedom and democracy," he told a questioner at a news conference in October 1979. "The Soviets subjugate the rights of an individual human being to the rights of the state; we do just the opposite. The Soviets are an atheistic nation; we have deep and fundamental religious beliefs." A month later, an emotional Carter charged that the new Islamic government of Iran's part in the seizure of American hostages "violates not only the most fundamental precepts of international law but the common ethical and religious heritage of humanity. There is no recognized religious faith on Earth which condones kidnapping. There is no recognized religious faith on Earth which condones blackmail. There is certainly no religious faith on Earth which condones the sustained abuse of innocent people." But to

Christian conservatives in America, none of this mattered at all. The damage had already been done.[9]

To evangelicals, America's national and international weaknesses were inextricably linked. Communists abroad and their allies at home were weakening the nation. "In the late seventies," recalled a Moral Majority official,

> the threat of communism was great, whether it was seen as a "hot" war or an undermining action to take over this country by giving away our freedoms and our rights, including the freedom to preach and the freedom to have a church and be separate and be different. Now whether that was real or not, it was perceived as real by fundamentalist people. We felt a threat. We really had a fortress mentality: "Let's hang on. We are losing ground every day to society, to the world, to bureaucracy, to the federal government." It was a very real threat, and Falwell had an easy time rallying people for a strong America.

Christian conservatives had had enough. It was time for America to be America again. Accordingly, in time for the 1980 election, groups like Moral Majority and Christian Voice came out with vigorous foreign policy platforms that criticized Carter's continuation of Nixon and Ford's détente, especially nuclear disarmament negotiations with the Soviet Union (the Strategic Arms Limitation Treaty, SALT II under Carter); the recognition of the People's Republic of China (Nixon had never established official ties; it was Carter who normalized relations, in 1979); and the handing over of the Panama Canal.[10]

In 1979, after an unproductive fence-mending meeting with Carter, Tim LaHaye expressed the frustrations of many Christian conservatives. "We had a man in the White House who professed to be a Christian, but didn't understand how un-Christian his administration was." After the meeting, while waiting outside the White House for his car, a bewildered and angry LaHaye made a vow to defeat Carter in the next year's election. "I stood there and I prayed this prayer," he recalled: "God, we have got to get this man out of the White House and get someone in here who will be aggressive about bringing back traditional moral values." That man, he believed, was Ronald Reagan.[11]

REAGAN'S FAITH WAS eclectic rather than systematic, lived rather than learned. He was a devout, Bible-believing Christian, but he also harbored a rather more unorthodox spiritualism, such as a belief in ghosts; his wife, Nancy, dabbled in astrology. In this sense, Reagan's devout but unconventional beliefs had more in common with those of George Washington, John Quincy Adams, or Abraham Lincoln than they did with Harry

Truman, Dwight Eisenhower, or John Kennedy. Even Lyndon Johnson and Richard Nixon were more mainstream than Reagan, at least in their religious practices. But Reagan's enigmatic syncretism was a strength rather than a weakness for, in the hands of a politician of Reagan's gifts, it afforded his stewardship of America's civil religion an almost limitless flexibility.

Reagan was raised in Dixon, Illinois, in a religiously divided household. His father was a lapsed Irish Catholic who expressed little outward sign of faith. But his mother, Nelle, who was to leave a strong imprint on her son, was a member of the evangelical Disciples of Christ, otherwise known simply as the Christian Church. Nelle's faith, based on an unbridled, postmillennial optimism and a firm belief in the all-powerful goodness of God's providence, was typical of the Disciples. It was a fervently evangelical denomination, often bordering theologically on fundamentalism, yet it was grounded in a doctrine of good works and liberal politics. Recall other members of the Christian Church—Kirby Page, the interwar pacifist; Charles Clayton Morrison, the founding editor of *Christian Century*; Lyndon Johnson, who converted to the Disciples as a teenager—and then recall their progressivism. Young Reagan had an active church life as a boy: he chose to be baptized in 1922, at the age of eleven, and taught Sunday school as an adolescent. The Social Gospel was important to the Reagan family, as it was to most Disciples, but they supported a more conservative interpretation of progress. They believed in moral uplift, but more by voluntarism and individual faith, much as Herbert Hoover and Richard Nixon's western interpretations of Quakerism had informed their conservative politics. Despite their later support for the New Deal, the Reagans were not John Dewey pragmatists but temperance progressives, evangelicals who sought moral and spiritual uplift through clean living and traditional values. They were progressives, then, but conservative progressives—an oxymoron, perhaps, but the Reagans did not see it that way, and young Ronald learned the invaluable political skill of living comfortably with contradictions at an early age. After high school Reagan attended nearby Eureka College, which had official ties to the Disciples of Christ and where daily Bible reading was part of the curriculum. In this religious atmosphere, he formed an intense hostility to communism, a steadfast belief in the Bible, especially the inerrancy of the New Testament, and a firm belief in the guiding hand of providence.[12]

After his happy if sheltered Midwestern upbringing, Reagan's life in Hollywood could not have been more different. Initially, his faith receded, at least as part of his daily life. But it did not disappear. When his film career began to wane in the late 1950s, he turned to politics, and as he did, religion became important once again. Along the way, he traded his New Deal liberalism for staunch western conservatism and a suspicion of government, beliefs to which his Disciples faith could easily adapt. In 1964, no doubt with electoral strategy in mind but also out of genuine political and theological conviction, he began regularly attending services at the Bel Air Presbyterian Church in Los Angeles. Elected governor of California in 1966 and reelected in 1970, Reagan's faith returned in full force. "I have spent more time in prayer these past months than in any previous period I can recall," he confessed shortly after moving into the governor's mansion. "I've always believed there is a certain divine scheme of things," he said elsewhere. "Whatever I do has meaning, only if I ask that it serves His purpose." As governor, Reagan vigorously courted and associated with religious conservatives and invited Billy Graham to speak to the legislature on two separate occasions. He also began claiming born-again status, as in this statement from his 1976 bid for the Republican presidential nomination: "In my own experience there came a time when there developed a new relationship with God . . . So yes, I have had an experience that could be described as 'born again.' " But he also displayed a pragmatic streak, signing into law a relatively liberal abortion bill years before *Roe v. Wade.* His conservative supporters did not like it, but Reagan suffered no lasting damage as a result.[13]

That Reagan could bridge such a wide gap between rhetoric and reality was testament to his tremendous political skills. As Robert Dallek has pointed out, foremost among these skills was his mastery of "the politics of symbolism," which served him particularly well in presidential politics. Reagan was especially adept at deploying religious imagery and appealing to the patriotism of civil religion that linked together God and country, mission and nation. In 1980, he recognized the latent power of the Religious Right and moved swiftly to take advantage of it in ways nobody else could. After winning the Republican nomination, Reagan attended the National Affairs Briefing in Dallas. Organized by Religious Roundtable's Ed Robison, one of Christian conservatism's most militant leaders, the National Affairs Briefing was designed as a forum where politicians and the Religious Right could exchange ideas about domestic politics and foreign policy. Carter and independent candidate John Anderson declined Robison's invitation, but Reagan accepted. In speeches and study sessions on SALT II, Panama, and the Middle East, delegates propounded on the unilateralist Christian conservative worldview. In a speech delivered right before Reagan's keynote, Robison issued a call to arms that was shrill even by the rhetorical standards of the Religious Right. With the forces of secularism on the march at home and the communists rampaging abroad, the stakes could not be higher. "We'll either have a Hitler-type takeover, or Soviet domination, or God is going to take over this country," he railed. The audience, including Reagan, loved it. Reagan then followed with his own speech praising traditional morals and condemning the Supreme

Court for banning school prayer. The National Affairs Briefing was ostensibly apolitical, which is why Carter and Anderson had been invited in the first place, but it was clearly a showcase for the emerging alliance between Christian conservatives and the Republican Party. Reagan certainly knew it, and he said as much. "You can't endorse me, but I endorse you," he declared to his officially neutral but obviously supportive audience.[14]

Once elected president, Reagan made religious faith an important part of his political persona. This is not to say he was insincere: everything he did in the realm of political religion was consistent with what we know of his private beliefs. Unlike presidents before him, Reagan deployed religious rhetoric to rally his supporters rather than to bind the nation together as a whole behind a common cause. In a significant but little-noticed shift, Reagan reconfigured the Judeo-Christian civil religion from what it had been since the 1930s—a way to foster inclusiveness—into a rhetorical device to attack liberalism and secularism. "I know this may often be laughed and sneered at in some sophisticated circles, but ours is a Judeo-Christian heritage, and ours is a loving and living God, the fountain of truth and knowledge," he told the annual convention of the National Parent-Teacher Association. "I can't help but believe that He, who has so blessed this land and made us a good and caring people, should never have been expelled from our classrooms." This subtle recasting of the Judeo-Christian concept spoke to the core concerns of religious conservatives, Protestant and Catholic alike, who feared that the First Amendment was being used as a weapon against faith itself. As he argued before an evangelical audience in Dallas, "We establish no religion in this country, nor will we ever. We command no worship. We mandate no belief. But we poison our society when we remove its theological underpinnings. We court corruption when we leave it bereft of belief. All are free to believe or not believe; all are free to practice a faith or not. But those who believe must be free to speak of and act on their belief, to apply moral teaching to public questions."[15]

Throughout his presidency, Reagan promoted many of the causes of the Religious Right. In 1982, he submitted to Congress a constitutional amendment to legalize school prayer. In his 1983 State of the Union address, he urged passage of the school prayer amendment and defended the notorious Christian academies by urging "tuition tax credits for parents who want to send their children to private or religiously affiliated schools." Elsewhere, he criticized liberal theologians for portraying Jesus as "merely human" rather than the son of God who was crucified and rose from the dead. He also took issue with Darwinian theories of evolution and believed biblical creationism should have an equal opportunity to be taught in science classes. His views on creationism were characteristically expressed in one of his favorite jokes. As he told the 1988 Annual National

Prayer Breakfast, "I've had an unholy desire to invite some atheists to a dinner and then serve the most fabulous gourmet dinner that has ever been concocted and, after dinner, ask them if they believe there was a cook." He even repeated the joke to a gathering of dissidents while visiting the Soviet Union for his final summit with Gorbachev in May 1988.[16]

Reagan was also friendly to Catholics, who comprised many of his top-level appointees. Both of his secretaries of state (Alexander Haig and George Shultz), three national security advisers (Richard Allen, William Clark, and Robert McFarlane), and one director of Central Intelligence (William Casey), in addition to many lower-level aides and speechwriters, were Roman Catholics. And in 1984, Reagan fulfilled Harry Truman's goal and established normal diplomatic relations with the Holy See.[17]

Yet overall, when it came to actual policy Reagan delivered very little to religious conservatives. The school prayer amendment did not pass; Darwinism remained in the schools; abortion remained legal—in fact, Reagan appointed a known abortion-rights advocate, Sandra Day O'Connor, to the Supreme Court. The Religious Right grumbled, but it did not abandon him. Because the alternatives were far worse, there was simply nowhere else to turn. And at least Reagan promoted their causes, even if he was unsuccessful in doing so.[18]

REAGAN FULFILLED MUCH of the Religious Right's political platform in only one area: a hard-line anticommunist foreign policy. But this was more correlation than cause, for Reagan was already committed to ending détente and reigniting the Cold War. He could not undo some of the things Carter had done—for instance, he could not retake the Panama Canal, at least not without triggering a war—but he could increase defense spending, escalate his anti-Soviet rhetoric, and look for ways to contain and perhaps even roll back communist rule. He issued the Reagan Doctrine, which pledged U.S. political support and military aid (but, with the Vietnam trauma fresh in the collective memory, not troops) to "freedom fighters" resisting communist governments anywhere in the world. Behind the theory of the Reagan Doctrine lay the reality of Central America, specifically Nicaragua and El Salvador, where leftist and communist parties had either come to power (the Sandinistas in Nicaragua) or were threatening to (a Cuban-backed coalition in El Salvador). Though conflicts elsewhere were also critical, Nicaragua became the focal point of both the Reagan Doctrine and its domestic critics, including a majority in Congress. The Reagan administration funded and trained the Contras, a right-wing insurgency that aimed to topple the Sandinistas. In 1983, he also authorized the invasion of the Caribbean island of Grenada out of fear that communists were poised to take over the country.[19]

Religion did not cause or drive these events, or even shape U.S. policy toward them. But for many people in both North and Central America, religion helped frame their perceptions of, and political position on, the key issues. As we shall see, the Catholic Church was deeply involved in the Central American controversies. But religion played a broader role, as well. Symbolically, Reagan framed his reescalation of the Cold War in religious terms that bore striking resemblance to those once used by Truman, Eisenhower, and Dulles. Unlike Kennedy, Johnson, or Carter, Reagan was not squeamish about invoking God's name in America's crusade, and unlike Nixon, Reagan spoke as if he meant it.

Picking up from the Helsinki groups, Reagan attacked the Soviet Union for its systematic violations of religious freedom in the Soviet republics, such as Ukraine, and in Eastern Europe. "Two visions of the world remain locked in dispute," he proclaimed during Captive Nations Week in 1983. "The first believes all men are created equal by a loving God who has blessed us with freedom"; Abraham Lincoln was its most eloquent spokesman. The second vision, following the dictates of Lenin, "believes that religion is opium for the masses. It believes that eternal principles like truth, liberty, and democracy have no meaning beyond the whim of the state." In a speech before the Irish parliament, Reagan framed the Cold War in religious terms that would have been instantly familiar to Harry Truman; the only difference was that Reagan also aimed his message at the liberal and secular doubters in the United States and throughout Western Europe. "The struggle between freedom and totalitarianism today is not ultimately a test of arms or missiles, but a test of faith and spirit. And in this spiritual struggle, the Western mind and will is the crucial battleground," he told the Irish legislators. "We must not hesitate to express our dream of freedom; we must not be reluctant to enunciate the crucial distinctions between right and wrong—between political systems based on freedom and those based on a dreadful denial of the human spirit."[20]

Reagan's bellicose stance was controversial—three members of the Irish parliament stormed out in protest—but at least he had an ally. The United States and the Catholic Church had often shared a visceral anticommunist outlook, but they just as often differed about other priorities. But it was no coincidence that, forty-five years after FDR had first sent Myron Taylor to Rome, it was Reagan who normalized relations between the two leading voices of Christian anticommunism, the White House and the Vatican. In 1978, the College of Cardinals elected Karol Wojtyla, a Polish cardinal, as Pope John Paul II. Unlike John XXIII and Paul VI, this new pope—the first non-Italian in centuries—was committed to applying traditional solutions to modern problems. Coming from Poland, anticommunism was part of his political birthright. Such was the strength of the Catholic Church in Poland that the communist authorities had never been able to suppress it. Tacitly allowed to remain, the Polish Church became a quiet symbol of defiance, outwardly apolitical but representing a living, lasting blemish on the supposed purity of communist orthodoxy. "Imbued with a hatred of communism and a love of God," writes the Cold War historian Melvyn Leffler, John Paul II "was an omen of the times." In an increasingly interdependent world governed by standards set in Helsinki, Washington and the Vatican pressured communism from opposite ends, almost as if in tandem. In the end, Moscow could do little to resist.[21]

Reagan's most famous (or infamous, depending on the audience) use of religious anticommunism—branding the Soviet Union an "evil empire"—came in a widely reported speech to the 1983 annual meeting of the National Association of Evangelicals (NAE). While many Americans and Europeans were calling for a return to détente, Reagan called instead for eternal vigilance. In doing so, he held little back: "There is sin and evil in the world, and we're enjoined by Scripture and the Lord Jesus to oppose it with all our might." It was rare for a president to use as bracing and unequivocal a word as "evil," but Reagan knew his audience. "Evil" was not simply a concept to the pastors and evangelists gathered at the NAE convention, but a reality. Satan was real, not figurative, and he wrought mischief upon the world through his acolytes, the godless communists of the Soviet Union. Evil also had eschatological significance, especially for the premillennial dispensationalists who thought the end of the world was approaching. With all this in mind, Reagan's script returned to the theme of evil repeatedly. At times, he even sounded like a preacher himself: "Yes, let us pray for the salvation of all of those who live in that totalitarian darkness—pray they will discover the joy of knowing God. But until they do, let us be aware that while they preach the supremacy of the state, declare its omnipotence over individual man, and predict its eventual domination of all peoples on the Earth, they are the focus of evil in the modern world."

Reagan then quoted the *Screwtape Letters* by C. S. Lewis, a hero revered by evangelicals, to warn Americans not to be lulled into a false sense of security by the "quiet men," the outwardly bland but ruthless communist functionaries—supported by unwitting allies in America—who spoke of peace while waging war against freedom. Especially galling was the "nuclear freeze," a disarmament protest movement then gaining ground in the United States and Europe, especially in the Catholic Church. Because these quiet men "sometimes speak in soothing tones of brotherhood and peace," Reagan warned in an unmistakable reference to the liberal apostles of progress at home, "some would have us accept them at their word and accommodate ourselves to their aggressive impulses." Americans had learned this lesson once already, in the 1940s; they must not forget it now. If "history teaches anything," Reagan continued, "it teaches that simple-minded appeasement or wishful thinking about our adversaries is folly. It means the betrayal of our past, the squandering of our freedom." This was a pretty stern message, one that was already bound to be controversial, but Reagan did not stop there:

> So, I urge you to speak out against those who would place the United States in a position of military and moral inferiority. You know, I've always believed that old Screwtape reserved his best efforts for those of you in the church. So, in your discussions of the nuclear freeze proposals, I urge you to beware the temptation of pride—the temptation of blithely declaring yourselves above it all and label both sides equally at fault, to ignore the facts of history and the aggressive impulses of an evil empire, to simply call the arms race a giant misunderstanding and thereby remove yourself from the struggle between right and wrong and good and evil.

To his audience, the links between today's evil empire and tomorrow's Armageddon would have been obvious.[22]

Reagan's other major foray into religious geopolitics had even greater consequences. Following Brzezinski's lead, the Reagan administration, guided mostly by the enthusiasm of CIA director William Casey, significantly expanded U.S. support for the mujahedin resisting Soviet rule in Afghanistan. This meant working even more closely with conservative Islamists not only in Afghanistan, but Pakistan and Saudi Arabia as well. It required Casey convincing skeptical career CIA officers that arming Islamic radicals was a good idea. And it also involved the importation of fanatical Islamic warriors from elsewhere in the Muslim world, principally the Arab states of the Middle East.

Critics abounded, mostly within the State Department and CIA. But to its adherents on both sides, the alliance between the Reagan administration and the Muslim fighters made perfect sense: both hated the Soviet Union for its aggression, its communism—and its atheism. Casey, who often traveled secretly to Islamabad and Riyadh to solicit funds not only for the mujahedin in Afghanistan but the Contras in Nicaragua, found it easy to speak to devout, anticommunist Muslims on a gut level of basic faith and morality. Reagan's intelligence czar was a veteran of the wartime OSS as well as the Cold War CIA, and so brought to the task a formidable talent in the dark arts of intelligence. But he was also a fervent Catholic who rarely missed Sunday mass—even when traveling in Saudi Arabia, where Christian worship was officially illegal—and filled his house, which he named Maryknoll after the Catholic order, with religious relics and icons. He had thoroughly enjoyed his Jesuit education from elementary school right up through his undergraduate years at Fordham, the spiritual home of serious, intellectual, conservative Catholicism. During the Spanish Civil War, he was an outspoken supporter of Franco and the Nationalists who fought the fight of faith against communism. Like Reagan, then, Casey was a Christian anticommunist, a true believer who hesitated at nothing to beat back the Soviet menace. Through his contacts in the worldwide Catholic Church, he funneled funds and supplies to the Solidarity movement in Poland as well as the Contras and the right-wing government of El Salvador. But Afghanistan was his largest feat. In 1984, supported in public by the rowdy Texas Congressman Charlie Wilson, Casey transformed low-level U.S. support for the mujahedin into a massive and increasingly sophisticated military juggernaut. He did not worry that the United States was allying with Islamic fundamentalists. To Casey, it made perfect sense for the faithful, of whatever faith, to wage war together against godless communism.[23]

NOT EVERYONE SHARED Casey's commitment. Religious liberals did not recede with the coming of the age of Reagan but instead regrouped and maintained their own pressure on U.S. foreign policymakers. They continued to push for the adoption of a global Social Gospel and resisted Reagan's policies whenever they deviated from this vision (as they almost always did). Thus continued the great schism between religious liberals and conservatives that had emerged with the postwar world. The Social Gospelers had strong views on many topics, but the two aspects of Reagan's foreign policy that generated the most religious controversy were Central America and nuclear weapons. Both were essentially the continuation of struggles from earlier periods.

For many Americans, Nicaragua and El Salvador bore all the hallmarks of Vietnam. Though the situations in the two countries were fundamentally different—in Nicaragua, Reagan supported the insurgents, while in El Salvador he backed the government—they both seemed to share with Vietnam a dynamic in which the United States supported brutal right-wing thugs against the will of the majority of the people, all in the name of a reactionary anticommunism. The conflicts in Central America, liberals charged, committed American support for dictators who systematically violated the most basic human rights of their own people. They also pitted an all-powerful United States against some of the poorest people in the world. And both conflicts raised the possibility of gradual U.S. military escalation leading to a full-scale war in the jungles of Central America, something even Reagan wanted to avoid.

Religious Americans, particularly Christians, were in the vanguard of opposition to Reagan's policies partly because of their personal experiences or personal contacts in Central America. Though she tried to be balanced, Lisa Fitzgerald, a thirty-nine-year-old Nicaragua-based Catholic nun from Troy, New York, could not help but wonder why her country had picked a fight with a people mired in abject poverty. Should Reagan not instead help these people with humanitarian and economic aid rather than stocking right-wing militias with weapons to destabilize the Sandinista government? In 1983, Fitzgerald returned north to testify about her Nicaraguan experiences before Congress. She did not want to choose sides, she said, but circumstances were forcing her to. "It is harder and harder for people to express my views without being branded as a leftist, like the red-baiting of the 1950s," she complained to a reporter. Communism was an abstraction, she argued, a political luxury for a people struggling against poverty and hunger. What was important was sustainable, equitable development, not warmongering. "When I hear the Reagan people talk about this in terms of Communism, I get really mad." To see the conflict through "cold war eyes," she concluded, "is to distort it." That same year, Nicaragua-based missionaries from nineteen different American Catholic orders, supported by the ecumenical Inter-Religious Task Force on Central America, sent a letter of protest to Congress alleging that Reagan's policy was based on distortions of the true situation on the ground. Still, opposition to the Reagan administration's aid to the Contras was not widely shared within the Catholic hierarchy; after all, the Sandinistas were backed by the Soviets and Cubans and had clamped down on the Catholic Church. And the Church hierarchy in Nicaragua was firmly opposed to the Sandinista government, as was the Vatican.[24]

Liberal Protestants were a different story. Their critique of the oppressive nature of U.S. foreign policy had changed little since it had begun in earnest in the 1950s and escalated dramatically during the Vietnam War; Nicaragua was but the latest episode in a long sordid tale of global injustice. Taking advantage of a hemispheric network of Christian churches and missions, thousands of Americans headed to Nicaragua to witness the conflict for themselves. What they saw appalled them. Two members of the North Carolina–based Resource Center for Women and Ministry in the South, a mainline Protestant organization, spent two weeks in Nicaragua in the summer of 1985. They returned with horror stories of Contra brutality and U.S. support for it. The situation, they wrote to supporters in the United States, "inspires both hope and fear": hope from the perseverance of ordinary people, fear from the tyranny of the right-wing militias. Contrary to Reagan administration propaganda, the people supported the Sandinistas because "reforms are happening" that would bring about "impressive change in a poor country where most people still work with a hoe and machete to survive." The Nicaraguan government was certainly a threat, argued the women, but only to American corporations that wanted to keep Nicaraguans in a state of dependent destitution and virtual slavery. To religious liberals, freedom meant economic and social progress, not freedom from communism. "To stop these evil deeds being done in Nicaragua, we will need to persuade our fellow Americans that the threat of the Left is not automatically a threat to our economic or political security," explained Reverend William Sloane Coffin, a veteran of crusades against Vietnam and nuclear weapons. "Most of all we need to recognize that the real source of insurgency in all of Central America is not Moscow or Havana, but decades of economic inequality and political dictatorships."[25]

Opposition from mainline feminist peace activists and William Sloane Coffin were to be expected. More worrying for Reagan was the spread of opposition to normally supportive conservatives. Most Christian conservatives, Protestant and Catholic, firmly backed Reagan's policies. But not everyone did, especially those churches and denominations that had missionary contacts in Central America who could eyewitness events and relay information back home. In 1985, Bishop August E. Wenzel of the Texas-based Southern District of the American Lutheran Church wrote Reagan to convey the moral misgivings of his denomination. At its annual convention, the Southern District passed three resolutions declaring its opposition to U.S. policy in Central America. "You should know also that the Southern District . . . would, by most standards, be considered conservative theologically and politically but that these resolutions passed with a sizeable majority vote," Wenzel explained. "The experience of many of our people in these countries and our contact with refugees do not coincide with the kind of information that many of us believe is shaping our nation's policy."[26]

Actually, what concerned the Lutheran Church's Southern District even more than the Contras was U.S. support for the authoritarian regime in El Salvador, and especially the Reagan administration's obstructionist policy toward the refugees generated by the conflict there; two of the convention's three resolutions dealt with El Salvador. While religious opponents thought Reagan's Salvadoran policy of supporting right-wing dictators was grotesque, they were even more disturbed by the U.S. government's refusal to grant asylum to the thousands of refugees who fled the conflict and headed north. People fleeing communist countries were automatically granted asylum and residency in the United States; Cuban exiles and Vietnamese boat people were two recent examples. But refugees from El Salvador were instead turned away at the border and shipped back to their country, usually to face certain imprisonment, torture, and even death at the hands of a regime they had sought to escape. Reviving a tactic pioneered during the anti–Vietnam War movement, churches across the United States offered sanctuary to refugees and refused entry to immigration authorities seeking to deport them. The rhetoric of the sanctuary movement was emotional, and it cast the U.S. government not as a protector of human rights but as their worst violator. To do so, the sanctuary movement used the language of revolutionary patriotism normally confined to the extremist, anti-statist right. "When the laws of a nation underwrite genocide, and compassion becomes a subversive activity, it is time to change the laws of that nation," Reverend Lee Taylor of the Pilgrim Congregational Church in Anacortes, Washington, explained to the members of his church. "When a democratic nation no longer represents the interests of democracy, but chooses instead the interests of corporate greed and violence, it is time for the people of that democracy to take that government back into their own hands."[27]

Quakers, Unitarians, and mainline Presbyterians and Congregationalists were among the most common denominations to offer sanctuary, but in fact nobody had more sanctuary churches than Roman Catholics—by 1985, Catholic churches and organizations such as Catholic Worker accounted for nearly 10 percent of the four hundred sanctuary churches. The difference between El Salvador and Nicaragua was that the Salvadoran Catholic Church backed leftist revolution while the Nicaraguan Church opposed it. From their contacts in El Salvador, Catholic priests, nuns, and laypeople fed secular human rights groups with detailed and fairly precise information about the number of government death squads, right-wing militias, murders, and "disappearances" that occurred with American backing. In homage to those fighting for freedom and justice in Central America, more radical Catholics (and Protestants, especially feminists and Black Power advocates) turned to liberation theology, a fusion of Christianity and Marxism that explained the conflicts as struggles against the neocolonial ambitions of American corporations and the U.S. government.[28]

Domestic opposition to U.S. policy in Central America was passionate, broad-based, and continual, and as such it applied uncomfortable pressure on the Reagan administration. But so long as it was confined to the religious left, Reagan and his advisers were confident they could withstand it. More difficult was the issue of nuclear weapons, which provoked a much wider protest movement that voiced anger at Reagan's expensive military buildup and nuclear rearmament program at a time when he had also pushed through deep tax and spending cuts. "As military spending continues to grow, the ability to meet social needs declines," and the gap between rich and poor within America and between nations continued to grow, the Women's Missionary Society of the African Methodist Episcopal Church pointed out in 1984. In rare harmony, American Muslims and Jews joined Protestants and Catholics in the World Conference on Religion and Peace to urge Reagan to disarm America's nuclear arsenal, preferably under UN supervision. In a broadside typical of the religious left, the ecumenical Sacramento Religious Community for Peace linked "the problems of the arms race . . . with concerns about justice, hunger, poverty, war in Central America and our responsibility to our children." Such protests were part of the nuclear freeze movement Reagan had singled out for special condemnation in his "evil empire" speech. As with the anti–Vietnam War protests, religion was a significant but by no means sole influence within the nuclear freeze movement. But as during the Vietnam era, protest by otherwise respectable churches and clergy gave the movement a moral and political credibility it might otherwise have lacked.[29]

This was never more evident than during the deliberations of the National Conference of Catholic Bishops (NCCB). Normally one of the strongest bodies of support for U.S. foreign policy, particularly when it was directed against communism, the NCCB was having serious second thoughts about the nuclear basis of the Cold War. Crucially, the NCCB was no longer dominated by Cardinal Spellman's generation. By the 1980s, the formative experiences for most bishops were Vatican II, civil rights, Vietnam, and Watergate, not the anticommunist crusades of Pius XII and Bishop Fulton Sheen. From time to time, the bishops issued pastoral letters instructing the laity on the proper Catholic approach toward a wide variety of subjects. But in November 1980, alarmed by the breakdown of détente and the rise of international tensions, the bishops began drafting a pastoral letter on nuclear strategy. Judging the issue to be the most important facing humanity, they deliberately wrote their letter to be accessible to all Americans, not just Catholics. A handful of bishops, such as Archbishop Raymond Hunthausen of Seattle, were committed pacifists and were thus opposed to nuclear weapons on any grounds. Another group, led by Archbishop John O'Connor of New York, supported traditional deterrence theory. The majority of bishops stood between these two extremes but, guided by just war doctrine, found it difficult to imagine a circumstance in which the use of nuclear missiles would be proportionate, and therefore just. Father J. Bryan Hehir, the main author of the letter's final version, had to balance all these viewpoints, but in the end he followed the will of the clerical majority. This did not bode well for Reagan.[30]

In May 1983, following two years of wide-ranging consultation, including with Reagan administration officials, the NCCB published Hehir's conclusions in *The Challenge of Peace*. Because it involved the deliberate targeting of civilians, deterrence was immoral; obviously so was any recourse to actually waging nuclear war. Hehir and the bishops did not totally repudiate American nuclear strategy, but they came very close. "The nuclear age is an era of moral as well as physical danger," they concluded. "We are the first generation since Genesis with the power to virtually destroy God's creation. We cannot remain silent in the face of such danger." By every consideration, the bishops had determined that "good ends," such as national self-defense and protecting freedom, "cannot justify immoral means." In an unsubtle reference to Reagan's foreign policy stewardship, they expressed "fear that our world and our nation are headed in the wrong direction." The whole premise of U.S. foreign policy, indeed of the Cold War itself, was predicated upon deterrence and the threat of war. But the bishops had decided it was now time to end that system. "Peacemaking is not an optional commitment. It is a requirement of our faith. We are called to be peacemakers, not by some movement of the moment, but by our Lord Jesus."[31]

This was, of course, the very same Lord Jesus who had called Reagan to resist communism wherever it reared its satanic head. Thus it was no surprise that the White House could call upon a number of conservative Catholics to resist Hehir and the bishops. To combat the "leftward drift" in the Church, New York–area Catholics established the American Catholic Committee as a rival voice to the NCCB. William F. Buckley Jr., one of the leading lay Catholic writers in the country, warned the Church against being tempted by the sin of appeasement. In a similar spirit Michael Novak, the Catholic neoconservative and an editor at Buckley's *National Review*, founded his own journal to promote a more realistic application of Catholicism to world politics; in a nod to Niebuhr, he called it *Catholicism in Crisis*. With a foreword by Billy Graham and an introduction by Buckley, Novak then followed with *Moral Clarity in the Nuclear Age*, a book-length response to what he saw as the dangerous moral relativism found in the bishops' pastoral letter. (And after that, he published a scathing critique of liberation theology and anti-Contra protests.) In the usually more liberal pages of the *New Republic*, Patrick Glynn penned a critique of the NCCB's position that Assistant Secretary of State Elliott Abrams recommended to National Security Adviser William Clark, himself a Catholic, as "the best analysis I have ever seen of the recent political activism of the Church." Characteristically, Catholic traditionalists simply condemned the bishops' peace drive as the work of the Antichrist.[32]

But the most extraordinary response of all was a joint letter to Archbishop Joseph Bernardin of Chicago, sent under Illinois Congressman Henry Hyde's name and signed by twenty-three other Catholic members of Congress, that carefully attacked the bishops' terms point by point. As elected representatives, it was their job to ensure the security of the American people; if nuclear weapons served this purpose, argued the lawmakers, then so be it. Nuclear weapons kept in check "the very real threat of Soviet communism" and its "aggressive intentions." Arms control efforts had been sabotaged by Soviet recalcitrance and dishonesty. In any event, arms control would not itself lead to peace because nuclear weapons were a symptom of international tension, not a cause of it. The Catholic congressmen also rejected the bishops' implication that the nation's only Catholic president "was less than moral in defending our freedom during the Cuban missile crisis." And anyway, conventional weapons killed millions more people than nuclear arms, so surely the bishops should focus on a very real problem instead of a largely theoretical one. Rarely had the gap between clergy and laity been so wide.[33]

Even though they had not been able to bring an end to deterrence, the National Conference of Catholic Bishops had inflicted severe damage on the Reagan administration's foreign policy. If the nation's Catholic bishops, once the final defense of anticommunist forces in America, a body of clerics who did not come out against Vietnam until 1971 and tepidly at that, could condemn a staple of Cold War national security policy, then something had to be seriously wrong with U.S. foreign policy. And of course, the Catholic bishops were not isolated: just as Billy Graham and William F. Buckley had teamed up in a conservative alignment, mainline Protestants praised the NCCB pastoral letter and crusaded with liberal Catholics against the nuclear threat. Thus while Reagan found he could drastically escalate the Cold War, he also discovered that the Soviets were not his only opposition. With the evil empire speech, in Central America, and with rearmament, Reagan had taken the initiative. But he had also provoked an equally strong reaction, mostly at home. And by the time of his reelection, it was unclear how much longer he could keep waging this battle on two fronts.[34]

TO BREAK THE deadlock between East and West, peace and war, Reagan began to reach out, quietly at first, to Soviet leaders. Mikhail Gorbachev's rise to become general secretary of the Communist Party in 1985 provided a partner who was willing and able to do business with the West, but Reagan had already been moving toward a modification of his hard-line stance two years before. On two of the Cold War's most divisive issues, individual liberty and nuclear weapons, he eased off the extreme positions he had taken in order to create space for a new dialogue with Moscow. Central to both these issues, and thus at the very heart of the end of the process that led to the end of the Cold War, stood religion.

Thanks to his mother, Nelle, and the comforting evangelical faith of the Disciples of Christ, Reagan grew up believing in the literal truth of the word of God as laid down in the Bible. He held fast to this biblically inerrant outlook even as his faith began to wander off, amiably if aimlessly, in various spiritual directions. One book of the Bible particularly seized hold of his fertile imagination: the end times foretold in the Book of Revelation. And within Revelation, one episode in particular fascinated him: the battle of Armageddon. Christ's prophecy of the future, revealed after his death to the disciple John, describes a climactic battle with the Antichrist on the plains of Armageddon. Victory against Satan would eventually presage Christ's return to earth and give rise to a new heaven and a new earth.

Reagan referred to Armageddon on several occasions before his reelection in 1984—in other words, during the most dangerous phase of his presidency, when Cold War tensions reached levels unseen for decades—and clearly cast the Soviets in the role of the Antichrist. Unsurprisingly, many observers worried that their Bible-thumping commander-in-chief cited Revelation as a precursor to unleashing nuclear hell on the Soviet Union. An interfaith group of liberal clergy called upon Reagan not only to stop mentioning Armageddon but to repudiate its relevance to the modern world. "The president had fairly strong views about the parable of Armageddon," National Security Adviser Robert McFarlane later told an interviewer. "He believed that a nuclear exchange would be the fulfillment of that prophecy [and that] the world would end through a nuclear catastrophe." And soon, too. As Reagan revealed on televangelist Jim Bakker's program, *The PTL Club*, in 1980, "We may be the generation that sees Armageddon."[35]

Yet it was a different reading of the end times, largely unnoticed at the time, that was really guiding Reagan's thoughts. For Reagan was not only fascinated by the Book of Revelation, he was terrified of it. And though he did not doubt that the world would one day end, he wanted no part of it. We now know what Reagan knew then: that the year 1983 brought the superpowers closer to an exchange of nuclear weapons than they had been since the Cuban Missile Crisis. Tensions were already high thanks to Reagan's evil empire speech and the Soviet downing of a Korean passenger jet earlier in the year that killed all 269 people on board; 61 U.S. citizens died, including a member of Congress. Then in November, during NATO military exercises code-named Able Archer, the Soviets believed they were about to be attacked and mobilized their military, including their strategic nuclear arsenal, for a preemptive launch against the United States. Shaken by events that seemed to lead straight to Armageddon, Reagan began to step back from the brink. Already convinced that nuclear weapons were a menace to humanity, he became something of a nuclear abolitionist—thanks in part to his literal belief in the Bible's eternal truth.[36]

In fact, courtesy of the Vashchenkos, a family of Pentecostals from Siberia, Reagan had already been looking for a way out of the Cold War. On July 3, 1978, five members of the Vashchenko family and two others from their hometown of Chernogorsk, near the Mongolian border, barged their way past startled Soviet police officers guarding the U.S. Embassy entrance. They had tried the same tactic in January 1963, only to be turned away at the embassy doors. They made it through this time, though the U.S. foreign service officers in the embassy wished they had not. Despite the reluctance of U.S. officials to prolong an obvious irritant to the Soviets, and despite the lack of proper living quarters in the embassy, the Vashchenkos settled for an indefinite stay, all seven of them living together in a single twelve-by-fifteen-foot room. Embassy staff collected whatever blankets and bedding they could and made sure these religious refugees were well fed. But soon, some of the family went on a hunger strike; two had to be hospitalized. Their demand: exit visas so they could emigrate to America, where they could freely practice their faith.[37]

The Carter administration paid them little heed, but the "Siberian Seven" attracted widespread sympathy in the United States. Church groups called attention to their plight; so did a contingent of congressional representatives visiting the Soviet Union in 1979. The pace of protest quickened after Reagan's election as president, probably on the assumption that he would be more attentive to the Pentecostals' ordeal. Indeed he was, but there was little he felt he could do about it for now, especially with a reluctant State Department. Still, Americans kept up the pressure. The National Interreligious Task Force on Soviet Jewry informed Reagan it was "most anxious about the safety of the Pentecostal Seven." New York Representative Benjamin Gilman consulted with Ray Hughes, the general overseer of the Church of God, the nation's oldest Pentecostal denomination and one of its largest, to find a home for the Vashchenko family. A freshman lawmaker from Massachusetts, Barney Frank, was particularly indefatigable on behalf of the Siberian Seven. As the successor to Father Drinan in Massachusetts' Fourth District, Frank may have felt compelled to maintain pressure on the Soviet Union's appalling human rights record, especially on religious liberty. Perhaps, as a Jew, he empathized with people suffering communist tyranny for their religion. Whatever the reason, he urged Reagan to help. "The struggle of the Pentecostalists is a compelling human drama highlighting their fight to practice religious beliefs without harassment and intimidation," Frank wrote Reagan in May 1981, only a few months after being inaugurated into Congress. A year later, he and Tom Harkin of Iowa led the signatures of nearly eighty other congressmen and -women in a petition to Reagan to come up with a solution that would allow the Pentecostals to emigrate "so that they may be allowed to practice their religious beliefs in freedom."[38]

Reagan was not a policy wonk and was notorious for drifting off during detailed briefings, especially on technical matters of diplomacy or strategy. But as Barney Frank had guessed, the old actor was instinctively drawn to a "compelling human drama," and he followed the Pentecostals' story with great interest. Indeed, he had already done so before 1980 in radio broadcasts and his nationally syndicated newspaper column. After coming into office, he sent the hunger strikers a personal note expressing concern for their health, recommending that they begin to eat again, and urging them "to continue your courageous course, a struggle that is an inspiration to all who value religious freedom and individual human rights." In November 1981, Reagan summoned diplomat Jack Matlock to the Oval

Office to discuss Soviet affairs. Matlock had just returned from a stint in the Moscow embassy, and he had been there in 1978 when the Vashchenkos stormed through the embassy doors. Once it was clear the religious refugees would not leave, Matlock and his wife, Rebecca, made sure they were as well fed and decently housed as possible under the circumstances. Now, back home in 1981, Matlock expected Reagan to quiz him about the war in Afghanistan, unrest in Poland, or economic conditions in the Soviet Union. But Reagan only wanted to talk about the Pentecostals. "Why don't the Soviets let them go?" he asked, almost plaintively.[39]

Eventually, Reagan thought he might as well ask them himself. Just over a year after his meeting with Matlock, Secretary of State George Shultz discreetly escorted Soviet Ambassador Anatoly Dobrynin through the White House basement garage and into the president's private living quarters. Incredibly, two full years into the Reagan presidency, it was the first time the president had met the Soviet ambassador outside of crowded White House functions. Reagan wanted to begin a dialogue with the Kremlin, and he wanted to keep it quiet. Above all, he wanted to probe their sincerity, to see if they too wanted a new and more productive relationship. "Probably," Reagan said to Dobrynin, "people in the Soviet Union regard me as a crazy warmonger. But I don't want a war between us, because I know it would bring countless disasters. We should make a fresh start." He then suggested the place he would most like a fresh start: the Siberian Seven. Shultz noted the president's "sincere intensity" when he spoke about the Vashchenkos. For his part, Dobrynin was only just coming to realize that the Pentecostals were "Reagan's favorite subject." It was a bewildering turn of events—as Dobrynin put it, two full years in office "and at his first meeting with the Soviet ambassador, the president actually raised only one concrete issue . . . as if it were the most important issue between us."[40]

Dobrynin had not survived Soviet politics and Washington's bureaucratic battles for two decades for nothing, however, and he immediately recommended to the Politburo that they grant Reagan's request. It was obviously personally important to the president and would therefore be a gesture of good faith that could go a long way. The Soviet leadership agreed and sent Shultz a message hinting that the Vashchenkos would be allowed to emigrate, but only if they first returned home to Chernogorsk and applied for exit visas like everyone else. Shultz considered the oblique, subtly worded message "a significant overture" that "could open other avenues for progress." It was indeed significant, and not only for the concession on emigration, for it began a mutual exchange based solely on trust. The Soviets promised, if only implicitly, to allow the Pentecostals to leave the Soviet Union (via Israel, the same inconspicuous route that refusenik Jews had already traveled) while the Americans promised that they would, as Reagan later put it, "never mention it as an exchange or concession" and thus embarrass the Soviets. A few months later, both sides proved as good as their word, and the Vashchenkos left the Soviet Union forever. In fact, dozens more Siberian Pentecostals were allowed to leave with them. Reagan was delighted. "Quiet diplomacy is working," he exulted in his diary. When Indiana Senator Dan Quayle, who had close ties to the Religious Right, asked that the Pentecostals be hosted at the White House when they moved to the United States, Reagan demurred. It would not be "appropriate," said the official who replied to Quayle's letter on Reagan's behalf.[41]

Perhaps, Reagan surmised, the successful resolution of the Pentecostals' case could mark a new beginning. To Dobrynin, Shultz, and Matlock, it demonstrated that the White House and the Kremlin could work together, quietly and constructively, to ease tensions. It did to Reagan as well, but it also meant much more. To him, the Pentecostals might become the symbol of a new Soviet Union that tolerated its religious people. If so, it would be an important first step on the long road to reform. "Ronald Reagan was intensely interested in the fate of individuals in trouble," recalled Matlock. "He wanted to do everything in his power to help them. His harsh judgment of the Soviet leaders was based . . . on his perception of the way they treated their own people." If the Soviet leaders were going to treat their people better, perhaps they themselves deserved better treatment. Reagan sensed that religion had provided him with an opening, and he was determined to seize it.[42]

At the same time, Reagan encouraged his friend Billy Graham—who had also become a convinced nuclear abolitionist in recent years—to ignore the opposition of the State Department and most Christian conservatives and accept Moscow's invitation to take his crusade to the Soviet Union. "I believe God moves in mysterious ways," he told Graham at the White House in 1982, when criticism of the evangelist's Moscow trip was at its height. "I'll be praying for you every mile of the way." Billy Graham walking in the peacemaking footsteps of the National Council of Churches' 1963 exchange? These were strange times indeed. Graham traveled twice to the country he had spent a lifetime demonizing, in 1982 and 1984, and on both occasions he spoke the rhetoric of freedom but also the language of peace. He called for increased religious freedom, but he also called for mutual respect and understanding between the two sides of the Cold War. During his 1982 visit, he met with the Pentecostals in the U.S. Embassy, but they simply berated the evangelist for even coming to the Soviet Union in the first place. Behind the scenes, Graham urged Soviet officials to let the Pentecostals emigrate, not only in the name of human rights but in the name of Soviet-American harmony. Reagan, Shultz, and Dobrynin would later make the decisive intervention that led to the Vashchenkos' freedom, but Graham's private efforts certainly helped. Like Reagan, and with the president's support, he had come to the realization that the Cold War, especially the arms race, was futile, perhaps even meaningless.[43]

With understandable puzzlement, Dobrynin noted in his memoirs that it was "most difficult for us to fathom" why Reagan would keep delivering "vehement public attacks on the Soviet Union while he was secretly sending . . . quite different signals seeking more normal relations." After all, only three weeks after his first, secret meeting with the Soviet ambassador, Reagan delivered his incendiary "evil empire" speech to the National Association of Evangelicals. But to Reagan, this strategy was not contradictory or confused but a deliberate blend of offense and defense. Reagan's détente would not be a Nixonian or Kissingerian pact with the devil, in which human rights would be sacrificed upon the altar of Cold War stability. He wanted détente, but on terms that were conducive to American ideals that he assumed to be universal. Matlock noted that most people looking back at the 1980s and the end of the Cold War assumed there were two Reagans: the first, a bellicose cold warrior, gave way to the second, a congenial statesman, shortly after the 1984 election and the coming to power of Gorbachev. But Matlock found this a bit too facile, because "in Reagan's mind his policy was consistent throughout." Perhaps, then, he was not a crusader, but a missionary out to spread his values—America's values—as widely as possible and by whatever means necessary. "Unlike many of his advisers," Matlock concluded, Reagan "believed that, if given the chance, he could convince the Soviet leaders that these goals were in the Soviet Union's interest—provided, and only provided, they came to understand that military competition with the United States was a losing strategy."[44]

In the Vatican, Pope John Paul II shared Reagan's vision. From personal experience and years of bitter struggle, the pontiff knew the Polish people had retained their ancient faith. From little more than an optimistic hunch, the unfortunate Pentecostals, and some carefully selected anecdotes, Reagan believed the same was true of the people of the Soviet Union. After John Paul's remarkable homecoming to Poland in 1979, when he was greeted by millions of adoring Catholics and which the communist authorities were powerless to stop, Reagan had predicted that "religion might very well turn out to be the Soviets' Achilles' heel." But more important, he believed that if the suppression of Russian religion were lifted, it might just provide the path to world peace. As had most of his predecessors, Reagan assumed that religion provided a baseline for democracy and that once a state allowed its people to worship it could do little to hold back the swell of other freedoms. "The truth is, politics and morality are inseparable," he told an audience during the 1984 campaign. "And as morality's foundation is religion, religion and politics are necessarily related. We need religion as a guide. We need it because we are imperfect, and our government needs the church, because only those humble enough to admit they're sinners can bring to democracy the tolerance it requires in order to survive." Thus the easing of restrictions on religion in the Soviet Union would create the conditions for peaceful internal revolution—and perhaps even an end to the Cold War. "Like you," he wrote to a friend while watching the funeral of Soviet Premier Yuri Andropov on television in February 1984, "I continue to believe that the hunger for religion may yet be a major factor in bringing about a change in the present situation." He got his chance to convert Gorbachev during the 1988 summit in Moscow by making a case for the existence of God and urging the atheist leader to relax restrictions on the thousands of churches, synagogues, and mosques throughout the Soviet Union.[45]

"It's been said that an icon is a window between heaven and Earth through which the believing eye can peer into the beyond," Reagan told a gathering of religious leaders in Moscow in May 1988, when Gorbachev's reformist policies of glasnost and perestroika were at their height. Here, in a church in the middle of the capital of world communism, an American president could now address a religious audience on the importance of religious liberty to political freedom. It was their task, Reagan told the assembled clerics, to foster the spiritual bases of peace and freedom. He confessed to being moved by "the deep faith that lives in the hearts of the people of this land," a faith that had been "tested and tempered in the crucible of hardship. But in that suffering, it has grown strong, ready now to embrace with new hope the beginnings of a second Christian millennium." Speaking on behalf of the American people, he revealed his dream that one day, hopefully soon, the people of the Soviet Union could reclaim their golden religious heritage:

> We in our country share this hope for a new age of religious freedom in the Soviet Union. We share the hope that this monastery is not an end in itself but the symbol of a new policy of religious tolerance that will extend to all peoples of all faiths.
>
> Our people feel it keenly when religious freedom is denied to anyone anywhere and hope with you that soon all the many Soviet religious communities that are now prevented from registering, or are banned altogether, including the Ukrainian Catholic and Orthodox Churches, will soon be able to practice their religion freely and openly . . .
>
> We may hope that *perestroika* will be accompanied by a deeper restructuring, a deeper conversion, a *mentanoya*, a change in heart, and

that *glasnost*, which means giving voice, will also let loose a new chorus
of belief, singing praise to the God that gave us life.

Only with faith could the political and economic freedom promised by
glasnost and perestroika flourish. It was a moving message, but it was also
an example of Reagan's idealistic synthesis that deftly blended the promotion of ideals with the soothing, conciliatory tones of détente—albeit
strictly on American terms. With this in mind, he closed with a message
of America's hope: "In our prayers we may keep that image in mind: the
thought that the bells may ring again, sounding throughout Moscow and
across the countryside, clamoring for joy in their new-found freedom."[46]

The Last Crusade?

St. Paul's Chapel, New York City, December 2001. Three months after the terrorist attacks of September 11, Rudy Giuliani, New York's mayor for the past eight years, delivered his farewell address. Already something of a national figure by the time of 9/11, Giuliani had become internationally renowned as the public face of his stricken city. Though term limits prevented him from running for reelection, his newfound stature gave him a political and cultural platform to interpret the terrorist attacks and America's response to them. His choice of venue was revealing: St. Paul's Chapel on Church Street in Lower Manhattan. An Episcopal Church only a block from City Hall, St. Paul's is the oldest public building in New York. Built in 1766, a few years after the Seven Years' War had redrawn the map of colonial North America and only a year after the outbreak of protest against the Stamp Act, St. Paul's had been George Washington's place of worship on his—and the nation's—first presidential inauguration day in 1789. A special pew commemorating Washington's visit has remained in the church ever since.

But more important for Giuliani was the proximity of St. Paul's to the World Trade Center site, now ominously known as Ground Zero. The chapel stands directly across Church Street from Ground Zero, yet it suffered no damage—not even a broken stained-glass window—when the towers collapsed and other, more modern buildings were toppled or severely damaged. For many, including Giuliani, the incredible survival of St. Paul's—"miraculous may not be too strong a word," intoned the *New York Times*—symbolized the resilient power of both faith and nation. In the weeks and months after 9/11, St. Paul's served as a refuge and recovery coordinating center, a haven for weary rescue workers and, of course, a place of worship for bewildered New Yorkers. Exhausted firefighters, police officers, and rescuers slept on the pews of St. Paul's while others prayed beside them. All told, it was an eminently fitting location for the mayor of New York's farewell address.[1]

"The reason I chose this chapel is because this chapel is thrice-hallowed ground," Giuliani told his listeners. "This is a place of really special importance to people who have a feeling and a sense and an emotion and an

601

understanding of patriotism." The church was first hallowed when it was "consecrated as a house of God" in 1766. Its next sanctification came at the birth of the nation. In April 1789, Giuliani explained, "George Washington came and after he was inaugurated as the first president of our republic he prayed right here in this church, which makes it very sacred ground to people who feel what America is all about." And it was hallowed again, this time in tragedy, on September 11, 2001. Giuliani reminded his listeners of the extraordinary perseverance of St. Paul's under extraordinary pressures. The devastation obliterated much of the area, but the chapel, only a few hundred yards from the World Trade Center complex, was left untouched. "And," he continued,

> I think there's some very, very special significance in that. The place where George Washington prayed when he first became president of the United States stood strong, powerful, untouched, undaunted by the attacks of these people who hate what we stand for. Because what we stand for is so much stronger than they are.
>
> . . . So this chapel stands for our values. And it's a very important place. And I hope you return here often to reflect on what it means to be an American and a New Yorker.

Giuliani took the idea of hallowed ground seriously—and literally. Ground Zero and St. Paul's would be sacred sites of memory for all Americans for all time, for both religious and patriotic reasons. "Long after we are all gone, it's the sacrifice of our patriots and their heroism that is going to be what this place is remembered for. This is going to be a place that is remembered 100 and 1,000 years from now, like the great battlefields of Europe and of the United States. And we really have to be able to do with it what they did with Normandy or Valley Forge or Bunker Hill or Gettysburg. We have to be able to create something here that enshrines this forever and that allows people to build on it and grow from it."[2]

Rudy Giuliani's turn to religion for reassurance and resolve was not unusual in the months following 9/11. Many Americans from all walks of life, from coast to coast, from the policymaking elite to the modest local church, sought comfort in faith. Ministers, priests, and rabbis noted a surge in attendance at their services, especially in the weeks immediately after the attacks. Neither was Giuliani's mix of religious faith and patriotism out of the ordinary. The faith-based vision of a virtuous, tolerant, and democratic America was invoked constantly, even by those who were convinced that U.S. foreign policy was at least partly responsible for triggering the attacks. Americans, in other words, turned not simply to religion, but to civil religion. "As the horror of last week unfolded, people from every conceivable community of faith expressed an interest in doing something," observed a county official in Maryland. "People seem to want to be together. They want to touch each other and express both faith and patriotism." Reverend Leroy Bowman of the First Baptist Church in Annapolis, Maryland, agreed. "I think that the Lord intends for us to draw this nation closer together."[3]

Reverend Lloyd John Ogilvie, chaplain of the U.S. Senate, expressed these same feelings even more forcefully. But he also cast the basic issue in Niebuhrian terms of using just force in an unjust world. People might be moral, but international politics was often too rough for moral niceties, and justice had to be done. "I preach and teach and counsel forgiveness in personal relationships," Ogilvie told an interviewer. "There are times, however . . . when there must be a confrontation of force to bring justice." World War II, Reinhold Niebuhr's finest hour, was a case in point, because armed force was "the only way the evil of Nazism could be rooted out and defeated," despite the claims of Christian pacifists. "Almighty God," Ogilvie prayed at the start of Senate proceedings on September 12, "we praise You for the consistency and constancy of Your presence with us to help us confront and battle the forces of evil manifested in infamous, illusive, cowardly acts of terrorism." Ogilvie thanked God for having "been with us in trouble and tragedies of the past" and for giving America "victory over tyranny" in previous conflicts. Above all, he prayed that God would "Bless the women and men of this Senate today as they join with President Bush in decisive action. Guide them as they seek justice against the perpetrators of yesterday's evil destruction and seek to devise a long-range solution to the insidious problem of terrorism." When he finished, Senate Majority Leader Tom Daschle thanked Reverend Ogilvie and applauded his message: "I know he speaks for us all."[4]

He certainly spoke for President George W. Bush, whose use of both religion and civil religion was constant after 9/11. Perhaps this was because Bush, an evangelical Methodist, felt himself called by God at this moment in history. Shortly after the attacks, a leading cleric in the Lutheran Church (Missouri Synod) told him, "you are a servant of God called for such a time like this." Bush did not disagree and simply replied: "I accept the responsibility." In a rare quiet moment after 9/11 with his chief political aide Karl Rove, Bush confided his belief that "I'm here for a reason, and this is going to be how we're going to be judged."[5]

In deploying religion, Bush appealed to both the sword of the spirit and the shield of faith. He spoke of launching a "crusade" against Islamic terrorism, apparently unaware of the bitter historical memory of the medieval Christian Crusades that still lingered in the minds of Arabs. Yet on several occasions, he also invoked the Judeo-Christian tradition of religious tolerance to deflect Americans from seeking revenge against Muslims. "The face of terror is not the true faith of Islam. That's not what

Islam is all about," he said on September 17. Islam instead represented "peace" because it was "a faith that brings comfort to a billion people around the world . . . and that's made brothers and sisters out of every race—out of every race." But most of all, Bush blended the language of faith and nation to offer benediction to America's mission in the world—a mission that intended peace even when it resorted to war. Following the launch of the air war against Afghanistan, which continued to provide a base for al Qaeda, he explained that the Taliban was "hearing from a tolerant nation, a nation that respects Islam and values our many Muslim citizens. They are hearing from a prayerful nation, a nation that prays to an almighty God for protection and for peace. And they are hearing from a patient and determined nation, a nation that will continue this war for as long as it takes to win."[6]

Bush's words, all of them, rested comfortably within a bipartisan tradition of using religion to frame foreign policy. This was no coincidence. "Just 3 days removed from these events, Americans do not yet have the distance of history," he declared in one of his most important post-9/11 speeches, at the National Cathedral in Washington on September 14, which he had declared a National Day of Prayer and Remembrance. "But our responsibility to history is already clear: To answer these attacks and rid the world of evil." The National Cathedral address framed the morality of the terrorist attacks and America's response to them. And to do so, Bush touched on many of the themes that had animated the religious influence on American war and diplomacy during the previous four centuries: the links between religion and democracy; the importance of religious liberty; the blessing of America's errand to the world; the tragic necessity of using force for justice in an unjust world; the presence of evil as a test to the faithful; the responsibilities that come with power and wealth. God had given much to America; he expected much in return. But Bush's pronouncement at the National Cathedral had a harder edge to it, too, resolute but also defiant, even aggressive. And it was clear what would come next. "War has been waged against us by stealth and deceit and murder," he continued. "This Nation is peaceful, but fierce when stirred to anger. This conflict was begun on the timing and terms of others. It will end in a way and at an hour of our choosing." This was not Bush's will, but God's. "As we have been assured, neither death nor life, nor angels nor principalities nor powers, nor things present nor things to come, nor height nor depth, can separate us from God's love. May He bless the souls of the departed. May He comfort our own, and may He always guide our country. God bless America."[7]

The ecclesiastical setting was not incidental, and the address was not simply a foreign policy speech that just happened to be delivered in a place of worship. Bush intended the speech to be a statement of foreign policy, but he hoped it would also be something more profound. "I saw it as a moment to make sure that I helped comfort and helped get through the mourning process," he recalled in an interview with the journalist Bob Woodward. "I also really looked at it from a spiritual perspective, that it was important for the nation to pray." He confessed that the speech "really was a prayer. . . . I believed that the nation needed to be in prayer."[8]

Bush's speech—some called it a sermon—was widely hailed, but it did not sit well with everyone. Some worried about the appearance of a secular official, one charged with upholding the laws of the land that included the separation of church and state, using a religious setting to make a statement of government policy. Some objected to the use of a church to justify war, no matter how worthy or necessary it might be. Some objected to the impending war itself. And some objected to Bush's appropriation of the moral high ground by appealing to a religious faith they did not necessarily share. As one Christian commentator argued in the *Washington Post*, "A War President Shouldn't Ask What Jesus Would Do." The journalist E. J. Dionne, a close observer of American religion and its political role, was more subtle in issuing a similar rebuttal to those who would claim God's favor. "Faith is more credible when it stands as a challenge, when it insists on aspirations beyond those of our own political movements, communities or nations," Dionne wrote in response to Bush's National Cathedral speech. He concluded with an allusion to Lincoln: "The prayers of this faith do not express certainty that God is on our side, only the hope that this might prove to be true."[9]

At the time, many Americans, supporters and critics alike, thought of Bush's rhetoric as exceptional and that his use of religion to frame and justify foreign policy was a radical break with the American diplomatic tradition. Many also criticized his close political relationship with Christian conservatives as unusual. Bush's use of religion was certainly more pervasive than some of his predecessors'. But as we have seen, the religious influence on foreign relations has been a constant throughout American history. After all, only three years earlier, on September 11, 1998, President Bill Clinton delivered a strikingly similar speech from the very same spot—the pulpit of the National Cathedral—following the al Qaeda bombings of U.S. embassies in Kenya and Tanzania. Clinton called for a "common commitment to carry on the cause of peace and freedom," but he also promised "to find those responsible and bring them to justice" and "not to rest as long as terrorists plot to take more innocent lives." For America's "larger struggle, for hope over hatred and unity over division," he explained, "is a just one. And with God's help, it will prevail." Religion has not always been a determining or formative influence in the history of American foreign relations, but it has been consistent. Whether one supported or opposed Bush's particular foreign policies, his use of religion was entirely in keeping with American tradition.[10]

For better or worse, the last twenty-five years have followed in this tradition. The religious influence has sometimes stemmed from the personal beliefs of individual policymakers. But just as often, it has emerged as a result of political pressures emanating from below, as religious Americans—liberals and conservatives, Democrats and Republicans, Christians, Jews, Muslims, Buddhists, Hindus, and those of many other faiths—have organized, mobilized, and brought their views to bear on politicians and policymakers. Unlike intelligence data, weapons expertise, diplomatic experience, or fluency in a foreign language, anyone can possess a religious faith if they want to; and because religion can belong to everyone, it has provided a common denominator for dialogue between policymaking elites and the wider public. It has provided a shared language with which all Americans can negotiate the terms of their engagement with the rest of the world. If Bush had indeed launched the United States on a crusade, it was certainly not for the first time. Nor would it be the last.

IN THE 1988 ELECTION, Vice President George H. W. Bush campaigned like Ronald Reagan. He claimed born-again status, promised to support constitutional amendments on school prayer and abortion, and assiduously courted the Religious Right. But once in office, Bush governed like Richard Nixon, especially on foreign policy. "I and a lot of other evangelicals are getting fed up too soon with President Bush. I didn't expect much; we're getting less," one pastor complained to a White House aide. "I would suggest to you: don't unpack everything. Four years will pass all too soon." Evangelicals, who comprised much of Bush's electoral base, wanted him to launch a post–Cold War crusade for religious liberty and human rights, especially in the Balkans, China, Africa, and the Soviet Union. Instead, the arch-realist Bush administration prioritized order over justice, stability over human rights. The people of Ukraine, Tibet, and China got little support from Washington as they confronted war and oppression. When asked if Washington would intervene to halt genocide in Bosnia, Secretary of State James A. Baker summed up the Bush administration's attitude: "We have no dog in that fight."[11]

While evangelicals wanted a more activist foreign policy, many Catholics, Jews, and liberal Protestants wanted a more modest one. Bush's signature foreign policy achievement, victory over Iraq in the Gulf War, was at the time intensely controversial, especially among religious groups. Their criticism of his use of force followed from earlier misgivings about other episodes in the Bush foreign policy, especially the 1989 invasion of

Panama and the reluctance to engage in wider-ranging nuclear reduction talks with the Soviet Union. The Catholic hierarchy reacted to operations Desert Shield and Desert Storm cautiously. While the National Conference of Catholic Bishops told Bush they "strongly support and commend your efforts to build global solidarity," as the NCCB's head, Daniel Cardinal Pilarczyk, wrote, they also implored him to find "a peaceful solution that seeks to bring justice to the region without resort to war." The National Council of Churches expressed similar reservations, while the Most Reverend Edmond L. Browning, the presiding bishop of the Episcopal Church—the president's own denomination—met with Bush at the White House and bluntly told him, "In no way is the war option going to serve our national interest." It was, Bush recalled, "a very emotional meeting, at least for me."[12]

In the end, the Bush foreign policy pleased very few religious Americans. For most liberals, it was too robust; for most conservatives, too amoral; for others still, too vacillating and accommodating. Other problems abounded. Prophetic Christians and fundamentalists recoiled in horror from Bush's promise that America would build a "new world order," and from his deference to the United Nations, which all seemed suspiciously similar to the Antichrist's plans for world government. Christian Zionists refused to support Bush and Baker's attempts to use victory over Iraq to begin a peace process in the Middle East that would severely curtail Israeli ambitions. Overall, then, George H. W. Bush pleased nobody, and he paid for it at the ballot box in 1992. Even the evangelicals and fundamentalists of the Religious Right, who had closely allied with the Republican Party since 1980, deserted him. While 70 percent of white evangelicals had voted for Bush in 1988 (and 80 percent for Reagan in 1984), only a small majority—55 percent—voted for him in 1992 and many more stayed home; moreover, only 46 percent of Catholics voted for him, the lowest total for a Republican candidate in nearly two decades. Bush's realist foreign policy, which blended a willingness to use military force with an aversion to moral crusades, turned off religious liberals and religious conservatives almost in equal measure.[13]

CLINTON FACED SIMILAR problems throughout the 1990s, a decade in which public religiosity may not have reached the levels seen in the 1950s and 1970s but that did witness unusually high levels of faith-based political activism. It was also the scene of some of the most polarized, politicized religion since the Protestant-Catholic feuds of the interwar era, for the 1990s saw the revival of the culture wars between liberals and conservatives over school prayer, abortion, gender, race, and gay rights that had begun in the Sixties. On many issues, Christian conservatives gained predominance. A watershed year in conservatism, in 1992 the Religious

Right was able to use the Republican defeat to its advantage. Christian conservatives' defection from Bush illustrated their cohesive bloc voting power that future Republican candidates could not afford to ignore. Afterward, the Religious Right stood as one of the strongest groups in conservative politics.

On foreign policy, Christian conservatives pushed three big ideas particularly hard, though not always in sync. The first was unilateralism—not necessarily isolationism, but the safeguarding of American sovereignty while the nation involved itself in the world. The second, both cause and consequence of the first, was the zealous promotion of America as exceptional: different, virtuous, and strong, God's chosen nation. These two ideas, unilateralism and nationalism, found a wide audience through conservative commentators such as Pat Buchanan (Roman Catholic) and Pat Robertson (Pentecostal), whose 1991 bestseller *The New World Order* painted a dark picture of America subservient to the secular humanists, communists, and heathens of the United Nations.[14]

The third big conservative idea was the promotion of human rights, which mostly meant individual rights—especially religious liberty—but not group rights that would guarantee socioeconomic equality. As the editors of *Christianity Today* reminded their mostly evangelical readers, "Despite communism's decline, torture and persecution continue." And it was America's duty to do something about it.[15]

Enacted mostly by a Republican-dominated Congress whose leadership was sympathetic toward the Religious Right, many of these ideas became policy. Most important was the 1998 International Religious Freedom Act, which created an Office of International Religious Freedom in the State Department and the Commission on International Religious Freedom, an independent federal agency. Both would monitor global infringements upon religious liberty, with violators potentially subject to U.S. sanctions. Moreover, mission boards and faith-based aid organizations began receiving vastly larger amounts of public funding to dispense to poor countries and development projects around the world. Finally, Christian Zionists, including many members of Congress, helped renew and expand America's unwavering support for Israel.[16]

GEORGE H. W. BUSH's son would not commit the political sins of his father. Indeed, as George W. Bush told Bob Woodward, Bush Sr. "is the wrong father to appeal to in terms of strength. There is a higher father that I appeal to." Instead of ignoring the Religious Right, as his own father did, George W. Bush formed a tight bond with Christian conservatives. Richard Land, head of the Southern Baptist Convention's Ethics and Religious Liberty Commission and the leading SBC spokesman on foreign policy, observed that Bush the son not only listened to the views of evangelicals, he actively solicited them.[17]

As president, moreover, Bush surrounded himself with fellow devout Christians, including those who had a major hand in foreign policymaking. Michael Gerson, Bush's chief speechwriter, was a fellow evangelical who framed Bush's key speeches on world affairs around highly moralistic Christian themes of mission, charity, redemption, and crusade. Condoleezza Rice, national security adviser in Bush's first term and secretary of state in his second, was a devoted Presbyterian. Thanks to her father, Reverend John Wesley Rice, she had been literally raised in a church—a small, four-room apartment attached to the Westminster Presbyterian Church in Birmingham, Alabama—and absorbed its teachings, particularly its Calvinist ideas of sacrifice, chosenness, responsibility, and destiny. "The peace and love of God is real," she told an interviewer. "In fact, there's so much confirmation of Christ in my life that faith and reason don't conflict in very important ways. I have been religious all my life. I cannot remember when I did not believe." Colleagues observed that in moments of crisis, she prayed.[18]

Bush himself spoke of his own faith in similar terms—openly and unabashedly—perhaps more than any president before him. Just as he relied on religion to shape America's response to the 9/11 attacks, he used it to frame other aspects of policy, both foreign and domestic. At home, in the controversial "faith-based initiatives," he significantly increased the amount of public funding for charitable purposes received by churches and other religious organizations. Abroad, he discussed his own faith and the importance of religious liberty with world leaders, including Russia's Vladimir Putin and China's Jiang Zemin. Partly at the behest of Gerson, who was close to evangelical missionaries, Bush devoted more attention and funding to Africa, especially for AIDS treatment and prevention. He also was receptive to the Republican Congress' desire to rein in or deny foreign aid that would contribute to birth control and abortion programs. And of course, he turned to the language of faith to help launch the war against Iraq in 2003.[19]

Yet the United States did not have a monopoly on faith-based geopolitics. Beginning in the 1970s, most of the world had experienced a boom in religion, especially in countries—Russia, China, India, and Turkey—that had spent much of the previous century trying to restrain faith or even eradicate it altogether. In particular, Islam surged in popularity and replaced its secular rivals, such as pan-Arabism, Ba'athism, nationalism, and socialism, as the dominant ideology throughout the Middle East. Christianity soared as its center of gravity shifted from Europe and North America to the developing world, where the largest churches—Protestant and Catholic—could now be found in Africa. Evangelical Protestantism, especially Pentecostalism, won millions of converts in East Asia and Latin America. What was striking was not simply the growth of faith, but the growth of conservative and fundamentalist faith—particularly in Islam and Christianity, but also in Judaism and Hinduism—and its intimate role in politics, governance, and international relations. The world had become defined not only by George W. Bush, but also Osama bin Laden.[20]

Nor did Bush have a monopoly on faith at home, where his pious vision and sense of global mission were challenged by a wide array of religious Americans. The resurgence of Christian conservatism in the 1970s, the culture wars of the 1990s, and the crusading faith-based policies of Bush after 2001 triggered a reaction from the left. Progressive religious activists—Rabbi Michael Lerner; Catholic intellectuals E. J. Dionne and Garry Wills; and evangelical Protestant Jim Wallis, founder of the organization Sojourners—mounted countercrusades to reclaim faith from what they condemned as conservative extremes. Rather than war, they and others said, a penitent America should use its strength and wealth to bring food to the hungry, clean water to the thirsty, and peace to a war-torn world. Bush had not implemented the will of God, but subverted it. And if Bush enjoyed the support of Christian conservatives, he also often disappointed them when he was unable, or unwilling, to implement everything they wanted. Meanwhile, the nation's fastest-growing religious group, Muslims, were largely repelled by the Bush administration's foreign policy, especially its wars in Iraq and Afghanistan and its unbending support for Israel.[21]

Nor, finally, was Bush an aberration in the American diplomatic tradition. His strain of evangelicalism was not especially radical, and his application of religious principles and rhetoric to public policy, including foreign policy, was not unusual. No matter what their ideology or party affiliation, to some extent almost all presidents framed and justified their foreign policies in religious terms.[22]

THOUGH HIS POLITICS and policies differ sharply, the presidency of Barack Obama is showing every sign of continuing these religious traditions in U.S. foreign relations. Raised with the input of various intellectual, social, and cultural traditions on two continents, Obama's faith did not really coalesce until he moved to Chicago, in the 1980s, and joined Trinity United Church of Christ. Trinity's minister, Reverend Jeremiah Wright, was heavily influenced by Christian Black Power and liberation theology, especially the writings of James H. Cone, and these ideas formed the basis of Trinity's mission on Chicago's impoverished South Side. But as important as this milieu was, Obama's intellectual and spiritual curiosity led him to other theological influences, especially the Social Gospel ministry of Martin Luther King and the Christian realism of Reinhold Niebuhr. Jimmy Carter had found such combinations politically lethal, but Obama was not a born-again Christian and was thus unbound by normal conventions. He was, simply by virtue of who he was, free to be as ecumenical, syncretic, and experimental as he wished.[23]

With Obama, two things became clear. The first was the intellectual depth of his faith. The second, not unrelated, was the political relevance of his religion. He bridled at suggestions from conservatives that religion was no place for the progressive politics of liberalism. When Kansas Republican Senator Sam Brownback, a staunch Christian conservative, introduced Obama during a joint appearance at Rick Warren's Saddleback Church in California with the words "Welcome to my house," Obama was not slow to respond: "There is one thing I've gotta say, Sam, though: This is my house, too. This is God's house." But he was equally dismayed by his fellow liberal Democrats who felt there was no place for religion in politics at all. In the summer of 2006, he bluntly warned that "secularists are wrong when they ask believers to leave their religion at the door before entering into the public square. Frederick Douglass, Abraham Lincoln, William Jennings Bryan, Dorothy Day, Martin Luther King—indeed, the majority of great reformers in American history—were not only motivated by faith but repeatedly used religious language to argue for their cause." On this point, Obama would not be misunderstood. "So to say that men and women should not inject their 'personal morality' into public-policy debates is a practical absurdity. Our law is by definition a codification of morality, much of it grounded in the Judeo-Christian tradition."[24]

Like his heroes, Obama has used religious language to argue for his causes too, including those in the wider world. But, characteristically, he has put his own spin on longstanding traditions. Niebuhr's Christian realism is one, and perhaps the most important. In a play on Franklin D. Roosevelt's "good neighbor policy" toward Latin America, one commentator has even dubbed Obama's foreign policy the "Good Niebuhr Policy." Niebuhr may have been a realist, but he was unlike a Nixon or a Kissinger: he was instead a *Christian* realist for whom faith must provide the moral core of American foreign policy. Without religion, Niebuhr argued, realism would invariably lead the nation astray because it would lack a moral compass and thus lack moral purpose, but without realism, religion could also be damaging because of its tendency to veer off into destructive idealistic crusades. Niebuhr advised American leaders to be righteous without indulging in self-righteousness; he wanted them to be moral without being moralistic. This was a delicate balance to maintain, but it suited Obama perfectly. "He's one of my favorite philosophers," Obama told *New York Times* columnist David Brooks when asked about Niebuhr, because of his "compelling idea that there's serious evil in the world, and hardship and pain. And we should be humble and modest in our belief we can eliminate those things. But we shouldn't use that as an excuse for cynicism and inaction."[25]

In accepting the Nobel Peace Prize in December 2009, Obama invoked Niebuhrian realism and the timeless "notions of just war and the imperatives of a just peace." And while he recognized the heroic Christian pacifism of Martin Luther King, he also firmly rejected it:

> We must begin by acknowledging the hard truth: We will not eradicate violent conflict in our lifetimes. There will be times when nations—acting individually or in concert—will find the use of force not only necessary but morally justified.
>
> . . . I face the world as it is, and cannot stand idle in the face of threats to the American people. For make no mistake: Evil does exist in the world. A non-violent movement could not have halted Hitler's armies. Negotiations cannot convince al Qaeda's leaders to lay down their arms. To say that force may sometimes be necessary is not a call to cynicism—it is a recognition of history; the imperfections of man and the limits of reason.

"The spirit of Niebuhr presided over the Nobel address," observed George Packer.[26]

On a visit to China, Obama referred to a different concept from the canon on religion and foreign relations: the importance of religious liberty. In the American tradition, this was an even older concept than realism or the just war. In a November 2009 town hall meeting with "future Chinese leaders," Obama lectured his hosts on the principles of good governance. The United States was by no means perfect: Americans had tolerated the sin of slavery for far too long, and it took a civil war to eradicate it; it then took a civil rights movement to make good on the original promise of emancipation. But freedom prevailed nonetheless, and it ensured America's role as the guarantor of world freedom. "And that is why," Obama continued in a reiteration of the first two of Franklin Roosevelt's Four Freedoms,

> America will always speak out for these core principles around the world. We do not seek to impose any system of government on any other nation, but we also don't believe that the principles that we stand for are unique to our nation. These freedoms of expression and worship—of access to information and political participation—we believe are universal rights. They should be available to all people, including ethnic and religious minorities—whether they are in the United States, China, or any nation. Indeed, it is that respect for uni-

versal rights that guides America's openness to other countries; our respect for different cultures; our commitment to international law; and our faith in the future.

Religious liberty, Obama told the Chinese, was one of the preconditions for political liberty. And with political liberty would come peace, at home and abroad.[27]

Obama has also stressed the importance of religious pluralism to harmonious international relations. In perhaps his most famous foreign speech, in Cairo in June 2009, Obama conceded that the United States had made mistakes in the region but maintained that America's Judeo-Christian civil religion, and especially its grounding in religious tolerance, provided a path to peace. Echoing two centuries of American political thought, he told his Egyptian and largely Muslim audience that "freedom in America is indivisible from the freedom to practice one's religion." The universality of religious liberty and its centrality to the democratic peace meant that all faiths required accommodation. "People in every country should be free to choose and live their faith based upon the persuasion of the mind and the heart and the soul. This tolerance is essential for religion to thrive," while freedom of religion "is central to the ability of people to live together." The Golden Rule, Obama concluded in another nod to FDR, was common to every religion, not just Christianity. "It's a belief that pulsed in the cradle of civilization," he preached, "and that still beats in the hearts of billions around the world. It's a faith in other people, and it's what brought me here today." The importance of pluralism and tolerance have been common refrains in Obama's speeches since, particularly at moments, such as the "Ground Zero mosque" controversy and the anniversary of 9/11, when religious prejudice has flared in the United States.[28]

Thus continues the religious influence on American foreign relations. There will be American crusades in the future just as there have been in the past. Whether from the top down in the form of the personal piety of American leaders, or the bottom up in the form of pressure from religious groups and individuals, whether for peace or for war, religion remains, and will continue to remain, an integral part of foreign relations. It may not always determine the direction of policy, but it will be an ever-present factor. Those who conduct U.S. foreign policy ignore it at their peril.

ABBREVIATIONS

ABHS American Baptist Historical Society
AHJ *American Holiness Journal*
AHTL Andover-Harvard Theological Library, Harvard University
BC Burns Library, Boston College
BHL Bentley Historical Library, University of Michigan
CC *Christian Century*
C&C *Christianity and Crisis*
CEIP Records of the Carnegie Endowment for International Peace, Nicholas Murray Butler Library, Columbia University
CF Country File
CHS Connecticut Historical Society
CR *Congressional Record*
CRT *Current Religious Thought*
CT *Christianity Today*
DDEL Dwight D. Eisenhower Library
DHTP *Documentary History of the Truman Presidency*
DSB *Department of State Bulletin*
FCB *Federal Council Bulletin*
FCC Federal Council of Churches
FDRFA *Franklin D. Roosevelt and Foreign Affairs*
FDRL Franklin D. Roosevelt Library
FRUS *Foreign Relations of the United States*
GBL George Bush Library
GF General File
GRFL Gerald R. Ford Library
HL Houghton Library, Harvard University
HML Hagley Museum and Library
HSTL Harry S. Truman Library
IWPPC Issues of War and Peace Pamphlet Collection, Yale Divinity School
JFKL John F. Kennedy Library
JHL John Hay Library, Brown University
JTS Jewish Theological Seminary
LAT *Los Angeles Times*
LBJL Lyndon B. Johnson Library
LOC Library of Congress
Memcon Memorandum of conversation
MHS Massachusetts Historical Society
MNHS Minnesota Historical Society
MSCD Manuscript and Special Collections, William R. Perkins Library, Duke University

NAEC National Archives of the Episcopal Church, Booher Library, Episcopal Seminary of the Southwest
NCC National Council of Churches
NF Name File
NSF National Security Files
NYT *New York Times*
OF Official File
OHRO Oral History Research Office, Columbia University
PDDE *The Papers of Dwight David Eisenhower*
POF President's Office Files
PHS Presbyterian Historical Society
PPAFDR *The Public Papers and Addresses of Franklin D. Roosevelt*
PPP *Public Papers of the Presidents of the United States*
PSF President's Secretary's Files
PTS Special Collections, Henry Luce III Library, Princeton Theological Seminary
PWW *Papers of Woodrow Wilson*
RG Record Group
RM Religious Matters
RNL Richard Nixon Library
RRL Ronald Reagan Library
SF Subject File
SHC-UNC Southern Historical Collection, University of North Carolina
SMLP Seeley G. Mudd Manuscripts Library, Princeton University
UAD University Archives, Duke University
UEA *United Evangelical Action*
UTS Union Theological Seminary Archives, Burke Theological Library, Columbia University
UVA Albert and Shirley Small Special Collections Library, University of Virginia
UW Special Collections, Allen Library South, University of Washington
WCC Archives of the World Council of Churches, Geneva
WHCF White House Central Files
WHORM White House Office of Records Management
WP *Washington Post*
WSJ *Wall Street Journal*
YDS Special Collections, Yale Divinity School

NOTES

PREFACE

1. "Address Before a Joint Session of the Congress on the State of the Union," January 28, 2003, *PPP: George W. Bush, 2003*, Book 1, 90; "Remarks at the National Religious Broadcasters Convention in Nashville, Tennessee," ibid., 147, 150.
2. "Hardening His Tone, Hussein Challenges Inspectors and Talks of War Readiness," *NYT*, January 7, 2003; "Bin Laden's Message to Muslims in Iraq: Fight the 'Crusaders,' " *NYT*, February 15, 2003.
3. Though they are not all focused solely on connecting religion with foreign relations, for the broad overviews, see Tuveson, *Redeemer Nation*; Miscamble, "Catholics and American Foreign Policy"; Stephanson, *Manifest Destiny*; McDougall, *Promised Land, Crusader State*; and Phillips, *Cousins' Wars*. More recently, see the insightful and incisive surveys in Mead, "God's Country?"; and Mead, *God and Gold*.
4. Jacobs, "Our System Demands the Supreme Being"; a few years later, Jacobs included his important article in the 2004 book *America's Miracle Man*. McAlister, *Epic Encounters* (the first edition was published in 2001). Rotter, "Christians, Muslims, and Hindus"; Rotter, *Comrades at Odds*, 220–248.

INTRODUCTION

1. The works of Richard Hofstadter, who coined the phrase "paranoid style," did much to demonize religion in the American historical profession. See especially his *Anti-Intellectualism in American Life* and *Paranoid Style in American Politics*. For the absence of religion in diplomatic history, see Preston, "Bridging the Gap" or Preston, "Reviving Religion." For religion's absence in other branches of American history, see Boyer, "In Search of the Fourth 'R' "; Butler, "Jack-in-the-Box Faith"; Chappell, *Stone of Hope*; and Spickard, "Asian Americans, Religion, and Race." On various theories and methods of diplomatic history, see the essays in Hogan and Paterson, eds., *Explaining the History of American Foreign Relations*. For a synthesis of the cultural turn, see Hixson, *Myth of American Diplomacy*. For the internationalization of American history, see Bender, *Nation Among Nations*. My list of diplomatic history overviews that ignore or marginalize religion despite their focus on ideas and values refers to, in order, Osgood, *Ideals and Self-Interest in America's Foreign Relations*; Dallek, *American Style of Foreign Policy*; Hunt, *Ideology and U.S. Foreign Policy*; Smith, *America's Mission*; Steigerwald, *Wilsonian Idealism in America*; Walker, *National Security and Core Values in American History*; and Brewer, *Why America Fights*. More broadly, however, the separation of religion from the rest of American history has recently shown signs of ending. For surveys that take religion seriously and effectively integrate it into a larger

historical narrative, see McDougall, *Freedom Just Around the Corner* and *Throes of Democracy*; Howe, *What Hath God Wrought*; Kuklick, *Political History of the USA*; and Reynolds, *America, Empire of Liberty*.

2. This approach, of prioritizing the twentieth century, is not unusual for synthetic treatments of the history of American foreign relations. See, most recently, the structure of the superb one-volume account in Herring, *From Colony to Superpower*.

3. Iriye, "Culture and Power," 116.

4. This is not necessarily to say that U.S. foreign policy has been progressive. I use the term "progressive" throughout the book mostly to identify Americans who believed their country should be an agent of progress in the world. I therefore use it to describe people's intentions, not the results of their actions. That their universalistic visions of progress were in fact particularistic American visions is interesting, but not especially relevant for my purposes. Just as I do not intend to praise or condemn religion, I do not seek to evaluate the wisdom or morality of U.S. foreign policy; here, as with religion, I will pay readers the compliment of letting them decide for themselves.

5. On the development and impact of popular enfranchisement, see Wilentz, *Rise of American Democracy*. On its complications and limitations, see Keyssar, *Right to Vote*.

6. Tocqueville, *Democracy in America*, vol. 1, part 2, chap. 9, 279.

7. On free security, see Woodward, "Age of Reinterpretation." For the best recent account, from which I have learned a great deal, see Craig and Logevall, *America's Cold War*. This is not to say that free security was absolute or uncontroversial. As some historians have noted, through the nineteenth century and into the twentieth, Britain was one of America's greatest competitors as well as its most natural partner. Moreover, it is also important to remember that the idea of free security emerged, for political purposes, in the era of the world wars when internationalists were trying to discredit isolationists. Though both of these points have merit and must be taken into account, however, as long as we acknowledge free security's highly politicized origins the theory is still useful. At the very least, even when tensions between Britain and the United States were high, Americans still did not fear a British invasion and occupation of their country, let alone an invasion or attack by another country. And as historians now acknowledge, though Britain was often a rival, its statesmen found common ideological cause with their American counterparts much more often then not because they viewed the word largely from the same normative perspective. For the most persuasive and thoughtful critique of the free security concept, see Zakaria, "Myth of America's 'Free Security'"; and Zakaria, *From Wealth to Power*, 177–178. For the tacit partnership between British and American policymakers despite their frequent disagreements, see, most recently, Sexton, *Monroe Doctrine*.

8. See MacCulloch, *Reformation*, esp. xxii, 175–176, 390–391, 496, 533–545, 603–604, 700–701.

9. On the development of the American religious marketplace, see, among many others, Hatch, *Democratization of American Christianity*; Finke and Stark, *Churching of America*; Moore, *Selling God*; Stokes and Conway, eds., *Market Revolution in America*; Roof, *Spiritual Marketplace*; Noll, *America's God*, esp. 223–224; Wuthnow, *America and the Challenges of Religious Diversity*; and Lambert, *Religion in American Politics*.

10. On religion as a source of nationalism, see Hastings, *Construction of Nationhood*; Haas, *Nationalism, Liberalism, and Progress*, vol. 1, 53–57, passim in subsequent case studies; Roshwald, *Endurance of Nationalism*, 48–51, 134–149, 167–225; Smith, *Chosen Peoples*; and, specifically in the American context, Furstenberg, *In*

the Name of the Father. Significantly, and unusually, historians who link nationalism to religion often trace its rise well before the modern period. On religion as a source of American nationalism, see Vinz, *Pulpit Politics*; and Lieven, *America Right or Wrong.*

11. The very idea of a "civil religion" is, in American religious studies, complicated by the fact that it emerged at a certain time (the late 1960s) with a specific purpose (to rescue liberal religion from decline and use it to help solve the nation's social and political crises). But we can use the term in a more neutral way, simply to mean the use of faith to sustain and promote political ideas and national identity. In this sense, and certainly in the way I perceive it, "civil religion" is nothing more than a blend of faith and patriotism with overwhelming political resonance. On politics and religion as ceremonial, I am obviously following along a well-worn path first blazed by Émile Durkheim; see his book *Elementary Forms of the Religious Life,* originally published in 1912. For an insightful, more recent analysis from which I have also drawn, see Kertzer, *Ritual, Politics, and Power.* For the early versions of "civil religion" in the United States, see esp. Bellah, "Civil Religion in America" and Bellah, *Broken Covenant.* I am grateful to Leigh Schmidt for his advice on this problematic concept.

12. Tocqueville, *Democracy in America,* vol. 1, part 2, chap. 9, 275.

PART I. IN THE BEGINNING

1. Morgan, *American Slavery, American Freedom,* 98–99; Taylor, *American Colonies,* 134–135. On Virginia's population, see McCusker and Menard, *Economy of British America,* 118–119.

2. Rountree, "Powhatan Priests"; Rountree and Turner, *Before and After Jamestown,* 165–166; Shea, *Virginia Militia in the Seventeenth Century,* 25. On Pocahontas, see Townsend, *Pocahontas and the Powhatan Dilemma*; and Rountree, *Pocahontas.* On Powhatan religion, see Rountree, *Powhatan Indians of Virginia,* 126–139. On religion being a greater distinction than race in the early modern world, see Kidd, *Forging of Races,* 54–55.

3. Gray quoted in Craven, "Indian Policy in Early Virginia," 65; colonists quoted in Horn, *Adapting to a New World,* 412.

4. Morgan, *American Slavery, American Freedom,* 99–100; Vaughan, "Expulsion of the Salvages"; Kukla, "Order and Chaos," 284. Colonist quoted in Rountree, "Powhatans and the English," 191.

5. Horn, *Adapting to a New World,* 280; Rountree, "Powhatan Priests"; Billings, *Sir William Berkeley,* 96.

6. Games, *Web of Empire,* esp. 219–253. On the diversity of colonial American religion, see Pestana, "Religion"; and Butler, Wacker, and Balmer, *Religion in American Life,* 76–115. On the conflation of Catholicism with tyranny and Protestantism with liberty in early modern English political thought, and their impact on English imperialism, see Phillips, *Cousins' Wars,* 3–32; Fatovic, "Anti-Catholic Roots"; and Pestana, *Protestant Empire.* On the "Protestant Cause," see Milton, *Catholic and Reformed,* 503–515.

CHAPTER ONE. DEFENDERS OF THE FAITH

1. Kelsey, *Sir Francis Drake,* 9–10, 111, 393, 401–404; Drake quoted in Porter, *Inconstant Savage,* 186.

2. Taylor, *American Colonies,* 59–60; Bishop quoted in Porter, *Inconstant Savage,* 135.

3. This biographical portrait is based on Mancall, *Hakluyt's Promise*, esp. 72, 109–110, 162–163. On the uncertainty of religion as the main driver of Hakluyt's views, see Armitage, *Ideological Origins of the British Empire*, 71–81.

4. Hakluyt, *Discourse of Western Planting* (London, 1584), in Gaustad, *Documentary History of Religion in America to the Civil War*, 53. On the mercantilist imperative to overseas expansion, see McCusker and Menard, *Economy of British North America*, 35–38, 45. On religion complementing ideas of economic imperialism, see, albeit from different perspectives, Wright, *Religion and Empire*; Rabb, *Enterprise and Empire*, 86–89, 100; Lovejoy, *Religious Enthusiasm*, 11–13; Pagden, *Lords of All the Worlds*, 35–37, 88; and Mead, *God and Gold*.

5. Richard Hakluyt, preface to *Divers Voyages* (London, 1582), in Taylor, *Original Writings and Correspondence of the Two Richard Hakluyts*, 178. On the Black Legend, see Hillgarth, *Mirror of Spain*, esp. 3–68, 351–395; and Stevens, *Poor Indians*, 46–49.

6. Milton, *Catholic and Reformed*, 42–46; Maltby, *Black Legend in England*, 15–16; Wernham, *Making of Elizabethan Foreign Policy*, 45–48, 85–86; Guy, *Tudor England*, 343–345; Purkiss, *English Civil War*, 88–89. On the transnational waging of war on behalf of religion and ideology in the early modern world, see Owen, *Clash of Ideas*.

7. Gilbert to Elizabeth I, November 6, 1577, in Quinn, *Voyages and Colonising Enterprises of Sir Humphrey Gilbert*, 176–180.

8. Quoted in Armitage, *Ideological Origins of the British Empire*, 86.

9. Quoted in Jennings, *Invasion of America*, 81. On Purchas's justifications for English claims to "vacant" land, see Miller, *Errand Into the Wilderness*, 115–118; and Armitage, *Ideological Origins of the British Empire*, 96–97.

10. Bremer, *John Winthrop*, 4–5, 7, 92, 148.

11. Hakluyt, preface to *Divers Voyages*, 178; Virginian quoted in Mancall, *Hakluyt's Promise*, 164. On Roanoke, see Kupperman, *Roanoke*; and Stick, *Roanoke Island*.

12. Miller, *Errand Into the Wilderness*, 99–126; Governing Council quoted in Nash, "Image of the Indian," 210. On Hakluyt and Purchas, see, respectively, *Morgan, American Slavery, American Freedom*, 44; and Jennings, *Invasion of America*, 78–79.

13. Johnson, "John Donne and the Virginia Company"; Stubbs, *John Donne*, 226–227, 392–394; Morgan, *American Slavery, American Freedom*, 46–47, 151; Butler, *Awash in a Sea of Faith*, 38; Horn, *Adapting to a New World*, 383–385; Donne quoted in Fischer, *Albion's Seed*, 232.

14. Except for Smith, quotations from Porter, *Inconstant Savage*, 99, 104. For Smith, see *A Map of Virginia. With a Description of the Countrey, the Commodities, People, Government and Religion* (London, 1612), in Barbour, *Complete Works of Captain John Smith*, vol. I, 159.

15. Symonds, *A Sermon Preached at White-Chappel*, A3.

16. Hakluyt, "Epistle Dedicatory to the Council of Virginia," April 15, 1609, in Taylor, *Original Writings and Correspondence of the Two Richard Hakluyts*, vol. II, 503.

17. Quoted in Cave, *Pequot War*, 56. On religion as the primary factor in triggering the Puritan migration, see Breen and Foster, "Moving to the New World," esp. 201–205, 220–221; Anderson, *New England's Generation*, 37–46; Fischer, *Albion's Seed*, 18–24; and Moore, *Pilgrims*, 18–31. But it is also important to remember that in early modern England, and especially for the Puritans, religious and political motivations were inseparable. On this point, see Foster, *Long Argument*, 108–137. For a nuanced and balanced overview of Puritan motivations, see Cressy, *Coming Over*, 74–106, esp. 74–83 for religion.

18. Winthrop, "A Modell of Christian Charity," in Miller and Johnson, *Puritans*, 197–199.

19. Knight, *Orthodoxies in Massachusetts*. For an extremely insightful analysis of Win-

throp's sermon, see Bremer, *John Winthrop*, 173–184; see also Moseley, *John Winthrop's World*, 42–44.

20. Winthrop and Hooker quoted, respectively, in Zakai, *Exile and Kingdom*, 145, 64. On the initial unhappiness and homesickness of many Puritan migrants, see Fischer, *Albion's Seed*, 55–57. On purification and a return to the early church, see Bozeman, *To Live Ancient Lives*.

21. Settler (Francis Higginson) quoted in Fischer, *Albion's Seed*, 50. On the Book of Exodus, and of America as the Puritans' promised land, see Zakai, *Exile and Kingdom*, 144–155.

22. Johnson, *Wonder-Working Providence*, in Miller and Johnson, *Puritans*; Cotton, *God's Promise*, 3; Cotton to colleague quoted in Guyatt, *Providence and the Invention of the United States*, 27. For the importance of providential thinking in England, see Walsham, *Providence in Early Modern England*. For New England, see Winship, *Seers of God*, 9–28.

23. Axtell, *Invasion Within*, 218–241; Company charter quoted in Thomas, "Puritans, Indians, and the Concept of Race," 5; Company seal quoted in Lepore, *Name of War*, xvii; Winthrop quoted in Bozeman, *To Live Ancient Lives*, 96. For the link to the Macedonians and Alexander the Great, see Richter, *Facing East from Indian Country*, 100.

24. Bercovitch, *American Jeremiad*; Butler, *Awash in a Sea of Faith*, 42; Horn, *Adapting to a New World*, 385; Bonomi, *Under the Cope of Heaven*, 16–17; Hambrick-Stowe, *Practice of Piety*, 246–256.

25. For Virginia, see Rountree and Turner, "On the Fringe," 366; Bond, *Damned Souls in a Tobacco Colony*, 75–77, 196–197, 201; Jennings, *Invasion of America*, 53–54; and Perry, *Formation of a Society on Virginia's Eastern Shore*, 38–39. For Harvard's Indian College, see Lepore, *Name of War*, 33, 44. For Eliot, see Cogley, *John Eliot's Mission*. For Martha's Vineyard and its syncretism, see Silverman, *Faith and Boundaries*. Axtell, *After Columbus*, 47–57, 100–121, argues that European missionaries met mostly with success and that Indian conversions were mostly genuine. But for the larger, unsuccessful pattern of conversion in colonial America, see Richter, *Ordeal of the Longhouse*, 109.

26. Canny, "Ideology of English Colonization," esp. 583–585, 588, 596; Nash, *Wilderness and the American Mind*, 34–35.

27. Lepore, *Name of War*, 79–89, 93; Lovejoy, "Satanizing the American Indian"; Axtell, *Invasion Within*, 167–178; Morgan, *American Slavery, American Freedom*, 44–70; Sheehan, *Savagism and Civility*; Simmons, "Cultural Bias." For the "social mirror," which also applied to Africans, see Wood, *Origins of American Slavery*, 21–22. On the overriding distinction of religion, see Kidd, *Forging of Races*, 54–55.

28. Hall, *Worlds of Wonder*, 90–92, 167; New England Confederation quoted in Carroll, *Puritanism and the Wilderness*, 78.

CHAPTER TWO. GOD IS AN EXCELLENT MAN OF WAR

1. Steele, *Warpaths*, 96–98; Starkey, *European and Native American Warfare*, 61–63; Elliott, *Empires of the Atlantic World*, 190.

2. Breen, *Character of the Good Ruler*, 121; Cotton quoted in Hall, *Faithful Shepherd*, 131; Sibbes quoted in Walzer, *Revolution of the Saints*, 285. On militia membership, see Breen, "English Origins," 83–84. On the simultaneity of radicalism and conservatism within Puritan thought, see Pocock, *Machiavellian Moment*, 336–337.

3. O'Brien, *Conduct of Just and Limited War*, 13–70; Walzer, *Just and Unjust Wars*, 21–47; Parker, "Early Modern Europe," 42–51.

4. Johnson, *Just War Tradition*, 4–10, 150–165, 172–179; MacCulloch, *Reformation*, 69–70; Markus, "Saint Augustine's Views on the 'Just War,' " 1–13; Miller, *Interpretations of Conflict*, 18–27, 54–61; Hartle, *Moral Issues in Military Decision Making*, 94–95.

5. Donagan, "Did Ministers Matter?," 129–135; Lepore, *Name of War*, 107.

6. Parker, "Early Modern Europe," 40–58; Bobbitt, *Shield of Achilles*, 508–518; Tyerman, *Fighting for Christendom*, 95–124.

7. Leighton, *Speculum Belli Sacri*, 6–7, 48. See also Walzer, *Revolution of the Saints*, 268–270, 280–283; and George, "War and Peace in the Puritan Tradition," 493–497. For the New England Puritans' hostility toward other reformed Protestant denominations, especially the Quakers, see Emerson, *Puritanism in America*, 135–136; Ahlstrom, *Religious History*, 166–178; Bremer, *Puritan Experiment*, 115–124; and Foster, *Long Argument*, 189–190. It is important to recognize that the Puritans were not the only ones in Europe, or even in England, to argue for aggressive holy war during this era. Advocates of holy war could be found across the Christian spectrum. See Johnson, *Ideology, Reason, and the Limitation of War*, 10, 81–117.

8. Sutton, *Good Fight of Faith*, 7–8; Johnson, *Ideology, Reason, and the Limitation of War*, 117–129; Walzer, *Revolution of the Saints*, 277–278, 281. For anti-Catholic invocations, see Leighton, *Speculum Belli Sacri*, 40–41.

9. For the radicalization of Puritan military doctrine in the era of the English Civil War, see Donagan, *War in England*, 15–23, 128–129.

10. Walzer, *Just and Unjust Wars*, 21; Donagan, "Atrocity, War Crime, and Treason," 1137–1166. On Puritans and Machiavelli, see Mosse, "Assimilation of Machiavelli in English Thought"; George, "War and Peace in the Puritan Tradition," 499; and Riebling, "Milton on Machiavelli."

11. Cressy, *England on Edge*, 184–185, 217, 226–227; Donagan, "Did Ministers Matter?," 124, 126; Bremer, *John Winthrop*, 332–333; Cotton, *God's Promise*, 4. For Cotton on Charles I, see Bremer, "In Defense of Regicide."

12. Quoted in Lepore, *Name of War*, 121.

13. For the best history of the conflict, see Cave, *Pequot War*. For more concise overviews, see Bourne, *Red King's Rebellion*, 41–84; and Bourne, *Gods of War*, 51–67. On the secular causes of the war, see Cronon, *Changes in the Land*, 96–97; and Drinnon, *Facing West*, 35–45.

14. Cave, *Pequot War*, 109–110; Jennings, *Invasion of America*, 209–211; Winthrop quoted in Bremer, *John Winthrop*, 269.

15. Quoted in Cave, *Pequot War*, 124. On Williams' diplomacy, see Bourne, *Gods of War*, 55–62.

16. Puritan minister quoted in Cave, *Pequot War*, 136. Hooker quoted in Karr, "Why Should You Be So Furious?" 904. Shuffelton, *Thomas Hooker*, 236–237. For a contemporary account, see also Vincent, *True Relation of the Late Battell*, esp. 11, 15, 20.

17. Quoted in Winship, *Times and Trials of Anne Hutchinson*, 83.

18. Delbanco, *Puritan Ordeal*, 106; Breen, *Transgressing the Bounds*, 64, 73–74; Underhill quoted in Karr, "Why Should You Be So Furious?," 877. For "imps" and "lions," see Hirsch, "Collision of Military Cultures," 1206.

19. Cave, *Pequot War*, 85–86, 88, 99, 111, 124, 134, 136, 150, 161–163. On Hutchinson, see LaPlante, *American Jezebel*, 6–7; and Winship, *Making Heretics*, 139–140.

20. For an argument that the war did in fact amount to genocide, see Freeman, "Puritans and Pequots." Arguing that it did not is Katz, "Pequot War Reconsidered"; and Katz, "Pequots and the Question of Genocide."

21. Bremer, *Puritan Crisis*, 97–129, 328–349; Pestana, *English Atlantic in an Age of Revolution*, 38–42, 56–58, 65–66, 102–103, 115–117, 214–217; Bliss, *Revolution and*

Empire, 73–102; Stout, *New England Soul*, 50–53; Braddick, *God's Fury*, 222, 340–341; Horn, *Adapting to a New World*, 180, 390–392. On the centrality of religion in the Civil Wars, see Morrill, "Religious Context."

22. Pestana, *English Atlantic in an Age of Revolution*, 58, 60; Lovejoy, *Religious Enthusiasm*, 90–91; Guyatt, *Providence and the Invention of the United States*, 30–34; Cressy, *England on Edge*, 184–185. On Peter's travels, see Games, *Migration and the Origins of the English Atlantic World*, 166. On the outflow of people from New England, see Moore, *Pilgrims*, 54–73 (page 66 for Cromwell and Massachusetts).

23. Capp, *Fifth Monarchy Men*; Maclear, "New England and the Fifth Monarchy"; Lovejoy, *Religious Enthusiasm*, 100–110; Delbanco, *Puritan Ordeal*, 202–203.

24. Phillips, *Cousins' Wars*, 55–63; Randolph quoted in Lovejoy, *Religious Enthusiasm*, 109.

25. On this interregnum between the Puritan-Indian wars, see Jennings, *Invasion of America*, 227.

26. The best overall account is Lepore, *Name of War*. But see also Bourne, *Red King's Rebellion*; and Drake, *King Philip's War*.

27. Slotkin, *Regeneration Through Violence*, 78–93; Bourne, *Red King's Rebellion*, 144; "Backsliding" quoted in Lepore, *Name of War*, 102, 100; Massachusetts Council minutes, Boston, September 17, 1675, in Slotkin and Folsom, *So Dreadfull a Judgment*, 102–103; Increase Mather, *An Earnest Exhortation to the Inhabitants of New-England* (Boston, 1676), in ibid., 172.

28. For "Passions," see Slotkin, *Regeneration Through Violence*, 88; "Gods marsi" quoted in Lepore, *Name of War*, 78; Mather, *Earnest Exhortation* and *A Brief History of the Warr With the Indians in Newe England* (Boston, 1676), in Slotkin and Folsom, *So Dreadfull a Judgment*, 191, 142.

29. Bourne, *Red King's Rebellion*, 145–146, 151–160.

30. Mather, *Earnest Exhortation* and *Brief History*, in Slotkin and Folsom, *So Dreadfull a Judgment*, 171, 86; Rowlandson, *The Soveraignty & Goodness of God* (Cambridge, Mass., 1682), in Vaughan and Clark, *Puritans Among the Indians*, 34–35, 63–64. For faces, see Lepore, *Name of War*, 93; for torture of livestock, see ibid., 96; for taunts and disemboweling, see ibid., 104–105.

31. Lepore, *Name of War*, 102, 106–107, 119 (captain quoted on 104); Slotkin, *Regeneration Through Violence*, 79–80; Bourne, *Red King's Rebellion*, 99–100, 104, 107–108; Pestana, *Quakers and Baptists in Colonial Massachusetts*, 147, 154–155; Cogley, *John Eliot's Mission*, 200–206, 237–239.

32. For Indian population and battle deaths, see Cook, "Interracial Warfare and Population Decline," 21. For Saltonstall's estimate, see Lepore, *Name of War*, 71. For the population of New England in 1670—where the figure of "approximately 50,000" comes from, although it was surely higher by 1675–76—see McCusker and Menard, *Economy of British America*, 103; and Fischer, *Albion's Seed*, 226n3.

33. Morone, *Hellfire Nation*, 100–101, 114–116; McKenna, *Puritan Origins*.

34. Lepore, *Name of War*, 173–240; and McWilliams, *New England's Crises and Cultural Memory*, 106–133.

CHAPTER THREE. WARS OF PERMANENT REFORMATION

1. Richter, *Facing East from Indian Country*, 155; Richter, "Native Peoples of North America."

2. Bremer, *Puritan Experiment*, 211; Chet, *Conquering the American Wilderness*, 74–75. On Protestant liberty as central to the British self-conception, see Colley, *Britons*, 18–54; and Greene, "Empire and Identity," 213–215.

3. Butler, *Awash in a Sea of Faith*, 177; Butler, *Huguenots in America*, 73, 75, 162–165; Bosher, "Huguenot Merchants and the Protestant International." Increase Mather quoted in Hall, *Worlds of Wonder*, 105.

4. Miller, *Popery and Politics*, 154–188; Greaves, *Secrets of the Kingdom*, 5–52, 332–333; and Marotti, *Religious Ideology and Cultural Fantasy*, 158–200.

5. "Declaration of the Gentlemen, Merchants, and Inhabitants of Boston," April 18, 1689, quoted in Kidd, *Protestant Interest*, 5–6; Hall, *Last American Puritan*, 210–254.

6. The best single overview of the Glorious Revolution is Vallance, *Glorious Revolution*. Historian quoted is Lenman, "Providence, Liberty, and Prosperity," 144; Mather quoted in Pole, *Gift of Government*, 52.

7. Breen, *Character of the Good Ruler*, 150–167; Lovejoy, *Glorious Revolution in America*, 235–293 (Boston bystander quoted on 243); Bliss, *Revolution and Empire*, 219–247. On Leisler, see Balmer, *Perfect Babel of Confusion*, 30–34; Voorhees, "fervent Zeale" (quotations from 469, 470); and Duncan, *Citizens or Papists?*, 6–11.

8. Leach, *Northern Colonial Frontier*, 109–117.

9. French misdeeds are from Peckham, *Colonial Wars*, 29, 32, 48, except for: assassination of minister, from Johnson, "Growth and Mastery," 281; and Puritan captives, from Foster, *Captors' Narrative*, 1–2, 37, 83, 100. English misdeeds are from Chet, *Conquering the American Wilderness*, 80, 83. Mather quoted in Slotkin, *Regeneration Through Violence*, 120. On colonial gender and captivity, see also Namias, *White Captives*, 21–112.

10. Lovejoy, "Between Hell and Plum Island," 359–360; Kences, "Some Unexplored Relationships"; Godbeer, *Devil's Dominion*, 182–204; Norton, *In the Devil's Snare*, 82–111.

11. Peckham, *Colonial Wars*, 51–52; Steele, *Warpaths*, 146–147; Namias, *White Captives*, 29–30; Cotton Mather, "A Narrative of Hannah Dustan's Notable Deliverance from Captivity," in Vaughan and Clark, *Puritans Among the Indians*, 162–164.

12. Lenman, "Colonial Wars and Imperial Instability"; Simms, *Three Victories*, 49–76.

13. Marsden, *Jonathan Edwards*, 12–13; Peckham, *Colonial Wars*, 61, 67, 71; Foster, *Captors' Narrative*, 70, 83, 100. Clough quoted in Kidd, *Protestant Interest*, 142–143.

14. Weber, *Spanish Frontier*, 142–145 (quotations from, respectively, 142, 144); Gold, "Departure of Spanish Catholicism from Florida," 387–388.

15. Demos, *Unredeemed Captive*.

16. Bourne, *Gods of War*, 172; Vaughan and Clark, *Puritans Among the Indians*, 167.

17. Demos, *Unredeemed Captive*, 17–20; Peckham, *Colonial Wars*, 63–64.

18. Haefeli and Sweeney, *Captors and Captives*, 151–163, 177–181.

19. Slotkin, *Regeneration Through Violence*, 100–101; Demos, *Unredeemed Captive*, 51–52.

20. On the religious dimension to the Yamasee War, see Merrell, *Indians' New World*, 66–80; Steele, *Warpaths*, 165–166; Bonomi, *Under the Cope of Heaven*, 58; Ramsey, "Something Cloudy in Their Looks"; Oatis, *Colonial Complex*, 91–95, 288; and Laing, "Heathens and Infidels," 202. For the northern fighting, see Steele, *Warpaths*, 161–162; and Calloway, *Western Abenakis of Vermont*, 113–131. Confusingly, the northern conflict was also known to some colonists as Dummer's War, after Massachusetts Lieutenant-Governor William Dummer. Rale's name occurs in about a dozen different spellings; mine follows the most common English-language practice.

21. Leach, *Northern Colonial Frontier,* 131–132; Kidd, *Protestant Interest,* 91–114 (Mather quoted on 108); historian quoted is Clark, "Church at Nanrantsouak," 229; Rale quoted in Slotkin, *Regeneration Through Violence,* 127.

22. Kidd, *Protestant Interest.* See also Marsden, *Jonathan Edwards,* 90; and, for an earlier period, Games, *Web of Empire,* 219–253.

23. Miller, *Errand Into the Wilderness,* 164–165; Noll, *America's God,* 22–25 (Edwards quoted on 23); Marsden, *Jonathan Edwards,* 88–89, 134, 198, 219–224, 336–338, 415–416; Bremer, *Puritan Experiment,* 228. Contemporary (Benjamin Trumbull) quoted in Conforti, *Jonathan Edwards,* 19.

24. Sermon by Jonathan Edwards, "The Duties of Christians in a Time of War," April 4, 1745, in *Works of Jonathan Edwards,* vol. 25, 134; sermon by Edwards, "God's People Tried by a Battle Lost," August 28, 1755, in ibid., 689; Marsden, *Jonathan Edwards,* 15–17, 415–416 (quotation from 196); McDermott, *One Holy and Happy Society,* 133, 144–151.

25. Stout, *Divine Dramatist,* 40–44, 79–81, 93–95, 151–154; Lambert, *Inventing the "Great Awakening,"* 97; Kidd, *Great Awakening,* 44, 48–49, 51.

26. On Whitefield's anti-Catholicism, see Stout, *Divine Dramatist,* 57, 217–218; and Mahaffey, *Preaching Politics,* 147–183 (Whitefield quoted on 147).

27. O'Brien, "Transatlantic Community of Saints"; Lambert, *Inventing the "Great Awakening."*

28. For overall accounts of the war, see Anderson, *War of the Austrian Succession;* and Simms, *Three Victories,* 274–354. For an excellent social history of the colonists' wartime motivations and experiences, including religion, see Nash, *Urban Crucible,* 165–176.

29. Steele, *Warpaths,* 168–169; Bushnell, *Situado and Sabana,* 198; Berlin, *Many Thousands Gone,* 72–76; Thornton, "African Dimensions of the Stono Rebellion"; Laing, "Heathens and Infidels?"; Landers, "Traditions of African American Freedom," 28. For the history of Portuguese Catholicism in Africa and among African slaves, see Frey and Wood, *Come Shouting to Zion,* 3–30.

30. Hatch, *Sacred Cause of Liberty,* 39–40; Selesky, *War and Society in Colonial Connecticut,* 78; Marsden, *Jonathan Edwards,* 196–197, 306.

31. On Stoddard, see Marcus, "Connecticut Valley," 240; Demos, *Unredeemed Captive,* 113–119; and Marsden, *Jonathan Edwards,* 316, 343–345. On Pepperrell, see Marsden, *Jonathan Edwards,* 310.

32. For the scene, see Nash, *Urban Crucible,* 170–171; Stout, *New England Soul,* 233–235; Stout, *Divine Dramatist,* 195–196; and Mahaffey, *Preaching Politics,* 139. Whitefield and motto quoted in Kidd, *Great Awakening,* 172; historian quoted is Peckham, *Colonial Wars,* 100.

33. Hatch, *Sacred Cause of Liberty,* 6–8, 36–37, 40–41; Stout, *New England Soul,* 233–238. Tennent and Prince quoted respectively in Noll, *America's God,* 78, 79; Chauncy quoted in Kidd, *Great Awakening,* 172.

34. Edwards quoted in Marsden, *Jonathan Edwards,* 313; Franklin, *Benjamin Franklin's Autobiography,* 93; "A Proclamation for a General Fast," December 9, 1747, *Papers of Benjamin Franklin,* vol. 3, 228–229; Coalter, *Gilbert Tennent,* 131; Morgan, *Benjamin Franklin,* 67–68. On the appeasement of the Quakers, see A Tradesman of Philadelphia [Benjamin Franklin], "Plain Truth," November 17, 1747, *Papers of Benjamin Franklin,* vol. 3, 200–201. On the Whitefield-Franklin relationship, see Lambert, *Inventing the "Great Awakening,"* 120; and Lemay, *Life of Benjamin Franklin,* vol. 2, 420–451. On Franklin's fears and support for the war and the opposition this generated among some Pennsylvanians, see Middlekauff, *Benjamin Franklin and His Enemies,* 37–39.

35. For Edwards, see Marsden, *Jonathan Edwards,* 318. For the addition of republi-

canism to Protestant liberty during King George's War, see Noll, *America's God*, 78–80.

36. The best overall account of the conflict is Anderson, *Crucible of War*. But for an excellent treatment of the war as it was fought in Europe and connected to America, see Simms, *Three Victories*, 387–498. For the war as it was fought in North America, see also Steele, *Warpaths*, 188–221.

37. Heimert, *Religion and the American Mind*, 323–324, 376; Hatch, *Sacred Cause of Liberty*, 5–8 and passim; Marietta, *Reformation of American Quakerism*, 150–186; Seeman, *Pious Persuasions*, 196–200; Steele, *Warpaths*, 176, 198. Anonymous [Benjamin Franklin], "A DIALOGUE between X, Y, and Z, concerning the present State of Affairs in Pennsylvania," December 18, 1755, in *Papers of Benjamin Franklin*, vol. 6, 302. See also Franklin, *Benjamin Franklin's Autobiography*, 123; Davidson, *War Comes to Quaker Pennsylvania*, 113–196; and Wood, *Americanization of Benjamin Franklin*, 78–81.

38. On the colonists' strategic and cultural fears of encirclement, see Anderson, *Crucible of War*, 22–41; and Weeks, *Building the Continental Empire*, 5. Stiles quoted in Selesky, *War and Society in Colonial Connecticut*, 146. Burr quoted in Davidson, *Logic of Millennial Thought*, 197. On New York, see Duncan, *Citizens or Papists?*, 26; on Virginia, see Pilcher, *Samuel Davies*, 113.

39. Hatch, *Sacred Cause of Liberty*, 41; Davidson, *Logic of Millennial Thought*, 202–205; Guyatt, *Providence and the Invention of the United States*, 63–64, 82–83. Hobby quoted in Berens, *Providence and Patriotism*, 38.

40. Sermon by Joseph Parsons, ca. 1756, Parsons papers, RG30, Box 214, YDS; sermon by Joseph Lathrop, April 6, 1758, Lathrop papers, Box 1, Folder 2, AHTL; Coalter, *Gilbert Tennent*, 153–154. Edwards quoted in Marsden, *Jonathan Edwards*, 415. See also Berens, *Providence and Patriotism*, 41–44; and Davidson, *Logic of Millennial Thought*, 205–212.

41. Hatch, *Sacred Cause of Liberty*, 34–35; Bloch, *Visionary Republic*, 25–40; Anderson, *People's Army*, 213–222; Anderson, *Crucible of War*, 373–376; McKenna, *Puritan Origins of American Patriotism*, 67; Stout, "Puritans and Edwards," 155–156; Edwards, "God's People Tried by a Battle Lost," 694–697.

42. Mahaffey, *Preaching Politics*, 169–173; Heimert, *Religion and the American Mind*, 332–334.

43. Noll, *America's God*, 80–81; Hatch, *Sacred Cause of Liberty*, 43–44.

44. Anderson, *People's Army*, 155–157, 210–214; James Beebe, "An Address to the Soldiers," May 7, 1758, Beebe papers, RG30, Box 212, YDS.

45. Griffiths, *Contexts of Acadian History*, 74–87; Plank, *Unsettled Conquest*, 6, 59–61, 80, 94–95, 120, 139, 142; Jennings, *Empire of Fortune*, 175–182; Bell, *Foreign Protestants and the Settlement of Nova Scotia*; Rawlyk, *Nova Scotia's Massachusetts*, 201–202.

46. Steele, *Warpaths*, 224; Gold, "Departure of Spanish Catholicism from Florida."

47. On the wartime fall and rise of Indian missions, see Davidson, *Logic of Millennial Thought*, 208; Marsden, *Jonathan Edwards*, 420–427; Guyatt, *Providence and the Invention of the United States*, 78; and Kidd, *Great Awakening*, 203, 206, 270. On the broad effects of the war upon colonial religion, see Hatch, *Sacred Cause of Liberty*, 5.

48. On ecumenical unity, see Butler, *Awash in a Sea of Faith*, 177. Sermon by Izrahiah Wetmore, ca. 1761, Wetmore papers, RG30, Box 215, YDS. Forbes quoted in Guyatt, *Providence and the Invention of the United States*, 83. Horrocks quoted in Berens, *Providence and Patriotism*, 47.

49. Varg, "Advent of Nationalism," 169–171, 174–176; Bumsted, "Things in the Womb of Time," 543–563; Kidd, *British Identities Before Nationalism*, 263–269.

PART II. THE AMERICAN REVELATION

1. Quotations from Randall, *Benedict Arnold*, 155–156.
2. Royster, *Revolutionary People at War*, 23–24; Lambert, *"Pedlar in Divinity,"* 214–215; Kidd, *Great Awakening*, 288; Spring quoted in Randall, *Benedict Arnold*, 156; "precious relic" quoted in Martin, *Benedict Arnold*, 119.
3. Quoted in Royster, *Revolutionary People at War*, 361.
4. Lambert, *"Pedlar in Divinity,"* 210–214, 217–218, 222; Mahaffey, *Preaching Politics*, 199–200, 201–204; Whitefield quoted in Kenney, "George Whitefield, Dissenter Priest," 93.
5. On the strategic activism of revolutionary states, see Walt, *Revolution and War*. On the lack of difference between the foreign and the domestic, see Onuf, "Declaration of Independence," 76.
6. On the American Revolution as a foundational episode in American foreign relations, see Herring, *From Colony to Superpower*, 14–34. On the importance of American diplomacy from the very onset of the war, see Kaplan, ed., *American Revolution and "A Candid World"*; Dull, *Diplomatic History of the American Revolution*; Horsman, *Diplomacy of the New Republic*; Brecher, *Securing American Independence*; and Tudda, "Messiah that Will Never Come."
7. Isaac, *Transformation of Virginia*, 5. In navigating the sometimes treacherous historiographical waters of religion's causal relationship with the Revolution, I have relied in particular on the following essays: Goff, "Revivals and Revolution"; Guelzo, "God's Designs"; Gura, "Role of the 'Black Regiment' "; Kloppenberg, *Virtues of Liberalism*, 21–37; Noll, "American Revolution and Protestant Evangelicalism"; Rodgers, "Republicanism," 11–24; and Wood, "Religion and the American Revolution."
8. Wood, "Religion and the American Revolution," 180–181. On the Great Awakening's subversive "enthusiasm," and its applications to Whig ideology, see Lovejoy, *Religious Enthusiasm in the New World*, 195–214, 222–230. On the politically empowering effects of the Great Awakening, see McLoughlin, "Role of Religion in the Revolution," 197–202; Nash, *Urban Crucible*, 198–232; Royster, *Revolutionary People at War*, 152–153; Stout and Onuf, "James Davenport"; Bonomi, *Under the Cope of Heaven*; Ferguson, *American Enlightenment*, 49–60; and Noll, "American Revolution and Protestant Evangelicalism," 626–627. However, the causal linkages between the Awakening, and even religion more generally, and the Revolution are not uncontroversial. For incisive, at times compelling, critiques that complicate such linkages, see Butler, *Awash in a Sea of Faith*, 164–224; and Bailyn, *Faces of Revolution*, 104–149.
9. Morgan, *Challenge of the American Revolution*, 88–138; for another application, see Kramnick, *Republicanism and Bourgeois Radicalism*. Adams to Greene, March 18, 1780, *Papers of John Adams*, vol. 9, 62. On Calvinism and original sin, see Bailyn, *Ideological Origins of the American Revolution*, 60. On the covenant, see Stout, *New England Soul*, 7–8, 277–278, 296–299. On the blending of Locke and religion in American republicanism, see Pangle, *Spirit of Modern Republicanism*; and Zuckert, *Natural Rights and the New Republicanism*.
10. Noll, *Christians in the American Revolution*, 46–48. On Henry, see Isaac, *Transformation of Virginia*, 267–269.
11. Stout, "Religion, Communications, and the Ideological Origins of the American Revolution"; Weber, *Rhetoric and History*; Lambert, *Inventing the "Great Awakening"*; Stout, *New England Soul*, 6; Ferguson, *American Enlightenment*, 44.

CHAPTER FOUR. THE HARMONY OF THE
WORLD CONFOUNDED

1. White, *Middle Ground*, 269–314; Richter, *Facing East from Indian Country*, 191–201; Dowd, *War Under Heaven*, 94–105. On the influence of Indian spiritualism, see Dowd, *Spirited Resistance*, 27–37; and Steele, *Warpaths*, 234.

2. Richter, *Facing East from Indian Country*, 201–203, 206; Jennings, *Empire of Fortune*, 202; Clark, *Language of Liberty*, 258–260, 266–269; Silver, *Our Savage Neighbors*, 177–208; Marietta, *Reformation of American Quakerism*, 189–193; Kars, *Breaking Loose Together*, 126–128. Smith quoted in Kidd, *Great Awakening*, 279; Barton quoted in Griffin, *American Leviathan*, 67.

3. On the SPG controversy, see Fowler, *Samuel Adams*, 27–29; Bridenbaugh, *Mitre and Sceptre*, 178–183, 211–214, 263–265; Bailyn, *Ideological Origins of the American Revolution*, 95–97; Taylor, *Divided Ground*, 52, 59, 61, 65–68; and Griffin, *American Leviathan*, 36–37. On the Bishops Plot, see Bridenbaugh, *Mitre and Sceptre*, 144–166; Nash, *Urban Crucible*, 203–204; Curry, *First Freedoms*, 121–126; and Clark, *Language of Liberty*.

4. Stout, *New England Soul*, 259–264; Akers, *Called Unto Liberty*, 198–216; Bailyn, *Ordeal of Thomas Hutchinson*, 35–38; Heimert, *Religion and the American Mind*, 244–245; Akers, *Divine Politician*. Sons of Liberty quoted in Bloch, *Visionary Republic*, 54. On religious opposition beyond New England, see Bridenbaugh, *Mitre and Sceptre*, 257–258; and Morgan and Morgan, *Stamp Act Crisis*, 301–324.

5. Lambert, *"Pedlar in Divinity,"* 221–222; Alexander, *Samuel Adams*, 110; Mahaffey, *Preaching Politics*, 195–196; Nash, *Urban Crucible*, 361. Adams quoted in Hatch, *Sacred Cause of Liberty*, 74.

6. John Adams, *A Dissertation on the Canon and Feudal Law* (Boston, 1765), in *Papers of John Adams*, vol. I: 106, 108, 113–114, 115, 110, 126.

7. On the effective amalgam of classical republicanism, liberalism, virtue, and religion, see Kloppenberg, *Virtues of Liberalism*, 23–28. On colonial perceptions of official political and religious corruption, see Bonomi, *Under the Cope of Heaven*, 200–202, 208; and Butler, *Becoming America*, 120–123.

8. Chandler, *Friendly Address to All Reasonable Americans*, 5.

9. Quoted in Wood, *Creation of the American Republic*, 112.

10. Noll, *Christians in the American Revolution*, 103–114; Woolverton, *Colonial Anglicanism in North America*, 225–233; Potter, *Liberty We Seek*, 57–61, 144–149.

11. Isaac, *Transformation of Virginia*, 260–262; Noll, *Christians in the American Revolution*, 115–116, 146–147, 187; John Wesley, *A Calm Address to Our American Colonies* (London, 1775), in Sandoz, *Political Sermons of the American Founding Era*, vol. 1, 413–420; John Fletcher, *The Bible and the Sword* (London, 1776), in ibid., 563–578.

12. Brock, *Pacifism in the United States*, 183–284; Mekeel, *Relation of the Quakers to the American Revolution*; Marietta, *Reformation of American Quakerism*, 222–248. On the Quakers who supported the Revolution, and even fought in it, see Kashatus, *Conflict of Conviction*.

13. Engel, *Religion and Profit*; Brock, *Pacifism in the United States*, 303–321.

14. McLoughlin, *New England Dissent*, vol. 1, 547–587; Marini, *Radical Sects of Revolutionary New England*, 40–59; Noll, *Christians in the American Revolution*, 51–77; Clark, *Language of Liberty*, 335–381; Ferguson, *American Enlightenment*, 46–47; Cooper, *Tenacious of Their Liberties*.

15. Butler, *Awash in a Sea of Faith*, 203–206; Butler, *Becoming America*, 244; Noll, *Christians in the American Revolution*, 117–122.

16. Wilson, "Religion and Revolution," 600–601; Royster, *Revolutionary People at War*, 19–21. On the Lutherans, see Butler, *Awash in a Sea of Faith*, 202–203.

17. Butler, *Awash in a Sea of Faith*, 205–206; Kidd, *Great Awakening*, 291–293; Ferling, *Leap in the Dark*, 216–235.
18. For "black regiment," see Stout, *New England Soul*, 266. British officer and Ambrose Serle both quoted in Royster, *Revolutionary People at War*, 19. For Edwards Jr., see Weber, *Rhetoric and History*, 60–70; and Valeri, "New Divinity and the American Revolution," 742. For Hopkins, see Conforti, *Samuel Hopkins*, 126–141.
19. Crane, "Religion and Rebellion," 80–82. For Abigail Adams, see Keller, *Patriotism and the Female Sex*, 68–70. For early calls for independence, see Guyatt, *Providence and the Invention of the United States*, 86–88.
20. Royster, *Revolutionary People at War*, 16, 22, 27–28, 162–169; Jones, *Defensive War in a Just Cause Sinless*; George Washington, General Orders of May 2, 1778, *Papers of George Washington: Revolutionary War Series*, vol. 15, 13; Bolton, *Private Soldier Under Washington*, 159.
21. Jones quoted in Royster, *Revolutionary People at War*, 162. Corporal quoted in Bolton, *Private Soldier Under Washington*, 231.
22. Bloch, *Visionary Republic*, 75–76; see also 77–93. See also Hatch, *Sacred Cause of Liberty*, 55–96; Royster, *Revolutionary People at War*, 152–161; and Davis, "Religion and the American Revolution," 722.
23. Royster, *Revolutionary People at War*, 157; see also 108, 119–120, 157–159, 176–177. Washington, General Orders of May 5, 1778, *Papers of George Washington: Revolutionary War Series*, vol. 15, 39. Preachers quoted in Ferguson, *American Enlightenment*, 49. On Revolutionary providentialism, see also Berens, *Providence and Patriotism*, 51–111; and Guyatt, *Providence and the Invention of the United States*, 84–104.

CHAPTER FIVE. LIBERATION THEOLOGY

1. For insightful discussions of the Founders' faiths, see Gaustad, *Faith of Our Fathers*; West, *Politics of Revelation and Reason*, 11–78; Lambert, *Founding Fathers and the Place of Religion*; Meacham, *American Gospel*, 64–113; and Muñoz, *God and the Founders*.
2. On Washington's faith, see esp. Henriques, *Realistic Visionary*, 167–186; Smith, *Faith and the Presidency*, 21–52; Morrison, *Political Philosophy of George Washington*, esp. 135–172; and Thompson, *"In the Hands of a Good Providence."* For Washington as a political and religious symbol, see Furstenberg, *In the Name of the Father*, esp. 50–64. Washington quoted in Gaustad, *Faith of Our Fathers*, 77.
3. Middlekauff, *Glorious Cause*, 48. The term "religious Enlightenment" was coined for Europe, but it applies equally well to early America: see Sorkin, *Religious Enlightenment*; and, for America, Ferguson, *American Enlightenment*, esp. 44–79. On the Bible and freedom, see Davis, *Revolutions*, 15–18.
4. Van Alstyne, *Empire and Independence*, 55–139.
5. Herring, *From Colony to Superpower*, 21; Perkins, *Creation of a Republican Empire*, 24–31; Franklin quoted in Davis, *Revolutions*, 41.
6. Cogliano, *No King, No Popery*; Lawson, *Imperial Challenge*; Herring, *From Colony to Superpower*, 21; diary entry, August 1, 1761, *Diary and Autobiography of John Adams*, vol. 1, 219–220; Adams to Louisa Catherine Adams, May 17, 1821, in Hutson, *Founders on Religion*, 41; Dickinson quoted in Hutson, *John Adams*, 27; Stahr, *John Jay*, 2–3, 8, 88.
7. Diary entry, March–April 1776, *Diary and Autobiography of John Adams*, vol. 2, 236. On the Model Treaty, see Gilbert, *To the Farewell Address*, 48–56; Hutson, *John Adams*, 26–31; and Stinchcombe, "John Adams and the Model Treaty."
8. Butler, *Awash in a Sea of Faith*, 196.

9. Isaac, *Transformation of Virginia*, 246–247; Kloppenberg, *Virtues of Liberalism*, 23–28; Noll, *Christians in the American Revolution*, 53–54; Noll, *America's God*, 53–92; Wood, *Creation of the American Republic*, 59–60. See also Kidd, "Civil Theology and Church Establishments," 1010–1017.

10. For a discussion of the missing Christian dimension in the history and historiography of republicanism, see Black, "Christianity and Republicanism." On Calvin's injunction, see Skinner, *Foundations of Modern Political Thought*, vol. 2, 219–221, 230–233.

11. On the imperial sources of religious diversity in colonial America, see Pestana, "Religion."

12. Cooper, *Tenacious of Their Liberties*; Bell, *War of Religion*. On the memory of the English Civil War during the era of the American Revolution, see Heimert, *Religion and the American Mind*, 275, 357–358; Bailyn, *Ideological Origins of the American Revolution*, 34–35, 45; and Stout, *New England Soul*, 260, 268. On New England during the English Civil War, see Bremer, *Puritan Crisis*; Pestana, *English Atlantic in an Age of Revolution*; and Bliss, *Revolution and Empire*, 73–102. On the controversy in the 1640s and '50s over Paul's message about deference to authority in Romans 13, see Skinner, *Visions of Politics*, vol. 3, 287–307.

13. Milton, *Paradise Lost*, Book V, lines 822–825; Milton, in a substantial revision and misrepresentation of Machiavelli, quoted in Brown, "Great Senates and Godly Education," 43. On Milton's political distinction between "liberty" and "slavery," see Skinner, *Visions of Politics*, vol. 2, 297–307. On the centrality of Protestantism to Milton's writings, see Gregerson, *Reformation of the Subject*. For opposition to Anglican bishops, see Milton, *Of Reformation*; Bonomi, *Under the Cope of Heaven*, 189–190; and Knight, *Orthodoxies in Massachusetts*, 189–191.

14. Bonomi, *Under the Cope of Heaven*, 189–199; Stout, *New England Soul*, 266–267, 277–278, 273. On the popularity of Milton in late colonial America, see Sensabaugh, *Milton in Early America*, 97–183; Schulman, *Paradise Lost and the Rise of the American Republic*; Phillips, *Cousins' Wars*, 95; and Davies, "Borrowed Language," 256–263. For the political philosophy of *Paradise Lost*, see Revard, *War in Heaven*, esp. 264–306; and Himy, "*Paradise Lost*."

15. *Federalist* No. 2, October 31, 1787, in Hamilton, Madison, and Jay, *The Federalist*, 6; Washington quoted in Gaustad, *Faith of Our Fathers*, 77.

16. "Universal Peace," January 3, 1792, *Papers of James Madison*, vol. 14, 206–209. See also Gilbert, *To the Farewell Address*, 54–75; and Stuart, *War and American Thought*. For Montesquieu, see his *Spirit of the Laws* (1741), Part 2, Book 9, 132–133; for Kant, see the excerpts from his *Perpetual Peace* (1795) in Brown, Nardin, and Rengger, *International Relations in Political Thought*, 436–438.

17. Rush quoted in Watts, *Republic Reborn*, 133; Abraham Keteltas, *God Arising and Pleading His People's Cause; Or the American War in Favor of Liberty, Against the Measure and Arms of Great Britain, Shewn to be the Cause of God* (Newburyport, Mass., 1777), in Sandoz, *Political Sermons of the American Founding Era*, vol. 1, 595.

18. Robbins and poem quoted, respectively, in Royster, *Revolutionary People at War*, 99, 251.

19. Thomas Paine, *Common Sense* (1776), in Paine, *Political Writings*, 35–36; William Livingston, "A Plea for Liberty of Conscience," 1778, in Vaughan, *Chronicles of the American Revolution*, 318–321; Washington to Benedict Arnold, September 14, 1775, *Papers of George Washington: Revolutionary War Series*, vol. 1, 456; Washington, "Address to the Inhabitants of Canada," September 14, 1775, ibid., 461–462; Washington, "To the Hebrew Congregation in Newport, Rhode Island," August 18, 1790, *Papers of George Washington: Presidential Series*, vol. 6, 285.

20. "Memorial and Remonstrance against Religious Assessments," June 20, 1785, *Papers of James Madison*, vol. 8, 298–304, esp. 299–300; "The Virginia Statute for Religious Freedom," October 1785, in Morison, *Sources and Documents*, 206–208. On Madison, see Rakove, *James Madison*, 13; Rakove, *Original Meanings*, 40–42, 310–313; Morrison, *John Witherspoon*, 37–42; Buckley, *Church and State in Revolutionary Virginia*, 15, 99; and Banning, *Sacred Fire of Liberty*, 84–96. In general, see Ragosta, *Wellspring of Liberty*.

21. Hatch, *Democratization of American Christianity*. On the Northwest Ordinance and religious diversity in the Ohio country, see Morgan, *Birth of the Republic*, 115; and Hinderaker, *Elusive Empires*, 259. In addition to Hatch, on the decline of religious authority and the rise of the evangelical upstarts, see McLoughlin, "Role of Religion in the Revolution," 203–208; Wood, *Radicalism of the American Revolution*, 329–333; Marini, "Religion, Politics, and Ratification," 193–195; and Noll, *America's God*, 165–186. New Englander quoted in Kidd, *Great Awakening*, 317.

22. Isaac Backus to Simon Backus, February 13, 1806, Isaac Backus papers, Box 1, JHL. On Tennent, see McCrady, *History of South Carolina in the Revolution*, 206–207; and Levy, *Establishment Clause*, 5–6. On Parsons, see Heimert, *Religion and the American Mind*, 390. On the Baptists, see Isaac, *Transformation of Virginia*, 278–280; Lovejoy, *Religious Enthusiasm in the New World*, 216–220; and Ragosta, *Wellspring of Liberty*. In general, see also Curry, *First Freedoms*, 131–132, 149–150, 165–177.

23. On Henry, see Isaac, *Transformation of Virginia*, 278, 283–284; and Buckley, *Church and State in Revolutionary Virginia*, 73. For convincing arguments that the Founders had little intention to remove religion from public life in the First Amendment, see Curry, *First Freedoms* (Backus quoted on 169–170); and Hamburger, *Separation of Church and State*.

24. Quoted in Gaustad, *Faith of Our Fathers*, 78.

25. Hamilton, *Federalist No. 1*, October 27, 1787, in Hamilton, Madison, and Jay, *The Federalist*, 2; Madison, *Federalist No. 51*, February 6, 1788, ibid., 254. On the distinction between the states and the nation, see Wood, *Creation of the American Republic*, 427–428; and Kruman, *Between Authority and Liberty*, 45–49.

26. Calhoon, *Loyalist Perception*, 206–208. Marini, *Radical Sects of Revolutionary New England*, 116–171; Noll, "American Revolution and Protestant Evangelicalism," 635; Isaac, *Transformation of Virginia*, 295; Howe, "Protestantism, Voluntarism, and Personal Identity"; Noll, *America's God*, 182, 197–199; Bushman, *Joseph Smith and the Beginnings of Mormonism*; Bringhurst, *Brigham Young*, 1–49; Neem, "Elusive Common Good."

PART III. IMPERIAL DESTINIES

1. Adams, *Memoirs of John Quincy Adams*, vol. 12, 242.

2. "Proceedings for the House of Representatives," February 9, 1846, *Congressional Globe*, vol. 15, 339–342; Adams, *Memoirs of John Quincy Adams*, vol. 12, 243–244. For other accounts of this extraordinary political drama, see Bemis, *John Quincy Adams and the Union*, 489–491; Merk, *Oregon Question*, 227–229; and Richards, *Life and Times of Congressman John Quincy Adams*, 182–186.

3. Nagel, *John Quincy Adams*, 124, 202–204, 230–231, 235, 260–262, 308, 314; Remini, *John Quincy Adams*, 3–4, 43, 128–129; Weeks, *John Quincy Adams*, 10–11, 189–190.

4. Adams to Richard C. Anderson (Bogota), May 27, 1823, in LaFeber, ed., *John Quincy Adams*, 124; "President Adams' Message to the Senate of the United States," December 26, 1825, ibid., 133; Adams, "The Opium War and the Sanc-

tity of Commercial Reciprocity," ibid., 49. On their religious views, see, for example, John Adams to John Quincy Adams, January 3, 1817, *Selected Writings of John and John Quincy Adams*, 291–292.

5. Nagel, *John Quincy Adams*, 231, 407. On the lingering influence of Puritanism within the Adams family, see Brookhiser, *America's First Dynasty*, 13–15, 67, 209–210. Adams quoted, respectively, in LaFeber, ed., *John Quincy Adams*, 36–37; and Mayers, *Dissenting Voices*, 86.

6. Adams, *Memoirs of John Quincy Adams*, vol. 4, 274. See also Weeks, *John Quincy Adams*, 17–20.

7. On the partisan political dimension of Adams and expansion, see Weeks, *John Quincy Adams*, 35.

8. Neem, *Creating a Nation of Joiners*. On the two agendas of antebellum reform and progress, see Clark, *Social Change in America*.

9. On Adams and reform, see Howe, *Political Culture of the American Whigs*, 43–68 ("progressive improvement" quoted on 59). For the 1825 speeches, see "Inaugural Address," March 4, 1825, *Selected Writings of John and John Quincy Adams*, 353–360, esp. 359; and "First Annual Message," December 6, 1825, ibid., 360–367.

CHAPTER SIX. ABSOLUTIST APOSTASIES

1. On the European situation, see Schroeder, *Transformation of European Politics*, 67–150. On its general diplomatic implications and challenges for the United States, see Herring, *From Colony to Superpower*, 56–73; and Perkins, *Creation of a Republican Empire*, 82–87.

2. Bloch, *Visionary Republic*, 150–163, 168–179; Davis, *Revolutions*, 40–46; Lathrop, *Happiness of a Free Government*, 14.

3. Nash, "American Clergy and the French Revolution"; Hunt, *Ideology and U.S. Foreign Policy*, 97–100; Davis, *Revolutions*, 46–47.

4. Though they draw different conclusions, see Buel, *Securing the Revolution*, 28–49; Elkins and McKitrick, *Age of Federalism*, 303–373, esp. 354–365; and Sharp, *American Politics in the Early Republic*, 69–91.

5. For extended discussions of the events in this radically compressed summary of Federalist diplomacy, see Horsman, *Diplomacy of the New Republic*, 42–78; and Perkins, *Creation of a Republican Empire*, 87–110. For the domestic political dimensions of the Jay Treaty, see Buel, *Securing the Revolution*, 54–71; Elkins and McKitrick, *Age of Federalism*, 415–431; and Sharp, *American Politics in the Early Republic*, 113–137.

6. Bloch, *Visionary Republic*, 202–231; Buel, *Securing the Revolution*, 138, 167, 170–172, 232–233. On the basis of American fears over the violence and radicalism in France, see Cleves, *Reign of Terror in America*, 13–14, 20–57. On Hamilton, see Stourzh, *Alexander Hamilton*, 122, 125.

7. Waldstreicher, *In the Midst of Perpetual Fetes*, 145–152; Hatch, *Sacred Cause of Liberty*, 13–14; Kerber, *Federalists in Dissent*, 208–212. For reactions against the revolutionary violence in France as the source of reform movements in antebellum America, see Cleves, *Reign of Terror in America*.

8. DeConde, *Quasi War*, 6; Hunt, *Ideology and U.S. Foreign Policy*, 92–94.

9. Stahr, *John Jay*, 300–301 (quoted on 88); Combs, *Jay Treaty*, 18–19; West, *Politics of Revelation and Reason*, 53–56.

10. Field, *America and the Mediterranean World*, 27–38; Lambert, *Barbary Wars*, 17–41.

11. "Treaty of Peace and Friendship," signed November 4, 1796, and ratified June 10, 1797, *Treaties and Other International Agreements of the United States of America*, vol. 11, 1072; Eaton quoted in Oren, *Power, Faith, and Fantasy*, 65. On Jefferson, see Tucker and Hendrickson, *Empire of Liberty*, 294–299.

12. Grant, *John Adams*, 380–381; Hall, *Worlds of Wonder*, 87, 201; Bloch, *Visionary Republic*, 120, 122, 131, 145, 169; Oren, *Power, Faith, and Fantasy*, 27, 42–45, 59; Allison, *Crescent Obscured*, 35–59 (bestselling book and Eaton quoted, respectively, on 36, 53–54); Noah Webster, *The Revolution in France* (New York, 1794), in Sandoz, *Political Sermons of the American Founding Era*, vol. 2, 1263.

13. Lambert, *Barbary Wars*, 110; Peskin, *Captives and Countrymen*. On links between the Indian and Barbary captivity narratives, see also Baepler, "Barbary Captivity Narrative in Early America."

14. Cotton Mather, *The Glory of Goodness* (Boston, 1703), in Baepler, *White Slaves, African Masters*, 61; Barnby, *Prisoners of Algiers*, 44–46, 94–95; Davis, *Challenging the Boundaries of Slavery*, 10–12; Hassan quoted in Oren, *Power, Faith, and Fantasy*, 22. On the history of Islamic enslavement of Christians along the Barbary coast, see Davis, *Christian Slaves, Muslim Masters*.

15. Horsman, *Causes of the War of 1812*; and Hickey, *War of 1812*, 5–28.

16. Almost all accounts of the War of 1812 stress the importance of honor to some degree, but for the recourse to war as a way to protect American republicanism, see Brown, *Republic in Peril*.

17. "To Congress," June 1, 1812, *Papers of James Madison: Presidential Series*, vol. 4, 437; for the fast day message, see Gribbin, *Churches Militant*, 20–21. See also Moore, *One Nation Under God*, 83–84.

18. Watts, *Republic Reborn*, 131–160, 286–289 (Weems quoted on 151); Furstenberg, *In the Name of the Father*, 105–145.

19. Jones to Madison, September 15, 1812, and November 26, 1812, Jones papers, Box 1, ABHS. On Jones, see also Gribbin, *Churches Militant*, 81–82.

20. Isaac Backus to Simon Backus, January 31, 1814, Backus papers, Box 1, JHL; address to the General Assembly, October 1814, Smith papers, Supplement Box, CHS; "approbation" quoted in Stout, "Rhetoric and Reality," 75; Massachusetts minister quoted in Waldstreicher, *In the Midst of Perpetual Fetes*, 257. On religious Federalists and antiwar opposition, see also Gribbin, *Churches Militant*, 40–60; and Sassi, *Republic of Righteousness*, 101–105. On Republican charges about religious liberty in New England, see Stagg, *Mr. Madison's War*, 254–255. On the Baptists, see McLoughlin, *New England Dissent*, 831.

21. Porter, *Sermon, Delivered in Boston*, 13, 17; Cary, *Sermon Preached*, 3.

22. S. P. Robbins to Thomas Robbins, October 1, 1813, Robbins papers, Box 1, CHS. Both South Carolina Federalists quoted in Berens, *Providence and Patriotism*, 150. For the concept of a "greater New England," see Fischer, *Albion's Seed*, 812–898, esp. 847, 866, for its relevance to national divisions during the War of 1812.

23. Curti, *American Peace Crusade*, 3–41; Brock, *Pacifism in the United States*, 365–366, 449–481; Gribbin, *Churches Militant*, 124–125. For Jefferson and Madison on war, see Tucker and Hendrickson, *Empire of Liberty*, 16–17, 39–44.

24. Perkins, *Creation of a Republican Empire*, 141–146; Watts, *Republic Reborn*, 283–289 (quote on 283).

25. Berens, *Providence and Patriotism*, 149–166 (New Hampshire minister quoted in 159); Guyatt, *Providence and the Invention of the United States*, 161–168; Vermont newspaper quoted in Watts, *Republic Reborn*, 285; Methodist preacher quoted in Weeks, *Building the Continental Empire*, 31. On the war as a turning point for Indians, see Dippie, *Vanishing American*, 5–9.

CHAPTER SEVEN. THE BENEVOLENT EMPIRE,
AT HOME AND ABROAD

1. Sellers, *Market Revolution*; Meyer, *Roots of American Industrialization*. On the "communications revolution," see Howe, *What Hath God Wrought*, esp. 5–7, 44–50, 270–275, 525–569. On the healing of divisions in New England, see Sassi, *Republic of Righteousness*, 147–148.

2. The late nineteenth-century United States and post–World War II Japan are the classic examples of a prosperous economy failing to produce an activist foreign or military policy. Still, economics is important: no nation can be a great power for long without prosperity and financial stability. So too are state capabilities, especially a strong central government and bureaucracy. Given these complications, it is not surprising that the causal relationship between economics and geopolitics remains controversial. For an explanation of how military and diplomatic strength largely stem from economics, see Kennedy, *Rise and Fall of the Great Powers*. For the argument that while finance is vital, a nation's military and diplomatic power stem mostly from political rather than economic factors, see Ferguson, *Cash Nexus*. For the importance of a strong, centralized state, using the late nineteenth-century United States as a case study, see LaFeber, *American Search for Opportunity*; and Zakaria, *From Wealth to Power*.

3. Carwardine, *Evangelicals and Politics*, 58–68, 97–132; Howe, *Political Culture of the American Whigs*, 150–180; Johnson, *Redeeming America*, 150–154; Holt, *Rise and Fall of the American Whig Party*, 30–31, 117, 742.

4. Butler, *Awash in a Sea of Faith*, 225–256; Noll, *America's God*, 293–329. On American religion and the challenge of the market revolution, see Davenport, *Friends of the Unrighteous Mammon*. On religion and reform, see esp. Mintz, *Moralists and Modernizers*; Abzug, *Cosmos Crumbling*; and Matthews, *Toward a New Society*, 26–46. On the Second Great Awakening, see McLoughlin, *Revivals, Awakenings, and Reform*, 98–140. Historians had long argued that the religious reform movements were nothing more than a form of "social control," a ruse by elites to maintain their position at the head of society. But for persuasive critiques of the social control thesis, see Banner, "Religious Benevolence as Social Control"; and Cleves, *Reign of Terror in America*.

5. On Hopkins and Beecher, see Noll, *America's God*, 271–282, 290–297. On the New Haven Theology, see Kuklick, *Churchmen and Philosophers*, 94–111. On Finney, see Howe, *What Hath God Wrought*, 170–176. On both Taylor and Finney, see Noll, *America's God*, 279–281, 297–299, 306–308, 313–316; and Holifield, *Theology in America*, 354–368 (Taylor quoted on 354).

6. Mintz, *Moralists and Modernizers*, 16–49; Abzug, *Cosmos Crumbling*; Howe, *What Hath God Wrought*, 285–327.

7. On the Unitarians, see Howe, *Unitarian Conscience*; Howe, *Making the American Self*, 130–135, 197–202; Hutchison, *Modernist Impulse*, 12–40; and Kuklick, *Churchmen and Philosophers*, 80–93. On the Universalists, see Bressler, *Universalist Movement*, 54–96.

8. Ralph Waldo Emerson to Lidian Emerson, January 18, 1843, *Letters of Ralph Waldo Emerson*, vol. 3, 118. On the religious context of the Transcendentalists, see Hutchison, *Transcendentalist Ministers*; Schmidt, *Restless Souls*; and Gura, *American Transcendentalism*. See also Conkin, *American Originals*, 71–72, 77–81. On reformism as a central aspect, see Rose, *Transcendentalism as a Social Movement*, 217–223.

9. Brock, *Pacifism in the United States*, 482–522, 559–615. On Rush, see Watts, *Republic Reborn*, 131.

10. Baptist is Neale, *Fourth Annual Address of the Connecticut Peace Society*, 5; Boston minister is Sharp, *Obedience to Magistrates Inculcated*, 18; Emerson, "We Must All Appear before the Judgment Seat of Christ," preached fourteen times between November 1830 and March 1837, in *Complete Sermons of Ralph Waldo Emerson*, vol. 3, 37–38.

11. Kellogg, *War Contrary to the Gospel*; Channing, *Sermon on War*, 2, 8; Parker quoted in Chesebrough, *Theodore Parker*, 53. "Expenses of War," *Family Christian Almanack for the United States, 1844*, 28; "Change After Death," March 31, 1847, Montgomery sermons, Box 2, Folder 12, AHTL.

12. "Philanthropos," *Solemn Appeal to Christians of All Denominations*, 34; Graves, *Desire of All Nations*. On the "Evangelical United Front," see Foster, *Errand of Mercy*; and Howe, *What Hath God Wrought*, 192–195. For the Congress of Nations and League of Universal Brotherhood, see Curti, *American Peace Crusade*, 56, 143–165. More generally, see also Sexton, *Monroe Doctrine*, 115–116.

13. *Examination of the Principles of Peace and War*, 13, 18.

14. Field, *America and the Mediterranean World*, 120–122. On Winthrop, see Lovejoy, *Religious Enthusiasm*, 94; and Bremer, *John Winthrop*, 340–342.

15. Harvard professor and Brooklyn cross quoted in Mayers, *Dissenting Voices*, 57, 59; Dwight quoted in Field, *America and the Mediterranean World*, 129; Harrison quoted in Oren, *Power, Faith, and Fantasy*, 109.

16. "The Revolution in Greece," January 19, 1824, *Papers of Daniel Webster: Speeches and Formal Writings*, vol. 1, 100–101, 111. On Webster's religion, see Bartlett, *Daniel Webster*, 44. On religion as an important part of his rhetoric, see Remini, *Daniel Webster*, 54; and Smith, *Daniel Webster*, 66–67.

17. Field, *America and the Mediterranean World*, 126–128, 132–153; Sexton, *Monroe Doctrine*. For missionary opposition, see Finnie, *Pioneers East*, 192–194; Mayers, *Dissenting Voices*, 58; and Oren, *Power, Faith, and Fantasy*, 110.

18. The best single overview of Protestant American missions is Hutchison, *Errand to the World*. For the establishment and early career of the ABCFM, see Phillips, *Protestant America and the Pagan World*; Andrew, *Rebuilding the Christian Commonwealth*; and Kling, "New Divinity and the Origins of the American Board." The story of missions is perhaps best told through case studies. For China, see Varg, *Missionaries, Chinese, and Diplomats*, 3–30; Fairbank, *Missionary Enterprise in China and America*; Iriye, *Across the Pacific*, 18–22; and Hunt, *Making of a Special Relationship*, 24–32. For the Middle East, see Tibawi, *American Interests in Syria*; Finnie, *Pioneers East*, 112–136; Field, *America and the Mediterranean World*, 176–206; Grabill, *Protestant Diplomacy and the Near East*, 4–24; Oren, *Power, Faith, and Fantasy*, 80–173; Makdisi, *Artillery of Heaven*; and Sharkey, *American Evangelicals in Egypt*, 18–36. For Hawaii, see Smith, *Yankees in Paradise*; and Tate, "Sandwich Islands Missionaries." For Catholic missionaries, see Dolan, *Catholic Revivalism*.

19. Abeel, *Missionary Fortified Against Trials*, 6, 7, 9. For death rates and median age, see Finnie, *Pioneers East*, 119. For Niebuhr's theory, see Moessner, "Missionary Motivation."

20. Field, *America and the Mediterranean World*, 199–206; Oren, *Power, Faith, and Fantasy*, 95.

21. Webster to David Porter, February 2, 1842, *Papers of Daniel Webster: Diplomatic Papers*, vol. 1, 280–281; Repousis, "Devil's Apostle." On the antebellum missionary as hopeful imperialist, see Hunt, *Making of a Special Relationship*, 30–32; Oren, *Power, Faith, and Fantasy*, 129–132; and Greenberg, *Manifest Manhood*, 231–268. For a very perceptive discussion of the nature of American missions' relationship to empire, see Makdisi, *Artillery of Heaven*, esp. 9–11. For "world is

in arms," see Andrew, *Rebuilding the Christian Commonwealth*, 151. For "reforming the world" and "God's plan for this world's recovery," see, respectively, "Editor's Address," *Christian Almanack, 1823*; and Phelps, *Christian Character*, 3.

22. William Frederic Williams to Dwight W. Marsh, March 28, 1850, Williams papers, RG 30, Box 35, Folder 1, YDS; John T. Hargrave, "Missionary Sermon,"
January 7, 1847, Sermons Folder, Box 2, Shepherdstown (West Virginia) records, UVA.

23. Hutchison, *Errand to the World*, 77–90 (quotations from, respectively, 85, 88, 89);
Harris, *Nothing but Christ*, 96–132.

24. Cooke to Mary Keeler, November 28, 1837, July 27, 1838, and March 2, 1843;
Cooke to Aaron Seeley, October 12, 1841: all in Cooke papers, Box 1, CHS.

25. Van Alstyne, *Rising American Empire*, 129–130; Cohen, *America's Response to China*,
12; Bryson, *American Diplomatic Relations with the Middle East*, 21–22. Though
she does not make this argument, see also Greenberg, *Manifest Manhood*, 259–
261. French diplomat quoted in Finnie, *Pioneers East*, 129.

CHAPTER EIGHT. MANIFEST DESTINY AND
ITS DISCONTENTS

1. Stephanson, *Manifest Destiny*, 38–48 (quotations on 40, 42).
2. On the very long career of manifest destiny, particularly its religious foundations in the colonial period, see Tuveson, *Redeemer Nation*, 91–136; Stephanson,
Manifest Destiny, 3–27; Nobles, *American Frontiers*; and Guyatt, *Providence and
the Invention of the United States*. On the pressures created by the constant surging of Americans into land beyond their own—pressures that then led to official
policy—see Kagan, *Dangerous Nation*.
3. Bailey, *Shadow on the Church*, 224–228; Rothman, *Slave Country*, 64–65, 208;
Episcopal bishop quoted in *Journal of the Proceedings of the Bishops, Clergy, and
Laity of the Protestant Episcopal Church . . . 1847*, 209.
4. Stringfellow, "A Brief Examination of Scripture Testimony on the Institution of
Slavery," *Religious Herald*, February 25, 1841, in Faust, *Ideology of Slavery*, 154,
165; Thornwell quoted in Noll, *Civil War as a Theological Crisis*, 2. On evangelicalism as the South's social bond, see Mathews, *Religion in the Old South*; Boles,
Great Revival; and Crowther, "Holy Honor." For a thoughtful evaluation of the
evolving proslavery argument, see O'Brien, *Conjectures of Order*, vol. 2, 938–992,
and, for its religious bases, 1149–1157; see also Daly, *When Slavery was Called
Freedom*. On the uneasy mix of race and religion in manifest destiny, see Horsman, *Race and Manifest Destiny*, 126, 139–140. On religion as a basis for ideas
about racial equality, see Goodman, *Of One Blood*.
5. Calhoun quoted in Noll, *God and Race in American Politics*, 35; Rice quoted in
Noll, *Civil War as a Theological Crisis*, 5. On the Protestant schisms, see Goen,
Broken Churches; Snay, *Gospel of Disunion*, 113–180; Crowther, "Religion Has
Something"; and Genovese, "Religion in the Collapse of the American Union."
For "the foreign policy of slavery," see Kagan, *Dangerous Nation*, 181–223; see
also Crapol, "Foreign Policy of Antislavery." On competing republicanism and
territorial expansion as the central concerns, see Morrison, *Slavery and the American West*; and Fry, *Dixie Looks Abroad*, 40–74.
6. Elias Cornelius to Calhoun, July 10, 1818, Cornelius papers, Box 1, CHS; Mayers, *Dissenting Voices*, 86. For McCoy, see Schultz, *Indian Canaan*.
7. Jackson quoted, respectively, in Remini, *Andrew Jackson and the Course of American Freedom*, 218; and Remini, *Andrew Jackson and the Course of American Democracy*, 418. On Jackson's religious views, see Remini, *Andrew Jackson and the*

Course of American Empire, 7; Remini, *Andrew Jackson and the Course of American Freedom*, 10–11, 62–63, 331–333; and Remini, *Andrew Jackson and the Course of American Democracy*, 91, 226, 229, 251–252, 398–400, 443–447.

8. Phillips, *Jedidiah Morse*, 35–37, 129–160, 195–215; Snyder, "Foundations of Liberty"; Horsman, "Dimensions of an 'Empire for Liberty,' " 6; Guyatt, *Providence and the Invention of the United States*, 174–180; *American Geography* quoted in Drinnon, *Facing West*, 402. On Morse's religious orthodoxy, see Phillips, *Jedidiah Morse*.

9. On Samuel Morse, religion, and empire, see Mabee, *American Leonardo*; and Phillips, *Jedidiah Morse*, 220–222. On Romanticism and evangelicalism, see Goen, *Broken Churches*, 34, 153–164; and Gabriel, "Evangelical Religion and Popular Romanticism."

10. Howe, *What Hath God Wrought*, 1–3, 692–698.

11. Stegner, *Gathering of Zion*; Arrington, *Brigham Young*; Shipps, *Mormonism*, 25–65. On relations with the Indians, see Farmer, *On Zion's Mount*. On Mormon millennialism and expansionism, see Tuveson, *Redeemer Nation*, 175–186.

12. Brock, *Pacifism in the United States*, 523–558; Stewart, *Holy Warriors*, 32–43; and, for antislavery ideology's roots and fundamentals, Davis, *Problem of Slavery in Western Culture*, 382–390. Canfield sermon on Ezekiel 20:44, 1844, Canfield papers, Box 1, Folder 72, JHL.

13. McKanan, *Identifying the Image of God*; Carwardine, *Evangelicals and Politics*, 134–139; Goodman, *Of One Blood*; Sermon, George Kaercher, February 16, 1845, Kaercher and Packer Family papers, Box 2, Cornell; Channing to Clay, August 1, 1837, *Works of William E. Channing*, 752–781; Clay to John P. Kennedy, May 16, 1839, *Papers of Henry Clay*, vol. 9, 314. On Garrison's evangelicalism, see Abzug, *Cosmos Crumbling*, 129–162. On his pacifism, see Mayer, *All on Fire*, 120–122, 222–226, 237–238, 249–251, 360–361, 478–480. On women, see Walters, *American Reformers*, 101–121; and Jeffrey, *Great Silent Army*, 134–170.

14. Howe, *What Hath God Wrought*, 678; Crapol, "Foreign Policy of Antislavery"; Jordan, *Evangelical Alliance*. On the relationship between American and British evangelicals, see Carwardine, *Trans-Atlantic Revivalism*. On harmonious Anglo-American diplomacy, see Jones and Rakestraw, *Prologue to Manifest Destiny*.

15. Watson, *Liberty and Power*, 109–110; Wallace, *Long, Bitter Trail*, 46–47, 68–69; Mayers, *Dissenting Voices*, 87–89; Emerson to Van Buren, April 23, 1838, *Emerson's Antislavery Writings*, 2–3.

16. Fredrickson, *Black Liberation*, 61–68. On free blacks and antislavery, see Blackett, *Building an Antislavery Wall*; Gosse, "As a Nation, the English Are Our Friends"; Johnson, *Redeeming America*, 134–139; and Noll, *Civil War as a Theological Crisis*, 64–72.

17. Genovese, *Roll, Jordan, Roll*, 161–284; Raboteau, *Slave Religion*; Frey and Wood, *Come Shouting to Zion*, 118–208.

18. Blassingame, *Slave Community*, 126–130; Oakes, *Slavery and Freedom*, 22–24, 143–144; Berlin, *Generations of Captivity*, 159–244, esp. 206–209, 217; Rothman, *Slave Country*, 188–203. For the centrality of Baptist evangelicalism to Turner's radical protest and black dissent in general, see Scully, *Religion and the Making of Nat Turner's Virginia*.

19. Blake address at the Boston Lyceum, n.d., Blake-Clapp-Arguimbau Family papers, Box 1, Folder 15, MHS; Fogel, *Without Consent or Contract*, 251–254; Carwardine, *Evangelicals and Politics*, 141–142; Conforti, *Samuel Hopkins*, 142–158; Guyatt, *Providence and the Invention of the United States*, 183–194. On Lincoln's support for colonization, see Carwardine, *Lincoln*, 24–25, 30–31, 79, 199, 215; and Foner, *Fiery Trial*.

20. Beecher, *Discourse Delivered at the Plymouth Church*, 14–15. For Beecher's antipa-

thy to manifest destiny, see Clark, *Henry Ward Beecher*, 86. On Lyman Beecher and education, see Fraser, *Pedagogue for God's Kingdom*.

21. Knowles, *Perils and Safeguards*, 9, 18; Cheever quoted in Guyatt, *Providence and the Invention of the United States*, 280; Bushnell quoted in Edwards, "My God and My Good Mother," 117.

22. "The Young American," Boston, February 7, 1844, *Collected Works of Ralph Waldo Emerson*, vol. 1, 226, 229, 230. On Emerson, see also Gougeon, *Virtue's Hero*, 131–145; and Buell, *Emerson*, 250, 272–273. On Channing and Parker, see Stephanson, *Manifest Destiny*, 51–54.

23. Sampson, *John L. O'Sullivan*, 92, 194–207; Emerson quoted in Richardson, *Emerson*, 498.

24. McPherson, *Battle Cry of Freedom*, 3–5, 47–77; Anderson and Cayton, *Dominion of War*, 274–293. On the Mexican War as the essential causal event in the origins of the Civil War, see Kornblith, "Rethinking the Coming of the Civil War."

25. For overviews of the war and its causes, see Weems, *To Conquer a Peace*; Howe, *What Hath God Wrought*, 658–791; and, for its military history, Bauer, *Mexican War*. For the Mexican perspective, see Henderson, *Glorious Defeat*. For the Texas controversy, see Silbey, *Storm Over Texas*, 1–145.

26. Dusinberre, *Slavemaster President*; Bergeron, *Presidency of James K. Polk*, 51–136; Haynes, *James K. Polk and the Expansionist Impulse*. On the causal linkages between Texas, Oregon, and Mexico, see Pletcher, *Diplomacy of Annexation*.

27. Polk quoted in Price, *Origins of the War with Mexico*, 10. On Polk's religion, see Sellers, *James K. Polk*, 309; and Bergeron, *Presidency of James K. Polk*, 9–10, 137, 214, 239–241; and Sexton, *Monroe Doctrine*, 115.

28. Stewart quoted in Johannsen, *To the Halls of the Montezumas*, 49–50; Bellows quoted in Hixson, *Myth of American Diplomacy*, 68. For an overview of American religion and the war, see Ellsworth, "American Churches and the Mexican War."

29. Fleek, *History May Be Searched in Vain*; Schroeder, *Mr. Polk's War*, 108; Kirkham to his wife, June 1, 1847, and June 6, 1847, in Miller, ed., *Mexican War Journal and Letters of Ralph W. Kirkham*, 21, 27. On Mexican perceptions, see Brack, "Mexican Opinion," 170–171.

30. Quoted in Greenberg, *Manifest Manhood*, 99.

31. West, *Politics of Revelation*; Pinheiro, "Religion without Restriction," 69–70, 73–74; Noll, *Civil War as a Theological Crisis*, 130. On the emergence of nativism, see Wilentz, *Chants Democratic*, 266–270, 315–335; and Holt, *Rise and Fall of the American Whig Party*, 187–194, 203–207. On anti-Catholicism in antebellum culture and politics, see, respectively, Franchot, *Roads to Rome*; and Holt, *Forging a Majority*.

32. For Brownson, see Schroeder, *Mr. Polk's War*, 109–110; soldier quoted in Stevens, *Rogue's March*, xi; leaflet quoted in Miller, *Shamrock and Sword*, 162–163. See also Pinheiro, "Religion without Restriction." On the maltreatment of Catholic soldiers, see Foos, *Short, Offhand, Killing Affair*, 25–29.

33. Foos, *Short, Offhand, Killing Affair*, 26 (*Catholic Telegraph* quoted on 47); Schroeder, *Mr. Polk's War*, 107–108.

34. Thanksgiving sermon, 1847, Canfield papers, Box 1, JHL; Edward Warner Bentley's college journal, Bentley papers, RG30, Box 213, YDS; Episcopalian is Pyne, *Sermon Delivered on Thanksgiving Day*, 13.

35. For Gallatin, see Guyatt, *Providence and the Invention of the United States*, 224. For Calhoun, see Lander, *Reluctant Imperialists*, 63–64; and Hunt, *Ideology and U.S. Foreign Policy*, 34.

36. Beecher quoted in Clark, *Henry Ward Beecher*, 87; "The Mexican War," ca. 1848,

Parker papers, Sermons: vol. XI, Box 11, AHTL; Grodzins, *American Heretic*, 172–174, 333–340, 471–475, 498.

37. For Thoreau's tax resistance, see Howe, *Making the American Self*, 235–255, for the Christian context of his ideas and morals, 245–247.

38. Naval commander (Robert F. Stockton) quoted in *Niles National Register*, January 22, 1848, in Graebner, *Manifest Destiny*, 210; Kalloch, *National Fast-Day Sermon*, 6; Polk quoted in Price, *Origins of the War with Mexico*, 11.

39. "Speech at a Meeting to Aid John Brown's Family," November 18, 1859, in *Emerson's Antislavery Writings*, 118; Garrison quoted in Mayer, *All on Fire*, 502–503; Child quoted in Brock, *Pacifism in the United States*, 682. For Parker, see Albrecht, *Theodore Parker*, 133–134. For "violent messiahs," see McKanan, *Identifying the Image of God*, 174–217. For a balanced examination of the Christian faith at the heart of Brown's revolt and the rejection of pacifism, see McGlone, *John Brown's War Against Slavery*.

PART IV. AMERICA'S MISSION

1. Quoted in Olcott, *Life of William McKinley*, vol. 2, 109–111.

2. Iriye, "Imperialism and Sincerity," 119. Similarly, not all historians accept the authenticity of the quotation itself. See Gould, *Spanish-American War*, 109; and Smith, "A Question from Which We Could Not Escape," 364. For an exception to Iriye's verdict, see Miller, *"Benevolent Assimilation,"* 24.

3. McKinley quoted in Olcott, *Life of William McKinley*, vol. 2, 368; verse from Micah quoted in Leech, *In the Days of McKinley*, 132.

4. Leech, *In the Days of McKinley*, 4–8, 11–13; Morgan, *William McKinley*, 17–18, 24–26, 31–32, 45–46, 50–52, 67–68; McSeveney, *Politics of Depression*, 164; Kelly, "Election of 1896," 190–191.

5. On McKinley's domestic policies, see Gould, *Presidency of William McKinley*, 21–32, 40–48, 153–177. For his about-face silence on Jim Crow as a way to placate the South, see Williamson, *Crucible of Race*, 342–345; Perman, *Struggle for Mastery*, 116–123; and Blight, *Race and Reunion*, 350–352. For his new conservatism on matters economic and industrial, see McSeveney, *Politics of Depression*, 163–221.

6. On McKinley in control of foreign policy, see Beisner, *From the Old Diplomacy to the New*, 120–144.

CHAPTER NINE. ABRAHAM LINCOLN AND THE FIRST WAR OF HUMANITARIAN INTERVENTION

1. Much has been written on America's Civil War diplomacy, but see esp. Jones, *Blue & Gray Diplomacy*; for a briefer overview, see Herring, *From Colony to Superpower*, 224–250. On the Union's foreign policy, see Mahin, *One War at a Time*; and on the Confederacy's, Fry, *Dixie Looks Abroad*, 75–105. See also Jones, *Union in Peril*; and McPherson, "No Peace without Victory." On the Civil War as an episode in world history, see Bender, *Nation Among Nations*, 116–181; and Bayly, *Birth of the Modern World*, 161–165.

2. Paludan, *People's Contest*, 339–340; Noll, *Civil War as a Theological Crisis*, 11–14 (figures on 12–13).

3. Surprisingly, there is relatively little scholarship on religion and the Civil War. For an excellent overview, see the various essays in Miller, Stout, and Wilson, eds., *Religion and the American Civil War*. On the lack of theological innovation,

see Noll, *Civil War as a Theological Crisis*. On the sectional church schisms, see Snay, *Gospel of Disunion*. On the clergy's role in advocating total war, see Stout, *Upon the Altar*. On the Christian Commission, see Moorhead, *American Apocalypse*, 65–70; and Paludan, *People's Contest*, 351–354. On the soldiers' faith, see McPherson, *For Cause and Comrades*, 62–76; Woodworth, *While God is Marching On*; and Manning, *What This Cruel War Was Over*, 113–145.

4. Quoted in Paludan, *People's Contest*, 371; see also Niebuhr, *Children of Light and the Children of Darkness*, 181; and Niebuhr, *Irony of American History*, 171–173. Because of the importance of his presidency and the ambiguity of his religious beliefs, Lincoln's faith—indeed, whether he even had any faith—is historically controversial. My own account draws especially heavily upon Carwardine, *Lincoln*, 32–44, 56–58, 123–124, 146–147, 221–229, 233–235, 274–282, 313–314. But, from a wide range of perspectives, see also Wolf, *Almost Chosen People*; Guelzo, *Abraham Lincoln*; Noll, *America's God*, 425–435; Miller, *Lincoln's Virtues*, 42–43, 49–50, 83–90, 294–296, 365; Jacoby, *Freethinkers*, 104–123; and Smith, *Faith and the Presidency*, 91–127.

5. This is a radically compressed treatment of a complex subject. For recent, more thorough discussions, see Gates, ed., *Lincoln on Race and Slavery*; and Foner, *Fiery Trial*.

6. Lincoln to Gillespie quoted in Carwardine, *Lincoln*, 43; Lincoln to Hodges, April 4, 1864, *Collected Works of Abraham Lincoln*, vol. 7, 281. Lincoln's belief that "If slavery is not wrong, nothing is wrong" likely owed much to the writings of the Reverend Leonard Bacon, a Congregationalist from New Haven, Conn., who had condemned slavery in similar terms in the 1840s and whose writings Lincoln had read. See Carwardine, *Lincoln*, 32–33. On Lincoln's long-standing belief that slavery itself was immoral and unjust, see Miller, *Lincoln's Virtues*; and McPherson, "Who Freed the Slaves?"

7. Quoted in Carwardine, *Lincoln*, 231.

8. On the egalitarian core of evangelical abolitionism, see Goodman, *Of One Blood*. On Catholics, see Curran, "Rome, the American Church, and Slavery"; McGreevey, *Catholicism and American Freedom*, 49–66; and Noll, *Civil War as a Theological Crisis*, 125–132. On Jews, see Korn, *American Jewry and the Civil War*, 15–31; and Sarna, *American Judaism*, 112–113.

9. Howard, *Religion and the Radical Republican Moment*; Tyng and Read both quoted in Tuveson, *Redeemer Nation*, 192–193; soldier is from Rankin, ed., *Diary of a Christian Soldier*, 110.

10. Payne quoted in Noll, *Civil War as a Theological Crisis*, 6; *Christian Recorder* quoted in Stout, *Upon the Altar*, 179. On the Civil War as an African American war of liberation, see Tuck, *We Ain't What We Ought To Be*, 11–36. On emancipation as a slave rebellion, see Hahn, *Political Worlds of Slavery and Freedom*, 55–114. For black soldiers, see Manning, *What This Cruel War Was Over*, 125–131.

11. Tuveson, *Redeemer Nation*, 190–191; Wilson, *Patriotic Gore*, 3–58. On Stowe's religious background and beliefs, see Hedrick, *Harriet Beecher Stowe*, 40–42, 143–157, 215.

12. "Battle Hymn" quoted in Tuveson, *Redeemer Nation*, 198; on "John Brown's Body," see Paludan, *People's Contest*, 350–351. See also Wilson, *Patriotic Gore*, 91–98; and Stout, *Upon the Altar*, 115–116.

13. Paludan, *People's Contest*, 342–347; Fredrickson, "Coming of the Lord," 114–119; Stout, *Upon the Altar*, 140–141, 167–190 (Carden quoted on 248); Manning, *What This Cruel War Was Over*, 115–116, 118–119, 121–125.

14. McPherson, *Battle Cry of Freedom*, 490–510, 538–544, 557–567; Donald, *Lincoln*, 362–376; diary entry, September 22, 1862, *Diary of Gideon Welles*, vol. 1, 143.

15. Annual Message to Congress, December 1, 1862, *Collected Works of Abraham*

Lincoln, vol. 5, 537; Lincoln to Speed quoted in Donald, *Lincoln,* 377; Pittsburgh preacher quoted in Moorhead, *American Apocalypse,* 103.

16. Lincoln after Gettysburg quoted in Stout, *Upon the Altar,* 241; Lincoln to Gurney quoted in White, "Lincoln's Sermon," 219. On the relationship between emancipation and Lincoln's growing faith, see Stampp, "Lincoln's History," 29–30; and Carwardine, *Lincoln,* 228, 233–234. On Lincoln and the Thirteenth Amendment, see Vorenberg, *Final Freedom,* 123–127, 176–182, 198–199, 208–210, 223–227.

17. Douglass quoted in, respectively, Oakes, *Radical and the Republican,* 242, and White, "Lincoln's Sermon," 223; Noll, *America's God,* 426 (Schaff quoted on 6–7); White, "Lincoln's Sermon."

18. Lincoln, Second Inaugural Address, March 4, 1865, *Collected Works of Abraham Lincoln,* vol. 8, 332–333.

19. Seward quoted in Guyatt, *Providence and the Invention of the United States,* 259. On the new strain of American nationalism produced by the Civil War, particularly in the North, see also Foner, *Reconstruction,* 24, 29–30.

20. On the important role of preachers, see Fredrickson, "Coming of the Lord"; and Stout, *Upon the Altar.* On the clergy and Northern nationalism before 1861, see Grant, *North Over South.* For after 1861, see Kirby, "Matthew Simpson and the Mission of America."

21. Pennsylvania soldier quoted in McPherson, *For Cause and Comrades,* 71; Bushnell quoted in Noll, *America's God,* 432; Payne quoted in Noll, *Civil War as a Theological Crisis,* 78.

22. Miller, "Catholic Religion, Irish Ethnicity, and the Civil War"; Noll, *Civil War as a Theological Crisis,* 125–132; Dolan, *Immigrant Church,* 162; Samito, *Becoming American Under Fire.* On Catholicism's role in the draft riots, see Bernstein, *New York City Draft Riots.*

23. Korn, *American Jewry and the Civil War,* 122–155, 217–219; Stout, *Upon the Altar,* 199–200, 208; Lincoln quoted in Sarna, *American Judaism,* 121.

24. On the wartime upsurge in providential thinking, see Guyatt, *Providence and the Invention of the United States,* 259–298. On its crisis, see Noll, *Civil War as a Theological Crisis,* 75–94. On Jackson, see Stowell, "Stonewall Jackson."

25. Carwardine, *Lincoln,* 39–40, 225–228, 233–235, 246–247, 278–279; Guelzo, *Lincoln's Emancipation Proclamation,* 6–7, 149–151; Noll, *America's God,* 430–432. On Lincoln's "fatalism" as opposed to providentialism, see Donald, *Lincoln,* 14–15.

26. For "angels," see Paludan, *People's Contest,* 351. On patriotism, civil religion, and the idea of "martyrdom," see Stout, *Upon the Altar,* xvii–xxii, 28–29, 82–94, 248–251 (Schaff quoted on 250; Beecher quoted on 90). On death as divine sacrifice for a noble cause, see Faust, *This Republic of Suffering,* esp. 7–9, 23–26. On the Christian imagery of the Gettysburg Address, see Wolf, *Almost Chosen People,* 169–172; Wills, *Lincoln at Gettysburg,* 88; and Guelzo, *Abraham Lincoln,* 372–373.

27. Lincoln, Gettysburg Address (George Bancroft copy), November 19, 1863, *Collected Works of Abraham Lincoln,* vol. 7, 22.

CHAPTER TEN. MISSIONARIES AND THE IMPERIALISM OF HUMAN RIGHTS

1. LaFeber, *American Search for Opportunity*; Zakaria, *From Wealth to Power.*

2. Kennedy, *Rise and Fall of the Great Powers,* 242–249 (quotation from 243).

3. On the emergence of American internationalism in this era, see Ninkovich, *Global Dawn*; and Tyrrell, *Reforming the World.* On the link between material goods and empire, see Rosenberg, *Spreading the American Dream,* 3–62; and Ho-

ganson, *Consumers' Imperium*. On the inadequacy of economic factors alone in explaining America's rise to global power, see May, *Imperial Democracy*.

4. On the stagnation and resumption of missions, see Rabe, *Home Base of American China Missions*. Figures from Hutchison, *Errand to the World*, 91, 93; and Young, *Rhetoric of Empire*, 76–77, 142.

5. Hutchison, *Modernist Impulse*, 44–47, 87–94; Varg, *Missionaries, Chinese, and Diplomats*, 68–76, 86–98; Hutchison, *Errand to the World*, 103–111. On Protestants and Darwin, see Roberts, *Darwinism and the Divine*; and Moore, *Post-Darwinian Controversies*.

6. LaFeber, *New Empire*, 72–80; Curtis, "Son of Man and God the Father"; Edwards, "Forging an Ideology." On Catholic missionaries, see Donovan, *Pagoda and the Cross*; Breslin, *China, American Catholicism, and the Missionary*; and Dries, *Missionary Movement in American Catholic History*, 22–61.

7. Fishburn, "Social Gospel as Missionary Ideology"; Xing, *Baptized in the Fire of Revolution*; Hutchison, *Errand to the World*, 104; Mead, *Special Providence*, 132–162; missionary quoted in Varg, *Missionaries, Chinese, and Diplomats*, 64. The classic account of the Social Gospel is May, *Protestant Churches and Industrial America*; but for more recent overviews, see White and Hopkins, *Social Gospel*; Gorrell, *Age of Social Responsibility*; and, especially, Curtis, *Consuming Faith*. On the shared crusading spirit of both secular and religious Progressives, see Crunden, *Ministers of Reform*.

8. L. W. Munhall, "The Coming of the Lord and World-Wide Evangelization," in Dayton, ed., *Prophecy Conference Movement*, vol. 3, 111; Hutchison, *Modernist Impulse*, 155, 258–261; Marsden, *Fundamentalism and American Culture*, 68–70, 97–98; Hutchison, *Errand to the World*, 112–118 (missionary quoted on 116). On the initial support for reform among both modernists and conservatives, see Wacker, "Holy Spirit and the Spirit of the Age."

9. Hill, *World Their Household*, 3 and passim; Robert, *American Women in Mission*, 130–137, 188; Beaver, *American Protestant Women in World Mission*, 87–143; Hunter, *Gospel of Gentility*.

10. Speer, "Foreign Missions or World-Wide Evangelism," in *The Fundamentals*, 70; Parliament organizer quoted in Rosenberg, *Spreading the American Dream*, 8. On missionaries and late nineteenth-century U.S. empire, see May, *Imperial Democracy*, 25–29; Schlesinger, "Missionary Enterprise and Theories of Imperialism"; and, in Japan, Henning, *Outposts of Civilization*. See Reed, *Missionary Mind*, for its continuation into the twentieth.

11. Newspaper quoted in Young, *Rhetoric of Empire*, 155; booklet, "Quarter Centennial Union Missionary Training Institute, 1885–1910," Francis Brown papers, Series 3, Box 1, Folder 10, UTS; Bachman, *Triumph of Foreign Missions*, 3.

12. On Turner's frontier thesis and expansionism, see LaFeber, *New Empire*, 63–72.

13. For the inherently international outlook of Catholics and Jews, see Jacobson, *Special Sorrows*; and D'Agostino, *Rome in America*.

14. Walls, "World Christianity"; Hawaiian missionary is Egbert C. Smyth, "Report of Committee on Missions in the Pacific Islands," *Missionary Herald*, November 1892, 501; Clarke quoted in Hutchison, *Errand to the World*, 105.

15. Beardsley, *Sermon Preached in St. Thomas's Church*, 13; Andover professor quoted in Walls, "World Christianity," 150; Speer, "Foreign Missions or World-Wide Evangelism," in *The Fundamentals*, 64.

16. On postbellum secularization among intellectuals, see Fredrickson, *Inner Civil War*, 199–216; Turner, *Without God*, 171–261; and Meyer, "American Intellectuals and the Victorian Crisis of Faith." On Holmes, see Menand, *Metaphysical Club*, 36–37. For the *Nation*, see Grabill, *Protestant Diplomacy*, 31. On Twain and the missionaries, see Young, *Rhetoric of Empire*, 193–195; and Hunt, *Making of*

a Special Relationship, 287–288. Du Bois quoted in Gaines, "Black Americans' Racial Uplift Ideology," 436. For an excellent analysis of race and Du Bois's anti-imperialism, see Kaplan, *Anarchy of Empire*, 171–212.

17. Collins Denny, "Around the World," *Episcopal Methodist*, March 16, 1887. For the racial tolerance of home missions, see Richardson, *Christian Reconstruction*; and Robertson, *Christian Sisterhood*, 11–44. On the Exclusion Acts, see McKee, *Chinese Exclusion*, 113–115.

18. B. C. Atterbury, "Lay Missionaries in China," *Missionary Review of the World*, June 1889, 438; Brent to John Wood, September 20, 1902, RG76, Records of the Domestic and Foreign Missionary Society: Philippine Mission Records, Box 2, Folder 10, NAEC. On Chinese dress, see Hunter, *Gospel of Gentility*, 138–140.

19. Brent to Wood, September 20, 1902, RG76, Box 2, Folder 10, NAEC; Episcopal missionary is Walter Clapp, private newsletter to friends, November 20, 1901, RG76, Box 5, Folder 27, NAEC.

20. Quoted in Grabill, *Protestant Diplomacy*, 24. On Korea, see Davies, "Building a City on a Hill in Korea"; and Manela, *Wilsonian Moment*, 124–129.

21. Quoted in Muller, "Josiah Strong," 495.

22. Mott quoted in Hopkins, *John R. Mott*, 83, 329; pamphlet, "Recent comments on Mr. John R. Mott and his work," March 1914, Francis Brown papers, Series 1, Box 2, Folder 27, UTS.

23. Cavert, "Missionary Enterprise as the Moral Equivalent of War." For "moral equivalent for imperialism," see Hutchison, *Errand to the World*, 92. For "converting colonialism," see Robert, "Introduction," 4. On Strong, see Muller, "Josiah Strong." On missionaries themselves changing, see Knox, "What Modifications in Western Christianity May Be Expected"; and Lian, *Conversion of Missionaries*. On both, see Dunch, "Beyond Cultural Imperialism." My interpretation of American missions has been influenced by a similar argument regarding the ambivalent relationship between British missions and the British Empire: see Stanley, *Bible and the Flag*; Porter, *Religion Versus Empire?*; and Etherington, ed., *Missions and Empire*. For a similar reading of missionaries and the American Empire, see Tyrrell, *Reforming the World*. Similarly, for Catholic missionaries and the French Empire, see Ramsay, *Mandarins and Martyrs*.

24. Morgenthau quoted in Oren, *Power, Faith, and Fantasy*, 333; Charles Denby to Jason Shackleford, March 20, 1886, reprinted as "A Noble Testimony to American Missionaries: Letter from the American Minister to China," *Missionary Review of the World*, February 1888, 117. On the empowering appropriation of Christianity by indigenous populations, see Sanneh, "World Christianity and the New Historiography."

25. Minutes of the Synod of Atlantic, Rock Hill, S.C. (Report by the Synod's Committee on Foreign Missions), 1904, RG395, African American Presbyteries and Synods Collection, Box 1, Folder 4, PHS. On African American missions to Africa, see Williams, *Black Americans and the Evangelization of Africa*; Adeleke, *UnAfrican Americans*, esp. 70–110, 114–115, 132–135; Little, *Disciples of Liberty*, 62–83; Killingray, "Black Atlantic Missionary Movement and Africa"; and, esp. for the antebellum period, Sanneh, *Abolitionists Abroad*.

26. Campbell, *Songs of Zion*; Gaines, "Black Americans' Racial Uplift Ideology," 444–447; hymn quoted in Williams, *Black Americans and the Evangelization of Africa*, 180.

27. "Girls in China," *Missionary Herald*, December 1881, 519–522 (quoted on 522).

28. Quoted in Sharkey, *American Evangelicals in Egypt*, 5.

29. J. Lamb Doty (French Tahiti) to Edwin F. Uhl (State Department, Washington), May 11, 1895, *FRUS, 1898*, 349. On the Mormon missionaries, see also Uhl to Doty, June 25, 1895, ibid., 352; John Sherman to U.S. Legation in Turkey, Janu-

ary 11, 1898, ibid., 1112; Laurits S. Swenson (Copenhagen) to Hay, March 29, 1900, *FRUS, 1900*, 413–414; David J. Hill (Berlin) to Elihu Root, September 22, 1908, *FRUS, 1908*, 366; Hill to Root, December 1, 1908, ibid., 370; Hill to the German Foreign Office, November 30, 1908, ibid., 370–371; Royal Legation of the Netherlands to State Department, September 30, 1908, ibid., 659; Alvey A. Adee to the Netherlands Embassy, October 10, 1908, ibid., 659–660; and Glad, *Mission of Mormonism in Norway.*

30. Hay to U.S. legation in La Paz, September 1, 1899, *FRUS, 1899*, 112; Harrison quoted in "Religious Liberty: Methodist Ministers Are Working for Changes in South America," *Daily Northwestern* (Oshkosh, Wis.), March 21, 1898. For the dispute, see "Marriage Laws in South America," *Chicago Daily Tribune*, May 29, 1896; "Church Folk on a Trip," *Chicago Daily Tribune*, July 13, 1897; "South American Marriage Laws," *Nebraska State Journal*, May 15, 1900. On the changing of the Bolivian constitution to widen protections of religious freedom, see William B. Sorsby (La Paz) to Elihu Root, September 12, 1906, *FRUS, 1906*, part 1, 107. For continuing protection, see Huntington Wilson (State Department) to Fox (Quito), June 19, 1909, *FRUS, 1909*, 245–246.

31. Dennis, "The American Missionary in the Orient," *Missionary Review of the World*, November 1889, 809. See also Dennis, *Islam and Christian Missions.*

32. Quoted in Rabe, *Home Base of American China Missions*, 63.

33. Warnshuis interview, 9, OHRO; Eddy to H. C. Price, December 5, 1934, Eddy papers, Box 2, Folder 33, YDS.

34. Varg, *Missionaries, Chinese, and Diplomats*, 31–41 (leaflet and motto quoted on 38, 124); Hunt, *Making of a Special Relationship*, 154–162, 285–286. See also Wehrle, *Britain, China, and the Antimissionary Riots*. On this pattern more generally, see Plesur, *America's Outward Thrust*, 74–86. On its emergence in China, see Cohen, *China and Christianity.*

35. Reid and Rockhill quoted in Young, *Rhetoric of Empire*, 187, 214. For the estimate, see Beisner, *From the Old Diplomacy to the New*, 60.

36. Conger to Tsung-li Yamen, August 25, 1898, *FRUS, 1898*, 215. On passport renewal, see John Hay to E. H. Conger (U.S. Consul, Beijing), January 18, 1900, *FRUS, 1900*, 393–394; and, on a more general level, Scully, *Bargaining with the State*, 56–59. On missionaries and military force, see Miller, "Ends and Means." For "righteous vengeance," see Frederick C. Copper (Shanghai) to John Wood, July 13, 1900, RG64, Records of the Domestic and Foreign Missionary Society: China Mission Records, Box 4, Folder 19, NAEC.

37. Reed, *Missionary Mind*, passim; Varg, *Missionaries, Chinese, and Diplomats*, 114–116; Hunt, *Making of a Special Relationship*, 160, 166.

38. Dunch, *Fuzhou Protestants and the Making of a Modern China*; Lian, *Redeemed by Fire*; Lutz, *China and the Christian Colleges*; Iriye, *Pacific Estrangement*, 123; Cohen, "Littoral and Hinterland," 218–220; Garrett, *Social Reformers in Urban China*; Rankin, "Social and Political Change in Nineteenth-Century China," 50, 56. On Taiping, see Spence, *God's Chinese Son*; and O'Brien, *Intellectual Life and the American South*, 46–47. For the missionary influence on Sun Yat-sen, see Schiffrin, *Sun Yat-sen and the Origins of the Chinese Revolution*, 14–18, 89–90; and Bergère, *Sun Yat-sen*, 26–28, 31–32. On Wellington Koo, see Manela, *Wilsonian Moment*, 113.

39. Merguerian, "Missions in Eden"; Fleischmann, "Evangelization or Education"; Grabill, *Protestant Diplomacy*, 24–34, 40–57; Sharkey, *American Evangelicals in Egypt*, 48–95.

40. Notes, "The Armenian Question," July 25, 1896, Denny papers, Box 66, UVA. See also Grabill, *Protestant Diplomacy*, 40–57.

41. J. Williams to Joseph Cheshire, with anonymous enclosure, January 16, 1896,

and "Confidential: Attacks on Christianity in Turkey," January 23, 1896, both in Cheshire papers, Box 1, Folder 11, SHC-UNC. On the ABCFM's role, see Reed, "American Foreign Policy," 230–245.

42. Alexander Stevenson Twombly to his children, February 2, 1894; Twombly to "Ned," February 5, 1894, both in RG30, Twombly papers, Box 109, YDS.

CHAPTER ELEVEN. AN ALSO CHOSEN PEOPLE

1. Sarna, *American Judaism*, 151–159; Raphael, *Judaism in America*, 50–56.
2. Jacobson, *Special Sorrows*, 43–53; Sarna, *American Judaism*, 135–138.
3. Brooks Adams to Henry Adams, February 14, 1898 (letter 96) and May 22, 1898 (letter 101), Brooks Adams letters, Box 1, HL; Henry Adams to Brooks Adams, June 12, 1899, in Carter, *Henry Adams and His Friends*, 467. Historian quoted is Dinnerstein, *Antisemitism in America*, 35–57 (quoted on 35). On the anti-Semitism of Brooks and Henry Adams, see Brookhiser, *America's First Dynasty*, 165–166, 195.
4. Hale to Henry Cabot Lodge, December 16, 1901, Lodge papers, Box 6/Reel 16, MHS.
5. Diary entry, September 4, 1920, 54, Castle diary, Volume 2, HL.
6. W. H. Cooke to Gustav Gottheil, December 15, 1876, Gottheil papers, Box 1, JTS; "The Dreyfus Case," in Kilgo, *Chapel Talks*, 139.
7. Vogel, *To See a Promised Land*; Obenzinger, *American Palestine*, esp. 39–58, from which "Peaceful Crusade" and "sacred geography" are quoted; Oren, *Power, Faith, and Fantasy*, 161–166, 238–244, 280–283.
8. William G. Moorehead address at the International Prophetic Conference, "The Conversion of the World After the Conversion of the Jews," December 10–15, 1901, in Dayton, ed., *Prophecy Conference Movement*, vol. 3, 45. On the emergence and theology of Christian Zionism, see Ariel, *On Behalf of Israel*, 11–54; and Merkley, *Politics of Christian Zionism*, 54–58.
9. Plesur, *America's Outward Thrust*, 70–73; Oren, *Power, Faith, and Fantasy*, 219, 276–280; Ariel, *On Behalf of Israel*, 55–96; Robert, *Occupy Until I Come*, 276–277; Goldman, *God's Sacred Tongue*, 235–252.
10. Gaddis, *Russia, the Soviet Union, and the United States*, 28–29; Jelavich, *Russia and the Formation of the Romanian National State*, 285, 289; Oren, *Power, Faith, and Fantasy*, 279; Diner, *Jews of the United States*, 96. On anti-Semitism in Romania and its causes during this period, see Iancu, *Jews in Romania*, 90–153; and Butnaru, *Silent Holocaust*, 16–26. In Russia, see Klier, *Imperial Russia's Jewish Question*, 285–449; and Nathans, *Beyond the Pale*, 186–198, 257–307.
11. Hay to McCormick, August 11, 1902, *FRUS, 1902*, 43–45.
12. Hay to McCormick, July 1, 1904, *FRUS, 1904*, 790; Foglesong, *American Mission and the "Evil Empire,"* 23–25. On the meeting and the petition, see Clymer, *John Hay*, 79–80; and Gaddis, *Russia, the Soviet Union, and the United States*, 42–43.
13. Hay to Charles L. Wilson, July 17, 1902, *FRUS, 1902*, 911; "Annual Message to Congress," December 6, 1904, *NYT*, December 7, 1904, 3. For the congressional resolution, see Hay to McCormick, July 1, 1904, *FRUS, 1904*, 790; "Russia's Exclusion of Jews," *NYT*, April 22, 1904, 1; and "Our Request to Russia," *NYT*, August 22, 1904, 2. Diplomat quoted in "President's Criticism May Offend Russia," *NYT*, December 7, 1904, 1. For the abrogation of the 1832 treaty, see Laserson, *American Impact on Russia*, 353–371.
14. Root to G. v. L. Meyer (St. Petersburg), November 22, 1905, *FRUS, 1905*, 831; Foglesong, *American Mission and the "Evil Empire,"* 28; Fink, *Defending the Rights of Others*, 51–57.
15. Hay to McCormick, August 11, 1902, *FRUS, 1902*, 43–45. On Hay's attitudes

toward American Jews, see Clymer, *John Hay*, 75–81. For examples of State Department antipathy to European Jews, see John B. Jackson (Athens) to Hay, March 21, 1903, *FRUS, 1903*, 702–703; and Wilson to Hay, November 15, 1903, ibid., 706–707.

16. Memorial quoted in Clymer, *John Hay*, 81.

CHAPTER TWELVE. CUBA, THE PHILIPPINES, AND THE FIRST CRUSADE

1. For muscular Christianity, see Putney, *Muscular Christianity*; Kimmel, *Manhood in America*, 175–181; and Prothero, *American Jesus*, 87–97 (Episcopal priest quoted on 89). For the revival of Puritan ideas, see Matarese, *American Foreign Policy and the Utopian Imagination*, 20–22 (Denver writer quoted on 21); and McKenna, *Puritan Origins*, 176–180. For Anglo-Saxonism, see Anderson, *Race and Rapprochement*; Hunt, *Ideology and U.S. Foreign Policy*, 77–81; Perkins, *Great Rapprochement*, 76–84; and, in deeper historical perspective, Horsman, *Race and Manifest Destiny*.

2. Jessup, *Elihu Root*, vol. 1, 39–40, 57–60 (quoted on 58); Zimmermann, *First Great Triumph*, 123–148. On the burned-over district, see Barkun, *Crucible of the Millennium*; and Wellman, *Grass Roots Reform*.

3. On Mahan's theory of sea power from a variety of perspectives, see Livezey, *Mahan on Sea Power*; Kennedy, *Rise and Fall of British Naval Mastery*, 1–9; Seager, *Alfred Thayer Mahan*, 191–218; Sumida, *Inventing Grand Strategy and Teaching Command*; and Zimmermann, *First Great Triumph*, 85–122.

4. Mahan to Silas McBee, September 1899, *Letters and Papers of Alfred Thayer Mahan*, vol. 2, 661. For Mahan's integration of religion and history, see Seager, *Alfred Thayer Mahan*, 64–80, 574–581; Livezey, *Mahan on Sea Power*; Sumida, *Inventing Grand Strategy and Teaching Command*, 76–79.

5. Mahan to the Editor of the *New York Times*, August 14, 1914, *Letters and Papers of Alfred Thayer Mahan*, vol. 3, 539; Mahan to Ellen Evans Mahan, January 28, 1894, ibid., vol. 2, 218. On the mission school, see Taylor, *Life of Admiral Mahan*, 264.

6. Marks, "Morality as a Drive Wheel," 44, 47; Smith, *Faith and the Presidency*, 130–138 (quoted on 134); Hawley, *Theodore Roosevelt*, 13–18, 73.

7. "A Confession of Faith," Chicago, August 6, 1912, in Roosevelt, *Progressive Principles*, 173. On Roosevelt's domestic Progressivism as president and candidate in 1912, see Cooper, *Warrior and the Priest*, 76–86, 189–191, 216–218.

8. Marks, "Morality as a Drive Wheel"; Ninkovich, "Theodore Roosevelt"; "We cannot help playing" quoted in Cooper, *Warrior and the Priest*, 112; Roosevelt to Mott, October 12, 1908, Mott papers, Box 76, Folder 1383, YDS.

9. For a succinct overview, see Herring, *From Colony to Superpower*, 309–319. On the history and historiography of the war, see Pérez, *War of 1898*. Especially good on the psychological and ideological causes of the U.S. decision to go to war is Ninkovich, *United States and Imperialism*, 9–30. On international progressivism as a form of imperialism, see also Pérez, *Cuba in the American Imagination*.

10. Clebsch, "Christian Interpretations."

11. On the role of religious newspapers, see Pratt, *Expansionists of 1898*, 279–316. *Congregationalist* quoted in Healy, *US Expansionism*, 134; *California Christian Advocate* quoted in MacKenzie, *Robe and the Sword*, 72; *Methodist Review* quoted in Varg, *Missionaries, Chinese, and Diplomats*, 82; *Evangelist* quoted in Handy, *Undermined Establishment*, 78.

12. Dorn, *Washington Gladden*, 407–409 (quoted on 408, 409). For the WCTU and

CRTU, see Tyrrell, *Woman's World/Woman's Empire*, 176, 183; and Hoganson, *Fighting for American Manhood*, 18–19, 33–34, 58, 60, 125. For Allen, see Mc-Dowell, *Social Gospel in the South*, 73. For Rauschenbusch, see Evans, *Kingdom Is Always but Coming*, 139.

13. Brown, *Lyman Abbott*, 161–169 (quoted on 168).

14. Kazin, *Godly Hero*, 7–8, 86–89, 123–127.

15. Ahlstrom, *Religious History of the American People*, 878.

16. On the evolution of Methodism, see Norwood, *Story of American Methodism*, 239–354. For its role in the origins of Pentecostalism, see Blumhofer, *Restoring the Faith*, 26–29; and Wacker, *Heaven Below*, 2–6.

17. MacKenzie, *Robe and the Sword*; Shankman, "Southern Methodist Newspapers." For a good discussion of the initial ambivalence of some clergy, see Hudson, "Protestant Clergy Debate," 110–113.

18. "The President's Message," *NYT*, April 12, 1898, 1. For congressional fury, see "An Angry Congress," ibid.

19. For Catholics on the *Maine*, see Handy, *Undermined Establishment*, 78–79.

20. Cross, *Emergence of Liberal Catholicism*; Gillis, *Roman Catholicism in America*, 65–67.

21. For the peace mission and Ireland's views on the war, see Offner, "Washington Mission"; Moynihan, *Life of Archbishop John Ireland*, 162–176; and O'Connell, *John Ireland*, 444–454. Ireland and Knights of Columbus quoted in Marty, *Modern American Religion*, vol. 1, 307; Fitzgerald quoted in Hoganson, *Fighting for American Manhood*, 81. On immigrants, see Jacobson, *Special Sorrows*, 141–176.

22. Quinn, "Mormon Church and the Spanish-American War"; Arrington and Bitton, *Mormon Experience*, 251.

23. Casualty figures from Ninkovich, *United States and Imperialism*, 27.

24. On the war, see esp. Welch, *Response to Imperialism*, 24–42; and Linn, *Philippine War*.

25. On arbitration, see May, *Imperial Democracy*, 62–65.

26. Woolsey, *Peaceful Mission of America*, 6, 7–8. On the WCTU, see Tyrrell, *Woman's World/Woman's Empire*, 184–186; and Hoganson, *Fighting for American Manhood*, 177–178, 190.

27. Little, *Disciples of Liberty*, 113–134; Gatewood, *Black Americans and the White Man's Burden*, 162, 200, 235–236; Litwack, *Trouble in Mind*, 463–470.

28. Simmons, *History of Our Philippine Relations*, 10–11. For a balanced discussion of mainline anti-imperialism and its critics, see Welch, *Response to Imperialism*, 94–100.

29. Jacobson, *Special Sorrows*, 177–216; Dries, *Missionary Movement in American Catholic History*, 63–64. Spalding quoted in Marty, *Modern American Religion*, vol. 1, 187.

30. Atkinson, *Criminal Aggression*, 13; Hoar, *Speech of Hon. George F. Hoar*, 16; Hoar, "nature's God," quoted in Beisner, *Twelve Against Empire*, 161. On Hoar's faith as an influence on his politics, see Welch, *George Frisbie Hoar*, 313–315.

31. Tillman quoted in Fairclough, *Better Day Coming*, 13. For Hoar's lament, see Hoar, *Autobiography of Seventy Years*, 305. On imperialism as a facilitator of segregation, see Woodward, *Strange Career of Jim Crow*, 72–74.

32. Quoted in Hoganson, *Fighting for American Manhood*, 184. On the racism of anti-imperialism, see Love, *Race Over Empire*.

33. Coletta, *William Jennings Bryan*, vol. 1, 233–237; Kazin, *Godley Hero*, 89–108. On the politics of imperialism, see Miller, *"Benevolent Assimilation,"* 13–30, 129–149; and Brands, *Bound to Empire*, 20–35.

34. "Mr. Bryan's Speech of Acceptance," *NYT*, August 9, 1900, 1. For McKinley's resentment, see Kazin, *Godley Hero*, 104.

35. Brands, *Bound to Empire*, 60–84.
36. Miller, *"Benevolent Assimilation,"* 17–19. For the poll, see Young, *Rhetoric of Empire*, 142–143. *Broadside* quoted in Tompkins, *Anti-Imperialism in the United States*, 11.
37. Clymer, *Protestant Missionaries in the Philippines*, 93–113, 153–173; Williams, "United States Indian Policy"; YMCA newsletter, "First Impressions of the Philippines," April 10, 1911, Eddy papers, Box 3, Folder 59, YDS.
38. Parker, *Kingdom of Character*, 114–115; Hopkins, *John R. Mott*, 309–310, 320; Strong, *Expansion Under New-World Conditions*, 301; Varg, *Missionaries, Chinese, and Diplomats*, 83.
39. Dorn, *Washington Gladden*, 412–415; Minus, *Walter Rauschenbusch*, 107–109; Evans, *Kingdom Is Always but Coming*, 139. Gladden quoted in Hudson, "Protestant Clergy Debate," 116; Abbott quoted in Brown, *Lyman Abbott*, 172. On the WCTU, see Bordin, *Woman and Temperance*, 155; Tyrrell, *Woman's World/Woman's Empire*, 213–217; and Foster, *Moral Reconstruction*, 146–147.
40. Anti-imperialist quoted in Tompkins, *Anti-Imperialism in the United States*, 12; Strong, *Expansion Under New-World Conditions*, 287, 292; Lawrence, "Sermon Preached at the Old South Church," 379; "Proceedings of the Church Club of New York in the Matter of the Establishment of an Episcopate in the Philippine Islands," March 27, 1901, RG76, Records of the Domestic and Foreign Missionary Society: Philippine Mission Records, Box 32, Folder 2, NAEC.
41. Quoted in Healy, *US Expansionism*, 131. On Platt's religion, see Coolidge, *Old-Fashioned Senator*, 591.
42. Quoted in Miller, *"Benevolent Assimilation,"* 27.
43. Strong, *Expansion Under New-World Conditions*, 288–289, 297; Gladden quoted in Dorn, *Washington Gladden*, 412.
44. Hoganson, *Fighting for American Manhood*, 192–193; Roosevelt quoted in Ninkovich, *United States and Imperialism*, 52.
45. Kramer, *Blood of Government*, 161–162, 192, 208–214; Clymer, "Humanitarian Imperialism." On the "hierarchy of race," see Hunt, *Ideology and U.S. Foreign Policy*, 46–91.
46. Quoted in Ninkovich, *United States and Imperialism*, 57. The best detailed examination of these issues is found in Reuter, *Catholic Influence on American Colonial Policies*.
47. Quoted in Smith, *Faith and the Presidency*, 143. On Roosevelt and American Catholics, see Reuter, *Catholic Influence on American Colonial Policies*, 106–136; and Miller, *"Benevolent Assimilation,"* 136–140.
48. Alvarez, "Purely a Business Matter"; Ninkovich, *United States and Imperialism*, 62–64; Handy, *Undermined Establishment*, 86–88; Kramer, *Blood of Government*, 357–360; Reuter, "William Howard Taft" (Vatican quoted on 117); Stanley, *Nation in the Making*, 82, 185–187. On Taft in the Philippines, see also Anderson, *William Howard Taft*, 66–78. On Filipino religion, see Gowing, "Disentanglement of Church and State"; Clifford, *"Iglesia Filipina Independiente,"* 224–248; and Deats, *Nationalism and Christianity in the Philippines*.
49. Dewey quoted in Hixson, *Myth of American Diplomacy*, 97; *Tribune* quoted in Hoganson, *Fighting for American Manhood*, 175; Taft quoted in Varg, *Missionaries, Chinese, and Diplomats*, 80.
50. For "doubtful," see Mahan to Henry Cabot Lodge, July 27, 1898, *Letters and Papers of Alfred Thayer Mahan*, vol. 2, 569; for "calling of God," see Mahan to McBee, September 1899, ibid., 662; for "Personal Will," see Livezey, *Mahan on Sea Power*, 26; for "Deus vult," see Mahan to George Sydenham Clarke, August 17, 1898, *Letters and Papers of Alfred Thayer Mahan*, vol. 2, 580.
51. Braeman, *Albert J. Beveridge*, 6–13 (quoted on 9).

52. Beveridge quoted, respectively, in Braeman, *Albert J. Beveridge*, 23; and Brewer, *Why America Fights*, 14.
53. First McKinley quote and newspaper quote are from, respectively, Miller, *"Benevolent Assimilation,"* ii, 17; other two McKinley quotes are from Ninkovich, *United States and Imperialism*, 38.

PART V. WOODROW WILSON AND THE SECOND CRUSADE

1. "Clergymen Call for World Peace," *NYT*, December 28, 1914, 1, 3; Coffin, *Preparedness of a Christian Nation*, 2, 12. Background details from Hutchison, *Modernist Impulse*, 234–236. Reverend William Sloane Coffin's protest against Vietnam is examined in a later chapter, but see also Goldstein, *William Sloane Coffin, Jr.* However, it does not seem that William was much influenced or guided by his uncle's pre-1917 antiwar dissent.
2. Sermon, January 7, 1917, and sermon, "The Cross as a Disclosure," March 25, 1917, both in Coffin papers, Box 7, Folder 117, UTS.
3. Easter Day sermon, April 8, 1917, ibid.
4. "General War-Time Commission of the Churches," *War-Time Agencies of the Churches*, 150; Abrams, *Preachers Present Arms*, 172; sermon, November 10, 1918, and sermon, November 17, 1918, both in Coffin papers, Box 7, Folder 120, UTS.
5. "Nations Catholics Unite in Peace Plea," *NYT*, March 22, 1915, 5; "See Happier World in Year to Come," *NYT*, December 31, 1916, 7; "Mgr. Lavelle Blesses Service Flag," *NYT*, November 17, 1917, 13; "Lavelle Says Back Wilson," *NYT*, May 7, 1918, 12. For Farley, see Abrams, *Preachers Present Arms*, 23, 73, 129.
6. Wise to Wilson, November 12, 1915, in Voss, *Stephen S. Wise*, 68; "served the interests" quoted in Abrams, *Preachers Present Arms*, 180; Urofsky, *Voice That Spoke for Justice*, 134–151; Shapiro, *Reform Rabbi in the Progressive Era*, 326–357.
7. There are only a handful of good studies that focus exclusively on the role of American religion during World War I. See especially Piper, *American Churches in World War I*; McKeown, *War and Welfare*; Schweitzer, *Cross and the Trenches*; Gamble, *War for Righteousness*; and Ebel, *Faith in the Fight*. On the role of religion in wartime Europe, see Becker, *War and Faith*; and Hoover, *God, Germany and Britain in the Great War*. In Canada, see Vance, *Death So Noble*, esp. 35–72. The "Protestant-Catholic-Jew" formula for examining "the American Creed" was first set forth in Herberg, *Protestant, Catholic, Jew*.

CHAPTER THIRTEEN. THE IDEALISTIC SYNTHESIS

1. Gamble, *War for Righteousness*, 25–67, esp. 30–31; Chatfield, *For Peace and Justice*, 15–41 (esp. 30–31); Marchand, *American Peace Movement*, esp. 323–342. On Carnegie's humanism and radical ecumenism, see Wall, *Carnegie*, 367–369, 971, 1009–1011. On the secular peace movement before 1914, see Patterson, *Toward a Warless World*.
2. Chatfield, *For Peace and Justice*, 19–21, 32–33; Marchand, *American Peace Movement*, 350–359, 364, 370–376; Early, *World Without War*, 14.
3. Chatfield, *For Peace and Justice*, 17, 35, 43–49, 62–63; Hentoff, *Peace Agitator*, 42–46; Robinson, *Abraham Went Out*, 19–31.
4. Thomas oral history, 22–23, OHRO; Swanberg, *Norman Thomas*, 10–15, 23–28, 43–75. On the mood at Union, see Handy, *History of Union Theological Seminary*, 139–144.
5. Farrell, *Beloved Lady*, 29–31, 34–35, 40–42, 45–47, 60–70, 141, 199–200; Elshtain,

Jane Addams, 72–76; Brown, *Education of Jane Addams*, 271–274; Chatfield, *For Peace and Justice*, 38–39.

6. Hopkins, *John R. Mott*, 439–446, 469–470 (quotations from 446).

7. Sermon, "Memorabilia for Year 1916," Stocker sermons and manuscripts, Box 1, UVA.

8. Gladden, *Recollections*, 385; Dorn, *Washington Gladden*, 419–429; Hutchison, *Modernist Impulse*, 238–239.

9. "Extension of Remarks of Hon. Warren Worth Bailey," including address by Martin Hardin, "Civilization at the Cross-Roads," February 26, 1916, *CR*, vol. 53, 408–416.

10. Quoted in Wacker, *Heaven Below*, 238.

11. Niebuhr, "The Failure of German-Americanism," *Atlantic Monthly*, July 1916, 13–18; Capozzola, *Uncle Sam Wants You*, 192–195; Conley, "Priest, Chaplain, Soldier."

12. Rauschenbusch to Hall, November 10, 1914, Rauschenbusch papers, Box 1, UTS; Wendte to Rauschenbusch, September 25, 1915, Rauschenbusch papers, Box 29, ABHS. On Rauschenbusch's anguish during the war, see Minus, *Walter Rauschenbusch*, 177–189; and Evans, *Kingdom Is Always but Coming*, 263–311. For Hall's dismissal, see Hutchison, *Modernist Impulse*, 238–239; and Handy, *History of Union Theological Seminary*, 140–142.

13. Miller, *Emigrants and Exiles*, 533–535, 542–543; Jacobson, *Special Sorrows*, 223–226; McKeown, *War and Welfare*, 36–40 (Gibbons quoted on 38).

14. Thompson, *Woodrow Wilson*, 107–122.

15. "An Address in Philadelphia to Newly Naturalized Citizens," May 10, 1915, *PWW*, vol. 33, 149.

16. Marsden, *Fundamentalism and American Culture*, 132–135; Kazin, *Godly Hero*, 215–242. On the Peace Treaties, see Coletta, *William Jennings Bryan*, vol. 2, 239–249. For "missionary isolationism," see Clements, *William Jennings Bryan*, esp. 57–58 for a definition.

17. Medford and Parkhurst sermons quoted in *Sixty American Opinions on the War*, 118–121; Walton to Rauschenbusch, September 9, 1915, Rauschenbusch papers, Box 29, ABHS; Stimson, *While the War Rages*, 12–13.

18. Roosevelt, *Fear God and Take Your Own Part*, 15, 17, 28, 21, 26, 57.

19. Cooper, *Woodrow Wilson*, 4; Gamble, *War for Righteousness*; Abbott, *Twentieth Century Crusade*. Most historians forget that Wilson was not immune to the constraints of politics. For an insightful reminder, see Thompson, *Woodrow Wilson*.

20. Strong, *Our Country*, 13–15; Fosdick, *Challenge of the Present Crisis*, 10. On the effects of interconnectedness, see Ninkovich, *Modernity and Power*, xi–xviii, 1–68; and, in terms of religion and foreign policy, Preston, "Religion and World Order at the Dawn of the American Century."

21. "International Friendship in the Church: Program and Methods," October 1–4, 1917, 8–9, FCC Records, RG18, Box 44, Folder 11, PHS.

22. Wiebe, *Search for Order*; speech notes, "Interdenominational," ca. 1907, Barbour papers, Box 1, ABHS. On ecumenism and the founding of the FCC, see Hutchison, *We Are Not Divided*; Lee, *Social Sources of Church Unity*; Smith, "Ecclesiastical Politics"; Marchand, *American Peace Movement*, 342–347; and Schneider, "Voice of Many Waters."

23. Rauschenbusch, *Dare We Be Christians?*, 17, 43; Rauschenbusch, *Theology for the Social Gospel*, 4–5, 64–66, 255–256.

24. Eddy, *Suffering and the War*, 85; Brown, "Devotional Meeting, Part IV: Intercession for Those for Whom We Are Working," William Adams Brown papers, Series 3, Box 3, Folder 12, UTS. On the pre-1917 cult of sacrifice and suffering among the mainline clergy, see Marchand, *American Peace Movement*, 362–363.

CHAPTER FOURTEEN. ONWARD CHRISTIAN SOLDIERS

1. "An Address to a Joint Session of Congress," April 2, 1917, *PWW*, vol. 41, 520, 525, 527.
2. "Remarks to Confederate Veterans in Washington," June 5, 1917, *PWW*, vol. 42, 452–453.
3. "Preface" in Batten, *Moral Meaning of the War.* For Wilson's call to the clergy, see "An Appeal to the American People," April 15, 1917, *PWW*, vol. 42, 75.
4. Marsden, *Fundamentalism and American Culture*, 141–153; Wacker, *Heaven Below*, 240–250.
5. Both quotations from Ruotsila, *Origins of Christian Anti-Internationalism*, 36, 61.
6. Quoted in Abrams, *Preachers Present Arms*, 79, 106. My portrait of Sunday is based on Dorsett, *Billy Sunday*, esp. 17–32, 70–74.
7. Sermon, "Is God on the Side of Autocracy or Democracy in this War?" ca. 1917, John Roach Straton papers, Box 10, ABHS.
8. Straton, letter to the editor of the *New York Times*, ca. 1918, John Roach Straton papers, Box 10, ABHS; Torrey, *What the War Teaches*, 8, 9, 11.
9. Torrey, *What the War Teaches*, 2–8. On premillennialist wartime excitement, see also Sandeen, *Roots of Fundamentalism*, 233–234; Weber, *Living in the Shadow of the Second Coming*, 105–117; Marsden, *Fundamentalism and American Culture*, 143–144, 150–152; and Boyer, *When Time Shall Be No More*, 93, 100–104.
10. Merkley, *Politics of Christian Zionism*, 75–94 (Brandeis to Blackstone quoted on 89); Ariel, *On Behalf of Israel*, 46–48, 85–93; Oren, *Power, Faith, and Fantasy*, 359.
11. Weber, *Living in the Shadow of the Second Coming*, 117–122; Marsden, *Fundamentalism and American Culture*, 141–153; Carpenter, *Revive Us Again*, 41, 102.
12. Chatfield, *For Peace and Justice*, 25–30, 43–49, 62–63; Marchand, *American Peace Movement*, 376–380; Dunham, "The Narrative of a Conscientious Objector" (1921), in Brock, ed., *"These Strange Criminals,"* 128–148; Norman Thomas, "The Religion of Free Men," *New Republic*, May 26, 1917, 109–111. On Wilson and the church service, see diary entry, June 3, 1917, in Cronon, ed., *Cabinet Diaries of Josephus Daniels*, 161.
13. Chambers, *To Raise an Army*, 205–222; Chatfield, *For Peace and Justice*, 50–55; Capozzola, *Uncle Sam Wants You*, 56–64, 71 (figures from 56); Early, *World Without War*, 93, 216n7; Forbes, *Quaker Star under Seven Flags*. On Mennonites, see Homan, *American Mennonites and the Great War*; and Bush, *Two Kingdoms, Two Loyalties*, 27–32. On the shared Quaker activism of Hoover and the AFSC, see Burner, "Quaker Faith of Herbert Hoover," 60; and Fausold, *Presidency of Herbert C. Hoover*, 11.
14. Chatfield, *For Peace and Justice*, 40; Bacon, *Non-Resistance: Christian or Pagan?*, 5, 28.
15. Fosdick, *Challenge of the Present Crisis*, 26; Coffin, *In a Day of Social Rebuilding*, 14; Mathews, *Patriotism and Religion*, 99; Mathews, "Religion and War"; Mathews to Page quoted in Chatfield, *For Peace and Justice*, 46.
16. Hardin to Julia Hardin, March 17, 1918, Hardin papers, Box 1, Folder 1, Cornell; Eddy, *Right to Fight*, 4; Hopkins, *John R. Mott*, 470–471, 528–530; Lynch, *President Wilson and the Moral Aims of the War*; Dorn, *Washington Gladden*, 429–436. On Bryan, see Levine, *Defender of the Faith*, 90–94; and Kazin, *Godly Hero*, 254–255.
17. Sermon by John D. Reid, "The Defence of Our Heritage," Unity Church, St. Paul, Minnesota, in *Soul of America in Time of War*, 54; Speer, *Christian Man, the Church, and the War*, 15. On Southern Methodists, see McDowell, *Social Gospel in the South*, 73–77.
18. Sermon, February 18, 1917, Hussey papers, Box 10, Folder 3, AHTL.

19. Quoted in Abrams, *Preachers Present Arms*, 110. For the Speer incident, see Piper *American Churches in World War I*, 49–61.

20. Mathews, *Patriotism and Religion*, 4, 70, 124.

21. Magee, *What the World Should Be*, 73–74.

22. "A Brief Historical Statement of the Enlistments and Activities of the Second Presbyterian Church, Richmond, Virginia, in the World War of 1917–8," December 21, 1920, Cecil papers, Box 1, UVA.

23. Estimates of FCC membership from Noll, *History of Christianity in the United States and Canada*, 307; and Handy, *Undermined Establishment*, 166–167.

24. Marchand, *American Peace Movement*, 339–355; Meyer, *Protestant Search for Political Realism*, 46–48. On ecumenism as an expression of the Social Gospel, see Carter, *Decline and Revival of the Social Gospel*; Curtis, *Consuming Faith*; Dorrien, *Making of American Liberal Theology*; and Rossinow, "Radicalization of the Social Gospel," 64, 69–73.

25. "Peace Prayers Sent to 130,000 Churches," *NYT*, September 20, 1914, 15; Shailer Mathews, et al., to Wilson, August 18, 1914, *PWW*, vol. 30, 396–398; Macfarland, *Across the Years*, 101–112. Generally on FCC activities, see Gamble, *War for Righteousness*, 55–63, 84–94, 127–132.

26. Newton Diehl Baker to Wilson, March 7, 1917, and enclosed telegram, Worth M. Tippy to Wilson, March 7, 1917, *PWW*, vol. 41, 353; Piper, *American Churches in World War I*, 35–48, 179–186.

27. Marchand, *American Peace Movement*, 351–354, 366–370; Early, *World Without War*, 19; Gamble, *War for Righteousness*, 192–193; Lynch, *President Wilson and the Moral Aims of the War*, 7.

28. Bryan to Mott, May 3, 1915, Box 12, Folder 220, Mott papers, YDS; Lansing to Mott, November 8, 1917, Mott papers, Box 48, Folder 900, YDS; "Somewhere in France," ca. 1917, Eddy papers, Box 3, Folder 64, YDS. See also Eddy, *With Our Soldiers in France*. On Bolshevism, see Frank L. Polk to Paris, December 24, 1918, *FRUS: Paris Peace Conference*, vol. II, 477–478. For Mott, the Y, and Wilson, see Hopkins, *John R. Mott*, 450–452, 474–475, 522–528, 532–535; General Order No. 57 quoted in Piper, *American Churches in World War I*, 19.

29. Mott to E. C. Carter, August 13, 1914, Mott papers, Box 14, Folder 259, YDS; Murray, *Call of a World Task in War Time*, ix; *Christian Students and World Problems*, iii. On the decline of the SVM, see Showalter, *End of a Crusade*; and Parker, *Kingdom of Character*.

30. Marchand, *American Peace Movement*, 355–357; Piper, *American Churches in World War I*, 43, 77–83; Hopkins, *John R. Mott*, 535–544.

31. All quoted in Piper, *American Churches in World War I*, 21–22.

32. Ibid., 23–30. On the diversity and tensions within American Catholicism, see Greeley, *American Catholic*, 33–34; Orsi, *Madonna of 115th Street*, 16–17, 56–57; Dolan, *In Search of an American Catholicism*, 71–126; and O'Toole, *Faithful*, 94–144.

33. Miller, *Emigrants and Exiles*, 370–371, 569–571; McKeown, *War and Welfare*, 35, 40–45.

34. Quoted in McKeown, *War and Welfare*, 49. On Ireland, see O'Connell, *John Ireland*, 517; and Moynihan, *Life of Archbishop John Ireland*, 267–272.

35. Piper, *American Churches in World War I*, 88–106 (Burke quoted on 96); McKeown, *War and Welfare*, 45–53; "Day of Celebration in Churches Here," *NYT*, October 29, 1917, 13.

36. Piper, *American Churches in World War I*, 100–103, 178; Pollard, *Unknown Pope*; D'Agostino, *Rome in America*, 111–120.

37. Piper, *American Churches in World War I*, 5–6, 69–87; McKeown, *War and Welfare*, 71–126.

38. Urofsky, *American Zionism from Herzl to the Holocaust*, 5–116; Raider, *Emergence of American Zionism*.

39. Marchand, *American Peace Movement*, 298–303; Sterba, *Good Americans*, 155–163.

40. Wise to Maurice Leon, November 18, 1914, in Voss, *Stephen S. Wise*, 62; Adler to Schechter, March 4, 1915, *Cyrus Adler: Selected Letters*, vol. 1, 265.

41. Oren, *Power, Faith, and Fantasy*, 363; Schlossberg quoted in Sterba, *Good Americans*, 165; "Jewish Welfare Board, United States Army and Navy," *War-Time Agencies of the Churches*, 50–52; Adler, *I Have Considered the Days*, 300.

42. Sterba, *Good Americans*, 169–172.

43. Wise to Israel Zangwill, April 29, 1917, in Voss, *Stephen S. Wise*, 78; Marx to Harry Friedenwald, November 8, 1918, Friedenwald papers, Box 2, Vol. I, JTS.

CHAPTER FIFTEEN. THE WILSONIAN CREED

1. "An Address to a Joint Session of Congress," January 8, 1918, *PWW*, vol. 45, 534–539; Clemenceau quoted in Magee, *What the World Should Be*, 98.

2. Mott quoted in Hopkins, *John R. Mott*, 531; Mathews, *Spiritual Interpretation of History*, vii; Fosdick, *Challenge of the Present Crisis*, 20–22; Mathews on nonresistance quoted in Gamble, *War for Righteousness*, 75; FCC quoted in Marchand, *American Peace Movement*, 368. Mathews linked the purposes of the Great War to emancipation in the Civil War in his *Patriotism and Religion*, 75.

3. Curti, *American Peace Crusade*, 56, 143–165; Lynch quoted in Gamble, *War for Righteousness*, 77; "With New Year's Greetings from Andrew Carnegie: War Abolished—Peace Enthroned," January 1915, Mott papers, Box 14, Folder 255, YDS.

4. Lyon, *Christian Equivalent of War*, 34–36, 50–51; "The Church and Permanent Peace," 1916, FCC Records, RG18, Box 44, Folder 11, PHS.

5. Ainslie, *Towards Christian Unity*, 92; Gladden, *Ruling Ideas of the Present Age*, 71; Rauschenbusch, *Theology for the Social Gospel*, 111; *One Hundred Fifteenth Annual Report of the Board of Home Missions of the Presbyterian Church*, 5–6; *Journal of the General Convention of the Protestant Episcopal Church in the United States of America, 1916*, 55; Floyd L. Carr, "The World-Task" (Boston, ca. 1918), Pamphlet Collection, Box 77, ABHS. For the Jim Crow clergy, see Harrington, "Unification and the Negro." However, among nonecumenists, even Social Gospelers, Southern ministers' views on desegregation were generally mixed, and often hostile. For an overview, see Harvey, *Freedom's Coming*, 47–106.

6. "Kingdom of God on earth" quoted in Marty, *Modern American Religion*, vol. 2, 230; "The Heroism of Faith," September 15, 1918, Denison papers, RG30, Box 195, YDS.

7. Gamble, *War of Righteousness*, 89–95.

8. Gordon to Sidney L. Gulick, April 1, 1919, FCC Records, RG18, Box 44, Folder 10, PHS; Marchand, *American Peace Movement*, 180, 361–370; Gamble, *War of Righteousness*, 231, 239–243.

9. "Movements of Promise Within Organized Christianity," ca. 1918, William Adams Brown papers, Series 3, Box 3, Folder 12, UTS; Ashworth, "Christian Union After the War"; Speer, *War and the Religious Outlook*, 26–27; Hopkins, "Federated Church the Next Great Forward Movement." On Korea, see Lee, "A Political Factor in the Rise of Protestantism in Korea"; and Manela, *Wilsonian Moment*, 197–199, 211.

10. "United Churches of the World," quoted in Marchand, *American Peace Movement*, 355; Rockefeller speech to the Civic and Commercial Club of Denver, "Brotherhood of Men and Nations," June 13, 1918, Mott Papers, Box 76, Folder 1380, YDS; William G. Shepherd, "An Outside View of the Interchurch," *Chris-*

tian Herald, May 22, 1920, 613; Curtis Lee Laws, "Baptists and the Interchurch Movement," *Christian Index*, June 24, 1920, 20; "Rockefeller Drops Baptist Gifts in Favor of Non-Sectarian Aid," *NYT*, November 15, 1935. On the Interchurch Movement, see also Marty, *Modern American Religion*, vol. 1, 278–281; and Harvey, "John D. Rockefeller, Jr."

11. Notes of a meeting, and appendix 1, May 1, 1919, *FRUS: Paris Peace Conference*, vol. V, 393–399; notes of a meeting, May 17, 1919, ibid., 679–680; notes of a meeting, June 6, 1919, *FRUS: Paris Peace Conference*, vol. VI, 221–222; Edward M. House to Wilson, May 22, 1919, *FRUS: Paris Peace Conference*, vol. XI, 586. For the final treaty, see Treaty of Versailles, *FRUS: Paris Peace Conference*, vol. XIII, 230; and Treaty with Poland, ibid., 798–801. On Wilson and religious liberty at Paris, see also Knock, *To End All Wars*, 206.

12. Hopkins, *John R. Mott*, 561; "War Council of the Home Mission Board of the Southern Baptist Convention," *War-Time Agencies of the Churches*, 18–19; FCC Administrative Committee resolution of February 13, 1919, in Macfarland to Alfred Williams Anthony, March 10, 1919, FCC Records, RG18, Box 18, Folder 15, PHS; Taft, "The League of Nations and Religious Liberty," December 17, 1918, and "Religious and Racial Freedom," April 24, 1919, both in *Collected Works of William Howard Taft*, vol. 7, 154–156, 283–284. On the internationalism of Southern Baptists in the World War I era, see Queen, *In the South the Baptists Are the Center of Gravity*, 59–60; and Flynt, *Alabama Baptists*, 298–302. Yet it is important to remember that there was a large discrepancy of opinion between the clergy and the much more conservative laity. See Harvey, *Redeeming the South*, 222.

13. Baker to Wilson, January 15, 1924, *PWW*, vol. 68, 531; "Wilson Thanks Churches," *NYT*, February 25, 1919, 3; Joseph P. Tumulty to Wilson, October 6, 1920, *PWW*, vol. 66, 201–204. For similar but nonetheless distinct outlines of the argument that Wilson's religious faith and background offer a blueprint for understanding his diplomacy, see Link, *Higher Realism*, 3–20; Mulder, *Woodrow Wilson*, esp. 269–277; Mulder, "Gospel of Order"; Crunden, *Ministers of Reform*, 225–273; Gamble, *War for Righteousness*, 224–231; Magee, *What the World Should Be*; and Benbow, *Leading Them to the Promised Land*. This is not to say, of course, that religion was the sole or even predominant influence on Wilson's diplomatic thought. For other, mostly secular influences, see Thompson, *Reformers and War*, 177–258; Knock, *To End All Wars*; and Kennedy, *Will to Believe*.

14. "There is a spirit that rules us" in "A Campaign Address in Jersey City, New Jersey," May 25, 1912, *PWW*, vol. 24, 443; "If I were not a Christian" quoted in Grayson, *Woodrow Wilson*, 106; "I believe that God" in "A Campaign Address in Jersey City," May 25, 1912, *PWW*, vol. 24, 443.

15. The most thorough discussions of Wilson and covenant theology are found throughout Mulder, *Woodrow Wilson*, esp. 7–8, 18–19, 34–37, 56–58, 80, 99, 103–107, 124–125, 139, 160–161, 191, 269–277; Magee, *What the World Should Be*, esp. 14–15, 17–19, 29–30, 33, 74, 100, 105–106, 110; and Benbow, *Leading Them to the Promised Land*.

16. Except for Houston, Keynes, and Clemenceau, all quotes are from Crunden, *Ministers of Reform*, 229, 229, 251, 252. For the others, see Houston, *Eight Years with Wilson's Cabinet*, vol. 2, 159; Keynes, *Economic Consequences of the Peace*, 38, 46; and Clemenceau quoted in Magee, *What the World Should Be*, 98.

17. Diary entry, July 9, 1918, in Cronon, ed., *Cabinet Diaries of Josephus Daniels*, 318; biographer is Mulder, *Woodrow Wilson*, 180; "A Fourth of July Address," Philadelphia, July 4, 1914, *PWW*, vol. 30, 254.

18. "Each man a magistracy" and student are from Mulder, *Woodrow Wilson*, 104, 124.

19. Wilson in 1900 quoted in Mulder, *Woodrow Wilson*, 151; Wilson to Mott, May 1, 1908, Mott papers, Box 100, Folder 1760, YDS; "A Religious Address at McCormick Theological Seminary," Chicago, November 2, 1909, *PWW*, vol. 19, 472. On Wilson's support for missions, see Varg, *Missionaries, Chinese, and Diplomats*, 80–81; and Smith, *Faith and the Presidency*, 167–168. More generally on Wilson's religion and progressivism, see Link, *Wilson*, vol. 1, 321–322; Link, *Wilson*, vol. 3, 64–66; and Crunden, *Ministers of Reform*, 39.

20. Wilson, notes for an address at Carnegie Hall, "Mediation of Youth in Christian Progress," November 19, 1905, *PWW*, vol. 16, 227; "Two News Reports of an Address in New York on Youth and Christian Progress," November 20, 1905, ibid., 228–229; Wilson address to the FCC, Columbus, Ohio, December 10, 1915, ibid., vol. 35, 330, 332. For "spiritual mediation," see Magee, *What the World Should Be*, 76, 82.

21. Quoted in Mulder, *Woodrow Wilson*, 270.

22. "An Address at Mansion House," London, December 28, 1918, *PWW*, vol. 53, 534; "An Address in Free Trade Hall," Manchester, December 30, 1918, ibid., 552. For Smuts, see Crunden, *Ministers of Reform*, 258. On the Covenant, see also Mulder, *Woodrow Wilson*, 269–277; and Magee, *What the World Should Be*, 14–15, 100, 105–106, 110.

23. Kerby quoted in Piper, *American Churches in World War I*, 104; Baroway to his family, November 14, 1918, Baroway papers, Box 1, JTS.

24. Maxwell, "Irish-Americans and the Fight for Treaty Ratification"; Jacobson, *Special Sorrows*, 226–227; O'Connell quoted in McKeown, *War and Welfare*, 52–53; Wise to Wilson, April 11, 1917, in Voss, *Stephen S. Wise*, 76–77; McKillen, "Ethnicity, Class, and Wilsonian Internationalism Reconsidered."

25. Oren, *Power, Faith, and Fantasy*, 351–366; Berkowitz, *Western Jewry and the Zionist Project*, 40–45.

26. Brandeis to Bernard Flexner, February 12, 1919, *Letters of Louis D. Brandeis*, vol. 4, 381; meeting notes, May 17, 1919, *FRUS: Paris Peace Conference*, vol. V, 680; Gelfand, *Inquiry*, 248; Wise, *Challenging Years*, 182–201 (for the letter, see 194). On Progressivism as central to Brandeis's Zionism, see Urofsky, *Mind of One Piece*, 95–115. For Lansing's unease with Wilson's Zionism, see minutes of daily meeting, April 12, 1919, *FRUS: Paris Peace Conference*, vol. XI, 150; and Lansing, *Peace Negotiations*, 97–98.

27. "From World War to World Brotherhood," *Federal Council Bulletin*, June 1919, 91; Cooper, *Breaking the Heart of the World*, 302–303; Gamble, *War for Righteousness*, 228–231. For the best account of the Paris Peace Conference, including Wilson's role, see MacMillan, *Paris 1919*.

28. Brandeis to Federation of English Zionists, May 8, 1919, *Letters of Louis D. Brandeis*, vol. 4, 393; Wilson quoted in Wise, *Challenging Years*, 186–187; Grabill, *Protestant Diplomacy*, 155–185; MacMillan, *Paris 1919*, 410–423, 434–436, 444; Oren, *Power, Faith, and Fantasy*, 376–393.

29. Cooper, "A Friend in Power?"; Hovannisian, "Armenian Genocide," 260–261; Duff, "Versailles Treaty and the Irish-Americans."

30. Church service program, Calvary Baptist Church, New York, June 8, 1924, Straton papers, Box 7, ABHS; Horsh, *Modern Religious Liberalism*, 196–198. For opposition to the IWM, see I. M. Haldeman, "Why I Am Opposed to the Interchurch World Movement," in Carpenter, ed., *Fundamentalist-Modernist Conflict*. On these elements within fundamentalist theology, see Ammerman, "North American Protestant Fundamentalism," esp. 14–16; and Marsden, *Understanding Fundamentalism and Evangelicalism*, esp. 67–68.

31. Gray, "The Proposed World Church Union—Is It of God or Man?" May 1919,

in Carpenter, ed., *Fundamentalist-Modernist Conflict*; Sandeen, *Roots of Fundamentalism*, 235; Marsden, *Fundamentalism and American Culture*, 154–156 (Gray quoted on 154).

32. Gaebelein and Massee quoted in Ruotsila, *Origins of Christian Anti-Internationalism*, 38–39.

33. Smith, *Robert Lansing*, 5–6, 147–148; Crunden, *Ministers of Reform*, 231; Walworth, *Wilson and His Peacemakers*, 42–43, 109–110; Knock, *To End All Wars*, 205. Lansing defined his own faith in these terms: "I consider myself of the orthodox school which look upon the Bible as containing the history of the true religion, and of God's relation to man, and which consider repentance toward God and belief in Jesus Christ to be the only means of salvation." Quoted in Reed, *Missionary Mind*, 195.

PART VI. FRANKLIN ROOSEVELT AND THE THIRD CRUSADE

1. Memcon, Henry-Haye and Hull, January 18, 1941, *FRUS, 1941*, vol. II: 102; Hull, *Memoirs*, vol. 1, 847.

2. Memcon, Henderson and Rajchman, February 29, 1940, *FRUS, 1940*, vol. II: 756; Leopold III to Roosevelt, in William C. Bullitt (Paris) to Hull, May 21, 1940, *FRUS, 1940*, vol. I: 204; René de Saint-Quentin to Hull, August 6, 1940, *FRUS, 1940*, vol. II: 538–540; Pétain to Roosevelt, August 27, 1940, ibid., 541; memcon, Welles and Henry-Haye, September 20, 1940, ibid., 549–550. However, some observers in 1940–41 doubted that Europe was on the brink of starvation, indeed, thought that it had more than enough resources to feed itself. See, for example, Brandt, "How Europe Is Fighting Famine."

3. Aide-Mémoire, British Embassy in Washington to the Department of State, July 17, 1940, ibid., 537; Hull to U.S. Embassy in London, February 15, 1940, ibid., 753.

4. Hoover speech at Vassar College, November 15, 1940, and *Collier's* article, November 23, 1940, both reprinted in Hoover, *American Epic*, vol. 4, 32–33. On Hoover and Quaker relief in Nazi-occupied Europe, see Schmitt, *Quakers and Nazis*, 176–177. On Quaker religion as a major source of Hoover's outlook, see Houck, *Rhetoric as Currency*, 55–59; Fausold, *Presidency of Herbert C. Hoover*, 18–19, 244–245; Burner, "Quaker Faith of Herbert Hoover," 60–63; and Burner, *Herbert Hoover*, 8–16, 253. On his relief efforts in World War II, see George, "Another Chance."

5. Hull, *Memoirs*, vol. 1, 804; diary entry, December 7, 1939, Israel, *War Diary of Breckenridge Long*, 40; diary entry, December 1, 1940, Ickes, *Secret Diary*, vol. 3, 385.

6. "10,000 pulpits" from Medlicott, *Economic Blockade*, vol. 1, 576; "spiritual and moral forces" quoted in Hoover to William Barrow Pugh (Secretary of the Presbyterian Church USA), October 19, 1940, Coffin papers, Box 3, Folder 32, UTS; partial Committee membership list in Hoover, *American Epic*, vol. 4, 30. On Mooney, see Flynn, *Roosevelt and Romanism*, 79. On Mott, see Hoover to Mott, December 5, 1940, Mott papers, Box 42, Folder 766, YDS. On Poling, see Poling, *Mine Eyes Have Seen*, 179–193; Poling, presidential address to the International Society of Christian Endeavor, "Always—For Christ and the Church," July 9, 1941, Pamphlets Collection, Box 134, ABHS; and Poling, *Preacher Looks at War*. On the Four Chaplains and the sinking of the *Dorchester*, see Morison, *History of United States Naval Operations in World War II*, vol. 1, 331–334.

7. James P. Alter to Coffin, October 23, 1940, Coffin papers, Box 3, Folder 32, UTS. For the FCC, see "What the Churches Are Doing About Relief Needs

Abroad," *FCB*, October 1940, 7–8. For Tittle, see Miller, *How Shall They Hear,* 437–438; and Marty, *Modern American Religion,* vol. 3, 30–31.

8. Tuttle, "Aid-to-the-Allies," 844–846.

9. "15 Leaders Oppose Feeding of Europe," *NYT,* October 6, 1940, 1; "Group Opposes Sending Food to Europeans," *WP,* October 6, 1940, 12; "American Christians and the Feeding Proposals," December 2, 1940, Coffin papers, Box 3, Folder 32, UTS; Cavert to Edwin M. Watson, Presidential Papers: OF 213, FDRL; Friedlander, *Years of Extermination,* 304; Wise, *Challenging Years,* 178.

10. For Coffin and the British, see Coffin to Lord Lothian, November 18, November 27, and December 4, 1940, all in Coffin papers, Box 3, Folder 32, UTS; and Coffin to Dean Acheson, November 18, 1941, Coffin papers, Box 3, Folder 35, UTS. For the Inter-Faith Committee, see "3 Faiths' Leaders Plea for Britain," *NYT,* December 29, 1940, 14; and "Jewish Congress Plans British Aid," *NYT,* December 30, 1940, 9. For Wise, see "U.S. Jews Praised for Aid to Britain," *NYT,* September 21, 1941, 38; "$18,000 in vitamins Donated to British," *NYT,* March 1, 1941, 5; "$69,000 Contributed for British Children," *NYT,* July 2, 1941, 5; "Mrs. Stephen S. Wise 'Adopts' British Boy," *NYT,* June 23, 1941, 9.

CHAPTER SIXTEEN. PRINCES OF PEACE AND PROPHETS OF REALISM

1. The relevant literature is large, but for a recent account see Kosek, *Acts of Conscience.*

2. Brown, *Statement of the Church Peace Union on the Japan-China Conflict,* 3–4. See also, for example, Merrill, *Christian Internationalism;* and Tufts, "Religion's Place in Securing a Better World-Order." Though their perspectives are often sharply different, the best secondary accounts of the interwar peace movement are Chatfield, *For Peace and Justice* (Thomas quoted on 321); and Meyer, *Protestant Search for Political Realism.* On the internationalism of the American peace movement, see also Lynch, *Beyond Appeasement,* 125–171.

3. On Quakers, see Jones, *Swords Into Ploughshares;* and Forbes, *Quaker Star Under Seven Flags.* On Mennonites, see Bush, *Two Kingdoms, Two Loyalties,* 32–57.

4. Page, *Sword or the Cross,* 40, 49. See also Eddy and Page, *Abolition of War.*

5. "Extract from letter by G. Sherwood Eddy," October 28, 1935, Eddy papers, Box 2, Folder 33, YDS; see also Nutt, *Whole Gospel for the Whole World,* 284–294. Thomas quoted in Chatfield, *For Peace and Justice,* 243.

6. Sermon, "The Peacemakers," November 11, 1934, Fitt papers, Box 1, BHL. Especially good on the political influence of religious noninterventionism are Divine, *Illusion of Neutrality;* and Doenecke, *Storm on the Horizon.*

7. Talbot to William Floyd, April 29, 1940, *America* Magazine Archives, Box 5, Folder 14, Georgetown; Talbot to Louis C. Haggerty, May 9, 1941, *America* Magazine Archives, Box 6, Folder 1, Georgetown. On the 1936 election, see Flynn, *American Catholics and the Roosevelt Presidency,* 233–234. On Coughlin, see Brinkley, *Voices of Protest,* 96, 134–137, 151–152, 267; and Marcus, *Father Coughlin,* 83–84, 196–204. On Smith, see Ribuffo, *Old Christian Right,* 157–159.

8. For examples of CAIP thinking on war in the 1930s and in 1940, see Moon, *Causes of War;* Emanuel, et al., *Ethics of War;* and Ryan, et al., *Obligation of Catholics to Promote Peace.* On the Catholic Worker movement, see Segers, "Equality and Christian Anarchism," 196–202. On both CAIP and CW, see McNeal, *Harder Than War,* 1–48. For an incisive analysis of Ryan's anti-fascism, see Miscamble, "Limits of American Catholic Antifascism."

9. Edgar Jones and Joseph Sizoo to Roosevelt, February 15, 1938, Presidential Papers: OF 213, FDRL.

10. Fey to Wygal, October 23, 1937, Niebuhr papers, Box 6, LOC. On CORE, see Chatfield, *For Peace and Justice*, 214–220; Branch, *Parting the Waters*, 171–173; and Kosek, "Richard Gregg, Mohandas Gandhi, and the Strategy of Nonviolence," 1319–1321, 1342–1343. This is not to say that civil rights groups discovered Gandhi only through the FOR and white Christians. On the many pre–World War II links between Indian nationalists and African Americans, see Horne, *End of Empires*.

11. Van Kirk, *Religion Renounces War*; Van Kirk, "The ABC of American Neutrality," 1935, FCC Records, RG18, Box 38, Folder 1, PHS; Meyer, *Protestant Search for Political Realism*, 370.

12. Notes from the annual and general assemblies of the PCUSA (1934), Evangelical Synod of North America (1934), Methodist Episcopal Church (1936), Northern Baptist Convention (1936), Southern Baptist Convention (1934), all in FCC Records, RG18, Box 34, Folder 11, PHS; *Lambeth Conference, 1930*, 46.

13. Buttrick and Cavert to Roosevelt, October 9, 1939, Presidential Papers: OF 213, FDRL.

14. *Churches Survey Their Task*, 48–50; notes of discussion of the Church and War Committee, Oxford Conference on Church and Society, July 15, 1937, Box 301.002, Folder 1, WCC; William Adams Brown to Nicholas Murray Butler, October 1938, Box 225, Folder 3, CEIP; Provisional Committee of the World Council of Churches, "The Churches and the International Situation," July 1939, FCC Records, RG18, Box 34, Folder 17, PHS.

15. Charles Aldrich to Niebuhr, December 17, 1940, Box 2; Ansley to Niebuhr, February 4, 1941, Box 2; Brandon to Niebuhr, January 13, 1941, Box 2; Lyttle to Niebuhr, May 10, 1941, Box 8; Day to Niebuhr, January 18, 1941, Box 3: all in Niebuhr papers, LOC.

16. Frankfurter to Niebuhr, December 24, 1941, Niebuhr papers, Box 6, LOC.

17. Fox, *Reinhold Niebuhr*, 174–178, 193–197; Stone, *Reinhold Niebuhr*, 54–69. On Niebuhr's place in the liberal theological tradition, see Dorrien, *Making of American Liberal Theology*, vol. 2, 435–521: rather than "realist" or "neo-orthodox," Dorrien classifies Niebuhr as "neoliberal." On Niebuhr's place in the liberal tradition in political thought, see Halliwell, *Constant Dialogue*.

18. For a detailed examination, see esp. Lovin, *Reinhold Niebuhr and Christian Realism*.

19. The previous paragraphs are based on Fox, *Reinhold Niebuhr*, 154–159; and Thompson, "Exception to Exceptionalism," 838–842. For a penetrating and thorough analysis on Niebuhr's transition throughout the period, see Meyer, *Protestant Search for Political Realism*.

20. Goldman, *God's Sacred Tongue*, 260–262; Craig, *Glimmer of a New Leviathan*, 38–45.

21. Fox, *Reinhold Niebuhr*, 187–192.

22. Eddy, *Eighty Adventurous Years*, 104.

23. Zietsma, "Sin Has No History," 536–538. For the realist turn to theology, see Bennett, "Outlook for Theology."

24. Lovin, *Reinhold Niebuhr and Christian Realism*; Zietsma, "Sin Has No History," 544–546; Gilkey, *On Niebuhr*, 130–141, 151–154, 224–225; Niebuhr, *Moral Man and Immoral Society*; Niebuhr, "Why the Christian Church Is Not Pacifist," in Brown, *Essential Reinhold Niebuhr*, 102–103. On neo-orthodox theology and its American application, see Ahlstrom, *Religious History of the American People*, 932–948. A transcendent, entirely spiritual God and a belief that everyone was a sinner had profound implications for evangelical and fundamentalist theology, although conservatives could never wholly accept neo-orthodoxy because they rejected Barth's claim that the Bible was not necessarily the literal word of God.

See Balmer and Winner, *Protestantism in America*, 31–32. Niebuhr remained a political liberal, but theologically he stood somewhere between the opposing ends of conservative fundamentalism and liberal modernism (albeit much, much closer to modernism). For a fuller analysis of *Moral Man* and its context, see Meyer, *Protestant Search for Political Realism*, 227–232; Craig, *Glimmer of a New Leviathan*, 33–37; and Danielson, "In My Extremity I Turned to Gandhi," 369–373.

25. Lovin, *Reinhold Niebuhr and Christian Realism*, 1–3; Bennett, "After Liberalism— What?" *CC*, November 8, 1933, 1403–1406; Horton, *Realistic Theology*; Niebuhr, "Man the Sinner"; Bennett, *Social Salvation*, esp. 10–19. For fuller discussions, see Meyer, *Protestant Search for Political Realism*, 240–246; Marty, *Modern American Religion*, vol. 2, 303–320; and Dorrien, *Making of American Liberal Theology*, vol. 2, 459–464.

26. Childress, "Reinhold Niebuhr's Critique of Pacifism," esp. 488; Haas, "Reinhold Niebuhr's 'Christian Pragmatism' "; McKeogh, *Political Realism of Reinhold Niebuhr*, 71–94. Niebuhr later expanded upon his earlier inchoate thinking on just war theory: see Craig, *Glimmer of a New Leviathan*, 40–41, 80–83.

27. Bennett, *Christianity—And Our World*, 58–59; Van Dusen to Cavert, September 12, 1939, FCC Records, RG18, Box 6, Folder 10, PHS. For the FCC statement, see Hutchison, *We Are Not Divided*, 218–219.

28. Niebuhr to Bennett, May 31, 1940, Niebuhr papers, Series 2, Box 1, Folder III-3, UTS.

29. *Church and Industrial Reconstruction*, 114–115.

30. "The Church and World Problems," Brown essay for the Federal Council Biennial Meeting, New York, December 6, 1938, FCC Records, RG18, Box 27, Folder 15, PHS; Handy, *History of Union Theological Seminary*, 189–202; Warren, *Theologians of a New World Order*, esp. 59–75.

31. Niebuhr, "Christian Faith and the Common Life"; Bennett, "Causes of Social Evil"; Aubrey, "Oxford Conference," 380. See also Warren, *Theologians of a New World Order*, 77–83.

32. Statement of purpose, "Christianity and Crisis," December 1940, Mott papers, Box 62, Folder 1149, YDS. On the UDA, see Fox, *Reinhold Niebuhr*, 197–199. On *C&C*, see Hulsether, *Building a Protestant Left*, 24–48.

33. Shafer, "What Should Be the Bearing of the Foreign Missionary Enterprise on World Peace?" in *Foreign Missions Conference of North America . . . 1938*, 107–108.

34. Phillips, "Can Pacifism Save Democracy," *CRT*, February 1941, 14–15.

35. Attebery speech to the Rotary Club of Portland, "The United States Faces Up to the World Crisis," January 12, 1941, Attebery papers, Box 2, Folder 3, UW.

36. On the sharp swing of American public opinion toward the Allies, especially Britain, see the polling data in Cantril, "America Faces the War"; and Cantril, Rugg, and Williams, "America Faces the War."

CHAPTER SEVENTEEN. THE SIMPLE FAITH OF FRANKLIN ROOSEVELT

1. Meyer, *Protestant Search for Political Realism*, 40–43; Hein and Shattuck, *Episcopalians*, 97–99, 116–117; Albright, *History of the Protestant Episcopal Church*, 312–325.

2. Roosevelt, *Affectionately, F.D.R.*, 106, 99; Perkins, *Roosevelt I Knew*, 141; Roosevelt, *This I Remember*, 67, 346. For Eleanor's spiritual differences with FDR, see Roosevelt, *This Is My Story*, 149–150.

3. Davis, *FDR*, 57–59, 101–128, 192–193; Smith, *Faith and the Presidency*, 193.

4. Sherwood, *Roosevelt and Hopkins*, 9. My description of FDR in these paragraphs is culled mainly from the religious portrait found in Smith, *Faith and the Presidency*, 191–220, esp. 192–199 ("very Low Church" quoted on 195). But see also Maney, *Roosevelt Presence*, 4–6, 56, 79, 117 ("What I am more interested in" quoted on 117); Goodwin, *No Ordinary Time*, 393–394; Meacham, *Franklin and Winston*, 17, 27–29, 119; and Smith, *FDR*, 24.

5. Badger, *New Deal*, 248–249; Kennedy, *Freedom from Fear*, 285. On Catholics, see Barone, "Franklin D. Roosevelt"; O'Brien, *American Catholics and Social Reform*, 51–69; Flynn, *American Catholics and the Roosevelt Presidency*, 36–60; Cohen, *Making a New Deal*, 224–226, 269–270; Heineman, *Catholic New Deal*; McShane, *"Sufficiently Radical"*; Brown and McKeown, *Poor Belong to Us*, 151–192; and, for a prominent Catholic social theorist at the time, Ryan, "Roosevelt and Social Justice." "Jew Deal" quoted in Novick, *Holocaust in American Life*, 33, 42. On Jews, see Feingold, *Time for Searching*, 211–220.

6. "Moses," O'Connell, and Baker quoted in Maney, *Roosevelt Presence*, 70; Coughlin quoted in Kennedy, *Freedom from Fear*, 231; Gray quoted in Carpenter, *Revive Us Again*, 94; Winrod quoted in Ribuffo, *Old Christian Right*, 104, 106.

7. Smith, *Faith and the Presidency*, 197–203; Weigle and Cavert to Roosevelt, January 2, 1942, Presidential Papers: OF 213, FDRL.

8. Farley, *Jim Farley's Story*, 36.

9. Hull, *Memoirs*, vol. 1, 292–301; Farley, *Jim Farley's Story*, 43–44; Dallek, *Franklin Roosevelt and American Foreign Policy*, 39, 78–80; Foglesong, *American Mission and the "Evil Empire,"* 77–78; William C. Bullitt to Hull, October 4, 1933, *FRUS: The Soviet Union, 1933–1939*, 16–17. On Farley's Catholicism, see Scroop, *Mr. Democrat*, 35, 39, 102, 178–183.

10. See the remarkable exchange of seven letters between Roosevelt and Litvinov, all dated November 16, 1933, in *FRUS: The Soviet Union, 1933–1939*, 28–34 (Roosevelt quoted on 30, 34).

11. Perkins, *Roosevelt I Knew*, 143. FDR also told the story to Jim Farley, who tells a similar version with only slight variation. See Farley, *Jim Farley's Story*, 44–45.

12. Speech to the Inter-American Conference for the Maintenance of Peace, December 1, 1936, *FDRFA*, Series 1, vol. III: 521. On religion as a theme in FDR's anti-Nazi speeches, see also Moore, *Know Your Enemy*, 90–91.

13. "Radio address on Brotherhood Day," February 23, 1936, *PPAFDR, 1936*, 85.

14. Buttrick to Roosevelt, February 27, 1940, and Roosevelt to Buttrick, March 14, 1940, both in Mott papers, Box 14, Folder 263, YDS.

15. "Address at the University of Virginia," June 10, 1940, *PPAFDR, 1940*, 261. On American perceptions of vulnerability from being surrounded in a hostile world, see Leffler, *Specter of Communism*, 29–30.

16. "Annual Message to the Congress," January 4, 1939, *PPAFDR, 1939*, 1–2.

17. "Annual Message to the Congress," January 3, 1940, *PPAFDR, 1940*, 4; Radio Address Before the Eighth Pan American Scientific Congress, Washington, D.C., May 10, 1940, ibid., 185; Radio Address Announcing the Proclamation of an Unlimited National Emergency, May 27, 1941, *PPAFDR, 1941*, 192; Navy and Total Defense Day Address, October 27, 1941, ibid., 440; "Annual Message to the Congress," January 6, 1942, *PPAFDR, 1942*, 35. Many historians now agree with Roosevelt that Nazism constituted a political religion and that Hitler intended to replace Christianity as the traditional standard for ethical and moral norms. See, for example, Burleigh, "National Socialism as a Political Religion"; and Burleigh, *Sacred Causes*, 94–122.

18. "Annual Message to the Congress," January 6, 1941, *PPAFDR, 1940*, 672; Joint

Declaration by the United Nations, January 1, 1942, *FRUS, 1942,* vol. I: 25; Hull, *Memoirs,* vol. 2, 1120.

19. Hull, *Memoirs,* vol. 2, 1733; speech at Columbia University, February 12, 1942, Berle papers, Box 145, FDRL; Welles press conference, enclosure within Welles to Laurence A. Steinhardt (Moscow), June 23, 1941, *FRUS, 1941,* vol. I: 767; "Third Meeting of Ministers of Foreign Affairs of the American Republics: Address by the Under Secretary of State," *DSB,* January 17, 1942, 62.

20. U.S. Delegation meeting minutes, May 16, 1945, *FRUS, 1945,* vol. I: 752; "Radio Report to the American People on the Potsdam Conference," August 9, 1945, *PPP: Truman, 1945,* 206–207.

CHAPTER EIGHTEEN. THE HOLOCAUST AND
THE MORAL MEANING OF THE WAR

1. Abrams, *Preachers Present Arms,* 255. For a thorough examination of American attitudes, including religious ones, to the rise of Nazism, see Moore, *Know Your Enemy.*
2. Holmes and Page both quoted in Chatfield, *For Peace and Justice,* 247.
3. On Jewish support for Britain, see, for example, "Jewish Congress Plans British Aid," *NYT,* December 30, 1940, 9.
4. Wise to Holmes, 1938, *Personal Letters of Stephen Wise,* 250–251.
5. "Religion: As to War," *Time,* June 10, 1940; Feely, *Nazism versus Religion,* 3; Moore, *Know Your Enemy,* 57–60, 151. Polling data from "American Institute of Public Opinion–Surveys, 1938–1939," 598. On Nazi hostility to religion in general—that is, to Christianity as well as Judaism—see Burleigh, *Sacred Causes,* 168–213. On American Catholics' ambivalence toward fascism in Italy and Spain, see Flynn, *American Catholics and the Roosevelt Presidency;* Diggins, *Mussolini and Fascism;* D'Agostino, *Rome in America,* 158–193, 230–257; and Traina, *American Diplomacy and the Spanish Civil War.*
6. Frankfurter to Astor, June 2, 1938, in Freedman, ed., *Roosevelt and Frankfurter,* 475; Wise to his daughter, 1933, *Personal Letters of Stephen Wise,* 223.
7. Cyrus Adler to Maurice William, February 24, 1936, *Cyrus Adler: Selected Letters,* vol. 2, 311–312; Goldman, *God's Sacred Tongue,* 253–262; Holmes, *Through Gentile Eyes;* Fosdick, *Living of These Days,* 281–282; diary entry, November 15, 1938, Ickes, *Secret Diary of Harold L. Ickes,* vol. 2, 503. For Christian appeals on behalf of Jewish refugees, see "200 Join in Appeal for Jewish Exiles," *NYT,* October 7, 1935, 15; "How Christians May Show Sympathy for Jews," *FCB,* October 1935, 4–5; "Americans Appeal for Jewish Refuge," *NYT,* May 31, 1936, 14; meeting minutes, Joint Meeting of the American sections of the World Conference on Faith and Order and the Universal Christian Council for Life and Work, New York, October 28, 1941, Box 301.002, Folder 8, WCC. On the problem of religious refugees, see Nichols, *Uneasy Alliance,* 41–51.
8. Memcon, Kellogg, Wise, and Milton Strasburger, February 12, 1927, *FRUS, 1927,* vol. III: 638–640; Hull to London, August 24, 1938, *FRUS, 1938,* vol. I: 771; Wallace Murray (Near Eastern Affairs, State Department) to Jerusalem, July 2, 1938, ibid., 752. On the Roosevelt administration, Évian, European Jewish refugees, and the voluntarist response, see Offner, *American Appeasement,* 60–61, 68, 80–93; Feingold, *Time for Searching,* 226–239; and Nichols, *Uneasy Alliance,* 47–48. On the DR, see Wells, *Tropical Zion.*
9. Caro, *Years of Lyndon Johnson: The Path to Power,* 481–482; Dallek, *Lone Star Rising,* 169–170; Woods, *LBJ,* 139–140. Another rescue operation saw Jews flee to

the Philippines, then an American colony, with help from the High Commissioner to the Philippines (and former governor of Indiana) Paul V. McNutt. See Kotlowski, "Breaching the Paper Walls."

10. Dinnerstein, *Antisemitism in America*, 105–127; MacLean, *Behind the Mask of Chivalry*, 6, 8, 91–97; Trollinger, *God's Empire*, 68–82; Smith, *To Save a Nation*, 122–138; Cole, *America First*, 131–154. Coughlin quoted in Brinkley, *Voices of Protest*, 266; Nye quoted in Hixson, *Charles A. Lindbergh*, 125.

11. Meeting minutes, Committee of Catholics for Human Rights, New York, January 18, 1940, Hans Reinhold papers, Box 3, Folder 15, BC; Curti, *American Philanthropy Abroad*, 361–390; Carpenter, *Revive Us Again*, 98–99; Flynt, *Alabama Baptists*, 397–398.

12. Silk, "Notes on the Judeo-Christian Tradition," 66; Wall, *Inventing the "American Way,"* 77–87 ("Nazis vs. Civilization" quoted on 84). On interventionist efforts to discredit isolationism by linking it to anti-Semitism and demagoguery at home, see Smith, *To Save a Nation*, 139–157; and Kazin, *Populist Persuasion*, 127–128.

13. "Through a Glass Darkly," Church Newsletter, September 1939, Records of the First Baptist Church of Seattle, Box 16, UW. For the American Alliance of Christians and Jews, see Alson J. Smith to Herman F. Reissig, n.d. [ca. March 1940], Box 2, Niebuhr papers, LOC.

14. Silver, "Preserving the Genius of Americanism," *CRT*, March 1941, 20–23.

15. "The President Greets the Jewish Theological Seminary on Its Fifty-fifth Anniversary," November 11, 1942, *PPAFDR, 1942*, 467; "3 Faiths Allied by Year of War," *NYT*, December 26, 1942, 13. For the congressional resolutions, see *Rescue of the Jewish and Other Peoples in Nazi-Occupied Territory*. My view here of religion, politics, and American identity owes much to the more general discussion in Wall, *Inventing the "American Way,"* 103–159.

16. "Questions Turned In to a Chaplain," April 2, 1943, University of Michigan War Historian records, Box 12, BHL; Maurin quoted in Marty, *Modern American Religion*, vol. 3, 18.

17. Sheen, "What This War Is Not and What It Is," *CRT*, February 1943, 14–16; Cannon quoted in "Wallace Addresses 500 Presenting Petition for Help," *WP*, October 7, 1943, 1; listener figures for the *Catholic Hour* from Dolan, *American Catholic Experience*, 392–393.

18. Wallace quoted in "Wallace Addresses 500 Presenting Petition for Help," *WP*, October 7, 1943, 1; "250 Notables Join Persecution Fight," *NYT*, August 13, 1944, 19; "Save Doomed Jews, Huge Rally Pleads," *NYT*, March 2, 1943, 1, 4.

19. Duker, "Political and Cultural Aspects of Jewish Post-War Problems," 2–3, 5. Criticism of American Jewry has been one of the more emotional themes in an already controversial historiography. For leading examples, see Lookstein, *Were We Our Brothers' Keepers?*; Medoff, *Deafening Silence*; and Leff, *Buried by the Times*. For a vigorous rebuttal, see Novick, *Holocaust in American Life*, 30–46.

20. Taylor to Roosevelt and Hull, October 20, 1942, Welles papers, Box 84, Folder 18, FDRL; Welles to A. L. Easterman, ibid.; Welles, *Time for Decision*, 71, 76, 96–97, 117, 158, 251, 262–263, 266; Hull to Roosevelt, May 7, 1943, *FRUS, 1943*, vol. I: 176–178; Roosevelt to Hull, May 14, 1943, ibid., 179; Hull to Roosevelt, March 23, 1943, ibid., 146; Admiral Leahy to Hull, April 26, 1943, ibid., 296–297. For a powerful indictment of American inaction during the Holocaust, see Wyman, *Abandonment of the Jews*. But on the practical and political difficulties of mounting an Allied rescue mission for Jews in Nazi-occupied Europe, see Novick, *Holocaust in American Life*, 47–59.

21. Pioneer Women's Organization to Truman, March 1, 1943, U.S. Senator and Vice President papers, Box 92, HSTL; "Findings and Recommendations of the

Emergency Conference to Save the Jewish People of Europe," July 20–25, 1943, Box 228, Folder 9, CEIP; Wise to Welles, August 25, 1943, Welles papers, Box 93, Folder 12, FDRL.

22. Atkinson, " 'The Jewish Problem' Is a Christian Problem," *C&C*, June 28, 1943, 3–4.

23. Council on Foreign Relations, Studies of American Interests in the War and the Peace, Peace Aims Series, Hamilton Fish Armstrong–rapporteur, "Future of the Jews in Europe with Special Relation to Palestine," May 31, 1943, Welles papers, Box 190, Folder 11, FDRL; Weizmann, "Palestine's Role in the Solution of the Jewish Problem," 338.

24. Roosevelt to King Saud, January 9, 1939, *FDRFA*, series 2, vol. 13, 88; Welles, *Time for Decision*, 267; "Press Release Issued by the Department of State," October 14, 1938, *FRUS, 1938*, vol. II: 953–955; Roosevelt to Wagner, October 15, 1944, *FRUS, 1944*, vol. V: 615; "Tripartite Dinner Meeting," February 10, 1945, *FRUS: Conferences at Malta and Yalta*, 924. For the geopolitical considerations, see Dallek, *Franklin Roosevelt and American Foreign Policy*, 446–448.

25. William A. Eddy to Hull, January 5, 1945, *FRUS, 1945*, vol. VIII: 679; James M. Landis to Roosevelt, January 17, 1945, ibid., 681; William Eddy to Hull, February 1, 1945, ibid., 687; memcon, Roosevelt and Abdul Aziz Al Saud, February 14, 1945, ibid., 2–3; Harold B. Hoskins to Paul H. Alling, March 5, 1945, ibid., 690–691.

26. "President Again Asks Palestine's Freedom," *NYT*, March 17, 1945, 13.

27. Advertisement by the Committee for a Jewish Army of Stateless and Palestinian Jews, *NYT*, December 7, 1942, 14–15; Truman speech before the United Rally "To Demand Rescue of Doomed Jews," Chicago, April 14, 1943, U.S. Senator and Vice President papers, Box 283, HSTL; Truman, *Memoirs*, vol. 1, 69.

28. Truman to Churchill, July 24, 1945, *FRUS: Conference of Berlin*, vol. II: 1402; "President's News Conference," August 16, 1945, *PPP: Truman, 1945*, 228; Truman to Attlee, August 31, 1945, *FRUS, 1945*, vol. VIII: 738; Truman to Walter F. George, October 8, 1946, PSF/SF, Box 161, Palestine: Jewish Immigration Folder, HSTL; "President's News Conference," September 26, 1945, *PPP: Truman, 1945*, 347; Truman to Eisenhower, August 31, 1945, and "Report of Earl G. Harrison," *DSB*, September 30, 1945, 455–463. On these early Anglo-American tensions, see Dinnerstein, "America, Britain, and Palestine."

CHAPTER NINETEEN. SPIRITUAL DIPLOMACY

1. Quoted in Churchill, *Second World War: The Gathering Storm*, 135.

2. Hull, *Memoirs*, vol. 1, 713–715; William Phillips (Rome) to Hull, February 28, 1940, *FRUS, 1940*, vol. I: 126–127; Kennedy to Taylor, April 23, 1940, Taylor papers, Box 2, Cornell; Cooney, *American Pope*, 113–117; Fogarty, "Roosevelt and the American Catholic Hierarchy," 23–25.

3. Conway, "Myron C. Taylor's Mission," 85–89; Badger, *New Deal*, 129–130.

4. Roosevelt to Pius XII, December 23, 1939, *Wartime Correspondence between President Roosevelt and Pope Pius XII*, 19. On Ready, see Ready to Amleto Cicognani, April 15, 1939, *Records and Documents of the Holy See Relating to the Second World War*, 103; and Cicognani to Maglione, June 27, 1939, ibid., 179–180. On Hurley, see Gallagher, *Vatican Secret Diplomacy*, 93–130. On Hopkins, see Plokhy, *Yalta*, 372–373.

5. Welles, *Time for Decision*, 142; Welles memos, both March 18, 1940, *FRUS, 1940*, vol. I: 106–109; Maglione's notes, March 18, 1940, *Records and Documents of the Holy See Relating to the Second World War*, 376. On the Welles mission, see also Rofe, *Franklin Roosevelt's Foreign Policy and the Welles Mission*, 164–165. On

Vatican efforts to use the United States to restrain Italy, and for FDR's letters to Mussolini, see notes of the Secretary of State, March 15, 1940, *Records and Documents of the Holy See Relating to the Second World War*, 368–369; Phillips to Hull, April 19, 1940, *FRUS, 1940*, vol. II: 686; Taylor to Roosevelt, April 19, 1940, ibid., 686–688; Taylor to Roosevelt, April 20, 1940, ibid., 688–689; Pius XII to Mussolini, April 24, 1940, *Records and Documents of the Holy See Relating to the Second World War*, 395; Hull to Phillips (with Roosevelt to Mussolini enclosure), April 29, 1940, *FRUS, 1940*, vol. II: 691–692; Taylor to Roosevelt, April 30, 1940, ibid., 692–693; and Roosevelt to Mussolini, May 14, 1940, ibid., 704–705.

6.   Roosevelt to Berle, March 15, 1940, Presidential Papers: OF 213, FDRL; Berle to Roosevelt, March 18, 1940, *FRUS, 1940*, vol. I: 129–130; memcon, Berle and Ertegün, April 5, 1940, ibid., 132; Hull, *Memoirs*, vol. 1, 715–716.

7.   Conway, "Myron C. Taylor's Mission," 90–98. For a firsthand account, see Tittmann, *Inside the Vatican of Pius XII.*

8.   Taylor to Pius XII, September 19, 1942, Taylor Papers, Box 1, Cornell.

9.   Addison, "Destiny, History, and Providence"; Williamson, "Christian Conservatives and the Totalitarian Challenge," 607–609.

10. McKibbin, *Classes and Cultures*, 272–295.

11. "A Total and Unmitigated Defeat," October 5, 1938, James, ed., *Winston S. Churchill: His Complete Speeches*, vol. 6, 6011; "Their Finest Hour," June 18, 1940, ibid., 6238; "War of the Unknown Warriors," July 14, 1940, ibid., 6248; "United States Cooperation," January 9, 1941, ibid., 6327.

12. This is a radical compression of complex events. For a fuller treatment, see Reynolds, *Creation of the Anglo-American Alliance.*

13. Churchill, *Second World War: The Grand Alliance*, 23; Moran, *Winston Churchill*, 6; Sherwood, *Roosevelt and Hopkins*, 247.

14. Iriye, *Origins of the Second World War in Asia and the Pacific*, 155; Atlantic Charter quoted in Borgwardt, *New Deal for the World*, 304; Roosevelt to Congress, August 21, 1941, *PPAFDR, 1941*, 334; Roosevelt, "Fireside Chat on Progress of the War," February 23, 1942, *PPAFDR, 1942*, 115.

15. Borgwardt, *New Deal for the World*, 1–3; Meacham, *Franklin and Winston*, 113–115; hymns and prayer quoted in Morton, *Atlantic Meeting*, 100–102. For the 1934 and 1939 services, see Roosevelt, *Affectionately, F.D.R.*, 100–101, 105.

16. Morton, *Atlantic Meeting*, 102; Meacham, *Franklin and Winston*, 115–116; FDR to Elliott Roosevelt quoted in Roosevelt, *As He Saw It*, 33. On Morton's career, see Bartholomew, *In Search of H. V. Morton.*

17. "Day of Prayer for Great Britain Set Tomorrow," *WP*, September 28, 1940, 2.

18. Coffin to Morgan P. Noyes, September 30, 1940, Coffin papers, Box 3, Folder 32, UTS; Niebuhr, *Children of Light and the Children of Darkness*, 183–185; Niebuhr quoted in Craig, *Glimmer of a New Leviathan*, 44.

19. Radio broadcast, "Prayers for Great Britain and All Civilization," September 29, 1940, WJZ–New York and NBC Blue network, and "A Message from an American Churchman," n.d., both in Coffin papers, Box 3, Folder 33, UTS; Coffin, "Talk to Be Given over the BBC," January 4, 1942, Coffin papers, Box 3, Folder 34, UTS; Coffin, "A Broadcast to Britain," *CRT*, March 1942; "3 Faiths' Leaders Plead for Britain," *NYT*, December 29, 1940, 14; Kallen, "National Solidarity and the Jewish Minority," 27–28.

20. Diary entry, May 26, 1940, *Journals of Thomas Merton*, vol. 1, 221; Nesbitt to Cavert, January 5, 1943, FCC Records, RG18, Box 11, Folder 23, PHS; Jones, "Imperialism or Democracy?" *CRT*, March 1944, 6.

21. Judd to Reverend J. Paul Tatter, April 10, 1943, Judd papers, Box 22, MNHS.

22. Truman quoted in Hamby, *Man of the People*, 270.

23. Welles press conference, June 23, 1941, *FRUS, 1941*, vol. I: 767–768; Fox,

Reinhold Niebuhr, 200. On the decision to extend Lend-Lease to the USSR, see Herring, *Aid to Russia*, 2–48.

24. Harriman and Abel, *Special Envoy to Churchill and Stalin*, 103; diary entry, July 5, 1940, Ickes, *Secret Diary of Harold L. Ickes*, vol. 3, 229; Hopkins to Bracken quoted in Sherwood, *Roosevelt and Hopkins*, 372.

25. American Institute of Public Opinion poll, June 24, 1941, Table 1–8; Hero, *American Religious Groups View Foreign Policy*, 286; Dawson, *Decision to Aid Russia*, 91–95; Chen, "Religious Liberty in U.S. Foreign Policy," 132–134.

26. *Qui Pluribus*, Encyclical on Faith and Religion, November 9, 1846, in Carlen, ed. *Papal Encyclicals*, vol. 1, 280; *Divini Redemptoris*, Encyclical on Atheistic Communism, March 19, 1937, ibid., vol. 3, 537, 549. On the popes, see Kent, *Lonely Cold War of Pope Pius XII*, 11–18. For a nuanced discussion of the "structure" of the Catholic Church, see Greeley, *Catholic Imagination*, 137–157.

27. Preston, "Death of a Peculiar Special Relationship," 210.

28. Sherwood, *Roosevelt and Hopkins*, 384.

29. Phillips to Hull, July 24, 1941, *FRUS, 1941*, vol. I: 999; Ready to Welles, August 23, 1941, and Welles to Roosevelt, August 25, 1941, both in Taylor papers, Box 10, FDRL.

30. Welles, *Where Are We Heading?*, 37–38. For discussions of FDR and his theory of "convergence," see Gaddis, *United States and the Origins of the Cold War*, 41; Kimball, *Juggler*, 198–199; and Preston, "Death of a Peculiar Special Relationship," 208–209. More generally, see Engerman, *Modernization from the Other Shore*; and Engerman, "To Moscow and Back." On the liberalization of religion in the wartime Soviet Union, see Miner, *Stalin's Holy War*. On U.S. optimism about it, see Hollander, *Political Pilgrims*; Mark, "October or Thermidor?", 945–951; and Foglesong, *American Mission and the "Evil Empire,"* 90–93.

31. Roosevelt to Pius XII, September 3, 1941, *Wartime Correspondence between President Roosevelt and Pope Pius XII*, 61–62; memcon, Pius XII and Taylor, September 9, 1941, and "Monsignor Tardini's confidential memorandum on the religious situation in Russia," September 20, 1941, both in Taylor papers, Box 10, FDRL.

32. Memcon, Roosevelt, Hull, Hopkins, and Oumansky, September 11, 1941, *FRUS, 1941*, vol. I: 832–833. See also Hull, *Memoirs*, vol. 2, 976–977.

33. Steinhardt to Hull, with Harriman October 2 memo enclosed, October 4, 1941, *FRUS, 1941*, vol. I: 1001; Oumansky quoted in Miner, *Stalin's Holy War*, 217; Braun to Taylor, October 3, 1941, Taylor papers, Box 10, FDRL. See also Sherwood, *Roosevelt and Hopkins*, 391–393; Harriman and Abel, *Special Envoy to Churchill and Stalin*, 102–104; and Braun, *In Lubianka's Shadow*, 245–246.

34. Dawson, *Decision to Aid Russia*, 237–238, 266–267; Jan Ciechanowski to Hull, September 29, 1941, reprinted in *DSB*, October 4, 1941, 245; Steinhardt to Hull, October 6, 1941, *FRUS, 1941*, vol. I: 1002–1003.

35. Roosevelt press conference, October 2, 1941, enclosed within Hull to Steinhardt, October 2, 1941, *FRUS, 1941*, vol. I: 1000–1001. For the clerical advice that Americans would accept Lend-Lease aid to the Soviets in order to defeat Germany, see Dawson, *Decision to Aid Russia*, 234, 264.

36. Walsh quoted in "Catholic Leader Assails 'Mockery,' " *NYT*, October 6, 1941, 4; Knights of Columbus quoted in "Soviet's 'Freedom' Defined," *NYT*, October 6, 1941, 4; Wade and Weigle quoted in "God & Lend-Lease," *Time*, October 13, 1941; Fish quoted in Dallek, *Franklin D. Roosevelt and American Foreign Policy*, 297.

37. Dallek, *Franklin D. Roosevelt and American Foreign Policy*, 297–299 (Kennan quoted on 298).

38. Miner, *Stalin's Holy War*, 164–168; Ready quoted in "Local Boy Makes Good," *Time*, May 8, 1944.

39. Gaddis, *United States and the Origins of the Cold War*, 34–42; Heale, *American Anticommunism*, 129–132 (Roosevelt and Willkie quoted on 130); Foglesong, *American Mission and the "Evil Empire*,*"* 83–92, 260n2; Plokhy, *Yalta*, 371–375.

40. Kennan to Taylor, October 2, 1942, Taylor Papers, Box 8, Cornell; Kennan to Stettinius, February 3, 1945, *FRUS, 1945*, vol. V: 1115.

41. Kennan, "Russia's International Position at the Close of the War with Germany," May 1945, in Kennan, *Memoirs, 1925–1950*, 541–542.

42. "Summary of Opinion and Ideas on International Post-War Problems," November 4, 1942, Welles papers, Box 190, Folder 1, FDRL; "Notes of meeting on 'Peace Aims,'" Oxford, July 15–16, 1942, FCC Records, RG18, Box 29, Folder 6, PHS; Carpenter, *Revive Us Again*, 149; Niebuhr to Van Kirk, November 6, 1944, FCC Records, RG18, Box 40, Folder 8, PHS; Divine, *Second Chance*, 230, 251; Ward, *CC*, October 28, 1942.

43. Mooney to Taylor, November 30, 1942, Taylor papers, Box 8, Cornell. For the continuation of religious anti-communism through the war, see Preston, "Death of a Peculiar Special Relationship," 210–213.

CHAPTER TWENTY. THE CHURCH UNMILITANT

1. "Into the Way of Peace," May 13, 1945, Hersey papers, Box 3, AHTL.

2. The phrase comes from Adams, *Best War Ever*. The title is ironic, a satirical stab at the myth that the war was free of internal tension, corruption, and social problems at home.

3. These phrases come from two books that also challenge the idea that the war was consensual, bipartisan, and unproblematic at home: Casey, *Cautious Crusade*; and Sittser, *Cautious Patriotism*. See also Abrams, "Churches and the Clergy in World War II"; O'Neill, *Democracy at War*; Marty, *Modern American Religion*, vol. 3, 17–53; Jeffries, *Wartime America*; Erenberg and Hirsch, eds., *War in American Culture*; Bess, *Choices Under Fire*; and Alvarez, *Power of the Zoot*. For recent challenges to the dominant view of the war as a necessary and just war, see Baker, *Human Smoke*; and Hixson, *Myth of American Diplomacy*, 154–170. On the civilian suffering caused by Allied war strategy, see Hitchcock, *Bitter Road to Freedom*.

4. "A United Nations Prayer–Radio Address on United Flag Day," June 14, 1942, *PPAFDR, 1942*, 288; "D-Day Prayer on the Invasion of Normandy," June 6, 1944, *PPAFDR, 1944–45*, 153. For days of prayer, see, for example, "Proclamation No. 2571: Thanksgiving Day Proclamation in Services Broadcast to the Nation," November 26, 1942, *PPAFDR, 1942*, 495–496; "Churches Prepare New Year Services," *NYT*, December 31, 1942, 18; and "Worshipers Pray for Armed Forces," *NYT*, January 1, 1943, 21.

5. "The Century of the Common Man," May 8, 1942, in Wallace, *Century of the Common Man*, 13–20. For an example of Wallace's Christian progressivism, see Wallace, *Statesmanship and Religion*. On Wallace's religion, especially his Social Gospel roots and later eclectic spirituality, see Walker, *Henry A. Wallace*, 50–63; White and Maze, *Henry A. Wallace*, 5–10, 15–43; and Culver and Hyde, *American Dreamer*, 25, 31–32, 49–50, 76–82, 95–99, 128–131.

6. "To Troops of A.E.F.," June 6, 1944, *PDDE*, vol. 3, 1913.

7. Sermon, "The Christian Church and the War of Aggression," December 14, 1941, FCC Records, RG18, Box 6, Folder 10, PHS; "Un-Christian Co-Prosperity," *Time*, August 24, 1942; Hull to Leland Harrison, December 12, 1942, *FRUS, 1942*, vol. I: 835–836.

8. "Chaplain Hits Assailers of Song in Letter," *Seattle Post-Intelligencer*, February 5, 1943, 4; "God Is My Co-Pilot" quoted in Sherry, *Rise of American Air Power*, 134.

9. "D.C. Clergy Join Other Protestant Leaders Throughout U.S. in Calling for

Axis Defeat," *WP*, August 19, 1942, 9; "Axis Defeat Held Key to Freedom," *WP*, December 11, 1942, 16; Annual Meeting of the Church Peace Union, Report by General Secretary Henry A. Atkinson, January 20, 1944, Box 225, Folder 3, CEIP; "Methodists Score War Plant Strikes," *NYT*, May 26, 1944, 16; "Catholic Appeal for 'Victory, Peace,' " *NYT*, November 15, 1942, 1; " 'Victory and Peace' Statement of Catholic Prelates," *NYT*, November 15, 1942, 52. On the Catholic repudiation of Catholic isolationism, see Francis E. McMahon, "Catholics and Isolationism," *PM*, November 22, 1943, 4.

10. Spellman, *Road to Victory*, x, 116–117. On Spellman during the war, see Cooney, *American Pope*, 120–145.

11. Oswald W. S. McCall, "The Bandits Must Be Stopped!" *CRT*, January 1942, 1; Chatfield, *For Peace and Justice*, 114.

12. Manning, "The Message of the Church to Our Nation at War," August 23, 1942, Presidential Papers: Vertical File, World War, Religious Aspects, FDRL.

13. Ryan, "The Patriotic Citizen," *CRT*, March 1942, 17, 19; Cyprian Emanuel, "The Conscientious Objector to War," *Catholic Mind*, October 22, 1940, 393–406; Emanuel, *Morality of Conscientious Objection to War*; "Seminary Scores Draft Objectors," *NYT*, October 15, 1940, 17; Handy, *History of Union Theological Seminary*, 199–202.

14. Carpenter, *Revive Us Again*, 166–167; Sutton, *Aimee Semple McPherson*, 258–266; McPherson quoted in Thomas, *Storming Heaven*, 334; Riley, "Hitlerism; or, The Philosophy of Evolution in Action," 1941, in Trollinger, ed., *Antievolution Pamphlets of William Bell Riley*, 207–218 (quotes from 207, 214).

15. Charles P. Proudfit to Niebuhr, December 21, 1940, Niebuhr papers, Box 10, LOC.

16. Johnson, "Impact of the War on Religion in America," 359; Herbert Agar to Coffin, December 16, 1943, and Coffin article, "Religion and the War," n.d., both in Coffin papers, Box 15, Folder 193, UTS; Eddy, *Why America Fights*. On evangelicals seeing the armed forces as mission field, see Loveland, *American Evangelicals and the U.S. Military*.

17. "Broadcast to the American People Announcing the Surrender of Germany," May 8, 1945, *PPP: Truman, 1945*, 48–50; "Proclamation 2660: Victory in the East—Day of Prayer," August 16, 1945, ibid., 223–224.

18. "The Church Unmilitant," *New Republic*, June 22, 1942, 850. On faith and pacifism during the war, see Wittner, *Rebels Against War*, 40–45.

19. Department of State, Division of Special Research, "Summary of Opinion and Ideas on International Post-War Problems," July 15, 1942, Welles papers, Box 190, Folder 1, FDRL; Washington Embassy to Foreign Office, March 20, 1943, and July 19, 1943, both in Nicholas, ed., *Washington Despatches*, 168, 222; Fosdick to Sayre, February 16, 1944, Fosdick papers, Series IIB, Box 1, Folder 8, UTS.

20. "The Just War of Unjust Nations," *C&C*, February 8, 1943, 2; "Baptists Modify Stand On War," *NYT*, May 27, 1944, 16.

21. Memcon, Jones and Maxwell M. Hamilton, September 17, 1941, *FRUS, 1941*, vol. IV: 455–457; Jones to Hamilton, October 8, 1941, ibid., 501–502; Jones to Hamilton, October 26, 1941, ibid., 555–557; Jones to Roosevelt, October 27, 1941, ibid., 557–558; memcon, Jones and Hamilton, December 1, 1941, ibid., 702–703; 1942 Foreign Missions Conference quoted in "Missions Show the Way," *CC*, February 3, 1943, 126. On the Catholic peace initiative, see Butow, *John Doe Associates*. In the interwar years right up to the bombing of Pearl Harbor, it was not uncommon for American missionaries to Japan to take a Japanese perspective in their pursuit of peace. See Taylor, "Japan's Missionary to the Americans."

22. "Our Country Passes from Undeclared to Declared War," *Catholic Worker*, January 1942, 1; McNeal, *Harder Than War*, 26, 41–44.
23. "Position of the Brethren," *Conscientious Objector*, February 1943, 1; O'Toole, *War and Conscription at the Bar of Christian Morals*; Chatfield, *For Peace and Justice*, 304–309, 326–327.
24. Sittser, *Cautious Patriotism*, 130–133; Handy, *History of Union Theological Seminary*, 200; "U.S. Urged to Delay Compulsory Bill," *NYT*, November 2, 1944, 11; Flynn, "Lewis Hershey and the Conscientious Objector."
25. "Massacre by Bombing," *Catholic C.O.*, April–June 1944, 1; "Obliteration Raids on German Cities Protested in U.S.," *NYT*, March 6, 1944, 1; Van Roey quoted in "An American Atrocity," *Catholic C.O.*, October 1944, 2; J. Frank Bucher to the FCC, January 6, 1943, FCC Records, RG18, Box 11, Folder 23, PHS. On Allied bombing strategy, see Sherry, *Rise of American Air Power*, 116–176, esp. 138–143; and Weinberg, *World at Arms*, 574–581. On the Allied destruction of occupied Europe, see Hitchcock, *Bitter Road to Freedom*.
26. "Peace Views of Vatican Contrary to Allied Aims," *NYT*, July 16, 1944, E6; Pius XII to Roosevelt, July 19, 1943, *Wartime Correspondence between President Roosevelt and Pope Pius XII*, 95–97; Vatican quoted in Phayer, *Pius XII, the Holocaust, and the Cold War*, 135.
27. McCawley, "Bombing of Civilians"; Ford, "Morality of Obliteration Bombing."
28. "An Interpretation," July 7, 1943, Andrews papers, Series 3, Box 2, Folder 13, UW; *Japanese in Our Midst*; Niebuhr to Bennett, April 21, 1942, Niebuhr papers, Box 2, LOC. For a more general discussion of both pro- and anti-internment views among American Christians, see Sittser, *Cautious Patriotism*, 169–178. The literature on Japanese internment is vast, but for a good overview, see Kashima, *Judgment Without Trial*. However, historians have mostly overlooked religious opposition.
29. Boyer, *By the Bomb's Early Light*, 200; see also Wittner, *Rebels Against War*, 126–127. For an excellent discussion of Truman's reaction, see Miscamble, *From Roosevelt to Truman*, 243–245.
30. Minister quoted in "Use of Atomic Bomb Criticized in Several Capital Pulpits," *WP*, August 13, 1945, 1; open letter quoted in "Truman Is Urged to Bar Atom Bomb," *NYT*, August 20, 1945, 21; Axling to Van Kirk, August 7, 1945, FCC Records, RG18, Box 24, Folder 12, PHS.
31. Leahy quoted in Miscamble, *From Roosevelt to Truman*, 243. For Axling's views, see his books *Kagawa* and *Toward an Understanding of the Far Eastern Crisis*.
32. "Oxnam, Dulles Ask Halt in Bomb Use," *NYT*, August 10, 1945, 6; Cavert to Truman, August 9, 1945, FCC Records, RG18, Box 3, Folder 20, PHS; "Clergyman Warns on Atomic Power," *NYT*, August 30, 1945, 4. For the FCC's most comprehensive statement, see Commission on the Relation of the Church to the War in the Light of the Christian Faith, *Atomic Warfare and the Christian Faith*. In general, see also Inboden, *Religion and American Foreign Policy*, 31–33.
33. *L'Osservatore Romano* quoted in Boyer, *By the Bomb's Early Light*, 14; Ryan quoted in "Use of Atomic Bomb Criticized in Several Capital Pulpits," *WP*, August 13, 1945, 2; "Peace or Truce," *Catholic C.O.*, July-September 1945, 1. See also Flynn, *Roosevelt and Romanism*, 209–211.
34. McIntire, *For Such a Time as This*, 132; "Atomic Apocalypse," *CC*, September 25, 1946, 1146; *Fortune* quoted in Boyer, *By the Bomb's Early Light*, 212; sermon, "A Different World," September 9, 1945, Hersey papers, Box 3, AHTL. On nuclear weapons as a spur to prophecy belief, see Boyer, *When Time Shall Be No More*.
35. Handy, "American Religious Depression." For an excellent portrait of religion in the interwar era, see Dumenil, *Modern Temper*, 169–200. On fundamentalists and evangelicals, see esp. Carpenter, "Fundamentalist Institutions"; see also Car-

penter, *Revive Us Again*. On Pentecostals, see Wacker, *Heaven Below*. On Catholics, see Hennesey, *American Catholics*, 234–279. On Jews, see Moore, *At Home in America*.

36. Carpenter, *Revive Us Again*, 144–146, 158; Murch, *Cooperation Without Compromise*; Stone, *On the Boundaries of American Evangelicalism*, 83.

37. Carpenter, *Revive Us Again*, 168–169; U.S. Delegation meeting minutes, June 18, 1945, *FRUS, 1945*, vol. I: 1339–1340; U.S. Delegation meeting minutes, June 20, 1945, ibid., 1391–1392. On the controversy of youth culture during the war, see Alvarez, *Power of the Zoot*.

38. Roland Bahnsen to Aubrey, August 1, 1943, Aubrey papers, Box 1, ABHS; Fosdick to Truman, March 20, 1943, Fosdick papers, Series IIA, Box 10, Folder 11, UTS; "VJ Day Radio Address," WPAG Radio, Ann Arbor, August 15, 1945, Carpenter papers, Box 1, BHL; Dower, *War Without Mercy*, 168–169.

CHAPTER TWENTY-ONE. JOHN FOSTER DULLES AND THE QUEST FOR A JUST AND DURABLE PEACE

1. Divine, *Second Chance*, 22.
2. Eden's "pontificating American," Churchill, and special assistant quoted in Hoopes, *Devil and John Foster Dulles*, 53, 169, 221; "preacher in a world of politics" quoted in Eden, *Full Circle*, 64; "The Peacemaker," *Time*, August 13, 1951.
3. Pruessen, *John Foster Dulles*, 1–15, 58–75 (Dulles quoted on 10).
4. "Assembly Awaits Fosdick Decision," *NYT*, May 28, 1924, 12; "J. F. Dulles Proposal Linked with British Manifesto," *The Witness*, January 30, 1947, 3; Dulles, "As Seen by a Layman," in Van Dusen, ed., *Spiritual Legacy of John Foster Dulles*, 13–22.
5. Pruessen, *John Foster Dulles*, 29–57; Brands, *Cold Warriors*, 3–6.
6. Dulles NBC Radio address, "The Church and International Peace," May 20, 1937, Coffin papers, Box 15, Folder 197, UTS.
7. Dulles, "Problem of Peace in a Dynamic World," esp. 146–149, 152–155, 168 ("canalize" quoted on 148). Dulles elaborated on these themes at greater length in his 1938 book *War, Peace and Change*. On Dulles and the realists at Oxford, see also Warren, *Theologians of a New World Order*, 78.
8. Dulles to Williams Adams Brown, June 3, 1940, FCC Records, RG18, Box 7, Folder 30, PHS; untitled essay by Dulles, October 7, 1921, Dulles papers, Box 279, SMLP. For an example of his earlier interwar views on war, change, and peaceful alternatives, see Dulles, *Peaceful Change within the Society of Nations*.
9. Dulles speech, "America's Role in World Affairs," YMCA National Council, Detroit, October 28, 1939, Dulles papers, Box 289, SMLP; Dulles speech, "The United States and the World of Nations," National Study Conference on The Churches and the International Situation, Philadelphia, February 27, 1940, Dulles papers, Box 290, SMLP; participant is Visser 't Hooft, *Memoirs*, 111; Dulles to Coffin, May 20, 1940, FCC Records, RG18, Box 7, Folder 30, PHS.
10. Dulles, "Christianity—Solvent of World Conflict," January 1943, Dulles Papers, Box 283, SMLP; Dulles, *War, Peace and Change*, 18–19.
11. FCC statement, drafted by Dulles, "The American Churches and the International Situation," December 1940, Box 301.73, Folder 1, WCC; "one man show" quoted in Hoopes, *Devil and John Foster Dulles*, 55; Van Dusen to Visser 't Hooft, November 27, 1941, Box 301.009, Folder 9, WCC.
12. Divine, *Second Chance*, 31–32, 36–37 (Van Kirk quoted on 45); Van Kirk to Niebuhr, April 4, 1941, Niebuhr Papers, Box 5, LOC; Warren, *Theologians of a New World Order*, 98–100. For more detailed accounts of Dulles's leadership of

the Commission, see Pruessen, *John Foster Dulles*, 190–217; Toulouse, *Transformation of John Foster Dulles*, 61–86; and Nurser, *For All Peoples and All Nations*, 49–68.

13. Meeting minutes, Committee of Direction, March 21, 1941, FCC Records, RG18, Box 29, Folder 6, PHS; Warren, *Theologians of a New World Order*, 100.

14. Dulles, *War, Peace, and Change*, 124–127, 136, 157–158; Fagley, *Study of Peace Aims in the Local Church*, 8; Justin Wroe Nixon, "Power Politics Within World Government," *C&C*, November 1, 1943, 4. "Transcending" is from the March 1942 Commission on a Just and Durable Peace study conference, Delaware, Ohio, quoted in Warren, *Theologians of a New World Order*, 101.

15. "Long Range Peace Objectives," September 18, 1941, 8, 5, 9, 10, FCC Records, RG18, Box 29, Folder 6, PHS; Divine, *Second Chance*, 44–45. For an extended discussion of the Atlantic Charter, see Borgwardt, *New Deal for the World*, 14–45.

16. Study Department of the WCC, No. 7/E44: "Analysis of the Christian Attitude to the Social and Economic Bases of a Just and Durable Peace," June 1944, Box 301.010, Folder 6, WCC.

17. "Confidential Memorandum Prepared by John Foster Dulles and Walter W. Van Kirk on Their Recent Visit to England," July 1942, Dulles papers, Box 282, SMLP.

18. "Notes of meeting on 'Peace Aims,'" Oxford, July 15–16, 1942, FCC Records, RG18, Box 29, Folder 6, PHS.

19. Commission to Study the Bases of a Just and Durable Peace, *Six Pillars of Peace*; Divine, *Second Chance*, 88–89.

20. "Council of Churches Advocates World-Wide Post-War Alliance," *New York Herald Tribune*, March 19, 1943, 1; "Churchmen Detail 'Pillars of Peace': Six Political Principles Aimed at Meeting Post-War Needs Outlined to Leaders," *NYT*, March 19, 1943, 1; Dulles, "Six Pillars of Peace Program of Federal Council of Churches," *NYT*, May 20, 1943, 23; Fosdick, *NYT*, July 4, 1943, 10; Ball, *NYT*, June 20, 1943, 36; Welles, *NYT*, May 30, 1943, 17; Dewey, *NYT*, June 27, 1943, 18; "U.S. Churches' Peace Plan," *The Times*, March 19, 1943, 3; "Pillars of Peace," *Time*, March 29, 1943; Washington Embassy to Foreign Office, November 14, 1943, in Nicholas, ed., *Washington Despatches*, 273.

21. Memo of conference with the President at the White House (drafted by Dulles), March 26, 1943, Dulles papers, Box 283, SMLP. On Roosevelt's emphasis for a realistic plan for the UN, which meant placing a priority on cooperation with the Soviet Union, see Gaddis, *United States and the Origins of the Cold War*, 27–29; Dallek, *Franklin Roosevelt and American Foreign Policy*, 283–284, 358–359; Hoopes and Brinkley, *FDR and the Creation of the U.N.*; and Miscamble, *From Roosevelt to Truman*, 39–42.

22. Conference document 42, Joint British-Soviet-American Communiqué, October 30, 1943, *FRUS, 1943*, vol. I: 741–744; Divine, *Second Chance*, 162–163 (including Dulles quotes).

23. Divine, *Second Chance*, 189, 216–217; Hull, *Memoirs*, vol. 2, 1686.

24. Hull, *Memoirs*, vol. 1, 174, and vol. 2, 1689–1692; Dulles quoted in Pruessen, *John Foster Dulles*, 228.

25. Hull, *Memoirs*, vol. 2, 1692–1695, 1708 (quoted on 1691); diary entry, August 25, 1944, in Israel, ed., *War Diary of Breckenridge Long*, 376; Divine, *Second Chance*, 217–220, 227–228.

26. "Comments on Current Discussions of International Order," September 21, 1944, FCC Records, RG18, Box 29, Folder 7, PHS; Dulles quoted in Divine, *Second Chance*, 230. On Dumbarton Oaks, see Hoopes and Brinkley, *FDR and the Creation of the U.N.*, 133–158; and Borgwardt, *New Deal for the World*, 142–168, 172–176, 181–186, 191–193.

27. "A Superstate of Free Peoples," *CRT*, January 1942, 19–20; "A World Brotherhood in God," ibid., 22; *Minutes of the General Assembly of the Presbyterian Church in the United States of America*, May 25–31, 1944, 100–101; sermon, Dwight Place Congregational Church, New Haven, Conn., August 19, 1945, Pickett papers, RG30, Box 315, Folder 4, YDS; journal of Bishop Paul Neff Garber, March 7, 1945, James Cannon III papers, Box 9, UAD.

28. Divine, *Second Chance*, 160–161; "Role of Church in Promoting World Peace Forms Topic of Many Sermons," *WP*, November 8, 1943, 8.

29. Miller, *Bishop G. Bromley Oxnam*, 282–286; Sittser, *Cautious Patriotism*, 234–237; Nurser, *For All Peoples and All Nations*, 69–78; Oxnam, "The Crusade for a New World Order," *C&C*, July 26, 1943, 12–13; "World Order Crusade Sunday: Your Duty as a Christian Citizen," March 1944, Lenox papers, main folder, ABHS; Northern Baptist Convention leaflet, "Postwar Objectives, Concerns, Hopes," ca. 1943, Pamphlet Collection, Box 151, ABHS; Walter Horton, "Wartime Decisions and Peacetime Consequences," *Social Action*, October 15, 1942, 5–6.

30. "The Churches and World Order: World Order Day, November 12, 1944," Presidential Papers: OF 213, FDRL. For the United Council of Church Women, see UCCW press release, June 22, 1944, FCC Records, RG18, Box 27, Folder 13, PHS; and Harper Sibley to the Carnegie Endowment, August 7, 1945, Box 263, Folder 7, CEIP. For the WCC, see Visser 't Hooft, *Memoirs*, esp. 152–155, 173–176; and Visser 't Hooft, "The Ecumenical Church and the International Situation," April 1940, Box 301.008, Folder 3, WCC.

31. Wallace, "Practical Religion in the World of Tomorrow"; John Frazer to James T. Shotwell, March 28, 1944, and undated SCC pamphlet, both in Box 261, Folder 11, CEIP; "To Enforce Peace," *Jackson Daily News*, March 18, 1945, 6; "Churchmen Launch War Against Pacifism," *Montgomery Advertiser*, June 1, 1945, 1.

32. Open letter by Fellowship of Southern Churchmen Chairman T. B. Cowan, n.d. [ca. 1943], Niebuhr papers, Box 5, LOC; notes on SBC annual meeting, Atlanta, May 1944, FCC Records, RG18, Box 27, Folder 13, PHS; Lawrence Lay to the Commission on the Relation of the Church to the War in Light of the Christian Faith, July 23, 1943, Aubrey papers, Box 1, ABHS.

33. "Bishops' Statement on International Order," November 16, 1944, IWPPC, Box 1, Folder 23, YDS; Martin, "Integrating Forces for an International Community"; Ross, "Sociologist's Contribution to Postwar Reconstruction"; Ross, "Towards Postwar Social Cooperation." On Catholics at the UN, see Rossi, *American Catholics and the Formation of the United Nations*.

34. Quoted in Cohen, *Americanization of Zionism*, 206.

35. G. Ashton Oldham to Roosevelt, September 30, 1943, Presidential Papers: Personal File, Folder 1627, FDRL; "Interfaith Declaration on World Peace," *FCB*, November 1943, 7; Wall, *Inventing the "American Way,"* 136, 143–148, 157–158.

36. Boyer, *When Time Shall Be No More*, 111; M. G. Hatcher, "Why I Am Opposed to the United World Federalists," May 23, 1943, Brasher papers, Box 46, MSCD.

37. "Showers of Blessing: A Weekly Paper in Loyalty to Christ," vol. 2, no. 2, February 12, 1943, FCC Records, RG18, Box 8, Folder 24, PHS; Smith quoted in Borgwardt, *New Deal for the World*, 147; Dan Gilbert, "Christian Youth's Window to the World," *Congregational Christian Beacon*, March 1943, 5; Dan Gilbert, "The Federal Council and the San Francisco Conference," *The Voice*, vol. 24, no. 1, July 1945, FCC Records, RG18, Box 8, Folder 24, PHS.

38. H. Richard Niebuhr to Richard Fagley, n.d. [ca. August 1945], FCC Records, RG18, Box 24, Folder 15, PHS.

39. Niebuhr, "The Atomic Issue," *C&C*, October 15, 1945, 6; Niebuhr, "American Power and World Responsibility," *C&C*, April 5, 1943, 2, 4. For Dumbarton

Oaks, see Stone, *Reinhold Niebuhr,* 116–118; and Nurser, *For All Peoples and All Nations,* 103.

40. *C&C* flyer, ca. 1940, Niebuhr Papers, Box 11, LOC; Niebuhr quoted in meeting minutes, FCC Commission on the Church and War, December 28–29, 1945, Aubrey Papers, Box 1, ABHS; Niebuhr, "Prayer and a Global Civilization," *C&C,* September 18, 1944, 1. For some of the articles, see Rhoda McCulloch, "Toward a United Nations Council," *C&C,* February 22, 1943, 1–2; George Stewart, "Why the League Failed," ibid., 3–7; Van Dusen, "Six Pillars of Peace," *C&C,* March 22, 1943, 1–2; William Adams Brown, "Mutual Security Comes First," ibid., 5–6; John Crosby Brown, "Christianity and International Order," *C&C,* December 27, 1943, 5–7; and Bennett, "Establish World Organization Now," *C&C,* June 12, 1944, 1–2. For explicit links between ecumenism and collective security, see Edward L. Parsons, "Church Unity and World Unity," *C&C,* May 31, 1943, 1–2; Bennett, "An Ecumenical Consensus," *C&C,* July 26, 1943, 4–6; Oxnam, "The Crusade for a New World Order," ibid., 12–13; Leiper, "Christian Unity Must Be Maintained," *C&C,* January 24, 1944, 1–2.

41. Diary entry, May 28, 1944, Israel, ed., *War Diary of Breckenridge Long,* 350; diary entries, June 26–29, 1944, and March 27, 1945, *Private Papers of Senator Vandenberg,* 87, 160; Pruessen, *John Foster Dulles,* 235–237.

42. Dulles to Van Kirk, April 5, 1945, and attached prayer, "To the United States Delegation at the San Francisco Conference," FCC Records, RG18, Box 29, Folder 7, PHS; Joint Committee on Religious Liberty statement, November 30, 1944, ibid., Box 18, Folder 15, PHS. For the best account of religious NGOs and Nolde's important role, see Nurser, *For All Peoples and All Nations,* esp. 106, 111–125.

43. Diary entry, May 19, 1945, *Private Papers of Senator Vandenberg,* 194–195; "Mr. Dulles' Draft Statement," section g., U.S. Delegation meeting minutes, June 1, 1945, *FRUS, 1945,* vol. I: 1066.

44. Diary entry, May 19, 1945, *Private Papers of Senator Vandenberg,* 195.

45. Pruessen, *John Foster Dulles,* 220–226, 232–237, 248–250.

46. For Dulles's defense of regional security arrangements, including the Monroe Doctrine, see U.S. Delegation meeting minutes, April 16, 1945, *FRUS, 1945,* vol. I: 302–304; U.S. Delegation meeting minutes, May 4, 1945, ibid., 596; U.S. Delegation meeting minutes, May 8, 1945, ibid., 644, 648–649; U.S. Delegation meeting minutes, May 11, 1945, ibid., 667; memcon, U.S. and U.K. Delegations, May 12, 1945, ibid., 700–701. For "compulsory jurisdiction," see U.S. Delegation meeting minutes, April 30, 1945, ibid., 492.

47. U.S. Delegation meeting minutes, April 16, 1945, *FRUS, 1945,* vol. I: 308–309 (including Dulles-Vandenberg exchange); meeting minutes, Four-Power Consultative Meeting, May 3, 1945, ibid., 582–583; U.S. Delegation meeting minutes, May 23, 1945, ibid., 852–856; U.S. Delegation meeting minutes, June 14, 1945, ibid., 1301–1302. On the problem of domestic jurisdiction, see also Anderson, *Eyes Off the Prize,* 48–50; and Borgwardt, *New Deal for the World,* 192.

48. Dulles broadcast on WOR Radio, New York, June 24, 1947, Dulles Papers, Box 294, SMLP; Divine, *Second Chance,* 251–252; Washington Embassy to Foreign Office, January 28, 1945, in Nicholas, ed., *Washington Despatches,* 505. For the Gallup poll, see Borgwardt, *New Deal for the World,* 156.

49. Warren, *Theologians of a New World Order,* 107; Nurser, *For All Peoples and All Nations,* 111–125.

PART VII. THE COLD WAR AND THE FOURTH CRUSADE

1. Truman to Jesse Bader, September 29, 1947, OF 213, Box 803, HSTL.
2. Truman to Pius XII, August 6, 1947, and Pius XII to Truman, August 26, 1947, Taylor papers, Box 1, HSTL.
3. Harry Truman to Bess Truman, October 2, 1947, in Ferrell, ed., *Dear Bess*, 551. For the most thorough accounts of the Taylor mission under Truman, on which my own radically condensed version draws, see Kirby, "Harry Truman's Religious Legacy"; and Inboden, *Religion and American Foreign Policy*, 119–155. But see also Kirby, "Truman's Holy Alliance"; Kirby, "Divinely Sanctioned"; and Preston, "Death of a Peculiar Special Relationship." The Taylor mission has not received much attention from historians of European religion, but for British and Vatican perspectives, see, respectively, Kirby, *Church, State and Propaganda*; and Kent, *Lonely Cold War of Pope Pius XII*.
4. Blanshard, *American Freedom and Catholic Power*; memo for the file on Oxnam, June 13, 1949, OF 1766, Box 1676, HSTL; all quotes from Taylor memo for the record, October 26, 1948, Taylor papers, Box 3, Cornell.
5. Acheson, *Present at the Creation*, 574–575; "Confidential Memorandum by Department of State Regarding United States Representation to the Holy See," January 18, 1951, Taylor papers, Box 2, HSTL. For Acheson's Episcopal upbringing, see Rotter, *Comrades at Odds*, 221; and McMahon, *Dean Acheson*, 5–9.
6. Acheson, *Present at the Creation*, 575; Dahlberg quoted in "Meeting of Protestant Clergymen with Myron C. Taylor at Union Club, New York," October 20, 1947, Taylor Papers, Box 1, HSTL; Fosdick to Truman, October 22, 1951, Fosdick papers, Series IIA, Box 10, Folder 11, UTS; "violently bigoted" quoted in unsent letter, Truman to Irvin Harlamert, January 3, 1952, in Poen, ed., *Strictly Personal*, 44; Truman, *Mr. Citizen*, 119–120. On the protest mail, see Gustafson, "Religion of a President," 385; and McCoy, *Presidency of Harry S. Truman*, 277. For two early warnings that reveal Protestant concerns about Catholic "clericalism," excessive anticommunism, and authoritarianism, see the letters of Oxnam to Taylor, May 12, 1945, and January 21, 1947, both in the folder marked "Correspondence Between Bishop Oxnam and Mr. Myron Taylor, 1945–1950," Taylor papers, Box 7, Cornell.

CHAPTER TWENTY-TWO. THE FAITH OF HARRY TRUMAN AND THE THEOLOGY OF GEORGE KENNAN

1. The phrase comes from a book on the CIA's funding of cultural programs in Europe: Saunders, *Cultural Cold War*.
2. Biographer is Hamby, *Man of the People*, 474; "Fundamentalist" is from Gustafson, "Religion of a President," 380. For his Bible reading as a child, see Truman, *Harry S. Truman*, 52. Oddly, Truman's religion has been mostly ignored by his biographers. But for two especially perceptive analyses, see Spalding, *First Cold Warrior*, 199–222; and Inboden, *Religion and American Foreign Policy*, esp. 105–116. The only other historians who pay it much attention examine U.S. policy toward the Middle East. See Benson, *Harry S. Truman and the Founding of Israel*, 30–37; Anderson, *Biblical Interpretation and Middle East Policy*, 87–89; and Oren, *Power, Faith, and Fantasy*, 475–477.
3. "Common man" quoted in Spalding, *First Cold Warrior*, 206; diary entry, April 13, 1952, in Ferrell, ed., *Off the Record*, 247; "underdog" quoted in Hillman, ed., *Mr. President*, 88.

4. Hamby, *Man of the People*, 114, 264–265.
5. Harry Truman to Bess Truman, June 22, 1936, in Ferrell, ed., *Dear Bess*, 388; "Address in Kansas City at a Dinner Honoring Democratic National Chairman, William M. Boyle, Jr.," September 29, 1949, *PPP: Truman, 1949*, 494; "fundamental basis" quoted in Spalding, *First Cold Warrior*, 219.
6. "Annual Message to the Congress on the State of the Union," January 7, 1948, *PPP: Truman, 1948*, 2–3; "Address on Foreign Policy at the Navy Day Celebration in New York City," October 27, 1945, *PPP: Truman, 1945*, 435; "Address in Little Rock at the Dedication of the World War Memorial Park," June 11, 1949, *PPP: Truman, 1949*, 286; "Remarks in Chicago at the Shriners Diamond Jubilee Banquet," July 19, 1949, ibid., 390.
7. Truman, *Mr. Citizen*, 119. For the Judeo-Christian concept's emergence in the 1930s and its culmination in the early Cold War, see Wall, *Inventing the "American Way,"* 9–10, 77–87, 143–148, 177–187, 222–227, 243, 283–284. For just the Cold War, see Silk, *Spiritual Politics*, 40–53; Hollinger, *Science, Jews, and Secular Culture*, 23; Suri, *Henry Kissinger and the American Century*, 59–65; and Inboden, *Religion and American Foreign Policy*.
8. "Address at the Unveiling of a Memorial Carillon in Arlington National Cemetery," December 21, 1949, *PPP: Truman, 1949*, 582–583; diary entry, February 26, 1952, in Ferrell, ed., *Off the Record*, 241–242.
9. Spalding, *First Cold Warrior*, 212–213, 220.
10. "Address at the Cornerstone Laying of the New York Avenue Presbyterian Church," April 3, 1951, *PPP: Truman, 1951*, 211–212.
11. For a diplomat who never rose above the middle ranks of the foreign policy bureaucracy, the literature on Kennan is inordinately large. Though they do not agree on everything, for Kennan's background and the outlines of containment I have relied especially upon Gaddis, *Strategies of Containment*, 24–52; Isaacson and Thomas, *Wise Men*; and Lukacs, *George Kennan*.
12. Kennan, "Sources of Soviet Conduct," 581. On the variations of containment throughout the Cold War, see Gaddis, *Strategies of Containment*.
13. For "legalistic-moralistic," see Kennan, *American Diplomacy*, 95; "universalistic" quoted in Gaddis, *Strategies of Containment*, 27–29. On Kennan and Vietnam, see Hixson, "Containment on the Perimeter."
14. Kennan, "The Relation of Religion to Government," *Princeton Seminary Bulletin*, Winter 1969, 45–46; Kennan, "Foreign Policy and Christian Conscience," *Atlantic Monthly*, May 1959, 48–49; Kennan to Toynbee, March 31, 1952, Kennan papers, Box 29, Folder 2-A-1952 O-Z, SMLP. See also Kennan, *Around the Cragged Hill*, 37–52. Kennan's religious beliefs, and their role in shaping his diplomatic thought, have been almost completely ignored. But for brief examinations, see Stephanson, *Kennan and the Art of Foreign Policy*, 248–250; and Lukacs, *George Kennan*, 176–189.
15. Kennan sermon, April 15, 1962, Kennan papers, Box 20, Folder 1-C-115, SMLP.
16. Kennan sermon, April 15, 1962; Milton, *Paradise Lost*, Book XII, lines 561–564; "With regard" quoted in Gaddis, *Strategies of Containment*, 130n.
17. Fox, *Reinhold Niebuhr*, 238; Gaddis, *Strategies of Containment*, 31n; "father of us all" quoted in Stone, *Reinhold Niebuhr*, 169; all other Kennan quotes from sermon, Protestant Church Service, Belgrade, March 17, 1963, Kennan papers, Box 20, Folder 1-C-120, SMLP; Niebuhr quoted in "Foreign Policy and Moral Problems," in Davis and Good, eds., *Reinhold Niebuhr on Politics*, 331–332. For Niebuhr's praise of Kennan, see also Niebuhr, *Irony of American History*, 147–149.
18. Kennan sermon, "To Be or Not to Be a Christian," October 18, 1953, Kennan papers, Box 3, Folder 1-B-27, SMLP. A version of this sermon was reprinted in *C&C*, May 3, 1954, 51–53.

19. Kennan, "Sources of Soviet Conduct," 582. The religious element to Kennan's article has been almost completely overlooked. For an insightful exception, see Inboden, *Religion and American Foreign Policy*, 17–18.

20. Inboden, *Religion and American Foreign Policy*, 107.

21. Forrestal to Lippmann, January 7, 1946, in Millis, ed., *Forrestal Diaries*, 128. Similarly, as the historian Odd Arne Westad has observed on a more secular note, Soviet communism and Americanism represented two opposite, and therefore oppositional, visions of modernity. See his *Global Cold War*, 8–72.

22. Preston, "Death of a Peculiar Special Relationship," 214; Kent, *Lonely Cold War of Pope Pius XII*, 96, 167; note for the file on Bishop Holt, March 23, 1946, OF 76-A, Box 428, HSTL; note for the file on Clark Buckner and other clergymen, June 1, 1945, OF 1766, Box 1676, HSTL.

23. "The President's News Conference," June 14, 1946, *PPP: Truman, 1946*, 302.

24. Churchill to Taylor quoted in Kirby, "Divinely Sanctioned," 391; "The Sinews of Peace," Fulton, Missouri, March 5, 1946, in James, ed., *Winston S. Churchill: His Complete Speeches*, vol. 7, 7291. Event details from "The Red Riddle," *NYT*, March 10, 1946, E1; see also Wright, *Iron Curtain*, 21–45.

25. "Address in Columbus at a Conference of the Federal Council of Churches," March 6, 1946, *PPP: Truman, 1946*, 141.

26. Prayer from House proceedings, *CR*, March 12, 1947, 1997; "Special Message to Congress on Greece and Turkey: The Truman Doctrine," March 12, 1947, *PPP: Truman, 1947*, 178–179; Lippmann, "Policy or Crusade?" *WP*, March 15, 1947, 7. For two accounts that convincingly place the rhetoric of the Truman Doctrine in a tradition of American Puritanism, especially the jeremiad, see Rosenberg, "U.S. Cultural History," in May, ed., *American Cold War Strategy*, 160–164; and Stephanson, "Liberty or Death."

27. NSC-68 has been analyzed exhaustively, but see esp. Gaddis, *Strategies of Containment*, 88–115; Leffler, *Preponderance of Power*, 355–360; May, ed., *American Cold War Strategy*; and Craig and Logevall, *America's Cold War*, 108–114. On the document's overwhelmingly Protestant themes, see Kuklick, "U.S. Intellectual History," in May, ed., *American Cold War Strategy*, 156–159; and Stephanson, "Liberty or Death."

28. NSC-68, April 14, 1950, *FRUS, 1950*, vol. I: 237–240.

29. Sullivan, "Politics of Altruism," 762–764; Inboden, *Religion and American Foreign Policy*, 116–119 (PSB quoted on 118); U.S. Delegation meeting minutes, April 13, 1949, *FRUS, 1949*, vol. II: 78. On Elsey, see Benson, *Harry S. Truman and the Founding of Israel*, 33; and Spalding, *First Cold Warrior*, 292n22.

30. See, for example, Stanton Griffis (Warsaw) to Marshall, November 15, 1947, *FRUS, 1947*, vol. IV: 458; Walter Bedell Smith (Moscow) to Marshall, August 26, 1947, ibid., 584–585; Smith to Marshall, October 29, 1947, ibid., 602–604; Eldridge Durbrow (Moscow) to Marshall, December 2, 1947, ibid., 628–630; Selden Chapin (Budapest) to Marshall, November 17, 1948, *FRUS, 1948*, vol. IV: 389–390; Acheson to "certain diplomatic missions," January 31, 1949, *FRUS, 1949*, vol. V: 224–226; Department of State policy statement, June 25, 1949, ibid., 503; and Department of State policy statement, November 27, 1950, *FRUS, 1950*, vol. IV: 1041.

31. Chapin to Marshall, December 29, 1948, *FRUS, 1948*, vol. IV: 393–394; Chapin to Marshall, December 30, 1948, *FRUS, 1949*, vol. V: 452–453; Dulles memo, March 24, 1948, *FRUS, 1948*, vol. I: 544. On Stepinac, see Gallagher, "United States and the Vatican in Yugoslavia," 126–136.

32. Spellman quoted in Jacobs, *America's Miracle Man*, 82–83; "Mindszenty Case Is Put to Truman," *NYT*, January 17, 1949, 2; "Lovett Deplores Cardinal's Arrest in Budapest as a Sickening Sham," *NYT*, December 30, 1948, 1; Acheson to

London, February 12, 1949, *FRUS, 1949*, vol. V: 227; "The President's News Conference," December 30, 1948, *PPP: Truman, 1948*, 968. On the Vatican, see Kent, *Lonely Cold War of Pope Pius XII*, 155–176, 226–229. For examples of Protestant fundamentalism, see Markham, *Rumania Under the Soviet Yoke*; and Markham, ed., *Communists Crush Churches in Eastern Europe*. The papal encyclicals are *Luctuosissimi Eventus*, Encyclical Urging Public Prayers for Peace and Freedom for the People of Hungary, October 28, 1956, in Carlen, ed. *Papal Encyclicals*, vol. 4, 315–316; *Laetamur Admodum*, Encyclical Renewing Exhortation for Prayers for Peace in Poland, Hungary, and the Middle East, November 1, 1956, ibid., 317–318; and *Datis Nuperrime*, Encyclical Lamenting the Sorrowful Events in Hungary and Condemning the Ruthless Use of Force, November 5, 1956, ibid., 319–320.

33. Judt, *Postwar*, 207. This is a radical compression of a complex and thoroughly researched subject. For more comprehensive accounts, see Warner, *Confessions of an Interest Group*; and Kisatsky, *United States and the European Right*. On Christian Democracy in Italy, including the U.S. role in the 1948 elections, see Miller, *United States and Italy*, 223–235, 243–249; Lucas, *Freedom's War*, 43–47; Pollard, "Vatican, Italy and the Cold War"; Kent, *Lonely Cold War of Pope Pius XII*, 196–201; and Mistry, "Case for Political Warfare." On West Germany, see Lappenküper, "Between Concentration Movement and People's Party." On Spellman's efforts, see Cooney, *American Pope*, 157–161.

34. Truman to Douglas Horton, October 16, 1945, OF 76-A, Box 428, HSTL; note for the file on FCC, October 4, 1945, OF 213, Box 803, HSTL; Grew to Pew, October 5, 1949, Pew papers, Box 22, Folder 5, HML; diary entry, July 10, 1946, in Millis, ed., *Forrestal Diaries*, 177–178; Goodman, *America's Japan*, 66–67; Garner, "Global Feminism." On the private religious efforts, see Shibusawa, *America's Geisha Ally*, 184–204, 213–254.

35. Clifford quoted in Little, *American Orientalism*, 86; "political implications" is from Truman to Lovett, August 16, 1948, PSF/SF, Box 157, Israel Folder, HSTL. On the State and Defense Departments' objections, see Brands, *Inside the Cold War*, 165–192; and Hahn, *Caught in the Middle East*, 28–31, 35–51.

36. Baruch and Truman quoted in Little, *American Orientalism*, 82, 81; "embarrassing" referred to Zionist support in the Senate and is in Grew to Truman, May 26, 1945, PSF/SF, Box 160, Palestine Folder, HSTL. For Zionist pressure and Truman's resentment, see Oren, *Power, Faith, and Fantasy*, 487–488, 492–493; and Benson, *Harry S. Truman and the Founding of Israel*, 191–199.

37. Merkley, *American Presidents, Religion, and Israel*, 1–22; Clifford quoted in Anderson, *Biblical Interpretation and Middle East Policy*, 88; Truman quoted in Oren, *Power, Faith, and Fantasy*, 501.

38. Truman speech at Passover, March 26, 1945, U.S. Senator and Vice President papers, Box 289, HSTL; "are all cousins" quoted in Benson, *Harry S. Truman and the Founding of Israel*, 35–36.

39. Truman quoted in Oren, *Power, Faith, and Fantasy*, 483; Taylor to Truman, July 30, 1947, Taylor papers, Box 3, HSTL.

40. "Statement by the President Following the Adjournment of the Palestine Conference in London," October 4, 1946, *PPP: Truman, 1946*, 442–444; "Exchange of Messages Between the King of Saudi Arabia and the President," *DSB*, November 10, 1946, 848–849.

41. Clifford, *Counsel to the President*, 4.

42. Quoted in Cohen, *Truman and Israel*, 209. See also Spalding, *First Cold Warrior*, 95–99.

CHAPTER TWENTY-THREE. HIGH PRIESTS
OF THE COLD WAR

1. Herberg, *Protestant-Catholic-Jew*; church figures from Ribuffo, "God and Contemporary Politics," 1518; Miller quoted in Smith, *Faith and the Presidency*, 232. Particularly good on the postwar boom in religion are Oakley, *God's Country*, 319–327; Wuthnow, *Restructuring of American Religion*; Silk, *Spiritual Politics*; and Marty, *Modern American Religion*, vol. 3, 277–330. On the 1950s as another great awakening, see Ribuffo, "Religion in the History of U.S. Foreign Policy," 14, which calls the decade the Fifth Great Awakening; and Jacobs, *America's Miracle Man*, 60–87, which calls it the Third.

2. McAlister, *Epic Encounters*, 43–83 (DeMille quoted on 44); Jacobs, *America's Miracle Man*, 62–71 (Bible sales figures quoted on 66).

3. Silk, *Spiritual Politics*, 99–100; Marty, *Modern American Religion*, vol. 3, 298–301 (Eisenhower quoted on 300); Douglas quoted in Jacobs, "Our System Demands the Supreme Being," 621.

4. Schlesinger, *Cycles of American History*, 394.

5. Neely quoted in Smith, *Faith and the Presidency*, 226; Eisenhower to Benson quoted in Lyon, *Eisenhower*, 497n; "goddammit" quoted in Oakley, *God's Country*, 153.

6. Jacobs, "Our System Demands the Supreme Being," 594.

7. Eisenhower to Clifford Roberts, July 29, 1952, *PDDE*, vol. 13, 1284; Eisenhower to Archibald Bennett, January 23, 1954, *PDDE*, vol. 15, 845; Lyon, *Eisenhower*, 33–34, 38–39 (quoted on 38); Inboden, *Religion and American Foreign Policy*, 264–265; Smith, *Faith and the Presidency*, 222.

8. Eisenhower to James Mintener, March 28, 1952, *PDDE*, vol. 13, 1142; Eisenhower press conference, Columbia University, May 3, 1948, Pre-Presidential papers, Principal File, Box 156, DDEL.

9. Press conference, Columbia University; Eisenhower to Roberts, July 29, 1952, *PDDE*, vol. 13, 1285.

10. Eisenhower quoted in Jacobs, *America's Miracle Man*, 67; High quoted in Jacobs, "Our System Demands the Supreme Being," 593; Fox quoted in Inboden, *Religion and American Foreign Policy*, 267. On Luce and Fox, see Smith, *Faith and the Presidency*, 223–224, 239.

11. "Statement for American Bible Society," October 28, 1943, Pre-Presidential papers, Principal File, Box 149, DDEL. On Eisenhower reinventing American civil religion for the Cold War, see also Inboden, *Religion and American Foreign Policy*, 257–309.

12. Text of Eisenhower speech in "President-Elect Says Soviet Demoted Zhukov Because of Their Friendship," *NYT*, December 23, 1952, 1, 16. For a brilliant discussion of the historical controversy surrounding this quotation, see Henry, "And I Don't Care What It Is."

13. Eisenhower to Anton Lorenzen, September 9, 1953, *PDDE*, vol. 14, 508–509; draft Eisenhower statement, "Message of Israel," July 1954, WHCF/GF 118-B, Box 682, DDEL.

14. Diary entry, July 2, 1953, *PDDE*, vol. 14, 358–362; Griffith, "Dwight D. Eisenhower and the Corporate Commonwealth" ("danger arises" quoted on 90); Chernus, "Operation Candor," 785–786; "Protestant beliefs" quoted in Smith, *Faith and the Presidency*, 248.

15. "Remarks at the Cornerstone-Laying Ceremony for the Interchurch Center," New York, October 12, 1958, *PPP: Eisenhower, 1958*, 732; Smith quoted in Jacobs, *America's Miracle Man*, 69; Eisenhower quoted in "Remark Called Casual," *NYT*, July 11, 1952, 10.

16. "Address at the Tenth Anniversary Meeting of the United Nations," San Francisco, June 20, 1955, *PPP: Eisenhower, 1955,* 607; "Address and Remarks at the Baylor University Commencement Ceremonies," May 25, 1956, *PPP: Eisenhower, 1956,* 528.
17. "Inaugural Address," January 20, 1953, *PPP: Eisenhower, 1953,* 2–4; "Farewell Radio and Television Address to the American People," January 17, 1961, *PPP: Eisenhower, 1960–61,* 1037.
18. Eisenhower to Willard Stewart Paul, March 27, 1954, *PDDE,* vol. 15, 985; "Address and Remarks at Baylor," 528; "Radio and Television Address to the American People Prior to Departure for the Big Four Conference at Geneva," July 15, 1955, *PPP: Eisenhower, 1955,* 704–705.
19. "Statement by the President: National Day of Prayer," September 21, 1954, *PPP: Eisenhower, 1954,* 852; "Eisenhower Statement to Peoples of Iron Curtain countries" and Eisenhower to Knowland, September 20, 1954, both in WHCF/OF 144-F (1), Box 737, DDEL.
20. "Address at the Second Assembly of the World Council of Churches," Evanston, August 19, 1954, *PPP: Eisenhower, 1954,* 739–740; "Eisenhower Asks Prayer for Peace," *NYT,* Aug 20, 1954, 20; Washburn to L. Arthur Minnich, Jr., November 2, 1954, WHCF/OF 144-H, Box 738, DDEL.
21. Memcon of NSC meeting, November 1, 1956, *FRUS, 1955–1957,* vol. XXV: 359; "Closed Circuit Television Remarks to a Group in Boston, Massachusetts, on Election Eve," November 5, 1956, *PPP: Eisenhower, 1956,* 1085. On Diem, see Jacobs, *America's Miracle Man.* On Mindszenty, see also Granville, *First Domino,* 171–175, 192–193. On religion in official U.S. propaganda, see Osgood, *Total Cold War,* 248, 256–257, 290, 310–314, 320; Inboden, *Religion and American Foreign Policy,* 299–308; Cull, *Cold War and the United States Information Agency,* 103, 113, 127, 163–164; and Belmonte, *Selling the American Way,* 58, 103–107.
22. Diary entry, January 10, 1956, in Ferrell, ed., *Eisenhower Diaries,* 306; exchange of letter between Eisenhower and High, November 11 and November 16, 1952, *PDDE,* vol. 13, 1433–1434.
23. "Evil" quoted in Gaddis, *Strategies of Containment,* 154; "Bible" and "terrible things" quoted in Jacobs, *America's Miracle Man,* 72, 77.
24. Historians are still coming to grips with Dulles, overall an important but rather unlikable figure who is easy to deride and mischaracterize. Most accounts of Dulles correctly emphasize his commitment to anticommunism and his aggressive strategic posture—massive retaliation, brinkmanship, and so forth—but ignore his contradictions and complexities. But for more nuanced portraits that avoid caricature, see Pruessen, *John Foster Dulles;* Gaddis, *United States and the End of the Cold War,* 65–86; and Immerman, *John Foster Dulles.*
25. U.S. Delegation meeting minutes, May 8, 1945, *FRUS, 1945,* vol. I: 644.
26. Pruessen, *John Foster Dulles,* 263–276. For Lansing and communism, see Gardner, *Safe for Democracy,* 156–161 (Lansing quoted on 159, 161); and Levin, *Woodrow Wilson and World Politics,* 51, 57, 64–69.
27. "The Churches and World Order," FCC Records, RG18, Box 40, PHS.
28. Dulles, "Thoughts on Soviet Foreign Policy and What to Do about It," *Life,* June 3, 1946, 113–126, and June 10, 1946, 118–130. Biographer is Pruessen, *John Foster Dulles,* 267, 285, 287–288. On Americans wanting to expand their own system as a way to enhance security, see Leffler, *Preponderance of Power.*
29. Commission on a Just and Durable Peace meeting notes, afternoon and evening sessions, June 6, 1946, FCC Records, RG18, Box 40, Folder 14, PHS. For the security dilemma in international relations theory, see Jervis, *Perception and Misperception,* 58–95; and Jervis, "Cooperation Under the Security Dilemma."

On whether the Cold War was caused by the security dilemma, see Leffler, "Cold War," 512–513, 516; and Jervis, "Was the Cold War a Security Dilemma?"

30. Commission on a Just and Durable Peace meeting notes, afternoon and evening sessions, June 6, 1946, FCC Records, RG18, Box 40, Folder 14, PHS.

31. Address at *New York Herald Tribune* Forum, "Our Spiritual Heritage," October 21, 1947, in Van Dusen, ed., *Spiritual Legacy of John Foster Dulles*, 64.

32. Address under the auspices of The Brotherhood of St. Andrew, "World Brotherhood Through the State," Convention Hall, Philadelphia, September 8, 1946, ibid., 111–112; U.S. Delegation meeting minutes, November 19, 1946, *FRUS, 1946*, vol. I: 1015.

33. Dulles quoted in Hoopes, *Devil and John Foster Dulles*, 64; Crain to Van Kirk, June 14, 1946, FCC Records, RG18, Box 40, Folder 14, PHS; McIntire quoted in "Dulles Attacked by Church Council," *NYT*, October 30, 1948, 16.

34. Commission on a Just and Durable Peace statement, "Soviet-American Relations," October 11, 1946, Dulles Papers, Box 284, SMLP; memcon, Dulles and Gromyko, November 15, 1947, *FRUS, 1947*, vol. I: 225; Dulles, "How Should the United States Confront the Soviet Communist Party," *CRT*, May 1948, 1–2; "War With Russians Not an Inevitability, Protestants Told on Eve of Reorganization," *WP*, November 28, 1950, 2; Statement for Brotherhood Week, February 5, 1947, Dulles papers, Box 294, SMLP; Dulles press statement, October 13, 1947, in editorial note, *FRUS, 1947*, vol. I: 297.

35. On Dumbarton Oaks, see Warren, *Theologians of a New World Order*, 105. On Dulles's views on the Soviets and the UN, see Pruessen, *John Foster Dulles*, 277–278, 289–290.

36. Address at the Assembly of the World Council of Churches, August 24, 1948, Box 31.004, WCC; address at First Presbyterian Church, Watertown, N.Y., "Faith of Our Fathers," August 28, 1949, in Van Dusen, ed., *Spiritual Legacy of John Foster Dulles*, 8.

37. U.S. Delegation meeting minutes, April 11, 1945, *FRUS, 1945*, vol. I: 256; "Curb on U.N. Veto Is Urged by Dulles," *NYT*, August 7, 1947, 8; Dulles lecture at the Carnegie Endowment for International Peace, September 29, 1948, Dulles papers, Box 295, SMLP.

38. U.S. Delegation meeting minutes, April 13, 1949, *FRUS, 1949*, vol. II: 77; Dulles statement to the press, January 16, 1949, Dulles papers, Box 297, SMLP; State Department press release of NBC News Transcript, March 18, 1949, *DHTP*, vol. 17, 72; Pruessen, *John Foster Dulles*, 261.

39. Quoted in Guhin, *John Foster Dulles*, 55.

40. Quoted in Gaddis, *Strategies of Containment*, 145, 149.

41. Quoted in Inboden, *Religion and American Foreign Policy*, 249. On the gulf between the bellicosity of Secretary of State Dulles's public rhetoric and the more reasonable inclinations of his private views, see Gaddis, *United States and the End of the Cold War*, 65–86; and Tudda, *Truth Is Our Weapon*.

42. Gaddis, *United States and the End of the Cold War*, 66–73, 82 (Dulles quoted on 71, 69).

43. Trachtenberg, *Constructed Peace*, 121–125, 150–151. On Dulles and Monnet, see Hoopes, *Devil and John Foster Dulles*, 29, 67; and Pruessen, *John Foster Dulles*, 118–119, 309. On the Eisenhower administration's support for European integration, see Giauque, *Grand Designs*.

44. Inboden, *Religion and American Foreign Policy*, 239, 247–248 (quoted on 239); Brands, *Cold Warriors*, 23.

45. Quoted in Inboden, *Religion and American Foreign Policy*, 250.

46. Dulles, "The Cost of Peace," *DSB*, June 18, 1956, 999–1000; Dulles, "Policy

for Security and Peace," 355; State Department press release of NBC News Transcript, March 18, 1949, *DHTP,* vol. 17, 69. See also Dulles, "Challenge and Response," 28–35.

47. Dulles, address to the San Francisco Council of Churches, "The Moral Foundations of the United Nations," June 19, 1955, in Van Dusen, ed., *Spiritual Legacy of John Foster Dulles,* 1301–31.

48. Dulles, "Challenge and Response," 29, 41, 42.

CHAPTER TWENTY-FOUR. THE GREAT SCHISM AND THE MYTH OF CONSENSUS

1. Political historians have begun to challenge the myth of bipartisan consensus. My thinking on this point has been particularly influenced by Gerstle, "Race and the Myth of the Liberal Consensus"; Craig and Logevall, *America's Cold War;* and Zelizer, *Arsenal of Democracy.*

2. These are enormously complicated topics, each with its own rich literature. But on the gradual postwar decline of anti-Catholicism and anti-Semitism, see Ribuffo, *Right, Center, Left,* 59–66; and Dinnerstein, *Antisemitism in America,* 150–174. On secularization, see Bruce, ed., *Religion and Modernization;* Hollinger, " 'Secularization' Question"; Smith, "Introduction"; and O'Brien, "American Experience of Secularisation."

3. On the relatively recent hardening of the wall of separation, see esp. Hamburger, *Separation of Church and State.* On Jewish litigation on church-state issues, see Ivers, *To Build a Wall.*

4. The seminal analysis of these changes is Wuthnow, *Restructuring of American Religion.*

5. Most histories of religion and the Cold War present faith-based anticommunism as somewhat consensual, even monolithic. But for two excellent examples of the diversity of the religious influence on foreign policy, see Marty, *Modern American Religion,* vol. 3; and Inboden, *Religion and American Foreign Policy,* esp. 29–102.

6. "Inaugural Address," January 20, 1949, *PPP: Truman, 1949,* 112.

7. Chambers, *Witness,* 449. For an excellent discussion of Chambers's religion and its role in his anticommunism, see Tanenhaus, *Whittaker Chambers,* esp. 165, 171–172, 453, 467–468.

8. Whitfield, *Culture of the Cold War,* 77–100; Morone, *Hellfire Nation,* 380–384; Lahr, *Millennial Dreams.* On the political emergence of conservative Protestantism between the 1920s and 1950s, see Carpenter, *Revive Us Again;* and Williams, *God's Own Party,* 11–48.

9. Martin, *With God On Our Side,* 25–46; Graham quoted in Marty, *Modern American Religion,* vol. 3, 151–152. The story and significance of Graham's L.A. revival is well-told in Martin, *Prophet with Honor,* 106–120; Carpenter, *Revive Us Again,* 217–226; and Dochuk, "They Locked God Outside the Iron Curtain."

10. Graham, *America's Hour of Decision,* 150–151. On the emergence and popularity of the neo-evangelicals, see Carpenter, *Revive Us Again,* 211–232.

11. Fox handwritten notes April 9 and May 8, 1959, WHCF/OF 144-B, Box 736, DDEL; McIntire, *Author of Liberty,* 158, 163; McIntire, "The Communist Party Line in the Churches," May 8, 1953, WHCF/GF 118, Box 679, DDEL.

12. Sheen, "The Philosophy of Communism," *CRT,* April 1947, 13. For a superb analysis of Catholicism, Americanism, and Cold War anti-communism, see Jacobs, *America's Miracle Man,* 77–87; see also Schrecker, *Many Are the Crimes,* 72–75. For Buckley and Mindszenty, see Allitt, *Catholic Intellectuals and Conservative Politics,* 20–31, 60–70. For Joseph McCarthy, see Crosby, *God, Church, and Flag.*

For Spellman, see Cooney, *American Pope*, 146–245. For Joseph McCarthy's Catholic critics, see Marty, *Modern American Religion*, vol. 3, 356–358; Whitfield, *Culture of the Cold War*, 40–41; and Sandbrook, *Eugene McCarthy*, 61–63.

13. Appelman, *Christianity or Communism*; Schwarz, *You Can Trust the Communists (to Be Communists)*. For Schwarz sales figure, see Marty, *Modern American Religion*, vol. 3, 371.

14. National Opinion Research Center polls, April 22, 1948, Table 3-8, and November 26, 1954, Table 3-9, Hero, *American Religious Groups View Foreign Policy*, 309, 311; Jeansonne, *Gerald L. K. Smith*, 80–114.

15. Oshinsky, *Conspiracy So Immense*, 204–205, 428n (McCarthy quoted on 205n); von Hoffman, *Citizen Cohn*, 107–109, 138–139; Belmonte, *Selling the American Way*, 55.

16. Shapiro, *Time for Healing*, 23–26; Friedman, *Neoconservative Revolution*, 36–38, 62–79; Bloom, *Prodigal Sons*, 27–50; Dalin, "Will Herberg's Path"; Gerstenfeld, "The Spiritual Challenge of Communism to America," *CRT*, February 1951, 20–21. On Judaism and neoconservatism, see Friedman, *Neoconservatism Revolution*.

17. McIntire, *Rise of the Tyrant*, vii; McIntire, *Author of Liberty*, 155–156.

18. "Church and Industry Face a Common Foe," *Understanding*, September 1946, 1; "Communist Infiltration in Christian Service Agencies," *Economic Council Papers*, February 1948. On the links between business and religious conservatism, see Moreton, *To Serve God and Wal-Mart*; and Phillips-Fein, *Invisible Hands*, esp. 68–77, 225–235.

19. McIntire booklet, "Bishop Oxnam: Prophet of Marx," n.d., Smith papers, Box 42, BHL; McIntire, *Truth About the Federal Council of Churches*; members of the ACCC of California to William Martin, March 10, 1953, WHCF/GF 118, Box 679, DDEL.

20. Gillon, *Politics and Vision*, 9–11, 28; Fox, *Reinhold Niebuhr*, 230–231.

21. Peale to Pew, October 3, 1945, Pew papers, Box 7, HML; Peale sermon, "Perils to Freedom," October 12, 1947, Pew papers, Box 14, HML; American Council of Christian Laymen pamphlet, "Shall Our Churches Teach Christianity or Communism?" ca. 1949, RG17, NCC Records, Special Topics, Series III, Box 6, Folder 2, PHS; Glenwood Blackmore, "Is God a 'Collectivist' or a 'Communist'?" *UEA*, January 15, 1947, 3; NSC-68, *FRUS, 1950*, vol. I: 263. In general, see Whitfield, *Culture of the Cold War*, 77–100.

22. "Branded at Last!" *Methodist Challenge*, January 1949, 5; "A Personal Word," *One Methodist Voice*, January 1954, 2a; Miller, *Bishop G. Bromley Oxnam*, 519–531.

23. On the development of conservative ecumenism, see Wuthnow, *Restructuring of American Religion*; Van Engen, "Broadening Vision"; and Carpenter, 141–176, 211–232.

24. Niebuhr, "The Fight for Germany," *Life*, October 21, 1946, 65–72.

25. Luce to Niebuhr, January 8, 1949, Niebuhr papers, Box 8, LOC. On Luce's missionary upbringing and sense of religious mission, see Herzstein, *Henry R. Luce*, 24–29; and Herzstein, *Henry R. Luce*.

26. Melton to Senator Clyde Hoey, April 29, 1951, Melton volumes, Box 3, Volume 8, SHC-UNC. For conservative concerns about sovereignty and identity, see Carpenter, *Revive Us Again*, 105; and Lahr, *Millennial Dreams*, 39, 44–45. For fundamentalist concerns about prophecy, see Boyer, *When Time Shall Be No More*, 119–121. For the liberal Christian realist critique, see Niebuhr, "Illusion of World Government."

27. Anonymous missionary quoted in confidential memo, "Christian Interests and the Communist State in China," n.d., Box 301.014, Folder 3, WCC; McCulloch newsletter, January 11, 1948, McCulloch papers, Box 1, ABHS; Beijing convert

in letter to John Foster, January 26, 1948, Foster papers, Box 4, MNHS; Herzstein, *Henry R. Luce*, 63; Everett Drumright to Hull, March 16, 1944, *FRUS, 1944*, vol. VI: 378–381. On the missionary influence on America's China policy in the early Cold War, see Inboden, *Religion and American Foreign Policy*, 157–189 (Presbyterian Foreign Missions quoted on 170).

28. Shaw, *American Missionary in China*, 152–263; Inboden, *Religion and American Foreign Policy*, 160–161, 164–169 (Stuart quoted on 165).

29. Judd to Robbins Strong, May 30, 1946, Judd papers, Box 39, MNHS; Judd interview, 20–21, OHRO; Judd, *Autopsy on Our Blunders in Asia*. See also Inboden, *Religion and American Foreign Policy*, 161–163, 171–172.

30. Graham quoted in Martin, *Prophet with Honor*, 147; "Church Group Heads Laud U.N. on Korea," *NYT*, July 7, 1950, 5; Thanksgiving sermon, November 23, 1950, Coffin papers, Box 11, Folder 157, UTS; *World Alliance News Letter*, January 1953, 1. For an excellent overview on the Korean War and its effect on the Cold War as a whole, see Stueck, *Rethinking the Korean War*.

31. "Arise altogether" quoted in "World Revolution Is Called Danger," *NYT*, July 15, 1949, 15; Korean evangelical quoted in Lahr, *Millennial Dreams*, 59.

32. "Father of His Country?" *Time*, October 16, 1950; Jacobs, *America's Miracle Man*, 122–123; Luce quoted in Herzstein, *Henry R. Luce*, 114.

33. Carpenter, *Revive Us Again*, 177–186; Pierard, "Pax Americana"; Whaites, "Pursuing Partnership," 412–413 (Pierce quoted on 412); Van Engen, "Broadening Vision," 206–211.

34. Laubach, *World Is Learning Compassion*, 173, 190, 245.

35. Newton, *American Churchman in the Soviet Union*, 5. In general, see also Hollander, *Political Pilgrims*.

36. Casey, "Cultural Mission of Russian Orthodoxy," 257–258, 275; Oxnam, "Communism, Capitalism, and the Church," *CRT*, April 1946, 21.

37. "Report Urges Churches to Reject Both Communism and Capitalism," *NYT*, September 2, 1948, 1; WCC report quoted in "No Pentecost," *Time*, September 13, 1948; Hromadka quoted in "Argument at Amsterdam," *Time*, September 6, 1948. On the WCC's differences with the Truman administration, see Inboden, *Religion and American Foreign Policy*, 41–49, 128–137.

38. "The Churches and Human Rights," December 1948, FCC Records, RG18, Box 18, Folder 16, PHS; Nurser, *For All Peoples and All Nations*, 143–171; Niebuhr quoted in "Church Too Aloof, C. P. Taft Asserts," *NYT*, December 3, 1948, 52.

39. Leiper, "God's Design in This Atomic Age," *C&C*, March 17, 1947, 1–2; Herklots and Leiper, *Pilgrimage to Amsterdam*; Fosdick, "Prayer for Universal Peace," in promotional flyer for the World Congress of Religion, October 23–27, 1948, Box 225, Folder 4, CEIP; Nixon, *United Nations and Our Religious Heritage*, 64.

40. "U.S. Women Called to Pray for the U.N.," *NYT*, October 18, 1946, 2; United Church Women press release, "The Christian Woman's Action Program for World Peace," May 16, 1951, OF 2953, Box 1743, HSTL; "Women Answering Anti-U.N. Campaign," *NYT*, April 5, 1953, 17; "World Order Day in City Churches," *NYT*, October 23, 1948, 16; "8,000 Christians Support Making UN World Government," *Oklahoma Citizen*, November 1, 1950, 1, found in Holmes papers, Box 33, Folder 2, AHTL (the *Oklahoma Citizen* was not a regular community newspaper but the in-house organ of the Oklahoma World Federation Referendum Committee); Howard Carroll to Eisenhower, November 14, 1956, WHCF/OF 137, Box 687, DDEL; "Text of Statement on World Crisis by Catholic Bishops of U.S.," *NYT*, November 18, 1956, 84. On Catholics, see also Rossi, *Uncharted Territory*. On the support, see the polls in Table 2–5, Hero, *American Religious Groups View Foreign Policy*, 294–295.

41. "Church Group Favors Power to Discourage Russian Use of Force," *WP*, March

11, 1949, 1; National Study Conference quoted in Inboden, *Religion and American Foreign Policy*, 50; "Churchmen Argue on Atlantic Pact," *NYT*, March 11, 1949, 4.

42. Grace Wilson, newsletters from Hiroshima, February 9, 1950, and March 6, 1950, both in Andrews papers, Box 1, Folder 37, UW; Parsons, Conway, and Mahony, *Peace in the Atomic Age*, esp. 16; journal entries, May 20, 1948, and October 9, 1948, *Journals of David E. Lilienthal*, vol. 2, 347, 419; Boyer, *By the Bomb's Early Light*, 218; Muste to John Stamm, March 6, 1950, FCC Records, RG18, Box 11, Folder 6, PHS.

43. Danielson, "Christianity, Dissent, and the Cold War"; Muste quoted in Wittner, *Rebels Against War*, 185. More generally, see Kosek, *Acts of Conscience*, 191–227.

44. "Instead of Rearmament and War," pamphlet for the Conference of Church People on World Peace, Washington, D.C., April 6–7, 1948, FCC Records, RG18, Box 27, Folder 11, PHS; "The Methodist Church and War and Peace," adopted by the General Conference of the Methodist Church, May 7, 1948, FCC Records, RG18, Box 71, Folder 3, PHS.

45. Niebuhr, "Our Chance for Peace," *C&C*, February 17, 1947, 1.

46. Pamphlet of the Commission on a Just and Durable Peace, "Problems of Peace in East Asia," ca. 1947, FCC Records, RG18, Box 26, Folder 9, PHS; FCC Records, RG18, Box 32, Folder 4, PHS.

47. Rowland M. Cross to Van Kirk, November 4, 1949, with enclosed Foreign Missions Conference draft statement, "The Churches and American Policy in the Far East," FCC Records, RG18, Box 40, PHS.

48. East Harlem Peace Council flyer, October 1950, East Harlem Protestant Parish records, Box 29, UTS; Foreign Policy Commission of Christian Action draft policy statement, "The People's Republic of China and the United Nations," October 28, 1955, Niebuhr papers, Box 2, LOC; Eleanor Roosevelt to Truman, July 20, 1951, OF 2953, Box 1743, HSTL; "Mrs. Roosevelt Finds Need for Peiping in U.N.," *NYT*, October 14, 1959, 3.

49. The Oblate Fathers and Brothers of Pass Christian, Mississippi, to Eisenhower, November 11, 1956, WHCF/OF 137, Box 687, DDEL.

50. Draft of "ADA Statement on Foreign Policy," November 1955, Box 1, and Niebuhr to Ernest Lefever, June 19, 1956, Box 8, both in Niebuhr papers, LOC.

51. Donald Tewksbury, "The Significance of the Bandung Conference," *World Alliance News Letter*, June 1955, 3; American Baptist Women circular, "Are Your Attitudes Showing and Growing?" April 1957, Martin papers, Box 2, ABHS; Ekbladh, *Great American Mission*, 105–108, 144, 171, 175–176, 188.

52. Race Relations Sunday quotes from "Churches Give Day to Race Relations," *NYT*, February 14, 1949, 17; "The Service for World Day of Prayer," United Church Women, March 5, 1954, McConnell papers, Box 1, MNHS.

53. Findlay, *Church People in the Struggle*, 11–27. On the causal links between the civil rights movement and the Cold War, see Dudziak, *Cold War Civil Rights*; and Borstelmann, *Cold War and the Color Line*.

54. King, *Stride Toward Freedom*, 145; Mays, *Born to Rebel*, 260–261; Dorrien, *Making of American Liberal Theology*, vol. 2, 415–434. On Mays's influence on King, see also Sitkoff, *King*, 11–14, 45.

55. On these earlier tensions arising from blacks campaigning for freedom abroad while enduring oppression at home, see Slotkin, *Lost Battalions*; and Lentz-Smith, *Freedom Struggles*.

56. "Report of Committee on Social Education and Action," minutes of the Synod of Catawba, Danville, Va., October 21–23, 1947, 18, African-American Presbyteries and Synods Collection, RG395, Series IV, Box 1, Folder 19, PHS.

57. *A.M.E. Church Year Book of Negro Churches, 1948–1949*, 17, 38–39; "A Ray of

Light in African Race Relations," *World Associates Newsletter*, June 1954, Mott papers, Box 52, Folder 958, YDS.

58. McMullen to Niebuhr, April 2, 1954, Niebuhr papers, Box 8, LOC; "A Christian Looks at the Atomic Age," *Social Action*, October 1957, 9; Jane Evans to Eisenhower and attached resolutions of the National Federation of Temple Sisterhoods 20th Biennial Assembly, February 13–16, 1955, WHCF/GF 118-B, Box 682, DDEL.

59. King, *Stride Toward Freedom*, 95; Wittner, *Rebels Against War*, 187, 190, 232–235.

60. "7 Pacifists Insist on Guilty Pleas," *NYT*, September 29, 1955, 14; "9 Pacifists Seized in Defying Alert," *NYT*, May 7, 1958, 30.

61. Craig, *Glimmer of a New Leviathan*, 82–86; Niebuhr to Bennett, December 16, 1957, Niebuhr papers, Series 2, Box 1, Folder III-3, UTS.

PART VIII. REFORMATION AND COUNTERREFORMATION

1. Stewart Herman, "Christian Responsibility and International Affairs," March 9, 1963, NCC Records, RG17, Box 5, Folder 8, PHS.

2. "Protestant Unit Will Visit Soviet," *NYT*, March 1, 1962, 10; NCC quoted in "Churchmen Report on Moscow Visit," *United Church Herald*, October 4, 1962, 26; Blake quoted in "O.K. on Red-U.S. Church Visits," *Kansas City Times*, March 1, 1962, 2.

3. Endy, *Cold War Holidays*; Osgood, *Total Cold War*, 214–252 (USIA quoted on 216); "Discussions Held at Seabury House Between US & USSR Churchmen," *The Witness*, March 21, 1963, 5–6; R. H. Edwin Espy to NCC members, April 2, 1963, NCC Records, RG17, Box 5, Folder 16, PHS; "Baptist Call for Talks with China," *San Francisco Chronicle*, May 23, 1965, 26.

4. "Soviet Presses War on Religion," *NYT*, Jan 7, 1963, 7; "What's News," *WSJ*, Jan 4, 1963, 1; "Siberians Ask U.S. Help in 'Persecution,' " *WP*, January 4, 1963, A1; "Stoyan Revealed as Secret Police, KGB Members," *Christian Beacon*, March 14, 1963, 1, 8; K. N. Calkin to Radio Station WHHH in Warren, Ohio, February 3, 1963, and George McMillin to NCC, March 26, 1963, both in NCC Records, RG17, Box 5, Folder 16, PHS.

CHAPTER TWENTY-FIVE. THE REVOLUTIONARY CHURCH IN A REVOLUTIONARY AGE

1. "Inaugural Address," January 20, 1961, *PPP: John F. Kennedy, 1961*, 1, 3.

2. "Inaugural Address," January 20, 1965, *PPP: Lyndon B. Johnson, 1965*, Book I, 73.

3. Salinger, *With Kennedy*, 70.

4. Dallek, *Unfinished Life*, 23–30, 86–87, 146–148; Smith, *Faith and the Presidency*, 260–266 (Eunice Kennedy quoted on 260); Sorensen, *Kennedy*, 17, 19; Schlesinger, *Thousand Days*, 107–108.

5. Morrison quoted in Smith, *Faith and the Presidency*, 269; Oxnam and Blake quoted in Silk, *Spiritual Politics*, 121; letters to Wine, August 26, 1960, and September 7, 1960, both in Wine papers, Series 1, Box 1, JFKL.

6. "Transcript of Kennedy Talk to Ministers and Questions and Answers," *NYT*, September 13, 1960, 22. On Kennedy's religion and the 1960 election, see Carty, *Catholic in the White House?*; and Casey, *Making of a Catholic President*.

7. Moyers to O'Donnell, February 2, 1961, POF/SF, Box 96, JFKL; election analysis from Smith, *Faith and the Presidency*, 271.

8. Resident quoted in Caro, *Years of Lyndon Johnson*, 92; Valenti, *Very Human President*, 17–18; Califano, *Triumph and Tragedy of Lyndon Johnson*, 334–335.

See also the impressions of LBJ's brother Sam Houston Johnson in Johnson, *My Brother Lyndon*, 35–37. On Johnson's upbringing and religious habits, see Woods, *LBJ*, 41, 685, 688, 799; and Woods, "Conflicted Hegemon," 749. On the Graham-Johnson relationship, see Gibbs and Duffy, *Preacher and the Presidents*, 113–156, esp. 118–125.

9. On the Rights Revolution, see Patterson, *Grand Expectations*, 562–592, 637–648; Garrow, *Liberty and Sexuality*; Walker, *Rights Revolution*; and Skrentny, *Minority Rights Revolution*.

10. Historians quoted are Isserman and Kazin, *America Divided*, 249. For a similar perspective, see Silk, *Spiritual Politics*, 108–135; Wuthnow, *Restructuring of American Religion*; Ellwood, *Sixties Spiritual Awakening*; and Allitt, *Religion in America since 1945*.

11. On the Court's decisions, see Zimmerman, *Whose America?*, 160–185; Dierenfield, *Battle over School Prayer*; and Viteritti, *Last Freedom*, 100–107.

12. Vahanian, *Death of God*, xxxii; Van Buren, *Secular Meaning of the Gospel*; Cox, *Secular City*; Cox, *God's Revolution*, 105; Altizer and Hamilton, *Radical Theology and the Death of God*; "Is God Dead?" *Time*, April 8, 1966. On Christian existentialism and anxiety, see Rossinow, *Politics of Authenticity*, esp. 53–84; and, related, on the widespread acceptance of the doctrine of original sin, see Finstuen, *Original Sin and Everyday Protestants*, esp. 13–46; and Stevens, *God-Fearing and Free*. On Cold War disillusionment and its effects in a more secular context, see Suri, *Power and Protest*.

13. Rose, *Grass Roots Church*, 3; Fletcher, *Situation Ethics*.

14. Cone, *Black Theology and Black Power*, 39, 41; Cone, *Black Theology of Liberation*; Cleage, *Black Messiah*; Hough, *Black Power and White Protestants*. On the Black Power moment in black Protestantism, see Ellwood, *Sixties Spiritual Awakening*, 272–277; and Allitt, *Religion in America since 1945*, 111–115.

15. Greeley, *Catholic Revolution*; Dillon, *Catholic Identity*, 45–53; O'Toole, *Faithful*, 199–265.

16. On the new pluralism, see Hutchison, *Religious Pluralism in America*, 222–224; and Wuthnow, *America and the Challenges of Religious Diversity*. On the growth of New Age and other spiritualisms, see Clecak, *America's Quest for the Ideal Self*, 125–156; and Wuthnow, *After Heaven*, 52–84. On the complex mix of Islam, traditional African religion, pan-Africanism, and Black Power, see Ellwood, *Sixties Spiritual Awakening*, 179–180; Jackson, *Islam and the Blackamerican*, esp. 131–170; McCloud, *Transnational Muslims in American Society*; Gomez, *Black Crescent*, 203–370; and Joseph, *Waiting 'Til the Midnight Hour*, 18–19, 101–113, 222–226.

17. "Nationalism Held Peril to Church," *NYT*, January 11, 1960, 11; Cameron Hall (NCC Executive Director) to Kennedy, August 13, 1962, WHCF, Box 885, JFKL.

18. On the Kennedy administration and modernization, see Latham, *Modernization as Ideology*. On Rostow, see Preston, *War Council*, 75–100; and Milne, *America's Rasputin*, esp. 41–72.

19. "Remarks at the Dedication Breakfast of International Christian Leadership, Inc.," February 9, 1961, *PPP: John F. Kennedy, 1961*, 77; "Remarks at the 10th Annual Presidential Prayer Breakfast," March 1, 1962, *PPP: John F. Kennedy, 1962*, 175.

20. Harlan Cleveland, "The Ethics of Mutual Development," n.d. [ca. 1961], Cleveland personal papers, Box 38, JFKL; Moyers to O'Donnell, January 28, 1961, WHCF/RM 3-3, Box 887, JFKL.

21. *Mater et Magistra*, "Christianity and Social Progress," May 15, 1961, in Carlen, ed. *Papal Encyclicals*, vol. 5, 63–64, 67.

22. *Pacem in Terris*, "Establishing Universal Peace in Truth, Justice, Charity, and

Liberty," April 11, 1963, in Carlen, ed. *Papal Encyclicals*, vol. 5, 125; Reinhardt (Rome) to Rusk, March 8, 1963, NSF/CF/Vatican, Box 191A, JFKL.

23. "U.S. Ponders Role of Pope in Cold War," *WP*, April 7, 1963, A1; Cousins memcon, n.d., attached to Dungan to Kennedy, January 19, 1963, Thomas L. Hughes (INR) to Rusk, April 27, 1963, CIA Office of National Estimates, staff memo 27–63, "Change in the Church," May 13, 1963, all in NSF/CF/Vatican, Box 191A, JFKL. For other exploratory contacts, see Schlesinger to Kennedy, November 2, 1962, NSF/CF/Vatican, Box 191A, JFKL; and Dungan to Kennedy, June 22, 1963, Dungan personal papers, Box 11, JFKL. Cleverly, in calling for a "peace race," the pope was simply quoting Kennedy's own words. See "Address in New York City before the General Assembly of the United Nations," September 25, 1961, *PPP: John F. Kennedy, 1961*, 620.

24. "Text of Catholic Bishops' Statement Issued at Close of Annual Meeting," *NYT*, November 19, 1961, 82. On leftist Catholic social thought in the middle Cold War, both liberal and radical, see Prentiss, *Debating God's Economy*.

25. Shaull, "Revolutionary Change in Theological Perspective," 31; Cox, *God's Revolution*, 53, 104.

26. Henry Cadbury to Kennedy, "Memorandum on World Order and Disarmament," May 1, 1962, POF/SF, Box 106, JFKL; Sidney Regner to Kennedy, and attached "Report of the Committee on Justice and Peace" from 1962 annual convention, WHCF/SF, Box 359, JFKL; Merton to Hans Reinhold, June 6, 1962, Reinhold papers, Box 7, Folder 5, BC; Merton, et al., *Breakthrough to Peace*; order of service for churches nationwide on World Community Day, November 6, 1964, Martin papers, Box 1A, ABHS. On the sources of Merton's antinuclear activism, see Powaski, *Thomas Merton on Nuclear Weapons*; and Farrell, "Thomas Merton and the Religion of the Bomb."

27. Cox newsletter, June 8, 1970, Lehmann papers, Box 22, Folder 37, PTS.

28. "2 Methodists Bid Missions Change," *NYT*, January 11, 1969, 19; "U.S. Catholics Raise Missions' Goal to $22-Million," *NYT*, October 3, 1968, 30; Novak, *Theology for Radical Politics*; *Populorum Progressio*, "The Development of Peoples," March 26, 1967, in Carlen, ed., *Papal Encyclicals*, vol. 5, 183–201; World Council of Churches, "Towards Justice and Peace in International Affairs," 254, 256; Welch, "Mobilizing Morality"; Sweeney to Blake, January 4, 1968, Sweeney papers, Box 10, Folder 26, BC. On Catholic opposition to world population control, see Connelly, *Fatal Misconception*.

29. Schlesinger, *Thousand Days*, 298.

30. State Department to Walter Rogers, June 28, 1962, WHCF, Box 885, JFKL; NSC to Peter Haas, November 1, 1963, WHCF/SF, Box 375, Folder HU 4-3, JFKL; State Department to Steven Derounian, July 9, 1962, WHCF/SF, Box 375, Folder HU 4-3, JFKL.

31. Quoted in Preston, *War Council*, 120.

32. Rusk, *As I Saw It*, 34–35, 51–52, 61–62, 188 (quoted on 61, 71); Schoenbaum, *Waging Peace and War*, 35–37, 40–41, 53; Zeiler, *Dean Rusk*, 4–6.

33. Rusk, *As I Saw It*, 389–390.

34. For Kennedy's commitment to détente, see Trachtenberg, *Constructed Peace*, 352–402. For Johnson's, see Costigliola, "Lyndon B. Johnson, Germany, and 'the End of the Cold War,'" 192–208; Schwartz, *Lyndon Johnson and Europe*; Suri, "Lyndon Johnson and the Global Disruption of 1968," 58–77; and Preston, *War Council*, 69–74.

35. Thich, *Vietnam*. On Buddhist political activism in South Vietnam during the war, see Topmiller, *Lotus Unleashed*. On Diem's Catholicism, see Jacobs, *America's Miracle Man*.

CHAPTER TWENTY-SIX. THE VALLEY OF THE SHADOW OF DEATH

1. Quoted in Levy, *Debate Over Vietnam*, 95.
2. On these points, see especially Logevall, *Choosing War.*
3. Levy, *Debate Over Vietnam*, 92–93 (Heschel quoted on 93).
4. Merton to Johnson, February 20, 1965, WHCF/NF, Folder: Merti, LBJL; Catholic Peace Fellowship pamphlet, "Peace on Earth, Peace in Vietnam," ca. December 1965, IWPPC, Box 2, Folder 27, YDS. The most thorough account of Catholic antiwar activism is McNeal, *Harder Than War*, 131–172.
5. On the radical and socioeconomic aspects of the civil rights movement, see Hall, "Long Civil Rights Movement"; Jackson, *From Civil Rights to Human Rights*; Lassiter, "De Jure/De Facto Segregation"; Gilmore, *Defying Dixie*; Sugrue, *Sweet Land of Liberty*; and Tuck, *We Ain't What We Ought to Be*, 281–325. On the Poor People's Campaign, see Garrow, *Bearing the Cross*, 575–624.
6. King on the Peace Corps quoted in Jackson, *From Civil Rights to Human Rights*, 130; King on the Bay of Pigs quoted in Hall, *Peace and Freedom*, 8–9.
7. Garrow, *Bearing the Cross*, 394, 428–430, 436–461, 538–578; Hall, *Peace and Freedom*, 26, 34–35, 108; Jackson, *From Civil Rights to Human Rights*, 308–328 ("$53" and "Negro" quoted on 264, 337); Rieder, *Word of the Lord*, 132–133.
8. "A Time to Break Silence," April 4, 1967, in Washington, ed., *Testament of Hope*, 234; "Remaining Awake Through a Great Revolution," March 31, 1968, ibid., 275; "racist decision-making" quoted in Hall, *Peace and Freedom*, 10. For King's general critique of U.S. foreign policy, see Sitkoff, *King*, 218–219.
9. For Coffin, see Goldstein, *William Sloane Coffin, Jr.*, esp. 145–224. For Johnson, see sermon, "God's Gift to Us," Memorial Methodist Church, Asbury, N.C., December 18, 1966, Johnson papers, Box 6, Folder 521, MSCD. For Pike, see Robertson, *Passionate Pilgrim*, 195–198 (quoted on 195–196).
10. Bennett, "View of an American Theologian," 36; Bennett testimony before the Senate Foreign Relations Committee, "The Moral Effects of the War on the Life of Our Country," May 7, 1970, Lehmann papers, Box 56, Folder 17, PTS.
11. Quotations are from letters by Niebuhr to Bennett, all in Niebuhr papers, Series 2, Box 1, Folder II-3, UTS: "futile and cruel" from letter of September 12, 1967; "whole argument" from August 31, 1967; "Nixon's madness" from April 6, 1970. On *C&C*, see Hulsether, *Building a Protestant Left*, 125–134.
12. "Clerics Accuse U.S. of War Crimes," *NYT*, February 4, 1968, 1, 6; Drinan, *Democracy, Dissent, and Disorder*, 67–68; Waldemar Argow sermon, "The Larger Implications of Vietnam," First Unitarian Church of Toledo, September 19, 1965, Pamphlet Collection, Box 1, AHTL.
13. "Clergymen Protest Court-Martial of Marine," *LAT*, August 16, 1968, 3; "Court Bars Service by Antiwar Clergy," *WP*, February 6, 1968, B1.
14. Wells, *War Within*, 192; Foley, *Confronting the War Machine*, 76–109, 272–282, 308–322; Robinson, *Abraham Went Out*, 131–134, 194–220. For a contemporary view on conscientious objection, see also Minear, "Conscience and the Draft."
15. Philip Berrigan interview 1, 31, and interview 2, 62, OHRO; Berrigan, *Prison Journals*, 19. For the Berrigans' story and Vietnam, see McNeal, *Harder Than War*, 173–210; Polner and O'Grady, *Disarmed and Dangerous*, 166–250; and Bivins, *Fracture of Good Order*, 115–151.
16. Hall, *Because of Their Faith*; Hall, "CALCAV and Religious Opposition to the Vietnam War," 35–45. For Bennett, see Roger Shinn to UTS colleagues, October 12, 1967, Lehmann papers, Box 56, Folder 18, PTS. For CALCAV affiliates, see, for example, Ernst and Baldwin, "Not So Silent Minority," 119–120, 138–141.

17. Fernandez quoted in Wells, *War Within*, 74; "National Fast Will Be Extended in Southland," *LAT*, April 6, 1968, B7.

18. Buddhist crisis is from Forrestal to Bundy, June 28, 1963, NSF/CF/Vatican, Box 191A, JFKL; "deeply worried" from Reinhardt to Rusk, February 10, 1965, *FRUS, 1964–1968*, vol. XII: 641; Rusk to Johnson, September 25, 1965, NSF/CF/Vatican, Vol. 1, Box 231, LBJL. For the Vatican's peace moves, see Rusk to Reinhardt, November 17, 1966, NSF/CF/Vatican, Vol. 1, Box 231, LBJL; Rusk to Johnson, January 3, 1967, *FRUS, 1964–1968*, vol. V: 10–13; Reinhardt to Rusk, February 3, 1967, NSF/CF/Vatican, Vol. 1, Box 231, LBJL; memcon, Paul VI and Johnson, Vatican, December 23, 1967, *FRUS, 1964–1968*, vol. XII: 660–666; Rostow to Johnson, March 11, 1968, *FRUS, 1964–1968*, vol. VI: 365; memcon, March 18, 1968, ibid., 406–407; Rusk to Bunker, March 21, 1968, NSF/CF/Vietnam, Box 94, Folder 6B, LBJL. For Ho Chi Minh, see "Ho Appeals to Pope for Peace Help," *WP*, February 14, 1967, 1.

19. Shapley, *Promise and Power*, 407–437, 443–444, 498–553 ("McNamara's War" and secretary quoted on 299, 444); Hendrickson, *Living and the Dead*, 333–334. On McNamara's turn against the war while still at the Pentagon, see Gardner, *Pay Any Price*, 378–406.

20. Shapley, *Promise and Power*, 6–8, 354–355.

21. McNamara, *In Retrospect*, 216; Karnow, *Vietnam*, 512; details on Morrison's death from Hendrickson, *Living and the Dead*, 187–191. Incredibly, Morrison had Emily, his year-old baby daughter, in his arms just before he struck the match that would light the kerosene that covered his body. At the last moment, he let her go, and she fell to the ground, unharmed.

22. Torgersen statement at City Hall, Worcester, Mass., May 8, 1970, Torgersen papers, Box 1, ABHS.

23. Board of Deacons of the First Baptist Church, Holden, Mass., to Torgersen, May 26, 1970, ibid.; Torgersen statement at Annual Meeting of the First Baptist Church of Worcester, May 19, 1970, ibid.; sermon, "A Minister's Response to President Nixon," First Baptist Church of Worcester, April 15, 1971, ibid.

24. Levy, *Debate Over Vietnam*, 95–96; 1968 poll and Lutheran magazine quoted in Hall, "CALCAV and Religious Opposition to the Vietnam War," 44.

25. Levy, *Debate Over Vietnam*, 94; Loveland, *American Evangelicals and the U.S. Military*, 118–138; Granberg and Campbell, "Certain Aspects of Religiosity."

26. "Angels in Viet Nam," *AHJ*, January 1967, 23–24; Resolutions No. 10 and 12, adopted at the ACCC Convention, Harrisburg, Penn., April 27, 1967, Hall-Hoag Collection, Christian Religious Right, Box 15:1:148/5/1, JHL; "Why Lose" quoted in "McIntire Puts Blame on Nixon," *Courier-Post* (Camden, N.J.), September 29, 1970; McIntire and Hargis quoted in Allitt, *Religion in America since 1945*, 100.

27. On Graham's ambivalence about Vietnam, see Martin, *Prophet with Honor*, 343–348, 422–424 (Graham quoted on 345).

28. "All-out war with Red China" and "I have no sympathy" quoted in Martin, *Prophet with Honor*, 311–312; "Never!" quoted in Frady, *Billy Graham*, 426.

29. Graham quoted in Frady, *Billy Graham*, 422, 424; Wirt, *Social Conscience of the Evangelical*, 125.

30. Ramsey, "Ethics of Intervention," 291; Ramsey, *Just War*, 497; Hulsether, *Building a Protestant Left*, 125–128; McKenzie, *Paul Ramsey's Ethics*, 109–130.

31. Nichols, *Uneasy Alliance*, 101–107; Gill, "Politics of Ecumenical Disunity," 179–187; Loveland, *American Evangelicals and the U.S. Military*, 139–164.

32. Levy, *Debate Over Vietnam*, 96–100; Jacobs, *America's Miracle Man*; Fisher, "Second Catholic President."

33. Philip Berrigan interview 1, 43–44, OHRO; "Catholic Bishops Back War Policy," *NYT,* November 22, 1966, 1, 18; "Text of Bishops' Pastoral Statement on Peace and Vietnam," *NYT,* November 22, 1966, 18; Morgan, "Change of Course."

34. Miscamble, "Francis Cardinal Spellman"; Jacobs, *America's Miracle Man,* 32, 134–135, 185–188, 233, 260–261; Polner and O'Grady, *Disarmed and Dangerous,* 122–132; Cooney, *American Pope,* 240–245, 286–294, 298–299; Westmoreland, *Soldier Reports,* 368.

35. Quoted in Lienesch, *Redeeming America,* 202, 204.

CHAPTER TWENTY-SEVEN. GET THEE BEHIND ME, SATAN

1. On Nixon and Kissinger's response to the crises, see Logevall and Preston, eds., *Nixon in the World.*

2. Woodward and Bernstein, *Final Days,* 422–424 (Nixon quoted on 423, Kissinger on 424); Nixon, *Memoirs,* 1076–1077; Kissinger, *Years of Upheaval,* 1207–1210. See also Isaacson, *Kissinger,* 597–600.

3. Morris, *Richard Milhous Nixon,* 21–31, 52–53, 84–87 (Morris and friend quoted on 31, 85); Ambrose, *Nixon,* vol. 1, 30–31.

4. Ambrose, *Nixon,* vol. 1, 57–58; Brodie, *Richard Nixon,* 162–164; campaign ad quoted in Greenberg, *Nixon's Shadow,* 19.

5. "Inaugural Address," January 20, 1969, *PPP: Richard Nixon, 1969,* 1–2; Domke and Coe, *God Strategy,* 61; Graham, *Just As I Am,* 440–442. On the Nixon-Graham relationship, including Graham's disillusionment, see Gibbs and Duffy, *Preacher and the Presidents,* 157–231. On Nixon's desire to emulate his mother's faith, at least rhetorically, see also Brodie, *Richard Nixon,* 62–63; and Greenberg, *Nixon's Shadow,* 273. On his "evangelical strategy," see Williams, *God's Own Party,* 89–103.

6. Suri, *Henry Kissinger and the American Century,* 16–51 (Kissinger quoted on 269). On Kissinger's German-Jewish upbringing, see also Isaacson, *Kissinger,* 17–32.

7. Martin, *With God on Our Side,* 75–76 (Kennedy quoted on 75); Kruse, "Beyond the Southern Cross," 291; Overstreet, *Strange Tactics of Extremism,* 143–148; CACC newsletter, February 1962, Smith papers, Box 56, BHL; Feldman to Kennedy, August 15, 1963, POF/SF, Box 106, JFKL. On the dramatic but not always straightforward growth of conservatism in the 1960s, religious or otherwise, see Isserman and Kazin, *America Divided,* 213–228; Klatch, *Generation Divided*; Schoenwald, *Time for Choosing*; and Lichtman, *White Protestant Nation,* 232–280. On religious conservatism specifically, see Williams, *God's Own Party,* 49–88.

8. Henry, *Faith at the Frontiers,* 47; Munn, Life Line Freedom Talk radio transcript, October 31, 1971, Vice Presidential papers, Box 172, GRFL.

9. Henry, *Plea for Evangelical Demonstration,* 7. On the Christian schools controversy, see Crespino, "Civil Rights and the Religious Right." The best overall accounts of the rise of the Religious Right are Martin, *With God on Our Side*; and Dochuk, *From Bible Belt to Sunbelt.* For an excellent survey that analyzes religion within a range of other conservative issues, see Micklethwait and Wooldridge, *Right Nation.*

10. "Text of Proclamation by Gov. Wallace," *NYT,* June 12, 1963, 20; Carter, *Politics of Rage,* 298–299; Link, *Righteous Warrior,* 125–127, 176–182 (Helms quoted on 179); Harding, *Book of Jerry Falwell.*

11. Isserman and Kazin, *America Divided,* 253–255; Wolfe, *Mauve Gloves & Madmen,* 117–155; Boyer, "Evangelical Resurgence" (*Newsweek* and church figures quoted on 29, 33); Manza and Brooks, "Changing Political Fortunes of Mainline Protestants"; Kell and Camp, *In the Name of the Father.*

12. Kruse, "Beyond the Southern Cross," esp. 292–295, 298–301; Dochuk, "They Locked God Outside the Iron Curtain"; Dochuk, "Evangelicalism Becomes Southern"; Dochuk, *From Bible Belt to Sunbelt.*

13. Steffgen to Otto Zink, March 27, 1961, Smith papers, Box 53, BHL.

14. Kellstedt, et al., "Faith Transformed," 272–273, 277–278; Boyer, "Evangelical Resurgence," 36–37; Wuthnow, *Restructuring of American Religion*, 84–86; Allitt, *Catholic Intellectuals*, 121–162, 252–261, 270–278, 286–288; Steinfels, "Roman Catholics and American Politics"; McGirr, *Suburban Warriors*, 50, 107; Isserman and Kazin, *America Divided*, 221–222; Patterson, *Restless Giant*, 132–133. On Catholic traditionalism, see Dinges and Hitchcock, "Roman Catholic Traditionalism," 66–74, 78–97; Komonchak, "Interpreting the Council"; and Cuneo, *Smoke of Satan.*

15. John R. Brown III to Harry Dent, December 19, 1969, WHCF/RM 3-1, Box 18, RNL.

16. Martin, *Prophet With Honor*, 312; Wirt, *Social Conscience of the Evangelical*, 136.

17. Robert Goepfert to Dirksen, May 21, 1968, WHCF/SF/RM, Box 1, LBJL. On the intimate relationship between anti-statist views on religion and economics, see Moreton, *To Serve God and Wal-Mart.* For an intriguing explanation on how evangelicals made a peace (of sorts) with the Cold War state, see Schäfer, "What Marx, Lenin, and Stalin Needed."

18. Emerson and Smith, *Divided by Faith*; Wuthnow, *Restructuring of American Religion*, 146–148; Crespino, *In Search of Another Country*, 63–73, 144–172; *Christian Beacon* and Falwell quoted in Martin, *With God on Our Side*, 79, 69. My thinking on the nonracial sources of the New Right, especially the anti-statism of conservative views on political economy, has been shaped by Durr, *Behind the Backlash*; Shafer and Johnston, *End of Southern Exceptionalism*; Lassiter, *Silent Majority* (Book quoted on 285–286); Shermer, "Origins of the Conservative Ascendancy"; and Phillips-Fein, *Invisible Hands.*

19. Formisano, *Boston Against Busing*, 10–15, 19, 41–43, 72–73, 110–120 ("Mother Superior" quoted on 2).

20. Graham, *World Aflame*, 1; Henry, *Faith at the Frontiers*, 47, 50.

21. Graham, *World Aflame*, 9; Reynolds quoted in ACCC fund-raising letter, May 1965, Hall-Hoag Collection, Christian Religious Right, Box 15:1:148/2/1, JHL; Hargis, *Communist America*, vii; Hargis, *Far Left*; "The Russian Space Ships," *The Herald*, September 19, 1962, 1; Charles Robertson newsletter, ca. 1962, Smith papers, Box 53, BHL; P. S. Lipscombe and Henry Patten, on behalf of the Missionary Baptist Pastors' Conference of Philadelphia, to Kennedy, June 26, 1962, WHCF/RM 2, Box 886, JFKL.

22. Kirk, "Struggle for Power with Communism," 3–5.

23. Doris Phillips, et al, to Kennedy, with Peale sermon attached, both September 24, 1961, WHCF/SF, Box 920, JFKL.

24. Memcon, June 24, 1959, *FRUS, 1958–1960*, vol. VI: 540; Walsh, "Cuban Refugee Children," a firsthand account by a priest who took part in refugee relief; Martin, *With God on Our Side*, 77.

25. Moyers to O'Donnell, August 22, 1962, WHCF, Box 885, JFKL; "Peace Corps Ties Stir Church Issue," *NYT*, June 19, 1961, 1; Nichols, *Uneasy Alliance*, 95–99.

26. "Anti-Red Dispute Grips Illinoisans," *NYT*, May 21, 1961, 54; Loveland, *American Evangelicals and the U.S. Military*, 100–117; Bacevich, *New American Militarism*, 138–146.

27. Hargis quoted in Morris, *Preachers*, 300; Christian Nationalist Crusade booklet, "Kissinger—A National Disaster," ca. 1975, Smith papers, Box 92, BHL; Schlafly and Ward, *Kissinger on the Couch*, 16, 17.

28. Martin, *With God on Our Side*, 203–204; Falwell to Marrs, July 10, 1975, Marrs papers, Box 25, GRFL.

29. Gergen to Rhatican and Brannon, and attached questions from *Christianity Today*, September 23, 1976, Gergen files, Box 8, GRFL; "What Is Communism?" *Applied Christianity*, November 1973, 6. On Christian anti-statism and foreign policy, see also Preston, "Universal Nationalism."

30. Bundy quoted in Overstreet, *Strange Tactics of Extremism*, 182; "U.N.'s Yule Cards Decried in D.A.R.," *NYT*, November 23, 1961, 13; 20th Century Reformation Hour pamphlet, "UNICEF Trick: The Spy Treatment," ca. 1966, McIntire papers, Box 1, Folder 5, PTS; "Battle Flags," *AHJ*, May 1963, 12.

31. "Metropolitan Nikodim," ca. 1975, McIntire papers, Box 1, Folder 4, PTS; Ashbrook, "World Council of Churches: A Case of Pinkeye," *CR*, December 18, 1975, H-13022.

32. Boyer, *When Time Shall Be No More*, 262–266, 276–278 (fundamentalist quoted on 264); Lienesch, *Redeeming America*, 237–238; "Common Market" quoted in R. S. McGrew, "Christ's Return Before the Great Tribulation," *AHJ*, June 1963, 57; Lindsey, *Late Great Planet Earth*, 94–96. On LaHaye's worldview, especially as it is expressed in his novels, see McAlister, "Prophecy, Politics, and the Popular."

33. Dobson quoted in *With God on Our Side*, 236. On the bases of evangelicalism and fundamentalism, see Ammerman, "North American Protestant Fundamentalism," 14–16; Marty, "Fundamentals of Fundamentalism," esp. 21; Marsden, *Understanding Fundamentalism and Evangelicalism*, 67–68; and Owen, Wald, and Hill, "Authoritarian or Authority-Minded?"

34. Quoted in Boyer, *When Time Shall Be No More*, 263. On the 1970s as a transitional era for economics, see Maier, "Consigning the Twentieth Century to History"; and Sargent, "United States and Globalization."

35. UN General Assembly Resolution 3379, November 10, 1975, *United Nations Resolutions*, Series 1, vol. 15, 524; "Huge Rally Here Condemns U.N. Anti-Zionism Move," *NYT*, November 12, 1975, 1; Moynihan quoted in "A Moment of Truth," *WSJ*, October 24, 1975, 16; Roland Elliott to NCCJ, December 15, 1975, WHCF/Name File, Box 2295, GRFL; "Senate to Reassess Membership in U.N.," *WP*, November 12, 1975, 1; "Congress Explores Pullout of U.S. from U.N. Units," *WP*, November 27, 1975, K22.

36. "News Summary and Index," *NYT*, July 3, 1975, 33; Edmondson and Schlafly quoted in Critchlow, *Phyllis Schlafly*, 245, 247–248.

CHAPTER TWENTY-EIGHT. A JUDEO-CHRISTIAN FOREIGN POLICY

1. Quoted in Allitt, *Religion in America since 1945*, 94–95.

2. Novick, *Holocaust in American Life*, 127–142.

3. Tanenbaum lecture, "The Meaning of Israel: A Jewish View," Southern Baptist Theological Seminary, August 18, 1969, Drinan papers, Box 1, BC; Shapiro, *Time for Healing*, 201–213 (Liebman quoted on 201).

4. Allitt, *Religion in America since 1945*, 98; Shapiro, *Time for Healing*, 184–185; Jacobson, *Roots Too*; McAlister, *Epic Encounters*, 155–197.

5. Smith, *Foreign Attachments*, 57–58, 110–113; Shapiro, *Time for Healing*, 211 (for Himmelfarb, see 219). For a much stronger argument that assigns predominant influence to the Israel lobby, see Mearsheimer and Walt, *Israel Lobby*. For a critique of Mearsheimer and Walt, see Preston, "Israel Lobby." On Jews as loyal Democrats, see Zeitz, "If I Am Not for Myself."

6. Lindsey, *Late Great Planet Earth*, esp. 42–58. On Christian Zionism, see Boyer, *When Time Shall Be No More*, 181–224; and Lienesch, *Redeeming America*, 229–237.
7. CCI Notebook No. 14, October 1973, Cushman papers, Box 11, UAD.
8. The standard work remains Garthoff, *Détente and Confrontation*. But see also Gaddis, *Strategies of Containment*, 272–341.
9. On the issue of Soviet Jewry before the 1970s, see Ro'i, *Struggle for Soviet Jewish Emigration*. On the emergence of a global human rights discourse in the 1970s, see Morgan, "Seventies and the Rebirth of Human Rights"; and Moyn, *Last Utopia*.
10. "B'nai B'rith Tells of Mob Action Against Jews in Soviet," *WP*, January 24, 1963, A18; Paul D'Ortona to Kennedy, October 28, 1963, WHCF/SF, Box 375, Folder HU 4–3, JFKL; "Jews' Treatment by Soviet Scored," *NYT*, October 19, 1964, 2; "Soviet U.N. Mission Is Picketed by 700 over Anti-Semitism," *NYT*, May 2, 1964, 2; Seymour Cohen to Lee White, August 18, 1965, WHCF/SF/RM, Box 6, LBJL; "Nixon Scores Soviet for Policy on Jews," *NYT*, October 2, 1968, 14.
11. Lewis Weinstein to Nixon, March 12, 1969, WHCF/RM 3-2, Box 19, RNL; "Protest Backs Soviet Jews on Eve of Israel's Birthday," *NYT*, May 7, 1973, 81; "Brezhnev's Visit and the Jews," *WP*, March 30, 1973, A15; NCCB newsletter, "Catholics Speak Out for Soviet Jews," June 1971, Lerman papers, Box 9, MNHS; copy of Local 250 newsletter about resolution on Mikhail Shtern, February 24, 1975, Lissy files, Box 42, GRFL; advertisement, "An Interfaith Appeal for the Life of Dr. Mikhail Shtern," *WP*, June 17, 1975, A16; Leonard Garment to Morgenthau, May 30, 1972, WHCF/RM 3-2, Box 20, RNL.
12. Tolstoy to Nixon, December 9, 1970, WHCF/RM 3-3, Box 20, RNL; William Baroody and Myron Kuropas to Ford, September 17, 1976, WHCF/RM 3-1, Box 2, GRFL; "Report on the Implementation of the Helsinki Final Act in Soviet Occupied Latvia," August 1980, Jackson papers, Series 6, Box 29, Folder 10, UW; *Chronicle of the Catholic Church in Lithuania*, 1972, Jackson papers, Series 6, Box 31, Folder 30, UW; "Soviet Persecution of Christians Continues," *Applied Christianity*, March 1973, 35–37; "Soviet Baptists Try a Dash Into U.S. Embassy for Visas," *NYT*, September 6, 1975, 22; "Soviet Pentecostals Stage Sit-in in U.S. Embassy," *NYT*, July 4, 1978, 2; John Dunlop, report to the House Subcommittee on International Organizations, "The Contemporary Russian Orthodox Church," June 30, 1976, Jackson papers, Series 6, Box 49, Folder 13, UW.
13. Kaufman, *Henry M. Jackson*, 48–49, 110–111, 143–148, 162–163; Heilbrunn, *They Knew They Were Right*, 114–125; Kissinger, *Years of Upheaval*, 984; "man of high principle" from Kissinger, *Years of Renewal*, 113.
14. Kaufman, *Henry M. Jackson*, 124 (Jackson quoted on 13); Javits, *Javits*, 472–474.
15. Kaufman, *Henry M. Jackson*, 83–85; Jackson observers are Prochnau and Larsen, *Certain Democrat*, 188; Dorothy Fosdick, "What Youth Expects of the Oxford Conference," May 27, 1937, Coffin papers, Box 15, Folder 197, UTS.
16. Dow to Nixon, May 26, 1971, WHCF/RM 3-2, Box 19, RNL; "2 Congressmen Petition Soviet Envoys on Jews," *WP*, August 13, 1976, C2; Tanenbaum to Kissinger, March 19, 1973, WHCF/RM 3-3, Box 18, RNL.
17. Kissinger to Hugh Sloan, April 22, 1969, WHCF/RM 3-2, Box 19, RNL; Kissinger to Riesman, October 1, 1973, ibid.; memcon, Kissinger and State Department officials, March 18, 1974, in Burr, ed., *Kissinger Transcripts*, 225.
18. Kissinger to Moynihan, September 26, 1969, WHCF/RM 3-2, Box 19, RNL. For Kissinger's reasoning, see also Kissinger, *Years of Upheaval*, 254, 979–983, 986–989. This was also Nixon's view. See Nixon, *Memoirs*, 876.
19. "Statement issued by the National Conference on Soviet Jewry after meeting with Senator Henry M. Jackson," May 8, 1973, Lerman papers, Box 9, MNHS;

press release of Jackson statement in Denver, March 31, 1973, Jackson papers, Series 6, Box 10, Folder 13, UW.

20. Jackson staff paper, "Trade and Détente," n.d., Jackson papers, Series 6, Box 10, Folder 138, UW.

21. Hartke and Jackson quoted in "Some Senators Not Convinced by Brezhnev on Jews," *NYT*, June 20, 1973, 20. On official Israeli support for Jackson-Vanik, see Kochavi, "Idealpolitik in Disguise."

22. Memcon, Kissinger, Brezhnev, et al., Moscow, October 24, 1974, in Burr, ed., *Kissinger Transcripts*, 333; Kissinger to Ford, December 20, 1974, WHCF/RM 3-2, GRFL. For a persuasive critique of Kissinger's handling of the Jewish emigration issue along these lines, see Kochavi, "Insights Abandoned." More generally, see Hanhimäki, *Flawed Architect*; and Sandbrook, "Salesmanship and Substance."

23. Dobrynin, *In Confidence*, 339; Kissinger, *Years of Renewal*, 302–309; Kissinger, *Years of Upheaval*, 256, 983.

24. Thomas, *Helsinki Effect*, 55–88; Morgan, "United States and the Making of the Helsinki Final Act"; Sandbrook, "Salesmanship and Substance," 99–101; Snyder, *Human Rights Activism and the End of the Cold War*.

25. Snyder, *Human Rights Activism and the End of the Cold War*, 66; Thomas, *Helsinki Effect*, 121–194; Foglesong, *American Mission and the "Evil Empire,"* 161–163; Moyn, *Last Utopia*, 166, 172; Drinan travelogue, "Conversations in Rumania and Israel," August 13–31, 1975, Drinan papers, Box 1, BC.

26. Jackson speech to the National Council of Jewish Women, Washington, D.C., October 17, 1979, Jackson papers, Series 6, Box 13, Folder 38, UW; Helsinki Watch press release, December 7, 1979, and Christian Solidarity International press release, April 9, 1980, both in Jackson papers, Series 6, Box 29, Folder 41, UW; Senate Concurrent Resolution 118, "Resolution Urging the Soviet Union to Permit Religious Freedom," *CR*, May 19, 1976, 14560–14562; Vins prayer and Jackson Senate remarks, *CR*, June 7, 1979, 13811, 13814.

CHAPTER TWENTY-NINE. RONALD THE LIONHEART

1. "Address to the Nation on the Soviet–United States Summit Meeting," December 10, 1987, *PPP: Ronald Reagan, 1987*, Book II, 1501–1504.

2. Biographical details here and elsewhere from Kaufman, *Presidency of James Earl Carter, Jr.*, 5–18.

3. The best portrait of Carter's faith is Ribuffo, *Right Center Left*, 214–248. But see also Smith, *Faith and the Presidency*, esp. 294–300.

4. "Machiavellian tactics" quoted in Smith, *Faith and the Presidency*, 303; "laws of the prophets" quoted in Ribuffo, *Right Center Left*, 233; Brzezinski, *Power and Principle*, 49. On Carter's initial attempt to transcend the Cold War, see Dumbrell, *Carter Presidency*.

5. Smith, *Faith and the Presidency*, 322–323 ("Christ admonishes us" quoted on 305, "no special claim" on 300); Powell quoted in Martin, *With God on Our Side*, 150–151; inaugural prayer quoted in Allitt, *Religion in America since 1945*, 148.

6. "Remarks and a Question-and-Answer Session at a Town Meeting," October 29, 1980, *PPP: Jimmy Carter, 1980–81*, Book III, 2506.

7. Coll, *Ghost Wars*, 42–46; Brzezinski, *Power and Principle*, 434–435; official quoted in Rubin, *Paved With Good Intentions*, 215; Iranian revolutionary quoted in Oren, *Power, Faith, and Fantasy*, 545. The Carter administration's consistent underestimation and misreading of religion in Iran is a central theme in Farber, *Taken Hostage*. For an excellent comparative analysis of American, Iranian, and other kinds of religious fundamentalism, see Almond, Appleby, and Sivan, *Strong Re-*

ligion; and for comparisons between Egyptian Islamic and American Christian fundamentalism in this period, see Chamberlin, "World Restored." For an insightful examination of the centrality of religion in Iranian political ideology, see Takeyh, *Guardians of the Revolution*, 11–33; and not just on Iran but Afghanistan as well, Westad, *Global Cold War*, 288–330, esp. 294.

8. Smith, *Faith and the Presidency*, 318.

9. "The President's News Conference," October 9, 1979, *PPP: Jimmy Carter, 1979*, Book II, 1838; "The President's News Conference," November 28, 1979, ibid., 2167–2168. On Carter's rearmament program and Cold War turn, see Auten, *Carter's Conversion*.

10. Quoted in Martin, *With God On Our Side*, 210.

11. Quoted in ibid. 189.

12. Vaughn, "Moral Inheritance"; Smith, *Faith and the Presidency*, 326–327.

13. Reagan quoted in Smith, *Faith and the Presidency*, 327–328, 336.

14. Dallek, *Ronald Reagan*; Martin, *With God on Our Side*, 214–217 (quotes from 216, 217). On Reagan's partnership with the Religious Right, see also Williams, *God's Own Party*, 187–211.

15. "Remarks at the Annual Convention of the National Parent-Teacher Association," Albuquerque, June 15, 1983, *PPP: Ronald Reagan, 1983*, Book I, 871; "Remarks at an Ecumenical Prayer Breakfast," Dallas, August 23, 1984, *PPP: Ronald Reagan, 1984*, Book II, 1167.

16. "Message to the Congress Transmitting a Proposed Constitutional Amendment on Prayer in School," May 17, 1982, *PPP: Ronald Reagan, 1982*, Book I, 647–648; "Address before a Joint Session of the Congress on the State of the Union," January 25, 1983, *PPP: Ronald Reagan, 1983*, Book I, 106–107; "merely human" quoted in Smith, *Faith and the Presidency*, 330; "Remarks at the Annual National Prayer Breakfast," February 4, 1988, *PPP: Ronald Reagan, 1988*, Book I, 172–173; "Remarks to Soviet Dissidents at Spaso House in Moscow," May 30, 1988, ibid., 677.

17. Smith, *Faith and the Presidency*, 340.

18. Martin, *With God On Our Side*, 221–237.

19. See LaFeber, *Inevitable Revolutions*, 271–339; and LeoGrande, *Our Own Backyard*. Both are also excellent on the role of the Catholic Church.

20. "Remarks at a Ceremony Marking the Annual Observance of Captive Nations Week," July 19, 1983, *PPP: Ronald Reagan, 1983*, Book II, 1053; "Address before a Joint Session of the Irish National Parliament," Dublin, June 4, 1984, *PPP: Ronald Reagan, 1984*, Book I, 811.

21. Leffler, *For the Soul of Mankind*, 325; Gaddis, *Cold War*, 192–194, 195–236 passim.

22. "Remarks at the Annual Convention of the National Association of Evangelicals," March 8, 1983, *PPP: Ronald Reagan, 1983*, Book I, 362–364; for eschatology, see FitzGerald, *Way Out There in the Blue*, 25–27.

23. Persico, *Casey*, 17, 19–32, 42–43, 109, 113, 573–574; Coll, *Ghost Wars*, 89–107.

24. "Nun Sees a 'Big Truth' in Nicaragua," *NYT*, July 4, 1983, 8; "Statement by U.S. Missionaries in Nicaragua in Response to Address by President Reagan to Joint Session of Congress," Managua, April 29, 1983, Resource Center for Women and Ministry in the South records, Box 1, MSCD.

25. "Dear Friends" newsletter from "Cathy and Linda," August 29, 1985, Resource Center for Women and Ministry in the South records, Box 1, MSCD; Coffin, "Nicaragua on the Brink of War: An Eyewitness Report," *Disarming: The Newsletter for the Riverside Church Disarmament Program*, vol. 4 (September 1982), Hall-Hoag Collection, Christian Religious Left, Box 59:7:2147, JHL.

26. Wenzel to Reagan, July 2, 1985, WHORM/RM 033-08, Box 7, File 317779, RRL.

27. Pilgrim Congregational Church newsletter, July 1983, University Baptist Church records, Box 2, Folder 1, UW; Allitt, *Religion in America since 1945*, 174–180.

28. National denominational figures from Sanctuary Media Packet, April 1985, University Baptist Church records, Box 2, Folder 7, UW; "Two Groups in U.S. Contend El Salvador Violates Civil Rights," *NYT*, January 27, 1982, A10; "Salvador Rights Violations Charged," *NYT*, September 13, 1985, A3. On the transmission of liberation theology to America, see Dorrien, *Reconstructing the Common Good*, 101–126; Wogaman, *Christian Perspectives on Politics*, 79–101; and Allitt, *Religion in America since 1945*, 113–114, 127–128, 174–175.

29. Women's Missionary Society and Young People's Division of the AME Church, 1984 Yearbook, Robinson papers, Box 1, BHL; Malcolm Sutherland (WCRP) to Frederick J. Ryan, Jr., August 25, 1982, WHORM/RM, Box 1, File 078672, RRL; "Church Leaders Ask for A-Arms Freeze and Aid for the Poor," *NYT*, April 2, 1982, A21; Sacramento Religious Community for Peace pamphlet, "Faith, War, and Peace in the Nuclear Age," June 1985, Hall-Hoag Collection, Christian Religious Left, Box 59:7:3874, JHL.

30. Allitt, *Catholic Intellectuals*, 289–296.

31. National Conference of Catholic Bishops, *Challenge of Peace*, 331–333 (note that this refers to paragraphs, not pages).

32. "Bishops' Stand Stirs Catholic Protest," *NYT*, November 13, 1982, 26; Allitt, *Catholic Intellectuals*, 291–293; Novak, *Will It Liberate?*; Glynn, "Pulpit Politics," *New Republic*, March 14, 1983, 11–14; Abrams to Clark, March 8, 1963, WHORM/RM 031, Box 6, File 134023, RRL; Christian counterrevolution pamphlet, "The Truth About Vatican II," September 1985, Hall-Hoag Collection, Catholic Traditionalism, Box 97:1:310, JHL.

33. Hyde et al. to Bernardin, December 15, 1982, WHORM/RM 031, Box 6, File 121164, RRL.

34. For Protestant support of the NCCB, see "Arms Stand of Bishops Praised," *NYT*, May 14, 1983, 9; and "Presbyterians Hail Message of Catholic Bishops on War," *NYT*, May 30, 1983, 21.

35. "Does Reagan Expect a Nuclear Armageddon?" *WP*, April 8, 1984, C1, C4; "President Has No Plans for Day of Judgment," *WSJ*, February 8, 1985, 1; "Armageddon," *WP*, October 24, 1984, A6; McFarlane and Reagan quoted in Fischer, *Reagan Reversal*, 107.

36. Fischer, *Reagan Reversal*, 106–143, 147–149; Rhodes, *Arsenals of Folly*, 172–174, 178–179. More generally for Reagan as a nuclear abolitionist, see Gaddis, *Strategies of Containment*, 356–367.

37. "Soviet Pentecostals Stage Sit-in in U.S. Embassy," *NYT*, July 4, 1978, 2; "Pentecostalists Continue Sit-in at U.S. Embassy," *WP*, July 19, 1978, A17; "U.S. Asylum Like a Prison for Soviet 7," *WP*, March 9, 1979, C1. The Pentecostals' case has been mostly ignored by historians, but for an excellent exception see Snyder, *Human Rights Activism and the End of the Cold War*, 141–146.

38. "Churches in U.S. Back Christians Who Seek to Quit Soviet Union," *NYT*, February 26, 1979, A9; "U.S. Legislators End 3-Day Visit with Soviet Leaders and Dissidents," *NYT*, August 23, 1979, A3; Sister Ann Gillen to Reagan, June 4, 1981, WHORM/CO 165, Box 1, File 027723, RRL; Gilman to Richard Allen, January 15, 1981, WHORM/CO 165, Box 1, File 006491, RRL; Frank to Reagan, May 27, 1981, WHORM/CO 165, Box 1, File 026802, RRL; Frank et al. to Reagan, February 4, 1982, WHORM/CO 165, Box 4, File 059403, RRL.

39. Reeves, *President Reagan*, 138; Reagan to Augustina and Lidiya Vashchenko, n.d., Matlock files, Box 30, Folder 2/4, RRL; Matlock, *Reagan and Gorbachev*, 55–56.

40. Dobrynin, *In Confidence*, 522–527, 540; Shultz, *Turmoil and Triumph*, 165; Oberdorfer, *Turn*, 19–21.

41. Shultz, *Turmoil and Triumph*, 166; Reagan, *American Life*, 558; diary entry, July 20, 1983, in Brinkley, ed., *Reagan Diaries*, 168; draft of White House letter to Quayle, n.d. [ca. August 1983], Matlock files, Box 30, Folder 4/4, RRL.

42. Shultz, *Turmoil and Triumph*, 168–171, 281, 469, 1094; Matlock, *Reagan and Gorbachev*, 55.

43. Graham, *Just as I Am*, 499–527 (Reagan quoted on 502); Martin, *Prophet with Honor*, 491–524; Gibbs and Duffy, *Preacher and the Presidents*, 254–275.

44. Dobrynin, *In Confidence*, 532; Matlock, *Reagan and Gorbachev*, xiv.

45. "Ecumenical Prayer Breakfast," 1167; "Achilles' Heel," letter and conversation with Gorbachev quoted in Mann, *Rebellion of Ronald Reagan*, 87, 88, 294–296.

46. "Remarks to Religious Leaders at the Danilov Monastery," Moscow, May 30, 1988, *PPP: Ronald Reagan, 1988*, Book I, 674–675.

EPILOGUE. THE LAST CRUSADE?

1. "Amid the Rubble, A Steeple Stands," *NYT*, September 17, 2001, A8; "Near Ground Zero, Unbowed Spires," *NYT*, September 30, 2001, RE1. The church itself has a website with several links for more information and photos from its role in the post-9/11 recovery process: http://www.saintpaulschapel.org/

2. "Giuliani Talks of a City's Spirit, and a Grand Monument to Those Who Died," *NYT*, December 28, 2001, D6.

3. On the surge in religious attendance, see "In a Needy Time, America Seeks Spiritual Solace," *LAT*, September 14, 2001, A50; "Comfort Sought in Houses of Worship," *WP*, September 20, 2001, T14; and "Attacks Spur a Surge of Interest in Religion," *NYT*, September 30, 2001, A33. County official and Bowman quoted in "Houses of Worship Offering Solace," *WP*, September 20, 2001, T11.

4. "I preach and teach" quoted in "Many Attempt to Reconcile the Horror with Their Faith," *WP*, September 13, 2001, B4; Ogilvie prayer and Daschle quoted in Senate proceedings, *CR—Senate*, September 12, 2001, S9283.

5. Lutheran and Bush exchange quoted in Smith, *Faith and the Presidency*, 397; Bush to Rove quoted in Woodward, *Plan of Attack*, 91.

6. "Remarks on Arrival at the White House and an Exchange With Reporters," September 16, 2001, *PPP: George W. Bush, 2001*, Book II, 1116; "Remarks at the Islamic Center of Washington," September 17, 2001, ibid., 1121; "Remarks at the California Business Association Breakfast in Sacramento," October 17, 2001, ibid., 1254.

7. "Remarks at the National Day of Prayer and Remembrance Service," Washington, D.C., September 14, 2001, ibid., 1108–1109.

8. Quoted in Woodward, *Bush at War*, 67–68.

9. "A War President Shouldn't Ask What Jesus Would Do," *WP*, September 30, 2001, B5; Dionne, "The Question of Faith," *WP*, September 18, 2001, A31. For a more thorough version of Dionne's views, which provides an excellent summation of views by the progressive religious left during the Bush era, see Dionne, *Souled Out*.

10. "Remarks at a Memorial Service for the Victims of the Embassy Bombings in Kenya and Tanzania," Washington, D.C., September 11, 1998, *PPP: Bill Clinton, 1998*, Book II, 1567.

11. Lon E. Calloway to Doug Wead, May 22, 1989, Doug Wead files, Correspondence File, Box 3, GBL; Preston, "Politics of Realism and Religion" (Baker quoted on 103).

12. Pilarczyk to Bush, November 15, 1990, Presidential Records, Office of Public Liaison, Leigh Ann Metzger files, Box 63, GBL; Browning quoted in "U.S.

Church Leaders Urge Against Gulf War," *WP*, December 22, 1990, A11; Bush and Scowcroft, *World Transformed*, 427.

13. Preston, "Politics of Realism and Religion," 117–118. On Christian conservative reaction to Bush's "new world order," see Lienesch, *Redeeming America*, 237–241; and Barkun, *Culture of Conspiracy*, 39–78. 1992 polling data from "Religious Right Regroups after Loss at the Polls," *St. Petersburg Times*, November 7, 1992, 1E; Kim A. Lawton, "Seeking Common Ground," *CT*, December 14, 1992, 41; and Kellstedt, Green, Smidt, and Guth, "Faith Transformed," 273. Polling data for 1988 and 1984 from Kellstedt, Smidt, and Kellstedt, "Religious Tradition, Denomination, and Commitment," 142, 147. Another survey puts Bush's share of the born-again vote in 1988 as high as 80 percent: see Kosmin and Lachman, *One Nation Under God*, 184. Even by the more capacious definition of "conservative Protestants," in 1992 Bush won only 60 percent of the conservative Protestant vote. See Table 14.2 in Emerson and Hawkins, "Viewed in Black and White," 340.

14. Robertson, *New World Order*.

15. "Freedoms Under Fire," *CT*, July 20, 1992, 29.

16. Farr, *World of Faith and Freedom*; Hertzke, *Freeing God's Children*; Marsden, *For God's Sake*. On Christian Zionism, see Clark, *Allies for Armageddon*; and Spector, *Evangelicals and Israel*.

17. Woodward, *Plan of Attack*, 421. For Land, see Smith, *Faith and the Presidency*, 383.

18. On Gerson, see Jeffrey Goldberg, "The Believer," *New Yorker*, February 13, 2006, 56; "Mr. Compassionate Conservatism," *WSJ*, October 21, 2006; and Lindsay, *Faith in the Halls of Power*, 24–26. On Rice, see Bumiller, *Condoleezza Rice*, 8–23; Montgomery, *Faith of Condoleezza Rice* (Rice quoted on 119, 198).

19. Lindsay, *Faith in the Halls of Power*, 47–49. Because it avoids both polemics and hagiography, the best overview of Bush's faith is Smith, *Faith and the Presidency*, 365–413, esp. 372–394, 399–404 for foreign policy.

20. On the resurgence of global faith and the expansion of Christianity, see Jenkins, *New Faces of Christianity*; Jenkins, *Next Christendom*; Noll, *New Shape of World Christianity*; and Micklethwait and Wooldridge, *God Is Back*. On its implications for world politics, see Thomas, "Globalized God"; and Toft, Philpott, and Shah, *God's Century*.

21. Lambert, *Religion in American Politics*, 218–250; Abdo, *Mecca and Main Street*, 29, 84–86; Barrett, *American Islam*, 15–61, 280–283. For Lerner, see his *Left Hand of God*. For Dionne, see his *Souled Out*. For Wallis, see his *God's Politics* and *Great Awakening*. For Wills, see his *Head and Heart*, 495–552. On Bush's sometimes difficult relationship with the Religious Right, see Williams, *God's Own Party*, 245–267.

22. On Bush's faith as typical, see Ribuffo, "George W. Bush."

23. Remnick, *Bridge*, 169–176; Kloppenberg, *Reading Obama*, 202–209.

24. Kloppenberg, *Reading Obama*, 33–34, 142–144, 198–201; Remnick, *Bridge*, 440–442 ("secularists" quoted on 440); Lisa Miller and Richard Wolfe, "Finding His Faith," *Newsweek*, July 21, 2008, 27–32; Obama to Brownback quoted in Heilemann and Halperin, *Game Change*, 69; E. J. Dionne Jr., "Obama's Eloquent Faith," *WP*, June 30, 2006.

25. Matthew Continetti, "A Good Niebuhr Policy," *Weekly Standard*, July 13, 2009; Brooks, "Obama, Gospel and Verse," *NYT*, April 26, 2007. See also Brian Urquhart, "What You Can Learn from Reinhold Niebuhr," *New York Review of Books*, March 26–April 8, 2009, 22–24; and Kloppenberg, *Reading Obama*, 16–17, 22, 26, 119–121, 142–143, 215, 243–244, 250, 260.

26. "Remarks by the President at the Acceptance of the Nobel Peace Prize," December 10, 2009, http://www.whitehouse.gov/the-press-office/remarks-president-acceptance-nobel-peace-prize; Packer, "Peace and War," *New Yorker*, December 21, 2009. See also David Brooks, "Obama's Christian Realism," *NYT*, December 15, 2009; E. J. Dionne Jr., "A Culture War Cease-Fire," *WP*, December 24, 2009, A15; and Kloppenberg, *Reading Obama*, 242–244.

27. "Remarks by President Barack Obama at Town Hall Meeting with Future Chinese Leaders," Shanghai, November 16, 2009, http://www.whitehouse.gov/the-press-office/remarks-president-barack-obama-town-hall-meeting-with-future-chinese-leaders.

28. "Remarks by the President on a New Beginning," Cairo, June 4, 2009, http://www.whitehouse.gov/the-press-office/remarks-president-cairo-university-6-04-09; "Remarks by the President at Iftar Dinner," August 13, 2010, http://www.whitehouse.gov/the-press-office/2010/08/13/remarks-president-iftar-dinner-0; "Remarks by the President at the Pentagon Memorial," September 11, 2010, http://www.whitehouse.gov/the-press-office/2010/09/11/remarks-president-pentagon-memorial.

BIBLIOGRAPHY

PRIMARY SOURCES
UNPUBLISHED MANUSCRIPTS AND ARCHIVES

AMERICAN BAPTIST HISTORICAL SOCIETY, ATLANTA, GA.
MANUSCRIPT COLLECTIONS
Edwin Ewart Aubrey papers
Thomas S. Barbour papers
Samuel Zane Batten papers
Edwin T. Dahlberg papers
David Jones papers
G. Merrill Lenox papers
Gertrude F. McCulloch papers
Mabel Martin papers
Pamphlet Collection
Orlo J. Price papers
Mildred Proctor papers
Walter Rauschenbusch papers
Hillyer Hawthorne Straton papers
John Roach Straton papers
Gordon M. Torgersen papers

BOSTON COLLEGE, CHESTNUT HILL, MASS.
BURNS LIBRARY
Robert F. Drinan papers
Hans Reinhold papers
Francis Sweeney papers

BROWN UNIVERSITY, PROVIDENCE, R.I.
JOHN HAY LIBRARY
Isaac Backus papers
Hall-Hoag Collection of
Dissenting and Extremist
Propaganda
    Catholic Traditionalism
    Christian Identity
    Christian Religious Left
    Christian Religious Right
Eli Hawley Canfield papers

COLUMBIA UNIVERSITY, NEW YORK, N.Y.

BURKE THEOLOGICAL LIBRARY

Union Theological Seminary Archives
Francis Brown papers
William Adams Brown papers
Henry Sloane Coffin papers
East Harlem Protestant Parish records
Harry Emerson Fosdick papers
Reinhold Niebuhr papers
Walter Rauschenbusch papers
Philip Schaff papers

ORAL HISTORY RESEARCH OFFICE,

NICHOLAS MURRAY BUTLER LIBRARY

Philip Berrigan
Walter Judd
Norman Thomas
A. L. Warnshuis

RARE BOOKS AND MANUSCRIPTS,

NICHOLAS MURRAY BUTLER LIBRARY

Carnegie Endowment for International Peace records

CONNECTICUT HISTORICAL SOCIETY, HARTFORD, CONN.

MANUSCRIPT COLLECTIONS

Amos Starr Cooke papers
Elias Cornelius papers
Thomas Robbins papers
John Cotton Smith papers

CORNELL UNIVERSITY, ITHACA, N.Y.

RARE AND MANUSCRIPT COLLECTIONS, CARL A. KROCH LIBRARY

Martin D. Hardin papers
Kaercher and Packer Family papers
Hugh Anderson Moran papers
Myron C. Taylor papers

DWIGHT D. EISENHOWER LIBRARY, ABILENE, KAN.

Pre-Presidential papers
Principal File
White House Central Files
Official File
General File

DUKE UNIVERSITY, DURHAM, N.C.

MANUSCRIPT AND SPECIAL COLLECTIONS, WILLIAM R. PERKINS LIBRARY

John Larkin Brasher papers
Kenneth M. Johnson sermons
Carlyle Marney papers

Resource Center for Women and
Ministry in the South records
John Jacob Scherer papers

UNIVERSITY ARCHIVES, WILLIAM R. PERKINS LIBRARY

James Cannon III papers
James T. Cleland papers
Robert Earl Cushman papers
John C. Kilgo records and papers
Creighton Lacy papers
Hiram Earl Myers papers
Hilrie Shelton Smith papers

EPISCOPAL SEMINARY OF THE SOUTHWEST, AUSTIN, TEX.

NATIONAL ARCHIVES OF THE EPISCOPAL CHURCH, BOOHER LIBRARY

Records of the Domestic and Foreign Missionary Society
China Mission records
Japan Mission records
Mexico Mission records
Philippine Mission records

FRANKLIN D. ROOSEVELT LIBRARY, HYDE PARK, N.Y.

Adolf A. Berle papers
Good Neighbor League records
R. Walton Moore papers
Presidential Papers
Official File
Personal File
Vertical File
Myron C. Taylor papers
Sumner Welles papers

GEORGETOWN UNIVERSITY, WASHINGTON, D.C.

SPECIAL COLLECTIONS DIVISION, GUNLOCKE RARE BOOK ROOM,
LAUINGER LIBRARY

America magazine archives

GERALD R. FORD LIBRARY, ANN ARBOR, MICH.

David Gergen files
David H. Lissy files
Theodore C. Marrs files
National Security Adviser files
Vice Presidential papers
White House Central File
Name File
Religious Matters

HAGLEY MUSEUM AND LIBRARY, WILMINGTON, DEL.

MANUSCRIPTS AND ARCHIVES, SODA HOUSE

J. Howard Pew papers

HARRY S. TRUMAN LIBRARY, INDEPENDENCE, MO.

Federal Records
    Committee on Religion and Welfare in the Armed Forces
Official File
President's Secretary's Files
    Subject File
Myron C. Taylor papers
U.S. Senator and Vice President papers

HARVARD UNIVERSITY, CAMBRIDGE, MASS.
MANUSCRIPTS AND ARCHIVES, ANDOVER-HARVARD THEOLOGICAL LIBRARY

Joseph Barth papers
William Ellery Channing papers
William Wallace Fenn papers
Dana McLean Greeley papers
Edward Everett Hale papers
Edward Everett Hale sermons
Benjamin B. Hersey papers
Frank Orville Holmes papers
Alfred Rodman Hussey papers
Joseph Lathrop papers
George Washington Montgomery sermons
Pamphlet collection (882: American sermons)
David Boynton Parke papers
Theodore Parker papers
John Van Schaik, Jr. papers

HOUGHTON LIBRARY

Brooks Adams letters
William R. Castle diary

JEWISH THEOLOGICAL SEMINARY OF AMERICA, NEW YORK, N.Y.
SPECIAL COLLECTIONS

Moses Baroway papers
Harry Friedenwald papers
Gustav Gottheil papers

JOHN F. KENNEDY LIBRARY, BOSTON, MASS.

Harlan Cleveland personal papers
Ralph A. Dungan personal papers
National Security Files
    Country File
    Departments and Agencies File
President's Office Files
    Subject File
White House Central Files
    Subject File
James Wine personal papers

LIBRARY OF CONGRESS, WASHINGTON, D.C.
MANUSCRIPTS DIVISION
Reinhold Niebuhr papers

LYNDON B. JOHNSON LIBRARY, AUSTIN, TEX.
National Security File
   Country File
White House Central File
   Name File
   Subject File

MASSACHUSETTS HISTORICAL SOCIETY, BOSTON, MASS.
MANUSCRIPT COLLECTIONS
Blake-Clapp-Arguimbau Family papers
Henry Cabot Lodge papers

MINNESOTA HISTORICAL SOCIETY, ST. PAUL, MINN.
MANUSCRIPT COLLECTIONS
Viola C. McConnell papers
John B. Foster papers
Walter Judd papers
Louis E. Lerman papers
Harold E. Stassen papers

PRESBYTERIAN HISTORICAL SOCIETY, PHILADELPHIA, PA.
ARCHIVAL RECORDS
American and Foreign Christian Union records
Federal Council of Churches records
National Council of Churches records
   Division of Overseas Ministries
   Special Topics
Presbyterian Church in the USA records
   African-American Presbyteries and Synods collection

PRINCETON THEOLOGICAL SEMINARY, PRINCETON, N.J.
SPECIAL COLLECTIONS, HENRY LUCE III LIBRARY
Maitland Alexander papers
Carlton C. Allen papers
E. Theodore Bachmann papers
Adolph H. Behrenberg papers
Eugene Carson Blake papers
Bryant Kirkland papers
Walter Frederick and Agnes
McAlphine Douglas Kuentzel papers
Paul Lehmann papers
Carl McIntire papers
Richard Shaull papers

PRINCETON UNIVERSITY, PRINCETON, N.J.

SEELEY G. MUDD MANUSCRIPT LIBRARY

John Foster Dulles papers
George F. Kennan papers

RICHARD M. NIXON LIBRARY, YORBA LINDA, CALIF.

White House central file
Religious Matters

RONALD REAGAN LIBRARY, SIMI VALLEY, CALIF.

White House Office of Records Management
Countries: USSR
Religious Matters
Jack F. Matlock, Jr., files

UNIVERSITY OF MICHIGAN, ANN ARBOR, MICH.

BENTLEY HISTORICAL LIBRARY

Charles William Carpenter papers
Richard S. M. Emrich papers
Frank Fitt papers
St. Matthew's and St. Joseph's
Episcopal Church records
Gerald L. K. Smith papers
John B. Trevor, Jr., papers
University of Michigan War
Historian records

UNIVERSITY OF NORTH CAROLINA, CHAPEL HILL, N.C.

SOUTHERN HISTORICAL COLLECTION, LOUIS ROUND WILSON LIBRARY

Thomas N. Carruthers papers
Boyd D. Cathey papers
Joseph Blount Cheshire papers
Silas McBee papers
Anson Gustavus Melton volumes

UNIVERSITY OF VIRGINIA, CHARLOTTESVILLE, VA.

ALBERT AND SHIRLEY SMALL SPECIAL COLLECTIONS LIBRARY

Russell Cecil papers
Collins Denny papers
Harry Emilius Stocker sermons and manuscripts
Shepherdstown (West Virginia) records

UNIVERSITY OF WASHINGTON, SEATTLE, WASH.

SPECIAL COLLECTIONS, ALLEN LIBRARY SOUTH

Emery E. Andrews papers
E. Raymond Attebery papers
Henry M. Jackson papers
Seattle First Baptist Church records
University Baptist Church records

WORLD COUNCIL OF CHURCHES, GENEVA, SWITZERLAND

PAPER COLLECTION, ECUMENICAL CENTRE LIBRARY

World Council of Churches records

YALE UNIVERSITY, NEW HAVEN, CONN.

SPECIAL COLLECTIONS, DIVINITY SCHOOL LIBRARY

George Sherwood Eddy papers

Issues of War and Peace Pamphlet collection

Miscellaneous Personal Papers (Record Group 30)

James Beebe

Edward Warner Bentley

David G. Colwell

Howard J. Conn

Robert C. Denison

Henry Smith Leiper

Oscar Maurer

Joseph Parsons

Warren W. Pickett

Alexander Stevenson Twombly

Izrahiah Wetmore

William Frederic Williams

John R. Mott papers

PRIMARY SOURCES: PUBLISHED DOCUMENTS

CHURCH AND MISSIONARY RECORDS AND PROCEEDINGS

A.M.E. Church Year Book of Negro Churches, 1948–1949, ed. Reverdy C. Ransom. Nashville, Tenn.: A.M.E. Sunday School Union, 1948.

Carlen, Claudia, ed. *The Papal Encyclicals,* 5 vols. Ann Arbor, Mich.: Pierian Press, 1990.

Christian Students and World Problems: Report of the Ninth International Convention of the Student Volunteer Movement for Foreign Missions, Indianapolis, Indiana, December 28, 1923, to January 1, 1924, ed. Milton T. Stauffer. New York: Student Volunteer Movement for Foreign Missions, 1924.

The Church and Industrial Reconstruction. New York: Association Press, 1920.

The Churches Survey Their Task: The Report of the Conference at Oxford, July 1937, on Church, Community, and State. London: Allen & Unwin, 1937.

Commission on the Relation of the Church to the War in the Light of the Christian Faith. *Atomic Warfare and the Christian Faith.* New York: Federal Council of the Churches of Christ in America, 1946.

Commission to Study the Bases of a Just and Durable Peace. *Six Pillars of Peace: A Study Guide Based on "A Statement of Political Propositions."* New York: Federal Council of the Churches of Christ in America, 1943.

Dayton, Donald W., ed. *The Prophecy Conference Movement,* 4 vols. New York: Garland, 1988.

Foreign Missions Conference of North America: Report of the Forty-Fifth Annual Meeting of the Conference of Foreign Mission Boards in Canada and the United States, Royal York Hotel, Toronto, Canada, January 4–6, 1938, ed. Leslie B. Moss and Mabel H. Brown. New York: Foreign Missions Conference of North America, 1938.

Journal of the General Convention of the Protestant Episcopal Church in the United States of America, 1916. New York: Sherwood Press, 1917.

Journal of the Proceedings of the Bishops, Clergy, and Laity of the Protestant Episcopal Church in the United States of America, Assembled in a General Convention, 1847. New York: Daniel Dana, Jr., 1847.

The Lambeth Conference, 1930: Encyclical Letter from the Bishops, with Resolutions and Reports. London: Society for Promoting Christian Knowledge, 1930.

Minutes of the General Assembly of the Presbyterian Church in the United States of America. Philadelphia: Office of the Presbyterian General Assembly, 1944.

National Conference of Catholic Bishops. *The Challenge of Peace: God's Promise and Our Response: A Pastoral Letter on War and Peace, May 3, 1983.* Washington, D.C.: United States Catholic Conference Office of Publishing Services, 1983.

One Hundred Fifteenth Annual Report of the Board of Home Missions of the Presbyterian Church in the United States of America. New York: Presbyterian Church in the United States of America, 1917.

War-Time Agencies of the Churches: Directory and Handbook. New York: General War-Time Commission of the Churches, 1919.

World Council of Churches. "Towards Justice and Peace in International Affairs [Report Adopted by the Assembly of the World Council of Churches, July 16, 1968, Uppsala, Sweden]." *Journal of Church and State* 11 (1969): 253–264.

OFFICIAL GOVERNMENT DOCUMENTS

Burr, William, ed. *The Kissinger Transcripts: The Top Secret Talks with Beijing and Moscow.* New York: New Press, 1998.

Congressional Globe/Congressional Record. Washington, D.C.: Government Printing Office, 1831–.

Documentary History of the Truman Presidency, 35 vols. Bethesda, Md.: University Publications of America, 1995–2002.

Franklin D. Roosevelt and Foreign Affairs, series 1, vols. 1–3. Cambridge, Mass.: Harvard University Press, 1969.

Franklin D. Roosevelt and Foreign Affairs, series 2, vols. 4–17. New York: Clearwater Publishing, 1979–1983.

Rescue of the Jewish and Other Peoples In Nazi-Occupied Territory. Hearings before the Committee on Foreign Affairs, House Of Representatives, Seventy-Eighth Congress, First Session, on H. Res. 350 and H. Res. 352, November 26, 1943. Washington, D.C.: Government Printing Office, 1943.

Nicholas, H. G., ed. *Washington Despatches, 1941–1945: Weekly Political Reports from the British Embassy.* London: Weidenfeld and Nicholson, 1981.

The Public Papers and Addresses of Franklin D. Roosevelt, 1928–1945, 13 vols. New York: Random House/Harper & Brothers, 1938–1950.

Public Papers of the Presidents of the United States: Dwight D. Eisenhower, 1953–1961. Washington, D.C.: Government Printing Office, 1958–1961.

Public Papers of the Presidents of the United States: George W. Bush, 2001–2005. Washington, D.C.: Government Printing Office, 2003–2007.

Public Papers of the Presidents of the United States: Harry S. Truman, 1945–1953. Washington, D.C.: Government Printing Office, 1961–1966.

Public Papers of the Presidents of the United States: Jimmy Carter, 1977–1981. Washington, D.C.: Government Printing Office, 1977–1980.

Public Papers of the Presidents of the United States: John F. Kennedy, 1961–1963. Washington, D.C.: Government Printing Office, 1962–1964.

Public Papers of the Presidents of the United States: Lyndon B. Johnson, 1963–1969. Washington, D.C.: Government Printing Office, 1965–1970.

Public Papers of the Presidents of the United States: Richard Nixon, 1969–1974. Washington, D.C.: Government Printing Office, 1971–1975.

Public Papers of the Presidents of the United States: Ronald Reagan, 1981–1989. Washington, D.C.: Government Printing Office, 1982–1991.

Public Papers of the Presidents of the United States: William J. Clinton, 1993–2001. Washington, D.C.: Government Printing Office, 1994–2002.

Records and Documents of the Holy See Relating to the Second World War: The Holy See and the War in Europe, ed. Gerald Noel. London: Herder, 1968.

Treaties and Other International Agreements of the United States of America, 1776–1949, 12 vols. Washington, D.C.: Department of State, 1968–1974.

United Nations Resolutions, series 1, 24 vols., ed. Dusan J. Djonovich. Dobbs Ferry, N.Y.: Oceana Publications, 1972–1988.

U.S. Department of State. *Department of State Bulletin,* 89 vols. Washington, D.C.: Government Printing Office, 1938–1989.

———. *Foreign Relations of the United States, 1898.* Washington, D.C.: Government Printing Office, 1901.

———. *Foreign Relations of the United States, 1899.* Washington, D.C.: Government Printing Office, 1901.

———. *Foreign Relations of the United States, 1900.* Washington, D.C.: Government Printing Office, 1902.

———. *Foreign Relations of the United States, 1902.* Washington, D.C.: Government Printing Office, 1903.

———. *Foreign Relations of the United States, 1903.* Washington, D.C.: Government Printing Office, 1904.

———. *Foreign Relations of the United States, 1904.* Washington, D.C.: Government Printing Office, 1905.

———. *Foreign Relations of the United States, 1905.* Washington, D.C.: Government Printing Office, 1906.

———. *Foreign Relations of the United States, 1906,* 2 parts. Washington, D.C.: Government Printing Office, 1909.

———. *Foreign Relations of the United States, 1908.* Washington, D.C.: Government Printing Office, 1912.

———. *Foreign Relations of the United States, 1909.* Washington, D.C.: Government Printing Office, 1914.

———. *Foreign Relations of the United States: The Paris Peace Conference, 1919,* 13 vols. Washington, D.C.: Government Printing Office, 1942–1947.

———. *Foreign Relations of the United States, 1927,* 3 vols. Washington, D.C.: Government Printing Office, 1942.

———. *Foreign Relations of the United States: The Soviet Union, 1933–1939.* Washington, D.C.: Government Printing Office, 1952.

———. *Foreign Relations of the United States, 1938,* 5 vols. Washington, D.C.: Government Printing Office, 1955–1956.

———. *Foreign Relations of the United States, 1940,* 5 vols. Washington, D.C.: Government Printing Office, 1959–1961.

———. *Foreign Relations of the United States, 1941,* 7 vols. Washington, D.C.: Government Printing Office, 1958–1963.

———. *Foreign Relations of the United States, 1942,* 6 vols. Washington, D.C.: Government Printing Office, 1960–1963.

———. *Foreign Relations of the United States, 1943,* 6 vols. Washington, D.C.: Government Printing Office, 1963–1965.

———. *Foreign Relations of the United States, 1944,* 7 vols. Washington, D.C.: Government Printing Office, 1965–1967.

———. *Foreign Relations of the United States, 1945,* 9 vols. Washington, D.C.: Government Printing Office, 1967–1969.

————. *Foreign Relations of the United States: The Conferences at Malta and Yalta, 1945.* Washington, D.C.: Government Printing Office, 1955.

————. *Foreign Relations of the United States: The Conferences of Berlin (The Potsdam Conference), 1945,* 2 vols. Washington, D.C.: Government Printing Office, 1960.

————. *Foreign Relations of the United States, 1946,* 11 vols. Washington, D.C.: Government Printing Office, 1969–1972.

————. *Foreign Relations of the United States, 1947,* 8 vols. Washington, D.C.: Government Printing Office, 1971–1973.

————. *Foreign Relations of the United States, 1948,* 9 vols. Washington, D.C.: Government Printing Office, 1972–1976.

————. *Foreign Relations of the United States, 1949,* 9 vols. Washington, D.C.: Government Printing Office, 1974–1978.

————. *Foreign Relations of the United States, 1950,* 7 vols. Washington, D.C.: Government Printing Office, 1976–1981.

————. *Foreign Relations of the United States, 1955–1957,* 27 vols. Washington, D.C.: Government Printing Office, 1985–1993.

————. *Foreign Relations of the United States, 1958–1960,* 19 vols. Washington, D.C.: Government Printing Office, 1986–1996.

————. *Foreign Relations of the United States, 1964–1968,* 34 vols. Washington, D.C.: Government Printing Office, 1992–2006.

Wartime Correspondence Between President Roosevelt and Pope Pius XII. New York: Macmillan, 1947.

ANTHOLOGIES, LETTERS, AND PERSONAL PAPERS

Baepler, Paul, ed. *White Slaves, African Masters: An Anthology of American Barbary Captivity Narratives.* Chicago: University of Chicago Press, 1999.

Barbour, Philip L., ed. *The Complete Works of Captain John Smith (1580–1631),* vol. I. Chapel Hill: University of North Carolina Press, 1986.

Berrigan, Philip. *Prison Journals of a Priest Revolutionary.* New York: Holt, Rinehart and Winston, 1970.

Brinkley, Douglas, ed. *The Reagan Diaries.* New York: HarperCollins, 2007.

Brock, Peter, ed. *"These Strange Criminals": An Anthology of Prison Memoirs by Conscientious Objectors from the Great War to the Cold War.* Toronto: University of Toronto Press, 2004.

Brown, Chris, Terry Nardin, and Nicholas Rengger, eds. *International Relations in Political Thought: Texts from the Ancient Greeks to the First World War.* Cambridge: Cambridge University Press, 2002.

Brown, Robert McAfee, ed. *The Essential Reinhold Niebuhr: Selected Essays and Addresses.* New Haven: Yale University Press, 1986.

Carpenter, Joel A., ed. *The Fundamentalist-Modernist Conflict: Opposing Views on Three Major Issues.* New York: Garland, 1988.

Carter, H. D., ed. *Henry Adams and His Friends: A Collection of His Unpublished Letters.* Boston: Houghton Mifflin, 1947.

The Collected Works of Abraham Lincoln, 8 vols. New Brunswick, N.J.: Rutgers University Press, 1953.

The Collected Works of Ralph Waldo Emerson, 7 vols. Cambridge, Mass.: Harvard University Press, 1971–2008.

The Collected Works of William Howard Taft, 8 vols. Athens: Ohio University Press, 2002–2004.

Cronon, E. David, ed. *The Cabinet Diaries of Josephus Daniels, 1913–1921.* Lincoln: University of Nebraska Press, 1963.

Davis, Harry R., and Robert C. Good, eds. *Reinhold Niebuhr on Politics: His Political*

Philosophy and Its Application to Our Age as Expressed in His Writings. New York: Simon & Schuster, 1960.

Cyrus Adler: Selected Letters, 2 vols. Edited by Ira Robinson. Philadelphia and New York: Jewish Publication Society of America/Jewish Theological Seminary of America, 1985.

Diary and Autobiography of John Adams, 4 vols. Edited by L. H. Butterfield. Cambridge, Mass.: Harvard University Press, 1961.

Diary of Gideon Welles, Secretary of the Navy under Lincoln and Johnson, 3 vols. Boston: Houghton Mifflin, 1911.

Ellsberg, Robert, ed. *The Duty of Delight: The Diaries of Dorothy Day.* Milwaukee, Wis.: Marquette University Press, 2008.

Faust, Drew Gilpin, ed. *The Ideology of Slavery: Proslavery Thought in the Antebellum South, 1830–1860.* Baton Rouge: Louisiana State University Press, 1981.

Ferrell, Robert H., ed. *Off the Record: The Private Papers of Harry S. Truman.* New York: Harper & Row, 1980.

———. *The Eisenhower Diaries.* New York: W. W. Norton, 1981.

———. *Dear Bess: The Letters from Harry to Bess Truman, 1910–1959.* New York: W. W. Norton, 1983.

Freedman, Max, ed. *Roosevelt and Frankfurter: Their Correspondence, 1928–1945.* Boston: Little, Brown, 1968.

The Fundamentals: A Testimony to Truth, 4 vols. Edited by George M. Marsden. New York: Garland, 1988.

Gaustad, Edwin S., ed. *A Documentary History of Religion in America to the Civil War,* 2nd ed. Grand Rapids, Mich.: Eerdmans, 1993.

Gougeon, Len, and Joel Myerson, eds. *Emerson's Antislavery Writings.* New Haven: Yale University Press, 1995.

Graebner, Norman A., ed. *Manifest Destiny.* Indianapolis: Bobbs-Merrill, 1968.

Hamilton, Alexander, James Madison, and John Jay. *The Federalist, with Letters of "Brutus."* Edited by Terence Ball. Cambridge: Cambridge University Press, 2003.

Hillman, William, ed. *Mr. President: The First Publication from the Personal Diaries, Private Letters, Papers, and Revealing Interviews of Harry S. Truman, Thirty-Second President of the United States of America.* New York: Farrar, Straus and Young, 1952.

Hutson, James H., ed. *The Founders on Religion: A Book of Quotations.* Princeton: Princeton University Press, 2005.

Ickes, Harold L. *The Secret Diary of Harold L. Ickes,* 3 vols. New York: Simon & Schuster, 1953–1954.

Israel, Fred L., ed. *The War Diary of Breckenridge Long: Selections from the Years 1939–1944.* Lincoln: University of Nebraska Press, 1966.

James, Robert Rhodes, ed. *Winston S. Churchill: His Complete Speeches,* 8 vols. New York and London: Chelsea House/R. R. Bowker, 1974.

The Journals of David E. Lilienthal, 7 vols. New York: Harper & Row, 1964–1983.

The Journals of Thomas Merton, 7 vols. San Francisco: HarperSanFrancisco, 1995–1998.

Koch, Adrienne, and William Peden, eds. *The Selected Writings of John and John Quincy Adams.* New York: Alfred A. Knopf, 1946.

LaFeber, Walter, ed. *John Quincy Adams and American Continental Empire: Letters, Speeches, and Papers.* Chicago: Quadrangle Books, 1965.

Letters and Papers of Alfred Thayer Mahan, 3 vols. Edited by Robert Seager and Doris D. Maguire. Annapolis, Md.: Naval Institute Press, 1975.

Letters of Louis D. Brandeis, 5 vols. Edited by Melvin I. Urofsky and David W. Levy. Albany: State University of New York Press, 1971–1978.

The Letters of Ralph Waldo Emerson, 6 vols. Edited by Ralph L. Rusk. New York: Columbia University Press, 1939.

Millis, Walter, ed. *The Forrestal Diaries.* New York: Viking Press, 1951.

Miller, Perry, and Thomas H. Johnson, eds. *The Puritans: A Sourcebook of Their Writings*, rev. ed., 2 vols. New York: Harper & Row, 1963.

Miller, Robert Ryal, ed. *The Mexican War Journal and Letters of Ralph W. Kirkham*. College Station: Texas A&M University Press, 1991.

Moran, Charles McMoran Wilson. *Winston Churchill: The Struggle for Survival, 1940–1965, Taken from the Diaries of Lord Moran*. London: Constable, 1966.

Morison, Samuel Eliot. *Sources and Documents Illustrating the American Revolution, 1764–1788*, 2nd ed. New York: Oxford University Press, 1965.

Papers of John Adams, 14 vols. Cambridge, Mass.: Harvard University Press, 1977–2008.

The Papers of Benjamin Franklin, 38 vols. New Haven: Yale University Press, 1959–2006.

The Papers of Daniel Webster: Diplomatic Papers, 2 vols. Hanover, N.H.: University Press of New England, 1983–1987.

The Papers of Daniel Webster: Speeches and Formal Writings, 2 vols. Hanover, N.H.: University Press of New England, 1986–1988.

The Papers of Dwight David Eisenhower, 21 vols. Baltimore: Johns Hopkins University Press, 1970–2001.

The Papers of George Washington: Revolutionary War Series, 18 vols. Charlottesville: University Press of Virginia, 1985–2008.

The Papers of George Washington: Presidential Series, 14 vols. Charlottesville: University Press of Virginia, 1987–2008.

The Papers of Henry Clay, 11 vols. Lexington: University Press of Kentucky, 1959–1992.

The Papers of James Madison, 17 vols. Chicago and Charlottesville: University of Chicago Press and University Press of Virginia, 1962–1991.

The Papers of James Madison: Presidential Series, 5 vols. Charlottesville: University Press of Virginia, 1984–2004.

The Papers of Woodrow Wilson, 69 vols. Princeton: Princeton University Press, 1966–1994.

The Personal Letters of Stephen Wise. Edited by Justine Wise Polier and James Waterman Wise. Boston: Beacon Press, 1956.

Poen, Monte M., ed. *Strictly Personal and Confidential: The Letters Harry Truman Never Mailed*. Boston: Little, Brown, 1982.

The Private Papers of Senator Vandenberg. Edited by Arthur H. Vandenberg Jr. Boston: Houghton Mifflin, 1952.

Quinn, David Beers, ed. *The Voyages and Colonising Enterprises of Sir Humphrey Gilbert*. London: Hakluyt Society, 1940.

Rankin, David C., ed. *Diary of a Christian Soldier: Rufus Kinsley and the Civil War*. New York: Cambridge University Press, 2004.

Reception and Entertainment of the Honourable Artillery Company of London. Boston: Norwood Press, 1904.

Roosevelt, Theodore. *Progressive Principles: Selections from Addresses Made During the Presidential Campaign of 1912*. Edited by Elmer H. Youngman. New York: Progressive National Service, 1913.

Slotkin, Richard, and James K. Folsom, eds. *So Dreadfull a Judgment: Puritan Responses to King Philip's War, 1676–1677*. Middletown, Conn.: Wesleyan University Press, 1978.

Strachey, William. *The Historie of Travell into Virginia Britania*. Edited by Louis B. Wright and Virginia Freund. London: Hakluyt Society, 1953.

Taylor, E. G. R., ed. *The Original Writings and Correspondence of the Two Richard Hakluyts*, 2 vols. London: Hakluyt Society, 1935.

Trollinger, William Vance, ed. *The Antievolution Pamphlets of William Bell Riley*. New York: Garland, 1995.

Van Dusen, Henry P., ed. *The Spiritual Legacy of John Foster Dulles: Selections from His Articles and Addresses.* Philadelphia: Westminster Press, 1960.

Vaughan, Alden T., ed. *Chronicles of the American Revolution.* New York: Grosset and Dunlap, 1965.

Vaughan, Alden T., and Edward W. Clark, eds. *Puritans Among the Indians: Accounts of Captivity and Redemption, 1676–1724.* Cambridge, Mass.: Harvard University Press, 1981.

Voss, Carl Hermann, ed. *Stephen S. Wise: Servant of the People.* Philadelphia: Jewish Publication Society of America, 1969.

Wallace, Henry A. *The Century of the Common Man.* Edited by Russell Lord. New York: Reynal and Hitchcock, 1943.

Washington, James Melvin, ed. *A Testament of Hope: The Essential Writings of Martin Luther King, Jr.* San Francisco: Harper & Row, 1986.

The Works of Jonathan Edwards, 26 vols. New Haven: Yale University Press, 1957–2008.

The Works of William E. Channing. New York: B. Franklin, 1970.

MEMOIRS AND AUTOBIOGRAPHIES

Acheson, Dean. *Present at the Creation: My Years in the State Department.* New York: W. W. Norton, 1969.

Adams, John Quincy. *Memoirs of John Quincy Adams, Comprising Portions of His Diary from 1795 to 1848,* 12 vols. Edited by Charles Francis Adams. Philadelphia: Lippincott, 1874–1877.

Adler, Cyrus. *I Have Considered the Days.* Philadelphia: Jewish Publication Society of America, 1941.

Braun, Leopold L. S. *In Lubianka's Shadow: The Memoirs of an American Priest in Stalin's Moscow, 1934–1945.* Edited by G. M. Hamburg. Notre Dame, Ind.: University of Notre Dame Press, 2006.

Brzezinski, Zbigniew. *Power and Principle: Memoirs of the National Security Advisor, 1977–1981.* New York: Farrar, Straus and Giroux, 1983.

Bush, George, and Brent Scowcroft. *A World Transformed.* New York: Alfred A. Knopf, 1998.

Califano, Joseph A., Jr. *The Triumph and Tragedy of Lyndon Johnson: The White House Years.* New York: Simon & Schuster, 1991.

Chambers, Whittaker. *Witness.* New York: Random House, 1952.

Churchill, Winston S. *The Second World War: The Gathering Storm.* Boston: Houghton Mifflin, 1948.

———. *The Second World War: The Grand Alliance.* Boston: Houghton Mifflin, 1950.

Clifford, Clark, with Richard Holbrooke. *Counsel to the President: A Memoir.* New York: Random House, 1991.

Dobrynin, Anatoly. *In Confidence: Moscow's Ambassador to America's Six Cold War Presidents (1962–1986).* New York: Times Books, 1995.

Eddy, Sherwood. *Eighty Adventurous Years: An Autobiography.* New York: Harper, 1955.

Eden, Anthony. *Full Circle: The Memoirs of the Rt. Hon. Sir Anthony Eden.* London: Cassell, 1960.

Farley, James A. *Jim Farley's Story: The Roosevelt Years.* New York: Whittlesey House, 1948.

Fosdick, Harry Emerson. *The Living of These Days: An Autobiography.* New York: Harper & Row, 1956.

Franklin, Benjamin. *Benjamin Franklin's Autobiography: An Authoritative Text, Backgrounds, Criticism.* Edited by J. A. Leo Lemay and P. M. Zall. New York: W. W. Norton, 1986.

Gladden, Washington. *Recollections.* Boston: Houghton Mifflin, 1909.

Goodman, Grant K. *America's Japan: The First Year, 1945–1946*. New York: Fordham University Press, 2005.

Graham, Billy. *Just as I Am: The Autobiography of Billy Graham*. San Francisco: HarperSanFrancisco, 1997.

Grayson, Cary T. *Woodrow Wilson: An Intimate Memoir*. New York: Holt, Rinehart and Winston, 1960.

Harriman, W. Averell, and Elie Abel. *Special Envoy to Churchill and Stalin, 1941–1946*. New York: Random House, 1975.

Hoar, George F. *Autobiography of Seventy Years*, 2 vols. New York: Charles Scribner's Sons, 1903.

Hoover, Herbert. *An American Epic*, 4 vols. Chicago: Regnery, 1959–1964.

Houston, David F. *Eight Years with Wilson's Cabinet, 1913 to 1920: With a Personal Estimate of the President*, 2 vols. Garden City, N.Y.: Doubleday, Page & Company, 1926.

Hull, Cordell. *The Memoirs of Cordell Hull*, 2 vols. New York: Macmillan, 1948.

Javits, Jacob K., with Rafael Steinberg. *Javits: The Autobiography of a Public Man*. Boston: Houghton Mifflin, 1981.

Johnson, Sam Houston. *My Brother Lyndon*. New York: Cowles Book Co., 1970.

Kennan, George F. *Memoirs, 1925–1950*. Boston: Little, Brown, 1967.

Keynes, John Maynard. *The Economic Consequences of the Peace*. London: Macmillan, 1919.

Kissinger, Henry. *Years of Upheaval*. Boston: Little, Brown, 1982.

———. *Years of Renewal*. New York: Simon and Schuster, 1999.

King, Martin Luther, Jr. *Stride Toward Freedom: The Montgomery Story*. New York: Harper, 1958.

Lansing, Robert. *The Peace Negotiations: A Personal Narrative*. Boston: Houghton Mifflin, 1921.

Macfarland, Charles Stedman. *Across the Years*. New York: Macmillan, 1936.

McNamara, Robert S., with Brian VanDeMark. *In Retrospect: The Tragedy and Lessons of Vietnam*. New York: Times Books, 1995.

Matlock, Jack F., Jr. *Reagan and Gorbachev: How the Cold War Ended*. New York: Random House, 2004.

Mays, Benjamin E. *Born to Rebel: An Autobiography*. New York: Scribner's, 1971.

Morton, H. V. *Atlantic Meeting: An Account of Mr. Churchill's Voyage in H.M.S. Prince of Wales, in August, 1941, and the Conference with President Roosevelt which Resulted in the Atlantic Charter*. London: Methuen, 1943.

Nixon, Richard. *The Memoirs of Richard Nixon*. New York: Grosset & Dunlap, 1978.

Perkins, Frances. *The Roosevelt I Knew*. New York: Viking, 1946.

Poling, Daniel A. *Mine Eyes Have Seen*. New York: McGraw-Hill, 1959.

Reagan, Ronald. *An American Life*. New York: Simon & Schuster, 1990.

Roosevelt, Eleanor. *This Is My Story*. New York: Harper & Brothers, 1937.

———. *This I Remember*. New York: Harper & Brothers, 1949.

Roosevelt, Elliott. *As He Saw It*. New York: Duell, Sloan and Pearce, 1946.

Roosevelt, James, and Sidney Shalett. *Affectionately, F.D.R.: A Son's Story of a Lonely Man*. New York: Harcourt, Brace, 1959.

Rusk, Dean, with Richard Rusk. *As I Saw It*. New York: W. W. Norton, 1990.

Salinger, Pierre. *With Kennedy*. New York: Doubleday, 1966.

Schlesinger, Arthur M., Jr. *A Thousand Days: John F. Kennedy in the White House*. Boston: Houghton Mifflin, 1965.

Shultz, George P. *Turmoil and Triumph: My Years as Secretary of State*. New York: Charles Scribner's Sons, 1993.

Sorensen, Theodore C. *Kennedy*. New York: Harper & Row, 1965.

Tittmann, Harold H., Jr. *Inside the Vatican of Pius XII: The Memoir of an American Diplomat during World War II.* Edited by Harold H. Tittmann III. New York: Image Books/Doubleday, 2004.

Truman, Harry S. *Memoirs,* 2 vols. New York: Doubleday, 1955–1956.

———. *Mr. Citizen.* New York: Geis Associates, 1960.

Truman, Margaret. *Harry S. Truman.* New York: William Morrow, 1973.

Valenti, Jack. *A Very Human President.* New York: W. W. Norton, 1975.

Visser 't Hooft, W. A. *Memoirs.* Philadelphia: Westminster Press, 1973.

Welles, Sumner. *The Time for Decision.* New York: Harper & Brothers, 1944.

Westmoreland, William C. *A Soldier Reports.* Garden City, N.Y.: Doubleday, 1976.

Wise, Stephen S. *Challenging Years: The Autobiography of Stephen Wise.* New York: G. P. Putnam's Sons, 1949.

PERIODICALS

NEWSPAPERS AND MAGAZINES

The Atlantic Monthly
Chicago Daily Tribune/Chicago Tribune
The Conscientious Objector
Courier-Post (Camden, N.J.)
Daily Northwestern (Oshkosh, Wis.)
Economic Council Papers
Foreign Policy
Jackson Daily News (Miss.)
Kansas City Times
Life
Los Angeles Times
Montgomery Advertiser (Ala.)
Nebraska State Journal
The New Republic
Newsweek
New York Herald Tribune
New York Review of Books
New York Times
The New Yorker
Oklahoma Citizen
PM
St. Petersburg Times
San Francisco Chronicle
Seattle Post-Intelligencer
Time
The Times (London)
Wall Street Journal
Washington Post
The Weekly Standard

RELIGIOUS PERIODICALS

America (Catholic)
American Holiness Journal (Pentecostal)
Applied Christianity (nondenominational Protestant)
The Catholic C.O.
The Catholic Mind

Catholic News
The Catholic Worker
Christian Beacon (nondenominational Protestant)
Christian Century (nondenominational Protestant)
Christian Herald (nondenominational Protestant)
Christian Index (nondenominational Protestant)
Christianity and Crisis (nondenominational)
Christianity Today (nondenominational Protestant)
Commonweal (Catholic)
Congregational Christian Beacon
Current Religious Thought (nondenominational)
The Episcopal Methodist
Federal Council Bulletin (nondenominational Protestant)
The Herald (Pentecostal)
The Methodist Challenge
Missionary Herald (nondenominational Protestant)
Missionary Review of the World (nondenominational Protestant)
One Methodist Voice
Our Sunday Visitor (Catholic)
Princeton Seminary Bulletin (Presbyterian)
Social Action (Congregational)
Understanding (nondenominational Protestant)
United Church Herald (United Church of Christ)
United Evangelical Action (nondenominational Protestant)
The Witness (Episcopal)
World Alliance News Letter (nondenominational Protestant)
The World Tomorrow (nondenominational Protestant)
Zion's Herald (Methodist)

SERIALS

Family Christian Almanack for the United States, Calculated for the Horizons and Meridians of Boston, New-York, Baltimore, and Charleston, 1844. New York: American Tract Society, 1843.
The Christian Almanack, 1823. Boston: Lincoln and Edmands, 1822.
The Christian Almanack, 1825. Boston: Lincoln and Edmands, 1824.

SERMONS

Bachman, R. L. *The Triumph of Foreign Missions: Sermon Preached in First Presbyterian Church, Utica, N.Y., March 30, 1895.* Utica, N.Y.: n.p., 1895.
Bacon, Leonard Woolsey. *The Peaceful Mission of America: A Sermon to Citizens.* Norwich, Conn.: Cranston & Co., 1898.
Beardsley, William A. *A Sermon Preached in St. Thomas's Church, Whitsunday, 1901, In Commemoration of the Two Hundredth Anniversary of the Founding of the Society for the Propagation of the Gospel in Foreign Parts.* New Haven: n.p., 1901.
Beecher, Henry Ward. *A Discourse Delivered at the Plymouth Church, Brooklyn, N.Y., Upon Thanksgiving Day, November 25th, 1847.* New York: Cady and Burgess, 1848.
Cary, Samuel. *A Sermon Preached Before the Ancient and Honorable Artillery Company.* Boston: Thomas Wells, 1814.
Channing, William Ellery. *A Sermon on War.* Boston: Wells and Lilly, 1816.
Coffin, Henry Sloane. *The Preparedness of a Christian Nation.* New York: Madison Avenue Presbyterian Church, 1916.
The Complete Sermons of Ralph Waldo Emerson, 4 vols. Columbia: University of Missouri Press, 1989–1992.

Cotton, John. *God's Promise to His Plantations*. London: William Jones for John Bellamy, 1634.

Graves, J. R. *The Desire of All Nations*. Nashville: Graves and Shankland, 1853.

Jones, David. *Defensive War in a Just Cause Sinless*. Philadelphia: Henry Miller, 1775.

Kalloch, A. *National Fast-Day Sermon: Delivered before the Members of the Legislature of the State of Maine*. Augusta, Me.: William T. Johnson, 1849.

Kellogg, Ezra B. *War Contrary to the Gospel*. Providence, R.I.: H. H. Brown, 1830.

Kilgo, John Carlisle. *Chapel Talks, by John Carlisle Kilgo*, ed. D. W. Newsom. Nashville, Dallas, and Richmond: Methodist Episcopal Church, South, 1922.

Knowles, James D. *Perils and Safeguards of American Liberty*. Boston: Lincoln and Edmands, 1828.

Lawrence, William. "A Sermon Preached at the Old South Church on the 266th Anniversary of the Ancient and Honorable Artillery Company, June 6, 1904." In *Reception and Entertainment of the Honourable Artillery Company of London*. Boston: Norwood Press, 1904.

Lathrop, Joseph. *The Happiness of a Free Government, and the Means of Preserving It*. Springfield, Mass.: James R. Hutchins, 1794.

Leighton, Alexander. *Speculum Belli Sacri: Or the Looking-Glasse of the Holy War wherein Is Discovered: The Evill of War. The Good of Warr. The Guide of War*. Amsterdam: Printed by the successors of Giles Thorp, 1624.

Phelps, Austin. *Christian Character a Power in the Redemption of the World*. Andover, Mass.: W. F. Draper and Brother, 1854.

Porter, Eliphalet. *A Sermon, Delivered in Boston, June 1st, 1812, before the Ancient and Honorable Artillery Company*. Boston: Munroe and Francis, 1812.

Pyne, Smith. *A Sermon Delivered on Thanksgiving Day*. Washington, D.C.: C. Alexander, 1846.

Sandoz, Ellis, ed. *Political Sermons of the American Founding Era, 1730–1805*, 2nd ed., 2 vols. Indianapolis: Liberty Fund, 1998.

Sharp, Daniel. *Obedience to Magistrates Inculcated: A Discourse Delivered before the Ancient and Honorable Artillery Company*. Boston: Gould, Kendall and Lincoln, 1840.

The Soul of America in Time of War: Representative Sermons by Fifteen Unitarian Ministers. Boston: Beacon Press, 1918.

Sutton, Thomas. *The Good Fight of Faith*. London: Printed by Samuel Man, 1652; 1624.

Symonds, William. *A Sermon Preached at White-Chappel, in the Presence of Many, Honourable and Worshipfull, the Adventurers and Planters for Virginia*. London: Printed by I. Windet for Eleazar Edgar and William Welby, 1609.

BOOKS

Abbott, Lyman. *The Twentieth Century Crusade*. New York: Macmillan, 1918.

Abeel, David. *The Missionary Fortified Against Trials*. Boston: Perkins, Marvin, and Co., 1835.

Ainslie, Peter. *Towards Christian Unity*. Baltimore: Association for the Promotion of Christian Unity, 1918.

Altizer, Thomas J. J., and William Hamilton. *Radical Theology and the Death of God*. Indianapolis: Bobbs-Merrill, 1966.

Appelman, Hyman J. *Christianity or Communism—Which?* Grand Rapids, Mich.: Zondervan, 1956.

Atkinson, Edward. *Criminal Aggression: By Whom Committed?* Boston: Allied Printing Trades Council, 1899.

Axling, William. *Kagawa*, 2nd ed. New York: Harper & Brothers, 1932.

———. *Toward an Understanding of the Far Eastern Crisis*. Tokyo: n.p., 1938.

Bacon, Benjamin W. *Non-Resistance: Christian or Pagan?* New Haven: Yale University Press, 1918.

Batten, Samuel Zane, ed. *The Moral Meaning of the War: A Prophetic Interpretation.* Philadelphia: American Baptist Publication Society, 1919.

Bennett, John C. *Social Salvation: A Religious Approach to the Problems of Social Change.* New York: Charles Scribner's Sons, 1935.

———. *Christianity—And Our World.* New York: Association Press, 1936.

Blanshard, Paul. *American Freedom and Catholic Power.* Boston: Beacon Press, 1949.

Brown, Arthur J., et al. *Statement of the Church Peace Union on the Japan-China Conflict.* New York: Church Peace Union, 1938.

Chandler, Thomas Bradbury. *A Friendly Address to All Reasonable Americans, on the Subject of Our Political Confusions, in which the Necessary Consequences of Violently Opposing the King's Troops, and of a General Non-Importation Are Fairly Stated.* New York: James Rivington, 1774.

Cleage, Albert B., Jr. *The Black Messiah.* New York: Sheed and Ward, 1968.

Coffin, Henry Sloane. *In a Day of Social Rebuilding: Lectures on the Ministry of the Church.* New Haven, Conn.: Yale University Press, 1918.

Cone, James H. *Black Theology and Black Power.* New York: Seabury Press, 1969.

———. *A Black Theology of Liberation.* Philadelphia: Lippincott, 1970.

Cox, Harvey. *God's Revolution and Man's Responsibility.* Valley Forge, Pa.: Judson Press, 1965.

———. *The Secular City: Secularization and Urbanization in Theological Perspective.* New York: Macmillan, 1965.

Dennis, James S. *Islam and Christian Missions.* New York: Funk & Wagnalls, 1889.

Dionne, E. J., Jr. *Souled Out: Reclaiming Faith and Politics after the Religious Right.* Princeton: Princeton University Press, 2008.

Drinan, Robert F. *Democracy, Dissent, and Disorder: The Issues and the Law.* New York: Seabury Press, 1969.

Dulles, John Foster. *Peaceful Change within the Society of Nations.* Washington, D.C.: Government Printing Office, 1936.

———. *War, Peace and Change.* New York: Harper & Brothers, 1939.

Eddy, Sherwood. *Suffering and the War.* London and New York: Longmans, Green and Company, 1916.

———. *With Our Soldiers in France.* New York: Association Press, 1917.

———. *The Right to Fight: The Moral Grounds of War.* New York: Association Press, 1918.

———. *Why America Fights.* New York: International Committee of the Young Men's Christian Association, 1942.

Eddy, Sherwood, and Kirby Page. *The Abolition of War: The Case Against War and Questions and Answers Concerning War.* New York: George H. Doran, 1924.

Emanuel, Cyprian, et al. *The Ethics of War.* Washington, D.C.: Catholic Association for International Peace, 1932.

———. *The Morality of Conscientious Objection to War.* Washington, D.C.: Catholic Association for International Peace, 1941.

An Examination of the Principles of Peace and War, as Connected with Religion and Morality; Particularly in Reference to the Formation of Peace Societies. Philadelphia: Joseph Rakestraw, 1821.

Fagley, Richard M. *The Study of Peace Aims in the Local Church: Why? What? How?* New York: Church Peace Union and World Alliance for International Friendship through the Churches, 1943.

Farr, Thomas F. *World of Faith and Freedom: Why International Religious Liberty Is Vital to American National Security.* New York: Oxford University Press, 2008.

Feely, Raymond T. *Nazism versus Religion.* New York: Paulist Press, 1940.

Fletcher, Joseph. *Situation Ethics: The New Morality.* Philadelphia: Westminster Press, 1966.

Fosdick, Harry Emerson. *The Challenge of the Present Crisis.* New York: Association Press, 1918.

Gladden, Washington. *Ruling Ideas of the Present Age.* Boston: Houghton Mifflin, 1895.

Graham, Billy. *America's Hour of Decision.* Wheaton, Ill.: Van Kampen Press, 1951.

———. *World Aflame.* Garden City, N.Y.: Doubleday, 1965.

Gulick, Sidney L. *American Democracy and Asiatic Citizenship.* New York: Scribner's, 1918.

Hargis, Billy James. *Communist America: Must It Be?* Tulsa, Okla.: Christian Crusade, 1960.

———. *The Far Left.* Tulsa, Okla.: Christian Crusade, 1964.

Henry, Carl F. H. *Faith at the Frontiers.* Chicago: Moody Press, 1969.

———. *A Plea for Evangelical Demonstration.* Grand Rapids, Mich.: Baker Book House, 1971.

Herklots, H. G. G., and Henry Smith Leiper. *Pilgrimage to Amsterdam.* New York: Morehouse-Gorham, 1947.

Hertzke, Allen D. *Freeing God's Children: The Unlikely Alliance for Global Human Rights.* Lanham, Md.: Rowman & Littlefield, 2004.

Hoar, George F. *Speech of Hon. George F. Hoar, of Massachusetts, in the Senate of the United States.* Washington, D.C.: Allied Printing Trades Council, 1902.

Holmes, John Haynes. *Through Gentile Eyes: A Plea for Tolerance and Good Will.* New York: Jewish Opinion Publishing Corporation, 1938.

Horsh, John. *Modern Religious Liberalism: The Destructiveness and Irrationality of the New Theology.* Scottdale, Pa.: Fundamental Truth Depot, 1921.

Horton, Walter Marshall. *Realistic Theology.* New York: Harper & Brothers, 1934.

Hough, Joseph C., Jr. *Black Power and White Protestants: A Christian Response to the New Negro Pluralism.* New York: Oxford University Press, 1968.

The Japanese in Our Midst. Denver: Colorado Council of Churches, 1943.

Judd, Walter H. *Autopsy on Our Blunders in Asia.* New York: National Industrial Conference/American Affairs Pamphlets, 1950.

Kennan, George F. *American Diplomacy, 1900–1950.* Chicago: University of Chicago Press, 1951.

———. *Around the Cragged Hill: A Personal and Political Philosophy.* New York: W. W. Norton, 1993.

Laubach, Frank C. *The World Is Learning Compassion.* New York: Fleming H. Revell, 1958.

Lerner, Michael. *The Left Hand of God: Taking Back Our Country from the Religious Right.* San Francisco: HarperSanFrancisco, 2006.

Lindsey, Hal, with C. C. Carlson. *The Late Great Planet Earth.* Grand Rapids, Mich.: Zondervan, 1970.

Lynch, Frederick. *President Wilson and the Moral Aims of the War.* New York: Fleming H. Revell, 1918.

Lyon, D. Willard. *The Christian Equivalent of War.* New York: Association Press, 1915.

McIntire, Carl. *The Rise of the Tyrant: Controlled Economy vs. Private Enterprise.* Collingswood, N.J.: Christian Beacon Press, 1945.

———. *Author of Liberty.* Collingswood, N.J.: Christian Beacon Press, 1946.

———. *For Such a Time as This.* Collingswood, N.J.: Christian Beacon Press, 1946.

———. *The Truth about the Federal Council of Churches and the Kingdom of God.* Collingswood, N.J.: Christian Beacon Press, 1950.

Markham, Reuben H. *Rumania Under the Soviet Yoke.* Boston: Meador Publishing Co., 1949.

———, ed. *Communists Crush Churches in Eastern Europe.* Boston: Meador Publishing Co., 1950.

Mathews, Shailer. *The Spiritual Interpretation of History*, 2nd ed. Cambridge, Mass.: Harvard University Press, 1917.

———. *Patriotism and Religion.* New York: Macmillan, 1918.

Merrill, William P. *Christian Internationalism.* New York: Macmillan, 1919.

Merton, Thomas, et al. *Breakthrough to Peace.* Norfolk, Conn.: J. Laughlin/New Directions, 1962.

Milton, John. *Of Reformation Touching Church-Discipline in England: And the Cases that Hitherto Have Hindered It.* London: Thomas Underhill, 1641.

———. *Paradise Lost.* Edited by Stephen Orgel and Jonathan Goldberg. Oxford: Oxford University Press, 2004.

Montesquieu, Charles de Secondat, Baron de. *The Spirit of the Laws.* Edited by Anne M. Cohler, Basia Carolyn Miller, and Harold Samuel Stone. Cambridge: Cambridge University Press, 1989.

Moon, Parker Thomas. *Causes of War: A Preliminary Report of the Committee on Sources of International Enmity.* Washington, D.C.: Catholic Association for International Peace, 1930.

Murray, J. Lovell. *The Call of a World Task in War Time*, rev. ed. New York: Student Volunteer Movement, 1918.

Neale, R. H. *The Fourth Annual Address of the Connecticut Peace Society.* Hartford: William Watson, 1835.

Newton, Louie D. *An American Churchman in the Soviet Union.* New York: American Russian Institute, 1946.

Niebuhr, Reinhold. *Moral Man and Immoral Society: A Study in Ethics and Politics.* New York: Scribner's, 1932.

———. *The Children of Light and the Children of Darkness: A Vindication of Democracy and a Critique of Its Traditional Defence.* New York: Scribner's, 1944.

———. *The Irony of American History.* New York: Scribner's, 1952.

Nixon, Justin Wroe. *The United Nations and Our Religious Heritage.* New York: Church Peace Union, 1953.

Novak, Michael. *A Theology for Radical Politics.* New York: Herder and Herder, 1969.

———. *Will It Liberate? Questions about Liberation Theology.* New York: Paulist Press, 1986.

O'Toole, George Barry. *War and Conscription at the Bar of Christian Morals.* New York: Catholic Worker Press, 1941.

Page, Kirby. *The Sword or the Cross: An Examination of War in the Light of Jesus' Way of Life.* New York: George H. Doran Company, 1921.

Paine, Thomas. *Political Writings.* Edited by Bruce Kuklick. Cambridge: Cambridge University Press, 1989.

Parsons, Wilfrid, Edward A. Conway, and Thomas H. Mahony. *Peace in the Atomic Age: Three Reports.* Washington, D.C.: Catholic Association for International Peace, 1947.

"Philanthropos." *A Solemn Appeal to Christians of All Denominations in Favor of the Cause of Permanent and Universal Peace.* Boston: American Peace Society, 1836.

Poling, Daniel A. *A Preacher Looks at War.* New York: Macmillan, 1943.

Ramsey, Paul. *The Just War: Force and Political Responsibility.* New York: Scribner's, 1968.

Rauschenbusch, Walter. *Dare We Be Christians?* Boston: Pilgrim Press, 1914.

———. *A Theology for the Social Gospel.* New York: Macmillan, 1917.

Robertson, Pat. *The New World Order.* Dallas: Word Publishing, 1991.

Roosevelt, Theodore. *Fear God and Take Your Own Part.* New York: George H. Doran Company, 1916.

Rose, Stephen C. *The Grass Roots Church: A Manifesto for Protestant Renewal.* New York: Holt, Rinehart and Winston, 1966.

Ryan, John A., et al. *The Obligation of Catholics to Promote Peace.* Washington, D.C.: Catholic Association for International Peace, 1940.

Schlafly, Phyllis, and Chester Ward. *Kissinger on the Couch.* New Rochelle, N.Y.: Arlington House, 1975.

Schwarz, Fred. *You Can Trust the Communists (to Be Communists).* Englewood Cliffs, N.J.: Prentice-Hall, 1960.

Simmons, Henry M. *History of Our Philippine Relations as Told in Official Records.* Minneapolis: Minneapolis Anti-Imperialist League, 1899.

Sixty American Opinions on the War. London: T. Fisher Unwin, 1915.

Speer, Robert E. *The Christian Man, the Church, and the War.* New York: Macmillan, 1918.

———. *The War and the Religious Outlook.* New York: Association Press, 1919.

Spellman, Francis J. *The Road to Victory.* New York: Scribner's, 1942.

Stimson, Henry A. *While the War Rages: An Appraisal of Some Ethical Factors.* New York: Abingdon Press, 1915.

Strong, Josiah. *Our Country: Its Possible Future and Its Present Crisis.* Edited by Jurgen Herbst. Cambridge, Mass.: Harvard University Press, 1963 [1885; 1891].

———. *Expansion Under New-World Conditions.* New York: Baker and Taylor, 1900.

Thich Nhat Hanh. *Vietnam: Lotus in a Sea of Fire.* New York: Hill and Wang, 1967.

Tocqueville, Alexis de. *Democracy in America.* Edited by Harvey C. Mansfield and Delba Winthrop. Chicago: University of Chicago Press, 2000.

Torrey, R. A. *What the War Teaches, or The Great Lessons of 1917.* In *Conservative Call to Arms,* ed. Joel A. Carpenter. New York: Garland, 1988.

Vahanian, Gabriel. *The Death of God: The Culture of Our Post-Christian Era.* New York: George Braziller, 1961.

Van Buren, Paul. *The Secular Meaning of the Gospel, Based on an Analysis of Its Language.* New York: Macmillan, 1963.

Van Kirk, Walter W. *Religion Renounces War.* Chicago: Willet, Clark and Company, 1934.

Vincent, Philip. *A True Relation of the Late Battell Fought in New England, between the English, and the Salvages.* London: M.P. for Nathanael Butter and John Bellamie, 1637.

Wallace, Henry A. *Statesmanship and Religion.* New York: Round Table Press, 1934.

Wallis, Jim. *God's Politics: Why the Right Gets It Wrong and the Left Doesn't Get It.* San Francisco: HarperSanFrancisco, 2005.

———. *The Great Awakening: Reviving Faith and Politics in a Post-Religious Right America.* New York: HarperOne, 2008.

Welles, Sumner. *Where Are We Heading?* New York: Harper & Brothers, 1946.

Wills, Garry. *Head and Heart: American Christianities.* New York: Penguin Press, 2007.

Wirt, Sherwood Eliot. *The Social Conscience of the Evangelical.* New York: Harper & Row, 1968.

Wolfe, Tom. *Mauve Gloves & Madmen, Clutter & Vine, and Other Stories, Sketches, and Essays.* New York: Farrar, Straus and Giroux, 1976.

JOURNAL ARTICLES AND BOOK CHAPTERS

"American Institute of Public Opinion-Surveys, 1938–1939." *Public Opinion Quarterly* 3 (October 1939): 581–607.

Ashworth, Robert A. "Christian Union after the War." *Biblical World* 52 (November 1918): 290–295.

Aubrey, Edwin Ewart. "The Oxford Conference, 1937." *Journal of Religion* 17 (October 1937): 379–396.

Bennett, John C. "The Causes of Social Evil." In Nils Ehrenström, et al., *Christian Faith and the Common Life*. London: Allen & Unwin, 1938: 175–196.

———. "The Outlook for Theology." *Journal of Religion* 21 (October 1941): 341–353.

———. "The View of an American Theologian." In John C. Bennett, et al., *The Road to Peace: Christian Approaches to Defence and Disarmament*. London: SCM Press, 1965: 32–41.

Brandt, Karl. "How Europe Is Fighting Famine." *Foreign Affairs* 19 (July 1941): 806–817.

Cantril, Hadley. "America Faces the War: A Study in Public Opinion." *Public Opinion Quarterly* 4 (September 1940): 387–407.

Cantril, Hadley, Donald Rugg, and Frederick Williams. "America Faces the War: Shifts in Opinion." *Public Opinion Quarterly* 4 (December 1940): 651–656.

Casey, Robert P. "The Cultural Mission of Russian Orthodoxy." *Harvard Theological Review* 40 (October 1947): 257–275.

Cavert, Samuel McCrea. "The Missionary Enterprise as the Moral Equivalent of War." *Biblical World* 50 (December 1917): 348–352.

Duker, Abraham G. "Political and Cultural Aspects of Jewish Post-War Problems." *Jewish Social Service Quarterly* 19 (September 1942): 2–12.

Dulles, John Foster. "The Problem of Peace in a Dynamic World." In Marquess of Lothian, et al., *The Universal Church and the World of Nations*. London: Allen & Unwin, 1938: 143–168.

———. "Policy for Security and Peace." *Foreign Affairs* 32 (April 1954): 353–364.

———. "Challenge and Response in United States Policy." *Foreign Affairs* 36 (October 1957): 25–43.

Farr, Thomas F. "Diplomacy in an Age of Faith." *Foreign Affairs* 87 (March/April 2008): 110–124.

Ford, John C. "The Morality of Obliteration Bombing." *Theological Studies* 5 (1944): 261–309.

Granberg, Donald, and Keith E. Campbell. "Certain Aspects of Religiosity and Orientations toward the Vietnam War among Missouri Undergraduates." *Sociological Analysis* 34 (Spring 1973): 40–49.

Harrington, Karl P. "Unification and the Negro." *Methodist Review Quarterly* 68 (July 1919): 468–476.

Hopkins, W. H. "The Federated Church the Next Great Forward Movement." *Christian Union Quarterly* 9 (July 1919): 35–37.

Johnson, F. Ernest. "The Impact of the War on Religion in America." *American Journal of Sociology* 48 (November 1942): 353–360.

Kallen, H. M. "National Solidarity and the Jewish Minority." *Annals of the American Academy of Political and Social Science* 223 (September 1942): 17–28.

Kennan, George F. "The Sources of Soviet Conduct." *Foreign Affairs* 25 (July 1947): 566–582.

Kirk, Russell. "The Struggle for Power with Communism." In *Christianity and World Revolution*. Edited by Edwin H. Rian. New York: Harper & Row, 1963: 3–12.

Knox, George William. "What Modifications in Western Christianity May Be Expected from Contact with Oriental Religions on the Mission Field?" *American Journal of Theology* 11 (October 1907): 569–579.

McCawley, James. "The Bombing of Civilians." *Catholic World* 162 (October 1945): 11–19.

Martin, Leo J. "Integrating Forces for an International Community." *American Catholic Sociological Review* 4 (December 1943): 194–204.

Mathews, Shailer. "Religion and War." *Biblical World* 52 (September 1918): 163–176.

Minear, Lawrence. "Conscience and the Draft." *Theology Today* 23 (April 1966): 60–72.

Niebuhr, H. Richard. "Man the Sinner." *Journal of Religion* 15 (July 1935): 272–280.

Niebuhr, Reinhold. "The Christian Faith and the Common Life." In Nils Ehrenström, et al., *Christian Faith and the Common Life*. London: Allen & Unwin, 1938: 67–97.

———. "The Illusion of World Government." *Foreign Affairs* 27 (April 1949): 379–388.

Ramsey, Paul. "The Ethics of Intervention." *Review of Politics* 27 (July 1965): 287–310.

Ross, Eva J. "The Sociologist's Contribution to Postwar Reconstruction." *American Catholic Sociological Review* 4 (March 1943): 3–9.

———. "Towards Postwar Social Cooperation." *American Catholic Sociological Review* 6 (June 1945): 91–96.

Ryan, John A. "Roosevelt and Social Justice." *Review of Politics* 7 (July 1945): 297–305.

Shaull, Richard. "Revolutionary Change in Theological Perspective." In *The Church Amid Revolution: A Selection of the Essays Prepared for the World Council of Churches Geneva Conference on Church and Society*. Edited by Harvey G. Cox. New York: Association Press, 1967: 27–47.

Tufts, James H. "Religion's Place in Securing a Better World-Order." *Journal of Religion* 2 (March 1922): 113–128.

Wallace, Henry A. "Practical Religion in the World of Tomorrow." In *Christian Bases of World Order: The Merrick Lectures for 1943*. New York: Abingdon-Cokesbury Press, 1943: 9–20.

Walsh, Bryan O. "Cuban Refugee Children." *Journal of Interamerican Studies and World Affairs* 13 (July-October 1971): 378–415.

Weizmann, Chaim. "Palestine's Role in the Solution of the Jewish Problem." *Foreign Affairs* 20 (January 1942): 324–338.

SECONDARY SOURCES
BOOKS

Abdo, Geneive. *Mecca and Main Street: Muslim Life in America after 9/11*. New York: Oxford University Press, 2006.

Abrams, Ray H. *Preachers Present Arms: A Study of the War-Time Attitudes and Activities of the Churches and the Clergy in the United States, 1914–1918*. New York: Round Table Press, 1933.

Abzug, Robert H. *Cosmos Crumbling: American Reform and the Religious Imagination*. New York: Oxford University Press, 1994.

Adams, Michael C. C. *The Best War Ever: America and World War II*. Baltimore: Johns Hopkins University Press, 1994.

Adeleke, Tunde. *UnAfrican Americans: Nineteenth-Century Black Nationalists and the Civilizing Mission*. Lexington: University Press of Kentucky, 1998.

Ahlstrom, Sydney E. *A Religious History of the American People*. New Haven: Yale University Press, 1972.

Akers, Charles W. *Called unto Liberty: A Life of Jonathan Mayhew, 1720–1766*. Cambridge, Mass.: Harvard University Press, 1964.

———. *The Divine Politician: Samuel Cooper and the American Revolution in Boston*. Boston: Northeastern University Press, 1982.

Albright, Raymond W. *A History of the Protestant Episcopal Church*. New York: Macmillan, 1964.

Alexander, John K. *Samuel Adams: America's Revolutionary Politician*. Lanham, Md.: Rowman & Littlefield, 2002.

Allison, Robert J. *The Crescent Obscured: The United States and the Muslim World, 1776–1815*. New York: Oxford University Press, 1995.

Allitt, Patrick. *Catholic Intellectuals and Conservative Politics in America, 1950–1985*. Ithaca: Cornell University Press, 1993.

———. *Religion in America since 1945: A History*. New York: Columbia University Press, 2003.

Almond, Gabriel A., R. Scott Appleby, and Emmanuel Sivan. *Strong Religion: The Rise of Fundamentalisms Around the World*. Chicago: University of Chicago Press, 2003.

Alvarez, Luis. *The Power of the Zoot: Youth Culture and Resistance During World War II*. Berkeley: University of California Press, 2008.

Ambrose, Stephen E. *Nixon*, 3 vols. New York: Simon and Schuster, 1987–1991.

Anderson, Carol. *Eyes Off the Prize: The United Nations and the African American Struggle for Human Rights, 1944–1955*. New York: Cambridge University Press, 2003.

Anderson, Fred. *A People's Army: Massachusetts Soldiers and Society in the Seven Years' War*. Chapel Hill: University of North Carolina Press, 1984.

———. *Crucible of War: The Seven Years' War and the Fate of Empire in British North America, 1754–1766*. New York: Alfred A. Knopf, 2000.

Anderson, Fred, and Andrew Cayton. *The Dominion of War: Empire and Liberty in North America, 1500–2000*. New York: Viking, 2005.

Anderson, Irvine H. *Biblical Interpretation and Middle East Policy: The Promised Land, America, and Israel, 1917–2002*. Gainesville: University Press of Florida, 2005.

Anderson, Judith Icke. *William Howard Taft: An Intimate History*. New York: W. W. Norton, 1981.

Anderson, M. S. *The War of the Austrian Succession, 1740–1748*. London: Longman, 1995.

Anderson, Stuart. *Race and Rapprochement: Anglo-Saxonism and Anglo-American Relations, 1895–1904*. Rutherford, N.J.: Fairleigh Dickinson University Press, 1981.

Anderson, Virginia DeJohn. *New England's Generation: The Great Migration and the Formation of Society and Culture in the Seventeenth Century*. Cambridge: Cambridge University Press, 1991.

Andrew, John A. *Rebuilding the Christian Commonwealth: New England Congregationalists and Foreign Missions, 1800–1830*. Lexington: University Press of Kentucky, 1976.

Ariel, Yaakov. *On Behalf of Israel: American Fundamentalist Attitudes toward Jews, Judaism, and Zionism, 1865–1945*. New York: Carlson Publishing, 1991.

Armitage, David. *Ideological Origins of the British Empire*. Cambridge: Cambridge University Press, 2000.

Arrington, Leonard J. *Brigham Young: American Moses*. New York: Alfred A. Knopf, 1985.

Arrington, Leonard J., and Davis Bitton. *The Mormon Experience: A History of the Latter-day Saints*. New York: Alfred A. Knopf, 1979.

Atwood, Craig D. *Community of the Cross: Moravian Piety in Colonial Bethlehem*. University Park: Pennsylvania State University Press, 2004.

Auten, Brian J. *Carter's Conversion: The Hardening of American Defense Policy*. Columbia: University of Missouri Press, 2008.

Axtell, James. *After Columbus: Essays in the Ethnohistory of Colonial North America*. New York: Oxford University Press, 1988.

Bacevich, Andrew J. *The New American Militarism: How Americans Are Seduced by War*. New York: Oxford University Press, 2005.

Badger, Anthony J. *The New Deal: The Depression Years, 1933–1940*. Basingstoke, U.K.: Macmillan, 1989.

Bailey, David T. *Shadow on the Church: Southwestern Evangelical Religion and the Issue of Slavery, 1783–1860*. Ithaca, N.Y.: Cornell University Press, 1985.

Bailyn, Bernard. *The Ideological Origins of the American Revolution*. Cambridge, Mass.: Harvard University Press, 1967.

———. *The Ordeal of Thomas Hutchinson*. Cambridge, Mass.: Harvard University Press, 1974.

————. *Faces of Revolution: Personalities and Themes in the Struggle for American Independence.* New York: Alfred A. Knopf, 1990.

Baker, Nicholson. *Human Smoke: The Beginnings of World War II, the End of Civilization.* New York: Simon & Schuster, 2008.

Balmer, Randall H. *A Perfect Babel of Confusion: Dutch Religion and English Culture in the Middle Colonies.* New York: Oxford University Press, 1989.

Balmer, Randall, and Lauren F. Winner. *Protestantism in America.* New York: Columbia University Press, 2002.

Banning, Lance. *The Sacred Fire of Liberty: James Madison and the Founding of the Federal Republic.* Ithaca, N.Y.: Cornell University Press, 1995.

Barkun, Michael. *Crucible of the Millennium: The Burned-Over District of New York in the 1840s.* Syracuse, N.Y.: Syracuse University Press, 1986.

————. *A Culture of Conspiracy: Apocalyptic Visions in Contemporary America.* Berkeley: University of California Press, 2003.

Barnby, H. G. *The Prisoners of Algiers: An Account of the Forgotten American-Algerian War, 1785–1797.* London: Oxford University Press, 1966.

Barrett, Paul M. *American Islam: The Struggle for the Soul of a Religion.* New York: Farrar, Straus and Giroux, 2007.

Bartholomew, Michael. *In Search of H. V. Morton: The Authorised Biography of H. V. Morton.* London: Methuen, 2004.

Bartlett, Irving H. *Daniel Webster.* New York: W. W. Norton, 1978.

Bauer, K. Jack. *The Mexican War, 1846–1848.* New York: Macmillan, 1974.

Bayly, C. A. *The Birth of the Modern World, 1780–1914: Global Connections and Comparisons.* Malden, Mass.: Blackwell, 2004.

Beaver, R. Pierce. *American Protestant Women in World Mission: History of the First Feminist Movement in North America.* Grand Rapids, Mich.: Eerdmans, 1980.

Becker, Annette. *War and Faith: The Religious Imagination in France, 1914–1930.* Translatead by Helen McPhail. Oxford: Berg, 1998.

Beisner, Robert L. *Twelve Against Empire: The Anti-Imperialists, 1898–1900.* New York: McGraw-Hill, 1968.

————. *From the Old Diplomacy to the New, 1865–1900,* 2nd ed. Arlington Heights, Ill.: Harlan Davidson, 1986.

Bell, James. *A War of Religion: Dissenters, Anglicans and the American Revolution.* New York: Palgrave Macmillan, 2008.

Bell, Winthrop Pickard. *The Foreign Protestants and the Settlement of Nova Scotia: The History of a Piece of Arrested British Colonial Policy in the Eighteenth Century.* Toronto: University of Toronto Press, 1961.

Bellah, Robert N. *The Broken Covenant: American Civil Religion in Time of Trial.* New York: Seabury Press, 1975.

Belmonte, Laura A. *Selling the American Way: U.S. Propaganda and the Cold War.* Philadelphia: University of Pennsylvania Press, 2008.

Bemis, Samuel Flagg. *John Quincy Adams and the Union.* New York: Alfred A. Knopf, 1956.

Benbow, Mark. *Leading Them to the Promised Land: Woodrow Wilson, Covenant Theology, and the Mexican Revolution, 1913–1915.* Kent, Ohio: Kent State University Press, 2010.

Bender, Thomas. *A Nation among Nations: America's Place in World History.* New York: Hill and Wang, 2006.

Benson, Michael T. *Harry S. Truman and the Founding of Israel.* Westport, Conn.: Praeger, 1997.

Bercovitch, Sacvan. *The American Jeremiad.* Madison: University of Wisconsin Press, 1978.

————. *Rites of Assent: Transformations in the Symbolic Construction of America.* New York: Routledge, 1993.

Berens, John F. *Providence and Patriotism in Early America, 1640–1815.* Charlottesville: University Press of Virginia, 1978.

Bergère, Marie-Claire. *Sun Yat-sen.* Translated by Janet Lloyd. Stanford, Calif.: Stanford University Press, 1998.

Bergeron, Paul H. *The Presidency of James K. Polk.* Lawrence: University Press of Kansas, 1987.

Berkowitz, Michael. *Western Jewry and the Zionist Project, 1914–1933.* Cambridge: Cambridge University Press, 1997.

Berlin, Ira. *Many Thousands Gone: The First Two Centuries of Slavery in North America.* Cambridge, Mass.: Harvard University Press, 1998.

————. *Generations of Captivity: A History of African-American Slaves.* Cambridge, Mass.: Harvard University Press, 2003.

Bernstein, Iver. *The New York City Draft Riots: Their Significance in American Society and Politics in the Age of the Civil War.* New York: Oxford University Press, 1990.

Bess, Michael. *Choices under Fire: Moral Dimensions of World War II.* New York: Alfred A. Knopf, 2006.

Bivins, Jason C. *The Fracture of Good Order: Christian Antiliberalism and the Challenge to American Politics.* Chapel Hill: University of North Carolina Press, 2003.

Blackett, R. J. M. *Building an Antislavery Wall: Black Americans in the Atlantic Abolitionist Movement, 1830–1860.* Baton Rouge: Louisiana State University Press, 1983.

Blassingame, John W. *The Slave Community: Plantation Life in the Antebellum South.* New York: Oxford University Press, 1972.

Blight, David W. *Race and Reunion: The Civil War in American Memory.* Cambridge, Mass.: Harvard University Press, 2001.

Bliss, Robert M. *Revolution and Empire: English Politics and the American Colonies in the Seventeenth Century.* Manchester: Manchester University Press, 1990.

Bloch, Ruth. *Visionary Republic: Millennial Themes in American Thought, 1756–1800.* Cambridge: Cambridge University Press, 1985.

Bloom, Alexander. *Prodigal Sons: The New York Intellectuals and Their World.* New York: Oxford University Press, 1986.

Blumhofer, Edith L. *Restoring the Faith: The Assemblies of God, Pentecostalism, and American Culture.* Urbana: University of Illinois Press, 1993.

Bobbitt, Philip. *The Shield of Achilles: War, Peace, and the Course of History.* New York: Alfred A. Knopf, 2002.

Boles, John B. *The Great Revival, 1787–1805: The Origins of the Southern Evangelical Mind.* Lexington: University Press of Kentucky, 1972.

Bolton, Charles Knowles. *The Private Soldier under Washington.* New York: Scribner's, 1902.

Bond, Edward L. *Damned Souls in a Tobacco Colony: Religion in Seventeenth-Century Virginia.* Macon, Ga.: Mercer University Press, 2000.

Bonomi, Patricia U. *Under the Cope of Heaven: Religion, Society, and Politics in Colonial America,* rev. ed. New York: Oxford University Press, 2003.

Bordin, Ruth. *Woman and Temperance: The Quest for Power and Liberty, 1873–1900.* Philadelphia: Temple University Press, 1981.

Borgwardt, Elizabeth. *A New Deal for the World: America's Vision for Human Rights.* Cambridge, Mass.: Harvard University Press, 2005.

Borstelmann, Thomas. *The Cold War and the Color Line: American Race Relations in the Global Arena.* Cambridge, Mass.: Harvard University Press, 2001.

Bourne, Russell. *The Red King's Rebellion: Racial Politics in New England, 1675–1678.* New York: Oxford University Press, 1990.

————. *Gods of War, Gods of Peace: How the Meeting of Native and Colonial Religions Shaped Early America.* New York: Harcourt, 2002.

Boyer, Paul. *By the Bomb's Early Light: American Thought and Culture at the Dawn of the Atomic Age.* New York: Pantheon, 1985.

————. *When Time Shall Be No More: Prophecy Belief in Modern American Culture.* Cambridge, Mass.: Harvard University Press, 1992.

Bozeman, Theodore Dwight. *To Live Ancient Lives: The Primitivist Dimension in Puritanism.* Chapel Hill: University of North Carolina Press, 1988.

Braddick, Michael. *God's Fury, England's Fire: A New History of the English Civil Wars.* London: Allen Lane, 2008.

Braeman, John. *Albert J. Beveridge: American Nationalist.* Chicago: University of Chicago Press, 1971.

Branch, Taylor. *Parting the Waters: America in the King Years, 1954–1963.* New York: Simon & Schuster, 1988.

Brands, H. W. *Cold Warriors: Eisenhower's Generation and American Foreign Policy.* New York: Columbia University Press, 1988.

————. *Inside the Cold War: Loy Henderson and the Rise of the American Empire, 1918–1961.* New York: Oxford University Press, 1991.

————. *Bound to Empire: The United States and the Philippines.* New York: Oxford University Press, 1992.

Brecher, Frank W. *Securing American Independence: John Jay and the French Alliance.* Westport, Conn.: Praeger, 2003.

Breen, Louise A. *Transgressing the Bounds: Subversive Enterprises among the Puritan Elite in Massachusetts, 1630–1692.* New York: Oxford University Press, 2001.

Breen, T. H. *The Character of the Good Ruler: A Study of Puritan Political Ideas in New England, 1630–1730.* New Haven: Yale University Press, 1970.

Bremer, Francis J. *Puritan Crisis: New England and the English Civil Wars, 1630–1670.* New York: Garland, 1989.

————. *The Puritan Experiment: New England Society from Bradford to Edwards.* Hanover, N.H.: University Press of New England, 1995.

————. *John Winthrop: America's Forgotten Founding Father.* New York: Oxford University Press, 2003.

Breslaw, Elaine G. *Tituba, Reluctant Witch of Salem: Devilish Indians and Puritan Fantasies.* New York: New York University Press, 1996.

Breslin, Thomas A. *China, American Catholicism, and the Missionary.* University Park: Pennsylvania State University Press, 1980.

Bressler, Ann Lee. *The Universalist Movement in America, 1770–1880.* New York: Oxford University Press, 2001.

Brewer, Susan A. *Why America Fights: Patriotism and War Propaganda from the Philippines to Iraq.* New York: Oxford University Press, 2009.

Bridenbaugh, Carl. *Mitre and Sceptre: Transatlantic Faiths, Ideas, Personalities, and Politics, 1689–1775.* New York: Oxford University Press, 1962.

Bringhurst, Newell G. *Brigham Young and the Expanding American Frontier.* Boston: Little, Brown, 1986.

Brinkley, Alan. *Voices of Protest: Huey Long, Father Coughlin, and the Great Depression.* New York: Alfred A. Knopf, 1982.

Brock, Peter. *Pacifism in the United States: From the Colonial Era to the First World War.* Princeton: Princeton University Press, 1968.

Brodie, Fawn M. *Richard Nixon: The Shaping of His Character.* New York: W. W. Norton, 1981.

Brookhiser, Richard. *America's First Dynasty: The Adamses, 1735–1918.* New York: Free Press, 2002.

Brown, Dorothy M., and Elizabeth McKeown. *The Poor Belong to Us: Catholic Charities and American Welfare*. Cambridge, Mass.: Harvard University Press, 1997.

Brown, Ira. V. *Lyman Abbott, Christian Evolutionist: A Study in Religious Liberalism*. Cambridge, Mass.: Harvard University Press, 1953.

Brown, Roger H. *The Republic in Peril: 1812*. New York: Columbia University Press, 1964.

Brown, Victoria Bissell. *The Education of Jane Addams*. Philadelphia: University of Pennsylvania Press, 2004.

Bruce, Steve, ed. *Religion and Modernization: Sociologists and Historians Debate the Secularization Thesis*. New York: Oxford University Press, 1992.

Bryson, Thomas A. *American Diplomatic Relations with the Middle East, 1784–1975*. Metuchen, N.J.: Scarecrow Press, 1977.

Buckley, Thomas E. *Church and State in Revolutionary Virginia, 1776–1787*. Charlottesville: University Press of Virginia, 1977.

Buel, Richard. *Securing the Revolution: Ideology in American Politics, 1789–1815*. Ithaca, N.Y.: Cornell University Press, 1972.

Buell, Lawrence. *Emerson*. Cambridge, Mass.: Harvard University Press, 2003.

Burleigh, Michael. *Sacred Causes: Religion and Politics from the European Dictators to Al Qaeda*. London: HarperCollins, 2006.

Burner, David. *Herbert Hoover: A Public Life*. New York: Alfred A. Knopf, 1979.

Bush, Perry. *Two Kingdoms, Two Loyalties: Mennonite Pacifism in Modern America*. Baltimore: Johns Hopkins University Press, 1998.

Bush, Sargent, Jr. *The Writings of Thomas Hooker: Spiritual Adventure in Two Worlds*. Madison: University of Wisconsin Press, 1980.

Bushman, Richard Lyman. *Joseph Smith and the Beginnings of Mormonism*. Urbana: University of Illinois Press, 1984.

Bushnell, Amy Turner. *Situado and Sabana: Spain's Support System for the Presidio and Mission Provinces of Florida*. New York: American Museum of Natural History, 1994.

Butler, Jon. *Huguenots in America: A Refugee People in New World Society*. Cambridge, Mass.: Harvard University Press, 1983.

———. *Awash in a Sea of Faith: Christianizing the American People*. Cambridge, Mass.: Harvard University Press, 1990.

———. *Becoming America: The Revolution Before 1776*. Cambridge, Mass.: Harvard University Press, 2000.

Butler, Jon, Grant Wacker, and Randall Balmer. *Religion in American Life: A Short History*. New York: Oxford University Press, 2003.

Butnaru, I. C. *The Silent Holocaust: Romania and Its Jews*. New York: Greenwood Press, 1992.

Butow, R. J. C. *The John Doe Associates: Backdoor Diplomacy for Peace, 1941*. Stanford, Calif.: Stanford University Press, 1974.

Calhoon, Robert M. *The Loyalist Perception, and Other Essays*. Columbia: University of South Carolina Press, 1989.

Calloway, Colin G. *The Western Abenakis of Vermont, 1600–1800: War, Migration, and the Survival of an Indian People*. Norman: University of Oklahoma Press, 1990.

Campbell, James T. *Songs of Zion: The African Methodist Episcopal Church in the United States and South Africa*. New York: Oxford University Press, 1995.

Capozzola, Christopher. *Uncle Sam Wants You: World War I and the Making of the Modern American Citizen*. New York: Oxford University Press, 2008.

Capp, B. S. *The Fifth Monarchy Men: A Study in Seventeenth-Century English Millenarianism*. London: Faber and Faber, 1972.

Caro, Robert A. *The Years of Lyndon Johnson: The Path to Power*. New York: Alfred A. Knopf, 1982.

Carpenter, Joel A. *Revive Us Again: The Reawakening of American Fundamentalism*. New York: Oxford University Press, 1997.

Carroll, Peter N. *Puritanism and the Wilderness: The Intellectual Significance of the New England Frontier, 1629–1700*. New York: Columbia University Press, 1969.

Carter, Dan T. *The Politics of Rage: George Wallace, the Origins of the New Conservatism, and the Transformation of American Politics*. New York: Simon & Schuster, 1995.

Carter, Paul A. *The Decline and Revival of the Social Gospel: Social and Political Liberalism in American Protestant Churches, 1920–1940*. Ithaca, N.Y.: Cornell University Press, 1954.

Carty, Thomas J. *A Catholic in the White House? Religion, Politics, and John F. Kennedy's Presidential Campaign*. New York: Palgrave Macmillan, 2004.

Carwardine, Richard J. *Trans-Atlantic Revivalism: Popular Evangelicalism in Britain and America, 1790–1865*. Westport, Conn.: Greenwood Press, 1978.

———. *Evangelicals and Politics in Antebellum America*. New Haven, Conn.: Yale University Press, 1993.

———. *Lincoln: A Life of Purpose and Power*. New York: Alfred A. Knopf, 2006.

Casey, Shaun A. *The Making of a Catholic President: Kennedy vs. Nixon, 1960*. New York: Oxford University Press, 2009.

Casey, Steven. *Cautious Crusade: Franklin D. Roosevelt, American Public Opinion, and the War against Nazi Germany*. New York: Oxford University Press, 2001.

Cave, Alfred A. *The Pequot War*. Amherst: University of Massachusetts Press, 1996.

Chambers, John Whiteclay. *To Raise an Army: The Draft Comes to Modern America*. New York: Free Press, 1987.

Chappell, David L. *A Stone of Hope: Prophetic Religion and the Death of Jim Crow*. Chapel Hill: University of North Carolina Press, 2004.

Chatfield, Charles. *For Peace and Justice: Pacifism in America, 1914–1941*. Knoxville: University of Tennessee Press, 1971.

Chernow, Ron. *Alexander Hamilton*. New York: Penguin Press, 2004.

Chesebrough, David B. *Theodore Parker: Orator of Superior Ideas*. Westport, Conn.: Greenwood Press, 1999.

Chet, Guy. *Conquering the American Wilderness: The Triumph of European Warfare in the Colonial Northeast*. Amherst: University of Massachusetts Press, 2003.

Clark, Christopher. *Social Change in America: From the Revolution through the Civil War*. Chicago: Ivan R. Dee, 2006.

Clark, Clifford E. *Henry Ward Beecher: Spokesman for a Middle-Class America*. Urbana: University of Illinois Press, 1978.

Clark, J. C. D. *The Language of Liberty, 1660–1832: Political Discourse and Social Dynamics in the Anglo-American World*. Cambridge: Cambridge University Press, 1994.

Clark, Victoria. *Allies for Armageddon: The Rise of Christian Zionism*. New Haven: Yale University Press, 2007.

Clecak, Peter. *America's Quest for the Ideal Self: Dissent and Fulfillment in the '60s and '70s*. New York: Oxford University Press, 1983.

Clements, Kendrick A. *William Jennings Bryan: Missionary Isolationist*. Knoxville: University of Tennessee Press, 1982.

Cleves, Rachel Hope. *The Reign of Terror in America: Visions of Violence from Anti-Jacobinism to Antislavery*. New York: Cambridge University Press, 2009.

Clymer, Kenton J. *John Hay: The Gentleman as Diplomat*. Ann Arbor: University of Michigan Press, 1975.

———. *Protestant Missionaries in the Philippines, 1898–1916*. Urbana: University of Illinois Press, 1986.

Coalter, Milton J., Jr. *Gilbert Tennent, Son of Thunder: A Case Study of Continental Pietism's Impact on the First Great Awakening in the Middle Colonies*. New York: Greenwood Press, 1986.

Coffman, Ralph J. *Solomon Stoddard*. Boston: Twayne, 1978.

Cogley, Richard W. *John Eliot's Mission to the Indians before King Philip's War*. Cambridge, Mass.: Harvard University Press, 1999.

Cogliano, Francis D. *No King, No Popery: Anti-Catholicism in Revolutionary New England*. Westport, Conn.: Greenwood Press, 1995.

Cohen, Lizabeth. *Making a New Deal: Industrial Workers in Chicago, 1919–1939*. New York: Cambridge University Press, 1990.

Cohen, Michael J. *Truman and Israel*. Berkeley: University of California Press, 1990.

Cohen, Naomi W. *The Americanization of Zionism, 1897–1948*. Hanover, N.H.: Brandeis University Press/University Press of New England, 2003.

Cohen, Paul A. *China and Christianity: The Missionary Movement and the Growth of Chinese Antiforeignism, 1860–1870*. Cambridge, Mass.: Harvard University Press, 1963.

Cohen, Warren I. *America's Response to China: A History of Sino-American Relations*, 4th ed. New York: Columbia University Press, 2000.

Cole, Wayne S. *America First: The Battle Against Intervention, 1940–41*. Madison, Wis.: University of Wisconsin Press, 1953.

Coletta, Paolo E. *William Jennings Bryan*, 3 vols. Lincoln: University of Nebraska Press, 1964–1969.

Coll, Steve. *Ghost Wars: The Secret History of the CIA, Afghanistan, and Bin Laden, from the Soviet Invasion to September 10*. New York: Penguin Press, 2004.

Colley, Linda. *Britons: Forging the Nation, 1707–1837*. New Haven: Yale University Press, 1992.

Combs, Jerald A. *The Jay Treaty: Political Battleground of the Founding Fathers*. Berkeley: University of California Press, 1970.

Conforti, Joseph A. *Samuel Hopkins and the New Divinity Movement: Calvinism, the Congregational Ministry, and Reform in New England between the Great Awakenings*. Grand Rapids, Mich.: Christian University Press, 1981.

———. *Jonathan Edwards, Religious Tradition, and American Culture*. Chapel Hill: University of North Carolina Press, 1995.

Conkin, Paul K. *American Originals: Homemade Varieties of Christianity*. Chapel Hill: University of North Carolina Press, 1997.

Connelly, Matthew. *Fatal Misconception: The Struggle to Control World Population*. Cambridge, Mass.: Harvard University Press, 2008.

Coolidge, Louis A. *An Old-Fashioned Senator: Orville H. Platt of Connecticut*. New York: G. P. Putnam's Sons, 1910.

Cooney, John. *The American Pope: The Life and Times of Francis Cardinal Spellman*. New York: Times Books, 1984.

Cooper, James F., Jr. *Tenacious of Their Liberties: The Congregationalists in Colonial Massachusetts*. New York: Oxford University Press, 1998.

Cooper, John Milton, Jr. *The Warrior and the Priest: Woodrow Wilson and Theodore Roosevelt*. Cambridge, Mass.: Harvard University Press, 1983.

———. *Breaking the Heart of the World: Woodrow Wilson and the Fight for the League of Nations*. New York: Cambridge University Press, 2001.

———. *Woodrow Wilson: A Biography*. New York: Alfred A. Knopf, 2009.

Craig, Campbell. *Glimmer of a New Leviathan: Total War in the Realism of Niebuhr, Morgenthau, and Waltz*. New York: Columbia University Press, 2003.

Craig, Campbell, and Fredrik Logevall. *America's Cold War: The Politics of Insecurity*. Cambridge, Mass.: Harvard University Press, 2009.

Crespino, Joseph. *In Search of Another Country: Mississippi and the Conservative Counterrevolution*. Princeton: Princeton University Press, 2007.

Cressy, David. *Coming Over: Migration and Communication between England and New*

England in the Seventeenth Century. Cambridge: Cambridge University Press, 1987.

———. *England on Edge: Crisis and Revolution, 1640–1642*. Oxford: Oxford University Press, 2006.

Critchlow, Donald T. *Phyllis Schlafly and Grassroots American Conservatism: A Woman's Crusade*. Princeton, N.J.: Princeton University Press, 2001.

Cronon, William. *Changes in the Land: Indians, Colonists, and the Ecology of New England*. New York: Hill and Wang, 1983.

Crosby, Donald F. *God, Church, and Flag: Senator Joseph R. McCarthy and the Catholic Church, 1950–1957*. Chapel Hill: University of North Carolina Press, 1978.

Cross, Robert D. *The Emergence of Liberal Catholicism in America*. Cambridge, Mass.: Harvard University Press, 1958.

Crunden, Robert M. *Ministers of Reform: The Progressives' Achievement in American Civilization, 1889–1920*. New York: Basic Books, 1982.

Cull, Nicholas J. *The Cold War and the United States Information Agency: American Propaganda and Public Diplomacy, 1945–1989*. New York: Cambridge University Press, 2008.

Culver, John C., and John Hyde. *American Dreamer: The Life and Times of Henry A. Wallace*. New York: W. W. Norton, 2000.

Cuneo, Michael W. *The Smoke of Satan: Conservative and Traditionalist Dissent in Contemporary American Catholicism*. New York: Oxford University Press, 1997.

Curry, Thomas J. *The First Freedoms: Church and State in America to the Passage of the First Amendment*. New York: Oxford University Press, 1986.

Curti, Merle. *The American Peace Crusade, 1815–1860*. Durham, N.C.: Duke University Press, 1929.

———. *American Philanthropy Abroad: A History*. New Brunswick, N.J.: Rutgers University Press, 1963.

Curtis, Susan. *A Consuming Faith: The Social Gospel and Modern American Culture*. Baltimore: Johns Hopkins University Press, 1991.

D'Agostino, Peter R. *Rome in America: Transnational Catholic Ideology from the Risorgimento to Fascism*. Chapel Hill: University of North Carolina Press, 2004.

Dallek, Robert. *Franklin Roosevelt and American Foreign Policy, 1932–1945*. New York: Oxford University Press, 1979.

———. *The American Style of Foreign Policy: Cultural Politics and Foreign Affairs*. New York: Alfred A. Knopf, 1983.

———. *Ronald Reagan: The Politics of Symbolism*. Cambridge, Mass.: Harvard University Press, 1984.

———. *Lone Star Rising: Lyndon Johnson and His Times, 1908–1960*. New York: Oxford University Press, 1991.

———. *An Unfinished Life: John F. Kennedy, 1917–1963*. Boston: Little, Brown, 2003.

Daly, John. *When Slavery Was Called Freedom: Evangelicalism, Proslavery, and the Causes of the Civil War*. Lexington: University Press of Kentucky, 2002.

Davenport, Stewart. *Friends of the Unrighteous Mammon: Northern Christians and Market Capitalism, 1815–1860*. Chicago: University of Chicago Press, 2008.

Davidson, James West. *The Logic of Millennial Thought: Eighteenth-Century New England*. New Haven, Conn.: Yale University Press, 1977.

Davidson, Robert L. D. *War Comes to Quaker Pennsylvania, 1682–1756*. New York: Columbia University Press, 1957.

Davis, David Brion. *The Problem of Slavery in Western Culture*. Ithaca, N.Y.: Cornell University Press, 1966.

———. *Revolutions: Reflections on American Equality and Foreign Liberations*. Cambridge, Mass.: Harvard University Press, 1990.

———. *In the Image of God: Religion, Moral Values, and Our Heritage of Slavery.* New Haven, Conn.: Yale University Press, 2001.

———. *Challenging the Boundaries of Slavery.* Cambridge, Mass.: Harvard University Press, 2003.

Davis, Kenneth S. *FDR: The Beckoning of History, 1882–1928.* New York: G. P. Putnam's Sons, 1972.

Davis, Robert C. *Christian Slaves, Muslim Masters: White Slavery in the Mediterranean, the Barbary Coast, and Italy, 1500–1800.* New York: Palgrave Macmillan, 2003.

Dawson, Raymond H. *The Decision to Aid Russia, 1941: Foreign Policy and Domestic Politics.* Chapel Hill: University of North Carolina Press, 1959.

Deats, Richard L. *Nationalism and Christianity in the Philippines.* Dallas: Southern Methodist University Press, 1967.

DeConde, Alexander. *The Quasi-War: The Politics and Diplomacy of the Undeclared War with France 1797–1801.* New York: Scribner's, 1966.

Delbanco, Andrew. *The Puritan Ordeal.* Cambridge, Mass.: Harvard University Press, 1989.

Demos, John. *The Unredeemed Captive: A Family Story from Early America.* New York: Alfred A. Knopf, 1994.

Dierenfield, Bruce J. *The Battle over School Prayer: How Engel v. Vitale Changed America.* Lawrence: University Press of Kansas, 2007.

Diggins, John P. *Mussolini and Fascism: The View from America.* Princeton, N.J.: Princeton University Press, 1972.

Dillon, Michele. *Catholic Identity: Balancing Reason, Faith, and Power.* New York: Cambridge University Press, 1999.

Diner, Hasia R. *The Jews of the United States, 1654 to 2000.* Berkeley: University of California Press, 2004.

Dinnerstein, Leonard. *Antisemitism in America.* New York: Oxford University Press, 1994.

Dippie, Brian W. *The Vanishing American: White Attitudes and U.S. Indian Policy.* Middletown, Conn.: Wesleyan University Press, 1982.

Divine, Robert A. *The Illusion of Neutrality.* Chicago: University of Chicago Press, 1962.

———. *Second Chance: The Triumph of Internationalism in America During World War II.* New York: Atheneum, 1967.

Dochuk, Darren. *From Bible Belt to Sunbelt: Plain-Folk Religion, Grassroots Politics, and the Rise of Evangelical Conservatism.* New York: W. W. Norton, 2010.

Doenecke, Justus D. *Storm on the Horizon: The Challenge to American Intervention, 1939–1941.* Lanham, Md.: Rowman & Littlefield, 2000.

Dolan, Jay P. *The Immigrant Church: New York's Irish and German Catholics, 1815–1865.* Baltimore: Johns Hopkins University Press, 1975.

———. *Catholic Revivalism: The American Experience, 1830–1900.* Notre Dame, Ind.: University of Notre Dame Press, 1978.

———. *The American Catholic Experience: A History from Colonial Times to the Present.* Garden City, N.Y.: Doubleday, 1985.

———. *In Search of an American Catholicism: A History of Religion and Culture in Tension.* New York: Oxford University Press, 2002.

Domke, David, and Kevin Coe. *The God Strategy: How Religion Became a Political Weapon in America.* New York: Oxford University Press, 2008.

Donald, David Herbert. *Lincoln.* New York: Simon & Schuster, 1995.

Donagan, Barbara. *War in England, 1642–1649.* Oxford: Oxford University Press, 2008.

Donovan, John F. *The Pagoda and the Cross: The Life of Bishop Ford of Maryknoll.* New York: Scribner's, 1967.

Dorn, Jacob H. *Washington Gladden: Prophet of the Social Gospel.* Columbus: Ohio State University Press, 1966.

Dorrien, Gary J. *Reconstructing the Common Good: Theology and the Social Order.* Maryknoll, N.Y.: Orbis, 1990.

————. *The Making of American Liberal Theology,* 3 vols. Louisville, Ky.: Westminster John Knox Press, 2001–2006.

Dorsett, Lyle W. *Billy Sunday and the Redemption of Urban America.* Grand Rapids, Mich.: Eerdmans, 1991.

Dowd, Gregory Evans. *A Spirited Resistance: The North American Indian Struggle for Unity, 1745–1815.* Baltimore: Johns Hopkins University Press, 1991.

————. *War under Heaven: Pontiac, the Indian Nations, and the British Empire.* Baltimore: Johns Hopkins University Press, 2002.

Dower, John W. *War without Mercy: Race and Power in the Pacific War.* New York: Pantheon, 1986.

Drake, James D. *King Philip's War: Civil War in New England, 1675–1676.* Amherst: University of Massachusetts Press, 1999.

Dries, Angelyn. *The Missionary Movement in American Catholic History.* Maryknoll, N.Y.: Orbis Books, 1998.

Drinnon, Richard. *Facing West: The Metaphysics of Indian-Hating and Empire-Building.* Norman: University of Oklahoma Press, 1997.

Dudziak, Mary L. *Cold War Civil Rights: Race and the Image of American Democracy.* Princeton, N.J.: Princeton University Press, 2000.

Dull, Jonathan R. *A Diplomatic History of the American Revolution.* New Haven, Conn.: Yale University Press, 1985.

Dumbrell, John. *The Carter Presidency: A Re-Evaluation,* 2nd ed. Manchester: Manchester University Press, 1995.

Dumenil, Lynn. *The Modern Temper: American Culture and Society in the 1920s.* New York: Hill and Wang, 1995.

Duncan, Jason K. *Citizens or Papists? The Politics of Anti-Catholicism in New York, 1685–1821.* New York: Fordham University Press, 2005.

Dunch, Ryan. *Fuzhou Protestants and the Making of a Modern China, 1857–1927.* New Haven, Conn.: Yale University Press, 2001.

Durkheim, Émile. *The Elementary Forms of the Religious Life.* Translated by Carol Cosman. New York: Oxford University Press, 2001.

Durr, Kenneth D. *Behind the Backlash: White Working-Class Politics in Baltimore, 1940–1980.* Chapel Hill: University of North Carolina Press, 2003.

Dusinberre, William. *Slavemaster President: The Double Career of James Polk.* New York: Oxford University Press, 2003.

Early, Frances H. *A World Without War: How U.S. Feminists and Pacifists Resisted World War I.* Syracuse, N.Y.: Syracuse University Press, 1997.

Ebel, Jonathan H. *Faith in the Fight: Religion and the American Soldier in the Great War.* Princeton, N.J.: Princeton University Press, 2010.

Ekbladh, David. *The Great American Mission: Modernization and the Construction of an American World Order.* Princeton, N.J.: Princeton University Press, 2010.

Elkins, Stanley, and Eric McKitrick. *The Age of Federalism: The Early American Republic, 1788–1800.* New York: Oxford University Press, 1993.

Elliott, J. H. *Empires of the Atlantic World: Britain and Spain in America, 1492–1830.* New Haven, Conn.: Yale University Press, 2006.

Ellwood, Robert S. *The Sixties Spiritual Awakening: American Religion Moving from Modern to Postmodern.* New Brunswick, N.J.: Rutgers University Press, 1994.

Elshtain, Jean Bethke. *Jane Addams and the Dream of American Democracy: A Life.* New York: Basic Books, 2002.

Emerson, Everett. *Puritanism in America, 1620–1750.* Boston: Twayne, 1977.

Emerson, Michael O., and Christian Smith. *Divided by Faith: Evangelical Religion and the Problem of Race in America*. New York: Oxford University Press, 2000.

Endy, Christopher. *Cold War Holidays: American Tourism in France*. Chapel Hill: University of North Carolina Press, 2004.

Engel, Katherine Carté. *Religion and Profit: Moravians in Early America*. Philadelphia: University of Pennsylvania Press, 2008.

Engerman, David C. *Modernization from the Other Shore: American Intellectuals and the Romance of Russian Development*. Cambridge, Mass.: Harvard University Press, 2003.

Erenberg, Lewis A., and Susan E. Hirsch, eds. *The War in American Culture: Society and Consciousness during World War II*. Chicago: University of Chicago Press, 1996.

Etherington, Norman, ed. *Missions and Empire*. Oxford: Oxford University Press, 2005.

Evans, Christopher H. *The Kingdom Is Always but Coming: A Life of Walter Rauschenbusch*. Grand Rapids, Mich.: Eerdmans, 2004.

Fairbank, John K., ed. *The Missionary Enterprise in China and America*. Cambridge, Mass.: Harvard University Press, 1974.

Fairclough, Adam. *Better Day Coming: Blacks and Equality, 1890–2000*. New York: Viking, 2001.

Farber, David. *Taken Hostage: The Iran Hostage Crisis and America's First Encounter with Radical Islam*. Princeton, N.J.: Princeton University Press, 2005.

Farmer, Jared. *On Zion's Mount: Mormons, Indians, and the American Landscape*. Cambridge, Mass.: Harvard University Press, 2008.

Farrell, John C. *Beloved Lady: A History of Jane Addams' Ideas on Reform and Peace*. Baltimore: Johns Hopkins University Press, 1967.

Fausold, Martin L. *The Presidency of Herbert C. Hoover*. Lawrence: University Press of Kansas, 1985.

Faust, Drew Gilpin. *This Republic of Suffering: Death and the American Civil War*. New York: Alfred A. Knopf, 2008.

Feingold, Henry L. *A Time for Searching: Entering the Mainstream, 1920–1945*. Baltimore: Johns Hopkins University Press, 1992.

Ferguson, Niall. *The Cash Nexus: Money and Power in the Modern World, 1700–2000*. New York: Basic Books, 2001.

Ferguson, Robert A. *The American Enlightenment, 1750–1820*. Cambridge, Mass.: Harvard University Press, 1997.

Ferling, John. *A Leap in the Dark: The Struggle to Create the American Republic*. New York: Oxford University Press, 2003.

Field, James A., Jr. *America and the Mediterranean World, 1776–1882*. Princeton, N.J.: Princeton University Press, 1969.

Findlay, James F., Jr. *Church People in the Struggle: The National Council of Churches and the Black Freedom Movement, 1950–1970*. New York: Oxford University Press, 1993.

Fink, Carole. *Defending the Rights of Others: The Great Powers, the Jews, and International Minority Protection, 1878–1938*. Cambridge: Cambridge University Press, 2004.

Finke, Roger, and Rodney Stark. *The Churching of America, 1776–1990: Winners and Losers in Our Religious Economy*. New Brunswick, N.J.: Rutgers University Press, 1992.

Finnie, David H. *Pioneers East: The Early American Experience in the Middle East*. Cambridge, Mass.: Harvard University Press, 1967.

Finstuen, Andrew S. *Original Sin and Everyday Protestants: The Theology of Reinhold Niebuhr, Billy Graham, and Paul Tillich in an Age of Anxiety*. Chapel Hill: University of North Carolina Press, 2009.

Fischer, Beth A. *The Reagan Reversal: Foreign Policy and the End of the Cold War*. Columbia: University of Missouri Press, 1997.

Fischer, David Hackett. *Albion's Seed: Four British Folkways in America*. New York: Oxford University Press, 1989.

FitzGerald, Frances. *Way Out There in the Blue: Reagan, Star Wars, and the End of the Cold War*. New York: Simon & Schuster, 2000.

Fleek, Sherman L. *History May be Searched in Vain: A Military History of the Mormon Battalion*. Spokane, Wash.: Arthur H. Clark, 2006.

Flynn, George Q. *American Catholics and the Roosevelt Presidency, 1932–1936*. Lexington: University of Kentucky Press, 1968.

———. *Roosevelt and Romanism: Catholics and American Diplomacy, 1937–1945*. Westport, Conn.: Greenwood, 1976.

Flynt, Wayne. *Alabama Baptists: Southern Baptists in the Heart of Dixie*. Tuscaloosa: University of Alabama Press, 1998.

Fogel, Robert William. *Without Consent or Contract: The Rise and Fall of American Slavery*. New York: W. W. Norton, 1989.

Foglesong, David S. *The American Mission and the "Evil Empire": The Crusade for a "Free Russia" since 1881*. New York: Cambridge University Press, 2007.

Foley, Michael S. *Confronting the War Machine: Draft Resistance during the Vietnam War*. Chapel Hill: University of North Carolina Press, 2003.

Foner, Eric. *Reconstruction: America's Unfinished Revolution, 1863–1877*. New York: Harper & Row, 1988.

———. *The Fiery Trial: Abraham Lincoln and American Slavery*. New York: W. W. Norton, 2010.

Foos, Paul. *A Short, Offhand, Killing Affair: Soldiers and Social Conflict during the Mexican-American War*. Chapel Hill: University of North Carolina Press, 2002.

Forbes, John. *The Quaker Star under Seven Flags, 1917–1927*. Philadelphia: University of Pennsylvania Press, 1962.

Formisano, Ronald P. *Boston against Busing: Race, Class, and Ethnicity in the 1960s and 1970s*. Chapel Hill: University of North Carolina Press, 1991.

Foster, Charles I. *An Errand of Mercy: The Evangelical United Front, 1790–1837*. Chapel Hill: University of North Carolina Press, 1960.

Foster, Gaines M. *Moral Reconstruction: Christian Lobbyists and the Federal Legislation of Morality, 1865–1920*. Chapel Hill: University of North Carolina Press, 2002.

Foster, Stephen. *The Long Argument: English Puritanism and the Shaping of New England Culture, 1570–1700*. Chapel Hill: University of North Carolina Press, 1991.

Foster, William Henry. *The Captors' Narrative: Catholic Women and Their Puritan Men on the Early American Frontier*. Ithaca, N.Y.: Cornell University Press, 2003.

Fowler, William M., Jr. *Samuel Adams: Radical Puritan*. New York: Longman, 1997.

Fox, Richard Wightman. *Reinhold Niebuhr: A Biography*. New York: Pantheon, 1985.

Frady, Marshall. *Billy Graham: A Parable of American Righteousness*. New York: Simon & Schuster, 1979.

Franchot, Jenny. *Roads to Rome: The Antebellum Protestant Encounter with Catholicism*. Berkeley: University of California Press, 1994.

Fraser, James W. *Pedagogue for God's Kingdom: Lyman Beecher and the Second Great Awakening*. Lanham, Md.: University Press of America, 1985.

Frazier, Patrick. *The Mohicans of Stockbridge*. Lincoln: University of Nebraska Press, 1992.

Fredrickson, George M. *The Inner Civil War: Northern Intellectuals and the Crisis of the Union*. New York: Harper & Row, 1965.

———. *Black Liberation: A Comparative History of Black Ideologies in the United States and South Africa*. New York: Oxford University Press, 1995.

Frey, Sylvia R., and Betty Wood. *Come Shouting to Zion: African American Protestantism in the American South and British Caribbean to 1830*. Chapel Hill: University of North Carolina Press, 1998.

Friedlander, Saul. *The Years of Extermination: Nazi Germany and the Jews, 1939–1945*. New York: HarperCollins, 2007.

Friedman, Murray. *The Neoconservatism Revolution: Jewish Intellectuals and the Shaping of Public Policy*. New York: Cambridge University Press, 2005.

Fry, Joseph A. *Dixie Looks Abroad: The South and U.S. Foreign Relations, 1789–1973*. Baton Rouge: Louisiana State University Press, 2002.

Furstenberg, François. *In the Name of the Father: Washington's Legacy, Slavery, and the Making of a Nation*. New York: Penguin, 2006.

Gaddis, John Lewis. *The United States and the Origins of the Cold War, 1941–1947*. New York: Columbia University Press, 1972.

———. *Russia, the Soviet Union and the United States: An Interpretive History*, 2nd ed. New York: McGraw-Hill, 1990.

———. *The United States and the End of the Cold War: Implications, Reconsiderations, Provocations*. New York: Oxford University Press, 1992.

———. *The Cold War: A New History*. New York: Penguin Press, 2005.

———. *Strategies of Containment: A Critical Appraisal of American National Security Policy during the Cold War*, rev. ed. New York: Oxford University Press, 2005.

Gallagher, Charles R. *Vatican Secret Diplomacy: Joseph P. Hurley and Pope Pius XII*. New Haven, Conn.: Yale University Press, 2008.

Gallay, Alan. *The Indian Slave Trade: The Rise of the English Empire in the American South, 1670–1717*. New Haven, Conn.: Yale University Press, 2002.

Gamble, Richard M. *The War for Righteousness: Progressive Christianity, the Great War, and the Rise of the Messianic Nation*. Wilmington, Del.: ISI Books, 2003.

Games, Alison. *Migration and the Origins of the English Atlantic World*. Cambridge, Mass.: Harvard University Press, 1999.

———. *The Web of Empire: English Cosmopolitans in an Age of Expansion, 1560–1660*. New York: Oxford University Press, 2008.

Gardner, Lloyd C. *Safe for Democracy: The Anglo-American Response to Revolution, 1913–1923*. New York: Oxford University Press, 1984.

———. *Pay Any Price: Lyndon Johnson and the Wars for Vietnam*. Chicago: Ivan R. Dee, 1995.

Garrett, Shirley S. *Social Reformers in Urban China: The Chinese Y.M.C.A., 1895–1926*. Cambridge, Mass.: Harvard University Press, 1970.

Garrow, David J. *Bearing the Cross: Martin Luther King, Jr. and the Southern Christian Leadership Conference*. New York: William Morrow, 1986.

———. *Liberty and Sexuality: The Right to Privacy and the Making of Roe v. Wade*. New York: Macmillan, 1994.

Garthoff, Raymond L. *Detente and Confrontation: American-Soviet Relations from Nixon to Reagan*, rev. ed. Washington, D.C.: Brookings Institution Press, 1994.

Gates, Henry Louis, Jr., ed. *Lincoln on Race and Slavery*. Princeton, N.J.: Princeton University Press, 2009.

Gatewood, Willard B., Jr. *Black Americans and the White Man's Burden, 1898–1903*. Urbana: University of Illinois Press, 1975.

Gaustad, Edwin S. *Faith of Our Fathers: Religion and the New Nation*. San Francisco: Harper & Row, 1987.

Gelfand, Lawrence Emerson. *The Inquiry: American Preparations for Peace, 1917–1919*. New Haven, Conn.: Yale University Press, 1963.

Genovese, Eugene D. *Roll, Jordan, Roll: The World the Slaves Made*. New York: Pantheon, 1974.

Giauque, Jeffrey Glen. *Grand Designs and Visions of Unity: The Atlantic Powers and the*

Reorganization of Western Europe, 1955–1963. Chapel Hill: University of North Carolina Press, 2002.

Gibbs, Nancy, and Michael Duffy. *The Preacher and the Presidents: Billy Graham in the White House.* New York: Center Street, 2007.

Gilbert, Felix. *To the Farewell Address: Ideas of Early American Foreign Policy.* Princeton, N.J.: Princeton University Press, 1961.

Gilkey, Langdon. *On Niebuhr: A Theological Study.* Chicago: University of Chicago Press, 2001.

Gillis, Chester. *Roman Catholicism in America.* New York: Columbia University Press, 1999.

Gillon, Steven M. *Politics and Vision: The ADA and American Liberalism, 1947–1985.* New York: Oxford University Press, 1987.

Gilmore, Glenda Elizabeth. *Defying Dixie: The Radical Roots of Civil Rights, 1919–1950.* New York: W. W. Norton, 2008.

Glad, Johnnie. *The Mission of Mormonism in Norway, 1851–1920: A Study and Analysis of the Reception Process.* Frankfurt and Oxford: Peter Lang, 2006.

Godbeer, Richard. *The Devil's Dominion: Magic and Religion in Early New England.* Cambridge: Cambridge University Press, 1992.

Goen, C. C. *Broken Churches, Broken Nation: Denominational Schisms and the Coming of the American Civil War.* Macon, Ga.: Mercer University Press, 1985.

Goldman, Shalom. *God's Sacred Tongue: Hebrew and the American Imagination.* Chapel Hill: University of North Carolina Press, 2004.

Goldstein, Warren. *William Sloane Coffin, Jr.: A Holy Impatience.* New Haven, Conn.: Yale University Press, 2004.

Gomez, Michael A. *Black Crescent: The Experience and Legacy of African Muslims in the Americas.* New York: Cambridge University Press, 2005.

Goodman, Paul. *Of One Blood: Abolitionism and the Origins of Racial Equality.* Berkeley: University of California Press, 1998.

Goodwin, Doris Kearns. *No Ordinary Time: Franklin and Eleanor Roosevelt: The Home Front in World War II.* New York: Simon & Schuster, 1994.

Gorrell, Donald K. *The Age of Social Responsibility: The Social Gospel in the Progressive Era, 1900–1920.* Macon, Ga.: Mercer University Press, 1988.

Gougeon, Len. *Virtue's Hero: Emerson, Antislavery, and Reform.* Athens: University of Georgia Press, 1990.

Gould, Lewis L. *The Presidency of William McKinley.* Lawrence: University Press of Kansas, 1980.

———. *The Spanish-American War and President McKinley.* Lawrence: University Press of Kansas, 1982.

Grabill, Joseph L. *Protestant Diplomacy and the Near East: Missionary Influence on American Policy, 1810–1927.* Minneapolis: University of Minnesota Press, 1971.

Grant, Susan-Mary. *North over South: Northern Nationalism and American Identity in the Antebellum Era.* Lawrence: University Press of Kansas, 2000.

Granville, Johanna. *The First Domino: International Decision Making during the Hungarian Crisis of 1956.* College Station: Texas A&M University Press, 2004.

Greaves, Richard L. *Secrets of the Kingdom: British Radicals from the Popish Plot to the Revolution of 1688–89.* Stanford, Calif.: Stanford University Press, 1992.

Greeley, Andrew M. *The American Catholic: A Social Portrait.* New York: Basic Books, 1977.

———. *The Catholic Imagination.* Berkeley: University of California Press, 2000.

———. *The Catholic Revolution: New Wine, Old Wineskins, and the Second Vatican Council.* Berkeley: University of California Press, 2004.

Greenberg, Amy S. *Manifest Manhood and the Antebellum American Empire.* Cambridge: Cambridge University Press, 2005.

Greenberg, David. *Nixon's Shadow: The History of an Image.* New York: W. W. Norton, 2003.

Gregerson, Linda. *The Reformation of the Subject: Spenser, Milton, and the English Protestant Epic.* Cambridge: Cambridge University Press, 1995.

Gribbin, William. *The Churches Militant: The War of 1812 and American Religion.* New Haven, Conn.: Yale University Press, 1973.

Griffin, Patrick. *American Leviathan: Empire, Nation, and Revolutionary Frontier.* New York: Hill and Wang, 2007.

Griffiths, Naomi E. S. *The Contexts of Acadian History, 1686–1784.* Montreal and Kingston, Ont.: Centre for Canadian Studies, Mount Allison University/McGill-Queen's University Press, 1992.

Grodzins, Dean. *American Heretic: Theodore Parker and Transcendentalism.* Chapel Hill: University of North Carolina Press, 2002.

Guelzo, Allen C. *Abraham Lincoln: Redeemer President.* Grand Rapids, Mich.: Eerdmans, 1999.

———. *Lincoln's Emancipation Proclamation: The End of Slavery in America.* New York: Simon & Schuster, 2004.

Guhin, Michael A. *John Foster Dulles: A Statesman and His Times.* New York: Columbia University Press, 1972.

Gura, Philip F. *American Transcendentalism: A History.* New York: Hill and Wang, 2007.

Guy, John. *Tudor England.* Oxford: Oxford University Press, 1988.

Guyatt, Nicholas. *Providence and the Invention of the United States, 1607–1876.* Cambridge: Cambridge University Press, 2007.

Haas, Ernst B. *Nationalism, Liberalism, and Progress,* 2 vols. Ithaca, N.Y.: Cornell University Press, 1997–2000.

Haefeli, Evan, and Kevin Sweeney. *Captors and Captives: The 1704 French and Indian Raid on Deerfield.* Amherst: University of Massachusetts Press, 2003.

Hahn, Peter L. *Caught in the Middle East: U.S. Policy toward the Arab-Israeli Conflict, 1945–1961.* Chapel Hill: University of North Carolina Press, 2004.

Hahn, Steven. *The Political Worlds of Slavery and Freedom.* Cambridge, Mass.: Harvard University Press, 2009.

Hall, David D. *The Faithful Shepherd: A History of the New England Ministry in the Seventeenth Century.* Chapel Hill: University of North Carolina Press, 1972.

———. *Worlds of Wonder, Days of Judgment: Popular Religious Belief in Early New England.* New York: Alfred A. Knopf, 1989.

Hall, Michael G. *The Last American Puritan: The Life of Increase Mather.* Middletown, Conn.: Wesleyan University Press, 1988.

Hall, Mitchell K. *Because of Their Faith: CALCAV and Religious Opposition to the Vietnam War.* New York: Columbia University Press, 1990.

Halliwell, Martin. *The Constant Dialogue: Reinhold Niebuhr and American Intellectual Culture.* Lanham, Md.: Rowman & Littlefield, 2005.

Hambrick-Stowe, Charles E. *The Practice of Piety: Puritan Devotional Disciplines in Seventeenth-Century New England.* Chapel Hill: University of North Carolina Press, 1982.

Hamburger, Philip. *Separation of Church and State.* Cambridge, Mass.: Harvard University Press, 2002.

Hamby, Alonzo L. *Man of the People: A Life of Harry S. Truman.* New York: Oxford University Press, 1995.

Handy, Robert T. *A History of Union Theological Seminary in New York.* New York: Columbia University Press, 1987.

———. *Undermined Establishment: Church-State Relations in America, 1880–1920.* Princeton, N.J.: Princeton University Press, 1991.

Hanhimäki, Jussi. *The Flawed Architect: Henry Kissinger and American Foreign Policy.* New York: Oxford University Press, 2004.

Harding, Susan Friend. *The Book of Jerry Falwell: Fundamentalist Language and Politics.* Princeton, N.J.: Princeton University Press, 2000.

Harris, Paul William. *Nothing but Christ: Rufus Anderson and the Ideology of Protestant Foreign Missions.* New York: Oxford University Press, 1999.

Hartle, Anthony E. *Moral Issues in Military Decision Making*, 2nd ed. Lawrence: University Press of Kansas, 2004.

Harvey, Paul. *Redeeming the South: Religious Cultures and Racial Identities among Southern Baptists, 1865–1925.* Chapel Hill: University of North Carolina Press, 1997.

———. *Freedom's Coming: Religious Culture and the Shaping of the South from the Civil War through the Civil Rights Era.* Chapel Hill: University of North Carolina Press, 2005.

Hastings, Adrian. *The Construction of Nationhood: Ethnicity, Religion, and Nationalism.* Cambridge: Cambridge University Press, 1997.

Hatch, Nathan O. *The Sacred Cause of Liberty: Republican Thought and the Millennium in Revolutionary New England.* New Haven, Conn.: Yale University Press, 1977.

———. *The Democratization of American Christianity.* New Haven, Conn.: Yale University Press, 1989.

Hawley, Joshua David. *Theodore Roosevelt: Preacher of Righteousness.* New Haven, Conn.: Yale University Press, 2008.

Haydon, Colin. *Anti-Catholicism in Eighteenth Century England, c. 1714–80: A Political and Social Study.* Manchester: Manchester University Press, 1993.

Haynes, Sam W. *James K. Polk and the Expansionist Impulse*, 2nd ed. New York: Longman, 2001.

Heale, M. J. *American Anticommunism: Combating the Enemy Within, 1830–1970.* Baltimore: Johns Hopkins University Press, 1990.

Healy, David. *U.S. Expansionism: The Imperialist Urge in the 1890s.* Madison: University of Wisconsin Press, 1970.

Hedrick, Joan D. *Harriet Beecher Stowe: A Life.* New York: Oxford University Press, 1994.

Heilbrunn, Jacob. *They Knew They Were Right: The Rise of the Neocons.* New York: Doubleday, 2008.

Heilemann, John, and Mark Halperin. *Game Change: Obama and the Clintons, McCain and Palin, and the Race of a Lifetime.* New York: Harper, 2010.

Heimert, Alan. *Religion and the American Mind: From the Great Awakening to the Revolution.* Cambridge, Mass.: Harvard University Press, 1966.

Hein, David, and Gardiner H. Shattuck Jr. *The Episcopalians.* Westport, Conn.: Praeger, 2004.

Heineman, Kenneth J. *A Catholic New Deal: Religion and Reform in Depression Pittsburgh.* University Park: Pennsylvania State University Press, 1999.

Henderson, Timothy J. *A Glorious Defeat: Mexico and Its War with the United States.* New York: Hill and Wang, 2007.

Hendrickson, Paul. *The Living and the Dead: Robert McNamara and Five Lives of a Lost War.* New York: Alfred A. Knopf, 1996.

Hennesey, James. *American Catholics: A History of the Roman Catholic Community in the United States.* New York: Oxford University Press, 1981.

Henning, Joseph M. *Outposts of Civilization: Race, Religion, and the Formative Years of American-Japanese Relations.* New York: New York University Press, 2000.

Henriques, Peter R. *Realistic Visionary: A Portrait of George Washington.* Charlottesville: University of Virginia Press, 2006.

Hentoff, Nat. *Peace Agitator: The Story of A. J. Muste.* New York: Macmillan, 1963.

Herberg, Will. *Protestant, Catholic, Jew: An Essay in American Religious Sociology*. Garden City, N.Y.: Doubleday, 1955.

Hero, Alfred O., Jr. *American Religious Groups View Foreign Policy: Trends in Rank-and-File Opinion, 1937–1969*. Durham, N.C.: Duke University Press, 1973.

Herring, George C. *Aid to Russia, 1941–1946: Strategy, Diplomacy, the Origins of the Cold War*. New York: Columbia University Press, 1973.

———. *From Colony to Superpower: U.S. Foreign Relations since 1776*. New York: Oxford University Press, 2008.

Herzstein, Robert E. *Henry R. Luce: A Political Portrait of the Man Who Created the American Century*. New York: Charles Scribner's Sons, 1994.

———. *Henry R. Luce, Time, and the American Crusade in Asia*. New York: Cambridge University Press, 2005.

Hickey, Donald R. *The War of 1812: A Forgotten Conflict*. Urbana: University of Illinois Press, 1989.

Hill, Patricia R. *The World Their Household: The American Woman's Foreign Mission Movement and Cultural Transformation, 1870–1920*. Ann Arbor: University of Michigan Press, 1985.

Hillgarth, J. N. *The Mirror of Spain, 1500–1700: The Formation of a Myth*. Ann Arbor: University of Michigan Press, 2000.

Hinderaker, Eric. *Elusive Empires: Constructing Colonialism in the Ohio Valley, 1673–1800*. Cambridge: Cambridge University Press, 1997.

Hitchcock, William I. *The Bitter Road to Freedom: A New History of the Liberation of Europe*. New York: Free Press, 2008.

Hixson, Walter L. *Charles A. Lindbergh: Lone Eagle*, 2nd ed. New York: Longman, 2002.

———. *The Myth of American Diplomacy: National Identity and U.S. Foreign Policy*. New Haven, Conn.: Yale University Press, 2008.

Hofstadter, Richard. *Anti-Intellectualism in American Life*. New York: Alfred A. Knopf, 1963.

———. *The Paranoid Style in American Politics, and Other Essays*. New York: Alfred A. Knopf, 1965.

Hogan, Michael J., and Thomas G. Paterson, eds. *Explaining the History of American Foreign Relations*, 2nd ed. New York: Cambridge University Press, 2004.

Hoganson, Kristin L. *Fighting for American Manhood: How Gender Politics Provoked the Spanish-American and Philippine-American Wars*. New Haven: Yale University Press, 1998.

———. *Consumers' Imperium: The Global Production of American Domesticity, 1865–1920*. Chapel Hill: University of North Carolina Press, 2007.

Holifield, E. Brooks. *Theology in America: Christian Thought from the Age of the Puritans to the Civil War*. New Haven, Conn.: Yale University Press, 2003.

Hollander, Paul. *Political Pilgrims: Travels of Western Intellectuals to the Soviet Union, China, and Cuba, 1928–1978*. New York: Oxford University Press, 1981.

Hollinger, David A. *Science, Jews, and Secular Culture: Studies in Mid-Twentieth-Century American Intellectual History*. Princeton, N.J.: Princeton University Press, 1996.

Holt, Michael F. *Forging a Majority: The Formation of the Republican Party in Pittsburgh, 1848–1860*. New Haven, Conn.: Yale University Press, 1969.

———. *The Rise and Fall of the American Whig Party: Jacksonian Politics and the Onset of the Civil War*. New York: Oxford University Press, 1999.

Homan, Gerlof D. *American Mennonites and the Great War, 1914–1918*. Scottdale, Pa.: Herald Press, 1994.

Hoopes, Townsend. *The Devil and John Foster Dulles*. Boston: Little, Brown, 1973.

Hoopes, Townsend, and Douglas Brinkley. *FDR and the Creation of the U.N.* New Haven, Conn.: Yale University Press, 1997.

Hoover, A. J. *God, Germany and Britain in the Great War*. New York: Praeger, 1989.

Hopkins, C. Howard. *John R. Mott, 1865–1955: A Biography.* Grand Rapids, Mich.: Eerdmans, 1979.

Horn, James. *Adapting to a New World: English Society in the Seventeenth-Century Chesapeake.* Chapel Hill: University of North Carolina Press, 1994.

Horne, Gerald. *The End of Empires: African Americans and India.* Philadelphia: Temple University Press, 2008.

Horsman, Reginald. *The Causes of the War of 1812.* Philadelphia: University of Pennsylvania Press, 1962.

———. *Race and Manifest Destiny: The Origins of American Racial Anglo-Saxonism.* Cambridge, Mass.: Harvard University Press, 1981.

———. *The Diplomacy of the New Republic, 1776–1815.* Arlington Heights, Ill.: Harlan Davidson, 1985.

Houck, Davis W. *Rhetoric as Currency: Hoover, Roosevelt, and the Great Depression.* College Station: Texas A&M University Press, 2001.

Howard, Victor B. *Religion and the Radical Republican Movement, 1860–1870.* Lexington: University Press of Kentucky, 1990.

Howe, Daniel Walker. *The Unitarian Conscience: Harvard Moral Philosophy, 1805–1861.* Cambridge, Mass.: Harvard University Press, 1970.

———. *The Political Culture of the American Whigs.* Chicago: University of Chicago Press, 1979.

———. *Making the American Self: Jonathan Edwards to Abraham Lincoln.* Cambridge, Mass.: Harvard University Press, 1997.

———. *What Hath God Wrought: The Transformation of America, 1815–1848.* New York: Oxford University Press, 2007.

Hulsether, Mark. *Building a Protestant Left: Christianity and Crisis Magazine, 1941–1993.* Knoxville: University of Tennessee Press, 1999.

Hunt, Michael H. *The Making of a Special Relationship: The United States and China to 1914.* New York: Columbia University Press, 1983.

———. *Ideology and U.S. Foreign Policy.* New Haven, Conn.: Yale University Press, 1987.

Hunter, Jane. *The Gospel of Gentility: American Women Missionaries in Turn-of-the-Century China.* New Haven, Conn.: Yale University Press, 1984.

Hutchison, John Alexander. *We Are Not Divided: A Critical and Historical Study of the Federal Council of the Churches of Christ in America.* New York: Round Table Press, 1941.

Hutchison, William R. *The Transcendentalist Ministers: Church Reform in the New England Renaissance.* New Haven, Conn.: Yale University Press, 1959.

———. *The Modernist Impulse in American Protestantism.* Cambridge, Mass.: Harvard University Press, 1976.

———. *Errand to the World: American Protestant Thought and Foreign Missions.* Chicago: University of Chicago Press, 1987.

———. *Religious Pluralism in America: The Contentious History of a Founding Ideal.* New Haven, Conn.: Yale University Press, 2003.

Hutson, James H. *John Adams and the Diplomacy of the American Revolution.* Lexington: University Press of Kentucky, 1980.

Iancu, Carol. *Jews in Romania, 1866–1919: From Exclusion to Emancipation.* Boulder, Colo.: East European Monographs, 1996.

Immerman, Richard H. *John Foster Dulles: Piety, Pragmatism, and Power in U.S. Foreign Policy.* Wilmington, Del.: Scholarly Resources, 1999.

Inboden, William. *Religion and American Foreign Policy, 1945–1960: The Soul of Containment.* New York: Cambridge University Press, 2008.

Iriye, Akira. *Pacific Estrangement: Japanese and American Expansion, 1897–1911.* Cambridge, Mass.: Harvard University Press, 1972.

————. *The Origins of the Second World War in Asia and the Pacific.* London: Longman, 1987.

Isaac, Rhys. *The Transformation of Virginia, 1740–1790.* Chapel Hill: University of North Carolina Press, 1982.

Isaacson, Walter. *Kissinger: A Biography.* New York: Simon & Schuster, 1992.

Isaacson, Walter, and Evan Thomas. *The Wise Men: Six Friends and the World They Made.* New York: Simon & Schuster, 1986.

Isserman, Maurice, and Michael Kazin. *America Divided: The Civil War of the 1960s,* 2nd ed. New York: Oxford University Press, 2004.

Ivers, Gregg. *To Build a Wall: American Jews and the Separation of Church and State.* Charlottesville: University Press of Virginia, 1995.

Jackson, Sherman A. *Islam and the Blackamerican: Looking Toward the Third Resurrection.* New York: Oxford University Press, 2005.

Jackson, Thomas F. *From Civil Rights to Human Rights: Martin Luther King, Jr., and the Struggle for Economic Justice.* Philadelphia: University of Pennsylvania Press, 2007.

Jacobs, Seth. *America's Miracle Man in Vietnam: Ngo Dinh Diem, Religion, Race, and U.S. Intervention in Southeast Asia, 1950–1957.* Durham, N.C.: Duke University Press, 2004.

Jacobson, Matthew Frye. *Special Sorrows: The Diasporic Imagination of Irish, Polish, and Jewish Immigrants in the United States.* Cambridge, Mass.: Harvard University Press, 1995.

————. *Roots Too: White Ethnic Revival in Post-Civil Rights America.* Cambridge, Mass.: Harvard University Press, 2006.

Jacoby, Susan. *Freethinkers: A History of American Secularism.* New York: Metropolitan Books, 2004.

Jeansonne, Glen. *Gerald L. K. Smith, Minister of Hate.* New Haven, Conn.: Yale University Press, 1988.

Jeffrey, Julie Roy. *The Great Silent Army of Abolitionism: Ordinary Women in the Antislavery Movement.* Chapel Hill: University of North Carolina Press, 1998.

Jeffries, John W. *Wartime America: The World War II Home Front.* Chicago: Ivan R. Dee, 1996.

Jelavich, Barbara. *Russia and the Formation of the Romanian National State, 1821–1878.* Cambridge: Cambridge University Press, 1984.

Jenkins, Philip. *The New Faces of Christianity: Believing the Bible in the Global South.* New York: Oxford University Press, 2006.

————. *The Next Christendom: The Coming of Global Christianity,* rev. ed. New York: Oxford University Press, 2007.

Jennings, Francis T. *The Invasion of America: Indians, Colonialism, and the Cant of Conquest.* New York: W. W. Norton, 1975.

————. *Empire of Fortune: Crowns, Colonies, and Tribes in the Seven Years War in America.* New York: W. W. Norton, 1988.

Jervis, Robert. *Perception and Misperception in International Politics.* Princeton, N.J.: Princeton University Press, 1976.

Jessup, Philip C. *Elihu Root,* 2 vols. New York: Dodd, Mead, 1938.

Jewett, Robert, and John Shelton Lawrence. *Captain America and the Crusade against Evil: The Dilemma of Zealous Nationalism.* Grand Rapids, Mich.: Eerdmans, 2003.

Johannsen, Robert W. *To the Halls of the Montezumas: The Mexican War in the American Imagination.* New York: Oxford University Press, 1985.

Johnson, Curtis D. *Redeeming America: Evangelicals and the Road to the Civil War.* Chicago: Ivan R. Dee, 1993.

Johnson, James Turner. *Ideology, Reason, and the Limitation of War: Religious and Secular Concepts, 1200–1740.* Princeton, N.J.: Princeton University Press, 1975.

———. *Just War Tradition and the Restraint of War: A Moral and Historical Inquiry*. Princeton, N.J.: Princeton University Press, 1981.

Jones, Howard. *Union in Peril: The Crisis over British Intervention in the Civil War*. Chapel Hill: University of North Carolina Press, 1992.

———. *Blue and Gray Diplomacy: A History of Union and Confederate Foreign Relations*. Chapel Hill: University of North Carolina Press, 2010.

Jones, Howard, and Donald A. Rakestraw. *Prologue to Manifest Destiny: Anglo-American Relations in the 1840s*. Wilmington, Del.: Scholarly Resources, 1997.

Jones, Mary Hoxie. *Swords into Ploughshares: An Account of the American Friends Service Committee, 1917–1937*. Westport, Conn.: Greenwood Press, 1971.

Jordan, Philip D. *The Evangelical Alliance for the United States of America, 1847–1900: Ecumenism, Identity, and the Religion of the Republic*. New York: Edwin Mellen, 1982.

Joseph, Peniel E. *Waiting 'Til the Midnight Hour: A Narrative History of Black Power in America*. New York: Henry Holt, 2006.

Judt, Tony. *Postwar: A History of Europe since 1945*. New York: Penguin Press, 2005.

Kagan, Robert. *Dangerous Nation: America's Place in the World from Its Earliest Days to the Dawn of the Twentieth Century*. New York: Alfred A. Knopf, 2006.

Kaplan, Amy. *The Anarchy of Empire in the Making of U.S. Culture*. Cambridge, Mass.: Harvard University Press, 2002.

Kaplan, Lawrence S., ed. *The American Revolution and "A Candid World."* Kent, Ohio: Kent State University Press, 1977.

Karnow, Stanley. *Vietnam: A History*, rev. ed. New York: Penguin, 1991.

Kars, Marjoleine. *Breaking Loose Together: The Regulator Rebellion in Pre-Revolutionary North Carolina*. Chapel Hill: University of North Carolina Press, 2002.

Kashatus, William C. *Conflict of Conviction: A Reappraisal of Quaker Involvement in the American Revolution*. Lanham, Md.: University Press of America, 1990.

Kashima, Tetsuden. *Judgment without Trial: Japanese American Imprisonment during World War II*. Seattle: University of Washington Press, 2003.

Kaufman, Burton I. *The Presidency of James Earl Carter, Jr.* Lawrence: University Press of Kansas, 1993.

Kaufman, Robert G. *Henry M. Jackson: A Life in Politics*. Seattle: University of Washington Press, 2000.

Kazin, Michael. *The Populist Persuasion: An American History*, rev. ed. Ithaca, N.J.: Cornell University Press, 1998.

———. *A Godly Hero: The Life of William Jennings Bryan*. New York: Alfred A. Knopf, 2006.

Kell, Carl L., and L. Raymond Camp. *In the Name of the Father: The Rhetoric of the New Southern Baptist Convention*. Carbondale: Southern Illinois University Press, 1999.

Kellaway, William. *The New England Company, 1649–1776: Missionary Society to the American Indians*. London: Longmans, Green and Company, 1961.

Keller, Rosemary. *Patriotism and the Female Sex: Abigail Adams and the American Revolution*. New York: Carlson, 1994.

Kelsey, Harry. *Sir Francis Drake: The Queen's Pirate*. New Haven, Conn.: Yale University Press, 1998.

Kennedy, David. *Freedom from Fear: The American People in Depression and War, 1929–1945*. New York: Oxford University Press, 1999.

Kennedy, Paul. *The Rise and Fall of British Naval Mastery*. London: Allen Lane, 1976.

———. *The Rise and Fall of the Great Powers: Economic Change and Military Conflict from 1500 to 2000*. New York: Random House, 1987.

Kennedy, Ross A. *The Will to Believe: Woodrow Wilson, World War I, and America's Strategy for Peace and Security*. Kent, Ohio: Kent State University Press, 2009.

Kent, Peter C. *The Lonely Cold War of Pope Pius XII: The Roman Catholic Church and the Division of Europe, 1943–1950*. Montreal and Kingston, Ont.: McGill-Queen's University Press, 2002.

Kerber, Linda K. *Federalists in Dissent: Imagery and Ideology in Jeffersonian America*. Ithaca, N.Y.: Cornell University Press, 1970.

Kertzer, David I. *Ritual, Politics, and Power*. New Haven, Conn.: Yale University Press, 1988.

Keyssar, Alexander. *The Right to Vote: The Contested History of Democracy in the United States*, rev. ed. New York: Basic Books, 2009.

Kidd, Colin. *British Identities before Nationalism: Ethnicity and Nationhood in the Atlantic World, 1600–1800*. Cambridge: Cambridge University Press, 1999.

———. *The Forging of Races: Race and Scripture in the Protestant Atlantic World, 1600–2000*. Cambridge: Cambridge University Press, 2006.

Kidd, Thomas S. *The Protestant Interest: New England after Puritanism*. New Haven, Conn.: Yale University Press, 2004.

———. *The Great Awakening: The Roots of Evangelical Christianity in Colonial America*. New Haven, Conn.: Yale University Press, 2007.

Kimball, Warren F. *The Juggler: Franklin Roosevelt as Wartime Statesman*. Princeton, N.J.: Princeton University Press, 1991.

Kimmel, Michael. *Manhood in America: A Cultural History*. New York: Free Press, 1996.

Kirby, Dianne. *Church, State and Propaganda: The Archbishop of York and International Relations, A Political Study of Cyril Forster Garbett, 1942–1955*. Hull, U.K.: University of Hull Press, 1999.

Kisatsky, Deborah. *The United States and the European Right, 1945–1955*. Columbus: Ohio State University Press, 2005.

Klatch, Rebecca E. *A Generation Divided: The New Left, the New Right, and the 1960s*. Berkeley: University of California Press, 1999.

Klier, John Doyle. *Imperial Russia's Jewish Question, 1855–1881*. Cambridge: Cambridge University Press, 1995.

Kloppenberg, James T. *The Virtues of Liberalism*. New York: Oxford University Press, 1998.

———. *Reading Obama: Dreams, Hope, and the American Political Tradition*. Princeton, N.J.: Princeton University Press, 2010.

Knight, Janice. *Orthodoxies in Massachusetts: Rereading American Puritanism*. Cambridge, Mass.: Harvard University Press, 1994.

Knock, Thomas J. *To End All Wars: Woodrow Wilson and the Quest for a New World Order*. New York: Oxford University Press, 1992.

Korn, Bertram W. *American Jewry and the Civil War*. New York: Atheneum, 1970.

Kosek, Joseph Kip. *Acts of Conscience: Christian Nonviolence and Modern American Democracy*. New York: Columbia University Press, 2009.

Kosmin, Barry A., and Seymour P. Lachman. *One Nation under God: Religion in Contemporary American Society*. New York: Harmony Books, 1993.

Kramer, Paul A. *The Blood of Government: Race, Empire, the United States, and the Philippines*. Chapel Hill: University of North Carolina Press, 2006.

Kramnick, Isaac. *Republicanism and Bourgeois Radicalism: Political Ideology in Late Eighteenth-Century England and America*. Ithaca, N.Y.: Cornell University Press, 1990.

Kruman, Marc W. *Between Authority and Liberty: State Constitution Making in Revolutionary America*. Chapel Hill: University of North Carolina Press, 1997.

Kuklick, Bruce. *Churchmen and Philosophers: From Jonathan Edwards to John Dewey*. New Haven, Conn.: Yale University Press, 1985.

———. *A Political History of the USA: One Nation under God*. New York: Palgrave Macmillan, 2009.

Kupperman, Karen Ordahl. *Roanoke: The Abandoned Colony.* Totawa, N.J.: Rowman & Allanheld, 1984.

LaFeber, Walter. *The New Empire: An Interpretation of American Expansion, 1860–1898.* Ithaca, N.Y.: Cornell University Press, 1963.

———. *The Cambridge History of American Foreign Relations,* vol. 2: *The American Search for Opportunity, 1865–1913.* Cambridge: Cambridge University Press, 1993.

———. *Inevitable Revolutions: The United States in Central America,* 2nd ed. New York: W. W. Norton, 1993.

Lahr, Angela M. *Millennial Dreams and Apocalyptic Nightmares: The Cold War Origins of Political Evangelicalism.* New York: Oxford University Press, 2007.

Lambert, Frank. *"Pedlar in Divinity": George Whitefield and the Transatlantic Revivals, 1737–1770.* Princeton, N.J.: Princeton University Press, 1994.

———. *Inventing the "Great Awakening."* Princeton, N.J.: Princeton University Press, 1999.

———. *The Founding Fathers and the Place of Religion in America.* Princeton, N.J.: Princeton University Press, 2003.

———. *The Barbary Wars: American Independence in the Atlantic World.* New York: Hill and Wang, 2005.

———. *Religion in American Politics: A Short History.* Princeton, N.J.: Princeton University Press, 2008.

Lander, Ernest McPherson, Jr. *Reluctant Imperialists: Calhoun, the South Carolinians, and the Mexican War.* Baton Rouge: Louisiana State University Press, 1980.

LaPlante, Eve. *American Jezebel: The Uncommon Life of Anne Hutchinson, the Woman Who Defied the Puritans.* San Francisco: HarperSanFrancisco, 2004.

Laserson, Max M. *The American Impact on Russia: Diplomatic and Ideological, 1784–1917.* New York: Macmillan, 1950.

Lassiter, Matthew D. *The Silent Majority: Suburban Politics in the Sunbelt South.* Princeton, N.J.: Princeton University Press, 2006.

Latham, Michael E. *Modernization as Ideology: American Social Science and "Nation Building" in the Kennedy Era.* Chapel Hill: University of North Carolina Press, 2000.

Lawson, Philip. *The Imperial Challenge: Quebec and Britain in the Age of the American Revolution.* Montreal and Kingston, Ont.: McGill-Queen's University Press, 1989.

Lawson, Steven. *Running for Freedom: Civil Rights and Black Politics in America since 1941,* 3rd ed. Malden, Mass.: Wiley-Blackwell, 2009.

Lee, Robert. *The Social Sources of Church Unity: An Interpretation of Unitive Movements in American Protestantism.* New York: Abingdon Press, 1960.

Leech, Margaret. *In the Days of McKinley.* New York: Harper, 1959.

Leff, Laurel. *Buried by the Times: The Holocaust and America's Most Important Newspaper.* New York: Cambridge University Press, 2005.

Leffler, Melvyn P. *A Preponderance of Power: National Security, the Truman Administration, and the Cold War.* Stanford, Calif.: Stanford University Press, 1992.

———. *The Specter of Communism: The United States and the Origins of the Cold War, 1917–1953.* New York: Hill and Wang, 1994.

———. *For the Soul of Mankind: The United States, the Soviet Union, and the Cold War.* New York: Hill and Wang, 2007.

Lemay, J. A. Leo. *The Life of Benjamin Franklin,* 3 vols. Philadelphia: University of Pennsylvania Press, 2005–2008.

Lentz-Smith, Adriane. *Freedom Struggles: African Americans and World War I.* Cambridge, Mass.: Harvard University Press, 2009.

LeoGrande, William M. *Our Own Backyard: The United States in Central America, 1977–1992.* Chapel Hill: University of North Carolina Press, 1998.

Lepore, Jill. *The Name of War: King Philip's War and the Origins of American Identity.* New York: Alfred A. Knopf, 1998.

Levin, N. Gordon, Jr. *Woodrow Wilson and World Politics: America's Response to War and Revolution.* New York: Oxford University Press, 1968.

Levine, Lawrence W. *Defender of the Faith: William Jennings Bryan: The Last Decade, 1915–1925.* New York: Oxford University Press, 1965.

Levy, David W. *The Debate over Vietnam,* 2nd ed. Baltimore: Johns Hopkins University Press, 1995.

Levy, Leonard W. *The Establishment Clause: Religion and the First Amendment.* Chapel Hill: University of North Carolina Press, 1994.

Lian Xi. *The Conversion of Missionaries: Liberalism in American Protestant Missions in China, 1907–1932.* University Park: Pennsylvania State University Press, 1997.

———. *Redeemed by Fire: The Rise of Popular Christianity in Modern China.* New Haven, Conn.: Yale University Press, 2010.

Lichtman, Allan J. *White Protestant Nation: The Rise of the American Conservative Movement.* New York: Atlantic Monthly Press, 2008.

Lienesch, Michael. *Redeeming America: Piety and Politics in the New Christian Right.* Chapel Hill: University of North Carolina Press, 1993.

Lieven, Anatol. *America Right or Wrong: An Anatomy of American Nationalism.* New York: Oxford University Press, 2004.

Lindsay, D. Michael. *Faith in the Halls of Power: How Evangelicals Joined the American Elite.* New York: Oxford University Press, 2007.

Link, Arthur S. *Wilson,* 5 vols. Princeton, N.J.: Princeton University Press, 1947–1965.

———. *The Higher Realism of Woodrow Wilson.* Nashville, Tenn.: Vanderbilt University Press, 1971.

Link, William A. *Righteous Warrior: Jesse Helms and the Rise of Modern Conservatism.* New York: St. Martin's, 2008.

Linn, Brian McAllister. *The Philippine War, 1899–1902.* Lawrence: University Press of Kansas, 2000.

Little, Douglas. *American Orientalism: The United States and the Middle East since 1945.* Chapel Hill: University of North Carolina Press, 2002.

Little, Lawrence S. *Disciples of Liberty: The African Methodist Episcopal Church in the Age of Imperialism, 1884–1916.* Knoxville: University of Tennessee Press, 2000.

Litwack, Leon F. *Trouble in Mind: Black Southerners in the Age of Jim Crow.* New York: Alfred A. Knopf, 1998.

Livezey, William E. *Mahan on Sea Power,* rev. ed. Norman: University of Oklahoma Press, 1981.

Logevall, Fredrik. *Choosing War: The Lost Chance for Peace and the Escalation of War in Vietnam.* Berkeley: University of California Press, 1999.

Logevall, Fredrik, and Andrew Preston, eds. *Nixon in the World: American Foreign Relations, 1969–1977.* New York: Oxford University Press, 2008.

Lookstein, Haskel. *Were We Our Brothers' Keepers? The Public Response of American Jews to the Holocaust, 1938–1944.* New York: Hartmore House, 1985.

Love, Eric T. L. *Race over Empire: Racism and U.S. Imperialism, 1865–1900.* Chapel Hill: University of North Carolina Press, 2004.

Lovejoy, David S. *The Glorious Revolution in America.* New York: Harper & Row, 1972.

———. *Religious Enthusiasm in the New World: Heresy to Revolution.* Cambridge, Mass.: Harvard University Press, 1985.

Loveland, Anne C. *American Evangelicals and the U.S. Military, 1942–1993.* Baton Rouge: Louisiana State University Press, 1996.

Lovin, Robin W. *Reinhold Niebuhr and Christian Realism.* Cambridge: Cambridge University Press, 1995.

Lucas, Scott. *Freedom's War: The American Crusade against the Soviet Union.* New York: New York University Press, 1999.

Lukacs, John. *George Kennan: A Study of Character.* New Haven, Conn.: Yale University Press, 2007.

Lutz, Jessie Gregory. *China and the Christian Colleges, 1850–1950.* Ithaca, N.Y.: Cornell University Press, 1971.

Lynch, Cecelia. *Beyond Appeasement: Interpreting Interwar Peace Movements in World Politics.* Ithaca: Cornell University Press, 1999.

Lyon, Peter. *Eisenhower: Portrait of the Hero.* Boston: Little, Brown, 1974.

Mabee, Carleton. *The American Leonardo: A Life of Samuel F. B. Morse.* New York: Alfred A. Knopf, 1943.

MacCulloch, Diarmaid. *Reformation: Europe's House Divided, 1490–1700.* London: Allen Lane, 2003.

MacKenzie, Kenneth M. *The Robe and the Sword: The Methodist Church and the Rise of American Imperialism.* Washington, D.C.: Public Affairs Press, 1961.

MacLean, Nancy. *Behind the Mask of Chivalry: The Making of the Second Ku Klux Klan.* New York: Oxford University Press, 1994.

MacMillan, Margaret. *Paris 1919: Six Months that Changed the World.* New York: Random House, 2002.

McAlister, Melani. *Epic Encounters: Culture, Media, and U.S. Interests in the Middle East since 1945,* rev. ed. Berkeley: University of California Press, 2005.

McCloud, Aminah Beverly. *Transnational Muslims in American Society.* Gainesville, Fla.: University Press of Florida, 2006.

McCoy, Donald R. *The Presidency of Harry S. Truman.* Lawrence: University Press of Kansas, 1984.

McCusker, John J., and Russell R. Menard. *The Economy of British North America, 1607–1789.* Chapel Hill: University of North Carolina Press, 1985.

McDougall, Walter A. *Promised Land, Crusader State: The American Encounter with the World since 1776.* Boston: Houghton Mifflin, 1997.

———. *Freedom Just Around the Corner: A New American History, 1585–1828.* New York: HarperCollins, 2004.

———. *Throes of Democracy: The American Civil War Era, 1829–1877.* New York: HarperCollins, 2008.

McDowell, John Patrick. *The Social Gospel in the South: The Woman's Home Mission Movement in the Methodist Episcopal Church, South, 1886–1939.* Baton Rouge: Louisiana State University Press, 1982.

McGirr, Lisa. *Suburban Warriors: The Origins of the New American Right.* Princeton, N.J.: Princeton University Press, 2001.

McGlone, Robert E. *John Brown's War Against Slavery.* New York: Cambridge University Press, 2009.

McGreevy, John T. *Catholicism and American Freedom: A History.* New York: W. W. Norton, 2003.

McKanan, Dan. *Identifying the Image of God: Radical Christians and Nonviolent Power in the Antebellum United States.* New York: Oxford University Press, 2002.

McKee, Delber L. *Chinese Exclusion versus the Open Door Policy, 1900–1906: Clashes over China Policy in the Roosevelt Era.* Detroit: Wayne State University Press, 1977.

McKenna, George. *The Puritan Origins of American Patriotism.* New Haven, Conn.: Yale University Press, 2007.

McKenzie, Michael C. *Paul Ramsey's Ethics: The Power of "Agape" in a Postmodern World.* Westport, Conn.: Praeger, 2001.

McKeogh, Colm. *The Political Realism of Reinhold Niebuhr: A Pragmatic Approach to the Just War.* New York: St. Martin's Press, 1997.

McKeown, Elizabeth. *War and Welfare: American Catholics and World War I.* New York: Garland, 1988.

McKibbin, Ross. *Classes and Cultures: England, 1918–1951*. Oxford: Oxford University Press, 1998.

McLoughlin, William G. *New England Dissent, 1630–1833: The Baptists and the Separation of Church and State*, 2 vols. Cambridge, Mass.: Harvard University Press, 1971.

———. *Revivals, Awakenings, and Reform: An Essay on Religion and Social Change in America, 1607–1977*. Chicago: University of Chicago Press, 1978.

McMahon, Robert J. *Dean Acheson and the Creation of an American World Order*. Washington, D.C.: Potomac Books, 2009.

McNeal, Patricia. *Harder Than War: Catholic Peacemaking in Twentieth-Century America*. New Brunswick, N.J.: Rutgers University Press, 1992.

McPherson, James M. *Battle Cry of Freedom: The Civil War Era*. New York: Oxford University Press, 1988.

———. *For Cause and Comrades: Why Men Fought in the Civil War*. New York: Oxford University Press, 1997.

McSeveney, Samuel. *The Politics of Depression: Political Behavior in the Northeast, 1893–1896*. New York: Oxford University Press, 1972.

McShane, Joseph M. *"Sufficiently Radical": Catholicism, Progressivism, and the Bishops' Program of 1919*. Washington, D.C.: Catholic University of America Press, 1986.

McWilliams, John. *New England's Crises and Cultural Memory: Literature, Politics, History, Religion, 1620–1860*. New York: Cambridge University Press, 2004.

Magee, Malcolm D. *What the World Should Be: Woodrow Wilson and the Crafting of a Faith-Based Foreign Policy*. Waco, Tex.: Baylor University Press, 2008.

Mahaffey, Jerome Dean. *Preaching Politics: The Religious Rhetoric of George Whitefield and the Founding of a New Nation*. Waco, Tex.: Baylor University Press, 2007.

Mahin, Dean B. *One War at a Time: The International Dimensions of the American Civil War*. Washington, D.C.: Brassey's, 1999.

Makdisi, Ussama. *Artillery of Heaven: American Missionaries and the Failed Conversion of the Middle East*. Ithaca, N.Y.: Cornell University Press, 2008.

Maltby, William S. *The Black Legend in England: The Development of Anti-Spanish Sentiment, 1558–1660*. Durham, N.C.: Duke University Press, 1971.

Mancall, Peter C. *Hakluyt's Promise: An Elizabethan's Obsession for an English America*. New Haven, Conn.: Yale University Press, 2006.

Manela, Erez. *The Wilsonian Moment: Self-Determination and the International Origins of Anticolonial Nationalism*. New York: Oxford University Press, 2007.

Maney, Patrick J. *The Roosevelt Presence: A Biography of Franklin Delano Roosevelt*. New York: Twayne, 1992.

Mann, James. *The Rebellion of Ronald Reagan: A History of the End of the Cold War*. New York: Viking, 2009.

Manning, Chandra. *What This Cruel War Was Over: Soldiers, Slavery, and the Civil War*. New York: Alfred A. Knopf, 2007.

Marchand, C. Roland. *The American Peace Movement and Social Reform, 1898–1918*. Princeton, N.J.: Princeton University Press, 1972.

Marcus, Sheldon. *Father Coughlin: The Tumultuous Life of the Priest of the Little Flower*. Boston: Little, Brown, 1973.

Marietta, Jack D. *The Reformation of American Quakerism, 1748–1783*. Philadelphia: University of Pennsylvania Press, 1984.

Marini, Stephen A. *Radical Sects of Revolutionary New England*. Cambridge, Mass.: Harvard University Press, 1982.

Marotti, Arthur F. *Religious Ideology and Cultural Fantasy: Catholic and Anti-Catholic Discourses in Early Modern England*. Notre Dame, Ind.: University of Notre Dame Press, 2005.

Marsden, George M. *Fundamentalism and American Culture: The Shaping of Twentieth-Century Evangelicalism, 1870–1925*. New York: Oxford University Press, 1980.

———. *Understanding Fundamentalism and Evangelicalism*. Grand Rapids, Mich.: Eerdmans, 1991.

———. *Jonathan Edwards: A Life*. New Haven, Conn.: Yale University Press, 2003.

Marsden, Lee. *For God's Sake: The Christian Right and US Foreign Policy*. London: Zed Books, 2008.

Martin, James Kirby. *Benedict Arnold, Revolutionary Hero: An American Warrior Reconsidered*. New York: New York University Press, 1997.

Martin, William. *A Prophet with Honor: The Billy Graham Story*. New York: William Morrow, 1991.

———. *With God on Our Side: The Rise of the Religious Right in America*. New York: Broadway Books, 1996.

Marty, Martin E. *Modern American Religion*, 3 vols. Chicago: University of Chicago Press, 1986–1996.

Matarese, Susan M. *American Foreign Policy and the Utopian Imagination*. Amherst: University of Massachusetts Press, 2001.

Mathews, Basil. *John R. Mott, World Citizen*. New York: Harper & Brothers, 1934.

Mathews, Donald G. *Religion in the Old South*. Chicago: University of Chicago Press, 1977.

Matthews, Jean V. *Toward a New Society: American Thought and Culture, 1800–1830*. Boston: Twayne, 1991.

May, Ernest R. *Imperial Democracy: The Emergence of America as a Great Power*. New York: Harcourt, Brace & World, 1961.

———, ed. *American Cold War Strategy: Interpreting NSC 68*. Boston: Bedford/St. Martin's, 1993.

May, Henry F. *Protestant Churches and Industrial America*. New York: Harper & Row, 1949.

Mayer, Henry. *All on Fire: William Lloyd Garrison and the Abolition of Slavery*. New York: St. Martin's Press, 1998.

Mayers, David. *Dissenting Voices in America's Rise to Power*. New York: Cambridge University Press, 2007.

Meacham, Jon. *American Gospel: God, the Founding Fathers, and the Making of a Nation*. New York: Random House, 2006.

———. *Franklin and Winston: An Intimate Portrait of an Epic Friendship*. New York: Random House, 2003.

Mead, Walter Russell. *Special Providence: American Foreign Policy and How It Changed the World*. New York: Alfred A. Knopf, 2003.

———. *God and Gold: Britain, America, and the Making of the Modern World*. New York: Alfred A. Knopf, 2007.

Mearsheimer, John J., and Stephen M. Walt. *The Israel Lobby and U.S. Foreign Policy*. New York: Farrar, Straus and Giroux, 2007.

Medlicott, W. N. *The Economic Blockade*, 2 vols. London: Her Majesty's Stationery Office/Longmans, Green and Co., 1952–1959.

Medoff, Rafael. *The Deafening Silence*. New York: Shapolsky Publishers, 1987.

Mekeel, Arthur J. *The Relation of the Quakers to the American Revolution*. Washington, D.C.: University Press of America, 1979.

Menand, Louis. *The Metaphysical Club*. New York: Farrar, Straus and Giroux, 2001.

Merk, Frederick. *The Oregon Question: Essays in Anglo-American Diplomacy and Politics*. Cambridge, Mass.: Harvard University Press, 1967.

Merkley, Paul Charles. *The Politics of Christian Zionism, 1891–1948*. London: Frank Cass, 1998.

———. *American Presidents, Religion, and Israel: The Heirs of Cyrus*. Westport, Conn.: Praeger, 2004.

Merrell, James H. *The Indians' New World: Catawbas and Their Neighbors from Euro-*

pean Contact through the Era of Removal. Chapel Hill: University of North Carolina Press, 1989.

Meyer, David R. *The Roots of American Industrialization.* Baltimore: Johns Hopkins University Press, 2003.

Meyer, Donald. *The Protestant Search for Political Realism, 1919–1941,* 2nd ed. Middletown, Conn.: Wesleyan University Press, 1988.

Micklethwait, John, and Adrian Wooldridge. *The Right Nation: Conservative Power in America.* New York: Penguin Press, 2004.

———. *God Is Back: How the Global Revival of Faith Is Changing the World.* New York: Penguin Press, 2009.

Middlekauff, Robert. *The Glorious Cause: The American Revolution, 1763–1789.* New York: Oxford University Press, 1982.

———. *Benjamin Franklin and His Enemies.* Berkeley: University of California Press, 1996.

Miller, James Edward. *The United States and Italy, 1940–1950: The Politics and Diplomacy of Stabilization.* Chapel Hill: University of North Carolina Press, 1986.

Miller, John. *Popery and Politics in England, 1660–1688.* Cambridge: Cambridge University Press, 1973.

Miller, Kerby A. *Emigrants and Exiles: Ireland and the Irish Exodus to North America.* New York: Oxford University Press, 1985.

Miller, Perry. *Errand into the Wilderness.* Cambridge, Mass.: Harvard University Press, 1956.

Miller, Randall M., Harry S. Stout, and Charles Reagan Wilson, eds. *Religion and the American Civil War.* New York: Oxford University Press, 1998.

Miller, Richard B. *Interpretations of Conflict: Ethics, Pacifism, and the Just-War Tradition.* Chicago: University of Chicago Press, 1991.

Miller, Robert J. *Both Prayed to the Same God: Religion and Faith in the American Civil War.* Lanham, Md.: Lexington Books, 2007.

Miller, Robert Moats. *How Shall They Hear Without a Preacher? The Life of Ernest Fremont Tittle.* Chapel Hill: University of North Carolina Press, 1971.

———. *Bishop G. Bromley Oxnam: Paladin of Liberal Protestantism.* Nashville, Tenn.: Abingdon Press, 1990.

Miller, Robert Ryal. *Shamrock and Sword: The Saint Patrick's Battalion in the U.S.-Mexican War.* Norman: University of Oklahoma Press, 1989.

Miller, Stuart Creighton. *"Benevolent Assimilation": The American Conquest of the Philippines, 1899–1903.* New Haven, Conn.: Yale University Press, 1982.

Milne, David. *America's Rasputin: Walt Rostow and the Vietnam War.* New York: Hill and Wang, 2008.

Milton, Anthony. *Catholic and Reformed: The Roman and Protestant Churches in English Protestant Thought, 1600–1640.* Cambridge: Cambridge University Press, 1995.

Miner, Steven Merritt. *Stalin's Holy War: Religion, Nationalism, and Alliance Politics, 1941–1945.* Chapel Hill: University of North Carolina Press, 2003.

Mintz, Steven. *Moralists and Modernizers: America's Pre–Civil War Reformers.* Baltimore: Johns Hopkins University Press, 1995.

Minus, Paul M. *Walter Rauschenbusch: American Reformer.* New York: Macmillan, 1988.

Miscamble, Wilson D. *From Roosevelt to Truman: Potsdam, Hiroshima, and the Cold War.* New York: Cambridge University Press, 2007.

Montgomery, Leslie. *The Faith of Condoleezza Rice.* Wheaton, Ill.: Crossway Books, 2007.

Moore, Deborah Dash. *At Home in America: Second Generation New York Jews.* New York: Columbia University Press, 1981.

Moore, James P., Jr. *One Nation under God: The History of Prayer in America.* New York: Doubleday, 2005.

Moore, James R. *The Post-Darwinian Controversies: A Study of the Protestant Struggle to Come to Terms with Darwin in Great Britain and America, 1870–1900.* Cambridge: Cambridge University Press, 1979.

Moore, Michaela Hoenicke. *Know Your Enemy: The American Debate on Nazism, 1933–1945.* New York: Cambridge University Press, 2010.

Moore, R. Laurence. *Selling God: American Religion in the Marketplace of Culture.* New York: Oxford University Press, 1994.

Moore, Susan Hardman. *Pilgrims: New World Settlers and the Call of Home.* New Haven, Conn.: Yale University Press, 2007.

Moorhead, James H. *American Apocalypse: Yankee Protestants and the Civil War, 1860–1869.* New Haven, Conn.: Yale University Press, 1978.

Moreton, Bethany. *To Serve God and Wal-Mart: The Making of Christian Free Enterprise.* Cambridge, Mass.: Harvard University Press, 2009.

Morgan, Edmund S. *The Birth of the Republic, 1763–1789.* Chicago: University of Chicago Press, 1956.

———. *American Slavery, American Freedom: The Ordeal of Colonial Virginia.* New York: W. W. Norton, 1975.

———. *The Challenge of the American Revolution.* New York: W. W. Norton, 1976.

———. *Benjamin Franklin.* New Haven, Conn.: Yale University Press, 2002.

Morgan, Edmund S., and Helen M. Morgan. *The Stamp Act Crisis: Prologue to Revolution,* rev. ed. New York: Collier, 1962.

Morgan, H. Wayne. *William McKinley and His America.* Syracuse, N.Y.: Syracuse University Press, 1964.

Morison, Samuel Eliot. *History of United States Naval Operations in World War II,* 15 vols. Boston: Little, Brown, 1947–1962.

Morone, James A. *Hellfire Nation: The Politics of Sin in American History.* New Haven, Conn.: Yale University Press, 2003.

Morris, James. *The Preachers.* New York: St. Martin's, 1973.

Morris, Roger. *Richard Milhous Nixon: The Rise of an American Politician.* New York: Henry Holt, 1990.

Morrison, Jeffry H. *John Witherspoon and the Founding of the American Republic.* Notre Dame, Ind.: University of Notre Dame Press, 2005.

———. *The Political Philosophy of George Washington.* Baltimore: Johns Hopkins University Press, 2009.

Morrison, Michael A. *Slavery and the American West: The Eclipse of Manifest Destiny and the Coming of the Civil War.* Chapel Hill: University of North Carolina Press, 1997.

Morse, James King. *Jedidiah Morse: A Champion of New England Orthodoxy.* New York: Columbia University Press, 1939.

Moseley, James G. *John Winthrop's World: History as a Story, the Story as History.* Madison: University of Wisconsin Press, 1992.

Moyn, Samuel. *The Last Utopia: Human Rights in History.* Cambridge, Mass.: Harvard University Press, 2010.

Moynihan, James H. *The Life of Archbishop John Ireland.* New York: Harper, 1953.

Mulder, John M. *Woodrow Wilson: The Years of Preparation.* Princeton, N.J.: Princeton University Press, 1978.

Muñoz, Vincent Phillip. *God and the Founders: Madison, Washington, and Jefferson.* New York: Cambridge University Press, 2009.

Murch, James DeForest. *Cooperation without Compromise: A History of the National Association of Evangelicals.* Grand Rapids, Mich.: Eerdmans, 1956.

Nagel, Paul C. *John Quincy Adams: A Public Life, A Private Life.* New York: Alfred A. Knopf, 1997.

Namias, June. *White Captives: Gender and Ethnicity on the American Frontier.* Chapel Hill: University of North Carolina Press, 1993.

Nash, Gary B. *The Urban Crucible: Social Change, Political Consciousness, and the Origins of the American Revolution*. Cambridge, Mass.: Harvard University Press, 1979.

Nash, Roderick. *Wilderness and the American Mind*, rev. ed. New Haven, Conn.: Yale University Press, 1973.

Nathans, Benjamin. *Beyond the Pale: The Jewish Encounter with Late Imperial Russia*. Berkeley: University of California Press, 2001.

Neem, Johann N. *Creating a Nation of Joiners: Democracy and Civil Society in Early National Massachusetts*. Cambridge, Mass.: Harvard University Press, 2008.

Nichols, J. Bruce. *The Uneasy Alliance: Religion, Refugee Work, and U.S. Foreign Policy*. New York: Oxford University Press, 1988.

Ninkovich, Frank. *Modernity and Power: A History of the Domino Theory in the Twentieth Century*. Chicago: University of Chicago Press, 1994.

———. *The United States and Imperialism*. Oxford: Blackwell, 2001.

———. *Global Dawn: The Cultural Foundation of American Internationalism, 1865–1890*. Cambridge, Mass.: Harvard University Press, 2009.

Nobles, Gregory H. *American Frontiers: Cultural Encounters and Continental Conquest*. New York: Hill and Wang, 1997.

Noll, Mark A. *Christians in the American Revolution*. Washington, D.C.: Christian University Press, 1977.

———. *A History of Christianity in the United States and Canada*. Grand Rapids, Mich.: Eerdmans, 1992.

———. *America's God: From Jonathan Edwards to Abraham Lincoln*. New York: Oxford University Press, 2002.

———. *The Civil War as a Theological Crisis*. Chapel Hill: University of North Carolina Press, 2006.

———. *God and Race in American Politics: A Short History*. Princeton, N.J.: Princeton University Press, 2008.

———. *The New Shape of World Christianity: How American Experience Reflects Global Faith*. Downers Grove, Ill.: IVP Academic, 2009.

Norton, Mary Beth. *In the Devil's Snare: The Salem Witchcraft Crisis of 1692*. New York: Alfred A. Knopf, 2002.

Norwood, Frederick A. *The Story of American Methodism: A History of the United Methodists and Their Relations*. Nashville, Tenn.: Abingdon Press, 1974.

Novick, Peter. *The Holocaust in American Life*. Boston: Houghton Mifflin, 1999.

Nurser, John S. *For All Peoples and All Nations: The Ecumenical Church and Human Rights*. Washington, D.C.: Georgetown University Press, 2005.

Nutt, Rick L. *The Whole Gospel for the Whole World: Sherwood Eddy and the American Protestant Mission*. Macon, Ga.: Mercer University Press, 1997.

Oakes, James. *Slavery and Freedom: An Interpretation of the Old South*. New York: Alfred A. Knopf, 1990.

———. *The Radical and the Republican: Frederick Douglass, Abraham Lincoln, and the Triumph of Antislavery Politics*. New York: W. W. Norton, 2007.

Oakley, J. Ronald. *God's Country: America in the Fifties*. New York: Dembner Books, 1986.

Oatis, Steven J. *A Colonial Complex: South Carolina's Frontiers in the Era of the Yamasee War, 1680–1730*. Lincoln: University of Nebraska Press, 2004.

Obenzinger, Hilton. *American Palestine: Melville, Twain, and the Holy Land Mania*. Princeton, N.J.: Princeton University Press, 1999.

Oberdorfer, Don. *The Turn: From the Cold War to a New Era, 1983–1990: The United States and the Soviet Union*. New York: Poseidon Press, 1991.

O'Brien, David J. *American Catholics and Social Reform: The New Deal Years*. New York: Oxford University Press, 1968.

O'Brien, Michael. *Conjectures of Order: Intellectual Life and the American South, 1810–1860*, 2 vols. Chapel Hill: University of North Carolina Press, 2004.

———. *Intellectual Life and the American South, 1810–1860*. Chapel Hill: University of North Carolina Press, 2010.

O'Brien, William V. *The Conduct of Just and Limited War.* New York: Praeger, 1981.

O'Connell, Marvin R. *John Ireland and the American Catholic Church.* St. Paul: Minnesota Historical Society Press, 1988.

Offner, Arnold A. *American Appeasement: United States Foreign Policy and Germany, 1933–1938.* Cambridge, Mass.: Harvard University Press, 1969.

Olcott, Charles S. *The Life of William McKinley*, 2 vols. Boston: Houghton Mifflin, 1916.

O'Neill, William L. *A Democracy at War: America's Fight at Home and Abroad in World War I.* Cambridge, Mass.: Harvard University Press, 1993.

Oren, Michael B. *Power, Faith, and Fantasy: America in the Middle East, 1776 to the Present.* New York: W. W. Norton, 2007.

Orsi, Robert Anthony. *The Madonna of 115th Street: Faith and Community in Italian Harlem, 1880–1950.* New Haven, Conn.: Yale University Press, 1985.

Osgood, Kenneth. *Total Cold War: Eisenhower's Secret Propaganda Battle at Home and Abroad.* Lawrence: University Press of Kansas, 2006.

Osgood, Robert Endicott. *Ideals and Self-Interest in America's Foreign Relations: The Great Transformation of the Twentieth Century.* Chicago: University of Chicago Press, 1953.

Oshinsky, David M. *A Conspiracy So Immense: The World of Joe McCarthy.* New York: Free Press, 1983.

O'Toole, James M. *The Faithful: A History of Catholics in America.* Cambridge, Mass.: Harvard University Press, 2008.

Overstreet, Harry, and Bonaro Overstreet. *The Strange Tactics of Extremism.* New York: W. W. Norton, 1964.

Owen, Richard M. *The Clash of Ideas in World Politics: Transnational Networks, States, and Regime Change, 1510–2010.* Princeton, N.J.: Princeton University Press, 2011.

Pagden, Anthony. *Lords of All the Worlds: Ideologies of Empire in Spain, Britain and France c. 1500–c. 1850.* New Haven, Conn.: Yale University Press, 1995.

Paludan, Phillip Shaw. *"A People's Contest": The Union and Civil War, 1861–1865.* New York: Harper & Row, 1988.

Pangle, Thomas L. *The Spirit of Modern Republicanism: The Moral Vision of the American Founders and the Philosophy of Locke.* Chicago: University of Chicago Press, 1988.

Parker, Michael. *The Kingdom of Character: The Student Volunteer Movement for Foreign Missions, 1886–1926.* Lanham, Md.: University Press of America, 1998.

Patterson, David S. *Toward a Warless World: The Travail of the American Peace Movement, 1887–1914.* Bloomington, Ind.: Indiana University Press, 1976.

Peckham, Howard H. *The Colonial Wars, 1689–1762.* Chicago: University of Chicago Press, 1964.

Pérez, Louis A., Jr. *The War of 1898: The United States and Cuba in History and Historiography.* Chapel Hill: University of North Carolina Press, 1998.

———. *Cuba in the American Imagination: Metaphor and the Imperial Ethos.* Chapel Hill: University of North Carolina Press, 2008.

Perkins, Bradford. *The Great Rapprochement: England and the United States, 1895–1914.* New York: Atheneum, 1968.

———. *The Cambridge History of American Foreign Relations*, vol. 1: *The Creation of a Republican Empire, 1776–1865.* Cambridge: Cambridge University Press, 1993.

Perman, Michael. *Struggle for Mastery: Disfranchisement in the South, 1888–1908.* Chapel Hill: University of North Carolina Press, 2001.

Perry, James R. *The Formation of a Society on Virginia's Eastern Shore, 1615–1655.* Chapel Hill: University of North Carolina Press, 1990.

Persico, Joseph E. *Casey: From the OSS to the CIA.* New York: Viking, 1990.

Peskin, Lawrence A. *Captives and Countrymen: Barbary Slavery and the American Public, 1785–1816.* Baltimore: Johns Hopkins University Press, 2009.

Pestana, Carla Gardina. *Quakers and Baptists in Colonial Massachusetts.* Cambridge: Cambridge University Press, 1991.

———. *The English Atlantic in an Age of Revolution, 1640–1661.* Cambridge, Mass.: Harvard University Press, 2004.

———. *Protestant Empire: Religion and the Making of the British Atlantic World.* Philadelphia: University of Pennsylvania Press, 2009.

Phayer, Michael. *Pius XII, the Holocaust, and the Cold War.* Bloomington: Indiana University Press, 2008.

Phillips, Clifton Jackson. *Protestant America and the Pagan World: The First Half Century of the American Board of Commissioners for Foreign Missions, 1810–1860.* Cambridge, Mass.: East Asian Research Center, Harvard University, 1969.

Phillips, Joseph W. *Jedidiah Morse and New England Congregationalism.* New Brunswick, N.J.: Rutgers University Press, 1983.

Phillips, Kevin. *The Cousins' Wars: Religion, Politics, and the Triumph of Anglo-America.* New York: Basic Books, 1999.

Phillips-Fein, Kim. *Invisible Hands: The Making of the Conservative Movement from the New Deal to Reagan.* New York: W. W. Norton, 2009.

Pilcher, George William. *Samuel Davies: Apostle of Dissent in Colonial Virginia.* Knoxville: University of Tennessee Press, 1971.

Piper, Robert F., Jr. *The American Churches in World War I.* Athens: Ohio University Press, 1985.

———. *Robert E. Speer: Prophet of the American Church.* Louisville, Ky.: Geneva Press, 2000.

Plank, Geoffrey. *An Unsettled Conquest: The British Campaign against the Peoples of Acadia.* Philadelphia: University of Pennsylvania Press, 2001.

———. *Rebellion and Savagery: The Jacobite Rising of 1745 and the British Empire.* Philadelphia: University of Pennsylvania Press, 2006.

Plesur, Milton. *America's Outward Thrust: Approaches to Foreign Affairs, 1865–1890.* DeKalb: Northern Illinois University Press, 1971.

Pletcher, David M. *The Diplomacy of Annexation: Texas, Oregon, and the Mexican War.* Columbia: University of Missouri Press, 1973.

Plokhy, S. M. *Yalta: The Price of Peace.* New York: Viking Press, 2010.

Pocock, J. G. A. *The Machiavellian Moment: Florentine Political Thought and the Atlantic Republican Tradition.* Princeton, N.J.: Princeton University Press, 1975.

Pole, J. R. *The Gift of Government: Political Responsibility from the English Restoration to American Independence.* Athens: University of Georgia Press, 1983.

Pollard, John F. *The Unknown Pope: Benedict XV (1912–1922) and the Pursuit of Peace.* London: Geoffrey Chapman, 1999.

Polner, Murray, and Jim O'Grady. *Disarmed and Dangerous: The Radical Lives and Times of Daniel and Philip Berrigan.* New York: Basic Books, 1997.

Porter, Andrew. *Religion versus Empire? British Protestant Missionaries and Overseas Expansion, 1700–1914.* Manchester: Manchester University Press, 2004.

Porter, H. C. *The Inconstant Savage: England and the North American Indian, 1500–1660.* London: Duckworth, 1979.

Potter, Janice. *The Liberty We Seek: Loyalist Ideology in Colonial New York and Massachusetts.* Cambridge, Mass.: Harvard University Press, 1983.

Powaski, Ronald E. *Thomas Merton on Nuclear Weapons.* Chicago: Loyola University Press, 1988.

Pratt, Julius W. *Expansionists of 1898: The Acquisition of Hawaii and the Spanish Islands.* Baltimore: Johns Hopkins University Press, 1936.

Prentiss, Craig R. *Debating God's Economy: Social Justice in America on the Eve of Vatican II.* University Park: Pennsylvania State University Press, 2008.

Preston, Andrew. *The War Council: McGeorge Bundy, the NSC, and Vietnam.* Cambridge, Mass.: Harvard University Press, 2006.

Price, Glenn W. *Origins of the War with Mexico: The Polk-Stockton Intrigue.* Austin: University of Texas Press, 1967.

Prochnau, William W., and Richard W. Larsen. *A Certain Democrat: Senator Henry M. Jackson, A Political Biography.* Englewood Cliffs, N.J.: Prentice-Hall, 1972.

Prothero, Stephen. *American Jesus: How the Son of God Became a National Icon.* New York: Farrar, Straus and Giroux, 2003.

Pruessen, Ronald W. *John Foster Dulles: The Road to Power.* New York: Free Press, 1982.

Purkiss, Diane. *The English Civil War: A People's History.* London: Harper Perennial, 2006.

Putney, Clifford. *Muscular Christianity: Manhood and Sports in Protestant America, 1880–1920.* Cambridge, Mass.: Harvard University Press, 2001.

Queen, Edward L. *In the South the Baptists Are the Center of Gravity: Southern Baptists and Social Change, 1930–1980.* New York: Carlson, 1991.

Rabb, Theodore K. *Enterprise and Empire: Merchant and Gentry Investment in the Expansion of England, 1575–1630.* Cambridge, Mass.: Harvard University Press, 1967.

Rabe, Valentin H. *The Home Base of American China Missions, 1880–1920.* Cambridge, Mass.: Council on East Asian Studies, Harvard University, 1978.

Raboteau, Albert J. *Slave Religion: The "Invisible Institution" in the Antebellum South.* New York: Oxford University Press, 1978.

Ragosta, John A. *Wellspring of Liberty: How Virginia's Religious Dissenters Helped Win the American Revolution and Secured Religious Liberty.* New York: Oxford University Press, 2010.

Raider, Mark A. *The Emergence of American Zionism.* New York: New York University Press, 1998.

Rakove, Jack N. *James Madison and the Creation of the American Republic.* Boston: Little, Brown, 1990.

———. *Original Meanings: Politics and Ideas in the Making of the Constitution.* New York: Alfred A. Knopf, 1996.

Ramsay, Jacob. *Mandarins and Martyrs: The Church and the Nguyen Dynasty in Early Nineteenth-Century Vietnam.* Stanford, Calif.: Stanford University Press, 2008.

Randall, Willard Sterne. *Benedict Arnold: Patriot and Traitor.* New York: William Morrow, 1990.

Raphael, Marc Lee. *Judaism in America.* New York: Columbia University Press, 2003.

Rawlyk, George A. *Nova Scotia's Massachusetts: A Study of Massachusetts–Nova Scotia Relations, 1630 to 1784.* Montreal and Kingston, Ont.: McGill-Queen's University Press, 1973.

Reed, James. *The Missionary Mind and American East Asia Policy, 1911–1915.* Cambridge, Mass.: Council on East Asian Studies, Harvard University, 1983.

Reeves, Richard. *President Reagan: The Triumph of Imagination.* New York: Simon & Schuster, 2005.

Remini, Robert V. *Andrew Jackson and the Course of American Empire, 1767–1821.* New York: Harper & Row, 1977.

———. *Andrew Jackson and the Course of American Freedom, 1822–1832.* New York: Harper & Row, 1981.

———. *Andrew Jackson and the Course of American Democracy, 1833–1845.* New York: Harper & Row, 1984.

———. *Daniel Webster: The Man and His Time.* New York: W. W. Norton, 1997.

————. *John Quincy Adams*. New York: Times Books, 2002.

Remnick, David. *The Bridge: The Life and Rise of Barack Obama*. New York: Alfred A. Knopf, 2010.

Reuter, Frank T. *Catholic Influence on American Colonial Policies, 1898–1904*. Austin: University of Texas Press, 1967.

Revard, Stella Purce. *The War in Heaven: "Paradise Lost" and the Tradition of Satan's Rebellion*. Ithaca, N.Y.: Cornell University Press, 1980.

Reynolds, David. *The Creation of the Anglo-American Alliance, 1937–41: A Study in Competitive Co-operation*. London: Europa, 1981.

————. *America, Empire of Liberty: A New History of the United States*. New York: Basic Books, 2009.

Rhodes, Richard. *Arsenals of Folly: The Making of the Nuclear Arms Race*. New York: Alfred A. Knopf, 2007.

Ribuffo, Leo P. *The Old Christian Right: The Protestant Far Right from the Great Depression to the Cold War*. Philadelphia: Temple University Press, 1983.

————. *Right Center Left: Essays in American History*. New Brunswick, N.J.: Rutgers University Press, 1992.

Richards, Leonard L. *The Life and Times of Congressman John Quincy Adams*. New York: Oxford University Press, 1986.

Richardson, Joe M. *Christian Reconstruction: The American Missionary Association and Southern Blacks, 1861–1880*. Athens: University of Georgia Press, 1986.

Richardson, Robert D., Jr. *Emerson: The Mind on Fire*. Berkeley: University of California Press, 1995.

Richter, Daniel K. *The Ordeal of the Longhouse: The Peoples of the Iroquois League in the Era of European Colonization*. Chapel Hill: University of North Carolina Press, 1992.

————. *Facing East from Indian Country: A Native History of Early America*. Cambridge, Mass.: Harvard University Press, 2001.

Rieder, Jonathan. *The Word of the Lord Is Upon Me: The Righteous Performance of Martin Luther King, Jr*. Cambridge, Mass.: Harvard University Press, 2008.

Robert, Dana L. *American Women in Mission: A Social History of Their Thought and Practice*. Macon, Ga.: Mercer University Press, 1997.

————. *Occupy until I Come: A. T. Pierson and the Evangelization of the World*. Grand Rapids, Mich.: Eerdmans, 2003.

Roberts, Jon H. *Darwinism and the Divine in America: Protestant Intellectuals and Organic Evolution, 1859–1900*. Madison: University of Wisconsin Press, 1988.

Robertson, David M. *A Passionate Pilgrim: A Biography of Bishop James A. Pike*. New York: Alfred A. Knopf, 2004.

Robertson, Nancy Marie. *Christian Sisterhood, Race Relations, and the YWCA, 1906–1946*. Urbana: University of Illinois Press, 2007.

Robinson, Jo Ann Ooiman. *Abraham Went Out: A Biography of A. J. Muste*. Philadelphia: Temple University Press, 1981.

Rofe, J. Simon. *Franklin Roosevelt's Foreign Policy and the Welles Mission*. New York: Palgrave Macmillan, 2007.

Ro'i, Yaacov. *The Struggle for Soviet Jewish Emigration, 1948–1967*. Cambridge: Cambridge University Press, 1991.

Roof, Wade Clark. *Spiritual Marketplace: Baby Boomers and the Remaking of American Religion*. Princeton, N.J.: Princeton University Press, 1999.

Rose, Anne C. *Transcendentalism as a Social Movement, 1830–1850*. New Haven, Conn.: Yale University Press, 1981.

Rosenberg, Emily S. *Spreading the American Dream: American Economic and Cultural Expansion, 1890–1945*. New York: Hill and Wang, 1982.

Roshwald, Aviel. *The Endurance of Nationalism: Ancient Roots and Modern Dilemmas.* Cambridge: Cambridge University Press, 2006.

Rossi, Joseph S. *American Catholics and the Formation of the United Nations.* Lanham, Md.: University Press of America, 1993.

———. *Uncharted Territory: The American Catholic Church at the United Nations, 1946–1972.* Washington, D.C.: Catholic University of America Press, 2006.

Rossinow, Doug. *The Politics of Authenticity: Liberalism, Christianity, and the New Left in America.* New York: Columbia University Press, 1998.

Rothman, Adam. *Slave Country: American Expansion and the Origins of the Deep South.* Cambridge, Mass.: Harvard University Press, 2005.

Rotter, Andrew J. *Comrades at Odds: The United States and India, 1947–1964.* Ithaca, N.Y.: Cornell University Press, 2000.

Rountree, Helen C. *The Powhatan Indians of Virginia: Their Traditional Culture.* Norman: University of Oklahoma Press, 1989.

———. *Pocahontas, Powhatan, Opechancanough: Three Indian Lives Changed by Jamestown.* Charlottesville: University of Virginia Press, 2005.

Rountree, Helen C., and E. Randolph Turner III. *Before and after Jamestown: Virginia's Powhatans and Their Predecessors.* Gainesville: University Press of Florida, 2002.

Royster, Charles. *A Revolutionary People at War: The Continental Army and American Character, 1775–1783.* Chapel Hill: University of North Carolina Press, 1979.

Rubin, Barry. *Paved with Good Intentions: The American Experience and Iran.* New York: Oxford University Press, 1980.

Ruotsila, Markku. *The Origins of Christian Anti-internationalism: Conservative Evangelicals and the League of Nations.* Washington, D.C.: Georgetown University Press, 2008.

Samito, Christian G. *Becoming American under Fire: Irish Americans, African Americans, and the Politics of Citizenship during the Civil War Era.* Ithaca, N.Y.: Cornell University Press, 2009.

Sampson, Robert. *John L. O'Sullivan and His Times.* Kent, Ohio: Kent State University Press, 2002.

Sandbrook, Dominic. *Eugene McCarthy: The Rise and Fall of Postwar American Liberalism.* New York: Alfred A. Knopf, 2004.

Sandeen, Ernest R. *The Roots of Fundamentalism: British and American Millenarianism, 1800–1930.* Chicago: University of Chicago Press, 1970.

Sanneh, Lamin. *Abolitionists Abroad: American Blacks and the Making of Modern West Africa.* Cambridge, Mass.: Harvard University Press, 1999.

———. *Disciples of All Nations: Pillars of World Christianity.* New York: Oxford University Press, 2008.

Sarna, Jonathan D. *American Judaism: A History.* New Haven: Yale University Press, 2004.

Sassi, Jonathan D. *A Republic of Righteousness: The Public Christianity of the Post-Revolutionary New England Clergy.* New York: Oxford University Press, 2001.

Saunders, Frances Stonor. *The Cultural Cold War: The CIA and the World of Arts and Letters.* New York: New Press, 1999.

Schiffrin, Harold Z. *Sun Yat-sen and the Origins of the Chinese Revolution.* Berkeley: University of California Press, 1968.

Schlesinger, Arthur M., Jr. *The Cycles of American History.* Boston: Houghton Mifflin, 1986.

Schmidt, Leigh E. *Restless Souls: The Making of American Spirituality.* San Francisco: HarperSanFrancisco, 2005.

Schmitt, Hans A. *Quakers and Nazis: Inner Light in Outer Darkness.* Columbia: University of Missouri Press, 1997.

Schoenbaum, Thomas J. *Waging Peace and War: Dean Rusk in the Truman, Kennedy, and Johnson Years*. New York: Simon & Schuster, 1988.

Schoenwald, Jonathan M. *A Time for Choosing: The Rise of Modern American Conservatism*. New York: Oxford University Press, 2001.

Schrecker, Ellen. *Many Are the Crimes: McCarthyism in America*. Boston: Little, Brown, 1998.

Schroeder, John H. *Mr. Polk's War: American Opposition and Dissent, 1846–1848*. Madison: University of Wisconsin Press, 1973.

Schroeder, Paul W. *The Transformation of European Politics, 1763–1848*. Oxford: Oxford University Press, 1994.

Schulman, Lydia Dittler. *Paradise Lost and the Rise of the American Republic*. Boston: Northeastern University Press, 1992.

Schultz, George A. *An Indian Canaan: Isaac McCoy and the Vision of an Indian State*. Norman: University of Oklahoma Press, 1972.

Schwartz, Thomas Alan. *Lyndon Johnson and Europe: In the Shadow of Vietnam*. Cambridge, Mass.: Harvard University Press, 2003.

Schweitzer, Richard. *The Cross and the Trenches: Religious Faith and Doubt among British and American Great War Soldiers*. Westport, Conn.: Praeger, 2003.

Scroop, Daniel. *Mr. Democrat: Jim Farley, the New Deal, and the Making of Modern American Politics*. Ann Arbor: University of Michigan Press, 2006.

Scully, Eileen P. *Bargaining with the State from Afar: American Citizenship in Treaty Port China, 1844–1942*. New York: Columbia University Press, 2001.

Scully, Randolph Ferguson. *Religion and the Making of Nat Turner's Virginia: Baptist Community and Conflict, 1740–1840*. Charlottesville: University of Virginia Press, 2008.

Seager, Robert. *Alfred Thayer Mahan: The Man and His Letters*. Annapolis, Md.: Naval Institute Press, 1977.

Seeman, Erik R. *Pious Persuasions: Laity and Clergy in Eighteenth-Century New England*. Baltimore: Johns Hopkins University Press, 1999.

Selesky, Harold E. *War and Society in Colonial Connecticut*. New Haven, Conn.: Yale University Press, 1990.

Sellers, Charles. *James K. Polk, Jacksonian, 1795–1843*. Princeton, N.J.: Princeton University Press, 1957.

———. *The Market Revolution: Jacksonian America, 1815–1846*. New York: Oxford University Press, 1991.

Sensabaugh, George Frank. *Milton in Early America*. Princeton, N.J.: Princeton University Press, 1964.

Sexton, Jay. *The Monroe Doctrine: Empire and Nation in Nineteenth-Century America*. New York: Hill and Wang, 2011.

Shafer, Byron E., and Richard Johnston. *The End of Southern Exceptionalism: Class, Race, and Partisan Change in the Postwar South*. Cambridge, Mass.: Harvard University Press, 2006.

Shapiro, Edward S. *A Time for Healing: American Jewry since World War II*. Baltimore: Johns Hopkins University Press, 1992.

Shapiro, Robert D. *A Reform Rabbi in the Progressive Era: The Early Career of Stephen S. Wise*. New York: Garland, 1988.

Shapley, Deborah. *Promise and Power: The Life and Times of Robert McNamara*. New York: Simon & Schuster, 1993.

Sharkey, Heather J. *American Evangelicals in Egypt: Missionary Encounters in an Age of Empire*. Princeton, N.J.: Princeton University Press, 2008.

Sharp, James Roger. *American Politics in the Early Republic: The New Nation in Crisis*. New Haven, Conn.: Yale University Press, 1993.

Shaw, Yu-ming. *An American Missionary in China: John Leighton Stuart and Chinese-*

American Relations. Cambridge, Mass.: Council on East Asian Studies, Harvard University, 1992.

Shea, William L. *The Virginia Militia in the Seventeenth Century.* Baton Rouge: Louisiana State University Press, 1983.

Sheehan, Bernard W. *Savagism and Civility: Indians and Englishmen in Colonial Virginia.* Cambridge: Cambridge University Press, 1980.

Sherry, Michael S. *The Rise of American Air Power: The Creation of Armageddon.* New Haven: Yale University Press, 1987.

Sherwood, Robert. *Roosevelt and Hopkins: An Intimate History.* New York: Harper, 1948.

Shibusawa, Naoko. *America's Geisha Ally: Reimagining the Japanese Enemy.* Cambridge, Mass.: Harvard University Press, 2006.

Shipps, Jan. *Mormonism: The Story of a New Religious Tradition.* Urbana: University of Illinois Press, 1985.

Showalter, Nathan D. *The End of a Crusade: The Student Volunteer Movement for Foreign Missions and the Great War.* Lanham, Md.: Scarecrow Press, 1998.

Shuffelton, Frank. *Thomas Hooker, 1586–1647.* Princeton, N.J.: Princeton University Press, 1977.

Silbey, Joel H. *Storm over Texas: The Annexation Controversy and the Road to Civil War.* New York: Oxford University Press, 2005.

Silk, Mark. *Spiritual Politics: Religion and America since World War II.* New York: Simon & Schuster, 1988.

Silver, Peter. *Our Savage Neighbors: How Indian War Transformed Early America.* New York: W. W. Norton, 2008.

Silverman, David J. *Faith and Boundaries: Colonists, Christianity, and Community among the Wampanoag Indians of Martha's Vineyard, 1600–1871.* New York: Cambridge University Press, 2005.

Simms, Brendan. *Three Victories and a Defeat: The Rise and Fall of the First British Empire, 1714–1783.* London: Allen Lane, 2007.

Sitkoff, Harvard. *King: Pilgrimage to the Mountaintop.* New York: Hill and Wang, 2008.

Sittser, Gerald L. *A Cautious Patriotism: The American Churches and the Second World War.* Chapel Hill: University of North Carolina Press, 1997.

Skinner, Quentin. *The Foundations of Modern Political Thought,* 2 vols. Cambridge: Cambridge University Press, 1978.

———. *Visions of Politics,* 3 vols. Cambridge: Cambridge University Press, 2002.

Skrentny, John D. *The Minority Rights Revolution.* Cambridge, Mass.: Harvard University Press, 2002.

Slotkin, Richard. *Regeneration through Violence: The Mythology of the American Frontier, 1600–1800.* Middletown, Conn.: Wesleyan University Press, 1973.

———. *Lost Battalions: The Great War and the Crisis of American Nationality.* New York: Henry Holt, 2005.

Smith, Anthony D. *Chosen Peoples.* Oxford: Oxford University Press, 2003.

Smith, Bradford. *Yankees in Paradise: The New England Impact on Hawaii.* Philadelphia: Lippincott, 1956.

Smith, Craig R. *Daniel Webster and the Oratory of Civil Religion.* Columbia: University of Missouri Press, 2005.

Smith, Daniel M. *Robert Lansing and American Neutrality, 1914–1917.* Berkeley: University of California Press, 1958.

Smith, Gary Scott. *Faith and the Presidency: From George Washington to George W. Bush.* New York: Oxford University Press, 2006.

Smith, Geoffrey S. *To Save a Nation: American "Extremism," the New Deal, and the Coming of World War II,* rev. ed. Chicago: Ivan R. Dee, 1992.

Smith, Jean Edward. *FDR.* New York: Random House, 2007.

Smith, Tony. *America's Mission: The United States and the Worldwide Struggle for Democracy in the Twentieth Century*. Princeton, N.J.: Princeton University Press, 1994.

———. *Foreign Attachments: The Power of Ethnic Groups in the Making of American Foreign Policy*. Cambridge, Mass.: Harvard University Press, 2000.

Snay, Mitchell. *Gospel of Disunion: Religion and Separatism in the Antebellum South*. New York: Cambridge University Press, 1993.

Snyder, Sarah B. *Human Rights Activism and the End of the Cold War: A Transnational History of the Helsinki Network*. New York: Cambridge University Press, 2011.

Sorkin, David. *The Religious Enlightenment: Protestants, Jews, and Catholics from London to Vienna*. Princeton, N.J.: Princeton University Press, 2008.

Spalding, Elizabeth Edwards. *The First Cold Warrior: Harry Truman, Containment, and the Remaking of Liberal Internationalism*. Lexington: University Press of Kentucky, 2006.

Spector, Stephen. *Evangelicals and Israel: The Story of American Christian Zionism*. New York: Oxford University Press, 2008.

Spence, Jonathan D. *God's Chinese Son: The Taiping Heavenly Kingdom of Hong Xiuquan*. New York: W. W. Norton, 1996.

Stagg, J. C. A. *Mr. Madison's War: Politics, Diplomacy, and Warfare in the Early American Republic, 1783–1830*. Princeton, N.J.: Princeton University Press, 1983.

Stahr, Walter. *John Jay: Founding Father*. New York: Hambledon and London, 2005.

Stanley, Brian. *The Bible and the Flag: Protestant Missions and British Imperialism in the Nineteenth and Twentieth Centuries*. Leicester, U.K.: Apollos, 1990.

Stanley, Peter W. *A Nation in the Making: The Philippines and the United States, 1899–1921*. Cambridge, Mass.: Harvard University Press, 1974.

Starkey, Armstrong. *European and Native American Warfare, 1675–1815*. London: UCL Press, 1998.

Steele, Ian K. *Warpaths: Invasions of North America*. New York: Oxford University Press, 1994.

Stegner, Wallace. *The Gathering of Zion: The Story of the Mormon Trail*. Lincoln: University of Nebraska Press, 1964.

Steigerwald, David. *Wilsonian Idealism in America*. Ithaca, N.Y.: Cornell University Press, 1994.

Stephanson, Anders. *Kennan and the Art of Foreign Policy*. Cambridge, Mass.: Harvard University Press, 1989.

———. *Manifest Destiny: American Expansion and the Empire of Right*. New York: Hill and Wang, 1995.

Sterba, Christopher M. *Good Americans: Italian and Jewish Immigrants during the First World War*. New York: Oxford University Press, 2003.

Stevens, Jason W. *God-Fearing and Free: A Spiritual History of America's Cold War*. Cambridge, Mass.: Harvard University Press, 2010.

Stevens, Laura M. *The Poor Indians: British Missionaries, Native Americans, and Colonial Sensibility*. Philadelphia: University of Pennsylvania Press, 2004.

Stevens, Peter F. *The Rogue's March: John Riley and the St. Patrick's Battalion*. Washington, D.C.: Brassey's, 1999.

Stewart, James Brewer. *Holy Warriors: The Abolitionists and American Slavery*, rev. ed. New York: Hill and Wang, 1996.

Stick, David. *Roanoke Island: The Beginnings of English America*. Chapel Hill: University of North Carolina Press, 1983.

Stokes, Melvyn, and Stephen Conway, eds. *The Market Revolution in America: Social, Political and Religious Expressions, 1800–1880*. Charlottesville: University Press of Virginia, 1996.

Stone, Jon R. *On the Boundaries of American Evangelicalism: The Postwar Evangelical Coalition*. New York: St. Martin's Press, 1997.

Stone, Ronald H. *Reinhold Niebuhr: Prophet to Politicians.* Nashville, Tenn.: Abingdon Press, 1972.

Stourzh, Gerald. *Alexander Hamilton and the Idea of Republican Government.* Stanford, Calif.: Stanford University Press, 1970.

Stout, Harry S. *The New England Soul: Preaching and Religious Culture in Colonial New England.* New York: Oxford University Press, 1986.

———. *The Divine Dramatist: George Whitefield and the Rise of Modern Evangelicalism.* Grand Rapids, Mich.: Eerdmans, 1991.

———. *Upon the Altar of the Nation: A Moral History of the American Civil War.* New York: Viking Press, 2006.

Stubbs, John. *John Donne: The Reformed Soul.* London: Viking Press, 2006.

Stueck, William. *Rethinking the Korean War: A New Diplomatic and Strategic History.* Princeton, N.J.: Princeton University Press, 2002.

Sugrue, Thomas J. *Sweet Land of Liberty: The Forgotten Struggle for Civil Rights in the North.* New York: Random House, 2008.

Sumida, Jon Tetsuro. *Inventing Grand Strategy and Teaching Command: The Classic Works of Alfred Thayer Mahan Reconsidered.* Baltimore: Johns Hopkins University Press, 1997.

Suri, Jeremi. *Power and Protest: Global Revolution and the Rise of Détente.* Cambridge, Mass.: Harvard University Press, 2003.

———. *Henry Kissinger and the American Century.* Cambridge, Mass.: Harvard University Press, 2007.

Sutton, Matthew Avery. *Aimee Semple McPherson and the Resurrection of Christian America.* Cambridge, Mass.: Harvard University Press, 2007.

Swanberg, W. A. *Norman Thomas: The Last Idealist.* New York: Charles Scribner's Sons, 1976.

Takeyh, Ray. *Guardians of the Revolution: Iran and the World in the Age of the Ayatollahs.* New York: Oxford University Press, 2009.

Tanenhaus, Sam. *Whittaker Chambers: A Biography.* New York: Random House, 1997.

Taylor, Alan. *American Colonies.* New York: Viking Press, 2001.

———. *The Divided Ground: Indians, Settlers, and the Northern Borderland of the American Revolution.* New York: Alfred A. Knopf, 2006.

Taylor, Charles Carlisle. *The Life of Admiral Mahan, Naval Philosopher, Rear-Admiral United States Navy.* New York: George H. Doran Company, 1920.

Thomas, Daniel C. *The Helsinki Effect: International Norms, Human Rights, and the Demise of Communism.* Princeton, N.J.: Princeton University Press, 2001.

Thomas, Lately. *Storming Heaven: The Lives and Turmoils of Minnie Kennedy and Aimee Semple McPherson.* New York: Morrow, 1970.

Thompson, John A. *Reformers and War: American Progressive Publicists and the First World War.* Cambridge: Cambridge University Press, 1987.

———. *Woodrow Wilson.* London: Longman, 2002.

Thompson, Mary V. *"In the Hands of a Good Providence": Religion in the Life of George Washington.* Charlottesville: University of Virginia Press, 2008.

Tibawi, A. L. *American Interests in Syria, 1800–1901: A Study of Educational, Literary and Religious Work.* Oxford: Clarendon, 1966.

Toft, Monica Duffy, Daniel Philpott, and Timothy Samuel Shah. *God's Century: Resurgent Religion and Global Politics.* New York: W. W. Norton, 2011.

Tompkins, E. Berkeley. *Anti-imperialism in the United States: The Great Debate, 1898–1920.* Philadelphia: University of Pennsylvania Press, 1970.

Topmiller, Robert J. *The Lotus Unleashed: The Buddhist Peace Movement in South Vietnam.* Lexington: University Press of Kentucky, 2002.

Toulouse, Mark G. *The Transformation of John Foster Dulles: From Prophet of Realism to Priest of Nationalism.* Macon, Ga.: Mercer University Press, 1985.

Townsend, Camilla. *Pocahontas and the Powhatan Dilemma: An American Portrait*. New York: Hill and Wang, 2004.

Trachtenberg, Marc. *A Constructed Peace: The Making of the European Settlement, 1945–1963*. Princeton, N.J.: Princeton University Press, 1999.

Traina, Richard P. *American Diplomacy and the Spanish Civil War*. Bloomington: Indiana University Press, 1968.

Trollinger, William Vance, Jr. *God's Empire: William Bell Riley and Midwestern Fundamentalism*. Madison: University of Wisconsin Press, 1990.

Tuck, Stephen. *We Ain't What We Ought to Be: The Black Freedom Struggle from Emancipation to Obama*. Cambridge, Mass.: Harvard University Press, 2010.

Tucker, Robert W., and David C. Hendrickson. *Empire of Liberty: The Statecraft of Thomas Jefferson*. New York: Oxford University Press, 1990.

Tudda, Chris. *The Truth Is Our Weapon: The Rhetorical Diplomacy of Dwight D. Eisenhower and John Foster Dulles*. Baton Rouge: Louisiana State University Press, 2006.

Turner, James. *Without God, Without Creed: The Origins of Unbelief in America*. Baltimore: Johns Hopkins University Press, 1985.

Tuveson, Ernest Lee. *Redeemer Nation: The Idea of America's Millennial Role*. Chicago: University of Chicago Press, 1968.

Tyerman, Christopher. *Fighting for Christendom: Holy War and the Crusades*. Oxford: Oxford University Press, 2004.

Tyrrell, Ian. *Woman's World/Woman's Empire: The Woman's Christian Temperance Union in International Perspective, 1880–1930*. Chapel Hill: University of North Carolina Press, 1991.

———. *Reforming the World: The Creation of America's Moral Empire*. Princeton, N.J.: Princeton University Press, 2010.

Urofsky, Melvin I. *A Mind of One Piece: Brandeis and American Reform*. New York: Charles Scribner's Sons, 1971.

———. *American Zionism from Herzl to the Holocaust*. Garden City, N.Y.: Anchor Press/Doubleday, 1975.

———. *A Voice That Spoke for Justice: The Life and Times of Stephen S. Wise*. Albany: State University of New York Press, 1982.

Vallance, Edward. *The Glorious Revolution: 1688, Britain's Fight for Liberty*. London: Little, Brown, 2006.

Van Alstyne, Richard W. *The Rising American Empire*. New York: Oxford University Press, 1960.

———. *Empire and Independence: The International History of the American Revolution*. New York: Wiley, 1965.

Vance, Jonathan F. *Death So Noble: Memory, Meaning, and the First World War*. Vancouver: UBC Press, 1997.

Varg, Paul A. *Missionaries, Chinese, and Diplomats: The American Protestant Missionary Movement in China, 1890–1952*. Princeton, N.J.: Princeton University Press, 1958.

Vinz, Warren L. *Pulpit Politics: Faces of American Protestant Nationalism in the Twentieth Century*. Albany: State University of New York Press, 1997.

Viteritti, Joseph P. *The Last Freedom: Religion from the Public School to the Public Square*. Princeton, N.J.: Princeton University Press, 2007.

Vogel, Lester I. *To See a Promised Land: Americans and the Holy Land in the Nineteenth Century*. University Park: Pennsylvania State University Press, 1993.

Von Hoffman, Nicholas. *Citizen Cohn*. New York: Doubleday, 1988.

Vorenberg, Michael. *Final Freedom: The Civil War, the Abolition of Slavery, and the Thirteenth Amendment*. New York: Cambridge University Press, 2001.

Wacker, Grant. *Heaven Below: Early Pentecostals and American Culture*. Cambridge, Mass.: Harvard University Press, 2001.

Waldstreicher, David. *In the Midst of Perpetual Fetes: The Making of American Nationalism, 1776–1820*. Chapel Hill: University of North Carolina Press, 1997.

Walker, J. Samuel. *Henry A. Wallace and American Foreign Policy*. Westport, Conn.: Greenwood Press, 1976.

Walker, Samuel. *The Rights Revolution: Rights and Community in Modern America*. New York: Oxford University Press, 1998.

Walker, William O., III. *National Security and Core Values in American History*. New York: Cambridge University Press, 2009.

Wall, Joseph Frazier. *Andrew Carnegie*. New York: Oxford University Press, 1970.

Wall, Wendy L. *Inventing the "American Way": The Politics of Consensus from the New Deal to the Civil Rights Movement*. New York: Oxford University Press, 2008.

Wallace, Anthony F. C. *The Long, Bitter Trail: Andrew Jackson and the Indians*. New York: Hill and Wang, 1993.

Walsham, Alexandra. *Providence in Early Modern England*. Oxford: Oxford University Press, 1999.

Walt, Stephen M. *Revolution and War*. Ithaca, N.Y.: Cornell University Press, 1997.

Walters, Ronald G. *American Reformers, 1815–1860*. New York: Hill and Wang, 1978.

Walworth, Arthur. *Wilson and His Peacemakers: American Diplomacy at the Paris Peace Conference, 1919*. New York: W. W. Norton, 1986.

Walzer, Michael. *The Revolution of the Saints: A Study in the Origins of Radical Politics*. Cambridge, Mass.: Harvard University Press, 1965.

———. *Just and Unjust Wars: A Moral Argument with Historical Illustrations*, 2nd ed. New York: Basic Books, 1992.

Warner, Carolyn M. *Confessions of an Interest Group: The Catholic Church and Political Parties in Europe*. Princeton, N.J.: Princeton University Press, 2000.

Warren, Heather A. *Theologians of a New World Order: Reinhold Niebuhr and the Christian Realists, 1920–1948*. New York: Oxford University Press, 1997.

Watson, Harry L. *Liberty and Power: The Politics of Jacksonian America*. New York: Hill and Wang, 1990.

Watts, Jill. *God, Harlem U.S.A.: The Father Divine Story*. Berkeley: University of California Press, 1992.

Watts, Steven. *The Republic Reborn: War and the Making of Liberal America, 1790–1820*. Baltimore: Johns Hopkins University Press, 1987.

Weber, David J. *The Spanish Frontier in North America*. New Haven, Conn.: Yale University Press, 1992.

Weber, Donald. *Rhetoric and History in Revolutionary New England*. New York: Oxford University Press, 1988.

Weber, Timothy P. *Living in the Shadow of the Second Coming: American Premillennialism, 1875–1925*. New York: Oxford University Press, 1979.

Weeks, William Earl. *John Quincy Adams and American Global Empire*. Lexington: University Press of Kentucky, 1992.

———. *Building the Continental Empire: American Expansion from the Revolution to the Civil War*. Chicago: Ivan R. Dee, 1996.

Weems, John Edward. *To Conquer a Peace: The War between the United States and Mexico*. College Station: Texas A&M University Press, 1974.

Wehrle, Edmund S. *Britain, China, and the Antimissionary Riots, 1891–1900*. Minneapolis: University of Minnesota Press, 1966.

Weinberg, Gerhard L. *A World at Arms: A Global History of World War II*. Cambridge: Cambridge University Press, 1994.

Welch, Richard E., Jr. *George Frisbie Hoar and the Half-Breed Republicans*. Cambridge, Mass.: Harvard University Press, 1971.

———. *Response to Imperialism: The United States and the Philippine-American War, 1899–1902*. Chapel Hill: University of North Carolina Press, 1979.

Wellman, Judith. *Grass Roots Reform in the Burned-Over District of Upstate New York: Religion, Abolitionism, and Democracy.* New York: Garland, 2000.

Wells, Allen. *Tropical Zion: General Trujillo, FDR, and the Jews of Sosúa.* Durham, N.C.: Duke University Press, 2009.

Wells, Tom. *The War Within: America's Battle over Vietnam.* Berkeley: University of California Press, 1994.

Wernham, R. B. *The Making of Elizabethan Foreign Policy, 1558–1603.* Berkeley: University of California Press, 1980.

West, John G., Jr. *The Politics of Revelation and Reason: Religion and Civic Life in the New Nation.* Lawrence: University Press of Kansas, 1996.

Westad, Odd Arne. *The Global Cold War: Third World Interventions and the Makings of Our Times.* Cambridge: Cambridge University Press, 2005.

White, Graham, and John Maze. *Henry A. Wallace: His Search for a New World Order.* Chapel Hill: University of North Carolina Press, 1995.

White, Richard. *The Middle Ground: Indians, Empires, and Republics in the Great Lakes Region, 1650–1815.* Cambridge: Cambridge University Press, 1991.

White, Ronald C., Jr., and C. Howard Hopkins. *The Social Gospel: Religion and Reform in Changing America.* Philadelphia: Temple University Press, 1976.

Whitefield, Stephen J. *The Culture of the Cold War,* 2nd ed. Baltimore: Johns Hopkins University Press, 1996.

Wilentz, Sean. *Chants Democratic: New York City and the Rise of the American Working Class, 1788–1850.* New York: Oxford University Press, 1984.

———. *The Rise of American Democracy: Jefferson to Lincoln.* New York: W. W. Norton, 2005.

Williams, Daniel K. *God's Own Party: The Making of the Christian Right.* New York: Oxford University Press, 2010.

Williams, Walter L. *Black Americans and the Evangelization of Africa 1877–1900.* Madison: University of Wisconsin Press, 1982.

Williamson, Joel. *The Crucible of Race: Black/White Relations in the American South since Emancipation.* New York: Oxford University Press, 1984.

Wills, Garry. *Lincoln at Gettysburg: The Words that Remade America.* New York: Simon & Schuster, 1992.

Wilson, Edmund. *Patriotic Gore: Studies in the Literature of the American Civil War.* New York: Oxford University Press, 1966.

Winship, Michael P. *Seers of God: Puritan Providentialism in the Restoration and Early Enlightenment.* Baltimore: Johns Hopkins University Press, 1996.

———. *Making Heretics: Militant Protestantism and Free Grace in Massachusetts, 1636–1641.* Princeton, N.J.: Princeton University Press, 2002.

———. *The Times and Trials of Anne Hutchinson: Puritans Divided.* Lawrence: University Press of Kansas, 2005.

Wittner, Lawrence S. *Rebels against War: The American Peace Crusade, 1941–1960.* New York: Columbia University Press, 1969.

Wogaman, J. Philip. *Christian Perspectives on Politics,* rev. ed. Louisville, Ky.: Westminster John Knox Press, 2000.

Wolf, William J. *The Almost Chosen People: A Study of the Religion of Abraham Lincoln.* Garden City, N.Y.: Doubleday, 1959.

Wood, Betty. *The Origins of American Slavery: Freedom and Bondage in the English Colonies.* New York: Hill and Wang, 1997.

Wood, Gordon S. *The Creation of the American Republic, 1776–1787.* Chapel Hill: University of North Carolina Press, 1969.

———. *The Americanization of Benjamin Franklin.* New York: Penguin Press, 2004.

Woods, Randall B. *LBJ: Architect of American Ambition.* New York: Free Press, 2006.

Woodward, Bob. *Bush at War.* New York: Simon & Schuster, 2002.

————. *Plan of Attack.* New York: Simon & Schuster, 2004.

Woodward, Bob, and Carl Bernstein. *The Final Days.* New York: Simon & Schuster, 1976.

Woodward, C. Vann. *The Strange Career of Jim Crow,* 3rd ed. New York: Oxford University Press, 1974.

Woodworth, Steven E. *While God Is Marching On: The Religious World of Civil War Soldiers.* Lawrence: University Press of Kansas, 2001.

Woolverton, John Frederick. *Colonial Anglicanism in North America.* Detroit: Wayne State University Press, 1984.

Wright, Louis B. *Religion and Empire: The Alliance between Piety and Commerce in English Expansion, 1558–1625.* Chapel Hill: University of North Carolina Press, 1943.

Wright, Patrick. *Iron Curtain: From Stage to Cold War.* Oxford: Oxford University Press, 2007.

Wuthnow, Robert. *The Restructuring of American Religion: Society and Faith since World War II.* Princeton, N.J.: Princeton University Press, 1988.

————. *After Heaven: Spirituality in America since the 1950s.* Berkeley: University of California Press, 1998.

————. *America and the Challenges of Religious Diversity.* Princeton, N.J.: Princeton University Press, 2005.

Wyman, David S. *The Abandonment of the Jews: America and the Holocaust, 1941–1945.* New York: Pantheon, 1984.

Xing, Jun. *Baptized in the Fire of Revolution: The American Social Gospel and the YMCA in China, 1919–1937.* Bethlehem, Pa.: Lehigh University Press, 1996.

Young, Marilyn Blatt. *The Rhetoric of Empire: American China Policy, 1895–1901.* Cambridge, Mass.: Harvard University Press, 1968.

Zakai, Avihu. *Exile and Kingdom: History and Apocalypse in the Puritan Migration to America.* Cambridge: Cambridge University Press, 1992.

Zakaria, Fareed. *From Wealth to Power: The Unusual Origins of America's World Role.* Princeton, N.J.: Princeton University Press, 1998.

Zeiler, Thomas W. *Dean Rusk: Defending the American Mission Abroad.* Wilmington, Del.: Scholarly Resources, 1999.

Zelizer, Julian E. *Arsenal of Democracy: The Politics of National Security—From World War II to the War on Terrorism.* New York: Basic Books, 2009.

Zimmerman, Jonathan. *Whose America? Culture Wars in the Public Schools.* Cambridge, Mass.: Harvard University Press, 2002.

Zimmermann, Warren. *First Great Triumph: How Five Americans Made Their Country a World Power.* New York: Farrar, Straus and Giroux, 2002.

JOURNAL ARTICLES AND BOOK CHAPTERS

Abrams, Ray H. "The Churches and the Clergy in World War II." *Annals of the American Academy of Political and Social Science* 256 (March 1948): 110–119.

Addison, Paul. "Destiny, History, and Providence: The Religion of Winston Churchill." In *Public and Private Doctrine.* Edited by Michael Bentley. Cambridge: Cambridge University Press, 1993: 236–250.

Alvarez, David. "Purely a Business Matter: The Taft Mission to the Vatican." *Diplomatic History* 16 (Summer 1992): 357–369.

Ammerman, Nancy T. "North American Protestant Fundamentalism." In *Fundamentalisms Observed.* Edited by Martin E. Marty and R. Scott Appleby. Chicago: University of Chicago Press, 1991: 1–65.

Baepler, Paul. "The Barbary Captivity Narrative in Early America." *Early American Literature* 30 (Fall 1995): 95–120.

Banner, Lois W. "Religious Benevolence as Social Control: A Critique of an Interpretation." *Journal of American History* 60 (June 1973): 23–41.

Barone, Michael. "Franklin D. Roosevelt: A Protestant Patrician in a Catholic Party." In *FDR, the Vatican, and the Roman Catholic Church in America, 1933–1945*. Edited by David B. Woolner and Richard G. Kurial. New York: Palgrave Macmillan, 2003: 3–10.

Bellah, Robert N. "Civil Religion in America." *Daedalus* 96 (Winter 1967): 1–21.

Black, Antony. "Christianity and Republicanism: From St. Cyprian to Rousseau." *American Political Science Review* 91 (September 1997): 647–656.

Bosher, J. F. "Huguenot Merchants and the Protestant International in the Seventeenth Century." *William and Mary Quarterly*, 3rd series, 52 (January 1995): 77–102.

Boyer, Paul. "In Search of the Fourth 'R': The Treatment of Religion in American History Textbooks and Survey Courses." *History Teacher* 29 (February 1996): 195–216.

———. "The Evangelical Resurgence in 1970s American Protestantism." In *Rightward Bound: Making America Conservative in the 1970s*. Edited by Bruce J. Schulman and Julian E. Zelizer. Cambridge, Mass.: Harvard University Press, 2008: 29–51.

Brack, Gene M. "Mexican Opinion, American Racism, and the War of 1846." *Western Historical Quarterly* 1 (April 1970): 161–174.

Breen, T. H. "English Origins and New World Development: The Case of the Covenanted Militia in Seventeenth-Century Massachusetts." *Past and Present* 57 (November 1972): 74–96.

Breen, T. H., and Stephen Foster. "Moving to the New World: The Character of Early Massachusetts Immigration." *William and Mary Quarterly*, 3rd series, 30 (April 1973): 190–222.

Bremer, Francis J. "In Defense of Regicide: John Cotton and the Execution of Charles I." *William and Mary Quarterly*, 3rd series, 37 (January 1980): 103–124.

Brown, Cedric C. "Great Senates and Godly Education: Politics and Cultural Renewal in Some Pre- and Post-Revolutionary Texts of Milton." In *Milton and Republicanism*, ed. David Armitage, Armand Himy, and Quentin Skinner. Cambridge: Cambridge University Press, 1995: 43–60.

Bumsted, J. M. " 'Things in the Womb of Time': Ideas of American Independence, 1633 to 1763." *William and Mary Quarterly*, 3rd series, 31 (October 1974): 534–564.

Burleigh, Michael. "National Socialism as a Political Religion." *Totalitarian Movements and Political Religions* 1 (Autumn 2000): 1–26.

Burner, David. "The Quaker Faith of Herbert Hoover." In *Understanding Herbert Hoover: Ten Perspectives*. Edited by Lee Nash. Stanford: Hoover Institution Press, 1987: 53–64.

Butler, Jon. "Jack-in-the-Box Faith: The Religion Problem in Modern American History." *Journal of American History* 90 (March 2004): 1357–1378.

Canny, Nicholas P. "The Ideology of English Colonization: From Ireland to America." *William and Mary Quarterly*, 3rd series, 30 (October 1973): 575–598.

Carpenter, Joel A. "Fundamentalist Institutions and the Rise of Evangelical Protestantism, 1929–1942." *Church History* 49 (March 1980): 62–75.

Chamberlin, Paul. "A World Restored: Religion, Counterrevolution, and the Search for Order in the Middle East." *Diplomatic History* 32 (June 2008): 441–469.

Chernus, Ira. "Operation Candor: Fear, Faith, and Flexibility." *Diplomatic History* 29 (November 2005): 779–809.

Childress, James F. "Reinhold Niebuhr's Critique of Pacifism." *Review of Politics* 36 (October 1974): 467–491.

Clark, William A. "The Church at Nanrantsouak: Sébastien Râle, S.J., and the Wabanaki of Maine's Kennebec River." *Catholic Historical Review* 92 (July 2006): 225–251.

Clebsch, William A. "Christian Interpretations of the Civil War." *Church History* 30 (June 1961): 212–222.

Clifford, Dorita. "*Iglesia Filipina Independiente*: The Revolutionary Church." In *Studies in Philippine Church History*. Edited by Gerald H. Anderson. Ithaca, N.Y.: Cornell University Press, 1969: 223–255.

Clymer, Kenton J. "Humanitarian Imperialism: David Prescott Barrows and the White Man's Burden in the Philippines." *Pacific Historical Review* 45 (November 1976): 495–517.

Cohen, Paul A. "Littoral and Hinterland in Nineteenth Century China: The 'Christian' Reformers." In *The Missionary Enterprise in China and America*. Edited by John K. Fairbank. Cambridge, Mass.: Harvard University Press, 1974: 196–225.

Conley, Rory T. "Priest, Chaplain, Soldier . . . Spy? Father Franz J. Feinler and the Experience of German American Catholics during World War I." In *Building the Church in America*. Edited by Joseph C. Linck and Raymond J. Kupke. Washington, D.C.: Catholic University of America, 1999: 140–160.

Conway, John S. "Myron C. Taylor's Mission to the Vatican, 1940–1950." *Church History* 44 (March 1975): 85–99.

Cook, Sherburne F. "Interracial Warfare and Population Decline among the New England Indians." *Ethnohistory* 20 (Winter 1973): 1–24.

Cooper, John Milton, Jr. "A Friend in Power? Woodrow Wilson and Armenia." In *America and the Armenian Genocide of 1915*. Edited by Jay Winter. Cambridge: Cambridge University Press, 2003: 103–112.

Costigliola, Frank. "Lyndon B. Johnson, Germany, and 'the End of the Cold War.' " In *Lyndon Johnson Confronts the World: American Foreign Policy, 1969–1977*. Edited by Warren I. Cohen and Nancy Bernkopf Tucker. New York: Cambridge University Press, 1994: 173–210.

Crane, Elaine Forman. "Religion and Rebellion: Women of Faith in the American War for Independence." In *Religion in a Revolutionary Age*, ed. Ronald Hoffman and Peter J. Albert. Charlottesville: University Press of Virginia, 1994: 52–86.

Crapol, Edward P. "The Foreign Policy of Antislavery, 1833–1846." In *Redefining the Past: Essays in Diplomatic History in Honor of William Appleman Williams*. Edited by Lloyd C. Gardner. Corvallis: Oregon State University Press, 1986: 85–103.

Craven, Wesley Frank. "Indian Policy in Early Virginia." *William and Mary Quarterly*, 3rd series, 1 (January 1944): 65–82.

Crespino, Joseph. "Civil Rights and the Religious Right." In *Rightward Bound: Making America Conservative in the 1970s*. Edited by Bruce J. Schulman and Julian E. Zelizer. Cambridge, Mass.: Harvard University Press, 2008: 90–105.

Crowther, Edward R. "Holy Honor: Sacred and Secular in the Old South." *Journal of Southern History* 58 (November 1992): 619–636.

———. " 'Religion Has Something . . . to Do with Politics': Southern Evangelicals and the North, 1845–1860." In *Religion and the Antebellum Debate over Slavery*. Edited by John R. McKivigan and Mitchell Snay. Athens: University of Georgia Press, 1998: 317–342.

Curran, Robert Emmett. "Rome, the American Church, and Slavery." In *Building the Church in America*. Edited by Joseph C. Linck and Raymond J. Kupke. Washington, D.C.: Catholic University of America, 1999: 30–49.

Curtis, Susan. "The Son of Man and God the Father: The Social Gospel and Victorian Masculinity." In *Meanings for Manhood: Constructions of Masculinity in Victorian America*. Edited by Mark C. Carnes and Clyde Griffen. Chicago: University of Chicago Press, 1990: 67–78.

Dalin, David G. "Will Herberg's Path from Marxism to Judaism: A Case Study in the Transformation of Jewish Belief." In *The Americanization of the Jews*. Edited by Robert M. Seltzer and Norman J. Cohen. New York: NYU Press, 1995: 119–132.

Danielson, Leilah C. " 'In My Extremity I Turned to Gandhi': American Pacifists, Christianity, and Gandhian Nonviolence, 1915–1941." *Church History* 72 (June 2003): 361–388.

———. "Christianity, Dissent, and the Cold War: A. J. Muste's Challenge to Realism and U.S. Empire." *Diplomatic History* 30 (September 2006): 645–669.

Davies, Daniel M. "Building a City on a Hill in Korea: The Work of Henry G. Appenzeller." *Church History* 61 (December 1992): 422–435.

Davies, Tony. "Borrowed Language: Milton, Jefferson, Mirabeau." In *Milton and Republicanism*. Edited by David Armitage, Armand Himy, and Quentin Skinner. Cambridge: Cambridge University Press, 1995: 254–271.

Davis, Derek H. "Religion and the American Revolution." *Journal of Church and State* 36 (Autumn 1994): 709–724.

Dinges, William D., and James Hitchcock. "Roman Catholic Traditionalism and Activist Conservatism in the United States." In *Fundamentalisms Observed*. Edited by Martin E. Marty and R. Scott Appleby. Chicago: University of Chicago Press, 1991: 66–141.

Dinnerstein, Leonard. "America, Britain, and Palestine: The Anglo-American Committee of Inquiry and the Displaced Persons, 1945–46." *Diplomatic History* 4 (Summer 1980): 283–301.

Dochuk, Darren. "Evangelicalism Becomes Southern, Politics Becomes Evangelical: From FDR to Reagan." In *Religion and American Politics: From the Colonial Period to the Present*, 2nd ed. Edited by Mark A. Noll and Luke E. Harlow. New York: Oxford University Press, 2007: 297–325.

———. " 'They Locked God Outside the Iron Curtain': The Politics of Anticommunism and the Ascendancy of Plain-Folk Evangelicalism in the Postwar West." In *The Political Culture of the New West*. Edited by Jeff Roche. Lawrence: University Press of Kansas, 2008: 97–131.

Donagan, Barbara. "Did Ministers Matter? War and Religion in England, 1642–1649." *Journal of British Studies* 33 (April 1994): 119–156.

———. "Atrocity, War Crime, and Treason in the English Civil War." *American Historical Review* 99 (October 1994): 1137–1166.

Duff, John B. "The Versailles Treaty and the Irish-Americans." *Journal of American History* 55 (December 1968): 582–598.

Dunch, Ryan. "Beyond Cultural Imperialism: Cultural Theory, Christian Missions, and Global Modernity." *History and Theory* 41 (October 2002): 301–325.

Edwards, Wendy J. Deichmann. "Forging an Ideology for American Missions: Josiah Strong and Manifest Destiny." In *North American Foreign Missions, 1810–1914*. Edited by Wilbert R. Shenk. Grand Rapids, Mich.: Eerdmans, 2004: 163–191.

Ellsworth, Clayton Sumner. "The American Churches and the Mexican War." *American Historical Review* 45 (January 1940): 301–326.

Emerson, Michael O., and J. Russell Hawkins. "Viewed in Black and White: Conservative Protestantism, Racial Issues, and Oppositional Politics." In *Religion and American Politics: From the Colonial Period to the Present*, 2nd ed. Edited by Mark A. Noll and Luke E. Harlow. New York: Oxford University Press, 2007: 327–343.

Engerman, David C. "To Moscow and Back: American Social Scientists and the Concept of Convergence." In *American Capitalism: Social Thought and Political Economy in the Twentieth Century*. Edited by Nelson Lichtenstein. Philadelphia: University of Pennsylvania Press, 2006: 47–69.

Ernst, John, and Yvonne Baldwin. "The Not So Silent Minority: Louisville's Antiwar Movement, 1960–1975." *Journal of Southern History* 73 (February 2007): 105–142.

Farrell, James J. "Thomas Merton and the Religion of the Bomb." *Religion and American Culture* 5 (Winter 1995): 77–98.

Fatovic, Clement. "The Anti-Catholic Roots of Liberal and Republican Conceptions of Freedom in English Political Thought." *Journal of the History of Ideas* 66 (January 2005): 37–58.

Fishburn, Janet F. "The Social Gospel as Missionary Ideology." In *North American Foreign Missions, 1810–1914*. Edited by Wilbert R. Shenk. Grand Rapids, Mich.: Eerdmans, 2004: 218–242.

Fisher, James T. "The Second Catholic President: Ngo Dinh Diem, John F. Kennedy, and the Vietnam Lobby, 1954–1963." *U.S. Catholic Historian* 15 (Summer 1997): 119–137.

Fleischmann, Ellen. "Evangelization or Education: American Protestant Missionaries, the American Board, and the Girls and Women of Syria." In *New Faith in Ancient Lands: Western Missions in the Middle East in the Nineteenth and Early Twentieth Centuries*. Edited by Heleen Murre–van den Berg. Leiden: Brill, 2006: 263–280.

Flynn, George Q. "Lewis Hershey and the Conscientious Objector: The World War II Experience." *Military Affairs* 47 (February 1983): 1–6.

Fogarty, Gerald P. "Roosevelt and the American Catholic Hierarchy." In *FDR, the Vatican, and the Roman Catholic Church in America, 1933–1945*. Edited by David B. Woolner and Richard G. Kurial. New York: Palgrave Macmillan, 2003: 11–43.

Fredrickson, George M. "The Coming of the Lord: The Northern Protestant Clergy and the Civil War Crisis." In *Religion and the American Civil War*. Edited by Randall M. Miller, Harry S. Stout, and Charles Reagan Wilson. New York: Oxford University Press, 1998: 110–130.

Freeman, Michael. "Puritans and Pequots: The Question of Genocide." *New England Quarterly* 68 (June 1995): 278–293.

Furstenberg, François. "The Significance of the Trans-Appalachian Frontier in Atlantic History." *American Historical Review* 113 (June 2008): 647–677.

Gabriel, Ralph H. "Evangelical Religion and Popular Romanticism in Early Nineteenth-Century America." *Church History* 19 (March 1950): 34–47.

Gaines, Kevin. "Black Americans' Racial Uplift Ideology as 'Civilizing Mission': Pauline E. Hopkins on Race and Imperialism." In *Cultures of United States Imperialism*. Edited by Amy Kaplan and Donald E. Pease. Durham, N.C.: Duke University Press, 1993: 433–455.

Gallagher, Charles R. "The United States and the Vatican in Yugoslavia, 1945–50." In *Religion and the Cold War*. Edited by Dianne Kirby. Basingstoke, U.K.: Palgrave Macmillan, 2003: 118–144.

Garner, Karen. "Global Feminism and Postwar Reconstruction: The World YWCA Visitation to Occupied Japan, 1947." *Journal of World History* 15 (June 2004): 191–227.

Genovese, Eugene D. "Religion in the Collapse of the American Union." In *Religion and the American Civil War*. Edited by Randall M. Miller, Harry S. Stout, and Charles Reagan Wilson. New York: Oxford University Press, 1998: 74–88.

George, Jr., James H. "Another Chance: Herbert Hoover and World War II Relief." *Diplomatic History* 16 (Summer 1992): 389–407.

George, Timothy. "War and Peace in the Puritan Tradition." *Church History* 53 (December 1984): 492–503.

Gerstle, Gary. "Race and the Myth of the Liberal Consensus." *Journal of American History* 82 (September 1995): 579–586.

Gill, Jill K. "The Politics of Ecumenical Disunity: The Troubled Marriage of Church World Service and the National Council of Churches." *Religion and American Culture* 14 (Summer 2004): 175–212.

Goff, Philip. "Revivals and Revolution: Historiographic Turns since Alan Heimert's *Religion and the American Mind*." *Church History* 67 (December 1998): 695–721.

Gold, Robert L. "The Departure of Spanish Catholicism from Florida, 1763–1765." *The Americas* 22 (April 1966): 377–388.

Gosse, Van. " 'As a Nation, the English Are Our Friends': The Emergence of African American Politics in the British Atlantic World, 1772–1861." *American Historical Review* 113 (October 2008): 1003–1028.

Gowing, Peter G. "The Disentanglement of Church and State Early in the American Regime in the Philippines." In *Studies in Philippine Church History*. Edited by Gerald H. Anderson. Ithaca, N.Y.: Cornell University Press, 1969: 203–222.

Greene, Jack P. "Empire and Identity from the Glorious Revolution to the American Revolution." In *The Oxford History of the British Empire*, Vol. II: *The Eighteenth Century*. Edited by P. J. Marshall. Oxford: Oxford University Press, 1998: 208–230.

Griffith, Robert. "Dwight D. Eisenhower and the Corporate Commonwealth." *American Historical Review* 87 (February 1982): 87–122.

Guelzo, Allen C. "God's Designs: The Literature of the Colonial Revivals of Religion, 1735–1760." In *New Directions in American Religious History*. Edited by Harry S. Stout and D. G. Hart. New York: Oxford University Press, 1997: 141–172.

Gura, Philip F. "The Role of the 'Black Regiment': Religion and the American Revolution." *New England Quarterly* 61 (September 1988): 439–454.

Gustafson, Merlin. "The Religion of a President." *Journal of Church and State* 10 (Autumn 1968): 379–387.

Haas, Mark L. "Reinhold Niebuhr's 'Christian Pragmatism': A Principled Alternative to Consequentialism." *Review of Politics* 61 (Autumn 1999): 605–636.

Hall, Jacquelyn Dowd. "The Long Civil Rights Movement and the Political Uses of the Past." *Journal of American History* 91 (March 2005): 1233–1263.

Hall, Mitchell K. "CALCAV and Religious Opposition to the Vietnam War." In *Give Peace a Chance: Exploring the Vietnam Antiwar Movement*. Edited by Melvin Small and William D. Hoover. Syracuse, N.Y.: Syracuse University Press, 1992: 35–52.

Handy, Robert T. "The American Religious Depression, 1925–1935." *Church History* 29 (March 1960): 3–16.

Harvey, Charles E. "John D. Rockefeller, Jr., and the Interchurch World Movement of 1919–1920: A Different Angle on the Ecumenical Movement." *Church History* 51 (June 1982): 198–209.

Henry, Patrick. " 'And I Don't Care What It Is': The Tradition-History of a Civil Religion Proof-Text." *Journal of the American Academy of Religion* 49 (March 1981): 35–49.

Himy, Armand. "*Paradise Lost* as a Republican 'Tractatus Theologico-Politicus.' " In *Milton and Republicanism*. Edited by David Armitage, Armand Himy, and Quentin Skinner. Cambridge: Cambridge University Press, 1995: 118–134.

Hirsch, Adam J. "The Collision of Military Cultures in Seventeenth-Century New England." *Journal of American History* 74 (March 1988): 1187–1212.

Hixson, Walter L. "Containment on the Perimeter: George F. Kennan and Vietnam." *Diplomatic History* 12 (April 1988): 149–164.

Hollinger, David A. "The 'Secularization' Question and the United States in the Twentieth Century." *Church History* 70 (March 2001): 132–143.

Horsman, Reginald. "The Dimensions of an 'Empire for Liberty': Expansion and Republicanism, 1775–1825." *Journal of the Early Republic* 9 (Spring 1989): 1–20.

Hovannisian, Richard G. "The Armenian Genocide and US Post-War Commissions." In *America and the Armenian Genocide of 1915*. Edited by Jay Winter. Cambridge: Cambridge University Press, 2003: 257–275.

Howe, Daniel Walker. "Protestantism, Voluntarism, and Personal Identity in Antebellum America." In *New Directions in American Religious History*. Edited by Harry S. Stout and D. G. Hart. New York: Oxford University Press, 1997: 206–235.

Hudson, Winthrop S. "Protestant Clergy Debate the Nation's Vocation, 1898–1899." *Church History* 42 (March 1973): 110–118.

Iriye, Akira. "Imperialism and Sincerity." *Reviews in American History* 1 (March 1973): 119–125.

———. "Culture and Power: International Relations as Intercultural Relations." *Diplomatic History* 3 (Spring 1979): 115–128.

Jacobs, Seth. " 'Our System Demands the Supreme Being': The U.S. Religious Revival and the 'Diem Experiment,' 1954–55." *Diplomatic History* 25 (Fall 2001): 589–624.

Jervis, Robert. "Cooperation under the Security Dilemma." *World Politics* 30 (January 1978): 167–214.

———. "Was the Cold War a Security Dilemma?" *Journal of Cold War Studies* 3 (Winter 2001): 36–60.

Johnson, Richard R. "Growth and Mastery: British North America, 1690–1748." In *The Oxford History of the British Empire*, Vol. II: *The Eighteenth Century*. Edited by P. J. Marshall. Oxford: Oxford University Press, 1998: 276–299.

Johnson, Stanley. "John Donne and the Virginia Company." *ELH* 14 (June 1947): 127–138.

Karr, Ronald Dale. " 'Why Should You Be So Furious?': The Violence of the Pequot War." *Journal of American History* 85 (December 1998): 876–909.

Katz, Steven T. "The Pequot War Reconsidered." *New England Quarterly* 64 (June 1991): 206–224.

———. "Pequots and the Question of Genocide: A Reply to Michael Freeman." *New England Quarterly* 68 (December 1995): 641–649.

Kellstedt, Lyman, John Green, Corwin Smidt, and James Guth. "Faith Transformed: Religion and American Politics from FDR to George W. Bush." In *Religion and American Politics: From the Colonial Period to the Present*, 2nd ed. Edited by Mark A. Noll and Luke E. Harlow. New York: Oxford University Press, 2007: 269–295.

Kelly, Patrick J. "The Election of 1896 and the Restructuring of Civil War Memory." In *The Memory of the Civil War in American Culture*. Edited by Alice Fahs and Joan Waugh. Chapel Hill: University of North Carolina Press, 2004: 180–212.

Kences, James. "Some Unexplored Relationships of Essex County Witchcraft to the Indian Wars of 1675 and 1689." *Essex Institute Historical Collections* 120 (1984): 181–211.

Kenney, William Howland. "George Whitefield, Dissenter Priest of the Great Awakening, 1739–1741." *William and Mary Quarterly*, 3rd series, 26 (January 1969): 75–93.

Kidd, Colin. "Civil Theology and Church Establishments in Revolutionary America." *Historical Journal* 42 (December 1999): 1007–1026.

Killingray, David. "The Black Atlantic Missionary Movement and Africa, 1780s–1920s." *Journal of Religion in Africa* 33 (February 2003): 3–31.

Kirby, Dianne. "Truman's Holy Alliance: The President, the Pope and the Origins of the Cold War." *Borderlines* 4 (1997): 1–17.

———. "Divinely Sanctioned: The Anglo-American Cold War Alliance and the Defence of Western Civilization and Christianity, 1945–48." *Journal of Contemporary History* 35 (July 2000): 385–412.

———. "Harry Truman's Religious Legacy: The Holy Alliance, Containment, and the Cold War." In *Religion and the Cold War*. Edited by Dianne Kirby. Basingstoke, U.K.: Palgrave Macmillan, 2003: 77–102.

Kirby, James E. "Matthew Simpson and the Mission of America." *Church History* 36 (September 1967): 299–307.

Kling, David W. "The New Divinity and the Origins of the American Board of Commissioners for Foreign Missions." In *North American Foreign Missions, 1810–1914*. Edited by Wilbert R. Shenk. Grand Rapids, Mich.: Eerdmans, 2004: 11–38.

Kochavi, Noam. "Insights Abandoned, Flexibility Lost: Kissinger, Soviet Jewish Emigration, and the Demise of Détente." *Diplomatic History* 29 (June 2005): 503–530.

————. "Idealpolitik in Disguise: Israel, Jewish Emigration from the Soviet Union, and the Nixon Administration, 1969–1974." *International History Review* 29 (September 2007): 550–572.

Komonchak, Joseph A. "Interpreting the Council: Catholic Attitudes toward Vatican II." In *Being Right: Conservative Catholics in America.* Edited by Mary Jo Weaver and R. Scott Appleby. Bloomington: Indiana University Press, 1995: 17–36.

Kornblith, Gary J. "Rethinking the Coming of the Civil War: A Counterfactual Exercise." *Journal of American History* 90 (June 2003): 76–105.

Kosek, Joseph Kip. "Richard Gregg, Mohandas Gandhi, and the Strategy of Nonviolence." *Journal of American History* 91 (March 2005): 1318–1348.

Kotlowski, Dean J. "Breaching the Paper Walls: Paul V. McNutt and Jewish Refugees to the Philippines, 1938–1939." *Diplomatic History* 33 (November 2009): 865–896.

Kruse, Kevin M. "Beyond the Southern Cross: The National Origins of the Religious Right." In *The Myth of Southern Exceptionalism.* Edited by Matthew D. Lassiter and Joseph Crespino. New York: Oxford University Press, 2010: 286–307.

Kukla, Jon. "Order and Chaos in Early America: Political and Social Stability in Pre-Restoration Virginia." *American Historical Review* 90 (April 1985): 275–298.

Laing, Annette. " 'Heathens and Infidels'? African Christianization and Anglicanism in the South Carolina Low Country, 1700–1750." *Religion and American Culture* 12 (Summer 2002): 197–228.

Landers, Jane L. "Traditions of African American Freedom and Community in Spanish Colonial Florida." In *The African American Heritage of Florida.* Edited by David R. Colburn and Jane L. Landers. Gainesville: University Press of Florida, 1995: 17–41.

Lappenküper, Ulrich. "Between Concentration Movement and People's Party: The Christian Democratic Union in Germany." In *Christian Democracy in Europe since 1945.* Edited by Michael Gehler and Wolfram Kaiser. London: Routledge, 2004: 25–37.

Lassiter, Matthew D. "De Jure/De Facto Segregation: The Long Shadow of a National Myth." In *The Myth of Southern Exceptionalism.* Edited by Matthew D. Lassiter and Joseph Crespino. New York: Oxford University Press, 2010: 25–48.

Lee, Timothy S. "A Political Factor in the Rise of Protestantism in Korea: Protestantism and the 1919 March First Movement." *Church History* 69 (March 2000): 116–142.

Leffler, Melvyn P. "The Cold War: What Do 'We Now Know'?" *American Historical Review* 104 (April 1999): 501–524.

Lenman, Bruce. "Providence, Liberty, and Prosperity: An Aspect of English Thought in the Era of the Glorious Revolution." In *The World of William and Mary: Anglo-Dutch Perspectives on the Revolution of 1688–89.* Edited by Dale Hoak and Mordechai Feingold. Stanford, Calif.: Stanford University Press, 1996: 135–151.

————. "Colonial Wars and Imperial Instability, 1688–1793." In *The Oxford History of the British Empire*, Vol. II: *The Eighteenth Century.* Edited by P. J. Marshall. Oxford: Oxford University Press, 1998: 151–168.

Lovejoy, David S. "Satanizing the American Indian." *New England Quarterly* 67 (December 1994): 603–621.

————. "Between Hell and Plum Island: Samuel Sewall and the Legacy of the Witches, 1692–97." *New England Quarterly* 70 (September 1997): 355–367.

McAlister, Melani. "Prophecy, Politics, and the Popular: The Left Behind Series and Christian Fundamentalism's New World Order." *South Atlantic Quarterly* 102 (Fall 2003): 773–798.

Maclear, J. F. "New England and the Fifth Monarchy: The Quest for the Millennium in Early American Puritanism." *William and Mary Quarterly*, 3rd series, 32 (April 1975): 223–260.

McDermott, Gerald R. "Jonathan Edwards and American Indians: The Devil Sucks Their Blood." *New England Quarterly* 72 (December 1999): 539–557.

McKillen, Elizabeth. "Ethnicity, Class, and Wilsonian Internationalism Reconsidered: The Mexican-American and Irish-American Immigrant Left and U.S. Foreign Relations, 1914–1922." *Diplomatic History* 25 (Fall 2001): 553–587.

McLoughlin, William G. "The Role of Religion in the Revolution: Liberty of Conscience and Cultural Cohesion in the New Nation." In *Essays on the American Revolution*. Edited by Stephen G. Kurtz and James H. Hutson. Chapel Hill: University of North Carolina Press, 1973: 197–255.

McPherson, James M. "Who Freed the Slaves?" *Proceedings of the American Philosophical Society* 139 (March 1995): 1–10.

————. "No Peace without Victory, 1861–1865." *American Historical Review* 109 (February 2004): 1–18.

Maier, Charles S. "Consigning the Twentieth Century to History: Alternative Narratives for the Modern Era." *American Historical Review* 105 (June 2000): 807–831.

Manza, Jeff, and Clem Brooks. "The Changing Political Fortunes of Mainline Protestants." In *The Quiet Hand of God: Faith-Based Activism and the Public Role of Mainline Protestantism*. Edited by Robert Wuthnow and John H. Evans. Berkeley: University of California Press, 2002: 159–178.

Marcus, Richard H. "The Connecticut Valley: A Problem in Intercolonial Defense." *Military Affairs* 33 (April 1969): 230–242.

Marini, Stephen A. "Religion, Politics, and Ratification." In *Religion in a Revolutionary Age*. Edited by Ronald Hoffman and Peter J. Albert. Charlottesville: University Press of Virginia, 1994: 184–217.

Mark, Eduard. "October or Thermidor? Interpretations of Stalinism and the Perception of Soviet Foreign Policy in the United States, 1927–1947." *American Historical Review* 94 (October 1989): 937–962.

Marks, Frederick W., III. "Morality as a Drive Wheel in the Diplomacy of Theodore Roosevelt." *Diplomatic History* 2 (Winter 1978): 43–62.

Markus, R. A. "Saint Augustine's Views on the 'Just War.'" In *The Church and War*. Edited by W. J. Sheils. Oxford: Blackwell/Ecclesiastical History Society, 1983.

Marty, Martin E. "Fundamentals of Fundamentalism." In *Fundamentalism in Comparative Perspective*. Edited by Lawrence Kaplan. Amherst: University of Massachusetts Press, 1992: 15–23.

Maxwell, Kenneth R. "Irish-Americans and the Fight for Treaty Ratification." *Public Opinion Quarterly* 31 (Winter 1967–1968): 620–641.

Mead, Walter Russell. "God's Country?" *Foreign Affairs* 85 (September/October 2006): 24–43.

Merguerian, Barbara J. "'Missions in Eden': Shaping an Educational and Social Program for the Armenians in Eastern Turkey (1885–1895)." In *New Faith in Ancient Lands: Western Missions in the Middle East in the Nineteenth and Early Twentieth Centuries*. Edited by Heleen Murre–van den Berg. Leiden: Brill, 2006: 241–262.

Meyer, D. H. "American Intellectuals and the Victorian Crisis of Faith." In *Victorian America*. Edited by Daniel Walker Howe. Philadelphia: University of Pennsylvania Press, 1976: 59–77.

Miller, Perry. "Solomon Stoddard, 1643–1729." *Harvard Theological Review* 34 (October 1941): 277–320.

Miller, Randall M. "Catholic Religion, Irish Ethnicity, and the Civil War." In *Religion and the American Civil War*. Edited by Randall M. Miller, Harry S. Stout, and Charles Reagan Wilson. New York: Oxford University Press, 1998: 261–296.

Miller, Stuart Creighton. "Ends and Means: Missionary Justification of Force in Nineteenth Century China." In *The Missionary Enterprise in China and America*. Edited by John K. Fairbank. Cambridge, Mass.: Harvard University Press, 1974: 249–282.

Miscamble, Wilson D. "Catholics and American Foreign Policy from McKinley to McCarthy: A Historiographical Survey." *Diplomatic History* 4 (Summer 1980): 223–240.

———. "The Limits of American Catholic Antifascism: The Case of John A. Ryan." *Church History* 59 (December 1990): 523–538.

———. "Francis Cardinal Spellman and 'Spellman's War.' " In *The Human Tradition in the Vietnam Era*. Edited by David L. Anderson. Wilmington, Del.: Scholarly Resources, 1999: 3–22.

Mistry, Kaeten. "The Case for Political Warfare: Strategy, Organization and US Involvement in the 1948 Italian Election." *Cold War History* 6 (August 2006): 301–329.

Moessner, Jeanne Stevenson. "Missionary Motivation." *Sociological Analysis* 53 (Summer 1992): 189–200.

Moorhead, James H. "The Erosion of Postmillennialism in American Religious Thought, 1865–1925." *Church History* 53 (March 1984): 61–77.

Morgan, Joseph G. "A Change of Course: American Catholics, Anticommunism, and the Vietnam War." *U.S. Catholic Historian* 22 (Fall 2004): 117–130.

Morgan, Michael Cotey. "The United States and the Making of the Helsinki Final Act." In *Nixon in the World: U.S. Foreign Relations, 1969–1977*. Edited by Fredrik Logevall and Andrew Preston. New York: Oxford University Press, 2008: 164–182.

———. "The Seventies and the Rebirth of Human Rights." In *The Shock of the Global: The 1970s in Perspective*. Edited by Niall Ferguson, Charles S. Maier, Erez Manela, and Daniel J. Sargent. Cambridge, Mass.: Harvard University Press, 2010: 237–250.

Morrill, John. "The Religious Context of the English Civil War." *Transactions of the Royal Historical Society*, 5th series, 34 (1984): 155–178.

Mosse, George L. "The Assimilation of Machiavelli in English Thought: The Casuistry of William Perkins and William Ames." *Huntington Library Quarterly* 17 (August 1954): 315–326.

Mulder, John M. " 'A Gospel of Order': Woodrow Wilson's Religion and Politics." In *The Wilson Era: Essays in Honor of Arthur S. Link*. Edited by John Milton Cooper Jr. and Charles E. Neu. Arlington Heights, Ill.: Harlan Davidson, 1991: 223–247.

Muller, Dorothea R. "Josiah Strong and American Nationalism: A Reevaluation." *Journal of American History* 53 (December 1966): 487–503.

Nash, Gary B. "The American Clergy and the French Revolution." *William and Mary Quarterly*, 3rd series, 22 (July 1965): 392–412.

———. "The Image of the Indian in the Southern Colonial Mind." *William and Mary Quarterly*, 3rd series, 29 (April 1972): 197–230.

Neem, Johann N. "The Elusive Common Good: Religion and Civil Society in Massachusetts, 1780–1833." *Journal of the Early Republic* 24 (Autumn 2004): 381–417.

Ninkovich, Frank. "Theodore Roosevelt: Civilization as Ideology." *Diplomatic History* 10 (July 1986): 221–245.

Noll, Mark A. "The American Revolution and Protestant Evangelicalism." *Journal of Interdisciplinary History* 23 (Winter 1993): 615–638.

O'Brien, Michael. "The American Experience of Secularisation." In *Religion and the Political Imagination*. Edited by Ira Katznelson and Gareth Stedman Jones. Cambridge: Cambridge University Press, 2010: 132–149.

O'Brien, Susan. "A Transatlantic Community of Saints: The Great Awakening and the First Evangelical Network, 1735–1755." *American Historical Review* 91 (October 1986): 811–832.

Offner, John. "Washington Mission: Archbishop Ireland on the Eve of the Spanish-American War." *Catholic Historical Review* 73 (October 1987): 562–575.

Onuf, Peter S. "A Declaration of Independence for Diplomatic Historians." *Diplomatic History* 22 (Winter 1998): 71–83.

Owen, Dennis E., Kenneth D. Wald, and Samuel S. Hill. "Authoritarian or Authority-Minded? The Cognitive Commitments of Fundamentalists and the Christian Right." *Religion and American Culture* 1 (Winter 1991): 73–100.

Paludan, Phillip Shaw. "Religion and the American Civil War." In *Religion and the American Civil War.* Edited by Randall M. Miller, Harry S. Stout, and Charles Reagan Wilson. New York: Oxford University Press, 1998: 21–40.

Parker, Geoffrey. "Early Modern Europe." In *The Laws of War: Constraints on Warfare in the Western World.* Edited by Michael Howard, George J. Andreopoulos, and Mark R. Shulman. New Haven, Conn.: Yale University Press, 1994: 40–58.

Pencak, William. "Perspectives on Britain's First Ethnically Diverse Empire." *Ethnohistory* 48 (Winter-Spring 2001): 323–336.

Pestana, Carla Gardina. "Religion." In *The British Atlantic World, 1500–1800.* Edited by David Armitage and Michael J. Braddick. New York: Palgrave, 2002: 69–89.

Pierard, Richard V. "Pax Americana and the Evangelical Missionary Alliance." In *Earthen Vessels: American Evangelicals and Foreign Missions, 1880–1980.* Edited by Joel A. Carpenter and Wilbert R. Shenk. Grand Rapids, Mich.: Eerdmans, 1990: 155–179.

Pinheiro, John C. " 'Religion without Restriction': Anti-Catholicism, All Mexico, and the Treaty of Guadalupe Hidalgo." *Journal of the Early Republic* 23 (Spring 2003): 69–96.

Pollard, John. "The Vatican, Italy and the Cold War." In *Religion and the Cold War.* Edited by Dianne Kirby. Basingstoke, U.K.: Palgrave Macmillan, 2003: 103–117.

Preston, Andrew. "Bridging the Gap between Church and State in the History of American Foreign Relations." *Diplomatic History* 30 (November 2006): 783–812.

———. "The Israel Lobby and U.S. Foreign Policy: Roundtable Review." *H-Diplo Roundtable Reviews* 8 (December 2007): http://www.h-net.org/~diplo/roundtables/PDF/IsraelLobby-Preston.pdf

———. "The Death of a Peculiar Special Relationship: Myron Taylor and the Religious Roots of America's Cold War." In *America's Special Relationships: Foreign and Domestic Aspects of the Politics of Alliance.* Edited by John Dumbrell and Axel R. Schäfer. New York and London: Routledge, 2009: 202–216.

———. "Religion and World Order at the Dawn of the American Century." In *The U.S. Public and American Foreign Policy.* Edited by Andrew Johnstone and Helen Laville. New York and London: Routledge, 2010: 73–86.

———. "Reviving Religion in the History of American Foreign Relations." In *God and Global Order: The Power of Religion in American Foreign Policy.* Edited by Jonathan Chaplin and Robert Joustra. Waco, Tex.: Baylor University Press, 2010: 25–44.

———. "The Politics of Realism and Religion: Christian Responses to Bush's New World Order." *Diplomatic History* 34 (January 2010): 95–118.

———. "Universal Nationalism: Christian America's Response to the Years of Upheaval." In *The Shock of the Global: The 1970s in Perspective.* Edited by Niall Ferguson, Charles S. Maier, Erez Manela, and Daniel J. Sargent. Cambridge, Mass.: Harvard University Press, 2010: 306–318.

Quinn, D. Michael. "The Mormon Church and the Spanish-American War: An End to Selective Pacifism." *Pacific Historical Review* 43 (August 1974): 342–366.

Ramsey, William L. " 'Something Cloudy in Their Looks': The Origins of the Yamasee War Reconsidered." *Journal of American History* 90 (June 2003): 44–75.

Rankin, Mary Backus. "Social and Political Change in Nineteenth-Century China." In *Historical Perspectives on Contemporary East Asia.* Edited by Merle Goldman and Andrew Gordon. Cambridge, Mass.: Harvard University Press, 2000: 42–84.

Reed, James Eldin. "American Foreign Policy, the Politics of Missions and Josiah Strong, 1890–1900." *Church History* 41 (June 1972): 230–245.

Repousis, Angelo. " 'The Devil's Apostle': Jonas King's Trial against the Greek Hierarchy in 1852 and the Pressure to Extend U.S. Protection for American Missionaries Overseas." *Diplomatic History* 33 (November 2009): 807–837.

Reuter, Frank T. "William Howard Taft and the Separation of Church and State in the Philippines." *Journal of Church and State* 24 (Winter 1982): 105–117.

Ribuffo, Leo P. "God and Contemporary Politics." *Journal of American History* 79 (March 1993): 1515–1533.

———. "Religion in the History of U.S. Foreign Policy." In *The Influence of Faith: Religious Groups and U.S. Foreign Policy.* Edited by Elliott Abrams. Lanham, Md.: Rowman & Littlefield, 2001: 1–27.

———. "George W. Bush, the 'Faith-Based' Presidency, and the Latest 'Evangelical Menace.' " *Journal of American and Canadian Studies* 24 (2006): 17–37.

Richter, Daniel K. "Native Peoples of North America and the Eighteenth-Century British Empire." In *The Oxford History of the British Empire*, Vol. II: *The Eighteenth Century.* Edited by P. J. Marshall. Oxford: Oxford University Press, 1998: 347–371.

Riebling, Barbara. "Milton on Machiavelli: Representations of the State in *Paradise Lost.*" *Renaissance Quarterly* 49 (Autumn 1996): 573–597.

Robert, Dana L. "Introduction." In *Converting Colonialism: Visions and Realities in Mission History, 1706–1914.* Edited by Dana L. Robert. Grand Rapids, Mich.: Eerdmans, 2008: 1–20.

Rodgers, Daniel T. "Republicanism: The Career of a Concept." *Journal of American History* 79 (June 1992): 11–38.

Rotter, Andrew J. "Christians, Muslims, and Hindus: Religion and U.S.–South Asian Relations, 1947–1954." *Diplomatic History* 24 (Fall 2000): 593–613.

Rountree, Helen C. "Powhatan Priests and English Rectors: World Views and Congregations in Conflict." *American Indian Quarterly* 16 (Autumn 1992): 485–500.

———. "The Powhatans and the English: A Case of Multiple Conflicting Agendas." In *Powhatan Foreign Relations, 1500–1722.* Edited by Helen C. Rountree. Charlottesville: University Press of Virginia, 1993: 173–205.

Rountree, Helen C., and E. Randolph Turner III. "On the Fringe of the Southeast: The Powhatan Paramount Chiefdom in Virginia." In *The Forgotten Centuries: Indians and Europeans in the American South, 1521–1704.* Edited by Charles Hudson and Carmen Chaves Tesser. Athens: University of Georgia Press, 1994: 355–372.

Sandbrook, Dominic. "Salesmanship and Substance: The Influence of Domestic Policy and Watergate." In *Nixon in the World: U.S. Foreign Relations, 1969–1977.* Edited by Fredrik Logevall and Andrew Preston. New York: Oxford University Press, 2008: 85–105.

Sanneh, Lamin. "World Christianity and the New Historiography: History and Global Interconnections." In *Enlarging the Story: Perspectives on Writing World Christian History.* Edited by Wilbert R. Shenk. Maryknoll, N.Y.: Orbis Books, 2002: 94–114.

Sargent, Daniel J. "The United States and Globalization in the 1970s." In *The Shock of the Global: The 1970s in Perspective.* Edited by Niall Ferguson, Charles S. Maier, Erez Manela, and Daniel J. Sargent. Cambridge, Mass.: Harvard University Press, 2010: 49–64.

Schäfer, Axel R. " 'What Marx, Lenin, and Stalin Needed Was . . . to Be Born Again': Evangelicals and the Special Relationship between Church and State in U.S. Cold War Foreign Policy." In *America's Special Relationships: Foreign and Domestic Aspects of the Politics of Alliance.* Edited by John Dumbrell and Axel R. Schäfer. New York and London: Routledge, 2009: 223–241.

Schlesinger, Arthur M., Jr. "The Missionary Enterprise and Theories of Imperialism."

In *The Missionary Enterprise in China and America.* Edited by John K. Fairbank. Cambridge, Mass.: Harvard University Press, 1974: 336–373.

Schneider, Robert A. "Voice of Many Waters: Church Federation in the Twentieth Century." In *Between the Times: The Travail of the Protestant Establishment in America, 1900–1960.* Edited by William R. Hutchison. New York: Cambridge University Press, 1990: 95–121.

Segers, Mary C. "Equality and Christian Anarchism: The Political and Social Ideas of the Catholic Worker Movement." *Review of Politics* 40 (April 1978): 196–230.

Shankman, Arnold M. "Southern Methodist Newspapers and the Coming of the Spanish-American War: A Research Note." *Journal of Southern History* 39 (February 1973): 93–96.

Shermer, Elizabeth Tandy. "Origins of the Conservative Ascendancy: Barry Goldwater's Early Senate Career and the De-legitimization of Organized Labor." *Journal of American History* 95 (December 2008): 678–709.

Silk, Mark. "Notes on the Judeo-Christian Tradition in America." *American Quarterly* 36 (Spring 1984): 65–85.

Simmons, William S. "Cultural Bias in the New England Puritans' Perception of Indians." *William and Mary Quarterly,* 3rd series, 38 (January 1981): 56–72.

Smith, Christian. "Introduction: Rethinking the Secularization of American Public Life." In *The Secular Revolution: Power, Interests, and Conflict in the Secularization of American Life.* Edited by Christian Smith. Berkeley: University of California Press, 2003: 1–96.

Smith, Ephraim K. " 'A Question from Which We Could Not Escape': William McKinley and the Decision to Acquire the Philippine Islands." *Diplomatic History* 9 (Fall 1985): 363–375.

Smith, John Abernathy. "Ecclesiastical Politics and the Founding of the Federal Council of Churches." *Church History* 43 (September 1974): 350–365.

Snyder, K. Alan. "Foundations of Liberty: The Christian Republicanism of Timothy Dwight and Jedidiah Morse." *New England Quarterly* 56 (September 1983): 382–397.

Spickard, Paul. "Asian Americans, Religion, and Race." In *From Arrival to Incorporation: Migrants to the U.S. in a Global Era.* Edited by Elliott R. Barkan, Hasia Diner, and Alan M. Kraut. New York: New York University Press, 2008: 94–117.

Stampp, Kenneth M. "Lincoln's History." In *"We Cannot Escape History": Lincoln and the Last Best Hope of Earth.* Edited by James M. McPherson. Urbana: University of Illinois Press, 1995: 17–32.

Steinfels, Peter. "Roman Catholics and American Politics, 1960–2004." In *Religion and American Politics: From the Colonial Period to the Present,* 2nd ed. Edited by Mark A. Noll and Luke E. Harlow. New York: Oxford University Press, 2007: 345–366.

Stephanson, Anders. "Liberty or Death: The Cold War as U.S. Ideology." In *Reviewing the Cold War: Approaches, Interpretations, Theory.* Edited by Odd Arne Westad. London: Frank Cass, 2000: 81–100.

Stinchcombe, William C. "John Adams and the Model Treaty." In *The American Revolution and "A Candid World."* Edited by Lawrence S. Kaplan. Kent, Ohio: Kent State University Press, 1977: 69–84.

Stout, Harry S. "The Puritans and Edwards." In *Jonathan Edwards and the American Experience.* Edited by Nathan O. Hatch and Harry S. Stout. New York: Oxford University Press, 1988: 142–159.

———. "Rhetoric and Reality in the Early Republic: The Case of the Federalist Clergy." In *Religion and American Politics: From the Colonial Period to the Present,* 2nd ed. Edited by Mark A. Noll and Luke E. Harlow. New York: Oxford University Press, 2007: 65–78.

Stout, Harry S., and Peter Onuf. "James Davenport and the Great Awakening in New London." *Journal of American History* 70 (December 1983): 556–578.

Stowell, Daniel W. "Stonewall Jackson and the Providence of God." In *Religion and the American Civil War.* Edited by Randall M. Miller, Harry S. Stout, and Charles Reagan Wilson. New York: Oxford University Press, 1998: 187–207.

Sullivan, Robert R. "The Politics of Altruism: An Introduction to the Food-for-Peace Partnership between the United States Government and Voluntary Relief Agencies." *Western Political Quarterly* 23 (December 1970): 762–768.

Suri, Jeremi. "Lyndon Johnson and the Global Disruption of 1968." In *Looking Back at LBJ: White House Politics in a New Light.* Edited by Mitchell B. Lerner. Lawrence: University Press of Kansas, 1996: 53–77.

Tate, Merze. "The Sandwich Islands Missionaries Create a Literature." *Church History* 31 (June 1962): 182–202.

Taylor, Sandra C. "Japan's Missionary to the Americans: Sidney L. Gulick and America's Interwar Relationship with the Japanese." *Diplomatic History* 4 (Fall 1980): 387–407.

Thomas, G. E. "Puritans, Indians, and the Concept of Race." *New England Quarterly* 48 (March 1975): 3–27.

Thomas, Scott M. "A Globalized God: Religion's Growing Influence in International Politics." *Foreign Affairs* 89 (November/December 2010): 93–101.

Thompson, Michael G. "An Exception to Exceptionalism: A Reflection on Reinhold Niebuhr's Vision of 'Prophetic' Christianity and the Problem of Religion and U.S. Foreign Policy." *American Quarterly* 59 (September 2007): 833–855.

Thornton, John K. "African Dimensions of the Stono Rebellion." *American Historical Review* 96 (October 1991): 1101–1113.

Tudda, Chris. " 'A Messiah That Will Never Come': A New Look at Saratoga, Independence, and Revolutionary War Diplomacy." *Diplomatic History* 32 (November 2008): 779–810.

Tuttle, William M., Jr. "Aid-to-the-Allies Short-of-War versus American Intervention, 1940: A Reappraisal of William Allen White's Leadership." *Journal of American History* 56 (March 1970): 840–858.

Valeri, Mark. "The New Divinity and the American Revolution." *William and Mary Quarterly,* 3rd series, 46 (October 1989): 741–769.

Van Engen, Charles E. "A Broadening Vision: Forty Years of Evangelical Theology of Mission, 1946–1986." In *Earthen Vessels: American Evangelicals and Foreign Missions, 1880–1980.* Edited by Joel A. Carpenter and Wilbert R. Shenk. Grand Rapids, Mich.: Eerdmans, 1990: 203–232.

Varg, Paul A. "The Advent of Nationalism, 1758–1776." *American Quarterly* 16 (Summer 1964): 169–181.

Vaughan, Alden T. " 'Expulsion of the Salvages': English Policy and the Virginia Massacre of 1622." *William and Mary Quarterly,* 3rd series, 35 (January 1978): 57–84.

Vaughn, Stephen. "The Moral Inheritance of a President: Reagan and the Dixon Disciples of Christ." *Presidential Studies Quarterly* 25 (Winter 1995): 109–127.

Voorhees, David William. "The 'fervent Zeale' of Jacob Leisler." *William and Mary Quarterly,* 3rd series, 51 (July 1994): 447–472.

Wacker, Grant. "The Holy Spirit and the Spirit of the Age in American Protestantism, 1880–1910." *Journal of American History* 72 (June 1985): 45–62.

Walls, A. F. "World Christianity, the Missionary Movement and the Ugly American." In *World Order and Religion.* Edited by Wade Clark Roof. Albany: State University of New York Press, 1991: 147–172.

Welch, Claude E., Jr. "Mobilizing Morality: The World Council of Churches and its Program to Combat Racism, 1969–1994." *Human Rights Quarterly* 23 (November 2001): 863–910.

Whaites, Alan. "Pursuing Partnership: World Vision and the Ideology of Development: A Case Study." *Development in Practice* 9 (August 1999): 410–423.

White, Ronald C., Jr. "Lincoln's Sermon on the Mount: The Second Inaugural." In *Religion and the American Civil War.* Edited by Randall M. Miller, Harry S. Stout, and Charles Reagan Wilson. New York: Oxford University Press, 1998: 208–225.

Williams, Walter L. "United States Indian Policy and the Debate over Philippine Annexation: Implications for the Origins of American Imperialism." *Journal of American History* 66 (March 1980): 810–831.

Williamson, Philip. "Christian Conservatives and the Totalitarian Challenge, 1933–40." *English Historical Review* 115 (June 2000): 607–642.

Wilson, John F. "Religion and Revolution in American History." *Journal of Interdisciplinary History* 23 (Winter 1993): 597–613.

Wood, Gordon S. "Religion and the American Revolution." In *New Directions in American Religious History.* Edited by Harry S. Stout and D. G. Hart. New York: Oxford University Press, 1997: 173–205.

Woods, Randall B. "Conflicted Hegemon: LBJ and the Dominican Republic." *Diplomatic History* 32 (November 2008): 749–766.

Woodward, C. Vann. "The Age of Reinterpretation." *American Historical Review* 66 (October 1960): 1–19.

Zakaria, Fareed. "The Myth of America's 'Free Security.' " *World Policy Journal* 14 (Summer 1977): 35–43.

Zeitz, Joshua Michael. " 'If I am not for myself . . .': The American Jewish Establishment in the Aftermath of the Six Day War." *American Jewish History* 88 (June 2000): 253–286.

Zietsma, David. " 'Sin Has No History': Religion, National Identity, and U.S. Intervention, 1937–1941." *Diplomatic History* 31 (June 2007): 531–565.

ACKNOWLEDGMENTS

Unsurprisingly, in writing a book that covers four centuries and two subjects as enormous as foreign relations and religion, I have accumulated numerous debts—indeed, far too many to mention here. Nonetheless, some thanks are in order.

This book has been planned, researched, and written under the aegis of three institutions, each remarkable in its own way. I first began the book at Yale University, where I spent three years as an Olin Fellow. My main base at Yale, International Security Studies, was (and remains) a wonderfully nurturing environment where scholars from a wide variety of disciplines can exchange and debate ideas. At ISS, I am especially grateful to its directors, Paul Kennedy and John Lewis Gaddis, and its teaching and support staff (as they were then constituted) of Ted Bromund, Charlie Hill, Minh Luong, Ann Carter Drier, and Susan Hennigan. I also learned a great deal from fellow Fellows Ray Takeyh, Peter Westwick, and especially Jeff Engel. At the History Department, where I taught, Jon Butler and Skip Stout generously met with me to discuss American religious history and gave me advice on how to manage my approach to it. Ceara Donnelley provided excellent research assistance even as she began her legal career at the Law School.

I then moved to the University of Victoria, in British Columbia, where the Baird clan made me feel right at home. UVic is a special place, and a part of me has never left. I would especially like to thank those colleagues who took a special interest in my work: Sara Beam, Greg Blue, Martin Bunton, Simon Devereaux, Brian Dippie, Karen McIvor, Andrea McKenzie, Lynne Marks, Eric Sager, Tom Saunders, and Liz Vibert. I will particularly miss the late Ted Wooley, whose generosity of spirit and intellectual curiosity remain an inspiration.

Finally, my home institution, Cambridge University, where I teach American and international history, has been a uniquely stimulating environment. My bases there, the History Faculty and Clare College, have both been wonderfully supportive. My debts are many, but in particular I would like to thank those who have taken the time to discuss my book with me: Tony Badger, Duncan Bell, Bill Foster, Roger Greeves, John Guy, Joel Isaac, Sophie King, Barak Kushner, Gideon Mailer, Peter Mandler, Dan Matlin, Terry Moore, Michael O'Brien, William O'Reilly, Richard Rex, David Reynolds, Greg Seach, Mike Sewell, Ellie Shermer, Brendan Simms, Sujit Sivasundaram, John Swenson-Wright, John Thompson, and Betty Wood. One of the pleasures of being an Americanist at Cambridge is the arrival, every two years, of a visiting Pitt Professor of American History. In my time at Cambridge, I have been fortunate to work with three friendly and generous Pitts—Nancy Hewitt, Jim Kloppenberg, and Mills Thornton—all of whom discussed my project at length and offered helpful advice. I am also thankful to my graduate students who specialize on some aspect of the linkage between religion and American public life: Jonathan Bronitsky, Phil Dow, Naama Gaathon, John Heavens, Charlie Laderman, and Olivia Sohns. To an extent unlike anywhere else, Cambridge has an astonishing variety of forums in which academics can present their work. For this privilege, I am grateful to the American History Research Seminar in the History Faculty, the Cambridge History Society, the History of Christianity Research Seminar in the Divinity Faculty, the International History Research Seminar in the Centre of International Studies, the Trinity Hall History Society, and the history societies of Churchill, Corpus Christi, Magdalene, Murray Edwards, Queens', St. John's, and Trinity colleges.

I am immensely grateful to those colleagues who closely and critically read draft chapters that cover their own areas of expertise: Tim Borstelmann, Richard Carwardine, Darren Dochuk, Jeff Engel, Susan Ferber, Andy Fry, Malcolm Gaskill, Will Inboden, Joel Isaac, Richard King, Malcolm Magee, David Milne, Mark Noll, Michael O'Brien, David Reynolds, Leo Ribuffo, Brendan Simms, and John Thompson. Not all of them will agree with the final product, but I'm confident they'll recognize that the book is much improved for their reading of it.

I would be remiss if I did not also mention those who have discussed the connections between religion and foreign relations with me and generously offered their time and advice, often in response to a question or plea for help, or invited me to their university to present my work: Brooke Blower, Liz Borgwardt, Paul Boyer, Mark Bradley, Aron Burke, Dan Carter, Frank Costigliola, Mario Del Pero, Mike Desch, John Dumbrell, Kate Carté Engel, Kate Epstein, Charlie Gallagher, Eric Gregory, Jonathan Hagel, Simon Hall, Jussi Hanhimäki, Michael Hopkins, Seth Jacobs, Sheyda Jahanbani, Andrew Johnstone, Matthew Jones, Charles Keith, Dianne Kirby, Scott Kleeb, Sandra Kraft, Melissa Lane, Helen Laville, Mark Lawrence, Steven Lawson, Mel Leffler, Fred Logevall, Lorenz Lüthi, Erez Manela, Marco Mariano, Kaeten Mistry, Mike Morgan, Catherine Morley, Sam Moyn, Hang Nguyen, Jolie Olcott, Devin Pendas, Helle Porsdam, Doug Rossinow, Andy Rotter, Dom Sandbrook, Axel Schäfer, Bruce Schulman, Bevan Sewell, Sarah Snyder, Gagan Sood, Anders Stephanson, Stephen Tuck, Ian Tyrrell, Molly Worthen, Marilyn Young, Julian Zelizer, and David Zietsma. In addition, I would like to thank the following for their comments when I presented work-in-progress at various conferences: Frank Gavin, Will Inboden, Mark Kramer, Bill Miscamble, Emily Rosenberg, Leigh Schmidt, Tom Schwartz, Jeremi Suri, and Monica Toft. Tragically, my good friend Jon Persoff died as this book was nearing completion; after our countless conversations in New Haven and Los Angeles, I know he would have loved to see it in print. He was One Strong Dude and will be missed.

I would also like to thank the scholars and students at various institutions for inviting me to present my work and for offering critical feedback to it: in Denmark, at the University of Copenhagen; in Germany, at the Westfälische Wilhelms-Universität, Münster; in Ireland, at the Clinton Institute, University College Dublin; in Italy, at the universities of Bologna and Turin; in Switzerland, at the Graduate Institute of International and Development Studies, Geneva; in the United Kingdom, at the Institute of Historical Research in London, the London School of Economics, the Rothermere American Institute in Oxford, St. Antony's College, Oxford, and the universities of East Anglia, Keele, Leeds, Leicester, Liverpool, and Nottingham; and, in the United States, at Boston College, the Camden Conference, the Council on Foreign Relations, the Lone Star Conference, the Lyndon B. Johnson Presidential Library, Boston, Harvard, Princeton, Texas A&M, and Yale universities, and the universities of Connecticut and Notre Dame. I must also thank the U.K.'s Arts and Humanities Research Council for funding a sabbatical period that allowed me to finish writing a draft of the manuscript.

In every way, this book has been the product of three Andrews, and simply could not have been written without the other two. My literary agent, Andrew Wylie, showed enthusiasm at the very earliest stages and encouraged me to conceive of the book as broadly and ambitiously as possible. At the Wylie Agency, I would also like to thank Rebecca Nagel (in New York) and James Pullen (in London). Andrew then placed the book with my superb editor, Andrew Miller, who showed monastic levels of (nearly) infinite patience as the book assumed a life of its own, became much bigger, and took much longer to complete than either of us had ever imagined. I would also like to thank yet another namesake in New York, Andrew Carlson, who shepherded the manuscript through production, as well as Paul Taunton at Random House Canada in Toronto.

Last but not least comes my family. No longer will they need to ask, as has been their wont, "So . . . is the book finished yet?" The Patricks were, typically, warmly supportive. My brother Kevin was a steady source of ideas and feedback. My wife, Fran, and children, Rosie and Lizzie, have had to put up with my heading out of town for research trips, lectures, and conferences and, when I was finally home, usually found me hunched over my laptop at the kitchen table. If anyone has shown more patience than my editor, it is Fran, who has, characteristically, been a constant source of love and support and, not least of all, the book's title. Finally, I am enormously grateful to my parents, Harry and Mary Preston, who have always led by example rather than admonition. It is no exaggeration to say that without their unconditional generosity, encouragement, and love of reading, this book could not have been written. It is entirely appropriate that I dedicate it to them.

INDEX

Abbott, Lyman, 213–14, 225, 249, 262
Abenaki Indians, 49, 51, 53–4, 55
Abington Township v. Schemp, 506
Able Archer exercise, 594
abolitionism, 106, 112, 124, 140–2, 153, 166–7
  Civil War and, 160–5
  expansion opposed by, 140–6, 152
  foreign policy and, 141–2
abortion issue, 544, 546, 547, 554, 557, 558, 578, 581, 583, 607, 609
Abraham (prophet), 437
Abrams, Elliott, 566, 592
Abrams, Ray, 327
Acadia, 67–8
Acheson, Dean, 414, 434, 477
Acts, Book of, 27
Adam, 425
Adams, Abigail, 85
Adams, Brooks, 199–200
Adams, Henry, 199–200
Adams, John, 74, 80, 90–1, 95, 99, 105
  Model Treaty of, 91, 112, 130
Adams, John Quincy, 103–8, 112, 122–3, 130, 138, 199, 579
  religion and worldview of, 105–6
Adams, Louisa, 90
Adams, Samuel, 78, 99
Addams, Jane, 178, 242, 259
Adler, Cyrus, 272, 273–4
Advance, 273
Afghanistan, x, 586, 587, 596, 604, 610
  Soviet invasion of, x, 578
African Americans, 182, 383, 491–2, 505, 523, 591–2
  Black Power movement and, 508–9
  Christianity and, 165–6
  in missionary movement, 186–7
  western expansion opposed by, 142–3
  see also race, racism
African embassies bombing, 605

African Methodist Episcopal Church (AME), 187, 492, 590
Agency for International Development, 553
Aguinaldo, Emilio, 219, 222–3, 226, 228
Ahlstrom, Sydney, 215
AIDS, 609
Alabama, 136, 143
Alaska, 103, 155
  U.S. purchase of, 176
Albania, 196
Alexander II, Czar of Russia, 198
Alexander III (the Great), King of Macedonia, 28
Algiers, 113, 115
Allen, Emily, 213
Allen, Richard, 583
Alliance for Progress, 510
al Qaeda, x, 604, 605
Altizer, Thomas, 507
America, 299, 360
America First, 332
American Alliance of Christians and Jews, 333
American Baptist Foreign Mission Society, 277
American Baptist Women, 490
American Bible Society, 105, 112
American Board of Commissioners for Foreign Missions (ABCFM), 130–1, 133, 137, 138, 142, 181, 188, 191, 196, 224
American Catholic Committee, 592
American Christian Committee for German Refugees, 332
American Colony, 201
American Council for Judaism, 560
American Council of Christian Churches, 382, 468, 473, 533, 551
American Federation of Catholic Societies, 269
American Federation of Labor, 335
American Fellowship of Reconciliation, 241–4
American Freedom and Catholic Power (Blanshard), 413

ABOUT THE AUTHOR

ANDREW PRESTON teaches American history and international relations history at Cambridge University, where he is a fellow of Clare College. Before Cambridge, he taught history and international studies at Yale University. He has also taught at universities in Canada and Switzerland, and has been a fellow at the Cold War Studies Program at the London School of Economics. He is the author of *The War Council: McGeorge Bundy, the NSC, and Vietnam.*

A NOTE ON THE TYPE

This book was set in Janson, a typeface long thought to have been made by the Dutchman Anton Janson, who was a practicing typefounder in Leipzig during the years 1668–1687. However, it has been conclusively demonstrated that these types are actually the work of Nicholas Kis (1650–1702), a Hungarian, who most probably learned his trade from the master Dutch typefounder Dirk Voskens. The type is an excellent example of the influential and sturdy Dutch types that prevailed in England up to the time William Caslon (1692–1766) developed his own incomparable designs from them.

Composed by North Market Street Graphics, Lancaster, Pennsylvania

Printed and bound by Berryville Graphics, Berryville, Virginia

Book design by Robert C. Olsson